1995

Mobil Travel Guide.

Mid-Atlantic

Delaware

District of Columbia

Maryland

New Jersey

North Carolina

Pennsylvania

South Carolina

Virginia

West Virginia

D1264940

Fodor's Travel Publications, Inc.

This series of regional guides is published by Fodor's Travel Publications, Inc., in collaboration with Mobil Corporation, which has sponsored the books since 1958. The aim of the *Mobil Travel Guide* is to provide the most comprehensive, up-to-date, and useful regional guides at the lowest possible price. All properties listed are inspected by trained, experienced field representatives. There is no charge to any establishment for inclusion in these guides, and only establishments that meet the *Mobil Travel Guide* criteria are listed.

Every effort has been made to select a variety of all types of lodging and dining establishments available in a given locale. However, space limitations make it impossible to include every fine establishment, and the fact that some omissions occur does not imply adverse criticism or inferiority to listed establishments.

Information in the *Mobil Travel Guide* is revised and updated yearly. Ratings are reviewed annually on the basis of reports from our field representatives, senior staff evaluators and careful analysis of all available relevant material, including more than 100,000 opinions from users of the *Mobil Travel Guide*. All ratings are impartial, and every effort is made to rate fairly and consistently.

At the time of inspection, all establishments were clean, well-managed and met *Mobil Travel Guide* standards. Occasionally an establishment may go out of business or change ownership after date of publication. By calling ahead readers can avoid the disappointment of a closed or changed establishment.

By revising our listings yearly, we hope to make a contribution to maintaining and raising the standards of restaurants and accommodations available to travelers across the country. We are most interested in hearing from our readers about their experiences at the establishments we list, as well as any other comments about the quality and usefulness of the *Mobil Travel Guide*. Every communication from our readers is carefully studied with the object of making the *Mobil Travel Guide* better. Please address suggestions or comments about attractions, accommodations, or restaurants to *Mobil Travel Guide,* Fodor's Travel Publications, Inc., 4709 W. Golf Road, Suite 803, Skokie, IL 60076.

THE EDITORS

Guide Staff

Managing Director and Editor-in-Chief: Alice M. Wisel
Inspection Manager: Diane E. Connolly
Editorial Coordinator: Thomas W. Grant
Inspection Assistant: Adam Blieberg
Editorial Assistant: Mary Beth Doyle
Staff Assistant: Douglas M. Weinstein
Creative Director: Fabrizio LaRocca
Cover Design: John Olenyik
Cover Photograph: Pamela Zilly/Image Bank

Acknowledgements

We gratefully acknowledge the help of our 100 field representatives for their efficient and perceptive inspection of every hotel, motel, motor hotel, inn, resort and restaurant listed; the proprietors of these establishments for their cooperation in showing their facilities and providing information about them; our many friends and users of previous editions of *Mobil Travel Guide;* and the thousands of Chambers of Commerce, Convention and Visitors' Bureaus, city, state and provincial tourism offices and government agencies for their time and information.

Mobil

Published in 1995 by Fodor's Travel Publications, Inc.
201 E. 50th St.
New York, NY 10022

ISBN 0-679-02853-6
ISSN 0076-9797

Manufactured in the United States of America
10 9 8 7 6 5 4 3 2 1

MAP SYMBOLS

▬▬	Freeway	⓪⓪	Interstate route	**Boston**®	City over 500,000	⋯⋯	Time zone boundary
◄◄◄◄	Under construction	⓪⓪	U.S. route	Worcester®	City 100,000-499,999	-----	Trail
══	Tollway	⓪	State route	Bangor®	City 25,000-99,999	- - -	Ferry
══	Divided highway	⓪	Other route	Houlton○	City 5,000-24,999		
──	Primary road	▲2▲	Mileage between points	Mars Hill○	City 0-4,999		National park
──	Secondary road	▬▬	Interchanges	⊛	Capital city		Other recreation area
──	Other road	•	Point of interest	▬▬	International boundary		Built-up area
-----	Unpaved road	+	Mountain peak	▬▬	State boundary		Indian reservation

Contents

Mid-Atlantic

Introduction

Maps

A map of each state covered in this volume precedes the introduction. Larger, more detailed maps are available at many Mobil service stations.

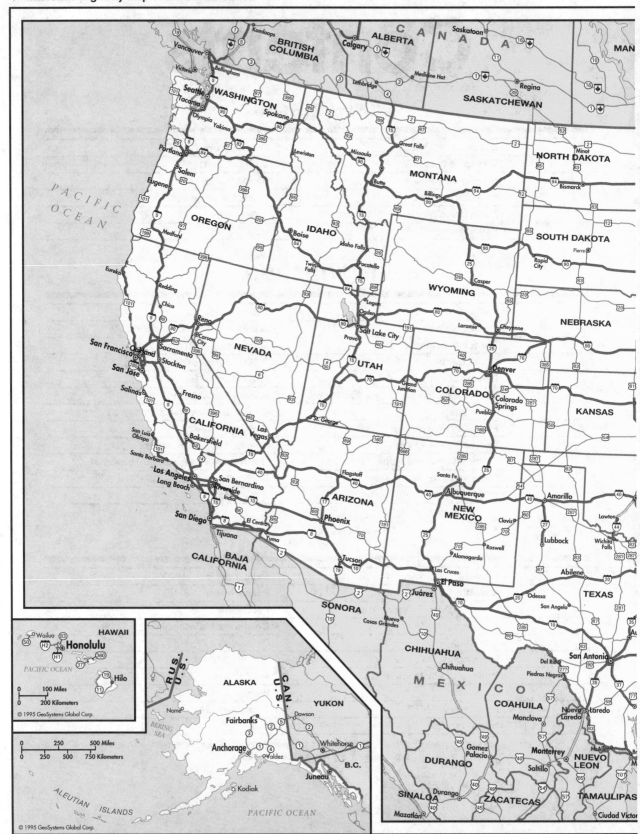

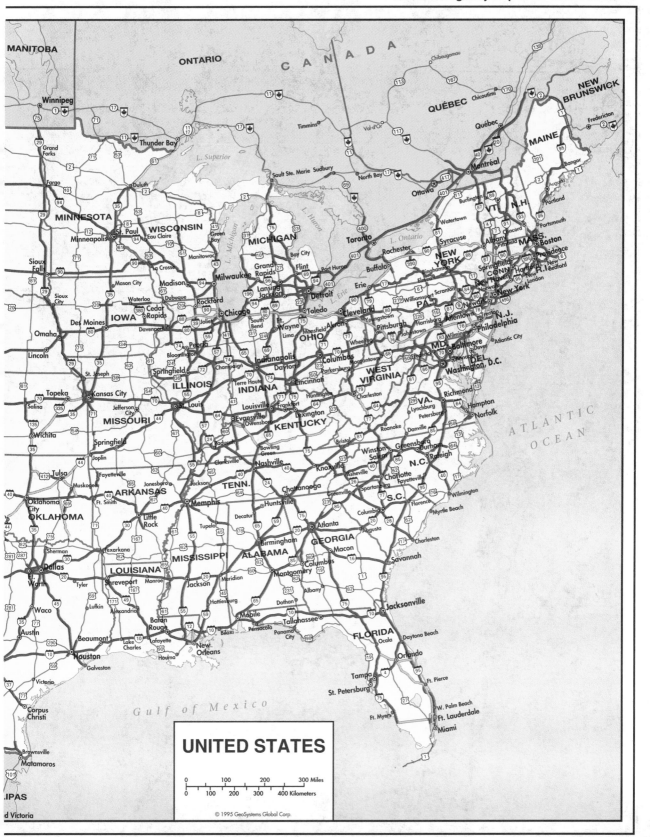

UNITED STATES

0   100   200   300 Miles
0   100   200   300   400 Kilometers

© 1995 GeoSystems Global Corp.

MASS.

95

Springfield

CONN.

Hartford

New Haven

New York

Albany

7

4

87

Norwalk

495

NEW JERSEY

Atlantic City

DELAWARE

Washington, D.C.

13

Hampton

17

80

Newark

78

Trenton

Philadelphia

Dover

Annapolis

Baltimore

Binghamton

88

84

9

Allentown

76

Wilmington

Maryland

70

95

64

Richmond

Syracuse

81

NEW YORK

Scranton

81

83

Harrisburg

Frederick

66

VIRGINIA

81

Rochester

Elmira

390

6

PENNSYLVANIA

Williamsport

15

220

50

29

L. Ontario

90

Johnstown

219

68

Buffalo

17

80

Pittsburgh

70
76

WEST VIRGINIA

64

Toronto

400

401

ONTARIO

Erie

79

Youngstown

Morgantown

79

Charleston

64

Port Huron

L. Erie

90

Cleveland

Akron

77

Canton

Wheeling

Columbus

70

Parkersburg

50

Detroit

401

71

23

Huntington

64

Flint

69

94

Toledo

75

Mansfield

OHIO

Ohio R.

23

L. Huron

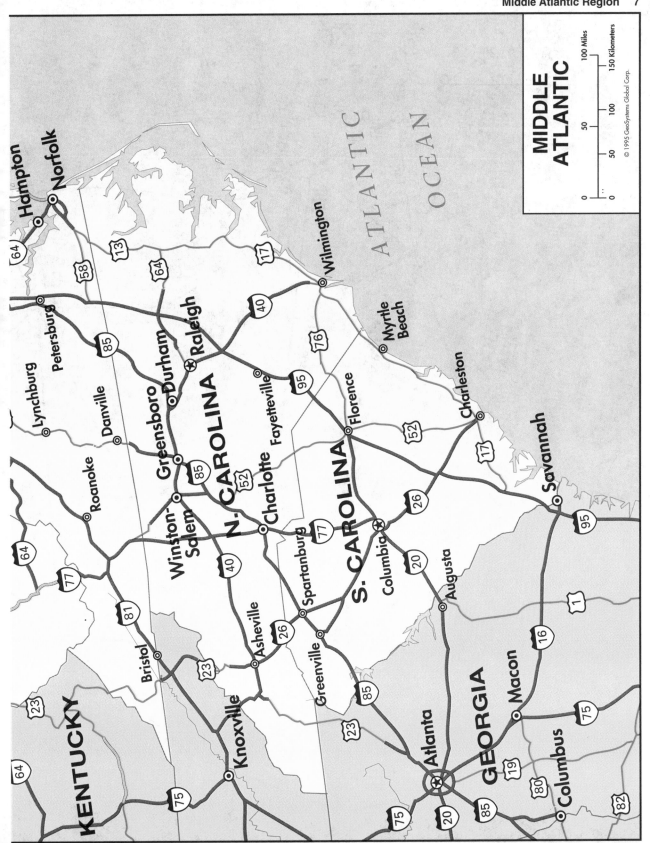

MIDDLE ATLANTIC

© 1995 GeoSystems Global Corp.

ATLANTIC

OCEAN

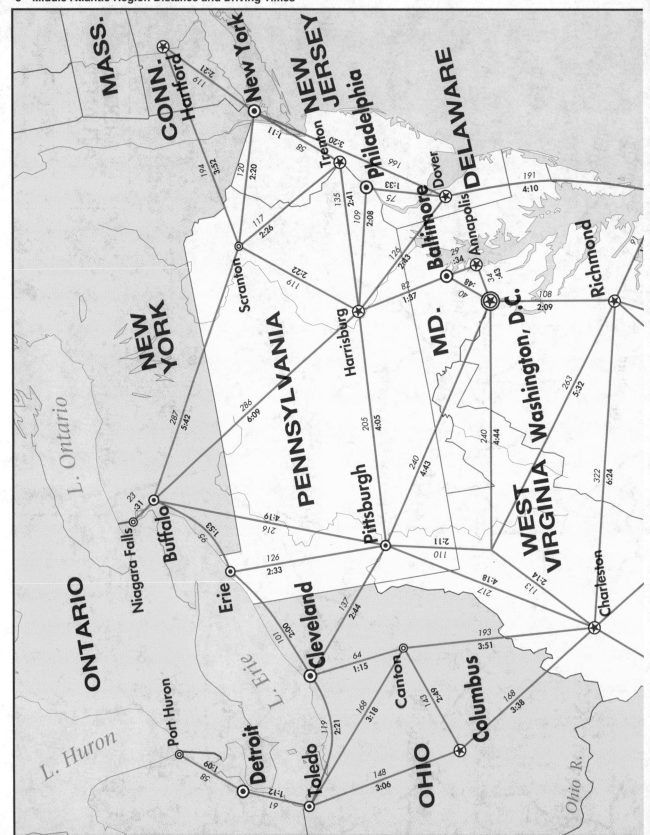

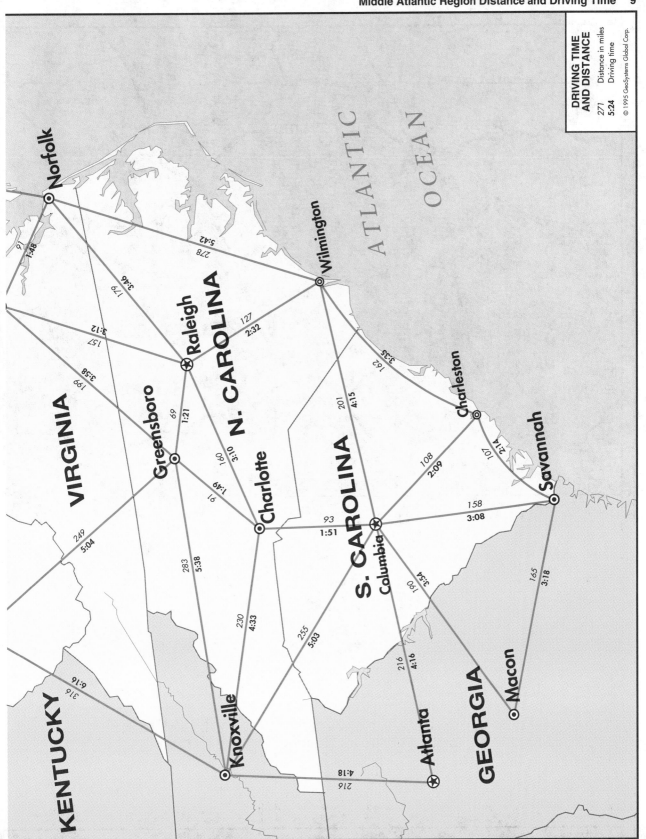

ATLANTIC

OCEAN

Norfolk

Wilmington

91
1:48

278
5:42

179
3:46

157
3:12

199
3:58

Raleigh

N. CAROLINA

127
2:32

Charleston

162
3:35

201
4:15

VIRGINIA

Greensboro

69
1:21

90
3:10

108
2:09

107
2:14

Savannah

Charlotte

91
1:49

93
1:51

158
3:08

S. CAROLINA

Columbia

249
5:04

283
5:38

160
3:54

165
3:18

230
4:33

255
5:03

216
4:16

Macon

KENTUCKY

316
6:16

GEORGIA

Knoxville

216
4:18

Atlanta

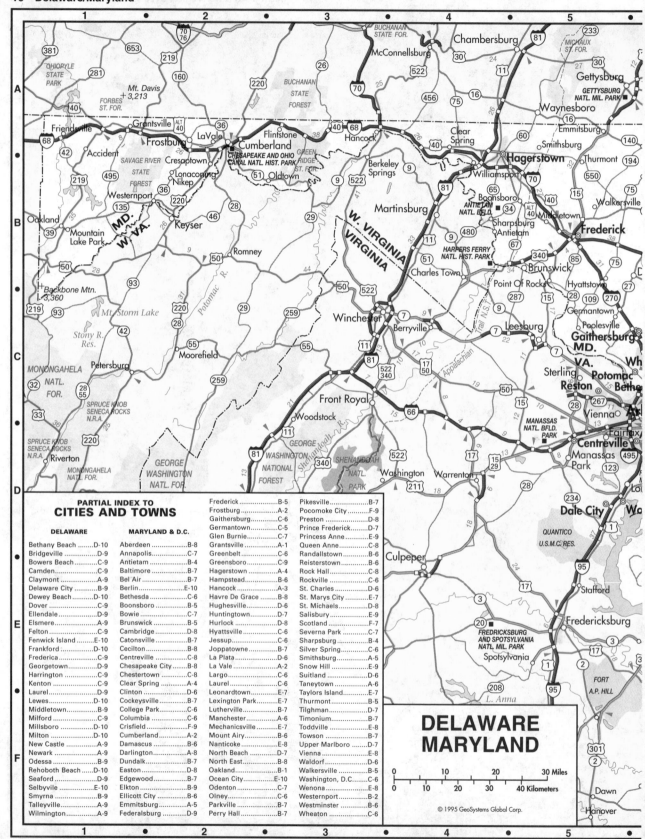

DELAWARE
MARYLAND

0   10   20   30 Miles

0 10 20 30 40 Kilometers

© 1995 GeoSystems Global Corp.

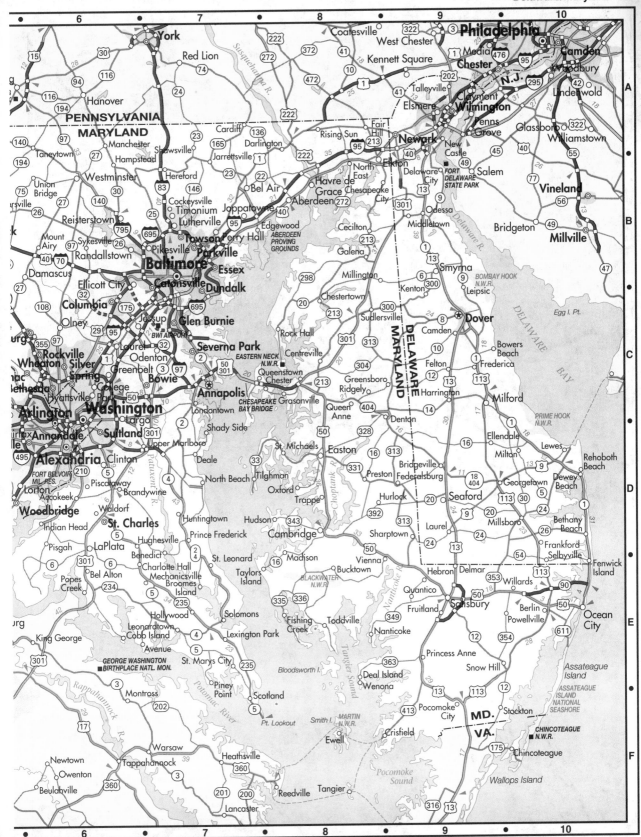

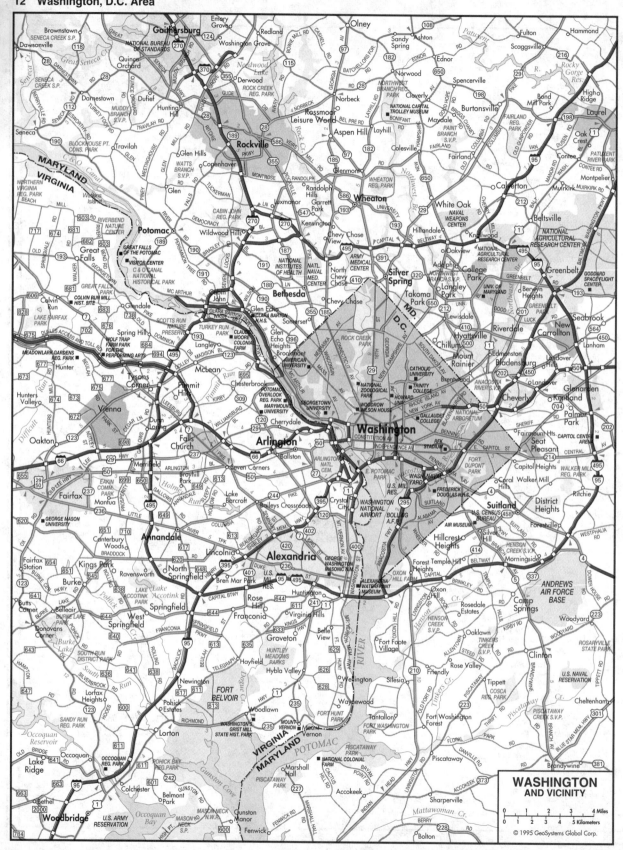

WASHINGTON AND VICINITY

0 1 2 3 4 Miles
0 1 2 3 4 5 Kilometers

© 1995 GeoSystems Global Corp.

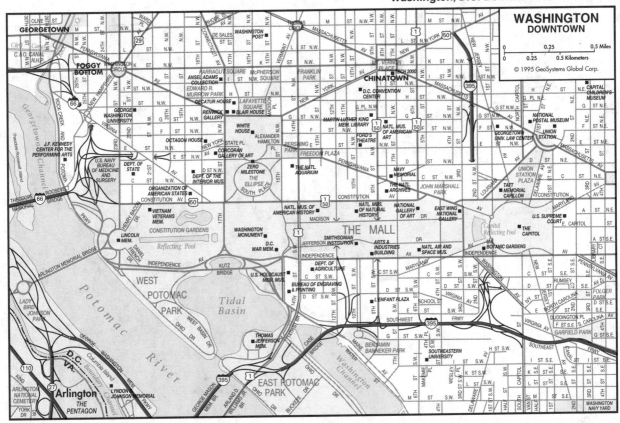

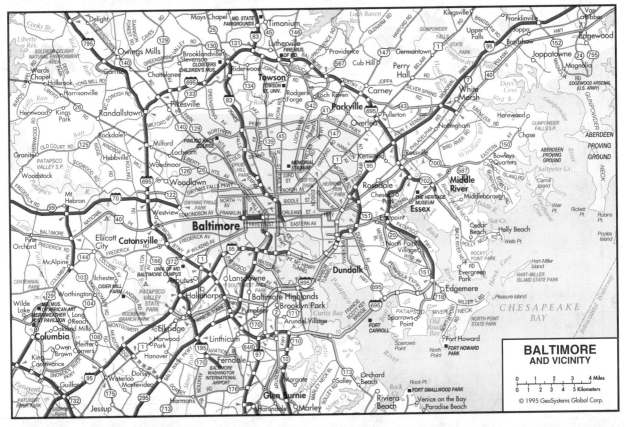

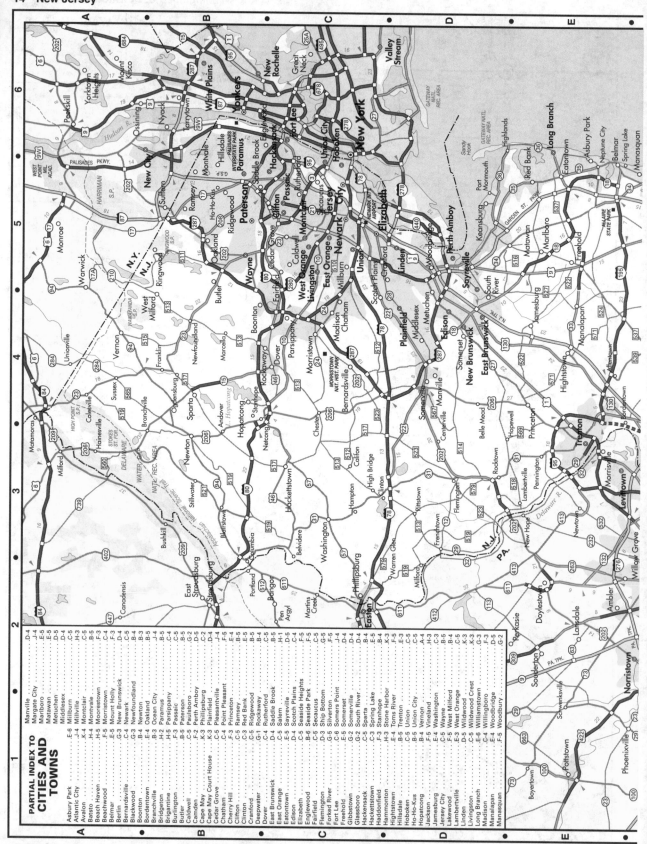

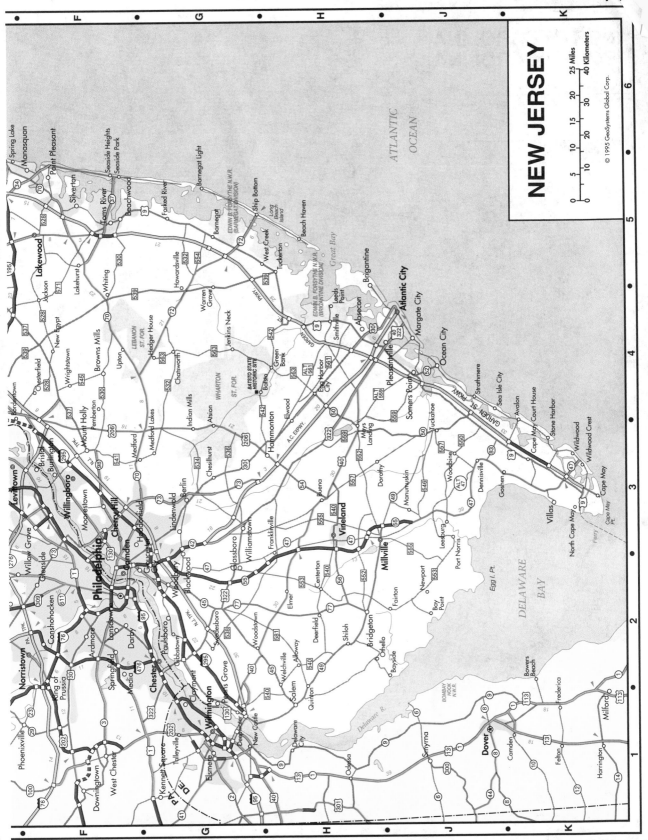

NEW JERSEY

25 Miles
40 Kilometers

© 1995 GeoSystems Global Corp.

ATLANTIC OCEAN

DELAWARE BAY

Great Bay

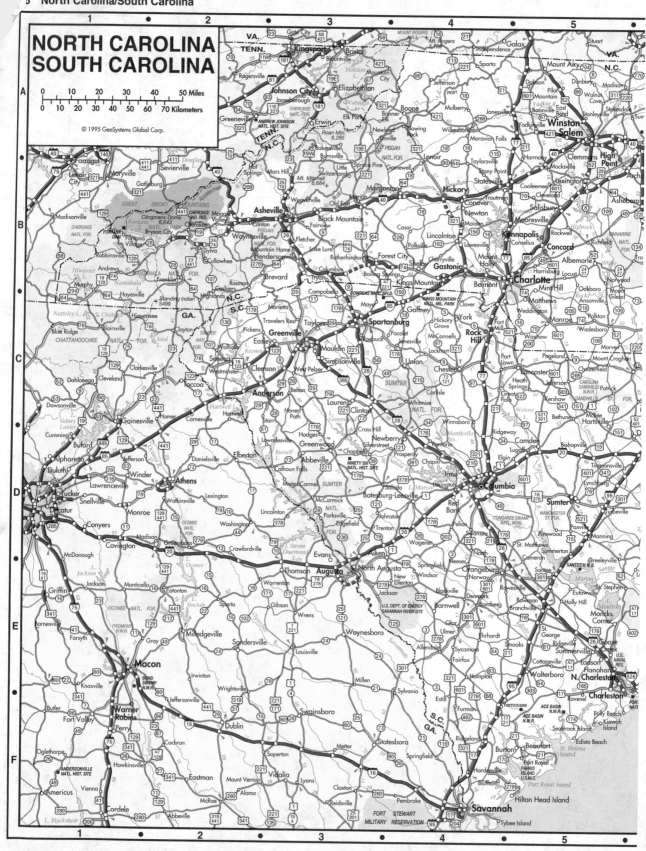

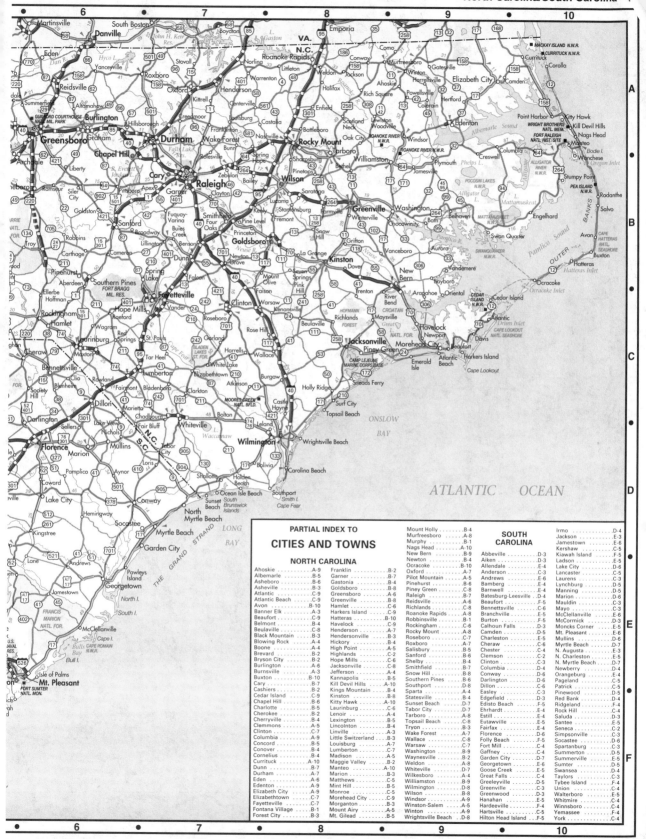

PARTIAL INDEX TO CITIES AND TOWNS

NORTH CAROLINA

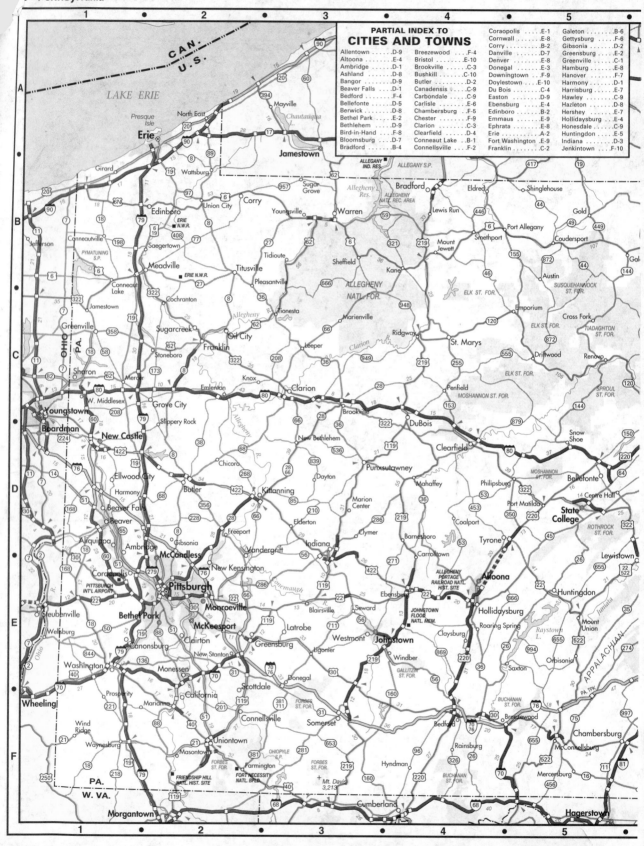

PENNSYLVANIA

0 10 20 30 40 50 Miles

0 10 20 30 40 50 60 70 Kilometers

© 1995 GeoSystems Global Corp.

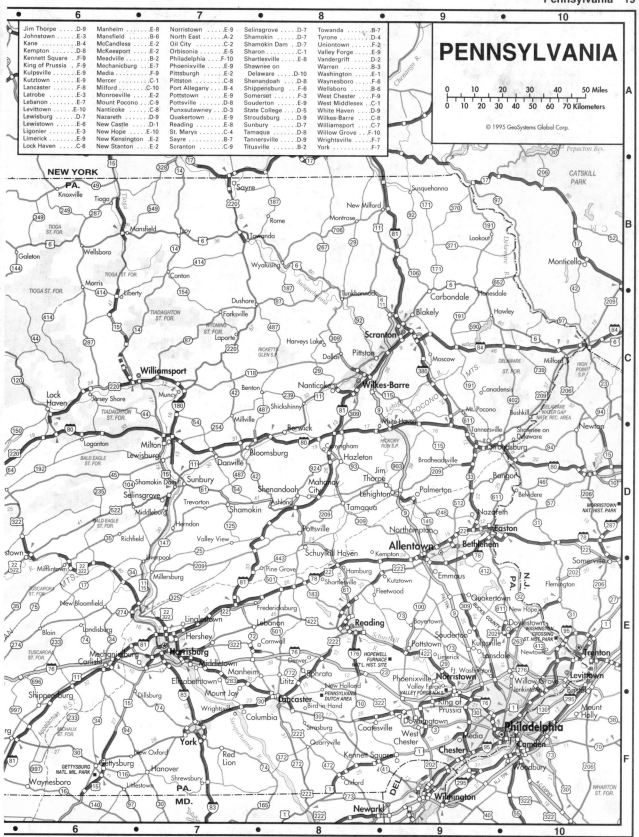

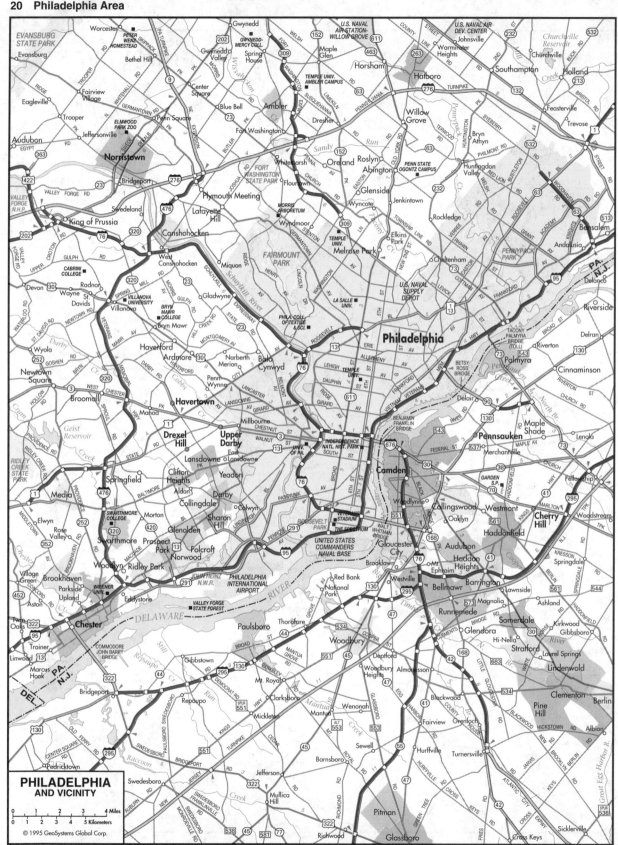

PHILADELPHIA
AND VICINITY

0 1 2 3 4 Miles
0 1 2 3 4 5 Kilometers

© 1995 GeoSystems Global Corp.

PHILADELPHIA
DOWNTOWN

0   0.1   0.2 miles
0   0.1   0.2   0.3 Kilometers

© 1995 GeoSystems Global Corp.

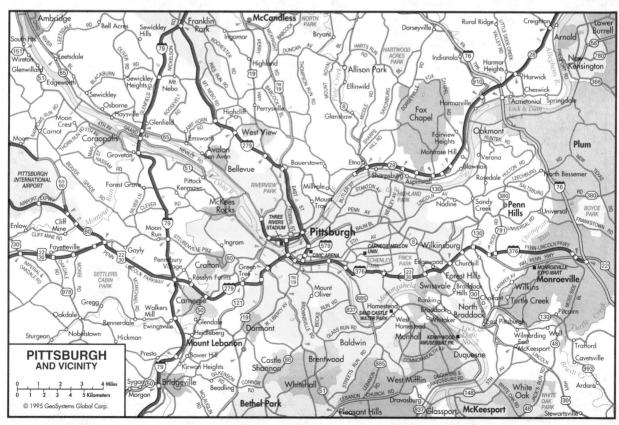

PITTSBURGH
AND VICINITY

0   1   2   3   4 Miles
0   1   2   3   4   5 Kilometers

© 1995 GeoSystems Global Corp.

VIRGINIA
WEST VIRGINIA

0 10 20 30 40 50 Miles
0 10 20 30 40 50 60 70 Kilometers

© 1995 GeoSystems Global Corp.

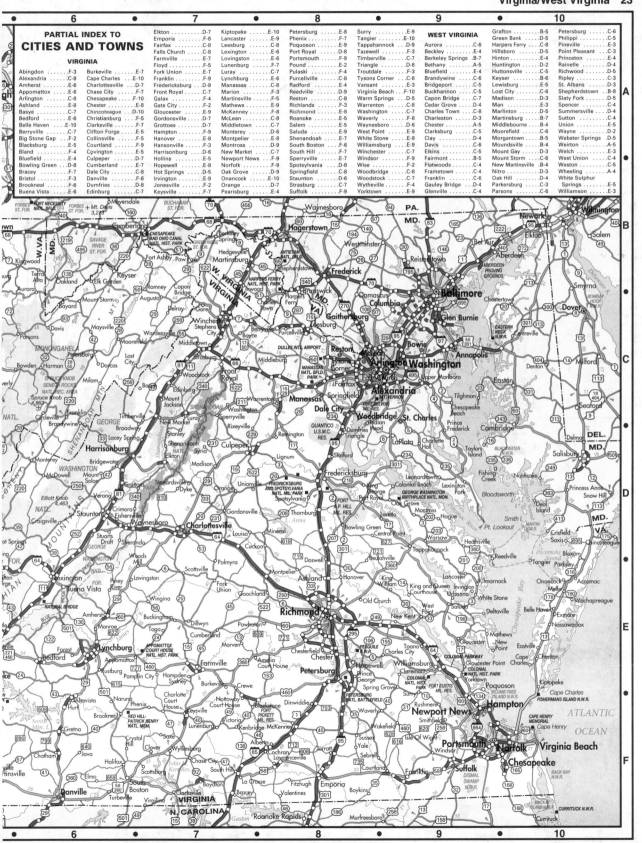

PARTIAL INDEX TO CITIES AND TOWNS

VIRGINIA

Abingdon	F-3
Alexandria	C-8
Amherst	E-6
Appomattox	E-6
Arlington	C-8
Ashland	E-8
Basye	C-7
Bedford	E-6
Belle Haven	E-10
Berryville	C-8
Big Stone Gap	F-2
Blacksburg	E-5
Bland	E-4
Bluefield	E-4
Bowling Green	D-8
Bracey	F-7
Bristol	F-3
Brookneal	F-6
Buena Vista	E-6
Burkeville	E-7
Cape Charles	E-10
Chase City	F-7
Chesapeake	F-10
Chester	E-8
Chincoteague	D-10
Christiansburg	F-5
Clarksville	F-7
Clifton Forge	E-5
Collinsville	F-5
Courtland	F-9
Covington	D-7
Culpeper	D-7
Cumberland	E-7
Dale City	C-8
Danville	F-6
Dumfries	D-8
Edinburg	C-7
Elkton	D-7
Emporia	F-8
Fairfax	C-8
Falls Church	C-8
Farmville	E-7
Floyd	F-5
Fork Union	E-7
Franklin	F-9
Fredericksburg	C-7
Front Royal	C-7
Galax	F-4
Gate City	F-2
Gloucester	E-9
Gordonsville	D-7
Grottoes	D-7
Hampton	F-9
Hanover	E-8
Hansonville	F-3
Harrisonburg	D-6
Hollins	E-5
Hopewell	E-8
Hot Springs	E-9
Irvington	E-9
Jonesville	F-2
Keysville	F-7
Kiptopeke	E-10
Lancaster	E-9
Leesburg	C-8
Lexington	E-6
Lovingston	E-6
Lunenburg	F-7
Luray	D-7
Lynchburg	E-6
Manassas	C-8
Marion	F-3
Martinsville	F-5
Mathews	E-9
McKenney	F-8
McLean	C-8
Middletown	C-7
Monterey	D-6
Montpelier	E-7
Montross	D-8
New Market	C-7
Newport News	F-9
Norfolk	F-9
Oak Grove	D-9
Onancock	E-10
Orange	D-7
Pearisburg	E-4
Petersburg	E-8
Phenix	F-7
Poquoson	F-9
Port Royal	D-8
Portsmouth	F-9
Pound	F-2
Pulaski	F-4
Purcellville	C-8
Radford	E-4
Reedville	D-9
Reston	C-8
Richlands	F-3
Richmond	E-8
Roanoke	E-5
Salem	E-5
Saluda	E-9
Shenandoah	D-7
South Boston	F-6
South Hill	F-7
Sperryville	D-7
Springfield	C-8
Staunton	D-6
Strasburg	C-7
Suffolk	F-9
Surry	E-9
Tangier	E-10
Tappahannock	D-9
Tazewell	F-3
Timberville	C-7
Triangle	D-8
Troutdale	F-3
Tysons Corner	C-8
Vansant	E-3
Virginia Beach	F-10
Warm Springs	D-5
Warrenton	C-8
Washington	C-7
Waverly	F-8
Waynesboro	D-6
West Point	E-9
White Stone	E-9
Williamsburg	E-9
Winchester	C-7
Windsor	F-9
Wise	F-2
Woodbridge	C-8
Woodstock	C-7
Wytheville	F-4
Yorktown	E-9

WEST VIRGINIA

Aurora	C-6
Beckley	D-4
Berkeley Springs	B-7
Bethany	A-5
Bluefield	E-4
Brandywine	C-5
Bridgeport	C-5
Buckhannon	C-5
Capon Bridge	C-7
Cedar Grove	D-4
Charles Town	C-8
Charleston	D-3
Chester	A-5
Clarksburg	C-5
Clay	D-4
Davis	C-5
Elkins	C-5
Fairmont	B-5
Flatwoods	C-5
Frametown	C-4
Franklin	C-5
Gauley Bridge	D-4
Glenville	C-4
Grafton	B-5
Green Bank	D-5
Harpers Ferry	C-8
Hillsboro	D-5
Hinton	D-5
Huntington	D-2
Huttonsville	C-5
Keyser	B-6
Lewisburg	E-5
Lost City	C-7
Madison	D-3
Man	E-3
Marlinton	D-5
Martinsburg	B-7
Middlebourne	B-4
Moorefield	C-6
Morgantown	B-5
Moundsville	B-4
Mount Gay	D-3
Mount Storm	C-6
New Martinsville	B-4
Nitro	D-3
Oak Hill	D-4
Parkersburg	C-3
Parsons	C-6
Petersburg	C-6
Philippi	C-5
Pineville	E-3
Point Pleasant	C-3
Princeton	E-4
Rainelle	D-4
Richwood	D-5
Ripley	C-3
St. Albans	D-3
Shepherdstown	B-8
Slaty Fork	D-5
Spencer	C-4
Summersville	D-4
Sutton	C-4
Union	E-5
Wayne	D-2
Webster Springs	D-5
Weirton	A-5
Welch	E-3
West Union	C-4
Weston	C-4
Wheeling	A-4
White Sulphur Springs	E-5
Williamson	E-3

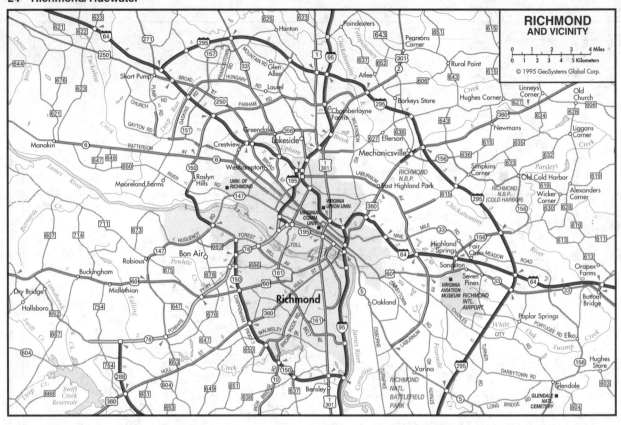

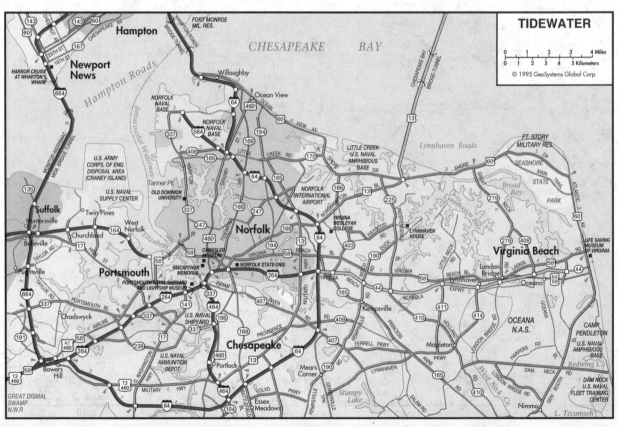

Introduction

The *Mobil Travel Guide* offers complete travel planning information for recreational and business travelers alike. Whether you are planning an extended trip, getting away for the weekend or dining close to home, you will find all the current detailed information you need to know in this guide. By planning ahead, you can save money, and when you arrive you won't waste valuable time deciding what to do.

An outstanding feature of the *Mobil Travel Guide* is its valuable quality ratings and information on more than 20,000 lodgings and restaurants. **There is no charge to an establishment for inclusion in** *Mobil Travel Guide* **publications.**

The 7 regional editions of the *Mobil Travel Guide* cover the 48 contiguous states and selected cities in 8 Canadian provinces. In each book the information is organized in the same easy-to-follow format: The states are arranged alphabetically and begin with a general introduction covering vital statistics, historical and geographical data, hunting, fishing, and seat belt regulations, visitor centers, and listings of state recreational areas, national forests, National Park Service Areas, interstate highways and ski areas (where applicable).

Cities are arranged alphabetically within each state. Maps are discussed below. Under the bold rule you will find population figures taken from the most recent census of the Bureau of Census, Department of Commerce. You will also find the city's elevation, area code, and zip code. Following city names are brief descriptions of the city, a "What to See and Do" section and listings of annual and seasonal events. Some 16,000 attractions and more than 5,500 events are highlighted. A mailing address and phone number for the local chamber of commerce or office of tourism is given whenever possible, as are cross-references, for example (See Havana, Petersburg), to nearby towns and cities with either additional things to see and do or with accommodations and/or restaurants. The quality-rated listings of lodgings and restaurants follow this information.

The Introduction below explains the features of the guide in more detail and provides useful travel advice.

Please keep in mind that every effort has been made to ensure that the information in this publication was accurate at the time it was printed. Neither Fodor's Travel Publications, Inc., nor Mobil Corporation can be held responsible for changes that occurred after publication. We regret any inconvenience you may incur due to improper information being listed.

Rating System

The star symbols and check marks are used in rating hotels, motor hotels, lodges, motels, inns, resorts, and restaurants:

★ **Good, better than average**
★★ **Very good**
★★★ **Excellent**
★★★★ **Outstanding—worth a special trip**
★★★★★ **One of the best in the country**
✔ **In addition, an unusually good value, relatively inexpensive**

Listing Symbols

Ⓟ Pegasus, the Flying Red Horse, is a trademark of Mobil Oil Corporation. This symbol next to a town name indicates the presence of one or more Mobil service stations in the area.

Ⅾ Disabled facilities available

🐾 Pets allowed

🎣 Fishing on property

🏇 Horseback riding on premises

⛷ Snow skiing nearby

🏌 Golf, 9-hole minimum, on premises or privileges within 10 miles

🎾 Tennis court(s) on premises or privileges within 5 miles

🏊 Swimming on premises

🏋 Exercise equipment or room on premises

🏃 Jogging on premises

✈ Major commercial airport within 2 miles of premises

🚭 No-smoking rooms

SC Senior citizen rates

🔥 Smoke detector and/or sprinkler system

Note: During the inspection of establishments, field representatives identify fire protection equipment in lodgings. The inspection does not extend to every room nor does it determine whether the equipment is working properly. The 🔥 symbol appearing at the end of a lodging listing indicates the presence of smoke detectors and/or sprinkler systems. This symbol does not appear in our restaurant listings because the presence of this equipment is assumed. Travelers wishing to gain more information on fire protection systems at properties should contact the establishment directly to verify the installation and working condition of their systems.

Attraction Symbols

Each attraction has a fee code that translates as follows:

Free	=	no charge
¢	=	up to $2
¢¢	=	$2.01 to $5
¢¢¢	=	$5.01 to $10
¢¢¢¢	=	$10.01 to $15
¢¢¢¢¢	=	over $15

Credit Cards

The major credit cards honored by each establishment are indicated by initials at the end of the listing. When credit cards are not accepted, the listing will say "no cr cds accepted." Please remember that Mobil Corporation credit cards cannot be used for payment of meals and room charges. Be sure the credit cards you plan to use in your travels are current and will not expire before your trip is over. If you should lose one, report the loss immediately.

The following letters indicate credit cards that are accepted by the listed establishments:

A-American Express
C-Carte Blanche
D-Diners Club
DS-Discover
ER-En Route
MC-MasterCard
V-Visa
JCB-Japanese Credit Bureau

Discount Coupons

The *Mobil Travel Guide* is pleased to offer discounts from major companies for products and services. These coupons can be found at the back of this book.

The *Mobil Travel Guide* and Fodor's Travel Publications, Inc., may not be held responsible for the failure of any participating company to honor these discounts

How to Read the Lodging & Restaurant Listings

Each listing of a motel, lodge, motor hotel, hotel, inn and resort gives the quality rating, name, address, directions (when there is

no street address), phone number (local and 800), room rates, seasons open (if not year-round) and number and type of rooms available. Facsimile (FAX) numbers appear immediately following an establishment's phone number for properties offering this service to all of their guests.

Listings in major cities include the neighborhood and/or directions from downtown as an aid to finding your way around. Maps showing these neighborhoods can be found immediately following the city name. Geographic descriptions of the neighborhoods are given under the "City Neighborhoods" heading. These are followed by a list of restaurants arranged by neighborhood, in alphabetical order. The listings also include information on recreational and dining facilities on or adjacent to the establishment and credit card information. Some hotels and motor hotels offer *LUXURY LEVELS*. You will find specific information on these special accommodations within the listing.

Restaurant listings give the quality rating, name, address, directions (when there is no street address), phone number, hours and days of operation, price range for each meal served and cuisine specialties. Additionally, special features such as chef ownership, ambience, entertainment, and credit card information are noted.

When a listing is located in a town that does not have its own city heading, it will appear under the city nearest its location. In these cases, the address and town appear in parentheses immediately following the name of the establishment.

When looking for a specific establishment, use the index at the back of this guide. You will find the establishment name, the city and state under which it is listed, and also the page number.

In large cities, lodgings located within 5 miles of major, commercial airports are listed under a separate "Airport" heading, following the city listings.

Mobil Travel Guide makes every effort to select a variety of lodging and dining establishments in a given locale. Occasionally, an establishment may go out of business or change ownership just after our publication deadline. By calling ahead for reservations, you can avoid the disappointment of discovering a closed or changed establishment. Space limitations necessitate the omission of many fine places; however, no adverse criticism is implied or should be inferred.

Neither Fodor's Travel Publications, Inc., nor Mobil Corporation can be held responsible for changes in prices, name, management or deterioration in services. There is no contractual agreement between management and the *Mobil Travel Guide* to guarantee prices or services. **There is no charge to an establishment for inclusion in *Mobil Travel Guide* publications.**

Motels and Lodges

Motels and lodges provide accommodations in low-rise structures with rooms easily accessible to parking areas. They have outdoor room entry and small, functional lobbies. Shops and businesses will be found only in the higher-rated properties.

Service is often limited and dining may not be offered in lower-rated motels and lodges. However, higher-rated properties will offer such services as bellmen, room service and restaurants serving three meals daily.

Lodges differ from motels primarily in their emphasis on outdoor recreational activities and in location. They are often found in resort and rural areas rather than in major cities and along highways.

Motor Hotels

Motor hotels offer the convenience of motels as well as many of the services of hotels. They range from low-rise structures offering limited services to multistoried buildings with a wide range of services and facilities. Dual building entry, elevators, inside hallways and parking areas near access doors are some of the features of a motor hotel.

Lobbies offer sitting areas and 24-hour desk and switchboard services. Often bellman and valet services are found in motor hotels as well as restaurants serving three meals a day. Expanded recreational facilities and more than one restaurant will be available in higher-rated properties. Because the following features and services apply to most establishments, they are not shown in the listing of motels and motor hotels:

- Year-round operation with a single rate structure
- European plan (meals not included in room rate)
- Bathroom with tub and/or shower in each room
- Air-conditioned/heated, often with individual room control
- Cots
- Daily maid service
- Free parking
- Phones in rooms
- Elevators

The distinction between motor hotels and hotels in metropolitan areas is minor.

Hotels

To be categorized as a hotel, the establishment must have most of the following facilities and services: multiple floors, a restaurant and/or coffee shop, elevators, room service, bellhops, valet services, spacious lobby and some recreational facilities.

A hotel offers its guests a broad spectrum of lodging experiences. Because the following features and services apply to most establishments, they are not shown in the listing:

- Year-round operation with a single rate structure
- European plan (meals not included in room rate)
- Bathroom with tub and/or shower in each room
- Air-conditioned/heated, often with individual room control
- Daily maid service
- Valet service (one-day laundry/cleaning service)
- Room service during hours restaurant is open

- Elevator
- Phones in rooms
- Bellhops
- Oversize beds available

LUXURY LEVEL: Many hotels offer their guests increased luxury accommodations on floors or towers that operate as a separate unit from the main establishment.

A boldface title, *LUXURY LEVEL(S),* follows the principal hotel listing with information pertinent to that level. There is no separate rating for this listing; the rating given applies to the overall hotel.

The criteria used to determine the qualifications for this distinctive listing are:

1. A minimum of one entire floor of the total structure must be devoted to the luxury level.

2. Management must provide no less than three of these four services:

- Separate check-in and check-out services
- Concierge services
- Private lounge
- Private elevator service (key access)

Complimentary breakfast and snacks are commonly offered on these floors as well as upscale amenities and services.

Resorts

Resorts are establishments specializing in stays of three days or more. They usually offer American Plan and/or housekeeping accommodations, with an emphasis on recreational facilities, and often provide the services of a social director.

Food services are of primary importance at a resort. Guests must be able to obtain three meals a day on the premises or be provided with grocery stores to enable them to obtain food for meal preparation without leaving the premises.

When horseback riding is indicated, phone ahead to inquire about English saddle availability; Western style is assumed.

Inns

Frequently thought of as a small hotel, an inn is a place of homelike comfort and warm hospitality. It is often a structure of historic significance, located in an equally interesting setting.

Meals are a special occasion at an inn and frequently tea and drinks are served in the late afternoon. Rooms are usually individually decorated, featuring antiques or furnishings representative of the locale. Phones, bathrooms, and TVs may not be available in every room.

Guest Ranches

Like resorts, guest ranches specialize in stays of three days or more. Guest ranches also offer meal plans and extensive outdoor activities such as horseback riding. There are stables and trails on the ranch property; daily, expert instruction is part of the program. Many guest ranches are working ranches, ranging from casual to rustic, and guests are encouraged to participate in various aspects of ranch life. Eating is often family style and may also include cookouts as part of morning, midday or evening trail rides. Phone ahead to inquire about English saddle availability; Western style is assumed.

Cottage Colonies

Cottage colonies are housekeeping cottages and cabins that are usually found in recreational areas. When dining or recreational facilities are available on the premises, you will find it noted in the listing.

Restaurants

Unless otherwise specified, restaurants listed:

- Are open daily, year-round
- Offer chiefly American cooking

Prices for an *a la carte* menu are given for entrees or main dishes only. Prices for *semi-a la carte* meals include vegetable, salad, soup, appetizer or other accompaniments to the main dish. *Table d'hôte* means a full meal for a stated price, with no *a la carte* selections available. *Prix fixe* indicates a fixed price for any meal on the menu.

By carefully reading the detailed restaurant information and comparing prices, you can easily determine whether the restaurant is formal and elegant or informal and comfortable for families. When children's meals are offered, you will find it noted in the listing.

Unrated Dining Spots

Chosen for their unique atmosphere, specialized menu and local flavor, restaurants listed under the Unrated Dining Spots category appear without a *Mobil Travel Guide* rating. However, they have been inspected by our team of field representatives and meet our high standards of cleanliness and maintenance.

These establishments feature a wide range of dining, from pizza, ice cream, sandwiches and health food to cafeterias and English tea service in fine hotels. They often offer extraordinary values, quick service and regional flavor and are worth a visit when traveling to a city offering these special listings. Unrated Dining Spots can be found after restaurant listings in many cities.

Prices and Taxes

All prices quoted in *Mobil Travel Guide* publications are expected to be in effect at the time of publication and during the entire year; however, prices cannot be guaranteed.

In some localities there may be short-term price variations because of special events or holidays. Whenever possible, these price changes are noted. Certain resorts have compli-

cated rate structures that vary with the time of year; it's a good idea to contact the management to confirm specific rates.

State and city sales taxes as well as special room taxes can increase your room rates as much as 25% per day. We are unable to bring this specific information into the listings, but we strongly urge that you ask about these taxes when placing reservations with establishments. Another charge that is often overlooked by travelers is that of telephone usage. Frequently, hotels charge a service fee for unanswered phone calls and credit card calls as well as long distance calls. It is advised that you read the information offered by the establishment before placing phone calls from your room. It is not unusual for a hotel to send bills for telephone calls to your home after you have checked out. Be certain to take the time to read your bill carefully before checking out. You will not be expected to pay for charges that were not explained in the printed matter given to you at the time of check-in. The use of public telephones in hotel lobbies should not be overlooked since the financial benefits may outweigh the inconvenience.

Explaining the Ratings

The *Mobil Travel Guide* has been rating motels, lodges, motor hotels, hotels, inns, resorts and restaurants since the first edition was published in 1958. For years it was the only guidebook to provide such ratings on a national basis, and *Mobil Travel Guide* remains one of the few guidebooks to rate restaurants across the country.

The rating categories, ★ through ★★★★★, apply nationally. The rating for each establishment—motel, lodge, motor hotel, hotel, inn, resort, guest ranch, or restaurant—is measured against others of the same type. The criteria for rating accommodations are related to the number and quality of facilities, guest services, luxury of appointments and attitude and professionalism of staff and management. Restaurant evaluations emphasize quality of food, preparation, presentation, freshness of ingredients, quality of service, attitude and professionalism of staff/management. Each type of establishment is viewed also in terms of its own style, unique characteristics, decor and ambience. Climate, historic, cultural and artistic variations representative of regional differences are also major factors in each rating. No rating is ever final and, since each is subject to annual review, each establishment must continue to earn its rating and has a chance to improve it as well.

Every establishment listed in *Mobil Travel Guide* publications is inspected by experienced field representatives who submit detailed reports to the editorial offices. From these reports, the editors extract information for listings and ascertain that establishments to be recommended are clean, well-maintained, well-managed and above average.

Ratings are based upon the inspection reports, written evaluations of staff members who stay and dine anonymously at establishments throughout the year, and an extensive review of guest comments received by the *Mobil Travel Guide*.

Every effort is made to assure that ratings are fair and accurate; the designated ratings are published to serve as an aid to travelers and should not be used for any other purpose.

A further rating designation exists: <u>Unrated</u>. When major changes have occurred during the one-year period prior to publication, there will be no star rating. These changes may be in management, ownership, general manager and master chef. If an establishment is undergoing major renovation/refurbishment or has been in operation less than one year, it will also appear unrated. The decision to list an establishment "unrated" is the responsibility of the Rating Committee.

Good Value Check Mark

The check mark (✔) designation appearing in front of the star rating of an establishment listing indicates "an unusually good value, relatively inexpensive." It will appear with the listing in the following manner:

✔ ★ FODOR'S MOTOR INN

Lodging establishments rated with a good value check mark have been determined to be clean and well-maintained, offering some appointments such as room phones, free television, pools and breakfast on or adjacent to the premises, at economical prices. Restaurants rated with a good value check mark have been determined to be clean and well-maintained, offering good food at economical prices.

Because prevailing rates vary regionally, we are able to be more selective in our good value rated establishments in some areas than in others. However, you will find a wide range of these properties to visit in all locales.

In major cities and resort areas, prices tend to be higher than in outlying areas. The following price range has been used to determine those properties awarded the good value check mark:

Major City and Resort Area Listings

Lodging—single, average $75–$90 per night
double, average $90–$105 per night

Restaurants—lunch, average $18, complete meal
dinner, exclusive of beverages and gratuities, average $30, complete meal

Local Area Listings

Lodging—single, average $45–$55 per night
double, average $55–$70 per night

Restaurants—lunch, average $9, complete meal
dinner, exclusive of beverages and gratuities, average $18, complete meal

Terms and Abbreviations

The following terms and abbreviations are used consistently throughout the listings.

AP   American plan (lodging plus all meals)

Bar   Liquor, wine and beer are served at a bar or in a cocktail lounge and usually with meals unless otherwise indicated (e.g., "wine, beer")

Ck-in; ck-out   Check-in time; check-out time

Coin lndry   Self-service laundry

Complete meal   Soup and/or salad, entree, dessert and non-alcoholic beverage

Continental bkfst   Usually coffee and a roll or doughnut

Cover   "Cover" is a fee added to the actual cost of food and drink in restaurants

D   Followed by a price; indicates room rate for two people in one room (one or two beds; charge may be higher if two double beds are offered)

Each addl   Extra charge for each additional person beyond the stated number of persons for a given price

Early   In referring to season openings or closings, approximately the first third of a month (May 1 to May 10); check with management for exact date

Early-bird dinner   A meal served at specified hours, at a reduced price

EP   European plan (lodging only)

Exc   Except

Exercise equipt   Two or more pieces of exercise equipment on the premises

Exercise rm   Both exercise equipment and room, with an instructor on the premises

FAX   Facsimile machines available to all guests

Golf privileges   Privileges at a course within 10 miles

Hols   Holidays

In-rm movies   Video cassette player available for use with video tapes

Kit. or kits.   A kitchen or kitchenette with stove or microwave, sink, and refrigerator that is either part of the room or a separate room. If the kitchen is not fully equipped, the listing will indicate "no equipt" or "some equipt"

Late   In referring to season openings or closings, approximately the last third of a month (May 21 to May 31); check with management for exact date

MAP   Modified American plan (lodging plus two meals)

Mid   In referring to season openings or closings, approximately the middle third of a month (May 11 to May 20); check with management for exact date

No elvtr   In a hotel with more than two stories, it is assumed there is an elevator, so it is not noted; only its absence is noted

No phones   Only the absence of phones is noted

Parking   There is a parking lot on the premises

Private club   A cocktail lounge or bar available to members and their guests (in motels and hotels where these clubs exist, registered guests can usually use the club as guests of the management; frequently the same is true of restaurants)

Prix fixe   A full meal for a stated price; usually one price is quoted

Res   Reservations

S   Followed by a price; indicates room rate for one person

Serv bar   A service bar, where drinks are prepared for dining patrons only

Serv charge   Service charge is the amount added to the restaurant check in lieu of a tip

Snow skiing downhill/x-country   Downhill and/or cross-country skiing within 20 miles of property

Table d'hôte   A full meal for a stated price dependent upon entree selection

Tennis privileges   Privileges at tennis courts within 5 miles

TV   Indicates color television; B/W indicates black-and-white television

Under 18 free   Children under a specific age not charged if staying in room with one or both parents

Valet parking   An attendant is available to park and retrieve a car

Maps and Map Coordinates

There is a map of each state in the front of the *Mobil Travel Guide.* Following each city or town listing in the guide are map coordinates (for example, Boston, B-4). There are corresponding coordinates on the appropriate state map. You'll find neighborhood and airport maps in the text of selected larger cities.

What to See and Do

This section appears at the beginning of each city and town listing and provides concise descriptions of notable attractions in the area—museums, art galleries, amusement parks, universities, historic sites and houses, plantations, churches, state parks, ski areas and so on. Municipal parks, public tennis courts, swimming pools, golf courses, and small educational institutions are generally excluded, since these are common to most towns. *Mobil Travel Guide* editors strive for a balance of recreational, athletic, cultural, historical and educational activities.

Following the name of the attraction is the street address or location. Directions are given from the center of the town under which the attraction is listed; please note that this may not be the town in which the attraction is located. For instance, directions for an attraction listed under Springfield may state "225 W Hawthorne, 12 mi N off US 42 in Zionsville."

Area codes are not provided for each attraction if the code is the same as that shown in the city statistics. Similarly, zip codes are given only if they differ from the one listed in the city statistics.

Next comes a brief description of the attraction, the months and days it is open, facilities for travelers with disabilities (if any), phone number and admission costs.

Events

Immediately following the "What To See and Do" section is the name, address and phone number of the local chamber of commerce or tourist bureau you may contact for further information. Following this are listings of annual, seasonal, and special events. An annual event is one that is held every year for a period of usually no longer than a week to 10 days. A seasonal event is one that may or may not be annual and that is held for a number of weeks or months in the year, such as horse racing, summer theater, concert or opera festivals, and professional sports. Special event listings occur infrequently and mark a certain date or event, such as a centennial or other commemorative celebration.

Additional Visitor Information

In larger cities, you are given the names of magazines or guides to the city, location of visitor centers, information on public transportation, and other helpful information.

Information for Travelers with Disabilities

The *Mobil Travel Guide* symbol Ⓓ shown in accommodation and restaurant listings indicates establishments that are at least partially accessible to people with mobility problems. Facilities providing for the needs of travelers with disabilities are noted in the listings.

The *Mobil Travel Guide* Criteria for accessibility are unique to our publication and were designed to meet the standards developed by our editorial staff. Please do not confuse them with the universal symbol for wheelchair accessibility. Travelers wishing to gain more information on facilities and services for travelers with disabilities should contact the establishments directly.

When the Ⓓ symbol appears following a listing, the establishment is equipped with facilities to accommodate persons in wheelchairs as well as on crutches and the aged in need of easy access to doorways and restroom facilities. Persons with severe mobility problems, as well as the hearing and visually impaired, should not assume establishments bearing our symbol will offer facilities to meet their needs. We suggest travelers with disabilities phone an establishment before their visit to ascertain if their particular needs will be met.

The following facilities must be available at all lodging properties bearing our Ⓓ symbol:

Public Areas

- ISA-designated parking near access ramps
- Level or ramped at entryways to buildings
- Swinging entryway doors minimum 3'-0"
- Restrooms on main level with room to operate a wheelchair; handrails at commode areas
- Elevators equipped with grab bars and lowered control buttons
- Restaurants with accessible doorways; restrooms with room to operate wheelchair; handrails at commode areas

Rooms

- Minimum 3'-0" width entryway to rooms
- Low-pile carpet
- Telephone at bedside and in bathroom
- Bed placed at wheelchair height
- Minimum 3'-0" width doorway to bathroom
- Bath with open sink—no cabinet; room to operate wheelchair
- Handrails at commode areas; tub handrails
- Wheelchair accessible "peep" hole in room entry door
- Wheelchair accessible closet rods and shelves

Restaurants

- ISA-designated parking beside access ramps
- Level or ramped front entryways to building
- Tables to accommodate wheelchairs
- Main-floor restrooms; minimum 3'-0" width entryway
- Restrooms with room to operate wheelchair; handrails at commode areas

Tips for Travel

The passage of the Americans with Disabilities Act (ADA) of 1990 means that all hotels and motels in the US have to make their facilities and services accessible to all guests. Although this law went into effect early in 1992, it will take some time for the more than 40,000 hotels and motels to implement the renovation programs and make their facilities totally accessible to every guest.

Any facility opened after January 26, 1993, must be designed and built totally in accordance with ADA Accessibility Guidelines. This means that a certain percentage of the rooms must be accessible to guests who have mobility, vision, hearing or speech impairments. In addition, all public spaces must be accessible to all guests to use and enjoy.

While all existing hotels and motels will not be totally accessible, you can expect all properties to be aware of the ADA and to make efforts to accommodate the special needs of any guest who has a physical disability.

To get the kind of service you need and have a right to expect, do not hesitate when making a reservation to:

- Ask about the availability of accessible rooms, parking, entrances, restaurants, lounges or any other facilities that are important to you.
- Inquire about any special equipment, transportation or services you may need.
- Ask for details about the accessibility of the room. For example, do both the room entry and bathroom doors have 30" of clear width? Is there a 5' diameter turning space in the bedroom and bathroom? For the hearing impaired, are fire alarms indicated by blinking lights?

When your stay is over, fill out the guest comment card and let the management know about the facilities, equipment and services that worked for you and those that need to be improved.

Additional Publications

Fodor's *Great American Vacations for Travelers with Disabilities* ($18) covers 38 top US travel destinations, including parks, cities and popular tourist regions. It's available from bookstores or by calling 1-800/533-6478.

The most complete listing of published material for travelers with disabilities is available from *The Disability Bookshop,* Twin Peaks Press, PO Box 129, Vancouver, Washington 98666; phone 206/694-2462.

A comprehensive guidebook to the national parks is a 1992 publication, *Easy Access to National Parks: The Sierra Club Guide for People with Disabilities;* Sierra Club, distributed by Random, $16 (paperback). Local public libraries should have relevant books on travel for people with disabilities. Individuals should contact the reference librarian at their public library for assistance.

The Reference Section of the National Library Service for the Blind and Physically Handicapped (NLS), Library of Congress, provides information and resources for persons with mobility problems and hearing and vision impairments, as well as information about the NLS talking-book program. For further information, contact: Reference Section, National Library Service for the Blind and Physically Handicapped, Library of Congress, Washington, DC 20542; phone 202/707-9275 or 202/707-5100.

Travel Tips

Lodging

Many hotels in major metropolitan areas have special weekend package plans. These plans offer considerable savings on rooms and may include breakfast, cocktails and some meal discounts as well. Prices for these specials are not included because they change frequently throughout the year. We suggest you phone to obtain such information prior to your trip.

LUXURY LEVEL accommodations, which appear within some hotel and motor hotel listings, frequently offer good value because many of them provide breakfast, cocktails, newspapers and upgraded amenities in the price of the room.

Dining

Reservations are important at most major city restaurants. Many restaurants will ask you to confirm your reservation by calling back the day you are to dine. Should you fail to do so, your reservation will not be held for you.

In fine restaurants the pace is leisurely, the service is professional and the prices are above average. Most of the dishes are cooked to order, and patrons' requests for special preparation are handled graciously.

Four-Star and Five-Star establishments are usually quite expensive because they offer higher quality food, superior service and distinctive decor. Read the listing and see if they are open for lunch. While the lunch prices are considerably higher than those at other restaurants, you may still enjoy the ambience, service and cuisine of a famous establishment for about half the cost of a dinner.

"Early bird" dinners are popular in many parts of the country and offer considerable savings on dinner prices. Information on the availability of these dinners has been given to us by restaurant management, but we suggest you phone ahead and ask if they still offer this special plan.

Tipping

Lodgings: Doormen in major city hotels are usually given $1 for getting you into a cab. Bellmen expect $1 per bag, usually never less than a $2 tip if you have only one bag. Concierges are tipped according to the service they perform. Suggestions on sightseeing or restaurants, as well as making reservations for dining, are standard services often requiring no tip. However, when reservations are obtained at restaurants known to be difficult to get into, a gratuity of $5 should be considered. If theater or sporting event tickets are obtained, a tip is expected, often $5 to $10. Maids, often overlooked by guests, may be tipped $1 to $2 per each day of your stay.

Restaurants: Coffee shop and counter service wait staff are usually given 8 to 10 percent of the bill. In full service restaurants, 15 percent of the bill, before sales tax, is suggested. In fine dining restaurants, where the staff is large and share the gratuity, 18 to 20 percent is recommended. The number of restaurants adding service charges to the bill is increasing. Carefully review your bill to make certain an automatic gratuity was not charged.

Airports: Curbside luggage handlers expect $1 per bag. Car rental shuttle drivers who help with your luggage appreciate a $1 or $2 tip. **Remember, tipping is an expression of appreciation for good service. You need not tip if service is poor—tipping is discretionary.**

10 Tips for Worry-Free Travel

1. Be sure to notify local police and leave a phone number where you can be contacted in case of emergency.

2. Lock doors and windows, but leave shades up and lights on (or on an automatic timer).

3. Stop newspaper deliveries and discontinue garbage pickups.

4. Remove food and defrost refrigerator; store valuables in a safe place; disconnect electrical appliances; turn off gas jets, including hot water heater; turn off water faucets and drain pipes in severe weather.

5. Remember to pack personal medicines and duplicate prescriptions; spare eyeglasses or the prescription; sunglasses; suntan lotion; first-aid kit; insect spray; towels and tissues; writing materials.

6. Make sure that proof of car insurance is in your glove compartment; also take along your driver's license and those of other passengers (check expiration dates); car registration; copies of birth certificates (if driving outside US); traveler's checks. Be sure you have a duplicate set of car keys.

7. Check to see that you have a jack, spare tire, repair kit, emergency tools, flashlights, tire chains, spare fan belt, windshield scraper, auto fuses, lug wrench and work gloves. A pre-trip tune-up won't hurt—and, of course, be sure to "fill up" before you start out.

8. Also check vehicle's battery, oil and air filters, cooling system, brakes and lights.

9. Remember "extras" like hunting/fishing licenses and equipment; camera and film; bathing suits, beach accessories, sports equipment; portable radio and/or TV; picnic accessories.

10. Buckle up your seat belt, and have a nice trip!

Special Park Passes

Federal Recreation Areas

While many national parks and recreation areas may be entered and used free of charge, others require an entrance fee (ranging from $1 to $4/person to $3 to $10/carload) and/or a "use fee" for special services and facilities. Those travelers who plan to make several visits to federal recreation areas will be dollars ahead if they investigate several money-saving programs coordinated by the National Park Service, US Department of the Interior.

Park Pass. This is an annual entrance permit to a specific park, monument, historic site or recreation area in the National Park System that normally charges an entrance fee. The Pass costs $10 or $15, depending upon the area, and is neither refundable nor transferrable.

The Pass admits the permit holder and any accompanying passengers in a private noncommercial vehicle or, in the case of walk-in facilities, the holder's spouse, children and parents. It is valid for entrance fees only and does not cover use fees, such as those for cave tours, camping or parking.

A Park Pass may be purchased in person or by mail from the National Park Service unit at which the pass will be honored.

Golden Eagle Passport. This pass, issued to persons 17 to 61 years of age, is good for one calendar year and costs $25. It entitles the purchaser and up to 6 people accompanying him or her in a private noncommercial vehicle to enter any federal outdoor recreation area that charges an entrance fee. These include national parks, monuments, historic and memorial parks and seashores. The passport will also admit the purchaser and family to most walk-in admission fee areas such as historical houses, buildings and museums in federal areas. However, it does not cover use fees, such as fees for camping, boat-launching equipment, parking, or cave tours.

The Golden Eagle Passport may be purchased in person or by mail from: the National Park Service, Office of Public Inquiries, Room 1013, US Department of the Interior, 18th and C Streets NW, Washington, DC 20240, or phone 202/208-4747; at any of the 10 regional offices throughout the country; and at any area of the National Park System. The Golden Eagle Passport is not transferrable, nor is the $25 refundable if the passport is stolen, lost or not used.

Golden Age Passport. Issued to citizens and permanent residents of the United States 62 years or older, this passport is a free lifetime entrance permit to fee-charging recreation areas. The fee exemption extends to those accompanying the permit holder in a private noncommercial vehicle or, in the case of walk-in facilities, to the holder's spouse and children. The passport entitles the holder to a 50% discount on use fees charged in park areas, but not to fees charged by concessionaires.

Golden Age Passports must be obtained in person; mail requests will not be honored. The applicant must show proof of age, i.e., a driver's license, a birth certificate or a signed affidavit attesting to one's age (Medicare cards are not acceptable proof). Passports are available at most federally operated recreation areas where they are used. They may be obtained at the National Park Service Headquarters in Washington, DC (see preceding Golden Eagle Passport section), at any of the park system's regional offices, at National Forest Supervisors' offices and at most Ranger Station offices (for location see NATIONAL PARK SERVICE AREAS AND NATIONAL FORESTS in the state introductory section of the guide).

Golden Access Passport. Issued to citizens and permanent residents of the United States who are physically disabled or visually impaired, this passport is a free lifetime entrance permit to fee-charging federal recreation areas. The fee exception extends to those accompanying the permit holder in a private noncommercial vehicle or, in the case of walk-in facilities, to the holder's spouse, children and parents. The passport entitles the holder to a 50% discount on use fees charged in park areas, but not to fees charged by concessionaires.

Golden Access Passports must be obtained in person; mail requests will not be honored. Proof of eligibility to receive federal benefits is required (under programs such as Disability Retirement, Compensation for Military Service-Connected Disability, Coal Mine Safety and Health Act, etc.), or an affidavit must be signed attesting to eligibility. These passports are available at the same outlets as Golden Age Passports.

Savings for Seniors

Mobil Travel Guide publications note senior citizen rates in lodgings, restaurants and attractions. Always call ahead to con-

firm that the discount is being offered. Carry proof of age, such as a passport, birth certificate or driver's license. Medicare cards are often accepted as proof. Contact the following organizations for additional information:

1. American Association of Retired Persons (AARP)
   Financial and Special Services Dept
   601 E Street NW
   Washington, DC 20049
   Phone 202/434-2277

2. National Council of Senior Citizens
   1331 F Street NW
   Washington, DC 20004
   Phone 202/347-8800

The mature traveler on a limited budget should look for the senior citizen discount symbol in Lodging and Restaurant listings. Also, pay special attention to all listings in the guide highlighted by a check mark (✓). (See Federal Recreation Areas for Golden Age Passport information.)

Border Crossing Regulations

Canada

Citizens of the United States do not need visas to enter Canada, but proof of citizenship is required. Proof of citizenship includes a passport, birth certificate or voter's registration card. A driver's license is not acceptable. Naturalized citizens should carry their naturalization certificates or their US passport, because these documents will be necessary for a return to the United States. People under 18 years of age who are traveling on their own should carry a letter from parents or guardian giving them permission to travel in Canada.

Travelers entering Canada in automobiles licensed in the United States may tour the provinces for up to three months without fee. Drivers are advised to carry their motor vehicle registration card and, if the car is not registered in the driver's name, a letter from the registered owner authorizing use of the vehicle.

If the car is rented, carry a copy of the rental contract stipulating use in Canada. For your protection, ask your car insurer for a Canadian Non-resident Interprovince Motor Vehicle Liability Insurance Card. This card ensures that your insurance company will meet minimum insurance requirements in Canada.

The use of seat belts by drivers and passengers is compulsory in all provinces. For additional information, see individual provinces. A permit is required for the use of citizens' band radios. Rabies vaccination certificates are required for dogs or cats.

No handguns may be brought into Canada. If you plan to hunt, sporting rifles and shotguns, plus 200 rounds of ammunition per person, will be admitted duty-free. Hunting and fishing licenses must be obtained from the appropriate province. Each province has its own regulations concerning the transportation of firearms.

The Canadian dollar's rate of exchange with the US dollar varies. For specific information on rate of exchange, contact your nearest bank. Since customs regulations can change, the guide recommends that you contact the Canadian consulate or embassy in your area. Offices are located in Atlanta, Boston, Buffalo, Chicago, Dallas, Detroit, Los Angeles, Minneapolis, New York City, Seattle and Washington, DC. For the most current and detailed listing of regulations and sources, ask for the annually revised brochure "Canada: Travel Information," which is available upon request.

Mexico

Proof of citizenship is required for travel into Mexico; a passport or certified birth certificate are acceptable. Aliens must carry their alien registration cards. Naturalized citizens should carry their certificates. If you take your car for the day, you may find it more convenient to unload all baggage before crossing than to go through a thorough customs inspection upon your return. Your automobile insurance is not valid in Mexico; for short visits get a one-day policy before crossing. US currency is accepted in all border cities.

You will not be permitted to bring any plants, fruits or vegetables into the United States.

Federal regulations permit each US citizen, 21 years of age or older, to bring back one quart of alcoholic beverage, duty-free. However, state regulations vary and may be more strict; check locally before entering Mexico. New regulations may be issued at any time, so be sure to check further if you have any questions. Mexico does not observe Daylight Saving Time.

If you are planning to stay more than 24 hours or if you are a naturalized citizen or resident alien, get a copy of current border regulations from the nearest Mexican consulate or Tourism Office before crossing and make sure you understand them. A helpful booklet, "Know Before You Go," may be obtained free of charge from the nearest office of the US Customs Service.

Car Care

Familiarize yourself with the owner's manual for your car. It provides valuable advice for service and maintenance. Before you travel, get a lubrication and oil change, an inspection of tires, fan belts and cooling system, and a check of engine performance, lights and brakes. Other inspections recommended by the car manufacturer should be made as well.

Once your car is ready for the road, make certain your insurance is paid up—and don't forget your registration certificate, insurance information, driver's license and an extra set of keys.

Keep your seat belt and harness fastened. Watch your instrument panel closely—your panel gauges or indicators will alert you to potential problems. If a problem arises, get to a service station as soon as possible.

A world of convenience is yours with a Mobil credit card. Mobil's gasoline, oil and tires, as well as many other products and services, may be charged at Mobil dealers in the United States as well as at certain other dealers throughout Canada.

Road Emergencies

The best insurance against an emergency is proper maintenance of your car. Despite care, however, the unexpected can happen. Here are a few tips for handling emergencies:

Accidents. If you should have an accident, observe the following:

- Do not leave accident scene
- Help the injured but don't move them unless necessary
- Call police—ask for medical help if needed
- Get names, addresses, license numbers and insurance companies of persons involved
- Get names and addresses of at least two witnesses
- Get description and registration number(s) of car(s) involved
- Report accident to your insurance company
- Diagram the accident, showing cars involved

Breakdowns. If your car breaks down, get out of traffic as soon as possible, pulling off the road if you can. Turn on your emergency flashers and raise the hood. If you have no flashers, tie a white cloth to the roadside door handle or antenna. Stay near your car but off the road. Carry and use flares or reflectors to keep your car from being hit.

Blowout. Do not overreact if you have a tire blowout. Hold the wheel steady—do not jerk it. Gradually let up on the gas pedal, steer straight and coast to a stop. If you have to brake, do so very gently.

Collision. "If a collision is imminent, you will need to make these split-second decisions," advises the National Safety Council's Defensive Driving Course. "Drive right, away from the oncoming vehicle. Drive with control, don't skid off the road. If you are forced to drive off the road, look for either something soft, like bushes or small trees, or something fixed, like a breakaway pole or a fence to break your impact. A fixed object has no momentum, and the crash will be less intense than if you had hit the oncoming vehicle. If you are unable to ride off the road, try to collide with the oncoming vehicle at an angle. A glancing blow is less dangerous than hitting a vehicle head on."

Flat tire. Drive off the road, even if you risk ruining your tire. Set the parking brake firmly, but remember it may not hold if a rear wheel is off the ground. Put wooden blocks, bricks or stones tightly against the front and rear of the tire diagonally opposite the flat. After removing the hubcap, loosen each wheel nut about one-half turn. Position the jack exactly as the instructions indicate, then raise the car an inch or two to determine how the jack fits. (If it appears to be about to slip, stop and wait for help.)

Jack the car until the flat is about three inches off the ground, remove the wheel nuts and put them in the hubcap. Keep your body away from the car. Handle the tire from the sides; never put your hand above or underneath the tire.

Slide the spare tire into place, using the wrench as a lever. You may have to raise the jack a little farther. Screw the nuts on firmly, and jack the car down, standing at the side, not in front of the car. Finally, fully tighten the wheel nuts and leave the hubcap off as a reminder to have the flat fixed.

Skids. When your car skids, let up on the gas gently, keeping some power going to the wheels. Steer into the direction of the skid, and brake only after you have the car under complete control.

Stuck wheels. If you get stuck in the mud or snow, don't spin the wheels. Rock the car by gently accelerating ahead and back in rhythm with the car's natural tendency.

Equipment. The following checklist describes the necessary equipment to carry at all times:

- ☐ Spare tire; tool kit; first-aid kit; flashlight
- ☐ Road flares; jumper cables; gloves
- ☐ Container of motor oil; a can opener
- ☐ Empty one-gallon container (Note: Check local laws governing type of container to use for gasoline.)
- ☐ Spare parts, fan belt and fuses
- ☐ In winter: chains, ice scraper, de-icer in spray can, shovel, "liquid chain" or a bag of sand
- ☐ Major credit card and auto club identification

HOW TO SURVIVE A HOTEL FIRE

The chances are quite slim that you will ever encounter a hotel or motel fire. In addition, should you hear an alarm or see smoke, the danger is almost always less than you think it to be. But in the event you do encounter a fire, **ENSURE YOUR SURVIVAL WITH BASIC PREPARATION AND CALM ACTION.**

PREPARATION IS QUICK AND EASY

WHEN YOU CHECK INTO YOUR ROOM, DO THE FOLLOWING SAFETY CHECK:
- *Where are the fire exits?* Walk to at least two, counting the doors along the way in case you need to find the exit in the dark.
- *Where are the fire extinguishers and alarms?* Walk to them quickly.
- *Where is the "off switch" on your room's air conditioner?* In case of fire, turn off the air conditioner to prevent smoke from being sucked into your room.
- *Where is your room key?* Keep your key with you so you may reenter your room.

IF THERE'S A FIRE . . . STAY CALM

Keep in mind that smoke, poisonous gases, and panic are the greatest threats. The fresh air you need to breathe is at or near the floor. Get on your hands and knees; stay low, keep calm and react as follows:

If you find a fire,
- pull the nearest fire alarm;
- then use a fire extinguisher *if the fire is small;*
- leave the building through the fire exit.

  Never enter an elevator when fire is threatening.

If you hear an alarm from your room,
- take your room key;
- check the door for heat, but *do not open a hot door;*
- open the door a crack if it is cool;
- use the fire exit if the hall is clear of thick smoke, but *slam the door shut if the hall is smoky.*

If your exit is blocked,
- try another exit;
- or if all exits are smoky, go back to your room—it's the safest place;
- and if you cannot get to your room, go to the roof.

If you must stay in your room because thick smoke blocks the fire exits,
- turn off the air conditioner;
- stuff wet towels under the door and in air vents to keep smoke out;
- fill your bathtub with water and keep wastebaskets or ice buckets nearby to remoisten the clothes or toss water on heating walls;
- phone your location to the front desk or directly to the fire department;
- *stay low, below smoke and poisonous gases, and await assistance;*
- tie a wet towel around your nose and mouth—it's an effective filter.

Hotel/Motel Toll-Free '800' Numbers

This selected list is a handy guide for hotel/motel toll-free reservation numbers. You can save time and money by using them in the continental United States and Canada; Alaska and Hawaii are not included. Although these '800' numbers were in effect at press time, the *Mobil Travel Guide* cannot be responsible should any of them change. Many establishments do not have toll-free reservation numbers. Consult your local telephone directory for regional listings. The toll-free numbers designated 'TDD' are answered by a telecommunications service for the deaf. *Don't forget to dial "1" before each number.*

Best Western International, Inc.
800-528-1234 Cont'l USA & Canada
800-528-2222 TDD

Budgetel Inns
800-4-BUDGET Cont'l USA

Budget Host
800-BUD-HOST

Clarion Hotels
800-CLARION

Comfort Inns
800-228-5150 Cont'l USA

Courtyard by Marriott
800-321-2211 Cont'l USA

Days Inn
800-325-2525 Cont'l USA

Doubletree Hotels
800-222-8733 Cont'l USA

Drury Inns
800-325-8300 Cont'l USA

Econo Lodges of America
800-446-6900 Cont'l USA & Canada

Embassy Suites
800-362-2779 Cont'l USA

Exel Inns of America
800-356-8013 Cont'l USA

Fairfield Inn by Marriott
800-228-2800

Fairmont Hotels
800-527-4727 Cont'l USA

Four Seasons Hotels
800-332-3442 Cont'l USA & Canada

Friendship Inns of America Int'l
800-453-4511 Cont'l USA

Guest Quarters
800-424-2900 Cont'l USA
800-PICKETT

Hampton Inn
800-HAMPTON Cont'l USA

Hilton Hotels Corp
800-HILTONS Cont'l USA
800-368-1133 TDD

Holiday Inns
800-HOLIDAY Cont'l USA & Canada
800-238-5544 TDD

Howard Johnson
800-654-2000 Cont'l USA & Canada
800-654-8442 TDD

Hyatt Corp
800-228-9000 Cont'l USA & Canada

Inns of America
800-826-0778 USA

Inter-Continental Hotels
800-327-0200 Cont'l USA, HI & Canada

La Quinta Motor Inns, Inc.
800-531-5900 Cont'l USA
800-426-3101 TDD

Loews Hotels
800-223-0888 Cont'l USA exc NY

Marriott Hotels
800-228-9290 Cont'l USA

Master Hosts Inns (Hospitality)
800-251-1962 Cont'l USA & Canada

Omni Hotels
800-843-6664 Cont'l USA & Canada

Park Inns Int'l
800-437-PARK

Quality Inns
800-228-5151 Cont'l USA & Canada

Radisson Hotel Corp
800-333-3333 Cont'l USA & Canada

Ramada Inns
800-2-RAMADA Cont'l USA
800-228-3232 TDD

Red Carpet/Scottish Inns (Hospitality)
800-251-1962 Cont'l USA & Canada

Red Lion-Thunderbird
800-547-8010 Cont'l USA & Canada

Red Roof Inns
800-843-7663 Cont'l USA & Canada

Residence Inn By Marriott
800-331-3131

Ritz-Carlton
800-241-3333 Cont'l USA

Rodeway Inns International
800-228-2000 Cont'l USA

Sheraton Hotels & Inns
800-325-3535 Cont'l USA & Canada

Shilo Inns
800-222-2244

Signature Inns
800-822-5252

Stouffer Hotels and Resorts
800-HOTELS-1 Cont'l USA & Canada

Super 8 Motels
800-843-1991 Cont'l USA & Canada
800-800-8000 Cont'l USA & Canada

Susse Chalet Motor Lodges & Inns
800-258-1980 Cont'l USA & Canada

Travelodge International Inc./Viscount Hotels
800-255-3050 Cont'l USA & Canada

Trusthouse Forte Hotels
800-225-5843 Cont'l USA & Canada

Vagabond Hotels Inc.
800-522-1555 Cont'l USA

Westin Hotels
800-228-3000 Cont'l USA & Canada

Wyndham Hotels
800-822-4200

Car Rental Toll-Free '800' Numbers

Advantage Rent A Car
800-777-5500 Cont'l USA

Agency Rent-A-Car
800-321-1972 Cont'l USA

Alamo Rent-A-Car
800-327-9633 Cont'l USA,
Canada

Allstate Rent-A-Car
800-634-6186 Cont'l USA

Avis-Reservations Center
800-331-1212 Cont'l USA,
Canada

Budget Rent-A-Car
800-527-0700 Cont'l USA,
Canada

Dollar Rent-A-Car
800-800-4000 Cont'l USA,
Canada

Enterprise Rent-A-Car
800-325-8007 Cont'l USA

Hertz Corporation
800-654-3131 Cont'l USA
800-654-3001 Canada

National Car Rental
800-CAR-RENT Cont'l USA,
Canada

Payless Rent-A-Car Inc.
800-237-2804 Cont'l USA

Sears Rent-A-Car
800-527-0770 Cont'l USA

Thrifty Rent-A-Car
800-367-2277 Cont'l USA,
Canada

U-Save Auto Rental of America
800-272-USAV

Value Rent-A-Car
800-327-2501 Cont'l USA,
Canada

Airline Toll-Free '800' Numbers

American Airlines, Inc. (AA)
800-433-7300

Canadian Airlines Intl, LTD
800-426-7000

Continental Airlines (CO)
800-231-0856

Delta Air Lines, Inc. (DL)
800-221-1212

Northwest Airlines, Inc. (NW)
800-225-2525

Southwest Airlines (WN)
800-435-9792

Trans World Airlines, Inc. (TW)
800-221-2000

United Air Lines, Inc. (UA)
800-241-6522

USAir (US)
800-428-4322

Delaware

Population: 666,168

Land area: 1,982 square miles

Elevation: 0-442 feet

Highest point: Ebright Road (New Castle County)

Entered Union: First state to ratify Constitution (December 7, 1787)

Capital: Dover

Motto: Liberty and Independence

Nicknames: First State, Small Wonder, Diamond State, Blue Hen State

State flower: Peach blossom

State bird: Blue hen chicken

State tree: American holly

State fair: July 20-29, 1995, in Harrington (see Dover)

Time zone: Eastern

Delaware ". . .is like a diamond, diminutive, but having within it inherent value," wrote John Lofland, the eccentric "Bard of Milford," in 1847. The state is 96 miles long and from 9 to 35 miles wide. With more than half of its 1,982 square miles (excluding marshes) used for farming, Delaware produces a flood of agricultural products. Poultry contributes approximately half of the state's total farm income, with soybeans, corn, tomatoes, strawberries, asparagus, fruit and other crops bringing in about $170 million more each year. Booming industry in northern and central Delaware balances the agricultural sector of the economy. Consistent state corporate policies have persuaded more than 183,000 corporations to make their headquarters in the "corporate capital of the world." Forty major US banks alone have established lending and credit operations in the state.

Compact but diverse, Delaware has rolling, forested hills in the north, stretches of bare sand dunes in the south and mile upon mile of lonely marsh along the coast. Visitors can tour a modern agricultural or chemical research center in the morning and search for buried pirate treasure in the afternoon. The *deBraak,* which foundered off Lewes in 1798, was raised in 1986 because of the belief that it may have had a fortune in captured Spanish coin or bullion aboard. The coins that frequently come ashore at Coin Beach below Rehoboth are believed to come from the *Faithful Steward,* a passenger vessel lost in 1785.

Delaware's history started on a grim note. The first colonists, 28 men under Dutch auspices, landed in the spring of 1631 near what is now Lewes. A year later, following an argument with a Lenni-Lenape chief, the bones of all 28 were found mingled with those of their cattle and strewn over their burned fields. In 1638 a group of Swedes established the first permanent settlement, Fort Christina, at a spot now in Wilmington. This was also the first permanent settlement of Swedes in North America. Dutch, English, Scottish and Irish colonists soon followed, with German, Italian and Polish groups coming in the late 19th century.

Henry Hudson, in Dutch service, discovered Delaware Bay in 1609. A year later Thomas Argall reported it to English navigators, naming it for his superior, Lord De La Warr, Governor of Virginia. Ownership changed rapidly from Swedish to Dutch to English hands. Later the area was claimed by both Lord Baltimore and the Penn family. The Maryland-Delaware boundary was set by British court order in 1750 and surveyed as part of the Mason-Dixon Line in 1763-67. The boundary with New Jersey, also long disputed, was confirmed by the Supreme Court in 1935.

The "First State" (first to adopt the Constitution—December 7, 1787) is proud of its history of sturdy independence, both military and political. During the Revolution, the "Delaware line" was a crack regiment of the Continental Army. After heavy casualties in 1780, the unit was reorganized. The men would "fight all day and dance all night," according to a dispatch by General Greene. How well they danced is open to question, but they fought with such gallantry that they were mentioned in nearly all of the General's dispatches.

Delaware statesman John Dickinson, "penman of the Revolution" and one of the state's five delegates to the Constitutional Convention, was instrumental in the decision to write a new document rather than simply patch up the Articles of Confederation. Later he effected the compromise on representation, a problem that had threatened to break up the convention completely.

In addition to Lofland and Dickinson, Delaware has produced many literary figures, including the 19th-century playwright and novelist Robert Montgomery Bird, writer and illustrator Howard Pyle, Henry Seidel Canby (founder of the *Saturday Review*) and novelist John P. Marquand.

A fine highway network tempts motorists to drive through diminutive Delaware without really seeing it. Those who take time to leave the major highways and explore the countryside will find much that is rewarding.

State Recreation Areas

The following towns list state recreation areas in their vicinity under What to See and Do; refer to the individual town for directions and park information.

Listed under **Bethany Beach:** see Holts Landing State Park.

Listed under **Dover:** see Killens Pond State Park.

Listed under **Fenwick Island:** see Fenwick Island State Park.

Listed under **Fort Delaware State Park:** see Fort Delaware State Park.

Listed under **Lewes:** see Cape Henlopen State Park.

Listed under **Newark:** see Walter S. Carpenter, Jr State Park.

Listed under **Odessa:** see Lums Pond State Park.

Listed under **Rehoboth Beach:** see Delaware Seashore State Park.

Listed under **Wilmington:** see Bellevue and Brandywine Creek state parks.

Water-related activities, hiking, riding, various other sports, picnicking and visitor centers are available in many of these areas. Delaware state parks are open all year, 8 am-sunset, except Fort Delaware (late Apr-late Sept). Most areas have fishing, boat ramps and picnicking. There is a $2.50 resident vehicle entrance fee and a $5 nonresident vehicle entrance fee from Memorial Day-Labor Day, daily; May & Sept-Oct, wkends & hols. Camping is available from mid-Mar-mid-Nov at Delaware Seashore; Apr-Oct at Lums Pond, Trap Pond and Cape Henlopen; year-round at Killens Pond (limited facilities during winter season.) There is a two-week maximum stay at campgrounds; no reservations are accepted; campsites run from $10-$19/night/site. For further information contact Department of Natural Resources & Environmental Control, Division of Parks & Recreation, PO Box 1401, Dover 19903; 302/739-4702.

Fishing & Hunting

Both fresh and saltwater fishing are excellent. The state owns, leases or licenses 33,000 acres of game and fish lands and waters. More than 50 well-stocked state and privately owned ponds are scattered throughout the state. Many miles of ocean shoreline between Rehoboth Beach and Indian River Inlet are ideal for surf fishing. Common saltwater fish include trout, bluefish, porgie, sea bass, flounder and croaker; freshwater fish include bass, bluegill, pickerel, crappie, perch and trout.

An annual resident hunting license is $12.50; resident trap license is $3. An annual nonresident hunting license is $45; nonresident 3-day small game license is $15. An annual resident freshwater fishing license is $8.50; nonresident license is $15; 7-day nonresident license is $5.20. A license is not required for tidal saltwater fishing. For further information on fishing or hunting contact the Department of Natural Resources & Environmental Control, Division of Fish & Wildlife, R & R Building, PO Box 1401, Dover 19903; 302/739-4431 or -5297.

Safety Belt Information

Safety belts are mandatory for all persons in front seat of vehicle. Children under 4 years and 40 pounds in weight must be in an approved safety seat anywhere in vehicle. For further information phone 302/739-5901.

Interstate Highway System

The following alphabetical listing of Delaware towns in *Mobil Travel Guide* shows that these cities are within 10 miles of the indicated interstate highway. A highway map, however, should be checked for the nearest exit.

INTERSTATE 95: Newark, New Castle, Wilmington.

Additional Visitor Information

Delaware Tourism Office, 99 Kings Highway, PO Box 1401, Dover 19903, will provide business and tourist information; phone 302/739-4271 or 800/441-8846.

Visitor centers also provide information and brochures on points of interest in the state. Their locations are as follows: Delaware Memorial Bridge Plaza, jct I-295 and the bridge at New Castle; I-95 rest area, Greater Wilmington Convention and Visitors Bureau, Wilmington; Delaware State Information Center, Duke of York & Federal Sts, Dover; Smyrna, 1 mi N on US 13; Bethany-Fenwick Area Chamber of Commerce, DE 1, north of Fenwick Island.

Bethany Beach (D-10)

Founded: 1901 **Pop:** 326 **Elev:** 8 ft **Area code:** 302 **Zip:** 19930

A quiet beach town on the Atlantic Ocean, Bethany Beach was started as a place for revival camp meetings; hence the Biblical name. Surf fishing and bathing are excellent here.

What to See and Do

1. **Prince George's Chapel** (1755). 11 mi W on DE 26 in Dagsboro. Restored chapel with beaded clapboard exterior. Interior temporarily closed. Call for appt. Phone 739-4266 or 645-9418. **Free.**
2. **Holts Landing State Park.** 8 mi NW via DE 26 & DE 346, N of Millville. A 203-acre park located along the Indian River Bay. Fishing, crabbing, clamming; sailing, boating (launch ramp providing access to bay). Picnicking, playground, ball fields. Standard hrs, fees. Phone 539-9060 or -1055 (summer).

(For further information contact Bethany-Fenwick Area Chamber of Commerce, Coastal Hwy/DE 1, PO Box 1450; 539-2100 or 800/962-7873.)

Annual Event

Boardwalk Arts Festival. The Boardwalk, Garfield Pkwy. Juried, original handmade works; woodcarving, photography, jewelry, batik, watercolor paintings. Last Sat Aug.

(See Fenwick Island, Lewes, Rehoboth Beach)

Motels

★ ★ **BETHANY ARMS.** *PO Box 1600, 99 Hollywood St.* 302/539-9603. 52 units, 2-3 story, 36 kit. units. No elvtr. Many rm phones. July-Aug: S, D $85-$135; each addl $5; under 4 free; wkly rates; lower rates rest of yr. Crib $5. TV; cable. Restaurant adj 7 am-9 pm. Ck-out 11 am. Some covered parking. Many refrigerators. Balconies. On ocean; beach, swimming. Cr cds: MC, V.

★ **BLUE SURF.** *PO Box 999, Garfield Pkwy at Boardwalk.* 302/539-7531. 35 units, 2 story, 29 kit. units. Mid-June-Labor Day: S, D $90-$115; each addl $8; under 7 free; lower rates rest of yr. Crib $5. TV; cable. Complimentary coffee in rms. Restaurant opp 7 am-10 pm. Ck-out 11 am. Refrigerators. Balconies. On beach; ocean swimming. Cr cds: MC, V.

★ **HARBOR VIEW.** *RD 1, Box 102, 3½ mi N on DE 1.* 302/539-0500; FAX 302/539-5170. 60 rms, 2 story, 8 kit. units. July-Aug: S, D $85-$95; each addl $10; kit. units $95-$115; under 14 free (off-season); wkly rates; lower rates rest of yr. Crib $5. TV; cable. Pool; lifeguard. Complimentary continental bkfst. Restaurant 11:30 am-10 pm; closed Dec-Jan. Ck-out 11 am. Coin lndry. Meeting rm. Some covered parking. Free bus depot, marina transportation. Some refrigerators. Balconies. Picnic tables, grills. On bay; swimming; crabbing and clamming. Cr cds: A, C, D, DS, MC, V.

Restaurant

✔ ★ **REUNION.** *214B Garfield Pkwy. 302/539-2336.* Hrs: 8 am-8 pm. Closed Thanksgiving, Dec 24 & 25. Res accepted. Continental menu. Semi-a la carte: bkfst $2.95-$5.95, lunch $3.95-$6.25, dinner $4.95-$12.95. Specializes in fresh seafood, prime rib. Salad bar. Cr cds: DS, MC, V.

Dover (C-9)

Founded: 1717 **Pop:** 27,630 **Elev:** 36 ft **Area code:** 302 **Zip:** 19901

The capital of Delaware since 1777, Dover was laid out by William Penn around the city's lovely green. For almost 200 years there were coach houses and inns on King's Road between Philadelphia and Lewes. Circling the green north and south on State Street are fine 18th- and 19th-century houses.

Today, because of Delaware's favorable corporation laws, more than 60,000 US firms pay taxes in Dover. At Dover Air Force Base, south off US 113, the Military Airlift Command operates one of the biggest air cargo terminals in the world, utilizing the giant C5-A aircraft. Dover is also the home of Delaware State College, Wesley College and the Terry campus of Delaware Technical and Community College.

What to See and Do

1. **Delaware State Museum.** 316 S Governors Ave. Complex of three buildings: Meetinghouse Gallery (1790) with an exhibit devoted to archaeology; 1880 Gallery with turn-of-the-century drugstore, blacksmith shop, general store, post office, shoemaker's shop and printer's shop; and Johnson building (see #4). (Tues-Sat; closed hols) Phone 739-4266. **Free.**

2. **State House** (1792). Federal St, The Green. Second oldest seat of government in continuous use in the US, the State House, restored in 1976, contains a courtroom, ceremonial governor's office, legislative chambers and county offices, including Levy Courtroom. A larger-than-life portrait of George Washington in the Senate Chamber was comissioned in 1802 by the legislature as a memorial to the nation's first president. Although Delaware's General Assembly moved to nearby Legislative Hall in 1934, the State House remains the state's symbolic capitol. (Daily exc Mon; closed state hols) For information phone 739-4266. **Free.**

3. **Visitor Center.** The Green. Administered by Division of Historical and Cultural Affairs, center offers information on attractions throughout state. Exhibit galleries; audiovisual show. (Daily; closed hols) Phone 739-4266. **Free.**

4. **Johnson Memorial.** Bank Lane & New St. Tribute to Eldridge Reeves Johnson, founder of the Victor Talking Machine Company. Collection of talking machines, Victrolas, early recordings and equipment. (Tues-Sat; closed hols) Phone 739-4266. **Free.**

5. **Hall of Records.** Court St & Legislative Ave. Delaware's historical public records; archive includes Royal Charter granted by King Charles II to James, Duke of York, for Delaware territory in 1682. (Mon-Fri; closed hols) Phone 739-5318. **Free.**

6. **Dover Heritage Trail.** Departs from State Visitor Center. Guided walking tour of historic areas, buildings and other attractions. (By appt only) Sr citizen rate. Phone 678-2040. **¢¢**

7. **Delaware Agricultural Museum and Village.** 866 N du Pont Hwy (US 13). Museum of farm life from early settlement to 1960. Main exhibition hall and historic structures representing a late 19th-century farming community; includes gristmill, blacksmith-wheel-wright shop, farmhouse, outbuildings, one-room schoolhouse, store and train station. Gift shop. (Apr-Dec, daily exc Mon; rest of yr, Mon-Fri) Sr citizen rate. Phone 734-1618. **¢¢**

8. **John Dickinson Plantation** (1740). 6 mi SE, near jct US 113 & DE 9 on Kitts Hummock Rd. Restored boyhood residence of Dickinson, the "penman of the Revolution." Reconstructed farm complex. (Mar-Dec, Tues-Sat, also Sun afternoons; rest of yr, Tues-Sat; closed hols) Phone 739-3277. **Free.**

9. **Killens Pond State Park.** 13 mi S via US 13. A 1,083-acre park with a 66-acre pond. Swimming pool; fishing; boating (rentals). Hiking and fitness trails; game fields. Picnicking. Camping (hookups, dump station). Standard hrs, fees. Phone 284-4526.

(For further information contact the Kent County Delaware Convention & Visitors Bureau, E Loockerman St, Treadway Towers, Ste 2-A, PO Box 576, 19903; 734-1736 or 800/233-KENT.)

Annual Events

Old Dover Days. Tours of historic houses and gardens not usually open to the public. Crafts exhibits, many other activities. For information & tickets contact Friends of Old Dover, PO Box 44; 674-2120. 1st wkend May.

Delaware State Fair. 17 mi S on US 13 in Harrington. Arts & crafts, home & trade show, carnival rides, shows; homemaking, agricultural and livestock exhibits. Phone 398-3269. July.

Seasonal Events

Harrington Raceway. 17 mi S on US 13, at fairgrounds in Harrington. Harness horse racing. Wagering most nights of the week. Phone 398-3269. Sept-Nov.

Dover Downs. 1131 N du Pont Hwy (US 13). Racing events include NASCAR Winston Cup auto racing (June, Sept); harness racing (mid-Nov-Mar). For fees and schedule, phone 674-4600.

(See Odessa, Smyrna)

Motels

✔ ★ **BUDGET INN.** *1426 N du Pont Hwy (US 13). 302/734-4433.* 68 rms, 2 story. May-Sept: S $42-$50; D $47-$55; each addl $5; lower rates rest of yr. Crib free. TV; cable. Pool; lifeguard. Complimentary coffee in lobby. Restaurant opp 8 am-9 pm. Ck-out 11 am. Coin lndry. Sundries. Cr cds: A, D, DS, MC, V.

★ **COMFORT INN.** *222 S du Pont Hwy (US 13). 302/674-3300; FAX 302/674-3300, ext. 190.* 94 rms, 2 story. May-Sept: S $47-$51; D $51-$55; each addl $5; kit. units $65; family, wkly rates; higher rates NASCAR races; lower rates rest of yr. Crib free. TV; cable. Pool; lifeguard. Complimentary continental bkfst, coffee. Restaurant adj 11 am-10 pm. Ck-out noon. Sundries. Some refrigerators. Grill. Cr cds: A, C, D, DS, ER, JCB, MC, V.

Motor Hotel

★ ★ ★ **SHERATON INN.** *1570 N du Pont Hwy (US 13). 302/678-8500; FAX 302/678-9073.* 152 rms, 7 story. S $79; D $86; each addl $5; under 18 free; higher rates NASCAR race. Crib free. TV; cable. Indoor pool; lifeguard. Restaurant 6:30 am-10 pm. Rm serv to 10:30 pm. Bars 11-1 am; entertainment exc Sun, dancing. Ck-out noon. Meeting rms. Bellhops. Sundries. Exercise equipt; treadmill, stair machine; whirlpool. Some refrigerators. Cr cds: A, D, DS, MC, V.

Restaurants

★ ★ ★ **BLUE COAT INN.** *800 N State St.* 302/674-1776. Hrs: 11:30 am-10 pm; Sat 11:30 am-3 pm, 4:30-10 pm; Sun noon-9 pm. Closed Mon; Dec 25. Res accepted. Bar. Semi-a la carte: lunch $4.25-$9.95, dinner $8.95-$24.95. Child's meals. Specializes in fresh seafood, colonial recipes. Own baking. Entertainment Sat. Parking. Early Amer decor. Lake setting. Cr cds: A, C, D, DS, MC, V.

★ ★ **CORAL REEF.** *(Box 375, Little Creek) On DE 9, 3 mi E of US 113.* 302/678-9175. Hrs: 11 am-9 pm; Sat 4-10 pm; Sun 1-9 pm. Closed Jan 1, Thanksgiving, Dec 25. Res accepted. Bar. Semi-a la carte: lunch $3.95-$7.25, dinner $4.95-$22.95. Child's meals. Specializes in steak, fresh local seafood. Parking. Nautical decor. Cr cds: A, D, MC, V.

★ ★ **PLAZA NINE.** *9 E Loockerman St, in Treadway Towers building.* 302/736-9990. Hrs: 11 am-2 pm, 5-10 pm; Sat from 5 pm. Closed Sun; Jan 1, Dec 25. Res accepted; required wkends & hols. Continental menu. Bar 11 am-midnight. Semi-a la carte: lunch $3.95-$7.95, dinner $10.95-$21. Child's meals. Specializes in fresh seafood, veal. Jazz Fri, Sat. Parking. Outdoor dining. Near State House and government buildings. Overlooks Mirror Lake. Cr cds: D, MC, V.

D

★ ★ **VILLAGE INN.** *(DE 9, Little Creek) On DE 9, 3 mi E of US 113.* 302/734-3245. Hrs: 11 am-2 pm, 4:30-10 pm; Sat 11 am-10 pm; Sun noon-9 pm. Closed Jan 1, Thanksgiving, Dec 25. Res accepted. Bar. Semi-a la carte: lunch $4.95-$9.95, dinner $12.95-$19.95. Specialties: stuffed flounder, prime rib. Parking. Colonial decor; fireplace, antiques. Cr cds: MC, V.

Fenwick Island (E-10)

Pop: 186 **Elev:** 4 ft **Area code:** 302 **Zip:** 19944

Fenwick Island, at the southeast corner of Delaware, was named after Thomas Fenwick, a wealthy Virginia landowner who purchased the land in 1686. For a time, a dispute raged over whether Fenwick Island was part of Maryland or Pennsylvania. It ended in 1751, when the Transpeninsular Line placed Fenwick Island in Delaware. In 1775, James and Jacob Brasure, residents of the island, began extracting salt from the ocean, and until 1825, "salt making" was big business. In the latter part of the 19th century, Fenwick Island grew as a religious-oriented summer campground. After World War I, Fenwick Island became fashionable as a summer resort.

What to See and Do

1. **Fenwick Island Lighthouse.** W of town via DE 54. Historic 87-foot-tall lighthouse; light was first turned on Aug 1, 1859. (June-Aug, 2 Wed afternoons per month; also by appt) Phone 410/250-1098.
2. **Fenwick Island State Park.** 1 mi N on DE 1. This 208-acre seashore park is located between the Atlantic Ocean and Little Assawoman Bay. Surfing, swimming, bathhouse; surf fishing; sailing (rentals). Standard hrs, fees. Phone 539-9060 or -1055 (summer).

(For further information contact the Bethany-Fenwick Area Chamber of Commerce, Coastal Hwy/DE 1, PO Box 1450, Bethany Beach 19930; 539-2100 or 800/962-7873.)

Annual Event

Surf-Fishing Tournament. Phone 539-2100. Columbus Day wkend.

(See Bethany Beach, Lewes, Rehoboth Beach; also see Ocean City, MD)

Motel

★ **ATLANTIC BUDGET INN.** *Jct DE 54, Ocean Hwy (DE 1).* 302/539-7673; res: 800/432-8038. 48 rms, 1-2 story, 3 kit. units. Memorial Day, July 4-Labor Day (3-day min): S, D $65-$95; each addl $6; kit. units for 2, $85; lower rates mid-Apr-June, after Labor Day-Oct. Closed rest of yr. Crib free. TV; cable. Pool; lifeguard. Complimentary coffee in lobby. Restaurant nearby. Ck-out 11 am. Refrigerators. Beach 1 blk. Cr cds: A, D, DS, MC, V.

≈ ⊠ ⊠ SC

Restaurants

✔ ★ ★ **HARPOON HANNA'S.** *DE 54 at the bay.* 302/539-3095. Hrs: 11-1 am; Sun from 10 am; Sun brunch 10 am-3 pm. Bar. A la carte entrees: lunch $3.95-$7.95, dinner $7.95-$18.95. Sun brunch $3.95-$7.95. Child's meals. Specializes in fresh seafood. Entertainment Fri & Sat. Parking. Outdoor dining. Casual-contemporary decor; fireplace. On waterfront. Cr cds: A, MC, V.

D

★ ★ **TOM & TERRY'S.** *DE 54 & The Bay.* 302/436-4161. Hrs: 11:30 am-10 pm; early-bird dinner 5-6 pm. Closed Dec 25. Bar. Semi-a la carte: lunch $5.95-$9.50, dinner $15.95-$22.95. Specializes in fresh local seafood, prime rib. Parking. Outdoor dining; view of Ocean City & Assawoman Bay. Cr cds: MC, V.

Fort Delaware State Park (B-9)

(On Pea Patch Island, opposite Delaware City)

A must for the Civil War buff, this grim gray fort was built as a coastal defense in 1859. The island was used as a prisoner of war depot for 3 years, housing up to 12,500 Confederate prisoners at a time. The damp, insect-infested terrain encouraged epidemics, leading to some 2,400 deaths. The fort remained in commission through World War II.

Restoration of the site is a continuing process. Available are nature trails, picnicking. Museum has scale models of fort, Civil War relics. Special events throughout summer. Boat trip to island from Delaware City (mid-June-Aug, Wed-Sun; last wkend Apr-mid-June & Sept, Sat, Sun & hols). No pets. For further information contact the Park Manager, PO Box 170, Delaware City 19706; 302/834-7941. Round trip ¢¢

(For accommodations see Newark, New Castle, Wilmington, also see Odessa)

Lewes (D-10)

Settled: 1631 **Pop:** 2,295 **Elev:** 10 ft **Area code:** 302 **Zip:** 19958

Lewes (LOO-is) has been home base to Delaware Bay pilots for 300 years. Weather-beaten, cypress-shingled houses still line the streets where privateers plundered and Captain Kidd bargained away his loot. The treacherous sandbars outside the harbor have claimed their share of ships, and stories of sunken treasure have circulated for centuries. Some buildings show the trace of cannonballs that hit their mark when the British bombarded Lewes in the War of 1812. Traces of the original stockade were discovered in 1964.

What to See and Do

1. **Zwaanendael Museum.** Savannah Rd & Kings Hwy. Adaptation of Hoorn, Holland Town Hall was built in 1931 as memorial to original Dutch founders of Lewes (1631). Highlights the town's maritime heritage with colonial, Native American and Dutch exhibits. (Daily exc Mon; closed hols) Phone 645-9418. **Free.**

2. **Restored buildings.** Maintained by the Lewes Historical Society. Cannon Ball House and US Lifesaving Station have marine exhibits and lightship *Overfalls*. Other buildings open are Thompson country store, Plank house, Rabbit's Ferry house, Burton-Ingram house, Ellegood house, Hiram R. Burton house and old doctor's office. (June-Labor Day, Tues-Sat) Tickets at Thompson Country Store. Guided walking tours (July-mid-Sept, Tues, Thurs & Fri). Varied events take place during summer season. Phone 645-7670. Tour ¢¢

3. **Cape Henlopen State Park.** 1 mi E on Cape Henlopen Dr. More than 3,000 acres at confluence of Delaware Bay and Atlantic Ocean; site of decommissioned Fort Miles, part of coastal defense system during World War II. Supervised swimming; fishing. Nature center, programs and trails. Picnicking, concession. Camping (water hookups, dump station). Standard hrs, fees. Phone 645-8983.

4. **Lewes-Cape May, NJ Ferry.** Sole connection between US 13 (Ocean Hwy) on the Delmarva Peninsula and southern terminus of Garden State Pkwy (NJ). Trip across Delaware Bay (16 mi) takes 70 minutes. (Daily; 22 crossings in summer, 10 in winter, 14-18 in spring & fall) Phone 645-6313. Per person, one way ¢¢¢¢-¢¢¢¢¢

(For further information contact the Lewes Chamber of Commerce, Fisher-Martin House, 120 Kings Hwy, PO Box 1; 645-8073.)

Annual Events

Great Delaware Kite Festival. Cape Henlopen State Park (see #3). Festival heralding the beginning of spring. Fri before Easter.

Coast Day. University of Delaware Marine Studies Complex. Facilities and research vessel open to public; marine exhibits, research demonstrations, nautical films. Phone 645-4346. 1st Sun Oct.

(See Bethany Beach, Fenwick Island, Rehoboth Beach)

Motel

★ **ANGLER'S.** 110 Anglers Rd, ¹/₂ blk NE of Canal Bridge. 302/645-2831. 25 rms, 1-2 story, 2 kits. Mid-May-mid-Sept (2-day min wkends, hols): S, D $55-$80; each addl $5; kit. units $65-$75; lower rates rest of yr. Crib free. TV; cable. Restaurant nearby. Ck-out 11 am. Picnic tables, grills. Sun deck. Overlooks canal, marina opp. Boat docking. Cr cds: A, DS, MC, V.

Hotel

★ ★ ★ **NEW DEVON INN.** Box 516, 142 2nd St. 302/645-6466; res: 800/824-8754. 26 rms, 3 story. Late May-mid-Oct: S, D $105; suites $145; package plans; lower rates rest of yr. TV avail. Restaurant 7 am-10 pm. Ck-out 11 am. Meeting rms. Shopping arcade. Built 1926. Cr cds: A, D, DS, MC, V.

Inn

★ ★ **INN AT CANAL SQUARE.** 122 Market St. 302/645-8499. 22 rms, 3 story. Late June-early Sept: D $125-$150; each addl $15; 2-bed rm houseboat $225 ($400 wkend); wkly rates; higher rates hols, wkends (2-night min); lower rates rest of yr. Crib $15. TV; cable. Complimentary continental bkfst. Complimentary coffee in lobby. Res-

taurant nearby. Ck-out 11 am. Concierge. Bellhop. Meeting rm. Balconies. On canal. Cr cds: A, D, DS, MC, V.

Restaurants

★ **ASHBY'S OYSTER HOUSE.** *DE 24, at Peddler's Village.* 302/945-4070. Hrs: 11-1 am; Sat & Sun from 9 am. Closed Thanksgiving, Dec 25. Bar. Semi-a la carte: lunch $3.95-$6.45, dinner $11.95-$19.95. Sat & Sun bkfst buffet $5.95. Child's meals. Raw bar. Parking. Casual dining. Cr cds: A, MC, V.

★ **GILLIGAN'S.** *134 Market St.* 302/645-7866. Hrs: 11 am-3:30 pm, 5-10 pm; Fri & Sat to 11 pm. Closed Oct-Apr. Continental menu. Bar. Semi-a la carte: lunch $6.50-$8.50, dinner $11.50-$19. Specialties: crab cakes, crab in artichoke hearts. Entertainment Sun evening. Outdoor dining. Part of exterior resembles the "good ship Minnow." View of harbor. Cr cds: A, MC, V.

★ ★ **KUPCHICK'S.** *3 East Bay Ave.* 302/645-0420. Hrs: 4:30-10 pm. Closed Dec 25; early Jan-mid-Feb. Res accepted; required summer wkends. Continental menu. Bar. A la carte entrees: dinner $11.95-$23.95. Child's meals. Specializes in fresh seafood, Angus beef. Jazz Fri & Sat. Parking. Victorian atmosphere. Original art, antiques. Cr cds: A, C, D, DS, MC, V.

★ **LIGHTHOUSE.** *Savannah Rd at Anglers Rd, just over the drawbridge.* 302/645-6271. Hrs: 4 am-10 pm; Sept-Mar 7 am-9 pm. Closed Thanksgiving, Dec 24-25. Bar 10:30-1 am. Semi-a la carte: bkfst $2.25-$7.50, lunch $2.50-$15, dinner $10.95-$25. Child's meals. Specialties: sticky buns, prime rib, fresh seafood. Entertainment wkends. Parking. Outdoor dining. Overlooks Lewes Harbor. Cr cds: MC, V.

Newark (A-9)

Settled: 1685 **Pop:** 25,098 **Elev:** 124 ft **Area code:** 302

Newark grew up at the crossroads of two well-traveled Indian trails. The site of the only Revolutionary battle on Delaware soil is at nearby Cooch's Bridge, southeast of Newark. According to tradition, Betsy Ross's flag was first raised in battle at Cooch's Bridge on September 3, 1777.

What to See and Do

1. **University of Delaware** (1743). (18,000 students) Founded as a small private academy; stately elm trees, fine lawns and Georgian-style brick buildings adorn the central campus. Tours from Visitors Center, 196 S College Ave (Mon-Fri, also Sat mornings). Phone 831-8123. On campus is

   University of Delaware Mineral Collection. Penny Hall, Academy St. Also fossil exhibit. (Mon-Fri, by appt only; closed hols) Phone 831-2569. **Free.**

2. **Walter S. Carpenter, Jr State Park.** 3 mi NW via DE 896. A 1,483-acre day park with farmlands, forest and streams. Fishing. Nature, fitness trails. Picnicking. Standard hrs, fees. Phone 368-6900.

(For further information contact the Greater Wilmington Convention & Visitors Bureau, 1300 Market St, Suite 504, Wilmington 19801; 652-4088.)

(See New Castle, Wilmington)

Motels

★ ★ **BEST WESTERN.** 260 Chapman Rd (19702), at I-95. 302/738-3400; FAX 302/738-3400, ext. 334. 99 rms, 2 story. S $55-$65; D $60-$75; each addl $5; under 18 free; wkend rates. Crib free. TV; cable. Pool; lifeguard. Restaurant 5-9 pm. Rm serv. Bar 4 pm-1 am. Ck-out noon. Meeting rms. Sundries. Cr cds: A, C, D, DS, MC, V.

✅ 🏊 ⛔ 🔥 SC

✔ ★ ★ **COMFORT INN.** 1120 S College Ave (DE 896) (19713). 302/368-8715; FAX 302/368-6454. 102 rms, 2 story. S $48-$52; D $54-$58; each addl $6; under 18 free. Crib free. Pet accepted. TV; cable. Pool; lifeguard. Complimentary continental bkfst, coffee. Ck-out noon. Meeting rm. Some refrigerators. Cr cds: A, C, D, DS, ER, JCB, MC, V.

D 🐾 🏊 ⛔ 🔥 SC

★ ★ **HOLIDAY INN.** 1203 Christiana Rd (19713). 302/737-2700; FAX 302/737-3214. 144 rms, 2 story. S $63-$68; D $69-$74; each addl $6; under 18 free. Crib free. TV; cable. Pool; lifeguard. Restaurant 6:30 am-10 pm. Rm serv. Bar noon-1 am. Ck-out noon. Coin lndry. Meeting rms. Valet serv. Sundries. Cr cds: A, C, D, DS, JCB, MC, V.

D 🏊 ⛔ 🔥 SC

★ ★ **HOWARD JOHNSON.** 1119 S College Ave (DE 896) (19713). 302/368-8521; FAX 302/368-9868. 142 rms, 2 story. S $55; D $70; each addl $10; under 18 free. Crib free. Pet accepted. TV; cable. Pool; lifeguard. Ck-out noon. Meeting rms. Valet serv. Private patios, balconies. Cr cds: A, C, D, DS, ER, JCB, MC, V.

D 🐾 🏊 ⛔ 🔥 SC

✔ ★ **McINTOSH INN.** 100 McIntosh Plaza (19713). 302/453-9100; res: 800/444-2775. 108 rms. S $38.95; D $44.95; each addl $3. Crib free. TV. Restaurant adj open 24 hrs. Ck-out 11 am. Cr cds: A, C, D, MC, V.

D ⛔ 🔥 SC

Hotel

★ ★ ★ **HILTON INN CHRISTIANA.** 100 Continental Dr (19713), I-95 exit 4 B (Stanton). 302/454-1500; FAX 302/454-0233. 200 rms, 4 story. S $107-$125; D $117-$135; each addl $10; suites $185-$325; family plans; higher rates univ graduation. Crib free. TV; cable. Heated pool; whirlpool, poolside serv, lifeguard. Restaurant 6:30 am-10 pm. Bar 11-1 am. Ck-out 11:30 am. Meeting rms. Concierge. RR station transportation. Tennis, golf privileges. Exercise equipt; treadmill, bicycles. *LUXURY LEVEL : EXECUTIVE LEVEL.* 66 rms, 2 suites. S $130-$140; D $140-$150; suites $225-$325. Private lounge. Complimentary continental bkfst, refreshments, shoeshine. Cr cds: A, C, D, DS, ER, JCB, MC, V.

D 🏋 🏊 🎿 ⛔ 🔥 SC

Restaurants

✔ ★ **KLONDIKE KATE'S.** 158 E Main St. 302/737-6100. Hrs: 11-1 am; Sun from 10 am. Closed Thanksgiving, Dec 25. Mexican, Amer menu. Bar. Semi-a la carte: lunch, dinner $4.95-$12.95. Child's meals. Specializes in fresh seafood, Tex-Mex dishes. Outdoor dining. In former courthouse/jail. Cr cds: A, DS, MC, V.

★ ★ **MIRAGE.** 100 Elkton Rd. 302/453-1711. Hrs: 11:30 am-2:30 pm, 5:30-9 pm; Sat 5:30-10 pm. Closed Sun; some major hols. Res accepted. Bar. A la carte entrees: lunch $4.95-$6.25, dinner $12.95-$17.95. Specializes in fresh seafood, beef. Jazz Fri. Parking. Modern decor. Cr cds: D, DS, MC, V.

D

✔ ★ **SANTA FE BAR & GRILL.** Chapman Rd at DE 273, in University Plaza Shopping Center. 302/738-0758. Hrs: 11-1 am; Sat & Sun from noon. Closed Dec 25. Res accepted. Mexican, Amer menu. Bar. Semi-a la carte: lunch $3.95-$5.50, dinner $5.95-$12.25. Specializes in mesquite-grilled dishes, Tex-Mex dishes. Magician Fri. Mexican decor. Cr cds: A, MC, V.

New Castle (A-9)

Settled: 1651 **Pop:** 4,837 **Elev:** 19 ft **Area code:** 302 **Zip:** 19720

New Castle—meeting place of the colonial assemblies, first capital of the state and an early center of culture and communication—was one of Delaware's first settlements. Its fine harbor made it a busy port in the 18th century until its commerce was taken over by Wilmington, which is closer to Philadelphia. Today, New Castle is a historian's and architect's delight—charming, mellow and relaxed. Three signers of the Declaration of Independence made their homes here: George Read, Thomas McKean and George Ross, Jr (considered a Pennsylvanian by some). New Castle lies at the foot of the Delaware Memorial Bridge, which connects with the southern end of the New Jersey Turnpike.

What to See and Do

1. **The Green.** Delaware & 3rd Sts. Laid out by direction of Peter Stuyvesant, this public square of the old town is surrounded by dozens of historically important buildings.

2. **Amstel House Museum** (1730). 2 E 4th St at Delaware St. Restored brick mansion of seventh governor of Delaware; an earlier structure was incorporated into the service wing. Houses colonial furnishings and arts; complete colonial kitchen. (Mar-Dec, daily exc Mon; rest of yr, Sat & Sun; closed major hols) Combination ticket available with Old Dutch House (see #4). Phone 322-2794. ¢

3. **Old New Castle Court House** (1732). 2nd & Delaware Sts, between the Green & Market Square. Original colonial capitol and oldest surviving courthouse in the state; furnishings and exhibits on display; cupola is the center of a 12-mile circle that delineates Delaware-Pennsylvania border. (Daily exc Mon; closed hols). Phone 323-4453. **Free.**

4. **Old Dutch House** (late 17th century). 32 E 3rd St. Thought to be Delaware's oldest dwelling in its original form; Dutch colonial furnishings; decorative arts. (Mar-Dec, daily exc Mon; rest of yr, Sat & Sun; closed major hols) Combination ticket available with Amstel House Museum (see #2). Phone 322-2794. ¢

5. **Old Library Museum** (1892). 40 E 3rd St. Unusual semi-octagonal Victorian building houses temporary exhibits relating to area. (Thurs-Sun) Phone 322-2794. **Free.**

6. **George Read II House** (1804). 42 The Strand. Federal-style house with elegant interiors: gilded fanlights; silver door hardware; carved woodwork; relief plasterwork. Furnished with period antiques; garden design dates from 1847. (Mar-Dec, daily exc Mon; Jan-Feb, Sat & Sun) Phone 322-8411. ¢¢

(For further information contact the Mayor and Council Office, 220 Delaware St; 322-9802.)

Annual Event

Separation Day. Battery Park. Observance of Delaware's declaration of independence from Great Britain. Regatta, shows, bands, concerts, fireworks. June.

Seasonal Event

Band concerts. Battery Park. Wed evenings, June-early Aug.

(See Newark, Wilmington)

Motels

★ QUALITY INN SKYWAYS. *147 N du Pont Hwy.* 302/328-6666; FAX 302/322-3791. 100 rms, 2 story. May-Oct: S $45-$62; D $53-$76; each addl $5; under 18 free; higher rates: U of D graduation, Dover Downs; lower rates rest of yr. Crib avail. Pet accepted. TV; cable. Pool; lifeguard. Restaurant adj 6 am-10 pm. Bar 11-1 am; entertainment. Ck-out noon. Meeting rm. Valet serv. Health club privileges. Lawn games. Some refrigerators. Cr cds: A, C, D, DS, ER, JCB, MC, V.

★★ RAMADA INN. *Box 647, Manor Branch, 1 mi S of DE Memorial Bridge at jct US 13, I-295.* 302/658-8511; FAX 302/658-3071. 131 rms, 2 story. S $67-$75; D $69-$85; each addl $6; under 18 free. Crib free. Pet accepted. TV; cable. Pool; poolside serv, lifeguard. Restaurant 6:30 am-10 pm; Sun to 9 pm. Rm serv from 7 am. Bar 4:30 pm-midnight. Ck-out noon. Meeting rms. Valet serv. Sundries. RR station, bus depot transportation. Cr cds: A, C, D, DS, MC, V.

✔ ★ RODEWAY INN. *111 S du Pont Hwy (US 13/40/301).* 302/328-6246; FAX 302/328-9493. 40 rms. S $39-$44; D $43-$50; each addl $5; under 18 free. Crib $5. Pet accepted. TV; cable. Restaurant adj 11 am-10 pm. Ck-out noon. Some refrigerators. Cr cds: A, C, D, DS, MC, V.

Restaurants

★★ AIR TRANSPORT COMMAND. *143 N du Pont Hwy (US 13).* 302/328-3527. Hrs: 11 am-4 pm, 5-11 pm; Fri to midnight; Sat 4:30 pm-midnight; Sun 4-10 pm; Sun brunch 10 am-3 pm. Res accepted; required Sat. Bar to 1 am. Semi-a la carte: lunch $4.50-$8.95, dinner $9.95-$23.95. Child's meals. Specializes in prime rib. Parking. Outdoor dining. Replica of WW II-era Scottish farmhouse; war memorabilia. Overlooks airfield. Cr cds: A, C, D, DS, MC, V.

★★ CASABLANCA. *4010 N du Pont Hwy (US 13).* 302/652-5344. Hrs: 5:30 pm-midnight. Closed Thanksgiving. Res accepted; required Fri & Sat. Moroccan menu. Bar. Complete meals: 7-course dinner $18 (serv charge 15%). Belly dancers Fri & Sat. Parking. Moroccan decor. Jacket. Cr cds: A, DS, MC, V.

★★★ LYNNHAVEN INN. *154 N du Pont Hwy (US 13/40/301).* 302/328-2041. Hrs: 11:30 am-9:30 pm; Sat 4-10 pm; Sun 1-9 pm. Closed Jan 1, Dec 24-25. Res accepted. Bar. Semi-a la carte: lunch $4.95-$10.75, dinner $10.95-$25.95. Child's meals. Specializes in imperial crab, prime rib, fresh local seafood. Parking. Early Amer decor. Cr cds: A, C, D, DS, MC, V.

★★ NEWCASTLE INN. *1 Market St, in historic district.* 302/328-1798. Hrs: 11:30 am-2:30 pm, 5-9 pm; Sun 11:30 am-2 pm, 4-8 pm. Res accepted. Semi-a la carte: lunch $4.75-$13.95, dinner $11.95-$21.95. Specialties: Delaware crab cakes, chicken & oyster pie. Building constructed in 1809 by the Federal government; originally used as arsenal. Colonial decor. Cr cds: A, C, D, DS, MC, V.

Odessa (B-9)

Settled: 1721 **Pop:** 303 **Elev:** 50 ft **Area code:** 302 **Zip:** 19730

Once a prosperous grain-shipping center, Odessa tried to protect its shipping trade by haughtily telling the Delaware Railroad, in 1855, to lay its tracks elsewhere. To glorify itself that same year, the town changed its name from Cantwell's Bridge to that of the Russian grain port on the Black Sea. But the sloops and schooners that transported grain even-

tually found less shortsighted ports of call. Odessa was an important station on the Underground Railroad for many years before the Civil War. Now it is a crossroads town, at the junction of US 13 and DE 299. The town exhibits numerous fine examples of 18th- and 19th-century domestic architecture.

What to See and Do

1. Historic Houses of Odessa. Main St. (Daily exc Mon; closed major hols; also Jan-Feb). Individual house tickets available. Phone 378-4069. Combination ticket ¢¢¢

Corbit-Sharp House (1774). Georgian house built by William Corbit, Odessa's leading citizen, was lived in by his family for 150 years. Restored and furnished with many family pieces, the interior reflects period from 1774 to 1818. Maintained by Winterthur Museum, Garden and Library (see WILMINGTON).

Wilson-Warner House (1769). Handsome red-brick Georgian house, with L-shape plan typical of early Delaware architecture, is accurately furnished to portray life in early 19th century. Maintained by Winterthur Museum, Garden and Library.

Brick Hotel Gallery & Manney Collection of Belter Furniture. Federal-style, 19th-century building was a hotel and tavern for nearly a century. Gallery houses the largest private collection of Belter furniture in existence. Very high-styled Victorian furniture, Belter parlor and bedroom suites, made in New York in the mid 19th century, were famous for craftsmanship, particularly the elaborate carvings. Individual ticket ¢¢

2. Lums Pond State Park. Approx 3 mi W on DE 299 to Middletown, then 8 mi N on US 301 & DE 71. More than 1,800-acre park centered around 200-acre pond. Supervised swimming; fishing; boating (rentals). Hiking and fitness trails, game courts. Picnicking, concessions. Camping (showers, dump station; Apr-Oct). Standard hrs, fees. Phone 368-6989. Per vehicle ¢¢

3. Fort Delaware State Park (see). Approx 9 mi NE on Pea Patch Island, opposite Delaware City.

(For accommodations see New Castle, Wilmington, also see Smyrna)

Rehoboth Beach (D-10)

Settled: 1872 **Pop:** 1,234 **Elev:** 16 ft **Area code:** 302 **Zip:** 19971

The "nation's summer capital" got its nickname by being a favorite with Washington diplomats and legislators. A two-and-one-half-hour drive from Washington, DC, the largest summer resort in Delaware began as a spot for camp-meetings amid sweet-smelling pine groves. In the 1920s, real estate boomed, triggering Rehoboth Beach's rebirth as a resort town. Deep-sea and freshwater fishing, sailing, swimming, biking and strolling along the boardwalk have kept it a favorite retreat from Washington's summer heat.

What to See and Do

Delaware Seashore State Park. 6 mi S on DE 1. Seven-mile strip of land separates Rehoboth and Indian River bays from the Atlantic. Bay and ocean swimming, fishing, surfing and boating (marina, launch, rentals). Picnicking, concession. Primitive & improved campsites (hookups). Standard hrs, fees. Phone 227-2800.

(For further information contact the Rehoboth Beach-Dewey Beach Chamber of Commerce, 501 Rehoboth Ave, PO Box 216; 227-2233 or 800/441-1329.)

Annual Events

Art League Cottage Tour. Tours of local houses. Phone 227-8408. July.

Sandcastle Contest. Fisherman's Beach. Castle, whale and free-form sculpture divisions. 1st Sat Aug.

Nanticoke Indian Pow-Wow. Phone 945-7022. Early Sept.

Seasonal Event

Bandstand Concerts. Bandstand, Rehoboth Ave. Open-air concerts. Sat & Sun evenings, Memorial Day-Labor Day.

(See Bethany Beach, Fenwick Island, Lewes)

Motels

★ ★ **ADAMS OCEAN FRONT RESORT.** *(4 Read St, Dewey Beach) 1 mi S on DE 1. 302/227-3030; res: 800/448-8080 (exc DE).* 23 rms, 3 story, 12 villas. No elvtr. Late June-Aug: S, D $95-$130; each addl $5; villas (up to 8) $250-$310 (3-day min); lower rates mid-Mar-late June, Sept-Oct. Closed rest of yr. Crib $5. TV; cable. Pool. Complimentary continental bkfst. Ck-out 11 am; villas 10 am. Refrigerators. Picnic tables, grills, On beachfront. Cr cds: MC, V.

★ ★ **ATLANTIC BUDGET INN.** *154 Rehoboth Ave. 302/227-9446; res: 800/245-2112 (MD, OH, PA & VA).* 97 rms, 1-4 story, 10 kits. Mid-July-late Aug, hol wkends: D $95-$110; each addl $6; kits. $135; under 11 free; lower rates rest of yr. Crib $6. Pet accepted, some restrictions. $25 deposit and $10 fee. TV; cable. Pool. Complimentary coffee. Restaurant nearby. Ck-out 11 am. Meeting rms. Some refrigerators. Cr cds: A, C, D, DS, MC, V.

✔ ★ **ATLANTIC VIEW.** *(2 Clayton St, North Dewey Beach) 1 mi S on DE 1. 302/227-3878; res: 800/777-4162.* 35 rms, 4 story. No elvtr. Mid-June-Labor Day (2-4 night min): S, D $89-$115; each addl $7; lower rates Apr-mid-June, after Labor Day-mid-Oct. Closed rest of yr. Crib $5. TV; cable. Pool; lifeguard. Complimentary coffee. Restaurant nearby. Ck-out 11 am. Coin lndry. Refrigerators. Balconies. Cr cds: DS, MC, V.

★ **BAY RESORT.** *Box 461, Bellevue St, on the bay. 302/227-6400; res: 800/922-9240.* 68 rms, 3 story, 58 kit. units. July-Labor Day: D $99-$109; each addl $10; kit. units $109-$125; under 12 free; wkend, wkly rates; lower rates May-June & rest of Sept. Closed rest of yr. Crib $10. TV; cable. Pool; lifeguard. Complimentary continental bkfst. Ck-out 11 am. Coin lndry. Many refrigerators. Some private patios, balconies. On bay. Cr cds: DS, MC, V.

★ **BAY VIEW INN.** *(1409 DE 1, Dewey Beach) 2 mi S on DE 1. 302/227-4343.* 33 kit. units, 3 story. July-Aug: S, D $85-$95; each addl $10; under 12 free; lower rates Apr-June & Sept-Oct. Closed rest of yr. Crib $5. TV. Complimentary coffee in lobby. Restaurant nearby. Ck-out 11 am. Covered parking. Balconies. Ocean 1 blk; swimming beach. Cr cds: MC, V.

★ **BEACH VIEW.** *6 Wilmington Ave. 302/227-2999; res: 800/288-5962.* 38 rms, 4 story. Mid-June-early Sept: D $94-$119; each addl $7; lower rates Apr-mid-June, early Sept-mid-Oct. Closed rest of yr. Crib $5. TV; cable. Pool; lifeguard. Complimentary continental bkfst. Restaurant adj 8 am-11 pm. Ck-out 11 am. Coin lndry. Refrigerators. Some balconies. Cr cds: DS, MC, V.

★ ★ **BEST WESTERN GOLD LEAF.** *(1400 DE 1, Dewey Beach) 2 mi S on DE 1. 302/226-1100; FAX 302/226-9785.* 75 rms, 4 story. July-Aug: S, D $108-$168; each addl $10; under 12 free; lower rates rest of yr. Crib $10. TV; cable. Pool; lifeguard. Complimentary coffee in lobby. Restaurant opp 8 am-9 pm. Ck-out 11 am. Coin lndry.

Meeting rms. Covered parking. Refrigerators. Balconies. Ocean ½ blk; swimming beach. Cr cds: A, C, D, DS, ER, JCB, MC, V.

★ ★ **DINNER BELL.** *2 Christian St, off Rehoboth Ave. 302/227-2561.* 27 rms, 2 story, 4 kit. cottages. Late June-Aug: D $95-$100; each addl $10; suites $115; kit. cottages $495/wk; under 12 free; lower rates Apr-late June & Sept. Closed rest of yr. Crib free. TV; cable. Restaurant noon-2 pm, 5-10 pm. Bar. Ck-out 11 am. Individually decorated rms. Ocean 2 blks. Cr cds: MC, V.

✔ ★ **ECONO LODGE RESORT.** *4361 DE 1. 302/227-0500; FAX 302/227-2170.* 79 rms, 3 story. June-Aug: S, D $75-$125; each addl $5; under 16 free; lower rates rest of yr. Crib free. TV; cable. Pool; lifeguard. Complimentary coffee. Restaurant nearby. Ck-out 11 am. Coin lndry. Some refrigerators. Balconies. Cr cds: A, C, D, DS, ER, JCB, MC, V.

★ ★ **OCEANUS.** *Box 324, 6 2nd St. 302/227-9436; res: 800/852-5011.* 38 rms, 3 story. No elvtr. July-Aug: D $99-$129; each addl $10; lower rates late Apr-June, Sept-early Oct. Closed rest of yr. Crib $7. TV; cable. Pool; lifeguard. Complimentary continental bkfst. Restaurant opp 8-2 am. Ck-out noon. Refrigerators. Cr cds: DS, MC, V.

★ ★ **SANDCASTLE.** *123 2nd St. 302/227-0400; res: 800/372-2112.* 60 rms, 3 story. Memorial Day-Labor Day: S, D $90-$106; each addl $7; under 11 free; lower rates rest of yr. Crib $5. TV. Indoor pool; whirlpool, sauna, lifeguard. Complimentary coffee. Ck-out 11 am. Meeting rms. Refrigerators. Balconies. Cr cds: A, DS, MC, V.

Motor Hotels

★ ★ **BRIGHTON SUITES.** *34 Wilmington Ave. 302/227-5780; res: 800/227-5788; FAX 302/227-6815.* 66 suites, 4 story. July-Aug: suites $129-$189; each addl $10; under 16 free; mid-wk rates; package plans; lower rates rest of yr. Crib $6. TV; cable. Heated pool; lifeguard. Complimentary coffee in lobby. Restaurant opp 11 am-9 pm. Ck-out 11 am. Meeting rms. Bellhops in season. Sundries. Garage parking. Exercise equipt; weight machines, bicycles. Refrigerators, wet bars. Cr cds: A, C, D, DS, MC, V.

★ ★ **HENLOPEN.** *511 N Boardwalk. 302/227-2551; res: 800/441-8450; FAX 302/227-8147.* 93 rms, 8 story. June-Aug (2-3-day min wkends): S, D $130-$185; each addl $10; under 16 free; varied lower rates Apr-May & Sept-Oct. Closed rest of yr. Crib free. TV; cable. Coffee in rms. Restaurant 8-11 am, 5-10 pm. Ck-out 11 am. Meeting rms. Bellhops. Sundries. Some refrigerators. Balconies. On beach; ocean views. Cr cds: A, C, D, DS, MC, V.

Hotel

★ ★ ★ **BOARDWALK PLAZA.** *2 Olive Ave. 302/227-7169; res: 800/332-3224; FAX 302/227-0561.* 84 units, 4 story, 45 suites, 6 kit. units. Memorial Day-Labor Day: S, D $125-$210; each addl $10; suites $185-$240; kit. units $1,800-$2,600/wk (Memorial Day-Labor Day 1-wk min); under 6 free; lower rates rest of yr. Crib free. TV; cable. Indoor/outdoor pool; poolside serv, lifeguard. Supervised child's activities (Memorial Day-Labor Day). Restaurant open 24 hrs in season; off season 7 am-10 pm. Rm serv 24 hrs. Ck-out 11 am. Meeting rms. Concierge. Exercise equipt; weight machines, bicycles. Refrigerators. Minibars. Some balconies. On beach; ocean swimming. Victorian decor & architectural detail in modern structure; antiques, period furnishings; glass-encased oceanview elvtr; rooftop sun deck. Cr cds: A, D, DS, MC, V.

Restaurants

★ ★ **1776.** *DE 1N, in Midway Shopping Center.* 302/226-1776. Hrs: 5-10 pm. Res accepted. Continental menu. Serv bar. Complete meal: dinner $20. Child's meals. Specializes in duckling, veal. Casual dining among 18th-century decor; period pieces. Cr cds: MC, V.

D

✔ ★ ★ **ADRIATICO RISTORANTE.** *6 N 1st St.* 302/227-9255. Hrs: 4:30-9 pm; summer to 10 pm. Res accepted. Italian menu. Bar. Semi-a la carte: dinner $8.25-$16.95. Child's meals. Specializes in veal, chicken, pasta. Cr cds: A, C, D, DS, MC, V.

D

★ ★ **BLUE MOON.** *35 Baltimore Ave.* 302/227-6515. Hrs: 6-11 pm; Sun brunch 11 am-2 pm. Closed Jan, Dec. Res accepted. Bar 4 pm-1 am. A la carte entrees: dinner $8.50-$26. Sun brunch $12.95. Child's meals. Outdoor dining. Innovative gourmet menu. Cr cds: A, C, D, DS, MC, V.

★ ★ **CHEZ LA MER.** *210 2nd St.* 302/227-6494. Hrs: 5:30-10 pm; Fri, Sat to 10:30 pm. Closed Mon-Wed off season; Thanksgiving; also Dec-Mar. Res accepted. Continental menu. Bar to 1 am. Semi-a la carte: dinner $15-$24. Child's meals. Specializes in fresh seafood, veal. Outdoor dining. Restored house with French provincial decor. Sun porch. Cr cds: A, D, MC, V.

✔ ★ **THE CRAB HOUSE.** *DE 1 and Phillips St.* 302/227-9007. Hrs: 4-11 pm. Closed mid-Sept-mid-May. Res accepted. Serv bar. Semi-a la carte: dinner $9.95-$16.95. Child's meals. Specializes in seafood, crab cakes, crab imperial. Salad bar. Parking. Casual atmosphere. Cr cds: A, C, D, MC, V.

D

★ ★ **FRAN O'BRIEN'S BEACH HOUSE.** *59 Lake Ave.* 302/227-6121. Hrs: 5 pm-1 am. Closed Oct-Apr; also Mon-Wed, May. Res accepted. Bar. Semi-a la carte: dinner $14-$28. Child's meals. Specializes in prime rib, seafood, steak. Salad bar. Pianist. Parking. Cr cds: A, MC, V.

★ ★ **GARDEN GOURMET.** *4121 DE 1.* 302/227-4747. Hrs: 5 pm-1 am. Closed 2 wks mid-Dec. Res accepted. Continental menu. Bar. Wine list. Semi-a la carte: dinner $12.50-$30. Complete meals: dinner $26-$43. Specializes in fresh local seafood, beef, veal. Parking. Renovated farm homestead (1898). Cr cds: DS, MC, V.

★ **IRISH EYES.** *15 Wilmington Ave.* 302/227-2888. Hrs: 5-10 pm; Sat, Sun from noon; Memorial Day-Labor Day to 11 pm. Closed Thanksgiving, Dec 25. Bar to 1 am. Semi-a la carte: lunch $4.75-$6.75, dinner $8.75-$19 (cover charge $5 during comedy club). Child's meals. Specializes in overstuffed sandwiches, steak, seafood. Irish music in season. Irish pub atmosphere. Cr cds: MC, V.

★ ★ **LA LA LAND.** *22 Wilmington Ave.* 302/227-3887. Hrs: 11 am-2:30 pm, 6-11 pm. Closed Jan 1, Thanksgiving, Dec 24, 25; also Nov-Mar. Res accepted. Bar 5 pm-1 am. A la carte entrees: lunch $5-$7.50, dinner $17-$24. Specialties: grilled Thai spiced swordfish, grilled mahi mahi with corn salsa. Outdoor dining. Artistic atmosphere; hand-painted walls & chairs; bamboo garden. Cr cds: DS, MC, V.

★ ★ **LAMP POST.** *4534 DE 1.* 302/645-9132. Hrs: 7-10 am, 11:30 am-10 pm; Fri, Sat 7 am-10:30 pm; Sun & Mon 7 am-10 pm; hrs vary Nov-Apr. Closed Dec 25. Bar. Semi-a la carte: bkfst $3.25-$8.95, lunch $3.95-$12, dinner $8.95-$23. Child's meals. Specializes in fresh seafood, veal, bottomless salad. Parking. Rustic decor. Cr cds: A, DS, MC, V.

★ ★ **RUSTY RUDDER.** *Dewey Beach, 2 mi S on DE 1, on bay.* 302/227-3888. Hrs: 11:30 am-9 pm, Fri, Sat to 10 pm; Memorial Day-Labor Day to 11 pm; Sun to 9 pm; Sun brunch 10 am-2 pm. Bar to 1 am. Semi-a la carte: lunch $3.95-$6.95, dinner $12.95-$25.95. Sun brunch $11.95. Child's meals. Specializes in prime rib, seafood. Salad bar. Entertainment. Parking. Outdoor dining. Nautical decor; view of bay. Cr cds: A, D, DS, MC, V.

D

★ ★ **SEA HORSE.** *330 Rehoboth Ave at State Rd.* 302/227-7451. Hrs: 11:30 am-10 pm; Fri-Sun to 11 pm. Res accepted. Bar. Semi-a la carte: lunch $4-$12, dinner $9-$19. Child's meals. Specializes in seafood, prime rib, steak. Parking. Cr cds: A, C, D, DS, MC, V.

D

✔ ★ **SIR BOYCE'S PUB.** *31 Robinson Dr, at DE 1.* 302/227-8600. Hrs: 11 am-10 pm; Memorial Day-mid-Sept Sat, Sun 8 am-midnight. Closed some major hols; also Mon Nov-late May. Res accepted. Bar 11-1 am. Semi-a la carte: bkfst $2.50-$4.75, lunch $3-$5.25, dinner $8.95-$18.95. Complete meals: dinner $8.95-$10.95. Child's meals. Specializes in king-cut prime rib, fresh seafood. Salad bar. Parking. Fireplace. Cr cds: D, DS, MC, V.

★ ★ **SQUARE ONE.** *37 Wilmington Ave.* 302/227-1994. Hrs: 6-11 pm. Closed Jan & Dec. Res accepted Fri-Sun. Bar 6 pm-1 am. A la carte entrees: dinner $17-$25. Specializes in fresh seafood, lamb, veal. Outdoor dining. Changing artwork. Patio with pool & fountain. Cr cds: A, C, D, DS, MC, V.

★ ★ **SYDNEY'S SIDE STREET.** *25 Christian St.* 302/227-1339. Hrs: 5:30-10 pm; Fri, Sat to 11 pm. Closed Thanksgiving, Dec 25; also days vary Nov-Apr. Res accepted. Bar 4 pm-1 am. Semi-a la carte: dinner $13-$20. Specializes in Cajun, Creole dishes. Own desserts. Blues & jazz evenings. Outdoor dining. Restored old schoolhouse. Cr cds: A, D, DS, MC, V.

Unrated Dining Spot

SURFSIDE DINER. *137 Rehoboth Ave.* 302/226-0700. Hrs: 8 am-4 pm; Fri-Sun to 11 pm; summer to 1 am. Serv bar 9-1 am. Semi-a la carte: bkfst $2.25-$6.95, lunch $2.99-$6.95, dinner $4.99-$10. Child's meals. 50s-style diner in converted movie theater. Cr cds: A, C, D, DS, MC, V.

D

Smyrna (B-9)

Founded: 1768 **Pop:** 5,231 **Elev:** 36 ft **Area code:** 302 **Zip:** 19977

Named in 1806 for the chief seaport of Turkish Asia Minor, Smyrna in the 1850s was an active shipping center for produce grown in central Delaware.

What to See and Do

1. **Historic Buildings.** Many historic houses and public edifices in what was originally Duck Creek Village (1½ mi N) and Duck Creek Cross Roads (now Smyrna) are well-preserved; some are open to public. (By appt) Contact Duck Creek Historical Society, 653-8844. **Free.**

2. **Smyrna Museum.** 11 S Main St. Furnishings and memorabilia from early Federal to late Victorian periods; changing exhibits. (Sat, limited hrs) Phone 653-8844. **Free.**

3. **Bombay Hook National Wildlife Refuge.** 5 mi E on DE 6, then 3 mi S on DE 9. Annual fall and spring resting and feeding spot for migratory waterfowl, including a variety of ducks and tens of thousands of snow geese and Canada geese; also home for bald eagles, shorebirds, deer, fox and muskrat. Auto tour route (12 mi),

wildlife foot trails, observation towers; visitor center offering interpretive and environmental education programs. (Spring & fall, daily, summer & winter, Mon-Fri) Golden Eagle, Golden Age and Golden Access passports accepted (see INTRODUCTION). Phone 653-6872. Per vehicle **¢¢**

(For further information contact the Smyrna Chamber of Commerce, 211 N du Pont Hwy, PO Box 126; 653-9291.)

(For accommodations see Dover, also see Odessa)

Restaurants

★ ★ **THOMAS ENGLAND HOUSE.** *662 S du Pont Hwy (US 13). 302/653-1420.* Hrs: 4-10 pm; wkends to 11 pm; early-bird dinner 4-7 pm. Res accepted; required Sat. Continental menu. Bar. Semi-a la carte: dinner $9.95-$29.95. Child's meals. Specializes in fresh seafood, prime rib. Parking. Colonial building that housed troops during Revolutionary War and was a stop on Underground Railroad. Cr cds: MC, V.
SC

✔ ★ **WAYSIDE INN.** *du Pont Hwy (US 13), at Mt Vernon, 1 blk S of DE 300. 302/653-8047.* Hrs: 11 am-9 pm; Fri, Sat to 9:30 pm; Sun noon-8 pm. Closed Mon; Jan 1, Dec 24-25. Res accepted. Semi-a la carte: lunch $4.25-$8.50, dinner $9.95-$16.95. Child's meals. Specializes in seafood, prime rib. Parking. Early Amer decor. Cr cds: DS, MC, V.

Wilmington (A-9)

Settled: 1638 **Pop:** 71,529 **Elev:** 120 ft **Area code:** 302

Wilmington, the "chemical capital of the world," international hub of industry and shipping, is the largest city in Delaware. The Swedish, Dutch and British have all left their mark on the city. The first settlement was made by Swedes seeking their fortunes; they founded the colony of New Sweden. In 1655 the little colony was taken without bloodshed by Dutch soldiers under Peter Stuyvesant, governor of New Amsterdam. Nine years later the English became entrenched in the town, which grew under the influence of wealthy Quakers as a market and shipping center. Abundant water power in creeks of the Brandywine River Valley, plus accessibility to other Eastern ports, stimulated early industrial growth. When Eleuthère du Pont built his powder mill on Brandywine Creek in 1802, the valley had already known a century of industry. From here come vulcanized fiber, glazed leathers, dyed cotton, rubber hose, autos and many other products.

What to See and Do

1. **Holy Trinity (Old Swedes) Church and Hendrickson House.** 606 Church St. Founded by Swedish settlers in 1698, the church stands as originally built and still has regular services. The house, a Swedish farmhouse built in 1690, is now a museum containing 17th- and 18th-century artifacts. (Mon, Wed, Fri & Sat afternoons; closed major hols) Phone 652-5629. **Free.**

2. **Fort Christina Monument.** Foot of E 7th St. Monument marks location where Swedes settled in 1638. Presented in 1938 to Wilmington by the people of Sweden, monument consists of black granite plinth surmounted by pioneers' flagship, the *Kalmar Nyckel*, sculpted by Carl Milles. Complex includes nearby log cabin, moved to this location as a reminder of Finnish and Swedish contributions to our nation.

3. **Grand Opera House** (1871). 818 Market St Mall. Historic landmark built by Masons, this restored Victorian theater now serves as Delaware's Center for the Performing Arts, home of Grand Opera (Sept-May), Opera Delaware (Nov-May) and Delaware Symphony. Facade is fine example of style of the Second Empire interpreted in cast iron. Open house (Thurs; fee for out-of-state visitors). Phone 658-7898.

4. **Amtrak Station.** Martin Luther King Dr & French St. Victorian railroad station, which continues to function as such, designed by master architect Frank Furness. Restored. (Daily)

5. **Willingtown Square.** 500 block Market St Mall. Historic square surrounded by four 18th-century houses moved to this location between 1973-1976. One houses museum gift shop for the Historical Society of Delaware; others serve as office and conference space.

6. **Old Town Hall Museum** (1798). 512 Market St, near Willingtown Sq. Georgian-style town hall served as city's meeting chambers, offices, jail, subscription library and headquarters for nearly all civic organizations in late 18th and early 19th centuries. Now a museum displaying items relating to Delaware history, including decorative arts, furniture and silver. Restored jail cells in basement; children's room. (Tues-Sat; closed hols & during exhibit changes) Phone 655-7161. **Free.**

7. **Delaware Art Museum.** 2301 Kentmere Pkwy. Expanded facility features Howard Pyle Collection of American illustrations, with works by Pyle, N.C. Wyeth and Maxfield Parrish; American painting collection, with works by West, Homer, Church, Glackens and Hopper; Bancroft Collection of English Pre-Raphaelite art, with works by Rossetti and Burne-Jones; and Phelps Collection of Andrew Wyeth works; also changing exhibits, children's participatory gallery; store. (Daily exc Mon; closed major hols) Guided tours by appt. Phone 571-9590. **¢¢**

8. **Rockwood Museum.** 610 Shipley Rd. A 19th-century Gothic-revival estate with gardens in English-Romantic style. On grounds are manor house, conservatory, porter's lodge and other outbuildings. Museum furnished with English, European and American decorative arts of the 17th through 19th centuries. Guided tours (Tues-Sat). (See ANNUAL EVENTS) Phone 761-4340. **¢¢**

9. **Brandywine Zoo and Park.** On both sides of Brandywine River, from Augustine to Market St bridges. Designed by Frederick Law Olmstead, the park includes Josephine Garden with fountain and roses; stands of Japanese cherry trees. The zoo, along North Park Drive, features animals from North and South America (daily). Picnicking; playgrounds. Sr citizen rate. Phone 571-7747. Zoo **¢¢;** Nov-Mar **free.**

10. **Winterthur Museum, Garden and Library.** 6 mi NW on DE 52. Museum houses decorative arts representing period from 1640 to 1860; collection of over 89,000 objects is displayed in two buildings. First floor exhibition introduces 200 years of American antiques. The Period Rooms (seen on guided tours) were arranged by Henry Francis du Pont in his 9-story country house. Museum is surrounded by 200 acres of naturally landscaped garden, also arranged by du Pont, on a 980-acre estate. The Galleries at Winterthur offer self-guided tours. (Daily exc Mon; closed hols) Admission varies with tour. Phone 888-4600 or 800/448-3883. General admission **¢¢¢**

11. **Hagley Museum.** 3 mi NW off DE 141. Old riverside stone mill buildings, one-room schoolhouse and millwright shop highlight 19th-century explosive manufacturing and community life; 240-acre historic site of E.I. du Pont's original black powder mills, including exhibit building with working models and dioramas, operating water wheel, stationary steam engine and a fully operable 1875 machine shop. Admission includes bus ride along river for tour of 1803 "Eleutherian Mills," residence with antiques reflecting five generations of du Ponts, a 19th-century garden and a barn with collection of antique wagons. Museum store. (Mid-Mar-Dec, daily; rest of yr, Sat & Sun, limited hrs Mon-Fri; closed Thanksgiving, Dec 25 & 31) Sr citizen rate. Phone 658-2400. **¢¢¢**

12. **Delaware Museum of Natural History.** 5 mi NW on DE 52 in Greenville. Exhibits of shells, birds, mammals; also largest bird egg and 500-pound clam. (Daily; closed major hols) Sr citizen rate. Phone 658-9111. **¢¢**

13. **Brandywine Springs Park.** 4 mi W on DE 41, 3300 Faulkland Rd. Site of a once-famous resort hotel (1827-45) for southern planters and politicos. Here Lafayette met Washington under the Council Oak before the Battle of Brandywine in 1777. Picnicking, fire-

places, pavilions, baseball fields. Pets on leash only. (Daily) Phone 323-6422. **Free.**

14. **Banning Park.** 2 mi S on DE 4. Middleboro Rd & Maryland Ave. Fishing. Tennis, playing fields. Picnicking; pavilions. (Daily) Phone 323-6422. **Free.**

15. **Brandywine Creek State Park.** 4 mi N on DE 100. A 841-acre day-use park. Fishing. Nature and fitness trails. Cross-country skiing. Picnicking. Nature center. Standard hrs, fees. Phone 577-3534.

16. **Bellevue State Park.** 4 mi NE via I-95, Marsh Rd exit. Fishing. Nature and fitness trails, bicycling, horseback riding trails; tennis, game courts. Picnicking (pavilions). Standard hrs, fees. Phone 577-3390.

17. **Fort Delaware State Park** (see). Approx 15 mi S on Pea Patch Island, opposite Delaware City.

18. **Nemours Mansion and Gardens.** Rockland Rd between DE 141 & US 202. Country estate (300 acres) of Alfred I. du Pont. Mansion (1910) is modified Louis XVI, by Carrère and Hastings, with 102 rooms of rare antique furniture, Oriental rugs, tapestries and paintings dating from 15th century. Formal French gardens extend one-third of a mile along main vista from house with terraces, statuary and pools. Tours (May-Nov, daily exc Mon; res required) Over 16 yrs only. Phone 651-6912. ¢¢¢

19. **Wilmington & Western Railroad.** 4 mi SW, near jct DE 2 & DE 41 at Greenbank Station. Round-trip steam-train ride (9 mi) to and from Mt Cuba picnic grove. (May-Oct, Sun; rest of yr, schedule varies) Phone 998-1930. ¢¢¢

(For further information contact the Greater Wilmington Convention & Visitors Bureau, 1300 Market St, Suite 504, 19801; 652-4088.)

Annual Events

Hagley's Irish Festival. Hagley Museum (see #11). Irish dancers, singers, bagpipes, traditional food. Last Sat Apr.

Wilmington Garden Day. Tour of famous gardens and houses. 1st Sat May.

Victorian Ice Cream Festival. Rockwood Museum (see #8). Victorian festival featuring high-wheeled bicycles, hot-air balloons, marionettes, old-fashioned medicine show, baby parade, crafts; homemade ice cream. Mid-July.

Delaware Nature Society Harvest Moon Festival. 3 mi NW via US 41, at Ashland Nature Center in Hockessin. Cider-pressing demonstrations, hay rides, nature walks, farm animals, arts & crafts, musical entertainment, pony rides, games. Phone 239-2334. 2nd wkend Oct.

Seasonal Event

Horse racing. Delaware Park. 7 mi S on I-95 exit 4B. Thoroughbred racing. Phone 994-2521. Mid-Mar-early Nov.

(In PA see Chester, Kennett Square & Philadelphia)

Motels

✔ ★ ★ ★ **BEST WESTERN BRANDYWINE VALLEY INN.** *1807 Concord Pike (US 202) (19803).* 302/656-9436; FAX 302/656-8564. 95 rms, 2 story, 12 kit. suites. S $67; D $73; each addl $5; kit. suites $85; under 18 free; wkend package. Crib $5. Pet accepted. TV; cable. Pool; lifeguard. Complimentary coffee in rms. Restaurant adj 7 am-11 pm. Ck-out noon. Meeting rms. Bellhops. Valet serv. Sundries. Cr cds: A, C, D, DS, MC, V.

D 🐾 🏊 🛇 🔥 SC

★ ★ **HOLIDAY INN NORTH.** *4000 Concord Pike (US 202) (19803).* 302/478-2222; FAX 302/479-0850. 141 rms, 2 story. S $66-$79; D $72-$84; each addl $6; under 18 free; wkend rates. Crib free. Pet accepted, some restrictions. TV; cable. Pool; lifeguard. Restaurant

6 am-10 pm. Rm serv. Bar 4 pm-1 am. Ck-out noon. Coin lndry. Meeting rms. Bellhops. Sundries. Cr cds: A, C, D, DS, JCB, MC, V.

D 🐾 🏊 🛇 🔥 SC

Hotels

★ ★ **COURTYARD BY MARRIOTT.** *1102 West St (19801).* 302/429-7600; FAX 302/429-9167. 125 rms, 10 story. S $95-$115; D $105-$125; each addl $10; under 18 free; wkend rates. Crib free. Garage $8.50. TV; cable, in-rm movies. Bkfst avail. Ck-out noon. Meeting rms. Airport, RR station, bus depot transportation. Exercise equipt; bicycle, stair machine. Refrigerators, wet bars. Cr cds: A, C, D, DS, MC, V.

D 🛇 🔥 SC

★ ★ ★ **GUEST QUARTERS.** *707 King St (19801).* 302/656-9300; FAX 302/656-2459. 49 suites, 4 story. S, D $79-$119; under 12 free; wkend rates. Crib free. Valet parking $7.50. TV; cable. Complimentary full bkfst buffet. Restaurant 7-10 am, 11:30 am-2:30 pm, 5-10 pm; Sat 8-10 am, 5-10 pm. Bar 11:30 am-10 pm. Ck-out noon. Meeting rms. Free local airport, RR station, bus depot transportation. Exercise equipt; bicycles, stair machine. Health club privileges. Bathrm phones, minibars. Modern decor with European accents; atrium. Cr cds: A, C, D, DS, MC, V.

D 🏃 🛇 🔥 SC

✔ ★ ★ **HOLIDAY INN-DOWNTOWN.** *700 King St (19801).* 302/655-0400; FAX 302/655-5488. 217 rms, 9 story. S $65-$115; D $65-$125; each addl $10; suites $275-$395; under 18 free; wkend rates. Parking $6 wkdays; $2 wkends. Pet accepted, some restrictions. TV; cable. Indoor pool. Restaurant 6:30 am-midnight; Sat, Sun from 7 am. Bar 11:30-1 am. Ck-out noon. Meeting rms. Gift shop. Beauty shop. Airport transportation. Exercise equipt; weights, bicycles, whirlpool. Some rms overlook pool, garden court. Cr cds: A, C, D, DS, JCB, MC, V.

D 🐾 🏊 🏃 🛇 🔥 SC

★ ★ ★ **HOTEL DU PONT.** *11th & Market Sts (19899).* 302/594-3100; res: 800/441-9019; FAX 302/656-2145. 216 rms, 12 story, 10 suites. S, D $123-$209; suites $285-$385; under 12 free; wkend rates. Crib free. Valet parking $11.50. TV; cable, in-rm movies. Restaurant (see GREEN ROOM). Rm serv 24 hrs. Bar; entertainment. Ck-out 1 pm. Convention facilities. Concierge. Shopping arcade. Barber, beauty shop. Airport transportation. Tennis privileges. 54-hole golf privileges, greens fee $25-$45, pro, putting green, driving range. Exercise rm; instructor, weight machine, bicycles. Minibars. An architectural landmark, this hotel has undergone a major renovation, resulting in an elegant world-class hotel that offers a blend of Old World tradition with contemporary amenities. Cr cds: A, C, D, DS, ER, JCB, MC, V.

D 🏃 🏃 🏃 🛇 🔥

★ ★ ★ **SHERATON SUITES.** *422 Delaware Ave (19801).* 302/654-8300; FAX 302/654-6036. 230 suites, 15 story. S $135; D $155; each addl $20; under 18 free; wkend rates. Crib free. Garage $8; Fri-Sat free. TV; cable. Indoor pool; lifeguard. Complimentary full bkfst buffet. Complimentary coffee in rms. Restaurant 6:30-9:30 am, 11:30 am-11 pm; Sun 6:30 am-11 pm. Bar. Ck-out noon. Coin lndry. Meeting rms. Free RR station, bus depot transportation. Exercise equipt; weight machine, bicycles, sauna. Health club privileges. Refrigerators. Cr cds: A, C, D, DS, ER, JCB, MC, V.

D 🏊 🏃 🛇 🔥 SC

Inn

✔ ★ ★ ★ **BOULEVARD BED & BREAKFAST.** *1909 Baynard Blvd (19802).* 302/656-9700. 6 rms (2 with shower only, 2 share bath), 3 story. Some rm phones. S $55-$70; D $60-$75; each addl $5. TV;

cable. Complimentary full bkfst, afternoon refreshments. Ck-out 11 am, ck-in noon. Brick house built 1913. Antiques. Cr cds: A, MC, V.

Restaurants

✔ ★ **CANTINA.** *729 N Union St.* 302/658-4758. Hrs: 11 am-11:30 pm; Fri to midnight; Sat & Sun from 4 pm. Closed most major hols. Mexican, Amer menu. Bar. Semi-a la carte: lunch, dinner $5.50-$15.25. Casual atmosphere; cantina decor. Cr cds: A, MC, V.

D

✔ ★ **CHINA ROYAL.** *1845 Marsh Rd.* 302/475-3686. Hrs: 11 am-10 pm; Fri, Sat to 11 pm. Closed Mon; Thanksgiving, Dec 25. Res accepted. Chinese menu. Bar. Semi-a la carte: lunch $4.25-$7.25, dinner $8.25-$16.95. Specializes in fresh seafood, Hunan dishes. Parking. Casual dining. Cr cds: A, MC, V.

D

★ ★ ★ **COLUMBUS INN.** *2216 Pennsylvania Ave.* 302/571-1492. Hrs: 11 am-11 pm. Closed most major hols. Res accepted; required Sat. Continental menu. Bar. Wine cellar. A la carte entrees: lunch $6-$12, dinner $14-$20. Child's meals. Specializes in fresh seafood, beef. Pianist Fri, Sat. Valet parking. Early American decor in 200-yr-old house. Fireplaces. Family-owned since 1957. Jacket (dinner). Cr cds: A, D, DS, MC, V.

D

★ ★ **CONSTANTINOU'S BEEF & SEAFOOD.** *1616 Delaware Ave.* 302/652-0653. Hrs: 11:15 am-9:30 pm; Thurs-Fri to 10:30 pm; Sat to 11 pm. Closed Dec 25. Res accepted. Bar. A la carte entrees: lunch $5.95-$11.95, dinner $16.95-$46. Specializes in steak, prime rib, seafood. Entertainment Fri, Sat. Old World atmosphere; antiques, stained-glass windows. Cr cds: A, C, D, DS, MC, V.

D

✔ ★ ★ **CYNTHIA'S.** *2006 Pennsylvania Ave, in shopping center.* 302/575-0300. Hrs: 11:30-1 am. Closed Sun; major hols. Res accepted. Italian menu. Bar to 1 am. Semi-a la carte: lunch $5.95-$9.50, dinner $8.95-$14.95. Specializes in Northern Italian cuisine. Entertainment Thurs-Sat. Cr cds: A, DS, MC, V.

D

★ ★ ★ **GREEN ROOM.** *(See Hotel Du Pont)* 302/594-3154. Hrs: 6:30 am-2:30 pm; Fri 6:30 am-2:30 pm, 6-10 pm; Sat 6-10 pm; Sun brunch 10 am-2 pm. Res accepted; required Sun brunch. Continental menu. Bar. Wine list. Semi-a la carte: bkfst $6.50-$12. A la carte entrees: lunch $14-$20, dinner $25-$35. Sun brunch $27. Child's meals. Specialities: lobster ravioli, rack of lamb, Dover sole. Harpist Fri & Sat. Valet parking. Elegant dining rm in historic hotel. Cr cds: A, C, D, DS, ER, JCB, MC, V.

D

★ ★ ★ **GREENERY.** *1001 Jefferson St, in Jefferson St Plaza.* 302/652-1404. Hrs: 11 am-9 pm; Fri, Sat to 10 pm. Closed Sun; major hols. Res accepted. Continental menu. Bar to 10 pm. Semi-a la carte: lunch $5.95-$9.95, dinner $11.95-$15.95. Specializes in fresh seafood, veal. Own baking. Comedy club Thurs-Sat. Outdoor dining. Garden atmosphere. Cr cds: A, C, D, DS, MC, V.

D

★ ★ ★ **GRIGLIA TOSCANA.** *1412 N Dupont St.* 302/654-8001. Hrs: 11:30 am-2 pm, 5:30-10 pm; wkends to 11 pm. Closed major hols. Res accepted; required wkends. Italian menu. Bar. A la carte entrees: lunch $8-$12, dinner $10-$18. Specializes in hand-rolled pasta, pizza baked in wood-burning oven. Parking. Atmosphere of European bistro. Cr cds: A, D, DS, MC, V.

D

★ ★ **HARRY'S SAVOY GRILL.** *2020 Naaman's Rd.* 302/475-3000. Hrs: 11 am-10:30 pm; Fri to 11:30 pm; Sat 5- 11:30 pm; Sun 4-10:30 pm; Sun brunch 10:30 am-3 pm. Closed Dec 25. Res accepted. Bar to 1 am. A la carte entrees: lunch $4.95-$9.95, dinner $10.95-$16.95. Sun brunch $6.95-$12.95. Specializes in prime rib, fresh seafood. Pianist Thurs-Sat; magicians perform at tables Tues evenings. Parking. Outdoor dining. Fireplaces. Cr cds: A, D, DS, MC, V.

D

★ **INDIA PALACE.** *101 N Maryland Ave.* 302/655-8772. Hrs: 11:30 am-2:30 pm, 5-10 pm; Fri & Sat to 10:30 pm. Closed Mon. Res accepted. Indian menu. Wine, beer. Semi-a la carte: lunch $5.95, dinner $6.95-$15.95. Specializes in vegetarian and tandoori meals. Indian art. Cooking observed behind glass wall. Cr cds: D, DS, MC, V.

D

✔ ★ **KID SHELLEENS.** *1801 W 14th St.* 302/658-4600. Hrs: 11 am-midnight; Sun brunch 10 am-3 pm. Closed Dec 25. Bar. A la carte entrees: lunch $4.95-$8.95, dinner $7.95-$13.95. Child's meals. Specializes in grilled dishes, fresh seafood. Parking. Outdoor dining. Casual atmosphere. Cr cds: A, D, DS, MC, V.

D

★ **PAN TAI.** *837 N Union St.* 302/652-6633. Hrs: 11:30 am-2:30 pm, 5-10 pm; Sat 5-10:30 pm. Closed Sun; major hols. Pan Asian menu. Wine, beer. A la carte entrees: lunch $6.50-$9.25, dinner $7.95-$17.95. Specializes in Vietnamese, Thai dishes. Small, intimate dining area. Cr cds: A, MC, V.

D

★ ★ ★ **POSITANO.** *2401 Pennsylvania Ave, in Devon Bldg.* 302/656-6788. Hrs: 11:30 am-2 pm, 5:30-10 pm; Sat from 5:30 pm. Closed Sun; major hols. Res required. Northern Italian menu. Wine list. Semi-a la carte: lunch $8.50-$15.95, dinner $14.95-$32.95. Specializes in veal, fresh seafood. Parking. Elegant and intimate dining. Jacket. Totally nonsmoking. Cr cds: A, D, DS, MC, V.

D

★ ★ ★ **SILK PURSE.** *1307 N Scott St.* 302/654-7666. Hrs: 5:30-9:30 pm. Closed Sun & Mon; major hols. Res accepted. French menu. Wine list. A la carte entrees: dinner $13.50-$23.50. Specializes in fresh seasonal ingredients, game, fish. Own baking, pasta, desserts. In converted town house; bistro on 2nd floor. Cr cds: A, MC, V.

D

★ ★ ★ **VINCENTE'S.** *4th & Lincoln Sts.* 302/652-5142. Hrs: 11 am-2 pm, 4:30-11 pm; Sat from 4:30 pm. Closed Sun; Jan 1, Thanksgiving, Dec 25. Res accepted. Italian menu. Bar. Wine list. Semi-a la carte: lunch $7.95-$14.95, dinner $8.95-$26.95. Child's meals. Specializes in veal, seafood, steak. Own baking. Valet parking. Jacket. Cr cds: A, C, D, DS, MC, V.

D

★ ★ **WATERWORKS CAFE.** *16th & French Sts.* 302/652-6022. Hrs: 11:30 am-2:30 pm, 5:30-10 pm; Sat from 5:30 pm. Closed Sun, Mon; major hols. Res accepted. Bar to 1 am. A la carte entrees: lunch $5.95-$14.95, dinner $13.95-$26.95. Specializes in fresh seafood. Parking. Outdoor dining. Old waterworks on Brandywine River. Cr cds: A, MC, V.

D

District of Columbia

Population: 606,900	
Land area: 63 square miles	
Elevation: 1-410 feet	
Highest point: Tenleytown	
District flower: American Beauty rose	
District bird: Wood thrush	
Founded: 1790	
Time zone: Eastern	

Washington

(see C-8 VA-WV map; C-6 DE-MD map)

Area code: 202

Washington, designed by Major Pierre Charles L'Enfant in about 1791, was the first American city ever planned for a specific purpose. It is a beautiful city, with wide, tree-lined streets laid out according to a design that is breathtaking in its scope and imagination. For its purpose the broad plan still works well even though L'Enfant could not have foreseen the automobile or the fact that the United States would come to have a population of more than 230 million people. Nevertheless, L'Enfant's concept was ambitious, allowing for vast growth. Washington, named for the first US president, has been the nation's capital since 1800. The city's business is centered around government and tourism; there is little heavy industry.

The District of Columbia and Washington are one and the same. Originally the District was a 10-mile square crossing the Potomac River into Virginia, but the Virginia portion (31 sq mi) was turned back to the state in 1846. Residences of federal workers spill into Virginia and Maryland; so do government offices. At the beginning, in 1800, there were 130 federal employees; at the end of the Civil War there were 7,000; now there are well over half a million. Although the city was a prime Confederate target in the Civil War, it was barely damaged. The assassination of Abraham Lincoln, however, struck a blow to the nation and drove home to Americans the fact that Washington was not merely a center of government. What happened here affected everyone.

This is a cosmopolitan city. Perhaps no city on earth has a populace with so many different origins. Representatives from all nations and men and women from every state work here—and vote in their home states by absentee ballot. It is a dignified, distinguished capital. Many who visit the city go first to the House of Representatives or Senate office buildings and chat with their representatives, who receive constituent visitors when they can. At these offices visitors obtain tickets to the Senate and House galleries. From the top of the Washington Monument there is a magnificent view of the capital. The Lincoln Memorial and the Jefferson Memorial cannot fail to capture the imagination.

Visitor Information

Washington DC Convention and Visitors Association, 1212 New York Ave NW, Suite 600, Washington, DC 20005, has brochures and schedules of events; phone 202/789-7000 (Mon-Fri, 9 am-5 pm). For daily recorded calendar of events phone 202/789-7000. In town, the Washington Visitor Information Center, 1455 Pennsylvania Ave NW, in the Willard Collection of Shops, provides literature, maps and touring information (daily exc Sun; closed major hols).

The National Park Service maintains information kiosks at several key points in the city.

Note: By writing to your representative or senator ahead of time, tickets can be obtained for two Congressional Tours: a guided White House tour that differs slightly from the normal tour (see #24) and begins at 8:15, 8:30 or 8:45 am (Tues-Sat; specific times are assigned); or passes to the House and Senate visitors' galleries to watch Congressional sessions in progress. Without this ticket, the chambers can only be viewed when Congress is not in session (see #1).

Write your senator at the United States Senate, Washington, DC 20510. Address your representative at the United States House of

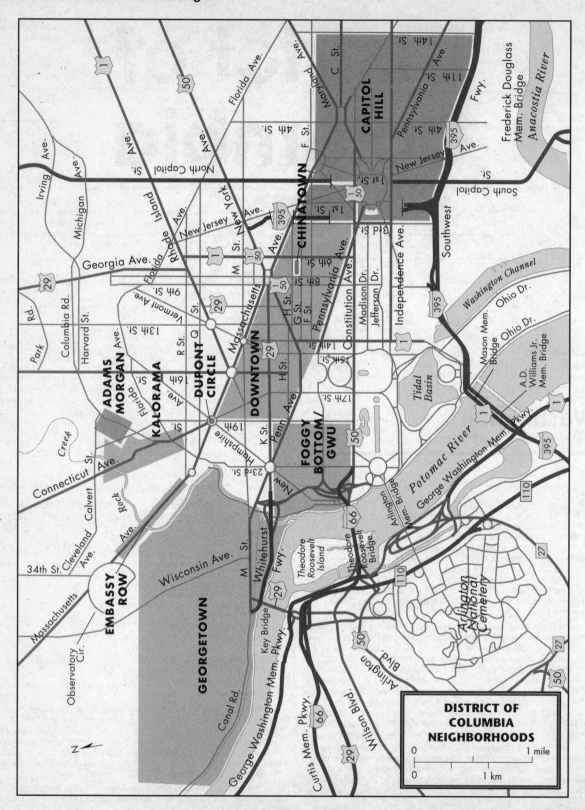

DISTRICT OF
COLUMBIA
NEIGHBORHOODS

0 ————————— 1 mile
0 ————————— 1 km

Representatives, Washington, DC 20515. All tickets are free, but in peak season, which starts in spring, White House tickets may be limited. In the letter, include the date you will be in Washington, first and second-choice dates for the tours and the number of people in your party. Also include your home phone number, should your representative's or senator's aide need to contact you. You can also get tickets, if available, directly from the office of your senator or representative after you arrive in Washington.

Transportation

Airports: *National,* 3 mi S in Virginia (see ARLINGTON COUNTY-NATIONAL AIRPORT AREA under Virginia), phone 703/419-8000; *Dulles Intl,* 26 mi W in Virginia (see DULLES INTL AIRPORT AREA under Virginia), phone 703/419-8000; *Baltimore/Washington Intl,* 32 mi NE in Maryland (see BALTIMORE/WASHINGTON INTL AIRPORT AREA under Maryland), phone 410/859-7100.

Car Rental Agencies: See toll-free numbers under Introduction.

Public Transportation: The Metrorail system is the least expensive means of getting around the capital. Metro (as it is called) provides a coordinated transportation system between buses and rail. The rapid rail system links the major commercial districts and neighborhoods, from the Capitol to the Pentagon and from the National Zoo to the National Airport and beyond. Trains operate every 6-12 minutes on the average: Monday-Friday, 5:30 am-midnight; Saturday & Sunday from 8 am. Phone 637-7000.

Rail Passenger Service: Amtrak 800/872-7245.

Driving in Washington

Since the city is divided into four quarters, or quadrants, emanating from the Capitol, driving may be confusing for the first-time visitor. The quadrants are northeast (NE), northwest (NW), southeast (SE) and southwest (SW). All Washington addresses have these designations listed after the street name. It is advisable to obtain a city map before attempting to drive through the city, especially during rush hours.

Safety Belt Information

Safety belts are mandatory for all persons in front seat of vehicle. All children under 3 years must be in an approved safety seat anywhere in vehicle. Children 3-16 years must be properly restrained in either a safety belt or child safety seat anywhere in the vehicle. For further information phone 202/939-8018.

What to See and Do

THE CAPITOL AREA

1. **The Capitol.** Between Constitution and Independence Aves, at Pennsylvania Ave, E end of Mall. The Capitol is the meeting place of Congress—the legislative branch of the government—as well as a symbol of the US government. George Washington laid the cornerstone in 1793, and part of the originally-planned building opened in 1800. Construction continued on and off over a number of years (including rebuilding after the British burned the Capitol in 1814) until the original building, which was crowned with a low copper-covered dome, was completed in 1826. Expansion in the 1850s and 1860s included the new wings, today's House and Senate chambers, and the cast iron dome seen today, which was completed during the Civil War. The Rotunda, in the center, is the main ceremonial room of the Capitol, where dignitaries have lain in-state. National Statuary Hall, just to the south, houses part of the state statue collection (each state can contribute two), but was originally built for the House as its chamber. (Tour every 15 min; closed Jan 1, Thanksgiving, Dec 25) Public dining room on 1st floor of Senate wing (Mon-Fri). Summer band concerts (see SEASONAL EVENTS). Phone 225-6827. **Free.**

   Congress. Tickets to the House and Senate visitors' galleries can be obtained from the office of your congressman or senator.

Foreign visitors can obtain passes to the Senate Gallery from the appointment desk, 1st floor, Senate Wing; and to the House of Representatives Gallery from the check stand, 3rd floor, House wing (identification required).

Old Senate Chamber. N of rotunda. Original Senate chamber has been restored to its 1850s appearance.

West Front. Along the Capitol's west front are terraces, gardens and lawns designed by Frederick Law Olmstead, who also planned New York City's Central Park. Halfway down the hill are the Peace Monument (on the north) and the Garfield Monument (on the south). At the foot of Capitol Hill is Union Square with a reflecting pool and Grant Monument. To the southwest is

2. **US Botanic Garden Conservatory.** Maryland Ave & 1st St SW, at base of Capitol Hill. The Botanic Garden, one of the oldest in the country, was established by Congress in 1820 for public education and exhibition. It features plants collected by the famous Wilkes Expedition of the South Seas. Conservatory has tropical, subtropical and desert plants; seasonal displays. Exterior gardens are planted for seasonal blooming; also here is Bartholdi Fountain, designed by sculptor of the Statue of Liberty. (Daily) Phone 225-8333 or -7099 (recording). **Free.** Up the hill, to the east of the conservatory are

3. **House Office Buildings.** Along Independence Ave, S side of Capitol grounds at Independence and New Jersey Aves. Pedestrian tunnel connects two of the oldest House Office Buildings with the Capitol. At corner of Independence and 1st St begin the buildings of the

4. **Library of Congress** (1800). 10 1st St SE. Treasures include a Gutenberg Bible, the first great book printed with movable metal type; the Giant Bible of Mainz, a 500-year-old illuminated manuscript. Collection includes books, manuscripts, newspapers, maps, recordings, prints, photographs, posters and more than 30 million books and pamphlets in 60 languages. In the elaborate Jefferson Building is the Great Hall, decorated with murals, mosaics and marble carvings; exhibition halls (some sections closed for renovation). In the Madison Building, a 22-minute audiovisual presentation, *America's Library,* provides a good introduction to the library and its facilities. (Daily; closed Jan 1, Dec 25) For reading room schedule, calendar of events, phone 707-6400; for information on exhibitions & free guided tours, phone 707-8000. **Free.** Library complex includes

   Folger Shakespeare Library (1932). 201 E Capitol St SE. Houses the finest collection of Shakespeare materials in the world, including the 1623 First Folio edition and large holdings of rare books and manuscripts of the English and continental Renaissance. The Great Hall offers year-round exhibits from the Folger's extensive collection. The Elizabethan Theatre, which was designed to resemble an innyard theater of Shakespeare's day, is the site of the Folger Shakespeare Library's series of museum and performing arts programs, which includes literary readings, drama, lectures and education and family programs. Guided tours (mornings). (Daily exc Sun; closed federal hols) Phone 544-7077. **Free.** North on 1st St is the

5. **Supreme Court of the United States.** 1st St NE at Maryland Ave, E of Capitol. Designed by Cass Gilbert in neo-classical style. Court is in session Oct-Apr (Mon-Wed, at 2-wk intervals from first Mon in Oct) and on the first workday of each week in May and June; court sessions are open to the public (10 am & 1 pm), on a first come basis; lectures are offered in the courtroom (Mon-Fri exc when court is in session; 20-min lectures hrly on half-hr); on ground floor are exhibits and film (23 min), cafeteria, snack bar, gift shop (Mon-Fri; closed hols). Phone 479-3000. **Free.** Continue north on 1st St to the

6. **Senate Office Buildings.** Constitution Ave on both sides of 1st St NE. Linked by private subway to Capitol. To the east on Consitution Avenue is

7. **Sewall-Belmont House** (1680 & 1800). 144 Constitution Ave NE. The Sewall-Belmont House is a living monument to Alice Paul, the author of the Equal Rights Amendment. From this house she

spearheaded the fight for the passage of the amendment. The house, now a national landmark, contains portraits and sculptures of women from the beginning of the suffrage movement; extensive collection of memorabilia of the suffrage and equal rights movements; headquarters of the National Woman's Party. (Daily exc Mon; closed Jan 1, Thanksgiving, Dec 25) Phone 546-3989 or -1210.   **Free.**   North of the Senate Office Bldgs, at the end of 1st St, is

8. **Union Station.** On Massachusetts Ave between 1st & 2nd Sts. Restored beaux-arts train station, designed by Daniel Burnham and completed in 1907, features lavish interior spaces under 96-foot-high, coffered, gold-leafed ceiling. Located within original station and train shed are 130 shops, restaurants and movie theater complex. Original spaces, such as the presidential suite, have been turned into restaurants without extensive alteration. Also located within the station are the Amtrak depot and Gray Line and Tourmobile Sightseeing operators (see SIGHTSEEING TOURS). (Daily)   **Free.**   Across N Capitol St is

9. **Government Printing Office.** On N Capitol St, between G and H Sts. Four buildings with 35 acres of floor space where most of the material issued by US Government, including production and distribution of the Congressional Record, Federal Register and US passports, is printed. (No public tours; to schedule private tours phone 512-1991.) Office includes the **Main Government Bookstore,** 710 N Capitol St NW. Nearly 20,000 publications available (Mon-Fri; closed hols). Phone 512-0132.

FEDERAL TRIANGLE

The Triangle consists of a group of government buildings, of which nine were built for $78 million in the 1930s in modern classic design. The apex of the triangle is at Pennsylvania and Constitution Aves NW.

10. **Labor Department.** Francis H. Perkins Building, 200 Constitution Ave NW. Lobby contains the Labor Hall of Fame, an exhibit depicting labor in United States; library on second floor is open to public. (Mon-Fri; closed major hols) Phone 219-5000 or -6992 (library).   **Free.**   At triangle apex is

11. **Federal Trade Commission Building** (1938). Pennsylvania Ave NW, between 6th & 7th Sts. (Mon-Fri; closed major hols) Phone 326-2222.   **Free.**   Directly west is

12. **The National Archives** (1934). Pennsylvania Ave between 7th & 9th Sts NW; exhibition entrance on Constitution Ave. Original copies of the Declaration of Independence, Bill of Rights, Constitution; a 1297 version of the Magna Carta and other historic documents, maps and photographs. Guided tours by appt only; phone 501-5205. Archives also available to public for genealogical and historical research (daily exc Sun; closed federal hols). (Daily; closed Dec 25) Phone 501-5000 (recording) or -5400 (research library and exhibition hall).   **Free.**

13. **United States Navy Memorial.** Pennsylvania Ave, at 7th & 9th Sts NW. Dedicated to those who have served in the Navy in war and in peacetime. A 100-foot diameter granite world map dominates the Plaza, where the *Lone Sailor,* a 7-foot bronze sculpture stands and the US Navy Band stages performances (Memorial Day-Labor Day, Tues evenings). Visitors Center features electronic kiosks with interactive video displays on naval history; also Navy Memorial Log Room and US Presidents Room. (Mon-Sat, also Sun afternoons) Phone 737-2300.   **Free.**   Also here is

   At Sea. Arleigh & Roberta Burke Theater. Underwritten by Mobil Corp, this is an award-winning high-resolution 70mm film that conveys the experience of being at sea aboard a US Navy aircraft carrier. The 241-seat theater employs a 2-story, 52-foot wide screen and 6-track digital audio to surround the audience with the sights and sounds of carrier operations. Showings (daily, every 45 min).   ¢¢

14. **Department of Justice Building** (1934). Pennsylvania Ave, between 9th & 10th Sts NW. (Not open to the public) Across Pennsylvania Ave is

   FBI Headquarters. J. Edgar Hoover Building, Pennsylvania Ave, between 9th and 10th Sts NW; tour entrance on 9th St NW. Tours of historical exhibits, including FBI laboratory; very large firearm collection; demonstration of firearms. (Mon-Fri; closed major hols) Phone 324-3447.   **Free.**   Across the street, in the next block to the west, is

15. **Pavilion at the Old Post Office** (1899). Pennsylvania Ave, between 11th & 12th Sts NW. Romanesque structure, which for years was headquarters of the US Postal Service, has been remodeled into a festival marketplace with 100 shops and restaurants, a miniature golf course and daily entertainment. In the 315-foot tower are replicas of the bells of Westminster Abbey, a Bicentennial gift from Great Britain; the tower, which is the second highest point in DC, offers spectacular views from an open-air observation deck (free). Above the Pavilion shops is the headquarters for the National Endowment for the Arts. (Daily; closed Jan 1, Thanksgiving, Dec 25) Phone 289-4224.   **Free.**   In the next blocks west are

16. **Department of Energy,** Pennsylvania Ave between 12th & 13th Sts NW; **Interstate Commerce Commission** (1934), Constitution Ave, between 12th & 13th Sts NW; **Customs Department,** Constitution Ave, between 13th & 14th Sts NW; and the **District Building,** Pennsylvania Ave, between 13th & 14th Sts NW, Washington's ornate 1908 city hall. The triangle ends at the

17. **Department of Commerce Building** (1932). Pennsylvania Ave, between 14th & 15th Sts NW. In the building is the

   National Aquarium. The nation's oldest public aquarium was established in 1873. It now exhibits more than 1,700 specimens representing approx 260 species, both freshwater and saltwater. Touch tank; theater. Shark feeding (Mon, Wed, Sat); piranha feeding Tues, Thurs, Sun. (Daily; closed Dec 25) Sr citizen rate. Phone 482-2825.   ¢

THE MALL AND TIDAL BASIN

18. **National Gallery of Art.** Constitution Ave, between 3rd & 7th Sts. The West Building (1941), designed by John Russell Pope, contains Western European and American art, spanning periods between the 13th and 20th centuries: highlights include the only Leonardo da Vinci painting in the western hemisphere, *Ginevra de' Benci;* a comprehensive collection of Italian paintings and sculpture; major French Impressionists; numerous Rembrandts and examples of the Dutch school; masterpieces from the Mellon, Widener, Kress, Dale and Rosenwald collections; special exhibitions. The East Building (1978), designed by architect I.M. Pei, houses the gallery's growing collection of 20th-century art, including Picasso's *Family of Saltimbanques* and Jackson Pollock's *Lavender Mist.* (Daily; closed Jan 1, Dec 25) Phone 737-4215.   **Free.**

19. **Smithsonian Institution.** The majority of Smithsonian museums are located on the National Mall. Smithsonian headquarters are located in the Smithsonian Institution Building, the "Castle" (1855), located at 1000 Jefferson Dr SW, on the Mall. The headquarters contain administrative offices, Smithson's crypt and the Smithsonian Information Center, which has information on all Smithsonian museums. Many visitors begin their day here. (All buildings open daily; closed Dec 25; Anacostia Museum and National Zoo hrs vary) For general information and schedule phone 357-2700.   **Free.**   Smithsonian museums on the Mall include

   National Museum of Natural History. Constitution Ave, between 9th & 12th Sts NW. Gems (including Hope Diamond), minerals; botanical, zoological and geological materials; live insect "zoo"; Dinosaur Hall, Discovery Room, with hand-on activities for children; living coral reef; cultures of Africa, Asia, the Pacific and the Americas are explored; Western civilization is traced to its roots. Cafeteria. Special Exhibition Hall.   **Free.**   To the west is

   National Museum of American History. Constitution Ave, between 12th & 14th Sts NW. Cultural and technological development of the US; Star-Spangled Banner; glass exhibit; numismatic exhibit; political history exhibits; gowns of First Ladies; interactive video stations; ship models; Railroad Hall. Cafeteria, snack bar, ice cream parlor. **Free.** Across the Mall is

Freer Gallery. Jefferson Dr at 12th St SW. Asian art with objects dating from Neolithic period to the early 20th century. Also works by late 19th- and early 20th-century American artists, including a major collection of James McNeill Whistler's work, highlighted by the famous Peacock Room. Phone 357-2700. **Free.** Next to the Freer is the Smithsonian Institution Building, or "the Castle." Connected to the Freer is the

Arthur M. Sackler Gallery. 1050 Independence Ave SW. Changing exhibitions of Asian art, both Near- and Far-Eastern, from major national and international collections. Permanent collection includes Chinese and South- and Southeast-Asian art objects presented by Arthur Sackler. **Free.** Between the Freer Gallery and the Arts and Industries Building is the **Enid A. Haupt Garden,** four acres that comprise the "roof" of the Sackler Gallery, the International Gallery, an underground Smithsonian research and education complex and

National Museum of African Art. 950 Independence Ave SW. Devoted to collection, study, research and exhibition of African art. The museum collection, numbering about 6,000 objects, is a primary source for the study of African art and culture; highlighted by traditional arts of sub-Saharan Africa, including collection of utilitarian ojects. Guided tours by appt. **Free.** To the east is

Arts and Industries Building. 900 Jefferson Dr SW. The exhibit *1876: A Centennial Exhibition* depicts the Victorian era via a re-creation of the 1876 Philadelphia exhibition, with machinery, exhibits from states and other countries. The south hall contains the Experimental Gallery, an exhibit space dedicated to innovative and creative exhibits from museums in the Smithsonian and from around the world. Discovery Theater (fee) hosts performances for children. **Free.** Directly to the east is

Hirshhorn Museum and Sculpture Garden. Independence Ave, between 7th & 9th Sts SW. Modern, circular museum houses a collection of more than 6,000 works of art donated by Joseph H. Hirshhorn. Emphasis on contemporary art, as well as 19th- and 20th-century painting and sculpture. Sculpture garden is on the Mall, between 7th & 9th Sts SW. **Free.** Directly east is

National Air and Space Museum. Independence Ave, between 7th & 4th Sts SW. Museum presents exhibits on history of aviation and space age; artifacts include the original *Kitty Hawk Flyer, Spirit of St Louis* and *Friendship 7;* also touchable moon rocks. In honor of the 500th anniversary of Columbus' voyage to the Western Hemisphere, the exhibit *Where Next, Columbus?* looks ahead to the next 500 years with a study of the scientific, technological, economic, ethical and political issues of future space travel. Five-story theater shows IMAX films on air and space travel (fee; for schedule phone 357-1686). Museum also encompasses Albert Einstein Planetarium (fee).

For a behind-the-scenes look at the restoration of the museum's reserve collection of approx 90 aircraft, spacecraft, engines, propellers and flight-related objects, visit the **Paul E. Garber Facility** in Suitland, MD (15 mi SE via Independence Ave to Pennsylvania Ave to Silver Hill Rd). Guided tours (daily; closed Dec 25; reservations must be made two wks in advance by contacting Tour Scheduler, Office of Volunteer Services, National Air and Space Museum, Smithsonian Institution, Washington, DC 20560; phone 357-1400). **Free.**

20. **Voice of America.** 330 Independence Ave SW between 3rd and 4th Sts SW; enter on C Street. Live radio broadcasts to foreign countries; 45-minute guided tours (Mon-Fri; closed major hols; reservations advised). Phone 619-3919. **Free.**

21. **Bureau of Engraving and Printing.** 14th and C Sts SW, S of Mall; enter on 14th St. Headquarters for making US paper money; self-guided tours (20 min). (Mon-Fri; closed hols & Dec 24-Jan 3) Phone 874-3019 or -3186. **Free.** Adj is

22. **US Holocaust Memorial Museum.** Entrances at Raoul Wallenberg Place (15th St SW) and at 14th St SW. Interprets the story of the Holocaust through modern exhibition techniques and authentic objects, including a railroad freight car used to transport Polish Jews from Warsaw, concentration camp uniforms, photographs, diaries. Visitors are taken from Hall of Witness directly to the fourth floor, and begin a chronological journey from the roots of the Holocaust to its aftermath. Changing exhibits include "Remember the Children," which interprets Holocaust events from a child's perspective. (Daily; closed Dec 25) Permanent exhibits recommended for ages 11 and over only. Phone 488-0400. **Free.**

23. **Washington Monument.** Mall at 15th St NW. Parking lot on N side, off Constitution Ave. The obelisk, tallest masonry structure in the world (555 ft), was dedicated in 1885 to the memory of the first US president. (Daily; extended hrs in summer) Elevator to observation room at 500 foot level. To take the 898 steps up or down, arrangements must be made in advance. Phone 426-6839 or -6841 (Visitor Center). **Free.** Directly north is

24. **Department of the Treasury.** Pennsylvania Ave at 15th St NW, E of White House. According to legend, this Greek-revival building, one of the oldest (1836-1869) in the city, was built in the middle of Pennsylvania Avenue because Andrew Jackson, tired of endless wrangling over the location, walked out of the White House, planted his cane in the mud and said, "Here." The building has been extensively restored. Tours (90 min) include office used by President Andrew Johnson after the Lincoln assassination, and the two-story marble Cash Room (Sat; by advance reservation). Phone 622-0896. **Free.** Next door is

25. **The White House** (1800). 1600 Pennsylvania Ave NW. Constructed under the supervision of George Washington, the house has been lived in by every president since John Adams. It was burned by the British during the War of 1812 and reconstructed under the guidance of James Monroe (1817-1825). The West Wing, which includes the oval office, was built during Theodore Roosevelt's administration (1901-1909); before its construction, executive offices shared the second floor with the president's private quarters. The interior of the White House was gutted and rebuilt, using modern construction techniques, during the Truman administration; President Truman and family resided at Blair House (see #28) for four years during the reconstruction. The Library and the Vermeil Room (on Ground Floor), the East Room, Green, Blue and Red rooms and the State Dining Room (on State Floor) are accessible to public. Tours (mid-March-Oct, Tues-Sat mornings; tickets avail on the Ellipse, the park S of White House; closed Jan 1, Dec 25 & presidential functions). Phone 456-7041 (recording). **Free.** West of White House is

26. **Old Executive Office Building** (1875). Pennsylvania Ave and 17th St NW. Second Empire/Victorian architecture. Built as War Office; was also home to State Department; now offices for president's staff. Closed to public. North of White House is

27. **Lafayette Square.** Statue of Andrew Jackson on horseback in center was first equestrian figure in Washington (1853). One of park benches was known as "Bernard Baruch's office" in 1930s and is dedicated to him. On square is

Decatur House Museum (1818). 748 Jackson Place NW. Federal town house built for naval hero Commodore Stephen Decatur by Benjamin H. Latrobe, second architect of the Capitol. After Decatur's death in 1820, the house was occupied by a succession of American and foreign statesmen and was a center of political and social life in the city. The ground floor family rooms reflect Decatur's federal-period lifestyle; the second-floor rooms retain their Victorian character. Operated by National Trust for Historic Preservation. (Daily exc Mon; closed Jan 1, Thanksgiving, Dec 25) Phone 842-0920. ¢¢ Around the corner is

28. **Blair House** (1824). 1651 Pennsylvania Ave NW. Guest house for heads of government and state who are visiting the US as guests of the president. Not open to public. Just west is

29. **Renwick Gallery.** Pennsylvania Ave NW at 17th St NW. American crafts from 1900 to the present. A department of the National Museum of American Art. (Daily; closed Dec 25) **Free.**

30. **Octagon House** (1798-1800). 1799 New York Ave NW, at 18th & E Sts NW. Federal town house built for Colonel John Tayloe III, based on designs by Dr. William Thornton. Served as temporary quarters for President and Mrs James Madison after White House was burned in War of 1812; also site of ratification of the Treaty of Ghent. Restored with period furnishings (1800-1828). Changing exhibits on architecture and allied arts. (Daily exc Mon; closed major hols) Sr citizen rate. Phone 638-3105. ¢¢

31. **Corcoran Gallery of Art** (1869). 17th St between New York Ave & E Street NW. Oldest and largest private gallery in the city has world's most comprehensive collection of 18th-20th-century American art; Walker and Clark collections of European art; changing exhibitions (fee) of painting, sculpture and photography. (Daily exc Tues; closed major hols) For general information phone 638-3211. **Free.** Across E St is

32. **American Red Cross.** 430 17th St NW. National headquarters includes three buildings bounded by 17th, 18th, D and E Sts NW. The 17th St building includes marble busts, *Faith, Hope* and *Charity,* by sculptor Hiram Powers and three original Tiffany stained-glass windows. (Mon-Fri) Phone 737-8300. **Free.** To the south is

33. **DAR Headquarters.** 1776 D Street NW. Includes Memorial Continental Hall (1904) and Constitution Hall (1920); DAR Museum Gallery, located in administration building, has 33 state period rooms; outstanding genealogical research library (fee for non-members). Guided tours (daily exc Sat). Phone 628-1776 or 879-3254. **Free.** Directly south is

34. **Organization of American States (OAS).** Constitution Ave & 17th St NW. Headquarters of OAS, set up to maintain international peace and security and to promote integral development in the Americas. Tropical patio, Hall of Heroes and Flags, Hall of the Americas, Aztec Garden, Council Chamber. (Mon-Fri; closed hols) Phone 458-3000. **Free.**

35. **Federal Reserve Building** (1937). C Street between 20th and 21st Sts NW. Primarily an office building, but noteworthy for its architecture; rotating art exhibits; film (20 min). Public tours (Thurs afternoons or by appt). Phone 452-3149. **Free.** Across the street is

36. **Constitution Gardens.** Along Constitution Ave between 18th & 22nd Sts NW. This 45-acre park, with a man-made lake, is also the site of the Signers of the Declaration of Independence Memorial. Phone 619-7222. **Free.**

37. **National Academy of Sciences** (1924). 2101 Constitution Ave, between 21st & 22nd Sts NW. Established in 1863 to stimulate research and communication among scientists and to advise the federal government in science and technology. A famous 21-foot bronze statue of Albert Einstein by Robert Berks is on the front lawn. Art exhibits, concerts. (Schedule varies) Phone 334-2436. **Free.** Across the street is

38. **Vietnam Veterans Memorial.** Constitution Ave between Henry Bacon Dr & 21st St NW. Designed by Maya Ying Lyn, the memorial's polished black granite walls are inscribed with the names of the 58,175 US citizens who died in or remain missing from the Vietnam War (a large directory helps visitors locate names). Also Statue of Three Servicemen. Built with private contributions of American citizens. (Daily) Phone 619-7222. **Free.** To the west is

39. **Lincoln Memorial.** 23rd St NW, at Daniel French & Henry Bacon Dr. Dedicated in 1922, Daniel Chester French's Lincoln looks across a reflecting pool to the Washington Monument and Capitol. Lincoln's Gettysburg Address and Second Inaugural Address are inscribed on the walls of the temple-like structure, which is particularly impressive at night. Tours. *(Interior to remain open to the public during restoration study.)* (Daily, 24 hrs) Phone 426-6895. **Free.** To the southeast is

40. **Potomac Park (East & West).** NW & SE of the Jefferson Memorial. On the banks of the Potomac River, park recreational activities include fishing, pedalboating; golf, tennis; picnicking. Washington's famous cherry trees can be found around the Tidal Basin.

Hundreds of **Yoshino and Akebono cherry trees**, a gift from Japan in 1912, come into full bloom in a celebration of spring (see ANNUAL EVENTS), an unforgettable floral display (late-Mar-early-Apr). West Potomac park is the site of the new Franklin Delano Roosevelt Memorial now under construction. For park information phone 619-7222. Within the park is

41. **Thomas Jefferson Memorial** (1943). S edge of Tidal Basin. Memorial honors the 2nd President of the United States and author of both the Declaration of Independence and Bill of Rights. Tours. (Daily, 24 hrs) *(Site to remain open to the public during restoration study.)* Phone 619-7222. **Free.**

NORTHWEST

The northwest quadrant of the city is north of the Mall and west of N Capitol St. Georgetown and Embassy Row are located within this section of Washington.

42. **Department of State Building.** 21st, 22nd, C and D Streets NW. The State Department's Diplomatic Reception Rooms, furnished with 18th-century American furniture and decorative art, are used by Secretary of State and cabinet members for formal entertaining. Tours (Mon-Fri; closed major hols & special events; 3-4 wks advance reservation suggested; children over 12 yrs preferred). Phone 647-3241. **Free.**

43. **Department of the Interior** (1938). C & D Streets NW, between 18th & 19th Sts NW. Within is museum with exhibits and dioramas depicting history and activities of the department and its various bureaus. Photo ID required. (Mon-Fri; closed major hols) Reference library open to public. Phone 208-4743. **Free.**

44. **Art Museum of the Americas, OAS.** 201 18th St NW. Dedicated to Latin American and Caribbean contemporary art; paintings, graphics, sculpture. (Tues-Sat; closed major hols) Phone 458-6016. **Free.**

45. **General Services Administration Building** (1917). 18th, 19th, E and F Sts NW. Was originally Department of Interior.

46. **George Washington University** (1821). (20,000 students) 19th to 24th Sts NW, F Street to Pennsylvania Ave. Theater; art exhibits in Dimock Gallery (Mon-Fri; closed hols) and University Library. Phone 994-6460.

47. **John F. Kennedy Center for the Performing Arts.** New Hampshire Ave at F Street NW. Official memorial to President Kennedy. Single structure, designed by Edward Durell Stone, incorporates opera house, concert hall, AFI movie theater, Eisenhower Theatre, Terrace Theatre and Theatre Lab; two restaurants; library. Tours (daily, limited hrs). Phone 416-8340 (tours) or 467-4600 (performance tickets).

48. **Theodore Roosevelt Memorial.** N end of Theodore Roosevelt Island, accessible only by footbridge from George Washington Memorial Pkwy, northbound lane, in Arlington, VA. The island is an 88-acre wilderness preserve; the 17-foot statue of Roosevelt was designed by Paul Manship. (Daily; closed Dec 25) Phone 703/285-2598. **Free.**

49. **Explorers Hall.** 17th & M Streets NW. National Geographic Society headquarters. Permanent science center shows the Society's explorations and exhibits on geography; Earth Station One; also a 1,100-pound, free-standing world globe 11 feet in diameter; changing exhibits. (Daily; closed Dec 25) Phone 857-7588 (recording). **Free.**

50. **B'nai B'rith Klutznick Museum.** B'nai B'rith International Center, 1640 Rhode Island Ave NW. Permanent exhibition of Jewish ceremonial and folk art. Changing exhibits. (Daily exc Sat; closed major Jewish hols, some legal hols) Phone 857-6583. **Free.**

51. **National Portrait Gallery.** 8th & F Sts NW. Portraits and statues of people who have made significant contributions to the history, development and culture of the US. (Daily; closed Dec 25) **Free.**

52. **National Museum of American Art.** 8th & G Sts NW, Gallery Place. American paintings, sculpture, prints and graphic art from the 18th century to the present. (Daily; closed Dec 25) **Free.**

53. **New York Ave Presbyterian Church.** 1313 New York Ave, at H Street NW. The church where Lincoln worshipped; rebuilt 1950-51 with Lincoln's pew. Dr. Peter Marshall was pastor 1939-49. Mementos on display include first draft of Emancipation Proclamation. (Daily, services Sun morning; closed hols) Phone 393-3700.

54. **National Museum of Women in the Arts.** 1250 New York Ave NW. Focus on women's contributions to history of art. More than 1,200 works by women artists from Renaissance to present. Paintings, drawings, sculpture, pottery, prints. Library, research center by appt. Guided tours (by appt). (Daily; closed Jan 1, Thanksgiving, Dec 25) Donation. Phone 783-5000.

55. **Martin Luther King Memorial Library** (1972). 901 G Street NW. Main branch of DC public library was designed by architect Mies van der Rohe. Martin Luther King mural. Books, periodicals, photographs, films, videocassettes, recordings, microfilms, Washingtoniana and the *Washington Star* collection. Library for the visually impaired; librarian for the hearing impaired; black studies division; AP wire service machine; community information service. Underground parking. (Mon-Sat, also Sun afternoons; closed hols) Phone 727-1111. **Free.**

56. **Ford's Theatre.** 511 10th St NW. Where John Wilkes Booth shot Abraham Lincoln on April 14, 1865. Restored as a functioning theater with Broadway and original productions offered throughout the year. Phone 347-4833 for tickets. Tours (daily; closed Dec 25). Phone 426-6924. Tours **free.** Performance tickets ¢¢¢¢-¢¢¢¢¢. In basement is

   Lincoln Museum. Exhibits and displays focus on Lincoln's life and assassination. (Daily; closed Dec 25) **Free.** Across the street is

   Petersen House (House where Lincoln died). 516 10th St NW. The house to where President Lincoln was carried after the shooting at Ford's Theatre; he died here the following morning. The house has been restored to its appearance at that time. (Daily; closed Dec 25) Phone 426-6830 or 619-7222. **Free.**

57. **Theaters. Shakespeare Theatre,** Lansburgh Theater 450 7th St NW, phone 393-2700. **The National,** 1321 Pennsylvania Ave NW, phone 628-6161. **Arena Stage,** 6th & Maine Ave SW, phone 488-3300. **The Warner,** 13th & E Sts NW, phone 703/824-1525. Also see Kennedy Center (#47).

58. **Shops at National Place.** National Press Building, F Street, between 13th & 14th Sts NW. Tri-level marketplace—at, above and below street grade—featuring more than 100 specialty shops and restaurants. (Daily) Phone 783-9090.

59. **Chinatown.** G & H Streets, between 6th & 8th Sts NW. Recognizable by the Chinatown Friendship Archway at 7th and H Sts. Archway is decorated in Chinese architectural styles of Qing and Ming dynasties and is topped with nearly 300 painted dragons.

60. **Judiciary Square.** D, E & F Streets, between 4th & 5th Sts NW. Two square blocks of judiciary buildings, including five federal and district courts and the US District Court (1820) and US Court of Appeals (1910). At D St halfway between 4th and 5th Sts is the first completed statue of Abraham Lincoln (1868). North of Judiciary Square is

61. **National Building Museum.** Housed in Old Pension Building, F St between 4th & 5th Sts NW. Deals with architecture, design, engineering and construction. Permanent exhibits include drawings, blueprints, models, photographs, artifacts; architectural evolution of Washington's buildings and monuments. The museum's enormous Great Hall is supported by eight of the world's largest Corinthian columns. Guided tours (afternoons: wkdays, 1 tour; wkends, 2 tours). Museum (Mon-Sat; also Sun afternoons) Phone 272-2448. **Free.**

62. **Howard University** (1867). (12,000 students) Main campus: 2400 6th St NW between W & Harvard Sts NW. West Campus: 2900 Van Ness St NW. Three other campuses in area. Main campus has Gallery of Fine Art, with permanent Alain Locke African Collection; changing exhibits (Sept-July, Mon-Fri). Phone 806-0970.

63. **Washington National Cathedral.** Massachusetts & Wisconsin Aves NW. Cornerstone of the Gothic cathedral was laid in 1907; final stone was set in 1990; structure, built entirely in the manner and materials of medieval cathedrals, took 83 years, 5 architects and the terms of 7 bishops to complete. Details are intentionally irregular to avoid uniform features typical of machine-age building. Tombs of Woodrow Wilson, Helen Keller and others are within structure. Pilgrim Observation Gallery overlooks Washington from city's highest geographic point. Within the grounds are tree grown from a cutting of England's Glastonbury Thorne, which by legend grew from the staff of Joseph of Arimathea; museum shop; Bishop's Garden, a medieval, walled garden; Herb Cottage; greenhouse with potted herbs for sale. Services (daily). Carillon recitals (Sat). Organ recitals (Sun). Tours (daily). Donation. Phone 537-6200 or -6207 (tours).

64. **National Presbyterian Church and Center.** 4101 Nebraska Ave NW. Chapel of the President contains memorabilia of past US presidents; faceted glass windows depict history of man and church. Self-guided tours (daily; no tours hols). Phone 537-0800.

65. **Hillwood Museum.** 4155 Linnean Ave NW. Opulent 25-acre estate was home of Marjorie Merriweather Post, heiress to the Post cereal fortune. Collection in 20-room house include works of 18th- and 19th-century Russian and French decorative arts; Russian collection is the most representative outside Russia. Tearoom. Tours (Tues-Sat, reservation required; closed hols & Feb). Grounds (daily). No children under 12 admitted. Phone 686-8500. Grounds ¢ Tours ¢¢¢

66. **Walter Reed Army Medical Center.** Alaska Ave and 16th St NW. On grounds is

   National Museum of Health and Medicine. Bldg #54, Walter Reed Army Medical Center. One of the most important medical collections in America. Interprets the link between history and technology; AIDS education exhibit; five interactive exhibits on human anatomy; collection of microscopes, medical teaching aids, tools and instruments (1862-1965) and the bullet that killed President Lincoln; *The Patient is Abraham Lincoln,* an interactive computer exhibit, deals with medical aspect of the assassination. (Daily; closed Dec 25) Phone 576-2348. **Free.**

67. **Fort Stevens Park.** Piney Branch Rd and Quackenbos St NW. General Jubal Early and his Confederate troops tried to invade Washington at this point on July 11 and 12, 1864. President Lincoln risked his life at the fort during the fighting. (Daily) Phone 282-1063. **Free.**

68. **Rock Creek Park.** NW on Beach Dr. More than 1,700 acres with working gristmill; 18-hole golf course, hiking, exercise course, historic sites, tennis courts, picnicking, self-guided nature trails, stables, bridle paths and biking trails, ball fields. Fee for some activities. Phone 282-1063. Also here are

   National Zoological Park. Main entrance at 3000 block of Connecticut Ave NW; other entrances at Beach Dr (Rock Creek Pkwy) and jct Adams Mill Rd & Harvard St. A branch of the Smithsonian Institution, the zoo features approx 5,000 animals of 500 species, including a giant panda; lions, tigers and cheetahs; great apes; elephants and rhinos; small mammals; reptiles and invertebrates; birdhouse and wetlands; rain forest exhibit. Picnicking, refreshments. Metrorail (Red Line) stop. Limited parking (fee). (Daily; closed Dec 25) Phone 673-4800. **Free.**

   Nature Center. 5200 Glover Rd NW. Planetarium, films, exhibits, nature demonstrations, self-guided walks. (Daily exc Mon; closed hols) Phone 426-6829. **Free.**

   Carter Barron Amphitheater. 16th St and Colorado Ave NW. This 4,200-seat outdoor theater in wooded area is setting for summer performances of symphonic, folk, pop and jazz music (see SEASONAL EVENTS) and Shakesperean theater. Some fees. Phone 426-6837; 421-6486 for tickets.

   Art Barn. Tilden St and Beach Dr NW. Historic carriage house (1831). Art exhibitions and demonstrations (Wed-Sun). Phone 244-2482. **Free.**

GEORGETOWN

Georgetown, a neighborhood within the city's northwest quadrant, is actually older than Washington. In colonial days, it was a busy commercial center along the Potomac. Today, Georgetown is an area of fine 18th- and 19th-century residences and fashionable shops and restaurants; the commercial center radiates from the intersection of Pennsylvania Ave and M St, northwest of the White House.

69. **Washington Harbour.** 30th & K Sts NW. This is a dining and shopping complex that features lavish fountains, life-size statuary and a boardwalk with view of Potomac River. Restaurants include China Regency and Tony & Joe's (see RESTAURANTS). Phone 944-4140.

70. **Chesapeake and Ohio Canal Boat Rides.** Departs from Lock 3, between 30th & Thomas Jefferson Sts NW. Narrated round-trip canal tours (1½ hrs) by park rangers in period clothing aboard mule-drawn boats. Ticket office adj. (Mid-Apr-Oct, Wed-Sun) Sr citizen rate. Phone 472-4376 or 653-5190.   ¢¢ (Also see CHESAPEAKE AND OHIO CANAL NATIONAL HISTORIC PARK in Maryland)

71. **Georgetown University** (1789). (12,000 students) Main entrance 37th & O Sts NW. Oldest Catholic college in US, a Jesuit school. Campus tours (daily exc Sun, by res) Phone 687-3600.

72. **St John's Church.** 3240 O St NW. Oldest Episcopal congregation in Georgetown, established 1796; original design of church by William Thornton, architect of the Capitol. Many presidents since Madison have worshiped here. Francis Scott Key was a founding member. Tours (daily, by appt). Phone 338-1796.

73. **Old Stone House** (1765). 3051 M St NW. Believed to be the oldest pre-Revolutionary building in Washington. Constructed on parcel No. 3 of the original tract of land that was then Georgetown, the house was used as both a residence and a place of business; five rooms are furnished with household items that reflect a middle-class residence of the late 18th century. The grounds are lush with fruit trees and seasonal blooms. (Wed-Sun; closed hols) Phone 426-6851 (also TTY service).   **Free.**

74. **Tudor Place** (1805). 1644 31st St NW. Twelve-room federal-style mansion was designed by William Thornton, architect of Capitol, for Martha Custis Peter, granddaughter of Martha Washington. Peter family lived in house for 180 years. All furnishings and objets d'art original. More than five acres of gardens. Docent tours (Tues-Sat, by reservation; closed hols). Phone 965-0400.   ¢¢

75. **Yellow House** (1733). 1430 33rd St NW. One of Georgetown's oldest homes, typical of the area's mansions. (Private residence)

76. **Dumbarton Oaks** (1800). 1703 32nd St NW; garden entrance 31st & R Sts NW. Famous gardens (16 acres) are both formal and Romantic in design. Mansion has antiques and European art, including El Greco's *The Visitation;* galleries of Byzantine art; library of rare books on gardening and horticulture. Museum of pre-Columbian artifacts housed in structure by Philip Johnson. Garden (daily; closed major hols); house & museum (Tues-Sun afternoons; closed major hols). Phone 338-8278 (recording) or 342-3200.   ¢

EMBASSY SECTION

This neighborhood, within the city's northwest quadrant, is centered around Sheridan Circle, at the intersection of Massachusetts Ave and 23rd St NW. Dozens of foreign legations can be found in the area and north along Massachusetts Ave.

77. **Dupont-Kalorama Museum Walk.** This is a joining of forces of seven museums to create an awareness of the area. Information and brochures are available at any of the museums concerned. The participating museums are

Textile Museum. 2320 S St NW. Founded in 1925 with the collection of George Hewitt Myers, the museum features changing exhibits of non-Western textiles, Oriental rugs and other handmade textile art. Guided tours (Wed, Sat & Sun; by appt). (Daily) Phone 667-0441.   **Free.**

Fondo del Sol. 2112 R St NW. Dedicated to presenting, promoting and preserving cultures of the Americas, the museum presents exhibitions of contemporary artists and craftsmen; holds special events; hosts traveling exhibits for museums and other institutions. (Tues-Sat afternoons; closed major hols) Phone 483-2777. ¢

Christian Heurich Mansion (1892). 1307 New Hampshire Ave NW, near Dupont Circle. Five-story, 31-room neo-Renaissance/late Victorian mansion has elaborate furnishings and garden; houses the Historical Society of Washington, DC and the society's Library of Washington History; changing exhibits. House tours (Wed-Sat afternoons; closed major hols). Library (Wed, Fri, Sat; closed major hols). Sr citizen rate. Phone 785-2068.   ¢¢

Phillips Collection. 1600 21st St NW. Oldest museum of modern art in the nation. Founded in 1918, the museum continues to emphasize the work of emerging as well as established international artists. Permanent collection of 19th- and 20th-century Impressionist, Post-Impressionist and modern painting and sculpture. (Daily; closed some major hols) Introductory tours (Wed & Sat). Concerts (Sept-May, Sun). Sr citizen rate. Wkday admission by donation. Phone 387-2151 or -0961. Wkend admission ¢¢¢

Anderson House Museum. 2118 Massachusetts Ave NW. Museum of the American Revolution and national headquarters of the Society of the Cincinnati has portraits by early American artists; 18th-century paintings; 17th-century tapestries; decorative arts of Europe and Asia; displays of books, medals and swords, silver, glass and china. (Tues-Sat; closed legal hols) Library (Mon-Fri). Free concert series. Donation. Phone 785-2040.

Woodrow Wilson House (1915). 2340 S St NW. Red-brick Georgian-revival town house to which President Wilson retired after leaving office; family furnishings and gifts-of-state. A National Trust for Historic Preservation property. (Daily exc Mon; closed Jan 1, Thanksgiving, Dec 25) Sr citizen rate. Phone 387-4062.   ¢¢

Meridian International Center. 1630 Crescent Place NW. Housed in two historic mansions designed by John Russell Pope; hosts international exhibits, concerts, lectures and symposia promoting international understanding. Period furnishings, Mortlake tapestry; gardens with linden grove. (Wed-Sun; closed major hols) Donation. Phone 939-5552.

78. **Islamic Center.** 2551 Massachusetts Ave NW. Leading mosque in the US has landscaped courtyard, intricate interior mosaics. (Daily; no tours during Fri Prayer service) Phone ahead for appropriate dress restrictions; 332-8343.

NORTHEAST

The northeast quadrant of the city is north of E Capitol St and east of N Capitol St.

79. **The Catholic University of America** (1887). (6,500 students) 620 Michigan Ave NE. Open to all faiths. Hartke Theatre (year-round). Phone 319-5000. Adj to campus is

80. **Basilica of the National Shrine of the Immaculate Conception.** On Metro Red Line stop. Largest Roman Catholic church in US and one of largest in the world. Byzantine and Romanesque architecture; extensive and elaborate collection of mosaics and artwork. (Daily) Carillon concerts (Sun afternoons); organ recitals (June-Aug, Sun evenings). Guided tours (daily). Phone 526-8300. Northeast of the campus is

81. **Franciscan Monastery.** 1400 Quincy St NE. Within the church and grounds is the "Holy Land of America"; replicas of sacred Holy Land shrines include the Manger at Bethlehem, Garden of Gethsemane and Holy Sepulchre. Also Grotto at Lourdes and Roman catacombs. Guided tours by the friars (daily). Phone 526-6800. **Free.**

82. **Kenilworth Aquatic Gardens.** Anacostia Ave and Douglas St NE. Water lilies, lotuses, other water plants bloom from mid-May until

frost. Gardens (daily). Guided walks (Memorial Day-Labor Day, Sat, Sun & hols or by appt). Phone 426-6905. **Free.** Adj is

83. **US National Arboretum.** 3501 New York Ave NE. Floral displays spring, summer, fall and winter on 444 acres; Japanese garden, National Bonsai & Penjing Museum (daily); National Herb Garden, major collections of azaleas (15,000), wildflowers, ferns, magnolias, crabapples, cherries, dogwoods; aquatic plantings; dwarf conifers (world's largest evergreen collection). (Daily; closed Dec 25) Under 16 years admitted only with adult. Phone 475-4815. **Free.**

84. **Capital Children's Museum.** 800 3rd St NE. Hands-on museum where children of all ages can explore exhibits on computers, human development and Mexican culture. (Daily; closed some major hols) Phone 543-8600. ¢¢¢

SOUTHEAST

The southeast quadrant of the city is south of E Capitol St and east of S Capitol St.

85. **Emancipation Statue.** Lincoln Park, E Capitol St NE between 11th and 13th Sts NE. Bronze work of Thomas Ball paid for by voluntary subscriptions from emancipated slaves, depicting Lincoln presenting Emancipation Proclamation to black man, was dedicated Apr 14, 1876, the 11th anniversary of Lincoln's assassination, with Fredrick Douglass in attendance. Also here is

Mary McLeod Bethune Memorial. Honors the noted educator and advisor to President Lincoln and founder of the National Council of Negro Women.

86. **Frederick Douglass National Historic Site, "Cedar Hill."** 1411 W St SE. This 21-room house on 9 acres is where Douglass, a former slave who became Minister to Haiti and a leading black spokesman, lived from 1877 until his death in 1895; visitor center with film, memorabilia. (Daily; closed Jan 1, Thanksgiving, Dec 25) Phone 426-5961. **Free.**

87. **Anacostia Museum**, Smithsonian Institution. 1901 Fort Place SE. An exhibition and research center for black heritage in the historic Anacostia section of southeast Washington. Changing exhibits. (Daily; closed Dec 25) Phone 357-2700. **Free.**

88. **Navy Yard.** M Street between 1st & 11th Sts SE. Along the Anacostia River, at a location chosen by George Washington, the yard was founded in 1799 and was nearly destroyed during the War of 1812. Outside the yard, at 636 G Street SE, is the John Phillip Sousa house, where the "march king" wrote many of his famous compositions; the house is private. One block east is

Marine Barracks. G Street between 8th & 9th Sts SE. Parade ground, more than two centuries old, is surrounded by handsome and historic structures, including the Commandant's House, facing G Street, which is said to be the oldest continuously occupied public building in the city. Spectacular parade is open to public Fri evenings in summer (see SEASONAL EVENTS). Entrance to Navy Yard is at end of 9th St at M Street SE. Inside is

Navy Museum. Bldg 76, Washington Navy Yard, 901 M Street SE. History of US Navy from the American Revolution to the space age. Dioramas depict achievements of early naval heroes; displays development of naval weapons; fully-rigged foremast fighting top and gun deck from frigate *Constitution* on display; World War II guns that can be trained and elevated; submarine room has operating periscopes. Approx 5,000 objects on display include paintings, ship models, flags, uniforms, naval decorations and the bathyscaphe *Trieste*. Two-acre outdoor park displays 19th- and 20th-century guns, cannon, other naval artifacts; US Navy destroyer *Barry* located on the waterfront. (Daily; closed Jan 1, Thanksgiving, Dec 24, 25) Tours (Mon-Fri). Phone 433-2651 or -4882. **Free.** Nearby is

Marine Corps Museum. Weapons, uniforms, maps, flags, and other artifacts describe the history of the US Marine Corps. Housed in restored 19th-century structure; also used as Marine barracks from 1941 to 1975. (Daily; closed Jan 1, Dec 25) Phone 433-3840 or -3841. **Free.**

89. **Fort Dupont Park.** Randle Circle & Minnesota Aves. Picnicking, hiking and bicycling in hilly terrain; cultural arts performances in summer (see SEASONAL EVENTS). Also films, slides and activities including natural science; environmental education programs; nature discovery room; summer day camp; programs for sr citizens and disabled persons; garden workshops and programmed activities by reservation. Phone 426-7723 or -7745. **Free.** Nearby is

Fort Dupont Sports Complex. E on Pennsylvania Ave SE; N on Minnesota Ave; E on Ely Pl. Skating, ice hockey (fee); tennis courts; basketball courts; ball fields (daily; free), jogging.

90. **Eastern Market.** 225 7th St SE. Meat, fish and produce sold. Also crafts & farmers market on Sat. (Daily exc Mon) Phone 546-2698.

NEARBY—IN THE AREA

91. **President Kennedy's Gravesite.** South Gate, Arlington National Cemetery. (See ARLINGTON COUNTY in Virginia)

92. **Iwo Jima Statue.** Across Theodore Roosevelt Bridge on Arlington Blvd. (See ARLINGTON COUNTY in Virginia)

93. **Mount Vernon.** 18 mi S via George Washington Memorial Pkwy. (See MOUNT VERNON in Virginia)

94. **Great Falls of the Potomac.** (See CHESAPEAKE AND OHIO CANAL NATIONAL HISTORICAL PARK in Maryland)

95. **Clara Barton National Historic Site.** 5801 Oxford Rd, 8 mi NW in Glen Echo, MD. Thirty-six room house (1891) of unusual architecture was both the national headquarters of the Red Cross and the home of Clara Barton for the last 15 years of her life. Contents include many items belonging to the founder of the American Red Cross. Period costumes worn during some special programs. (Daily; closed major hols) Phone 301/492-6245. **Free.**

96. **Washington Dolls' House & Toy Museum.** 5236 44th St NW. Splendid collection of antique doll houses, dolls, toys and games; museum shop. (Daily exc Mon; closed Jan 1, Thanksgiving, Dec 25) Sr citizen rate. Phone 363-6400. ¢¢

97. **Oxon Hill Farm.** Entrance from Oxon Hill Rd, 300 yds W of jct of MD 210 and I-95 in Oxon Hill, MD. "Living history" farm circa 1898-1914 located on working farm with livestock; participation activities. (Daily; closed Jan 1, Thanksgiving, Dec 25) Phone 301/839-1177. **Free.**

98. **National Colonial Farm.** I-95 exit 3A, then 10 mi S on MD 210, right on Bryan Point Rd, 3 mi in Accokeek, MD. Approx 150 acres in Piscataway National Park. A "living history" farm of mid-18th century; crops, herb garden, livestock, methods of the period are used; replicated farm buildings. (Daily exc Mon; closed Jan 1, Thanksgiving, Dec 25) Phone 301/283-2113. ¢

99. **Fort Washington National Park.** 4 mi S on MD 210, 3½ mi on Fort Washington Rd in Fort Washington, MD. Earliest defense of the city (1809), the original fort was destroyed in 1814; reconstructed by 1824. View of Potomac River; picnicking; history exhibits. (Daily) Phone 301/763-4600. Apr-Oct: per vehicle ¢¢; per person ¢

100. **Wild World.** E via Capital Beltway to exit 15A, then E on Central Ave (MD 214) in Mitchellville, MD, follow signs. Thrill rides, water attractions, children's rides; wave pool; Wild One Rollercoaster. Entertainment; game gallery. (Mid-May-Labor Day, schedule varies) Phone 301/249-1500. ¢¢¢¢¢

101. **Harness racing.** Rosecroft Raceway. 6336 Rosecroft Dr, 8 mi SE in Oxon Hill, MD. (Wed-Sun) Phone 301/567-4000. ¢

SIGHTSEEING TOURS

102. **Gray Line bus tours.** Tours of city and area attractions depart from terminal in Union Station (see #8). For information contact 5500 Tuxedo Rd, Tuxedo, MD 20781; 301/386-8300 or 800/862-1400.

103. **Tourmobile Sightseeing.** Narrated shuttle tours to 18 historic sites on the National Mall and in Arlington National Cemetery. Unlimited reboarding throughout day (daily; no tours Dec 25).

Additional tours separately or in combinations: Arlington National Cemetery; Mount Vernon (Apr-Oct) and Frederick Douglass Home (mid-June-Labor Day). Phone 554-7950 or -7020. ¢¢¢

Fourteen or more different gardens open to the public. Proceeds go to Georgetown Children's House; includes "Evermay" garden, which features grand expanses, fountains and sculptures. Self-guided tours. Phone 333-4953. Late Apr or early May.

104. CCInc Auto Tape Tours. This 90-minute cassette offers a mile-by-mile self-guided tour of the Washington, DC area. Written by knowledgeable guides, it covers Arlington Cemetery, Washington, Lincoln and Jefferson memorials, the White House, the Mall and Capitol, Embassy Row, National Cathedral, Georgetown, Old Alexandria, Mount Vernon. Tapes can be purchased locally at gift shops of the Air & Space Museum and Museum of American History or at the Lincoln and Jefferson memorials. Tapes may also be purchased directly from CCInc, PO Box 227, 2 Elbrook Dr, Allendale, NJ 07401; 201/236-1666. ¢¢¢¢

Annual Events

Cherry Blossom Festival. Celebrates the blooming Japanese cherry trees. Also Japanese Lantern Lighting ceremony and marathon run; parade. Phone 619-7275. Late Mar-early Apr.

Easter Egg Roll. White House Lawn. First introduced to Washington by Dolley Madison. Phone 456-2200 (recording). Mon after Easter.

Georgetown House Tour. Held since 1927, participants view 12 well-known and less well-known houses in Georgetown. St John's Episcopal Church members serve as hosts, guides and serve tea in the Parish Hall in the afternoon. Phone 338-1796. Late Apr.

Georgetown Garden Tour. Fourteen or more different gardens open to the public. Proceeds go to Georgetown Children's House; includes "Evermay" garden, which features grand expanses, fountains and sculptures. Self-guided tours. Phone 333-4953. Late Apr or early May.

Goodwill Industries Embassy Tour. Six to eight embassies are open to the public; only time embassies are open to public; visitors can view artifacts and design peculiar to each government's legation. Complimentary refreshments and illustrated tour booklet. Walking tour with shuttle bus between embassies. Tickets limited. No children under age 10. Phone 636-4225. 2nd Sat May.

Memorial Day Ceremony. Arlington National Cemetery (See ARLINGTON COUNTY in Virginia). Wreaths placed at Tomb of the Unknown Soldier. The National Symphony Orchestra gives a concert later in the evening on the lawn of the Capitol.

Festival of American Folklife. The Mall. Festival of folklife traditions from America and abroad. Sponsored by the Smithsonian Institution and National Park Service. Phone 357-2700 or 619-7222. Late June-early July.

July 4 Celebration. Washington Monument and Capitol west steps. Music, celebrations.

Washington National Cathedral Open House. Washington National Cathedral (see #63). Special tours, entertainment, food; demonstrations of cathedral arts. Only day of the year when central tower is open to the public. Phone 537-6200. Sat nearest Sept 29.

Pageant of Peace. Ellipse, S of White House. Seasonal music, caroling, the giant Christmas tree near the White House is lit by the President. Dec.

New Year's Eve Celebration. Old Post Office Pavilion.

Seasonal Events

Friday Evening Parade. US Marine Barracks (see #88), I Street between 8th and 9th Sts SE. Spectacular parade with Marine Band, US Marine Drum and Bugle Corps, Color Guard, Silent Drill Team and marching companies. Reservations suggested at least three weeks in advance. Phone 433-6060. Fri evenings, early-May-late Aug.

Concerts. Sylvan Theater, Washington Monument grounds, June-Aug, Sun, Tues-Fri, phone 619-7222. US Capitol, west terrace, June-Aug, Mon-Wed, Fri, Sun, phone 619-7222. Natl Gallery of Art, west garden court (#18), Oct-June, Sun evenings; passes required, phone 842-6941. Phillips Collection, a Dupont-Kalorama museum (see #77), Sept-May, Sun, phone 387-2151.

Wolf Trap Farm Park for the Performing Arts. In Vienna, VA, 14 mi NW via Washington Memorial Pkwy, VA 123, US 7, then S on Towlston Rd (Trap Rd), (VA 676), then follow signs. Phone 703/255-1900. (See FAIRFAX in Virginia) Late May-Sept.

Musical programs. In Carter Barron Amphitheater, Rock Creek Park (see #68). Phone 619-7222. Mid-June-Aug.

Fort Dupont Summer Theatre. Fort Dupont Park (see #89). Musicals, concerts, plays, dancing. Phone 426-7723 or 485-9660. Fri evenings, late June-late Aug.

Professional sports. Redskins (football), Robert F. Kennedy Memorial ("RFK") Stadium, 22nd and E Capitol Sts. Bullets (basketball) and Capitals (hockey), Capital Centre, 9 mi E in Landover, MD.

Washington Area Suburbs

The following suburbs and towns in the Washington, DC area are included in the *Mobil Travel Guide.* For information on any one of them, see the individual alphabetical listing. In Virginia: Alexandria, Arlington County (National Airport area), Fairfax, Falls Church, McLean, Springfield, Tysons Corner. In Maryland: Bethesda, Bowie, College Park, Laurel, Rockville, Silver Spring.

Airport Areas

For additional attractions and accommodations, see ARLINGTON COUNTY (NATIONAL AIRPORT AREA) and DULLES INTL AIRPORT AREA in Virginia. Also see BALTIMORE/WASHINGTON INTL AIRPORT AREA in Maryland.

City Neighborhoods

Many of the restaurants, unrated dining establishments and some lodgings listed under Washington include neighborhoods as well as exact street addresses. A map showing these neighborhoods can be found immediately following the city map. Geographic descriptions of these areas are given, followed by a table of restaurants arranged by neighborhood.

Adams Morgan: North of·Dupont Circle; along Columbia Rd between 18th Street NW and Kalorama, NW/Kalorama Park.

Capitol Hill: Both the Hill upon which the Capitol is built (south of Constitution Ave, west of 1st Street NE & SE, north of Independence Ave and east of 1st Street NW & SW) and the surrounding area south of F Street NW & NE, west of 14th Street NE & SE, north of the Southwest Frwy (I-395) and east of 3rd Street NW & SW.

Chinatown: Area of Downtown along G and H Streets NW between 6th and 8th Streets NW.

Downtown: South of Massachusetts Ave, west of N Capitol Street, north of Pennsylvania Ave and east of 19th Street. **North of Downtown:** North of Massachusetts Ave. **South of Downtown:** South of Independence Ave. **West of Downtown:** West of 19th St.

Dupont Circle: On and around the circle where Massachusetts, New Hampshire, Connecticut Aves and 19th and P Streets NW intersect.

Embassy Row: Area north of Dupont Circle; along Massachusetts Ave between Observatory Circle on the north and Sheridan Circle on the south.

Foggy Bottom: Area along the Potomac River south of K Street NW (US 29), west of 19th Street NW and north of Constitution Ave and I-66 interchange.

Georgetown: Northwest of Downtown; south of the Naval Observatory and W Street NW, west of Rock Creek Park and north and east of the Potomac River; area around intersection of Wisconsin Ave and M Street NW.

Kalorama: East and west of Connecticut Ave NW, south of Rock Creek Park and Calvert Street, west of Columbia Rd and north of R Street.

DISTRICT OF COLUMBIA
RESTAURANTS BY
NEIGHBORHOOD AREAS

(For full description, see alphabetical listings under Restaurants)

ADAMS MORGAN

Cafe Atlantico. 1819 Columbia Rd NW

Cities. 2424 18th St NW

I Matti Trattoria. 2436 18th St NW

Meskerem. 2434 18th St NW

Saigonnais. 2307 18th St NW

Stetson's. 1610 U Street NW

CAPITOL HILL

Head's. 400 1st St SE

La Colline. 400 N Capitol St NW

Monocle on Capitol Hill. 107 D Street NE

Sfuzzi. 50 Massachusetts Ave NE

CHINATOWN

China Inn. 631 H Street NW

Hunan Chinatown. 624 H Street NW

Mr. Yung's. 740 6th St NW

Tony Cheng's Mongolian Barbecue and Chinese Seafood Restaurant. 619 H Street NW

DOWNTOWN

701. 701 Pennsylvania Ave NW

Bice. 601 Pennsylvania Ave NW (entrance on Indiana Ave)

Bombay Club. 815 Connecticut Ave NW

Bombay Palace. 2020 K St NW

Dominique's. 1900 Pennsylvania Ave NW

Gary's. 1800 M Street NW

Gerard's Place. 915 15th St NW

German Deli-Cafe Mozart. 1331 H Street NW

I Ricchi. 1220 19th St NW

The Jefferson (Jefferson Hotel). 16th & M Sts

La Fonda. 1639 R Street NW

Le Lion d'Or. 1150 Connecticut Ave NW (entrance on 18th St)

Maison Blanche/Rive Gauche. 1725 F Street NW

Notte Luna. 809 15th St NW

Occidental Grill. 1475 Pennsylvania Ave NW

Old Ebbitt Grill. 675 15th St NW

Prime Rib. 2020 K Street NW

Primi Piatti. 2013 I Street NW

Red Sage. 605 14th St NW

Sichuan Pavilion. 1820 K Street NW

Taberna del Alabardero. 1776 I Street NW

Thai Kingdom. 2021 K Street NW

Tiberio. 1915 K Street NW

Willard Room (Willard Inter-Continental Hotel). 1401 Pennsylvania Ave NW

NORTH OF DOWNTOWN

Armand's Chicago Pizzeria. 4231 Wisconsin Ave NW

Fio's. 3636 16th St

Gaby's. 3311 Connecticut Ave NW

Guapo's. 4515 Wisconsin Ave NW

Lavandou. 3321 Connecticut Ave NW

Le Caprice. 2348 Wisconsin Ave NW

Murphy's of D.C. 2609 24th St NW,

New Heights. 2317 Calvert St NW

Old Europe Restaurant & Rathskeller. 2434 Wisconsin Ave NW

Petitto's Ristorante d'Italia. 2653 Connecticut Ave NW

Thai Taste. 2606 Connecticut Ave NW

Tucson Cantina. 2605 Connecticut Ave NW

SOUTH OF DOWNTOWN

Hogate's. 9th St & Maine Ave SW

Market Inn. 200 E Street SW

Phillips Flagship. 900 Water St SW

WEST OF DOWNTOWN

Colonnade (Ana Hotel). 2401 M Street NW

Melrose (Park Hyatt Hotel). 24th & M Street NW

DUPONT CIRCLE

Alekos. 1732 Connecticut Ave NW

Bacchus. 1827 Jefferson Place NW

Bua. 1635 P Street NW

C.F. Folks. 1225 19th St NW

Cafe Petitto. 1724 Connecticut Ave NW

Donna Adele. 2100 P Street NW

Kramerbooks & Afterwords. 1517 Connecticut Ave

Nora. 2132 Florida Ave NW

Obelisk. 2029 P Street NW

Palm. 1225 19th St NW

Pizzeria Paradiso. 2029 P Street NW

Sam & Harry's. 1200 19th St NW

Vincenzo. 1606 20th St NW

EMBASSY ROW

Jockey Club (The Ritz-Carlton Hotel). 2100 Massachusetts Ave NW

FOGGY BOTTOM

Galileo. 1110 21st St NW

Jean-Louis at The Watergate Hotel (The Watergate Hotel). 2650 Virginia Ave NW

Kinkead's. 2000 Pennsylvania Ave NW

Palladin by Jean-Louis (The Watergate Hotel). 2650 Virginia Ave NW

Roof Terrace. 2700 F Street NW

Sholl's Colonial Cafeteria. 1990 K Street NW

GEORGETOWN

1789. 1226 36th St NW

Aditi. 3299 M Street NW

Austin Grill. 2404 Wisconsin Ave NW

Billy Martin's Tavern. 1264 Wisconsin Ave NW

Bistro Francais. 3128 M Street NW

Busara. 2340 Wisconsin Ave NW

China Regency. 3000 K Street NW

El Caribe. 3288 M Street

Filomena Ristorante. 1063 Wisconsin Ave NW

Garrett's. 3003 M Street NW

Germaine's. 2400 Wisconsin Ave NW

Guards. 2915 M Street NW

J Paul's. 3218 M Street NW

Japan Inn. 1715 Wisconsin Ave NW

La Chaumière. 2813 M Street NW

Las Pampas. 3291 M Street NW

Madurai. 3316 M Street NW

Morton's of Chicago. 3251 Prospect St NW

Mr. Smith's. 3104 M Street NW

Nathans. 3150 M Street NW

Paolo's. 1303 Wisconsin Ave NW

Patisserie-Cafe Didier. 3206 Grace St NW

River Club. 3223 K Street NW

Sea Catch. 1054 31st St NW

Seasons (Four Seasons Hotel). 2800 Pennsylvania Ave NW

Sequoia. 3000 K Street NW

Tony and Joe's. 3000 K Street NW

KALORAMA

Katmandu. 2100 Connecticut Ave NW

Note: When a listing is located in a town that does not have its own city heading, it will appear under the city nearest to its location. In these cases, the address and town appear in parenthesis immediately following the name of the establishment.

Motel

★ ★ **CHANNEL INN.** *650 Water St SW (20024), south of downtown.* 202/554-2400; *res:* 800/368-5668; *FAX* 202/863-1164. 100 rms, 3 story. S $100-$125; D $110-$135; each addl $10; suites $175; studio rms $125-$150; under 13 free; wkend rates. Crib free. Pool; poolside serv, lifeguard. Restaurant 7 am-11 pm; Sun to 10 pm. Rm serv. Bar 11:30-1 am, Fri & Sat to 2 am, Sun to 10 pm; entertainment, dancing exc Mon. Ck-out noon. Meeting rms. Bellhops. Garage parking. Balconies. At waterfront, near piers. Cr cds: A, C, D, DS, JCB, MC, V.

Motor Hotels

★ ★ **HOLIDAY INN GOVERNOR'S HOUSE.** *1615 Rhode Island Ave (20036), at 17th St NW (20036), downtown.* 202/296-2100; *FAX* 202/331-0227. 152 units, 9 story, 24 kits. Mar-June, Sept-Oct: S $115-$155; D $130-$170; each addl $15; suites $175-$225; kit. units $145-$155; under 19 free; wkend, monthly rates; higher rates Cherry Blossom Festival; lower rates rest of yr. Crib free. Valet parking $14. TV; cable. Pool; lifeguard. Restaurant 7 am-midnight. Rm serv. Bar from 11:30 am. Ck-out noon. Meeting rms. Bellhops. Valet serv. Health

club privileges. On original site of Governor of Pennsylvania Gifford Pinchot's house. Cr cds: A, C, D, DS, JCB, MC, V.

★ ★ **HOWARD JOHNSON DOWNTOWN AT KENNEDY CENTER.** *2601 Virginia Ave NW (20037), in Foggy Bottom.* 202/965-2700; *FAX* 202/965-2700, ext. 7910. 192 rms, 8 story. Mid-Mar-Oct: S $82-$99; D $90-$99; each addl $5; under 18 free; lower rates rest of yr. Crib free. TV; in-rm movies. Rooftop pool; lifeguard (Memorial Day-Labor Day). Restaurant 6 am-11 pm. Ck-out noon. Meeting rm. Gift shop. Free covered parking. Game rm. Rec rm. Refrigerators. Some balconies. Cr cds: A, C, D, DS, ER, JCB, MC, V.

★ ★ **QUALITY HOTEL DOWNTOWN.** *1315 16th St NW (20036), downtown.* 202/232-8000; *FAX* 202/667-9827. 135 kit. units, 10 story. S $110-$130; D $130-$160; each addl $10; under 18 free; wkend rates. Crib free. Garage $8.50. TV; cable. Pool privileges. Restaurant 7 am-10 pm. Rm serv 7 am-2 pm, 5-9:30 pm. Bar 11:30 am-midnight. Ck-out noon. Meeting rms. Bellhops. Health club privileges. Cr cds: A, C, D, DS, ER, JCB, MC, V.

Hotels

★ ★ ★ ★ **ANA.** *2401 M Street NW (20037), west of downtown.* 202/429-2400; *res:* 800/228-3000; *FAX* 202/457-5010. 415 rms, 10 story. S $220-$255; D $250-$285; each addl $30; suites $600-$1,450; under 18 free; wkend, summer rates. Crib free. TV; cable. Indoor pool. Cafe 6:30 am-11 pm (also see COLONNADE). Rm serv 24 hrs. Bar 4 pm-midnight; entertainment. Ck-out 1 pm. Convention facilities. Concierge. Gift shop. Local shopping transportation. Exercise rm; instructor, weight machines, bicycles, whirlpool, sauna, steam rm. Massage. Squash & racquetball courts. Bathrm phones, refrigerators, minibars. Some balconies. Lobby and public areas with many antiques, old Italian statuary, 400-yr-old tapestries; distinctive decor with glass loggia creating a garden setting in lobby. *LUXURY LEVEL : EXECUTIVE CLUB FLOOR.* 202/429-2400. 50 rms, 10 suites. S $255; D $285; suites $600-$1,450. Concierge. Private lounge. Minibars. Complimentary continental bkfst, refreshments, newspaper, shoeshine. Cr cds: A, C, D, DS, ER, JCB, MC, V.

★ ★ **BARCELO-GEORGETOWN.** *2121 P Street NW (20037), in Dupont Circle area.* 202/293-3100; *res:* 800/257-5432; *FAX* 202/857-0134. 294 rms, 10 story. S $160-$190; D $180-$210; each addl $20; suites $175-$450; under 17 free; wkend rates. Crib free. Valet parking $13. TV; cable. Pool; lifeguard. Restaurant 7 am-midnight; Fri & Sat to 1 am. Bar noon-1 am. Ck-out noon. Meeting rms. Concierge. Gift shop. Exercise equipt; weights, bicycles, sauna. Bathrm phones, minibars. Cr cds: A, C, D, DS, ER, JCB, MC, V.

★ ★ **BELLEVUE.** *15 E Street NW (20001), in Capitol Hill area.* 202/638-0900; *res:* 800/372-6667; *FAX* 202/638-5132. 140 rms, 8 story. S $99.50; D $114.50; each addl $15; suites $175-$250; under 18 free; wkend rates. Crib free. TV; cable. Complimentary full bkfst. Restaurant 7 am-midnight. Bar 11:30-3 am. Ck-out noon. Meeting rms. Concierge. Free garage parking (overnight). Some refrigerators, wet bars. Old-World style hotel. Cr cds: A, C, D, DS, MC, V.

★ ★ **BEST WESTERN SKYLINE INN.** *10 I Street SW (20024), in Capitol Hill area.* 202/488-7500; *FAX* 202/488-0790. 203 rms, 7 story. Apr-Oct: S $79; D $89; each addl $10; under 18 free; wkend rates; lower rates rest of yr. Crib free. TV. Pool; poolside serv, lifeguard. Restaurant 7 am-10 pm. Bar 11:30 am-midnight. Ck-out noon. Coin

Indry. Meeting rms. Gift shop. Free garage parking. Cr cds: A, C, D, DS, ER, JCB, MC, V.

⊠ ⊠ ⊠ 🔥 SC

★ ★ **CANTERBURY.** *1733 N Street NW (20036), downtown. 202/393-3000; res: 800/424-2950; FAX 202/785-9581.* 99 rms, 10 story. S $140-$175; D $160-$195; each addl $20; under 12 free; wkend plans. Crib free. Garage $10. TV; cable. Complimentary continental bkfst, refreshments. Restaurant 7-10 am, 11 am-2:30 pm, 5:30-10 pm. wkend hrs vary. Bar 5-11 pm; closed Sun. Ck-out noon. Meeting rms. Health club privileges. Many refrigerators. On site of "Little White House," the Theodore Roosevelt house during his vice-presidency and first weeks of his presidency. Cr cds: A, C, D, DS, ER, JCB, MC, V.

⊠ ⊠ 🔥 SC

★ ★ ★ **THE CAPITAL HILTON.** *16th & K Streets NW (20036), downtown. 202/393-1000; FAX 202/639-5784.* 543 rms, 15 story. S $185-$295; D $210-$295; each addl $20; suites $495-$1,100; family, wkend rates; honeymoon plans. Crib free. TV; cable. Restaurants 6:30 am-midnight. Rm serv 24 hrs. Bar 11-2 am; entertainment Tues-Sat. Ck-out noon. Convention facilities. Concierge. Shopping arcade. Barber, beauty shop. Valet parking 24 hrs. Exercise equipt; weights, bicycles, sauna, steam rm. Minibars; many wet bars; some refrigerators. Tour desk. Foreign serv guide. *LUXURY LEVEL : THE TOWERS.* 71 rms, 6 suites, 4 floors. S, D $295; suites $650-$1,375. Private lounge. Some full wet bars. In-rm movies, tape library. Complimentary continental bkfst, afternoon tea, cocktails. Cr cds: A, C, D, DS, ER, JCB, MC, V.

D 🍴 ⊠ ⊠ 🔥 SC

★ ★ ★ ★ **THE CARLTON.** *923 16th St NW (20006), downtown. 202/638-2626; FAX 202/638-4231.* 197 rms, 8 story. S $240-$280; D $265-$305; each addl $25; suites $500-$1,600; under 18 free; wkend rates. Crib free. Covered valet parking $22. Pet accepted, some restrictions. TV; cable. Pool privileges. Restaurant 6:30-1 am. Afternoon tea 2:30-5:30 pm. Rm serv 24 hrs. Bar; entertainment. Ck-out 1 pm. Meeting rms. Concierge. Gift shop. Barber, beauty shop. Tennis privileges. 18-hole golf privileges 12 mi, greens fee $36, pro, putting green, driving range. Exercise room; bicycles, treadmill, weight machine. Massage. Bathrm phones, refrigerators, minibars. Courtyard terrace. Historic Renaissance-style building (1926). 2 blks from the White House. Cr cds: A, C, D, DS, ER, JCB, MC, V.

D 🍴 ⊠ 🍴 ⊠ 🔥 SC

⊯ ★ **CENTER CITY.** *1201 13th St NW (20005), north of downtown. 202/682-5300; FAX 202/371-9624.* 100 rms, 8 story. Apr-Sept: S $85-$115; D $95-$125; each addl $10; under 14 free; wkend rates; lower rates rest of yr. Parking $9 in/out. TV; cable. Complimentary continental bkfst. Restaurant nearby. Ck-out 11 am. Coin Indry. Exercise equipt; weight machine, bicycles, whirlpool, sauna. Cr cds: A, C, D, DS, MC, V.

D 🍴 ⊠ 🔥 SC

⊯ ★ **COMFORT INN.** *500 H Street NW (20001), downtown. 202/289-5959; FAX 202/682-9152.* 197 rms, 10 story. Apr-May, Sept-Oct: S, D $69-$139; each addl $5; under 18 free; wkend rates; lower rates rest of yr. Crib free. Garage $10. TV; cable. Coffee in rms. Restaurant 6:30 am-9 pm. Bar from 4:30 pm. Ck-out noon. Meeting rms. Coin Indry. Exercise equipt; weight machine, bicycles, sauna. Cr cds: A, C, D, DS, ER, JCB, MC, V.

D 🍴 ⊠ 🔥 SC

★ ★ ★ **COURTYARD BY MARRIOTT.** *1900 Connecticut Ave NW (20009), in Kalorama. 202/332-9300; res: 800/842-4211; FAX 202/328-7039.* 147 rms, 9 story. S $59-$135; D $69-$170; each addl $15; under 18 free; wkend rates (2-night min). Crib free. Pet accepted, some restrictions. Garage parking, valet $10. TV; cable. Pool; lifeguard. Restaurant 7 am-10:30 pm. Bar 5 pm-11 pm. Ck-out 1 pm. Coin Indry. Meeting rms. Health club privileges. Some minibars. Cr cds: A, C, D, DS, MC, V.

D 🐾 ⊠ ⊠ 🔥 SC

⊯ ★ **DAYS INN-DOWNTOWN.** *1201 K Street NW (20005), downtown. 202/842-1020; FAX 202/289-0336.* 220 rms, 9 story, 10 kit. units. Mar-May, Aug-Oct: S $75-$105; D $85-$115; each addl $10; suites $120-$150; family, wkend rates; higher rates Cherry Blossom Festival; lower rates rest of yr. Crib free. Garage $8.50. Pet accepted, some restrictions. TV; cable. Pool; lifeguard. Restaurant 7 am-10 pm; Sat, Sun 7-10:30 am, 5-10 pm. Bar noon-midnight. Ck-out noon. Meeting rms. Exercise equipt; weight machines, treadmill. Cr cds: A, C, D, DS, JCB, MC, V.

D 🐾 ⊠ 🍴 ⊠ 🔥 SC

★ **DUPONT PLAZA.** *1500 New Hampshire Ave NW (20036), in Dupont Circle area. 202/483-6000; res: 800/421-6662; FAX 202/328-3265.* 314 rms, 8 story. S $145-$195; D $165-$205; each addl $20; suites $195-$375; under 18 free. Crib free. Garage $13; valet parking. TV; cable. Restaurant 6:30 am-10:30 pm. Bar 11-1 am. Ck-out 1 pm. Meeting rms. Health club privileges. Bathrm phones, refrigerators, wet bars. Cr cds: A, C, D, ER, MC, V.

⊠ 🔥 SC

★ ★ **EMBASSY SQUARE SUITES.** *2000 N Street NW (20036), in Dupont Circle area. 202/659-9000; res: 800/424-2999; FAX 202/429-9546.* 250 kit. units, 10 story, 80 suites. Mar-mid-June, mid-Sept-mid-Dec: S $109-$135; D $119-$159; each addl $20; suites $139-$229; under 19 free; wkly, wkend rates; lower rates rest of yr. Crib free. Garage $10. TV; cable, in-rm movies. Pool; poolside serv, lifeguard. Complimentary continental bkfst. Rm serv noon-11 pm. Ck-out noon. Coin Indry. Meeting rms. Concierge in summer. Exercise equipt; bicycles, stair machine. Minibars. Some balconies. Cr cds: A, C, D, DS, MC, V.

D ⊠ 🍴 ⊠ 🔥 SC

★ ★ **EMBASSY SUITES.** *1250 22nd St NW (20037), west of downtown. 202/857-3388; FAX 202/293-3173.* 318 suites, 9 story. S $189-$279; D $209-$299; each addl $20; 2-bedrm suites $600-$1,200; under 13 free; wkend rates. Crib free. Garage $14. TV; cable, in-rm movies avail. Indoor pool; lifeguard. Complimentary full bkfst 6-9:30 am; Sat, Sun & hols 7-10:30 am. Complimentary coffee in rms. Restaurant 11 am-11 pm. Bar. Ck-out noon. Meeting rms. Exercise equipt; weight machine, bicycles, whirlpool, sauna. Game rm. Refrigerators. Cr cds: A, C, D, DS, JCB, MC, V.

D ⊠ 🍴 ⊠ 🔥 SC

★ ★ **EMBASSY SUITES CHEVY CHASE PAVILION.** *4300 Military Rd NW (20015), north of downtown. 202/362-9300; FAX 202/686-3405.* 198 suites, 9 story. S, D $145-$175; under 18 free; wkend rates. Crib avail. Pet accepted, some restrictions; $10 per day. Garage $10. TV; cable, in-rm movies avail. Indoor pool. Complimentary full bkfst. Complimentary coffee in rms. Restaurants 7 am-midnight. Ck-out noon. Coin Indry. Meeting rms. Exercise rm; instructor, weight machine, bicycles, whirlpool, sauna. Health club privileges. Refrigerators, wet bars. Atrium. Connected to shopping center. Cr cds: A, C, D, DS, MC, V.

D 🐾 ⊠ 🍴 ⊠ 🔥 SC

★ ★ ★ **FOUR SEASONS.** *2800 Pennsylvania Ave NW (20007), in Georgetown. 202/342-0444; res: 800/332-3442; FAX 202/944-2076.* 196 rms, 6 story. S $265-$310; D $295-$340; each addl $30; suites $575-$975; under 18 free; wkend rates. Crib free. Valet parking $22. Pet accepted. TV; cable. Indoor pool. Afternoon tea. Restaurant 7-2 am (also see SEASONS). Rm serv 24 hrs. Bar 11-2 am. Ck-out noon. Meeting rms. Concierge. Complimentary limo serv in DC area Mon-Fri. Exercise rm; instructor, weight machine, bicycles, steam rm. Massage. Full service health club & spa. Bathrm phones, minibars. Some balconies. Tastefully appointed rooms and public areas. Luxury hotel overlooking Rock Creek Park, at entrance to historic Georgetown. Cr cds: A, C, D, ER, JCB, MC, V.

D 🐾 ⊠ ⊠ 🍴 ⊠ 🔥 SC

★ **GEORGETOWN DUTCH INN.** *1075 Thomas Jefferson St NW (20007), in Georgetown. 202/337-0900; res: 800/388-2410; FAX 202/333-6526.* 47 kit. suites, 7 story. Feb-mid-June, Sept-mid-Nov: S

$110-$140; D $120-$160; each addl $20; suites (for 4) $210-$300; under 16 free; wkly, monthly rates; higher rates Cherry Blossom season; lower rates rest of yr. Crib free. TV; cable. Complimentary continental bkfst. Ck-out noon. Limited free covered parking. Bathrm phones. Some private patios. Cr cds: A, C, D, MC, V.

★ ★ ★ **GRAND.** *2350 M Street NW (20037), west of downtown.* 202/429-0100; res: 800/848-0016; FAX 202/429-9759. 262 rms, 32 suites. Sept-June: S $220-$240; D $240-$260; each addl $20; suites $450-$2,500; under 18 free; wkend packages; lower rates rest of yr. Crib free. Covered valet parking $18/day. TV; cable, in-rm movies avail. Heated pool; poolside serv, lifeguard. Restaurant 6:30 am-10:30 pm. Rm serv 24 hrs. Bar; pianist, chamber music. Ck-out 1 pm. Meeting rms. Concierge. Exercise equipt; weight machines, bicycles. Bathrm phones; some fireplaces; minibar, whirlpool in suites. Some balconies. Many rms with view of landscaped interior courtyard. Amenities package; 3 phones in each rm. Cr cds: A, C, D, JCB, MC, V.

★ ★ ★ **GRAND HYATT WASHINGTON.** *1000 H Street NW (20001), opp Washington Convention Center, downtown.* 202/582-1234; FAX 202/637-4781. 889 rms, 12 story. S $224; D $249; each addl $25; suites $425-$1,500; under 18 free; wkend rates. Crib free. Garage $12. TV; cable, in-rm movies. Supervised child's activities (Fri, Sat eves). Indoor pool; poolside serv. Restaurant 6:30-1 am. Rm serv 24 hrs. Bar; entertainment, dancing. Ck-out noon. Convention facilities. Exercise equipt; weights, bicycles, whirlpool, steam rm, sauna. Minibars. 12-story atrium lobby; 3-story cascading waterfall. **LUXURY LEVEL : REGENCY CLUB.** 63 rms, 3 suites. S $245; D $270. Concierge. Private lounge. Wet bar in suites. Complimentary continental bkfst, refreshments. Cr cds: A, C, D, DS, ER, JCB, MC, V.

★ **GUEST QUARTERS.** *2500 Pennsylvania Ave NW (20037), in Foggy Bottom.* 202/333-8060; FAX 202/338-3818. 123 kit. suites, 10 story. S $99-$159; D $99-$174; each addl $15; under 18 free. Crib free. Pet accepted; $12 per day. Garage $13. TV; cable, in-rm movies. Restaurant adj 11 am-midnight. Ck-out noon. Health club privileges. Cr cds: A, C, D, DS, MC, V.

★ ★ **HAMPSHIRE.** *1310 New Hampshire Ave NW (20036), in Dupont Circle area.* 202/296-7600; res: 800/368-5691; FAX 202/293-2476. 82 rms, 10 story. Mid-Mar-June, early Sept-mid-Nov: S $120; D $140; each addl $15; suites, kit. units $140-$179; under 13 free; wkend, monthly rates; lower rates rest of yr. Crib free. Garage $10. TV; cable. Complimentary coffee in rms. Restaurant 7-10 am, 11:30 am-2:30 pm, 5:30-10:30 pm; wkend hrs vary. Bar 5-10:30 pm, Sat, Sun from 6 pm. Ck-out noon. Meeting rms. Health club privileges. Refrigerators, minibars. Some balconies. Cr cds: A, C, D, DS, ER, JCB, MC, V.

HAY-ADAMS. *(Renovation incomplete when inspected, therefore not rated)* 800 16th St NW (20006), opp White House, downtown. 202/638-6600; res: 800/424-5054; FAX 202/638-2716. 143 rms, 8 story. S, D $210-$375; each addl $30; suites $450-$1,200; under 13 free; wkend package. Pet accepted. some restrictions. TV; cable. Restaurant 6:30-1 am. Afternoon tea 3-5 pm. Rm serv 24 hrs. Bars 11-1 am. Ck-out noon. Concierge. Valet parking $18. Health club privileges. Bathrm phones, refrigerators, minibars; some fireplaces. Some balconies. English country house atmosphere. Built 1927, on site of John Hay and Henry Adams mansions. Cr cds: A, C, D, ER, JCB, MC, V.

★ ★ ★ **HENLEY PARK.** *926 Massachusetts Ave NW (20001), 1 blk from Washington Convention Center, downtown.* 202/638-5200; res: 800/222-8474; FAX 202/638-6740. 96 rms, 8 story. S $165-$215; D $185-$235; each addl $20; suites $295-$675; under 16 free; wkend rates. Crib free. Valet parking $15. TV; in-rm movies avail. Afternoon tea 4-6 pm. Restaurant 7-10:30 am, 11:30 am-2 pm, 6-10 pm. Rm serv

24 hrs. Bar 11-12:30 am; entertainment Fri, Sat. Ck-out noon. Meeting rms. Health club privileges. Bathrm phones, refrigerators, minibars. Wet bar in suites. Tudor detailing; 1918 structure. Cr cds: A, C, D, DS, ER, JCB, MC, V.

★ ★ ★ **HILTON AND TOWERS.** *1919 Connecticut Ave NW (20009), in Kalorama.* 202/483-3000; FAX 202/265-8221. 1,123 rms, 10 story. S $140-$236; D $160-$256; each addl $20; suites $434-$791; wkend rates. Crib free. Pet accepted, some restrictions. Garage $12. TV; cable. Heated pool; poolside serv, lifeguard (in season). Restaurants 6:30 am-11 pm. Bar 11:30-2 am; entertainment. Ck-out noon. Convention facilities. Gift shop. Drugstore. Lighted tennis, pro. Exercise rm; instructor, weight machines, bicycles, steam rm. Minibars. Some balconies. Resort atmosphere; on 6½ landscaped acres. **LUXURY LEVEL : THE TOWERS.** 95 rms, 18 suites. S $247; D $267; suites $600-$1,400. Concierge. Private lounge. Reference library. Some bathrm phones. Complimentary continental bkfst, afternoon refreshments. Cr cds: A, C, D, DS, ER, JCB, MC, V.

★ **HOLIDAY INN GEORGETOWN.** *2101 Wisconsin Ave NW (20007), in Georgetown.* 202/338-4600; FAX 202/333-6113. 296 rms, 7 story. S $110-$140; D $120-$140; each addl $10; suites $200; under 19 free. Crib free. Parking in/out $10. TV; cable. Pool; lifeguard. Restaurant 6:30 am-10 pm; Sat & Sun from 7 am. Bar 11 am-midnight. Ck-out noon. Coin lndry. Meeting rms. Gift shop. Exercise equipt; weight machine, treadmill. Health club privileges. Refrigerators avail. Cr cds: A, C, D, DS, JCB, MC, V.

★ ★ **HOLIDAY INN-CAPITOL.** *550 C Street SW (20024), 2 blks from Mall museums, south of downtown.* 202/479-4000; FAX 202/479-4353. 529 rms, 9 story. S, D $149-$169; suites $199-$219; under 20 free; wkend packages. Crib free. Pet accepted. Garage $9. TV; cable. Pool; lifeguard. Restaurant 6 am-10 pm. Bar 11-1 am. Ck-out noon. Coin lndry. Convention facilities. Shopping arcade. Barber, beauty shop. Exercise equipt; weight machine, bicycles. Cr cds: A, C, D, DS, JCB, MC, V.

✔ ★ ★ **HOLIDAY INN-CENTRAL.** *1501 Rhode Island Ave NW (20005), north of downtown.* 202/483-2000; FAX 202/797-1078. 213 rms, 10 story. Apr-May & Oct: S, D $69-$119; each addl $14; suites $150; family, wkly, wkend rates; lower rates rest of yr. Crib free. Covered parking $8.90. TV; cable. Pool; lifeguard. Restaurant 6:30 am-10 pm. Bar; entertainment. Ck-out noon. Coin lndry. Meeting rms. Gift shop. Exercise equipt; weight machine, stair machine. Game rm. Some refrigerators. Balconies. Cr cds: A, C, D, DS, JCB, MC, V.

★ ★ ★ **HOTEL SOFITEL.** *1914 Connecticut Ave NW (20009), in Kalorama area.* 202/797-2000; res: 800/424-2464; FAX 202/462-0944. 145 units, 9 story, 40 suites. S $175-$205; D $195-$225; each addl $20; suites $255-$550; under 18 free; wkend rates; lower rates late June-Labor Day. Crib free. Garage parking; valet $15. TV; cable. Restaurant 6:30 am-10:30 pm. Rm serv 24 hrs. Bar noon-11:30 pm; Fri, Sat to 1 am. Meeting rms. Concierge. Health club privileges. Bathrm phones, minibars. Refurbished apartment building; built 1904. Cr cds: A, C, D, JCB, MC, V.

★ ★ **HOWARD JOHNSON.** *1430 Rhode Island Ave NW (20005), downtown.* 202/462-7777; FAX 202/332-3519. 186 units, 10 story, 158 kit. units. S $89-$99; D $99-$119; each addl $10; under 18 free; wkend rates. Crib free. Garage parking; valet $7. TV; cable. Pool; lifeguard. Restaurant 7-11 am; 11:30 am-2:30 pm, 5-10:30 pm. Bar 5 pm-midnight. Ck-out noon. Coin lndry. Health club privileges. Cr cds: A, C, D, DS, ER, JCB, MC, V.

★ ★ ★ **HYATT REGENCY WASHINGTON ON CAPITOL HILL.** *400 New Jersey Ave NW (20001), 2 blks N of Capitol, downtown.* *202/737-1234; FAX 202/347-2861.* 834 rms; 11 story. S $189; D $214; each addl $25; under 18 free; wknd rates. Crib free. Garage $16. TV; cable, in-rm movies. Indoor pool. Restaurants 6:30 am-11 pm. Bar 11-2 am. Ck-out noon. Meeting rms. Concierge. Gift shop. Barber, beauty shop. Exercise rm; instructor, weight machines, bicycles, steam rm, sauna. Minibars; some refrigerators. ***LUXURY LEVEL : REGENCY CLUB.*** 44 rms, 4 suites. S $224; D $249; each addl $25; suites $350-$1,025. Private lounge. Wet bar in suites. Complimentary continental bkfst, evening refreshments. Cr cds: A, C, D, DS, ER, JCB, MC, V.

★ ★ ★ **J.W. MARRIOTT.** *1331 Pennsylvania Ave NW (20004), at National Pl, 2 blks E of White House, downtown.* *202/393-2000; FAX 202/626-6991.* 772 rms, 12 story. S, D $224-$244; each addl $20; suites $275-$1,550; family, wknd rates. Crib free. Limited valet parking $16. TV; cable, in-rm movies. Indoor pool. Restaurant 7 am-11 pm. Rm serv 24 hrs. Bars; entertainment. Ck-out noon. Convention facilities. Concierge. Shopping arcade. Exercise rm; instructor, weights, bicycles, whirlpool, sauna. Game area. Some bathrm phones. Refrigerator in suites. Private patios on 7th & 12th floors. Luxurious hotel with elegant interior detail; extensive use of marble & mirrors; a large collection of artwork is displayed throughout the lobby. ***LUXURY LEVEL : CONCIERGE FLOOR.*** 96 rms, 2 floors. S, D $230-$250. Private lounge, honor bar. Complimentary continental bkfst, refreshments. Cr cds: A, C, D, DS, ER, JCB, MC, V.

★ ★ ★ **JEFFERSON.** *16th & M Streets NW (20036), downtown.* *202/347-2200; res: 800/368-5966; FAX 202/331-7982.* 100 rms, 8 story. Jan-June, Sept-Nov: S $220-$260; D $235-$275; each addl $25; suites $320-$1,000; under 15 free; wknd plans. Crib free. Garage, valet parking $20. TV; cable, in-rm movies. Pool privileges. Restaurants 6:30 am-11 pm. Rm serv 24 hrs. Afternoon tea 3-5 pm. Bar 10-2 am. Ck-out 1 pm. Concierge. Health club privileges. Some private patios. Individually decorated rms; some four-poster and canopy beds, antiques. In operation since 1923. Cr cds: A, C, D, DS, ER, JCB, MC, V.

★ ★ **THE LATHAM.** *3000 M Street NW (20007), in Georgetown.* *202/726-5000; res: 800/368-5922 (exc DC), 800/LATHAM-1; FAX 202/337-4250.* 143 rms, 10 story. S $155-$190; D $175-$210; each addl $20; suites $250-$450; under 16 free; wknd rates. Valet parking $15. TV; cable. Pool. Restaurant 6:30 am-10:30 pm. Bar 11 am-1 am, Fri & Sat to 2 am. Ck-out noon. Meeting rms. Health club privileges. Some minibars. Refrigerators avail. Sun deck. Overlooks historic Chesapeake & Ohio Canal. Cr cds: A, C, D, DS, ER, JCB, MC, V.

★ ★ ★ **LOEWS L'ENFANT PLAZA.** *480 L'Enfant Plaza SW (20024), south of downtown.* *202/484-1000; FAX 202/646-4456.* 370 rms on floors 11-15. S $165-$205; D $185-$225; each addl $20; suites $370-$1,200; under 18 free; wknd rates. Crib free. Valet parking $16. TV; cable, in-rm movies. Pool; poolside serv, lifeguard. Restaurant 6:30 am-midnight. Bar 11:30-1:30 am. Ck-out 1 pm. Meeting rms. Concierge. Underground shopping arcade with Metro subway stop. Gift shop. Exercise rm; instructor, weights, bicycles. Refrigerators, minibars. Many balconies. Cr cds: A, C, D, DS, MC, V.

★ ★ **LOMBARDY.** *2019 I Street NW (20006), downtown.* *202/828-2600; res: 800/424-5486; FAX 202/872-0503.* 126 units, 11 story, 106 kits. Apr-May, Sept-Oct: S $115; D $130; each addl $10; suites $150-$165; under 16 free; wknd rates; lower rates rest of yr. Crib free. TV; cable. Coffee in rms. Restaurant 7-10:30 am, 11:30 am-2:30 pm, 5-9:30 pm; Sat, Sun 8 am-1 pm, 5-9:30 pm. Ck-out noon.

Coin lndry. Meeting rm. Health club privileges. Refrigerators, minibars. Cr cds: A, C, D, DS, ER, MC, V.

★ ★ ★ **MADISON.** *15th & M Streets NW (20005), downtown.* *202/862-1600; res: 800/424-8577; FAX 202/785-1255.* 353 rms, 14 story. S $235-$395; D $250-$395; each addl $30; suites $395-$3,000; wknd packages. Crib $25. Garage $14. TV; cable, in-rm movies avail. Restaurant 6:30 am-11 pm. Rm serv 24 hrs. Bar 11-2 am. Ck-out 1 pm. Meeting rms. Concierge. Exercise equipt; weight machine, bicycles, sauna. Bathrm phones, refrigerators, minibars. Original paintings, antiques, Oriental rugs. Cr cds: A, C, D, DS, ER, JCB, MC, V.

★ ★ **MARRIOTT.** *1221 22nd St NW (20037), at M St, west of downtown.* *202/872-1500; FAX 202/872-1424.* 418 rms, 9 story. S, D $167-$182; each addl $15; suites $250-$500; under 18 free; wknd rates. Crib free. Pet accepted, some restrictions; $50. Garage $12; valet $14. TV; cable. Heated pool; poolside serv, lifeguard. Complimentary morning coffee. Restaurant 6:30 am-10 pm; Fri, Sat to 11 pm. Rm serv to midnight. Bars 11:30 am-midnight. Ck-out noon. Meeting rms. Concierge. Gift shop. Exercise equipt; weight machines, bicycles, whirlpool, sauna. Refrigerators avail. ***LUXURY LEVEL : CONCIERGE LEVEL.*** 62 rms, 2 suites. S, D $185-$200; suites from $275. Private lounge, honor bar. Bathrm phones in suites. Complimentary continental bkfst, refreshments, newspaper. Cr cds: A, C, D, DS, ER, JCB, MC, V.

✔ ★ ★ **NORMANDY INN.** *2118 Wyoming Ave NW (20008), in Kalorama.* *202/483-1350; res: 800/424-3729; FAX 202/387-8241.* 75 rms, 6 story. S $97; D $107; each addl $10; under 12 free. Crib free. Pet accepted, some restrictions. Garage $10. TV; cable. Continental bkfst. Complimentary coffee in rms. Restaurant nearby. Ck-out noon. Meeting rm. Refrigerators. In quiet residential neighborhood. Cr cds: A, C, D, DS, MC, V.

★ ★ **OMNI SHOREHAM.** *2500 Calvert St NW (20008), north of downtown.* *202/234-0700; FAX 202/332-1373.* 770 rms, 8 story. S, D $195-$220; each addl $20; suites $275-$1,200; under 18 free; wknd, hol packages. Crib free. Pet accepted, some restrictions. Garage $12. TV; cable. Pool; wading pool, poolside serv, lifeguard. Restaurant 6:30 am-11 pm. Bar 11-2 am; entertainment. Ck-out noon. Meeting rms. Shopping arcade. Lighted tennis, pro. Exercise equipt; weight machines, bicycles, sauna. Lawn games. Cr cds: A, C, D, DS, JCB, MC, V.

★ ★ ★ **ONE WASHINGTON CIRCLE.** *One Washington Circle NW (20037), in Foggy Bottom.* *202/872-1680; res: 800/424-9671; FAX 202/887-4989.* 151 kit. suites, 9 story. S $135-$275; D $145-$300; each addl $15; under 12 free; wknd plans. Pet accepted, some restrictions. Garage $15. TV; cable. Pool. Restaurant 7 am-11:30 pm; Fri & Sat to midnight. Bar; entertainment. Ck-out noon. Meeting rms. Concierge. Health club privileges. Some bathrm phones. Many balconies. Elegant furnishings; landscaped grounds in residential neighborhood. Cr cds: A, C, D, MC, V.

★ ★ ★ **PARK HYATT.** *24th & M Street NW (20037), west of downtown.* *202/789-1234; res: 800/922-PARK; FAX 202/457-8823.* 224 units, 10 story, 133 suites. S $265; D $290; each addl $25; suites $295-$1,975; under 18 free; wknd rates; lower rates July, Aug. Crib free. TV; cable. Indoor pool; poolside serv. Restaurant (see MELROSE). Afternoon tea 3-5 pm. Rm serv 24 hrs. Bar 11:30-1 am, Fri & Sat to 2 am; pianist. Ck-out noon. Meeting rms. Concierge. Gift shop. Barber, beauty shop. Covered parking; valet. Tennis & golf privileges. Exercise rm; instructor, weight machines, bicycles, whirlpool, steam rm, sauna.

Massage. Bathrm phones, refrigerators. Daily newspapers. Cr cds: A, C, D, DS, JCB, MC, V.

[icons]

★ ★ **PHOENIX PARK.** *520 N Capitol St (20001), opp Union Station, on Capitol Hill.* 202/638-6900; *res:* 800/824-5419; *FAX* 202/393-3236. 84 rms, 9 story. S $159-$199; D $179-$219; each addl $20; suites $300-$475; under 15 free; wkend package plans. Crib free. Valet parking $15. TV; cable. Coffee in rms. Restaurants 7-2 am. Bar from 11 am; Fri, Sat to 3 am; entertainment. Ck-out 1 pm. Meeting rms. Health club privileges. Minibars; some refrigerators. Older hotel near Capitol; traditional European, Irish decor. Cr cds: A, C, D, MC, V.

[icons]

✔ ★ **QUALITY HOTEL-CAPITOL HILL.** *415 New Jersey Ave NW (20001), on Capitol Hill.* 202/638-1616; *FAX* 202/638-0707. 341 rms, 10 story. Feb-May, Sept-Nov: S, D $79-$159; each addl $20; suites $130-$375; under 18 free; wkend rates; lower rates rest of yr. Crib free. TV; cable, in-rm movies. Rooftop pool; poolside serv, lifeguard. Restaurant 6:30 am-10 pm. Bar 11-2 am. Ck-out noon. Gift shop. Free covered parking. Cr cds: A, C, D, DS, ER, JCB, MC, V.

[icons]

★ ★ ★ ★ **THE RITZ-CARLTON.** *2100 Massachusetts Ave NW (20008), 1 blk NW of Dupont Circle, in Embassy Row Area.* 202/293-2100; *res:* 800/241-3333; *FAX* 202/293-0641. 206 rms, 8 story. S, D $250-$340; suites $350-$2,000; under 18 free; wkend rates. Crib free. Valet parking $20. TV; cable. Restaurant 6:30 am-10:30 pm (also see JOCKEY CLUB). Bar 11:30-1 am; entertainment. Ck-out noon. Meeting rms. Concierge. Tennis, golf privileges. Health club privileges. Bathrm phones, minibars; some bathrm TVs. Complimentary newspapers. Elegant ballroom. Classic 18th-century decor, restored. Within 10 minutes of Georgetown. *LUXURY LEVEL :* THE RITZ-CARLTON CLUB. 66 rms, 12 suites, 2 floors. S, D $345; suites $350-$2,000. Concierge. Private lounge. Complimentary continental bkfst. Five complimentary food and beverage presentations daily. Cr cds: A, C, D, DS, ER, JCB, MC, V.

[icons]

★ ★ **RIVER INN.** *924 25th St NW (20037), 2 blks from Kennedy Center, in Foggy Bottom.* 202/337-7600; *res:* 800/424-2741; *FAX* 202/337-6520. 127 kit. suites. S $125-$175; D $140-$190; each addl $15; under 13 free; wkend rates. Crib free. Parking $14. TV; cable. Restaurant 7-10:30 am, 11:30 am-2:30 pm, 5-10 pm; Sat 8-10:30 am, 11 am-2:30 pm, 5:30-11:30 pm; Sun 8 am-3 pm, 5-10 pm. Bar. Ck-out noon. Meeting rms. Health club privileges. Some bathrm phones. Quiet residential area. Cr cds: A, C, D, MC, V.

[icons]

★ ★ **SHERATON CITY CENTRE.** *1143 New Hampshire Ave NW (20037), at 21st & M Sts, west of downtown.* 202/775-0800; *FAX* 202/331-9491. 351 rms, 9 story. S $165-$210; D $180-$225; each addl $15; suites $250-$600; under 18 free. Crib free. Parking $14. TV; cable. Restaurant 6 am-10 pm. Bar noon-1 am; entertainment Mon-Fri. Ck-out noon. Meeting rms. Concierge. Gift shop. Health club privileges. Some bathrm phones, refrigerators. *LUXURY LEVEL:* CLUB LEVEL. 40 rms, 2 suites. S $185-$225; D $200-$250; addl bedrm $175. Private lounge. Some wet bars. Bathrm phone in suites. Complimentary continental bkfst. Cr cds: A, C, D, DS, ER, JCB, MC, V.

[icons]

★ ★ **ST. JAMES.** *950 24th St NW (20037), in Foggy Bottom.* 202/457-0500; *res:* 800/852-8512; *FAX* 202/659-4492. 196 kit. suites, 12 story. Feb-June & Sept-Oct: suites $139-$169; under 16 free; wkend rates; higher rates: Cherry Blossom Festival; lower rates rest of yr. Crib free. Garage parking $15; valet. TV; cable, in-rm movies. Pool; lifeguard. Complimentary continental bkfst. Coffee in rms. Restaurant nearby. Ck-out noon. Coin lndry. Meeting rms. Concierge. Exercise equipt; weights, rower. Cr cds: A, C, D, DS, MC, V.

[icons]

★ ★ **STATE PLAZA.** *2117 E Street NW (20037), in Foggy Bottom.* 202/861-8200; *res:* 800/424-2859; *FAX* 202/659-8601. 221 kit. suites, 8 story. S $95-$140; D $115-$160; each addl $20; under 18 free; wkend rates. Crib free. Garage $12. TV; cable. Restaurant 6:30 am-10 pm. Bar from 11:30 am. Ck-out noon. Coin lndry. Meeting rms. Exercise equipt; bicycles, treadmills. Minibars. Complimentary newspaper, shoeshine. Two rooftop sun decks. Cr cds: A, C, D, DS, ER, JCB, MC, V.

[icons]

★ ★ ★ **STOUFFER-MAYFLOWER.** *1127 Connecticut Ave NW (20036), 4 blks northwest of White House, downtown.* 202/347-3000; *FAX* 202/466-9082. 659 rms, 10 story, 78 suites. S, D $250-$290; each addl $30; suites $450-$2,500; under 19 free; wkend plans. Pet accepted, some restrictions. Garage adj $11.50. TV; cable. Complimentary coffee in rms. Restaurant 6:30 am-11:30 pm. Rm serv 24 hrs. Bar 11-1:30 am; entertainment. Ck-out 1 pm. Convention facilities. Concierge. Exercise equipt; weight machine, sauna. Health club privileges. Bathrm phones; refrigerators avail. Foreign currency exchange. Historic grand hotel (1925) with ornate interior details; gilded moldings, stained-glass skylights, lavish use of marble. Cr cds: A, C, D, DS, ER, JCB, MC, V.

[icons]

★ ★ **WASHINGTON.** *515 15th St NW (20004), at Pennsylvania Ave, 1 blk from White House, downtown.* 202/638-5900; *res:* 800/424-9540; *FAX* 202/638-4275. 350 rms, 11 story. S $155-$209; D $170-$209; each addl $18; suites $400-$609; under 14 free; wkend rates. Crib free. TV; cable. Restaurant 7 am-10 pm. Bar 11-1 am. Ck-out 1 pm. Meeting rms. Gift shop. Exercise equipt; weight machine, bicycles, sauna. Bathrm phones. Original Jardin D'Armide murals (1854). One of the oldest continuously-operated hotels in the city. Cr cds: A, C, D, MC, V.

[icons]

★ ★ ★ **THE WASHINGTON COURT ON CAPITOL HILL.** *525 New Jersey Ave NW (20001), on Capitol Hill.* 202/628-2100; *res:* 800/321-3010; *FAX* 202/879-7918. 266 rms, 15 story, 11 suites. S $175-$250; D $195-$300; each addl $25; suites $360-$1,500; under 16 free; wkend rates. Crib free. Pet accepted, some restrictions. Valet parking $15. TV; cable. Restaurant 6:30 am-11 pm. Bar; pianist. Ck-out noon. Meeting rooms. Concierge. Exercise equipt; weight machines, bicycles, sauna. Bathrm phones, refrigerators. Large atrium lobby. Cr cds: A, C, D, DS, JCB, MC, V.

[icons]

★ ★ **WASHINGTON RENAISSANCE.** *999 9th St NW (20001), across from Convention Center, downtown.* 202/898-9000; *FAX* 202/789-4213. 800 rms, 16 story. S, D $175-$225; each addl $20; suites $260-$2,000; under 18 free; wkend rates. Crib free. Pet accepted, some restrictions. Garage $14; valet parking $14. TV; cable. Indoor pool; lifeguard. Restaurant 6:30 am-11 pm. Rm serv 24 hrs. Bar 10-1 am; entertainment. Ck-out noon. Convention facilities. Concierge. Shopping arcade. Barber, beauty shop. Exercise rm; instructor, weight machine, bicycles, whirlpool, sauna. Minibars; some bathrm phones. *LUXURY LEVEL:* RENAISSANCE CLUB. 166 rms, 26 suites, 16 floors. S, D $225-$245; suites $300-$2,000. Private lounge, honor bar. Wet bar. Bathrm phones. Complimentary continental bkfst, refreshments. Cr cds: A, C, D, DS, ER, JCB, MC, V.

[icons]

★ ★ **WASHINGTON VISTA.** *1400 M Street NW (20005), downtown.* 202/429-1700; *res:* 800/VISTA-DC; *FAX* 202/785-0786. 399 rms, 14 story. S $165-$205; D $190-$230; each addl $25; suites $350-$975; family, wkend rates. Crib free. Pet accepted. Valet parking $14. TV; cable, in-rm movies avail. Restaurant 6:30 am-10:30 pm; Sat, Sun from 7 am. Rm serv 24 hrs. Bars 11:30-1 am. Ck-out noon. Convention facilities. Concierge. Gift shop. Exercise equipt; weights, bicycles, sauna. Refrigerators, minibars. Some balconies. *LUXURY LEVEL:* EXECUTIVE FLOOR. 60 rms, 3 suites. S, D $175-$240. Private lounge. Some wet bars, in-rm whirlpools. Complimentary continental bkfst, refreshments. Cr cds: A, C, D, DS, ER, JCB, MC, V.

D 🐾 🏋 🏊 🔥 SC

★ ★ ★ ★ **THE WATERGATE.** *2650 Virginia Ave NW (20037), in Foggy Bottom.* 202/965-2300; res: 800/424-2736; FAX 202/337-7915. 235 rms, 13 story. S $275-$410; D $300-$435; each addl $25; suites $550-$1,885; under 18 free; wkend, hol rates. Crib free. Valet parking $15. TV; cable, in-rm movies. Indoor pool; lifeguard. Restaurant 7 am-10:30 pm (also see JEAN-LOUIS AT THE WATERGATE HOTEL and PALLADIN BY JEAN-LOUIS). Rm serv 24 hrs. Bar 11:30-1 am; pianist. Ck-out noon. Meeting rms. Concierge. Shopping arcade. Barber, beauty shop. Complimentary downtown & Capitol transportation. Health club & fitness center: instructor, weight machines, bicycles, whirlpool, sauna, steam rm. Massage. Bathrm phones, minibars. Many balconies. Furnished with many fine antiques. Many extras. Landmark hotel, part of condominium complex overlooking Potomac River; most rooms overlook river. Kennedy Center adj. Cr cds: A, C, D, DS, JCB, MC, V.

D 🏊 🏋 🏊 🔥 SC

★ ★ ★ **WILLARD INTER-CONTINENTAL.** *1401 Pennsylvania Ave NW (20004), 2 blks E of White House, downtown.* 202/628-9100; res: 800/327-0200; FAX 202/637-7326. 340 units, 12 story, 36 suites. S $255-$350; D $285-$380; each addl $30; suites $495-$2,900; under 14 free; wkend rates. Crib free. Pet accepted, some restrictions. Covered parking, valet $16. TV; cable. Swimming privileges. Restaurant 6:30 am-11 pm (also see WILLARD ROOM). Rm serv 24 hrs. Bar 11-1 am, Sun 11:30 am-midnight; entertainment. Ck-out noon. Meeting rms. Concierge. Shopping arcade. Exercise equipt; weight machines, treadmill. Bathrm phones, minibars. Historic hotel (1847) (present building completed 1904), restored to original Edwardian elegance; turn-of-the-century decor; stately columns, mosiac floors. Famous "Peacock Alley" runs the length of the hotel, connecting Pennsylvania Ave and F St. Host to many presidents on the eves of their inaugurations. Cr cds: A, C, D, DS, ER, JCB, MC, V.

D 🐾 🏋 🏊 🔥 SC

★ ★ ★ **WYNDHAM BRISTOL.** *2430 Pennsylvania Ave NW (20037), west of downtown.* 202/955-6400; FAX 202/955-5765. 240 kit. units, 8 story, 37 suites. S $179-$209; D $199-$229; each addl $20; suites $285-$850; under 17 free; monthly rates; wkend plans. Crib free. Valet garage parking $15. TV; cable. Complimentary coffee in rms. Restaurant 7 am-11 pm. Rm serv 24 hrs. Bar 11-2 am. Ck-out noon. Meeting rms. Concierge. Exercise equipt; weight machines, treadmills. Bathrm phones. Classic English furnishings, art. Cr cds: A, C, D, DS, ER, JCB, MC, V.

D 🏋 🏊 🔥 SC

Inns

✔ ★ **EMBASSY.** *1627 16th St NW (20009), in Dupont Circle area.* 202/234-7800; res: 800/423-9111; FAX 202/234-3309. 38 rms, 5 story. S $69-$99; D $79-$99; each addl $10; under 14 free. Crib free. TV. Complimentary continental bkfst, coffee & tea/sherry. Ck-out noon, ck-in 1 pm. Valet serv. Antiques. Originally a boarding house (1922). Cr cds: A, C, D, MC, V.

🏊 🔥 SC

✔ ★ **KALORAMA GUEST HOUSE AT KALORAMA PARK.** *1854 Mintwood Pl NW (20009), in Kalorama.* 202/667-6369. 31 rms, some share bath, 3 story. No rm phones. S $45-$95; D $50-$100; each addl $5; suites $75-$115; wkly rates. Complimentary continental bkfst, sherry & lemonade. Ck-out 11 am, ck-in noon. Limited parking avail. Created from 4 connecting Victorian town houses (1890s); rms individually decorated, antiques. Garden. Cr cds: A, C, D, DS, MC, V.

🏊 🔥 SC

✔ ★ **KALORAMA GUEST HOUSE AT WOODLEY PARK.** *2700 Cathedral Ave NW (20008), north of downtown.* 202/328-0860. 19 rms, 12 with bath, 4 story, 2 suites. No rm phones. Mar-mid-June,

Sept-Nov: S $45-$90; D $55-$95; each addl $5; wkly rates; lower rates rest of yr. Children over 5 yrs only. Some B/W TV; TV in sitting rm. Complimentary continental bkfst, tea/sherry. Restaurant nearby. Ck-out 11 am, ck-in noon. Free lndry facilities. Limited off-street parking. Sitting rm; antiques. Early 20th-century town house (1910). Cr cds: A, C, D, DS, MC, V.

🏊 🔥 SC

★ ★ **MORRISON CLARK.** *1015 L Street NW (20001), at Massachusetts Ave, downtown.* 202/898-1200; res: 800/332-7898; FAX 202/289-8576. 54 units, 5 story, 14 suites. Mar-June, Sept-Nov: S $125-$175; D $145-$195; each addl $20; suites $145-$185; under 12 free; wkend rates; lower rates rest of yr. Crib free. TV. Complimentary continental bkfst. Dining rm 11:30 am-2 pm, 6-10 pm; Sat from 6 pm. Rm serv. Ck-out noon, ck-in 3 pm. Bellhops. Valet serv. Exercise equipt; weight machine, treadmills. Underground parking. Restored Victorian mansion (1864); two-story veranda; period furnishings. Cr cds: A, C, D, DS, ER, JCB, MC, V.

🏋 🏊 🔥 SC

✔ ★ **WINDSOR.** *1842 16th St NW (20009), north of downtown.* 202/667-0300; res: 800/423-9111; FAX 202/667-4503. 46 rms, 4 story, 9 suites. No elvtr. S $69-$89; D $79-$99; each addl $10; suites $105-$150; under 15 free; wkend rates. Crib free. TV. Complimentary continental bkfst, coffee, tea & evening sherry. Restaurant nearby. Ck-out noon, ck-in 1 pm. Refrigerator in suites. Originally a boarding house (1922); bed & breakfast atmosphere. Cr cds: A, C, D, MC, V.

🔥 SC

Restaurants

★ ★ ★ **1789.** *1226 36th St NW, in Georgetown.* 202/965-1789. Hrs: 6-10 pm; Fri, Sat to 11 pm. Res accepted. Bar. Extensive wine list. Semi-a la carte: dinner $16-$26. Prix fixe: pre-theater dinner $25. Specializes in seafood, rack of lamb. Own baking. Valet parking. In restored mansion; 5 dining rms on 3 levels. Federal-period decor. Fireplace. Jacket. Cr cds: A, D, DS, MC, V.

★ ★ ★ **701.** *701 Pennsylvania Ave NW, downtown.* 202/393-0701. Hrs: 11:30 am-3 pm, 5:30-10:30 pm; Wed, Thurs to 11 pm; Fri to 11:30 pm; Sun 5:30-9:30 pm. Closed major hols. Res accepted. Continental menu. Bar. Wine list. Semi-a la carte: lunch $7.50-$16.95, dinner $12.50-$22.50. Specializes in seafood, lamb chops, charred rib steak. Pianist Sun-Thurs, Jazz combo Fri-Sat. Valet parking. Outdoor dining. Overlooks fountain at Navy Memorial. Cr cds: A, C, D, MC, V.

D

✔ ★ ★ **ADITI.** *3299 M Street NW, in Georgetown.* 202/625-6825. Hrs: 11:30 am-2:30 pm, 5:30-10 pm; Fri, Sat to 10:30 pm. Closed Labor Day, Thanksgiving. Res accepted. Indian menu. Serv bar. Semi-a la carte: lunch $4.95-$7.95, dinner $4.95-$13.95. Specializes in barbecued meats, vegetarian dishes, tandoori-roasted butter chicken. Cr cds: A, C, D, DS, MC, V.

✔ ★ ★ **ALEKOS.** *1732 Connecticut Ave NW, in Dupont Circle.* 202/667-6211. Hrs: 11:30 am-11 pm. Closed Dec 25. Res accepted. Greek menu. Bar. Semi-a la carte: lunch $6.95-$9.95, dinner $7.95-$15.95. Specializes in seafood, moussaka. Greek Islands ambience. Cr cds: A, MC, V.

✔ ★ ★ **BACCHUS.** *1827 Jefferson Place NW (20036), in Dupont Circle.* 202/785-0734. Hrs: noon-2:30 pm, 6-10 pm; Fri to 10:30 pm; Sat 6-10:30 pm. Closed Sun; most major hols. Res accepted. Lebanese menu. A la carte entrees: lunch $6.50-$10.75, dinner $11.75-$14.75. Specializes in authentic Lebanese cuisine. Valet parking. Cr cds: A, MC, V.

★ ★ ★ **BICE.** *601 Pennsylvania Ave NW (Entrance on Indiana Ave), downtown.* 202/638-2423. Hrs: 11:30 am-3 pm, 5:30-10:30 pm; Fri to 11:30 pm; Sat 5:30-11:30 pm; Sun 5:30-10 pm. Closed Jan 1, Thanksgiving, Dec 25. Res accepted. Northern Italian menu. Bar. Extensive wine list. Semi-a la carte: lunch $11-$21, dinner $12-$25. Specializes in pasta, risotto, veal. Valet parking (dinner). Outdoor dining. Bright, modern Italian decor; windows on 3 sides of dining rm. Jacket. Cr cds: A, C, D, MC, V.

D

★ **BILLY MARTIN'S TAVERN.** *1264 Wisconsin Ave NW, in Georgetown.* 202/333-7370. Hrs: 8-1 am; Fri, Sat to 2:30 am; Sun brunch to 5:30 pm. Closed Dec 25. Res accepted. Bar. Semi-a la carte: bkfst $2.95-$11.50, lunch $5.95-$8.95, dinner $5.75-$18.95. Sat, Sun brunch $5.95-$12.95. Specializes in steak, seafood, chops. Outdoor dining. Established 1933. Family-owned. Cr cds: A, C, D, DS, MC, V.

★ **BISTRO FRANCAIS.** *3128 M Street NW, in Georgetown.* 202/338-3830; FAX 202/338-1421. Hrs: 11-3 am; Fri, Sat to 4 am; early-bird dinner 5-7 pm; Sat, Sun brunch 11 am-4 pm. Closed Dec 24, 25. Res accepted. Country French menu. Semi-a la carte: lunch $6.95-$11.95, dinner $12.95-$17.95. Sat, Sun brunch $13.95. Specializes in rotisserie chicken, fresh seafood. Cr cds: A, C, D, JCB, MC, V.

★ ★ **BOMBAY CLUB.** *815 Connecticut Ave NW, near White House, downtown.* 202/659-3727. Hrs: 11:30 am-2:30 pm, 6-10:30 pm; Fri, Sat 6-11 pm; Sun 5:30-9 pm; Sun brunch 11:30 am-2:30 pm. Closed some major hols. Res accepted. Indian cuisine. Bar 11:30 am-3 pm, 5-11 pm. A la carte entrees: lunch, dinner $7-$18.50. Sun brunch $14.95. Complete meals: pre-theater dinner (6-7 pm) $21.50. Specialties: tandoori salmon, thali, lamb Roganjosh, chicken Tikka Makhani. Pianist evenings, Sun brunch. Valet parking (dinner). Outdoor dining. Extensive vegetarian menu. Elegant club-like atmosphere. Cr cds: A, C, D, MC, V.

D

✔ ★ ★ **BOMBAY PALACE.** *2020 K St NW, downtown.* 202/331-4200. Hrs: 11:30 am-2:30 pm, 5:30-10 pm; Fri, Sat to 10:30 pm. Res accepted. Northern Indian menu. Bar. A la carte entrees: lunch, dinner $6.50-$14.95. Complete meals: lunch, dinner $13.95-$31.95. Specialties: butter chicken, gosht patiala. Indian decor and original art. Totally nonsmoking. Cr cds: A, D, MC, V.

✔ ★ **BUA.** *1635 P Street NW, in Dupont Circle.* 202/265-0828. Hrs: 11:30 am-2:30 pm, 5-10:30 pm; Fri to 11 pm; Sat noon-4 pm, 5-11 pm; Sun brunch noon-4 pm. Closed Thanksgiving, Dec 25. Res accepted. Thai menu. Bar. A la carte entrees: lunch $4.95-$7.50, dinner $7.25-$12.95. Specializes in seafood, Thai noodles, crispy flounder. Outdoor dining on 2nd-floor balcony. In town house on quiet side street; fireplace. Cr cds: A, D, MC, V.

★ ★ **BUSARA.** *2340 Wisconsin Ave NW, in Georgetown.* 202/337-2340. Hrs: 11:30 am-3 pm, 5-11 pm; Fri to midnight; Sat 5 pm-midnight; Sun 5-11 pm. Closed some major hols. Res accepted. Thai menu. Bar. Semi-a la carte: lunch $5.95-$7.95, dinner $6.95-$15.95. Specialties: panang gai, crispy whole flounder, pad Thai. Outdoor dining. Modern atmosphere. Cr cds: A, C, D, DS, MC, V.

D

★ **CAFE ATLANTICO.** *1819 Columbia Rd NW, in Adams Morgan area.* 202/328-5844. Hrs: 5:30-10 pm; Thurs-Sat to 12:30 am; Sun 5:30-10 pm. Closed Jan 1, July 4, Dec 24-25. Caribbean menu. Bar to 1:30 am; Fri, Sat to 2:30 am. Semi-a la carte: dinner $9.25-$13.95. Specialties: jerk chicken, coconut grouper, grilled fresh fish, curried lamb. Entertainment. Valet parking Tues-Sat (dinner). Outdoor dining. Modern, bi-level dining area. Cr cds: A, D, DS, MC, V.

★ **CHINA INN.** *631 H Street NW, in Chinatown.* 202/842-0909. Hrs: 11-1 am; Fri, Sat to 2 am. Res accepted. Chinese menu. Semi-a la carte: lunch $7.50-$20.95, dinner $9.50-$24.75. Specialties: wor hip har (butterfly shrimp), chow mai foon (fried rice noodles). Modern decor. Cr cds: A, MC, V.

★ ★ **CHINA REGENCY.** *3000 K Street NW, Suite 30, Washington Harbour complex, in Georgetown.* 202/944-4266. Hrs: 11:30 am-11 pm; Fri, Sat to midnight; Sun noon-11 pm. Closed Thanksgiving, Dec 25. Res accepted. Chinese menu. Bar. Semi-a la carte: lunch $6-$16, dinner $8-$20. Specializes in Szechuan and Hunan dishes.

Outdoor dining. Chinese artifacts. Overlooks fountains and Potomac River. Cr cds: A, C, D, MC, V.

D

★ ★ **CITIES.** *2424 18th St NW, in Adams Morgan area.* 202/328-7194. Hrs: 6-11 pm; Fri, Sat to 11:30 pm; Sun brunch 11 am-3:30 pm. Res accepted. Bar 5 pm-2 am; Fri & Sat to 3 am. A la carte entrees: dinner $10-$19. Sun brunch $4.50-$12.50. Valet parking (dinner). Located in 1930s hardware store. Menu and decor change every year to feature cuisine of different cities around the world. Cr cds: A, D, MC, V.

★ ★ **COLONNADE.** *(See Ana Hotel)* 202/457-5000. Hrs: 11:30 am-2:30 pm, 6-10 pm; Sun brunch 10:30 am-2:30 pm. Closed Sat; Jan 1. Res accepted. Continental menu. A la carte entrees: lunch $10.75-$17.50, dinner $18-$26. Buffet: lunch (Mon-Fri) $16.50. Sun brunch $30-$35. Specializes in rack of lamb, fresh seafood, veal. Own baking, pasta. Pianist (brunch). Valet parking. Garden atmosphere; gazebo; dining rm overlooks courtyard garden. Cr cds: A, C, D, DS, ER, JCB, MC, V.

D

★ ★ **DOMINIQUE'S.** *1900 Pennsylvania Ave NW, downtown.* 202/452-1126. Hrs: 11:30 am-2:30 pm, 5:30-10:30 pm; Fri, Sat 5:30 pm-midnight; Sun 5-9:30 pm. Closed some major hols. Res accepted. French, continental menu. Bar. Semi-a la carte: lunch $9.95-$18.95, dinner $17.95-$25.95. Prix fixe: lunch $13.95, dinner (before & after theater) $18.95. Specializes in rack of lamb, seafood, seasonal game, exotic game such as rattlesnake. Own baking. Pastry chef. Valet parking (dinner). Cr cds: A, D, MC, V.

★ ★ **DONNA ADELE.** *2100 P Street NW, in Dupont Circle.* 202/296-1142. Hrs: 11:30 am-2:30 pm, 5:30-10:30 pm; Fri to 11 pm; Sat 5:30-11 pm; Sun 5:30-9:30 pm. Closed Jan 1, Thanksgiving, Dec 25. Res accepted. Northern Italian menu. Bar. Semi-a la carte: lunch $15-$20, dinner $25-$35. Child's meals. Specializes in fresh game, fresh whole fish. Own pasta. Parking. Outdoor dining. Contemporary decor. Cr cds: A, D, ER, MC, V.

D

★ ★ **EL CARIBE.** *3288 M Street, in Georgetown.* 202/338-3121. Hrs: 11:30 am-11 pm; Fri, Sat to 11:30 pm; Sun to 10 pm. Res accepted. South Amer, Spanish menu. Bar. Semi-a la carte: lunch $6.95-$12.95, dinner $9.95-$19.50. Specialties: fritadas con Llapingachos, paella, seafood. Spanish decor. Family-owned. Cr cds: A, C, D, DS, MC, V.

★ ★ **FILOMENA RISTORANTE.** *1063 Wisconsin Ave NW, in Georgetown.* 202/338-8800; FAX 202/338-8806. Hrs: 11:30 am-11 pm. Closed Jan 1, Dec 24-25. Res accepted. Italian menu. Bar. A la carte entrees: lunch $5.95-$9.95, dinner $11.95-$29.95. Lunch buffet $6.95. Prix fixe: pre-theater dinner (exc Sun) $19.95. Specializes in pasta, seafood, regional Italian dishes. Own baking, pasta. Italian garden-like atmosphere; antiques. Overlooks Chesapeake & Ohio Canal. Cr cds: A, D, MC, V.

✔ ★ **FIO'S.** *3636 16th St, at Woodner Apts, north of downtown.* 202/667-3040. Hrs: 5-10:45 pm. Closed Mon; some major hols; last 2 wks Aug. Italian menu. Bar. Semi-a la carte: dinner $4.50-$11. Specializes in seafood, veal, pasta. Garage parking. Informal atmosphere; building overlooks Rock Creek Park. Cr cds: A, C, D, DS, MC, V.

★ ★ **GABY'S.** *3311 Connecticut Ave NW, north of downtown.* 202/364-8909. Hrs: 11:30 am-2:30 pm, 5-10 pm; Fri, Sat to 11 pm. Res accepted. French menu. Semi-a la carte: lunch $6.50-$15, dinner $14-19. Complete meals: dinner $24.50. Specializes in fresh seafood, breast of duck. Menu changes daily. Modern French decor. Cr cds: A, C, D, DS, MC, V.

★ ★ **GALILEO.** *1110 21st St NW, in Foggy Bottom.* 202/293-7191. Hrs: 11:30 am-2, 5:30-10 pm; Fri to 10:30 pm; Sat from 5:30 pm; Sun 5:30-8:30 pm. Closed some major hols. Res accepted. Northern Italian menu. Bar. Wine cellar. A la carte entrees: lunch $10.95-

$17.95, dinner $16.95-$29.95. Specializes in game & seasonal dishes, pasta, seafood. Valet parking (dinner). Outdoor dining. Light Mediterranean decor; reminiscent of an Italian trattoria. Cr cds: A, C, D, DS, MC, V.

D

✔ ★ **GARRETT'S.** 3003 M Street NW, in Georgetown. 202/333-1033. Hrs: 11:30 am-10:30 pm; Fri, Sat to 12:30 am. Res accepted. Bars 11:30-2 am; Fri, Sat to 3 am. Semi-a la carte: lunch $3.95-$8.50, dinner $4.75-$13.95. Specializes in steaks, hamburgers, pasta. 1794 landmark bldg; originally house of MD governor T.S. Lee. Cr cds: A, C, D, DS, MC, V.

★ ★ **GARY'S.** 1800 M Street NW, at 18th St in the Courtyard, downtown. 202/463-6470. Hrs: 11:30 am-10:30 pm; Sat 6-11 pm. Closed Sun; major hols. Res accepted. American, Italian menu. Bar. Semi-a la carte: lunch $10-$17. A la carte entrees: dinner $17-$35. Specializes in dry-aged prime beef, fresh seafood. Pianist Mon-Fri. Cr cds: A, C, D, DS, MC, V.

D

★ ★ ★ **GERARD'S PLACE.** 915 15th St NW (20005), downtown. 202/737-4445. Hrs: 11:30 am-2:30 pm, 5:30-9:30 pm; Fri to 10:30 pm; Sat 5:30-10:30 pm. Closed Sun; most major hols. Res accepted. French menu. Wine list. A la carte entrees: lunch $13-$15.50, dinner $16-$32. Prix fixe: dinner $50. Specializes in contemporary French cooking. Valet parking (dinner). Outdoor dining. Casual atmosphere. Some modern art. Cr cds: A, C, D, MC, V.

★ ★ ★ **GERMAINE'S.** 2400 Wisconsin Ave NW, in Georgetown. 202/965-1185. Hrs: 11:30 am-2:30 pm, 5:30-10 pm; Fri to 11 pm; Sat 5:30-11 pm; Sun 5:30-10 pm. Closed Jan 1, Dec 25. Res accepted. Pan-Asian menu. Bar. A la carte entrees: lunch $7.25-$12.95, dinner $12.25-$25.95. Specializes in grilled Asian dishes, seafood. Skylighted atrium dining rm. Cr cds: A, C, D, MC, V.

★ **GERMAN DELI-CAFE MOZART.** 1331 H Street NW, downtown. 202/347-5732. Hrs: 7:30 am-10 pm; Sat from 9 am; Sun from 11 am. Closed Jan 1, Thanksgiving, Dec 25. Res accepted. German, Austrian menu. Bar. Semi-a la carte: bkfst $3.10-$7.95, lunch $4.65-$18.95, dinner $8.45-$19.95. Child's meals. Specialties: Wienerschnitzel, pork roast, Kasseler rippchen. Entertainment Wed-Sat. Cr cds: A, C, D, DS, JCB, MC, V.

D

✔ ★ **GUAPO'S.** 4515 Wisconsin Ave NW, north of downtown. 202/686-3588. Hrs: 11:30 am-10:30 pm; Fri, Sat to midnight. Res accepted. Latin American, Mexican menu. Bar. Semi-a la carte: lunch $3.95-$10.25, dinner $4.95-$11.95. Specializes in combination platters, fajitas, tamales. Outdoor dining. Small, colorful dining rms. Cr cds: A, DS, MC, V.

★ ★ **GUARDS.** 2915 M Street NW, in Georgetown. 202/965-2350. Hrs: 11:30-2 am; Fri, Sat to 3 am; Sun brunch 11:30 am-4 pm. Res accepted. Continental menu. Bar. Semi-a la carte: lunch $4.50-$10.95, dinner $8.95-$18. Sun brunch $6-$12. Specializes in rack of lamb, Angus beef, fresh seafood. Atrium dining rm; country-English decor. Cr cds: A, C, D, DS, MC, V.

✔ ★ **HEAD'S.** 400 1st St SE, corner of D St SE, adj to Capitol South Metro stop, on Capitol Hill. 202/546-4545. Hrs: 11:30 am-10:30 pm. Closed Sun; Memorial Day, Dec 25. Bar. Semi-a la carte: lunch, dinner $5.75-$12.50. Specializes in barbecued beef, ribs, chicken. Eclectic decor. Cr cds: A, C, D, DS, MC, V.

★ ★ **HOGATE'S.** 9th St & Maine Ave SW, on the waterfront, south of downtown. 202/484-6300. Hrs: 11 am-10 pm; Sat noon-11 pm; Sun 10:30 am-10 pm; Sun brunch to 2:30 pm. Closed Dec 25. Res accepted. Bar. Semi-a la carte: lunch $6-$12, dinner $13-$35. Sun brunch $16.95. Child's meals. Specialties: mariner's platter, clam bake, rum buns. Indoor parking. Outdoor dining. Overlooks Potomac River. Cr cds: A, C, D, DS, MC, V.

D

★ ★ **HUNAN CHINATOWN.** 624 H Street NW, in Chinatown. 202/783-5858. Hrs: 11 am-11 pm; Fri, Sat to midnight. Closed Thanksgiving, Dec 25. Hunan, Szechwan menu. Serv bar. Semi-a la carte: lunch $6.50-$12, dinner $7.50-$20. Specialties: General Tso's chicken, tea-smoked half-duck, crispy prawns with walnuts. Parking (dinner). Modern, bi-level dining room. Cr cds: A, C, D, DS, MC, V.

✔ ★ ★ **I MATTI TRATTORIA.** 2436 18th St NW, in Adams Morgan area. 202/462-8844. Hrs: noon-2:30 pm, 6-10:30 pm; Fri to 11 pm; Sat noon-4:30 pm, 6-11 pm; Sun 5:30-10 pm; Sun brunch 11:30 am-3 pm. Closed Jan 1, Thanksgiving, Dec 25. Res accepted. Northern Italian menu. Bar. A la carte entrees: lunch, dinner $10-$15. Sun brunch $3.95-$12. Specializes in pasta, pizza, grilled dishes. Valet parking Tues-Sat. Upscale dining; lower dining area less formal. Cr cds: A, D, MC, V.

★ ★ ★ **I RICCHI.** 1220 19th St NW, downtown. 202/835-0459. Hrs: 11:30 am-2:30 pm, 5:30-11 pm; Sat from 5:30 pm. Closed Sun; major hols. Res accepted. Italian menu. Bar. Semi-a la carte: lunch $11.95-$19.95, dinner $13.95-$24.95. Specializes in traditional Tuscan dishes. Own baking, pasta. Valet parking (dinner). Tuscan villa decor; Italian artifacts. Cr cds: A, C, D, MC, V.

D

★ **J PAUL'S.** 3218 M Street NW, in Georgetown. 202/333-3450. Hrs: 11:30-2 am; Fri, Sat to 3 am; Sun 10:30-2 am; Sun brunch to 4 pm. Bar. Semi-a la carte: lunch, dinner $4.95-$19.95. Sun brunch $4.95-$16.95. Child's meals. Specializes in ribs, crab cakes. Turn-of-the-century saloon decor; antique bar from Chicago's old Stockyard Inn. Cr cds: A, C, D, DS, MC, V.

★ ★ **JAPAN INN.** 1715 Wisconsin Ave NW, in Georgetown. 202/337-3400. Hrs: noon-2 pm, 6-10 pm; Fri to 10:30 pm; Sat 6-10:30 pm; Sun 5:30-9:30 pm. Closed some major hols; also lunch all major hols. Res accepted. Japanese menu. Semi-a la carte: lunch $8-$12.50, dinner $12-$28. Specializes in tempura, sushi, shabu-shabu. Parking. Traditional Japanese decor. Four dining areas, each with different menu. Family-owned. Cr cds: A, C, D, JCB, MC, V.

★ ★ ★ ★ **JEAN-LOUIS AT THE WATERGATE HOTEL.** (See The Watergate Hotel) 202/298-4488. Hrs: 5:30-10 pm. Closed Sun. Res accepted. French menu. Serv bar. Extensive wine cellar. Table d'hôte: dinner $85-$95. Prix fixe: pre-theater dinner (5-6:30 pm) $50. Specialties: crispy Vancouver shrimp, duck foie gras, turbot with potato crust, seaweed salad. Own baking. Valet parking. Recessed lighting on mirrored ceiling; silk wall hangings; exotic flowers. Artistic food presentation. Pastry chef. Jacket. Cr cds: A, C, D, DS, JCB, MC, V.

★ ★ ★ **THE JEFFERSON.** (See Jefferson) 202/347-2200. Hrs: 6:30-10:30 am, 11:30 am-2:30 pm, 6-10:30 pm. Sun brunch 11 am-3 pm. Res accepted. Bar 10:30-1 am. Semi-a la carte: bkfst $4.50-$12.50, lunch $12-$24, dinner $22.50-$26. Sun brunch $21.50-$25.75. Specializes in New Virginia cuisine, seafood. Soft jazz Thurs-Sat evenings. Valet parking. Intimate club-style atmosphere. Cr cds: A, C, D, DS, ER, JCB, MC, V.

★ ★ ★ **JOCKEY CLUB.** (See The Ritz-Carlton Hotel) 202/659-8000. Hrs: 6:30-11 am, noon-2:30 pm, 6-10:30 pm. Res accepted. Classic French, international menu. Serv bar. Semi-a la carte: bkfst $3.75-$13.50, lunch $5.50-$25, dinner $21.50-$34. Specializes in veal, fresh seafood, Jockey Club crab cakes. Own baking. Valet parking. Tableside cooking. Club-like atmosphere in 1928 landmark building. Jacket, tie. Cr cds: A, C, D, DS, ER, JCB, MC, V.

✔ ★ **KATMANDU.** 2100 Connecticut Ave NW, in Kalorama. 202/483-6470. Hrs: 11:30 am-2:30 pm, 5:30-10:30 pm; Sun 5:30-10 pm. Res accepted. Nepalese, Kashmiri menu. Bar. Semi-a la carte: lunch $5.25-$8.75, dinner $7.50-$12. Specialties: mutton biriani, Katmandu chicken. Far Eastern decor. Cr cds: A, D, DS, MC, V.

★ ★ ★ **KINKEAD'S.** 2000 Pennsylvania Ave NW (20006), in Foggy Bottom. 202/296-7700. Hrs: 11:30 am-10:30 pm. Closed Jan 1, Thanksgiving, Dec 25. Res accepted. Bar to midnight. Semi-a la carte: lunch $10-$14, dinner $14-$19. Sun brunch $8-$12. Specialties: pepita crusted salmon, pepper-seared tuna, grilled squid. Valet parking (dinner). Outdoor dining. Three levels of dining areas. Cr cds: A, C, D, DS, JCB, MC, V.

D

★ ★ **LA CHAUMIÈRE.** *2813 M Street NW, in Georgetown.* *202/338-1784.* Hrs: 11:30 am-2:30 pm, 5:30-11 pm; Sat from 5:30 pm. Closed Sun; major hols. Res accepted. Country French menu. A la carte entrees: lunch $7.75-$11.95, dinner $9.95-$17.95. Specializes in seafood, veal, duck. Intimate room with beamed ceiling, open-hearth fireplace. Cr cds: A, C, D, MC, V.

D

★ ★ ★ **LA COLLINE.** *400 N Capitol St NW, on Capitol Hill.* *202/737-0400.* Hrs: 7-10 am, 11:30 am-3 pm, 6-10 pm; Sat from 6 pm. Closed Sun; major hols. Res accepted. French menu. Bar. Semi-a la carte: bkfst $2.50-$5, lunch $9-$17, dinner $14-$21. Complete meals: dinner $17.50. Specializes in seasonal foods, duck, seafood. Outdoor dining. Across from Union Station. Cr cds: A, C, D, MC, V.

D

✔ ★ ★ **LA FONDA.** *1639 R Street NW, downtown.* *202/232-6965.* Hrs: 11:30 am-3 pm, 5-11 pm; Fri, Sat to midnight; Sun 11:30 am-10 pm. Closed Labor Day, Thanksgiving, Dec 25. Mexican, Spanish menu. Bar. Semi-a la carte: lunch $5.25-$10.50, dinner $6.95-$13.95. Specialties: enchiladas, carne asada, fajitas. Outdoor dining. Cr cds: A, D, DS, MC, V.

SC

★ **LAS PAMPAS.** *3291 M Street NW, in Georgetown.* *202/333-5151.* Hrs: 11 am-11 pm; Fri, Sat to 3 am. Res accepted. Argentinean, Tex-Mex menu. Serv bar. Semi-a la carte: lunch $4.95-$8.95, dinner $6.95-$19.95. Specializes in grilled steak, boneless chicken, Argentinean empanadas, fajitas. Cr cds: A, C, D, MC, V.

✔ ★ ★ **LAVANDOU.** *3321 Connecticut Ave NW, north of downtown.* *202/966-3003.* Hrs: 11:30 am-2:30 pm, 5-10 pm; Fri to 11 pm; Sat 5-11 pm; Sun 5-10 pm; Mon from 5 pm. Closed most major hols. Res accepted. Southern French menu. Serv bar. Semi-a la carte: lunch $9.95-$12.95, dinner $11.95-$15.95. Specialties: clam á l'ail, truite saumonée, daube Provençale. French bistro atmosphere. Cr cds: A, D, MC, V.

★ ★ **LE CAPRICE.** *2348 Wisconsin Ave NW, north of downtown.* *202/337-3394.* Hrs: 6-10 pm. Res accepted. French menu. Bar. Semi-a la carte: dinner $17-$24. Prix fixe: dinner $29.50. Specialties: sliced breast of duck with glazed fruit, boneless breast of chicken in pastry crust. Own pasta, pâté. Outdoor dining. French provincial decor. Extensive wine selection. Cr cds: A, C, D, MC, V.

★ ★ ★ **LE LION D'OR.** *1150 Connecticut Ave NW (Entrance on 18th St), downtown.* *202/296-7972.* Hrs: noon-2 pm, 6-10 pm; Sat from 6 pm. Closed Sun; major hols; also last 3 wks Aug-Labor Day. Res accepted. Classical French menu. Bar. Wine list. A la carte entrees: lunch $15-$27, dinner $25-$36. Specialties: soufflé de homard, gateau de crab. Own baking. Gracious dining. Elegant French decor, original artwork, antiques. Chef-owned. Jacket, tie. Cr cds: A, C, D, MC, V.

★ ★ ★ **MAISON BLANCHE/RIVE GAUCHE.** *1725 F Street NW, downtown.* *202/842-0070.* Hrs: 11:45 am-2 pm, 6-9:30 pm; Sat from 6 pm. Closed Sun; major hols. French menu. Bar. Semi-a la carte: lunch $12-$25, dinner $16.50-$32.50. Prix fixe: lunch $19, dinner $24.95. Specialties: lobster with saffron pasta, Dover sole, rack of lamb. Pastry chef. Complimentary valet parking from 5 pm. European decor; four seasons tapestry. Jacket recommended. Cr cds: A, C, D, DS, MC, V.

D

★ **MARKET INN.** *200 E Street SW, south of downtown.* *202/554-2100.* Hrs: 11 am-midnight; Fri to 1 am; Sat 10:30-1 am; Sun 10:30 am-midnight; major hols from 4 pm. Closed Dec 25. Res accepted. Bar. Semi-a la carte: lunch $6-$13.50, dinner $10.95-$24.95. Sat, Sun brunch $6-$13. Child's meals. Specializes in she-crab soup, Maine lobster, beef. Pianist, bass noon-midnight; jazz Sun brunch.

Free valet parking. Outdoor dining. Display of drawings, photographs, newspaper headlines. Family-owned. Cr cds: A, C, D, DS, JCB, MC, V.

D

★ ★ ★ **MELROSE.** *(See Park Hyatt Hotel)* *202/955-3899.* Hrs: 6:30-11 am, 11:30 am-2:30 pm, 6-10:30 pm; Fri & Sat to 11 pm; Sun brunch 11:30 am-2:30 pm. Res accepted. Contemporary Amer menu. Bar 11-1 am. Wine cellar. Semi-a la carte: bkfst $5.50-$12.75, lunch $12-$18, dinner $19-$25. Chef's 7-course tasting dinner $48. Pre-theater dinner (5:30-7:30 pm) $22.95. Sun brunch $28; with champagne $31. Child's meals. Specializes in fresh fish, seafood, beef, veal and chicken. Own baking. Pianist. Valet parking. Outdoor dining. Sunlit atrium, fountain. Cr cds: A, C, D, DS, JCB, MC, V.

D

✔ ★ ★ **MESKEREM.** *2434 18th St NW, in Adams Morgan area.* *202/462-4100.* Hrs: noon-midnight; Fri-Sun noon-1 am. Closed Thanksgiving, Dec 25. Res accepted. Ethiopian menu. Bar. Semi-a la carte: lunch, dinner $8.50-$11.95. Specializes in lamb, beef, chicken, seafood. Own Ethiopian breads. Ethiopian band Fri, Sat. Tri-level dining rm; traditional Ethiopian decor. Cr cds: A, C, D, MC, V.

★ ★ **MONOCLE ON CAPITOL HILL.** *107 D Street NE, adj to US Senate Office Bldg, on Capitol Hill.* *202/546-4488.* Hrs: 11:30 am-midnight; Sat 6-11 pm. Closed Sun; major hols; also Sat Memorial Day-Labor Day. Res accepted. Bar. A la carte entrees: lunch $6-$15, dinner $10.50-$20. Child's meals. Specializes in seafood, aged beef. Valet parking. Located in 1865 Jenkens Hill building; fireplace. Close to Capitol; frequented by members of Congress and other politicians. Family-owned. Cr cds: A, C, D, MC, V.

★ ★ ★ **MORTON'S OF CHICAGO.** *3251 Prospect St NW, in Georgetown.* *202/342-6258.* Hrs: 5:30-11 pm; Sun 5-10 pm. Closed some major hols. Res accepted. Bar. Wine list. A la carte entrees: dinner $15.95-$28.95. Specializes in steak, lobster, seafood. Valet parking. Collection of Leroy Neiman paintings. Cr cds: A, C, D, MC, V.

D

✔ ★ **MR. SMITH'S.** *3104 M Street NW, in Georgetown.* *202/333-3104.* Hrs: 11:30-2 pm; Fri, Sat to 3 am; Sat, Sun brunch 11 am-4:30 pm. Bar. Semi-a la carte: lunch, dinner $4.95-$14.95. Sat, Sun brunch $4.50-$8. Specializes in seafood, pasta, hamburgers. Pianist 9 pm-1:30 am. Old tavern atmosphere. Outdoor dining. Family-owned. Cr cds: A, C, D, MC, V.

★ ★ **MR. YUNG'S.** *740 6th St NW, in Chinatown.* *202/628-1098.* Hrs: 11 am-11 pm. Chinese, Cantonese menu. Serv bar. Semi-a la carte: lunch $5.95-$7.95, dinner $8.95-$25.95. Specialties: silver snapper with ginger, bean cake, eggplant and green pepper stuffed with shrimp in black bean sauce. Oriental decor. Cr cds: A, C, D, DS, MC, V.

✔ ★ **MURPHY'S OF D.C.** *2609 24th St NW, (20008), at Calvert St, north of downtown.* *202/462-7171.* Hrs: 11-2 am. Closed some major hols. Irish, Amer menu. Semi-a la carte: lunch $5.95-$7.95, dinner $6.95-$11.95. Child's meals. Specialties: meat & potato pie, Irish stew, corned beef & cabbage. Traditional Irish music. Patio dining. Wood-burning fireplace. Cr cds: A, D, MC, V.

★ ★ **NATHANS.** *3150 M Street NW, in Georgetown.* *202/338-2000.* Hrs: 11 am-3 pm, 6-11 pm; Thurs, Fri to midnight; Sat 6 pm-midnight; Sun 6-11 pm; Sat, Sun brunch 9 am-3 pm. Res accepted. Northern Italian, Amer menu. Bar 11-2 am; Fri & Sat to 3 am. Semi-a la carte: lunch $5.25-$11.50, dinner $14.50-$26.50. Sat, Sun brunch $5.25-$10.50. Specializes in fish, poultry, veal. Own pasta. Disc jockey Fri, Sat. Antiques. Family-owned. Cr cds: A, C, D, MC, V.

★ ★ **NEW HEIGHTS.** *2317 Calvert St NW, north of downtown.* *202/234-4110.* Hrs: 5:30-10 pm; Fri, Sat to 11 pm; Sun brunch 11 am-2:30 pm. Closed major hols. Res accepted. New Amer cuisine. Bar from 5 pm. Semi-a la carte: dinner $12-$22. Sun brunch $8-$15. Specializes in calamari fritti, grilled salmon, fresh mozzarella. Menu changes seasonally; some entrees offered in half-portions. Outdoor dining. Main dining rm on 2nd floor overlooks Rock Creek Park. Cr cds: A, C, D, DS, MC, V.

★ ★ ★ **NORA.** 2132 Florida Ave NW, in Dupont Circle. 202/462-5143. Hrs: 6-10 pm; Fri, Sat to 10:30 pm. Closed Sun; major hols; also last 2 wks Aug. Res accepted. Bar. Semi-a la carte: dinner $15.95-$23.95. Specializes in healthy dining, additive-free meats, organic produce. Menu changes daily. Own desserts. Atrium dining. In 1890 building with American folk art, Amish quilts on walls. Totally nonsmoking. Cr cds: MC, V.

★ ★ **NOTTE LUNA.** 809 15th St NW, downtown. 202/408-9500. Hrs: 11 am-11 pm; Fri to midnight; Sat 5 pm-1 am; Sun 5-11 pm. Closed Easter, Dec 25. Res accepted. Italian menu. Bar. Semi-a la carte: lunch, dinner $8.95-$15.95. Specializes in pizza, grilled meats & fish. Own pasta. Valet parking (dinner exc Sun). Outdoor dining. Wood-burning oven. Lively atmosphere. Cr cds: A, C, D, DS, MC, V.

[D]

★ ★ **OBELISK.** 2029 P Street NW, in Dupont Circle. 202/872-1180. Hrs: 6-10 pm. Closed Sun; major hols. Res accepted; required Fri & Sat. Italian menu. Serv bar. Complete meals: dinner $35-$37. Specializes in seasonal dishes. Menu changes daily. Intimate dining rm on 2nd floor of town house. Totally nonsmoking. Cr cds: D, MC, V.

★ ★ **OCCIDENTAL GRILL.** 1475 Pennsylvania Ave NW, downtown. 202/783-1475. Hrs: 11:30 am-11:30 pm; Sun noon-9 pm. Closed major hols. Res accepted. Bar. A la carte entrees: lunch $9.50-$16.95, dinner $11-$19. Specializes in grilled seafood, beef. Own baking. Turn-of-the-century Victorian decor with autographed photos of celebrities; originally opened 1906. Cr cds: A, C, D, MC, V.

[D]

✔ ★ ★ **OLD EBBITT GRILL.** 675 15th St NW, downtown. 202/347-4801. Hrs: 7:30-1 am; Sat from 8 am; Sun from 9:30 am; Sun brunch to 4 pm. Res accepted. Bar to 2 am; Fri, Sat to 3 am. Semi-a la carte: bkfst $4.95-$7.95, lunch $5-$10, dinner $5-$15.95. Sun brunch $5.95-$10. Specializes in seafood, hamburgers. Own pasta. In old vaudeville theater built in early 1900s. Victorian decor, gaslights; atrium dining. Cr cds: A, D, DS, MC, V.

[D]

★ ★ **OLD EUROPE RESTAURANT & RATHSKELLER.** 2434 Wisconsin Ave NW, north of downtown. 202/333-7600. Hrs: 11:30 am-3 pm, 5-10:30 pm; Fri, Sat to 11 pm; Sun 4-10 pm. Closed Dec 24, 25. Res accepted. German menu. Serv bar. Semi-a la carte: lunch $5-$10.50, dinner $10-$20. Child's meals. Specialties: schnitzel Old Europe, Wienerschnitzel, sauerbraten. Pianist; polka band Fri, Sat evenings. Cr cds: A, C, D, MC, V.

★ ★ **PALLADIN BY JEAN-LOUIS.** (See The Watergate Hotel) 202/298-4455. Hrs: 7 am-2:30 pm, 5:30-10:30 pm. Sun brunch 11:30 am-2:30 pm. Res accepted; required Fri & Sat. French menu. Bar. Semi-a la carte: bkfst $4.50-$17, lunch $6.50-$26, dinner $7.50-$26. Pre-theater dinner: $35. Sun brunch $38. Specializes in southern French cooking with Italian and Spanish touches. Overlooking Potomac River. Jacket (dinner). Cr cds: A, C, D, DS, JCB, MC, V.

[D]

★ ★ **PALM.** 1225 19th St NW, in Dupont Circle. 202/293-9091. Hrs: 11:45 am-10:30 pm; Sat from 6 pm; Sun 5:30-9:30 pm. Closed major hols. Res accepted. Bar. A la carte entrees: lunch $7.50-$17, dinner $14-$45. Specializes in steak, lobster. Valet parking (dinner). 1920s New York-style steak house. Family-owned. Cr cds: A, C, D, MC, V.

[D]

★ ★ **PAOLO'S.** 1303 Wisconsin Ave NW, in Georgetown. 202/333-7353. Hrs: 11:30-2 am; Fri, Sat to 3 am; Sun 11 am-2 am; Sat, Sun brunch to 4 pm. Italian menu. Bar. Semi-a la carte: lunch, dinner $7.95-$18.95. Sun brunch $8.95-$10.95. Specializes in pizza, pasta, seafood. Jazz combo Sun afternoons. Patio dining; wood-burning pizza oven. Cr cds: A, C, D, DS, MC, V.

★ ★ **PETITTO'S RISTORANTE D'ITALIA.** 2653 Connecticut Ave NW, north of downtown. 202/667-5350. Hrs: 11:30 am-2:30 pm, 6-10:30 pm; Sat from 6 pm; Sun 6-9:30 pm. Closed major hols; also Christmas wk. Res accepted. Italian menu. Bar. A la carte entrees: lunch $6.50-$11, dinner $10-$18. Specializes in pasta, fish, veal. Valet parking from 6 pm. Outdoor dining. Dessert & cappuccino rm downstairs. Washington town house overlooking Connecticut Ave; fireplaces. Cr cds: A, C, D, DS, MC, V.

★ **PHILLIPS FLAGSHIP.** 900 Water St SW, on waterfront, south of downtown. 202/488-8515. Hrs: 11 am-11 pm; Fri, Sat to midnight. Closed Dec 24 & 25. Bar. Semi-a la carte: lunch, dinner $4.95-$25.95. Buffet: lunch (exc Sun) $12.95. Sun brunch $17.95. Child's meals. Specializes in crab Imperial, Eastern Shore seafood dishes. Sushi bar. Garage parking. Outdoor dining. Antiques; Tiffany lamps, stained glass. In clement weather, exterior wall is rolled up, opening dining rm to marina. Cr cds: A, C, D, DS, MC, V.

[D]

✔ ★ **PIZZERIA PARADISO.** 2029 P Street NW, in Dupont Circle. 202/223-1245. Hrs: 11 am-11 pm; Fri, Sat to midnight; Sun noon-10 pm. Closed some major hols. Italian menu. Wine, beer. A la carte entrees: lunch, dinner $3.25-$15.75. Specializes in pizza, salads, sandwiches. Lively, colorful atmosphere; pizza-makers visible from dining area. Totally nonsmoking. Cr cds: MC, V.

★ ★ ★ **PRIME RIB.** 2020 K Street NW, downtown. 202/466-8811. Hrs: 11:30 am-3 pm, 5-11 pm; Fri to 11:30 pm; Sat 5-11:30 pm. Closed Sun; major hols. Res accepted. Bar. Semi-a la carte: lunch $7-$17. A la carte entrees: dinner $16.50-$24. Specializes in roast prime rib, Chesapeake seafood, aged thick-cut steak. Pianist at noon, pianist & bass at night. Valet parking. Art deco decor; 1920s lithographs. Jacket & tie. Cr cds: A, D, MC, V.

✔ ★ ★ **PRIMI PIATTI.** 2013 I Street NW, downtown. 202/223-3600. Hrs: 11:30 am-2:30 pm, 5:30-10:30 pm; Fri, Sat 5:30-11:30 pm; Sun 5-9:30 pm. Closed some major hols. Res accepted; required Fri, Sat. Italian menu. Bar. Semi-a la carte: lunch, dinner $7.95-$16.95. Specializes in grilled fish & meat. Own pasta. Outdoor dining. Cr cds: A, C, D, MC, V.

[D]

★ ★ ★ **RED SAGE.** 605 14th St NW, in Westory Bldg, downtown. 202/638-4444. Hrs: 11:30 am-2 pm, 5:30-10:30 pm; Sun 5-10 pm. Closed Dec 25. Res accepted. Southwestern menu. Bar. Wine cellar. A la carte entrees: lunch $8.50-$15.50, dinner $16.75-$25. Specialties: herb-roasted breast of chicken, cowboy ribeye steak, grilled Atlantic salmon. Validated parking. Two-story restaurant composed of a large street-level bar and a series of dining rms below. Designed as a contemporary interpretation of the American West, each of dining level's four major spaces exhibits a particular scale and mood. Cr cds: A, D, MC, V.

[D]

★ ★ ★ **RIVER CLUB.** 3223 K Street NW, in Georgetown. 202/333-8118. Hrs: 7 pm-2 am; Fri & Sat to 3 am. Closed Sun & Mon; major hols. Res accepted. Continental menu. Bar. Semi-a la carte: dinner $16-$26. Specialties: smoked salmon, smoked lobster, roast rack of lamb. Entertainment. Elegant supper club atmosphere with lively bar area. Jacket. Cr cds: A, C, D, DS, MC, V.

[D]

★ ★ **ROOF TERRACE.** 2700 F Street NW, within Kennedy Center, in Foggy Bottom. 202/416-8555. Hrs: (open only on days of Kennedy Center performances) 11:30 am-3 pm, 5:30-9 pm. Sun brunch 11:30 am-3 pm. Res accepted. Semi-a la carte: lunch $10-$14, dinner $22-$24. Sun brunch $19.95. Child's meals. Specializes in regional American cooking. Pastry chef. Garage parking. Contemporary decor; floor-to-ceiling windows offer views of Lincoln Memorial, Georgetown, Potomac River and Virginia. Totally nonsmoking. Cr cds: A, C, D, MC, V.

[D]

✔ ★ ★ **SAIGONNAIS.** *2307 18th St NW, in Adams Morgan area.* 202/232-5300. Hrs: 11:30 am-3 pm, 5-11 pm; Fri to 11 pm; Sat 5:30-11 pm; Sun 5:30-10:30 pm. Closed Jan 1, Thanksgiving, Dec 25. Res accepted. Vietnamese menu. Semi-a la carte: lunch, dinner $7.95-$14.95. Specialties: lemongrass beef, shrimp on sugar cane stick, catfish. Vietnamese artwork. Cr cds: A, C, D, DS, MC, V.

★ ★ ★ **SAM & HARRY'S.** *1200 19th St NW, in Dupont Circle.* 202/296-4333. Hrs: 11:30 am-2:30 pm, 5:30-11 pm; Sat 5:30-11 pm. Closed Sun; major hols. Res accepted. Bar. A la carte entrees: lunch $8.95-$20.95, dinner $17.95-$28.95. Specializes in dry prime aged beef, Maine lobster, grilled fresh seafood. Valet parking (dinner). Club-like atmosphere with mahogany paneling, paintings of jazz legends. Cr cds: A, C, D, DS, MC, V.

🅳

★ ★ ★ **SEA CATCH.** *1054 31st St NW, in Georgetown.* 202/337-8855. Hrs: noon-3 pm, 5:30-10 pm. Closed Sun. Res accepted. Bar. Wine list. Semi-a la carte: lunch $4.75-$12, dinner $14-$22. Specializes in lobster, crab cakes. Own pastries. Raw bar. Valet parking. Outdoor dining on deck overlooking historic Chesapeake & Ohio Canal. Cr cds: A, D, DS, MC, V.

🅳

★ ★ ★ **SEASONS.** *(See Four Seasons Hotel)* 202/342-0444. Hrs: 7-11 am, noon-2:30 pm, 6:30-10:30 pm; Sun brunch 10 am-2:30 pm. Res accepted. Bar 11-2 am. Extensive wine list. Semi-a la carte: bkfst $7-$19, lunch $14-$29, dinner $23-$32. Child's meals. Specializes in regional and seasonal dishes. Own baking. Pianist. Valet parking. Overlooks Rock Creek Park. Cr cds: A, C, D, ER, JCB, MC, V.

🅳

★ ★ **SEQUOIA.** *3000 K Street NW, Washington Harbour complex, in Georgetown.* 202/944-4200. Hrs: 11:30 am-midnight; Fri & Sat to 1 am; Sat, Sun brunch 11 am-4 pm. Res accepted. Bar. Semi-a la carte: lunch, dinner $6.95-$20.95. Sun brunch $6.95-$11.95. Outdoor dining. Terrace and multi-story dining rm windows overlook Kennedy Center, Potomac River and Roosevelt Bridge & Island. Cr cds: A, D, MC, V.

🅳

★ ★ **SFUZZI.** *50 Massachusetts Ave NE, in Union Station, on Capitol Hill.* 202/842-4141. Hrs: 11:30 am-10 pm; Fri, Sat to 11 pm; Sun to 9 pm; Sun brunch 11 am-3 pm. Closed Dec 25. Res accepted. Italian, Amer menu. Bar. Semi-a la carte: lunch $8.50-$11, dinner $12-$20. Sun brunch $14.50. Specializes in veal, pasta, seafood. Outdoor dining. Tri-level dining room in restored 1907 railroad station. Cr cds: A, C, D, MC, V.

🅳

★ ★ **SICHUAN PAVILION.** *1820 K Street NW, downtown.* 202/466-7790. Hrs: 11:30 am-10:30 pm. Res accepted. Chinese menu. Bar. A la carte entrees: lunch $8-$16, dinner $25-$30. Complete meals: dinner $25-$30. Specializes in Szechwan dishes. Valet parking after 6 pm. Oriental decor; original Chinese art. Artistic food preparation. Cr cds: A, C, D, DS, JCB, MC, V.

✔ ★ **STETSON'S.** *1610 U Street NW, in Adams Morgan area.* 202/667-6295. Hrs: 4 pm-2 am; Fri to 3 am; Sat 5 pm-3 am; Sun 5 pm-2 am. Tex-Mex menu. Bar. Semi-a la carte: lunch, dinner $2.95-$9.95. Specializes in chili, fajitas, chimichangas. Outdoor dining. Old West saloon-like decor and atmosphere; antique bar; Western artifacts. Cr cds: A, MC, V.

★ ★ ★ **TABERNA DEL ALABARDERO.** *1776 I Street NW, entrance on 18th St, downtown.* 202/429-2200. Hrs: 11:30 am-2:30 pm, 6-10 pm; Fri to 11 pm; Sat 6-11 pm. Closed Sun; major hols. Res accepted. Basque, Spanish menu. Bar. Semi-a la carte: lunch $6.25-$14.50, dinner $14-$24. Complete meals: dinner $24.95. Specializes in beef, fish, rice. Tapas bar. Own baking. Flamenco dancers Apr & Oct.

Valet parking (dinner). Ornate, 19th-century Spanish decor. Cr cds: A, C, D, MC, V.

🅳

✔ ★ ★ **THAI KINGDOM.** *2021 K Street NW, downtown.* 202/835-1700. Hrs: 11:30 am-2:30 pm, 5-10:30 pm; Sat noon-11 pm; Sun noon-10 pm. Closed some major hols. Res accepted. Thai menu. Bar. A la carte entrees: lunch $6.50-$8.95, dinner $7.25-$9.95. Specialties: crispy chili fish, scallops wrapped in minced chicken, Thai Kingdom grilled chicken. Valet parking (dinner). Outdoor dining. Bi-level dining rm with full windows overlooking K St. Cr cds: A, C, D, MC, V.

🅳

★ **THAI TASTE.** *2606 Connecticut Ave NW, north of downtown.* 202/387-8876. Hrs: 11:30 am-10:30 pm; Fri, Sat to 11 pm. Closed some major hols. Res accepted. Sun-Thurs. Thai menu. A la carte entrees: lunch, dinner $7-$15.95. Specializes in crispy fish, chicken with basil, seafood combinations. Outdoor dining. Cr cds: A, C, D, MC, V.

★ ★ ★ **TIBERIO.** *1915 K Street NW, downtown.* 202/452-1915. Hrs: 11:45 am-2:30 pm, 6-11 pm; Sat from 5:30 pm. Closed Sun; major hols. Res accepted. Italian menu. Bar. Wine cellar. A la carte entrees: lunch $13-$15.95, dinner $16.95-$29.95. Specialties: agnolotti alla crema, osso buco alla Milanese. Own baking. Valet parking (dinner). Mediterranean decor. Jacket. Cr cds: A, C, D, MC, V.

★ ★ **TONY AND JOE'S.** *3000 K Street NW, at Washington Harbour complex, in Georgetown.* 202/944-4545. Hrs: 11 am-midnight; Sun to 10 pm; Sun brunch to 3 pm. Closed Dec 25. Res accepted. Bar. Semi-a la carte: lunch $6.95-$13.95, dinner $13.95-$25. Sun brunch $16.95. Specializes in seafood. Own desserts. Outdoor dining. Overlooks Potomac River. Cr cds: A, C, D, DS, JCB, MC, V.

🅳

★ ★ **TONY CHENG'S MONGOLIAN BARBECUE AND CHINESE SEAFOOD RESTAURANT.** *619 H Street NW, in Chinatown.* 202/842-8669. Hrs: 11 am-11 pm; Fri, Sat to midnight. Res accepted. Mongolian barbecue menu. Prix fixe: lunch $8.50, dinner $13.95 (serv charge 15%). Food bar surrounds Mongolian barbecue. Diners may prepare their meals in "hot pot." Oriental decor. Cr cds: A, MC, V.

★ **TUCSON CANTINA.** *2605 Connecticut Ave NW, north of downtown.* 202/462-6410. Hrs: noon-10:30 pm; Fri, Sat to 11 pm. Closed some major hols. Southwestern menu. Bar 4 pm-2 am; Fri, Sat to 3 am; Sun 6 pm-1 am. Semi-a la carte: lunch, dinner $4.25-$17.50. Child's meals. Specializes in wood-grilled meats. Patio dining. Cr cds: C, D, DS, MC, V.

★ ★ **VINCENZO.** *1606 20th St NW (20009), in Dupont Circle.* 202/667-0047. Hrs: noon-2 pm, 6-9:30 pm; Fri to 10 pm; Sat 6-10 pm. Closed Sun; major hols. Res accepted. Italian menu. Bar. Semi-a la carte: lunch, dinner $12.95-$19.95. Specializes in fresh seafood. Valet parking (dinner). Three dining rms, including atrium. Cr cds: A, C, D, MC, V.

★ ★ ★ **WILLARD ROOM.** *(See Willard Inter-Continental Hotel)* 202/637-7440. Hrs: 7:30-10 am, 11:30 am-2 pm, 6-10 pm; Sat, Sun from 6 pm; Sun brunch 11 am-2 pm; afternoon tea 3-5 pm. Res accepted. Bar 11-1 am. Extensive wine list. French, Amer regional cuisine. A la carte entrees: bkfst $7-$15.50, lunch $17-$28, dinner $18.50-$32. Afternoon tea $13. Sun brunch $28-$39. Child's meals. Specializes in seafood, lamb, veal. Seasonal specialties. Own pastries. Pianist. Valet parking. Elegant turn-of-the-century decor. Cr cds: A, C, D, DS, ER, JCB, MC, V.

🅳

Unrated Dining Spots

ARMAND'S CHICAGO PIZZERIA. *4231 Wisconsin Ave NW, north of downtown. 202/686-9450.* Hrs: 11:30 am-11 pm; Fri, Sat to 1 am. Closed Thanksgiving, Dec 25. Serv bar. A la carte entrees: lunch, dinner $4-$7. Buffet: lunch (pizza & salad) $4.49. Specializes in Chicago-style deep-dish pizza, sandwiches, salads, desserts. Outdoor dining. Cr cds: A, MC, V.

AUSTIN GRILL. *2404 Wisconsin Ave NW, in Georgetown. 202/337-8080.* Hrs: 11:30 am-11 pm; Fri, Sat 11:30 am-midnight; Sat brunch 11:30 am-3 pm, Sun brunch 11 am-3 pm. Closed Jan 1, Thanksgiving, Dec 24, Dec 25. Tex-Mex menu. Bar. Semi-a la carte: lunch, dinner $4.95-$12.95. Sat, Sun brunch $6.25-$6.95. Specializes in enchiladas, fajitas. Southwestern decor. Cr cds: A, D, DS, MC, V.

C.F. FOLKS. *1225 19th St NW, in Dupont Circle. 202/293-0162.* Hrs: 11:45 am-3 pm. Closed Sat, Sun; major hols. Semi-a la carte: lunch $4.95-$6.35. Complete meals: lunch $7-$10. Specializes in crab cakes, daily & seasonally changing cuisines. Outdoor dining. Old-fashioned lunch counter. No cr cds accepted.

CAFE PETITTO. *1724 Connecticut Ave NW, in Dupont Circle. 202/462-8771.* Hrs: 11:30 am-10:30 pm; Fri, Sat to 11 pm; Sun to 10 pm; Sat, Sun brunch to 2:30 pm. Italian menu. Bar. A la carte entrees: lunch, dinner $6-$13. Sat, Sun brunch $8.95. Specializes in pizza, pasta, hoagies. Cr cds: A, C, D, MC, V.

KRAMERBOOKS & AFTERWORDS. *1517 Connecticut Ave, in Dupont Circle. 202/387-1462.* Hrs: 7:30-1 am; wkends open 24 hrs; Sun brunch 9:30 am-3 pm. Closed Thanksgiving, Dec 25. Bar. Semi-a la carte: bkfst $3.95-$7.50, lunch, dinner $6.75-$12.75. Sun brunch $8.25-$10.75. Specializes in pasta, fresh seafood, Thai seafood salad, smoked chichen pita. Entertainment Thurs-Sun. Oudoor dining. Lively, entertaining spot in 2-story greenhouse & terrace behind Kramerbooks bookshop. Open continuously Fri morning to Mon night. Cr cds: A, DS, MC, V.

MADURAI. *3316 M Street NW, in Georgetown. 202/333-0997.* Hrs: 11:30 am-2:30 pm, 5:30-10 pm; Fri, Sat to 11 pm; Sun noon-4 pm, 5-10 pm. Vegetarian menu. Semi-a la carte: lunch, dinner $3.50-$9.95. Sun brunch $6.95. Specializes in curry, navratan garden vegetables. Cr cds: A, MC, V.

PATISSERIE-CAFE DIDIER. *3206 Grace St NW, in Georgetown. 202/342-9083.* Hrs: 8 am-7 pm; Sun to 5 pm. Closed Mon; Jan 1, Dec 25. Semi-a la carte: bkfst $1.10-$7.95, lunch, dinner $5.95-$8.95. Specializes in European desserts, quiche, pizza. European-style cafe and pastry house. Cr cds: C, D, DS, MC, V.

SHOLL'S COLONIAL CAFETERIA. *1990 K Street NW, in Esplanade Mall, in Foggy Bottom. 202/296-3065.* Hrs: 7 am-2:30 pm, 4-8 pm. Closed Sun; major hols. Avg ck: bkfst $3, lunch, dinner $5. Specializes in spaghetti, liver & onions, homemade pie. Family-owned. No cr cds accepted.

D

Maryland

Population:	4,917,269
Land area:	9,838 square miles
Elevation:	0-3,360 feet
Highest point:	Backbone Mountain (Garrett County)
Entered Union:	Seventh of original 13 states (April 28, 1788)
Capital:	Annapolis
Motto:	Manly deeds, womanly words
Nicknames:	Old Line State, Free State
State flower:	Black-eyed Susan
State bird:	Baltimore oriole
State tree:	Wye oak
State fair:	August 26-September 4, 1995, in Timonium (see Towson)
Time zone:	Eastern

Maryland prides itself on its varied terrain and diverse economy. Metropolitan life around the great cities of Baltimore and Washington, DC (the land was ceded from Maryland in 1791) is balanced by the rural atmosphere in central and southern Maryland and on the Eastern Shore, across Chesapeake Bay. Green mountains in the western counties contrast with white Atlantic beaches. A flourishing travel industry, agricultural and dairy wealth in central Maryland, the seafood industry of the Bay and its tidal rivers, manufacturing and commerce in the cities, plus federal government and defense contracts combine to make the state prosperous.

Maryland's three-and-one-half centuries of history began in March, 1634, when Lord Baltimore's brother, Leonard Calvert, solemnly knelt on tiny St Clements Island, near the wide mouth of the Potomac, and named his new province in honor of Henrietta Maria, wife of Charles I, King of England. Calvert's awkward little ships, the *Ark* and the *Dove,* then carried the 222 passengers, including religious refugees, to an Indian village a few miles away. They purchased the village and named it Saint Maries Citty (now St Mary's City). Religious toleration was practiced from the colony's founding and was assured by law in 1649. The land was cleared, tobacco was planted, and over the years, profits built elegant mansions, many of which still stand.

Maryland was one of the 13 original colonies. Its first capital was St Mary's City. In 1694 the capital was transferred to Annapolis, where it remains today.

Every war waged on US soil has seen major action by Marylanders. In 1755, British General Edward Braddock, assisted by Lt Colonel George Washington, trained his army at Cumberland for the fight against the French and Indians. In the Revolution, General William Howe invaded Maryland at the head of Chesapeake Bay, and a battle was joined at Brandywine Creek in Pennsylvania before the British moved on to capture Philadelphia. Maryland troops in the Battle of Long Island made a heroic bayonet coverage of the retreat. The courageous action of the "Old Line" gave the state one of its nicknames. The War of 1812 saw Fort McHenry at Baltimore withstand attack by land

and sea, with the action immortalized in the national anthem by Francis Scott Key, a Frederick lawyer. In the Civil War, Maryland was a major battleground at Antietam; troops moved back and forth through the state for the four bloody years of destruction.

A border state with commercial characteristics of both North and South, Maryland found its original dependence on tobacco relieved by the emerging Industrial Revolution. Modern factories, mills and ironworks around Baltimore became important to the state's economy. Educational institutions were established and the port of Baltimore, at the mouth of the Patapsco River, flourished. In the mid-19th century, with the Baltimore & Ohio Railroad and the Chesapeake & Ohio Canal carrying freight to the fast-developing western states, Maryland thrived.

Sportsmen have always thought well of Maryland. The state's thousands of miles of tidal shoreline allows plenty of elbow room for aquatic diversion. Maryland's race tracks include Pimlico (see BALTIMORE), featuring the nationally known Preakness Stakes, and Laurel, where the International Turf Festival is run. The "Maryland Million" is held alternately at Laurel and Pimlico. Deer hunting is allowed in most counties and goose hunting on the Eastern Shore. Historical sites cover the landscape, and more are constantly being opened up to the public by the state and National Park Service. Highways are good; reaching places in the Baltimore-Washington, DC area is simplified by direct, high-speed, four-lane highways constructed around, between and radiating from these cities.

National Park Service Areas

Maryland has Clara Barton National Historic Site (see DISTRICT OF COLUMBIA), Antietam National Battlefield (see), Fort McHenry National Monument and Historic Shrine (see BALTIMORE), Hampton National Historic Site (see TOWSON), Assateague Island National Seashore (see OCEAN CITY), the Chesapeake and Ohio Canal National Historical Park (see), Catoctin Mountain Park (see THURMONT), and Fort Washington National Park (see DISTRICT OF COLUMBIA).

State Recreation Areas

The following towns list state recreation areas in their vicinity under What to See and Do; refer to the individual town for directions and park information.

> Listed under **Annapolis:** see Sandy Point State Park.
>
> Listed under **Baltimore:** see Gunpowder Falls State Park (Hammerman Area).
>
> Listed under **Crisfield:** see Janes Island State Park.
>
> Listed under **Cumberland:** see Dans Mountain State Park, Green Ridge State Forest and Rocky Gap State Park.
>
> Listed under **Easton:** see Tuckahoe State Park.
>
> Listed under **Elkton:** see Elk Neck State Park and Elk Neck State Forest.
>
> Listed under **Ellicott City:** see Patapsco Valley State Park.
>
> Listed under **Frederick:** see Gambrill State Park.
>
> Listed under **Gaithersburg:** see Seneca Creek State Park.
>
> Listed under **Grantsville:** see New Germany State Park and Savage River State Forest.
>
> Listed under **Hagerstown:** see Fort Frederick and Greenbrier state parks.
>
> Listed under **Havre de Grace:** see Susquehanna State Park.
>
> Listed under **La Plate:** see Smallwood State Park.
>
> Listed under **Oakland:** see Deep Creek Lake State Park, Garrett State Forest, Herrington Manor State Park, Potomac State Forest and Swallow Falls State Park.
>
> Listed under **Ocean City:** see Assateague State Park.
>
> Listed under **St Mary's City:** see Point Lookout State Park.
>
> Listed under **Thurmont:** see Cunningham Falls State Park.
>
> Listed under **Waldorf:** see Cedarville State Forest.

Water-related activities, hiking, riding, various other sports, picnicking and visitor centers, as well as camping, are available in many of these areas. Most state-maintained areas have small charges for parking and special services. Camping: $6-$12/site/night, exc Assateague ($18) and Point Lookout ($18); stays limited to two wks; most areas are open late Mar-early Dec, but season varies from one park to the next; ck-out 3 pm; reservations for a stay of 1 wk are available at Assateague—they may be obtained by writing directly to the park (see OCEAN CITY). Pets allowed at the following parks (some special restrictions may apply; phone ahead): Green Ridge Forest, Elk Neck, Patapsco (Hollofield), Point Lookout, Rocky Gap, Savage River Forest, Susquehanna, Swallow Falls, Garrett Forest, Potomac Forest and Pocomoke River (Milburn Landing). Day use: 8 am-sunset; closed Dec 25; fee May-Sept. For complete information, including information on cabins, contact the Maryland Dept of Natural Resources, State Forest and Park Service, Tawes State Office Bldg E-3, 580 Taylor Ave, Annapolis 21401; 410/974-3771. It is advisable to call parks before visiting, as some may be closed during the off season.

Fishing & Hunting

Non-tidal, nonresident fishing license, $20; 5-day, $7; trout stamp, $5. Chesapeake Bay nonresident fishing license, $12; 5-day, $4.

Nonresident hunting licenses: consolidated, $83-$120.50, depending on state of residence; 3-day, $35; waterfowl stamp $6; regular deer stamp, $9.50; bow hunting deer stamp, $3.50; black powder deer stamp, $3.50; 2nd deer stamp, $10. For latest information, including *Maryland Sportfishing Guide* or the *Guide to Hunting, Trapping in Maryland,* contact Maryland Dept of Natural Resources, Sport Licensing Division, 580 Taylor Ave, Annapolis 21401; 410/974-3211.

Safety Belt Information

Safety belts are mandatory for driver and passengers in front seat of vehicle. Children 10 years and under must be in an approved passenger restraint anywhere in the vehicle. Children under 4 years or weighing 40 pounds or less must be in an approved safety seat. For further information phone 410/486-3101.

Interstate Highway System

The following alphabetical listing of Maryland towns in *Mobil Travel Guide* shows that these cities are within 10 miles of the indicated Interstate highways. A highway map should be checked, however, for the nearest exit.

INTERSTATE 68: Cumberland.

INTERSTATE 70: Baltimore, Columbia, Ellicott City, Frederick, Hagerstown.

INTERSTATE 81: Hagerstown.

INTERSTATE 83: Baltimore, Cockeysville, Towson.

INTERSTATE 95: Aberdeen, Baltimore, College Park, Elkton, Havre de Grace, Laurel, Silver Spring, Towson.

Additional Visitor Information

The *Maryland Travel and Outdoor Guide* and a calendar of events can be obtained from the Maryland Office of Tourism Development, 217 E Redwood St, Baltimore 21202; 800/543-1036.

There are several visitor information centers in Maryland; visitors who stop by will find information and brochures helpful in planning stops at points of interest. Their locations are as follows: on I-95 (N & S) near Laurel; on I-70 (E & W) between Hagerstown and Frederick; on US 15S at Emmitsburg; on I-95S near North East; on US 48E near Friendsville; on US 13N near Maryland-Virginia line; and in the State House, Annapolis. (Daily; closed some major hols)

Aberdeen (B-8)

Pop: 13,087 **Elev:** 83 ft **Area code:** 410 **Zip:** 21001

This is the home of the 75,000-acre Aberdeen Proving Grounds, a federal reservation along Chesapeake Bay. Various types of army materiel, ranging from gunsights to tanks, are tested under simulated combat conditions.

What to See and Do

1. **US Army Ordnance Museum.** At Aberdeen Proving Ground, off I-95 exit 85, 3 mi E on MD 22, follow signs. Tanks, self-propelled artillery, extensive small arms and ammunition collection. (Daily exc Mon; closed most major hols) Phone 278-3602. **Free.**

2. **Industrial tour. Philadelphia Electric Company.** 7 mi NE on US 40 or I-95, then 11 mi NW on US 222 to Conowingo. Hydroelectric plant on the Susquehanna River. Limited area of plant is open for guided tours (daily; reservations required wkdays; no tours Jan 1, Dec 25). For schedule and reservations phone 457-5011. **Free.** Nearby is

   Recreation area with 14-mi-long man-made lake; picnicking; hiking; swimming pool (fee); boating (ramps, marinas); waterskiing; fishing; fishermen's gallery (over 12 yrs only). Phone 457-5011. **Free.**

Motels

✔ ★ **DAYS INN.** *783 W Bel Air Ave, I-95 exit 85.* 410/272-8500; FAX 410/272-5782. 49 rms, 2 story. S $38; D $44; each addl $4;

under 16 free. Crib free. Pet accepted. TV; cable. Pool. Complimentary continental bkfst, coffee. Restaurant nearby. Ck-out 11 am. Cr cds: A, C, D, DS, MC, V.

★ ★ **HOLIDAY INN-CHESAPEAKE HOUSE.** *1007 Beards Hill Rd.* 410/272-8100; FAX 410/272-1714. 122 rms, 5 story. S $74-$84; D $84-$94; each addl $10; suites $125; kit. units $78-$88; under 18 free; wkend rates. Pet accepted. TV; cable. Indoor pool. Restaurant 6 am-2 pm, 5-10 pm; Sat, Sun from 7 am. Bar. Ck-out noon. Meeting rms. Sundries. Some refrigerators. Balconies. Cr cds: A, C, D, DS, JCB, MC, V.

D ✦ ≈ ⋈ ⋈ SC

Motor Hotel

★ ★ **SHERATON.** *PO Box V, 980 Beard's Hill Rd, W off I-95 exit 85.* 410/273-6300; FAX 410/575-7195. 131 rms, 4 story. Mid-Mar-mid-Nov: S, D $73-$99; each addl $10; suites $129; under 18 free; package plans; lower rates rest of yr. Crib free. Pet accepted, some restrictions. TV; cable. Pool. Restaurant 6:30 am-10 pm. Rm serv. Bar 10-2 am; entertainment, dancing Tues-Sat. Ck-out 11 am. Coin lndry. Meeting rms. Valet serv. Sundries. Health club privileges. Some refrigerators. Wet bar in suites. Cr cds: A, C, D, DS, MC, V.

D ✦ ≈ ⋈ ⋈ SC

Annapolis (C-7)

Founded: 1649 **Pop:** 33,187 **Elev:** 57 ft **Area code:** 410

The capital of Maryland, gracious and dignified in the colonial tradition, Annapolis has had a rich history for more than 300 years. Planned and laid out as the provincial capital in 1695, it was the first peacetime capital of the United States (Congress met here November 26, 1783-August 13, 1784). In 1845 the US Naval Academy was established here, at the Army's Fort Severn. Town life centers on sport and commercial water-oriented activities, state government and the academy. Every May, at commencement time, thousands of visitors throng the narrow, twisting streets.

What to See and Do

1. **State House** (ca 1772-79). State Circle, center of town. Oldest state house in continuous legislative use in US, this was the first capitol of the US. Here in 1784, a few weeks after receiving George Washington's resignation as commander-in-chief, Congress ratified the Treaty of Paris, which officially ended the American Revolution. Visitors Information Center. Guide service (exc Jan 1, Thanksgiving). (Daily; closed Dec 25) Phone 974-3400. **Free.**

2. **Old Treasury** (ca 1735). Just S of State House. Oldest public building in the state. (Mon-Fri; closed Jan 1, Thanksgiving, Dec 25) Phone 267-8149. **Free.**

3. **Governor's Mansion** (1868). Between State & Church Circles. This Victorian structure was remodeled in 1935 into a five-part Colonial-revival mansion; furnishings reflect Maryland's history and culture. Tours by appt (Tues-Thurs). Phone 974-3531. **Free.**

4. **St John's College** (1784). (400 students) College Ave. Nonsectarian liberal arts college. This 36-acre campus, one of the oldest in the country, is a National Historic Landmark. The college succeeded King William's School, founded in 1696. George Washington's two nephews and step-grandson studied here; Francis Scott Key was an alumnus. For information phone 263-2371, ext 239. On campus are

Elizabeth Myers Mitchell Art Gallery. Displays museum quality traveling exhibitions. (Academic yr, daily exc Mon) For schedule phone 626-2556. **Free.**

McDowell Hall (begun 1742, finished 1789). Named for St John's first president; the main classroom building was originally built as the Governor's Palace. Lafayette was feted here in 1824. (Daily by appt; closed hols) **Free.**

Charles Carroll, Barrister House (1722). Birthplace of the author of the Maryland Bill of Rights; moved in 1955 to the campus and restored; now an administration building. Open upon request. **Free.**

Liberty Tree. Tulip poplar, thought to be more than 400 years old, under which the Sons of Liberty met during the Revolution.

5. **Hammond-Harwood House** (1774). 19 Maryland Ave, at King George St, 1 blk W of US Naval Academy. Georgian house designed by William Buckland; antique furnishings; garden. Matthias Hammond, a Revolutionary patriot, was its first owner. (Daily; closed Jan 1, Thanksgiving, Dec 25) Phone 269-1714. **¢¢**

6. **Walking tours.**

Historic Annapolis Foundation. Self-guided audio cassette walking tours. Tours leave from Maritime Museum, 77 Main St. Includes Historic District, State House (see #1), Old Treasury (see #2), US Naval Academy (see #7) and William Paca Garden (see #8). (Mar-Nov, daily) Phone tour director, 267-7619 or 269-0432. **¢¢¢**

Three Centuries Tours of Annapolis. Morning tour leaves from lobby of Marriott-Waterfront Hotel (see) at Compromise & St Mary Sts and afternoon tour leaves from City Dock Visitor's Center (Apr-Oct, daily). Walking tours of US Naval Academy and Historic District conducted by guides in colonial dress carrying baskets of everyday objects from the 18th century (daily). Other tours, including mansions (daily, by appt). For information contact Tour Director, PO Box 29, 21404. Phone 263-5401 to confirm departure points and schedule. **¢¢¢**

7. **United States Naval Academy** (1845). (4,300 students) Entrance for Visitor Information Center in Ricketts Hall; enter through Gate #1. World-renowned school for naval officers; three dress parades held in fall and spring, weather permitting. (Daily; bldgs Mon-Fri, limited hrs Sun; closed Jan 1, Thanksgiving, Dec 25) The remains of John Paul Jones, removed from their original burial place in France, lie here beneath the chapel in a crypt similar to Napoleon's in Paris. Naval Academy Museum exhibits 300 years of American naval history (daily). Before Bancroft Hall, dormitory for all midshipmen, stands a bust of Tamanend, replica of figurehead of USS *Delaware,* renamed *Tecumseh.* Tours leave Visitor Center (daily). Parades, concerts and other events are held annually and during "Commissioning Week" (late May), culminated by midshipmen's graduation. Phone 263-6933 or 267-3363. Grounds **free;** tours **¢¢**

8. **William Paca Garden.** 186 Prince George St. Faithful re-creation of the elaborate landscaped garden developed in 1765 by William Paca, a signer of the Declaration of Independence and governor of Maryland during the Revolutionary War. Includes waterways, formal parterres and a miniature wilderness. (Daily exc Tues; closed Thanksgiving, Dec 25) Also here is

William Paca House. Paca built this five-part Georgian mansion in 1765. (Daily exc Tues; closed Thanksgiving, Dec 25) Phone 263-5553. Combination ticket (includes house and garden) **¢¢¢**

9. **Boat trips.** From city dock at foot of Main St. 40-minute narrated tours of city harbor, USNA and Severn River aboard *Harbor Queen* (Memorial Day-Labor Day, daily); 90-minute cruises to same locations aboard *Providence* and *Rebecca* (Mar-Dec, daily); cruises to St Michaels aboard the *Annapolitan II* (Memorial Day-Labor Day, daily); 40-minute cruises up Spa Creek, residential areas, city harbor and USNA aboard the *Miss Anne* and *Miss Anne II* (Memorial Day-Labor Day). Some cruises early spring and late fall, weather permitting. Reservations usually required. Phone 268-7600, 269-6776 (Baltimore) or 202/261-2719 (DC).

10. **London Town Publik House and Gardens** (ca 1760). 8 mi SE via MD 2S, 253 (Mayo Rd) in Edgewater, at the end of Londontown Rd (#839). Georgian-style inn on banks of South River; 10 acres of woodland gardens; log tobacco barn (1720); boat docking. Changing exhibits, special events. Guided tours. (Mar-Dec, daily exc Mon; closed hols) Sr citizen rate. Phone 222-1919. ¢¢

11. **Chesapeake Bay Bridge.** 7¼-mi link of US 50 across the Bay. Toll (charged eastbound only) ¢¢

12. **Sandy Point State Park.** 7 mi E on US 50, at W end of Chesapeake Bay Bridge. 786 acres. The park's location on the Atlantic Flyway makes it a fine area for bird watching; view of Bay Bridge and oceangoing vessels. Swimming in bay at 2 guarded beaches, 2 bathhouses; surf fishing, crabbing; boating (rentals, launches). Concession. Standard fees. (See ANNUAL EVENTS) Phone 757-1841.

(For general touring information, contact the Annapolis and Anne Arundel County Conference and Visitors Bureau, 26 West St, 21401; 268-TOUR. Information is also available at the Visitor Information Booth located at the city dock.)

Annual Events

Maryland Renaissance Festival. Food, craftsmen, minstrels, dramatic productions. Usually last wk Aug-1st wk Oct.

Maryland Seafood Festival. Sandy Point State Park (see #12). Food; entertainment. Usually wkend after Labor Day.

US Sailboat Show. City dock & harbor. Features world's largest in-water display of sailboats; exhibits of related marine products. Phone 268-8828. Early-mid-Oct.

US Powerboat Show. City dock & harbor. Extensive in-water display of powerboats; exhibits of related marine products. Phone 268-8828. Mid-Oct.

Chesapeake Appreciation Days. Sandy Point State Park (see #12). Skipjack sailing festival honors state's oystermen. Usually last wkend Oct.

Annapolis by Candlelight. For information, reservations contact Historic Annapolis Foundation (see #6); for dates phone 267-8149. Usually early Nov.

Seasonal Event

Christmas in Annapolis. Features decorated 18th-century mansions, parade of yachts, private home tours, pub crawls, concerts, holiday meals, caroling by candlelight at the State House and other events. For free events calendar phone 268-8687. Thanksgiving-Jan 1.

(See Baltimore, Baltimore/Washington Intl Airport Area)

Motels

✔ ★ ★ **COMFORT INN.** 76 Old Mill Bottom Rd N (21401), US 50/301 exit 28 to Bay Dale Dr. 410/757-8500; FAX 410/757-4409. 60 rms, 2 story. Apr-Oct: S $55-$90; D $60-$90; each addl $8; under 18 free; lower rates rest of yr. Crib $10. TV; cable. Pool; lifeguard. Complimentary continental bkfst. Restaurant opp 7 am-10 pm. Ck-out 11 am. Coin lndry. Cr cds: A, C, D, DS, ER, JCB, MC, V.

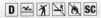

★ ★ ★ **COURTYARD BY MARRIOTT.** 2559 Riva Rd (21401). 410/266-1555; FAX 410/266-6376. 149 units, 3 story. S, D $80; suites $90-$119; under 12 free. Crib free. TV; cable. Indoor pool; lifeguard. Complimentary coffee in rms. Restaurant 6:30 am-2 pm, 5-10 pm; Sat, Sun from 7 am. Bar 4-11 pm. Ck-out noon. Coin lndry. Meeting rms. Valet serv. Sundries. Exercise equipt; weight machines, bicycles, whirlpool. Refrigerator in suites. Some balconies. Cr cds: A, C, D, DS, MC, V.

Motor Hotels

★ ★ ★ **HOLIDAY INN.** 210 Holiday Ct/Riva Rd (21401), MD 450 exit, entrance on Riva Rd. 410/224-3150; FAX 410/224-3413. 220 rms, 6 story. S $79-$119; D $89-$129; each addl $10; suites $139; under 18 free. Crib free. Pet accepted. TV; cable. Pool; lifeguard. Restaurant 6:30 am-2 pm, 5-10 pm. Rm serv. Bar 4 pm-midnight. Ck-out noon. Meeting rms. Bellhops. Valet serv. Sundries. Health club privileges. Cr cds: A, C, D, DS, JCB, MC, V.

✔ ★ ★ ★ **RAMADA.** 173 Jennifer Rd (21401). 410/266-3131; FAX 410/266-6247. 197 rms, 6 story. S $59-$109; D $79-$139; each addl $10; suites $175-$275; under 18 free; hol rates; higher rates special events. Crib free. TV; cable. Indoor pool; poolside serv, lifeguard. Restaurant 7 am-2 pm, 5-10 pm. Rm serv. Bar 2 pm-1 am; entertainment, dancing. Ck-out noon. Meeting rms. Free downtown transportation. Exercise rm: instructor, bicycles, rowing machine, whirlpool, sauna, steam rm. Health club privileges. Some refrigerators. Cr cds: A, C, D, DS, ER, MC, V.

Hotels

★ ★ ★ **LOEWS ANNAPOLIS.** 126 West St (21401). 410/263-7777; FAX 410/263-0084. 217 rms, 6 story, 23 suites. S $105-$145; D $125-$165; each addl $20; suites $185-$350; under 17 free. Crib free. Pet accepted. Valet parking $9. TV; cable. Pool privileges. Restaurant 6:30 am-10:30 pm; wkends to 11 pm. Bar 11-2 am. Ck-out noon. Meeting rms. Concierge. Gift shop. Barber, beauty shop. Lighted tennis privileges. Exercise equipt; weight machine, bicycle. Health club privileges. Bicycles avail. Minibars, refrigerators. Private patios, balconies. *LUXURY LEVEL : PLAZA CLUB.* 35 rms, 2 floors. S $135; D $165. Private lounge. Complimentary continental bkfst 7-10 am. Cr cds: A, C, D, MC, V.

★ ★ ★ **MARRIOTT-WATERFRONT.** 80 Compromise St (21401), opp Naval Academy. 410/268-7555; FAX 410/269-5864. 150 rms, 6 story. Apr-mid-Nov: S $135-$270; D $155-$290; each addl $20; family rates; lower rates rest of yr. Crib free. Garage $10, valet. TV; cable. Restaurant 7 am-10:30 pm. Bar 11-2 am. Ck-out 11 am. Meeting rms. Exercise equipt; weight machines, bicycles. Refrigerators avail. Some in-rm whirlpools. Some balconies. On waterfront; 250-ft dockage. Cr cds: A, C, D, DS, MC, V.

Inns

✔ ★ **THE CHARLES INN.** 74 Charles St (21401). 410/268-1451. 4 rms, 3 story. 1 rm phone. S $53.63-$99; D $84.53-$170; under 12 free; wkly, wkend rates. TV in some rms, some B/W; cable in sitting rm. Complimentary full bkfst, coffee. Restaurant nearby. Ck-in/ck-out times by arrangement. In-rm whirlpool avail. Built 1860; antiques. On Spa Creek; access to water taxi. Cr cds: A, MC, V.

★ **GIBSON'S LODGINGS.** 110 Prince George St (21401). 410/268-5555. 20 rms in 3 bldgs, 7 with bath, 3 story. Some rm phones. S $58-$110; D $68-$120; each addl $10. TV in some rms; cable. Complimentary continental bkfst, sherry. Restaurant nearby. Ck-out 11 am, ck-in 2 pm. Meeting rm. Antiques; library. Totally non-smoking. Cr cds: A, MC, V.

★ ★ **GOVERNOR CALVERT HOUSE.** Mailing address: 16 Church Circle (21401), 58 State Circle. 410/263-2641; res: 800/847-8882 (exc MD); FAX 410/268-3613. 51 rms, 4 story. S $115-$135; D $125-$155; each addl $10; suites $165-$240; under 18 free; higher rates special events. Crib free. Valet parking $10. TV; cable. Pool privileges. Restaurant nearby. Ck-out noon, ck-in 3 pm. Lighted tennis privileges. Golf privileges. Health club privileges. Refrigerators avail. Private patios, balconies. 18th-century state house; colonial gardens. Atrium. Cr cds: A, C, D, JCB, MC, V.

D 🏃‍♂️ 🎿 ⛵ 🔥 SC

★ ★ **MARYLAND.** *Church Circle & Main Street (21401), Church Circle & Main St.* 410/263-2641; *res:* 800/847-8882; *FAX* 410/268-3813. 44 rms, 4 story. S $95-$115; D $95-$145; each addl $10; suites $145-$260; under 18 free; higher rates special events. Crib free. Valet parking $10. Pool privileges. Bar; entertainment. Ck-out noon, ck-in 3 pm. Bellhops. Lighted tennis, golf privileges. Health club privileges. Some refrigerators. View of bay. Historic inn built 1776; many antique furnishings. Cr cds: A, C, D, JCB, MC, V.

🏃‍♂️ 🎿 ⛵ 🔥 SC

★ ★ **ROBERT JOHNSON HOUSE.** *Mailing address: 16 Church Circle (21401), 23 State Circle.* 410/263-2641; *res:* 800/847-8882; *FAX* 410/268-3613. 29 rms, 4 story. S $115-$135; D $125-$155; each addl $10; suites $260; under 18 free; higher rates special events. Crib free. Valet parking $10. TV; cable. Pool privileges. Restaurant nearby. Ck-out noon, ck-in 3 pm. Lighted tennis privileges. Golf privileges. Health club privileges. Refrigerators avail. Consists of 18th-century mansion plus 2 connecting town houses of the same period. Cr cds: A, C, D, JCB, MC, V.

D 🏃‍♂️ 🎿 ⛵ 🔥 SC

★ ★ **STATE HOUSE INN.** *16 Church Circle (21401), on State Circle, in Historic District.* 410/263-2641; *res:* 800/847-8882; *FAX* 410/268-3613. 9 rms, 3 story. S $95-$145; D $105-$165; each addl $10; under 18 free; higher rates special events. Crib free. Valet parking $10. TV; cable. Pool privileges. Restaurant nearby. Ck-out noon, ck-in 3 pm. Bellhops. Valet serv. Golf privileges. Health club privileges. Built 1820; remodeled interior. Antiques; sitting rm. Opp the State House. Cr cds: A, C, D, JCB, MC, V.

🏃‍♂️ ⛵ 🔥 SC

✔ ★ ★ **WILLIAM PAGE.** *8 Martin St (21401).* 410/626-1506; *FAX* 410/263-4841. 5 rms, 2 share bath, 3 story. S, D $65-$140; wkly rates. Complimentary full bkfst, coffee & tea. Restaurant nearby. Ck-out noon, ck-in 4-6 pm. Airport transportation. Former clubhouse (1908). Totally nonsmoking. Cr cds: MC, V.

⛵ 🔥

Restaurants

✔ ★ **BUDDY'S CRABS & RIBS.** *100 Main St.* 410/626-1100. Hrs: 11-1:30 am; Sun brunch 8:30 am-1 pm. Closed Dec 25. Bar. Semi-a la carte: lunch $3.95-$9, dinner $8.95-$15. Sun brunch $5.95. Child's meals. Specialties: Danish baby back ribs, steamed crabs. Entertainment. Dining on 2nd floor, overlooking waterfront. Cr cds: A, C, D, DS, MC, V.

D

★ ★ **BUSCH'S CHESAPEAKE INN.** *321 Busch's Frontage Rd (US 50/301).* 410/757-1717. Hrs: 11:30 am-9 pm; Fri to 10 pm, Sat to 11 pm; Sun 11 am-9 pm. Sun brunch to 3:30 pm. Closed Dec 23-26. Res accepted. Bar. Semi-a la carte: lunch $4.95-$9.95, dinner $14.95-$24.95. Lunch buffet $7.95. Sun brunch $12.95. Child's meals. Specializes in seafood. Parking. Nautical decor. Braille menu. Family-owned. Cr cds: A, C, D, DS, MC, V.

D SC

★ ★ **CAFE NORMANDIE.** *185 Main St, in Historic District.* 410/263-3382. Hrs: 8 am-10 pm; Fri, Sat to 10:30 pm. French menu. Serv bar. Semi-a la carte: bkfst $2.75-$5.50, lunch $4.25-$10.95, dinner $8.95-$18.50. Specializes in seafood, Maryland crab dishes. French-style cafe. Cr cds: A, MC, V.

★ ★ ★ **CARROL'S CREEK.** *(410 Severn Ave, Eastport)* 1/4 mi across Eastport Bridge. 410/263-8102. Hrs: 11:30 am-4 pm, 5-10 pm; Sun brunch 10 am-2 pm. Res accepted Mon-Thurs; required hols. Bar. Semi-a la carte: lunch $4.95-$9.95, dinner $14-$22. Sun brunch $15.95. Specializes in local seafood. Own baking. Parking. Outdoor dining. On water. Cr cds: A, D, DS, MC, V.

D

★ **DAMON'S-THE PLACE FOR RIBS.** *Severna Park (21146), 3 mi N of US 50/301; on MD 2 at Jones Station Rd.* 410/647-4300. Hrs: 11:30 am-10 pm; Fri & Sat to 11 pm; Sun 3-9 pm. Closed major hols. Bar. Semi-a la carte: lunch $3.95-$5.95, dinner $6.95-$17.95. Child's meals. Specializes in barbecued ribs, steak, chicken. Parking. Cr cds: C, D, DS, MC, V.

★ ★ **FRED'S.** *2348 Solomons Island Rd, MD 2 at Parole Plaza.* 410/224-2386. Hrs: 11 am-10 pm; Fri, Sat to 11 pm; early-bird dinner Mon-Fri 4-6 pm. Closed Thanksgiving, Dec 25. Res accepted. Continental menu. Bar. Semi-a la carte: lunch $4.25-$9.50, dinner $8.95-$33.95. Child's meals. Specializes in seafood, steak, Italian dishes. Parking. Victorian decor; antiques. Family-owned. Cr cds: A, C, D, DS, MC, V.

D

✔ ★ ★ **GRIFFINS.** *24 Market Space.* 410/268-2576. Hrs: 11 am-midnight; Fri & Sat to 1 am; Sun brunch 11 am-1 pm. Closed Dec 24, 25. Res accepted Mon-Thurs. Bar to 1:30 am. Semi-a la carte: lunch $5.95-$8.95, dinner $10.95-$15.95. Sun brunch $5.95-$7.95. Child's meals. Specializes in seafood, steak, pasta. Own desserts. Cr cds: A, D, DS, MC, V.

D

★ ★ **HARBOUR HOUSE.** *Dock St, on city dock.* 410/268-0771. Hrs: 11:30 am-10 pm. Closed Jan 1, Thanksgiving, Dec 25. Bar. Semi-a la carte: lunch $4.95-$7.75, dinner $12.95-$19.95. Child's meals. Specializes in seafood, prime rib. Outdoor dining May-Oct. Old dock warehouse. Family-owned. Cr cds: A, MC, V.

D

★ ★ **MIDDLETON TAVERN.** *2 Market Space.* 410/263-3323. Hrs: 11:30-2 am; Sat from 11 am; Sun from 10 am. Bar. Semi-a la carte: lunch $5.95-$9.95, dinner $11.95-$21.95. Specializes in seafood, crab dishes. Oyster bar; entertainment. Outdoor dining. Restored building (1750), traditional tavern decor. Overlooks harbor. Family-owned. Cr cds: DS, MC, V.

★ ★ ★ **NORTHWOODS.** *609 Melvin Ave.* 410/268-2609. Hrs: 5:30-10 pm; Sun 5-9 pm. Closed most major hols. Res required. Continental menu. Wine list. Semi-a la carte: dinner $15-$19. Complete meals: dinner $22.95. Specializes in fresh seafood, Italian dishes. Parking. Outdoor dining. Casual elegance in romantic setting. Cr cds: A, C, D, DS, MC, V.

D

★ ★ **O'LEARY'S.** *310 3rd St.* 410/263-0884. Hrs: 5:30-10 pm; Fri, Sat 5-11 pm; Sun 5-10 pm. Closed Thanksgiving, Dec 24, 25. Res accepted Sun-Thurs. Bar. Semi-a la carte: dinner $10.95-$24.95. Child's meals. Specializes in seafood. Own desserts. Parking. Cr cds: A, D, MC, V.

✔ ★ ★ ★ **RUSTIC INN.** *1803 West St.* 410/263-2626. Hrs: 5-10 pm; Fri, Sat to 11 pm. Closed some major hols. Res accepted; required Fri, Sat. Bar. Wine list. Semi-a la carte: dinner $10.75-$15.95. Child's meals. Specializes in seafood, veal, beef. Own baking. Parking. Cr cds: A, MC, V.

D

★ ★ ★ **TREATY OF PARIS.** *(See Maryland Inn)* 410/263-2641. Hrs: 7 am-2:30 pm, 5:30-10:30 pm; Fri & Sat to 11:30 pm; Sun to 9:30 pm; Sun brunch 10 am-2:30 pm. Closed Jan 1. Res accepted; required Fri & Sat. Continental menu. Bar 11-2 am; Sun to 1 am. Wine cellar.

Semi-a la carte: bkfst $3.50-$9, lunch $6.95-$10, dinner $14-$22. Complete meals: dinner $20 & $25. Sun brunch $15.95. Specializes in New American cuisine, fresh local seafood. Salad bar (lunch). Valet parking (dinner). Outdoor dining. Early American tavern atmosphere; fireplace. Cr cds: A, C, D, JCB, MC, V.

SC

Antietam National Battlefield (B-4)

(10 mi S of Hagerstown on MD 65)

On September 17, 1862, the bloodiest day in Civil War annals, more than 23,000 men were killed or wounded as Union forces blocked the first Confederate invasion of the North. A Union advantage was gained beforehand when a soldier accidentally found Lee's orders wrapped around some cigars. In spite of knowing Lee's tactical game plan, McClellan moved cautiously. The battle, critical because British aid to the Confederacy depended on the outcome, was a tactical draw but a strategic victory for the North. This victory allowed Lincoln to issue the Emancipation Proclamation, which expanded the war from simply re-uniting the country to a crusade to end slavery. The rebels withdrew across the Potomac on the night of September 18, but for some reason McClellan, with twice the manpower, delayed his pursuit. Lincoln relieved him of command of the Army of the Potomac seven weeks later.

Clara Barton, who was to found the Red Cross 19 years later, attended the wounded at a field hospital on the battlefield. Commissary Sgt William McKinley, later US president, served hot coffee and food to his men of Ohio during the battle.

Approximately 350 iron tablets, monuments and battlefield maps, located on eight miles of paved avenues, describe the events of the battle. The Visitor Center houses a museum and offers information, literature and a 26-minute orientation movie (shown on the hour). Visitor Center (daily; closed Jan 1, Thanksgiving, Dec 25); battlefield (daily); ranger-conducted walks, talks and demonstrations (Memorial Day-Labor Day, daily). Golden Age Passport (see INTRODUCTION). For information phone 301/432-5124. Entrance fee per person ¢, maximum per family ¢¢

Baltimore (B-7)

Settled: 1661 **Pop:** 736,014 **Elev:** 32 ft **Area code:** 410

Metropolis of Maryland and one of America's great cities, Baltimore is a city of neighborhoods built on strong ethnic foundations, a city of historic events that helped shape the nation and a city that has achieved an incredible downtown renaissance in the past 20 years. It is a major East Coast manufacturing center and, almost from its beginning, a world seaport. Several colleges and universities, foremost of which is Johns Hopkins, make their home here.

Lying midway between North and South and enjoying a rich cultural mixture of both, Baltimore is one of the nation's oldest cities. When British troops threatened Philadelphia during the Revolution, the Continental Congress fled to Baltimore, which served as the nation's capital for a little more than two months.

In October, 1814, a British fleet attacked the city by land and sea. The defenders of Fort McHenry withstood the naval bombardment for 25 hours until the British gave up. Francis Scott Key saw the huge American flag still flying above the fort and was inspired to pen "The Star-Spangled Banner."

Rapid growth in the early 19th century resulted from the opening of the National Road and then the nation's first railroad, the Baltimore & Ohio.

Politics was a preoccupation in those days, and the city hosted many national party conventions. At least seven presidents and three losing candidates were nominated here. Edgar Allan Poe's mysterious death in the city may have been at the hands of shady electioneers.

Untouched physically by the Civil War, effects came later when Southerners flooded in to rebuild their fortunes, and commerce was disrupted by the loss of Southern markets. A disastrous fire in 1904 destroyed 140 acres of the business district, but the city recovered rapidly and, during the two World Wars, was a major shipbuilding and naval repair center.

In the 1950s and early 60s Baltimore was the victim of apathy and the general decay that struck the industrial Northeast. But the city fought back, replacing hundreds of acres of slums, rotting wharves and warehouses with gleaming new office plazas, parks and public buildings. The Inner Harbor was transformed into a huge public area with shops, museums, restaurants and frequent concerts and festivals. Millions of tourists and proud Baltimoreans flock downtown to enjoy the sights and activities.

Famous residents and native sons include Babe Ruth, Edgar Allan Poe, H.L. Mencken, Mother Elizabeth Ann Seton, Eubie Blake, Ogden Nash, Thurgood Marshall, Wallis Warfield Simpson, who became the Duchess of Windsor, and more recent sports legends Brooks Robinson, Johnny Unitas and Jim Palmer.

Transportation

Airport: See BALTIMORE/WASHINGTON INTL AIRPORT AREA.

Car Rental Agencies: See toll-free numbers under Introduction.

Public Transportation: Bus & subway (Mass Transit Administration), phone 539-5000; trolley bus (Baltimore Trolley Works), phone 396-4259.

Rail Passenger Service: Amtrak 800/872-7245.

What to See and Do

MOUNT VERNON PLACE AREA

1. **Washington Monument** (1815-42). Charles & Monument Sts. First major monument to honor George Washington. Other monuments nearby honor Lafayette, Chief Justice Roger Brooke Taney, philanthropist George Peabody, lawyer Severn Teackle Wallis and Revolutionary War hero John Eager Howard.

2. **Walters Art Gallery.** 600 N Charles St, at Centre St. City-owned fine arts collection of paintings, sculpture, arms, armor, jewelry and manuscripts from antiquity through the 19th century. (Daily exc Mon; closed major hols) Phone 547-9000. ¢¢

3. **Peabody Institute of the Johns Hopkins University** (1857). (550 students) Mt Vernon Pl. Founded by philanthropist George Peabody; now affiliated with Johns Hopkins. Research and reference collection accessible to the public (Mon-Fri; closed hols). The Miriam A. Friedberg Concert Hall seats 800. The Conservatory holds orchestra concerts, recitals and operas. Box office phone 659-8124.

4. **Museum and Library of Maryland History, Maryland Historical Society.** 201 W Monument St, between Park Ave and Howard St. Original manuscript of "Star-Spangled Banner" is displayed; extensive displays of Maryland silver, furniture and painting; changing exhibits; maritime museum. Also within the museum is the **Darnall Young Peoples Museum**, a gallery with "hands-on" exhibits. Museum and gallery (Oct-Apr, daily exc Mon; rest of yr, Tues-Sat). Library (Tues-Sat). Sr citizen rate. Museum free on Wed. Phone 685-3750. ¢¢

5. **Asbury House** (ca 1850). 10 E Mt Vernon Pl. Brownstone with balcony and grillwork extending entire width of house; spiral staircase suspended from 3 floors; library with century-old painting on ceiling; drawing room. (Mon-Fri; closed hols and Mon after Easter) Phone 685-5290. **Free.**

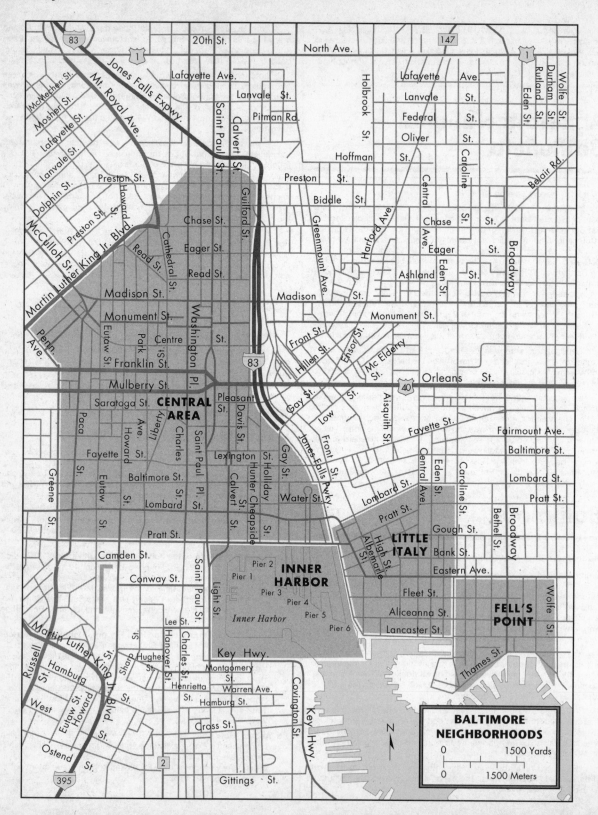

BALTIMORE
NEIGHBORHOODS

0   1500 Yards

0   1500 Meters

6. **First Unitarian Church** (1817). Charles & Franklin Sts. William Ellery Channing preached a sermon here that hastened the establishment of the Unitarian denomination. Example of Classic Revival architecture. Phone 685-2330.

DOWNTOWN AREA

7. **Basilica of the Assumption of the Blessed Virgin Mary.** Cathedral & Mulberry Sts. Now a co-cathedral, this was the first Roman Catholic cathedral in the US. Bishop John Carroll, head of the diocese of Baltimore from its establishment in 1789, blessed the cornerstone in 1806. The church was dedicated in 1821. Architectural design by B. H. Latrobe. Tours (2nd & 4th Sun each month or by appt). (Daily) Phone 727-3565.

8. **Enoch Pratt Free Library.** 400 Cathedral St, at Franklin St. City's public library. (Oct-Apr, daily exc Fri; rest of yr, Mon-Thurs & Sat; closed hols) Phone 396-5430.

9. **Battle Monument** (1815). Calvert & Fayette Sts. Memorial to those who fell defending the city in the War of 1812.

10. **City Hall.** 100 N Holliday St. Post-Civil War architecture, restored to original detail. Tours by appt, phone 396-4900. **Free.**

11. **City Court House** (1900). St Paul & Fayette Sts. On steps is statue of Cecil Calvert, brother of Leonard and founder of Maryland as the second Lord Baltimore.

12. **Peale Museum** (1814). 225 Holliday St. Built as Rembrandt Peale's "Baltimore Museum," it is the nation's oldest museum building. Later Baltimore's first city hall, it is now a history museum housing a collection of Baltimore photographs and paintings, including many by members of the Peale family, plus an exhibit on the evolution of American museums. Walled garden. (Daily exc Mon; closed hols) Phone 396-3523 or -1149. ¢

13. **Carroll Mansion** (ca 1810). 800 E Lombard St, at Front St. Residence of Charles Carroll. When he died here in 1832, he was the last surviving signer of Declaration of Independence. Period furnishings. (Daily exc Mon; closed hols) Phone 396-3523. ¢

14. **Shot Tower** (1829). Fayette & Front Sts. Tapering brick structure (234 feet) where molten lead was dropped to form round shot that hardened when it hit water at base. Self-activated film; exhibits. (Daily) Phone 396-5894. **Free.**

15. **Star-Spangled Banner Flag House and 1812 Museum.** 844 E Pratt St, at Albemarle St. The banner (30 by 42 feet) with 15 stars and 15 stripes that Key saw "by the dawn's early light" over Ft McHenry was hand-sewn here by Mary Young Pickersgill. The actual flag is in the Smithsonian. House (1793) is authentically restored and furnished in the Federal period. 1812 Museum contains relics, documents, weapons, memorabilia; audiovisual program; garden. Focal point of the garden is a stone map of the US; every state is represented by a stone native to and cut in the shape of each state. (Daily exc Sun; closed some hols) Sr citizen rate. Phone 837-1793. ¢¢

16. **Edgar Allan Poe House** (ca 1830). 203 N Amity St, off 900 blk W Lexington St. Poe's home from 1832-35. (Apr-July & Oct-mid-Dec, Wed-Sat, afternoons; Aug & Sept, Sat afternoon only) Also offered are tours of Westminster Cemetery and catacombs (evenings, by appt; fee). Phone 396-7932. ¢

17. **Edgar Allan Poe Grave.** At Westminster Burying Ground and Catacombs, Fayette & Greene Sts. Baltimore's oldest cemeteries also contain the graves of many prominent early Marylanders. Tour of catacombs by appt (Apr-Nov, 1st & 3rd Fri & Sat). Phone 706-7228. ¢¢

18. **Mother Seton House.** 600 N Paca St. Home of St Elizabeth Ann Bayley Seton from 1808-09. Here she established forerunner of the parochial school system. She also established an order of nuns here that eventualy became the Daughters & Sisters of Charity in the US and Canada. (Sat & Sun afternoons; also by appt; closed Jan 1, Easter, Dec 25) Phone 523-3443. **Free.**

19. **Lexington Market.** 400 W Lexington St, between Eutaw and Paca Sts. In continuous operation since 1782, this famous indoor marketplace houses more than 140 stalls run by independent merchants. (Daily exc Sun; closed major hols) Phone 685-6169. **Free.**

20. **Charles Center.** Bounded by Charles, Liberty, Saratoga and Lombard Sts. 33-acre business area with European-style plazas, part of an overhead walkway system, shops, restaurants and outdoor activities. Prize-winning office building by Mies van der Rohe borders center plaza. Also here is

    Baltimore Center for the Performing Arts-Morris Mechanic Theater. Hopkins Plaza. Hosts Broadway productions. For schedule, fees phone 625-1400.

21. **Jewish Historical Society of Maryland.** 15 Lloyd St. Buildings include Lloyd St Synagogue (1845), the oldest in Maryland; B'nai Israel Synagogue (1876); Jewish Museum of Maryland. (Tues-Fri & Sun afternoons; or by appt; closed Jewish hols) Research archives (Mon-Fri, by appt). Phone 732-6400. ¢

22. **Holocaust Memorial.** Water & Gay Sts. Simple stone memorial to the victims of the Holocaust.

23. **University of Maryland at Baltimore.** (5,000 students) Lombard, Greene & Redwood Sts. The 32-acre downtown campus includes 6 professional schools; the University of Maryland Medical System and the Graduate School. Davidge Hall (1812) is the oldest medical teaching building in continuous use in the Western Hemisphere. Phone 706-7820.

INNER HARBOR

24. **National Aquarium.** Pier 3, 501 E Pratt St. One of the most advanced facilities in US. Exhibits include a South American rain forest, Atlantic coral reef, shark tank; houses 5,000 specimens of 500 different types of mammals, fish, birds, reptiles, amphibians, invertebrates and plants. (Daily; closed Thanksgiving, Dec 25) Sr citizen rate. Phone 576-3810. ¢¢¢¢ Visitors cross an enclosed skywalk to reach the adj wing, which houses

    Marine Mammal Pavilion. Pier 4. This unique structure features a 1,300-seat amphitheater surrounding a 1.2-million-gallon pool, which houses Atlantic bottlenose dolphins; underwater viewing areas enable visitors to also observe the mammals from below the surface. (Daily) Special video programs about dolphins and whales; educational arcade with computerized video screens and other participatory exhibits around the upper deck of the pavilion. A visitor service area is located in the atrium. Gift shop. Cafe. A life-size replica of a humpback whale spans two levels of the atrium. A Discovery Room houses a collection of marine artifacts. The Resource Center is designed as an aquatic learning center for school visitors; a library boasts an extensive collection of marine science material. One ticket for admission to both buildings.

25. **Harborplace.** Light and Pratt Sts, at Inner Harbor. European-style marketplace comprised of two glass-enclosed pavilions; one featuring many eateries, including waterside cafes and restaurants, the other housing dozens of specialty shops arranged in Parisian style along a colonnade. Overhead walkway leads to **The Gallery at Harborplace**, with many additional top-name shops and eateries. Free summer concerts along waterfront. (Daily; closed Thanksgiving, Dec 25) Phone 332-4191.

26. **Maryland Science Center & Davis Planetarium.** 601 Light St. Home of the Maryland Academy of Sciences, the oldest scientific institution in the state. Features exhibits in areas such as energy, physics, the Chesapeake Bay, optical illusions & television production. Planetarium. Includes IMAX theater. Science demonstrations. (Daily; closed Thanksgiving, Dec 25) Sr citizen rate. Phone 685-5225 (recording). ¢¢¢

27. **Top of the World.** World Trade Center, Pratt St at the harbor. Observation deck and museum on the 27th floor of the World Trade Center, which was designed by I.M. Pei. Exhibits describe the city's history, famous residents and the activities of the port. (Daily) Sr citizen rate. Phone 837-4515. ¢

28. **US Frigate *Constellation*.** Pier 1 (Constellation Dock), Pratt St. National Naval Historic Shrine. First ship of US Navy (1797); oldest

warship in world still afloat; restored. Early Navy relics, self-guided tours. (Daily) Sr citizen rate. Phone 539-1797. ¢¢

29. **Baltimore Maritime Museum.** Pier 3, Pratt St. USS *Torsk,* WW II submarine, Coast Guard cutter *Taney* and lightship *Chesapeake.* Sr citizen rate. Phone 396-5528. ¢¢

30. *Minnie V.* Docks near Constellation Dock. Chesapeake Bay skipjack built in 1906. Harbor tours under sail (mid-June-Labor Day, daily exc Mon; May-mid-June & rest of Sept, Sat & Sun). Phone 522-4214. ¢¢¢¢

31. **Public Works Museum & Streetscape.** 751 Eastern Ave, at Inner Harbor East. Museum exhibits the history and artifacts of public works. Located in historic sewage pumping station. Streetscape sculpture outside depicts the various utility lines and ducts under a typical city street, in a walk-through model. (Mid-Apr-mid-Oct, daily; rest of yr, Wed-Sun) Phone 396-5565. ¢¢

32. **Pier 6 Concert Pavilion.** Pier 6. Summertime outdoor concerts and plays at the water's edge. Some covered seating. (June-Sept, evenings) (See SEASONAL EVENTS) Phone 625-1400 for schedule. ¢¢¢¢

33. **Federal Hill.** Warren St & Battery Ave. View of city harbor and skyline. Named after a celebration that occurred here in 1788 to mark Maryland's ratification of the Constitution.

34. **Old Otterbein United Methodist Church** (1785-86). Conway & Sharp Sts. Fine Georgian architecture; mother church of United Brethren. Tours of historic building (Apr-Oct, Sat). Phone 685-4703.

35. **Otterbein "Homesteading."** Area around S Sharp St. The original neighborhood dates back to 1785. Houses have been restored.

SOUTH

36. **Fort McHenry National Monument and Historic Shrine.** E end of Fort Ave. The flag flying over this five-pointed, star-shaped brick fort inspired Francis Scott Key to write the poem in 1814 that later became the lyrics to the national anthem. Named for James McHenry, Secretary of War (1796-1800). Replica flagpole on 1814 site. Restored powder magazine, guardroom, officers' quarters and barracks all contain exhibits. Cannons of War of 1812 and Civil War periods. Guided activities (mid-June-Aug, daily). The Fort McHenry Guard, in period uniform, reenacts life at the garrison (mid-June-Aug, Sat & Sun afternoons). Military ceremony (July-Aug, some Sun evenings). Visitor Center has exhibit area, film, gift shop. Special exhibits for visually and hearing impaired. (Daily; closed Jan 1, Dec 25) Phone 962-4299. ¢

   Narrated cruises depart from Inner Harbor Finger Pier to Fort McHenry and Fells Point (Memorial Day-Labor Day). Also departures from Fort McHenry and Fells Point. For other tours contact Maryland Tours, Inc, phone ticket office 685-4288 (Apr-Oct) or 745-9216 (rest of yr). Round-trip ¢¢

37. **Baltimore Museum of Industry.** 1415 Key Hwy. Exhibits trace the growth of Baltimore as an industrial center. Turn-of-the-century machine shop, print shop and garment loft. Hands-on exhibits; children's activities. Restored tugboat on waterfront behind museum. (Thurs-Sun; limited hrs, phone ahead; closed most hols) Sr citizen rate. Phone 727-4808. ¢¢

SOUTHWEST

38. **B & O Railroad Museum.** 901 W Pratt St, at Poppleton St. The museum includes the Mount Clare Station (1851), site of the nation's first passenger station, and the roundhouse (1884); original tracks and wooden turntable are fully preserved. Collection includes over 100 full-sized train cars. (Daily; closed major hols) Sr citizen rate. Phone 752-2393. ¢¢

39. **Babe Ruth Birthplace/Baseball Center.** 216 Emory St. Renovated house where Babe Ruth was born. Features memorabilia of Babe Ruth, Orioles and Maryland baseball; 25-min movie of the "Sultan of Swat" and many other audiovisual displays. (Daily) Sr citizen rate. Phone 727-1539. ¢¢

40. **Mount Clare Museum House** (1760). In Carroll Park at Monroe St & Washington Blvd. Oldest mansion in Baltimore, former home of Charles Carroll, barrister. 18th-century furnishings. Guided tours on the hr. (Daily exc Mon; closed some hols) Phone 837-3262. ¢¢

41. **H.L. Mencken House.** 1524 Hollins St, in historic Union Square. The "Sage of Baltimore" lived and wrote here for 68 years. Exhibits, furnishings. (Sat & Sun; Tues & Thurs by appt) Sr citizen rate. Phone 396-3524. ¢

NORTH

42. **Baltimore Museum of Art.** Art Museum Dr near N Charles & 31st Sts. Variety of collections, including American paintings, period rooms; African and Oceanian art. Noted for Cone collection of French Post-Impressionists, including Matisse and Picasso; Cheney miniature rooms; modern paintings; sculpture gardens; museum cafe and shop. (Wed-Sun) Sr citizen rate. Phone 396-7100 or -7101. ¢¢¢

43. **Johns Hopkins University** (1876). (4,600 students) Charles & 34th Sts, 2 mi N. Modern buildings in Georgian style on wooded 126-acre campus. Distinguished research school founded by wealthy merchant of the city. Phone 516-8000. On grounds are

   Lacrosse Hall of Fame Museum. 113 W University Pkwy. Team trophies, display of lacrosse artifacts and memorabilia; videotapes of championship games. (Mon-Fri; Sat during lacrosse season; closed hols) Phone 235-6882. ¢

   Bufano Sculpture Garden. Dunning Park, behind Mudd Hall. A wooded retreat with animals sculpted by artist Beniamino Bufano. **Free.**

   Evergreen House. 4545 N Charles St, approx 2 mi N of Homewood campus. On 26 wooded acres; features Classical-revival architecture and formal garden. Contains the Library (35,000 volumes). Post-Impressionist paintings, Japanese and Chinese collections and Tiffany glass. Tours (daily exc Sat). Phone 516-0341. ¢¢

   Homewood House Museum. On Charles St near 34th St. Former country home (1801) of Charles Carroll, Jr, whose father was a signer of the Declaration of Independence; period furnishings. (Tues-Sat, also Sun afternoons) Guided tours (hourly). Phone 516-5589. ¢¢

44. **Baltimore Zoo.** Druid Hill Park. Main zoo has collection of more than 1,500 animals. Includes 3-acre African elephant park; 6-acre African watering hole; hippo and African flamingo exhibit; 8-acre children's zoo (daily); track train & carousel (Apr-Sept; fee). Zoo (daily exc Dec 25). Sr citizen rate. Phone 366-5466. ¢¢¢

45. **City of Baltimore Conservatory.** Druid Hill Park. This graceful building (ca 1885) houses a large variety of tropical plants. Special shows during Easter, Nov and Christmas. (Daily) Phone 396-0180. **Free.**

46. **Maryland Institute, College of Art** (1826). (880 students) Main building 1300 Mt Royal Ave, at Lanvale St. Institute hosts frequent contemporary art exhibitions. Cafeteria. Campus distinguished by recycled buildings and white marble Italianate Main Building. (Daily) Phone 669-9200.

47. **Morgan State University** (1867). (5,100 students) Cold Spring Lane & Hillen Rd. The James E. Lewis Museum of Art has changing exhibits (Mon-Fri; wkends by appt; closed hols). Phone 319-3333.

48. **Meyerhoff Symphony Hall.** 1212 Cathedral St. Permanent residence of the Baltimore Symphony Orchestra. Phone 783-8000 or -8100.

49. **Cylburn Arboretum.** 4915 Greenspring Ave. Marked nature trails. Nature museum, ornithological room, horticultural library in restored mansion; shade and formal gardens, All-American Selection Garden, Garden of the Senses. (Daily) Phone 396-0180. **Free.**

50. **Sherwood Gardens.** Stratford Rd & Greenway, located in the residential community of Guilford in northern Baltimore. More than 6 acres in size, the gardens reach their peak of splendor in late Apr & early May, when thousands of tulips, azaleas and flowering shrubs bloom. Phone 366-2572.

51. **Baltimore Streetcar Museum.** 1901 Falls Rd, under North Ave Bridge. 11 electric streetcars and two horsecars used in city between 1859 and 1963; 1 1/4-mile rides (fee). (June-Oct, Sat & Sun afternoons; rest of yr, Sun afternoons only; also open Memorial Day, July 4, Labor Day) Phone 547-0264. **Free.**

52. **Cloisters Children's Museum.** 10440 Falls Rd, Brooklandville, 8 mi N. Museum in medieval-style mansion features weekly performances, tours, workshops, demonstrations, hands-on permanent and changing exhibits, and activities. (Wed-Sun) Sr citizen rate. Phone 823-2550 (recording) or -2551. **¢¢**

53. **Lovely Lane Museum.** 2200 St Paul St. Permanent and changing exhibits of items of Methodist church history since 1760. Guided tours (Mon-Fri; also Sun after services and by appt; closed hols). Phone 889-1512. **Free.**

EAST

54. **Fell's Point.** Broadway, S of Fleet St to the harbor. Shipbuilding and maritime center, this neighborhood dates back to 1730; approx 350 original residential structures. Working tugboats and tankers can be observed from docks.

55. **Johns Hopkins Medical Institutions** (1889). Broadway & Monument St. Widely known as a leading medical school, research center and teaching hospital. Victorian buildings.

56. **Old Town Mall.** 400 and 500 blocks of N Gay St. This 150-yr-old, brick-lined commercial area has been beautifully refurbished; closed to vehicular traffic. Nearby."

57. **Stirling Street "Homesteading."** 1000 block of Monument St, 1 blk W of mall. First community urban "homesteading" venture in the US. Renovated homes date back to the 1830s. Original façades have been maintained; the interior rehabilitation ranges in style from the antique to the avant garde.

58. **Church Home and Hospital.** Broadway & Fairmount Ave. Edgar Allan Poe died here in 1849.

59. **Theaters.**

   Vagabond Players. 806 S Broadway. Oldest continuously operating "little theater" in US. Recent Broadway shows, revivals and original scripts are performed. (Fri-Sun) Box office phone 563-9135.

   Cockpit in Court Summer Theatre. (See SEASONAL EVENTS)

HERE AND THERE

60. **Patterson Park.** Baltimore St, Eastern & Patterson Park Aves. Defenses here helped stop British attack in 1814. Breastworks, artillery pieces are displayed.

61. **Gunpowder Falls State Park.** Approx 17,000 acres, located in Gunpowder River Valley. **Hammerman Area**, E on US 40, right onto Ebenezer Rd, 5 mi to park entrance in Chase, is a developed day-use area. Offers swimming beach, windsurfing beach, boating, marina (Dundee Creek), picnicking, playground. Other areas offer hiking/biking trails, canoeing, trout fishing. Standard fees. Phone 592-2897.

62. **Harbor cruises.** Depart from Inner Harbor.

   MV *Lady Baltimore.* West Bulkhead, Light St. Round-trip cruises to Annapolis (June-Aug, Wed); also cruises to the Chesapeake & Delaware Canal (3 selected Sun in Oct). *Bay Lady* has lunch and dinner cruises (Apr-Oct, daily; limited schedule rest of yr). Phone 727-3113 or 800/695-LADY. **¢¢¢¢¢**

   Baltimore Patriot has 90-minute tours around Baltimore harbor. (Apr-Oct, daily) Phone 685-4288 (ticket office). **¢¢¢**

63. **Industrial tour. MPT (Maryland Public Television).** Tours of state's television network studios. (By appt) Phone 356-5600 or 800/223-3MPT (surrounding states). **Free.**

Annual Events

ACC Crafts Fair. Convention Center and Festival Hall. Featuring more than 800 artisans. Late Feb.

Maryland House and Garden Pilgrimage. More than 100 homes and gardens throughout the state are open. To purchase tour book contact 1105-A Providence Rd, 21286; 821-6933. Late Apr-early May.

Flower Mart. In Mt Vernon Place, at base of Washington Monument. Traditional spring festival with flowers, baked goods. Early May.

Maryland Preakness Celebration. Statewide festival; events include hot air balloon festival, parade, steeplechase, celebrity golf tournament, block parties and schooner race. Phone 837-3030. 10 days preceding Preakness Stakes (see SEASONAL EVENTS). Early to mid-May.

Harbor Expo. Middle Branch and Canton Waterfront. Boat parades; seafood festival; entertainment; events. Phone 732-8155. Mid-June.

Artscape. Salute to the arts & culture. Phone 396-4575. 3 days July.

Baltimore International Jumping Classic. Baltimore Arena. Grand Prix jumping, internationally known riders and horses. Phone 347-2020. Usually 1st wkend Oct.

New Year's Eve Extravaganza. Convention Center and Inner Harbor. Parties, entertainment, big bands, fireworks.

Seasonal Events

Pimlico Race Course. Hayward & Winner Aves, 2 mi W of Jones Falls Expy. Thoroughbred racing. **The Preakness**, the $500,000 middle jewel in Thoroughbred racing's Triple Crown, has been run here yearly since 1873 and is held the 3rd Sat in May. All seats reserved Preakness Day. Phone 542-9400. Late Mar-early June & early Aug-early Oct.

Cockpit in Court Summer Theatre. 7201 Rossville Blvd, use Beltway (I-695) exit 34, in Baltimore County. Theater in residence at Essex Community College. Four separate theaters offer a diverse collection of plays, including Broadway productions, contemporary drama, revues and Shakespeare. Box office phone 780-6369. Mid-June-mid-Aug.

Pier 6 Concert Pavilion. Evening concerts featuring big names in jazz, pop, classical and country music. For schedule phone 625-1400. Late June-Sept.

Showcase of Nations Ethnic Festivals. Presenting the food, music and crafts of a different culture each wkend. Various downtown locations. Phone 752-8632. June-Sept.

Professional sports. Blast (soccer), Skipjacks (hockey) and Thunder (box lacrosse) in Baltimore Arena; Orioles (baseball) in Oriole Park at Camden Yards.

Additional Visitor Information

Maps, brochures and calendars of events are available at the Baltimore Area Visitors Center, 300 W Pratt St, 21201, and at Inner Harbor Visitor Information Center; phone 837-INFO or 800/282-6632.

Baltimore Area Suburbs

The following towns and suburbs in the Baltimore area are included in the *Mobil Travel Guide*. For information on any one of them, see the individual alphabetical listing. Aberdeen, Cockeysville, Columbia, Ellicott City, Pikesville, Towson.

Baltimore/Washington Intl Airport Area

For additional accommodations, see BALTIMORE/WASHINGTON INTL AIRPORT AREA, which follows BALTIMORE.

City Neighborhoods

Many of the restaurants, unrated dining establishments and some lodgings listed under Baltimore include neighborhoods as well as exact street addresses. A map showing these neighborhoods can be found immediately following the city map. Geographic descriptions of these areas are given, followed by a table of restaurants arranged by neighborhood.

Central Area: South of Mt Royal Ave, west of I-83, north of the Inner Harbor and Pratt St and east of Martin Luther King Jr Blvd and Greene St. **North of Central Area:** North of Chase. **East of Central Area:** East of I-83.

Fell's Point: Waterfront area east of Inner Harbor; south of Eastern Ave, west of Wolfe St and east of Caroline St.

Inner Harbor: Waterfront area south of Central Area at Pratt St, west of Jones Fall Pkwy and east of Light St.

Little Italy: East of Inner Harbor; south of Lombard St, west of Caroline St, north of Lancaster St and the waterfront and east of Jones Fall Pkwy.

BALTIMORE RESTAURANTS BY NEIGHBORHOOD AREAS

(For full description, see alphabetical listings under Restaurants)

CENTRAL AREA

Light House. 10 Park Ave

Louie's Bookstore Cafe. 518 N Charles St

Maison Marconi's. 106 W Saratoga

Prime Rib. 1101 N Calvert St

Tio Pepe. 10 E Franklin St

NORTH OF CENTRAL AREA

Angelina's. 7135 Harford Rd

Brass Elephant. 924 N Charles St

Jeannier's. 105 W 39th St

Thai Restaurant. 3316 Greenmount Ave

EAST OF CENTRAL AREA

Haussner's. 3244 Eastern Ave

Ikaros. 4805 Eastern Ave

Karson's Inn. 5100 Holabird Ave

FELL'S POINT

Henninger's Tavern. 1812 Bank St

Obrycki's. 1727 E Pratt St

Waterfront Hotel. 1710 Thames St

INNER HARBOR

City Lights. 301 Light St

Hampton's (Harbor Court Hotel). 550 Light St

Taverna Athena. 201 E Pratt St

Water Street Exchange. 110 Water St

Wayne's Bar-B-Que. 301 Light St

LITTLE ITALY

Capriccio. 846 Fawn St

Chiapparelli's. 237 S High St

Dalesio's. 829 Eastern Ave

Germano's Trattoria. 300 S High St

Giuseppe Ristorante Italiano. 248 Albermarle St

Velleggia's. 829 E Pratt St

Note: When a listing is located in a town that does not have its own city heading, it will appear under the city nearest to its location. In these cases, the address and town appear in parenthesis immediately following the name of the establishment.

Motels

(In this area I-95 is Kennedy Memorial Hwy; I-695 is the Beltway)

(Rates may be much higher Preakness wkend, mid-May)

✔ ★ **CHRISTLEN.** 8733 Pulaski Hwy (US 40) (21237), I-695 exit 35B, east of Central Area. 410/687-1740. 28 rms. S $32-$38; D $38-$42; each addl $5. Crib $5. TV; cable. Restaurant adj open 24 hrs. Ck-out 11 am. Refrigerators. Picnic tables. Cr cds: A, D, DS, MC, V.

D 🐾 🔥

★ **ECONO LODGE.** 5801 Baltimore Natl Pike (21228), on US 40, just E of I-695 exit 15A, west of Central Area. 410/744-5000; FAX 410/788-5197. 217 rms, 2-3 story, 38 kits. No elvtr. S $42.95-$48.95; D $45.95-$55.95; each addl $5; kit. units $52.95; under 18 free. Crib free. Pet accepted. TV; cable. Pool; lifeguard. Restaurant 7 am-2 pm, 5-10 pm. Rm serv. Ck-out noon. Coin lndry. Meeting rms. Sundries. Cr cds: A, C, D, DS, JCB, MC, V.

D 🐾 ≈ 🔥 SC

★ ★ **HOLIDAY INN SECURITY/BELMONT.** 1800 Belmont Ave (21244), north of Central Area. 410/265-1400; FAX 410/281-9569. 135 units, 2 story. S, D $59-$83; each addl (after 3 persons) $10; under 18 free; monthly rates. Crib free. Pet accepted. TV; cable. Pool; wading pool, lifeguard. Restaurant 6 am-2 pm, 5-10 pm; Sat & Sun from 7 am. Rm serv. Bar 5 pm-midnight; Sun to 10 pm. Ck-out noon. Meeting rms. Valet serv. Sundries. Health club privileges. Some refrigerators. Cr cds: A, C, D, DS, ER, JCB, MC, V.

D 🐾 ≈ 🔥 SC

✔ ★ **SUSSE CHALET.** 4 Philadelphia Court (21237), I-695 exit 34, north of Central Area. 410/574-8100; FAX 410/574-8204. 132 rms, 5 story. S $48.70; D $55.70; each addl $3. Crib free. TV; cable. Pool; lifeguard. Complimentary continental bkfst. Restaurant nearby. Ck-out 11 am. Coin lndry. Sundries. Cr cds: A, C, D, DS, MC, V.

D ≈ 🔥 SC

Motor Hotels

★ ★ **BEST WESTERN-EAST.** 5625 O'Donnell St (21224), I-95 exit 57, east of Central Area. 410/633-9500; FAX 410/633-6314. 175 rms, 12 story. S $69-$74; D $79-$84; each addl $10; suites $189-$225. Crib avail. Pet accepted; some restrictions; $25 deposit. TV; cable. Indoor pool; lifeguard. Complimentary continental bkfst. Restaurant 6:30 am-10 pm. Rm serv. Bar. Ck-out noon. Coin lndry. Meeting rms. Gift shop. Airport, bus depot transportation. Exercise equipt; weights, treadmill, sauna. Game rm. Cr cds: A, DS, MC, V.

D 🐾 ≈ 🏋 🔥 SC

★ ★ **CROSS KEYS INN.** 5100 Falls Rd (21210), north of Central Area. 410/532-6900; res: 800/532-5397; FAX 410/532-2403. 148 rms, 4 story. S $79-$129; D $99-$139; each addl $10; suites $140-$340; under 16 free; wkend rates. Crib $10. TV; cable. Pool; poolside serv, lifeguard. Restaurant 7 am-10 pm. Rm serv. Bar 11 am-midnight. Ck-out noon. Meeting rms. Shopping arcade. Barber, beauty shop. Free city transportation. Tennis privileges. Bathrm phones. Some private balconies. Cr cds: A, C, D, DS, MC, V.

🇩 🏃 ≋ 🏌 ⊠ 🔥 SC

★★ **DAYS INN INNER HARBOR.** *100 Hopkins Pl (21201), in Central Area.* 410/576-1000; FAX 410/576-9437. 250 rms, 9 story. S $75-$95; D $85-$115; each addl $10; suites $115-$130; under 12 free. Crib free. Garage $7. TV; cable. Pool; poolside serv, lifeguard. Restaurant 7 am-10 pm. Rm serv. Bar. Ck-out noon. Meeting rms. Bellhops. Concierge. Sundries. Health club privileges. Some refrigerators. Cr cds: A, D, DS, MC, V.

🇩 ≋ ⊠ 🔥 SC

★★ **HOLIDAY INN TIMONIUM.** *(2004 Greenspring Dr, Timonium 21093) I-83 exit 16.* 410/252-7373; FAX 410/561-0182. 250 rms, 5 story. S $99; D $109; each addl $10; suites $150; family, wkly, wkend, hol rates. Crib free. TV; cable. Indoor/outdoor pool; whirlpool, sauna, poolside serv. Restaurant 6 am-10 pm. Bars; entertainment. Ck-out noon. Coin lndry. Meeting rms. Bellhops. Gift shop. Valet serv. Health club privileges. Cr cds: A, C, D, DS, JCB, MC, V.

🇩 ≋ ⊠ 🔥 SC

✔ **HOWARD JOHNSON.** *5701 Baltimore Natl Pike (21228), 1/2 mi E of I-695 exit 15A, west of Central Area.* 410/747-8900; FAX 410/744-3522. 145 rms, 7 story. S $40-$50; D $48-$60; each addl $8; under 18 free. Crib free. TV; cable. Pool; whirlpool, lifeguard. Restaurant open 24 hrs. Ck-out noon. Coin lndry. Meeting rms. Sundries. Some refrigerators, balconies. Cr cds: A, C, D, DS, ER, JCB, MC, V.

🇩 ≋ ⊠ 🔥 SC

Hotels

★★ **BROOKSHIRE INNER HARBOR SUITE HOTEL.** *120 E Lombard St (21202), Inner Harbor.* 410/625-1300; res: 800/647-0013 (exc MD); FAX 410/625-0912. 90 suites, 12 story. S $145-$185; D $155-$195; each addl $10; children free; wkend rates. Crib free. Valet parking $15. TV; cable. Restaurant 7 am-10 pm. Bar 11 am-9 pm. Ck-out noon. Meeting rms. Concierge. Health club privileges. Bathrm phones, refrigerators, minibars. Cr cds: A, C, D, DS, MC, V.

🇩 ⊠ 🔥 SC

★★★ **CLARION INN-HARRISON'S PIER 5.** *711 Eastern Ave (21202), Inner Harbor.* 410/783-5553; FAX 410/783-1787. 71 rms, 3 story. May-Oct: S $139-$169; D $149-$179; each addl $10; suites $199-$350; under 18 free; lower rates rest of yr. Crib free. TV; cable. Restaurant 7 am-11 pm. Bar 11-1 am; entertainment. Ck-out noon. Meeting rms. Shopping arcade. Airport transportation. Exercise equipt; weight machines, bicycles. Bathrm phones, minibars. Some balconies. Mahogany furnishings. Atrium lobby with 40-ft skipjack boat. On Inner Harbor. Cr cds: A, C, D, DS, ER, MC, V.

🇩 🏌 ⊠ 🔥 SC

✔ ★★ **DAYS HOTEL.** *(9615 Deereco Rd, Timonium 21093) I-83 exit 17, Padonia Rd.* 410/560-1000; FAX 410/561-3918. 146 rms, 7 story. S $45-$75; D $45-$90; each addl $5; suites $90-$125; family, hol rates. Crib avail. TV; cable. Pool. Complimentary continental bkfst. Restaurant open 24 hrs. Rm serv 7 am-10 pm. Bar. Ck-out noon. Lndry facilities. Meeting rms. Exercise equipt; weights, treadmill. Health club privileges. Game rm. Cr cds: A, C, D, DS, MC, V.

🇩 ≋ 🏌 ⊠ 🔥 SC

★★★ **DOUBLETREE INN AT THE COLONNADE.** *4 West University Pkwy (21218), north of Central Area.* 410/235-5400; FAX 410/235-5572. 125 units, 11 story, 31 suites. S, D $109-$149; each addl $15; suites $135-$475; family rates; wkend, honeymoon plans. Crib free. Pet accepted. TV; cable, in-rm movies. Indoor pool; whirlpool, poolside serv. Restaurant 6 am-11 pm. Rm serv to midnight. Ck-out noon. Meeting rms. Concierge. Gift shop. Barber, beauty shop. Free RR station, bus depot, downtown transportation. Exercise equipt; bicycles, treadmill. Video library. Some wet bars. Balconies. Bieder-

meier-inspired furnishings; extensive collection of 18th-century European masters. Adj to Johns Hopkins University. Cr cds: A, C, D, DS, ER, JCB, MC, V.

🇩 🍴 ≋ 🏌 ⊠ 🔥 SC

★★★ **EMBASSY SUITES.** *(213 International Circle, Hunt Valley 21030) I-83N to exit 20A, Shawan Rd E.* 410/584-1400; FAX 410/584-7306. 223 kit. suites, 8 story. S $109-139, D $119-149; each addl $5; under 12 free; wkend rates; higher rates special events. Crib free. Pet accepted. TV; cable. Indoor pool; whirlpool, sauna, steam rm. Complimentary full bkfst. Restaurant 11 am-10 pm. Bar to 2 am. Ck-out noon. Meeting rms. Gift shop. Built around 8-story atrium; glass-enclosed elvtrs. Cr cds: A, C, D, DS, JCB, MC, V.

🇩 🍴 ≋ ⊠ 🔥 SC

★★★ **HARBOR COURT.** *550 Light St (21202), Inner Harbor.* 410/234-0550; res: 800/824-0076; FAX 410/659-5925. 203 rms, 8 story, 25 suites. S $205-$245; D $220-$260; suites $375-$2,000; under 18 free; wkend rates; some package plans. Crib free. Covered parking: self-park $9; valet $12. TV; cable. Heated pool; poolside serv, lifeguard. Restaurant 7 am-11 pm (also see HAMPTON'S). Rm serv 24 hrs. Bar 11-2 am; entertainment exc Sun. Ck-out noon. Meeting rms. Concierge. Airport transportation. Tennis. Exercise rm; instructor, weight machines, bicycles, whirlpool, sauna. Massage. Handball, racquetball courts. Lawn games. Bathrm phones, refrigerators. Elegant retreat located on Inner Harbor; panoramic view of city. Cr cds: A, C, D, DS, ER, JCB, MC, V.

🇩 🏃 ≋ 🏌 ⊠ 🔥 SC

★★★ **HOLIDAY INN BALTIMORE-INNER HARBOR.** *301 W Lombard St (21201), in Central Area.* 410/685-3500; FAX 410/727-6169. 375 rms, 10 & 13 story. Apr-Sept: S $109; D $119; each addl $10; suites $250; under 12 free; lower rates rest of yr. Crib free. Pet accepted, some restrictions. Garage parking $6. TV; cable. Indoor pool; lifeguard. Complimentary coffee in rms. Restaurant 6:30 am-11 pm. Bar 11-1 am. Ck-out noon. Convention facilities. Gift shop. Exercise equipt; weight machine, bicycles, sauna. Some balconies. Cr cds: A, C, D, DS, ER, JCB, MC, V.

🇩 🍴 ≋ 🏌 ⊠ 🔥 SC

★★★ **HYATT REGENCY.** *300 Light St (21202), adj to Inner Harbor.* 410/528-1234; FAX 410/685-3362. 487 rms, 14 story. S $119-$180; D $145-$200; each addl $25; suites $250-$1,000; under 18 free; wkend plan. Crib free. Valet parking $12. TV; cable. Pool. Restaurant 6:30-1 am. Bar 11:30-2 am; entertainment. Ck-out noon. Convention facilities. Concierge. Gift shop. Tennis. Exercise rm; instructor, weight machines, bicycles, whirlpool, sauna. Minibars. *LUXURY LEVEL .* 54 rms. S, D $175-$225. Private lounge, honor bar. Complimentary continental bkfst, refreshments. Cr cds: A, C, D, DS, ER, JCB, MC, V.

🇩 🏃 ≋ 🏌 🏃 ⊠ 🔥 SC

★★★ **LATHAM.** *612 Cathedral St (21201), at Mt Vernon Pl, north of Central Area.* 410/727-7101; res: 800/528-4261; FAX 410/789-3312. 104 rms, 14 story, 2 suites, 5 kits. S $135-$155; D $155-$175; each addl $20; suites $250-$350; under 18 free; wkend, honeymoon packages. Crib free. Valet parking $10. TV; cable. Pool privileges. Restaurants 6:30 am-11 pm. Rm serv to midnight. Bar. Ck-out 1 pm. Meeting rms. Concierge. Health club privileges. Bathrm phones, minibars; some in-rm whirlpools. Restored hotel built 1927. Marble floors & stairs in lobby. Period furnishings, artwork, crystal chandeliers. Cr cds: A, C, D, DS, ER, JCB, MC, V.

🇩 ⊠ 🔥 SC

★★★ **MARRIOTT INNER HARBOR.** *Pratt & Eutaw Sts (21201), Inner Harbor.* 410/962-0202; FAX 410/962-0202, ext. 2044. 525 units, 10 story. S, D $195; suites $195-$650; under 18 free; wkend rates. Crib free. Pet accepted, some restrictions. Covered parking $8. TV; cable. Indoor pool; lifeguard. Restaurant 6 am-11 pm. Bar noon-2 am; entertainment, dancing. Ck-out noon. Convention facilities. Concierge. Exercise rm; instructor, weights, bicycles, whirlpool, sauna. Opp baseball stadium at Camden Yards. *LUXURY LEVEL : CONCIERGE FLOOR.* 70 units. S, D $195; suites $195-$625. Private lounge. Wet bars. Complimentary continental bkfst 7-10 am, refreshments. Cr cds: A, C, D, DS, ER, JCB, MC, V.

[D] [icons] [SC]

★ ★ ★ **OMNI INNER HARBOR.** 101 W Fayette St (21201), Inner Harbor. 410/752-1100; FAX 410/625-3805. 703 rms, 2 towers, 23 & 27 story. S $135-$160; D $155-$180; each addl $20; suites $200-$750; under 17 free; wkend rates. Crib free. Garage $9; valet parking $14. TV; cable. Pool; poolside serv, lifeguard. Restaurant 6:30 am-midnight. Bars noon-2 am. Ck-out noon. Convention facilities. Inner Harbor transportation. Exercise equipt; weights, bicycles. Minibars; some refrigerators. Cr cds: A, C, D, DS, ER, MC, V.

[D] [icons] [SC]

★ ★ **RADISSON PLAZA-LORD BALTIMORE.** 20 W Baltimore St (21201), in Central Area. 410/539-8400; FAX 410/625-1060. 419 rms, 23 story. S $129; D $144; each addl $15; suites $199-$350; kit. units $600-$800; under 17 free; wkend rates. Crib free. Valet parking $12. TV; cable. Restaurants 6:30 am-10 pm. Bar 11-2 am. Ck-out noon. Meeting rms. Concierge. Airport transportion. Exercise equipt; weight machines, bicycles, whirlpool, sauna. Historic landmark; near harbor. Cr cds: A, C, D, DS, ER, JCB, MC, V.

[D] [icons] [SC]

★ ★ **SHERATON INNER HARBOR.** 300 S Charles St (21201), in Inner Harbor. 410/962-8300; FAX 410/962-8211. 337 rms, 14 story. Mar-June & Sept-Dec: S, D $155-$185; each addl $15; suites $325-$1,300; under 17 free; wkly, wkend rates; lower rates rest of yr. Crib free. Pet accepted. Covered parking $10. TV; cable. Indoor pool; lifeguard. Restaurant 6:30 am-11 pm. Bar 11:30-2 am. Ck-out noon. Convention facilities. Concierge. Gift shop. Exercise equipt; bicycles, treadmill, sauna. Minibars; some bathrm phones, refrigerators. Cr cds: A, C, D, DS, ER, JCB, MC, V.

[D] [icons] [SC]

★ ★ ★ **STOUFFER HARBORPLACE.** 202 E Pratt St (21202), Inner Harbor. 410/547-1200; FAX 410/539-5780. 622 rms, 12 story. S $180-$210; D $200-$230; each addl $20; suites $300-$1,000; under 18 free; wkend rates. Covered parking $8; valet $11. Crib free. TV; cable. Indoor pool; poolside serv, lifeguard. Restaurant 6:30 am-11 pm. Rm serv 24 hrs. Bar 11-1:30 am; entertainment. Ck-out noon. Convention facilities. Concierge. Shopping arcade. Tennis privileges. Exercise rm; instructor, weight machines, bicycles, whirlpool, sauna. Minibars; many bathrm phones. Opp harbor. **LUXURY LEVEL : CLUB FLOOR.** 94 units, 7 suites. S $210-$230; D $230-$250; suites $300-$1,000. Private lounge. Complimentary bkfst, refreshments, newspaper. Cr cds: A, C, D, DS, ER, JCB, MC, V.

[D] [icons] [SC]

✔ ★ ★ **TREMONT.** 8 E Pleasant St (21202), in Central Area. 410/576-1200; res: 800/873-6668; FAX 410/244-1154. 58 kit. suites, 13 story. S $89-$119; D $109-$139; each addl $20; under 16 free; wkend rates. Crib free. Pet accepted; $3 per night. Valet parking $8.50. Pool privileges. TV; cable. Restaurant 7 am-2 pm, 5-10 pm. Bar 5 pm-2 am. Ck-out noon. Meeting rms. Health club privileges. Cr cds: A, C, D, DS, MC, V.

[D] [icons] [SC]

Inns

★ ★ ★ **ADMIRAL FELL.** 888 S Broadway (21231), in Fell's Point. 410/522-7377; res: 800/292-4667 (exc MD); FAX 410/522-0707. 37 rms, 4 story. S, D $115-$175; each addl $15; wkly rates. TV; cable. Complimentary continental bkfst 7-11 am. Dining rm 11 am-3 pm, 5-9 pm; Sat to 10 pm. Bar 11-2 am. Ck-out noon, ck-in 3 pm. Meeting rms. Concierge. Some in-rm whirlpools. Cr cds: A, D, DS, MC, V.

[D] [icons] [SC]

★ ★ ★ **CELIE'S WATERFRONT BED & BREAKFAST.** 1714 Thames St (21231), in Fell's Point. 410/522-2323; res: 800/432-0184;

FAX 410/522-2324. 7 rms (1 with shower only), 3 story. 2-day min: S $90-$140; D $100-$160; hol & wkend rates. Children over 9 yrs only. TV. Complimentary continental breakfast. Complimentary coffee in room. Restaurant adj 11 am-10 pm. Ck-out 11 am, ck-in 3 pm. Refrigerators. On harbor; many antiques. Totally nonsmoking. Cr cds: A, D, MC, V.

[D] [icons]

★ ★ ★ **GOVERNMENT HOUSE.** 1125 N Calvert St (21202), north of Central Area. 410/539-0566; FAX 410/539-0567. 20 rms, 4 story. S, D $125-$150; wkly rates; Preakness (2-day min). TV. Complimentary continental bkfst, afternoon tea & wine. Restaurant nearby. Ck-out noon, ck-in 2 pm. Part of complex of several Federal and Victorian mansions and town houses (1888). Totally nonsmoking. Cr cds: A, C, D, MC, V.

[icons] [SC]

★ ★ **THE INN AT HENDERSON'S WHARF.** 1000 Fell St (21231), in Fell's Point. 410/522-7777; res: 800/522-2088; FAX 410/522-7087. 38 rms. S, D $95-$135; each addl $15; under 16 free; higher rates special events. Crib free. TV; cable, in-rm movies avail. Complimentary continental bkfst. Restaurant nearby. Ck-out noon, ck-in 3 pm. Coin lndry. Meeting rms. Bellhops. Valet serv. Sundries. Gift shop. Exercise equipt; weight machine, bicycles. Some refrigerators, minibars. On waterfront. 19th-century tobacco warehouse. Cr cds: A, C, D, MC, V.

[D] [icons] [SC]

★ ★ ★ ★ **MR MOLE BED & BREAKFAST.** 1601 Bolton St (21217), north of Central Area. 410/728-1179; FAX 410/728-3379. 5 rms, 5 story, 2 suites. S $75-$100; D $90-$115; each addl $15; suites $100-$145; higher rates wkends (2-day min); children over 16 yrs only. Complimentary continental bkfst. Restaurant nearby. Ck-out 11 am, ck-in 4-6 pm. Free RR station transportation. Built 1867; furnished with 18th- and 19th-century antiques. Library in each rm. Totally nonsmoking. Cr cds: A, DS, MC, V.

[icons]

✔ ★ ★ **SOCIETY HILL-58 WEST.** 58 W Biddle St (21201), west of Central Area. 410/837-3630; res: 800/676-3630; FAX 410/837-4654. 15 rms, 4 story. S, D $90-$140. TV; cable. Complimentary continental bkfst. Dining rm 11 am-10 pm; Fri, Sat to midnight. Bar to midnight; Fri, Sat to 2 am; pianist Wed-Sat. Ck-out noon, ck-in 1 pm. Turn-of-the-century building in the heart of the Mt Vernon district; original antique furnishings. Cr cds: A, C, D, MC, V.

[icons] [SC]

★ ★ ★ **SOCIETY HILL-HOPKINS.** 3404 St Paul St (21218), north of Central Area. 410/235-8600; FAX 410/235-7051. 26 rms, 4 story. S, D $107-127; suites $127-$135; wkly rates. Crib free. TV. Complimentary continental bkfst, tea & wine. Restaurant nearby. Ck-out 11 am, ck-in 1 pm. Meeting rms. Covered parking. 1920's Spanish-revival apartment building. Rms individually furnished in variety of styles. Cr cds: A, C, D, MC, V.

[icons] [SC]

Restaurants

★ ★ **ANGELINA'S.** 7135 Harford Rd, north of Central Area. 410/444-5545. Hrs: 11:30 am-10 pm; Fri, Sat to 11:30 pm. Closed Mon; Thanksgiving, Dec 25. Italian menu. Bar. Semi-a la carte: lunch $5-$15, dinner $9-$26. Child's meals. Specializes in crab cakes, seafood. Entertainment Fri. Cr cds: A, DS, MC, V.

★ ★ **BRASS ELEPHANT.** 924 N Charles St, north of Central Area. 410/547-8480. Hrs: 11:30 am-2 pm, 5:30-9:30 pm; Fri to 11 pm; Sat 5:30-11 pm; Sun 5-9 pm. Closed major hols & Dec 24. Res accepted. Northern Italian menu. Bar 5 pm-1 am. Semi-a la carte: lunch $4.25-$10., dinner $10.50-$22. Complete meals: lunch $7, dinner $15.95. Specializes in homemade pasta, seafood, veal. Own pastries. Braille menu. Historic town house (1861); floor-to-ceiling stained-glass windows, marble fireplace. 6 dining areas, individually decorated. Totally nonsmoking. Cr cds: A, C, D, MC, V.

★ ★ **CAPRICCIO.** *846 Fawn St, Little Italy.* 410/685-2710. Hrs: 11:30 am-10:30 pm; Fri & Sat to 11:30 pm. Closed Thanksgiving, Dec 25. Res accepted. Northern Italian menu. Bar. Semi-a la carte: lunch $6.25-$12, dinner $9.95-$26. Child's meals. Specialties: fettucine frutta de mare (white or red), veal Capriccio, seafood. Own pasta. Cr cds: A, C, D, MC, V.

★ ★ **CHIAPPARELLI'S.** *237 S High St, Little Italy.* 410/837-0309. Hrs: 11 am-11 pm; Fri, Sat to midnight. Closed Thanksgiving, Dec 25. Res accepted. Italian menu. Semi-a la carte: lunch $7-$14, dinner $10-$24. Child's meals. Specialty: Piatto Napolitano. Built 1870; original brick walls, oak paneling. 7 dining rms on 2 levels. Family-owned. Cr cds: A, C, D, DS, MC, V.
D

★ ★ **CITY LIGHTS.** *301 Light St, Light St Pavilion, Inner Harbor.* 410/244-8811. Hrs: 11:30 am-10 pm; Fri & Sat to midnight. Closed Thanksgiving, Dec 24 & 25. Res accepted. Bar. A la carte entrees: lunch, dinner $5-$18. Child's meals. Specializes in Chesapeake Bay seafood. Own desserts. Outdoor dining. Cr cds: A, C, D, DS, MC, V.

★ ★ **DALESIO'S.** *829 Eastern Ave, Little Italy.* 410/539-1965. Hrs: 11:30 am-3 pm, 5-10 pm; Sun 4-9 pm. Closed Thanksgiving. Res accepted. Northern Italian menu. Bar. A la carte entrees: lunch $5.25-$10.95, dinner $9.75-$22.95. Specializes in Northern Italian spa cuisine. Own cakes, pasta. Cr cds: A, D, MC, V.

★ ★ **GERMANO'S TRATTORIA.** *300 S High St, Little Italy.* 410/752-4515. Hrs: 11:30 am-11 pm; Fri, Sat to midnight. Closed Thanksgiving, Dec 25. Res accepted. Italian menu. Bar. Semi-a la carte: lunch $4-$8.95, dinner $7.50-$19.75. Child's meals. Specializes in Tuscan cuisine. Cr cds: A, C, D, MC, V.

★ ★ **GIUSEPPE RISTORANTE ITALIANO.** *248 Albermarle St, Little Italy.* 410/685-1859. Hrs: 11 am-11 pm. Closed Thanksgiving, Dec 25. Res accepted; required Fri & Sat. Italian menu. Bar. A la carte entrees: lunch $6.50-$13.50, dinner $8.50-$23. Child's meals. Specialties: linguine pescatore, veal involtino. Traditional decor. Cr cds: A, D, MC, V.
D

★ ★ ★ **HAMPTON'S.** *(See Harbor Court Hotel)* 410/234-0550. Hrs: 5:30-11 pm; Sun to 10 pm; Sun brunch 10:30 am-3 pm. Closed Mon. Res required. Serv bar. Wine list. A la carte entrees: dinner $20-$36. Sun brunch $19.95-$27.95. Specializes in seafood, veal, game, regional dishes. Own pastries. Valet parking $12. Dining rm decor similiar to that of 18th-century mansion. Scenic view of harbor. Jacket. Cr cds: A, C, D, DS, ER, JCB, MC, V.
D

★ ★ ★ **HAUSSNER'S.** *3244 Eastern Ave, east of Central Area.* 410/327-8365. Hrs: 11 am-10 pm. Closed Sun, Mon; Dec 25. Res accepted. German, Amer menu. Bar. Semi-a la carte: lunch, dinner $8-$24.50. Specializes in seafood, sauerbraten, strawberry pie. Own baking. Braille menu. Large display of original artwork. Old-world atmosphere. Family-owned. Cr cds: A, C, D, DS, MC, V.
D

★ **HENNINGER'S TAVERN.** *1812 Bank St, in Fell's Point.* 410/342-2172. Hrs: 5-10 pm; Fri, Sat to 11 pm. Closed Sun, Mon; Jan 1, Dec 25. Bar to 1 am. A la carte entrees: dinner $13.95-$18.95. Specializes in seafood. Late 1800s atmosphere. Cr cds: A, MC, V.

✔ ★ ★ **IKAROS.** *4805 Eastern Ave, east of Central Area.* 410/633-3750. Hrs: 11 am-10 pm; Fri, Sat to 11 pm. Closed Tues; Thanksgiving, Dec 25. Greek, Amer menu. Serv bar. Semi-a la carte: lunch $4-$9, dinner $8-$15. Specializes in lamb, squid, fresh whole fish. Cr cds: A, C, D, DS, MC, V.

★ ★ **JEANNIER'S.** *105 W 39th St, north of Central Area.* 410/889-3303. Hrs: 11:30 am-2:30 pm, 5:30-9:30 pm; Fri to 10 pm; Sat 5:30-10 pm; early-bird dinner 5:30-7 pm. Closed Sun; most major hols. French, continental menu. Bar 11:30 am-11 pm. Wine cellar. A la carte entrees: lunch $6-$11, dinner $13.95-$25. Complete meals: dinner $13 & $22. Specializes in seafood, country-French cuisine. Own pastries, desserts. Country chateau decor. Cr cds: A, MC, V.

★ ★ **KARSON'S INN.** *5100 Holabird Ave, east of Central Area.* 410/631-5400. Hrs: 11 am-10 pm; Sat 4-11 pm; Sun noon-9 pm. Closed major hols. Res accepted; required hols. Bar. Semi-a la carte: lunch $4.95-$10.50, dinner $10.95-$32. Child's meals. Specializes in steak, seafood. Parking. Family-owned. Cr cds: A, DS, MC, V.
D

✔ ★ **LIGHT HOUSE.** *10 Park Ave, in Central Area.* 410/727-3814. Hrs: 7-2 am. Closed Thanksgiving, Dec 25. Bar. Semi-a la carte: bkfst $3-$6, lunch $4.50-$9, dinner $9.95-$14. Child's meals. Specializes in Maryland seafood, Greek shish kebab. Valet parking. Built 1890; former hotel. Cr cds: A, C, D, MC, V.
SC

★ **MAISON MARCONI'S.** *106 W Saratoga, in Central Area.* 410/727-9522. Hrs: 11:30 am-3:30 pm, 5-8 pm; Fri & Sat to 9 pm. Closed Sun, Mon; major hols. Res accepted. Continental menu. Serv bar. A la carte entrees: lunch, dinner $7-$19. Specialties: lobster Cardinal, seafood. Complimentary valet parking. Early 19th-century town house. Jacket. Cr cds: A, MC, V.

★ ★ **OBRYCKI'S.** *1727 E Pratt St, in Fell's Point.* 410/732-6399. Hrs: noon-11 pm; Sun to 9:30 pm. Closed mid-Dec-Mar. Bar. Semi-a la carte: lunch $5.50-$17.95, dinner $13.25-$24.95. Child's meals. Specializes in steamed crab, crabmeat entrees. Cr cds: A, C, D, DS, MC, V.
D

★ ★ ★ **PRIME RIB.** *1101 N Calvert St (21202), in Central Area.* 410/539-1804. Hrs: 5 pm-midnight; Sun 4-11 pm. Closed Thanksgiving. Res accepted. Bar. Wine list. A la carte entrees: dinner $15-$25. Specializes in steak, seafood, lamb. Pianist. Parking. Black laquered walls. Paintings and prints displayed. Jacket. Family-owned. Cr cds: A, C, D, MC, V.

★ ★ **TAVERNA ATHENA.** *201 E Pratt St, in Pratt St Pavilion, Inner Harbor.* 410/547-8900. Hrs: 11:30 am-10:30 pm; wkends to 11 pm. Closed Thanksgiving, Dec 25. Res accepted; required July 4 & Dec 31. Greek menu. Bar to 11 pm. Semi-a la carte: lunch $4.95-$13.95, dinner $5.95-$26.95. Specializes in seafood, lamb, veal. Outdoor dining. Cr cds: A, C, D, DS, MC, V.

✔ ★ **THAI RESTAURANT.** *3316 Greenmount Ave, north of Central Area.* 410/889-7304. Hrs: 11:30 am-3 pm, 5-10:30 pm; Sun from 5 pm. Closed July 4 & Dec 25. Thai menu. Serv bar. Semi-a la carte: lunch $5.50-$7, dinner $6.95-$14. Specializes in traditional Thai curry dishes. Cr cds: A, MC, V.

★ ★ ★ **TIO PEPE.** *10 E Franklin St, in Central Area.* 410/539-4675. Hrs: 11:30 am-2:30 pm, 5-10:30 pm; Fri to 11:30 pm; Sat 5-11:30 pm; Sun 4-10:30 pm. Closed most major hols. Res required. Spanish, continental menu. Bar. Wine cellar. Semi-a la carte: lunch $7-$12, dinner $13.75-$22. Specialties: shrimp in garlic sauce, suckling pig. Spanish casa atmosphere. Jacket. Cr cds: A, C, D, DS, MC, V.
D

★ ★ **VELLEGGIA'S.** *829 E Pratt St, Little Italy.* 410/685-2620. Hrs: 11 am-11 pm; Fri, Sat to 1 am. Closed Dec 24 & 25. Res accepted. Italian menu. Bar. A la carte entrees: lunch $4.50-$9.50, dinner $8.50-$19.95. Child's meals. Specializes in veal, seafood. Own pasta. Family-owned. Cr cds: A, D, MC, V.

✔ ★ ★ **WATER STREET EXCHANGE.** *110 Water St, Inner Harbor.* 410/332-4060. Hrs: 11:30 am-11 pm. Closed Sun; major hols. Res accepted. Bar to 2 am. Semi-a la carte: lunch, dinner $5-$15. Specializes in salad, sandwiches. Own desserts. Outdoor dining. Victorian decor. Cr cds: A, C, D, DS, MC, V.

★ **WATERFRONT HOTEL.** *1710 Thames St, in Fell's Point.* 410/327-4886. Hrs: 11 am-10 pm; Fri, Sat to 11 pm. Closed Dec 25. Res accepted. Continental menu. Bar 10-2 am. Semi-a la carte: lunch $4.50-$9.95, dinner $11.95-$24.95. Child's meals. Specializes in seafood, beef. Restored building (1772) located on waterfront; 3-story brick fireplace, stained-glass windows. Cr cds: A, C, D, MC, V.

✔ ★ **WAYNE'S BAR-B-QUE.** *301 Light St, in Light St Pavilion, Inner Harbor.* 410/539-3810. Hrs: 8 am-midnight; Fri, Sat to midnight. Closed Thanksgiving. Res accepted. Bar to 2 am. A la carte entrees: bkfst $4.50-$7.95, lunch, dinner $5-$12.95. Child's meals. Specializes in barbecue dishes, desserts. Outdoor dining. Cr cds: A, C, D, MC, V.

[SC]

Unrated Dining Spot

LOUIE'S BOOKSTORE CAFE. *518 N Charles St, in Central Area.* 410/962-1224. Hrs: 11:30-1 am; Mon to midnight; Fri, Sat to 2 am; Sun 10:30 am-midnight; Sun brunch to 3:30 pm. Closed major hols. Bar. Semi-a la carte: lunch $3.50-$8.95, dinner $3.95-$14.75. Sun brunch $3.25-$7. Specializes in Maryland seafood, desserts. Own pastries. Chamber music. Enter through bookstore; cafe in rear. Original artwork. Cr cds: A, MC, V.

Baltimore/Washington Intl Airport Area (C-7)

Services and Information

Information: 410/859-7100.

Lost and Found: 410/859-7040.

Weather: 301/936-1212.

Cash Machines: Main Terminal, Pier C.

Club Lounges: Red Carpet Club (United), South Terminal, Pier A; USAir Club (US Air), North Terminal, Pier D.

Terminals

Pier A: United

Pier B: Air Canada, America West, Delta

Pier C: American, Continental, Northwest

Pier D: Cayman (departures), LADECO (departures), TWA, USAir

Pier E: Air Jamaica, Cayman (arrivals), El Al, Icelandair, KLM, LADECO (arrivals)

(Airlines and their terminal locations may change. Before leaving for the airport, you should phone the airline to confirm terminal location for your flight.)

(See Baltimore; also see District of Columbia)

Motel

✔ ★ **HOLIDAY INN-SOUTH.** *(6600 Ritchie Hwy, Glen Burnie 21061)* I-195 to I-695, E to MD 2 (Ritchie Hwy). 410/761-8300; FAX 410/760-4966. 100 rms, 3 story. S, D $69; each addl $10; under 18 free. Crib free. Pet accepted, some restrictions. TV; cable. Pool; lifeguard. Restaurant 6 am-2 pm, 5-10 pm; Sat, Sun from 7 am. Rm serv.

Bar 4 pm-midnight. Ck-out noon. Meeting rms. Valet serv. Mall opp. Cr cds: A, C, D, DS, ER, JCB, MC, V.

[D] [♦] [≈] [⚒] [🔥] [SC]

Motor Hotels

✔ ★ ★ **BEST WESTERN AT BWI AIRPORT.** *(6755 Dorsey Rd, Dorsey 21227)* I-295 S to MD 176. 410/796-3300; FAX 410/379-0471. 134 rms, 4 story. S $69; D $74; each addl $5; under 18 free. Crib free. TV; cable. Indoor pool; lifeguard. Complimentary coffee in lobby. Restaurant adj 7 am-11 pm; Sat, Sun to 10 pm. Ck-out noon. Meeting rms. Valet serv. Free airport transportation. Exercise equipt; weight machines, bicycles, whirlpool, sauna. Cr cds: A, C, D, DS, ER, MC, V.

[D] [≈] [🏃] [✈] [⚒] [🔥] [SC]

★ ★ **COMFORT INN-AIRPORT.** *(6921 Baltimore Annapolis Blvd, Baltimore 21225)* N on MD 170 to Baltimore Annapolis Blvd. 410/789-9100; FAX 410/355-2854. 188 rms, 6 story. S $70; D $78; each addl $8; suites $125-$225; studio rms $68-$78; under 12 free; wkend rates. Crib free. Pet accepted. TV; cable. Restaurant 6:30 am-11 pm. Bar 11 am-midnight. Ck-out 11 am. Meeting rms. Bellhops. Valet serv. Free airport transportation. Exercise equipt; weights, bicycles, whirlpool, sauna. Game rm. Cr cds: A, C, D, DS, ER, JCB, MC, V.

[D] [♦] [🏃] [✈] [⚒] [🔥] [SC]

✔ ★ **HAMPTON INN.** *(829 Elkridge Landing Rd, Linthicum 21090)* From I-95 or I-295 take I-195E to exit 1A (MD 170N). 410/850-0600; FAX 410/850-0600, ext. 607. 139 rms, 5 story. S $64; D $68; under 18 free. Crib free. TV; cable. Complimentary continental bkfst, coffee. Restaurant nearby. Ck-out noon. Meeting rms. Bellhops. Valet serv. Free airport, local transportation. Some refrigerators. Cr cds: A, C, D, DS, MC, V.

[D] [🏃] [✈] [⚒] [🔥] [SC]

★ ★ ★ **SHERATON INTERNATIONAL AT BWI AIRPORT.** *(7032 Elm Rd, Baltimore 21240)* N of terminal. 410/859-3300; FAX 410/859-0565. 196 rms, 2 story. S $117-$129; D $129-$149; each addl $10; suites $165-$225; under 16 free; wkend rates. Crib free. TV; cable. Pool; poolside serv, lifeguard. Coffee in rms. Restaurant 6:30 am-3 pm, 5-10:30 pm. Rm serv 24 hrs. Bar 11-2 am; entertainment, dancing. Ck-out noon. Meeting rms. Bellhops. Sundries. Gift shop. Free airport transportation. Exercise equipt; weights, bicycles. Cr cds: A, C, D, DS, MC, V.

[≈] [🏃] [✈] [⚒] [🔥] [SC]

★ **SUSSE CHALET.** *(1734 W Nursery Rd, Linthicum 21090)* 410/859-2333; FAX 410/859-2357. 128 rms, 5 story. S $58.70-$65.70; D $61.70-$76.70; each addl $5; suites $79.70-$104.70; under 18 free. Crib free. TV; cable. Pool; lifeguard. Complimentary continental bkfst. Restaurant nearby. Ck-out 11 am. Coin lndry. Meeting rms. Bellhops. Valet serv. Free airport, RR station transportation. Cr cds: A, C, D, DS, MC, V.

[D] [≈] [✈] [⚒] [🔥] [SC]

Hotel

★ ★ **GUEST QUARTERS-AIRPORT.** *(1300 Concourse Dr, Linthicum 21090)* N on MD 170 to Elkridge Landing Rd, NW 1 1/2 mi to Winterson Rd, W to Concourse Dr; or I-295 to W Nursery Rd exit, then to Winterson Rd. 410/850-0747; FAX 410/859-0816. 251 suites, 8 story. S $140-$170; D $160-$190; each addl $20; under 18 free; wkend rates. Crib free. TV; cable. Indoor pool; lifeguard. Complimentary coffee in rms. Restaurant 6:30 am-11 pm. Bar 11-1 am. Ck-out noon. Convention facilities. Gift shop. Airport transportation. Exercise equipt; weights, bicycles, whirlpool, sauna. Bathrm phones, refrigerators, wet bars. Cr cds: A, C, D, DS, ER, JCB, MC, V.

[D] [≈] [🏃] [✈] [⚒] [🔥] [SC]

Bethesda (C-6)

Pop: 62,936 **Elev:** 305 ft **Area code:** 301

A suburb of Washington, DC, Bethesda is the home of both the National Institutes of Health, research arm of the Public Health Service, and Bethesda Naval Hospital.

What to See and Do

1. **National Library of Medicine.** 8600 Rockville Pike. World's largest biomedical library; rare books, manuscripts, prints; medical art displays. (Daily exc Sun; closed hols & Sat before Mon hols) Visitors center & guided tour (Mon-Fri, 1 departure each day). Phone 496-6308. **Free.**

2. **Clara Barton National Historic Site.** 3 mi W via MD 191, Goldsboro Rd in Glen Echo (see DISTRICT OF COLUMBIA).

3. **Cabin John Regional Park.** Approx 3 mi N on MD 355 then W on Tuckerman Lane. This 551-acre park has playgrounds, miniature train ride; nature center; concerts (summer evenings; free); tennis courts, game fields, ice rink, nature trails, picnicking. Fee for some activities. (Mon-Fri) Phone 299-4555.

(For further information contact the Bethesda-Chevy Chase Chamber of Commerce, Landow Bldg, 7910 Woodmont Ave, Suite 1204, 20814; 652-4900.)

(See District of Columbia)

Motor Hotel

★ **AMERICAN INN OF BETHESDA.** *8130 Wisconsin Ave (20814). 301/656-9300; res: 800/323-7081; FAX 301/656-2907.* 76 rms, 5 story. S $80; D $90; each addl $5; under 18 free; wkend, wkly, monthly rates. Crib free. TV; cable. Pool; lifeguard. Complimentary continental bkfst. Restaurant 6:30-9:30 am, 11:30 am-10 pm; Fri, Sat to 11 pm; Sun to 9:30 pm. Ck-out 12:30 pm. Meeting rms. Sundries. Cr cds: A, C, D, DS, MC, V.

Hotels

✔ ★ ★ **HOLIDAY INN-CHEVY CHASE.** *(5520 Wisconsin Ave, Chevy Chase 20815) S on Wisconsin Ave. 301/656-1500; FAX 301/656-5045.* 216 rms, 12 story. S, D $69-$129; each addl $10; suites $99-$149; under 18 free. Crib free. Pet accepted, some restrictions. TV; cable. Pool. Restaurant 6:30 am-11 pm. Bar. Ck-out 1 pm. Free lndry facilities. Meeting rms. Health club privileges. Bathrm phones. Cr cds: A, C, D, DS, ER, JCB, MC, V.

★ ★ ★ **HYATT REGENCY.** *One Bethesda Metro Center (20814). 301/657-1234; FAX 301/657-6453.* 381 rms, 12 story. S $149; D $174; each addl $20; suites $175-$600; under 18 free; wkend rates. Crib free. Covered parking $10; valet $12. TV; cable. Indoor pool; lifeguard. Restaurant 6:30 am-11:30 pm. Bar 11:30-12:30 am. Ck-out noon. Convention facilities. Exercise equipt; bicycles, rowing machine, sauna. Bathrm phones. Private patios, balconies. 12-story atrium lobby; extensive collection of artwork. *LUXURY LEVEL :* **GOLD PASSPORT.** 657-1234, ext 6532. 50 rms, 2 floors. S, D $165-$190. Concierge. Private lounge. Cr cds: A, C, D, DS, ER, JCB, MC, V.

★ ★ ★ **MARRIOTT.** *5151 Pooks Hill Rd (20814), 1 blk S of I-495 exit 34. 301/897-9400; FAX 301/897-0192.* 407 rms, 4-16 story. S $95-$160; D $105-$180; each addl $10; suites $275-$700; under 18 free; wkend plan. Crib free. Pet accepted. TV; cable. 2 pools, 1 indoor; poolside serv, lifeguard. Restaurants 6:30 am-10 pm. Rm serv to 1 am.

Bar 11:30 am-midnight; entertainment. Ck-out noon. Convention facilities. Gift shops. Barber. Lighted tennis. Exercise equipt: weight machines, bicycles, whirlpool, sauna. Game rm. Some balconies. On 18 landscaped acres. *LUXURY LEVEL :* **CONCIERGE LEVEL.** 47 rms. S $145-$165; D $175-$185. Concierge. Private lounge, honor bar. Complimentary continental bkfst, refreshments, newspaper. Cr cds: A, C, D, DS, ER, JCB, MC, V.

★ ★ ★ **MARRIOTT SUITES.** *6711 Democracy Blvd (20817). 301/897-5600; FAX 301/530-1427.* 274 suites, 11 story. Suites $165-$250; family rates. Crib free. Pet accepted, some restrictions. TV; cable. Indoor/outdoor pool; poolside serv, lifeguard. Complimentary continental bkfst. Complimentary coffee in rms. Restaurant 6:30 am-10:30 pm. Bar noon-midnight. Ck-out 1 pm. Meeting rms. Metro station transportation. Tennis privileges. Exercise rm: instructor, weights, bicycles, whirlpool. Refrigerators, wet bars. Balconies. Cr cds: A, C, D, DS, ER, JCB, MC, V.

★ ★ **RESIDENCE INN BY MARRIOTT.** *7335 Wisconsin Ave (20814). 301/718-0200; FAX 301/718-0679.* 187 kit suites, 13 story. S, D $149-$199; each addl $5; under 16 free; wkend, wkly & extended stay rates. Crib free. Pet accepted; $100 and $5 per day. Valet parking $10. TV; cable. Pool; lifeguard. Complimentary continental bkfst. Complimentary coffee in rms. Restaurant adj 6:30 am-10 pm. Ck-out noon. Coin lndry. Meeting rms. Exercise equipt; weight machine, bicycles, sauna. Rec rm. Cr cds: A, C, D, DS, JCB, MC, V.

Restaurants

★ ★ **BACCHUS.** *7945 Norfolk Ave. 301/657-1722.* Hrs: noon-2:30 pm, 6-10 pm; Fri to 10:30 pm; Sat 6-10:30 pm; Sun 6-10 pm. Closed Jan 1, Labor Day. Res accepted; required Fri, Sat. Lebanese menu. Serv bar. Complete meals: lunch $8. A la carte entrees: dinner $16-$25. Specializes in falafel, shish kebab. Valet parking. Cr cds: A, MC, V.

★ ★ **BUON GIORNO.** *8003 Norfolk Ave. 301/652-1400.* Hrs: 11:30 am-2:30 pm, 5:30-10 pm; Fri to 10:30 pm; Sat 5:30-10:30 pm; Sun 5:30-10 pm. Closed Mon; Jan 1, Thanksgiving, Dec 25; also mid-Aug-mid-Sept. Res accepted; required Fri, Sat. Italian menu. Serv bar. Semi-a la carte: lunch $4.50-$13.95, dinner $5.25-$19.95. Specialties: veal Marsala, trenette alla Genovese, pappardelle alla contadina, fresh fish. Own pasta. Cr cds: A, C, D, MC, V.

★ ★ **COTTONWOOD CAFE.** *4844 Cordell Ave. 301/656-4844.* Hrs: 11:30 am-10 pm; Fri & Sat to 11 pm; Sun 5:30-10 pm. Closed Jan 1, July 4 & Thanksgiving. Res accepted. Southwestern menu. Bar. Semi-a la carte: lunch $5.75-$11.95, dinner $12.65-$19.75. Specializes in grilled meats, seafood. Valet parking (dinner). Outdoor dining. Southwestern atmosphere. Mural of adobe village. Cr cds: A, MC, V.

✔ ★ **FOONG LIN.** *7710 Norfolk Ave. 301/656-3427.* Hrs: 11 am-10:30 pm; Fri, Sat to 11 pm. Closed Thanksgiving. Res accepted. Chinese menu. Serv bar. Semi-a la carte: lunch $4.50-$7.50, dinner $7.25-$17.95. Specializes in fresh fish, Peking duckling, crispy beef. Cr cds: A, MC, V.

★ ★ **FRASCATI RISTORANTE ITALIANO.** *4806 Rugby Ave. 301/652-9514.* Hrs: 11 am-2:30 pm, 4-10:30 pm; Sat from 5 pm; Sun 4-9:30 pm; early-bird dinner Tues-Fri & Sun 4-6:30 pm. Closed Mon; Jan 1, Easter, Dec 25. Res accepted; required Fri, Sat. Italian menu.

Semi-a la carte: lunch $4.75-$8, dinner $9.75-$15.95. Child's meals. Specializes in fresh fish, veal, pasta. Cr cds: A, C, D, DS, MC, V.

★ ★ **LA MICHE.** 7905 Norfolk Ave. 301/986-0707. Hrs: 11:30 am-2:30 pm, 6-10 pm; Sat from 6 pm. Closed Sun; major hols. Res required Fri, Sat. French menu. Serv bar. A la carte entrees: lunch $6-$17, dinner $13-$24. Specialties: soufflés, fricassee of lobster, grilled breast of duck. Valet parking (dinner). Outdoor dining. Country French decor. Cr cds: A, C, D, MC, V.

★ ★ ★ **LA VIEUX LOGIS.** 7925 Old Georgetown Rd. 301/652-6816. Hrs: 11:30 am-2 pm, 5:30-10 pm; Sat from 5:30 pm. Closed Sun; Jan 1, Dec 25. Res accepted; required Sat. French, Scandinavian menu. Serv bar. Wine list. A la carte entrees: lunch $8.75-$13.75, dinner $11.75-$19.95. Specialties: rack of lamb, vol au vont with lobster & Swedish meatballs. Valet parking. Rustic French inn atmosphere. Cr cds: A, C, D, MC, V.

★ ★ **O'DONNELL'S.** 8301 Wisconsin Ave. 301/656-6200. Hrs: 11:30 am-10 pm; Fri, Sat to 10:30 pm; Sun noon-9:30 pm. Closed Dec 25. Res accepted. Bar. Semi-a la carte: lunch $4.95-$9.95, dinner $11.95-$28.95. Child's meals. Specializes in seafood, rum buns. Parking. Nautical theme. Family-owned. Cr cds: A, C, D, DS, MC, V.

✔ ★ ★ **PERSEPOLIS.** 7130 Wisconsin Ave. 301/656-9339. Hrs: noon-11 pm. Res accepted; required Fri & Sat. Persian menu. Bar. A la carte entrees: lunch, dinner $6.95-$12.95. Lunch buffet $6.95. Specializes in kebab, grilled meats, seafood. Cr cds: A, C, D, MC, V.

★ ★ ★ **ST ELMO'S CAFE.** 7820 Norfolk Ave. 301/657-1607. Hrs: 11:30 am-2 pm, 5:30-10 pm; Sat-Mon from 5:30 pm. Closed Jan 1, Dec 25. French menu. Serv bar. A la carte entrees: lunch $6-$14; dinner $12.95-$21.95. Complete meals: dinner $24.95 & $34.95. Specializes in grilled seafood, rack of lamb coated with mustard. Own desserts. Valet parking (dinner). Patio dining. Cr cds: A, C, D, DS, MC, V.

✔ ★ **TAKO GRILL.** 7756 Wisconsin Ave. 301/652-7030. Hrs: 11:30 am-2 pm, 5:30-9:45 pm; Fri & Sat to 10:15 pm. Closed Sun; most major hols. Japanese menu. Serv bar. Semi-a la carte: lunch $5.50-$8.75, dinner $7.95-$15.50. Specializes in seafood, sushi, robatayaki. Blend of Eastern and Western ambiance; Japanese prints. Cr cds: A, MC, V.

✔ ★ **TEQUILA SUNRISE CAFE.** 7940 Wisconsin Ave. 301/907-6536. Hrs: 11:30 am-10 pm; Fri, Sat to 11 pm. Closed Jan 1, Thanksgiving, Dec 25. Res accepted Fri, Sat. Mexican menu. Bar to 1 am; Fri, Sat to 2 am. Semi-a la carte: lunch $3.25-$13.95, dinner $3.50-$15.95. Child's meals. Specializes in fajitas, chimichangas. Entertainment. Outdoor dining. Mexican/Caribbean cantina atmosphere. Cr cds: A, C, D, MC, V.

★ ★ **TERRAMAR.** 7800 Wisconsin Ave. 301/654-0888. Hrs: 11:30 am-2:30 pm, 5-10 pm; Fri to 11 pm; Sat 5-11 pm; Sun 5-9 pm. Closed Mon; some major hols. Res accepted; required Fri, Sat. Nicaraguan, Latin American menu. Bar. A la carte entrees: lunch $5.95-$7.95, dinner $10.95-$18.50. Specializes in tapas, churrasco, grilled seafood. Entertainment Fri & Sat eves. Indoor courtyard dining. Cr cds: A, D, DS, MC, V.

✔ ★ **THAI PLACE.** 4828 Cordell Ave. 301/951-0535. Hrs: 11 am-3 pm, 5-10 pm; Fri, Sat to 10:30 pm; Sun 11 am-10 pm. Closed Thanksgiving, Dec 25. Thai menu. Serv bar. Semi-a la carte: lunch $5.75-$6.50, dinner $6.50-$11. Specializes in steamed fish, Thai curry, Pad Thai. Cr cds: A, MC, V.

★ ★ ★ **TRAGARA.** 4935 Cordell Ave. 301/951-4935. Hrs: 11:45 am-2:30 pm, 6-10:30 pm; Sat & Sun from 6 pm. Closed Dec 25. Res accepted; required Fri, Sat. Italian menu. Semi-a la carte: lunch $8.95-$10.95. A la carte entrees: dinner $15.95-$25. Specialties: veal scaloppini, linguine with Maine lobster, lamb chops sauteed with herbs and mustard. Own pastries. Valet parking (dinner). Italian marble, original paintings, chandelier. Cr cds: A, C, D, MC, V.

★ ★ **VAGABOND.** 7315 Wisconsin Ave. 301/654-2575. Hrs: 11:30 am-2:30 pm, 5:30-10 pm, Fri to 10:30 pm; Sat 6-10:30 pm. Closed Sun. Central European menu. Res accepted. Bar. Semi-a la carte: lunch $6.95-$9.95, dinner $9.95-$19.95. Specializes in Romanian, Austro-Hungarian & Russian dishes. Strolling musicians Fri, Sat. Parking. Old World atmosphere. Cr cds: A, C, D, DS, MC, V.

Unrated Dining Spot

BETHESDA CRAB HOUSE. 4958 Bethesda Ave. 301/652-3382. Hrs: 9 am-midnight. Closed Dec 25. Res accepted. Wine, beer. A la carte entrees: lunch, dinner $10-$30. Serves only spiced shrimp, steamed crab, crabcakes. Outdoor dining. Rustic decor; established 1961. No cr cds accepted.

Boonsboro (Washington County) (B-5)

Settled: 1787 **Pop:** 2,445 **Elev:** 591 ft **Area code:** 301 **Zip:** 21713

What to See and Do

1. **Crystal Grottoes Caverns.** 1 mi SW on MD 34. Limestone caverns may be viewed from walkways. Picnicking. Guided tours (Mar-Oct, daily; rest of yr by appt). Phone 432-6336. ¢¢¢
2. **Washington Monument State Park.** 3 mi SE off US 40A. 147 acres. A 34-foot tower of native stone (1827) was first completed monument to honor George Washington. Views of nearby battlefields, two states (PA & WV). History Center displays firearms and Civil War mementos (by appt). The Appalachian Trail leads through the park; hiking and picnicking. Park schedule varies, phone ahead; 791-4767. **Free.**
3. **Gathland State Park.** 8 mi S off MD 67, then 1 mi E, W of Burkittsville off MD 17. 140 acres. A site once owned by George Townsend, Civil War reporter. Monument built in 1896 to honor Civil War correspondents. Visitor center contains original papers. Picnicking. Walking tour. Winter sports. Park schedule varies, phone ahead; 791-4767.
4. **Antietam National Battlefield** (see). 8 mi SW on MD 34.

(For further information contact the Washington County Tourism Office, 1826 Dual Hwy, Hagerstown 21740; 791-3130; 24-hr recording 797-8800.)

(For accommodations see Frederick, Hagerstown)

Bowie (C-7)

Pop: 37,589 **Elev:** 150 ft **Area code:** 301

What to See and Do

Marietta Manor. 3 mi W in Glenn Dale, at 5626 Bell Station Rd. A modest Federal-style plantation house built by Gabriel Duvall, an associate justice of the US Supreme Court (1811-1835). Tours. (Mar-Dec, Sun afternoons; also by appt) Sr citizen rate. Phone 464-5291. ¢

(For further information contact the Bowie Chamber of Commerce, 6770 Race Track Rd, Hilltop Plaza, 20715; 262-0920. Information is also available from Prince George's Conference & Visitors Bureau, 9475 Lottsford Rd, #130, Landover 20785; 925-8300.)

Annual Event

Heritage Day. Belair Mansion. Performance by Congress's Own Regiment; tour of stables and grounds; battle reenactments; demonstrations of colonial crafts. Phone 262-6200. 3rd Sun May.

(For accommodations see College Park, Silver Spring; also see District of Columbia)

Cambridge (D-8)

Founded: 1684 **Pop:** 11,514 **Elev:** 14 ft **Area code:** 410 **Zip:** 21613

On the Eastern Shore, Cambridge is Maryland's second largest deepwater port. Boating and fishing opportunities are found in the Choptank and Honga rivers and Chesapeake, Tar and Fishing bays.

What to See and Do

1. **Old Trinity Church, Dorchester Parish** (ca 1675). 8 mi SW on MD 16 in Church Creek. One of the oldest churches in US still holding regular services; faithful restoration of interior. (Daily exc Tues) Phone 228-2940. **Free.**
2. **Blackwater National Wildlife Refuge.** 12 mi S via MD 16, 335. Approx 20,000 acres of rich tidal marsh, freshwater ponds and woodlands. One of the chief wintering areas for Canada geese and ducks using the Atlantic Flyway; in fall, as many as 33,000 geese and 17,000 ducks swell the bird population. Also a haven for the bald eagle, the Delmarva fox squirrel and the peregrine falcon, all three of which are endangered species. Scenic drive, woodland trails, observation tower. Visitor center (Sept-May, daily; rest of yr, Mon-Fri; closed hols & Labor Day wkend). Golden Age, Golden Eagle and Golden Access Passports (see INTRODUCTION). Phone 228-2677. Per vehicle ¢¢; Per hiker or cyclist ¢
3. **Spocott Windmill.** 7 mi W via MD 343. Reproduction of working post gristmill built on original site. Also colonial miller's house and restored 19th-century schoolhouse. Grounds and buildings (daily). Phone 228-7090. **Free.**

(For further information contact the Cambridge-Dorchester Chamber of Commerce, 203 Sunburst Hwy; 228-3575.)

Annual Events

National Outdoor Show. Goose & duck calling, log sawing, trap setting contests; entertainment. Last wkend Feb.

Antique Aircraft Fly-in. Dorchester Heritage Museum, 5 mi W on MD 343 at 1904 Horne Point Rd. Old and new planes on display. Phone 228-5530 or -1899. Sat & Sun, 3rd wkend May.

(For accommodations see Easton, Salisbury)

Chesapeake Bay Bridge Area (C-7)

The majestic twin spans of the Chesapeake Bay Bridge carry visitors to the Eastern Shore, a patchwork of small picturesque towns, lighthouses and fishing villages tucked away from the city. Scenic rivers and bays, wildlife, gardens and wildflowers fill the countryside. The main attractions of any visit, however, are the many fine inns and the restaurants specializing in local seafood.

What to See and Do

Wye Oak State Park. E on US 50 to Wye Mills. Official state tree of Maryland is in this 29-acre park; it is the largest white oak in the US (108 feet high, 28 feet around) and believed to be over 400 years old; a new tree has been started from an acorn. A restored 18th-century one-room schoolhouse and the Old Wye Mill (late 1600s) are nearby. Phone 410/479-1619.

Motels

(Distances given are from E end of Chesapeake Bay Bridge)

✔ ★ **CHESAPEAKE FRIENDSHIP INN.** *(Rte 1, Box 145, Grasonville 21638) 8 mi E on US 50, 301.* 410/827-7272; res: 800/822-7272. 42 rms. S, D $34.95-$69.95; each addl $8; under 15 free. Crib free. Pet accepted; $5. TV; cable. Ck-out 11 am. Cr cds: A, DS, MC, V.

★ **COMFORT INN.** *(3101 Main St, Grasonville 21638) E via US 50, 1st right after Kent Narrows Bridge (exit 42).* 410/827-6767; FAX 410/827-8626. 86 units, 4 story, 9 kit. suites. Apr-Nov: S $76-$95; D $86-$140; each addl $8; kit. suites $125-$155; under 18 free; higher rates special events; lower rates rest of yr. Crib $6. TV; cable. Indoor pool. Complimentary continental bkfst. Complimentary coffee in rms. Restaurant nearby. Ck-out 11 am. Coin lndry. Meeting rms. Valet serv. Sundries. Exercise equipt; weight machines, bicycles, whirlpool, sauna. Refrigerators. On Chesapeake Bay. Cr cds: A, C, D, DS, JCB, MC, V.

Inns

★ ★ **IMPERIAL.** *(208 High St, Chestertown 21620) US 301 to Chestertown exit.* 410/778-5000. 13 rms, 3 story. S, D $125; suites $200-$250; lower rates wkdays. Crib free. TV; cable. Continental bkfst. Dining rm 5:30-9 pm, wkend hrs may vary; closed Mon. Ck-out 11 am, ck-in 3 pm. Meeting rms. Refrigerator in suites. Built 1903. Victorian furnishings. Cr cds: DS, MC, V.

★ **INN AT MITCHELL HOUSE.** *(8796 Maryland Pkwy, Chestertown 21620) US 50/301, continue N on US 301, then N on MD 213 to Chestertown, then left on MD 291W, right on MD 20S, then right on MD 21S.* 410/778-6500. 5 rms, 3 story. No rm phones. S $70-$95; D $75-$100; each addl $5; under 5 free. TV in sitting rm. Complimentary full bkfst, coffee. Dinner avail Fri & Sat. Ck-out noon, ck-in 3 pm. Free marina transportation. Tennis privileges. Lawn games. Fireplaces. Picnic tables, grills. Manor house (1743). Antiques; sitting rms. Cr cds: DS, MC, V.

★ ★ **KENT MANOR.** *(500 Kent Manor Dr, Kent Island 21666)* 1/2 mi E on US 50/301, then S off MD 8. 410/643-5757; FAX 410/643-8315. 24 units, 3 story. No elvtr. S $79; D $109-$139. Children over 8 yrs only. TV. Pool. Complimentary continental bkfst. Restaurant 11:30

am-9:30 pm. Rm serv. Ck-out 11 am, ck-in 3 pm. Local airport transportation. Lawn games. Balconies. Former working estate. Original section built 1820, main section 1864; Victorian antique reproductions, original Italian marble fireplaces, four-poster beds. On 226 acres with 1¹/₂ mi of waterfront along Eastern Bay inlet; walking trails. Cr cds: A, D, DS, MC, V.

D ≈ 🐾 SC

★ ★ **WHITE SWAN TAVERN.** *(231 High St, Chestertown 21620) US 301 to Chestertown exit.* *410/778-2300.* 6 units, 2¹/₂ story, 2 suites. No rm phones. S, D $100-$130; suites $140-$150; under 3 free. Crib free. TV in sitting rm. Complimentary continental bkfst. Complimentary coffee in rms. Restaurant nearby. Ck-out noon, ck-in 3 pm. Game rm. Former house and tavern built 1733 and 1793; restored with antique furnishings, museum. No cr cds accepted.

Restaurants

★ **FISHERMAN'S INN & CRAB DECK.** *(US 50/301, Kent Narrows) E over bridge to exit 42, turn right and continue to end of road.* *410/827-8807.* Hrs: 11 am-10 pm. Closed Dec 24 & 25. Bar. Semi-a la carte: lunch $4.95-$7.95, dinner $6.95-$24.95. Specializes in fresh seafood. Parking. 2 dining areas; fireplace; display of antique oyster plates. Scenic view of the Kent Narrows of the Eastern Bay. Family-owned. Cr cds: A, DS, MC, V.

D

★ **HARRIS CRAB HOUSE.** *(433 Kent Narrows Way N, Grasonville) 4 mi E via US 50/301.* *410/827-9500.* Hrs: 11 am-10 pm; Fri & Sat to 11 pm. Closed Jan 1, Dec 25. Bar. Semi-a la carte: lunch, dinner $6-$21.95. Child's meals. Specializes in fresh seafood, barbecued ribs & chicken, steamed crabs. Parking. Outdoor dining. On waterfront; dockage. Cr cds: MC, V.

D

★ ★ **IRONSTONE CAFE.** *(236 Cannon St, Chestertown) NE on US 301, N on MD 213 to Chestertown, left at 1st light to High St, continue to Cannon St.* *410/778-0188.* Hrs: 11:30 am-2 pm, 5:30-8 pm; wkends to 9 pm. Closed Sun, Mon; some major hols; also mid-Feb-mid-Mar. Res accepted. Serv bar. Semi-a la carte: lunch $4-$7, dinner $14-$19. Child's meals. Specializes in Maryland crabcake, seasonal dishes. Located in the historic district, near the Chester River. Cr cds: MC, V.

D

★ ★ **NARROWS.** *(3023 Kent Narrows Way S, Grasonville) 4 mi E via US 50/301.* *410/827-8113.* Hrs: 11 am-9 pm; summer to 10 pm; Sun brunch to 2 pm. Closed Jan 1, Dec 24, 25. Res accepted. Regional Eastern Shore menu. Bar. Wine list. Semi-a la carte: lunch $6-$12, dinner $9.75-$19.75. Sun brunch $9.75. Child's meals. Specializes in seafood, traditional Maryland recipes. Parking. Outdoor waterfront dining. View of the Narrows. Cr cds: C, D, MC, V.

D

★ ★ **OLD WHARF INN.** *(Box 637, Chestertown 21620) US 50 to Chestertown exit, on Chester River.* *410/778-3566.* Hrs: 11 am-9 pm; Fri, Sat to 10 pm; Sun brunch 10 am-3 pm. Closed Dec 25. Bar; Sun from noon. Semi-a la carte: lunch $3-$8, dinner $6.25-$29.95. Sun brunch $2.50-$12.25. Child's meals. Specializes in steak, prime rib, fresh seafood. Salad bar. Parking. View of river. Cr cds: MC, V.

✔ ★ **WATERMAN'S CRAB HOUSE.** *(Sharp St Wharf, Rock Hall) US 301 to MD 213, N to MD 20 to Rock Hall.* *410/639-2261.* Hrs: 11 am-9 pm; Fri & Sat to 10 pm. Closed some major hols. Bar. Semi-a la carte: lunch, dinner $8.99-$16.95. Child's meals. Specializes in seafood, steamed crabs, barbecued ribs. Parking. Outdoor dining. On Rock Hall Harbor. Cr cds: MC, V.

D

Chesapeake and Ohio Canal National Historical Park (A-2 - C-6)

As early as 1754, the enterprising George Washington, only in his twenties, proposed a system of navigation along the Potomac River valley. His Potowmack Canal Company, organized in 1785, cleared obstructions and built skirting canals to facilitate the transportation of goods from settlements beyond the Allegheny Mountains to the lower Potomac River towns.

The eventual inadequacy of these improvements and the renowned success of the Erie Canal spurred the formation in 1828 of the Chesapeake and Ohio Canal Company, whose purpose was to connect Georgetown with the Ohio Valley by river and canal. On July 4, 1828, President John Quincy Adams led the traditional groundbreaking ceremony declaring, "To subdue the earth is preeminently the purpose of this undertaking." Unfortunately, the earth was not easily subdued. President Adams bent his shovel after several attempts before breaking into an energetic frenzy and successfully getting a shovelful of dirt.

The difficulty of the groundbreaking ceremony foreshadowed the canal's short-lived future as a major transportation artery. Completed in 1850 as far as Cumberland, MD (184¹/₂ miles from Georgetown), the waterway was used extensively for the transportation of coal, flour, grain and lumber. Financial and legal difficulties, the decline of commerce after the Civil War, the Baltimore and Ohio Railroad and the advent of improved roads cut deeply into the commerce of the waterway, and it gradually faded into obsolescence. The canal still had limited commercial use as late as 1924, when a flood destroyed many of the canal locks and nothing was restored.

The unfortunate demise of the C & O Canal is now a blessing for hikers, canoeists and bikers, who can find access to the towpath along the banks of the waterway. Remaining as one of the least altered of old American canals, the Chesapeake and Ohio is flanked by ample foliage throughout most of its 20,239 acres.

Many points of interest can be seen along the waterway. Exhibits are offered in Cumberland and Hancock and at a museum near the Great Falls of the Potomac. At the Great Falls there are interpretive programs, including a mule-drawn canal boat, self-guiding trails, picnic facilities and a working lock. At Lock 3 in Georgetown there is also a mule-drawn canal boat (adjacent to the Foundry Mall between 30th and Thomas Jefferson Streets, phone 202/472-4376). Although the canal is predominately dry, the towpath extends the entire length and many locks, lockhouses and aqueducts are still intact and extensive improvements have been made. Camping for hikers and bikers is available throughout the park.

For information about the canal contact the Chief of Visitor Services, C & O Canal National Historical Park, PO Box 4, Sharpsburg, MD 21782; 301/739-4200. Visitor centers are located in Cumberland, Great Falls and Hancock.

Cockeysville (B-7)

Pop: 18,668 **Elev:** 260 ft **Area code:** 410 **Zip:** 21030

What to See and Do

Ladew Topiary Gardens. 3535 Jarrettsville Pike, 5 mi E on MD 143 to Sunnybrook, then 6 mi N on MD 146. Extensive topiary gardens on 22 acres; 15 flower gardens. Also here is the Manor House (fee), with English antiques, fox-hunting memorabilia, paintings, unusual china, reconstructed Elizabethan room; Oval Library housing more than 3,000 volumes; carriage museum; cafe; gift shop. (Mid-Apr-Oct, daily exc Mon) Sr citizen rate. Phone 557-9466. Gardens ¢¢; Combination gardens & house ¢¢¢

(For further information contact the Baltimore County Chamber of Commerce, 102 W Pennsylvania Ave, Ste 402, Towson 21204; 825-6200.)

Annual Event

Point-to-point Steeplechase. 3 well-known meets on consecutive wkends: **My Lady's Manor.** In Monkton. Mid-Apr. **Grand National.** In Butler; phone 666-7777. Mid-Apr. **Maryland Hunt Cup.** In Glyndon; phone 666-7777. Late Apr.

(For accommodations see Baltimore, Towson)

Restaurants

★ ★ ★ **THE MILTON INN.** (14833 York Rd, Sparks 14833) 5 mi N on MD 45. 410/771-4366. Hrs: 11:30 am-2:30 pm, 5:30-9:30 pm; Sat from 5:30 pm; Sun 5-8 pm. Closed some major hols. Res accepted. Bar. Wine cellar. Semi-a la carte: lunch $10-$15, dinner $18.50-$25. Child's meals. Specializes in seasonal dishes, fresh seafood, poultry. Parking. Outdoor dining. Main part of building ca 1820; one section was stagecoach stop ca 1740. Colonial Williamsburg-style decor. Jacket (dinner). Cr cds: A, D, DS, MC, V.

[D]

★ ★ **YORK INN.** 10010 York Rd. 410/666-0006. Hrs: 11-2 am; Sun brunch 9 am-2 pm. Closed Memorial Day, Dec 25. Res accepted; required major hols. Continental menu. Bar to 2 am. Semi-a la carte: lunch $6.95-$10.95, dinner $11.95-$25.95. Sun brunch $11.95. Child's meals. Specializes in seafood, steak. Parking. Casual dining. Cr cds: A, C, D, DS, MC, V.

College Park (C-6)

Pop: 21,927 **Elev:** 190 ft **Area code:** 301 **Zip:** 20740

What to See and Do

1. **University of Maryland** (1865). (35,000 students) Tawes Fine Arts Theater has plays, musicals, concerts, dance, opera and music festivals. Tours. For information phone 405-1000.

2. **Greenbelt Park.** 6565 Greenbelt Rd, E off Kenilworth Ave, MD 201 exit 23. A 1,300-acre wooded park operated by the National Park Service. Nature trails. Picnicking. Camping (dump station; 7-day limit Memorial Day-Labor Day; 14-day limit rest of yr). Self-registration, first come, first served. Standard fees. Phone 344-3948.

3. **NASA/Goddard Visitor Center.** SE on I-95 to Baltimore-Washington Pkwy, exit 22-A Greenbelt, then follow signs. Satellites, rockets, capsules and exhibits in all phases of space research. (Daily) For tour information phone 286-8981. **Free.**

4. **College Park Airport Museum.** 6709 Corporal Frank Scott Dr. World's oldest operating airport, started by Wilbur Wright in 1909 to train 2 military officers in the operation of aircraft. First airplane machine gun and radio-navigational aids tested here; first air mail and controlled helicopter flights. Museum (Wed-Sun; closed major hols). Phone 864-1530 (recording). **Free.**

(For further information contact the Prince George's Conference & Visitors Bureau, 9475 Lottsford Rd, #130, Landover 20785; 925-8300.)

(See Bowie, Silver Spring; also see District of Columbia)

Motels

★ ★ ★ **COURTYARD BY MARRIOTT.** (8330 Corporate Dr, Landover 20785) 1/2 mi W of I-95 exit 19B, on US 50. 301/577-3373; FAX 301/577-1780. 150 rms, 3-4 story. S $92; D $102; each addl (over 4 persons) $10; suites $105-$115; under 12 free; wkly, wkend rates. Crib free. TV; cable. Indoor pool; lifeguard. Restaurant 6:30 am-2 pm, 5-10 pm. Bar. Ck-out 1 pm. Coin lndry. Meeting rms. Valet serv. Exercise equipt; weights, bicycles, whirlpool. Many private patios, balconies. Cr cds: A, C, D, DS, MC, V.

[D] [≈] [✕] [⤵] [🔥] [SC]

✔ ★ ★ **RAMADA INN-CALVERTON.** (4050 Powder Mill Rd, Beltsville 20705) Off I-95 exit 29B at MD 212. 301/572-7100; FAX 301/572-8078. 168 rms in 2 bldgs, 1-4 story, 11 kits. S $68-$79; D $75-$80; kit. units $75-$85; under 18 free; wkend plan. Crib free. Pet accepted. TV; cable. Pool; wading pool, poolside serv, lifeguard. Playground. Restaurant 6 am-11 pm; Sat from 7 am; Sun 7-11:30 am, 5-10 pm. Rm serv. Bar 11-2 am; Sun from noon. Ck-out 11 am. Meeting rms. Gift shop. Exercise equipt; weight machine, bicycles. Cr cds: A, C, D, DS, ER, JCB, MC, V.

[D] [✋] [≈] [✕] [⤵] [🔥] [SC]

Hotels

★ ★ **HOLIDAY INN.** 10000 Baltimore Blvd. 301/345-6700; FAX 301/441-4923. 222 rms in 2 bldgs, 4 story. S, D $74-$84; each addl $6; under 18 free. Crib free. Pet accepted, some restrictions; $50 refundable. TV; cable. Indoor pool; poolside serv, lifeguard. Restaurant 6:30 am-10 pm. Bar 11-2 am. Ck-out noon. Coin lndry. Meeting rms. Gift shop. Exercise equipt; weights, bicycles, whirlpool, sauna. Refrigerators avail. Cr cds: A, C, D, DS, ER, JCB, MC, V.

[D] [✋] [≈] [✕] [⤵] [🔥] [SC]

✔ ★ ★ **HOLIDAY INN-CALVERTON.** (4095 Powder Mill Rd, Beltsville 20705) I-95 exit 29B. 301/937-4422; FAX 301/937-4455. 206 rms, 9 story. S, D $70-$85; each $6; suites $150-$175; under 18 free; wkly, wkend rates; higher rates Cherry Blossom. Crib free. TV; cable. Pool; lifeguard. Complimentary coffee in rms. Restaurant 6:30 am-11:30 pm; wkends from 7 am. No rm serv 2-5 pm. Bar. Ck-out noon. Coin lndry. Meeting rms. Gift shop. 18-hole golf privileges. Game rm. Cr cds: A, C, D, DS, JCB, MC, V.

[D] [🎿] [≈] [⤵] [🔥] [SC]

★ ★ ★ **MARRIOTT GREENBELT.** (6400 Ivy Lane, Greenbelt 20770) 2 blks N of I-95 exit 23 (Kenilworth Ave N). 301/441-3700; FAX 301/474-9128. 283 rms, 18 story. S $80-$117; D $80-$127; family, wkend rates. Crib free. Pet accepted. TV; cable. 2 pools, 1 indoor; poolside serv, lifeguard. Restaurant 6:30 am-10:30 pm. Bar. Games. Ck-out noon. Convention facilities. Gift shop. Lighted tennis. Exercise equipt; weights, bicycles, whirlpool, sauna. Some bathrm phones, refrigerators. Elegantly appointed rms. *LUXURY LEVEL :* CONCIERGE FLOORS. 52 rms, 3 floors. S $114; D $129; suites $250-$350. Private lounge. Some wet bars. Complimentary continental bkfst, newspaper, refreshments. Cr cds: A, C, D, DS, ER, JCB, MC, V.

[D] [✋] [✕] [≈] [✕] [⤵] [🔥] [SC]

Restaurants

✔ ★ **ALAMO.** (5508 Kenilworth Ave, Riverdale) S on US 201; 3 mi S of I-95 exit 23. 301/927-8787. Hrs: 11 am-11 pm. Closed Thanksgiving. Res accepted. Mexican menu. Bar. Semi-a la carte: lunch $5-$7, dinner $8.30-$12.95. Child's meals. Specializes in tostadas, tacos, enchiladas. Entertainment Tues-Sat. Parking. Mexican decor. Cr cds: A, C, D, MC, V.

★ ★ ★ **CHEF'S SECRET.** (5810 Greenbelt Rd, Greenbelt) 301/345-6101. Hrs: 11:30 am-2:30 pm, 5-10 pm; Sat from 4:30 pm;

Sun 4:30-9 pm. Closed Thanksgiving, Dec 25; also Sun in July-Aug. Res accepted. Continental menu. Serv bar. Semi-a la carte: lunch $5.95-$12.95, dinner $9.95-$24.95. Specializes in seafood, veal, steak. Own desserts. Cr cds: A, C, D, MC, V.

Columbia (C-6)

Pop: 75,883 **Elev:** 402 ft **Area code:** 410

A planned city built on a tract of land larger than Manhattan Island, Columbia is comprised of nine villages surrounding a central downtown service area. Construction of the city began in 1966.

(For information about this area contact the Howard County Tourism Council, PO Box 9, Ellicott City 21041; 410/313-1900 or 800/288-TRIP.)

(See Baltimore)

Hotels

★ ★ **COLUMBIA INN HOTEL AND CONFERENCE CENTER.** *10207 Wincopin Circle (21044), opp Columbia Mall.* 410/730-3900; res: 800/638-2817; FAX 410/730-1290. 289 rms, 3-10 story. S $115-$130; D $130-$145; each addl $15; suites $225-$375; under 12 free; wkend plan. Crib free. Pet accepted, some restrictions; $75 refundable. TV; cable, in-room movies. Pool; poolside serv (in season), lifeguard. Restaurant 6:30 am-2:30 pm, 6-10:30 pm. Bar 4 pm-2 am. Ck-out noon. Lndry facilities. Meeting rms. Gift shop. Airport transportation. Tennis privileges. 18-hole golf privileges, greens fee $15.50-$18. Health club privileges. Some bathrm phones. Overlooks Lake Kittamaqundi; boat rides, entertainment on lake (summer). Cr cds: A, C, D, DS, MC, V.

★ ★ **HILTON.** *5485 Twin Knolls Rd (21045), at jct US 29 & MD 175.* 410/997-1060; FAX 410/997-0169. 152 rms. S, studio rms $91-$115; D $106-$130; under 18 free; suites $175-$250; wkend plans. Crib free. TV; cable. Indoor pool. Restaurant 6:30 am-11 pm. Rm serv. Bar noon-midnight, Fri & Sat to 1 am. Ck-out 11 am. Meeting rms. Golf privileges. Exercise equipt; weights, bicycle, whirlpool, sauna. Cr cds: A, C, D, DS, ER, MC, V.

Restaurants

✔ ★ ★ **CHINA CHEFS.** *10801 Hickory Ridge Rd.* 410/730-1200. Hrs: 11 am-11 pm. Res accepted. Chinese menu. Serv bar. Semi-a la carte: lunch $5-$9, dinner $7-$14.95. Specializes in Szechwan dishes. Parking. Cr cds: A, MC, V.

★ ★ ★ **KING'S CONTRIVANCE.** *10150 Shaker Dr, 2¹/₂ mi S on US 29, left on Seneca Dr, right on Shaker Dr.* 410/995-0500. Hrs: 11:30 am-2 pm, 5-9 pm; Fri to 9:30 pm; Sat 5-9:30 pm; Sun 4-8 pm. Res accepted; required Dec. Bar. Wine cellar. Semi-a la carte: lunch $7-$14, dinner $13-$22. Specializes in fresh seafood, rack of lamb. Own baking. Parking. Enclosed porch dining. Mansion built 1900s. Cr cds: A, DS, MC, V.

Crisfield (F-9)

Pop: 2,880 **Elev:** 4 ft **Area code:** 410 **Zip:** 21817

What to See and Do

1. **Tyler's Cruises.** Sommers Cove Marina. The *Betty Jo Tyler* and the *Capt Tyler II* make approx one-hour cruises to Smith Island. Bus tour of the two villages comprising the island, with spare time to visit the rest of the island; lunch avail (fee). Tour length approx 4¹/₂ hours. (Memorial Day wkend-Oct) Phone 425-2771. ¢¢¢¢¢

2. **Janes Island State Park.** Approx 2 mi NE via MD 413, then 1¹/₂ mi N on MD 358. These 3,147 acres are nearly surrounded by Chesapeake Bay and its inlets. Swimming; fishing; boat ramp (rentals). Cabins. Camping. Standard fees. Phone 968-1565.

(For further information contact the Crisfield Area Chamber of Commerce, PO Box 292; 968-2500.)

Annual Event

National Hard Crab Derby & Fair. Cooking, crab picking, boat docking contests; crab racing; fireworks and parade. Phone 968-2682. Fri-Sun, Labor Day wkend.

(See Pocomoke City)

Motels

✔ ★ **PADDLEWHEEL.** *701 W Main St.* 410/968-2220. 19 rms, 2 story. June-Aug: D $38-$65; each addl $5; under 12 free; wkly rates; higher rates special events; lower rates rest of yr. TV; cable. Restaurant nearby. Ck-out 11 am. Some refrigerators. Near marina. Cr cds: MC, V.

★ ★ **PINES.** *Box 106, N Somerset Ave, 3 blks E of MD 413.* 410/968-0900. 40 rms. July-Aug: S $43-$55; D $55-$70; each addl $5; kit. units $15 addl; under 11 free; higher rates: July 4, Labor Day, special events; lower rates rest of yr. TV; cable. Pool. Restaurant nearby. Ck-out 11 am. Picnic area. In scenic, wooded section. No cr cds accepted.

Cumberland (A-2)

Settled: 1750 **Pop:** 23,706 **Elev:** 688 ft **Area code:** 301 **Zip:** 21502

Far to the west in the state, Cumberland is nestled between Pennsylvania and West Virginia. The Potomac River and its tributary, Wills Creek, flow peaceably by this onetime western outpost of the colonies.

British General Edward Braddock was sent here to conquer the French and Indians in 1755; unprepared for the wilderness, he met with defeat and death. George Washington, who defended the town in that period, felt the main east-west route would pass through Cumberland eventually. In 1833 the National Road (US 40 Alternate) made the town a supply terminus for overland commerce. The road was extended farther west, the B & O Railroad reached here in 1842, and eight years later came the Chesapeake and Ohio Canal (see CHESAPEAKE AND OHIO CANAL NATIONAL HISTORICAL PARK), bringing prosperous business. Today's economy no longer depends on industry alone but includes services and recreational facilities.

What to See and Do

1. **George Washington's Headquarters** (ca 1755). In Riverside Park, downtown, on Greene St. His first military headquarters. Taped narration. **Free.**

2. **Fort Cumberland Trail.** Walking trail covers several city blocks downtown around the site of Ft Cumberland. Includes boundary markers, audio units, narrative plaques.

3. **Western Maryland Station Center.** Canal St. 1913 railroad station houses industrial and transportation museum; art gallery; C & O Canal National Historical Park Visitors Center. (Daily exc Mon; closed Good Friday & most major hols) Phone 777-2787. **Free.** This is also the departure point for

   Western Maryland Scenic Railroad. Excursion train makes scenic trip 17 mi to Frostburg and back. (May-Sept, Wed-Sun; Oct, daily exc Mon; Apr & Nov, wkends) For schedule and fees phone 800/TRAIN-50.

4. **History House** (ca 1865). 218 Washington St, in Victorian Historic District. Restored 18-room Victorian house with nine period rooms; medical instruments, costumes; research room. (May-Oct, daily exc Mon; rest of yr, Tues-Sat) Phone 777-8678. **¢¢**

5. **Old Toll Gate House** (1836). Approx 6 mi W on US 40A, in La Vale. Built to collect tolls from users of Cumberland Road (National Road); only remaining toll house in state; restored. (June-Aug, Fri-Sun; May & Sept-Oct, Sun; schedule may vary, phone ahead) Phone 777-5905. **¢**

6. **The Narrows.** Picturesque 1,000-foot gap through Alleghenies (US 40A) used by pioneers on their way to the West.

7. **Rocky Gap State Park.** 6 mi E on I-68, exit 50. Mountain scenery around 243-acre lake with three swimming beaches. Swimming; fishing; boating (electric motors only; rentals). Nature, hiking trails. Picnicking, cafe. Improved camping (res accepted 1 yr in advance). Winter activities. Standard fees. (See ANNUAL EVENTS) Phone 777-2138 or -2139. Per person **¢**

8. **Dans Mountain State Park.** 10 mi W on I-68, then 8 mi S on MD 36, 2 mi SE of Lonaconing. 481 acres. Nearby Dans Rock affords a panoramic view of surrounding region from a height of 2,898 feet. Swimming pool (fee); fishing. Picnicking. Playground. Hiking. Sledding. Schedule varies, phone ahead; 463-5564 or 777-2139.

9. **Green Ridge State Forest.** 21 mi E off I-68 at exit 64. These 38,811 acres of forest land stretch across mountains of Western Maryland and occupy portions of Town Hill, Polish Mt and Green Ridge Mt. Abundant wildlife. Fishing. Boat launch; canoeing. Hiking trails. Picnicking. Camping. Winter sports. C & O Canal runs through here into 3,118-foot Paw-Paw Tunnel. Phone 777-2345.

(For further information and a brochure for a self-guided walking tour of Cumberland's Historic District, contact Allegany County Visitors Bureau, Mechanic & Harrison Sts; 777-5905.)

Annual Events

Agricultural Expo & Fair. Allegany County Fairgrounds. Poultry, livestock, carnival, entertainment. Phone 777-1888. Mid-July.

C & O Canal Boat Festival. 5 mi S via MD 51, at North Branch C & O Canal Park. Arts and crafts, reenactments of frontier and Civil War life, carriage rides; tours of canal boat replica; country music. Phone 729-3136. 2nd wkend July.

Rocky Gap Music Festival. Rocky Gap State Park (see #7). Features bluegrass and country music; children's activities, crafts, workshops. Phone 724-2511. Fri-Sun, 1st wkend Aug.

Street Rod Roundup. 6 mi S on MD 220, at fairgrounds. Hundreds of pre-1950 hot-rods on display and in competitions. Phone 724-6368. Labor Day wkend.

Motels

★ ★ ★ **BEST WESTERN BRADDOCK MOTOR INN.** *(1268 National Hwy, La Vale)* 6 mi W on US 40, at jct MD 53; I-68 exit 39 or 40. 301/729-3300; FAX 301/729-3300, ext. 602. 108 rms, 1-2 story. S $42-$50; D $48-$60; each addl $6; suites $75-$95; under 18 free. TV; cable. Indoor pool; poolside serv. Restaurant 7 am-9 pm. Rm serv. Bar 4:30 pm-midnight; Fri & Sat to 1 am; closed Sun. Ck-out 11 am. Meeting rm. Sundries. Airport transportation. Exercise rm; instructor, weights, bicycles, whirlpool, sauna. Game rm. Cr cds: A, C, D, DS, MC, V.

✔ ★ **SUPER 8.** *(1301 National Hwy, La Vale)* I-68 exit 39. 301/729-6265; FAX 301/729-6265, ext. 400. 63 rms, 3 story. S $38.88; D $44.88; each addl $5; suites $39.88-$45.88; under 12 free. Crib free. TV; cable. Restaurant opp open 24 hrs. Ck-out 11 am. Meeting rms. Cr cds: A, C, D, DS, JCB, MC, V.

Motor Hotel

★ ★ **HOLIDAY INN.** 100 S George St, I-68 exit downtown. 301/724-8800; FAX 301/724-4001. 130 rms, 6 story. S $64-$68; D $70-$78; each addl $6; under 18 free; wkend plan. Crib free. Pet accepted. TV; cable. Pool; lifeguard. Restaurant 6:30 am-2 pm, 5-10 pm; Sun from 7 am. Rm serv. Bar noon-2 am; Sun from 1 pm; entertainment, dancing Fri, Sat. Ck-out noon. Meeting rms. Sundries. Cr cds: A, C, D, DS, JCB, MC, V.

Inn

★ ★ **INN AT WALNUT BOTTOM.** 120 Green St, I-68 exit 43A, left at light. 301/777-0003; res: 800/286-9718. 12 rms, 7 with bath, 5 share bath, 2 story, 2 suites. S, D $65-$95; each addl $10; suites $95-$120. Crib avail. TV. Complimentary full bkfst. Dining rm 7 am-10 pm. Ck-out 11 am, ck-in 3 pm. Two buildings (1820, 1890). Rms furnished with antiques, period reproductions. Totally nonsmoking. Cr cds: A, DS, MC, V.

Restaurants

★ ★ ★ **AU PETIT PARIS.** *(86 E Main St, Frostburg)* Exit 34 off I-68. 301/689-8946. Hrs: 6-9:30 pm. Closed Sun, Mon; major hols. Res accepted. French menu. Bar 5:30 pm-midnight. Extensive wine list. Semi-a la carte: dinner $10.50-$28.95. Child's meals. Specializes in fresh seafood, coq au vin, Dover sole. Tableside preparation. Cr cds: A, C, D, DS, MC, V.

✔ ★ ★ **FRED WARNER'S GERMAN RESTAURANT.** *(Box 5536, Cresaptown)* US 220S, off I-68. 301/729-2361. Hrs: 11:30 am-9 pm; Fri, Sat to 10 pm; Sun noon-7 pm. Closed Mon; Jan 1, July 4, Dec 25. German, Amer menu. Bar. Semi-a la carte: lunch $3-$7.45, dinner $5.95-$13.95. Child's meals. Specialties: sauerbraten, bratwurst, bienenstich. Parking. Outdoor dining. Old World Bavarian atmosphere; costumed waitresses. Family-owned. Cr cds: A, MC, V.

 ★ **PEKING PALACE.** *(1209 National Hwy, La Vale)* 6 mi W on US 40. 301/729-1400. Hrs: 11:30 am-10 pm. Chinese menu. Serv bar. Semi-a la carte: lunch $4-$5, dinner $5.50-$14.95. Specialties: Peking duck, jade shrimp. Parking. Mandarin decor. Cr cds: A, DS, MC, V.

Easton (D-8)

Settled: 1682 **Pop:** 9,372 **Elev:** 28 ft **Area code:** 410 **Zip:** 21601

What to See and Do

1. **Third Haven Friends Meeting House** (1682-84). 405 S Washington St. One of the oldest frame-construction houses of worship in US. (Daily) Phone 822-0293.   **Free.**
2. **Historical Society of Talbot County.** 25 S Washington St. A 3-gallery museum in a renovated early commercial building; changing exhibits, museum shop. Historic houses: 1810 Federal town house, 1700s Quaker cabinetmaker's cottage, period gardens; tours. (Daily exc Mon) Phone 822-0773. Museum ¢; Houses ¢
3. **Tuckahoe State Park.** 5 mi N of Queen Anne, off MD 404. A 60-acre lake and Tuckahoe Creek provide a secluded atmosphere in this 3,498-acre park. The Adkins Arboretum, 500 acres, propagates trees, plants and shrubs indigenous to Maryland. Fishing; hunting; boating. Hiking. Picnicking. Standard fees. For schedule phone 634-2810.

(For further information contact the Talbot County Chamber of Commerce, PO Box 1366; 822-4606.)

Annual Events

Tuckahoe Steam & Gas Show and Reunion. 5 mi N via US 50, opp Woodlawn Memorial Park. Old steam and gas engines; antique tractors and cars. Demonstrations in soap and broom making; flour milling. Gas and steam wheat threshing; sawmill working; flea market, crafts, parade, entertainment. Phone 643-6123. Usually wkend after July 4.

Waterfowl Festival. Downtown and various locations in and around town. Exhibits on waterfowl; pictures, carvings; food. Phone 822-4606. 1st or 2nd wkend Nov.

(See Cambridge, St Michaels)

Motel

✔ ★ **COMFORT INN.** *8523 Ocean Gateway, E on US 50.* 410/820-8333; FAX 410/820-8436. 84 units, 2 story, 15 suites. May-mid-Dec: S $62-$75; D $66-$95; each addl $8; under 18 free; higher rates special events; lower rates rest of yr. Crib free. TV; cable. Pool; whirlpool. Complimentary continental bkfst. Restaurant nearby. Ck-out 11 am. Meeting rms. Sundries. Some refrigerators. Picnic tables. Cr cds: A, C, D, DS, JCB, MC, V.

Hotel

★ ★ ★ **TIDEWATER INN.** *101 E Dover St.* 410/822-1300; res: 800/237-8775; FAX 410/820-8847. 114 rms, 4 story. June-Nov: S $85-$145; D $85-$160; each addl $10; under 13 free; wkly, wkend rates; package plans; higher rates Waterfowl Festival; lower rates rest of yr. Crib free. Free valet parking. TV; cable. Pool; poolside serv. Restaurant 7 am-9 pm; Fri & Sat to 10 pm. Bar 11-2 am; entertainment Fri & Sat. Ck-out noon. Meeting rms. Health club privileges. Restored turn-of-the-century hotel. Cr cds: A, C, D, MC, V.

Inn

★ ★ ★ **ROBERT MORRIS INN.** *(Box 70, 314 N Morris St, Oxford 21654)* 11 mi SW on MD 333. 410/226-5111; FAX 410/226-5744.

33 rms, 2-3 story, 2 kit. cottages. No rm phones. D $70-$185; kit. cottages for 2-4, $100-$160. Children over 10 yrs only. Dining rm 8-11 am, noon-9 pm; winter hrs vary; closed Tues. Bar noon-10 pm. Ck-out noon, ck-in 3 pm. Golf privileges. Private patios, balconies. Historic house (1710) built by ships' carpenters. Private beach on river. Totally nonsmoking. Cr cds: MC, V.

Restaurant

★ **LEGAL SPIRITS.** *42 E Dover St, at Harrison St.* 410/820-0033. Hrs: 11:30 am-10 pm; Fri & Sat to 11 pm. Closed Sun; most major hols. Bar. A la carte entrees: lunch $4.25-$8.95, dinner $6.95-$17. Specializes in monster salads, crab cakes, regional seafood, prime beef. Located in restored 1922 vaudeville theater. Casual, pub-style bistro with Prohibition theme decor; photo collection from the files of UPI; stained-glass window featuring Blind Justice from the New Jersey Senate Bldg (1850s); ornately hand-carved triple arch back bar (ca 1900) obtained from a St Louis riverfront tavern. Cr cds: A, MC, V.

Elkton (B-9)

Pop: 9,073 **Elev:** 30 ft **Area code:** 410 **Zip:** 21921

What to See and Do

1. **Elk Neck State Forest.** 4 mi W off MD 7, near North East. Has 3,165 acres. Forest wildlife, particularly white-tailed deer, can be seen; food plots have been established. Hunting. Hiking. Bridle trail. Picnicking. Primitive camping. Shooting range. Winter sports. Pets allowed. Phone 287-5675.
2. **Elk Neck State Park.** 14 mi SW via US 40, MD 272, near North East. Park has 2,188 acres of sandy beaches, marshlands and heavily wooded bluffs. Swimming; fishing; boating (launch, rentals). Miniature golf (fee). Hiking and nature trails. Picnicking. Concession. Winter sports. Camping; cabins. Standard fees. Phone 287-5333.

(For further information contact the Chamber of Commerce, 101 E Main St; 398-1640.)

(See Havre De Grace)

Motel

✔ ★ **ELKTON LODGE.** *200 Belle Hill Rd, I-95 exit 109A.* 410/398-9400. 32 rms, 2 story. S $32-$40; D $34-$40; each addl $4; under 15 free. Crib $5. TV; cable. Restaurant nearby. Ck-out 11 am. Some refrigerators. Cr cds: A, C, D, DS, MC, V.

Inns

★ ★ **INN AT THE CANAL.** *PO Box 187 (21915), 7 mi S on MD 213.* 410/885-5995; FAX 410/885-3585. 6 rms, 3 story. No rm phones. Apr-Nov: D $75-$105; each addl $25; higher rates Labor Day & Memorial Day (2-night min); lower rates rest of yr. Children over 10 yrs only. TV; cable. Complimentary full bkfst. Restaurant nearby. Ck-out 11 am, ck-in 2 pm. Bellhop. Lawn games. Mansion built 1870; antiques. Overlooks Chesapeake & Delaware Canal. Totally nonsmoking. Cr cds: A, DS, MC, V.

★ **KITTY KNIGHT HOUSE.** *(PO Box 97, Georgetown 21930) 20 mi S on MD 213, turn right after drawbridge.* 410/648-5777;

res: 800/404-8712; FAX 410/648-5890. 11 rms, 3 story. No rm phones. D $75-$125; each addl $10. TV. Complimentary continental bkfst. Dining rm 11:30 am-3 pm, 5-9 pm; Fri & Sat to 10:30 pm; Sun Noon-9 pm. Ck-out 11 am, ck-in 2 pm. Built ca 1755. Antiques. Cr cds: A, MC, V.

Restaurant

★ ★ ★ **GRANARY.** *(Foot of George St, Georgetown) 20 mi S on MD 213, turn right before the drawbridge.* 410/275-8177. Hrs: 4:30-9 pm; wkends noon-10 pm. Closed Jan 1, Thanksgiving, Dec 25; also Mon & Tues Nov-Mar. Res accepted Sun-Fri. Bar. Extensive wine list. Semi-a la carte: dinner $7.95-$19.95. Child's meals. Specializes in fresh seafood, steak. DJ & combo Fri, Sat (Memorial Day-Labor Day). Parking. 2 dining areas, one with deck overlooking river; both areas offer scenic view of Sassafras River, piers and wooded area. Cr cds: A, DS, MC, V.

Ellicott City (B-6)

Settled: 1774 **Pop:** 41,396 **Elev:** 233 ft **Area code:** 410

The town was originally named Ellicott Mills for the three Quaker brothers who founded it as the site of their gristmill. Charles Carroll of Carrollton, whose Doughoregan Manor can still be seen nearby, lent financial help to the Ellicotts and the town eventually became the site of ironworks, rolling mills and the first railroad terminus in the US. The famous Tom Thumb locomotive race with a horse took place here. Many of the town's original stone houses and log cabins, on hills above the Patapsco River, have been preserved.

What to See and Do

1. **Patapsco Valley State Park.** NE and SE of town; 5 mi from I-695 exits 12 & 15. Four of the recreation areas located within the 15,000 acres sprawling along the Patapsco River are as follows. Area 1: Glen Artney via South St from MD 1, in Relay; Baltimore County. Picnicking, fishing. Area 2: Hilton Ave, via Rolling Rd, S of Frederick Rd, in Catonsville; Baltimore County. Picnicking, camping. Area 3: Hollofield, adj to US 40, near Ellicott City; Howard County. Scenic overlook, camping. Pets allowed (in camping area). Area 4: McKeldin Area, off Marriottsville Rd; Carroll County. Picnicking, fishing. Hiking trails & pavilions available in all areas. Golden Age Passport (see INTRODUCTION). Phone 461-5005. Per person ¢¢

2. **Ellicott City B & O Railroad Station Museum.** 2711 Maryland Ave, at Main St. Two restored buildings (ca 1830 and 1885) house historic rooms, RR displays and memorabilia, operating HO model RR of the first 13 mi of the B & O track, photographs, dioramas. Full size B & O caboose and museum store. (Memorial Day-Labor Day, daily exc Tues; rest of yr, Fri-Mon) Phone 461-1944 (recording). ¢¢

3. **Cider Mill Farm.** 5012 Landing Rd, Elkridge; 5 mi SE via MD 29 and MD 103. Cider press operating most days. Bushels of pumpkins, apples and other foods and produce. Hayrides, storytelling, crafts, contests, apple butter-making. (Apr-May & mid-Sept-Dec, daily) Phone 788-9595. **Free.**

(For further information contact the Howard County Tourism Council, PO Box 9, 21041; 313-1900 or 800/288-TRIP.)

Annual Events

Sheep & Wool Festival. In West Friendship. Craftsmen sell products related to sheep and wool; spinning, weaving, and sheep-shearing contests; wool dyeing; entertainment. 1st wkend May.

Howard County Fair. In West Friendship. Rides, entertainment, concessions, 4-H exhibits, horse-pulling contests and other events. Mid-Aug.

(See Baltimore)

Hotel

★ ★ ★ **TURF VALLEY HOTEL & COUNTRY CLUB.** 2700 Turf Valley Rd (21042), approx 8 mi W via US 40. 410/465-1500; res: 800/666-8873; FAX 410/465-8280. 173 rms, 7 story, 14 suites. Apr-Nov: S $85-$135; D $95-$145; each addl $10; suites $200-$400; under 15 free; wkend packages; lower rates rest of yr. Crib free. TV; cable. Pool; poolside serv, lifeguard. Restaurant 7 am-10 pm. Bar 7 pm-2 am; entertainment, dancing Thurs-Sun. Ck-out noon. Convention facilities. Gift shop. Lighted tennis. 54-hole golf, greens fee $30-$50, pro, putting green, driving range. Exercise equipt; weight machine, bicycles. Bathrm phone, minibar in suites. Balconies. Cr cds: A, C, D, DS, MC, V.

Restaurant

★ ★ **CRAB SHANTY.** 3410 Plumtree Dr & US 40W. 410/465-9660. Hrs: 11:30 am-2:30 pm, 5-10 pm; Fri to 11 pm; Sat 5-11 pm; Sun 2-9 pm. Bar. Semi-a la carte: lunch $2.95-$8.50, dinner $8.75-$18.95. Child's meals. Specializes in seafood. Pianist Wed-Sat. Parking. Cr cds: A, C, D, MC, V.

Emmitsburg (A-5)

Settled: 1785 **Pop:** 1,688 **Elev:** 449 ft **Area code:** 301 **Zip:** 21727

What to See and Do

1. **Mount Saint Mary's College and Seminary** (1808). (1,800 students) 3 mi S on US 15. Oldest independent Catholic college in US. Liberal arts and sciences. Phone 447-6122. Near the campus is the

   National Shrine Grotto of Lourdes. Replica of the French shrine is 1/3 the size of the original; oldest replica in the Western Hemisphere. Pangborn Memorial Campanile, constructed of native stone and located at the entrance, is 120 feet tall and is surmounted by a 25-foot bronze gold-leaf statue of the Blessed Virgin Mary. (Apr-Oct, daily; rest of yr, daily exc Mon; closed last 2 wks Jan) **Free.**

2. **Seton Shrine Center.** South Seton Ave. National Shrine of Saint Elizabeth Ann Seton, first US female saint, canonized 1975. Includes Stone House (1809), White House (1810), home in which Mother Seton died; slide presentation, basilica, museum and cemetery. (May-Nov, daily; rest of yr, daily exc Mon; closed Dec 25; also last 2 wks Jan) Phone 447-6606. **Free.**

(For further information contact the Tourism Council of Frederick County, 19 E Church St, Frederick 21701; 663-8687.)

(For accommodations see Frederick, Hagerstown, also see Thurmont)

Frederick (B-5)

Settled: 1745 **Pop:** 40,148 **Elev:** 290 ft **Area code:** 301 **Zip:** 21701

Home of dauntless Barbara Fritchie, who reportedly spoke her mind to Stonewall Jackson and his "rebel hordes," Frederick is a town filled with history. Named for Frederick Calvert, 6th Lord Baltimore, it is the seat of one of America's richest agricultural counties. Francis Scott Key and Chief Justice Roger Brooke Taney made their homes here. Court House Square was the scene of several important events during the Revolutionary War, including the famed protest against the Stamp Act, in which an effigy of the stamp distributor was burned.

During the Civil War, Frederick was a focal point for strategic operations by both sides. In the campaign of 1862 the Confederacy's first invasions of the North were made at nearby South Mountain and Sharpsburg, at Antietam Creek. Wounded men by the thousands were cared for here. Troop movements continued for the duration of the war; cavalry skirmishes took place in the streets. In July, 1864, the town was forced to pay a $200,000 ransom to Confederate General Jubal Early before he fought the Battle of Monocacy a few miles south. Frederick today is an educational center, tourist attraction, location of Fort Detrick army installation and home of diversified small industry. A 33-block area has been designated an Historic District.

What to See and Do

1. **Barbara Fritchie House and Museum.** 154 W Patrick St. Exhibits include quilts, clothing made by Fritchie, her rocker and Bible, the bed in which she died and other items; 10-min film; also garden. (Apr-Sept, Thurs-Mon; Oct-Nov, Sat & Sun) Phone 698-0630. ¢¢

2. **Roger Brooke Taney Home** (1799) **and Francis Scott Key Museum.** 123 S Bentz St. Chief Justice of Supreme Court from 1835-64, Taney was chosen by Andrew Jackson to succeed John Marshall. He swore in seven presidents, including Abraham Lincoln, and issued the famous Dred Scott Decision. He is buried in the cemetery of St John's Catholic Church at E 3rd & East Sts. (Apr-Oct, wkends) Phone 663-8687. ¢¢

3. **Trinity Chapel** (1763). W Church St, near N Market St. Graceful colonial church; Francis Scott Key was baptized here. Steeple houses town clock and ten-bell chimes; chimes play every Sat evening. The chapel is now used as Sunday School for

   Evangelical Reformed Church, United Church of Christ (1848). Opp Trinity Chapel. A Grecian-style building modeled after the Erechtheum, with two towers resembling Lanterns of Demosthenes. Here Stonewall Jackson slept through pro-Union sermon before Battle of Antietam; Barbara Fritchie was a member. Phone 662-2762.

4. **Rose Hill Manor Children's Museum.** 1611 N Market St. Hands-on exhibits of 19th-century family life; carriage museum; colonial herb and fragrant gardens; farm museum; blacksmith shop; log cabin. (Apr-Oct, daily; Nov, Sat & Sun only) Phone 694-1648 or -1650. ¢¢

5. **Schifferstadt** (1756). Rosemont Ave & W 2nd St. Fine example of German-colonial farmhouse architecture. Tours of architectural museum. Gift shop. (Apr-mid Dec, daily exc Mon; closed Thanksgiving) Phone 663-3885. ¢

6. **Mt Olivet Cemetery** (1852). S end of Market St. Monuments mark graves of Francis Scott Key and Barbara Fritchie. Flag flies over Key's grave.

7. **Historical Society of Frederick County Museum.** 24 E Church St. House, built in early 1800s, shows both Georgian and Federal details; leaded side and fanlights, Doric columns inside, double porches in rear and boxwood gardens. Portraits of early Frederick residents. Genealogy library. (Tues-Sat; also Sun afternoons) Phone 663-1188. Museum tour · ¢

8. **Monocacy Battlefield.** 3 mi S on MD 355. On July 9, 1864, Union General Lew Wallace with 5,000 men delayed General Jubal Early

and his 23,000 Confederate soldiers for 24 hours, during which Grant was able to reinforce, and save, Washington, DC. New Jersey, Vermont, Pennsylvania and Confederate monuments mark the area. For tour information phone park ranger, 662-3515.

9. **Gambrill State Park.** 5 mi NW off US 40. Park has 1,136 acres with two developed areas. Fishing. Nature, hiking trails. Picknicking. Tent and trailer sites (standard fees). Tea room. Three overlooks. (Schedule varies, phone ahead) Phone 791-4767 or 974-3771.

10. **Brunswick Museum.** 23 mi SW via US 340, MD 17 in Brunswick, at 40 W Potomac St. Furnishings and clothing interpret life in turn-of-the-century railroad town; large HO model train exhibit; gift shop. Special events held on selected wkends. (June-Sept, Thurs-Sun; Apr-May & Oct-late Dec, Sat & Sun; limited hrs, phone ahead) Phone 834-7100. ¢¢

11. **Byrd Winery.** 10 mi W via I-70, exit 42, Main St to Church Hill Rd, turn right 1 mi. Slide presentation and wine samples; panoramic view of Catoctin Valley. (Sat & Sun) Wine Harvest Festival (1st wkend Oct; fee). Phone 293-1110. **Free.**

(For further information, including material relating to guided and self-guided cycling, driving and walking tours, contact the Tourism Council of Frederick County, 19 E Church St; 663-8687.)

Annual Events

Lotus Blossom Festival. Lilypons Water Gardens, 6800 Lilypons Rd, 10 mi S via MD 85. Endless blooms of water lilies and lotus, water garden; arts & crafts, food, entertainment, lectures. Phone 874-5133. First double-digit wkend July.

Great Frederick Fair. Frederick county fair. Mid-late Sept.

New Market Days. 8 mi E, in New Market. Nostalgic revival of the atmosphere of a 19th-century village; costumed guides, period crafts and events; held in New Market, the town dedicated to being the "Antiques Capital of Maryland." Phone 831-6755. Last full wkend Sept.

Fall Festival. Rose Hill Manor (see #4). Apple-butter making, music, crafts demonstrations, tractor pull, hay rides, country cooking. Early Oct.

(See Hagerstown, Thurmont)

Motel

✔ ★ **DAYS INN.** 5646 Buckeystown Pike. 301/694-6600; FAX 301/831-4242. 119 rms, 2 story. Apr-Oct: S, D $54-$67; under 12 free; some lower rates rest of yr. Crib free. TV; cable. Pool. Playground. Restaurant 5 am-10 pm; wkend hrs vary. Ck-out noon. Meeting rms. Sundries. Cr cds: A, C, D, DS, MC, V.

D ≈ ✕ 🔥 SC

Motor Hotels

★ ★ **HAMPTON INN.** 5311 Buckeystown Pike. 301/698-2500; FAX 301/695-8735. 160 rms, 6 story. S, D $57-$100; each addl $5; suites $100; under 18 free. Crib free. Pet accepted, some restrictions; $25 refundable. TV; cable. Pool; lifeguard. Complimentary continental bkfst. Restaurant 11:30 am-9 pm. Bar; entertainment, dancing Wed-Sat. Ck-out noon. Meeting rms. Sundries. Valet serv. Exercise equipt; bicycles, rowers. Some refrigerators. Cr cds: A, C, D, DS, MC, V.

D ✔ ≈ 🏃 ✕ 🔥 SC

★ ★ **HOLIDAY INN.** 5400 Holiday Dr, at Francis Scott Key Mall. 301/694-7500; FAX 301/694-0589. 155 rms, 2 story. S $83-$93; D $93-$103; each addl $10; suites $200; under 20 free. Crib free. Pet accepted. TV; cable. Indoor pool; poolside serv, lifeguard. Restaurant 6:30 am-9 pm; Sat & Sun from 7 am. Rm serv. Bar; entertainment Fri & Sat, dancing. Ck-out noon. Coin lndry. Meeting rms. Sundries. Valet serv. Exercise equipt; weight machine, bicycles, sauna, steam rm. Holidome. Rec rm. Picnic tables. Cr cds: A, C, D, DS, ER, JCB, MC, V.

Inns

★ ★ ★ **INN AT BUCKEYSTOWN.** (3521 Buckeystown Pike, Buckeystown 21717) 5 mi S on MD 85. 301/874-5755; res: 800/272-1190. 8 rms, 3 story. MAP: S $117-$178; D $167-$272. Children over 16 yrs only. TV in 3 suites. Setups. Ck-out noon, ck-in 4 pm. Meeting rm. Downhill ski 20 mi; x-country ski 1 mi. Restored Victorian mansion (1897). Near river. Cr cds: A, MC, V.

★ ★ ★ **TURNING POINT.** (3406 Urbana Pike, Urbana) 9 mi S. 301/874-2421. 5 rms (2 with shower only), 3 story, 1 kit. cottage. S, D $75-$85; kit. cottage $125-$150. TV avail. Complimentary full bkfst, refreshments. Dining rm 11:30 am-2 pm, 5:30-9 pm; wkend hrs vary; closed Mon. Rm serv. Ck-out 11 am, ck-in 3 pm. Built 1910; antiques. View of Sugarloaf Mt and adj farmland. Cr cds: DS, MC, V.

D 🔥

Restaurants

★ ★ **BROWN PELICAN.** 5 E Church St. 301/695-5833. Hrs: 11:30 am-3 pm, 5-9:30 pm; Fri to 10 pm; Sat 5-10 pm; Sun 5-9:30 pm. Closed Jan 1, Thanksgiving, Dec 25; also Super Bowl Sun. Res accepted; required Fri & Sat. Continental menu. Bar. Semi-a la carte: lunch $5.75-$11.95, dinner $12.95-$20.95. Specializes in fresh seafood, pasta, veal. In basement of antebellum bank. Cr cds: A, MC, V.

★ ★ **TAURASO'S.** 6 East St, Everedy Square. 301/663-6600. Hrs: 11 am-11 pm; Sun brunch to 2 pm. Closed Dec 25. Res accepted. Continental, Italian menu. Bar to midnight. Semi-a la carte: lunch $4.25-$8, dinner $7.95-$21.95. Sun brunch $8.95-$10.95. Child's meals. Specializes in fresh fish, veal, steak. Valet parking. Outdoor dining. In restored factory building (late 1800s). Cr cds: A, C, D, MC, V.

D **SC**

Gaithersburg (C-6)

Pop: 39,542 **Elev:** 508 ft **Area code:** 301

What to See and Do

Seneca Creek State Park. 2¹/₂ mi W of I-270 on MD 117. Stream valley park of 6,109 acres with 90-acre lake. Historic sites with old mills, an old schoolhouse, stone quarries. Fishing; boating (rentals). Winter sports. Picnicking. Hiking, bicycle and bridle trails. Standard fees. Phone 924-2127. ¢

(For further information contact the Chamber of Commerce, 9 Park Ave, 20877; 840-1400.)

Annual Event

Montgomery County Agricultural Fair. One of the East Coast's leading county fairs; emphasis on agriculture, 4-H activities; animal exhibits, home arts; antique farm equipment; tractor pull, horse pull, demolition derby; rodeo; entertainment. Phone 926-3100. Late Aug.

(See Rockville)

Motel

✔ ★ **COMFORT INN SHADY GROVE.** 16216 Frederick Rd (20877). 301/330-0023; FAX 301/258-1950. 127 rms, 7 story. Apr-Oct: S $45-$69; D $45-$79; each addl $6; suites $55-$89; under 18 free; monthly rates; lower rates rest of yr. Crib free. Pet accepted, some restrictions. TV; cable. Heated pool; lifeguard. Complimentary continental bkfst. Restaurant adj 11 am-9 pm. Ck-out 11 am. Meeting rms. Valet serv. Free Metro station transportation. Exercise equipt; weight machine, bicycles. Some refrigerators. Wet bar in suites. Picnic tables. Cr cds: A, C, D, DS, ER, JCB, MC, V.

Motor Hotels

★ ★ ★ **COURTYARD BY MARRIOTT.** 805 Russell Ave (20879). 301/670-0008; FAX 301/948-4538. 203 rms, 7 story. S $87; D $97; each addl $10; suites $145-$250. Crib free. TV; cable. Pool; lifeguard. Restaurant 6-10 am, 6-10 pm. Bar 5 pm-midnight. Ck-out 1 pm. Coin Indry. Meeting rms. Valet serv. Lighted tennis. Exercise equipt; bicycles, treadmill, whirlpool, steam rm. Some refrigerators. Some balconies. Cr cds: A, C, D, DS, JCB, MC, V.

★ ★ **HOLIDAY INN.** 2 Montgomerey Village Ave (20879). 301/948-8900; FAX 301/258-1940. 303 rms, 1-8 story. S $95; D $105; suites $300-$350; kit. units $95-$105; under 18 free. Crib free. Pet accepted. TV; cable. Indoor pool; poolside serv, lifeguard. Restaurant 6:30 am-2 pm, 5-10 pm. Rm serv 6:30 am-10 pm. Bar 2 pm-1 am; entertainment, dancing exc Sun. Ck-out 1 pm. Coin Indry. Convention facilities. Bellhops. Gift shop. Exercise equipt; weights, bicycles, whirlpool. Game rm. Some refrigerators. Balconies. Cr cds: A, C, D, DS, JCB, MC, V.

✔ ★ ★ **RAMADA INN GERMANTOWN.** (20260 Goldenrod Lane, Germantown 20876) 301/428-1300; FAX 301/428-9034. 176 rms, 5 story, 16 kit. units. S $66; D $72; each addl $6; kit. units $125-$131; under 16 free; wkend rates. Crib avail. TV; cable. Pool. Restaurant 7 am-2 pm, 5-10 pm. Ck-out noon. Coin Indry. Meeting rms. Bellhops. Sundries. Valet serv. Exercise equipt; weights, treadmill, sauna. Health club privileges. Cr cds: A, C, D, DS, ER, JCB, MC, V.

Hotels

★ ★ **HILTON.** 620 Perry Pkwy (20877), 1 blk E of I-270 exit 11. 301/977-8900; FAX 301/869-8597. 301 rms, 12 story. S, D $105-$115; suites $250; under 18 free; wkend rates. Crib free. TV; cable. Indoor/outdoor pool. Restaurant 6:30 am-11 pm. Bars 11-1 am. Convention facilities. Gift shop. Exercise equipt; weights, bicycles. Game rm. Refrigerators avail. Some private patios, balconies. Adj to Lake Forest shopping center. Cr cds: A, C, D, DS, ER, JCB, MC, V.

★ ★ ★ **MARRIOTT WASHINGTONIAN CENTER.** 9751 Washingtonian Blvd (20878). 301/590-0044; FAX 301/212-6155. 284 rms, 11 story. S $114; D $124; suites $250; under 18 free; wkend rates. Crib free. TV; cable. Indoor pool; poolside serv, lifeguard. Restaurant 6:30-9 am, 11 am-2 pm, 5-11pm; wkend hrs vary. Bar 4 pm-midnight. Ck-out noon. Convention facilities. Concierge. Gift shop. Exercise equipt; weight machine, stair machine, whirlpool, sauna. Health club privileges. **LUXURY LEVEL .** 47 rms, 2 story, 4 suites. S $134; D $144. Concierge. Private lounge, honor bar. Complimentary continental bkfst, refreshments. Cr cds: A, C, D, DS, ER, JCB, MC, V.

Restaurants

✔ ★ **ALOHA INN.** *608 Quince Orchard Rd (20878). 301/977-0057.* Hrs: 11 am-10 pm; wkend hrs vary. Closed July 4, Thanksgiving, Dec 25. Res accepted; required Fri & Sat. Chinese menu. Serv bar. Lunch buffet $6.95. Semi-a la carte: lunch $3.75-$5.50, dinner $3.95-$9.50. Specializes in seafood, General Tso's chicken, crispy beef Szechuan-style. Parking. Polynesian theme. Cr cds: A, C, D, DS, MC, V.

★ **BARE BONES.** *617 S Frederick Ave (20877). 301/948-4344.* Hrs: 11:30 am-10 pm; Fri & Sat to 11 pm; Sun noon-10 pm. Closed Thanksgiving, Dec 25. Bar. Semi-a la carte: lunch $5-$8, dinner $8-$15. Child's meals. Specializes in barbecue. Parking. Cr cds: A, MC, V.

D

★ ★ **FLAMING PIT.** *18701 N Frederick Ave (18701). 301/977-0700.* Hrs: 11:30 am-10:30 pm; Fri to 11:30 pm; Sat 4-11 pm; Sun 5-10 pm. Closed some major hols; also Sun June-Aug. Res accepted; required Fri, Sat. Bar to midnight; Fri, Sat to 1:30 am. Semi-a la carte: lunch $4.50-$11, dinner $13.95-$29.95. Complete meals: dinner $8.95. Child's meals. Specializes in prime rib, lamb, fresh seafood. Pianist. Parking. Skylight; hanging baskets. Original antique fireplaces. Cr cds: A, C, D, MC, V.

★ ★ **GOLDEN BULL.** *7 Dalamar St, I-270 exit 124E. 301/948-3666.* Hrs: 11 am-3 pm, 4:30-10 pm; Fri, Sat to 11 pm; Sun noon-10 pm; early-bird dinner 4:30-6:30 pm. Closed Dec 25. Bar 11-1 am. Semi-a la carte: lunch $4.95-$10.95, dinner $7.95-$19.95. Child's meals. Specializes in beef, seafood. Parking. Cr cds: A, C, D, DS, MC, V.

D

✔ ★ ★ **PANDA RESTAURANT.** *18204 Contour Rd (20879). 301/670-9805.* Hrs: 11:30 am-10 pm. Closed Thanksgiving. Res accepted. Chinese menu. Serv bar. Lunch buffet $5.95. Semi-a la carte: lunch $4.50-$10.95, dinner $5.75-$10.95. Specializes in Szechuan-style cooking, vegetarian dishes. Parking. Cr cds: A, DS, MC, V.

D **SC**

★ **PAT & MIKE'S.** *800 W Diamond Ave. 301/948-1500.* Hrs: 11:30 am-10 pm; Thurs-Sat to 11 pm; summer to midnight. Closed Thanksgiving, Dec 25. Bar. Semi-a la carte: lunch, dinner $4.95-$16.95. Child's meals. Specializes in grilled fish, marinated steak, barbecued ribs. Own desserts. Parking. Patio dining. Main dining area on 2nd floor. Casual atmosphere. Totally nonsmoking. Cr cds: A, MC, V.

D

★ **ROY'S PLACE.** *2 E Diamond Ave. 301/948-5548.* Hrs: 11 am-11 pm; Fri, Sat to midnight; Sun from 11:30 am. Closed Thanksgiving, Dec 24 & 25. Bar. A la carte entrees: lunch, dinner $4.50-$18. Extensive sandwich selection. Parking. 1920s tavern atmosphere; Tiffany-style lamps, beamed ceiling, period posters. Family-owned. Cr cds: A, C, D, DS, MC, V.

D

✔ ★ ★ **SIR WALTER RALEIGH.** *19100 Montgomery Village Ave (20879). 301/258-0576.* Hrs: 11:30 am-2 pm, 5-9 pm; Fri to 10 pm; Sat 5-10 pm; Sun 4-8:30 pm. Closed Thanksgiving, Dec 24 & 25. Bar. Semi-a la carte: lunch $7-$10, dinner $10.95-$18. Child's meals. Specializes in prime rib, seafood, crab cakes. Salad bar. Parking. Some raised dining areas. Brick fireplaces. Cr cds: A, C, D, DS, MC, V.

D

Grantsville (A-1)

Pop: 505 **Elev:** 2,300 ft **Area code:** 301 **Zip:** 21536

What to See and Do

1. **Spruce Forest Artisan Village.** 1 mi E on US 40, near Penn Alps. Six log houses plus other historic buildings serve as studios for a potter, internationally recognized bird carver, weaver, spinner, stained-glass maker and other artisans. Buildings (Memorial Day-last Sat Oct, daily exc Sun); grounds (all yr). Special events (summer; fee). Restaurant (see). (See ANNUAL EVENTS) Phone 895-3332. **Free.**

2. **Savage River State Forest.** W & S of town via US 40, 48. Largest of Maryland's state forests comprises about 52,800 acres of near wilderness. A strategic watershed area, the northern hardwood forest surrounds the Savage River Dam. Fishing, hunting. Hiking trails. Winter sports. Primitive camping (permit required). Phone 895-5759.

3. **New Germany State Park.** 5 mi S. A 13-acre lake built on site of a once prosperous milling center. Swimming; fishing; boating. Nature, hiking trails. Winter sports. Picnicking, playground, concession. Improved campsites, cabins (fee). Phone 895-5453. Admission (wkends & hols) per person ¢

4. **Springs Museum.** 2 mi N via MD 669, PA 669 in Springs, PA. Depicts life of settlers of Casselman Valley; 18th-century farming tools, fossil collection, other exhibits. (Memorial Day-mid-Oct, Wed-Sat afternoons) Phone 814/662-4159. ¢

(For further information contact the Deep Creek Lake/Garret County Promotion Council, Courthouse Building, 200 S Third St, Oakland 21550; 334-1948.)

Annual Events

Spruce Forest Summerfest and Quilt Show. Spruce Forest Artisan Village (see #1). More than 200 quilts on display; more than 70 mountain craftsmen demonstrate their various skills. Phone 895-3332. 2nd full Thurs, Fri & Sat wkend July.

Springs Folk Festival. On grounds of Springs Museum (see #4). Pennsylvania Dutch food, music. 1st Fri & Sat Oct.

(For accommodations see Cumberland, Oakland)

Restaurant

✔ ★ ★ **PENN ALPS.** *1 mi E on US 40 at Casselman River Bridge. 301/895-5985.* Hrs: 7 am-8 pm; Sun to 3 pm. Closed Dec 24, 25. Complete meals: bkfst $2.25-$5.95, lunch $4-$6.95, dinner $5.75-$14. Sunday brunch $7.95. Child's meals. Specializes in Dutch cooking. Salad bar. Parking. Colonial decor; 1818 stagecoach stop. Totally nonsmoking. Cr cds: MC, V.

Hagerstown (A-4)

Settled: 1762 **Pop:** 35,445 **Elev:** 552 ft **Area code:** 301 **Zip:** 21740

Within the city of Hagerstown, there is a walking tour with points of interest marked on downtown sidewalks and walking paths in city parks. South Prospect Street is one of the city's oldest neighborhoods, listed on the National Register of Historic Places. The tree-lined street is graced by homes dating back to the early 1800s.

What to See and Do

1. **Washington County Museum of Fine Arts.** City Park, S on US 11 (Virginia Ave). Paintings, sculpture, changing exhibits; concerts, lectures. (Daily exc Mon; closed major hols) Phone 739-5727. **Free.**

2. **Jonathan Hager House and Museum** (1739). 19 Key St, in City Park. Stone house in park setting; authentic 18th-century furnishings. (Apr-Dec, daily exc Mon) Phone 739-8393. ¢¢

3. **Hagerstown Roundhouse Museum.** 300 S Burhans Blvd, across the tracks from City Park. Museum houses photographic exhibits of the 7 railroads of Hagerstown; historic railroad memorabilia, tools and equipment; archives of maps, books, papers and related items. Gift shop. (May-Sept, Wed-Sun afternoons; rest of yr, Fri-Sun afternoons) (See ANNUAL EVENTS) Phone 739-4665. ¢

4. **Miller House.** 135 W Washington St. Washington County Historical Society Headquarters. Federal town house (ca 1820); 3-story spiral staircase; period furnishings; garden; clock, doll and Bell pottery collections; Chesapeake & Ohio Canal and Civil War exhibits; 19th-century country store display. (Apr-Dec, Wed-Sun; closed major hols; also 1st 2 wks Dec) Sr citizen rate. Phone 797-8782. ¢

5. **Antietam National Battlefield** (see). 11 mi S on MD 65.

6. **Greenbrier State Park.** 10 mi E via US 40. The Appalachian Trail passes near this 1,275-acre park and its 42-acre man-made lake. Swimming (Memorial Day-Labor Day, daily); fishing; boating (rentals; no gas motors). Nature, hiking trails. Picnicking. Standard fees. Phone 791-4767.

7. **Ft Frederick State Park.** 19 mi S & W via I-81 & I-70 to Big Pool, then 1 mi SE via MD 56, unnumbered road. Erected in 1756, during French and Indian War, the fort is considered a fine example of a pre-Revolutionary stone fort. Overlooks Chesapeake and Ohio Canal National Historical Park (see); barracks, interior and wall of fort restored; military reenactments throughout year. Fishing; boating (rentals). Nature & hiking trails. Picnicking (shelter), playground. Unimproved camping. Museum, orientation film, historical programs. Standard fees. Winter hours may vary. Phone 842-2155.

(For further information contact the Washington County Tourism Office, 1826 Dual Hwy; 791-3130; 24-hr recording 797-8800.)

Annual Events

Halfway Park Days. Helicopter rides, antique cars, dance bands, flea market, food. Late May.

Hagerstown Railroad Heritage Days. Special events centered on the Roundhouse Museum (see #3). For information and schedule phone 739-4665. Last wk May-early June.

Frontier Craft Day. Colonial crafts demonstrated and exhibited. Bluegrass music; food. 1st wkend Aug.

Leitersburg Peach Festival. Peach-related edibles, farmers' market, bluegrass music, military reenactments. 2nd wkend Aug.

Williamsport C & O Canal Days. Arts and crafts, Indian Village, National Park Service activities; food. Late Aug.

Alsatia Mummers Halloween Parade Festival. Sat, wkend closest to Halloween.

(See Boonsboro, Frederick, Thurmont)

Motels

✔ ★ ★ **HOLIDAY INN.** 900 Dual Hwy (US 40), I-70 exit 32B. 301/739-9050; FAX 301/739-8347. 140 rms, 2 story. May-Sept: S $45-$65; D $58-$75; each addl $8; under 19 free; wkend rates; lower rates rest of yr. Crib free. Pet accepted. TV; cable. Pool. Restaurant 6 am-2 pm, 5-10 pm. Rm serv. Bar 4 pm-2 am. Ck-out noon. Coin lndry. Meeting rms. Health club privileges. Cr cds: A, C, D, DS, JCB, MC, V.

D ✎ ≋ ⊠ ⌕ SC

★ ★ **SHERATON INN CONFERENCE CENTER.** 1910 Dual Hwy (US 40), I-70 exit 32B. 301/790-3010; FAX 301/733-4559. 108 rms, 2 story. S $58-$63; D $64-$69; each addl $8; suites $125; under 18 free. Crib free. Pet accepted. TV; cable. Pool. Restaurant 6:30 am-10 pm; Sun 7 am-9 pm. Rm serv. Bar 11-2 am. Ck-out noon. Meeting rms. Bellhops. Valet serv. Sundries. Beauty shop. Airport transportation. Exercise equipt; weights, bicycles, whirlpool, sauna. Cr cds: A, C, D, DS, MC, V.

D ✎ ≋ ⌿ ⊠ ⌕ SC

Motor Hotels

✔ ★ ★ **BEST WESTERN VENICE INN.** 431 Dual Hwy (US 40), I-70 exit 32B, I-81 exit 6A. 301/733-0830; FAX 301/733-4978. 220 rms, 2-5 story. Apr-Oct: S $56-$66; D $62-$72; each addl $6; suites $100-$250; under 18 free; lower rates rest of yr. Crib $6. TV; cable. Pool; whirlpools. Restaurant 6 am-10:30 pm. Rm serv. Bar; entertainment, dancing Tues-Sat. Ck-out noon. Meeting rms. Bellhops. Valet serv. Beauty shop. Game rm. Golf adj. Refrigerators avail. Cr cds: A, C, D, DS, MC, V.

D ≋ ⊠ ⌕ SC

★ ★ ★ **HOWARD JOHNSON PLAZA.** Halfway Blvd, at I-81 exit 5. 301/797-2500; FAX 301/797-6209. 165 units, 6 story. S $57; D $66; each addl $8; suites $68-$77; under 18 free. Crib free. TV; cable. Indoor pool; lifeguard. Restaurant 6:30 am-9 pm. Rm serv. Bar 11 am-11 pm. Ck-out noon. Meeting rms. Valet serv. Exercise equipt; weight machines, bicycles, whirlpool, sauna. Refrigerators. Cr cds: A, C, D, DS, JCB, MC, V.

D ≋ ⌿ ⊠ ⌕ SC

★ ★ **RAMADA INN CONVENTION CENTER.** 901 Dual Hwy (US 40), I-70 exit 32B. 301/733-5100; FAX 301/733-9192. 210 rms, 5 story. S $59-$64; D $64-$69; each addl $5; suites $95-$200; under 18 free. Crib free. Pet accepted. TV; cable. Indoor pool. Restaurant 6:30 am-10 pm; Sun to 9 pm. Rm serv. Bar noon-2 am; videos, dancing. Ck-out noon. Coin lndry. Meeting rms. Exercise equipt; weight machines, bicycles. Indoor putting green. Some refrigerators. Cr cds: A, C, D, DS, MC, V.

D ✎ ≋ ⌿ ⌃ ⊠ ⌕ SC

Hotel

✔ ★ **DAGMAR.** 50 Summit Ave, at Antietam St. 301/733-4363; FAX 301/733-5675. 74 rms, 7 story. S $35; D $42; suites $65-$85. Crib free. TV; cable, in-rm movies avail. Restaurant 7 am-7 pm; Sat to 6 pm. Ck-out noon. Barber. Historic hotel (ca 1920). Cr cds: DS, ER, MC, V.

D ⊠ ⌕ SC

Inn

★ ★ **BEAVER CREEK HOUSE.** 20432 Beaver Creek Rd (20432), 4 mi E on I-70, exit 32A or 35, in village of Beaver Creek. 301/797-4764. 5 rms, 3 with bath. No rm phones. S $65-$75; D $75-$85; lower rates mid-wk. Children over 10 yrs only. TV in sitting rm. Complimentary full bkfst, tea/sherry. Ck-out 11 am, ck-in 1 pm. Turn-of-the-century country home located in historic village; antique furnishings and family memorabilia; parlor with fireplace; library/sitting rm; scenic view of South Mountain. Cr cds: A, D, DS, MC, V.

⊠ ⌕

Restaurants

✔ ★ **RAILROAD JUNCTION.** *808 Noland Dr, at jct US 11 (Virginia Ave).* 301/791-3639. Hrs: 6 am-8:30 pm. Closed Sun; also wk of July 4 and Dec 24-26. Res accepted. Semi-a la carte: bkfst $1.50-$4.95, lunch $2.50-$3.75, dinner $4.95-$10.95. Child's meals. Specializes in seafood, lasagne, Cajun steak. Own pies. Located near railroad tracks. Fun atmosphere with railroad-theme decor and tapes of actual trains; model trains circle the room at the ceiling. Cr cds: MC, V.

SC

★ ★ **RED HORSE STEAK HOUSE.** *1800 Dual Hwy (US 40).* 301/733-3788. Hrs: 4-10 pm; Sun to 9 pm. Closed major hols. Res accepted; required Fri, Sat. Bar. Semi-a la carte: dinner $9.75-$19.95. Child's meals. Specializes in prime rib, broiled seafood, steak. Parking. Open-hearth grill. Western-style atmosphere. Family-owned. Cr cds: C, D, MC, V.

D

✔ ★ **RICHARDSON'S.** *710 Dual Hwy (US 40W).* 301/733-3660. Hrs: 7 am-10 pm; Fri, Sat to 11 pm. Closed half-day Dec 24, Dec 25. Res accepted. Bar. Semi-a la carte: bkfst $1.95-$4.95, lunch $3.75-$6.95, dinner $5.95-$14.95. Buffet: bkfst $4.35, lunch $4.49, dinner $7.95-$14.95. Child's meals. Specializes in fried chicken, seafood, crab cakes. Salad bar. Own pies, cakes. Parking. 3 dining areas; railroad theme, memorabilia. Cr cds: MC, V.

SC

Havre De Grace (B-8)

Settled: 1658 **Pop:** 8,952 **Elev:** 52 ft **Area code:** 410 **Zip:** 21078

What to See and Do

1. **Decoy Museum.** Giles and Market Sts, at the bay. Houses a collection of hand-carved waterfowl decoys and interprets this art form as it applies to the heritage of Chesapeake Bay. (Daily; closed major hols) (See ANNUAL EVENTS) Sr citizen rate. Phone 939-3739. ¢

2. **Susquehanna State Park.** 3 mi N via MD 155. A 2,639-acre park. Fishing. Boat launch. Nature, riding and hiking trails. Cross-country skiing. Picknicking. Camping (fee). (Schedule varies, phone ahead) Phone 557-7994. In the park is

    Steppingstone Museum. 461 Quaker Bottom Rd. Self-guided tour of museum grounds includes sites of a once working Harford County farm; farmhouse is furnished as a turn-of-the-century country home; nearby shops and barn hold many displays and exhibits of the 1880-1920 period; demonstrations of rural arts & crafts of the period. Also here are blacksmith, woodworking, cooper and dairy shops. (May-1st Sun Oct, Sat & Sun; limited hrs) Special events held throughout the year (see ANNUAL EVENTS). Phone 939-2299. ¢-¢¢

3. **Concord Point Lighthouse** (1827). At foot of Lafayette St. Built of granite, considered the oldest continually used lighthouse on the East Coast. It was automated in 1928. (May-Oct, wkends only) **Free.**

(For further information contact the Chamber of Commerce, 220 N Washington St, PO Box 339; 939-3303 or 800/851-7756.)

Annual Events

Decoy Festival. Decoys on display, auction. Carving, gunning & calling contests. Refreshments. Phone 939-3739. Fri-Sun early May.

Fall Harvest Festival. Steppingstone Museum (see #2). Features activities related to the harvest and preparation for winter: apple press-

ing, scarecrow stuffing and other events. Entertainment. Phone 939-2299. Last full wkend Sept.

(See Aberdeen, Elkton)

Inn

★ ★ ★ **VANDIVER.** *301 S Union Ave.* 410/939-5200; res: 800/245-1655. 8 rms, 3 story. S, D $65-$95; wkly rates. TV avail (by advance request). Complimentary bkfst. Dining rm Fri, Sat 5-9 pm. Ck-out 11 am, ck-in 3 pm. Some fireplaces. Some balconies. Queen Anne-style mansion (1886) with antique furnishings. Chesapeake Bay 2 blks. Cr cds: A, MC, V.

D **⊠** **⊁** **SC**

Restaurants

✔ ★ ★ **BAYOU.** *927 Pulaski Hwy (US 40).* 410/939-3565. Hrs: 11:30 am-10 pm. Closed Dec 24-26. Res accepted; required hols. Semi-a la carte: lunch $3-$6.25, dinner $7.50-$13.50. Child's meals. Specializes in seafood, veal. Parking. Cr cds: A, C, D, MC, V.

D

★ ★ **CRAZY SWEDE.** *400 N Union Ave.* 410/939-5440. Hrs: 11-2 am; Sun brunch 10 am-2:30 pm. Closed Thanksgiving, Dec 25. Res accepted; required Fri & Sat. Continental menu. Bar. Semi-a la carte: lunch $4.25-$6.95, dinner $11.95-$21. Sun brunch $3.50-$9. Child's meals. Specializes in seafood. Cr cds: A, C, D, MC, V.

D

La Plata (D-6)

Pop: 5,841 **Elev:** 193 ft **Area code:** 301 **Zip:** 20646

What to See and Do

1. **Doncaster Demonstration Forest.** 13 mi W on MD 6, near Doncaster. Heavily forested with yellow poplar, sweet gum, red and white oaks, and pine throughout its 1,477 acres. Hunting; 13 mi of hiking trails, bridle trails; picnic area. Cross-country skiing. Phone 934-2282.

2. **Smallwood State Park.** 16 mi W via MD 225, 224, near Rison. Restored home of Revolutionary General William Smallwood. Guided tour and historical program during summer. Hiking. Picnicking. Marina. Boating (launch, rentals). Fishing. Retreat House. Park (daily). Standard fees. Phone 743-7613.

3. **Port Tobacco.** 3 mi SW on MD 6. Infrared aerial photography and archaeological excavation revealed the site of one of the oldest continuously inhabited English settlements in North America. Appearing as a Native American village on Captain John Smith's map of the area (1608), the area was colonized by the English as early as 1638. The town was chartered in 1727, and the first courthouse was erected in 1729. Among the remaining buildings are the Chimney House (1765) and Stagg Hall (1732), an original colonial home still a private residence, Burch (Catslide) House (1700), the reconstructed Quenzel Store, house and a Federal period courthouse, with the Port Tobacco Museum on the second floor; archeological items on display, replicas of colonial houses; Civil War and John Wilkes Booth exhibits, 30-minute audiovisual film of *The Story of Port Tobacco.* (Apr-May & Sept-Dec, Sat & Sun afternoons; June-Aug, Wed-Sun afternoons; schedule may vary, phone ahead) Phone 934-4313. ¢¢

(For further information contact the Charles County Chamber of Commerce, 6360 Crain Hwy, phone 932-6500; or the Dept of Tourism, phone 934-9305.)

Annual Event

Charles County Fair. Phone 934-1234. Sept.

(See Waldorf; also see District of Columbia)

Motel

 ★ ★ **BEST WESTERN.** 6900 S US 301. 301/934-4900; FAX 301/934-5389. 74 rms, 2 story, 8 suites. Apr-Sept: S $50; D $56; each addl $5; suites $65-$80; under 13 free; lower rates rest of yr. Crib free. Pet accepted, some restrictions; non-refundable fee. TV; cable. Pool. Complimentary continental bkfst, coffee. Restaurant adj 11 am-11 pm. Ck-out noon. Coin lndry. Meeting rm. Refrigerators. Picnic table. Cr cds: A, C, D, DS, MC, V.

Laurel (C-6)

Pop: 19,438 **Elev:** 160 ft **Area code:** 301

What to See and Do

Montpelier Mansion (ca 1780). 3 mi SE on MD 197. Built and owned for generations by Maryland's Snowden family; Georgian architecture. George Washington and Abigail Adams were among its early visitors. On the grounds are boxwood gardens, an 18th-century herb garden and a small summer house. Tours; purchase ticket in gift shop. (Mar-Dec, Sun afternoons; closed major hols) Sr citizen rate. Candlelight tours held in early Dec. Phone 953-1376. ¢

(For further information contact the Corridor Information Centers, PO Box 288, Savage 20763; 490-2444. There are 2 information centers open daily all yr at the northbound and southbound rest areas on I-195 just outside of Laurel.)

Seasonal Event

Thoroughbred racing. Laurel Race Course, on MD 198. Entrances accessible from northbound or southbound on US 1, I-95 or from Baltimore-Washington Pkwy, MD 198 exit. The International Turf Festival is run here in Oct. Phone 725-0400. Jan-late Mar, June-July & Oct-Dec.

(See Bowie, College Park, Silver Spring; also see District of Columbia)

Motels

 ★ **BUDGET HOST VALENCIA.** 10131 Washington Blvd (US 1) (20723). 301/725-4200; res: 800/336-4366. 80 units in 5 bldgs, 1-2 story, 44 kits. S, D $30-$36; each addl $3; kit. units $40-$45; under 18 free. Crib free. TV. Complimentary coffee. Restaurant nearby. Ck-out 11 am. Cr cds: A, DS, MC, V.

★ ★ **HOLIDAY INN.** 3400 Ft Meade Rd (20724), MD 198 & Oak Lane. 301/498-0900; FAX 301/498-0900, ext. 160. 115 rms, 2 story. S $68-$74; D $74-$80; each addl $6; under 18 free. Crib free. Pet accepted; $100 refundable. TV; cable. Pool; lifeguard. Complimentary full bkfst (Mon-Fri). Restaurant 6:30 am-10 pm. Rm serv from 7 am. Bar 4 pm-midnight. Ck-out 11 am. Coin lndry. Meeting rms. Valet serv. Exercise equipt; weight machine, bicycle. Health club privileges. Cr cds: A, C, D, DS, ER, JCB, MC, V.

Motor Hotel

★ ★ **COMFORT SUITES.** 14402 Laurel Place (20707). 301/206-2600; FAX 301/725-0056. 119 rms, 5 story. S $70-$95; D $80-$100; each addl $10; kit. units $95-$125; under 18 free; wkly, wkend rates; higher rates: cherry blossom, Memorial Day wkend. Crib free. Pet accepted; $50 refundable. TV; cable. Indoor pool; lifeguard. Complimentary continental bkfst. Complimentary coffee in rms. Restaurant nearby. Ck-out noon. Coin lndry. Meeting rms. Sundries. Valet serv. Airport transportation avail. Exercise equipt; weight machine, bicycles, whirlpool. Refrigerators. Cr cds: A, C, D, DS, ER, JCB, MC, V.

Leonardtown (E-7)

Pop: 1,475 **Elev:** 87 ft **Area code:** 301 **Zip:** 20650

What to See and Do

1. **St Mary's County Historical Society Museum.** 11 Court House Dr. Local historical exhibits housed in old jail; also a genealogy library for researchers. A cannon from Leonard Calvert's ship, the *Ark,* is mounted in front. (Tues-Sat; closed Thanksgiving; also last wk Dec-1st wk Jan) Phone 475-2467. **Free.**

2. **Sotterley** (ca 1715). 9 mi E on MD 245. Overlooks Patuxent River. Working plantation; house in original condition. Chinese Chippendale staircase, antiques, original pine paneling in three rooms. Farming exhibit. (June-Oct, daily exc Mon; Apr-May & Nov, by appt) Phone 373-2280. ¢¢

3. **St Clements Island-Potomac River Museum.** 5 mi W via MD 234 to Clements, then 9 mi S on MD 242, in Colton Point. Maryland colonists first landed on the island in 1634. Exhibits trace 12,000 years of local history and pre-history. Excursion vessel (May-Sept, fee). Picnic area; fishing and crabbing. (Daily; closed major hols) Phone 769-2222. ¢

4. **Calvert Marine Museum.** 1 mi SE on MD 5, then 11 mi NE on MD 4, cross bridge and continue on MD 2, in Solomons; follow signs. Museum complex with exhibits relating to the culture and marine environment of Chesapeake Bay and Patuxent River estuary; fossils of marine life; estuarine biology displays, aquariums, touch-tank; maritime history exhibits, including boat-building gallery. Also here is the restored Drum Point Lighthouse, built 1883; 1/2 mi S is the Oyster House, with exhibits on the area's seafood industry. Gift shop. (Daily; closed Jan 1, Thanksgiving, Dec 25) Phone 410/326-2042. Main exhibit building ¢¢

(For further information contact the St Mary's County Division of Tourism, PO Box 653; 800/327-9023.)

Annual Events

St Mary's County Fair. Midway, seafood, horse shows. Late Sept.

Blessing of the Fleet & Historical Pageant. St Clements Island. Celebration commemorates first Roman Catholic Mass held on Maryland soil and Governor Leonard Calvert's proclamation of religious freedom. Blessing of oyster and clam fishing fleets. Folk dances, historical exhibits, concerts. 1st wkend Oct.

St Mary's County Oyster Festival. County Fairgrounds. National oyster shucking contest; oyster cook-off, seafood and crafts. 3rd wkend Oct.

(For accommodations see St Mary's City; also see District of Columbia)

Oakland (Garrett Co) (B-1)

Settled: 1851 **Pop:** 1,741 **Elev:** 2,384 ft **Area code:** 301 **Zip:** 21550

What to See and Do

1. **Garrett State Forest.** 5 mi NW on County 20. Approx 6,800 acres. The forest contains much wildlife. Fishing, hunting. Hiking and riding trails. Winter activities. Primitive camping. Forestry demonstration area. Phone 334-2038. Within the forest is

   Herrington Manor State Park. Well-developed 365-acre park with housekeeping cabins, 53-acre lake. Swimming, fishing, boating (launch, rentals). Hiking trails. Concession. Picnicking. Cross-country skiing (rentals). Interpretive programs (summer). No pets. Standard fees. Phone 334-9180.

2. **Swallow Falls State Park.** 9 mi NW on County 20. Surrounding 257 acres, the Youghiogheny River tumbles along the park's boundaries, passing through shaded rocky gorges and over sunny rapids. Muddy Creek produces a 51-foot waterfall. Here the last remaining stand of virgin hemlock dwarfs visitors. Fishing. Nature trails, hiking. Picnicking. Improved campsites. Pets at registered campsites only. Standard fees. Phone 334-9180.

3. **Potomac State Forest.** 9 mi SE off MD 560, along Potomac River. 10,685 acres for hiking, riding and hunting. Primitive camping. Timber is harvested regularly here and the area is important in the management of watershed and wildlife programs. Phone 334-2038.

4. **Deep Creek Lake State Park.** 10 mi NE off US 219. Approx 1,800 acres with 3,900-acre man-made lake. Swimming, bathhouse; fishing, boating (rowboat rentals). Nature, hiking trails. Picnicking (shelters), playground, concession. Improved campsites (fee). For general information phone 387-5563, for camping reservations phone 387-7877 (reservations accepted up to 1 yr in advance). Entrance for day-use area, per person ¢

5. **Backbone Mt.** 8 mi S on US 219, then 2 mi E on US 50. Highest point in the state (3,360 ft).

(For further information contact the Deep Creek Lake/Garrett County Promotion Council, Courthouse Building, 200 S Third St; 334-1948.)

Annual Events

Winterfest. Ski races, parade, fireworks. Late Feb or early Mar.

Garrett County Horse Shows. May, June, Aug & Sept.

Garrett County Fair. McHenry Fairgrounds. Early Aug.

Autumn Glory Festival. Celebrates fall foliage. Features arts & crafts, five-string banjo contest, state fiddle contest, western Maryland tournament of bands, parades, antique show. Phone 334-1948. Mid-Oct.

Motels

✔ ★ ★ **ALPINE VILLAGE.** *Rte 4, Box 5200, 7 mi N on US 219. 301/387-5534.* 29 motel rms, 2 story, 8 kits., 14 kit. chalets. June-Sept: S, D $50-$70; each addl $5; kit. units, studio rms $60; chalets for 1-6, $570-$670/wk; lower rates rest of yr. Crib free. TV; cable. Heated pool; wading pool. Continental bkfst avail for motel rms. Restaurant 5-10 pm; Sun from 4 pm. Bar 5-11 pm. Ck-out 11 am. Downhill/x-country ski 5 mi. On lake; private sand beach; dock. Some private patios. Picnic table, grills. Cr cds: A, D, DS, MC, V.

★ **LAKE BREEZ.** *Rte 6, Box 124, 9 mi N on US 219. 301/387-5566.* 10 rms. May-Nov 1: S, D $55-64; each addl $4; MAP avail. Closed rest of yr. Crib free. TV. Pool privileges. Restaurant adj 7 am-2 pm, 5-9:30 pm. Ck-out 11 am. Golf privileges, greens fee $35-$45. On lake; private beach, dock. Picnic tables. Cr cds: A, DS, MC, V.

★ **LAKE SIDE MOTOR COURT.** *Rte 4, Box 5251, 8 mi N on US 219. 301/387-5566.* 10 rms, 1 cottage. Mid-June-Labor Day: S, D $55-$80; each addl $5; cottage for 2-6, $400/wk; MAP avail; lower rates May-mid-June, after Labor Day-Oct. Closed rest of yr. TV; cable. Pool privileges. Playground. Restaurant adj 7 am-2 pm, 5-9:30 pm. Ck-out 11 am. Refrigerators. Picnic area, grills. Overlooks lake; private beach; dock. Cr cds: A, D, DS, MC, V.

Restaurants

★ ★ **POINT VIEW INN.** *(Deep Creek Dr, McHenry) 8 mi N on US 219. 301/387-5555.* Hrs: 8 am-10 pm; Sun to 9 pm; early-bird dinner 5-6:30 pm. Closed Easter, Dec 25. Res accepted. German, Amer menu. Bar 1 pm-2 am. Semi-a la carte: bkfst $2.75-$5.50, lunch $2.75-$6.50, dinner $6.50-$21. Child's meals. Specialities: veal Cordon Bleu, Rahmschnitzel, prime rib. Entertainment wkends. Parking. Patio dining. Elevated dining areas with view of Deep Creek Lake. Cr cds: A, MC, V.

★ ★ **SILVER TREE.** *Deep Creek Lake, 8 blks N on Glendale Rd. 301/387-4040.* Hrs: 5-10 pm; Sat to 11 pm; summer hrs: 5-11 pm. Italian, Amer menu. Bar to 2 am. Semi-a la carte: dinner $4.99-$19.95. Child's meals. Specializes in pasta, seafood, steak. Seafood bar. Parking. 1890s decor. Stone fireplaces. View of lake. Cr cds: A, C, D, DS, MC, V.

Ocean City (E-10)

Founded: 1869 **Pop:** 5,146 **Elev:** 7 ft **Area code:** 410 **Zip:** 21842

Deep-sea fishing is highly regarded in Maryland's only Atlantic Ocean resort. The white sand beach, 3-mile boardwalk, amusements, golf courses and boating draw thousands of visitors every summer.

What to See and Do

Assateague Island National Seashore. 1 mi W on US 50, then 7 mi S on MD 611. A 37-mile barrier strand that supports an intricate ecosystem, Assateague is also known for its population of ponies, Sika deer (miniature Oriental elk) and, in autumn, the migratory peregrine falcon. Campground (fee; phone 641-3030); hike-in and canoe-in campsites and day-use facilities; conducted walks and demonstrations in summer. Visitor center (daily; closed winter hols). For further information phone 641-1441 or -3030 (camping). (See CHINCOTEAGUE, VA) Per vehicle ¢¢ Also on the island is

   Assateague State Park. 755 acres with 2 miles of ocean frontage and gentle, sloping beaches. Swimming, fishing. Boat launch. Picnicking, concession (summer). Bicycle, hiking trails. Camping (Apr-Nov). Standard fees (summer). For reservations, contact 7307 Stephen Decatur Hwy, Berlin 21811. Phone 641-2120. Entrance fee (Memorial Day-Labor Day) per person ¢

(For further information contact the Chamber of Commerce, 12320 Ocean Gateway; 213-0552.)

Annual Events

Fishing contests and tournaments. Many held throughout the yr. For exact dates contact the Chamber of Commerce.

Seasonal Event

Harness racing. Delmarva Downs. 4 mi W on US 50. Nightly exc Mon. Children with adult only. Phone 641-0600. Early Apr-Labor Day.

Motels

★ **BEACHMARK.** *PO Box 540, 73rd St and Oceanside.* 410/524-7300; res: 800/638-1600. 96 kit. units, 3 story. No elvtr. July-Aug: S, D $88; under 6 free; each addl $6; wkly rates; higher rates wkends & hols (3-night min); lower rates May-June & Sept. Closed rest of yr. TV; cable. Pool. Restaurant 6 am-2 pm. Ck-out 11 am. Bellhops (in season). Beach ½ blk. Cr cds: MC, V.

★ ★ **CASTLE IN THE SAND.** *Oceanfront at 37th St.* 410/289-6846; res: 800/552-7263; FAX 410/289-9446. 36 rms, 5 story, 27 cottages, 108 kit. units. Early July-late Aug: S, D $140-$159; each addl $7; kit. units $149-$179; cottages $650-$1,125/wk; under 12 free; lower rates mid-Apr-early July & late Aug-late Oct. Closed rest of yr. Crib $5. TV; cable. Pool; lifeguard. Supervised child's activities (June-Aug). Restaurant 7:30 am-midnight. Bar 11-2 am; entertainment wkends. Ck-out 11 am. Meeting rm. Bellhops. Free airport transportation. Game rm. Some balconies. Cr cds: A, D, DS, MC, V.

✔ ★ **EXECUTIVE.** *Box 540, Baltimore Ave at 30th St.* 410/289-3101; res: 800/638-1600. 47 rms, 3 story. No elvtr. Memorial Day wkend & July-Labor Day (3-day min wkends): S, D $68; each addl $6; under 6 free; varied lower rates late May-June & after Labor Day-mid-Sept. Closed rest of yr. Crib $6. TV; cable. Restaurant nearby. Ck-out 11 am. Refrigerators. Ocean, beach ½ blk. Cr cds: MC, V.

★ **GATEWAY.** *4800 Coastal Hwy.* 410/524-6500; res: 800/382-2582. 59 kit. units, 3 story. July-mid-Aug: S, D $170-$200; each addl $10; suites $1,000/wk; under 6 free; higher rates hol wkends; varied lower rates rest of yr. Crib $10. TV; cable. Pool; wading pool, whirlpool, lifeguard (summer). Playground. Complimentary coffee in rms. Restaurant 11-2 am. Rm serv. Bar; entertainment, dancing (off-season, wkends only). Ck-out 11 am. Coin lndry. Lawn games. Balconies. Picnic tables. On ocean, swimming beach. Cr cds: A, C, D, MC, V.

★ **NASSAU.** *6002 Coastal Hwy.* 410/524-6451. 63 rms, 3 story, 42 kits. No elvtr. July-late Aug: S, D $83-$103; each addl $6; higher rates wkends; varied lower rates Apr-June & late Aug-Oct. Closed rest of yr. Crib avail. TV; cable. Pool. Restaurant opp 7 am-11 pm. Ck-out 11 am. Sun deck. On ocean, beach. Cr cds: MC, V.

★ ★ **QUALITY INN OCEANFRONT.** *5400 Coastal Hwy, Oceanfront & 54th St.* 410/524-7200; res: 800/638-2106. 130 kit. units, 3-5 story. Late May-Sept: kit. units $74-$209; each addl $5; under 6 free; wkly rates; package plans; higher rates hols; varied lower rates rest of yr. Crib free. TV; cable. 2 pools, 1 indoor; wading pool. Playground. Restaurant 8 am-9 pm. Bar 11 am-11 pm. Ck-out 11 am. Free lndry facilities. Bellhops (summer). Tennis. Exercise equipt; weights, bicycles, whirlpools, saunas. Game rm. Lawn games. Private patios, balconies. Picnic tables, grills. On ocean, swimming beach. Cr cds: A, C, D, DS, ER, JCB, MC, V.

★ ★ **RAMADA LIMITED OCEANFRONT.** *Box 160, 32nd St at oceanfront.* 410/289-6444. 76 kit. units, 3 story. No elvtr. July-Aug: S, D $144-$159; each addl $7; surcharge off-season wkends; varied lower rates Feb-June & Sept-Oct. Closed rest of yr. Over 21 yrs only (exc with parents). Crib free. TV; cable; in-rm movies avail. Pool; wading pool. Complimentary continental bkfst. Complimentary coffee,

refreshments in lobby. Ck-out 11 am. Guest lndry. Bellhops. Balconies overlook beach. Picnic area. Cr cds: A, C, D, DS, ER, MC, V.

★ **SAFARI.** *Boardwalk at 13th St.* 410/289-6411. 46 rms in 2 bldgs, 3 & 4 story. July-Aug (3-day min wkends): S, D $98; under 12 free; lower rates Apr-June & Sept-Oct. Closed rest of yr. Crib free. Pet accepted, some restrictions; $6. TV; cable. Restaurant opp from 8 am. Ck-out 11 am. Bellhops. Balconies. On ocean. Cr cds: A, C, D, DS, MC, V.

✔ ★ ★ **SAHARA.** *Box 540, 19th St at Boardwalk.* 410/289-8101; res: 800/638-1600. 161 rms in 4 bldgs, 3 & 4 story, 5 kits. Elvtr in Tower bldg. Late June-mid-Sept: S, D $68-$118; each addl $6; kit. units $78-$128; lower rates late Apr-late June & late Sept. Closed rest of yr. Crib $6. TV. 2 pools. Restaurant 6 am-3 pm. Ck-out 11 am. Refrigerators. Some balconies. On beach. Cr cds: MC, V.

★ ★ **SATELLITE.** *Box 386, 2401 Atlantic Ave, Oceanfront & 24th St.* 410/289-6401. 72 units, 4 story, 26 kits. July-Aug: S, D $95-$105; kit. units $100-$115; under 6 free; wkly rates; varied lower rates Mar-June & Sept-Oct. Closed rest of yr. Crib $5. TV; cable. Pool. Restaurant 7 am-2 pm. Ck-out 11 am. Bellhops. Balconies. On beach. Cr cds: A, MC, V.

★ ★ **SURF AND SANDS.** *Box 236, Boardwalk at 23rd St.* 410/289-7161. 95 rms, 2-3 story, 20 kits. July-late Aug: S, D $95-$105; each addl $7; suites $135; kit. units $105-$115; under 7 free; wkends in season 3-day min; varied lower rates Easter-June & late Aug-mid-Oct. Closed rest of yr. Crib $7. TV; cable. Pool; wading pool. Restaurant 7 am-2 pm. Ck-out 11 am. Balconies. On beach. Cr cds: MC, V.

★ **TIDES.** *PO Box 540, 71st St and Oceanside.* 410/524-7100; res: 800/638-1600. 54 kit. units, 3 story. No elvtr. Late June-late Aug: S, D $86; each addl $6; under 6 free; higher rates: wkends & hols (3-night min), July-Aug wkdays (2-night min), Memorial Day & Labor Day; lower rates May-late June & Sept. Closed rest of yr. Crib $6. TV; cable. Pool. Restaurant nearby. Ck-out 11 am. Bellhops (in season). Some balconies. Ocean ½ blk. Cr cds: MC, V.

Motor Hotels

★ ★ **BRIGHTON SUITES.** *12500 Coastal Hwy.* 410/250-7600; res: 800/227-5788; FAX 410/250-7603. 57 suites. July-Aug: suites $109-$179; each addl $10; under 16 free; wkly, mid-wk rates; lower rates rest of yr. Crib $6. TV; cable. Indoor pool. Complimentary coffee in lobby. Ck-out 11 am. Meeting rms. Bellhops (in season). Exercise equipt; weight machine, bicycles. Refrigerators, wet bars. Balconies. Near ocean beach. Cr cds: A, C, D, DS, MC, V.

★ ★ **CAROUSEL.** *11700 Coastal Hwy, (MD 528) at 118th St.* 410/524-1000; res: 800/641-0011; FAX 410/524-7766. 266 kit. units. Memorial Day-Labor Day: S, D $139-$189; each addl $12; suites $275-$350; under 17 free; varied lower rates rest of yr. Crib free. TV; cable. Pool; lifeguard. Free supervised child's activities (Memorial Day-Labor Day). Restaurant 7:30 am-10 pm. Rm serv. Bar; entertainment, dancing. Ck-out 11 am. Meeting rms. Bellhops. Concierge. Exercise equipt; weights, bicycles, whirlpool, sauna. Ice rink. Rec rm. Game rm. Private patios, balconies. Cr cds: A, C, D, DS, MC, V.

★ **COMFORT INN BOARDWALK.** *5th St and Oceanfront.* 410/289-5155; res: 800/282-5155. 84 kit. units in 2 bldgs, 5 story. June-Aug: S, D $130-$160; each addl $10; under 12 free; lower rates

Mar-May & Sept-Nov. Closed rest of yr. Crib free. TV; cable. Pool. Complimentary coffee in lobby. Restaurant nearby. Ck-out 11 am. Bellhops. Balconies. On ocean. Cr cds: A, C, D, DS, ER, JCB, MC, V.

★ ★ ★ **DUNES MANOR.** *28th St at Oceanfront. 410/289-1100; res: 800/523-2888; FAX 410/289-4905.* 160 rms, 11 story, 10 kit. suites. Mid-June-early Sept: S, D $129-$189; each addl $10; kit. suites $225-$280; under 17 free; wkly rates; lower rates rest of yr. TV; cable. Indoor/outdoor pool; wading pool. Restaurant 7:30 am-9 pm. Rm serv. Bar 11-2 am. Ck-out 11 am. Meeting rms. Bellhops. Sundries. Free parking, some covered. Exercise equipt; treadmill, bicycles, whirlpool. Refrigerators. Balconies. On ocean, swimming beach. Cr cds: A, D, DS, MC, V.

★ ★ ★ **HOLIDAY INN OCEANFRONT.** *6600 Coastal Hwy/Oceanfront, Oceanfront & 67th St. 410/524-1600; FAX 410/524-1135.* 216 kit. units, 8 story. July-Aug: S, D $150-$214; each addl $9; under 19 free; higher rates hol wkends; lower rates rest of yr. Crib free. TV; cable, in-rm movies. 2 pools, 1 indoor; wading pools, poolside serv. Restaurant 6:30 am-1 pm, 5-10 pm. Rm serv. Bar 5-11 pm. Ck-out 11 am. Free lndry facilities. Meeting rms. Bellhops. Tennis. Exercise equipt; weight machines, bicycle, whirlpool, sauna. Game rm. Balconies. Picnic tables. On ocean. Cr cds: A, C, D, DS, ER, JCB, MC, V.

★ ★ **HOWARD JOHNSON.** *1109 Atlantic Ave, 12th & Boardwalk. 410/289-7251; res: 800/926-1122; FAX 410/289-3435.* 90 rms, 7 story. Mid-June-Labor Day: S, D $109-$179; each addl $5; under 12 free; lower rates rest of yr. Crib free. TV; cable. Indoor pool. Restaurant 8 am-10 pm. Rm serv in season. Ck-out 11 am. Valet serv. Sundries. Gift shop. Free garage parking. Balconies. Some refrigerators. On ocean beach. Cr cds: A, C, D, DS, ER, JCB, MC, V.

★ ★ **PHILLIPS BEACH PLAZA.** *Box K, Oceanfront at 13th St. 410/289-9121; res: 800/492-5834; FAX 410/289-3041.* 86 units, 5 story, 26 kits. July-late Aug: S, D $100-$125; each addl $7.50; kit. units $110-$155; $10 surcharge wkends; package plans; lower rates rest of yr. Crib $7.50. TV; cable. Restaurant 8 am-noon, 5-10 pm. Bar 5 pm-2 am; entertainment 6-11 pm. Ck-out 11 am. Bellhops. Shopping arcade. On ocean. Cr cds: A, C, D, DS, MC, V.

✔ ★ ★ **PLIM PLAZA.** *Box 160, Boardwalk & 2nd St. 410/289-6181; res: 800/638-2106.* 181 units, 5 story. June-Aug: S, D $79-$128; wkly rates; package plans; lower rates mid-Apr-June & Sept. Closed rest of yr. Crib free. TV; cable. Pool privileges. Restaurant 4:30-9 pm. Ck-out 11 am. Meeting rms. Bellhops. Whirlpool. Rec rm. Refrigerators. Some private patios. On boardwalk. Cr cds: C, D, DS, MC, V.

Hotels

★ ★ ★ **COCONUT MALORIE.** *60th St in the Bay, on Isle of Wight Bay. 410/723-6100; res: 800/767-6060; FAX 410/524-9327.* 85 suites, 5 story. Memorial Day-Labor Day: S, D $109-$199; each addl $15; wkly rate; golf plan; lower rates rest of yr. Crib free. TV; cable. Pool; poolside serv. Complimentary coffee in rms. Restaurant adj 11 am-11 pm. Ck-out noon. Meeting rms. Concierge. Airport transportation. 18-hole golf privileges, greens fee, pro, putting green. Health club privileges. Whirlpools, refrigerators; many bathrm phones. Balconies. Original Haitian art; antique collection. Footbridge over marsh to dining facilities. Cr cds: A, C, D, MC, V.

★ ★ ★ **LIGHTHOUSE CLUB.** *56th St In The Bay, on the Isle of Wight Bay. 410/524-5400; res: 800/767-6060; FAX 410/524-9327.* 23 rms, 2 story. Memorial Day-Labor Day: S, D $129-$219; package plan;

lower rates rest of yr. TV; cable, in-rm movies avail. Pool privileges. Complimentary continental bkfst. Complimentary coffee in rms. Restaurant adj 11 am-11 pm. Ck-out noon. Meeting rm. Concierge. Airport transportation. Tennis privileges. Golf privileges. Health club privileges. Bathrm phones, in-rm whirlpools, refrigerators, wet bars; some fireplaces. Balconies. Unique octagonal structure; wedge-shaped rms provide spectacular view of bay. Luxurious appointments; antique collection. Footbridge over marsh provides access to adj recreational and dining facilities. Cr cds: A, C, D, MC, V.

★ ★ ★ **PRINCESS ROYALE.** *Oceanfront at 91st St, 3 mi N on Coastal Hwy. 410/524-7777; res: 800/476-9253; FAX 410/524-7787.* 310 kit. suites, 5 story. Mid-June-Labor Day: D $99-$209; under 12 free; wkly rates; lower rates rest of yr. Crib $10. TV; cable. Indoor pool; poolside serv. Supervised child's activities (mid-June-Labor Day). Complimentary coffee in rms. Restaurant 7-2 am. Bar 11-2 am; entertainment. Ck-out 11 am. Coin lndry. Convention facilities. Beauty shop. Lighted tennis. 18-hole golf privileges, greens fee $30, pro, putting green, driving range. Exercise equipt; weight machine, bicycles, whirlpool, sauna. Game rm. Rec rm. Lawn games. Balconies. On ocean; swimming beach, ocean deck, private boardwalk. All suites with ocean view. Cr cds: A, C, D, DS, MC, V.

★ ★ ★ **SHERATON FONTAINEBLEAU.** *10100 Ocean Hwy (MD 528). 410/524-3535; FAX 410/524-3834.* 250 rms, 16 story, 8 kits. June-Aug: S, D $130-$210; each addl $14; suites, kit. units $275-$700; studio rms $240; under 17 free; higher rates hol wkends (3-day min); lower rates rest of yr. Crib $14. Pet accepted; $14. TV; cable. Heated pool; poolside serv in season, lifeguard. Coffee in rms. Restaurant 6:30 am-11 pm. Bar to 2 am; entertainment, dancing nightly (wkends in winter). Ck-out 11 am. Meeting rms. Beauty shop. Airport, bus depot transportation. Exercise rm; instructor, weights, bicycles, whirlpool, steam rm, sauna. Tennis & golf privileges. Game rm. Refrigerators. Balconies. On ocean, beach. Cr cds: A, C, D, DS, ER, JCB, MC, V.

Inns

★ ★ ★ **ATLANTIC HOTEL.** *(2 N Main St, Berlin 21811) 8 mi W on MD 50 to MD 113, S to Berlin. 410/641-3589; FAX 410/641-4928.* 17 rms, 3 story. S, D $49-$125; golf packages. Crib free. TV avail. Complimentary bkfst. Dining rm 6-10 pm. Bar noon-1 am. Ck-out 11 am, ck-in 3 pm. 18-hole golf privileges, greens fee $30-$35, pro, putting green. Porch on each floor. Restored Victorian hotel (1895); rms furnished with antiques. 2nd-floor parlor. Cr cds: MC, V.

★ ★ **MERRY SHERWOOD PLANTATION.** *(8909 Worcester Hwy, Berlin 21811) 6 mi W on US 50, then 3 mi S on MD 113. 410/641-2112; FAX 410/641-3605.* 8 rms, 6 with bath. No rm phones. D $125-$150; wkly rates. Children over 12 yrs only. TV in library. Complimentary full bkfst, tea/sherry. Restaurant nearby. Ck-out 11 am, ck-in 2 pm. Built 1859; on grounds of former plantation; large variety of trees and shrubs. Totally nonsmoking. Cr cds: MC, V.

Restaurants

✔ ★ ★ **ANGELO'S.** *2706 Coastal Hwy. 410/289-6522.* Hrs: 4-10 pm. Closed Jan; also Tues Oct-Apr. Res accepted. Italian menu. Serv bar. Semi-a la carte: dinner $6.50-$15.95. Child's meals. Specializes in veal, seafood. Own ravioli, fettucine, gnocchi. Cr cds: A, C, D, DS, MC, V.

★ ★ **BONFIRE.** *71st St & Coastal Hwy. 410/524-7171.* Hrs: 5-11 pm; from 4:30 pm in season; early-bird dinner 4:30-6 pm. Closed

Tues in winter; also 10 days at Christmas. Res accepted. Bar to 2 am. Semi-a la carte: dinner $9.95-$25. Child's meals. Specializes in steak, prime rib, seafood. Cr cds: A, C, D, MC, V.

★ ★ **EMBERS.** *24th St & Philadelphia Ave. 410/289-3322.* Hrs: 3:30-10 pm; also 7 am-1 pm Memorial Day wknd-mid-Oct. Closed Dec-Feb. Res accepted. Bar to 2 am. Buffet: bkfst $6.50. Semi-a la carte: dinner $12-$22. Seafood buffet $18.50. Child's meals. Specializes in fresh seafood, steak, prime rib. Parking. Family-owned. Cr cds: A, D, DS, MC, V.

D

★ ★ **FAGER'S ISLAND.** *60th St, in the Bay. 410/524-5500.* Hrs: 11 am-11 pm. Res accepted. Bar to 2 am. Semi-a la carte: lunch $3.95-$10.50, dinner $16.50-$25. Specializes in seafood, beef, roast duckling. Band (off-season, wkends only). Parking. View of bay. Cr cds: A, C, D, MC, V.

D

★ ★ **HARRISON'S HARBOR WATCH.** *806 S Boardwalk. 410/289-5121.* Hrs: 5-10 pm; July-Aug from 4:30 pm. Closed Mon-Thurs Nov-Mar. Res accepted. Bar 11:30 am-11 pm. Wine list. Semi-a la carte: dinner $8.95-$24.95. Child's meals. Specializes in fresh seafood, fish. Raw bar. Own breads. Parking. View of inlet overlooking Assateague Island. Cr cds: A, DS, ER, MC, V.

D

★ ★ **HOBBIT.** *81st St & Bay. 410/524-8100.* Hrs: 11-2 am; early-bird dinner 5-6 pm. Closed Dec 24-25. Res accepted. French, Amer menu. Bar. Wine list. Semi-a la carte: lunch $3.95-$8.95, dinner $15.95-$21.95. Child's meals. Specializes in beef, seafood. Own baking. Parking. Outdoor dining. View of bay. Cr cds: A, MC, V.

D

✔ ★ **JR'S.** *131st St at Coastal Hwy. 410/250-3100.* Hrs: 4-10 pm; Sun from 3 pm. Closed Thanksgiving, Dec 24, 25; also Tues off-season. Bar. Semi-a la carte: dinner $8.95-$16.95. Child's meals. Specializes in barbecued ribs, steaks, seafood. Entertainment June-Aug. Parking. Cr cds: A, DS, MC, V.

D

✔ ★ **LA HACIENDA.** *8003 Coastal Hwy. 410/524-8080.* Hrs: 5-10 pm. Closed Thanksgiving, Dec 25. Mexican menu. Bar. Semi-a la carte: dinner $5.75-$16.95. Child's meals. Specializes in fajitas, burritos. Parking. Cr cds: A, MC, V.

D

★ ★ **MARINA DECK.** *306 Dorchester St. 410/289-4411.* Hrs: 11:30 am-11 pm; Sun from 10 am. Closed early Oct-Easter. Bar. Semi-a la carte: lunch $4.95-$7.95, dinner $7.95-$23.95. Child's meals. Specializes in fish, lobster, coconut muffins. Parking. On waterfront. Cr cds: A, MC, V.

★ ★ **MARIO'S.** *22nd & Philadelphia Ave. 410/289-9445.* Hrs: 5-10 pm. Closed 10 days beginning mid-Dec; also Mon Oct-Memorial Day. Res accepted. Italian, Amer menu. Bar. Semi-a la carte: dinner $6.95-$20. Child's meals. Specializes in steak. Parking. Family-owned. Cr cds: A, D, MC, V.

★ ★ **OCEAN CLUB.** *49th St at Oceanfront. 410/524-7500.* Hrs: 11:30-2 am; early-bird dinner 5-7 pm; Memorial Day-Labor Day & wkends rest of yr from 8 am. Closed Dec 25; Tues off-season. Res accepted. Bar. Semi-a la carte: bkfst $3.25-$9.95 lunch $5-$10, dinner $12-$21. Child's meals. Specializes in seafood. Entertainment Apr-Oct; rest of yr, wkends only. Parking. Outdoor dining. On ocean. Cr cds: A, C, MC, V.

D

★ ★ **PHILLIPS CRAB HOUSE.** *2004 Philadelphia Ave at 21st St. 410/289-6821.* Hrs: 5-9 pm; Sat, Sun noon-10 pm; summer noon-11 pm. Closed Nov-Mar. Serv bar. Semi-a la carte: lunch, dinner $4-$25. Seafood buffet $19.95. Child's meals. Specializes in crab

dishes, fresh seafood. Parking. Family-owned. Cr cds: A, D, DS, MC, V.

★ ★ **PHILLIPS SEAFOOD HOUSE.** *14101 Coastal Hwy, at 141st St. 410/250-1200.* Hrs: noon-10 pm; Fri, Sat to 11 pm; off-season Mon-Thurs 5-9 pm. Closed last wk Nov-Mar 1. Bar to 2 am. Semi-a la carte: lunch $4.50-$7.95, dinner $8.95-$24.95. Child's meals. Specializes in fresh seafood, crab, lobster. Entertainment from 6 pm, exc Mon; off-season Thurs-Sun. Parking. Cr cds: A, D, DS, MC, V.

D

✔ ★ **TALBOT STREET CAFE.** *7 Talbot St. 410/289-3806.* Hrs: noon-2 am; Sun brunch 11 am-3 pm. Res accepted. Bar. Semi-a la carte: lunch, dinner $3.95-$6.95. Sun brunch $4.95-$6.95. Cover charge (special events). Specialties: seafood chowder, shrimp salad, meatloaf. Entertainment. Outdoor dining. Cr cds: MC, V.

✔ ★ ★ **THOMPSON'S ORIGINAL SEA GIRT HOUSE.** *8203 Coastal Hwy. 410/723-2500.* Hrs: 4-10:30 pm; Sat & Sun from noon; early-bird dinner 4-6 pm. Closed Dec 25; also 3 wks Jan. Res accepted. Bar to 2 am. Semi-a la carte: lunch $5-$7, dinner $12-$16. Child's meals. Specializes in seafood. Entertainment Wed-Sun. Parking. Outdoor dining. Contemporary decor; casual elegance. Panoramic bayfront view. Family-owned. Cr cds: A, MC, V.

D

Pikesville (B-7)

Pop: 24,815 **Area code:** 410 **Zip:** 21208

(See Baltimore)

Motels

✔ ★ **COMFORT INN NORTHWEST.** *10 Wooded Way, at I-695 exit 20. 410/484-7700; FAX 410/653-1516.* 103 rms, 2-3 story. No elvtr. S $40-$69; D $53-$75; each addl $7; under 18 free; wkly, monthly rates. Crib free. TV; cable. Pool; wading pool, lifeguard. Complimentary continental bkfst. Restaurant adj 6:30 am-11:30 pm. Ck-out 11 am. Coin lndry. Meeting rms. Valet serv Mon-Fri. Cr cds: A, C, D, DS, ER, JCB, MC, V.

D ⊠ ⌇ ⌇ 🔥 🐾 SC

★ ★ **HOLIDAY INN PIKESVILLE.** *1721 Reisterstown Rd, at I-695 exit 20. 410/486-5600; FAX 410/484-9377.* 108 rms, 2 story. S, D $49-$79; under 18 free; higher rates Preakness. Crib free. Pet accepted. TV; cable. Pool; poolside serv, lifeguard. Restaurant 6:30 am-2 pm, 5-10 pm; Sat, Sun from 7 am. Rm serv. Bar 4 pm-midnight. Ck-out noon. Meeting rms. Valet serv. Some refrigerators. Cr cds: A, C, D, DS, ER, JCB, MC, V.

D 🐾 ⌇ ⌇ 🔥 SC

Motor Hotel

★ ★ ★ **HILTON INN.** *1726 Reisterstown Rd, at I-695 exit 20S. 410/653-1100; FAX 410/484-4138.* 165 rms, 5 story. S $72-$118; D $82-$128; each addl $10; suites $150-$425; wkend plans; family rates. Crib $10. TV; cable. Pool; lifeguard. Restaurant 7 am-11 pm. Rm serv. Bar 11-2 am; entertainment Fri & Sat, dancing. Ck-out noon. Meeting rms. Bellhops. Valet serv. Gift shop. Barber, beauty shop. Airport transportation. Indoor tennis, pro. Exercise rm; instructor, weight machines, bicycles, sauna. Bathrm phones. Cr cds: A, C, D, DS, ER, MC, V.

D 🏃 ⌇ 🎿 ⌇ 🔥 SC

Inn

★ ★ ★ **GRAMERCY.** *(1400 Greenspring Valley Rd, Stevenson 21153) I-695 exit 23N, Falls Rd to 2nd light, left on Greenspring Valley Rd. 410/486-2405.* 2 rms, 3 story, 2 suites. No rm phones. D $90-$150; each addl $25; suites $100-$150; family rates. Crib $10. TV. Pool; whirlpool. Complimentary full bkfst. Ck-out noon, ck-in after 3-6 pm. Bellhop. Tennis. Lawn games. Picnic tables. Mansion (1902) on 45-acre wooded estate. Flower, herb gardens. Totally nonsmoking. Cr cds: DS, MC, V.

Restaurant

★ ★ ★ **FIORI.** *(100 Painters Mill Rd, Owings Mills) From I-695 exit 19, 4 mi NW on MD 795, then right on Owings Mill Blvd, then right on Dolfield Rd S, at jct Painters Mill Rd. 410/363-3131.* Hrs: 11:30 am-2:30 pm, 5-9 pm; Sat 5-10 pm; Sun 4-8:30 pm; early-bird dinner Mon-Fri 5-6:30 pm. Closed Jan 1, July 4, Dec 25. Res accepted. Italian menu. Bar. Wine list. A la carte entrees: lunch $4.50-$8.25, dinner $14-$20. Specializes in fresh seafood, homemade pasta, veal. Parking. In Owings mansion (1767), house of proprietor of Owings mills, for which town was named. Cr cds: A, MC, V.

Pocomoke City (F-9)

Founded: 1670 **Pop:** 3,922 **Elev:** 22 ft **Area code:** 410 **Zip:** 21851

(For information contact the Chamber of Commerce, City Hall, 2nd floor, Clarke Ave & Vine St, PO Box 356; 957-1919.)

(See Crisfield)

Motels

★ **DAYS INN.** *1540 Ocean Hwy, on US 13S. 410/957-3000; FAX 410/957-3147.* 87 rms, 2 story. Mid-June-mid-Sept: S, D $63.95-$65.95; each addl $6; under 18 free; higher rates Pony Penning; lower rates rest of yr. Crib free. Pet accepted. TV; cable. Pool. Restaurant 6 am-2 pm, 5-9 pm; Sun 7 am-9 pm. Rm serv. Bar 5-11 pm. Ck-out 11 am. Meeting rms. Refrigerators. Cr cds: A, C, D, DS, MC, V.

✔ ★ ★ **QUALITY INN.** *825 Ocean Hwy, 2¹/₂ mi S on US 13. 410/957-1300; FAX 410/957-9329.* 64 rms. S $42-$56; D $46-$70; each addl $5; under 18 free; higher rates Pony Penning. Crib free. Pet accepted. TV; cable. Pool; wading pool. Restaurant 6 am-10 pm. Bar 11-1 am. Ck-out 11 am. Sundries. Some in-rm whirlpools, refrigerators. Picnic tables, grills. Cr cds: A, C, D, DS, ER, JCB, MC, V.

Restaurant

★ **UPPER DECK.** *1245 Ocean Hwy, 2 mi S of US 113. 410/957-3166.* Hrs: 11 am-10 pm; Sun noon-9 pm. Res accepted. Bar to 2 am; Sun to 11 pm. Semi-a la carte: lunch $3.25-$5.95, dinner $7.50-$20. Child's meals. Specializes in local seafood, steak. Own desserts. Entertainment Thurs-Sat. Parking. Antiques. Cr cds: MC, V.

Rockville (C-6)

Pop: 44,835 **Elev:** 451 ft **Area code:** 301

Second largest city in the state of Maryland, Rockville is the seat of Montgomery County, located at the north edge of the District of Columbia. The Great Falls of the Potomac are 9 miles south off MD 189. This series of small falls was pretty but unnavigable, so the Chesapeake and Ohio Canal (see CHESAPEAKE AND OHIO CANAL NATIONAL HISTORICAL PARK) was built from Washington, DC, to Cumberland to simplify travel. Stone locks and levels are still visible. The graves of F. Scott and Zelda Fitzgerald are in St Mary's Cemetery.

What to See and Do

Beall-Dawson House (1815). 103 W Montgomery Ave. Federal architecture; period furnishings; library; museum shop; 19th-century doctor's office. Tours guided by docents. (Tues-Sat; also 1st Sun of month; closed major hols) Sr citizen rate. Phone 762-1492. ¢

(For further information contact the Chamber of Commerce, 600 E Jefferson St, PO Box 4173, 20850; 424-9300.)

Annual Event

Scottish Festival. Indoor Scottish ceilidh; pipe bands; Highland and country dancers; fiddler, harper; food and crafts. Phone 279-8500. 1st Sat May.

(See Gaithersburg)

Motels

★ ★ ★ **COURTYARD BY MARRIOTT.** *2500 Research Blvd (20850). 301/670-6700; FAX 301/670-9023.* 147 rms, 3 story, 14 suites. S $89; D $99; each addl (over 4) $10; suites $108-$118; under 12 free; wkly rates. Crib free. TV; cable. Indoor pool; lifeguard. Complimentary coffee. Restaurant 6:30 am-2 pm, 5-10 pm, wknds to 2 pm. Rm serv from 5 pm. Bar 11 am-11 pm. Ck-out 1 pm. Coin lndry. Meeting rms. Valet serv. Sundries. Exercise equipt; weight machine, bicycles, whirlpool. Balconies. Refrigerators avail. Cr cds: A, C, D, DS, MC, V.

✔ ★ **DAYS INN.** *16001 Shady Grove Rd (20850). 301/948-4300.* 190 rms, 2 story. S, D $45-$70; each addl $5; under 18 free; wkend rates. Crib free. Pet accepted. TV; cable. Pool. Playground. Restaurant 6:30 am-10 pm. Bar 10-12:30 am, Sun from 11 am. Ck-out 11 am. Cr cds: A, C, D, DS, MC, V.

Motor Hotel

★ ★ ★ **WOODFIN SUITES.** *1380 Piccard Dr (20850). 301/590-9880; res: 800/237-8811; FAX 301/590-9614.* 203 suites, 3 story. S, D $120-$151; each addl $15; 2-bedrm suites $187; under 12 free. Crib $10. TV; in-rm movies. Pool; lifeguard. Complimentary full bkfst. Restaurant 6-9 am, 11:30 am-2 pm, 5-10 pm, wknd hrs vary. Bar from 5 pm. Ck-out noon. Meeting rms. Valet serv. Sundries. Free local transportation. Exercise equipt; weight machine, treadmill, whirlpool. Refrigerators. Cr cds: A, C, D, DS, ER, JCB, MC, V.

Hotel

★ ★ ★ **HOLIDAY INN CROWNE PLAZA.** *1750 Rockville Pike (20852). 301/468-1100; FAX 301/468-0163.* 315 rms, 8 story. S $130-$135; D $145-$155; each addl $10; suites $195-$300; under 19 free;

wkly, wkend rates. Crib free. TV; cable. Indoor/outdoor pool; lifeguard. Restaurant 6:30-1 am. Bar 11-1 am; Fri, Sat to 2 am. Ck-out noon. Convention facilities. Concierge. Gift shop. Beauty shop. Covered parking, valet. Exercise rm; instructor, weights, bicycles, whirlpool, sauna. Refrigerators avail. 8-story atrium; 20-ft waterfall. Gazebo. **LUXURY LEVEL : EXECUTIVE LEVEL.** 68 units. S $150-$160; D $165-$175; suites $250. Concierge. Private lounge. Free continental bkfst, refreshments. Cr cds: A, C, D, DS, ER, JCB, MC, V.

D ⚊ ⫟ ⩙ ⚐ SC

Restaurants

★ ★ **ANDALUCIA.** 12300 Wilkins Ave (20852). 301/770-1880. Hrs: 11:30 am-2:30 pm, 5:30-10 pm; Sat 5:30-10:30 pm; Sun 4:30-9:30 pm. Closed Mon; some major hols. Res accepted; required Fri & Sat. Spanish menu. Bar. Semi-a la carte: lunch $7.50-$10.95, dinner $11.50-$16.95. Specializes in seafood, lamb, paella zarzuela. Parking. Spanish decor, atmosphere. Cr cds: A, DS, MC, V.

D

★ ★ **COPELAND'S OF NEW ORLEANS.** 1584 Rockville Pike. 301/230-0968. Hrs: 11 am-11 pm; Fri, Sat to midnight; Sun to 10 pm. Closed Thanksgiving, Dec 25. Bar; Fri, Sat to 1 am. Semi-a la carte: lunch $5-$15.75, dinner $5.95-$15.75. Child's meals. Specializes in seafood, Creole & Cajun dishes. Parking. Art deco decor. Cr cds: A, C, D, DS, MC, V.

D

✔ ★ ★ **HOUSE OF CHINESE GOURMET.** 1485 Rockville Pike. 301/984-9440. Hrs: 11:30 am-10 pm; Fri, Sat to 11 pm. Chinese menu. Semi-a la carte: lunch $4.75-$7.50, dinner $6.50-$14.95. Specialties: Peking duck, seafood Shanghai style, vegetarian dishes. Parking. Decorated with Chinese art. Cr cds: A, DS, MC, V.

D

★ ★ **NORMANDIE FARM.** (10710 Falls Rd, Potomac) 3½ mi SW on MD 189, I-270 exit 5. 301/983-8838. Hrs: 11:30 am-2:30 pm, 6-10 pm; Sun 5-9 pm; Sun brunch 11 am-2 pm. Closed Mon. Res accepted. French menu. Bar. Semi-a la carte: lunch $6-$12.50, dinner $12-$23. Sun brunch $16.50. Specializes in seafood, veal. Entertainment Fri, Sat. Parking. French provincial decor. Cr cds: A, C, D, MC, V.

★ ★ ★ **OLD ANGLER'S INN.** 10801 MacArthur Blvd. 301/365-2425. Hrs: noon-2:30 pm, 6-10:30 pm. Closed Mon. Bar. Wine list. A la carte entrees: lunch $12-$16, dinner $22-$29. Specializes in seafood, rack of lamb. Parking. Patio dining overlooking wooded area. Stone inn (1860). Family-owned. Cr cds: A, C, D, MC, V.

✔ ★ **SILVER DINER.** 11806 Rockville Pike (MD 355) (20852), in Mid-Pike Plaza. 301/770-4166. Hrs: 7-2 am; Fri & Sat to 3 am; early-bird dinner Mon-Fri 4-6 pm. Closed Dec 25. Serv bar. Semi-a la carte: bkfst $3.95-$5.95, lunch $5.95-$7.95, dinner $5.95-$9.95. Child's meals. Specializes in meatloaf, chicken-pot pie, turkey. 1950s-style diner with jukeboxes. Servers dressed in period clothing. Cr cds: DS, MC, V.

D SC

✔ ★ ★ **SUNNY GARDEN.** 1302 E Gude Dr (20850), MD 28 to E Gude Dr. 301/762-7477. Hrs: 11:30 am-10 pm; Fri & Sat to 10:30 pm. Res accepted; required Fri & Sat. Chinese, Mandarin menu. Serv bar. Semi-a la carte: lunch $4.50-$9.95, dinner $5.95-$11.95. Specialties: General Tso's chicken, steak orange peal, soft-shell crab. Parking. Tropical fish tanks. Cr cds: A, MC, V.

D

★ ★ **THAT'S AMORE.** 15201 Shady Grove Rd (20850). 301/670-9666. Hrs: 11:30 am-10:30 pm; Fri to midnight; Sat 4 pm-midnight; Sun 4-9:30 pm. Italian menu. Bar. A la carte entrees: lunch $5.95-$11.95, dinner $12-$28. Specializes in pasta, veal, chicken Ve-

suvio. Parking. Stained-glass windows. Early 20th-century mens club atmosphere. Cr cds: A, C, D, DS, MC, V.

D

✔ ★ ★ **WÜRZBURG HAUS.** 7236 Muncaster Mill Rd, in Red Mill Shopping Center. 301/330-0402. Hrs: 11:30 am-9 pm; Fri to 10 pm; Sat noon-10 pm. Closed Sun. German menu. Wine, beer. A la carte entrees: lunch $7.50-$10.95, dinner $8.25-$12.95. Child's meals. Specializes in schnitzel, wurst. Accordionist Fri, Sat. 2 dining areas. German, Austrian atmosphere; collection of beer steins. Cr cds: A, DS, MC, V.

D

Unrated Dining Spot

HARD TIMES CAFE. 1117 Nelson St (20850). 301/294-9720. Hrs: 11:30 am-10 pm; Fri & Sat to 11 pm; Sun noon-9 pm. Closed Thanksgiving, Dec 25. Bar. A la carte entrees: lunch, dinner $4.50-$6. Child's meals. Specializes in chili, vegetarian dishes. Cr cds: A, MC, V.

D

St Mary's City (E-7)

Settled: 1634 **Pop:** 1,300 (est) **Elev:** 36 ft **Area code:** 301 **Zip:** 20686

Maryland's first colonists bought a Native American village on this site upon their arrival in the New World under Leonard Calvert. The settlement was the capital and hub of the area until 1694, when the colonial capital was moved to Annapolis. The town gradually disappeared. The city and county are still rich in historical attractions.

What to See and Do

1. **Historic St Mary's City.** MD 5 & Rosecroft Rd. Outdoor museum at site of Maryland's 1st capital (1634) includes reconstructed State House (1676), replica of the original capital bldg; other exhibits include the *Maryland Dove*, replica of a 17th-century ship, and archaeological exhibits. Also seasonal living history programs, a 17th-century tobacco plantation, reconstructed 17th-century inn; visitor center, outdoor cafe. Visitor center (all yr, Wed-Sun; closed Jan 1, Thanksgiving, Dec 25); outdoor museum (4th wkend Mar-Nov, Wed-Sun). Sr citizen rate. Phone 862-0990. ¢¢

2. **Leonard Calvert Monument.** Trinity Churchyard. Monument to Maryland's first colonial governor.

3. **Margaret Brent Memorial.** Gazebo overlooking the river; memorial to the woman who, being a wealthy landowner, requested the right to vote in the Maryland Assembly in 1648, in order to settle Leonard Calvert's affairs after his death.

4. **Point Lookout State Park.** 13 mi S on MD 5. Site of the Confederate Monument, the only memorial erected by the US government to honor the POWs who died in the Point Lookout Prison Camp during the Civil War (3,384 died here). Swimming, fishing, boating, hiking. Picnicking; improved camping (Apr-Oct; self-contained camping units yr round). Nature center. Civil War museum. Standard fees. Phone 872-5688. Day-use entrance fee ¢

(For further information contact the St Mary's County Division of Tourism, PO Box 653, Leonardtown 20650; 800/327-9023.)

Annual Events

Maryland Days. Boat rides, seafood, Seventeenth-century militia musters. Wkend Mar.

Crab Festival. June.

(See Leonardtown, Waldorf; also see District of Columbia)

Motor Hotel

✔ ★ ★ **PATUXENT INN.** *(Box 778, Lexington Park 20653) 11 mi NW on MD 235.* 301/862-4100; FAX 301/862-4673. 120 rms, 3 story. S $54; D $59; each addl $5; under 18 free; wkend rates. Crib free. TV; cable. Pool; poolside serv. Complimentary coffee in lobby. Restaurant adj 6-2 am. Ck-out 11 am. Coin lndry. Free Naval Air Station transportation. Lighted tennis. Golf privileges. Refrigerators, some wet bars. Cr cds: A, C, D, MC, V.

Restaurant

✔ ★ **ALOHA.** *(2025 Wildewood Ctr, California) 11 mi NW on MD 235, in shopping center.* 301/862-4838. Hrs: 10:30 am-11 pm; Sat from noon; Sun noon-9:30 pm; early-bird dinner Mon-Fri 4:30-6:30 pm; Sun buffet noon-3 pm. Closed Thanksgiving, Dec 25. Res accepted. Chinese menu. Bar. Semi-a la carte: lunch $3.95-$4.95, dinner $5.95-$19. Complete meals: lunch $4.95, dinner $7.25-$9.95. Sun buffet: $6.95. Child's meals. Specializes in Szechwan, Hunan dishes, international dishes. Polynesian atmosphere. Cr cds: A, DS, MC, V.

D

St Michaels (D-8)

Pop: 1,301 **Elev:** 7 ft **Area code:** 410 **Zip:** 21663

Chartered in 1804, St Michaels has become a boating and tourist center while its main industry continues to be the catching and processing of seafood. It is a town with a number of Federal and Victorian period buildings.

What to See and Do

1. **Chesapeake Bay Maritime Museum.** Mill St. Waterside museum consists of 12 buildings. Includes historic lighthouse, floating exhibits, boat-building shop with working exhibit, ship models, small boats; paintings; aquarium; waterfowling exhibits; workboats and mechanical propulsion. (Mid-Mar-Dec, daily; rest of yr, wkends only) Phone 745-2916. ¢¢¢

2. **St Mary's Square.** Public square laid out in 1770 by Englishman James Braddock. Several buildings date to the early 1800s, including the Cannonball House and Dr. Miller's Farmhouse. The Ship's Carpenter Bell was cast in 1842; across from the bell stand 2 cannons, one dating from the Revolution, the other from the War of 1812. Also here is

   St Mary's Square Museum. Mid-19th-century home of "half-timber" construction; one of the earliest buildings in St Michaels. Exhibits of historical and local interest. (1st wkend May-last wkend Oct, Sat & Sun; also by appt) Inquire about the town walking tour brochures. Contact the Town Office, phone 745-9535.

3. **The Footbridge.** Joins Navy Point to Cherry St. Only remaining bridge of three that once connected the town with areas across the harbor.

4. **The *Patriot*.** Berthed at Chesapeake Bay Maritime Museum. 1½-hr narrated cruise on Miles River. Three trips daily. (Apr-Oct) Phone 745-3100. ¢¢¢

(For further information contact the Talbot County Chamber of Commerce, PO Box 1366, Easton 21601; 822-4606.)

Motor Hotel

✔ ★ ★ **BEST WESTERN.** *1228 S Talbott St.* 410/745-3333; FAX 410/745-2906. 93 rms, 2 story. May-mid-Nov: S $65-$75; D $70-$82; each addl $8; under 18 free; higher rates Waterfowl Festival; lower rates rest of yr. Crib $5. Pet accepted, some restrictions. TV. Pool. Complimentary coffee in lobby. Restaurant adj 11 am-11 pm. Ck-out 11 am. Meeting rms. Refrigerators avail. Cr cds: A, D, DS, MC, V.

Inns

★ ★ **BLACK WALNUT POINT.** *(PO Box 308, Black Walnut Rd, Tilghman 21671)* 15 mi W on MD 33. 410/886-2452; FAX 410/886-2053. 7 rms, 3 bldgs, main bldg 3 story. No rm phones. D $120; each addl $15; kit. unit $140. Adults only. TV in sitting rm. Pool. Complimentary continental bkfst, coffee & tea/sherry. Ck-out 11 am, ck-in 3-7 pm. Lighted tennis. 18-hole golf privileges; greens fee $42, pro, putting green, driving range. Lawn games. Balconies. Picnic tables, grills. On Cheasapeake Bay. Built 1843; hand-hewn beams. Cr cds: MC, V.

★ ★ ★ **INN AT PERRY CABIN.** *308 Watkins Lane.* 410/745-2200; res: 800/722-2949; FAX 410/745-3348. 41 rms, 3 story, 6 suites. S, D $225-$525; suites $475-$525. Children over 10 yrs only. TV; cable. Pool. Complimentary full bkfst. Dining rm (see ASHLEY ROOM). Rm serv. Ck-out noon, ck-in 3 pm. Bellhops. Valet serv. Concierge. Golf privileges. Exercise equipt; weights, bicycles, whirlpool, sauna, steam rm. Massage. Lawn games. Columned, rambling white clapboard, dormered house grew from late 18th-century farmhouse named for Admiral Perry; structure refurbished in 1990 by Sir Bernard Ashley to showcase "Laura Ashley English-country look." On Miles River, Chesapeake Bay. Cr cds: A, D, MC, V.

★ ★ **PARSONAGE INN.** *210 N Talbot St, edge of historic district.* 410/745-5519; res: 800/394-5519. 8 rms, 2 story. No rm phones. May-Oct: D $108-$140; lower rates rest of yr. Crib free. TV in sitting rm and in 2 guest rms. Complimentary full bkfst, tea/sherry. Restaurant adj noon-10 pm. Ck-out 11 am, ck-in 2-7 pm. Balconies. Picnic table, grill. Built 1883 as a private residence; later used as a parsonage. Restored and furnished with period reproductions. The brick exterior is unusual, with many different inlay patterns, and along with the steeple and Victorian gingerbread trim on the porches, the house makes a unique architectural statement. Totally nonsmoking. Cr cds: MC, V.

✔ ★ ★ **THE PASADENA INN.** *(PO Box 187, Royal Oak 21662) 3 mi E on MD 329.* 410/745-5053. 27 rms, 19 with bath, 3 story. No rm phones. D $30-$130; each addl $15; suite $95-$130; under 12 free; higher rates Waterfowl Festival; lower rates mid-wk. TV in sitting rm. Pool. Complimentary full bkfst. Dining rm 6-9 pm. Ck-out 11 am, ck-in 3 pm. Lawn games. Picnic tables. Former plantation house (1748) on banks of Oak Creek; antiques. Cr cds: MC, V.

★ ★ **WADES POINT INN ON THE BAY.** *PO Box 7, 5 mi W via MD 33, right on Wades Point Rd, in McDaniel.* 410/745-2500. 24 rms, 15 with bath, 12 A/C, 2 & 3 story, 4 kits. No rm phones. D $75-$175; each addl $10; kit. units $175; under 12 free. Crib free. Complimentary continental bkfst. Restaurant nearby. Ck-out 11 am, ck-in 2-8 pm. 18-hole golf privileges, greens fee $52.50, pro, putting green, driving range. Balconies. Picnic tables. Main building (1819) with new guest house (1989) built in the same style. Both buildings surrounded by fields on one side and Chesapeake Bay on the other. Located on 120 acres; includes flower gardens, woods with nature trail. Totally nonsmoking. Cr cds: MC, V.

Resort

★ ★ **HARBOURTOWNE.** *Box 126, 3 mi W on MD 33.* 410/745-9066; res: 800/446-9066; FAX 410/745-9124. 81 rms in main buildings, 30 villas, 1-2 story. Mar-Nov: S, D $135-$175; each addl $15; under 12 free; golf plans; lower rates rest of yr. Crib free. Pool; poolside serv, lifeguard. Dining rm 7 am-10 pm. Ck-out 11 am, ck-in 3 pm. Grocery, package store 3 mi. Convention facilities. Tennis. 18-hole golf, greens fee $45, pro, driving range, putting green. Exercise equipt; weights, treadmill. Bicycles. Paddle boats. Lawn games. Private patios, balconies. Cr cds: A, D, MC, V.

[D] [icons] SC

Restaurants

★ ★ ★ **208 TALBOT.** *208 N Talbot St.* 410/745-3838. Hrs: noon-2 pm, 5-10 pm; Tues & Sat from 5 pm; Sun 5-9 pm; Sun brunch 11 am-2 pm. Closed Mon; Dec 25. Res accepted; required wknds. Bar. Semi-a la carte: lunch $7.50-$12.50, dinner $16.50-$22. Sun brunch $6.50-$12.50. Specializes in fresh seafood, rack of lamb. Own pastries, ice cream. Parking. Casual gourmet dining in a renovated mid-1800s brick house; many antiques; original fireplace. Cr cds: MC, V.

★ ★ ★ **ASHLEY ROOM.** *(See Inn At Perry Cabin)* 410/745-2200. Hrs: 8-10:30 am, 12:30-2:30 pm, 6-10:30 pm; afternoon tea 3-5 pm. Res accepted. Continental menu. Serv bar. Wine list. Prix fixe: bkfst $12.50, 5-course dinner $55. A la carte entrees: lunch $12.95-$18. Specializes in classical cuisine; menu changes daily. Own herb garden. Own baking. Valet parking. English-country style dining rm with fireplace; French doors open to terrace overlooking bay. Totally nonsmoking. Cr cds: A, D, MC, V.

[D]

✔ ★ **ST MICHAELS CRAB HOUSE.** *305 Mulberry St.* 410/745-3737. Hrs: 11 am-10 pm. Res accepted. Bar. Semi-a la carte: lunch $4.95-$9, dinner $9.50-$14. Child's meals. Specializes in steamed crab & shellfish. Outdoor dining. Overlooks harbor. Cr cds: MC, V.

★ ★ **TOWN DOCK.** *125 Mulberry St, at the harbor, in public dock area.* 410/745-5577. Hrs: 11:30 am-10 pm; early-bird dinner Sun-Fri 3:30-5:30 pm; Sun brunch to 2 pm. Closed Dec 25. Res accepted. Continental menu. Bar. Semi-a la carte: lunch $4.50-$8.50, dinner $11.90-$19. Sun brunch $11.50. Child's meals. Specializes in fresh seafood, Eastern Shore cuisine. Nightclub on 2nd floor; entertainment Fri-Sat evenings. Parking. Outdoor dining. 4-level dining; all face harbor. Cr cds: A, D, MC, V.

Salisbury (E-9)

Founded: 1732 **Pop:** 20,592 **Elev:** 33 ft **Area code:** 410 **Zip:** 21801

"Central City of the Eastern Shore" and of the Delmarva Peninsula, Salisbury has a marina on the Wicomico River providing access to Chesapeake Bay. It lies within 30 miles of duck-hunting and deep-sea fishing. Gasoline pumps, hydraulic lifts, canned and frozen foods, seafood and poultry come from this area.

What to See and Do

1. **Ward Museum of Wildfowl Art.** 909 S Schumaker Dr, at Beaglin Park Dr. Displays include the history of decoy and wildfowl carving in North America; wildfowl habitats; contemporary wildfowl art. Changing exhibits. Gift shop. (Mon-Sat, also Sun afternoons) Sr.citizen rate. Phone 742-4988. ¢¢

2. **Poplar Hill Mansion** (ca 1805). 117 Elizabeth St. Example of Georgian and Federal-style architecture; palladium and bull's-eye windows; large brass box locks on doors, woodwork, mantels and fireplaces. Period furniture; country garden. (Usually Sun afternoons; Tues-Sat by appt, phone ahead; closed hols) Phone 749-1776. Tour ¢

3. **Mason-Dixon Line Marker.** 5 mi N on US 13, 13A, then 7 mi W on MD 467. Bears coats of arms of Lord Baltimore and William Penn.

4. **Princess Anne.** 13 mi SW on US 13. This town was the home of Samuel Chase, signer of the Declaration of Independence. Buildings of the Colonial and Federal periods are of architectural interest.

5. **The Nassawango Iron Furnace.** 16 mi S via MD 12 to Old Furnace Rd. One of the oldest industrial sites in Maryland and one of the earliest hot-blast mechanisms still intact. The stack was restored in 1966; archaeological excavations were made and a canal, a dike and a portion of the old waterwheel used in the manufacturing process were found. The remains of the area are undergoing restoration. (Apr-Oct, daily) Phone 632-2032. ¢¢ Surrounding the iron furnace is

   Furnace Town. This 1840s industrial village occupies 22 acres around the iron furnace and also includes six historic structures; a working 19th-century blacksmith shop and broom-making shop has demonstrations on selected days; a museum and company store; archaeological excavations; a nature trail and picnic area. Special events take place throughout the season. (Same days & fees as furnace)

6. **Salisbury Zoological Park.** 755 S Park Dr. Natural habitats for almost 400 mammals, birds and reptiles. Major exhibits include bears, monkeys, jaguars, bison, waterfowl. Also exotic plants. (Daily) Donation. Phone 548-3188.

(For further information contact the Wicomico County Convention & Visitors Bureau, Civic Center, 500 Glen Ave; 548-4914 or 800/332-TOUR. Information is also available from the Chamber of Commerce, 300 E Main St, PO Box 510; 749-0144.)

(See Ocean City)

Motels

✔ ★ ★ **COMFORT INN.** *2701 N Salisbury Blvd, 4½ mi N on US 13.* 410/543-4666; FAX 410/749-2639. 96 units, 2 story, 24 suites. Mid-June-mid-Sept: S $45.95; D $55.95; each addl $8; suites $55.95-$79.95; under 18 free; lower rates rest of yr. Crib avail. Pet accepted. TV; cable. Free continental bkfst, coffee. Restaurant nearby. Ck-out 11 am. Meeting rm. Valet serv. Sundries. Refrigerator, wet bar in suites. Cr cds: A, C, D, DS, ER, JCB, MC, V.

[D] [icons] SC

★ **DAYS INN.** *2525 N Salisbury Blvd, 3 mi N on US 13.* 410/749-6200; FAX 410/749-7378. 98 units, 2 story. Mid-June-mid-Sept: S, D $59-$64; each addl $5; under 18 free; higher rates: Wildfowl Show, auto racing wknds; lower rates rest of yr. Crib free. Pet accepted; $5. TV; cable. Pool. Playground. Complimentary continental bkfst, coffee. Restaurant opp 6 am-10 pm. Ck-out 11 am. Meeting rms. Sundries. Tennis privileges. Health club privileges. Some refrigerators. Cr cds: A, D, DS, MC, V.

[D] [icons] SC

★ ★ **HOLIDAY INN.** *2625 N Salisbury Blvd., 3 mi N on US 13.* 410/742-7194; FAX 410/742-5194. 123 rms, 2 story. Mid-June-mid-Sept: S $49-$87; D $49-$97; each addl $8; under 18 free; lower rates rest of yr. Crib free. Pet accepted, some restrictions. TV; cable. Pool. Restaurant 6:30 am-2 pm, 5-10 pm. Rm serv. Bar 4:30 pm-midnight. Ck-out 11 am. Coin lndry. Meeting rms. Valet serv. Sundries. Cr cds: A, C, D, DS, JCB, MC, V.

[D] [icons] SC

Motor Hotel

★ ★ ★ **SHERATON.** *300 S Salisbury Blvd. 410/546-4400; FAX 410/546-2528.* 156 rms, 5 story. Late May-mid-Sept: S, D $76-$98; each addl $10; suites $150; under 18 free; lower rates rest of yr. Crib free. TV; cable. Indoor pool. Restaurant 6:30 am-2:30 pm, 5:30-10:30 pm; wkends from 7 am. Rm serv. Bar 4 pm-2 am; wkends from noon. Ck-out noon. Meeting rms. Bellhops. Free airport transportation. Exercise equipt; weight machine, bicycle. Wet bar in suites. On river. Cr cds: A, C, D, DS, MC, V.

D ≋ ⨇ ⊼ ⌦ SC

Silver Spring (C-6)

Pop: 76,046 **Elev:** 350 ft **Area code:** 301

What to See and Do

1. **National Capital Trolley Museum.** Northwest Branch Park, about 7 mi N on Bonifant Rd, just off MD 650 in Layhill. Rides on old-time American and European trolleys; exhibits depict history of streetcars. Special events during yr. (July-Aug, Sat-Sun & Wed; rest of yr, Sat & Sun only; also open Memorial Day, July 4, Labor Day) Phone 384-6088. Museum **Free.** Rides **¢**

2. **Brookside Gardens.** N on MD 97, right on Randolph Rd, right on Glenallan Ave, in Wheaton. A 50-acre display garden with two conservatories, flowering displays; variety of flowering plants in eight gardens; educational programs. (Daily; closed Dec 25) Phone 949-8230. **Free.**

(For further information contact Chamber of Commerce, 8601 Georgia Ave, Suite 202, 20910; 565-3777.)

(See Bowie, College Park, Rockville; also see District of Columbia)

Motel

★ ★ ★ **COURTYARD BY MARRIOTT.** *12521 Prosperity Dr (20904), 6 mi NE on US 29, then E on Cherry Hill Rd to Prosperity Dr. 301/680-8500; FAX 301/680-9232.* 146 units, 3 story. S $85-$95; D, suites $95-$105; wkly, wkend rates. Crib free. TV; cable. Indoor pool; lifeguard. Complimentary coffee in rms. Restaurant 6:30 am-2 pm, 5-10 pm; Sat, Sun from 7 am. Bar 4-11 pm. Ck-out 1 pm. Coin lndry. Meeting rms. Valet serv. Sundries. Exercise equipt; weights, bicycles, whirlpool. Refrigerator in suites. Cr cds: A, C, D, DS, ER, JCB, MC, V.

D ≋ ⨇ ⊼ ⌦ SC

Hotel

★ ★ **HOLIDAY INN-SILVER SPRING PLAZA.** *8777 Georgia Ave (20910). 301/589-0800; FAX 301/587-4791.* 226 rms, 16 story. S, D $85-$90; each addl $10; suites $125-$135; under 20 free. Crib free. Pet accepted, some restrictions. TV; cable. Pool; lifeguard. Restaurant 6 am-11 pm. Bar 11:30-1 am. Ck-out noon. Coin lndry. Meeting rms. Shopping arcade. Exercise equipt; weights, bicycles, sauna. Refrigerators avail. Cr cds: A, C, D, DS, ER, JCB, MC, V.

D ↙ ≋ ⨇ ⊼ ⌦ SC

Restaurants

★ ★ **BLAIR MANSION INN.** *7711 Eastern Ave. 301/588-1688.* Hrs: 11:30 am-9 pm; Sat from 5 pm; Sun from 2 pm. Res accepted. Italian, Amer menu. Bar. Semi-a la carte: lunch $5.95-$9.95, dinner $9.95-$19.95. Specializes in poultry, beef, crab Imperial. Parking. Murder mystery dinners. 1890s Victorian mansion; gaslight chandelier, 7 fireplaces. Family-owned. Cr cds: A, D, DS, MC, V.

✔ ★ **CHINA RESTAURANT.** *8411 Georgia Ave. 301/585-2275.* Hrs: 11:30 am-2:30 pm, 5-9:30 pm; Sat from 5 pm; Sun 4-9 pm. Closed Mon; Thanksgiving. Chinese menu. Wine, beer. Semi-a la carte: lunch $3.75-$6.50, dinner $4.95-$10.95. Specialties: Mongolian beef, moo shu pork, Peking duck. Family-owned. No cr cds accepted.

★ ★ **CRISFIELD AT LEE PLAZA.** *8606 Colesville Rd (MD 29), ground floor of high rise building. 301/588-1572.* Hrs: 11:30 am-10 pm; Fri to 11 pm; Sat 4-11 pm; Sun 4-10 pm. Closed Thanksgiving, Dec 25. Res accepted; required Fri & Sat. Bar. Semi-a la carte: lunch $4.50-$22, dinner $13-$22, Child's meals. Specializes in seafood, baked stuffed shrimp, crab Imperial. Parking (dinner). Art deco decor. Cr cds: A, D, MC, V.

D

★ ★ **MRS. K'S TOLL HOUSE.** *9201 Colesville Rd. 301/589-3500.* Hrs: 11:30 am-2:30 pm, 5-8:30 pm; Fri, Sat to 9 pm; Sun 11 am-8:30 pm; Sun brunch to 1:45 pm. Closed Mon; Dec 25. Serv bar. Complete meals: lunch $11.40-$13.25, dinner $14.75-$22. Sun brunch $15. Specialty: roast turkey. Century-old tollhouse; antique china, glass. Gardens. Totally nonsmoking. Cr cds: A, C, D, DS, MC, V.

Thurmont (B-5)

Settled: 1751 **Pop:** 3,398 **Elev:** 523 ft **Area code:** 301 **Zip:** 21788

What to See and Do

1. **Cunningham Falls State Park.** 4,950 acres in the Catoctin Mountains. Two recreation areas: Houck, 5 mi W of town, has swimming, fishing, boating (rentals); picnicking, camping; hiking trails lead to 78-foot falls and scenic overlooks. Manor Area, 3 mi S of town on US 15, has picnicking, camping, playground. Trout fishing in Big Hunting Creek. Ruins of Iron Masters Mansion and the industrial village that surrounded it are also here. (See ANNUAL EVENTS) Standard fees. Phone 271-7574.

2. **Catoctin Mountain Park.** 3 mi W on MD 77. A 5,770-acre area on a spur of the Blue Ridge Mountains. Self-guided nature trails; restored whiskey still; fishing, picnicking; camping (mid-Apr-mid-Nov; fee), cabins (mid-Apr-Oct; fee). Park (daily). A unit of the National Park Service. Phone 663-9388. **Free.**

(For further information contact the Tourism Council of Frederick County, 19 E Church St, Frederick 21701; 663-8687.)

Annual Events

Maple Syrup Demonstration. At Cunningham Falls State Park (see #1). Tree tapping, sap boiling; carriage rides; food; children's storytelling corner. Usually 2nd & 3rd wkend Mar.

Catoctin Colorfest. Fall foliage; arts & crafts show. Phone 271-4432. 2nd Sat & Sun Oct.

(For accommodations see Frederick, Hagerstown)

Restaurant

✔ ★ ★ **COZY.** *105 Frederick Rd (MD 806), 3 blks E of US 15. 301/271-7373.* Hrs: 11 am-8:30 pm; Fri to 9 pm; Sat & Sun from 8 am. Closed Dec 24, 25. Res accepted. Bar. Buffet: bkfst $5.69, lunch $5.19-$7.39, dinner $7.99-$15.99 (Fri & Sat $13.29-17.29, Sun $9.79). Semi-a la carte: lunch $3.29-$5.99, dinner $8.19-$12.79. Child's meals. Specializes in fresh fish & poultry. Own desserts. Parking. Patio dining (seasonal). Family-owned. Cr cds: A, DS, MC, V.

D SC

Towson (B-7)

Pop: 49,445 **Elev:** 465 ft **Area code:** 410 **Zip:** 21204

What to See and Do

1. **Towson State University** (1866). (15,000 students) York Rd. On campus are three art galleries, including Holtzman Art Gallery, with an extensive collection of art media (Sept-May, daily exc Wed). Concerts and sporting events are held in the Towson Center. For information on entertainment & events phone 830-ARTS.

2. **Hampton National Historic Site.** 535 Hampton Lane, 1/2 mi off Dulaney Valley Rd; I-695 exit 27B. Includes ornate Georgian mansion (ca 1790) (tours), formal gardens and plantation outbuildings. Gift shop. (Daily; closed Jan 1, Thanksgiving, Dec 25) Tea room open for luncheon (daily exc Mon; closed 6 wks mid-Jan-early Mar). Phone 962-0688. **Free.**

3. **Fire Museum of Maryland.** 1301 York Rd, 1 blk N of I-695 exit 26B, in Lutherville. More than 60 pieces of antique fire-fighting equipment; includes motorized and hand/horse-drawn units from 1822-1957. (May-Oct, Sun; limited hrs) Sr citizen rate. Phone 321-7500. **¢¢**

4. **Soldiers Delight Natural Environment Area.** 7 mi W on I-695, then W on MD 26, then 5 mi N on Deerpark Rd to overlook. 1,725-acre park has 19th-century chrome mines; restored log cabin; scenic overlook; hiking, nature trails; picnicking. It is the only undisturbed serpentine barren in the state. Phone 922-3044.

(For further information contact the Baltimore County Chamber of Commerce, 102 W Pennsylvania Ave, Ste 402; 825-6200.)

Annual Event

State Fair. Timonium Fairgrounds, 3 mi N on York Rd, in Timonium. Ten-day festival of home arts; entertainment, midway; agricultural demonstrations, thoroughbred horse racing, livestock presentations. Phone 252-0200. Late Aug-Labor Day.

(See Baltimore)

Motor Hotel

 ★ DAYS INN BALTIMORE-EAST. 8801 Loch Raven Blvd. 410/882-0900; FAX 410/882-4176. 180 rms, 5 story. S $48; D $56; each addl $5; under 13 free. Crib free. Pet accepted, some restrictions; $25 refundable. TV; cable. Restaurant 7 am-10 pm. Rm serv. Bar 11-2 am. Ck-out 11 am. Coin lndry. Meeting rms. Sundries. Cr cds: A, D, DS, MC, V.

Hotel

★ ★ SHERATON BALTIMORE NORTH. 903 Dulaney Valley Rd, I-695 exit 27A. 410/321-7400; FAX 410/296-9534. 284 units, 12 story. S $126-$146; D $138-$158; each addl $12; suites $175-$350; under 17 free; wkend plans; higher rates Preakness. Crib free. TV; cable. Indoor pool; poolside serv, lifeguard. Coffee in rms. Restaurant 6:30 am-10:30 pm. Bar 11:30-1 am; entertainment, dancing exc Sun. Ck-out noon. Convention facilities. Gift shop. Free valet parking. Airport transportation. Exercise equipt; weight machines, bicycles, whirlpool, sauna. Cr cds: A, C, D, DS, MC, V.

Restaurants

★ CAFE TROIA. 28 W Allegheny Ave. 410/337-0133. Hrs: 11 am-3 pm, 5-10 pm; Fri to 11 pm; Sat 5-11 pm; Sun 5-9 pm. Res accepted. Italian menu. Bar. Semi-a la carte: lunch $4-$12, dinner $9-$20. Specializes in regional Italian dishes. Outdoor dining. Cr cds: A, D, MC, V.

★ ★ ★ HERSH'S ORCHARD INN. 1528 E Joppa Rd. 410/823-0384. Hrs: 11:30 am-10 pm; Fri, Sat to 11 pm; Sun noon-9 pm. Closed Memorial Day, Dec 25. Res accepted. Continental menu. Bar to 1:30 am. Semi-a la carte: lunch $5-$12, dinner $11-$21. Specializes in seafood, beef, poultry. Own breads. Piano bar Tues-Sat. Valet parking. Braille menu. Cr cds: A, MC, V.

★ ★ PEERCE'S PLANTATION. (Dulaney Valley Rd, Phoenix 21131) 6 mi N of I-695 exit 27 N. 410/252-3100. Hrs: 11:30 am-3 pm, 5-10 pm; Fri, Sat to 11 pm; Sun 5-9 pm; Sun brunch 11:30 am-2 pm. Closed Dec 25. Res accepted. Continental menu. Bar 11:30-2 am. Semi-a la carte: lunch $6.25-$15, dinner $15.95-$25.95. Sun brunch $6.25-$12.95. Child's meals. Specialties: salmon ciresi, filet Chesapeake. Valet parking. Outdoor dining. Antebellum decor. Scenic view of countryside overlooking Loch Raven Reservoir. Family-owned. Jacket. Cr cds: A, D, DS, MC, V.

Waldorf (D-6)

Pop: 15,058 **Elev:** 215 ft **Area code:** 301

What to See and Do

1. **John Wilkes Booth Escape Route.** After shooting Abraham Lincoln on April 14, 1865, John Wilkes Booth fled south into Maryland to rendezvous with his accomplice, David Herold at

    Surratt House and Tavern (1852), 9110 Brandywine Rd, Clinton (then Surrattsville), where they recovered arms they had hidden there. Though she may have been innocent, Mary Surratt was hanged for conspiracy. Eight period rooms, museum; guides in period costumes; Dec candlelight tours; special events and exhibits throughout the year. (Mar-mid-Dec, Thurs-Sun) Sr citizen rate. Phone 868-1121. **¢** Booth and Herold next stopped at

    Dr. Samuel A. Mudd House Museum (ca 1830). From US 301, take MD 5, then left on MD 205, turn right on Poplar Hill Rd approx 4 mi, right on Dr Samuel Mudd Rd, continue to house; sign at entrance. Where Dr. Mudd set Booth's broken leg, unaware that Booth had just shot the president. Mudd was convicted and imprisoned for life, but pardoned four years later by President Andrew Johnson. Tours conducted by costumed docents, some of whom are Dr. Mudd's descendants. (Apr-Nov, Sat-Sun afternoons & Wed 11 am-3 pm; closed Easter Sun, Thanksgiving) Phone 934-8464 or 645-6870. **¢¢**

    Booth and Herold continued south, crossed the Potomac River and were captured at Garrett's farm, Virginia, on April 26; Booth was killed. (See ANNUAL EVENT)

2. **Cedarville State Forest.** 4 mi E off US 301 on Cedarville Rd. 3,697 acres of woodland, once home of the Piscataway Indians, who settled around the Zekiah Swamp. Fishing, hunting. Nature, hiking trails. Picnicking. Standard fees. Schedule varies, phone ahead; 856-8987 or 410/974-3771.

3. **Farmer's Market and Auction.** 13 mi SE on MD 5. Nearby Amish farms offer fresh baked goods and produce (auction Wed) for sale; more than 90 shops. Antique dealers. (Wed & Sat) Phone 884-3108.

(For further information contact the Tourism Special Events Coordinator, Rte 1, Box 1144, Port Tobacco 20677; 934-9305.)

Annual Event

John Wilkes Booth Escape Route Tour. Day-long bus tour of Booth's route from Ford's Theatre, Washington, through southern Maryland to site of Garrett's farm, Virginia, with expert commentary. For reservations phone 868-1121. Mid-Apr & early Sept.

(See La Plata; also see District of Columbia)

Motels

★ **DAYS INN.** *5043 US 301 (20603). 301/932-9200; FAX 301/843-9816.* 100 rms, 3 story. S $43.95-$50; D $48.95-$80; each addl $5; under 18 free; wkly, monthly rates. Crib free. TV; cable. Complimentary continental bkfst, coffee. Restaurant adj 11 am-10 pm. Ck-out 11 am. Coin lndry. Some refrigerators, in-rm whirlpools. Cr cds: A, C, D, DS, MC, V.

✔ ★ **HoJo INN.** *3125 S Crain Hwy (20602). 301/932-5090; res: 800/826-4504.* 109 rms. S $30-$45; D $30-$50; suites, kit. units $45-$60; under 18 free; wkly rates. Crib free. Pet accepted. TV; cable. Pool. Complimentary continental bkfst. Restaurant adj 11 am-10 pm. Ck-out 11 am. Meeting rms. Valet serv. Picnic tables, grills. Refrigerators avail. Cr cds: A, C, D, DS, JCB, MC, V.

D ✔ ≈ ⚏ 🔥 SC

★ ★ **HOLIDAY INN.** *1 St Patrick's Dr (20603). 301/645-8200; FAX 301/843-7945.* 192 rms, 3 story, 8 kit. units. S, D $58-$64; each addl $6; suites, kit. units $70-$90; under 19 free. Crib free. Pet accepted. TV; cable. Pool; lifeguard. Complimentary coffee in rms. Restaurant 6:30 am-2 pm, 5-10 pm. Rm serv. Bar noon-midnight; entertainment, dancing Tues-Sat. Ck-out 11 am. Coin lndry. Meeting rms. Bellhops. Valet serv. Beauty shop. Health club privileges. Refrigerators avail. Cr cds: A, C, D, DS, JCB, MC, V.

D ✔ ≈ ⚏ 🔥 SC

Westminster (B-6)

Founded: 1764 **Pop:** 13,068 **Elev:** 717 ft **Area code:** 410 **Zip:** 21157

Westminster, a Union supply depot at the Battle of Gettysburg, saw scattered action before the battle. It is the county seat of Carroll County, first in the US to offer complete rural free delivery mail service (started in 1899 with four two-horse wagons).

(See Baltimore, Frederick)

Motel

★ ★ **COMFORT INN.** *451 WMC Dr (MD 140), adj to Western Maryland College. 410/857-1900; FAX 410/857-9584.* 101 rms, 1-2 story. May-June: S $49-$60; D $55-$66; each addl $6; under 18 free; wkly rates; higher rates: WMC parents wkend, graduation, Dec 31; lower rates rest of yr. Crib free. Pet accepted, some restrictions; $25 refundable. TV; cable. Pool; whirlpool. Complimentary continental bkfst. Restaurant 11:30 am-10 pm; Sat & Sun from 8 am. Bar; entertainment Thur-Sun, dancing. Ck-out noon. Meeting rms. Sundries. Valet serv. Health club privileges. Cr cds: A, C, D, DS, ER, JCB, MC, V.

Restaurant

✔ ★ **BAUGHER'S.** *289 W Main St. 410/848-7413.* Hrs: 7:30 am-10 pm; Sun from 9 am; winter hrs vary. Closed most major hols. Semi-a la carte: bkfst $1.30-$3.25, lunch $1-$4.10, dinner $3.75-$9. Specializes in beef, ham, chicken. Parking. Country-style restaurant; adj to farmer's market. Family-owned. No cr cds accepted.

New Jersey

Population: 7,730,188

Land area: 7,504 square miles

Elevation: 0-1,803 feet

Highest point: High Point Mountain (Sussex County)

Entered Union: Third of original 13 states (December 18, 1787)

Capital: Trenton

Motto: Liberty and Prosperity

Nickname: Garden State

State flower: Purple violet

State bird: Eastern goldfinch

State tree: Red oak

State fair: Early August, 1995, in Cherry Hill

Time zone: Eastern

Tree-shaded 18th-century towns and history-hallowed grounds, on which Revolutionary battles were fought, make this state one of dignified beauty and democratic tradition. More than 800 lakes and ponds, 100 rivers and streams and 1,400 miles of freshly stocked trout streams are scattered throughout its wooded, scenic northwest corner. The swampy meadows west of the New Jersey Turnpike have been reclaimed and transformed into commercial and industrial areas. The Meadowlands, a multimillion-dollar sports complex, offers horse racing, the NY Giants and the NY Jets NFL football teams, the NJ Devils NHL hockey team, and the NJ Nets NBA basketball team. The coastline, stretching 127 miles from Sandy Hook to Cape May, offers excellent swimming and ocean fishing.

George Washington spent a quarter of his time here as Commander-in-Chief of the Revolutionary Army. On Christmas night in 1776, he crossed the Delaware and surprised the Hessians at Trenton. A few days later, he marched to Princeton and defeated three British regiments. He then spent the winter in Morristown, where the memories of his campaign are preserved in a national historical park.

New Jersey often is associated only with its factories, oil refineries, research laboratories and industrial towns. But history buffs, hunters, anglers, scenery lovers and amateur beachcombers need only to wander a short distance from its industrial areas to find whatever they like best.

National Park Service Areas

New Jersey has Morristown National Historical Park, the Sandy Hook Unit of Gateway National Recreation Area and Edison National Historic Site (see WEST ORANGE). In addition, parts of the Delaware Water Gap National Recreation Area (see DELAWARE WATER GAP, PA), the Delaware National Scenic River and the Appalachian National Scenic Trail are in New Jersey. The Statue of Liberty National Monument can be reached from here (see JERSEY CITY).

State Recreation Areas

The following towns list state recreation areas in their vicinity under What to See and Do; refer to the individual town for directions and park information.

Listed under **Allaire State Park:** see Allaire State Park.

Listed under **Batsto:** see Wharton State Forest.

Listed under **Branchville:** see Stokes State Forest and Swartswood State Park.

Listed under **Bridgeton:** see Parvin State Park.

Listed under **Clinton:** see Round Valley State Park and Spruce Run State Recreation Area.

Listed under **Deepwater:** see Fort Mott State Park.

Listed under **Hackettstown:** see Allamuchy Mountain State Park (Stephens Section).

Listed under **High Point State Park:** see High Point State Park.

Listed under **Jersey City:** see Liberty State Park.

Listed under **Lake Hopatcong:** see Hopatcong State Park.

Listed under **Long Beach Island:** see Barnegat Lighthouse State Park.

Listed under **Matawan:** see Cheesequake State Park.

Listed under **Ringwood State Park:** see Ringwood State Park.

Listed under **Seaside Park:** see Island Beach State Park.

Listed under **Trenton:** see Washington Crossing State Park.

Water-related activities, hiking, riding, various sports, picnicking, camping and visitor centers are available in many of these areas. There is a $1/person (12-62 yrs) walk-in fee in some areas; there is a parking fee ($1-$5) in many areas. In most areas, fees are collected Memorial Day wkend-Labor Day wkend; fees collected yr-round at Island Beach (see SEASIDE PARK). No pets in bathing or camping areas; in other day-use areas, pets must be attended and kept on a six-foot leash.

Bathing at inland beaches, Memorial Day-Labor Day; at ocean beaches from mid-June; cabins ($32-$100); campsites ($10-$12), lean-tos ($15-$18); reservations accepted ($10, non-refundable). Most areas are wildlife sanctuaries. In addition, 1,700 acres of Palisades Interstate Parks (see) on the Hudson are in New Jersey. There are also more than 20 state-owned historic sites (clearly marked); some with museums and guides. For detailed information contact Division of Parks and Forestry, CN 404, Trenton 08625; 609/292-2797.

Fishing & Hunting

Fishing opportunities abound in New Jersey's fresh and salt waters. No license is required for deep-sea or surf fishing along the 127-mile coastline; *however,* a license is required for taking shellfish. Nonresident clam license: $20; under age 14, $2. A license is required for freshwater fishing for everyone over 14 years of age. Nonresident fishing license: $23; nonresident trout stamp: $14; 7-day nonresident vacation fishing license: $15.

Hunting licenses are required for everyone over 14 years of age. Firearms or bow & arrow: nonresident, $100 each; small game only: nonresident, 2-day, $25; nonresident, 1-day, $7 (for commercial or semi-wild preserves only). Juveniles 10-13 with licensee over 21, $2.75. Woodcock stamp, $2.50; pheasant & quail stamp, $20 (for wildlife management areas only). Hunter Education Course or a previous year's resident license required to purchase license. For information contact Department of Environmental Protection and Energy, Division of Fish, Game and Wildlife, CN-400, Trenton 08625-0400; 609/292-2965.

Skiing

The following towns list ski areas in their vicinity under What to See and Do; refer to the individual town for directions and information.

Listed under **Newfoundland:** see Craigmeur Ski Area.

Listed under **Ramsey:** see Campgaw Mountain Ski Area†.

Listed under **Vernon:** see Vernon Valley/Great Gorge Ski Area.

† Also cross-country trails

Safety Belt Information

Safety belts are mandatory for all persons in front seat of vehicle. Children under 5 years must be in an approved passenger restraint anywhere in vehicle: ages 18 months-4 years may use a regulation safety belt in back seat, however, in front seat, children must use an approved safety seat; children under 18 months must use an approved safety seat anywhere in vehicle. For further information phone 609/633-9300.

Interstate Highway System

The following alphabetical listing of New Jersey towns in *Mobil Travel Guide* shows that these cities are within 10 miles of the indicated Interstate highways. A highway map should be checked, however, for the nearest exit.

INTERSTATE 78: Clinton, Plainfield, Scotch Plains, Somerville, Union.

INTERSTATE 80: Fort Lee, Hackensack, Hackettstown, Paramus, Parsippany, Rockaway, Saddle Brook, Wayne.

INTERSTATE 95: Elizabeth, Fort Lee, Newark, Trenton, Woodbridge.

Additional Visitor Information

The State Division of Travel and Tourism, CN-826, Trenton 08625, phone 609/292-2470 or 800/JERSEY-7, publishes a variety of materials for travelers. There are also two periodicals: *New Jersey Monthly*

(write Subscription Dept, Box 936, Farmingdale, NY 11737); *New Jersey Outdoors* (write Dept of Environmental Protection & Energy, CN-402, Trenton 08625).

There are eight tourist welcome centers and numerous information centers in New Jersey. At these centers visitors will find information racks with brochures to help plan trips to points of interest. For a publication with the locations of the centers contact the State Division of Travel and Tourism.

Allaire State Park (F-5)

(On County 524 between Farmingdale and Lakewood)

Allaire State Park has more than 3,000 acres and offers a fishing pond for children under 14; bridle trails; picnic facilities, playground; camping (dump station, summer); and the opportunity to visit a historic 19th-century village (see below). Park (daily). Standard fees when village buildings are open. Phone 908/938-2371. Parking fee (Memorial Day-Labor Day) ¢¢

What to See and Do

Historic Allaire Village. In 1822, James Allaire bought this site as a source of bog ore for his ironworks. Approximately 500 residents turned out hollow-ware caldrons, pots, kettles and pipes for New York City's waterworks. Today, visitors can explore the enameling furnace, a bakery, carriage house, general store, blacksmith and carpentry shops, workmen's houses, the community church and other buildings still much as they were in 1853. Village grounds (all yr); village buildings (May-Labor Day, wkends); special events (Feb-Dec). For information phone village office, 908/938-2253. **Free.**

Train Rides. Narrow-gauge steam locomotive rides (mid-June-Labor Day, daily; Apr-mid-June & after Labor Day-Nov, Sat & Sun). Phone 908/938-5524. ¢

(For accommodations see Asbury Park, Freehold)

Asbury Park (E-6)

Settled: 1871 **Pop:** 16,799 **Elev:** 21 ft **Area code:** 908 **Zip:** 07712

This popular shore resort was bought in 1871 by New York brush manufacturer James A. Bradley and named for Francis Asbury, first American Bishop of the Methodist Episcopal Church. Bradley established a town for temperance advocates and good neighbors; it was also a Methodist camp meeting resort. The beach and the three lakes proved so attractive that, by 1874, Asbury Park had grown into a borough, and by 1897, a city. It is the home of the famous boardwalk, Convention Hall and Paramount Theatre. In September 1934, the SS *Morro Castle* was grounded off this beach and burned with a loss of 122 lives. Asbury park became the birthplace of a favorite sweet when a local confectioner introduced "salt-water taffy" and watched the sales curve rise with the tide. Today, it is a popular resort area for swimming and fishing.

What to See and Do

Long Branch Historical Museum (Church of the Presidents). 3 mi N at 1260 Ocean Ave in Elberon section of Long Branch. Presidents Grant, Garfield, Arthur, McKinley, Hayes, Harrison and Wilson worshipped here. Museum contains items of interest from post-Civil War to the present; also records, pictures, relics of period between the Civil War and World War I when the resort was the playground of notables. (By appt) Phone 229-0600 or 222-9879. **Free.**

(For further information contact the Greater Asbury Park Chamber of Commerce, Lake & Ocean Aves, PO Box 649; 775-7676.)

Annual Events

Jazz Fest. June.

National Bocce Tournament. Late June.

Seasonal Events

Horse racing. Monmouth Park. Oceanport Ave in Oceanport via NJ 35 N to NJ 36; or via Garden State Pkwy exit 105, then E on NJ 36. Thoroughbred racing Tues-Wed, Fri-Sun & some major hols. Phone 222-5100. Memorial Day-Labor Day.

Metro Lyric Opera Series. At the Paramount Theater on the Boardwalk. Sat evenings. Phone 531-2378 for schedule, information. July-Aug.

Motel

★ **HoJo INN.** *(NJ 35, Asbury Park Circle, Neptune 07753)* 1 mi W at jct NJ 35, 66; 2 mi E of Garden State Pkwy exit 102. 908/776-9000; FAX 908/776-9014. 60 rms, 2 story. Memorial Day-Labor Day: S $55-$69; D $65-$85; each addl $5; under 18 free; higher rates: wkends, hols; lower rates rest of yr. Crib free. TV; cable, in-rm movies. Pool. Complimentary continental bkfst. Restaurant nearby. Bar adj 11-2 am. Ck-out noon. Refrigerators avail. Private patios, balconies. Cr cds: A, C, D, DS, MC, V.

Restaurant

★ ★ **CHRISTIE'S.** *(1 English Lane, Wanamassa)* N of Asbury Park Circle, off NJ 35. 908/776-8558. Hrs: 11:30 am-10 pm; Sat 5 pm-midnight; Sun 1-10 pm; early-bird dinner 4-6:30 pm. Closed Mon; Thanksgiving. Res accepted. Italian, Amer menu. Bar. Semi-a la carte: lunch $5.95-$9.95, dinner $9.95-$18.95. Child's meals. Specialties: sea feast Fra Diavolo, duckling à l'orange, saltimbocca a la Christie. Entertainment exc Mon. Valet parking. Spacious grounds with outdoor garden overlooking golf course. Family-owned. Cr cds: A, C, D, DS, MC, V.

Atlantic City (J-4)

Settled: 1854 **Pop:** 37,986 **Elev:** 8 ft **Area code:** 609

Honeymooners, conventioneers, Miss America and some 30 million annual visitors have made Atlantic City the best-known New Jersey beach resort. Built on Absecon Island, it is shielded by the curve of the coast from battering northeastern storms while the nearby Gulf Stream warms its waters, helping to make it a year-round resort. A 60-foot-wide boardwalk extends along five miles of beaches. Hand-pushed wicker rolling chairs take visitors up and down the Boardwalk. Absecon Lighthouse ("Old Ab"), a well-known landmark, was first lit in 1857 and now stands in an uptown city park. The game of Monopoly uses Atlantic City street names.

What to See and Do

1. **Recreation areas.** Beach (Memorial Day-mid-Oct; free), surfing at special areas (daily); boating (boats may be docked in State Marina and at public facilities along bayfront). Bicycling (rentals) and rolling chairs on Boardwalk (daily); golf, tennis.

2. **Fishing.** Surf fishing and deep-sea fishing. License may be required, check locally. Charter boats (Mar-Nov). Many tournaments are scheduled.

3. **Convention Center.** Seats 22,000; one of the world's largest pipe organs. Can accommodate small meetings as well as large conventions, sports events; site of the annual Miss America Pageant. Phone 348-7000.

4. **Amusement piers.**

   The Shops on Ocean One. Boardwalk at Arkansas Ave. A 900-foot 3-deck shopping pier houses shops, food court & restaurants. (Daily) Phone 347-8082.

   Garden Pier. Boardwalk & New Jersey Ave. Atlantic City Art Center and Atlantic City Historical Museum are located here (daily). Phone 347-5844. **Free.**

5. **Historic Town of Smithville and the Village Greene at Smithville** (1787). 7 mi W on US 30 to Absecon, then 6 mi N on US 9, at Moss Mill Rd. Restored 18th-century village with specialty shops and restaurants. Also carousel, horse-drawn carriage rides, train ride, paddle boats and miniature golf (Apr-Oct, fee for each). Village (daily).

6. **Historic Gardner's Basin.** 800 New Hampshire Ave, at N end of city. An eight-acre, sea-oriented park featuring the state's oldest tugboat; US Coast Guard Lightship; speed boat belonging to Guy Lombardo; aquarium. Picnicking. (Daily) Phone 348-2880.

7. **Storybook Land.** 10 mi W via US 40, 322. More than 50 storybook buildings and displays depicting children's stories; live animals; rides; picnic area, playground, concession. (May-mid-Sept, daily; Mar-Apr & mid-Sept-Thanksgiving, Sat & Sun only) Christmas Fantasy with lights and visiting with Mr. and Mrs. Santa (Thanksgiving-Dec 30, nightly). Admission includes attractions and unlimited rides. Sr citizen rate. Phone 641-7847. ¢¢¢

8. **Lucy, The Margate Elephant.** S via Atlantic Ave in Margate. Only elephant in the world you can walk through and come out alive. Guided tour and exhibit inside this six-story elephant-shaped building. Built 1881; spiral stairs in Lucy's legs lead to main hall & observation area on her back. Gift shop. Concession. (Mid-June-Labor Day, daily; Apr-mid-June & Sept-Oct, Sat & Sun only) Free outdoor concerts (July-Aug, Thurs evenings). Phone 823-6473. ¢

9. **Edwin B. Forsythe National Wildlife Refuge, Brigantine Division.** 9 mi N on US 9. Auto-tour route; interpretive nature trails (daily). Over the years, more than 200 species of birds have been observed at this 38,000-acre refuge. Public use area has an 8-mi wildlife drive through diversified wetlands and uplands habitat; most popular in the spring and fall, during the course of the waterbird migration. Refuge headquarters (Mon-Fri). Contact PO Box 72, Great Creek Rd, Oceanville 08231; 652-1665. Per vehicle ¢¢

10. **Marine Mammal Stranding Center & Museum.** Over bridge and 1 mi N, at 3625 Atlantic-Brigantine Blvd. One of few marine mammal rescue and rehabilitation centers in US. Injured dolphins, turtles and other marine animals are brought to center for treatment. Museum offers exhibits on mammal species; recuperating animals can be viewed at center. Guided nature tours. Dolphin & whale watch tours available (fee). Special presentations (fee). (Memorial Day-Labor Day, daily; rest of yr, wkends only; closed some hols) Phone 266-0538. **Free.**

11. **Noyes Museum.** 12 mi NW via US 9, on Lily Lake Rd in Oceanville. Rotating and permanent exhibits of American art; collection of working bird decoys. (Wed-Sun; closed major hols) Sr citizen rate. Phone 652-8848. ¢¢

12. **Renault Winery.** 16 mi W on US 30 in Egg Harbor City. Guided tour (approx 1 hr) includes wine-aging cellars; press room; antique wine-making equipment; free wine tasting. (Daily) Restaurant (Fri-Sun; res recommended); garden cafe (daily exc Sun). Phone 965-2111. Tour ¢

(For further information contact the Greater Atlantic City Convention & Visitors Authority, 2314 Pacific Ave, 08401; 348-7100.)

Annual Events

Boardwalk National Professional Fine Arts Show. Phone 347-5844. Father's Day wkend.

Miss America Pageant. Convention Center. Usually wkend after Labor Day.

Indian Summer Boardwalk Art & Craft Show. Phone 347-5844. Usually 3rd wkend Sept.

Atlantic City Marathon. Phone 822-6911. Mid-Oct or mid-Nov.

Seasonal Event

Horse racing. Atlantic City Race Course. 14 mi NW at jct Black Horse Pike & US 40 in McKee City. Thoroughbred racing Tues-Sat evenings. Phone 641-2190. June-Sept.

(See Ocean City)

Motels

★ **BEST WESTERN BAYSIDE RESORT.** *(8029 Black Horse Pike, West Atlantic City 08232) 2 mi W on US 40, 322.* 609/641-3546; FAX 609/641-4329. 110 rms, 2 story. July-mid-Sept: S, D $85-$125; each addl $10; under 12 free; lower rates rest of yr. TV. 2 pools; wading pool. Restaurant 7 am-10 pm. Serv bar. Ck-out 11 am. Coin lndry. Meeting rms. Casino transportation. Indoor & outdoor tennis, pro. Exercise rm; instructor, weight machines, bicycles, sauna. On bay. Cr cds: A, C, D, DS, MC, V.

✔ ★ ★ **COMFORT INN NORTH.** *(405 E Abescon Blvd, Abescon 08201) 3 mi W on US 30.* 609/646-5000; FAX 609/383-8744. 200 rms, 6 story. S, D $40-$109; each addl $10; suites $125-$150; under 18 free. Crib free. Pet accepted, some restrictions. TV; cable. Pool. Complimentary continental bkfst, coffee. Restaurant nearby. Ck-out noon. Meeting rms. Cr cds: A, C, D, DS, ER, MC, V.

★ ★ **HAMPTON INN.** *(240 E White Horse Pike, Absecon 08201) 7 mi W on US 30.* 609/652-2500; FAX 609/652-2212. 129 rms, 4 story. Memorial Day-Labor Day: S, D $78-$126; suites $100-$150; under 18 free; higher rates hols; lower rates rest of yr. Crib free. TV; cable. Pool; whirlpool, lifeguard. Complimentary continental bkfst. Restaurant adj open 24 hrs. Ck-out 11 am. Coin lndry. Meeting rms. Free Atlantic City transportation. Cr cds: A, C, D, DS, MC, V.

✔ ★ **SUPER 8-ABSECON.** *(229 E US 30, Absecon 08201) 6 mi W on US 30.* 609/652-2477; FAX 609/748-0666. 58 rms, 2 story. July 4-Sept 1: S, D $45-$110; suites $55-$130; under 12 free; lower rates rest of yr. TV; cable. Complimentary coffee in lobby. Restaurant opp open 24 hrs. Ck-out noon. Refrigerators avail. Cr cds: A, C, D, DS, MC, V.

Hotels

★ ★ ★ **BALLY'S PARK PLACE CASINO.** *Park Place at Boardwalk (08401).* 609/340-2000; res: 800/225-5977 (exc NJ); FAX 609/340-4713. 1,265 rms, 49 story. Mid-June-Sept: S, D $125-$215; each addl $15; under 13 free; lower rates rest of yr. Crib free. TV; cable, in-rm movies. 2 pools, 1 indoor; poolside serv, lifeguard. Restaurants, bars open 24 hrs. Ck-out noon. Convention facilities. Barber, beauty shop. Valet parking; self-park garage. Exercise rm; instructor, weight machines, bicycles, whirlpool, sauna, steam rm. Massage. Bathrm phones; refrigerators avail. On beach. Cr cds: A, C, D, DS, MC, V.

★ ★ ★ **CAESARS ATLANTIC CITY HOTEL/CASINO.** *Pacific & Arkansas Aves (08401).* 609/348-4411; res: 800/443-0104; FAX 609/347-8089. 641 rms, 19 story. June-Labor Day: S, D $130-$175; each addl $15; lower rates rest of yr. Crib avail. TV; cable. Pool; lifeguard. Restaurants, bars open 24 hrs. Ck-out noon. Convention facilities. Shopping arcade. Barber, beauty shop. Free valet parking. Tennis. Miniature golf. Exercise rm; instructor, weight machines, bicycles, whirlpool, steam rm, sauna. Miniature golf. On ocean. Cr cds: A, C, D, DS, MC, V.

★ ★ **CLARIDGE CASINO/HOTEL.** *Indiana at Boardwalk (08401).* 609/340-3400; res: 800/257-8585; FAX 609/345-8909. 504 rms, 24 story. July-early Sept: S, D $130-$165; each addl $10; under 12 free; lower rates rest of yr. TV; cable, in-rm movies. Indoor pool; lifeguard. Restaurant open 24 hrs. Rm serv 24 hrs. Bar open 24 hrs. Ck-out noon. Meeting rms. Concierge. Beauty shop. Exercise rm; instructor, weights, bicycles, whirlpool, steam rm, sauna. On ocean. Refrigerators avail. Cr cds: A, C, D, DS, MC, V.

★ ★ ★ **THE GRAND-BALLY'S CASINO.** *Boston at Pacific (08404).* 609/347-7111; res: 800/257-8677; FAX 609/340-4858. 508 rms, 22 story. Late June-Sept: S, D $125-$200; each addl $15; suites $210-$400; under 12 free; lower rates rest of yr. Crib free. TV; cable. Indoor pool; poolside serv, lifeguard. Free supervised child's activities (July-Aug). Restaurant, bar open 24 hrs; entertainment. Ck-out noon. Convention facilities. Concierge. Barber, beauty shop. Valet parking. Exercise rm; instructor, weights, bicycles, whirlpool, steam rm, sauna. Game rm. Bathrm phones. On beach. Cr cds: A, C, D, DS, MC, V.

★ ★ ★ **HARRAH'S CASINO HOTEL.** *1725 Brigantine Blvd (08401).* 609/441-5000; res: 800/2-HARRAH (exc NJ); FAX 609/344-2974. 760 rms, 16 story. Mid-June-mid-Sept: S, D $100-$190; each addl $10; under 18 free; lower rates rest of yr. Crib free. TV; cable, in-rm movies. Indoor pool; lifeguard. Restaurants, bars open 24 hrs. Ck-out noon. Convention facilities. Shopping arcade. Barber, beauty shop. Valet parking. Beach, boardwalk transportation. 18-hole golf privileges. Tennis. Exercise rm; instructor, weight machines, bicycles, whirlpool, sauna. Game rm. Rec rm. Refrigerators avail. Marina. Cr cds: A, C, D, DS, MC, V.

★ ★ **HOLIDAY INN-BOARDWALK.** *Chelsea Ave at Boardwalk (08401).* 609/348-2200; FAX 609/348-0168. 220 rms, 20 story. Mid-June-Labor Day: S, D $80-$170; each addl $10; under 19 free; lower rates rest of yr. Crib avail. TV; cable. Heated pool; poolside serv. Restaurant 7-2 am. Bar 11:30-2 am. Ck-out 11 am. Meeting rms. Tennis, golf privileges. Health club privileges. Wet bar in suites. On ocean. Cr cds: A, C, D, DS, JCB, MC, V.

✔ ★ ★ **HOWARD JOHNSON.** *(539 Absecon Blvd, Absecon 08201) 3 mi W on US 30.* 609/641-7272; FAX 609/646-3286. 205 rms, 7 story. S, D $55-$125; each addl $12; suites $65-$125; under 12 free; wkly rates. Crib avail. Restaurant 7 am-10 pm. Bar. Ck-out noon. Meeting rms. Cr cds: A, C, D, DS, MC, V.

★ ★ ★ **MERV GRIFFIN'S RESORTS CASINO HOTEL.** *N Carolina Ave at Boardwalk (08404).* 609/344-6000; res: 800/438-7424 (exc NJ); FAX 609/340-6284. 669 rms, 15 story. July-Labor Day: S, D $105-$225; each addl $10; lower rates rest of yr. Crib free. TV; cable. Indoor/outdoor pool. Restaurants, bars open 24 hrs. Ck-out noon. Convention facilities. Concierge. Shopping arcade. Valet parking. Exercise rm; instructor, weights, bicycles, whirlpool, steam rm, sauna. Game rm. Bathrm phones. Some balconies. First casino in Atlantic City. Cr cds: A, C, D, DS, MC, V.

★ **QUALITY INN BOARDWALK.** *S Carolina & Pacific Aves (08401).* 609/345-7070; *res:* 800/356-6044; *FAX* 609/345-0633. 203 units, 17 story. July-early Sept: S, D $90-$125; each addl $10; suites $135-$150; under 18 free; lower rates rest of yr. Crib free. TV; cable. Restaurant 7 am-noon, 5-10 pm; Sat, Sun to 2 am. Bar. Ck-out noon. Cr cds: A, D, DS, ER, JCB, MC, V.

D 🏊 🎿 🔥 SC

★★ **SANDS HOTEL CASINO.** *Indiana Ave at Brighton Park (08401).* 609/441-4000; *res:* 800/257-8580; *FAX* 609/441-4180. 534 rms, 21 story. July-Sept: S, D $139-$269; each addl $12; under 12 free; package plans; lower rates rest of yr. Crib free. TV; cable. Heated pool; lifeguard. Restaurant, bar open 24 hrs; entertainment. Ck-out noon. Convention facilities. Concierge. Valet, garage parking. Golf privileges. Exercise rm; instructor, weight machines, bicycles, whirlpool, sauna. Game rm. On ocean. Cr cds: A, C, D, DS, MC, V.

D 🏌 🏊 🎿 🏋 🎿 🔥 SC

★★★ **SHERATON-ATLANTIC CITY WEST.** *(6821 Black Horse Pike, West Atlantic City 08232)* 5 mi W on Black Horse Pike. 609/272-0200; *FAX* 609/646-3703. 213 rms, 6 story, 98 suites. Memorial Day-Labor Day: S, D $115; suites $135; under 19 free; package plans; lower rates rest of yr. Crib avail. TV; cable. Pool. Restaurant 6:30 am-10:30 pm. Bar; entertainment Tues, Thurs-Sat. Ck-out noon. Meeting rms. Free airport transportation. 9-hole golf; greens fee $10. Exercise equipt; weights, bicycles. Game rm. Refrigerators avail. Cr cds: A, C, D, DS, MC, V.

D 🏃 🏊 🎿 🏋 🎿 🔥 SC

★★ **SHOWBOAT CASINO HOTEL.** *Box 840 (08404), Delaware Ave at Boardwalk.* 609/343-4000; *res:* 800/621-0200; *FAX* 609/345-2334. 516 rms, 24 story. July-mid-Sept: S, D $142-$182; each addl $15; suites $252-$469; under 12 free; mid-wk packages; lower rates rest of yr. Crib free. TV; cable. Pool; lifeguard. Restaurant, bar open 24 hrs; entertainment. Ck-out noon. Convention facilities. Beauty shop. Bowling center. Game rm. Exercise rm; instructor, weights, stair machines, whirlpool, sauna. Bathrm phones. Some refrigerators. Some balconies. On ocean; ocean view from most rms. Cr cds: A, C, D, DS, MC, V.

D 🏊 🎿 🏋 🎿 🔥

★★ **TROPWORLD CASINO.** *Brighton at Boardwalk (08401).* 609/340-4000; *res:* 800/257-6227; *FAX* 609/343-5211. 1,020 rms, 23 story. Mid-June-Sept: S, D $125-$225; each addl $10; under 18 free; lower rates rest of yr. TV; cable. 2 pools, 1 indoor; poolside serv, lifeguard. Restaurants, bars open 24 hrs. Ck-out noon. Shopping arcade. Barber, beauty shop. Valet, garage parking. Lighted tennis. Exercise rm; instructor, weights, bicycles, whirlpool, sauna. Some bathrm phones. Indoor adult amusement park. On ocean. Cr cds: A, DS, JCB, MC, V.

D 🏃 🏊 🏋 🎿 🎿 🔥

★★★★ **TRUMP PLAZA HOTEL & CASINO.** *Mississippi & Boardwalk (08401).* 609/441-6000; *res:* 800/677-7378; *FAX* 609/441-6916. 557 rms, 38 story. June-Sept: S, D $175-$205; each addl $10; under 16 free; lower rates rest of yr. Crib avail. TV; cable, in-rm movies. Indoor pool; lifeguard. Restaurants open 24 hrs (also see IVANA'S). Bar open 24 hrs; entertainment. Ck-out noon. Concierge. Shopping arcade. Free garage parking. Tennis. Golf privileges. Exercise rm; instructor, weights, bicycles, whirlpool, sauna, steam rm. Massage. Game rm. Bathrm phones. On ocean. Cr cds: A, C, D, DS, MC, V.

D 🏌 🏃 🏊 🏋 🎿 🔥

★★ **TRUMP REGENCY.** *2500 Boardwalk (08401), at Florida Ave.* 609/344-4000; *res:* 800/234-5678; *FAX* 609/344-1663. 500 rms, 22 story. Memorial Day-Labor Day: S, D $150-$185; each addl $10; suites $195-$510; under 12 free; lower rates rest of yr. Crib free. TV; cable. Indoor pool; poolside serv, lifeguard. Restaurant 7 am-midnight. Bar from 10 am. Ck-out noon. Convention facilities. Concierge. Gift shop. Valet parking. Exercise rm; instructor, weights, bicycles, whirl-

pool, sauna, steam rm. Bathroom phones; refrigerators avail. On ocean; beach. Cr cds: A, C, D, DS, MC, V.

D 🏊 🏋 🎿 🔥 SC

★★★ **TRUMP TAJ MAHAL CASINO RESORT.** *1000 Boardwalk (08401), at Virginia Ave.* 609/449-1000; *res:* 800/825-8786; *FAX* 609/449-6817. 1,250 rms, 51 story, 237 suites. July-Labor Day: S, D $165-$225; each addl $25; suites $275-$800; lower rates rest of yr. Crib free. TV; cable, in-rm movies. Indoor pool; poolside serv, lifeguard. Restaurant open 24 hrs, dining rm 6 pm-midnight. Rm serv 24 hrs. Bar open 24 hrs; entertainment. Ck-out noon. Convention facilities. Concierge. Shopping arcade. Barber, beauty shop. Valet parking. Exercise rm; instructor, weights, bicycles, whirlpool, sauna, steam rm. Massage. Casino. Game rm. Bicycles avail. Minibars. Refrigerators avail. On Boardwalk facing ocean; stylized blend of east Indian and European design. Cr cds: A, C, D, DS, JCB, MC, V.

D 🏊 🏋 🎿 🔥

★★★ **TRUMP'S CASTLE CASINO RESORT.** *Huron Ave & Brigantine Blvd (08401), marina area.* 609/441-2000; *res:* 800/777-8477; *FAX* 609/441-8541. 725 rms, 27 story. July-mid-Sept: S, D $110-$165; each addl $15; suites $150-$265; under 12 free; package plans; lower rates rest of yr. Crib free. TV; cable, in-rm movies. Pool; wading pool, poolside serv, lifeguard. Restaurants, bars open 24 hrs; entertainment. Ck-out noon. Convention facilities. Shopping arcade. Barber, beauty shop. Free garage parking. Lighted tennis. Exercise rm; instructor, weights, bicycles, whirlpool, sauna, steam rm. Massage. Miniature golf. Basketball. Lawn games. Game rm. On ocean inlet; marina. Cr cds: A, C, D, DS, JCB, MC, V.

D 🚣 🏌 🏊 🏋 🎿 🎿 🔥

Resort

★★★ **MARRIOTT'S SEAVIEW RESORT.** *(401 S New York Rd, Absecon 08201)* 7 mi W on US 9, just N of Absecon. 609/748-1990; *FAX* 609/652-2307. 299 rms, 3 & 4 story. EP, May-Nov: S, D $159-$210; suites $250-$650; under 18 free; golf, package plans; lower rates rest of yr. Crib free. TV; cable, in-rm movies avail. 2 pools, 1 indoor; poolside serv, lifeguard. Dining rm 6:30 am-10 pm. Rm serv. Box lunches. Snack bar at pro shop. Bar noon-2 am. Ck-out 12:30 pm, ck-in 4 pm. Coin lndry. Convention facilities. Sports dir. 8 tennis courts, 4 lighted, pro. 36-hole golf, pro, 9-hole putting green; golf school. Paddle tennis. Rec rm. Game rm. Exercise equipt; weights, bicycles, whirlpool, sauna. Refrigerator, fireplace, private patio in suites. Located on 670-acre estate; turn-of-the-century elegance combined with spectacular golf & tennis facilities. Cr cds: A, C, D, DS, ER, JCB, MC, V.

D 🏌 🏃 🏊 🏋 🎿 🎿 🔥 SC

Restaurants

★★ **ABE'S LOBSTER & SEAFOOD HOUSE.** *2031 Atlantic Ave at Arkansas.* 609/344-7701. Hrs: noon-9 pm; early-bird dinner 4-6 pm. Closed Mon (ex July & Aug); also Oct-mid-May. Res accepted. Bar. Semi-a la carte: lunch from $5, dinner $10-$30. Child's meals. Specializes in lobster, soft-shell crab. Parking. Lobster tank. Family-owned. Cr cds: A, C, D, DS, MC, V.

★ **CAPTAIN YOUNG'S SEAFOOD EMPORIUM.** *1 Atlantic Ocean, on 3rd floor of The Shops on Ocean One Mall.* 609/344-2001. Hrs: 11:30 am-9 pm; Sat to 10 pm. Closed Thanksgiving, Dec 25. Bar. Semi-a la carte: lunch $5.95-$7.95, dinner $11.95-$19.95. Specializes in fresh fish, fresh lobster, crab legs. Overlooks beach and Boardwalk. Cr cds: A, C, D, DS, MC, V.

D

★★ **CHEF VOLA'S.** *111 S Albion Place (08400).* 609/345-2022. Hrs: 6-10 pm. Closed Mon; Thanksgiving, Dec 24 & 25. Res required. Italian menu. Semi-a la carte: dinner $13.95-$30. Specializes in steak, veal chops, veal Marsala. Italian decor. Photographs of celebrities. No cr cds accepted.

✔ ★ **CRAB POT.** *(9707 Amherst Ave, Margate) 5 mi S on Pacific Ave.* 609/823-1163. Hrs: 8 am-9:30 pm; Fri & Sat to 10 pm. Closed Nov-Mar. Bar. Semi-a la carte: bkfst $2.50-$7.95, lunch $3.95-$6.95, dinner $10.95-$17.95. Child's meals. Specializes in fresh seafood. Entertainment wkends (in season). Parking. Outdoor dining. Overlooks bay, marina. Family-owned. No cr cds accepted.
D

★ ★ **DOCK'S OYSTER HOUSE.** *2405 Atlantic Ave (08400).* 609/345-0092. Hrs: 5-10:30 pm. Closed Mon; also Jan & Dec. Res accepted. Bar. Semi-a la carte: dinner $11.95-$25.95. Child's meals. Specialties: imperial crab, fried oysters, oyster stew. Pianist Thurs & Fri. Parking. Casual atmosphere in family-owned restaurant since 1897. Cr cds: A, D, MC, V.
D

★ ★ ★ **IVANA'S.** *(See Trump Plaza Hotel & Casino)* 609/441-6400. Hrs: 6-10 pm; Sat 6-11 pm. Closed Wed-Fri. Res accepted. Bar. Wine list. Continental menu. A la carte entrees: dinner $23-$29. Specialties: rack of lamb, medallions of veal, lobster in champagne sauce. Own baking. Pianist. Valet parking. Tableside cooking. Cr cds: A, C, D, DS, MC, V.
D

★ ★ **KNIFE & FORK INN.** *Albany & Atlantic Ave.* 609/344-1133. Hrs: noon-2 pm, 5:30-10 pm; hrs vary Nov-Easter. Closed Sun; Yom Kippur, Dec 25. Bar. A la carte entrees: lunch, dinner $20-$30. Specializes in seafood, fresh vegetables. Family-owned. Jacket. Cr cds: A, D, DS, MC, V.

★ ★ **OLD WATERWAY INN.** *1700 W Riverside Dr.* 609/347-1793. Hrs: 5-11 pm. Closed Dec 25; also Mon & Tues Oct-Apr. Res accepted. Bar. Semi-a la carte: dinner $12-$23. Child's meals. Specializes in fresh seafood and Cajun specialities. Own pasta. Outdoor dining. Nautical decor. On waterfront; view of skyline. Cr cds: A, D, MC, V.
D

★ ★ **PEKING DUCK HOUSE.** *2801 Atlantic Ave, at Iowa.* 609/344-9090. Hrs: noon-11 pm; Fri, Sat to midnight; Sun 2-11 pm. Res accepted. Chinese menu. Bar. Semi-a la carte: lunch $4.95-$8.50. Complete meals: dinner $10.95-$19.95. Child's meals. Specializes in Peking duck, fresh seafood. Parking. Oriental porcelains; Chinese silk flowers. Cr cds: A, C, D, MC, V.
D

★ ★ ★ **RAM'S HEAD INN.** *(9 W White Horse Pike, Absecon, Galloway Township) On US 30 at Garden State Pkwy exit 40 S.* 609/652-1700. Hrs: noon-3 pm, 5-9:30 pm; Sat 5-10 pm; Sun 3:30-9:30 pm. Res accepted. Closed Mon; Labor Day, Dec 24. Continental menu. Bar. Semi-a la carte: lunch $6.95-$12.95, dinner $14.25-$25.95. Child's meals. Specializes in colonial Amer dishes, fresh southern New Jersey seafood, duckling. Own baking. Pianist. Valet parking. Outdoor dining. Colonial decor; gallery with paintings, plants. Jacket (dinner). Cr cds: A, C, D, DS, MC, V.
D

★ ★ ★ **RENAULT WINERY.** *(72 N Bremen Ave, Egg Harbor City) 16 mi W on US 30.* 609/965-2111. Hrs: Fri & Sat 5-8 pm; Sun from 4:30 pm; Sun brunch 10:30 am-2:30 pm. Closed Mon-Thurs; Dec 25. Res required. Wine list. Complete meals: dinner $26-$30. Sun brunch $12.95. Specializes in fresh seafood, poultry, beef. Menu changes wkly. Pianist/guitarist. Parking. Elegant dining in eclectic Methode Champenoise rm of winery founded in 1864. Cr cds: A, C, D, MC, V.
D

✔ ★ **SAIGON.** *3205 Atlantic Ave (08400).* 609/344-2282. Hrs: 11:30 am-9 pm. Vietnamese menu. Semi-a la carte: lunch, dinner

$3.50-$11.95. Specialties: shrimp on sugar cane stick, Vietnamese crêpe. No cr cds accepted.

★ ★ **SCANNICCHIO'S.** *119 S California Ave.* 609/348-6378. Hrs: 4 pm-midnight. Closed most major hols. Res required wkends. Italian menu. Bar. A la carte entrees: dinner $11.95-$19.95. Specializes in veal, fresh seafood. Intimate ambiance. Cr cds: A, C, D, DS, MC, V.
D

Unrated Dining Spot

IRISH PUB AND INN. *St James Place & Boardwalk.* 609/344-9063. Open 24 hrs. Irish, Amer menu. Bar. A la carte entrees: lunch $1.95-$3.95, dinner $2.95-$6.25. Complete meals: dinner $5.50. Specialty: Dublin beef stew. Irish balladeer Thurs-Sun (summer months). Patio dining. Informal, Irish pub atmosphere. No cr cds accepted.
D

Batsto (H-4)

Area code: 609 **Zip:** 08037

(Approx 10 mi E of Hammonton)

The Batsto Iron Works, established in 1766, made munitions for the Revolutionary Army from the bog iron ore found nearby. Its furnaces shut down for the last time in 1848. Eighteen years later, Joseph Wharton, whose immense estate totaled nearly 100,000 acres, bought the land. In 1954, the state of New Jersey bought nearly 150 square miles of land in this area, including the entire Wharton tract, for a state forest.

What to See and Do

1. **Batsto State Historic Site.** Restored early 19th-century iron and glassmaking community. General store, gristmill, blacksmith shop, wheelwright shop, sawmill, workers houses and visitor center are open seasonally to the public. Guided tours of the mansion. Parking fee (Memorial Day-Labor Day, wkends & hols). For further information and hours phone 561-3262. **Free.**

2. **Wharton State Forest.** Along US 206 near Atsion. Crossed by NJ 542, 563. Streams wind through 109,298 acres of wilderness. Swimming; fishing; hunting; canoeing. Limited picnicking. Tent & trailer sites, cabins. Standard fees. Phone 561-3262. Also here is

   Atsion Recreation Area. Swimming; canoeing (boat rentals). Picnicking. Camping. Standard fees. For information phone the Atsion Ranger Station, 268-0444.

(For accommodations see Atlantic City)

Beach Haven (H-5)

(see Long Beach Island)

Berlin (G-3)

Pop: 5,672 **Elev:** 155 ft **Area code:** 609 **Zip:** 08009

(For information about this area contact the Borough of Berlin, 59 S White Horse Pike; 767-7777.)

(For accommodations see Cherry Hill, also see Camden, Haddonfield)

Bernardsville (C-4)

Pop: 6,597 **Elev:** 400 ft **Area code:** 908 **Zip:** 07924

What to See and Do

1. **Great Swamp National Wildlife Refuge.** 1 mi N on US 202, W on North Maple Ave, 2 mi E on Madisonville Rd, then 1 1/2 mi NE on Lee's Hill Rd, then right on Long Hill Rd. Nature trails, boardwalk. Observation blind; wilderness area. More than 200 species of birds, fish, reptiles, frogs, ducks, geese and fox may be seen in this 7,300-acre refuge. Headquarters (Mon-Fri; closed hols). Trails and information booth (daily, dawn-dusk). Phone 201/425-1222. **Free.**

2. **Morristown National Historical Park** (see). Approx 5 mi N on US 202.

(See Morristown)

Hotel

★ ★ ★ **SOMERSET HILLS.** *(200 Liberty Corner Rd, Warren 07059)* SW on I-287 to I-78E, exit 33 (Martinsville-Bernardsvile), left at top of ramp, right at 3rd light. 908/647-6700; res: 800/688-0700; FAX 908/647-8053. 111 units, 4 story, 4 suites, 6 kits. S $95-$140; D $95-$150; each addl $10; suites $195-$300; kits. $95-$175. Crib free. TV; cable, in-rm movies avail. Pool; poolside serv. Restaurant 6:30 am-11 pm. Bar 11:30-1 am. Ck-out noon. Meeting rms. Concierge. Gift shop. Tennis privileges. 18-hole golf privileges, pro, putting green, driving range. Exercise equipt; weight machine, bicycles. Nestled in the Watchung Mountains near the crossroads of historical Liberty Corner. Cr cds: A, C, D, MC, V.

Inn

★ ★ ★ ★ **THE BERNARDS INN.** 27 Mine Brook Rd. 908/766-0002; FAX 908/766-4604. 21 rms, 1 with shower only, 5 story, 3 suites. No elvtr. S, D $95-$155; suites $135-$155. Crib $20. TV; cable. Complimentary continental bkfst. Restaurant (see THE BERNARDS INN RESTAURANT). Rm serv Mon-Fri. Bar. Ck-out 11 am, ck-in 2 pm. Concierge. Bellman. Completely renovated inn, built 1907, recaptures the grandeur of the past and offers services and amenities of the present. Luxurious accommodations and Old World hospitality. Cr cds: A, C, D, MC, V.

Restaurants

★ ★ ★ **THE BERNARDS INN.** *(See The Bernards Inn)* 908/766-0002. Hrs: 11:30 am-3 pm, 5:30-10 pm; Fri & Sat to 11 pm. Closed Sun; some major hols. Res accepted, required Fri & Sat. Bar. Wine list. A la carte entrees: lunch $9-$13, dinner $21-$28. Specializes in rack of lamb, red snapper, veal medallion. Pianist. Parking. Elegant dining, turn-of-the-century ambiance. Jacket (dinner). Cr cds: A, C, D, MC, V.

★ ★ ★ **GIRAFE.** *(95 Morristown Rd, Basking Ridge)* I-287 exit 26B, W to US 202S. 908/221-0017. Hrs: 11:30 am-2 pm, 5:30-9:30 pm; Fri to 10 pm; Sat 5:30-10 pm. Closed Sun; Jan 1, Dec 25. Res accepted. Wine cellar. A la carte entrees: lunch $6.50-$12.50, dinner $16-$24. Specializes in pasta, fresh fish, desserts. Own baking. Parking. Jacket. Cr cds: A, C, D, MC, V.

D

Bordentown (E-4)

Settled: 1682 **Pop:** 4,341 **Elev:** 72 ft **Area code:** 609 **Zip:** 08505

A long and honorable history has left an indelible stamp on this town. Bordentown was once a busy shipping center and a key stop on the Delaware and Raritan Canal. In January, 1778, Bordentown citizens filled numerous kegs with gun powder and sent them down the Delaware River to Philadelphia hoping to blow up the British fleet stationed there. But the plan was discovered, and British troops intercepted the kegs and discharged them. In 1816, Joseph Bonaparte, exiled king of Spain and brother of Napoleon, bought 1,500 acres and settled here.

What to See and Do

Clara Barton Schoolhouse. 142 Crosswicks St. Building was in use as a school in Revolutionary days. In 1851, Clara Barton, founder of the American Red Cross, established one of the first free public schools in the country in this building. (By appt) Phone 298-1740. **Free.**

(For further information, contact the Historical Society Visitors Center, Old City Hall, 13 Crosswicks St, PO Box 182; 298-1740.)

(See Trenton)

Motel

★ **DAYS INN.** 1073 US 206, just N of NJ Tpke exit 7. 609/298-6100; FAX 609/298-7509. 131 rms, 2 story. S, D $75-$85; each addl $10; under 12 free. Crib free. Pet accepted. TV; cable. Pool; lifeguard. Restaurant 6:30-10 am, 5-9 pm. Rm serv. Bar 5 pm-1:30 am; entertainment Fri & Sat. Ck-out noon. Coin lndry. Meeting rms. Sundries. Cr cds: A, C, D, DS, JCB, MC, V.

Branchville (B-3)

Pop: 851 **Elev:** 529 ft **Area code:** 201 **Zip:** 07826

This town in Sussex County is near many attractions in New Jersey's scenic northwest corner.

What to See and Do

1. **Space Farms Zoo & Museum.** 6 mi N on County 519. Collection of more than 500 wild animals; early American museum in main building, addl museums on grounds; picnic area, concession; gift shop. Zoo and museum (May-Oct, daily). Phone 875-5800 or -3223. ¢¢¢

2. **Peters Valley.** 8 mi NW via US 206, County 560, then S on County 615. Historic buildings in the Delaware Water Gap National Recreation Area (see DELAWARE WATER GAP, PA) serve as residences and studios for professional craftspeople and summer crafts workshops in blacksmithing, ceramics, fine metals, photography, fibers and woodworking. Contemporary craft store (all yr). Studios (June-Aug, Fri-Sun afternoons). Phone 948-5200. **Free.**

3. **Stokes State Forest.** 5 mi N on US 206. Located on the Kittatinny Ridge, this 15,328-acre forest includes some of the finest mountain country in New Jersey. Swimming; fishing, hunting. Picnicking. Camping. Scenic views from Sunrise Mt; Tillman Ravine, a natural gorge, is in the southern corner of the park. Standard fees. Phone 948-3820.

4. **Swartswood State Park.** 2 mi S on County 519, then continue 2 mi on County 627, left 3 mi on County 521 to Swartswood, left 1 mi on County 622, right on County 619, 1/2 mi to park entrance. A

1,470-acre park on Swartswood Lake. Swimming, bathhouse; fishing, hunting; boating (rentals). Picnicking, concession. Camping. Standard fees. Phone 383-5230.

(For further information contact the Sussex County Chamber of Commerce, 112 Hampton House Rd, Newton 07860; 579-1811.)

Annual Event

Peters Valley Craft Fair. Peters Valley (see #2). More than 150 juried exhibitors; demonstrations, music, food. Last wkend July.

(For accommodations see Vernon)

Bridgeton (H-2)

Settled: 1686 **Pop:** 18,942 **Elev:** 40 ft **Area code:** 609 **Zip:** 08302

The City of Bridgeton has been recognized as New Jersey's largest historic district, with more than 2,200 registered historical landmarks. There are many styles of architecture here, some of which date back nearly 300 years.

What to See and Do

1. **Old Broad St Church** (1792). W Broad St & West Ave. Outstanding example of Georgian architecture, with Palladian window, high-backed wooden pews, wine glass pulpit, brick-paved aisles and brass lamps that once held whale oil.

2. **City Park.** W Commerce St & Mayor Aitken Dr off NJ 49. A 1,100-acre wooded area with swimming (protected beaches, Memorial Day-Labor Day); fishing; boating (floating dock), canoeing. Picnic grounds, recreation center. Zoo (parking fee). (Daily) Phone 451-9208. Also here is

   New Sweden Farmstead-Museum. Reconstruction of first permanent European settlement in Delaware Valley. Seven log buildings including smokehouse/sauna; horse barn, cow and goat barn, threshing barn; storage house; blacksmith shop; family residence with period furnishings. Costumed guides. (Memorial Day-Labor Day, daily; mid-Apr-Memorial Day & after Labor Day-Oct, Fri-Sun) Phone 455-9785. ¢¢

3. **Parvin State Park.** 7 mi NE off NJ 77, near Centerton. This 1,125-acre park offers swimming, bathhouse; fishing; boating, canoeing (rentals). Picnicking, concessions, playgrounds. Camping (dump station), cabins. Standard fees. Phone 358-8616.

4. **Gibbon House** (1730). 7 mi SW in Greenwich, on Ye Greate St. Site of New Jersey's only 18th-century tea burning party; genealogical research library (Mar-Dec, Wed & Sun). Events scheduled throughout yr. Gibbon House (early Apr-late Nov, daily exc Mon; closed Sun in July, Aug); tours (wkdays). Donation. Phone 455-4055 or 451-8454.

5. **George J. Woodruff Museum of Indian Artifacts.** Bridgeton Free Public Library, 150 E Commerce St. Approx 20,000 local Native American artifacts, some up to 10,000 years old; clay pots, pipes, implements. (Mon-Fri afternoons; also by appt; closed some major hols) Phone 451-2620. **Free.**

(For further information contact the Bridgeton-Cumberland Tourist Association, 50 E Broad St; 451-4802.)

Annual Event

Victorian Faire. Victorian Bridgeton is re-created through music, games and contests, street vendors, crafts, costumes and city tours. Phone 451-9208. Labor Day.

Seasonal Event

Concerts. Riverfront. Performances by ragtime, military, country & western bands and others. Sun nights. Phone 451-9208. Nine wks June-Aug.

(For accommodations see Millville)

Burlington (F-3)

Settled: 1677 **Pop:** 9,835 **Elev:** 13 ft **Area code:** 609 **Zip:** 08016

In 1774 Burlington, along with New York, Philadelphia and Boston, was a thriving port. A Quaker settlement, it was one of the first to provide public education. A 1682 Act of Assembly gave Matinicunk (now Burlington) Island in the Delaware River to the town with the stipulation that the revenue it generated would be used for public schools; that act is still upheld. Burlington was the capital of West Jersey; the legislature met here, and in the East Jersey capital of Perth Amboy, from 1681 until after the Revolution. In 1776, the Provincial Congress adopted the State Constitution here.

What to See and Do

1. **Friends Meeting House** (1784). High St in 300 block. (By appt) Phone 386-3993. ¢¢

2. **Old St Mary's Church** (1703). W Broad & Wood Sts. The oldest Episcopal Church building in the state. (By appt) Phone 386-0902.

3. **Burlington County Historical Society.** 457 High St. The society maintains **D.B. Pugh Library**, genealogical and historical holdings; **James Fenimore Cooper House** (ca 1780), birthplace of the famous author, now the society headquarters; **Bard-How House** (ca 1740) with period furnishings; **Capt James Lawrence House,** birthplace of the commander of the *Chesapeake* during the War of 1812 and speaker of the immortal words "Don't give up the ship," contains 1812 objects and costume display. Tour of historic houses (Sun-Thurs). Phone 386-4773. ¢¢

4. **Thomas Revell House** (1685). 213 Wood St. The oldest building in Burlington County. (By appt and during Wood Street Fair; see ANNUAL EVENT) Phone 386-2426. **Free.**

5. **Historic tours.** Leave foot of High St. Guided walking tours of 33 historic sites (1685-1829), eight of which are open to the public. (Daily; no tours Easter, Dec 25) Sr citizen rate. Phone 386-3993. ¢¢

Annual Event

Wood Street Fair. Re-creation of colonial fair; crafts, antiques exhibits; food; entertainment. First Sat after Labor Day.

(For accommodations see Bordentown, Mount Holly; also see Philadelphia, PA)

Restaurant

★ ★ ★ **CAFE GALLERY.** *219 High St. 609/386-6150.* Hrs: 11:30 am-10 pm; Fri & Sat to 11 pm; Sun brunch 11:30 am-3 pm. Closed most major hols. Res accepted. Continental menu. Bar. Semi-a la carte: lunch $5.75-$9.75, dinner $13.50-$19.75. Sun brunch $15.75. Child's meals. Specializes in fresh seafood, veal. Restored Colonial building overlooking Delaware River. Cr cds: A, C, D, MC, V.

D

Caldwell (C-5)

Pop: 7,549 **Elev:** 411 ft **Area code:** 201 **Zip:** 07006

What to See and Do

Grover Cleveland Birthplace State Historic Site. 207 Bloomfield Ave. Built in 1832, this building served as the parsonage of the First Presbyterian Church. It is the birthplace of President Grover Cleveland, the only president born in New Jersey. He lived here from 1837-41. (Wed-Sat, also Sun afternoons; closed Jan 1, Thanksgiving, Dec 25, all state hols) Reservations recommended. Phone 226-1810. **Free.**

(For accommodations see Newark, Newark Intl Airport Area)

Camden (F-2)

Settled: 1681 **Pop:** 87,492 **Elev:** 23 ft **Area code:** 609

Camden's growth as the leading industrial, marketing and transportation center of southern New Jersey dates from post-Civil War days. Its location across the Delaware River from Philadelphia prompted large companies such as Campbell Soup (national headquarters) to establish plants here. Walt Whitman spent the last 20 years of his life in Camden.

What to See and Do

1. **New Jersey State Aquarium.** 1 Riverside Dr, I-676 exit Mickle Blvd. Features one of the largest "open ocean" tanks in the country. Other highlights include an underwater research station, aquatic nursery and the opportunity to touch sharks, rays and starfish in special tanks and pools. Gift shop. Cafeteria. (Daily; closed some hols) Sr citizen rate. Phone 365-3300. **¢¢¢**

2. **Walt Whitman House State Historic Site.** 330 Mickle St. The last residence of the poet and the only house he ever owned; he lived here from 1884 until his death on March 26, 1892. Contains original furnishings, books and mementos. (Wed-Sun; closed Jan 1, Thanksgiving, Dec 25) Phone 964-5383 or 541-8280. **Free.**

3. **Tomb of Walt Whitman.** Harleigh Cemetery, Haddon Ave & Vesper Blvd. The "good gray poet's" vault, designed by the poet himself, is of rough-cut stone with a grillwork door.

4. **Camden County Historical Society-Pomona Hall** (1726/1788). Park Blvd at Euclid Ave. Brick Georgian house that belonged to descendants of William Cooper, an early Camden settler; period furnishings. Museum exhibits focus on regional history and include antique glass, lamps, toys and early hand tools; fire-fighting equipment; Victor Talking Machines. Library (fee) has more than 20,000 books, as well as maps (17th century-present), newspapers (18th-20th century), oral history tapes, photographs and genealogical material. (Sat-Thurs; closed major hols; also Aug) Phone 964-3333. Museum **¢**

5. **Campbell Museum.** Campbell Pl. Features permanent exhibition "Kings and Queens and Soup Toureens." Collection of elaborate silver, faience and porcelain soup tureens, bowls, ladles used by European royalty during the 18th & 19th centuries. Also traveling exhibition. 20-minute film (by appt). (Mon-Fri; closed hols) Phone 342-6440. **Free.**

6. **Walt Whitman Cultural Arts Center.** 2nd & Cooper Sts. Poetry readings, concerts and plays (Sept-May). Outdoor music programs (June-Sept, Fri); outdoor children's theater (late June-Aug, Fri). Art gallery; statuary. Center (Mon-Fri). For schedule and fees phone 964-8300.

(For accommodations see Cherry Hill; also see Philadelphia, PA)

Cape May (K-3)

Settled: 1631 **Pop:** 4,668 **Elev:** 14 ft **Area code:** 609 **Zip:** 08204

Cape May, the nation's oldest seashore resort, is located on the southernmost tip of the state surrounded by the Atlantic Ocean and Delaware Bay. Popular with Philadelphia and New York society since 1766, Cape May has been host to Presidents Lincoln, Grant, Pierce, Buchanan and Harrison, as well as notables such as John Wanamaker and Horace Greeley. The entire town has been proclaimed a National Historic Landmark because it has more than 600 Victorian homes and buildings, many of which have been restored. The downtown Washington Street Victorian Mall features three blocks of shops and restaurants. Four miles of beaches and a one-and-one-quarter mile paved promenade offer vacationers varied entertainment. "Cape May diamonds," often found on the shores of Delaware Bay by visitors, are actually pure quartz, rounded by the waves.

What to See and Do

1. **Emlen Physick Estate** (1879). 1048 Washington St. Authentically restored 18-room Victorian mansion designed by Frank Furness. Mansion is also headquarters for the Mid-Atlantic Center for the Arts. (Apr-Nov, daily exc Fri; rest of yr, Tues-Thurs & Sat-Sun) Phone 884-5404. **¢¢**

2. **Historic Cold Spring Village.** 3 mi N via US 109. Restored 1870 South Jersey farm village. Craft shops; spinning, blacksmithing, weaving, pottery, broom making, ship modeling demonstrations; folk art; bakery and food shops; restaurant. (June-Sept, daily) Phone 898-2300. **¢¢**

3. **Tours.** The Mid-Atlantic Center for the Arts offers the following tours. For further information contact PO Box 340; 884-5404.

   Trolleys. Half-hour tours on enclosed trolley bus or open-air carriage; three routes beginning at Ocean St opp the Washington St Mall. (June-Oct, daily; reduced schedule rest of yr; no tours Thanksgiving) **¢¢**

   Mansions by Gaslight. Three-hour tour begins at Emlen Physick Estate (see #1). Visits four Victorian landmarks: Emlen Physick House (1879), the Abbey (1869), Mainstay Inn (1872) and Humphrey Hughes House (1903); shuttle bus between houses. (Mid-June-Sept, Wed evenings; rest of yr, hol and special tours) **¢¢¢¢**

   Cape May INNteriors Tour & Tea. Features a different group of houses each week, visiting five or more bed & breakfast inns and guesthouses. Innkeepers greet guests and describe experiences. (Summer, Mon; rest of yr, Sat; no tours Dec-Jan) **¢¢¢¢**

   Walking Tours of the Historic District. Begin at Information Booth on Washington St Mall at Ocean St. Three 1½-hour guided tours give historical insight into the customs and traditions of the Victorians and their ornate architecture. (June-Sept, daily; reduced schedule rest of yr) **¢¢**

   Ocean Walk Tours. Begins at Promenade & Beach Dr. A 1½-hr guided tour of Cape May's beaches. Guide discusses marine life and history of the beaches, including legends of buried treasure. (May-Sept, Tues-Sat) **¢¢**

   Combination Tours. Begin at Emlen Physick Estate (see #1). Approx two hours; includes trolley tour and guided tour of Physick House. (June-Oct, daily; rest of yr, Sat & Sun) Phone for schedule. **¢¢¢**

4. **Swimming, fishing, boating.** Beaches with lifeguards (fee). Fishing is very good at the confluence of the Atlantic and Delaware Bay. A large harbor holds boats of all sizes; excellent for sailboating and other small boat activity.

5. **Cape May-Lewes (DE) Ferry.** Sole connection between southern terminus of Garden State Pkwy and US 13 (Ocean Hwy) on the Delmarva Peninsula. 16-mi, 70-min trip across Delaware Bay.

(Daily) For schedule phone 800/64-FERRY (Cape May Terminal) or 302/645-6313 (Lewes Terminal). Per vehicle ¢¢¢¢¢

(For further information contact the Chamber of Commerce, PO Box 556, phone 884-5508; or the Welcome Center at 405 Lafayette St, phone 884-9562.)

Annual Events

Promenade Art Exhibit. July.

Victorian Week. Tours, antiques, crafts, period fashion shows. Mid-Oct.

(See Wildwood & Wildwood Crest)

Motels

★ ★ **COACHMAN'S MOTOR INN.** *205 Beach Dr. 609/884-8463.* 65 rms, 3 story, 45 kits. No elvtr. Late June-Labor Day (3-day min hols): S, D $125-$165; each addl $15; kit. units $130-$170; lower rates rest of yr. Crib free. TV. Pool; wading pool. Restaurant 7:30 am-10 pm. Bar; entertainment, dancing (in season). Ck-out 11 am. Tennis. Lawn games. Sun deck. On ocean. Cr cds: A, DS, MC, V.

★ ★ **LA MER.** *1317 Beach Ave. 609/884-9000; FAX 609/884-5004.* 68 rms, 2 story, 18 kits. July-Labor Day: S $100-$130; D $115-$150; each addl $10-$15; kit. units to 5, $145-$180; lower rates May-June, after Labor Day-mid-Oct. Closed rest of yr. TV. Pool; wading pool. Restaurant 8 am-10 pm. Bar 11-1 am. Ck-out 11 am. Coin lndry. Putting green, miniature golf. Bicycles. Picnic tables, grill. On ocean. Cr cds: A, D, DS, MC, V.

★ **MT VERNON.** *Beach & 1st Aves. 609/884-4665.* 25 units, 2 story, 12 kits. July-Labor Day: S, D $127; each addl $12-$15; kit. units $121-$132; lower rates Apr-June, after Labor Day-Oct. Closed rest of yr. Crib avail. TV. Pool; wading pool. Restaurant adj 8 am-midnight. Ck-out 11 am. Refrigerators. Sun deck. Opp ocean. No cr cds accepted.

★ ★ **PERIWINKLE INN.** *Box 220, 1039 Beach Ave. 609/884-9200.* 50 rms, 3 story, 14 kits. July-Aug: S, D $118-$126; each addl $15; suites, kit. units $126-$185; lower rates mid-Apr-June, Sept-mid-Oct. Closed rest of yr. Crib free. TV. Pool; wading pool. Restaurant adj 7 am-10 pm. Ck-out 11 am. Refrigerators. Balconies. Grills. On ocean. No cr cds accepted.

Motor Hotels

★ ★ **MARQUIS DE LAFAYETTE.** *501 Beach Dr. 609/884-3500; res: 800/257-0432; FAX 609/884-0669.* 73 units, 6 story, 43 kits. July-Labor Day: S, D $188-$248; each addl $18; kit. units $198-$258; 2 children under 8 free; package plans; wknd rates; varied lower rates rest of yr. Crib avail. Pet accepted, some restrictions; $20 per day. TV. Pool; sauna, poolside serv. Complimentary full bkfst. Restaurant 8 am-9 pm. Bar; entertainment, dancing (in season, wknds off season). Ck-out 1 pm. Coin lndry. Meeting rms. Bellhops. Valet serv. Golf privileges. Balconies. On ocean. Cr cds: A, C, D, DS, ER, MC, V.

★ ★ ★ **MONTREAL.** *Beach & Madison Aves. 609/884-7011; res: 800/525-7011; FAX 609/884-4559.* 70 units, 4 story, 42 kits. Mid-June-mid-Sept: S, D, suites $75-$118; each addl $5-$8; kit. units $80-$135; lower rates Mar-mid-June, mid-Sept-Dec. Closed rest of yr. Crib free. TV. Heated pool; wading pool, poolside serv, lifeguard. Restaurant 8 am-11 pm. Rm serv. Bar from 11 am. Ck-out 11 am. Coin lndry. Valet serv. Airport transportation. Putting green, miniature golf.

Exercise equipt; weight machine, stair machine, whirlpool, sauna. Game rm. Refrigerators. Balconies. Picnic tables, grills. On ocean. Cr cds: A, DS, MC, V.

Hotel

★ ★ **INN OF CAPE MAY.** *601 Beach Dr. 609/884-3500; res: 800/257-0432; FAX 609/884-0669.* 78 rms, 54 baths, some share bath, 5 story. No A/C. No rm phones. July-Aug: S, D $88-$255; each addl $18; MAP avail; package plans; lower rates mid-May-June, Sept-mid Oct. Closed rest of yr. Crib avail. TV in lobby. Pool; poolside serv. Restaurant 8 am-noon, 6-9 pm. No rm serv. Bar noon-1 am. Ck-out 1 pm. Meeting rms. On ocean. Opened 1894; antique furnishings. Cr cds: A, C, D, DS, ER, MC, V.

Inns

★ ★ ★ **THE ABBEY.** *34 Gurney St, at Columbia Ave. 609/884-4506.* 14 rms in 2 bldgs, 3 story. No rm phones. Apr-mid-Dec: S, D $90-$190. Closed rest of yr. Children over 12 yrs only. Full bkfst, afternoon tea. Ck-out 11 am, ck-in after 2 pm. Lawn games. Picnic table. Beach passes, chairs & towels. Refrigerators. Gothic-style inn with 60-ft tower; main house built 1869, cottage built 1873. Stenciled and ruby glass arched windows; library, antiques. Smoking on veranda only. Cr cds: DS, MC, V.

★ ★ ★ **ANGEL OF THE SEA.** *5 Trenton Ave. 609/884-3369; res: 800/848-3369; FAX 609/884-3331.* 27 rms, 3 story. No A/C. No elvtr. No rm phones. June-Oct: S, D $130-$250; each addl $35; lower rates rest of yr. Children over 8 yrs only. TV; cable. Complimentary full bkfst, tea/wine. Ck-out 11 am, ck-in 2 pm. Concierge. Some balconies. Picnic tables. Authentic Victorian house (1850); award-winning restoration. Originally located in center of town, in 1891 it was relocated to the beach; because of its size, the house had to be cut in half to make the move. In 1968 the building was moved once again, from the beach to its present location, where both halves remain disconnected, but side by side. Located opp ocean, swimming beach; bicycles, beach passes and equipment avail. Totally nonsmoking. No cr cds accepted.

✔ ★ ★ **CARROLL VILLA.** *19 Jackson St. 609/884-9619; FAX 609/884-0264.* 21 rms, most rms shower only, 3 story. Memorial Day-mid-Sept: S $81-$111; D $91-$121; each addl $20; under 2 free; wkly rates; hols, wkends (2-3 night min); lower rates rest of yr. Crib avail. TV in parlor. Complimentary full bkfst. Restaurant (see MAD BATTER). Ck-out 11 am, ck-in 2 pm. Ocean ½ blk. Victorian inn (1882) furnished with antiques. Cr cds: MC, V.

✔ ★ **CHALFONTE.** *301 Howard St, at Sewell St. 609/884-8409; FAX 609/884-8480.* 72 rms (58 share bath), 3 story. No A/C. No rm phones. July-Aug: S $53-$77; D $72-$154; each addl $5; family rates; higher rates wkend & hols (2-3 day min); lower rates late May-June & Sept-mid-Oct. Closed rest of yr. Crib $5. Playground. Restaurant 8:30-10 am, 6-8:30 pm. Ck-out noon, ck-in 2 pm. Bellhops. Some balconies. Ocean 3 blks. Victorian-style house built 1876; antiques. Totally nonsmoking. Cr cds: MC, V.

★ ★ ★ **COLVMNS BY THE SEA.** *1513 Beach Dr. 609/884-2228.* 11 air-cooled rms, 3 story. No rm phones. July-Aug: S $120-$180; D $130-$190; each addl $35; wkly rates; lower rates rest of yr. Children over 12 yrs only. TV in parlor. Whirlpool. Complimentary full bkfst, tea/sherry. Restaurant nearby. Ck-out 11 am, ck-in 2 pm. Bicycles avail. Library. Victorian furnishings, antiques. On beach. Totally nonsmoking. No cr cds accepted.

★ ★ ★ **MAINSTAY.** *635 Columbia Ave.* 609/884-8690. 12 rms, 3 story, 4 suites. Mar-Dec 2-3 day min: S, D $95-$190; each addl $20. Complimentary full bkfst, afternoon tea. Ck-out 11 am, ck-in 2 pm. Lawn games. Some balconies. Beach passes. Built in 1872 as a gentlemen's gambling house. Victorian decor; antiques; 14-ft ceilings. Veranda. Totally nonsmoking. No cr cds accepted.

★ ★ ★ **QUEEN VICTORIA.** *102 Ocean St.* 609/884-8702. 17 rms, 3 story. June-Sept: S $155-$200; D $165-$210; each addl $20; suites $220-$250; lower rates rest of yr. Bkfst, afternoon tea. Ck-out 11 am. Bicycles, beach passes. Whirlpool in suites. Restored Victorian villa; rms individually decorated with Victorian antiques. Cr cds: MC, V.

★ ★ ★ **VIRGINIA.** *25 Jackson St, in historic district.* 609/884-5700; res: 800/732-4236; FAX 609/884-1236. 24 rms, 3 story. No elvtr. Memorial Day-Labor Day: S, D $130-$250; each addl $20; under 5 free; wkly rates; lower rates rest of yr; Jan open wkends only. Crib free. TV; cable, in-rm movies. Complimentary continental bkfst 7:30-10 am. Dining rm 9 am-2 pm, 5:30-10 pm; brunch Sun. Rm serv. Bar 5 pm-midnight; Sat, Sun from noon. Ck-out noon, ck-in 3 pm. Meeting rms. Bellhops. Concierge. Balconies. Built 1879; restored. Furnishings and amenities are a wonderful blend of antique and modern. Located ¹/₂ blk from beach; ocean view from veranda. Cr cds: A, C, D, DS, MC, V.

Restaurants

★ ★ **410 BANK STREET.** *410 Bank St, adj to Welcome Center.* 609/884-2127. Hrs: 5-10:30 pm. Closed Nov-Apr. Res accepted. Louisana French menu. Setups. A la carte entrees: dinner $20-$25. Child's meals. Specializes in grilled fish steaks and seafood. Porch and garden dining. Restored 1840 Cape May residence. Island atmosphere. Cr cds: A, C, D, DS, MC, V.

★ ★ **ALEXANDER'S INN.** *653 Washington St.* 609/884-2555. Hrs: 6-9 pm; Sun brunch 10 am-1 pm. Closed Tues; Jan 1, Thanksgiving, Dec 25. Res accepted. French menu. Setups. Semi-a la carte: dinner $18.95-$28.95. Complete meals: dinner $29.95-$39.95. Specializes in sweet breads, rabbit, Angus beef. Own ice cream. Victorian decor; antiques. Totally nonsmoking. Cr cds: A, C, D, DS, MC, V.

★ ★ **FRESCOS.** *412 Bank St, 1 blk behind Victorian Mall, adj to Welcome Ctr.* 609/884-0366. Hrs: 5-10:30 pm. Closed Jan-Apr. Res accepted. Italian menu. A la carte entrees: dinner $12.50-$21.95. Child's meals. Specializes in fresh seafood, pasta, veal. Outdoor porch dining. 3 dining areas in restored Victorian summer cottage. Cr cds: A, C, D, DS, MC, V.

★ ★ **LOBSTER HOUSE.** *Fisherman's Wharf, turn E just S of bridge at end of Garden State Pkwy.* 609/884-8296. Hrs: 11:30 am-3 pm, 5-10 pm; Sun from 4:30 pm; Sun in winter 2-9 pm. Closed Dec 25. Bar. Semi-a la carte: lunch $4.75-$11.25, dinner $13.25-$37.50. Child's meals. Specializes in fresh fish, lobster, crabmeat. Parking. Outdoor dining. On wharf; nautical decor. Fireplace. Cocktail lounge & lunch on fishing schooner, noon-4 pm; entertainment. Raw seafood bars in main bar & dock. Cr cds: A, DS, MC, V.

★ ★ **MAD BATTER.** *(See Carroll Villa Inn)* 609/884-5970. Hrs: 8 am-2:30 pm, 5:30-10 pm; Fri, Sat to 11 pm. Closed Jan. Res accepted. Setups. A la carte entrees: bkfst, lunch $5-$9. A la carte entrees: dinner $15-$21. Child's meals. Specializes in fresh seafood, desserts. Outdoor dining. Victorian inn (1882). Cr cds: MC, V.

★ ★ **MERION INN.** *106 Decatur St.* 609/884-8363. Hrs: 11:30 am-2:30 pm, 5-10 pm. Closed Nov-Mar; also Mon-Thurs mid-Mar-May & Oct. Res accepted. Bar. Semi-a la carte: lunch, dinner $14.95-$28.95. Child's meals. Specializes in stuffed lobster tail, fresh broiled fish, steak. Own desserts. Outdoor dining. Turn-of-the-century Victorian decor. Built 1885. Family-owned. Cr cds: A, DS, MC, V.

★ **PEACHES AT SUNSET.** *1 Sunset Blvd.* 609/898-0100. Hrs: 5-10 pm; Sun 4:30-9 pm. Closed Dec 25. Res accepted. Continental menu. Semi-a la carte: dinner $16.95-$24.95. Child's meals. Specialties: baked halibut with caramelized vidalia onions, rack of lamb. Parking. Outdoor dining overlooking gardens. Local artwork displayed. Totally nonsmoking. Cr cds: MC, V.

★ ★ ★ **WASHINGTON INN.** *801 Washington St.* 609/884-5697. Hrs: 5-10 pm; hrs may vary wkends & off season. Closed Thanksgiving, Dec 24-25. Res accepted; required Sat. Continental menu. Bar. Wine cellar. Semi-a la carte: dinner $15.95-$23.95. Child's meals. Specializes in steak, veal, fresh seafood. Own baking. Patio dining. Former plantation house (1848). Cr cds: A, C, D, DS, MC, V.

★ ★ **WATER'S EDGE.** *Beach & Pittsburgh Aves.* 609/884-1717. Hrs: July-Aug 8 am-11 pm; hrs vary off season. Closed Thanksgiving, Dec. 25. Res accepted. Bar. A la carte entrees: bkfst $1.95-$6.95, lunch $6-$12.50, dinner $14-$23. Child's meals. Specializes in fresh local seafood, veal, Angus steak. Contemporary decor. Patio dining, ocean view. Cr cds: A, C, D, DS, MC, V.

Cape May Court House (K-3)

Pop: 4,426 **Elev:** 18 ft **Area code:** 609 **Zip:** 08210

To be accurately named, this county seat would have to be called Cape May Court Houses, for there are two of them—one is a white, 19th-century building now used as a meeting hall.

What to See and Do

1. **Cape May County Historical Museum.** Shore Rd, 1 mi N on US 9. Period dining room (pre-dating 1820), 18th-century kitchen, doctor's room, military room with Merrimac flag, Cape May diamonds. Barn exhibits; whaling implements; Indian artifacts; pioneer tools; lens from Cape May Point Lighthouse. Genealogical library. (Mid-June-Labor Day wkend, daily exc Sun; after Labor Day-Nov & Apr-mid-June, Tues-Sat; Dec-Mar, Sat only) Phone 465-3535. ¢

2. **Victorian houses.** Fine examples of 19th-century architecture located in the area. Information can be obtained at the Chamber of Commerce Information Center, Crest Haven Rd & Garden State Pkwy, milepost #11 (Easter-mid-Oct, daily; rest of yr, Mon-Fri; closed hols).

3. **Cape May County Park.** On US 9 at Crest Haven Rd. Zoo has over 100 types of animals. Jogging path, bike trail; tennis courts. Picnicking, playground. (Daily) Phone 465-5271. **Free.**

4. **Leaming's Run Gardens.** Approx 4 mi N on US 9, between Pkwy exits 13 & 17 in Swainton. Amid 20 acres of lawns, ponds and ferneries are 25 gardens, each with a separate theme. 18th-century colonial farm grows tobacco and cotton; farm animals. (Mid-May-mid-Oct, daily) Phone 465-5871. ¢¢

(For further information contact the Cape May County Chamber of Commerce, PO Box 74; 465-7181.)

(For accommodations see Cape May, Stone Harbor, Wildwood & Wildwood Crest)

Restaurant

★ **ASSELTAS ITALIAN VILLA.** *1206 US 9, 3 mi S on US 9, near Burleigh; 1 mi S of Garden State Pkwy exit 8. 609/463-0744.* Hrs: 4:30-9:30 pm. Complete meals: dinner $6.95-$19.95. Child's meals. Specializes in seafood. Parking. Cr cds: MC, V.

Cedar Grove (Essex Co) (C-5)

Pop: 12,053 **Elev:** 340 ft **Area code:** 201 **Zip:** 07009

Restaurant

★ ★ **FRIAR TUCK INN.** *691 Pompton Ave (Rt 23). 201/239-4500.* Hrs: noon-3 pm, 5-9 pm; Fri to 10 pm; Sat 5-10 pm; Sun noon-9 pm. Closed Mon; also first 2 wks in July. Bar. A la carte entrees: lunch $5.75-$14.75, dinner $9.75-$17.50. Complete meals: dinner $12-$14.75. Child's meals. Specializes in steak, prime rib, seafood. Salad bar. Entertainment Fri. Free dessert table Tues-Thurs evenings. Parking. Cr cds: A, C, D, MC, V.

Chatham (C-4)

Pop: 8,007 **Elev:** 244 ft **Area code:** 201 **Zip:** 07928

What to See and Do

Great Swamp National Wildlife Refuge. SW of city (see BERNARDSVILLE).

(For further information contact the Borough Hall, 54 Fairmount Ave; 635-0674.)

Hotel

★ ★ **GRAND SUMMIT.** *(570 Springfield Ave, Summit 07901) 1¹/₂ mi S of NJ 24, 124, Summit Ave exit. 908/273-3000; res: 800/346-0773 (exc NJ); FAX 908/273-4228.* 145 rms, 2-4 story. S $130; D $140; each addl $15; suites $180-$750; under 12 free; wknd rates; package plans. Crib free. TV; cable. Pool; poolside serv, lifeguard. Restaurant 7 am-10 pm; Sat 6:30-12:30 am. Bar 10 am-midnight, Fri, Sat to 1 am, Sun 12:30-10 pm; entertainment. Ck-out noon. Meeting rms. Concierge. Gift shop. Free airport transportation. Exercise equipt; weight machines, bicycles. Bathrm phones; some in-rm whirlpools; wet bar in suites. Cr cds: A, C, D, MC, V.

Restaurant

★ ★ ★ **DENNIS FOY'S TOWNSQUARE.** *6 Roosevelt Ave. 201/701-0303.* Hrs: noon-2:30 pm, 5:30-10 pm; Sat from 5:30 pm. Closed Sun; most major hols. Res accepted, required Sat. French, Amer menu. Bar. Wine list. A la carte entrees: lunch $9.95-$26, dinner $21.75-$33. Specializes in game dishes, red snapper, tian of crab. Jazz, pianist Fri & Sat. Parking. Elegant dining in friendly atmosphere. Original artwork by Dennis Foy. Jacket. Cr cds: A, C, D, DS, MC, V.

Cherry Hill (F-3)

Pop: 69,319 **Elev:** 30 ft **Area code:** 609

What to See and Do

Barclay Farmstead. 209 Barclay Lane. One of the earliest properties settled in what is now Cherry Hill; origins traced to 1684. The township-owned site consists of 32 acres of open space; restored Federal-style farmhouse; operating forge barn; corn crib; Victorian spring house. Grounds (all yr); house tours (Tues-Fri; also by appt). Phone 795-6225. ¢

Annual Event

State Fair. Garden State Racetrack. Phone 646-3340. Early Aug.

(See Camden, Haddonfield)

Motels

★ **DAYS INN-BROOKLAWN.** *(801 US 130, Brooklawn 08030) On US 130, 1 mi S of I-76, NJ 42 (North South Frwy). 609/456-6688; res: 800/325-2525; FAX 609/456-1413.* 116 rms, 3 story. S $44-$65; D $49-$69; each addl $5; under 12 free. Crib free. TV; cable. Pool; lifeguard. Complimentary continental bkfst. Restaurant nearby. Ck-out noon. Coin lndry. Sundries. Refrigerators avail. Cr cds: A, C, D, DS, MC, V.

★ ★ **LANDMARK INN MOTOR LODGE.** *Maple Shade (08052), at jct NJ 73, 38, ¹/₂ mi N of I-295, 1 mi N of NJ Tpke exit 4. 609/235-6400; res: 800/635-5917; FAX 609/727-1027.* 163 rms, 3 story. S $49-$54; D $52-$57; each addl $3; under 18 free. Crib free. TV; cable, in-rm movies avail. Pool; wading pool, lifeguard. Playground. Restaurant 6:30 am-10 pm; Sat & Sun 8 am-noon, 5-10 pm. Rm serv. Bar; entertainment, dancing Thurs-Sat. Ck-out noon. Coin lndry. Meeting rms. Valet serv. Sundries. Exercise equipt; weights, treadmills, sauna. Refrigerators avail. Private patios, balconies. Cr cds: A, C, D, DS, MC, V.

✔ ★ ★ **LAUREL INN.** *Mount Laurel (08054), NJ 73 at NJ Tpke exit 4. 609/235-7400; FAX 609/778-9729.* 240 rms, 2 story. S $37.95-$42.95; D $44.95-$46.95; each addl $5; under 12 free. Crib avail. TV; cable. Pool. Restaurant 6:30 am-10 pm. Rm serv. Bar noon-midnight. Coin lndry. Meeting rms. Valet serv. Game rm. Refrigerators avail. Cr cds: A, C, D, DS, MC, V.

✔ ★ **McINTOSH INN.** *(NJ 73 & Church Rd, Mount Laurel 08054) On NJ 73, ¹/₄ mi E of NJ Tpke exit 4. 609/234-7194; res: 800/444-2775.* 93 rms, 2 story. S $36.95; D $42.95; each addl $3. Crib free. TV; cable. Restaurant adj open 24 hrs. Ck-out 11 am. Cr cds: A, C, D, MC, V.

★ ★ **RESIDENCE INN BY MARRIOTT.** *1821 Old Cuthbert Rd (08034), I-295 exit 34A at jct NJ 70E. 609/429-6111; FAX 609/429-0345.* 96 kit. suites, 2 story. S $115; D $125; each addl $10; under 12 free; wkly rates. Crib free. Pet accepted; $50-$75 non-refundable. TV; cable, in-rm movies avail. Pool; whirlpool, poolside serv (in season), lifeguard. Complimentary continental bkfst. Complimentary coffee in rms. Restaurant nearby. Rm serv. Ck-out noon. Coin lndry. Meeting rms. Valet serv. Health club privileges. Grills. Tennis adj. Cr cds: A, C, D, DS, MC, V.

Motor Hotel

★ ★ **HOLIDAY INN.** *NJ 70 & Sayer Ave (08002), 3 mi W of I-295, 7 mi W of NJ Tpke exit 4, opp Garden State Racetrack.* 609/663-5300; FAX 609/663-5300, ext. 7731. 186 rms, 6 story. S $67-$86; D $75-$89; each addl $8; under 18 free; wkend rates. Crib free. Pet accepted. TV; cable. 2 pools, 1 indoor; wading pool. Restaurant 6 am-10 pm. Rm serv. Bar 11 am-11 pm. Ck-out noon. Coin lndry. Meeting rms. Valet serv. Exercise equipt; weights, bicycles, sauna. Cr cds: A, C, D, DS, ER, JCB, MC, V.

Hotels

★ ★ ★ **CLARION MOUNT LAUREL.** *(NJ 73 & I-295, Mount Laurel 08054)* 1/2 mi N of NJ Tpke exit 4. 609/234-7300; FAX 609/866-9401. 300 rms, 10 story. S $85-$106; D $98-$126; each addl $13; suites $200-$250; under 17 free; wkend rates. Crib free. TV; cable. Pool; poolside serv, lifeguard. Restaurant 6:30 am-10 pm; Sat, Sun from 7 am. Bar. Ck-out 11 am. Coin lndry. Convention facilities. Gift shop. Lighted tennis. Golf privileges. Health club privileges. Lawn games. Some in-rm steam baths, in-rm whirlpools, refrigerators. Picnic tables. Some private patios, balconies. *LUXURY LEVEL : CONCIERGE LEVEL.* 20 rms, 3 suites. S, D $113-$126. Concierge. Private lounge, honor bar. Complimentary continental bkfst, refreshments. Cr cds: A, C, D, DS, MC, V.

★ ★ ★ **HYATT CHERRY HILL.** *2349 W Marlton Pike (08002).* 609/662-1234; FAX 609/662-3676. 410 rms, 14 story. S $115-$150; D $135-$170; each addl $25; suites $250-$650; under 18 free; wkend rates. Crib free. TV; cable. Pool; lifeguard. Restaurant 6:30 am-11:30 pm. Bar 11-2 am; entertainment. Ck-out noon. Convention facilities. Gift shop. Lighted tennis. Exercise equipt; bicycles, treadmills. On lake. *LUXURY LEVEL : REGENCY CLUB.* 40 rms. S $145; D $165. Concierge. Private lounge, honor bar. Complimentary continental bkfst, refreshments. Cr cds: A, C, D, DS, ER, JCB, MC, V.

★ ★ ★ **SHERATON POSTE INN.** *1450 Rte 7 East (08034), NJ 70 & I-295.* 609/428-2300; FAX 609/354-7662. 213 rms, 4 story. S $88-$119; D $98-$139; each addl $10; suites from $250; under 18 free; wkend rates. Crib free. Pet accepted, some restrictions; non-refundable fee. TV; cable. Heated pool. Restaurants 6:30 am-10 pm. Bar 11-2 am; entertainment, dancing Fri-Sun. Ck-out noon. Meeting rms. Gift shop. Tennis. Exercise equipt; weights, bicycles. Cr cds: A, C, D, DS, ER, MC, V.

Restaurants

✔ ★ **COLONNADE.** *Maple Shade, on NJ 73, 1 mi W of NJ Tpke exit 4.* 609/235-8550. Hrs: 7-1 am. Closed Dec 25. Res accepted. Bar from 11 am. Semi-a la carte: bkfst $2.50-$5.30, lunch $4.75-$10.95, dinner $7.95-$13.95. Child's meals. Specializes in prime rib, seafood. Salad bar. Parking. Cr cds: A, D, MC, V.

★ ★ **THE GREENBRIER.** *NJ 70 at Haddonfield Rd, 3 mi W of I-295.* 609/662-0800. Hrs: 11-1:30 am; early-bird dinner Mon-Sat 4-6:30 pm, Sun 3-7 pm; Sat & Sun brunch 10 am-2 pm. Closed Dec 25. Bar. Res accepted. Semi-a la carte: lunch $4.75-$7.95, dinner $7.95-$15.95. Sun brunch $12.95-$13.95. Child's meals. Specializes in grilled fresh fish, pasta, prime rib. Jazz duo Fri, Sat. Parking. Family-owned. Cr cds: A, C, D, MC, V.

Clifton (C-5)

Pop: 71,742 **Elev:** 70 ft **Area code:** 201

What to See and Do

Hamilton House Museum. 971 Valley Rd. Early 19th-century sandstone farmhouse with period furniture; country store; exhibits. Open-hearth cooking demonstrations by costumed guides. (Mar-Dec, Sun afternoons) Phone 744-5707. **Free.**

(For further information contact the North Jersey Regional Chamber of Commerce, 1033 US 46E, PO Box 110, 07011; 470-9300.)

Motel

★ ★ **HOWARD JOHNSON.** *680 NJ 3 W (07014), NJ Tpke exit 16W.* 201/471-3800; FAX 201/471-3800, ext. 500. 116 rms, 4 story, 8 kits. (no oven, equipt). S $75.50-$105.50; D $85.50-$115.50; each addl $10; kit. units $85-$95; under 18 free; wkend rates. Crib free. Pet accepted, some restrictions. TV; cable. Pool; lifeguard. Restaurant 7 am-midnight. Bar 4 pm-2 am. Ck-out noon. Meeting rm. Sundries. Private patios, balconies. Cr cds: A, C, D, DS, ER, JCB, MC, V.

Motor Hotel

★ ★ **RAMADA INN.** *265 NJ 3E.* 201/778-6500; FAX 201/778-8724. 183 rms, 4 story. S, D $89-$99; each addl $15; suites $150; kit units $175; under 12 free; wkend rates; higher rates World Cup. Crib free. TV; cable. Indoor pool. Restaurant 6:30 am-10 pm; wknds from 7 am. Rm serv. Bar; entertainment. Ck-out noon. Meeting rms. Concierge. Sundries. Gift shop. Exercise equipt; weights, bicycles, sauna. Some refrigerators. Cr cds: A, C, D, DS, ER, JCB, MC, V.

Clinton (C-3)

Pop: 2,054 **Elev:** 195 ft **Area code:** 908 **Zip:** 08809

What to See and Do

1. **Clinton Historical Museum.** 56 Main St, off I-78. Four-story gristmill (ca 1810). Ten-acre park houses education center, quarry and lime kilns, blacksmith shop, general store, one-room schoolhouse, log cabin, machinery sheds, herb garden. Gift shop. (Apr-Oct, daily exc Mon) Outdoor concerts Sat evenings in summer. Phone 735-4101. ¢¢

2. **Round Valley State Park.** Off US 22, E of jct I-78; follow signs. A 4,003-acre park. Swimming; fishing; boating. Picnicking, concession. Wilderness camping (access to campsites via hiking or boating only). Standard fees. Phone 236-6355.

3. **Spruce Run State Recreation Area.** 3 mi NW off NJ 31. A 1,961-acre park. Swimming; fishing; boating (launch, rentals). Picnicking, concession. Camping (Apr-Oct). Standard fees. Phone 638-8572.

(See Flemington)

Motor Hotel

★ ★ **HOLIDAY INN.** *111 NJ 173, I-78 exit 15, then W on NJ 173.* 908/735-5111; FAX 908/730-9768. 142 units, 5 story. S, studio rms $80-$100; D $84-$108; each addl $8; suites $100-$150; under 18 free; wkend rates. Crib free. Pet accepted. TV; cable. Indoor pool. Restaurant 6:30 am-10 pm. Rm serv. Bar noon-midnight; entertainment, dancing Fri & Sat. Ck-out noon. Meeting rms. Sundries. Exercise equipt; weights, bicycles. Some balconies. Cr cds: A, C, D, DS, ER, MC, V.

Inn

★ ★ **STEWART INN.** *(RD 1, Box 571, Stewartsville 08886) I-78 exit 4 (westbound), on S Main St.* 908/479-6060; FAX 908/479-1259. 8 rms, 6 with bath, 2 story. S, D $85-$135; suite $105-$135. Children over 12 yrs only. TV. Pool. Complimentary full bkfst. Restaurant nearby. Ck-out noon, ck-in 2 pm. Picnic tables, grills. Stone manor house built 1770s, set amidst 16 acres of lawns, gardens, woods, stream and pasture. Trout stream, barns and outbuildings with farm animals create a pastoral setting. Totally nonsmoking. Cr cds: A, MC, V.

Restaurant

★ ★ **CLINTON HOUSE.** *2 W Main St.* 908/730-9300. Hrs: 11:30 am-2:30 pm, 5-9:30 pm. Closed Sun; Thanksgiving, Dec 25. Res accepted. Bar to 2 am. Semi-a la carte: lunch $6.95-$9.95, dinner $12.95-$22.50. Child's meals. Specializes in beef, seafood. Parking. Built 1743; former stagecoach stop. Family-owned. Cr cds: A, C, D, MC, V.

Deepwater (G-1)

Pop: 650 (est) **Elev:** 10 ft **Area code:** 609 **Zip:** 08023

What to See and Do

Fort Mott State Park. 4 mi S on NJ 49, then SW on Fort Mott Rd. A 104-acre park at Finns Point; established in 1837 as a defense of the Port of Philadelphia. North of the park is Finns Point National Cemetery, where more than 2,500 Union and Confederate soldiers are buried. Fishing; boating. Picnicking, playground; overlook. Phone 935-3218.

Seasonal Event

Cowtown Rodeo. 8 mi E on US 40, near Woodstown. PRCA sanctioned. Phone 769-3200. Sat evenings, late May-mid-Sept.

Motel

★ ★ **WELLESLEY INNS & SUITES.** *(614 Soders Rd, Carneys Point 08069) At I-295 & NJ Tpke Deepwater exit.* 609/299-3800; FAX 609/299-6982. 140 units, 2 story. S $50-$80; D $60-$95; each addl $10; under 18 free; some wkend rates. Crib free. TV; cable. Indoor pool. Complimentary continental bkfst. Restaurant 7 am-11 pm. Bar. Ck-out noon. Coin lndry. Meeting rms. Valet serv. Exercise equipt; weights, bicycles. Refrigerators. Cr cds: A, C, D, DS, ER, JCB, MC, V.

Eatontown (E-5)

Pop: 13,800 **Elev:** 46 ft **Area code:** 908 **Zip:** 07724

(See Red Bank)

Motels

✔ ★ **DAYS INN.** *(11 Centre Plaza, Tinton Falls) Off Garden State Pkwy exit 105, turn right on Hope Rd.* 908/389-4646; FAX 908/389-4509. 120 rms, 3 story. May-Labor Day: S, D $51.95-$65.95; each addl $6; under 18 free; lower rates rest of yr. Crib free. Pet accepted, some restrictions. TV; cable. Complimentary continental bkfst. Restaurant nearby. Ck-out noon. Valet serv. Cr cds: A, C, D, DS, MC, V.

★ ★ **RESIDENCE INN BY MARRIOTT.** *(90 Park Rd, Tinton Falls) Off Garden State Pkwy exit 105, left on Hope Rd, then 1st left on Park Rd.* 908/389-8100; FAX 908/389-1573. 96 kit. suites. S, D $112-$142. Crib free. Pet accepted; $150 non-refundable. TV; cable, in-rm movies avail. Pool; whirlpool, lifeguard. Complimentary continental bkfst. Restaurant nearby. Ck-out noon. Coin lndry. Meeting rms. Valet serv. Health club privileges. Balconies. Picnic tables, grills. Cr cds: A, C, D, DS, MC, V.

Motor Hotel

★ ★ ★ **HOLIDAY INN TINTON FALLS.** *(700 Hope Rd, Tinton Falls) At Garden State Pkwy exit 105.* 908/544-9300; FAX 908/544-0570. 171 rms, 5 story. S, D $75-$115; each addl $10; suites $95-$225; wkend rates. Crib free. TV; cable. Pool; poolside serv. Restaurant 6:30 am-11 pm. Rm serv. Bar 11:30-2 am. Ck-out noon. Lndry facilities avail. Meeting rms. Bellhops. Valet serv. Gift shop. Exercise equipt; weight machines, bicycles, sauna. Refrigerators avail. Cr cds: A, C, D, DS, MC, V.

Hotels

★ ★ ★ **HILTON-OCEAN PLACE.** *(1 Ocean Blvd, Long Branch 07740) Garden State Pkwy exit 105, E on NJ 36.* 908/571-4000; FAX 908/571-3314. 254 rms, 12 story. Memorial Day-Labor Day: S $170-$205; D $190-$225; each addl $20; suites $350-$1,000; family, wkend rates; lower rates rest of yr. Crib free. TV; cable. 2 pools, 1 indoor; poolside serv, lifeguard. Supervised child's activities (summer). Restaurants 6:30 am-10 pm; Sat & Sun from 7 am. Rm serv 24 hrs (in season). Bar 11-2 am; entertainment, dancing. Ck-out noon. Convention facilities. Concierge. Shopping arcade. Barber, beauty shop. Free garage parking. RR station transportation. Lighted tennis. Golf privileges. Exercise rm; instructor, weight machine, bicycles, whirlpools, steam rm, sauna. Massage therapy. Balconies. On ocean. Cr cds: A, C, D, DS, ER, MC, V.

★ ★ ★ **SHERATON-EATONTOWN HOTEL & CONFERENCE CENTER.** *NJ 35 & Industrial Way E, off Garden State Pkwy exit 105.* 908/542-6500; FAX 908/542-6607. 208 rms, 6 story. May-Sept: S $100-$125; D $110-$135; each addl $10; suites $225; wkend rates; lower rates rest of yr. Crib free. TV; cable, in-rm movies. Indoor/outdoor pool. Restaurant 6:30 am-11 pm. Bar; entertainment, dancing Fri-Sat. Ck-out noon. Meeting rms. Gift shop. Golf privileges. Exercise equipt; bicycles, stair machine, whirlpool. Health club privileges. Refrigerators avail. Cr cds: A, C, D, DS, MC, V.

Edison (D-4)

Pop: 88,680 **Elev:** 95 ft **Area code:** 908

Although Thomas A. Edison's house here has been destroyed, Edison State Park and the Edison Memorial Tower stand in tribute to the great American inventor. Here, on December 6, 1877, the 30-year-old Edison invented the phonograph. Two years later, he perfected the first practical incandescent light, designing and constructing various kinds of electrical equipment we now take for granted. His workshop has been moved to the Ford Museum in Dearborn, Michigan. Edison also built the first electric railway locomotive here in 1880; it ran one-and-one-half miles over the fields of Pumptown.

What to See and Do

Edison Memorial Tower. Christie St, 1/2 mi SW of Garden State Pkwy exit 131 off NJ 27 in Edison State Park. A 131-foot tower topped by a 13-foot-high electric light bulb stands on the spot where the first incandescent bulb was made. Museum contains some of Edison's inventions (Memorial Day-Labor Day, daily exc Mon; rest of yr, Wed-Sun afternoons). Phone 549-3299. **Free.**

(For further information contact the Chamber of Commerce, PO Box 281, 08818; 287-1951.)

(See Woodbridge)

Motor Hotels

★ ★ ★ **CLARION HOTEL.** *2055 Lincoln Hwy (08817), 1/2 mi S of I-287 on NJ 27.* 908/287-3500; FAX 908/287-8190. 125 suites, 5 story. S $79-$89; D $89-$99; each addl $10; under 18 free; wkend rates. Crib free. TV; cable. Complimentary full bkfst. Restaurant 7 am-10:30 pm; Fri, Sat to 11 pm. Rm serv. Bar 11-2 am; entertainment, dancing Tues-Sat. Ck-out noon. Meeting rms. Bellhops. Valet serv. Gift shop. Exercise equipt; weights, bicycles, sauna. Many refrigerators. *LUXURY LEVEL.* 42 units, 2 suites. S $89-$98; D $98-$109; suites $185-$215. Concierge. Private lounge. Complimentary refreshments. Cr cds: A, C, D, DS, ER, MC, V.

★ ★ **RAMADA INN.** *3050 Woodbridge Ave (08837), on NJ 514W, Tpke exit 10.* 908/494-2000; FAX 908/417-1811. 189 rms, 9 story. S, D $78; each addl $10; suites $125-$150; under 12 free; wkend rates. Crib free. Pet accepted, some restrictions. TV; cable. Indoor pool; lifeguard. Restaurant 6 am-10 pm. Rm serv. Bar 11-2 am. Ck-out noon. Meeting rms. Valet serv. Gift shop. Sundries. Exercise equipt; bicycle, treadmill, sauna. Game rm. Heliport. Cr cds: A, C, D, DS, MC, V.

Elizabeth (C-5)

Settled: 1664 **Pop:** 110,002 **Elev:** 36 ft **Area code:** 201 and 908

More than 1,200 manufacturing industries are located in Elizabeth and Union County. Long before the Revolution, Elizabeth was not only the capital of New Jersey, but also a thriving industrial town. The first Colonial Assembly met here from 1669 to 1692. Princeton University began in Elizabeth in 1746 as the College of New Jersey. More than 20 pre-Revolutionary buildings still stand. Many noteworthy people were citizens of Elizabeth: William Livingston, first governor of New Jersey; Elias Boudinot, first president of the Continental Congress; Alexander Hamilton; Aaron Burr; General Winfield Scott; John Philip Holland, builder of the first successful submarine; and Admiral William J. Halsey.

The Elizabeth-Port Authority Marine Terminal is the largest container port in the US.

What to See and Do

1. **First Presbyterian Church and Graveyard.** Broad St & Caldwell Pl. The first General Assembly of New Jersey convened in an earlier building in 1668. The burned-out church was rebuilt in 1785-87, and again in 1949. The Rev. James Caldwell was an early pastor. Alexander Hamilton and Aaron Burr attended an academy where the parish house now stands.

2. **Boxwood Hall State Historic Site.** 1073 E Jersey St, 1 1/2 blks W of US 1. Home of Elias Boudinot, lawyer, diplomat, president (1783) of the Continental Congress and director of the US Mint. Boudinot entertained George Washington here on April 23, 1789, when Washington was on his way to his inauguration. (Wed-Sun; closed Jan 1, Thanksgiving, Dec 25) Phone 201/648-4540.

3. **Warinanco Park.** St Georges & Linden Aves, W edge of city. One of the largest Union County parks. Fishing; boating (rentals June-Sept, daily). Running track; parcourse fitness circuit; tennis (late Apr-early Oct); handball; horseshoes. Indoor ice-skating (early Oct-early Apr, daily). Henry S. Chatfield Memorial Garden features tulip blooms each spring; azaleas and Japanese cherry trees; summer and fall flower displays. Some fees. Phone 908/527-4900. **Free.**

(For further information contact the Union County Chamber of Commerce, 135 Jefferson Ave, PO Box 300, 07207; 908/352-0900.)

(For accommodations see Jersey City, Newark, Newark Intl Airport Area)

Flemington (D-3)

Settled: 1738 **Pop:** 4,047 **Elev:** 160 ft **Area code:** 908 **Zip:** 08822

Originally a farming community, Flemington became a center for the production of pottery and cut glass at the turn of the century.

What to See and Do

1. **County Courthouse** (1828). Main St. For 46 days in 1935, world attention was focued on this Greek-revival building where Bruno Hauptmann was tried for the kidnapping and murder of the Lindbergh baby.

2. **Fleming Castle** (1756). 5 Bonnell St. Typical two-story Colonial house built as a residence and inn by Samuel Fleming, for whom the town is named. DAR headquarters. (By appt) Donation. Phone 782-6472 (days) or -4655 (evenings).

3. **Kase Cemetery.** Bonnell St, W of Fleming Castle. John Philip Kase, Flemington's first settler, purchased a tract from William Penn. His family's crumbling gravestones date from 1774 to 1856. Kase's Indian friend, Chief Tuccamirgan, is also memorialized here.

4. **Black River & Western Railroad.** Center Shopping Area. Excursion ride on old steam train, 11-mile round trip to Ringoes. Picnic area; museum. (July-Aug, daily; Apr-June & Sept-Nov, Sat, Sun & hols) Phone 782-9600. ¢¢

5. **Volendam Windmill Museum.** Approx 21 mi NW via NJ 12, County 519 to Adamic Hill Rd in Milford, follow signs. Named after a town in the northern Netherlands, this is an authentic reproduction of an old-time wind-driven mill used for grinding raw grain into flour. Mill stands 60 ft high with sail arms stretching 86 ft. Museum contains old milling and farm tools. (May-Sept, Sat & Sun afternoons) Phone 995-4365. ¢¢

(For further information contact the Hunterdon County Chamber of Commerce, 2200 NJ 31, Box 15, Lebanon 08833; 735-5955.)

Annual Event

Flemington Agricultural Fair. Phone 782-2413. Late Aug-early Sept.

Seasonal Event

Stock car racing. Flemington Fair Speedway. Sat, Apr-Nov.

(See Clinton, Somerville)

Motel

★ **BEL AIR INN.** *250 US 202, 1/2 mi S of jct NJ 31.* 908/782-7472; FAX 908/782-1975. 104 rms, 2 story, 24 kits. S, D $72; each addl $8; suites $85-$110; kit. units $72. Crib avail. TV; cable. Pool. Complimentary continental bkfst. Restaurant 11:30 am-midnight. Bar. Ck-out 11 am. Coin lndry. Meeting rms. Cr cds: A, C, D, DS, MC, V.

Restaurant

★ ★ **UNION HOTEL.** *76 Main St.* 908/788-7474. Hrs: 11 am-10 pm; Sun noon-8 pm. Closed some major hols. Res accepted. Bar to 2 am. Semi-a la carte: lunch $4.95-$8.95, dinner $8.95-$16.95. Child's meals. Specializes in fresh fish, steak, prime rib. Entertainment Thurs-Sat. Parking. In ornate Victorian hotel (1878) opp county courthouse. Cr cds: A, MC, V.

Forked River (G-5)

Pop: 4,243 **Elev:** 19 ft **Area code:** 609 **Zip:** 08731

Restaurant

★ ★ **CAPTAIN'S INN.** *Lacey Rd, 1/2 mi E of US 9, Garden State Pkwy exit 74S, 69N.* 609/693-3351. Hrs: 11:45 am-10 pm. Closed Dec 25. Continental menu. Bar. Semi-a la carte: lunch from $3.75, dinner $9.95-$17.50. Child's meals. Specialties: crab Imperial, filet de sole à la Bercy. Entertainment Fri-Sun evenings. Parking. Built in 1831. Overlooks river. Cr cds: A, C, D, MC, V.

Fort Lee (C-6)

Pop: 31,997 **Elev:** 314 ft **Area code:** 201 **Zip:** 07024

North and south of the George Washington Bridge, Fort Lee is named for General Charles Lee, who served in the Revolutionary Army under George Washington. Its rocky bluff achieved fame as the cliff from which Pearl White hung in the early movie serial "The Adventures of Pearl White." From 1907 to 1916, 21 companies and seven studios produced motion pictures in Fort Lee. Stars such as Mary Pickford, Mabel Normand, Theda Bara and Clara Kimball Young made movies here.

What to See and Do

Fort Lee Historic Park. (See PALISADES INTERSTATE PARKS)

(For further information contact the Greater Fort Lee Chamber of Commerce, 2357 Lemaine Ave; 944-7575.)

(See Hackensack)

Motor Hotels

★ **DAYS INN.** *2339 NJ 4E.* 201/944-5000; FAX 201/944-0623. 175 rms, 6 story. S $66-$80; D $76-$89; each addl $10; under 18 free. Crib free. TV; cable. Restaurant 7 am-2 pm. Rm serv. Bar 4 pm-midnight. Ck-out noon. Meeting rms. Sundries. Cr cds: A, C, D, DS, MC, V.

★ ★ ★ **HILTON.** *2117 NJ 4E, at jct I-95 Fort Lee exit.* 201/461-9000; FAX 201/461-6783. 235 rms, 15 story. S $110; D $122; under 12 free. Crib free. Pet accepted, some restrictions. TV; cable. Indoor pool. Restaurant 6:30 am-10:30 pm; Sat, Sun from 7 am. Rm serv. Bars 11-1 am. Ck-out noon. Meeting rms. Bellhops. Valet serv. Concierge. Gift shop. Covered parking. Exercise equipt; weight machine, bicycles, whirlpool, sauna. Cr cds: A, C, D, DS, JCB, MC, V.

Restaurants

★ ★ ★ **ARCHER'S.** *1310 Palisade Ave.* 201/224-5653. Hrs: 11:30 am-3 pm, 5-11 pm; Sat 5 pm-midnight; Sun 2-10 pm. Closed Jan 1, Dec 25. Res accepted. Italian, Amer menu. Bar. A la carte entrees: lunch $9.95-$15.95, dinner $11.95-$24.45. Specializes in pasta, seafood. Entertainment Wed, Fri, Sat. Jacket. Cr cds: A, C, D, MC, V.

★ ★ **PALISADIUM.** *(700 Palisadium Dr, Cliffside Park) S on NJ 67.* 201/224-2211. Hrs: 6-11 pm; Fri & Sat to 2 am; Sun brunch 11 am-2:30 pm. Closed Mon; Jan 1. Res required. Continental menu. Bar. A la carte entrees: dinner $17.95-$24.95. Sun brunch $19.95. Specializes in veal chops. Entertainment Wed & Fri-Sun. Valet parking. View of Hudson River and Manhattan. Cr cds: A, C, D, MC, V.

Freehold (E-5)

Founded: 1715 **Pop:** 10,742 **Elev:** 154 ft **Area code:** 908 **Zip:** 07728

George Washington and the Revolutionary Army defeated the British under General Sir Henry Clinton at the Battle of Monmouth near here on June 28, 1778. Molly Hays carried water to artillerymen in a pitcher and from that day on she has been known as "Molly Pitcher." Freehold is the seat of Monmouth County, and the community's principal industry is glass manufacturing.

What to See and Do

1. **Monmouth County Historical Museum and Library.** 70 Court St. Headquarters of Monmouth County Historical Assn. Large rooms and galleries with 17th-, 18th- and early 19th-century furniture; collections of silver, ceramics, paintings; attic museum with toys, dolls, doll houses; Civil and Revolutionary War weapons. Museum (Tues-Sat, also Sun afternoons); library (Wed-Sat; both closed major hols). Sr citizen rate. Phone 462-1466. ¢

2. **Covenhoven House.** 150 W Main St. 18th-century house with period furnishings; once occupied by General Sir Henry Clinton prior to the Battle of Monmouth in 1778. (May-Oct, Tues, Thur, Sat & Sun afternoons) Sr citizen rate. Phone 462-1466. ¢

3. **Turkey Swamp Park.** 2 mi SW via US 9, County 524, Georgia Rd. A 565-acre park with fishing; boating (rentals). Hiking trails. Ice-skating. Picnicking (shelter), playfields. Camping (Mar-Nov; fee; electric & water hookups). Special events. Phone 462-7286. **Free.**

(For further information contact the Western Monmouth Chamber of Commerce, 49 E Main St; 462-3030.)

Seasonal Event

Harness racing. Freehold Raceway, jct US 9, NJ 33. Daily exc Mon. Phone 462-3800. Mid-Aug-May.

(See Eatontown, Hightstown, Lakewood)

Motor Hotels

★ **COLTS NECK INN.** *(6 NJ 537W, Colts Neck 07722)* W on NJ 537, at jct NJ 34. 908/409-1200; res: 800/332-5578; FAX 908/431-6640. 49 rms, 2 story. S $65; D $75; each addl $10; suites $135; under 12 free. Crib free. TV; cable. Complimentary continental bkfst, coffee. Restaurant adj 11:30 am-10 pm. Bar to 1 am; entertainment Fri & Sat, dancing. Ck-out 11 am. Meeting rms. Valet serv. Refrigerators avail. Cr cds: A, C, D, MC, V.

★ ★ **FREEHOLD GARDENS.** NJ 537 & Gibson Pl, 1 mi W on NJ 537. 908/780-3870; FAX 908/780-8725. 114 rms, 5 story. S, D $84; each addl $10; under 18 free. Crib free. Pet accepted, some restrictions; $100 deposit. TV; cable. Pool. Complimentary continental bkfst. Restaurant 5-11 pm. Rm serv. Entertainment, dancing Fri-Sat. Ck-out noon. Meeting rms. Health club privileges. Refrigerators avail. Cr cds: A, C, D, MC, V.

Gateway National Recreation Area (Sandy Hook Unit) (D-6)

(5 mi E of Atlantic Highlands on NJ 36)

Sandy Hook is a barrier peninsula that was first sighted by the crew of Henry Hudson's *Half Moon* (1609). It once was (1692) owned by Richard Hartshorne, an English Quaker, but has been government property since the 18th century. Fort Hancock (1895) was an important harbor defense from the Spanish-American War through the cold war era. Among Sandy Hook's most significant features are the Sandy Hook Lighthouse (1764), the oldest operating lighthouse in the US, and the US Army Proving Ground (1874-1919), the Army's first new-weapons testing site.

The park offers swimming (lifeguards in summer), fishing, guided and self-guided walks, picnicking and a concession. Visitors are advised to obtain literature at the Visitor Center (daily) There is no charge for entrance and activities scheduled by the National Park Service. Parking fee, Memorial Day wkend-Labor Day. (Daily, sunrise-sunset; some facilities closed in winter) For further information contact Superintendant, PO Box 530, Ft Hancock 07732; 908/872-0115.

What to See and Do

Twin Lights State Historic Site (1862). A lighthouse built to guide ships into New York harbor; now a marine museum operated by the State Park Service. (May-Oct, daily; rest of yr, Wed-Sun) Donation. Phone 908/872-1814.

(For accommodations see Red Bank)

Restaurant

★ **BAHRS.** *(2 Bay Ave, Highlands)* Garden State Pkwy exit 117, then NJ 36 E to Highlands Bridge. 908/872-1245. Hrs: 11:30 am-9:30 pm; Fri, Sat to 10:30 pm; Sun brunch 11 am-2:30 pm. Closed Thanksgiving, Dec 25. Bar. A la carte entrees: lunch, dinner $14-$19.95. Sun brunch $5-$9.95. Child's meals. Specializes in fresh seafood. Parking. Located on the waterfront; scenic view of the channel. Family-owned. Cr cds: A, D, DS, MC, V.

D

Gibbstown (G-2)

Pop: 3,902 **Elev:** 15 ft **Area code:** 609 **Zip:** 08027

What to See and Do

1. **Hunter-Lawrence-Jessup House** (1765). Approx 7 mi NW via NJ 45, County 534 in Woodbury at 58 N Broad St. Headquarters of Gloucester County Historical Society. Museum contains 16 rooms of furnishings and memorabilia from 17th-19th-century New Jersey. (Afternoons: Wed & Fri, also 1st & 3rd Mon of each month; closed hols) Phone 845-7881. **Free.**

2. **Nothnagle Home** (1638-43). 406 Swedesboro Rd. America's oldest log house. (By appt) Phone 423-0916. **Free.**

(For further information contact the Chamber of Commerce, 152 Broad St; 423-1406.)

Motel

✔ ★ ★ **DUTCH INN.** Harmony Rd, just off I-295 at exit 17. 609/423-6600; FAX 609/423-0757. 124 rms, 2 story. S $40-$54; D $45-$50; each addl $5; under 12 free. Crib $6. TV. Pool; lifeguard. Restaurant open 24 hrs; dining rm 11:30 am-2 pm, 4:30-9:30 pm; wkend hrs vary. Bar 11-2 am; closed Sun; entertainment, dancing. Ck-out noon. Meeting rms. Cr cds: A, C, D, DS, MC, V.

Motor Hotel

★ ★ ★ **HOLIDAY INN.** *(Box 304, Bridgeport 08014)* 3 mi S at I-295 exit 10. 609/467-3322; FAX 609/467-3031. 149 rms, 4 story. S $59-$84; D $59-$94; each addl $10; suites $125-$170; under 19 free. Crib free. TV; cable. Indoor pool; poolside serv. Restaurant 6:30 am-10 pm. Rm serv. Bar 11 am-midnight; entertainment Mon-Fri. Ck-out noon. Coin lndry. Meeting rms. Bellhops. Valet serv. Sundries. Gift shop. Airport, industrial park transportation. Exercise equipt; weights, bicycles, whirlpool. Game rm. Some refrigerators. Some balconies. Cr cds: A, C, D, DS, ER, JCB, MC, V.

Hackensack (C-5)

Settled: 1647 **Pop:** 37,049 **Elev:** 20 ft **Area code:** 201

Hackensack was officially known as New Barbados until 1921 when it received its charter under its present name, thought to be derived from the Native American word Hacquinsacq. The influence of the original Dutch settlers who established a trading post here remained strong even after British conquest. A strategic point during the Revolution, the city contains a number of historical sites from that era. Hackensack isthe hub for industry, business and government in Bergen County. Edward Williams College is located here.

What to See and Do

1. **The Church on the Green.** 42 Court St, NE corner of the Green, S end of Main St, opp County Court House. Organized in 1686, the original building was built in 1696 (13 monogrammed stones preserved in east wall), and rebuilt in 1791 in Stone Dutch architectural style. It is the oldest church building in Bergen County. Museum contains pictures, books and colonial items. Enoch Poor, a Revolutionary War general, is buried in the cemetery. Tours (wkdays on request). Phone 845-0957. **Free.**

2. **Steuben House State Historic Site** (1713). Approx ¼ mi N of NJ 4, at 1209 Main St in River Edge, overlooking river. Museum of the Bergen County Historical Society. Enlarged in 1752 as home of Jan and his wife Annetie Zabriskie. The house was confiscated during the Revolutionary War because the Zabriskies were Loyalists; it was given to Baron von Steuben, by the state of New Jersey, as a reward for his military services. The Baron later sold it back to the original owners. Colonial furniture, glassware, china; Native American artifacts. (Wed-Sat & Sun afternoons; closed Jan 1, Thanksgiving, Dec 25) Phone 487-1739.

3. **USS** *Ling* **Submarine.** Docked at Court and River Sts. Restored World War II fleet submarine; New Jersey Naval Museum. (Wed-Sun; closed most major hols) Sr citizen rate. Phone 342-3268. ¢¢

(For further information contact the Chamber of Commerce, 140 Main St, 07601; 489-3700.)

(See Fort Lee, Paterson)

Motel

★★ **BEST WESTERN ORITANI.** *414 Hackensack Ave (07601).* 201/488-8900; FAX 201/488-5456. 127 units, 2-4 story. S, D $79-$100. Crib $8. TV. Pool; sauna. Restaurant 7 am-3 pm, 6-10 pm; Sat 8-11 am, 6-10 pm; Sun 8-11 am. Bar 5 pm-midnight, Sat from 6 pm, closed Sun. Ck-out noon. Meeting rms. Valet serv. Sundries. Cr cds: A, C, D, DS, MC, V.

Hotels

★★★ **MARRIOTT GLENPOINTE HOTEL.** *(100 Frank W. Burr Blvd, Teaneck 07666)* At I-80/I-95, local lanes exit 70/70B. 201/836-0600; FAX 201/836-0638. 341 rms, 14 story. S, D $145-$160; each addl $15; suites $300-$650; under 18 free; wkend rates. Crib free. TV; cable. Indoor pool. Restaurant 6:30 am-midnight. Bar 11-1 am. Ck-out noon. Concierge. Exercise rm; instructor, weight machines, bicycles, whirlpool, sauna. Some bathrm phones, refrigerators. Cr cds: A, C, D, DS, ER, JCB, MC, V.

★★ **SHERATON HASBROUCK HEIGHTS.** *(650 Terrace Ave, Hasbrouck Heights 07604)* At jct NJ 17N, I-80. 201/288-6100; FAX 201/288-4717. 350 rms, 12 story. S $99-$119; D $119-$139; each addl $10; suites $175-$305; under 17 free; wkend rates. Crib free. Pet accepted. TV; cable, in-rm movies. Heated pool; poolside serv, lifeguard. Restaurant 6:30 am-11 pm; wkends from 7 am. Bars 12:30 pm-1:30 am, Sat to 2:30 am; entertainment wkends, dancing. Ck-out 1 pm. Convention facilities. Gift shop. Exercise rm; instructor, weights, bicycles, whirlpool, sauna. Some in-rm steam baths. ***LUXURY LEVEL : EXECUTIVE LEVEL.*** 124 rms, 8 suites, 4 floors. S, D $109-$139; suites $175-$305. Concierge. Private lounge. Cr cds: A, C, D, DS, ER, MC, V.

Restaurant

★★★ **STONY HILL INN.** *231 Polifly Rd, I-80 jct NJ 17N.* 201/342-4085. Hrs: 11:30 am-3 pm, 5:30-10:30 pm; Sat from 5:30 pm; Sun 3-10 pm. Closed Dec 25. Continental menu. Bar to midnight. Wine cellar. A la carte entrees: lunch $12.95-$18.95, dinner $13.95-$31.50. Specializes in continental cusine. Own pastries. Entertainment exc Sun & Mon. Landmark house (1818); period furnishings. Jacket. Cr cds: A, C, D, MC, V.

Hackettstown (C-3)

Settled: ca 1760 **Pop:** 8,120 **Elev:** 571 ft **Area code:** 908 **Zip:** 07840

First called Helm's Mills and then Musconetcong, citizens renamed the town for Samuel Hackett, the largest local landowner. His popularity increased when he provided unlimited free drinks at the christening of a new hotel. Hackettstown is located in the Musconetcong Valley between Schooleys and Upper Pohatcong mountains.

What to See and Do

1. **Allamuchy Mountain State Park, Stephens Section.** Willow Grove St, 1½ mi N of US 46. Allamuchy Mountain State Park (7,263 acres) is divided into three sections. The Stephens Section (482 acres) is developed; the rest (Allamuchy) is natural. Fishing in Musconetcong River. Hiking. Picnicking, playground. Camping. Standard fees. Phone 852-3790 (Stephens).

2. **Land of Make Believe.** I-80 exit 12, on County 611, in Hope. Amusement park at foot of Jenny Jump Mountain includes the Himalaya Ride; Old McDonald's Farm; the Red Baron airplane; Santa Claus at the North Pole; a Civil War train; a maze; water activities; hayrides; picnic grove; fudge factory. (Mid-June-Labor Day, daily; Memorial Day wkend-mid-June, wkends; Sept, Sun only) Phone 459-5100. ¢¢¢¢

(For further information contact the Town Hall, 215 Stiger St; 852-3130.)

Motel

★★ **INN AT PANTHER VALLEY.** *(Box 183, Allamuchy 07820)* ¾ mi S of I-80 exit 19, on County 517. 908/852-6000; FAX 908/850-1503. 100 rms, 1-2 story, 7 kits. S $70-$80; D $75-$90; each addl $5; kit. units $10 addl; under 13 free. Crib $5. TV. Restaurant 6:30 am-10 pm. Bar 11:30 am-midnight. Ck-out noon. Health club privileges. Cr cds: A, C, D, MC, V.

Inn

★★★ **THE INN AT MILLRACE POND.** *(Box 359, Hope 07844)* Off I-80 exit 12, then 1 mi S to NJ 519, then left. 908/459-4884. 17 rms, 2 story, 3 bldgs. S, D $85-$150; each addl $20. Some TV; cable. Complimentary continental bkfst. Restaurant 5-9 pm; Sun noon-8 pm. Ck-out noon, ck-in 3 pm. Tennis. Library. Colonial gristmill (1769). Rms individually decorated with colonial antiques and period reproductions. Cr cds: A, MC, V.

Haddonfield (F-3)

Settled: ca 1713 **Pop:** 11,628 **Elev:** 95 ft **Area code:** 609 **Zip:** 08033

Named for Elizabeth Haddon, a Quaker girl of 20 whose father sent her here from England in 1701 to develop 400 acres of land. This assertive young woman built a house, started a colony and proposed to a Quaker missionary who promptly married her. The "Theologian's Tale" in Longfellow's *Tales of A Wayside Inn* celebrates Elizabeth Haddon's romance with the missionary.

What to See and Do

1. **Greenfield Hall.** 343 King's Hwy E (NJ 41). Haddonfield's Historical Society headquarters in old Gill House (1747-1841) contains personal items of Elizabeth Haddon; furniture; costumes; doll collection. Boxwood garden; library on local history. On grounds is a house (ca 1735) once owned by Elizabeth Haddon. (Mon-Fri, mornings, other days by appt; closed Aug) Phone 429-7375. ¢
2. **Indian King Tavern Museum State Historic Site.** 233 King's Hwy E. Built as an inn; state legislatures met here frequently, passing a bill (1777) substituting "State" for "Colony" in all state papers. Colonial furnishings. Guided tours. (Wed-Sun; closed Jan 1, Thanksgiving, Dec 25; also Wed`if following Mon or Tues hol) Donation. Phone 429-6792.
3. **The Site of the Elizabeth Haddon House.** Wood Lane & Merion Ave. Isaac Wood built this house in 1842, on the foundation of Elizabeth Haddon's 1713 brick mansion, immediately after it was destroyed by fire. The original brew house Elizabeth built (1713) and the English yew trees she brought over in 1712 are in the yard. Private residence; not open to the public.

(For accommodations see Cherry Hill, also see Camden)

High Point State Park (A-4)

(7 mi NW of Sussex on NJ 23)

High Point's elevation (1,803 ft), the highest point in New Jersey, gave this 15,000-acre park its name. The spot is marked by a 220-foot stone war memorial. The view is magnificent, overlooking Tri-State—the point where New Jersey, New York and Pennsylvania meet—with the Catskill Mountains to the north, the Pocono Mountains to the west, and hills, valleys and lakes all around. Elsewhere in the forests of this Kittatinny Mountain park are facilities for swimming; fishing; boating. Nature studies. Picnicking. Tent camping (no trailers). Standard fees. Phone 201/875-4800.

Hightstown (E-4)

Pop: 5,126 **Elev:** 84 ft **Area code:** 609 **Zip:** 08520

Motel

★ ★ **TOWN HOUSE.** *NJ Tpke exit 8, on NJ 33.* 609/448-2400; *res:* 800/922-0622; *FAX* 609/443-0395. 104 rms, 1-2 story. S $55-$125; D $58-$125; each addl $10; suites, studio rms $95-$150; under 12 free; package plans. Crib free. TV. Pool; wading pool, lifeguard. Complimentary continental bkfst. Restaurant 7 am-10 pm. Bar 11-1 am; entertainment, dancing Wed, Fri, Sat. Ck-out 1 pm. Meeting rms. Sundries. Refrigerators; whirlpool in some suites. Cr cds: A, C, D, DS, MC, V.

Restaurant

★ ★ **FORSGATE COUNTRY CLUB.** *(Forsgate Dr, Jamesburg) At NJ Tpke, exit 8A.* 908/521-0070. Hrs: noon-2:30 pm, 6-10:30 pm; Sun brunch 11 am-2:30 pm. Closed Jan 1, Dec 25. Bar. A la carte entrees: lunch $7.50-$18, dinner $14-$26. Sun brunch $21.95. Specializes in regional American dishes. Parking. Country club atmosphere; view of golf course. Cr cds: A, D, MC, V.

Hillsdale (B-5)

Pop: 9,750 **Elev:** 83 ft **Area code:** 201 **Zip:** 07642

Restaurant

★ **HONG HING.** *(65 Old Hook Rd, Westwood) S on NJ 502.* 201/666-5393. Hrs: noon-midnight; Fri to 1 am; Sat 1 pm-1 am; Sun 1 pm-midnight. Closed Thanksgiving. Chinese menu. Bar. Semi-a la carte: lunch $4.50-$8.75, dinner $9.95-$22.50. Specializes in barbecue shrimp, Peking chicken. Parking. Oriental decor. Cr cds: A, MC, V.

Hoboken (C-5)

Settled: 1640 **Pop:** 33,397 **Elev:** 5 ft **Area code:** 201 **Zip:** 07030

In the early 19th century, beer gardens and other amusement centers dotted the Hoboken shore, enticing New Yorkers across the Hudson. John Jacob Astor, Washington Irving, William Cullen Bryant and Martin Van Buren were among the fashionable visitors. By the second half of the century, industries and shipping began to encroach on the fun. In 1928-29, Christopher Morley and Cleon Throckmorton presented revivals of *After Dark* and *The Black Crook* to enchanted New Yorkers. Today Hoboken is known as a seaport, railroad terminal and industrial center.

What to See and Do

Stevens Institute of Technology (1870). (3,600 students) Castle Point, E of Hudson St between 5th & 9th Sts. A leading college of engineering, science, computer science management and the humanities; also a center for research. Campus tours. Phone 216-5105. On campus are

Stevens Center (1962). The 14-story hub of campus. Excellent view of Manhattan from George Washington Bridge to the Verrazano Bridge.

Samuel C. Williams Library (1969). Special collections include set of facsimiles of every drawing by Leonardo da Vinci; library of 3,000 volumes by and about da Vinci; Alexander Calder mobile; the Frederick Winslow Taylor Collection of Scientific Management. (Academic yr) Phone 216-5198.

Davidson Laboratory. W end of campus. One of the largest privately owned hydrodynamic labs of its kind in the world. Testing site for models of ships, hydrofoils, the America's Cup participants and the Apollo command capsule. (Limited public access) Phone 216-5290.

(For further information contact the Hudson County Chamber of Commerce, 574 Summit Ave, Suite 404, Jersey City 07306; 653-7400.)

(For accommodations see Jersey City, Secaucus)

Restaurants

★ **ARTHUR'S TAVERN.** *237 Washington St, at 3rd St.* 201/656-5009. Hrs: 11:30 am-11 pm; Fri, Sat to midnight; Sun 2-10 pm. Closed Thanksgiving, Dec 25. Bars. A la carte entrees: lunch $3.75-$10.95, dinner $3.75-$20.95. Specialties: 24-oz Delmonico steak, Maine lobster. Built 1850; old tavern decor, stained glass. Cr cds: A, C, D, DS, MC, V.

D

★ ★ ★ RISTORANTE GERRINO. 96 River St, 1 blk N of RR station. 201/656-7731. Hrs: noon-11 pm; Sat from 5 pm. Closed major hols. Res accepted. Northern Italian, Amer menu. Bar. A la carte entrees: lunch $9.50-$13.50, dinner $11-$23. Complete meals: dinner $28. Specializes in veal, fresh seafood. Own desserts. Rooftop dining & bar (seasonal). Stained-glass ceiling. Cr cds: A, C, D, MC, V.

Hohokus (B-5)

Pop: 3,935 **Elev:** 111 ft **Area code:** 201 **Zip:** 07423

In colonial times, Ho-Ho-Kus was known as Hoppertown. Its present name is derived from the Chihohokies Indians, who also had a settlement on this spot.

What to See and Do

The Hermitage. 335 N Franklin Tpke. Stone Victorian house of Gothic-revival architecture superimposed on original 18th-century house. Its span of history includes ownership by the Rosencrantz family for more than 150 years. Grounds consist of five wooded acres, including a second stone Victorian house. Costumed docents conduct tours of site and the Hermitage. Clothing exhibit (June-Sept). Special events held throughout the yr. Tours (mid-Apr-Sept & Dec, Thurs; also 1st & 3rd Sun of each month; closed hols). Phone 445-8311 for exact schedule, including events and productions. ¢¢

(For further information contact the Borough of Ho-Ho-Kus, 333 Warren Ave; 652-4400.)

(For accommodations see Paramus)

Jackson (F-5)

Pop: 33,233 **Elev:** 138 ft **Area code:** 908 **Zip:** 08527

What to See and Do

Six Flags Great Adventure. On County 537, 1 mi S of I-195. A family entertainment center, including 350-acre drive-through safari park with more than 1,400 free-roaming animals from 6 continents; theme park featuring rides, shows and continuous live entertainment; 15-acre area with 10 water rides. Safari and entertainment parks (late Mar-late Oct; schedule varies). For information phone 928-1821. ¢¢¢¢

(For further information contact the Chamber of Commerce, PO Box A-C; 928-0027.)

(For accommodations see Lakewood, Toms River)

Jersey City (C-5)

Settled: 1629 **Pop:** 228,537 **Elev:** 11 ft **Area code:** 201

Jersey City's location on the Hudson River, due west of the southern end of Manhattan Island, has aided its growth to such a degree that it is now the second largest city in New Jersey. Railroads, buses, motor freight lines and highways crisscross the city. New Yorkers across the

bay tell time by the Colgate-Palmolive Clock at 105 Hudson St; the dial is 50 feet across, and the minute hand, weighing 2,200 pounds, moves 23 inches each minute. Jersey City's major links with New York are the 8,557-foot Holland Tunnel, which is 72 feet below water level, and the Port Authority Trans-Hudson (PATH) rapid transit system.

What to See and Do

Liberty State Park. Off NJ Tpke, exit 14B; on the New York Harbor, less than 2,000 feet from the Statue of Liberty. Offers breathtaking view of New York City skyline; flag display including state, historic and US flags; swimming pool (fee); boat launch; fitness course; picnic area. Historic railroad terminal has been partially restored. The Interpretive Center houses an exhibit area; adj to the Center is a 60-acre natural area consisting mostly of salt marsh. Nature trails and observation points complement this wildlife habitat. (Daily) Boat tours and ferry service to Ellis Island and Statue of Liberty are available; for schedule and general information, phone 915-3400.

(For further information contact the Hudson County Chamber of Commerce, 574 Summit Ave, Suite 404, 07306; 653-7400.)

(See Newark, Newark Intl Airport Area)

Motor Hotel

★ ★ QUALITY INN-JERSEY CITY. 180 12th St (07302), at entrance to Holland Tunnel. 201/653-0300; FAX 201/659-1963. 150 rms, 3 story. No elvtr. S $70-$74; D $74-$81; each addl $5; under 18 free. Crib free. TV; cable. Pool. Restaurant 6:30 am-10 pm; Sun 7 am-2 pm. Rm serv. Bar 11 am-11 pm; Sat from 5 pm, Sun noon-2 pm. Ck-out noon. Meeting rms. Cr cds: A, C, D, DS, MC, V.

≈ ⊠ 🐾 SC

Lake Hopatcong (B-4)

Area code: 201

(Approx 15 mi N and W of Dover via NJ 15 & unnumbered road)

The largest lake in New Jersey, Hopatcong's popularity as a resort is second only to the seacoast spots. It covers 2,443 acres and has a hilly shoreline of approximately 40 miles. The area offers swimming, stocked fishing and boating.

What to See and Do

Hopatcong State Park. SW shore of lake, near Landing. A 113-acre park with swimming, bathhouse; fishing. Picnicking, playground, concession. Historic museum (wkend afternoons). Standard fees. Phone 398-7010.

Motel

★ ★ DAYS INN. (1691 Rte 46, Ledgewood 07852) On US 46E at I-80 exit 27. 201/347-5100; FAX 201/347-6356. 98 rms, 2 story. S $59-$75; D $65-$75; each addl $8; under 15 free. Crib free. TV. Pool; lifeguard. Restaurant 7 am-10 pm; Sun 8 am-1 pm. Rm serv. Bar 4 pm-2 am; entertainment, dancing Fri & Sat. Ck-out noon. Coin lndry. Meeting rms. Sundries. 2 tennis courts. Cr cds: A, C, D, DS, MC, V.

🚶 ≈ 🐾 SC

Motor Hotel

★ ★ ★ SHERATON. (15 Howard Blvd, Mount Arlington 07856) I-80 exit 30. 201/770-2000; FAX 201/770-2000, ext. 615. 124 rms, 5 story. S $85.50-$104.50; D $95.50-$109.50; each addl $10; suites $125-$150; under 18 free; wknd rates. Crib free. TV; cable. Indoor pool; lifeguard. Restaurant 6:30 am-10 pm. Rm serv. Bar 11-1 am; entertainment, dancing Apr-Oct wkends. Ck-out noon. Meeting rms. Valet serv. Exercise equipt; weight machine, bicycles. Refrigerators avail. Art deco decor. Extensive grounds. Cr cds: A, C, D, DS, JCB, MC, V.

Lakewood (F-5)

Settled: 1800 **Pop:** 26,095 **Elev:** 67 ft **Area code:** 908 **Zip:** 08701

A well-known winter resort in the 1890s, many socially prominent New Yorkers such as the Astors, the Goulds, the Rhinelanders, the Rockefellers and the Vanderbilts maintained large homes on the shores of Lake Carasaljo.

What to See and Do

Ocean County Park #1. 659 Ocean Ave, 1 mi E on NJ 88. The 325-acre former Rockefeller estate. Lake swimming; children's fishing lake. Tennis, platform tennis. Picnicking (grills), playground, athletic fields. (Daily) Entrance fee (July-Aug, wkends). Phone 370-7380. Per car ¢

(For further information contact the Chamber of Commerce, PO Box 656; 363-0012.)

(See Toms River)

Motel

★★ BEST WESTERN LEISURE INN. *1600 NJ 70, Garden State Pkwy exit 88. 908/367-0900; FAX 908/370-4928.* 105 rms. Memorial Day-Sept: S, D $70-$104; each addl $10; lower rates rest of yr. Crib free. TV; cable. Pool. Complimentary continental bkfst. Restaurant 6:30 am-10 pm. Bar 6-11 pm. Ck-out 11 am. Coin lndry. Meeting rm. Refrigerators avail. Cr cds: A, C, D, DS, MC, V.

Lambertville (E-3)

Settled: 1705 **Pop:** 3,927 **Elev:** 76 ft **Area code:** 609 **Zip:** 08530

What to See and Do

1. **John Holcombe House.** 260 N Main St. Washington stayed here just before crossing the Delaware. Privately owned residence.

2. **Marshall House** (1816). 62 Bridge St. James Marshall, who first discovered gold at Sutter's Mill in California in 1848, lived here until 1834. Period furnishings; memorabilia of Lambertville; small museum collection. (May-mid-Oct, Sun or by appt) Phone 397-0770. **Free.**

(For further information contact the Lambertville Area Chamber of Commerce, 4 S Union St; 397-0055.)

(See Trenton)

Inns

★★ CHIMNEY HILL FARM. *207 Goat Hill Rd, just off NJ 179 & 29. 609/397-1516.* 7 rms, 3 story. No rm phones. S, D $105-$150; wkly rates; some lower rates mid-wk. Children over 12 yrs only. Complimentary continental bkfst, tea/sherry. Ck-out 11 am, ck-in 3 pm.

Downhill ski 1/2 mi. Balcony. Picnic tables. Elegant stone and frame manor house built 1820; furnishings are antiques and period reproductions. Cr cds: MC, V.

★★★ INN AT LAMBERTVILLE STATION. *11 Bridge St. 609/397-4400; res: 800/524-1091 (exc NJ); FAX 609/397-9744.* 45 units, 3 story. S, D $80-$115; each addl $15; suites $150. Crib avail. TV; cable. Complimentary continental bkfst in rms. Dining rm 11:30 am-10 pm. Honor bar to 2 am. Ck-out noon. Meeting rms. Fireplace in suites. View of Delaware River. Colonial antiques. Cr cds: A, C, D, MC, V.

Restaurant

★★ LAMBERTVILLE STATION. *11 Bridge St. 609/397-8300.* Hrs: 11:30 am-3 pm, 4-10 pm; Fri, Sat to 11 pm; early-bird dinner Mon-Fri 4-6:30 pm; Sun brunch 10:30 am-3 pm. Res required hols. Bar. Semi-a la carte: lunch $5.95-$8.95, dinner $9.95-$19.95. Sun brunch $5.75-$7.95. Child's meals. Specializes in rack of lamb, buffalo. Entertainment Fri, Sat. Parking. Renovated railroad station with 3 dining areas; 1 dining rm is an old station platform. Victorian-style decor. Cr cds: A, C, D, MC, V.

Livingston (C-5)

Pop: 26,609 **Elev:** 307 ft **Area code:** 201 **Zip:** 07039

This suburban community in southwestern Essex County is named for William Livingston, the first governor of New Jersey.

Restaurant

★★ AFTON. *(2 Hanover Rd, Florham Park)* 4 1/2 mi E of I-287 at Columbia Tpke, NJ 510. 201/377-1871. Hrs: 11:30 am-2:30 pm, 5-9 pm; Sun noon-8 pm. Closed Mon; Dec 25. Bar to 11 pm. Complete meals: lunch $7.50-$11.95, dinner $12-$18.50. Specializes in prime rib, seafood. Family-owned. Cr cds: A, C, D, MC, V.

Long Beach Island (G-5 - H-5)

Area code: 609

Six miles out to sea, this island is separated from the New Jersey mainland by Barnegat and Little Egg Harbor Bays. NJ 72, going east from Manahawkin on the mainland, enters the island at Ship Bottom. The island is no more than three blocks wide in some places, and extends 18 miles from historic Barnegat Lighthouse to the north. It includes towns such as Loveladies, Harvey Cedars, Surf City, Ship Bottom, Brant Beach and the Beach Havens at the southern tip. The island is a popular family resort with excellent fishing, boating and other water sports. For swimming, the bay is calm, while the ocean offers a vigorous surf.

Tales are told of pirate coins buried on the island, and, over the years, silver and gold pieces occasionally have turned up. Whether they are part of pirate treasure or the refuse of shipwrecks remains a mystery.

What to See and Do

1. **Barnegat Lighthouse State Park.** At N end of island. Barnegat Lighthouse, a 167-foot red and white tower, was engineered by

General George G. Meade and completed in 1858; 217-step spiral staircase leading to lookout offering spectacular view. Fishing. Picnicking. Park (daily); lighthouse (Memorial Day-Labor Day, daily; May & Labor Day-Oct, wkends only). Standard fees. Phone 494-2016.

2. **Fantasy Island Amusement Park.** 7th St & Bay Ave, Beach Haven. Family-oriented amusement park featuring rides and games; adult casino arcade; miniature golf. (June-Aug, daily; May & Sept, wkends; schedule varies, phone for hrs) Phone 492-4000.

3. **Whale watching.** Six-hr cruises. (June-Sept) Phone 494-2094.

(For further information contact the Southern Ocean County Chamber of Commerce, 265 W 9th St, Ship Bottom 08008; 494-7211 or 800/292-6372.)

Seasonal Event

Surflight Theatre. Engleside & Beach Aves, Beach Haven. Broadway musicals every two weeks, nightly. Children's theater, Wed-Sat. Phone 492-9477. May-mid-Oct.

Motels

★ ★ **ENGLESIDE.** *(30 Engleside Ave, Beach Haven 08008)* 7 mi S of NJ 72. 609/492-1251; FAX 609/492-9175. 73 units, 3 story, 37 kits. No elvtr. July-Labor Day: S, D $125-$170; each addl $10; suites $195-$254; kit. units for 2-4, $145-$175; lower rates rest of yr. Crib avail. TV; cable, in-rm movies. Pool; poolside serv (in season), lifeguard. Restaurant 8 am-2 pm, 5-9 pm. Bar. Ck-out noon. Meeting rms. Sundries. Exercise equipt; weight machine, bicycle, whirlpool, sauna. Refrigerators. Private patios, balconies. On beach. Cr cds: A, C, D, DS, MC, V.

★ **SANDPIPER.** *(Boulevard at 10th St, Ship Bottom 08008)* NJ 72E to end. 609/494-6909. 20 rms, shower only. No rm phones. July-Aug: S, D $75-$98; each addl $5; wkly rates; higher rates wkends & hols (3-day min); lower rates May-June & Sept-Oct. Closed rest of yr. TV; cable. Pool. Restaurant adj 4-10 pm. Ck-out 11 am. Refrigerators. Ocean 1 blk. Cr cds: A, MC, V.

★ **SPRAY BEACH MOTOR INN.** *(24th St at Ocean, Spray Beach 08008)* 5 1/2 mi S of NJ 72. 609/492-1501; FAX 609/492-0504. 88 rms, 3 story, 10 kits. Late June-Labor Day: S, D $85-$155; each addl $10; kit. units $99-$165; family rates; packages; lower rates rest of yr. Closed Jan. Crib $5. TV; cable, in-rm movies avail. Heated pool; lifeguard. Restaurant 8 am-2:30 pm, 5-10 pm. Bar 10:30-2 am; entertainment wkends, hols in season. Ck-out noon. Sundries. Refrigerators. On beach. Cr cds: A, MC, V.

Restaurant

★ ★ **BAYBERRY INN.** *(Boulevard at 13th St, Ship Bottom)* 5 blks S of NJ 72. 609/494-8848. Hrs: 11:30 am-10 pm; Sun from 10 am; early-bird dinner Mon-Fri 4-6 pm, Sun 3-5 pm. Closed Dec 25. Continental menu. Bar 11:30-2 am. Semi-a la carte: lunch $2.75-$10.95, dinner $9.95-$25.95. Sun brunch $11.95. Child's meals. Specializes in fresh seasonal seafood. Pianist Fri, Sat. Parking. Outdoor dining. Williamsburg decor. Cr cds: A, C, D, DS, MC, V.

Madison (C-4)

Settled: ca 1685 **Pop:** 15,850 **Elev:** 261 ft **Area code:** 201 **Zip:** 07940

For many years, the quiet suburban town of Madison was called the "Rose City" because of the thousands of bouquets produced in its many greenhouses.

What to See and Do

1. **Museum of Early Trades and Crafts.** Main St (NJ 124) at Green Village Rd. Hands-on look at 18th & 19th century artisans. Special events include Spring Festival (June) and Bottle Hill Craft Festival (Sept). Tours. (Tues-Sat, also Sun afternoons; closed major hols) Sr citizen rate. Phone 377-2982. ¢

2. **Drew University** (1867). (2,100 students) Madison Ave, NJ 24. A 186-acre wooded campus west of town. College of Liberal Arts, Theological School and Graduate School. On campus are a Neoclassical administration building (1833), the United Methodist Archives and History Center and the Rose Memorial Library containing Nestorian Cross collection, government and UN documents and manuscripts and memorabilia of early Methodism. Tours (by appt). Phone 408-3000.

3. **Fairleigh Dickinson University-Florham-Madison Campus** (1958). (3,889 students) 285 Madison Ave, NJ 24. (1 of 3 campuses) On site of Twombly Estate (1895); many original buildings still in use. Friendship Library houses numerous special collections including Harry A. Chesler collection of comic art, archives of the Outdoor Advertising Assn of America and collections devoted to printing and the graphic arts. (Academic yr, Mon-Fri; closed school hols) Tours of campus by appt. Phone 593-8500.

(For further information contact the Chamber of Commerce, 155 Main St, PO Box 160; 377-7830.)

Seasonal Event

New Jersey Shakespeare Festival. In residence at Drew University (see #2). Professional theater company. Includes Shakespearean, classic and modern plays; special guest attractions and classic films. For schedule, reservations phone 408-5600. Early June-Sept.

(For accommodations see Chatham, Morristown)

Matawan (E-5)

Pop: 9,270 **Elev:** 55 ft **Area code:** 908 **Zip:** 07747

What to See and Do

Cheesequake State Park. Garden State Pkwy, exit 120, right at 1st traffic light and right at next traffic light onto Gordon Rd, 1/4 mi to entrance. This 1,300-acre park offers swimming, bathhouse; fishing. Nature tours. Picnicking, playground, concession. Camping (fee; dump station). Standard fees. Phone 566-2161.

(For further information contact the Chamber of Commerce, PO Box 522; 290-1125.)

Seasonal Event

Concerts. Garden State Arts Center, at Telegraph Hill Park on the Garden State Pkwy, exit 116. A 5,302-seat amphitheater; lawn area seats 4,500-5,500. Contemporary, classical, pop and rock concerts. Phone 442-9200. Mid-June-Sept.

(See Freehold)

Motels

★ ★ **RAMADA INN.** *(2870 NJ 35, Hazlet 07730) 2 mi S of Garden State Pkwy exit 117.* 908/264-2400; FAX 908/739-9735. 120 rms, 2 story. S $75; D $88; each addl $6; under 18 free; higher rates summer wkends. Crib free. TV; cable, in-rm movies avail. 2 pools, 1 indoor; lifeguard. Restaurant 6:30 am-10 pm. Rm serv. Bar noon-2 am; entertainment, dancing exc Mon. Ck-out noon. Meeting rms. Exercise equipt; weights, rower, sauna. Cr cds: A, D, DS, JCB, MC, V.

✔ ★ **WELLESLEY INN.** *(3215 NJ 35, Hazlet 07730) 1 mi S of Garden State Pkwy, exit 117, S on NJ 35.* 908/888-2800; FAX 908/888-2902. 89 rms, 3 story. S $43.99-$63.99; D $49.99-$69.99; each addl $5; under 18 free; higher rates summer wkends. Crib free. Pet accepted, some restrictions; $3. TV; cable. Complimentary continental bkfst, coffee. Restaurant nearby. Ck-out 11 am. Refrigerators avail. Cr cds: A, D, DS, JCB, MC, V.

Restaurant

★ ★ **BUTTONWOOD MANOR.** *On NJ 34, 1/2 mi N.* 908/566-6220. Hrs: 11:30 am-10 pm; Sat to 11 pm; Sun noon-9 pm. Res accepted. Bar. Semi-a la carte: lunch $5.25-$9.95, dinner $13.95-$24.95. Child's meals. Specializes in duckling, steak, fresh seafood. Entertainment Fri, Sat. Parking. Lakeside dining. Cr cds: A, MC, V.

Metuchen (D-5)

(see Woodbridge)

Millburn (C-5)

Settled: 1720s **Pop:** 18,630 **Elev:** 140 ft **Area code:** 201 **Zip:** 07041

Once bristling with paper mills and hat factories, Millburn is today a quiet residential town.

What to See and Do

1. **Paper Mill Playhouse.** Brookside Dr. State Theater of New Jersey. A variety of plays, musicals and children's theater (Wed-Sun); matinees (Thurs, Sat & Sun). Sr citizen rate. Phone 376-4343 (box office) or 379-3636 (information).
2. **Cora Hartshorn Arboretum and Bird Sanctuary.** 2 mi W on Forest Dr in Short Hills. A 17-acre sanctuary with nature trails; guided walks. Stone House Museum with nature exhibits (late Sept-mid-June, Tues, Thurs & Sat). Grounds (daily). Phone 376-3587. **Free.**

(For further information contact the Chamber of Commerce, 56 Main St, PO Box 651; 379-1198.)

(See Newark, Newark Intl Airport Area, Union)

Hotel

HILTON AT SHORT HILLS. *(4-Star 1994; New general manager, therefore not rated) (41 John F Kennedy Pkwy, Short Hills 07078) 3 mi W at jct NJ 24 Livingston exit, JFK Pkwy, opp Mall at Short Hills.* 201/379-0100; FAX 201/379-6870. 300 rms, 7 story, 37 suites. S $205-$235; D $225-$255; each addl $20; suites $235-$900; under 18 free; wkend rates. Crib free. TV; cable. 2 pools, 1 indoor; lifeguard. Restaurant 6:30 am-10:30 pm (also see THE DINING ROOM). Rm serv 24 hrs. Bar 11:30-1:30 am; entertainment, dancing (Fri & Sat). Ck-out 1 pm. Meeting rms. Concierge. Gift shop. Beauty shop. Valet parking avail. Complimentary airport transportation. Exercise rm; instructor, weight machines, bicycles, whirlpool, sauna, steam rm. Massage. Refrigerator in suites. *LUXURY LEVEL : THE TOWERS.* 96 rms, 2 floors. S $225; D $245; suites $245-$860. Concierge. Private lounge. Deluxe toiletry amenities. Complimentary continental bkfst, refreshments. Cr cds: A, C, D, DS, ER, JCB, MC, V.

Restaurants

★ ★ **40 MAIN STREET.** *40 Main St, downtown near Paper Mill Playhouse.* 201/376-4444. Hrs: 11:30 am-2 pm, 5:30-10 pm; Fri to 11 pm; Sat 5:30-11 pm. Closed Sun, Mon; major hols. Res accepted; required wkends. Creative American gourmet menu. Bar. A la carte entrees: lunch $9.95-$13.95, dinner $22.95-$28.95. Specialties: grilled Norwegian salmon with anise mustard & leeks, roast rack of lamb with garlic. Own ice cream. Seasonal menu; wine tasting dinners. Pianist, Tues evenings. Storefront location; decor features paintings by Barbara Dalton. Intimate atmosphere. Cr cds: A, D, MC, V.

D

★ ★ ★ **THE DINING ROOM.** *(See Hilton At Short Hills Hotel)* 201/379-0100. Hrs: 5:30-10:30 pm. Closed Sun & Mon. Bar. Complete meals: 3-course dinner $55, 4-course dinner $65. Specializes in seafood, chicken, veal. Seasonal menu. Own pastries. Harpist. Valet parking. English drawing room atmosphere. Jacket. Cr cds: A, C, D, DS, ER, JCB, MC, V.

D

Millville (H-3)

Pop: 25,992 **Elev:** 37 ft **Area code:** 609 **Zip:** 08332

What to See and Do

Wheaton Village. 2 mi NE via County 552. Tranquil lifestyle of an 1888 South Jersey glass town. Buildings include Museum of American Glass, which houses an extensive glass collection; working factory where demonstrations of glassmaking are given; general store; restored train station; 1876 one-room schoolhouse. Crafts demonstrations, arcade, shops. Restaurant, hotel. Self-guided tours. (Apr-Dec, daily; closed major hols) Phone 825-6800. ¢¢¢

(For further information contact the Chamber of Commerce, 13 S High St, PO Box 831; 825-7000, ext 396.)

(See Bridgeton)

Motel

★ ★ **COUNTRY INN BY CARLSON.** *1125 Village Dr.* 609/825-3100; res: 800/456-4000; FAX 609/825-1317. 100 rms, 2 story. S $61-$65; D $64-$69; each addl $5; suites $125; under 18 free. Crib free. TV; cable. Heated pool. Restaurant 7 am-9 pm; Fri & Sat to 10 pm. Bar 11-1 am. Meeting rms. Some refrigerators. Cr cds: A, C, D, DS, MC, V.

D

Montclair (C-5)

Settled: 1666 **Pop:** 37,729 **Elev:** 337 ft **Area code:** 201

Originally a part of Newark, the area that includes Montclair was purchased from Native Americans in 1678 for "two guns, three coats and thirteen cans of rum." The first settlers were English farmers from Connecticut who came here to form a Puritan church of their own. Shortly after, Dutch from Hackensack arrived, and two communities were created: Cranetown and Speertown. The two communities later were absorbed into West Bloomfield.

During the Revolutionary War, First Mountain served as a lookout point and as a barrier, preventing the British from crossing into the Upper Passaic valley. In the early 1800s, manufacturing began, new roads opened and the area grew. In 1856-57, a rail controversy arose: West Bloomfield citizens wanted a rail connection with New York City; Bloomfield residents saw no need for it. In 1868, the two towns separated and West Bloomfield became Montclair. This railroad helped to make Montclair the suburban, residential town it is today. One of the town's schools is named for painter George Inness, who once lived here.

What to See and Do

1. **The Montclair Art Museum.** 3 S Mountain Ave at Bloomfield Ave. American art; Native American gallery; changing exhibits. (Daily exc Mon; closed Thanksgiving, Dec 25) Sunday gallery lectures. Concerts; jazz; film series. Phone 746-5555. ¢¢

2. **Israel Crane House** (1796). 110 Orange Rd. Federal mansion with period rooms; working 18th-century kitchen; school room; special exhibits during the year. Country Store & Post Office have authentic items; old-time crafts demonstrations. Research library. (Sept-June, Wed & Sun afternoons; other times by appt; costumed tours Sun only) Phone 744-1796. ¢¢

3. **Eagle Rock Reservation.** 1/2 mi W on Bloomfield Ave, then S on Prospect Ave to Eagle Rock Ave in West Orange (see).

4. **Presby Iris Gardens.** In Mountainside Park, on Upper Mountain Ave in Upper Montclair. Height of bloom in late May or early June. Phone 783-5974.

(For further information contact the Chamber of Commerce, 50 Church St, 07042; 744-7660.)

Seasonal Event

Summerfun Theater Inc. Weiss Arts Center, Montclair-Kimberley Academy, Lloyd Rd. Professional summer stock company presents six productions. Tues-Sat. Phone 256-0576. Mid-June-mid-Aug.

(For accommodations see Newark, Newark Intl Airport Area)

Montvale (B-5)

Pop: 6,946 **Elev:** 187 ft **Area code:** 201 **Zip:** 07645

Motel

★ ★ **RAMADA INN.** 100 Chestnut Ridge Rd. 201/391-7700; FAX 201/391-6648. 187 rms, 3 story. S $59-$89; D $59-$99; each addl $8; under 18 free; wkend rates. Crib free. TV; cable. Heated pool; poolside serv. Restaurant 7 am-2 pm; dining rm 11:30 am-10:30 pm; Sat from 5:30 pm. Rm serv. Bar 11:30-2 am; entertainment, dancing. Ck-out noon. Meeting rms. Bellhops. Valet serv. Gift shop. Exercise equipt; weights, bicycles. Cr cds: A, C, D, DS, MC, V.

Hotel

★ ★ ★ **MARRIOTT-PARK RIDGE.** *(300 Brae Blvd, Park Ridge 07656) Garden State Pkwy exit 172N (Grand Ave), then first 3 right turns.* 201/307-0800; FAX 201/307-0859. 289 units, 4 story. S, D $79-$137; suites $275; under 18 free; wkly, wkend rates. Crib avail. Pet accepted, some restrictions. TV; cable. Indoor/outdoor pool; poolside serv. Restaurant 6:30 am-10 pm; dining rm 5:30-10 pm. Bars 4:30 pm-2 am; pianist, dancing. Ck-out noon. Meeting rms. Concierge. Gift shop. Exercise rm: instructor, weights, bicycles, whirlpool, sauna. Refrigerators avail. Many private patios, balconies. Extensive grounds; small lake. *LUXURY LEVEL :* 89 rms. S, D from $149. Private lounge. Complimentary continental bkfst, refreshments. Cr cds: A, C, D, DS, JCB, MC, V.

Restaurant

★ ★ **VALENTINO'S.** *(103 Spring Valley Rd, Park Ridge) Garden State Pkwy exit 172, right on Grand Ave to 2nd light, right on Spring Valley Rd, approx 1 mi.* 201/391-2230. Hrs: 11:30 am-2:30 pm, 5-10 pm; Fri to 11 pm, Sat 5-11 pm. Closed Sun; some major hols. Res accepted. Italian menu. Bar. A la carte entrees: lunch $11-$20, dinner $14.95-$35. Specializes in veal, pasta, fish. Guitarist Mon, Thurs & Sat. Jacket. Cr cds: A, D, MC, V.

Moorestown (F-3)

(see Camden)

Morristown (C-4)

Settled: ca 1710 **Pop:** 16,189 **Elev:** 327 ft **Area code:** 201

Today, Morristown is primarily residential, but the iron industry, so desperately needed during the Revolutionary War, was responsible for the development of the town and the surrounding county. George Washington and his army spent two winters here, operating throughout the area until the fall of 1781. The first successful experiments with the telegraph were made in Morristown by Samuel F.B. Morse and Stephen Vail. Cartoonist Thomas Nast, writers Bret Harte and Frank Stockton and millionaire Otto Kahn all lived here. Morristown rises to a 597-foot peak at Fort Nonsense; the Whippany River runs through the town.

What to See and Do

1. **Morris Museum.** 6 Normandy Heights Rd. Art, science and history exhibits; permanent and changing. Musical, theatrical events; lectures and films. (Daily; closed hols) Sr citizen rate. Phone 538-0454. ¢¢

2. **Macculloch Hall Historical Museum.** 45 Macculloch Ave. Restored 1810 house and garden; home of George P. Macculloch, initiator of the Morris Canal, and his descendants for more than 140 years. American, European decorative arts from the 18th and 19th centuries. Illustrations by Thomas Nast. Garden. (Apr-Nov, Thurs & Sun afternoons; closed hols) Sr citizen rate. Phone 538-2404. ¢¢

3. **Schuyler-Hamilton House** (1760). 5 Olyphant Pl. Former house of Dr. Jabez Campfield. Alexander Hamilton courted Betsy Schuyler here. Period furniture; colonial garden. (Tues & Sun afternoons; other times by appt; closed Easter, Dec 25) Phone 267-4039. ¢

4. **Morristown National Historical Park** (see). Approx 3 mi S on US 202.

5. **Historic Speedwell.** 333 Speedwell Ave. Home and factory of Stephen Vail, iron master, who in 1818 manufactured the engine

for the SS *Savannah,* first steamship to cross the Atlantic. In 1838, Alfred Vail (Stephen's son), and Samuel F.B. Morse perfected the telegraph and first publicly demonstrated it here in the factory. Displays include period furnishings in the mansion, exhibit on Speedwell Iron Works, exhibits on history of the telegraph; water wheel, carriage house & granary. Gift shop. (May-Oct, Thurs-Sun; rest of yr, by appt) Sr citizen rate. Phone 540-0211. ¢¢

6. **Acorn Hall** (1853). 68 Morris Ave. Victorian Italianate house; original furnishings; reference library; restored garden. (Mar-Dec, Thurs & Sun, limited hrs; closed major hols) Phone 267-3465. ¢¢

7. **Fosterfields Historical Farm.** Kahdena Rd & NJ 24. Turn-of-the-century living-history farm (200 acres). Self-guided trail; displays; audiovisual presentations; workshops, farming demonstrations; restored Gothic-revival house. Visitor center. (Apr-Oct, Wed-Sun) Phone 326-7645. ¢¢-¢¢¢

8. **Frelinghuysen Arboretum.** 1¹/₂ mi NE via Morris Ave, Whippany Rd; entrance from E Hanover Ave. Features 127 acres of forest and open fields; natural and formal gardens; spring and fall bulb displays; labeled collections of trees and shrubs; Braille trail; gift shop. Grounds (daily). Phone 326-7600. **Free.**

(For further information contact the Historic Morris Visitors Center, 14 Elm St, 07960; 538-4576.)

(See Madison)

Motel

★ ★ **BEST WESTERN MORRISTOWN INN.** *270 South St (07960).* 201/540-1700; FAX 201/267-0241. 59 rms, 3 story, 14 kits. S $85-$105; D $95-$110; each addl $10; kit. units $87-$110; under 12 free; wkend rates. Crib free. TV; cable. Restaurant 6:30 am-2 pm, 5:30-9:30 pm. Ck-out noon. Coin lndry. Airport transportation. Exercise equipt; weights, bicycles, sauna. Colonial decor. Cr cds: A, C, D, DS, ER, MC, V.

D 🏃 ✈ 🚭 🔥 SC

Hotels

★ ★ ★ **GOVERNOR MORRIS HOTEL & CONFERENCE CENTER.** *2 Whippany Rd (07960), off I-287 exit 36.* 201/539-7300; res: 800/221-0241; FAX 201/984-1036. 198 rms, 6 story. S, D $129-$149; each addl $10; suites $149-$350; under 18 free; wkend rates. Crib free. TV; cable. Heated pool; poolside serv, lifeguard. Restaurant 6:30-2 am. Bar 11-2 am; entertainment Tues-Sun. Ck-out noon. Meeting rms. Tennis privileges. Exercise equipt; weight machine, bicycles. Lawn games. Refrigerator, wet bar in suites. Cr cds: A, C, D, DS, ER, MC, V.

D 🏃 ≈ ✈ 🚭 🔥 SC

★ ★ ★ **HEADQUARTERS PLAZA.** *3 Headquarters Plaza (07960).* 201/898-9100; res: 800/225-1942 (exc NJ), 800/225-1941 (NJ); FAX 201/292-0112. 256 rms, 16 story. S $140-$150; D $160-$170; each addl $20; under 12 free; wkend rates. Crib free. TV; cable. Indoor pool privileges. Restaurants 6 am-11 pm. Bars 11-2 am; entertainment Wed-Sat. Ck-out 1 pm. Meeting rms. Shopping arcade. Airport transportation. Health club privileges. **LUXURY LEVEL : CEO CLUB.** 36 rms, 4 suites, 2 floors. S $155-$160; D $175-$180; suites avail. Concierge. Private lounge. Complimentary full bkfst, refreshments. Cr cds: A, C, D, MC, V.

D 🚭 🔥 SC

★ ★ ★ **MADISON.** *1 Convent Rd (07961), at Madison Ave (NJ 24).* 201/285-1800; res: 800/526-0729; FAX 201/540-8566. 190 rms, 4 story. S $150-$200; D $170-$200; under 18 free; wkend rates. Crib free. TV; cable, in-rm movies. Indoor pool; poolside serv. Complimentary continental bkfst. Restaurants 7 am-11 pm. Bar 11-2 am; entertainment, dancing. Ck-out noon. Meeting rms. Concierge. Tennis, golf privileges. Exercise equipt; weight machines, bicycles, whirlpool, sauna. Some bathrm phones. Cr cds: A, C, D, DS, MC, V.

D 🏃 ≈ 🏃 🚭 🔥 SC

Restaurants

★ ★ ★ ★ **LE DELICE.** *(302 Whippany Rd, Whippany) 2¹/₂ mi NE of I-287 exit 35 (N) or 35A (S); 1¹/₂ mi S of NJ 10 on Whippany Rd (NJ Secondary Rte 511).* 201/884-2727. Hrs: 11:30 am-2:30 pm, 6-9:30 pm; Fri 11:30 am-2 pm, 6-10 pm; Sat 6-10 pm. Closed Sun; major hols. Res accepted. Contemporary French menu with Mediterranean accents. Serv bar. Wine cellar. A la carte entrees: lunch $11-$19, dinner $19-$29. Prix fixe: lunch (Tues-Fri) $18, dinner $25-$32. Specializes in rack of lamb, fresh fish, fresh game. California & French wines. Own baking. Entertainment Fri, Sat. Parking. Grows own herbs in summer. Menu with four seasonal changes. Chef-owned. Jacket. Cr cds: A, D, DS, MC.

★ ★ **LE PAPILLON.** *142 South St.* 201/539-8088. Hrs: 11:30 am-2:30 pm, 5-9:30 pm; Fri, Sat to 10:30 pm; Sun 5-9:30 pm. Res accepted. French menu. Bar. Semi-a la carte: lunch $6.95-$11.50, dinner $15.95-$21.50. Specializes in fresh fish & game. Parking. Mirrors, paintings on walls. Jacket. Cr cds: A, D, MC, V.

D

★ ★ **ROD'S 1890s RESTAURANT.** *(NJ 24, Convent Station) Approx 2¹/₂ mi E on NJ 24.* 201/539-6666. Hrs: 11:30 am-11 pm; early-bird dinner Mon-Sat 4:30-6 pm, Sun 4-6 pm; Sun brunch 11 am-3 pm. Closed Dec 25. Bar. Semi-a la carte: lunch $7.95-$14.95, dinner $13.95-$24.95. Sun brunch from $9.95. Child's meals. Specializes in prime beef, seafood, lobster. Salad bar. Entertainment. Valet parking. Display of authentic Victorian antiques. Large antique bar with wooden chandelier. Private dining avail in renovated railway cars by res. Family-owned. Jacket. Cr cds: A, C, D, MC, V.

D

Morristown National Historical Park (C-4)

(Approx 3 mi S of Morristown on US 202)

This national historical park, the first to be established and maintained by the federal government, was created by an Act of Congress in 1933. Its three units cover more than 1,600 acres, all but Jockey Hollow and the NJ Brigade Area being within Morristown's limits. The main body of the Continental Army stayed here in the winter of 1779-80.

Headquarters and museum (daily); Jockey Hollow buildings (summer, daily; rest of yr schedule varies, phone ahead; closed Jan 1, Thanksgiving, Dec 25). For further information contact Chief of Interpretation, Washington Place, Morristown 07960; 201/539-2085.

What to See and Do

1. **Historical Museum.** Washington Place, directly to the rear of Ford Mansion. Contains Washington memorabilia; period weapons and 18th-century artifacts; audiovisual programs. Sr citizen rate. ¢ Admission includes

   Ford Mansion. One of the finest early houses in Morristown was built in 1772-1774 by Colonel Jacob Ford, Jr, who produced gunpowder for American troops during the Revolution. His widow rented the house to the army for General and Mrs. Washington when the Continental Army spent the winter of 1779-80 here.

2. **Ft Nonsense.** Ann St. Its name came long after residents had forgotten the real reason for earthworks constructed here in 1777. Overlook commemorates fortifications which were built at Washington's order to defend military supplies stored in the village. **Free.**

3. **Jockey Hollow.** 4 mi SW of Morristown. The site of the Continental Army's winter quarters in 1779-80 and the 1781 mutiny of the Pennsylvania Line. Signs indicate locations of various brigades.

There are typical log huts and an officer's hut among other landmarks. Demonstrations of military and colonial farm life (summer). Visitor center has exhibits and audiovisual programs. **Free.**

4. **Wick House.** Jockey Hollow. Farmer Henry Wick lived here with his wife and daughter. Used as quarters by Major General Arthur St Clair in 1779-80. Restored with period furnishings. **Free.**

(For accommodations see Bernardsville, Morristown)

Mount Holly (F-3)

Settled: 1676 **Pop:** 10,639 **Elev:** 52 ft **Area code:** 609 **Zip:** 08060

The mountain that gives this old Quaker town its name is only 183 feet high. For two months in 1779, Mount Holly was the capital of the state; today, it is the seat of Burlington County.

What to See and Do

1. **John Woolman Memorial** (1783). 99 Branch St, ½ mi E. John Woolman, the noted Quaker abolitionist whose *Journal* is still appreciated today, owned the property on which this small, three-story red brick house was built; garden. Picnicking. (Mon-Fri by appt) Phone 267-3226. **Free.**

2. **Mansion at Smithville** (1840). On NJ 537, ½ mi W of US 206. Victorian mansion and village of inventor/entrepreneur Hezekiah B. Smith; home of the "Star" hi-wheel bicycle. Guided tours (May-Oct, Wed & Sun). Victorian Christmas tours (Dec; fee). Sr citizen rate. Phone 265-5068. ¢¢

3. **Burlington County Prison-Museum** (1810). 128 High St. Robert Mills, architect of the Washington Monument, designed this jail, said to be first fireproof building in US. Donation. For guided tour information phone 265-5068.

4. **Mount Holly Library.** 307 High St. Chartered in 1765 by King George III, the library is presently housed in Georgian mansion built in 1830. Historic Lyceum contains original crystal chandeliers, blue marble fireplaces, boxwood gardens; archives date to original 1765 collection. (Mon-Thurs & Sat, limited hrs) Phone 267-7111. **Free.**

(See Burlington)

Motel

★ ★ **HOWARD JOHNSON.** *Box 73, on NJ 541 at NJ Tpke exit 5. 609/267-6550; FAX 609/267-2575.* 90 rms, 2 story. S $56-$90; D $60-$90; each addl $7; under 12 free. Crib free. Pet accepted. TV. Pool; lifeguard, whirlpool, sauna. Playground. Restaurant 6 am-11 pm. Bar from 5 pm. Ck-out noon. Meeting rms. Cr cds: A, C, D, DS, JCB, MC, V.

Motor Hotel

✔ ★ ★ **DAYS INN.** *(Wrightstown-Cookstown Rd, Cookstown 08511) NJ 537E to McGuire Access Rd, left at 2nd light. 609/723-6500; FAX 609/723-7895.* 100 rms, 2 story. Mid-June-Sept: S, D $39-$95; each addl $5; suites $85-$225; under 16 free; wkend rates; higher rates hols; lower rates rest of yr. Crib free. TV; cable. Pool; whirlpool. Restaurant 6 am-10 pm. Rm serv from 3 pm. Bar. Ck-out 11 am. Refrigerators avail. Cr cds: A, C, D, DS, ER, JCB, MC, V.

D 🖼 ⚓ ✕ 🔥 SC

Restaurants

★ ★ ★ **BEAU RIVAGE.** *(128 Taunton Blvd, Medford) S on NJ 541, just S of Tuckerton Rd. 609/983-1999.* Hrs: 11:30 am-2:30 pm, 5:30-9:30 pm; Sat from 5:30 pm; Sun 4-8 pm. Closed most major hols; also 2 wks before Labor Day. Res accepted. French menu. Serv bar. Extensive wine cellar. Semi-a la carte: lunch $8.50-$12.50, dinner $16-$22. Specialties: beef Wellington, pheasant, fresh seafood. Own pastries. Parking. 2 dining areas, 1 upstairs. Sophisticated cuisine and formal service in country atmosphere. Jacket (dinner). Cr cds: A, D, MC, V.

D

★ ★ ★ **BRADDOCK'S TAVERN.** *(39 S Main St, Medford Village) S on NJ 541. 609/654-1604.* Hrs: 11:30 am-2:30 pm, 5:30-10 pm; Sun 11 am-3 pm, 4-9 pm. Closed Jan 1, Dec 25. Res accepted. Bar to 2 am. Semi-a la carte: lunch $5.75-$8.95, dinner $14.95-$22.95. Sun brunch $13.95. Child's meals. Specializes in prime rib, fresh fish. Own baking. Parking. Cr cds: A, C, D, MC, V.

D

✔ ★ ★ **CHARLEY'S OTHER BROTHER.** *NJ 537, ½ mi W of US 206. 609/261-1555.* Hrs: 11:30 am-2:30 pm, 5-9:30 pm; Fri, Sat to 10:30 pm; Sun 4-9 pm. Closed Dec 25. Res accepted. Bar. Semi-a la carte: lunch $4.50-$7.95, dinner $9.95-$15.95. Child's meals. Specializes in fresh seafood, steak, prime rib. Victorian decor; Tiffany lamps. Cr cds: A, D, DS, MC, V.

SC

Newark (C-5)

Settled: 1666 **Pop:** 275,221 **Elev:** 146 ft **Area code:** 201

Once a strict Puritan settlement, Newark has grown to become the largest city in the state and one of the country's leading manufacturing cities. Major insurance firms and banks have large offices in Newark, dominating the city's financial life. Newark was the birthplace of Stephen Crane (1871-1900), author of *The Red Badge of Courage,* and Mary Mapes Dodge (1838-1905), author of the children's book *Hans Brinker, or the Silver Skates.* Newark is also an educational center with Newark College of Rutgers University, College of Medicine and Dentistry of New Jersey, New Jersey Institute of Technology, Seton Hall Law School and Essex County College.

Transportation

Airport: See NEWARK INTL AIRPORT AREA.

Car Rental Agencies: See toll-free numbers under Introduction.

Public Transportation: Trains, buses (NJ Transit), phone 762-5100.

Rail Passenger Service: Amtrak 800/872-7245.

What to See and Do

1. **The Newark Museum.** 49 Washington St. Museum of art and science, with changing exhibitions. American paintings and sculpture, American and European decorative arts, classical art, the arts of Asia, the Americas and the Pacific, numismatics and the natural sciences. Also here are the Junior Museum, Mini Zoo, Dreyfuss Planetarium, Garden, with its 1784 schoolhouse and the Newark Fire Museum. Special programs, lectures, concerts; cafe open lunch. (Wed-Sun, afternoons; closed some major hols) Phone 596-6550. **Free.**

2. **New Jersey Historical Society.** 230 Broadway, at Taylor St. Museum with collections of paintings, prints, furniture, decorative arts; period room; special exhibitions. Reference and research

library of state and local history; manuscripts, documents, maps. (Wed-Fri; also 3rd Sat each month) Phone 483-3939. ¢¢

3. **The Wars of America.** Military Park, bounded by Broad St, Park Pl, Rector St, Raymond Blvd. Sculptured bronze group by Gutzon Borglum features 42 human figures representing soldiers in the major conflicts in US history. Other works by Borglum are

Bridge Memorial. N of Washington Park (Broad St, Washington Pl & Washington St). This sculpture of an Indian and a Puritan stands on the site of a colonial marketplace.

Statue of Abraham Lincoln. Essex Co Courthouse, Springfield Ave & Market St.

4. **Old Plume House.** 407 Broad St. Now the rectory of the adjoining House of Prayer Protestant Episcopal Church, it is thought to have been standing as early as 1710, which would make it the oldest building in Newark.

5. **Catholic Cathedral of the Sacred Heart.** 89 Ridge St, at Clifton & 6th Aves. French Gothic in design, it resembles the cathedral at Rheims. Hand-carved reredos. (Daily) Donation.

6. **Symphony Hall** (1925). 1020 Broad St. A 2,811-seat auditorium; home of New Jersey State Opera and the New Jersey Symphony Orchestra; also here is the famous Terrace Ballroom. Phone 643-4550; box office 643-8009.

(For further information contact the Convention & Visitors Bureau, One Newark Center, 07102; 622-3010.)

Newark Intl Airport Area

For additional accommodations, see NEWARK INTL AIRPORT AREA, which follows NEWARK.

(See Elizabeth, Jersey City)

Motor Hotel

★ ★ ★ **HILTON GATEWAY.** *Gateway Center, Raymond Blvd, N of McCarter Hwy (NJ 21) at Raymond Blvd.* 201/622-5000; FAX 201/622-2644. 253 rms, 10 story. S, D $119-$165; each addl $15; suites $235-$500; under 18 free; wkend rates. Crib free. TV; cable. Rooftop pool; lifeguard. Restaurant 6:30 am-10 pm; Sat, Sun from 7 am. Rm serv. Bar 11 am-midnight, Sat & Sun from noon; entertainment, dancing Wed-Fri. Ck-out noon. Meeting rms. Bellhops. Valet serv. Shopping arcade. Barber. Garage parking. Free airport transportation. Covered walkways to RR station. *LUXURY LEVEL : EXECUTIVE FLOOR.* 29 rms. S, D $155-$180; suites $235-$500. Concierge. Private lounge. Complimentary continental bkfst, refreshments, bar. Cr cds: A, C, D, DS, ER, JCB, MC, V.

D ⊠ ⊠ ⊠ SC

Restaurant

★ ★ **DON'S 21.** *1034 McCarter Hwy.* 201/622-6221. Hrs: noon-10 pm. Res required Sat. Italian, Spanish, Portuguese menu. Bar to midnight. A la carte entrees: lunch $9.95-$20.95, dinner $11.95-$20.95. Italian band Sat. Parking. Jacket. Cr cds: A, D, MC, V.

Newark Intl Airport Area (C-5)

Services and Information

Information: 201/961-6000 or 800/247-7433.
Lost and Found: 201/961-6230.

Weather: 201/624-8118.

Club Lounges: Presidents Club (Continental); Ambassadors Club (TWA); Red Carpet Club (United); USAir Club (US Air).

(See Newark)

Motels

✔ ★ ★ **BEST WESTERN-NEWARK AIRPORT.** *(450 US 1S, Newark 07114)* Off NJ Tpke exit 14, S on US 1/9. 201/242-0900; FAX 201/242-8480. 191 rms, 8 story. S, D $55.95-$89.95; each addl $5; suites $99-$120; under 18 free; wkend rates. Crib free. TV; cable. Restaurant 6:30 am-midnight. Rm serv. Bar from noon. Ck-out noon. Coin lndry. Meeting rms. Sundries. Free airport transportation. Cr cds: A, C, D, DS, MC, V.

D ✈ ⊠ ⊠ SC

★ ★ ★ **COURTYARD BY MARRIOTT.** *(600 US 1/9, Newark 07114)* NJ Tpke exit 14, S on US 1/9. 201/643-8500; FAX 201/648-0662. 146 rms, 3 story. S $104; D $114; suites $125-$135; children free; wkly, wkend rates. Crib free. TV; cable. Indoor pool. Complimentary coffee in rms. Restaurant 6:30 am-11 pm. Bar from 4 pm. Ck-out noon. Coin lndry. Meeting rms. Valet serv. Sundries. Free airport, RR station transportation. Exercise equipt; weight machine, bicycles, whirlpool. Some balconies. Cr cds: A, C, D, DS, MC, V.

D ⊠ ⊠ ✈ ⊠ ⊠ SC

✔ ★ **HOWARD JOHNSON.** *(50 Port St, Newark 07114)* Off NJ Tpke exit 14, Frontage Rd. 201/344-1500; FAX 201/344-3311. 170 rms, 3 story. S, D $49.99-$99.99; children free; wkend rates. Crib free. TV; cable. Restaurant 6-1 am. Ck-out noon. Coin lndry. Meeting rms. Gift shop. Free airport transportation. Cr cds: A, C, D, DS, MC, V.

D ✈ ⊠ ⊠ SC

Motor Hotel

★ ★ **HOLIDAY INN INTL AIRPORT-NORTH.** *(160 Holiday Plaza, Newark 07114)* Off NJ Tpke exit 14, opp N terminal; use Service Rd. 201/589-1000; FAX 201/589-2799. 234 rms, 10 story. S $69-$93; D $79-$123; each addl $5; under 18 free; wkend rates by res. Crib free. Pet accepted, some restrictions. TV; cable. Pool; lifeguard. Restaurant 6:30 am-11 pm; Sat, Sun 7 am-10:30 pm. Rm serv. Bar 11-2 am; Sun from 1 pm; entertainment, dancing Wed-Sat. Ck-out noon. Meeting rms. Bellhops. Sundries. Gift shop. Free airport transportation. Tennis. Lawn games. Some in-rm steam baths. Cr cds: A, C, D, DS, JCB, MC, V.

D ⊠ ⊠ ⊠ ✈ ⊠ ⊠ SC

Hotels

★ ★ ★ **HILTON-NEWARK AIRPORT.** *(1170 Spring St, Elizabeth 07201)* Off NJ Tpke exit 13 A. 908/351-3900; FAX 908/351-9556. 374 rms, 12 story. S, D $125-$175; each addl $10; suites $225-$700; children free; wkend rates. Crib free. TV; cable. Indoor pool. Restaurant 6:30 am-11 pm. Bar 4 pm-2 am. Ck-out noon. Convention facilities. Gift shop. Free airport, RR station transportation. Exercise equipt; weight machines, bicycles, whirlpool, sauna. Cr cds: A, C, D, DS, ER, JCB, MC, V.

D ⊠ ⊠ ✈ ⊠ ⊠ SC

★ ★ ★ **MARRIOTT-AIRPORT.** *(Newark Intl Airport, Newark 07114)* On airport grounds; follow signs from main terminal. 201/623-0006; FAX 201/623-7618. 590 rms, 10 story. S, D $125-$150; suites $400-$500; under 18 free; wkend rates. Crib free. Pet accepted, some restrictions. TV; cable. Indoor/outdoor pool; poolside serv. Restaurants 6 am-11 pm. Rm serv 24 hrs. Bars 11:30-1:30 am. Ck-out noon. Convention facilities. Concierge. Free airport transportation. Exercise equipt; weights, bicycles, whirlpool, sauna. Some refrigerators. Oriental carpets in lobby. *LUXURY LEVEL : CONCIERGE FLOOR.* 60 rms,

3 suites. S, D $175. Private lounge, honor bar. Complimentary continental bkfst, refreshments. Cr cds: A, C, D, DS, ER, JCB, MC, V.

[icons] D ★ ≈ ✕ ✈ ⊠ ♨ SC

★ ★ ★ RADISSON-NEWARK AIRPORT. (128 Frontage Rd, Newark 07114) Off NJ Tpke exit 14; use Service Rd. 201/690-5500; FAX 201/465-7195. 502 rms, 12 story. S, D $99-$125; each addl $10; suites $325-$495; under 18 free; wkend rates. Crib free. TV; cable. Indoor pool; poolside serv, lifeguard. Restaurants 6:30 am-11 pm. Bar 2 pm-2 am; entertainment Mon-Fri. Ck-out noon. Convention facilities. Concierge. Gift shop. Free airport transportation. Exercise equipt; weights, bicycles, whirlpool. Game rm. Refrigerators avail. Balconies. Atrium. LUXURY LEVEL : PLAZA CLUB LEVEL. 45 rms. S $129; D $144. Private lounge. Complimentary continental bkfst, refreshments. Cr cds: A, C, D, DS, MC, V.

[icons] D ≈ ✕ ✈ ⊠ ♨ SC

New Brunswick (D-4)

Settled: 1681 **Pop:** 41,711 **Elev:** 42 ft **Area code:** 908

New Brunswick, the seat of Middlesex County, is on the south bank of the Raritan River. It is both a college town and a diversified commercial and retail city. Rutgers University, the eighth oldest institution of higher learning in the country and the only state university with a colonial charter, was founded in 1766 as Queens College, and opened in 1771 with a faculty of one—aged 18. Livingston College, Cook College and Douglass College (for women), all part of the university, are also located here. One of New Brunswick's most important industries is Johnson and Johnson; their company headquarters are located downtown. Joyce Kilmer, the poet, was born in New Brunswick; his house, at 17 Joyce Kilmer Avenue, is open to visitors.

What to See and Do

1. **Buccleuch Mansion.** George St & Easton Ave, in 78-acre Buccleuch Park. Built in 1739 by Anthony White, son-in-law of Lewis Morris, a colonial governor of New Jersey. Period rooms. (June-Oct, Sun afternoons; closed hols) Under 10 only with adult. Phone 297-2438. **Free.**

2. **Hungarian Heritage Center.** 300 Somerset St. Museum of changing exhibits that focus on Hungarian folk life, fine and folk art; library, archives. (Daily exc Mon; closed major hols) Donation. Phone 846-5777.

3. **Rutgers-The State University** (1766). (49,000 students) Multiple campuses include 26 colleges serving students at all levels through postdoctoral studies; main campus on College Ave. For general information phone 932-1766; for campus tours phone 932-7881. On campus are

   Jane Voorhees Zimmerli Art Museum. George & Hamilton Sts. Paintings from early 16th century through the present; changing exhibits. (Tues-Fri, also Sat & Sun afternoons; closed major hols) Donation. Phone 932-7237.

   Geology Museum. Displays of New Jersey minerals; dinosaur; mammals, including a mastodon; Egyptian exhibit with mummy. (Mon afternoons & Tues-Fri mornings; closed hols) Phone 932-7243. **Free.**

4. **Rutgers University Display Gardens.** Ryder's Lane (US 1). Features extensive display of American holly. (Daily; closed Dec) **Free.**

5. **George Street Playhouse.** 9 Livingston Ave. Regional theater; seven-show season of plays and musicals; touring Outreach program for students. A 367-seat house. Stage II Theater; cafe; cabaret. (Daily) Phone 246-7717 (box office).

6. **Crossroads Theatre.** 7 Livingston Ave. Professional African-American theater company offering plays, musicals, touring pro-

grams and workshops. (Sept-May, Tues-Sun) For schedule, information phone 249-5560.

(For further information contact the Middlesex County Chamber of Commerce, 1091 Aaron Rd, North Brunswick, 08902; 908/821-1700.)

Annual Event

Middlesex County Fair. Cranbury-South River Rd, in East Brunswick. Aug.

Seasonal Event

Rutgers SummerFest. Rutgers Arts Center. Features music, dance, visual arts exhibits and theater performances. June-Aug.

Motel

✔ ★ McINTOSH INN. (764 NJ 18, East Brunswick 08816) 6 mi S on NJ 18, 4 mi off NJ Tpke exit 9. 908/238-4900; FAX 908/257-2023. 107 rms, 2 story. S $41.95-$44.95; D $47.95-$56.95; each addl $3. TV; cable. Restaurant adj open 24 hrs. Ck-out 11 am. Cr cds: A, D, MC, V.

[icons] D ⊠ ♨ SC

Motor Hotels

★ ★ HOLIDAY INN-SOMERSET. (195 Davidson Ave, Somerset 08873) Off NJ 527 at I-287 exit 6. 908/356-1700; FAX 908/356-0939. 280 rms, 6 story. S, D $85-$105; under 19 free; wkend rates. Crib free. Pet accepted. TV; cable. Heated pool; poolside serv, lifeguard. Complimentary coffee in rms. Restaurant 6:30 am-2:30 pm, 5-10:30 pm. Rm serv. Bar 11:30-1 am. Ck-out noon. Convention facilities. Bellhops. Valet serv. Sundries. Gift shop. Airport transportation. Exercise equipt; weight machine, bicycles. Health club privileges. Cr cds: A, C, D, DS, ER, MC, V.

[icons] D ★ ≈ ✕ ⊠ ♨ SC

★ ★ MADISON SUITES. (11 Cedar Grove Ln, Somerset 08873) 1/2 mi SE of I-287, exit 6, just off Easton Ave. 908/563-1000; FAX 908/563-0352. 83 suites, 2 story. Suites $85-$110; under 17 free; wkend rates. TV. Complimentary full bkfst. Ck-out noon. Meeting rms. Valet serv. Health club privileges. Many refrigerators. Cr cds: A, C, D, MC, V.

[icons] ⊠ ♨ SC

★ ★ SHERATON INN. (195 Hwy 18, East Brunswick 08816) NJ 18 & Eggers St, at NJ Tpke exit 9. 908/828-6900; FAX 908/937-4838. 137 rms, 4 story. S $89.50-$119.50; D $89.50-$129.50; each addl $10; under 18 free. Crib free. Pet accepted, some restrictions. TV; cable, in-rm movies. Pool. Coffee in rms. Restaurant 7 am-10 pm. Rm serv. Bar 11:30-1:30 am; entertainment Fri & Sat. Ck-out noon. Meeting rms. Valet serv. Exercise equipt; weights, treadmill. Health club privileges. Cr cds: A, C, D, DS, ER, MC, V.

[icons] ★ ≈ ✕ ⊠ ♨ SC

Hotels

★ ★ ★ EMBASSY SUITES. (121 Centennial Ave, Piscataway 08854) Off I-287 exit 5. 908/980-0500; FAX 908/980-9473. 220 kit. suites, 5 story. Kit. suites $145; each addl $20; under 12 free; wkend rates. Crib free. TV; cable. Indoor pool; lifeguard. Complimentary full bkfst, refreshments. Restaurant 11 am-2 pm, 5-10 pm. Bar to midnight. Ck-out 1 pm. Coin lndry. Meeting rms. Gift shop. Exercise equipt; weight machine, bicycle, whirlpool, sauna. Game rm. Atrium. Cr cds: A, C, D, DS, MC, V.

[icons] D ≈ ✕ ⊠ ♨ SC

★ ★ ★ **HILTON AND TOWERS.** *(3 Tower Center Blvd, East Brunswick 08816) Off I-95 exit 9. 908/828-2000; FAX 908/828-6958.* 405 rms, 15 story. S $120-$140; D $135-$155; each addl $20; suites $250-$750; under 18 free; wkend rates. Crib free. TV; cable. Indoor pool. Restaurant 6:30 am-10 pm. Rm serv 24 hrs. Bar 11-2 am; entertainment, exc Sun. Ck-out noon. Convention facilities. Concierge. Gift shop. Local airport transportation. Exercise equipt; weight machine, bicycles, whirlpool, sauna. Some bathrm phones, minibars; refrigerators avail. *LUXURY LEVEL : TOWERS.* 38 rms, 2 suites. S $130-$150; D $145-$165; suites $250-$750. Private lounge. Complimentary continental bkfst, refreshments. Coffee in rms. Cr cds: A, C, D, DS, ER, MC, V.

[D] [icons] [SC]

★ ★ ★ **HYATT REGENCY.** *2 Albany St (08901). 908/873-1234; FAX 908/873-1382.* 286 rms, 6 story. S $150; D $170; suites $250-$400; under 18 free; wkend rates. Crib free. TV; cable, in-rm movies. Indoor pool. Restaurant 6:30 am-11 pm. Bar 11-1 am; pianist. Ck-out noon. Convention facilities. Gift shop. Garage. Tennis. Exercise equipt; weights, bicycles, whirlpool, sauna. Refrigerators avail. Some balconies. Cr cds: A, C, D, DS, ER, JCB, MC, V.

[D] [icons] [SC]

★ ★ ★ **MARRIOTT-SOMERSET.** *(110 Davidson Ave, Somerset 08873) On NJ 527 at I-287 exit 6. 908/560-0500; FAX 908/560-3669.* 434 rms, 11 story. S $120; D $135; each addl $15; under 17 free; wkend rates. Crib free. TV; cable. Indoor/outdoor pool; poolside serv (summer). Restaurant 6:30 am-11 pm; Sat, Sun from 7 am; dining room 6-10 pm, closed Sun. Bar noon-2 am; entertainment, dancing. Ck-out 1 pm. Meeting rms. Concierge. Gift shop. Beauty shop. Tennis. Exercise rm; instructor, weight machines, bicycles, whirlpool, sauna. Some bathrm phones. Refrigerators avail. Some balconies. Cr cds: A, C, D, DS, JCB, MC, V.

[D] [icons] [SC]

★ ★ ★ **RADISSON SOMERSET.** *(200 Atrium Dr, Somerset 08873) Off I-287 Easton Ave exit 6, left on Davidson Ave. 908/469-2600; FAX 908/560-8043.* 361 rms, 6 story. S, D $90; each addl $15; suites $165-$450; family, wkend rates. Crib free. Pet accepted, some restrictions; $15. TV; cable, in-rm movies. 2 pools, 1 indoor; poolside serv, lifeguard. Restaurant 6:30 am-2 pm; dining rm 5:30-10 pm. Bar 2 pm-1:30 am; entertainment, dancing Fri-Sat. Ck-out 1 pm. Gift shop. Tennis. Exercise equipt; weights, bicycles, whirlpool. Game rm. Refrigerator in suites. Private patios. Cr cds: A, C, D, DS, ER, JCB, MC, V.

[D] [icons] [SC]

Restaurants

★ ★ ★ **THE FROG AND THE PEACH.** *29 Dennis St. 908/846-3216.* Hrs: 11:30 am-2:30 pm, 5:30-10:30 pm; Sat from 5:30 pm; Sun 4:30-9:30 pm. Closed Dec 25. Res accepted. Bar 11:30-2 am. A la carte entrees: lunch $7-$15, dinner $17-$28.50. Specializes in fresh seasonal entrees. Own baking. Parking. Outdoor dining. 1876 newspaper print shop with contemporary decor. Antique bar from Brooklyn waterfront saloon. Cr cds: A, C, D, DS, MC, V.

[D]

★ ★ **LA FONTANA.** *120 Albany St. 908/249-7500.* Hrs: 11:30 am-2:30 pm, 5:30-10 pm; Fri to 11 pm; Sat 5:30-11 pm. Closed Sun. Res accepted. Italian menu. Bar. Wine cellar. A la carte entrees: lunch $15, dinner $18-$22. Child's meals. Specializes in aristocratic-style Italian cuisine. Valet parking. 1920s Old World elegance. Jacket. Cr cds: A, D, DS, MC, V.

[D]

✔ ★ **MARITA'S CANTINA.** *1 Penn Plaza. 908/247-3840.* Hrs: 11:30-2 am; Sun 3 pm-1 am. Closed Thanksgiving, Dec 25. Res accepted. Mexican menu. Bar to 2 am. Semi-a la carte: lunch, dinner $2.95-$10.95. Buffet (Mon-Fri): lunch $5.95. Child's meals. Own desserts. Entertainment Tues, Thurs. Parking. Outdoor dining. Cr cds: A, C, D, MC, V.

[D]

★ **RUSTY NAIL.** *(US 130 S, North Brunswick) 4 mi S on US 130, 1 1/2 mi S of jct US 1 & US 130. 908/821-4141.* Hrs: 11:30 am-10 pm; Sun from 12:30 pm. Res accepted. Semi-a la carte: lunch $4.25-$7.25, dinner $10.95-$16.95. Child's meals. Specializes in prime roast beef. Salad bar. Parking. Cr cds: A, C, D, DS, MC, V.

Newfoundland (B-4)

Pop: 900 (est) **Elev:** 756 ft **Area code:** 201 **Zip:** 07435

What to See and Do

1. **Craigmeur Ski Area.** 2 mi S on Green Pond Rd (NJ 513) off NJ 23. Area has 1 double chairlift, T-bar, 2 rope tows; patrol, school, rentals; snowmaking; restaurant, cafeteria, bar. Four runs, longest run one-third mile; vertical drop 250 feet. (Dec-Mar, daily) Phone 697-4500. ¢¢¢¢

2. **Fairy Tale Forest.** NW via NJ 23, Oak Ridge Rd exit. There are 20 acres of enchanted woodlands. Features life-size storybook characters; animated three-ring circus; Christmas town; Candy Rock Line train ride; picnic area. (June 15-Labor Day, daily; May-mid June & after Labor Day-Oct 30, Sat-Sun) Phone 697-5656. ¢¢¢

(For accommodations see Wayne, also see Paterson)

Ocean City (J-4)

Pop: 15,512 **Elev:** 4 ft **Area code:** 609 **Zip:** 08226

Families from all over the country come to this popular resort year after year, as do conventions and religious conferences. In accordance with its founder's instructions, liquor cannot be sold here. Ocean City is an island that lies between the Atlantic Ocean and Great Egg Harbor. It has eight miles of beaches, more than two miles of boardwalk, an enclosed auditorium on the pier and excellent swimming, fishing, boating, golf and tennis.

What to See and Do

1. **Ocean City Historical Museum.** 1735 Simpson Ave, at 17th St. Victorian furnishings and fashions; doll exhibit; local shipwreck; historical Ocean City photographic exhibit; gift shop. (Apr-Dec, Mon-Fri, also Sat afternoons; rest of yr, Tues-Sat afternoons) Donation. Phone 399-1801.

2. **Historic House.** 1139 Wesley Ave. Furnishings and fashions circa 1920-1930. (Apr-Dec, daily exc Sun) Tours. Donation. Phone 399-1801.

(For further information contact the Public Relations Dept, City of Ocean City, 9th & Asbury Ave; 399-6111, ext 222, or 800/BEACH-NJ.)

Annual Events

Flower Show. Music Pier. June.

Baseball Card Convention. June.

Night in Venice. Decorated boat parade. Mid-July.

Hermit Crab Race, Miss Crustacean Contest. 6th St Beach. Crab beauty pageant, races. Phone 399-6111, ext 222. Early Aug.

Boardwalk Art Show. International and regional artists. Aug.

Seasonal Event

Concerts. Music Pier. Pops orchestra and dance band. Sun-Wed. Late June-early Sept.

(See Atlantic City)

Motels

★ ★ ★ **BEACH CLUB HOTEL.** *1280 Boardwalk, at 13th St.* 609/399-8555; FAX 609/398-4379. 82 rms, 3 story. Mid-June-Labor Day: S, D $148-$205; each addl $10; higher rates wkends, May-mid-June, Labor Day-Nov. Closed rest of yr. Crib free. TV; cable . Pool; wading pool, lifeguard. Restaurant 7 am-9 pm. Rm serv. Ck-out 11 am. Coin lndry. Bellhops. Golf privileges. Refrigerators. Balconies. Sun deck. On beach. Cr cds: A, D, MC, V.

★ **DAYS INN.** *Box 415, 7th St & Boardwalk.* 609/398-2200; FAX 609/391-2050. 80 rms, 4 story, 39 kit. suites. June-Aug: S, D $55-$190; each addl $10; kit. suites $70-$205; wkly rates; higher rates sporting events; lower rates Apr-May & Sept-Oct. Closed rest of yr. Crib free. TV; cable. Heated pool; lifeguard. Restaurant nearby. Ck-out 11 am. Coin lndry. Bellhops. Balconies. Ocean ½ blk. Cr cds: A, DS, MC, V.

★ ★ **FORUM.** *Box 448, 8th St, Ocean to Atlantic.* 609/399-8700; res: 800/228-8703. 58 rms, 2-3 story. July-Aug (3-day min): S, D $46-$112; each addl $8; some wkend rates; lower rates Apr-May, Sept-Oct. Closed rest of yr. Crib avail. TV. Heated pool; wading pool, lifeguard. Ck-out noon. Coin lndry. Game rm. Rec rm. Refrigerators. Picnic tables. Sun deck. Cr cds: MC, V.

★ ★ **IMPALA.** *10th St at Ocean Ave.* 609/399-7500; FAX 609/398-4379. 109 units in 2 bldgs, 2 story. July-Aug; S, D $99-$130; kit. units $990-$1,500/wk; lower rates rest of yr. Crib free. TV; cable. 2 pools, 1 heated; wading pool, lifeguard. Restaurant 7 am-9 pm. Rm serv. Ck-out 11 am. Meeting rms. Refrigerators. Sun deck. Cr cds: A, D, MC, V.

★ **PAVILION.** *801 Atlantic Ave.* 609/399-2600; res: 800/523-5225. 80 rms, 3 story. Early July-early Sept (3-day min wkends): S, D $92-$106; kit. units $150; lower rates Mar-June & early Sept-Nov; closed rest of yr. Crib avail. TV; cable. Heated pool; wading pool, poolside serv, lifeguard. Restaurant 7:30 am-9 pm. Rm serv. Ck-out 11 am. Coin lndry. Refrigerators. On beach. Cr cds: A, DS, MC, V.

★ ★ **PIER 4 ON THE BAY.** *(6 Broadway Ave, Somers Point 08244)* 1 mi E of Garden State Pkwy exit 30. 609/927-9141. 72 kit. units, 4 story. Early July-early Sept (3-day min hols): S, D $99-$139; under 16 free; lower rates rest of yr. Crib avail. TV. Pool; wading pool, lifeguard. Complimentary continental bkfst. Restaurant adj 11:30 am-10 pm. Ck-out 11 am. Coin lndry. Balconies. On bay. Cr cds: A, C, D, DS, MC, V.

★ ★ **RESIDENCE INN BY MARRIOTT.** *(900 Mays Landing Rd, Somers Point 08244)* 3 mi NW on NJ 52, then W on Mays Landing Rd; E of Garden State Pkwy exits 29N, 30S. 609/927-6400; FAX 609/926-0145. 120 kit. suites, 2 story. Memorial Day-Labor Day: S, D $120-$180; each addl $10; under 12 free; wkly rates; lower rates rest of yr. Crib $10. TV; cable. Heated pool; lifeguard. Complimentary continental bkfst. Bar (wine, beer) 5-7 pm Mon-Thurs. Ck-out 11 am. Coin lndry. Meeting rms. Valet serv. Casino transportation. Golf. Health

club privileges. Rec rm. Some private patios, balconies. Picnic tables, grills. Cr cds: A, C, D, DS, JCB, MC, V.

★ ★ **SANTA BARBARA.** *10th St at Wesley Ave.* 609/398-4700; res: 800/262-4456; FAX 609/398-4710. 78 kit. suites, 5 story. July-Aug: S, D $128; wkly rates; lower rates rest of yr. Crib avail. TV; cable, in-rm movies avail. Pool; lifeguard. Complimentary coffee in lobby. Restaurant nearby. Ck-out 11 am. Coin lndry. Covered parking. Exercise equipt; weight machine, bicycles. Balconies. Ocean 1 blk. Cr cds: DS, MC, V.

Motor Hotel

★ ★ ★ **PORT-O-CALL.** *Box 89, 1510 Boardwalk.* 609/399-8812; res: 800/334-4546; FAX 609/399-0387. 99 rms, 9 story. June-Sept: S, D $144-$204; each addl $15; penthouse apt $500; under 12 free; lower rates rest of yr. Crib free. TV; cable. Pool; sauna, lifeguard. Free supervised child's activities (June-Aug). Coffee in rms. Restaurant 7 am-2 pm, 5-8 pm; Sun 8:30 am-1:30 pm, 5-8 pm. Rm serv. Ck-out 11 am. Coin lndry. Meeting rms. Bellhops. Sundries. Barber, beauty shop. Golf privileges. Refrigerators. Balconies. On ocean. Cr cds: A, C, D, DS, MC, V.

Hotel

★ ★ ★ **FLANDERS.** *PO Box 29, Boardwalk at 11th St.* 609/399-1000; res: 800/345-0211; FAX 609/399-0194. 204 rms, 6 story, some half-baths. Late June-early Sept: S $74-$84; D $114-$150; each addl $35; family rates; MAP avail; varied lower rates rest of yr. Crib free. Parking $3. TV. Heated pool; lifeguard. Restaurants 8-10 am, noon-1:30 pm, 6-8 pm (jacket & tie). Ck-out noon. Meeting rms. Concierge. Shopping arcade. Barber, beauty shop. Miniature golf. Rec rm. Lawn games. Well-maintained older resort-type hotel. On ocean. Cr cds: A, MC, V.

Restaurants

★ ★ **CRAB TRAP.** *(Somers Pt Circle, Somers Point)* 1 mi E of Garden State Pkwy exit 30. 609/927-7377. Hrs: 11-2 am. Closed Dec 24 & 25. Bar. Semi-a la carte: lunch $4.75-$9.95, dinner $10.25-$26.95. Child's meals. Specialties: stuffed lobster tail, prime rib. Entertainment. Parking. Nautical decor. On the bay. Family-owned. Cr cds: A, C, D, DS, MC, V.

★ ★ **MAC'S.** *(908 Shore Rd, Somers Point)* 1 blk N of Somers Pt Circle. 609/927-4360. Hrs: 3:30-11 pm. Closed Thanksgiving, Dec 25. Res accepted. Italian, Amer menu. Bar. Semi-a la carte: dinner $9.95-$19.95. Child's meals. Specializes in seafood, steak. Parking. Family-owned. Cr cds: A, C, D, DS, MC, V.

Palisades Interstate Parks (B-6)

(Reached via Palisades Interstate Pkwy, starting at New Jersey end of George Washington Bridge; US 9W, NJ/NY 17, Dewey Thrwy exit 13)

This 81,067-acre system of conservation and recreation areas extends along the west side of the Hudson River from the George Washington Bridge at Fort Lee, New Jersey (see) to Saugerties, New York. Its main unit is the 51,679-acre tract of Bear Mountain and Harriman (New York) state parks; the two are contiguous.

Bear Mountain (5,066 acres) extends westward from the Hudson River opposite Peekskill. Only 45 miles from New York City via the Palisades Interstate Parkway, this is one of the most popular recreation areas, with year-round facilities, mostly for one-day visits. Area includes swimming pool, bathhouse; fishing, small game fields; boating on Hessian Lake. Nature trails. Cafeteria. Inn. Ice-skating; square dances on the rink in July and August.

Perkins Memorial Drive leads to the top of Bear Mountain, where there is a picnic area and a sightseeing tower. Near the site of Fort Clinton, just west of Bear Mountain Bridge, is the Trailside Museum, with exhibits of local flora, fauna, geology and history (daily; free).

Harriman (46,613 acres), southwest of Bear Mountain, includes much wilder country with several lakes. Swimming beaches (Lakes Tiorati, Welch and Sebago); fishing; boating. Miles of scenic drives, Tent camping (Lake Welch), cabins (Lake Sebago).

Many smaller parks are located in the New Jersey section of the park system.

Alpine Area (12 acres), off Henry Hudson Drive, east of Alpine. This area has fishing; boat basin. Hiking. Picnicking, concession (seasonal). Outdoor concerts in summer. (Daily, weather permitting)

Englewood-Bloomers Area (13 acres), off Henry Hudson Drive, east of jct Palisades Interstate Parkway & NJ 505 in Englewood Cliffs. This area offers fishing; boat basin. Hiking. Picnicking, concession (seasonal). (Daily, weather permitting)

Ross Dock (14 acres), off Henry Hudson Drive, north of George Washington Bridge. Near the southern end of the park system, this area has fishing; boat launching ramp. Hiking. Picnicking, playgrounds. (Apr-Oct, daily, weather permitting)

Fort Lee Historic Park. Hudson Terrace. This 33-acre facility presents the story of Washington's retreat from Fort Lee in 1776. Visitor's Center/Museum (Mar-Dec, Wed-Sun) offers two floors of exhibits; audiovisual displays; a short film; general information; special events. On grounds (daily, daylight hrs) are 18th-century soldiers' hut, reconstructed gun batteries, a rifle parapet; overlooks with scenic views of the George Washington Bridge, the Palisades, the Hudson River and the New York skyline. Parking fee (May-Sept, daily; Apr & Oct-mid-Nov, wkends & hols). No pets, bicycles or fires. Phone 461-1776. ¢¢

There are fees for parking and special events. For further information on the New Jersey section contact Palisades Interstate Park Commission, PO Box 155, Alpine 07620; 201/768-1360. Further information on the New York section can be obtained from Palisades Interstate Park Commission, Administration Building, Bear Mountain, NY 10911; 914/786-2701.

(For accommodations see Fort Lee, Hackensack)

Paramus (B-5)

Settled: 1660 **Pop:** 25,067 **Elev:** 58 ft **Area code:** 201 **Zip:** 07652

This old Dutch farm community was an important hub of transportation as long ago as the Revolutionary War; western Paramus became headquarters for the Continental Army as a result. Paramus has grown as a residential community from 4,000 inhabitants in 1946, to its present size.

What to See and Do

1. **Bergen Museum of Art & Science.** Ridgewood & Farview Aves. Features Dwarkskill and Hackensack mastodons; nature room; birds and minerals of Bergen County; Native American artifacts; galleries with changing exhibits. (Daily exc Mon; closed major hols) Phone 265-1248. **Free.**

2. **New Jersey Children's Museum.** 599 Industrial Ave. Interactive displays in 30 rms. Includes aviation, firefighting, TV studio, hospital. Gift shop. (Daily; closed some hols) Phone 262-5151. ¢¢¢

3. **Schoolhouse Museum.** 650 E Glen Ave, at NJ 17, in Ridgewood. Exhibits in 1873 schoolhouse depict life from colonial times through 19th century, with emphasis on local history. Native American relics; early maps; Dutch genealogies; farm implements; doll and toy displays; clothing. Tours (by appt). (May-late Oct, Sun afternoons; closed hols) Phone 652-4584 or 447-3242 (recording). **Free.**

4. **Van Saun County Park.** 216 Forest Ave, 1½ mi N of NJ 4. Fishing lake. Bike trail; tennis (fee); horseshoes, shuffleboard. Ice-skating, sledding. Picnicking, concession, playgrounds, ball fields (permit). Zoo; train, pony rides (fees). Garden surrounding historic Washington Spring; farmyard. Park (daily). Phone 599-6124; zoo 262-3771. **Free.**

(For further information contact the Chamber of Commerce, 80 E Ridgewood Ave, PO Box 325; 261-3344.)

Motel

★★ **HOWARD JOHNSON LODGE.** *393 NJ 17S, Garden State Pkwy N exit 163.* 201/265-4200; FAX 201/265-0247. 81 rms, 3 story. S $67-$80; D $75-$85; each addl $7; under 18 free. Crib free. Pet accepted, some restrictions. TV; cable. Pool. Restaurant 7 am-11 pm; Fri, Sat to 1 am, Sun from 7:30 am. Ck-out noon. Coin lndry. Meeting rms. Private patios, balconies. Cr cds: A, C, D, DS, ER, JCB, MC, V.

Motor Hotel

★★★ **RADISSON.** *601 From Rd, adj to Paramus Park Mall, Garden State Pkwy exit 165.* 201/262-6900; FAX 201/262-4955. 120 rms, 2 story. S $105; D $120; each addl $10; wkend rates. Crib free. Pet accepted, some restrictions. TV; cable. Complimentary coffee in rms. Restaurant 6:30 am-10:30 pm; Sat & Sun from 7 am. Rm serv. Bar; entertainment, dancing Fri & Sat. Ck-out noon. Coin lndry. Meeting rms. Bellhops. Sundries. Refrigerators. Cr cds: A, C, D, DS, ER, MC, V.

Parsippany (C-4)

Pop: 48,478 **Elev:** 282 ft **Area code:** 201 **Zip:** 07054

Motel

 ★ **HoJo INN.** *625 US 46.* 201/882-8600; FAX 201/882-3493. 117 rms, 3 story. S $44.95-$49.95; D $49.95-$59.95; under 16 free; wkly rates. Crib $6. TV; cable. Complimentary continental bkfst Mon-Fri. Complimentary coffee in lobby. Restaurant nearby. Ck-out noon. Coin lndry. Meeting rm. Refrigerators avail. Cr cds: A, C, D, DS, ER, JCB, MC, V.

Motor Hotels

★★ **HAMPTON INN.** *3535 US 46 E, at Cherry Hill Rd.* 201/263-0095; FAX 201/263-6133. 100 rms, 4 story. 18 kits. S $69; D $79-$88; kit. units $89-$99; each addl $10; under 18 free; wkend rates. Crib free. TV; cable. Restaurant 5-10 pm. Rm serv. Bar 4:30 pm-1:30 am. Ck-out noon. Meeting rm. Valet serv (exc wkends). Exercise equipt; weights, bicycles, whirlpool, sauna. Cr cds: A, C, D, DS, ER, MC, V.

★ **HOLIDAY INN.** *707 US 46, I-80 exit 42 (eastbound) or exit 47 (westbound).* 201/263-2000; FAX 201/299-9029. 153 rms, 4 story. S, D $76-$86; under 18 free; lower rates wknds. Crib free. TV. Pool. Restaurant 7 am-11 pm. Ck-out noon. Coin lndry. Meeting rms. Sundries. Cr cds: A, C, D, DS, JCB, MC, V.

Hotels

★ ★ ★ **EMBASSY SUITES.** *909 Parsippany Blvd, I-80 exit 42 (eastbound) or exit 43 (westbound).* 201/334-1440; FAX 201/402-1188. 274 suites, 5 story. Suites $129-$159; each addl $20; under 12 free; wkly rates. Crib free. TV; cable. Indoor pool. Complimentary full bkfst. Complimentary coffee in rms. Restaurant 11 am-11 pm. Bar to midnight. Ck-out noon. Coin lndry. Meeting rms. Gift shop. Exercise equipt; weight machine, bicycle, whirlpool, sauna. Game rm. Cr cds: A, C, D, DS, JCB, MC, V.

★ ★ ★ **HILTON.** *1 Hilton Ct, jct NJ 10 & I-287.* 201/267-7373; FAX 201/984-6853. 508 rms, 6 story. S $135-$165; D $155-$185; each addl $20; suites $350-$675; family, wkend rates. Crib free. Pet accepted, some restrictions. TV; cable. Indoor pool; poolside serv, lifeguard. Playground. Restaurants 6:30 am-11 pm; wkends from 7 am. Rm serv Mon-Thurs 6:30-2 am. Bar 11-2 am; entertainment, dancing. Ck-out noon. Convention facilities. Concierge. Tennis. Exercise equipt; weights, bicycles, whirlpool. Health club privileges. Some bathrm phones. Wet bar, refrigerator in suites. Cr cds: A, C, D, DS, ER, JCB, MC, V.

★ ★ ★ **SHERATON TARA.** *199 Smith Rd, I-80 exit 43 (eastbound) or exit 42 (westbound).* 201/515-2000; FAX 201/515-9798. 383 units, 6 story. S $130-$160; D $150-$170; each addl $20; suites $250-$450; under 18 free; wkend rates. Crib free. TV; cable. 2 pools, 1 indoor; poolside serv, lifeguard. Restaurant 6:30 am-11 pm; dining rm from 5 pm, Sun 10 am-2 pm. Bars 11:30-2 am. Ck-out noon. Convention facilities. Concierge. Gift shop. Exercise rm; instructor, weight machines, bicycles, whirlpool, sauna, steam rm. Bathrm phones, refrigerators avail. Overlooks lake; extensive grounds. Cr cds: A, C, D, DS, ER, MC, V.

Restaurants

✔ ★ ★ **BLACK BULL INN.** *(US 46, Mountain Lakes)* I-80 exit 42 (W) or 39 (E). 201/335-8585. Hrs: 11 am-11 pm; Fri, Sat to midnight. Closed Sun exc Mother's Day; major hols. Bar. Semi-a la carte: lunch $4.95-$11.95, dinner $4.95-$13.95. Child's meals. Specializes in Delmonico steak, prime rib, fish. Salad bar. Entertainment Fri, Sat. Parking. Rustic interior; Scottish atmosphere. Cr cds: A, C, D, DS, MC, V.

★ ★ ★ **LLEWELLYN FARMS.** *Morris Plains, on NJ 10, at jct US 202.* 201/538-4323. Hrs: 11:30-2 am. Closed Mon; Dec 25. Res accepted. Bar. A la carte entrees: lunch $6.45-$9.45, dinner $13.95-$24.95. Child's meals. Specialties: prime rib, roast boned duckling, stuffed prawns. Entertainment Fri & Sat. Valet parking (dinner). Tudor decor. Family-owned. Cr cds: A, C, D, DS, MC, V.

Paterson (B-5)

Settled: 1711 **Pop:** 140,891 **Elev:** 100 ft **Area code:** 201

Named after Governor William Paterson, this city owes its present and historic eminence as an industrial city to Alexander Hamilton. He was the first man to realize the possibility of harnessing the Great Falls of the Passaic River (see #1) for industrial purposes. As Secretary of the Treasury, he helped form the Society for Establishing Useful Manufactures in 1791 and, a year later, was instrumental in choosing Paterson as the site of its initial ventures. Paterson was the country's major silk-producing town in the late 1800s. Today, it is a diversified industrial center. The area surrounding the Great Falls is now being restored and preserved as a historic district. Paterson is the seat of Passaic County.

What to See and Do

1. **Great Falls Historic District.** McBride Ave Ext. & Spruce St. Includes 77-foot high falls, park and picnic area, renovated raceway system, restored 19th-century buildings. For further information and tours phone 279-9587. ¢ Also here is

   Paterson Museum. Thomas Rogers Bldg, 2 Market St. Contains shell of original 14-foot submarine invented by John P. Holland in 1878; also his second submarine (31 ft), built in 1881. Paterson-Colt gun collection (1836-1840); mineral display; exhibits on Paterson history, including the silk and locomotive industries; two locomotives; Curtiss-Wright airplane engines; changing art exhibits. (Daily exc Mon; closed hols) Donation. Phone 881-3874.

2. **Garret Mountain Reservation.** Rifle Camp Rd & Mountain Ave. A 570-acre woodland park on a 502-foot-high plateau. Fishing pond (stocked with trout); boat dock, rowboats, paddleboats. Trails, stables. Picnic groves. Phone 881-4832. **Free.**

3. **Rifle Camp Park.** Rifle Camp Rd in West Paterson. This 158-acre park is 584 feet above sea level. Includes nature and geology trails, nature center with astronomical observatory; walking paths, fitness course. Picnic areas. **Free.**

4. **Lambert Castle.** 3 Valley Rd. Built by an immigrant who rose to wealth as a silk manufacturer. The 1893 castle of brownstone and granite houses a local history museum; two restored period rooms; changing exhibits; library (by appt). (Wed-Sun, afternoons; closed most major hols) Sr citizen rate. Phone 881-2761. ¢

5. **American Labor Museum-Botto House National Landmark.** N on NJ 504, at 83 Norwood St in Haledon. The history of the working class is presented through restored period rooms, changing exhibits and ethnic gardens. Tours, seminars and workshops are offered. (Wed-Sun; closed major hols exc Labor Day) Phone 595-7953. ¢

(For further information contact the Great Falls Visitor Center, 65 McBride Ave Ext, 07501-1715, phone 279-9587; or the Special Events office, 72 McBride Ave, 07501, phone 523-9201.)

(For accommodations see Clifton, Wayne)

Plainfield (D-4)

Settled: 1685 **Pop:** 46,567 **Elev:** 118 ft **Area code:** 908

Plainfield, directly south of the Watchung Mountains, is actually the center of a group of associated towns: Scotch Plains (see), Watchung, North and South Plainfield, Fanwood, Green Brook, Warren Township, Dunellen, Middlesex and Piscataway, all of which are mainly residential. Plainfield is also home to a number of industries.

What to See and Do

Drake House Museum (1746). 602 W Front St. General Washington's headquarters in 1777; now the Plainfield Historical Society headquarters. Period furnishings; diorama depicts Battle for the Watchungs. (Sat afternoons) Phone 755-5831. ¢

(For further information contact the Central Jersey Chamber of Commerce, 120 W 7th St, #217, 07060; 754-7250.)

Motor Hotel

★★ **HOLIDAY INN.** *(4701 Stelton Rd, South Plainfield 07080) At jct NJ 529, I-287.* 908/753-5500; FAX 908/753-5500, ext. 620. 173 rms, 4 story. S $77-$99; D $84-$106; each addl $7; under 18 free; wkend rates. Crib free. Pet accepted, some restrictions. TV; cable. Indoor pool; lifeguard. Restaurant 6:30 am-10 pm. Rm serv. Ck-out 1 am. Coin lndry. Meeting rms. Valet serv. Exercise equipt; weights, bicycles, whirlpool, sauna. Refrigerators. Cr cds: A, C, D, DS, JCB, MC, V.

Princeton (E-4)

Settled: 1685 **Pop:** 12,016 **Elev:** 215 ft **Area code:** 609

In 1776, the first State Legislature of New Jersey met in Princeton University's Nassau Hall. Washington and his troops surprised and defeated a superior British Army in the 1777 Battle of Princeton. From June to November, 1783, Princeton was the new nation's capital. Around the same time, Washington was staying at Rockingham in nearby Rocky Hill, where he wrote and delivered his famous "Farewell Orders to the Armies."

Princeton's life is greatly influenced by the university, which opened here in 1756; at that time it was known as the College of New Jersey. In 1896, on the 150th anniversary of its charter, the institution became Princeton University. Woodrow Wilson, the first president of the university who was not a clergyman, held the office from 1902 to 1910. Princeton is also the home of the Institute for Advanced Study, where Albert Einstein spent the last years of his life.

What to See and Do

1. **Princeton University** (1746). (4,500 undergraduate, 1,650 graduate students) An Ivy League college that has been co-educational since 1969. A campus guide service shows the visitor points of interest on the main campus; for tour information phone 258-3603. (Daily; closed major hols) On campus are

   Woodrow Wilson School of Public and International Affairs. Designed by Minoru Yamasaki; reflecting pool and "Fountain of Freedom" by James Fitzgerald.

   Nassau Hall (1756). Provided all college facilities, classrooms, dormitories, library and prayer hall for about 50 years. New Jersey's first legislature met here in 1776, and the Continental Congress met here in 1783, when Princeton was the capital. During the Revolution, it served as a barracks and hospital for Continental and British troops.

   The Putnam Sculptures. One of the largest modern outdoor sculpture showcases in the country, with 19 sculptures on display throughout the campus, including pieces by Picasso, Moore, Noguchi, Calder and Lipchitz.

   McCarter Theatre. Professional repertory company performs classical and modern drama; concerts; ballet; other special programs year-round. Phone 683-8000 (box office).

2. **Princeton Battle Monument.** On Monument Dr, off Stockton St, near Morven (see #4). The work of Frederick W. MacMonnies, this

50-foot block of Indiana limestone commemorates the famous 1777 battle when George Washington defeated the British.

3. **Princeton Cemetery.** Witherspoon & Wiggins Sts. Buried in the Presidents' Plot are 11 university presidents, including Aaron Burr Sr, Jonathan Edwards and John Witherspoon. Monument to Grover Cleveland and grave of Paul Tulane, in whose honor Tulane University was named.

4. **Morven** (1755). 55 Stockton St. House of Richard Stockton, signer of the Declaration of Independence. Used as a Revolutionary headquarters; was frequently visited by General Washington and other Colonial leaders.

5. **Bainbridge House** (ca 1766). 158 Nassau St. Birthplace of commander of the USS *Constitution* during War of 1812. Period rooms and changing exhibits on Princeton history; research library, photo archives. Donation. Also offers walking tours of historic district (Sun; phone ahead). For schedule phone 921-6748.

6. **Kuser Farm Mansion and Park.** 10 mi SE via US 206, I-295 to Olden Ave in Hamilton, then 1/2 mi W to Newkirk Ave. Farm and 1890s summer mansion of Fred Kuser; more than 20 rooms open; some original furnishings. Grounds consist of 22 acres with original buildings including coachman's house, chicken house; tennis pavilion; clay tennis court. Park with picnic area; quoit courts, lawn bowling, walking trails; formal garden, gazebo. Tours (May-Nov, Thurs-Sun; Feb-Apr, Sat & Sun; limited hrs, call for schedule and hol closings); self-guided tour maps of grounds. Phone 890-3630. **Free.**

7. **Rockingham State Historic Site.** 4 mi N on US 206, then 2 mi E on County 518 in Rocky Hill. On this 5-acre site are 3 buildings; a kitchen, a wash house and the main building. This was Washington's headquarters Aug 23-Nov 10, 1783, where he wrote his "Farewell Orders to the Armies"; 10 rooms with period furnishings. (Wed-Sat, also Sun afternoons; closed most major hols) Phone 921-8835. **Free.**

(For further information contact the Chamber of Commerce, PO Box 431, 08542; 520-1776.)

(See Trenton)

Motels

✔ ★ **DAYS INN.** *(4191 US 1, Monmouth Junction 08852) 2 mi N on US 1.* 908/329-4555; FAX 908/329-1041. 73 rms, 2 story, 7 suites. S $44.95-$54.95; D $59.95-$79.95; each addl $7; suites $95.95. Crib free. TV; cable, in-rm movies avail. Restaurant 7 am-7 pm. Ck-out 11 am. Meeting rm. Refrigerators avail. Cr cds: A, C, D, DS, MC, V.

★★ **RESIDENCE INN BY MARRIOTT.** *Box 8388 (08543), 4225 US 1, 4 mi NE, just S of Raymond Rd on US 1.* 908/329-9600; FAX 908/329-8422. 208 kit. suites, 2 story. S, D $109-$124; under 18 free; wkly, wkend rates. Crib free. Pet accepted, some restrictions; $10. TV; cable. Heated pool; whirlpool, lifeguard. Free supervised child's activities (Memorial Day-Labor Day). Complimentary continental bkfst. Ck-out noon. Coin lndry. Meeting rms. Valet serv. Tennis. Lawn games. Many fireplaces. Balconies. Picnic tables, grills. Cr cds: A, C, D, DS, ER, JCB, MC, V.

Motor Hotels

★★ **NOVOTEL.** *100 Independence Way (08540), jct NJ 522, US 1.* 609/520-1200; FAX 609/520-0594. 180 rms, 4 story. S $99; D $109; suites $120; under 16 free; wkend rates. Crib free. Pet accepted, some restrictions. TV; cable. Pool. Restaurant 6 am-midnight. Rm serv. Bar. Ck-out 1 pm. Coin lndry. Meeting rms. Valet serv. Free RR station transportation. Exercise equipt; weight machine, bicycles, whirlpool. Cr cds: A, C, D, DS, ER, JCB, MC, V.

★ ★ ★ **RAMADA.** *US 1 & Ridge Rd (08540).* 609/452-2400; FAX 609/452-2494. 244 rms, 6 story. S $135; D $150; each addl $15; suites from $225; under 18 free; wkend rates. Crib free. Pet accepted, some restrictions. TV; cable. Indoor pool. Restaurant 6 am-10 pm. Bar 11-1 am. Ck-out noon. Meeting rms. Refrigerators avail. Cr cds: A, C, D, DS, MC, V.

D 🏌 ≋ ⊠ 🎿 🔥 SC

Hotels

★ ★ ★ **HYATT REGENCY PRINCETON.** *102 Carnegie Center (08540), 2 mi E on US 1, at Alexander Rd.* 609/987-1234; FAX 609/987-2584. 348 rms, 4 story. S $145-$170; D $155-$185; suites $200-$375; under 18 free; wkend rates. Crib free. TV; cable. Indoor/outdoor pool; poolside serv. Restaurant 6:30 am-1 pm. Bar 11-2 am; entertainment Fri-Sun. Ck-out noon. Gift shop. Tennis. Exercise equipt; weights, bicycles, whirlpool, sauna. Some bathrm phones. Cr cds: A, C, D, DS, MC, V.

D 🏌 ≋ 🎿 🎿 🔥 SC

★ ★ ★ **MARRIOTT PRINCETON.** *201 Village Blvd (08540), in Forrestal Village, 8 mi S of NJ Tpke exit 9.* 609/452-7900; FAX 609/452-1123. 300 units, 6 story. S, D $125-$145; each addl $15; under 18 free; some wkend rates. Crib free. TV; cable. Indoor/outdoor pool; poolside serv, lifeguard. Restaurant 6:30 am-11 pm. Bar noon-2 am; entertainment, dancing exc Sun. Ck-out 11 am. Coin lndry. Meeting rms. Concierge. Gift shop. Exercise equipt; weights, bicycles, whirlpool, sauna. Refrigerators avail. Some private patios, balconies. Shopping center adj. Cr cds: A, C, D, DS, ER, JCB, MC, V.

D ≋ 🎿 🎿 🎿 🔥 SC

★ ★ ★ **NASSAU INN.** *10 Palmer Sq (08542).* 609/921-7500; res: 800/243-1166 (exc NJ); FAX 609/921-9385. 215 rms, 5 story. S $120-$170; D $135-$185; each addl $15; suites $160-$495; under 13 free. Crib free. TV. Pool privileges. Restaurant 7 am-10 pm. Bar 10-1 am; entertainment Fri-Sat. Ck-out noon. Health club privileges. Refrigerators avail. Colonial atmosphere, beamed ceilings, fireplaces in public rms. Cr cds: A, C, D, MC, V.

D ⊠ 🔥 SC

★ ★ ★ **SCANTICON PRINCETON.** *100 College Rd E (08540), off US 1, in Princeton Forrestal Center.* 609/452-7800; res: 800/222-1131; FAX 609/452-7883. 301 rms, 3-4 story. S $110-$145; D $135-$160; each addl $25; suites $160-$370; under 12 free; wkend rates. Crib free. TV; cable, in-rm movies. Indoor pool. Restaurant 7 am-9:30 pm. Bars 11-1 am; entertainment, dancing Fri, Sat. Ck-out 1 pm. Convention facilities. Gift shop. Free valet parking. Lighted tennis. Golf privileges. Exercise equipt; weight machines, bicycles, whirlpool, sauna. Lawn games. Refrigerators. Scandinavian contemporary design and furnishings. On 25 wooded acres. *LUXURY LEVEL : EXECUTIVE CLUB.* 25 rms, 1 suite. S $140-$185; D $145-$210; suite $280-$325. Private lounge. Cr cds: A, C, D, ER, JCB, MC, V.

D 🏌 🏌 ≋ 🎿 🎿 🎿 🔥

Inn

★ ★ **PEACOCK INN.** *20 Bayard Lane (08540).* 609/924-1707; FAX 609/924-0788. 17 rms, 10 with bath, 3 story. Some rm phones. S $80-$115; D $90-$125; each addl $15; higher rates graduation. Crib free. Pet accepted; $20. TV in some rms & lobby; cable. Complimentary buffet bkfst. Dining rm 11:45 am-2:30 pm, 5:30-9:30 pm. Ck-out noon, ck-in 3 pm. Health club privileges. Historic late Georgian colonial house, built 1775 and relocated from Nassau St to its present site. Antique furnishings; rms individually decorated. 1 blk from Princeton University campus. Cr cds: A, MC, V.

🏌 🔥 SC

Restaurants

★ ★ **ALCHEMIST AND BARRISTER.** *28 Witherspoon.* 609/924-5555. Hrs: 11:30 am-2:30 pm, 5-10 pm; Fri, Sat to 10:30 pm; Sun 11:30 am-3 pm, 5-10 pm. Closed Jan 1, July 4, Dec 25. Res accepted. Bar to 2 am. Semi-a la carte: lunch $6.95-$9.95, dinner $18-$25. Sun brunch $7.95-$12.95. Specializes in seafood, steak. Outdoor dining in season. Colonial decor. Cr cds: MC, V.

★ ★ **GOOD TIME CHARLEY'S.** *(40 Main St, Kingston)* 2 mi N on NJ 27. 609/924-7400. Hrs: 11:30 am-10 pm; Fri to 10:30 pm; Sat 5-10:30 pm; Sun 4:30-9:30 pm. Closed Dec 25; also lunch major hols. Res accepted. Bar 11:30-2 am. Semi-a la carte: lunch $4.95-$9.95, dinner $9.95-$21.95. Specializes in prime rib, fresh seafood. Musicians Fri & Sat. Parking. Victorian decor. Tiffany lamps; posters. Cr cds: A, C, D, DS, MC, V.

D

✔ ★ ★ **RUSTY SCUPPER.** *378 Alexander Rd.* 609/921-3276. Hrs: 11:30 am-2:30 pm, 5-10 pm; Fri to 11 pm; Sat 5-11 pm; Sun 4-9 pm. Closed Dec 25. Res accepted. Bar 11:30-1 am; Sat, Sun from 4 pm. Semi-a la carte: lunch $5.95-$9.95, dinner $10.95-$16.95. Child's meals. Specializes in seafood, prime rib, steak. Salad bar. Parking. Outdoor dining. Cr cds: A, C, D, DS, MC, V.

SC

Ramsey (B-5)

Pop: 13,228 Elev: 373 ft Area code: 201 Zip: 07446

What to See and Do

1. **Darlington Swim Area.** 600 Darlington Ave in Mahwah; follow signs on NJ 17 or 208 N. Two lakes provide swimming (fee); fishing (in 1 lake). Tennis, handball; shuffleboard, horseshoes. Picnicking (pavilion), playground. Park (Apr-Nov). Sr citizen rate. For opening swim date phone 646-2680 or 327-3500. Park admission during swim season ¢¢¢

2. **Campgaw Mountain Ski Area.** NJ 17 N, exit NJ 202 Suffern, 1.6 mi S on NJ 202, left on Darlington Ave 1 blk, stay to right, 1 mi on Campgaw Rd in Mahwah. 2 double chair lifts, T-bar; patrol, school, rentals; snowmaking; cafeteria. Eight runs, longest run 1,760 feet; vertical drop 275 feet. (Early Dec-mid-Mar, daily) Lighted cross-country trails; half-pipe; cross-country and snowboard rentals. Phone 327-7800. ¢¢¢¢¢

3. **James A McFaul Environmental Center.** 3 mi NW off NJ 208 on Crescent Ave in Wyckoff. An 81-acre wildlife sanctuary including museum with natural history displays, lectures, film programs (Tues, Sat & Sun afternoons); woodland trail; waterfowl pond; picnic area. Arboretum and perennial gardens. (Daily; closed morning wkends & major hols) Phone 891-5571. **Free.**

Motor Hotel

✔ ★ ★ **RAMADA INN MAHWAH.** *(180 NJ 17S, Mahwah 07430)* S of US 202 on NJ 17. 201/529-5880; FAX 201/529-4767. 128 rms, 4 story. S, D $64-$94; each addl $10; suites $99-$129; under 18 free; lower wkend rates. Crib free. Pet accepted, some restrictions. TV; cable. Indoor pool. Restaurant 6:30 am-10 pm; wkends from 7 am. Rm serv from 7 am. Bar. Ck-out noon. Coin lndry. Meeting rms. Bellhops. Valet serv. Sundries. Cr cds: A, C, D, DS, JCB, MC, V.

D ≋ ⊠ 🔥 SC

Hotel

★ ★ ★ **SHERATON CROSSROADS HOTEL & TOWERS.** *(Crossroads Corporate Center, Mahwah 07495) 2 mi N on NJ 17.* 201/529-1660; FAX 201/529-4709. 225 units, 14-22 story. S $119-$145; D $139-$165; each addl $20; suites $260-$750; under 18 free; wkend rates. Crib free. Pet accepted, some restrictions. TV; cable. Indoor pool; lifeguard. Restaurant 6:30 am-11 pm. Bar noon-2 am; entertainment exc Sun, dancing. Ck-out noon. Convention facilities. Concierge. Shopping arcade. Covered parking avail. Newark airport transportation. Exercise equipt; weights, bicycles, sauna. Refrigerators avail. *LUXURY LEVEL : THE TOWER ROOMS.* 48 units. S $139-$174; D $149-$179. Private lounge. Bathrm phones. Complimentary continental bkfst, refreshments. Cr cds: A, C, D, DS, ER, MC, V.

Red Bank (E-5)

Pop: 10,636 **Elev:** 35 ft **Area code:** 908 **Zip:** 07701

Red Bank, a historic community on the shores of the Navesink River, includes a central business area with shops, restaurants, brokerage firms and an antique center.

What to See and Do

1. **Holmes-Hendrickson House** (ca 1750). Longstreet Rd in Holmdel, W on NJ 520. A 14-room Dutch Colonial farmhouse with period furnishings. (May-Oct, Tues, Thurs & Sun afternoons; also Sat; closed hols) Sr citizen rate. Phone 462-1466. ¢

2. **Marlpit Hall** (1685). 137 Kings Hwy in Middletown, N on NJ 35. Enlarged Dutch cottage in 1740 English style; period furnishings. Closed at press time for renovation. (Days same as Holmes House) Sr citizen rate. Phone 462-1466. ¢

3. **Allen House** (ca 1750). 2 mi S on NJ 35, at jct Sycamore Ave in Shrewsbury. Lower floor restored as tavern of the Revolutionary period; two upstairs galleries have historical exhibits. (Days same as Holmes House) Sr citizen rate. Phone 462-1466. ¢

4. **Monmouth Museum.** 5 mi W on Newman Springs Rd; on campus of Brookdale Community College in Lincroft. Changing exhibits of art, science, nature and cultural history; children's hands-on wing. (Daily exc Mon; closed hols) Sr citizen rate. Phone 747-2266. ¢¢

5. **Spy House Museum Complex.** 4 mi NW on NJ 35 to Middletown, then 3 mi N to Port Monmouth, on the bayshore at the end of Wilson Ave. The haunted Whitlock-Seabrook-Wilson House cabin was built in 1663. It was named "Spy House" because it was used as the meeting place for both British and patriot spies. Includes Shoal Harbor Marine Museum with exhibits on area's fishing and shipping history; Penelope Stout Museum of the Crafts of Man with examples from 1663 through the 19th century. (Daily, afternoons) Donation. Phone 787-1807.

Motel

★ ★ **COURTYARD BY MARRIOTT.** *245 Half Mile Rd, off Garden State Pkwy exit 109.* 908/530-5552; FAX 908/530-5756. 146 rms, 3 story. S $84-$94; D $94-$104; wkend rates. Crib free. TV; cable. Indoor pool. Complimentary coffee in rms. Restaurant 6:30-9:30 am, 5-10 pm. Bar 4-11 pm. Ck-out noon. Coin lndry. Meeting rms. Valet serv. Exercise equipt; weight machines, bicycles, whirlpool. Some refrigerators. Balconies. Cr cds: A, C, D, DS, MC, V.

Hotel

★ ★ ★ **OYSTER POINT.** *146 Bodman Place.* 908/530-8200; res: 800/345-3484; FAX 908/747-1875. 58 units, 5 story. S, D $79-$110; suites $140-$440; under 16 free; wkend plans. Crib free. TV; cable. Restaurant 6:30 am-10 pm. Bar 11-2 am; entertainment Fri & Sat. Ck-out noon. Meeting rms. Exercise equipt; bicycles, rowers. Some refrigerators. Some private patios, balconies. View of Navesink River; marina. Atrium lobby. Cr cds: A, C, D, DS, MC, V.

Restaurants

★ ★ **FARM HOUSE.** *(438 Branch Ave, Little Silver) 4 mi SE of Garden State Pkwy, exit 109.* 908/842-5017. Hrs: 4:30-9 pm; Sun 9 am-1 pm, 4:30-9 pm; early-bird dinner Wed-Fri 4:30-6 pm. Closed Mon, Tues; Thanksgiving; also Jan. Res accepted. Setups. Semi-a la carte: dinner $13.95-$21.95. Sun bkfst $3.95-$7.95. Child's meals. Specializes in seafood, strip steak. Salad bar. Parking. 150-yr-old farmhouse; antiques. Cr cds: MC, V.

★ ★ ★ **FROMAGERIE.** *(26 Ridge Rd, Rumson) 7 mi E of Garden State Pkwy exit 109, end of River Rd then left 1/4 mi.* 908/842-8088. Hrs: 11:30 am-2:30 pm, 5-10 pm; Fri to 11 pm; Sat 5-11 pm; Sun from 4 pm. Closed Dec 25. Res accepted (exc Sat). French menu. Bar. Extensive wine cellar. Semi-a la carte: lunch $8.95-$13.95, dinner $19.50-$29.50. Specialties: smoked duck with baked lentils, grilled swordfish with roasted red pepper coulis, rack of lamb. Own baking. Valet parking. Family-owned. Jacket. Cr cds: A, C, D, MC, V.

★ ★ **SHADOWBROOK.** *Shrewsbury, just off NJ 35, 2 mi SE of Garden State Pkwy exit 109.* 908/747-0200. Hrs: 5:30-9 pm; Fri, Sat to 10 pm; Sun 3-9 pm. Closed Mon; Dec 24. Res accepted. Bar. Semi-a la carte: dinner $18.95-$29.95. Child's meals. Specialties: shellfish Fra Diavolo, veal Francaise. Valet parking. Fireplace; in Georgian mansion; Victorian antiques. Formal gardens. Family-owned. Jacket. Cr cds: A, C, D, MC, V.

Ringwood State Park (B-5)

(On the New Jersey, New York border)

Ringwood State Park lies in upper Passaic County, near the town of Ringwood, within the heart of the Ramapo Mountains. Consisting of 4,054 acres, the park is reached by NJ 23 and 511 from the west and NJ 17 and Sloatsburg Rd from the east.

Ringwood Manor Section. This section features a 78-room mansion containing a collection of Americana; relics of iron-making days (1740); formal gardens. Interpretive tours. Fishing in Ringwood River. Picnic facilities nearby. Tours (May-Oct, daily exc Mon).

Shepherd Lake Section. A 541-acre wooded area has trap and skeet shooting all year (fee). The 74-acre Shepherd Lake provides a swimming beach and bathhouse; fishing; boating (ramp). Also available is ice-skating; picnicking (fireplaces).

Skylands Section. Located here is a 44-room mansion modeled after an English baronial house (not open to the public). The gardens (90 acres) surrounding the manor house comprise the only botanical garden in the state park system (guided tours upon request). This 1,119-acre section also offers fishing, hunting. Hiking.

Standard fees are charged for each section. Phone 201/962-7031.

(For accommodations see Wayne)

Rockaway (B-4)

Pop: 6,243 **Elev:** 534 ft **Area code:** 201 **Zip:** 07866

Motels

★ ★ **HOWARD JOHNSON.** *Green Pond Rd, I-80 exit 37, left.* 201/625-1200. 64 rms, 2 story. June-Sept: S, D $68.50-$84.50; each addl $10; lower rates rest of yr. Crib free. TV; cable. Pool; wading pool. Complimentary continental bkfst. Restaurant 6:30-2 am. Rm serv. Bar; entertainment, dancing wkends. Ck-out noon. Downhill ski 12 mi. Some refrigerators. Balconies. Cr cds: A, C, D, DS, ER, MC, V.

★ ★ **THE MOUNTAIN INN.** *156 NJ 46E, approx 3 mi off I-80 exit 42W.* 201/627-8310; res: 800/537-3732; FAX 201/627-0556. 110 rms, 2 story, 16 kits. (no ovens), 22 kit. apts (4 1/2 rms). S, D $39.50-$59.50; each addl $5; kit. apts $64.50-$70; under 12 free; wkend rates. Crib free. TV; cable. Pool; lifeguard. Complimentary continental bkfst. Restaurant noon-1 am. Bar. Ck-out 11 am. Coin lndry. Meeting rms. Valet serv. Cr cds: A, C, D, DS, MC, V.

Restaurant

★ ★ ★ **ALDO'S.** *68 NJ 46E.* 201/586-3006. Hrs: 11:30 am-5 pm; Fri 11:30-1 am; Sat 5 pm-1 am; Sun 3-9 pm. Closed Mon; Thanksgiving, Dec 25. Res accepted. Italian menu. Bar. Semi-a la carte: lunch $6.95-$12.95, dinner $10.95-$24.95. Specializes in seafood. Parking. Walls covered with photographs of celebrities. Cr cds: A, C, D, MC, V.

Rutherford (C-5)

Pop: 17,790 **Elev:** 100 ft **Area code:** 201

What to See and Do

Fairleigh Dickinson University-Rutherford Campus (1942). (2,300 students) W Passaic & Montross Aves. On campus is the Kingsland House (1670), in which George Washington stayed in August, 1783; and the Castle, an 1888 copy of Chateau d'Amboise in France. Phone 460-5009.

Motel

★ ★ **QUALITY INN SPORTS COMPLEX.** *(10 Polito Ave, Lyndhurst 07071)* Jct NJ 3 & NJ 17, Lyndhurst Serv Rd exit off NJ 17S. 201/933-9800; FAX 201/933-0658. 150 rms, 2 story. S $65; D $75; each addl $6; under 18 free; wkend rates. Crib free. TV; cable. Pool; lifeguard. Restaurant 6:30 am-10 pm. Rm serv. Bar 11-2 am. Ck-out noon. Coin lndry. Meeting rms. Sundries. Airport transportation. Stadium, racetrack opp. Cr cds: A, C, D, DS, ER, JCB, MC, V.

Motor Hotel

★ **DAYS INN.** *(850 NJ 120, East Rutherford 07073)* On NJ 120, 1/4 mi E of NJ 17. 201/507-5222; FAX 201/507-0744. 139 rms, 5 story. S, D $59-$89; each addl $10; under 12 free. Crib avail. Pet accepted, some restrictions; $25. TV; cable. Restaurant 6-10 am, 5-11 pm. Bar to midnight. Ck-out noon. Meeting rms. Airport transportation.

Exercise equipt; weight machines, bicycles. Cr cds: A, C, D, DS, ER, MC, V.

Hotel

★ ★ ★ **SHERATON MEADOWLANDS.** *(2 Meadowlands Plaza, East Rutherford 07073)* 1/4 mi E of NJ Tpke exit 16W, opp Meadowlands Sports Complex. 201/896-0500; FAX 201/896-9696. 423 units, 20 story. S, D $130-$160; each addl $20; suites $230-$550; under 18 free; wknd rates. Crib free. Pet accepted, some restrictions. TV; cable. Indoor pool; poolside serv. Restaurant 6:30 am-11 pm. Bars noon-2 am. Ck-out 1 pm. Convention facilities. Concierge. Gift shop. Airport transportation. Exercise equipt; weights, bicycles, whirlpool, sauna. Bathrm phone, wet bar in suites. Cr cds: A, C, D, DS, ER, JCB, MC, V.

Restaurant

★ ★ **ROMANISSIMO.** *(1 Hoboken Rd, East Rutherford)* NJ 17S exit Paterson Plank Rd, follow signs. 201/939-1128. Hrs: 11:30 am-11 pm; Sat 5 pm-midnight; Sun 2-10 pm. Res accepted. Country Italian menu. Bar. A la carte entrees: lunch $10.95-$14.95, dinner $10.95-$20. Specializes in rabbit, seafood. Singer Fri & Sat. Valet parking. Glass enclosed patio. Contemporary decor. Cr cds: A, C, D, MC, V.

Saddle Brook (B-5)

Pop: 13,296 **Elev:** 90 ft **Area code:** 201 **Zip:** 07662

Motor Hotel

★ ★ **RAMADA HOTEL.** *(375 W Passaic St, Rochelle Park)* At Garden State Pkwy exit 160N. 201/845-3400; FAX 201/845-0412. 174 rms, 5 story. S $85-$97; D $85-$104; each addl $10; suites $150; wkend rates. Crib free. TV; cable. Indoor pool. Restaurant 6:30 am-11 pm; wkends from 7 am. Rm serv. Bar 11-2 am; entertainment, dancing Fri-Sat. Ck-out noon. Coin lndry. Meeting rms. Valet serv. Sundries. Health club privileges. Cr cds: A, C, D, DS, ER, JCB, MC, V.

Hotels

★ ★ **HOLIDAY INN.** *50 Kenney Place, at jct Garden State Pkwy exit 159, I-80 exit 62.* 201/843-0600; FAX 201/843-2822. 144 rms, 12 story. S, D $69-$150; each addl $10; under 18 free; wkend rates. Crib free. Pet accepted, some restrictions. TV; cable. Pool. Restaurant 6:30 am-10 pm, wkends from 7 am. Bar 11 am-midnight; dancing Fri-Sat. Ck-out noon. Meeting rms. Cr cds: A, C, D, DS, MC, V.

★ ★ ★ **MARRIOTT.** *At jct I-80, Garden State Pkwy exit 159.* 201/843-9500; FAX 201/843-3539. 281 rms, 12 story. S, D $115; suites $250-$450; wkend rates. Crib free. Pet accepted, some restrictions; $25. TV; cable. 2 pools, 1 indoor; poolside serv, lifeguard. Restaurant 6:30 am-10 pm; Fri, Sat to 11 pm; Sun 7 am-10 pm. Bar 11:30-1 am. Ck-out noon. Meeting rms. Free parking. Exercise equipt; weights, bicycles, whirlpool, sauna. Game rm. Refrigerators avail. Cr cds: A, C, D, DS, ER, JCB, MC, V.

Salem (H-1)

Founded: ca 1675 **Pop:** 6,883 **Elev:** 19 ft **Area code:** 609 **Zip:** 08079

Salem is said to be the oldest English settlement on the Delaware River. The town and its surrounding area have more than sixty 18th-century houses and buildings, as well as many points of historical interest. In the Friends Burying Ground on West Broadway is the 600-year-old Salem Oak, under which John Fenwick, the town's founder, signed a treaty with the Lenni-Lenape tribe.

What to See and Do

Alexander Grant House (1721). 79-83 Market St. Headquarters of Salem County Historical Society. Twenty rooms with period furniture; Wistarburg glass; Native American relics; dolls; paintings; genealogy library; stone barn. (Tues-Fri afternoons; also open 2nd Sat afternoon of each month) Phone 935-5004.   ¢¢

(For further information contact the Greater Salem Chamber of Commerce, 104 Market St; 935-1415.)

(See Deepwater; also see Wilmington, DE)

Inn

✔ ★ **BROWN'S HISTORIC HOME.** *41-43 Market St. 609/935-8595.* 6 rms, 3 with bath, 2 story. No rm phones. S, D $65; kit. unit $175/wk. Adults preferred. TV in lounge; cable. Complimentary full bkfst. Restaurant nearby. Ck-out noon, ck-in 2 pm. Pre-revolutionary house (1738) in historic district. Totally nonsmoking. Cr cds: DS, MC, V.

Sandy Hook (D-6)

(see Gateway National Recreation Area)

Scotch Plains (C-4)

Settled: 1684 **Pop:** 21,160 **Elev:** 119 ft **Area code:** 908 **Zip:** 07076

What to See and Do

1. **Watchung Reservation.** 1 mi NE. A 2,000-wooded-acre reservation in the Watchung Mts including the 25-acre Surprise Lake. Nature trails, bridle trails. Ice-skating. Picnic areas, playground. Ten-acre nursery and rhododendron display garden. Phone 527-4900. Also here is

   Trailside Nature and Science Center. Coles Ave & New Providence Rd in Mountainside. Nature exhibits; special programs; planetarium shows (Sun; over 6 yrs only; fee). Museum (late Mar-mid-Nov, daily; rest of yr, wkends only; closed some hols). Visitor Center with live reptile exhibit (daily, afternoons). Gift shop. Grounds (daily). Phone 789-3670.   **Free.**

2. **Terry Lou Zoo.** 1451 Raritan Rd. Zoo includes lions, tigers, giraffes and hippos. Pony rides. (Daily) Phone 322-7180.   ¢¢¢

(For further information contact the Suburban Chambers of Commerce, PO Box 824, Summit 07902-0824; 522-1700.)

(See Plainfield)

Motel

★ ★ **BEST WESTERN WESTFIELD INN.** *(435 North Ave W, Westfield 07090) 2 1/2 mi E on NJ 28, 2 mi NW of Garden State Pkwy exit 135. 908/654-5600; FAX 908/654-6483.* 40 rms, 3 story, 14 kits. S $82-$92; D $92-$102; each addl $10; kit. units $90-$100; under 13 free. Crib free. TV; cable. Complimentary continental bkfst. Restaurant noon-10 pm. Ck-out 11 am. Coin lndry. Meeting rm. Valet serv. Cr cds: A, C, D, DS, ER, MC, V.

 SC

Restaurants

★ ★ **SINCLAIRE'S.** *(240 North Ave, Westfield) Garden State Pkwy exit 135 to Central Ave, left on North Ave. 908/789-0344.* Hrs: 11:30 am-2:30 pm, 5:30-9 pm; Fri to 10 pm; Sat 5:30-10 pm; Sun 4-8 pm. Closed some major hols. Res accepted. Serv bar. Semi-a la carte: lunch $9.75-$16.50, dinner $18.75-$24.50. Specialties: blue fin tuna, Dover sole, swordfish chops. Own desserts. Valet parking (dinner). Cr cds: A, MC, V.

★ ★ **STAGE HOUSE INN.** *366 Park Ave. 908/322-4224.* Hrs: 11:30 am-2:30 pm, 5:30-10 pm; Sun 4-8 pm. Closed Mon; Dec 25. Bar. A la carte entrees: lunch $5-$13, dinner $17-$23. Specialties: charlotte of Maine crab, monkfish with lobster and basil. Parking. Outdoor dining. Operated as inn since 1737; in historic village. Cr cds: A, DS, MC, V.

D

Seaside Park (F-5)

Pop: 1,871 **Elev:** 6 ft **Area code:** 908 **Zip:** 08752

What to See and Do

Island Beach State Park. S on Central Ave. This strip of land (3,002 acres) is across the water, N of Long Beach Island (see) and faces Barnegat Lighthouse. There are two natural areas (Northern Area & Southern Area) and a recreational zone in the center. Excellent swimming and fishing in Atlantic Ocean (seasonal). Nature tours. Picnicking. (Daily) Standard fees. Phone 793-0506.

Motels

★ **ISLAND BEACH MOTOR LODGE.** *24th & Central Aves. 908/793-5400.* 59 rms, 2 story, 35 kits. Late June-Labor Day: S, D $80-$158; each addl $5; kit. units $735-$1,100/wk; lower rates rest of yr. Crib $5. TV; cable. Heated pool; wading pool, lifeguard. Restaurant nearby. Ck-out 11 am. Coin lndry. Refrigerators. Balconies. On private beach. Cr cds: MC, V.

★ ★ **WINDJAMMER.** *1st & Central Aves. 908/830-2555.* 63 rms, 3 story, 24 kits. June-Sept: S, D $90-$120; each addl $10; kit. units $120; lower rates rest of yr. Crib $5. TV; cable. Pool; poolside serv. Restaurant 8 am-10 pm. Bar 11 am-midnight. Ck-out 11 am. Coin lndry. Beach privileges. Cr cds: A, MC, V.

Secaucus (C-5)

Pop: 14,061 **Elev:** 12 ft **Area code:** 201 **Zip:** 07094

Motor Hotel

★ ★ **HOLIDAY INN.** 300 Plaza Dr. 201/348-2000; FAX 201/348-6035. 158 rms, 8 story. S, D $110-$150; each addl $10; suites $150-$170; under 18 free; wkend, wkly rates. Crib free. Valet parking $2. Restaurant 7 am-10 pm. Rm serv. Bar. Ck-out 1 pm. Coin lndry. Meeting rms. Bellhops. Gift shop. Exercise equipt; weights, bicycles. Refrigerators. *LUXURY LEVEL : EXECUTIVE LEVEL.* S, D $119. Complimentary coffee, newspaper in rms. Concierge. Cr cds: A, C, D, DS, JCB, MC, V.

Hotels

★ ★ ★ **EMBASSY SUITES.** 455 Plaza Dr. 201/864-7300; FAX 201/864-5391. 261 suites, 9 story. S, D $164-$184; each addl $20; under 12 free; wkend rates. Crib free. TV; cable. Indoor pool. Complimentary full bkfst. Restaurant 11:30 am-10 pm. Bar noon-midnight. Ck-out 1 pm. Coin lndry. Meeting rms. Gift shop. Exercise equipt; bicycles, stair machines, whirlpool, sauna. Refrigerators. Cr cds: A, C, D, DS, MC, V.

★ ★ ★ **HILTON-MEADOWLANDS.** 2 Harmon Plaza, NJ Tpke exit 16W, Meadowlands Pkwy. 201/348-6900; FAX 201/864-0963. 296 rms, 14 story. S, D $79-$135; each addl $20; suites $160-$275; family, wkend rates. Crib free. Pet accepted, some restrictions. TV; cable. Pool; poolside serv. Restaurant 6:30 am-11 pm; Sat, Sun from 7 am. Bars 11-2 am. Ck-out 1 pm. Convention facilities. Concierge. Gift shop. Valet parking avail. Newark airport transportation Mon-Fri. Health club privileges. Exercise equipt; weight machine, bicycles, whirlpool, sauna. Some refrigerators. Cr cds: A, C, D, DS, ER, JCB, MC, V.

Ship Bottom (G-5)

(see Long Beach Island)

Somerset (D-4)

(see New Brunswick)

Somerville (D-4)

Pop: 11,632 **Elev:** 54 ft **Area code:** 908 **Zip:** 08876

What to See and Do

1. **Wallace House State Historic Site.** 38 Washington Pl. General and Mrs. Washington made their headquarters here immediately after the house was built in 1778, while the army was stationed at Camp Middlebrook. Period furnishings. (Wed-Sun; closed hols; hrs may vary, phone ahead) Phone 725-1015.
2. **Old Dutch Parsonage State Historic Site** (1751). 65 Washington Pl. Moved from its original location, this brick building was the home of the Rev Jacob Hardenbergh from 1758-1781. He

founded Queens College, now Rutgers University, while residing in this building. Some furnishings and memorabilia on display. (Wed-Sun; closed hols; hrs may vary, phone ahead) Phone 725-1015.
3. **Duke Gardens.** On US 206, about 1¼ mi S of Somerville Circle. Features 11 gardens under glass, including colonial, desert, Italian, Oriental, English and tropical (closed Jan 1, Thanksgiving, Dec 25); 45-minute guided tour (Oct-May, daily). No high heels, no cameras. Advance reservation is required; contact Duke Gardens Foundation (Mon-Fri), phone 722-3700. ¢¢-¢¢¢

(For further information contact the Somerset County Chamber of Commerce, 64 W End Ave, PO Box 833; 725-1552.)

(See New Brunswick)

Motels

★ **DAYS INN-HILLSBOROUGH.** 118 US 206. 908/685-9000; FAX 908/685-0601. 100 rms, 2 story. S $60.95-$70.95; D $70.95-$80.95; each addl $10; suites $100-$170; under 17 free. Crib free. TV; cable, in-rm movies avail. Complimentary continental bkfst, coffee in lobby. Ck-out 11 am. Valet serv. Some refrigerators. Cr cds: A, C, D, DS, MC, V.

★ ★ **HOLIDAY INN-BRIDGEWATER.** (1260 US 22E, Bridgewater 08807) Just W of jct I-287. 908/526-9500; FAX 908/526-2538. 172 rms, 2 story. S $70-$90; D $80-$95; each addl $10; under 12 free. Crib free. TV; cable. Pool; wading pool, poolside serv, lifeguard. Restaurant 6:30 am-2 pm, 5-10 pm. Rm serv. Bar 4 pm-2 am. Ck-out noon. Meeting rms. Valet serv. Cr cds: A, C, D, DS, JCB, MC, V.

Restaurant

★ ★ **VILLA.** (476 NJ 28, Bridgewater) 1¼ mi W of Somerville Circle on NJ 28. 908/722-2828. Hrs: noon-2 pm, 5-9 pm; Sat 5-10 pm; Sun noon-8 pm. Closed July 4, Dec 25. Res accepted Mon-Fri. Continental menu. Bar from 11 am. Complete meals: lunch $6.95-$11. Semi-a la carte: dinner $9.95-$19.25. Child's meals. Specializes in fresh seafood. Parking. Family-owned. Cr cds: A, D, MC, V.

Spring Lake (E-5)

Pop: 3,499 **Elev:** 25 ft **Area code:** 908 **Zip:** 07762

(See Asbury Park)

Motels

★ **COMFORT INN.** Box 14, 1909 NJ 35, Garden State Pkwy exit 98. 908/449-6146. 70 rms, 2 story. Mid-June-Labor Day: S, D $99; each addl $10; suites from $120; lower rates rest of yr. Crib $5. TV; cable. Pool; lifeguard. Complimentary continental bkfst. Meeting rm. Exercise equipt; weights, bicycles. Refrigerator in suites. Cr cds: A, C, D, DS, ER, JCB, MC, V.

★ **DOOLAN'S.** (700 NJ 71, Spring Lake Heights) 4 mi E of Garden State Pkwy exit 98. 908/449-3666; FAX 908/449-2601. 60 rms, 2 story. Memorial Day wkend-Labor Day: S, D $80-$120; each addl $15; lower rates rest of yr. Crib $5. TV. Pool; lifeguard. Complimentary continental bkfst. Restaurant (summer) 8-10 am, 11:30 am-3 pm, 4:30-10 pm; closed for lunch Sat. Bar; entertainment Wed-Sun. Ck-out 11 am. Meeting rms. Cr cds: A, C, D, DS, MC, V.

★ **POINT BEACH.** *(Ocean & Trenton Aves, Point Pleasant Beach 08742) Ocean Rd to NJ 35S (Main Ave), follow signs to beach. 908/892-5100.* 24 rms, 2 story. July-Labor Day: S, D $110-$124; each addl $10; under 10 free; higher rates hols; lower rates May-June & Sept. Closed rest of yr. Crib $5. TV; cable. Pool; wading pool, lifeguard. Ck-out 11 am. Refrigerators. Opp Atlantic Ocean. Cr cds: MC, V.

Hotels

★★ **BREAKERS.** *1507 Ocean Ave. 908/449-7700; FAX 908/449-0161.* 64 units. Mid-June-Labor Day (hol wkends 3-day min): S, D $135-$160; each addl $20; suites $175-$275; family, wkly rates; lower rates rest of yr. Crib free. TV. Pool; whirlpool, poolside serv, lifeguard. Restaurant 8 am-3 pm, 5-10 pm. Ck-out noon. Meeting rms. Refrigerators. Private beach. Restored Victorian ocean-front hotel. Cr cds: A, C, D, MC, V.

★★★ **HEWITT WELLINGTON.** *200 Monmouth Ave. 908/974-1212; FAX 908/974-2338.* 12 rms, 3 story, 17 suites. Late June-Labor Day: S, D $110-$220; each addl $10 (up to 2 addl persons); suites $150-$220; wkly rates; higher rates: wkends (2-day min), hols (3-day min); lower rates rest of yr. Children over 12 yrs only. TV; cable. Heated pool. Complimentary continental bkfst 8-10 am. Restaurant 4:30-11 pm. Ck-out noon. Meeting rms. Refrigerators. Some balconies. On lake, 1½ blks to ocean. Free beach passes. Renovated Victorian hotel (1880). Cr cds: A, MC, V.

Inns

★ **ASHLING COTTAGE.** *106 Sussex Ave. 908/449-3553; res: 800/237-1877.* 10 rms, 5 with shower only, 2 share bath, 3 story. No rm phones. Mid-June-mid-Sept (2-night min): S $90-$135; D $95-$140; each addl $25; hols (3-night min); lower rates Apr-mid-June & mid-Sept-Dec; closed rest of yr. TV in lobby. Complimentary full bkfst. Restaurant nearby. Ck-out 11 am, ck-in 1 pm. Concierge. Free RR station, bus depot transportation. Bicycles. Picnic tables. 1 blk to ocean, ½ blk to lake. Victorian-style frame house (1877). Antiques. Totally nonsmoking. No cr cds accepted.

★★★ **CHATEAU.** *500 Warren Ave. 908/974-2000; FAX 908/974-0007.* 40 rms, 2 story. Late June-Labor Day: S $90-$125; D $120-$135; each addl $15; suites $160-$195; lower rates rest of yr. TV; cable, in-rm movies. Beach, pool privileges. Continental bkfst. Meeting rm. Free trolley to beach. Tennis, golf privileges. Bicycles. Refrigerators; some fireplaces. Private patios. Renovated Victorian hotel (1888). Overlooks parks, lake; ocean 4 blks. Cr cds: A, D, MC, V.

★★ **GRENVILLE HOTEL.** *(345 Main Ave, Bay Head 08742) Ocean Rd to NJ 35S (Main Ave). 908/892-3100; FAX 908/892-0599.* 33 rms, 4 story. Mid-June-mid-Sept: S $77-$202; each addl $25; suites $150-$350; lower rates rest of yr. TV; cable. Complimentary continental bkfst. Restaurant (see GRENVILLE HOTEL). Limited rm serv. Ck-out 11 am, ck-in 2 pm. Victorian inn (1890); antiques. 1 blk to ocean, swimming beach. Cr cds: A, C, D, DS, MC, V.

★★ **NORMANDY INN.** *21 Tuttle Ave, Garden State Pkwy exit 98. 908/449-7172; FAX 908/449-1070.* 18 rms, 3 story. Mid-June-mid-Sept: S $96-$148; D $106-$158; each addl $10; lower rates rest of yr. Crib free. TV avail, $2. Complimentary full bkfst 8:30-10:30 am. Bicycles. Porches. Garden. Built as private residence in 1888; 19th-century antiques. Ocean ½ blk. Cr cds: A, C, D, DS, MC, V.

Restaurants

★★ **GRENVILLE HOTEL.** *(See Grenville Hotel Inn) 908/892-3100.* Hrs: 11:30 am-2:30 pm, 5-9 pm; Fri & Sat to 9:30 pm; Sun 10:30 am-2:30 pm, 5-9 pm. Closed Dec 25; also Mon off season. Res accepted. Wine. Semi-a la carte: lunch $6.50-$11.50, dinner $14.95-$24.95. Sun brunch $12.95. Child's meals. Specializes in fresh seafood, veal, beef. Valet parking. Outdoor dining. In Victorian inn. Jacket. Cr cds: A, D, DS, MC, V.

★★★ **OLD MILL INN.** *(Old Mill Rd, Spring Lake Heights) Garden State Pkwy exit 98. 908/449-1800.* Hrs: 11:30 am-10 pm; Fri, Sat to 11 pm; Sun to 9 pm; early-bird dinner Mon-Fri 2:30-6 pm; Sun brunch 11 am-3 pm. Closed Dec 24. Res accepted. Bar. Semi-a la carte: lunch $8.25-$10.95, dinner $15.95-$25.95. Sun brunch $8.95-$13.95. Child's meals. Specializes in seafood. Own baking. Entertainment Fri, Sat. Valet parking. Lakeside view. Cr cds: A, C, D, MC, V.

Stanhope (B-4)

Pop: 3,393 **Elev:** 882 ft **Area code:** 201 **Zip:** 07874

What to See and Do

Waterloo Village Restoration. I-80 exit 25; follow signs. Known as the Andover Forge during the Revolutionary War, it was once a busy town on the Morris Canal. The 18th-century buildings include Stagecoach Inn, houses and craft barns, gristmill, apothecary shop, general store. Music festival during summer. (Mid-Apr-Dec, daily exc Mon; closed Thanksgiving, Dec 25) Sr citizen rate. Phone 347-0900. ¢¢¢

(See Lake Hoptacong, Rockaway)

Inn

★★ **WHISTLING SWAN.** *110 Main St. 201/347-6369.* 9 rms, 1 suite. Rm phones avail. S, D $75-$100. Children over 12 yrs only. TV avail, also in lobby; cable. Complimentary full bkfst, coffee, tea/sherry. Restaurant nearby. Ck-out 11 am, ck-in 1 pm. Airport, RR station, bus depot transportation. Victorian home built 1905 with open-air, wrap-around porch; winding staircase; antiques; rms individually decorated. Totally nonsmoking. Cr cds: A, DS, MC, V.

Restaurant

★★ **THE BLACK FOREST INN.** *249 US 206N. 201/347-3344.* Hrs: 11:30 am-2 pm, 5-10 pm; Sun 1-9 pm. Closed Tues; Jan 1, Dec 24 & 25. Res accepted. German, continental menu. Bar. A la carte entrees: lunch $6.50-$15.50, dinner $16.75-$22.50. Specializes in veal, seafood. Parking. Classic European elegance. Cr cds: A, D, MC, V.

Stone Harbor (K-3)

Pop: 1,025 **Elev:** 5 ft **Area code:** 609 **Zip:** 08247

What to See and Do

Wetlands Institute. 3 mi E off Garden State Pkwy exit 10, on Stone Harbor Blvd. Environmental center focusing on coastal ecology. Also includes observation tower; marsh trail; aquarium; films and guided walks (July & Aug, daily). Bookstore. (Mid-May-mid-Oct, daily; rest of yr, Tues-Sat; closed Easter, July 4, Thanksgiving; also 2 wks late Dec-early Jan) Phone 368-1211. ¢¢

(For further information contact the Stone Harbor Chamber of Commerce, PO Box 422, phone 368-6101; or the Cape May County Chamber of Commerce, PO Box 74, Cape May Court House 08210, phone 465-7181.)

Annual Event

Wings 'n Water Festival. Arts & crafts, decoys; entertainment; seafood. Phone 368-1211. 3rd full wkend Sept.

Motels

★ ★ **DESERT SAND RESORT COMPLEX.** *(79th St & Dune Dr, Avalon 08202)* Off Garden State Pkwy exit 13. 609/368-5133; res: 800/458-6008; FAX 609/368-1849. 90 units, 3 story, 15 suites, 31 kits. July-Aug: S, D $99-$114; each addl $10; suites $105-$128; kits. $107-$153; wkly rates; higher rates hols; lower rates mid-Apr-June, Sept-Oct. Closed rest of yr. Crib avail. TV; cable. 2 pools, 1 indoor; lifeguard. Restaurant 8:30 am-10 pm. Bar noon-midnight. Ck-out 11 am. Coin lndry. Meeting rms. Exercise equipt; weight machine, bicycles, whirlpool. Refrigerators. Ocean 1 blk. Cr cds: MC, V.

★ ★ ★ **GOLDEN INN.** *(Oceanfront at 78th St, Avalon 08202)* Off Garden State Pkwy exit 10. 609/368-5155; FAX 609/368-6112. 160 rms, 3 story, 76 kits. June-Labor Day: S, D $139-$197; each addl $15; suites (to 4) $267-$287; kit. units $162-$197; under 12 free; lower rates rest of yr. Crib avail. TV. Heated pool; wading pool; poolside serv, lifeguard. Restaurant 8 am-11 pm. Rm serv. Bar 11-2 am; entertainment, dancing wkends. Ck-out 11 am. Meeting rms. Bellhops. Valet serv. Social dir. Tennis & golf privileges. Exercise equipt; weight machine, bicycle. Refrigerators. Balconies. Picnic tables. On beach. Cr cds: MC, V.

Toms River (F-5)

Pop: 7,524 **Elev:** 40 ft **Area code:** 908

What to See and Do

Cooper Environmental Center. 1170 Cattus Island Blvd, E on NJ 37 to Fischer Blvd, follow signs. A 500-acre facility with three-mile bay front. Boat tours (summer; free). Ten miles of marked trails. Picnicking (grills), playground. Nature center. (Daily) Phone 270-6960. **Free.**

(For further information contact the Toms River-Ocean County Chamber of Commerce, 1200 Hooper Ave, 08753; 349-0220.)

Motels

★ ★ **HOLIDAY INN.** *290 NJ 37E (08753). 908/244-4000; FAX 908/244-4000.* 123 rms, 4 story. Memorial Day-Labor Day: S $89-$107; D $99-$117; each addl $10; higher rates wknds; lower rates rest of yr. Crib free. TV; cable, in-rm movies. Indoor pool; whirlpool, sauna, poolside serv. Restaurant 6:30 am-10 pm. Rm serv. Bar 11-2 am; entertainment, dancing Fri & Sat. Ck-out noon. Coin lndry. Valet serv. Meeting rms. Game rm. Refrigerators. Cr cds: A, C, D, DS, JCB, MC, V.

D ≈ ⚓ ⚒ 🔥 SC

★ ★ **HOWARD JOHNSON.** *955 Hooper Ave (08753). 908/244-1000.* 96 rms, 2 story. S $85-$98, D $98-$110; each addl $6; under 18 free; higher rates some hols. Crib free. Pet accepted, some restrictions; $10. TV; cable. Indoor/outdoor pool. Restaurant 11 am-9 pm. Bar. Ck-out noon. Meeting rms. Cr cds: A, C, D, DS, MC, V.

D 🐾 ≈ ⚒ 🔥 SC

★ ★ **QUALITY INN.** *815 NJ 37W (08755),* Garden State Pkwy exit 82. 908/341-2400; FAX 908/341-6469. 100 rms, 2 story. Memorial Day-Labor Day: S, D $67-$100; each addl $8; suites $110-$179; under 18 free; lower rates rest of yr. Crib free. TV; cable, in-rm movies avail. Pool; poolside serv, lifeguard. Playground. Complimentary continental bkfst. Restaurant 7 am-10 pm. Rm serv. Bar; entertainment, dancing Fri & Sat. Ck-out 11 am. Meeting rms. Valet serv. Sundries. Airport transportation. Exercise equipt; weight machine, bicycles, sauna. Refrigerators avail. Cr cds: A, C, D, DS, JCB, MC, V.

D ≈ 🏃 ⚒ 🔥 SC

Motor Hotel

★ ★ **RAMADA HOTEL.** *2373 NJ 9 (08755),* at jct NJ 70. 908/905-2626; FAX 908/905-8735. 102 rms, 3 story. Memorial Day-Labor Day: S, D $75-$105; each addl $10; under 12 free; lower rates rest of yr. Crib free. TV; cable. Pool; lifeguard. Complimentary continental bkfst. Restaurant 7 am-10 pm. Rm serv. Bar. Ck-out noon. Coin lndry. Meeting rms. Sundries. Exercise equipt; weight machine, bicycles, whirlpool. Game rm. Refrigerators avail. Cr cds: A, C, D, DS, JCB, MC, V.

D ≈ 🏃 ⚒ 🔥 SC

Restaurant

✔ ★ **OLD TIME TAVERN.** *N Main St, 1 mi N on NJ 166, just N of NJ 37.* 908/349-8778. Hrs: 11:30-1 am; Sun to midnight. Closed Dec 25. Bar. Complete meals: lunch $4.99-$7.99. A la carte: dinner $8.99-$15.99. Child's meals. Specializes in steak, seafood, selected Italian dishes. Parking. Cr cds: A, C, D, MC, V.

D

Trenton (E-3)

Settled: 1679 **Pop:** 88,675 **Elev:** 50 ft **Area code:** 609

The capital of New Jersey since 1790, Trenton is one of the fastest growing business and industrial areas in the country and a leading rubber manufacturing center since colonial times. After crossing the Delaware on December 26, 1776, George Washington attacked the British-held town eight miles to the northwest.

What to See and Do

1. **New Jersey State Museum.** 205 W State St, adj Capitol. For schedules phone 292-6464. Includes

Main Building. Fine art, cultural history, archaeology and natural science exhibits. (Daily exc Mon; closed state hols) **Free.**

Auditorium. Lectures; films; music; children's theater. Some fees. Phone 292-6308.

Planetarium. One of few Intermediate Space Transit planetaria (duplicates motions of space vehicles) in the world. Programs (wkends; July-Aug, daily exc Mon). Over 4 yrs only exc children's programs. Tickets one-half hr in advance. Phone 292-6333. ¢

2. **The Old Barracks Museum.** Barrack St, opp W Front St. One of the finest examples of colonial barracks in the US. Built in 1758-59, it housed British, Hessian and Continental troops during the Revolution. Museum contains restored soldiers' squad room; antique furniture; ceramics; firearms; dioramas. Guides in period costumes. (Daily exc Mon; closed most major hols & Dec 24) Sr citizen rate. Phone 396-1776. ¢

3. **William Trent House** (1719). 15 Market St. Trenton's oldest house is an example of Queen Anne architecture. It was the home of Chief Justice William Trent, for whom the city was named. Colonial garden; period furnishings. (Daily, limited hrs; closed major hols) Phone 989-3027. ¢

4. **Washington Crossing State Park.** 8 mi NW on NJ 29. (See WASHINGTON CROSSING STATE PARK, PA) This 841-acre park commemorates the famous crossing on Christmas night, 1776, by the Continental Army, under the command of General George Washington. Continental Lane, at the park, is the road over which Washington's army began its march to Trenton, December 26, 1776. Nature tours. Picnicking, playground. Visitor center and nature center (Wed-Sun); open-air summer theater (fee). Standard fees. (See ANNUAL EVENTS) Phone 737-0623. Also in park is

Ferry House State Historic Site. Building sheltered Washington and some of his men on Dec 25, 1776, after they had crossed the Delaware from the Pennsylvania side. It is believed that the strategy to be used for the attack on Trenton was discussed here. Restored as a living history colonial farmhouse; special programs throughout the yr. (Wed-Sun) Phone 737-2515.

5. **Trenton State College** (1855). (6,150 students) 4 mi N on NJ 31. A 250-acre wooded campus with 2 lakes. Tours of campus. Phone 771-1855. On campus is the

College Art Gallery. (Feb-May & Sept-Dec, daily exc Sat; closed hols) Phone 771-2198. **Free.**

6. **Sesame Place.** 6 mi NW via NJ 29, then 8 mi SW on I-95 to Langhorne (see BRISTOL, PA). A family play park.

(For further information and a brochure describing historic sites contact the Mercer County Chamber of Commerce, 214 W State St, 08608; 393-4143.)

Annual Events

Trenton Kennel Club Dog Show. Mercer County Central Park. Early May.

Reenactment of Crossing of the Delaware. Washington Crossing State Park (see #4). Departs Pennsylvania side on the afternoon of Dec 25.

(See Princeton)

Motel

★ ★ **HOWARD JOHNSON.** *2995 Brunswick Pike (08648), 5 mi N on US 1. 609/896-1100; FAX 609/895-1325.* 104 rms, 2 story. S $62.50-$84.50; D $68.50-$84.50; each addl $10; under 18 free. Crib free. TV; cable. Pool. Restaurant open 24 hrs. Ck-out noon. Meeting rm. Valet serv. Sundries. Private patios, balconies. Cr cds: A, C, D, DS, JCB, MC, V.

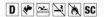

Restaurants

★ ★ **LA GONDOLA.** *762 Roebling Ave (08600). 609/392-0600.* Hrs: 11:30 am-3 pm, 4:30-10 pm; Fri to 11 pm; Sat 4:30-11 pm. Closed Sun; some major hols. Res accepted. Italian menu. Bar. Semi-a la carte: lunch $4.95-$14.95, dinner $12.95-$23.95. Child's meals. Specialties: saltimbocca alla Gondola, fussilli alla carbonara, fettine di pollo al carciofetto. Parking. Five dining rms. Dining in wine cellar. Mediterranean decor. Cr cds: A, C, D, MC, V.

★ ★ **LARRY PERONI'S WATERFRONT.** *1140 River Rd, 7 mi NW on NJ 29, 1/2 mi N of Scudder's Falls Bridge, I-95, exit 1. 609/882-0303.* Hrs: 11:30 am-10 pm; Sat 4-11 pm; early-bird dinner Mon-Fri 4-7 pm. Closed Dec 25. Res accepted. Bar. Semi-a la carte: lunch $4.95-$8.95, dinner $9.95-$18.95. Specializes in veal, beef, seafood. Parking. Paneled dining rms, fireplaces. Spacious grounds. Cr cds: A, C, D, DS, MC, V.

D

Union (C-5)

Settled: 1749 **Pop:** 50,024 **Elev:** 137 ft **Area code:** 908 **Zip:** 07083

(For information about this area contact the Union Township Chamber of Commerce, 355 Chestnut St; 688-2777.)

(See Elizabeth, Newark, Newark Intl Airport Area)

Motel

✔ ★ **UNION MOTOR LODGE.** *2735 US 22W. 908/687-8600; res: 800/526-4970; FAX 908/688-3660.* 98 rms, 2 story. S $39-$49; D $44-$49; each addl $6; under 12 free. Crib free. TV; cable. Restaurant 6 am-10 pm. Rm serv. Bar 11:30-2 am. Ck-out 11 am. Meeting rms. Free Newark airport transportation exc hols. Some in-rm steam baths. Cr cds: A, C, D, DS, MC, V.

Restaurants

★ ★ ★ **L'AFFAIRE.** *(1099 US 22E, Mountainside) On US 22E, 5 mi W of Garden State Pkwy exit 140, 140A. 908/232-4454.* Hrs: 11:30 am-3 pm, 4:30-10 pm; Fri to 11 pm; Sat 4:30-11 pm; Sun 12:30-9 pm; early-bird dinner Mon-Sat 4:30-6 pm. Closed major hols. Continental menu. Bar; entertainment Fri-Sat. Semi-a la carte: lunch $7.95-$12.95, dinner $16.25-$23.95. Specialties: lobster in whiskey, veal Oscar. Jacket (dinner). Cr cds: A, C, D, DS, MC, V.

D SC

★ ★ ★ **TOWER STEAK HOUSE.** *(1047 US 22E, Mountainside) 4 mi W of Garden State Pkwy exit 140. 908/233-5542.* Hrs: noon-3 pm, 5-9 pm; Sat 5-10 pm; Sun noon-9 pm. Closed Mon; Dec 25. Res accepted. Continental menu. Bar to 2 am. Semi-a la carte: lunch $6.95-$14.25, dinner $11.95-$27.95. Sun brunch $14.95. Specializes in steak, seafood, Italian dishes. Entertainment Sat. Jacket (dinner). Cr cds: A, C, D, DS, MC, V.

Vernon (A-4)

Pop: 1,696 **Elev:** 564 ft **Area code:** 201 **Zip:** 07462

What to See and Do

Action Park. NJ 94. Theme park includes 75 self-operative rides, shows and attractions. Action park has more than 40 water rides, including river rides and Tidal Wave Pool; also Grand Prix Race Cars, bungee jumping, miniature golf, children's park; food, picnic area. 3 daily shows, wkend festival series. (Mid-June-Labor Day, daily; late May-mid-June, Thurs-Sun) Phone 827-2000. ¢¢¢¢¢ Also here is

Vernon Valley/Great Gorge Ski Resort. NJ 94. Resort has 1 triple, 14 double chairlifts; 3 rope tows; school, rentals; 100% snowmaking; cafeterias, restaurants, bars, night club; nursery. 52 runs; vertical drop 1,040 feet. (Dec-Mar, daily) Night skiing. Health spa, country club (daily). For ski conditions phone 827-3900; general information and fees phone 827-2000. ¢¢¢¢¢

(For further information contact the Vernon Township Municipal Building, Church St; 764-4055.)

Resort

★ ★ ★ **SEASONS.** *(PO Box 637, Rte 517, McAfee 07428)* SW via NJ 94, at jct NJ 517. 201/827-6000; res: 800/835-2555; FAX 201/827-3767. 560 rms, 8 story, 18 kit. units. S $100-$140; D $120-$160; each addl $10; suites, kit. units $130-$550; under 18 free. Crib $10. TV; cable. 2 pools, one indoor; wading pool, whirlpool, sauna, poolside serv, lifeguard. Playground. Supervised child's activities (Memorial Day-Labor Day, wkends). Dining rms. Box lunches. Snack bar. Picnics. Rm serv. Bar 11-2 am; entertainment wkends, dancing. Ck-out noon, ck-in 3 pm. Convention facilities. Bellhops. Concierge. Gift shop. Airport, bus depot transportation. Sports dir. Indoor and outdoor tennis, pro. 27-hole golf, greens fee $43-$63, pro, putting green, driving range. Swimming. Downhill ski 1 mi; rentals. Sleighing. Hiking. Lawn games. Social dir. Rec rm. Game rm. Health club privileges. Balconies. Scenic view of mountains and golf course. Dinner theater. A four-season resort with excellent recreational facilities and tranquil environment. Cr cds: A, C, D, DS, MC, V.

Wayne (B-5)

Pop: 47,025 **Elev:** 200 ft **Area code:** 201 **Zip:** 07470

Wayne is the home of William Paterson College of New Jersey (1855).

What to See and Do

1. **Van Riper-Hopper (Wayne) Museum** (ca 1786). 533 Berdan Ave. Dutch Colonial farmhouse with 18th- and 19th-century furnishings; local historical objects; herb garden; bird sanctuary. Also here is **Mead Van Duyne House,** restored Dutch farmhouse. (Fri-Tues; closed Jan 1, Dec 25) Phone 694-7192. ¢

2. **Dey Mansion** (ca 1740). 199 Totowa Rd. Restoration of Washington's Headquarters (1780); period furnishings. Guided tours. Picnic tables. (Wed-Sun; closed major hols) Phone for hrs, 696-1776. ¢

3. **Terhune Memorial Park (Sunnybank).** 2¹/₂ mi N on US 202N. Estate of the late Albert Payson Terhune, author of *Lad, a Dog* and many other books about his collies. Scenic garden; picnic area, playground. (Daily) Phone 694-1800. **Free.**

(For further information contact the Tri-County Chamber of Commerce, 2055 Hamburg Tpke; 831-7788.)

Motels

★ ★ **HOLIDAY INN.** *334 US 46E, on Service Rd, I-80 exit S Verona.* 201/256-7000; FAX 201/890-5406. 140 rms, 2 story. S $78-$87; D $84-$93; each addl $6; under 18 free. Crib free. Pet accepted, some restrictions. TV; cable. Pool; poolside serv, lifeguard. Restaurant 6:30 am-11 pm. Rm serv. Bar 11-3 am; entertainment, dancing Tues-Sat. Ck-out noon. Meeting rms. Bellhops. Valet serv. Sundries. Health club privileges. Cr cds: A, C, D, DS, JCB, MC, V.

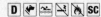

✔ ★ ★ **HOWARD JOHNSON.** *1850 NJ 23 and Ratzer Rd.* 201/696-8050; FAX 201/696-8050, ext. 555. 150 rms, 2 story. S $59.50-$67.50; D $65.50-$74.50; each addl $6; under 16 free. Crib free. Pet accepted, some restrictions. TV; cable. Pool. Ck-out noon. Coin lndry. Meeting rms. Valet serv. Health club privileges. Some refrigerators. Private patios, balconies. Cr cds: A, C, D, DS, JCB, MC, V.

Motor Hotels

★ ★ **HOLIDAY INN TOTOWA.** *(1 NJ 46, Totowa 07512)* On US 46 just E of Union Blvd in Totowa. 201/785-9000; FAX 201/785-3031. 154 rms, 5 story. S $87-$90; D $93-$96; each addl $6; under 18 free. Crib free. TV; cable. Pool. Restaurant 7 am-10 pm. Rm serv. Ck-out noon. Meeting rms. Bellhops. Valet serv. Sundries. Indoor parking. Indoor lighted tennis. Movie theater. Cr cds: A, C, D, DS, JCB, MC, V.

★ ★ ★ **RADISSON FAIRFIELD.** *(690 NJ 46E, Fairfield 07004)* ¹/₂ mi W of jct NJ 23. 201/227-9200; FAX 201/227-4308. 204 rms, 5 story, 61 suites. S $130-$150; D $135-$145; each addl $10; suites $140-$300; under 18 free. Crib $10. TV; cable. Indoor pool. Restaurant 6:30 am-10 pm. Rm serv. Bar 11-1:30 am; entertainment, dancing Fri, Sat. Ck-out noon. Meeting rms. Bellhops. Exercise rm; bicycles, rower, sauna. Bathrm phones, in-rm whirlpools; some refrigerators. Cr cds: A, C, D, DS, ER, JCB, MC, V.

West Orange (C-5)

Pop: 39,103 **Elev:** 368 ft **Area code:** 201 **Zip:** 07052

What to See and Do

1. **Edison National Historic Site.** Main St & Lakeside Ave. Phone 736-5050.

   Edison Laboratory. Built by Edison in 1887, it was his laboratory for 44 years. During that time, he was granted more than half of his 1,093 patents (an all-time record). Here he perfected the phonograph, motion picture camera and electric storage battery. One-hour lab tour (no video cameras, strollers) includes the chemistry lab and library; demonstrations of early phonographs. Visitor center has exhibits; films (daily; closed Jan 1, Thanksgiving, Dec 25). Sr citizens free. Phone 736-5050. ¢

2. **Eagle Rock Reservation.** NW via Main St & Eagle Rock Ave. A 644-foot elevation in the Orange Mts; visitors see a heavily populated area that stretches from the Passaic River Valley east to New York City. Hiking trails; carriage rides; restaurant. Picnicking. Bridle paths. (Daily) Phone 857-8530 or 731-3000.

3. **Turtle Back Zoo.** 560 Northfield Ave, 3 mi W on I-280, exit 10, in South Mountain Reservation. This 16-acre park features animals in natural surroundings; sea lion pool; miniature train ride (1 mi). Picnicking, concessions. (Daily; closed Jan 1, Thanksgiving, Dec 24, 25, 31; limited schedule Dec-Jan) Sr citizen rate. Phone 731-5800. ¢¢¢ Adj is

South Mountain Arena. Indoor ice rink. Hockey games, special events. Phone 731-3828.

(For further information contact the West Orange Chamber of Commerce, PO Box 83; 731-0360.)

(For accommodations see Livingston, Newark, Newark Intl Airport Area)

Restaurants

★ ★ ★ **HIGHLAWN PAVILION.** *Eagle Rock Reservation. 201/731-3463.* Hrs: noon-3 pm, 5:30-10 pm; Fri to 11:30 pm; Sat 5-11:30 pm; Sun 5-10 pm. Closed Dec 24. Res accepted. Bar to 2 am. A la carte entrees: lunch $6.95-$12.50, dinner $13.75-$22.50. Specializes in veal chop, steak, fresh seafood. Oyster bar. Pianist Wed-Sun. Valet parking. Outdoor dining. Located in county park on top of mountain; view of NY skyline. Food preparation visible from dining rm. Jacket. Cr cds: A, C, D, DS, MC, V.

D

★ ★ ★ **THE MANOR.** *111 Prospect Ave, I-280 exit 8B. 201/731-2360.* Hrs: noon-2:30 pm, 6-10 pm; Sat 6 pm-midnight; Sun to 8:30 pm. Closed Mon; Dec 24. Amer, continental menu. Bar to 2 am. Wine cellar. A la carte entrees: lunch from $8.50, dinner $18-$29. Lobster buffet Tues-Sat $33.95. Sun buffet $26.95. Wed lunch buffet $15.95. Specializes in rack of lamb, Dover sole, beef Wellington. Own baking. Pianist; band & vocalist Fri & Sat. Dining, cocktail terrace. Formal gardens, waterfalls, multicolored fountains. Jacket, tie. Cr cds: A, C, D, DS, MC, V.

D

Wildwood & Wildwood Crest (K-3)

Pop: Wildwood, 4,484; Wildwood Crest, 3,631 **Elev:** 8 ft **Area code:** 609 **Zip:** 08260

Wildwood's busy boardwalk extends for approximately two miles along the five miles of protected sandy beach it shares with North Wildwood and Wildwood Crest, two neighboring resorts. The area offers swimming, waterskiing, ocean and bay fishing, boating, sailing, bicycling, golf, tennis and shuffleboard.

What to See and Do

Boat trips. Capt Sinn's Dock, 6006 Park Blvd in Wildwood Crest. Sightseeing & whale watching cruises aboard *Big Flamingo*, (Apr-Nov, daily) For schedule, fees phone 522-3934.

(For further information, including other boat trips, contact the Greater Wildwood Chamber of Commerce, PO Box 823; 729-4000.)

(See Cape May)

Motels

(Rates quoted may be for advance reservation only; holiday rates may be higher)

★ ★ **AQUA BEACH RESORT.** *(5501 Ocean Ave, Wildwood Crest) On beach. 609/522-6507; res: 800/247-4776; FAX 609/522-8535.* 123 rms, 5 story, 113 kits. July-Aug (3-night min): S, D $114-

$144; each addl $10; kits. $128-$236; under 4 free; wkly, wkend rates; lower rates Mar-June & Sept-Oct. Closed rest of yr. Crib avail. TV; cable. Heated pool; wading pool, whirlpool, lifeguard. Supervised child's activities (June-Aug). Complimentary coffee in rms. Restaurant 6 am-4 pm. Rm serv. Ck-out 11 am. Coin lndry. Meeting rms. Valet serv. Game rm. Balconies. Grills. Cr cds: DS, MC, V.

D

★ ★ **ARMADA MOTOR INN.** *(6503 Ocean Ave, Wildwood Crest) On beach. 609/729-3000; res: 800/399-3001; FAX 609/729-7472.* 56 rms, 5 story, 40 kits. Mid-July-Aug: up to 4 persons $128-$136; each addl $10; kit. units up to 4 persons $140-$153; some lower rates rest of yr. Closed Oct-mid-Apr. Crib $5. TV. Heated pool; wading pool, sauna. Restaurant nearby. Ck-out 11 am. Coin lndry. Meeting rms. Valet serv. Sundries. Game rm. Refrigerators. Some balconies. Picnic tables, grill. Sun decks. Cr cds: A, DS, MC, V.

★ ★ **ASTRONAUT.** *(511 E Stockton Rd, Wildwood Crest) On beach. 609/522-6981.* 33 kit. units, 3 story. No elvtr. July-early Sept: up to 8 persons $125-$170; lower rates Apr-June, early Sept-mid-Oct. Closed rest of yr. Crib avail. TV. Pool; wading pool. Restaurant nearby. Ck-out 11 am. Coin lndry. Sundries. Shuffleboard. Refrigerators. Sun decks. Picnic tables, grills. Cr cds: MC, V.

★ ★ **ATTACHE.** *(Heather Rd & Beach, Wildwood Crest) On beach. 609/522-0241.* 42 rms, 3 story, 26 kits. Mid-July-late Aug: up to 4 persons $125-$165; each addl $10; kit. units for 4 persons $125-$165; family rates; lower rates mid-Apr-mid-July, late Aug-mid-Oct. Closed rest of yr. Crib avail. TV; cable. Heated pool; wading pool. Restaurant nearby. Ck-out 11 am. Lndry facilities. Refrigerators. Some balconies. Picnic tables, grill. Cr cds: A, D, DS, MC, V.

★ **BEACH COLONY.** *(500 E Stockton Ave, Wildwood Crest) At Ocean Ave. 609/522-4037.* 26 units, 2 story, 14 kits. Late June-Labor Day: S, D $85-$105; each addl $8; suites $96-$112; kit. units $95; lower rates early May-late June, after Labor Day-mid-Oct. Closed rest of yr. Crib avail. TV. Pool; wading pool. Restaurant adj 7 am-8 pm. Ck-out 11 am. Coin lndry. Sundries. Rec rm. Refrigerators. Picnic tables, grills. Cr cds: A, MC, V.

✔ ★ **CARIBBEAN.** *(5600 Ocean Ave, Wildwood Crest) At Buttercup Rd. 609/522-8292; res: 800/457-7040.* 30 rms, 2 story, 9 kits. July-Labor Day: up to 4 persons $85-$107; kit. units for 4 persons $90-$107; lower rates May-June, after Labor Day-Sept. Closed rest of yr. Crib avail. TV; cable. Heated pool; wading pool, lifeguard. Complimentary coffee in rms. Restaurant opp 7 am-10 pm. Ck-out 11 am. Coin lndry. Game rm. Lawn games. Refrigerators. Sun deck. Picnic tables, grills. Cr cds: MC, V.

✔ ★ **COMPASS MOTOR INN.** *(6501 Atlantic Ave, Wildwood Crest) 609/522-6948; res: 800/624-2530 Mid-Atlantic states only.* 50 rms, 3 story, 25 kits. No elvtrs. July-Aug: S, D $90-$112; each addl $8; family rates; wkly & wkend rates; higher rates hols (3-day min); lower rates May-June & Sept-Oct. Closed rest of yr. Crib $8. TV; cable. Heated pool; wading pool. Complimentary coffee in rms. Restaurant nearby. Ck-out 11 am. Meeting rms. Refrigerators. Ocean 1 blk. Cr cds: A, DS, MC, V.

★ ★ **CRUSADER RESORT MOTOR INN.** *(PO Box 1308, 6101 Ocean Ave, Wildwood Crest) At Cardinal Rd, on beach. 609/522-6991; res: 800/462-3260; FAX 609/522-2280.* 61 units, 3 story, 54 suites, 37 kits. July-Aug: S, D $120-$180; each addl $12; kit. units $148-$180; lower rates Apr-June & Sept-Oct. Closed Nov-Mar. Crib avail. TV; cable. Heated pool; wading pool, sauna, lifeguard. Restaurant 7 am-8 pm. Ck-out 11 am. Coin lndry. Meeting rms. Sundries. Gift shop. Game rm. Refrigerators. Some balconies. Picnic tables. Ocean beach; boardwalk. No cr cds accepted.

★ **IMPERIAL 500.** *(6601 Atlantic Ave at Forget-Me-Not Rd, Wildwood Crest)* 609/522-6063; res: 800/522-1255. 45 rms, 3 story, 26 kits. No elvtr. July-Labor Day: S, D for 4, $95-$105; each addl $5; kit. units $100-$105; lower rates May-June, after Labor Day-Sept. Closed rest of yr. Crib avail. TV; cable. Heated pool; wading pool. Restaurant nearby. Ck-out 11 am. Coin lndry. Meeting rm. Sundries. Shuffleboard. Rec rm. Lawn games. Refrigerators. Sun deck. Picnic tables, grills. Cr cds: MC, V.

★ **LONG BEACH LODGE.** *(9th Ave on Beach, North Wildwood)* 609/522-1520; FAX 609/523-1583. 24 kit. units, 3 story. No elvtrs. July-late Aug: S, D $60-$75; each addl $10; under 6 free; wkend, wkly rates; golf plan; higher rates hols (3-day min); lower rates Apr-June & late Aug-Oct. Closed rest of yr. Crib $8. TV; cable. Heated pool; wading pool. Complimentary coffee in lobby. Restaurant nearby. Ck-out 11 am. Coin lndry. Balconies. Swimming beach opp. Cr cds: A, DS, MC, V.

★ **MADRID OCEAN RESORT.** *(427 E Miami Ave, Wildwood Crest)* On beach. 609/729-1600; FAX 609/729-8483. 54 rms, 5 story, 24 kits. July-Labor Day: S, D $90-$115; each addl $10; suites $125; kit. units up to 4 persons $140; higher rates wkends; lower rates mid-May-June, after Labor Day-Sept. Closed rest of yr. Crib avail. TV. Heated pool; wading pool. Restaurant 7 am-11 pm. Ck-out 11 am. Coin lndry. Sundries. Rec rm. Sun deck. Refrigerators. Balconies. All oceanfront rms. Cr cds: A, MC, V.

★ ★ **OCEAN HOLIDAY.** *(6501 Ocean Ave, Wildwood Crest)* On beach. 609/729-2900; res: 800/321-6232; FAX 609/523-1024. 56 rms, 5 story, 40 kits. July-Aug (3-night min hol wkends): S, D $95-$115; each addl $10; kit. units (up to 4 persons) $100-$235; lower rates Apr-June, Sept-Oct. Closed rest of yr. Crib $5. TV. Pool; wading pool. Restaurant nearby. Ck-out 11 am. Coin lndry. Meeting rms. Sundries. Refrigerators. Some private patios, balconies. Picnic tables, grills. Cr cds: A, MC, V.

★ ★ **PAN AMERICAN HOTEL.** *(Crocus Rd & Ocean Ave, Wildwood Crest)* On beach. 609/522-6936; FAX 609/522-6937. 78 rms, 4 story, 39 kits. Early July-early Sept: up to 4 persons $145-$150; each addl $12; suites $172-$180; kit. units (up to 4 persons) $148-$151; lower rates mid-May-early June, early Sept-mid-Oct. Closed rest of yr. Crib free. TV. Heated pool; wading pool, sauna, lifeguard. Playground. Free supervised child's activities (July-Aug). Restaurant 7:30 am-8 pm. Rm serv. Ck-out 11 am. Meeting rm. Coin lndry. Sundries. Rec rm. Refrigerators. Sun deck. Balconies. Cr cds: MC, V.

★ ★ **PORT ROYAL.** *(6801 Ocean Ave, Wildwood Crest)* On beach. 609/729-2000. 100 rms, 6 story, 50 kits. Late June-Labor Day: S, D $145-$150; each addl $12; kit. units for 4 persons $170-$180; lower rates May-late June, after Labor Day-mid-Oct. Closed rest of yr. Crib avail. TV. Heated pool; wading pool, sauna. Playground. Free supervised child's activities (mid-June-Labor Day). Restaurant 8 am-8 pm in season. Ck-out 11 am. Coin lndry. Meeting rm (off-season). Sundries. Rec rm, game rm in season. Balconies. Cr cds: MC, V.

★ ★ **ROYAL HAWAIIAN.** *(Ocean & Orchid, Wildwood Crest)* 609/522-3414; FAX 609/522-1316. 88 rms, 5 story, 58 kits. Mid-July-Aug: S, D $98-$165; suites, kit. units for 4 $132-$230; each addl $10; higher rates conventions; lower rates mid-May-mid-July, Sept-Oct. Closed rest of yr. Crib avail. TV. Pool; wading pool, sauna, lifeguard. Playground. Restaurant 7 am-5 pm. Ck-out 11 am. Coin lndry. Valet

serv. Rec rm. Refrigerators. Balconies. Sun deck. Grills. On ocean. Cr cds: A, DS, MC, V.

Motor Hotels

★ ★ **BEACH TERRACE.** *PO Box 710, 3400 Atlantic Ave.* 609/522-8100; FAX 609/729-3336. 78 rms, 8 story, 24 kits. July-Aug: S, D $105-$115; each addl $10; kit. units $105-$115; lower rates Apr-June, Sept. Closed rest of yr. Crib avail. TV; cable. Pool; wading pool, lifeguard. Restaurant 8 am-noon, 5-10 pm. Ck-out 11 am. Refrigerators. Balconies. Cr cds: A, DS, MC, V.

★ **BRISTOL PLAZA.** *(6407 Ocean Ave, Wildwood Crest 08260-4195)* 609/729-1234; res: 800/433-9731; FAX 609/729-9363. 55 rms, 5 story, 41 kits. Mid-July-late Aug: S, D (up to 4) $116-162; family rates; wkly, wkend, hol rates; lower rates May-mid-July & late Aug-Oct. Closed rest of yr. Crib free. TV; cable. Heated pool; wading pool, sauna. Complimentary coffee in rms. Restaurant nearby. Ck-out 11 am. Coin lndry. Refrigerators. Balconies. Picnic tables. Opp ocean. Cr cds: A, DS, MC, V.

★ ★ ★ **EL CORONADO MOTOR INN.** *(8501 Atlantic Ave, Wildwood Crest)* On beach. 609/729-1000; res: 800/227-5302; FAX 609/729-6557. 113 rms, 6 story, 63 kit. suites. July-Aug: S, D $119-$129; each addl $10; kit. suites $140-$224; under 12 free; wkly, wkend (3-night min), hol rates; lower rates May-June & Sept-Oct. Closed rest of yr. Crib avail. TV; cable. Pool; wading pool, whirlpool, sauna, poolside serv, lifeguard. Restaurant 8 am-4 pm. Ck-out 11 am. Coin lndry. Meeting rms. Gift shop. Game rm. Refrigerators. Balconies. Cr cds: A, DS, MC, V.

★ ★ **WAIKIKI MOTOR INN.** *(6211 Ocean Ave, Wildwood Crest)* On beach at Wisteria. 609/522-0115; res: 800/622-5642; FAX 609/523-8817. 55 units, 6 story, 37 kits. S, D $139-$147; each addl after 4 $12; suites, kit units (1-2 bedrm) $139-$235; some wkend rates off season. Closed Dec-Feb. Crib $6. TV; in-rm movies. Heated pool; wading pool, sauna, Restaurant 8 am-3 pm. Ck-out 11 am. Coin lndry. Meeting rm. Sundries. Sun deck. Refrigerators. Balconies. Picnic tables, grills. Cr cds: A, C, D, DS, MC, V.

Inn

★ ★ **CANDLELIGHT INN.** *(2310 Central Ave, North Wildwood)* 609/522-6200; FAX 609/522-6125. 8 rms, 6 with A/C, 4 story. No rm phones. May-Oct: S $85-$100; D $100-$235; lower rates rest of yr. Adults preferred. Complimentary full bkfst, tea/sherry. Ck-out 11 am, ck-in 1 pm. Whirlpool, sun deck. Lawn games. Grills. Ocean, beach 3 blks. Queen Anne/Victorian-style house (ca 1905); restored. Antique furnishings include 1855 sofa and 1890 Eastlake piano. Large porch with swing and hammocks. Totally nonsmoking. Cr cds: A, DS, MC, V.

Restaurants

★ ★ **CAPTAIN'S TABLE.** *(Hollywood at Oceanfront, Wildwood Crest)* 609/522-2939. Hrs: 8 am-noon, 4:30-10 pm. Closed mid-Oct-Mother's Day. Res accepted. Buffet: bkfst $1.95-$7.95. Semi-a la carte: dinner $9.95-$25.95. Child's meals. Specializes in Maine lobster, steak. Parking. Nautical decor; ocean view. Family-owned. Cr cds: A, C, D, DS, MC, V.

D

★ ★ **GARFIELD GIARDINO.** *(3800 Pacific Ave, Wildwood) In Holly Beach Station Mall.* 609/729-0120. Hrs: 11:30 am-3 pm, 4 pm-midnight; early-bird dinner Mon-Sat 4-6:30 pm. Closed Dec 25. Res accepted. Italian menu. Bar. Semi-a la carte: lunch, dinner $10.95-$19.95. Child's meals. Specializes in fresh seafood, veal, poultry. 2 dining areas; roofed dining in garden setting & indoor. Cr cds: A, C, D, DS, MC, V.

[D] [SC]

★ ★ **LTE SEASONS.** *222 E Schellenger Ave.* 609/522-4400. Hrs: 11:30 am-3 pm, 4:30-10 pm; Sat from 4:30 pm; early-bird dinner 4:30-6 pm. Res accepted. Bar; entertainment Thur-Sat. Semi-a la carte: lunch, dinner $9.95-$19.95. Child's meals. Specializes in seafood, veal, steak. Valet parking. Cr cds: A, C, D, DS, MC, V.

[D]

★ ★ **LUIGI'S.** *4119 Pacific Ave.* 609/522-8571. Hrs: 4 pm-1 am; early-bird dinner to 6 pm. Closed mid-Oct-Easter. Res accepted. Italian, Amer menu. Bar. Semi-a la carte: dinner $8.95-$18.95. Child's meals. Specializes in veal Siciliano, fresh fish, pasta. Valet parking. Inviting, European-style dining. Family-owned. Cr cds: A, D, DS, MC, V.

[D]

★ **MENZ.** *(985 NJ 47S, Rio Grande) 5 mi NE.* 609/886-5691. Hrs: 4-9 pm; Sun, hols from noon. Closed Mid-Oct-Palm Sun; also wkends to Mother's Day. Res accepted. Semi-a la carte: dinner $8.50-$28.95. Child's meals. Specializes in seafood. Parking. Antique decor; music boxes, clocks, stained glass. No cr cds accepted.

[D]

✔ ★ **THE WHARF.** *(708 W Burk Ave, Wildwood)* 609/522-6336. Hrs: 4:30-10 pm; Fri & Sat to 11 pm; early-bird dinner Mon-Fri 4:30-6 pm. Closed Oct-mid-Apr. Res accepted. Bar to 3 am. Semi-a la carte: dinner $11.75-$16.95. Child's meals. Specializes in fresh seafood, steak, sauces. Entertainment. Parking. Outdoor dining overlooking waterway. Nautical decor. Cr cds: A, D, DS, MC, V.

[D]

Woodbridge (D-5)

Settled: 1664 **Pop:** 93,086 **Elev:** 21 ft **Area code:** 908 **Zip:** 07095

Here, where the first cloverleaf interchange in the US was constructed in 1929, cross two of the country's busiest roads—the Garden State Parkway and the New Jersey Turnpike. Also in Woodbridge are seaway and river port areas visited by thousands of vessels annually.

What to See and Do

Barron Arts Center. 582 Rahway Ave. Built in 1877 in Romanesque-revival style. Originally the first free public library in Middlesex County, now an arts and cultural center with art exhibits; workshops; lectures; poetry sessions; concerts; special events. Gallery (Mon-Fri; closed hols). Phone 634-0413. **Free.**

(For further information & details on a self-guided tour of Old Downtown contact the Chamber of Commerce Visitor Center, 52 Main St; 636-4040.)

Motel

✔ ★ ★ **BUDGET MOTOR LODGE.** *350 US 9N, off NJ Tpke exit 11 or Garden State Pkwy exit 127N.* 908/636-4000; FAX 908/636-0636. 168 rms, 5 story. S, D $48-$56; each addl $5; under 12 free. Crib free. TV; in-rm movies avail. Restaurant 6:30 am-10 pm. Rm serv. Bar 11:30-1 am. Coin lndry. Meeting rms. Valet serv. Sundries. Cr cds: A, D, DS, MC, V.

[D] [≈] [★] [≈] [SC]

Hotels

★ ★ ★ **HILTON.** *(120 Wood Ave S, Iselin 08830) W of Garden State Pkwy, exit 131A.* 908/494-6200; FAX 908/494-6200, ext. 240. 200 rms, 7-11 story. S $74-$129; D $86-$141; each addl $12; under 18 free; wkend packages. Crib free. TV; cable, in-rm movies. Indoor pool; lifeguard. Restaurant 6 am-midnight; dining rm 11 am-9:30 pm. Bar noon-1 am; entertainment, dancing Wed-Sat. Meeting rms. Gift shop. Exercise rm; instructor, weights, bicycles, whirlpool, steam rm. Bathrm phones; refrigerator in suites. Cr cds: A, C, D, DS, MC, V.

[D] [≈] [★] [≈] [≈] [SC]

★ ★ ★ **SHERATON AT WOODBRIDGE PLACE.** *(515 Rte 1 S, Iselin 08830) US 1 at Gill Lane, 1/2 mi N of Garden State Pkwy exit 130.* 908/634-3600; FAX 908/634-0258. 254 rms, 7 story. S, D $112; each addl $10; suites $165; under 18 free; wkend rates. Crib free. TV; cable. 2 pools, 1 indoor; poolside serv, lifeguard. Restaurants 6:30 am-10 pm; dining rm 11 am-3 pm, 6-11 pm. Bars 11-1 am; entertainment Fri-Sun. Ck-out noon. Convention facilities. Gift shop. Airport, Metro Park RR station transportation. Exercise equipt; weights, bicycles, whirlpool. Game rm. Wet bar in suites. 40-ft atrium lobby, marble fountain. Extensive grounds, attractive landscaping. **LUXURY LEVEL : THE TOWERS.** 36 units, 2 suites. S $125; D $135; suites $230. Concierge. Private lounge. Bathrm phones. Complimentary continental bkfst, refreshments. Cr cds: A, C, D, DS, ER, MC, V.

[D] [≈] [★] [≈] [≈] [SC]

North Carolina

Population: 6,628,637	
Land area: 48,843 square miles	
Elevation: 0-6,684 feet	
Highest point: Mount Mitchell (Yancey County)	
Entered Union: Twelfth of original 13 states (November 21, 1789)	
Capital: Raleigh	
Motto: To be rather than to seem	
Nicknames: Tar Heel State, Old North State	
State flower: American dogwood	
State bird: Cardinal	
State tree: Pine	
State fair: October 13-22, 1995, in Raleigh	
Time zone: Eastern	

North Carolina, besides being a wonderful place for a vacation, is a cross section of America—a state of magnificent variety with three distinctive regions: the coast, the heartland and the mountains. Its elevation ranges from sea level to 6,684 feet atop Mt Mitchell in the Black Mountain Range of the Appalachians. It has descendants of English, German, Scottish, Irish and African immigrants. It has Quakers, Moravians, Episcopalians and Calvinists. It produces two-thirds of our flue-cured tobacco, as well as cotton, peanuts and vegetables on its farms. Fabrics, furniture and many other products are made in its factories. It also has one of the finest state university systems in the nation with campuses at Chapel Hill, Raleigh, Greensboro, Charlotte, Asheville and Wilmington.

In 1585, the first English settlement was unsuccessfully started on Roanoke Island. Another attempt at settlement was made in 1587—but the colony disappeared, leaving only the crudely scratched word "CROATOAN" on a tree—perhaps referring to the Croatan Indians who may have killed the colonists or absorbed them into their own culture, leaving behind one of history's great mysteries. Here, in the Great Smoky Mountains, lived the Cherokee before the government drove them westward to Oklahoma over the Trail of Tears, on which a third of them died. Descendants of many members of this tribe, who hid in the inaccessible, rocky coves and forests, still live here. Some "mountain people," isolated, independent, still singing songs dating back to Elizabethan England, also live here. Few North Carolinians owned slaves, very few owned many, and, early on, the state accepted free blacks (in 1860 there were 30,463) as a part of the community.

Citizens take pride in being called "Tar Heels." During the Civil War, North Carolinians returning from the front were taunted by a troop from another state who had "retreated" a good deal earlier. The Carolinians declared that Jefferson Davis had decided to bring up all the tar from North Carolina to use on the heels of the other regiment to make them "stick better in the next fight." General Lee, hearing of the incident, said, "God bless the Tar Heel boys."

Individual and democratic from the beginning, this state refused to ratify the Constitution until the Bill of Rights had been added. Its western citizens strongly supported the Union in 1860. It did not join the Confederate States of America until after Fort Sumter had been fired upon and Lincoln had called for volunteers. Its independence was then challenged, and it furnished one-fifth of the soldiers of the Southern armies even though its population was only one-ninth of the Confederacy's. Eighty-four engagements (most of them small) were fought on its soil. Jealous of its rights, North Carolina resisted the authority of Confederate Army officers from Virginia and loudly protested many of the policies of Jefferson Davis; but its 125,000 men fought furiously, and 40,000 of them died for what they believed was right. For years after the Civil War North Carolina was a poverty-stricken state, although it suffered less from the inroads of carpetbaggers than did many of its neighbors.

The state seems designed for vacationers. Beautiful mountains and flowering plants, lake and ocean swimming and boating, hunting and fishing, superb golf courses, old towns, festivals, pageantry and parks are a few of the state's many attractions.

National Park Service Areas

North Carolina has Cape Hatteras National Seashore, Fort Raleigh National Historic Site and Great Smoky Mountains National Park (see all), Carl Sandburg Home National Historic Site (see HENDERSONVILLE), Guilford Courthouse National Military Park (see GREENSBORO), Moores Creek National Battlefield (see WILMINGTON), Wright Brothers National Memorial (see KILL DEVIL HILLS), part of the Blue Ridge Parkway (see in VIRGINIA) and Cape Lookout National Seashore (see BEAUFORT).

National Forests

The following is an alphabetical listing of some of the state's national forests and the towns they are listed under.

Croatan National Forest (see NEW BERN): Forest Supervisor in Asheville; Ranger office in New Bern.

Nantahala National Forest (see FRANKLIN): Forest Supervisor in Asheville; Ranger offices in Franklin, Highlands, Murphy*, Robbinsville.

Pisgah National Forest (see BREVARD): Forest Supervisor in Asheville; Ranger offices in Burnsville, Hot Springs*, Marion, Pisgah Forest*.

Uwharrie National Forest*: Forest Supervisor in Asheville; Ranger office in Troy*.

*Not described in text

State Recreation Areas

The following are some of the towns that list state recreation areas in their vicinity under What to See and Do; refer to the individual town for directions and park information.

Listed under **Albemarle:** see Morrow Mountain State Park.

Listed under **Edenton:** see Merchant's Millpond State Park.

Listed under **Goldsboro:** see Cliffs of the Neuse State Park.

Listed under **Henderson:** see Kerr Reservoir.

Listed under **Little Switzerland:** see Mt Mitchell State Park.

Listed under **Lumberton:** see Jones Lake State Park.

Listed under **Morehead City:** see Fort Macon State Park.

Listed under **Pilot Mountain:** see Pilot Mountain State Park.

Listed under **Raleigh:** see William B. Umstead State Park.

Listed under **Sanford:** see Raven Rock State Park.

Listed under **Statesville:** see Duke Power State Park.

Listed under **Wilkesboro:** see Stone Mountain State Park.

Listed under **Wilmington:** see Carolina Beach State Park.

Listed under **Winston-Salem:** see Hanging Rock State Park.

Water-related activities, hiking, riding, various other sports, picnicking and visitor centers, as well as camping, are available in many of these areas. Parks are open daily: June-Aug, 8 am-9 pm; Apr-May & Sept to 8 pm; Mar & Oct to 7 pm; Nov-Feb to 6 pm. Most parks have picnicking and hiking. Swimming ($2; 6-12, $1; under 6 free) and concessions open Memorial Day-Labor Day. Admission and parking free (exc reservoirs; $3); canoe and boat rentals ($2.50/hr first 2 hrs, $1/hr thereafter); fishing. Campgrounds: open all yr, limited facilities in winter; family of 6 for $9/day; hookups $5 more; primitive sites $5/day; youth group tent camping $1/person ($5 min). Dogs on leash only. Campgrounds are on first come, first served basis; reservations are allowed for minimum of 7 days, maximum of 14 days; write the Park Superintendent.

Information, including a comprehensive brochure, may be obtained from the Division of Parks & Recreation, Dept of Environment, Health and Natural Resources, PO Box 27687, Raleigh 27611; 919/733-7275 or -4181.

Fishing & Hunting

Nonresident fishing license $30; daily license $10; 3-day license $15. Nonresident 6-day and basic hunting license $40. Nonresident sportsman license (includes basic hunting and fishing, trout, big game hunting, game lands and primitive weapons; excludes special device) $130. Nonresident comprehensive hunting license (includes basic hunting, big game, game lands, primitive weapons) $80. **Note:** Both the nonresident sportsman and comprehensive hunt licenses are subject to significant additional fees based upon the visitor's home state. Nonresident trapping license $100. Nonresident comprehensive fishing license (includes basic fishing, trout and trout waters on gamelands) $50; 3-day license $25; daily license $15. Waterfowl stamp (mandatory) $5. Nonresident special device stamp (fishing: nets & baskets) $50.

For latest regulations contact License Section, Wildlife Resources Commission, Archdale Building, 512 N Salisbury St, Archdale Bldg, Raleigh 27604-1188; 919/662-4370.

Skiing

The following are some of the towns that list ski areas in their vicinity under What to See and Do; refer to the individual town for directions and information.

Listed under **Asheville:** see Wolf Laurel Ski Resort.

Listed under **Banner Elk:** see Ski Beech and Sugar Mt ski areas.

Listed under **Blowing Rock:** see Appalachian Ski Mountain and Hound Ears ski areas.

Listed under **Cashiers:** see Fairfield Sapphire Valley Ski Area.

Listed under **Highlands:** see Scaly Mountain Ski Area.

Listed under **Maggie Valley:** see Cataloochee Ski Area.

Safety Belt Information

Safety belts are mandatory for all persons in front seat of vehicle. Children under 6 years must be in an approved child passenger restraint system anywhere in vehicle; ages 3-6 may use a regulation safety belt; children under 3 years must use an approved child passenger restraint system. For further information phone 919/733-7952.

Interstate Highway System

The following alphabetical listing of North Carolina towns in *Mobil Travel Guide* shows that these cities are within 10 miles of the indicated Interstate highways. A highway map should, however, be checked for the nearest exit.

INTERSTATE 26: Asheville, Columbus, Hendersonville, Tryon.

INTERSTATE 40: Asheville, Burlington, Durham, Greensboro, Hickory, Maggie Valley, Marion, Morganton, Raleigh, Statesville, Waynesville, Wilmington, Winston-Salem.

INTERSTATE 77: Charlotte, Cornelius, Dobson, Statesville.

INTERSTATE 85: Burlington, Charlotte, Concord, Durham, Gastonia, Greensboro, Henderson, High Point, Lexington, Salisbury.

INTERSTATE 95: Dunn, Fayetteville, Lumberton, Roanoke Rapids, Rocky Mount, Smithfield, Wilson.

Additional Visitor Information

The North Carolina Gazetteer, by William S. Powell (University of North Carolina Press, Chapel Hill, 1968) lists over 20,000 entries that will enable the reader to find any place in the state, as well as information about size, history and derivation of name. The Travel and Tourism Division, 430 N Salisbury St, Raleigh 27611, 800/VISIT-NC, has free travel information, including brochures.

North Carolina Welcome Center locations are: I-85 North, Box 156, Norlina 27563; I-85 South, Box 830, Kings Mountain 28086; I-95 North, Box 52, Roanoke Rapids 27870; I-40, Box 809, Waynesville 28786; I-95 South, Box 518, Rowland 28383; I-26, Box 249, Columbus 28722; I-77 North, Box 1066, Dobson 27017; and I-77 South, Box 410724, Charlotte 28241-0724.

Ahoskie (A-9)

Pop: 4,391 **Elev:** 53 ft **Area code:** 919 **Zip:** 27910

Motel

✔ ★ **TOMAHAWK.** *601 N Academy. 919/332-3194; FAX 919/332-3194, ext. 232.* 58 rms. S $31.85; D $34.85; each addl $5. TV; cable. Pool. Restaurant opp 6 am-9 pm. Ck-out 11 am. Cr cds: A, C, D, DS, MC, V.

Motor Hotel

★ ★ **RAMADA INN.** *Rte 2, Box 3501, Jct NC 11 & 561. 919/332-4165; FAX 919/332-1632.* 98 rms, 2 story. S $42; D $51; each addl $10; suites $156; under 18 free. TV; cable. Indoor pool. Restaurant 6 am-2 pm, 5:30-10 pm. Bar 5:30-10 pm, Fri to 11 pm, Sat to 2 am; DJ, dancing Sat. Ck-out noon. Meeting rms. Valet serv. Cr cds: A, C, D, DS, MC, V.

Albemarle (B-5)

Founded: 1857 **Pop:** 14,939 **Elev:** 455 ft **Area code:** 704 **Zip:** 28001

Albemarle is in the gently rolling hills of the Uwharrie Mountains, in the Piedmont section of the state. It manufactures textiles, aircraft tires, automotive parts and aluminum.

What to See and Do

1. **Morrow Mountain State Park.** 7 mi E off NC 740, on Morrow Mountain Rd. Approx 4,700 acres of hilly forested terrain, touched on two sides by Lake Tillery. Swimming pool, bathhouse; fishing; boating (rentals, launching). Nature trails, hiking, riding. Picnic facilities, concessions. Camping (no hookups); 6 cabins, families only (Mar-Nov; advance reservation necessary). Natural history museum. Standard fees. Phone 982-4402.

2. **Town Creek Indian Mound State Historic Site.** 11 mi S on US 52, then 12 mi E on NC 731 to SR 1542. Reconstructed 16th-century Native American ceremonial center with stockade, temples and mortuary. Visitor center, audiovisual shows, exhibits (Apr-Oct, daily; rest of yr, daily exc Mon; closed hols in winter). Picnic area. Phone 919/439-6802. **Free.**

3. **Albemarle-Stanly County Historic Preservation Commission.** 112 N 3rd St. Originally built as a 3-room log cabin in the 1850s, the museum building has been enlarged and houses period artifacts. Research room. (Mon-Thurs; also wknds by appt; closed hols) Also on lot is Mark's House, town's oldest building (1850s) once used as residence/law office. Phone 983-7316. **Free.**

(For further information contact the Stanly County Chamber of Commerce, PO Box 909, 28002; 982-8116.)

(For accommodations see Concord)

Asheboro (B-6)

Founded: 1779 **Pop:** 16,362 **Elev:** 844 ft **Area code:** 910 **Zip:** 27203

Situated in the agriculturally and industrially rich Piedmont and the timber-covered Uwharrie Mountains, Asheboro has for over a century served as the seat of Randolph County. Planked roads, covered bridges and the waters of the Deep and Uwharrie rivers provided the impetus for industrial development late in the 19th century. Asheboro is in the heart of North Carolina's pottery-making country.

What to See and Do

North Carolina Zoological Park. 6 mi SE, off US 64. Over 700 African animals in 9 outdoor natural habitats; 37-acre plains exhibit; African Pavilion; free-flight aviary. (Daily) Sr citizen rate. Phone 879-7000. ¢¢¢

(For further information contact the Chamber of Commerce, PO Box 2007, 27204; 626-2626.)

Annual Event

Randolph County Fall Festival. Arts, crafts, food, music, entertainment. 1st wkend Oct.

(See Greensboro, High Point, Lexington)

Motel

✔ ★ ★ **DAYS INN.** *999 Albemarle Rd, at jct NC 49, US 220 Bypass. 910/629-2101; FAX 910/626-7944.* 138 rms, 2 story. S $38-$46; D $42-$50; each addl $4; suites $65-$90. Crib free. TV; cable. Pool. Complimentary continental bkfst. Restaurant 11:30 am-2 pm, 6-8 pm; Sun to 2 pm. Ck-out 11 am. Meeting rms. Valet serv. Cr cds: A, C, D, DS, MC, V.

Asheville (B-3)

Settled: 1794 **Pop:** 61,607 **Elev:** 2,134 ft **Area code:** 704

Thomas Wolfe came from Asheville, the seat of Buncombe County, as did the expression "bunkum" (nonsense). A local congressman, when asked why he had been so evasive during a masterful oration in which he said nothing, replied, "I did it for Buncombe." Wolfe wrote often of his hill-rimmed home, shrewdly observant of the people and life of Asheville.

Asheville is a vacation headquarters in the Blue Ridge Mountains, as well as a marketing and industrial city. It is the North Carolina city nearest Great Smoky Mountains National Park (see) and attracts many of the park's visitors with its annual mountain fetes, local handicrafts and summer theaters. It is the headquarters for the Uwharrie National Forest, Pisgah National Forest (see BREVARD), Nantahala National Forest (see FRANKLIN) and Croatan National Forest (see NEW BERN). The Blue Ridge Parkway brings many travelers to Asheville on their way south from the Shenandoah Valley of Virginia.

For further information about Croatan, Nantahala, Pisgah and Uwharrie National Forests contact the Supervisor, 100 Otis St, Box 2750, 28802; 253-2353.

What to See and Do

1. **Thomas Wolfe Memorial.** 48 Spruce St, between Woodfin & Walnut Sts. The state maintains the Wolfe boardinghouse as a literary shrine, restored and furnished to appear as it did in 1916. In

Asheville it is known as the "Old Kentucky Home." In *Look Homeward, Angel* it was referred to as "Dixieland"; Asheville was "Altamont." (Apr-Oct, daily; rest of yr, daily exc Mon; closed major hols) Phone 253-8304. ¢

2. **Biltmore Homespun Shops.** Grovewood Rd, near Macon Ave, 2 mi NE. At the turn of the century, Mrs. George W. Vanderbilt opened a school to keep alive the skills of hand-dyeing, spinning and hand-weaving wool into cloth. The business still has the old machinery and handlooms. An antique automobile museum and the North Carolina Homespun Museum are in an 11-acre park adjoining Grove Park Inn Resort (see RESORTS). (Apr-Oct, daily; rest of yr, daily exc Sun; closed Jan 1, Thanksgiving, Dec 25) Phone 253-7651. **Free.**

3. **Biltmore Estate.** S on US 25, 3 blks N of I-40 exit 50. The 8,000-acre country estate includes 75 acres of formal gardens, numerous varieties of azaleas and roses and the 250-room chateau (85 rooms are open for viewing), which is the largest house ever built in the New World. George W. Vanderbilt commissioned Richard Morris Hunt to design the house, which was begun in 1890 and finished in 1895. Materials and furnishings were brought from many parts of Europe and Asia; a private railroad was built to transport them to the site. Life here was lived in the grand manner. Vanderbilt employed Gifford Pinchot, later Governor of Pennsylvania and famous for forestry and conservation achievements, to manage his forests. Biltmore was the site of the first US forestry school. Tours of the original estate is now part of Pisgah National Forest. Tours of the estate include greenhouses and winery facilities; tasting. Two restaurants on grounds. (Daily; closed Jan 1, Thanksgiving, Dec 25) Guidebook (fee) is recommended. Phone 255-1700 or 800/543-2961. ¢¢¢¢

4. **Pack Place Education, Arts & Science Center.** 2 S Pack Square. This 92,000 square-foot complex features multiple museums and exhibit galleries as well as a state-of-the-art theater. A permanent exhibit entitled "Here is the Square..." describes the history of Asheville. Restaurant (lunch only); gift shop. (Tues-Sat, also some Sun afternoons; closed Jan 1, Thanksgiving, Dec 24-25) Sr citizen rate. For general information, phone 257-4500. Combination ticket ¢¢¢ Includes

   Asheville Art Museum. Permanent collection and changing exhibits. Phone 253-3227. ¢¢

   Colburn Gem and Mineral Museum. Displays of 1,000 minerals from around the world; includes information on mineral locations in state. Phone 254-7162. ¢¢

   The Health Adventure. Extensive collection of imaginative, educational exhibts on the human body; includes a talking transparent woman, a bicycle-pedaling skeleton and opportunity to hear sound of your own heartbeat. Also on premises is Creative PlaySpace, a special exhibit for young children. Phone 254-6373. ¢¢

   YMI Cultural Center. Galleries featuring permanent and rotating exhibts on African American art. Phone 252-4614. ¢¢

   Diana Wortham Theatre. This 500-seat theater hosts local, regional and national companies. For box office information, phone 257-4530.

5. **Graves of Thomas Wolfe** (1900-38) and **O. Henry** (William Sydney Porter) (1862-1910). Riverside Cemetery. Entrance on Birch St off Pearson Dr.

6. **Botanical Gardens of Asheville.** On campus of University of North Carolina. A 10-acre tract with thousands of flowers, trees and shrubs native to Southern Appalachia; 125-year-old "dog trot" log cabin. (Daily) Phone 252-5190. **Free.**

7. **Folk Art Center** of the Southern Highland Handicraft Guild. 5 mi E on US 70, then 1/2 mi N on the Blue Ridge Pkwy to Milepost 382. Stone and timber structure; home of Southern Highland Handicraft Guild, Blue Ridge Pkwy information center; craft exhibits, demonstrations, workshops, related programs. (Daily; closed Jan 1, Thanksgiving, Dec 25) Phone 298-7928. (See ANNUAL EVENTS) **Free.**

8. **Asheville Community Theatre.** 35 E Walnut St. Six comedies, musicals and dramas performed throughout year. (Aug-June, Fri & Sat evenings, also Sun matinee) Phone 254-1320. ¢¢¢-¢¢¢¢

9. **Zebulon B. Vance Birthplace State Historic Site.** 9 mi N on US 19/23, exit New-Stock Rd then 6 mi N on Reems Creek Rd in Weaverville. Log house (reconstructed 1961) and outbuildings on site where Civil War governor of North Carolina grew up. Honors Vance family, which was deeply involved with early history of state. Visitor center, exhibits. Picnic area. (Apr-Oct, daily; rest of yr, daily exc Mon; closed some hols) Phone 645-6706. **Free.**

10. **Western North Carolina Nature Center.** Gashes Creek Rd, 3 mi E on NC 81. Live animals, children's petting barnyard, natural history exhibits, nature trail, educational programs. (Memorial Day-Labor Day, daily; rest of yr, Tues-Sat & Sun afternoons) Sr citizen rate. Phone 298-5600. ¢¢

11. **Chimney Rock Park.** 25 mi SE on US 74, just past jct US 64, NC 9. Towering granite monolith Chimney Rock affords 75-mi view; 3 hiking trails lead to 404-ft Hickory Nut Falls, Moonshiner's Cave, Devil's Head balancing rock, Nature's Showerbath. Trails, stairs and catwalks; picnic areas, playground; nature center; observation lounge with snack bar, gift shop. 26-story elevator shaft through granite. (Daily, weather permitting; closed Jan 1, Dec 25) Phone 625-9611 or 800/277-9611. ¢¢¢

12. **Mt Mitchell State Park.** 27 mi NE on Blue Ridge Pkwy, then 5 mi N on NC 128 (see LITTLE SWITZERLAND).

13. **Wolf Laurel Ski Resort.** 27 mi N off US 23. Quad, double chairlifts, Mitey-mite; patrol, school, rentals; snowmaking; restaurant. Longest run 3/4 mi; vertical drop 700 ft. (Mid-Dec-mid-Mar, daily) Phone 689-4111. ¢¢¢¢

14. **River rafting. Carolina Wilderness Adventures.** Half- and full-day guided raft trips on the French Broad and Nolichucky Rivers. For information and reservations, contact PO Box 488, Hot Springs 28743; 800/872-7437. ¢¢¢¢

(For further information on fishing, industrial tours, and other attractions contact the Asheville Convention & Visitors Bureau, 151 Haywood St, PO Box 1010, 28802-1010; 258-3858 or 800/257-1300.)

Annual Events

   Shindig-on-the-Green. College & Spruce Sts, in front of City Hall. Mountain fiddling, dulcimer players, singing, square dancing. Sat evenings, July-Labor Day exc 1st wkend Aug.

   Southern Highland Handicraft Guild Fair. Civic Center, Haywood St, just off I-240. More than 175 craftsmen from 9 Southern states exhibit and demonstrate their skills. Folk and contemporary entertainment daily. Phone 298-7928. 3rd wkend July, 3rd wkend Oct.

   World Gee Haw Whimmy Diddle Competition. Folk Art Center (see #7). Competitions, demonstrations, storytelling, music, dance. Early Aug.

   Mountain Dance and Folk Festival. Civic Center. Folk songs and ballads. Finest of its kind for devotees of the 5-string banjo, gut-string fiddle, clogging and smooth dancing. 1st wkend Aug.

Seasonal Event

   Shakespeare in the Park. Montford Park Players. Wkends early June-late Aug. Phone 254-4540.

(See Maggie Valley, Waynesville)

Motels

   ✔ ★ **AMERICAN COURT.** *85 Merrimon Ave (28801). 704/253-4427; res: 800/233-3582.* 22 rms. S $36-$46; D $36-$58; each addl $3; under 12 free. Crib $2. TV; cable. Pool. Complimentary coffee.

Restaurant nearby. Ck-out 11 am. Coin lndry. Refrigerators avail. Cr cds: A, C, D, DS, MC, V.

≈ ⊠ ☇ SC

✔ ★ **BEST INNS OF AMERICA.** *1435 Tunnel Rd (28805).* 704/298-4000. 85 rms, 3 story. Apr-Oct: S $45.88-$50.88; D $51.88-$56.88; each addl $6; under 18 free; wkly rates; lower rates rest of yr. Crib free. TV; cable. Heated pool. Complimentary continental bkfst. Complimentary coffee in lobby. Restaurant nearby. Ck-out 1 pm. Some refrigerators. Cr cds: A, C, D, DS, MC, V.

D ≈ ⊠ ☇ SC

★ ★ **COMFORT INN.** *800 Fairview Rd (28803), I-240 exit 8.* 704/298-9141; FAX 704/298-6629. 178 rms, 3 story. Apr-Oct: S, D $55-$85; each addl $6; suites $125-$145; under 18 free; lower rates rest of yr. TV; cable. Pool. Playground. Complimentary continental bkfst. Restaurant opp 6 am-9 pm. Ck-out 11 am. Coin lndry. Meeting rms. Health club privileges. Refrigerator in suites. Cr cds: A, C, D, DS, ER, JCB, MC, V.

D ≈ ⊠ ☇ SC

★ ★ **COMFORT SUITES.** *890 Brevard Rd (28806), I-26 exit 2.* 704/665-4000; FAX 704/665-9082. 125 suites, 5 story. May-Oct: suites $63-$90; each addl $7; under 18 free; lower rates rest of yr. Crib free. TV; cable. Pool. Complimentary continental bkfst, coffee. Restaurant nearby. Ck-out noon. Coin lndry. Meeting rms. Valet serv. Free airport transportation. Exercise equipt; bicycles, stair machine, whirlpool. Refrigerators. Cr cds: A, C, D, DS, ER, JCB, MC, V.

D ★ ⊁ ≈ ⊠ ☇ SC

★ ★ **FOREST MANOR.** *866 Hendersonville Rd (28803), on US 25, 1 mi S of I-40 exit 50.* 704/274-3531. 21 rms. July, Aug & Oct: D $69-$119; kit. units $595-$695/wk; lower rates rest of yr. Crib $5. TV; cable. Heated pool. Complimentary continental bkfst. Restaurant nearby. Ck-out 11 am. Tennis privileges. Golf privileges. Lawn games. Located on 5 wooded acres. Cr cds: A, DS, MC, V.

D ★ ⊁ ≈ ⊠ SC

★ ★ **HAMPTON INN.** *1 Rocky Ridge Rd (28806), jct I-26 & NC 191.* 704/667-2022; FAX 704/665-9680. 121 rms, 5 story. June-Oct: S $59-$89; D $69-$89; suites $145; under 18 free. Crib free. TV; cable. Indoor pool. Complimentary continental bkfst, coffee. Ck-out noon. Meeting rms. Free airport transportation. Exercise equipt; bicycles, stair machine, whirlpool, sauna. Refrigerator in suites. Cr cds: A, C, D, DS, MC, V.

D ≈ ⊁ ⊠ ☇ SC

★ ★ **HOWARD JOHNSON-BILTMORE.** *190 Hendersonville Rd (28803).* 704/274-2300; FAX 704/274-2304. 68 rms, 2 story. Apr-Oct: S $54-$149; D $64-$149; each addl $8; higher rates: special events wkends & autumn foliage; lower rates rest of yr. Crib free. TV; cable. Pool. Restaurant 6:30 am-2 pm, 5:30-9 pm; Sat & Sun from 7 am. Ck-out noon. Meeting rms. Private patios, balconies. Cr cds: A, C, D, DS, JCB, MC, V.

D ≈ ⊠ ☇ SC

★ **MOUNTAIN SPRINGS.** *(US 151, Candler 28715) I-40 W to exit 44, S on US 151.* 704/665-1004; FAX 704/667-1581. 12 kit. cottages, 1-2 story. No rm phones. S, D $60-$115; each addl $10; family, wkly rates. Crib free. TV. Ck-out 10 am. Picnic tables. On river. Cr cds: MC, V.

☞ ☇

★ **NAKON.** *(US 19/23 S, Candler 28715) W on I-40 to exit 44, S on US 19/23.* 704/667-4543. 17 rms. May-Oct: S $28-$30; D $30-$35; each addl $8; under 12 free; higher rates wkends; lower rates rest of yr. Crib free. TV; cable. Ck-out 11 am. Refrigerators. Cr cds: MC, V.

⊠ ☇ SC

✔ ★ **RED ROOF INN.** *16 Crowell Rd (28806), I-40 exit 44.* 704/667-9803; FAX 704/667-9810. 109 rms, 3 story. May-Oct: S $49.99; D $54.99; under 18 free; lower rates rest of yr. Pet accepted, some restrictions. TV; cable. Complimentary morning coffee in lobby. Restaurant opp open 24 hrs. Ck-out noon. Cr cds: A, C, D, DS, MC, V.

D ☞ ⊠ ☇

Motor Hotels

★ ★ **BEST WESTERN-CENTRAL.** *22 Woodfin St (28801), 1 blk off I-240 at Merrimon Ave exit.* 704/253-1851; FAX 704/252-9205. 150 rms, 5 story. June-Sept: S $56-$89; D $61-$89; each addl $5; under 18 free; higher rates Oct; lower rates rest of yr. Crib free. TV; cable. Heated pool. Complimentary coffee in rms. Restaurant 6:30-10 am. Bar 5 pm-1 am. Ck-out noon. Meeting rm. Valet serv. Health club privileges adj. Cr cds: A, C, D, DS, MC, V.

D ≈ ⊠ ☇ SC

★ ★ **GREAT SMOKIES HILTON.** *1 Hilton Inn Dr (28806).* 704/254-3211; FAX 704/254-1603. 278 rms, 5 story. May-Oct: S $82-$122; D $92-$132; each addl $10; suites $175-$275; family, honeymoon rates; ski, golf plans; lower rates rest of yr. Crib free. TV; cable. 2 pools; wading pool. Restaurant 6:30 am-10 pm. Rm serv. Bar 11-1 am; entertainment, dancing Tues-Sat. Ck-out noon. Convention facilities. Bellhops. Valet serv. Indoor & outdoor tennis, pro. 18-hole golf, greens fee $26, pro, putting green, driving range. Health club privileges. Some wet bars. Refrigerator in suites. Private patios, balconies. Near shopping center. Cr cds: A, C, D, DS, ER, MC, V.

D ★ ⊁ ⊁ ≈ ⊠ ☇ SC

★ ★ **QUALITY INN-BILTMORE.** *115 Hendersonville Rd (28803).* 704/274-1800; FAX 704/274-5960. 160 rms, 5 story, 20 suites. Apr-Oct: S, D $88-$102; each addl $8; suites $95-$140; under 18 free; lower rates rest of yr. Crib free. TV; cable. Pool. Complimentary coffee in rms. Restaurant 6:30 am-8 pm. Rm serv. Bar 5-11 pm. Ck-out noon. Meeting rms. Bellhops. Valet serv. Some refrigerators. Cr cds: A, C, D, DS, MC, V.

D ≈ ⊠ ☇ SC

Hotels

★ ★ ★ **HAYWOOD PARK.** *One Battery Park Ave (28801).* 704/252-2522; res: 800/228-2522; FAX 704/253-0481. 33 suites, 4 story. S $98-$230; D $120-$280; each addl $15; under 12 free. TV; cable. Complimentary continental bkfst in rms. Restaurant 7 am-9:30 pm (also see 23 PAGE RESTAURANT). Bar. Ck-out noon. Meeting rms. Shopping arcade. Free valet parking. Exercise rm; instructor, weights, bicycle, sauna. Bathrm phones; refrigerators. Cr cds: A, C, D, DS, MC, V.

D ⊁ ⊠ ☇ SC

★ ★ **RADISSON.** *One Thomas Wolfe Plaza (28801).* 704/252-8211; FAX 704/254-1374. 281 rms, 12 story. Apr-mid-Nov: S $69-$99; D $79-$109; each addl $10; suites $195-$225; under 17 free; lower rates rest of yr. Crib free. TV; cable. Pool; poolside serv. Restaurant 6:30 am-10 pm. Bar 11-1 am. Ck-out noon. Convention facilities. Concierge. Gift shop. Exercise equipt; weight machine, bicycles. Game rm. Minibars. Refrigerators avail. Cr cds: A, C, D, DS, MC, V.

D ≈ ⊁ ⊠ ☇ SC

Inns

★ ★ **CAIRN BRAE.** *217 Patton Mountain Rd (28804).* 704/252-9219. 3 rms, 1 with shower only, 2 story, 1 suite. No rm phones. S $70-$85; D $85-$100; each addl $15; suite $130. Children over 10 yrs only. TV in sitting rm; cable. Complimentary full bkfst. Complimentary tea/sherry, coffee. Ck-out 11 am, ck-in 3 pm. Airport transportation. Rec rm. Picnic tables. Situated along mountainside. Totally nonsmoking. Cr cds: DS, MC, V.

⬛⬛ SC

★ ★ **CEDAR CREST.** *674 Biltmore Ave (28803). 704/252-1389.* 9 rms, 3 story, 2 cottage suites. S $109-$134; D $115-$140; each addl $20; suites $115-$185. Children over 10 yrs only. Complimentary continental bkfst. Ck-out 11 am, ck-in 3-10 pm. Lawn games. Balconies. Historic inn (1890); antiques. Flower gardens. Cr cds: A, DS, MC, V.

⬛⬛

★ **CORNER OAK MANOR.** *53 St Dunstang Rd (28803). 704/253-3525.* 4 air-cooled rms, 2 story, 1 kit. unit. No rm phones. S $65; D $85; kit. $100. Children over 12 yrs only. Complimentary full bkfst. Ck-out 11 am, ck-in 3 pm. Whirlpool on terrace. Picnic tables. English Tudor home (1924); antiques. Totally nonsmoking. Cr cds: A, DS, MC, V.

⬛⬛

✔ ★ ★ **FLINT STREET INNS.** *116 Flint St (28801). 704/253-6723.* 8 rms in 2 buildings, 2 story. S $65; D $85; each addl $25. Complimentary full bkfst, refreshments. Ck-out 11 am, ck-in noon-9 pm. Old home in Montford Historic District. Cr cds: A, DS, ER, MC, V.

⬛

★ ★ **LAKE LURE.** *(Box 10, Lake Lure 28746) 26 mi SE on US 74. 704/625-2525; res: 800/277-5873; FAX 704/625-9655.* 50 rms, 3 story. Mar-Oct: S $69-$79; D $79-$109; each addl $10; under 12 free. Crib free. TV; cable. Pool. Complimentary continental bkfst. Dining rm 5-9 pm; Sun 11 am-2:30 pm; closed Mon. Bar. Ck-out 11 am, ck-in 3 pm. On lake; view of Blue Ridge Mountains. Mediterranean-style hostelry (1927). Cr cds: A, D, DS, MC, V.

D ⬛⬛⬛ SC

★ **OLD REYNOLDS MANSION.** *100 Reynolds Heights (28804). 704/254-0496.* 10 rms, 8 with bath, 3 story. No rm phones. S, D $50-$90; cottage suite $110. Pool. Complimentary continental bkfst, tea/sherry. Restaurant nearby. Ck-out 11 am, ck-in 3 pm. Antebellum mansion (1855) on hill overlooking mountains; antiques, verandas. No cr cds accepted.

⬛

★ ★ ★ **RICHMOND HILL.** *87 Richmond Hill Dr (28806). 704/252-7313; res: 800/545-9238; FAX 704/252-8726.* 12 rms, 3 story, 9 cottages. S, D $140-$350; each addl $20. Crib $15. TV; cable. Complimentary full bkfst, afternoon tea service. Dining rm (see GABRIELLE'S). Ck-out 11 am, ck-in 3 pm. Queen Anne-style architecture; library, grand entrance hall. Former congressman's residence. Cr cds: A, MC, V.

D ⬛⬛

Resorts

★ ★ ★ ★ **GROVE PARK INN RESORT.** *290 Macon Ave (28804). 704/252-2711; res: 800/438-5800; FAX 704/253-7053.* 510 rms, 5-10 story. Apr-Dec: S, D $125-$199; each addl $25; under 16 free; golf, honeymoon packages; lower rates rest of yr. Crib free. TV; cable. 2 heated pools, 1 indoor; lifeguard. Supervised child's activities (May-Dec). Dining rms (public) 6:30 am-midnight (also see BLUE RIDGE DINING ROOM). Rm serv. Bar from 11 am; entertainment, dancing. Ck-out noon, ck-in 4 pm. Convention facilities. Bellhops. Valet serv. Shopping arcade. 9 lighted tennis courts, 3 indoor. Golf, greens fee $59 incl cart (cart required), nine holes $30, putting green. Rec rm. Exercise rm; instructor, weights, bicycles, whirlpool, sauna. Raquetball & squash courts. Massage. Fireplaces in lobby. Terraces overlook Blue Ridge Mts, golf course. Historic resort, renovated and expanded. *LUXURY LEVEL: CLUB LEVEL.* 28 rms. S, D $250. Concierge. Private

lounge. Bathrm phones, in-rm whirlpools. Complimentary continental bkfst, refreshments, newspaper. Cr cds: A, C, D, DS, JCB, MC, V.

D ⬛⬛⬛⬛⬛⬛⬛ SC

✔ ★ **PISGAH VIEW RANCH.** *(Rte 1, Candler 28715) Enka-Candler exit off I-40, S on US 19/23 4 mi to Candler, left on NC 151, 9 mi to ranch. 704/667-9100.* 47 units. May-Oct: AP: S $45-$100/person, $225-$390/wk; D $45-$78/person, $225-$390/wk; family rates. Closed rest of yr. Crib free. TV. Heated pool. Playground. Dining rm 8 am-7:15 pm. Ck-out 11 am, ck-in 2 pm. Coin lndry. Meeting rms. Gift shop. Airport, bus depot transportation. Tennis. Hiking trails. Rec rm. Lawn games. Entertainment. No cr cds accepted.

D ⬛⬛⬛⬛⬛

Restaurants

★ ★ ★ **23 PAGE.** *(See Haywood Park Hotel) 704/252-3685.* Hrs: 5:30-10 pm; early-bird dinner 5:30-6:30 pm. Closed some major hols. Res accepted. Continental menu. Bar. Extensive wine list. A la carte entrees: dinner $14.50-$22.50. Child's meals. Specializes in seafood, desserts, pasta. Parking. Intimate dining. Cr cds: A, D, MC, V.

D

★ ★ ★ **BLUE RIDGE DINING ROOM.** *(See Grove Park Inn Resort) 704/252-2711.* Hrs: 6:30 am-2 pm, 6:30-9:30 pm; Sun brunch 11:30 am-3 pm. Hrs may vary seasonally. Res accepted. Serv bar. Semi-a la carte: bkfst $4.95-$8.75, lunch $8.50-$11.75, dinner $16-$27. Buffet dinner: Fri (seafood) $25.54, Sat (prime rib) $29.26. Sun brunch $23.10. Child's meals. View of mountains. Cr cds: A, D, DS, ER, MC, V.

D

★ **FINE FRIENDS.** *946 Merrimon Ave, in Northland Shopping Center. 704/253-6649.* Hrs: 11:30 am-10 pm; Fri, Sat to 11 pm. Closed Thanksgiving, Dec 24 & 25. Res accepted. Bar to midnight. Semi-a la carte: lunch $6.85-$12.45, dinner $7.95-$18.75. Child's meals. Specializes in seafood, beef, pasta. Own desserts. Cr cds: A, D, DS, MC, V.

★ ★ ★ **GABRIELLE'S.** *(See Richmond Hill Inn) 704/252-7313.* Hrs: 6-10 pm; Sun 11 am-2 pm. Res required. Extensive wine list. Semi-a la carte: dinner $25-$35. Sun brunch $18.95. Child's meals. Specializes in fresh fish, beef, homemade pasta. Pianist Wed-Sun. Valet parking. Formal dining. Jacket. Totally nonsmoking. Cr cds: A, MC, V.

D

★ ★ **GREENERY.** *148 Tunnel Rd. 704/253-2809.* Hrs: 5-10 pm. Closed Jan 1. Res accepted. Bar. Semi-a la carte: dinner $12.95-$19.95. Specialty: Maryland crabcakes. Pianist wkends. Parking. Cr cds: A, MC, V.

✔ ★ **McGUFFEY'S.** *13 Kenilworth Knoll. 704/252-0956.* Hrs: 11-2 am; Sun brunch to 4 pm. Closed Thanksgiving, Dec 25. Bar. Semi-a la carte: lunch $4.99-$7.99, dinner $7.99-$14.99. Sun brunch $4.99-$10.99. Specializes in beef, seafood, chicken. Cr cds: A, MC, V.

D SC

★ ★ **VINCENZO'S.** *10 N Market St (28801). 704/254-4698.* Hrs: 6-10 pm. Closed Jan 1, Easter, Dec 25. Res accepted. Italian, continental menu. Bar. Semi-a la carte: $11.50-$17.50. Child's meals. Specializes in veal, pasta, seafood. Entertainment Fri & Sat. Parking. Extensive wine selection. Eclectic decor with art deco influence. Cr cds: A, DS, MC, V.

★ ★ **WINDMILL EUROPEAN GRILL.** *85 Tunnel Rd, at Innsbruck Mall. 704/253-5285.* Hrs: 5:30-9:30 pm; Fri, Sat to 10 pm. Closed Sun, Mon; most major hols. Res accepted. Continental menu. Bar. Complete meals: dinner $8.99-$17.99. Specializes in seafood, beef, pasta. Cr cds: A, MC, V.

Unrated Dining Spot

SMOKY MOUNTAIN BBQ. *20 Spruce St. 704/253-4871.* Hrs: 5-11 pm; Fri, Sat to midnight. Closed Sun, Mon; Jan 1, Dec 25. Res accepted. Bar. Semi-a la carte: dinner $5.95-$9.95. Child's meals. Specializes in barbecued chopped pork, fried chicken, barbecued chicken. Bluegrass band, clogging. Parking. Casual, family atmosphere. Cr cds: A, MC, V.

Atlantic Beach (C-9)

(see Morehead City)

Banner Elk (A-3)

Pop: 933 **Elev:** 3,739 ft **Area code:** 704 **Zip:** 28604

What to See and Do

1. **Grandfather Mountain.** 3 mi SW via US 221 (see LINVILLE).
2. **Skiing.**

Sugar Mt. Off NC 184. 5 chairlifts, 2 T-bars, rope tow; patrol, school, rentals, snowmaking; children's program; lodging, cafeteria; nursery. (Mid-Nov-mid-Mar, daily) Phone 898-4521. ¢¢¢¢

Ski Beech. 3 mi N on NC 184. 1 quad chairlift, 6 double chairlifts, 1 J-bar, 1 rope tow; patrol, school, rentals; snowmaking; restaurant, cafeteria; nursery, shopping. Vertical drop 830 ft. (Mid-Nov-mid-Mar, daily) Also ice-skating. For information phone 387-2011. ¢¢¢¢¢

(For further information contact the Chamber of Commerce, PO Box 335; 898-5605.)

(See Blowing Rock, Boone, Linville)

Motels

★ ★ **HOLIDAY INN.** *Box 1478, 1 mi S on NC 184 between NC 194 and NC 105. 704/898-4571; FAX 704/898-8437.* 101 rms, 2 story. Dec-Feb: S, D $95-$99; under 12 free; ski plans; lower rates rest of yr. Crib free. TV; cable. Pool; wading pool. Restaurant 7 am-2 pm, 5-9 pm. Rm serv. Ck-out 11 am. Meeting rms. Downhill/x-country ski 1 mi. Cr cds: A, C, D, DS, MC, V.

★ ★ **PINNACLE INN.** *Box 1136, off NC 184. 704/387-2231; res: 800/438-2097.* 242 kits., 3 story. No elvtr. Mid-Nov-mid-Mar: kit. units $70-$150; lower rates rest of yr. Crib $5. TV; cable. Indoor pool. Free supervised child's activities (mid-June-mid-Sept). Restaurant nearby. Ck-out 10 am. Coin lndry. Meeting rms. Tennis. Downhill ski ½ mi. Exercise equipt; weight machines, bicycles, whirlpool, sauna, steam rm. Game rm. Fireplaces. Balconies. Picnic tables, grills. Cr cds: A, MC, V.

Inn

✔ ★ **ARCHERS INN.** *Rte 2, Box 56-A, Beech Mt Pkwy, NC 184. 704/898-9004.* 14 rms, 2 story. Mid-Dec-mid-Mar: S, D $55-$125; each addl $10; lower rates rest of yr. Crib free. TV; cable. Complimentary full bkfst. Ck-out 11 am, ck-in 3-6 pm. Lighted tennis privileges.

Downhill ski 2 mi. Fireplaces; many refrigerators. Many balconies. Rustic decor. Cr cds: MC, V.

Beaufort (C-9)

Pop: 3,808 **Elev:** 7 ft **Area code:** 919 **Zip:** 28516

Beaufort, dating from the colonial era, is a seaport with more than 125 historic houses and sites.

What to See and Do

1. **Beaufort Historic Site.** Old Burying Ground, 1829 restored Old Jail, restored houses (1767-1830), courthouse (ca 1796), apothecary shop, art gallery. Obtain additional information, self-guided walking tour map from Beaufort Historical Assn, Inc, 138 Turner St, PO Box 1709. (Daily exc Sun; closed some major hols) Phone 728-5225. Admission to 6 buildings open to the public ¢¢

2. **North Carolina Maritime Museum.** 315 Front St. Natural & maritime history exhibits, field trips; special programs in maritime and coastal natural history. (Daily; closed Jan 1, Thanksgiving, Dec 25) Phone 728-7317. **Free.**

3. **Cape Lookout National Seashore.** This unit of the National Park System, on the outer banks of North Carolina, extends 55 miles south from Ocracoke Inlet and includes unspoiled barrier islands. There are no roads or bridges; access is by boat only (fee). Ferries from Harkers Island, Davis, Atlantic and Ocracoke (Apr-Nov). Excellent fishing & shell collecting; primitive camping; interpretive programs (seasonal). Lighthouse (1859) at Cape Lookout is still operational. Phone 728-2250.

(For further information contact the Carteret County Tourism Development Bureau, PO Box 1406, Morehead City 28557; 726-8148 or 800/SUNNY-NC.)

Annual Event

Old Homes Tour and Antiques Show. Private homes and historic public buildings; Carteret County Militia; bus tours & tours of old burying ground; historical crafts. Sponsored by the Beaufort Historical Assn, Inc, PO Box 1709. Last wknd June.

(See Morehead City)

Inns

★ ★ **CEDARS.** *305 Front St. 919/728-7036; res: 800/732-7036.* 7 rms, 5 suites, 2 story. Mid-Apr-mid-Oct: D, suites $85-$175; mid-wk rates; lower rates rest of yr. Complimentary bkfst. Ck-out 11 am, ck-in 1 pm. Private patios, balconies. Historic house (ca 1770) overlooking river; antiques. Cr cds: MC, V.

★ **DELAMAR INN.** *217 Turner St. 919/728-4300.* 3 rms (2 with shower only), 2 story. No rm phones. May-Sept: D $88; lower rates rest of yr. Children over 12 yrs only. Complimentary continental bkfst. Complimentary tea/sherry in drawing rm. Restaurant nearby. Ck-out noon, ck-in 1 pm. Built 1866; first and second floor porches. Many antiques. Totally nonsmoking. Cr cds: MC, V.

★ **PECAN TREE INN.** *116 Queen St. 919/728-6733.* 7 rms (6 with shower only), 2 story. No rm phones. Mid-Apr-mid-Sept: D $80-$120; each addl $15; wkly rates; lower rates rest of yr. Children over 12 yrs only. Complimentary continental bkfst. Restaurant adj 11 am-10 pm. Ck-out 11 am, ck-in 3 pm. Game rm. Built for sea captain in 1866. Many antiques. Totally nonsmoking. Cr cds: DS, MC, V.

Restaurant

✔ ★ ★ **BEAUFORT HOUSE.** *502 Front St, on the Waterfront.* *919/728-7541.* Hrs: 11 am-9 pm; hrs may vary Nov-Feb. Bar. Semi-a la carte: lunch $4.99-$8.95, dinner $8.99-$13.99. Buffet: lunch, dinner (Sun) $11.99. Child's meals. Specializes in fresh local seafood, prime rib. Parking. Williamsburg decor; overlooks harbor. Cr cds: DS, MC, V.

Blowing Rock (A-4)

Founded: 1880 **Pop:** 1,257 **Elev:** 3,579 ft **Area code:** 704 **Zip:** 28605

On the Blue Ridge Parkway, Blowing Rock was named for the cliff near town where lightweight objects thrown outward are swept back to their origin by the wind. It has been a resort area for more than 100 years; a wide variety of recreational facilities and shops can be found nearby.

What to See and Do

1. **Tweetsie Railroad.** 4 mi N on US 321. A three-mile excursion, with mock holdup and Indian raid, on old narrow-gauge railroad; Western Town with variety show at Tweetsie Palace; country fair, petting zoo; craft village; chairlift to Mouse Mt Picnic Area. (May-Oct, limited hrs) Phone 264-9061. ¢¢¢¢

2. **Blowing Rock.** 2 mi SE on US 321. Cliff (4,000 ft) hangs over Johns River Gorge 2,000-3,000 feet below. Scenic views of Grandfather, Grandmother, Table Rock and Hawksbill mountains. Observation deck. Gift shop. (Apr-Nov, daily) Phone 295-7111. ¢¢

3. **Moses H. Cone Memorial Park.** On Blue Ridge Pkwy. Former summer estate of textile magnate. Bridle paths, 2 lakes; 25 miles of hiking and cross-country skiing trails. (May-Oct, daily) Phone 295-7591. **Free.**

   Parkway Craft Center. Demonstrations of weaving, wood carving, pottery, jewelry making, other crafts. (May-Oct, daily) Handcrafted items for sale. Phone 295-7938. **Free.**

4. **Julian Price Memorial Park.** SW via US 221 and Blue Ridge Pkwy. Boating (hand-powered only, rentals). Picnicking. Camping (trailer facilities, no hookups; June-Oct only; fee). Amphitheater; evening interpretive programs (May-Oct). Park open yr-round (weather permitting). Phone 295-7591 or 963-5911. **Free.**

5. **Skiing.**

   Appalachian Ski Mountain. 3 mi N on US 321, near Blueridge Pkwy intersection. Quad & 2 double chairlifts, 2 rope tows, 1 handle-pull tow; patrol; French-Swiss Ski College; Ski-Wee children's program; equipment rentals; 100% snowmaking; restaurant; 8 runs; longest run 2,700 ft; vertical drop 365 ft. (Thanksgiving-mid-Mar, daily & nightly; closed Dec 24 evening-Dec 25) Night skiing (all slopes lighted); half-day and twilight rates. Phone 295-7828 or 800/322-2373 (res). ¢¢¢¢¢

   Hound Ears. 7 mi NW via NC 105. Chairlift, rope tow; patrol, school, rentals; snowmaking; concession area, restaurant. Lodge (see RESORTS). Longest run 1,200 ft; vertical drop 107 ft. (Mid-Dec-Feb, Fri-Sun, hols) Phone 963-4321. ¢¢¢¢¢

(For further information contact the Chamber of Commerce, PO Box 406; 295-7851.)

Annual Event

Tour of Homes. 4th Fri July.

(See Banner Elk, Boone, Linville)

Motels

★ ★ **BLOWING ROCK INN.** *Box 265, N Main St,* 1/4 *mi N on US 221/321 Business.* 704/295-7921. 24 rms. July-Nov: S, D $69; each addl $10; lower rates early-mid-Nov & Apr-May; also 1-bedrm villas avail at wkly rates. Closed mid-Nov-March. Crib $5. TV; cable. Heated pool. Complimentary morning coffee. Restaurant nearby. Ck-out 11 am. Picnic tables. Cr cds: A, DS, MC, V.

★ ★ **CLIFF DWELLERS INN.** *Box 366, 1 mi S, Blue Ridge Pkwy exit for US 321, across from Shoppes on the Pkwy.* 704/295-3121; res: 800/322-7380. 20 rms, 3 story, 3 suites, 2 kit. units. No elvtr. Mid-May-early Nov: S, D $75-$90; each addl $5-$10; suites, kit. units $115-$185; under 12 free; higher rates: ski season wkends, Dec 25; lower rates rest of yr. Crib $5. TV; cable. Heated pool; whirlpool. Complimentary coffee in rms. Restaurant nearby. Ck-out 11 am. Downhill ski 3 mi; x-country ski 2 mi. Balconies. View of mountains. Cr cds: A, C, D, MC, V.

✔ ★ **HOMESTEAD INN.** *Box 1030, Morris St.* 704/295-9559. 14 rms. No rm phones. Mid-June-Oct: S, D $47-$52; each addl $5; family, wkday, wkly rates; lower rates rest of yr. Crib free. TV; cable. Playground. Morning coffee in lobby. Restaurant nearby. Ck-out 11 am. Downhill ski 4 mi. Refrigerators avail. Picnic tables, grills. Cr cds: DS, MC, V.

Inns

★ ★ **GREEN PARK.** *Box 7, 2 mi SE on US 321.* 704/295-3141; res: 800/852-2462; FAX 704/295-3141, ext. 116. 85 rms, 3 story. No A/C. Mid-June-mid-Nov: S $94, D $104; suites $115-$160; lower rates rest of yr. Crib free. TV; cable. Pool. Dining rms 7:30-10 am, 6:30-10 pm. Bar 5 pm-midnight. Ck-out 11 am, ck-in 3 pm. Meeting rms. Bellhops. Tennis & 18-hole golf adj. Downhill ski 2 mi. Lawn games. Many private porches. Historic building (1882); library, fireplace. Cr cds: A, DS, MC, V.

★ ★ ★ **MEADOWBROOK.** *Box 2005, N Main St.* 704/295-9341; res: 800/456-5456; FAX 704/295-9341, ext. 118. 46 rms, 3 story. Apr-Nov: S, D $99; each addl $10; suites $139-$159; under 12 free; ski plans; lower rates rest of yr. TV; cable. Indoor pool. Complimentary continental bkfst. Dining rm 11 am-2 pm, 6-9 pm. Bar; entertainment. Ck-out 11 am, ck-in 3 pm. Meeting rms. Downhill ski 3 mi. Exercise rm; whirlpool. European style country inn. Cr cds: A, D, DS, MC, V.

✔ ★ ★ **RAGGED GARDEN.** *PO Box 1927, Sunset Dr.* 704/295-9703. 7 rms, 2 story. No A/C. S, D $55-$90; higher rates wkends. Children over 12 yrs only. Closed Jan & Mar. Complimentary full bkfst, coffee & tea. Ck-out 11 am, ck-in after 1 pm. Built 1900; gardens. Totally nonsmoking. Cr cds: MC, V.

Resorts

★ ★ ★ **CHETOLA.** *Box 17, N Main St.* 704/295-5500; res: 800/243-8652; FAX 704/295-5529. 42 rms, 1-3 story. May-Oct: S, D $98-$189; lower rates rest of yr. Crib $8. TV; cable. Indoor pool. Playground. Supervised child's activities (June-Aug). Dining rm (public by res) 7:30-10 am, 11:30 am-2 pm, 5:30-9:30 pm. Ck-out 11 am, ck-in 3 pm. Coin lndry. Meeting rms. Grocery, package store ½ mi. Sports dir. Lighted tennis. Boating, fishing. Downhill/x-country ski 3 mi. Hiking. Bicycles. Soc dir. Entertainment. Racquetball court. Game rm. Exercise rm; instructor, weight machines, bicycles, whirlpool, sauna. Refrigerators. Some private balconies. Picnic tables, grills. Seven-acre lake. Adj to Moses Cone Natl Park. Cr cds: A, DS, MC, V.

★ ★ ★ **HOUND EARS LODGE & CLUB.** *Box 188, 7 mi W, ½ mi off NC 105.* 704/963-4321; FAX 704/963-8030. 27 rms in lodge & club house, 2 story. MAP, mid-June-Oct: S $150; D $244; each addl $48; suites $268; under 11, $22; lower rates rest of yr. Serv charge 17%. TV; cable. Heated pool; poolside serv, lifeguard. Free supervised child's activities (June-Sept). Dining rm 7-10 am, noon-2:30 pm, 6:30-9:30 pm (res required; jacket, tie at dinner). Rm serv. Setups; entertainment, dancing. Ck-out noon, ck-in 1:30 pm. Meeting rms. Bellhops. Valet serv. Airport transportation. 6 tennis courts, pro. 18-hole golf, greens fee $25, pro. Downhill ski on site. Sleigh rides in winter. Exercise equipt; weight machines, bicycle, steam rm. In Blue Ridge Mountain Valley; named after rock formation overlooking club. Cr cds: A, MC, V.

Restaurants

★ ★ **BEST CELLAR.** *On Little Springs Rd, behind Food Lion Shopping Center.* 704/295-3466. Hrs: 6-9:30 pm; Nov-mid-May, Fri & Sat only. Closed Sun. Res accepted. No A/C. Continental menu. Wine, beer. Semi-a la carte: dinner $10.95-$17.95. Specializes in roast duckling, poached salmon, banana cream pie. Valet parking. Rustic decor; pine floor, stone walls, 3 fireplaces. Cr cds: A, C, D, DS, MC, V.

★ ★ **RIVERWOOD.** *US 231, at jct Blue Ridge Pkwy.* 704/295-4162. Hrs: 5:30 pm-closing. Closed Tues; Labor Day; mid-Nov-mid-Mar. Res accepted. No A/C. Bar. Semi-a la carte: dinner $12.95-$19.95. Specialties: stuffed rainbow trout, marinated beef tenderloin. Own desserts. Parking. Rustic decor. Cr cds: DS, MC, V.

✔ ★ **SPECKLED TROUT CAFE.** *Main St & US 221.* 704/295-9819. Hrs: 8 am-3 pm, 5-9:30 pm. Closed Dec 25. Res accepted. Bar from 5 pm. Semi-a la carte: bkfst $1.95-$4.50, lunch $2.95-$6.95, dinner $9.95-$16.95. Specializes in rainbow trout, roast duckling, beef. Parking. Outdoor dining. Cr cds: A, MC, V.

★ ★ **TWIG'S.** *US 321 Bypass.* 704/295-5050. Hrs: 5:30-9:30 pm; Fri, Sat to 10 pm. Closed Dec 24-25; Mon early Nov-late May. Res accepted. No A/C. Continental menu. Bar 5:30 pm-1 am. A la carte entrees: dinner $8.95-$18.95. Specializes in fowl, lamb, fresh seafood. Parking. Porch dining (summer). Cr cds: A, DS, MC, V.

Blue Ridge Parkway (B-2 - A-4)

(see Virginia)

Boone (A-4)

Settled: 1772 **Pop:** 12,915 **Elev:** 3,266 ft **Area code:** 704 **Zip:** 28607

Boone, the seat of Watauga County, was named for Daniel Boone, who had a cabin and hunted here in the 1760s. This "heart of the High Country" sprawls over a long valley, which provides a natural pass through the hills. Watauga County boasts several industrial firms providing its economic base, in addition to tourism, agriculture and Appalachian State University. Mountain crafts are featured in a variety of craft fairs, festivals and shops.

What to See and Do

1. **Appalachian State University** (1899). (11,500 students) Atop Blue Ridge Mountains. Offers 90 undergraduate and 12 graduate majors. Dark Sky Observatory. Phone 262-2000 or -2179. (See SEASONAL EVENTS)

2. **Daniel Boone Native Gardens.** Horn in the West Dr, 1 mi E off US 421, adj to Daniel Boone Theater (see SEASONAL EVENTS). Native plants in informal setting; Squire Boone Cabin, wishing well, fern garden. (May-Sept, daily; Oct, wkends) Phone 264-6390. ¢

(For further information contact the Convention & Visitors Bureau, 208 Howard St, 262-3516 or 800/852-9506; or North Carolina High Country Host, 1700 Blowing Rock Rd, 264-1299.)

Seasonal Events

Horn in the West. Daniel Boone Amphitheatre, 1 mi E off US 421. Outdoor drama depicts Daniel Boone and settlers of the mountain during the Revolutionary War. Nightly exc Mon. Contact PO Box 295; 264-2120. Mid-June-mid-Aug.

An Appalachian Summer. Appalachian State University. Concerts, drama, art exhibits. Phone 800/841-2787.

(See Banner Elk, Blowing Rock, Linville)

Motels

★ ★ **BROYHILL INN & CONFERENCE CENTER.** *96 Bodenheimer Dr.* 704/262-2204; res: 800/951-6048; FAX 704/262-2946. 83 rms, 2 story, 7 suites. S $56; D $60; each addl $4; suites $85-$150; under 12 free. Crib free. TV; cable. Free coffee in rms. Restaurant 7-10 am, 11:30 am-1:30 pm, 5:30-9 pm; Sun brunch 11 am-2 pm. Bar. Ck-out noon. Coin lndry. Meeting rms. Refrigerators avail. Picnic tables. Cr cds: A, MC, V.

★ **ECONO LODGE.** *2419 NC 105, 3 mi S on NC 105.* 704/264-4133; FAX 704/262-0101. 100 rms, 4 story. Mid-June-late Oct & late Dec-Feb: S, D $47-$67; each addl $4; under 18 free; lower rates rest of yr. Crib free. TV; cable. Indoor pool. Complimentary continental bkfst, coffee. Restaurant nearby. Ck-out 11 am. Downhill/x-country ski 8 mi. Game rm. Cr cds: A, C, D, DS, MC, V.

✔ ★ **HIGH COUNTRY INN.** *Box 1339, NC 105S.* 704/264-1000; res: 800/334-5605. 120 rms, 3 story. Late Dec-Feb, mid-June-Oct: S $27-$64; D $32-$69; each addl $5; under 16 free; golf, ski, rafting plans; lower rates rest of yr. Crib free. TV; cable. Indoor/outdoor pool; whirlpool, sauna. Restaurant 7 am-2 pm, 5-9 pm. Rm serv. Bar 6 pm-1 am. Ck-out 11 am. Lndry facilities. Downhill ski 8 mi. Some fireplaces. Picnic tables, grills. Cr cds: A, DS, MC, V.

✔ ★ **HOLIDAY INN EXPRESS.** *1855 Blowing Rock Rd.* 704/264-2451; FAX 704/265-3861. 138 rms, 2 story. June-Oct, ski season: S $40-$69; D $49-$79; each addl $8; under 19 free; lower rates rest of yr. Crib free. TV; cable. Heated pool. Complimentary continental bkfst. Ck-out 11 am. Coin lndry. Meeting rms. Downhill ski 5 mi. Cr cds: A, C, D, DS, JCB, MC, V.

Motor Hotel

★ ★ **HAMPTON INN.** *1075 NC 105.* 704/264-0077; res: 800/888-6867; FAX 704/264-4600. 95 rms, 5 story. June-Oct: S $60-$70; D $66-$75; under 18 free; lower rates rest of yr. Crib free. TV; cable. Indoor pool. Complimentary continental bkfst. Complimentary coffee in lobby. Restaurant adj 11 am-10 pm. Ck-out 11 am. Meeting rms. Exercise equipt; weight machine, bicycles, whirlpool. Cr cds: A, C, D, DS, ER, JCB, MC, V.

Hotel

★ ★ ★ **QUALITY INN APPALACHIAN CONFERENCE CEN-TER.** 344 Blowing Rock Rd, 1 mi S at jct US 321, NC 105. 704/262-0020; FAX 704/262-0020, ext. 132. 134 rms, 7 story. Mid-June-Oct: S $64-$76; D $70-$80; each addl $6; suites $80-$150; under 18 free; ski, golf packages; higher rates late Dec-Feb; lower rates rest of yr. TV; cable. Indoor pool. Restaurant 7 am-2 pm, 5:30-10 pm. Bar 5 pm-1 am. Ck-out 11 am. Lndry facilities. Meeting rms. Golf privileges. Downhill ski 8 mi; x-country ski 9 mi. Exercise equipt; weights, bicycles. Refrigerator in suites. Cr cds: A, C, D, DS, ER, JCB, MC, V.

Restaurants

★ **CHUCK'S STEAK HOUSE.** 644 Blowing Rock Rd. 704/262-1666. Hrs: 4:30-10 pm. Closed Easter, Dec 25. Res accepted. Semi-a la carte: dinner $5.95-$19.95. Child's meals. Specializes in steak, fresh fish, chicken. Salad bar. Parking. Cr cds: A, MC, V.

✔ ★ **DAN'L BOONE INN.** 130 Hardin St, at jct US 421 & US 321. 704/264-8657. Hrs: 11 am-9 pm; Sat, Sun from 8 am; Nov-Mar from 5 pm. Closed 2 days at Christmas. No A/C. Family style: bkfst $6, lunch, dinner $9.95. Specializes in fried chicken. Parking. In one of oldest buildings in Boone; country atmosphere. Family-owned. No cr cds accepted.

★ ★ **MAKOTO.** 815 Blowing Rock Rd. 704/264-7976. Hrs: 11:30 am-2 pm, 5-9 pm; Fri, Sat to 10 pm. Closed Thanksgiving, Dec 24-25. Res accepted. Japanese menu. Serv bar. Complete meals: lunch $3.75-$9.50, dinner $8.95-$22.95. Serv charge 15%. Child's meals. Specializes in seafood, beef, poultry. Tableside preparation. Parking. Cr cds: A, C, D, DS, MC, V.

Brevard (B-2)

Settled: 1861 **Pop:** 5,388 **Elev:** 2,230 ft **Area code:** 704 **Zip:** 28712

An industrial and mountain resort center near the entrance to Pisgah National Forest, Brevard has several industries, including E.I. du Pont, Coats American Company and the Ecusta division of P.H. Glatfelter.

What to See and Do

1. **Mt Pisgah** (5,749 ft). Blue Ridge Pkwy, US 276 to within 1 mi of summit, trail rest of way.
2. **Pisgah National Forest.** NW of town, via US 276. A 499,816-acre, 4-district forest. The Cradle of Forestry Visitor Center (summer, daily) is at site of first forestry school in the US. The forest surrounds Mt Mitchell State Park (see LITTLE SWITZERLAND), which contains the highest point in the US east of the Mississippi (6,684 ft). Linville Gorge Wilderness is 10,975 acres of precipitous cliffs and cascading falls (permit required May-Oct for overnight camping, contact the Grandfather Ranger District in MARION). Wiseman's View looks into Linville Gorge. Shining Rock Wilderness contains 18,500 acres of rugged alpine scenery. The forest shares with Cherokee National Forest in Tennessee the 6,286-foot Roan Mountain, with its purple rhododendron and stands of spruce and fir. Offers swimming and boating sites; good fishing for trout, bass and perch; hunting for deer, bear and small game; miles of hiking

and riding trails; picnic sites; campgrounds (fee). For further information contact the Supervisor, 100 Otis St, Box 2750, Asheville 28802; 257-4200.

(For further information contact the Chamber of Commerce, PO Box 589; 883-3700 or 800/648-4523.)

Annual Event

Festival of the Arts. Music, crafts, art, sporting events. 2nd wk July.

Seasonal Event

Summer Festival of Music. Brevard Music Center. Whittington-Pfhol Auditorium. More than 50 programs presented, including symphonic, choral, chamber, recital; musical comedy and operatic performances; guest artists. Mon-Sat evenings; Sun afternoons. Contact Box 592; 884-2019 or -2011. Late June-early Aug.

(See Asheville, Hendersonville)

Motels

★ ★ **IMPERIAL MOTOR LODGE.** Box 586, 1/2 mi N on US 64, 276. 704/884-2887. 95 rms, 1-2 story. June-Oct: S, D $50-$70; each addl $5; under 12 free; lower rates rest of yr. Crib $5. TV; cable. Pool. Restaurant opp 6 am-midnight. Ck-out 11:30 am. Refrigerators. Grill. Cr cds: A, C, D, MC, V.

★ **SUNSET.** 415 S Broad St. 704/884-9106. 18 rms. June-Oct: S $48; D $58; each addl $5; lower rates rest of yr. Crib free. TV; cable. Restaurant opp 11 am-10 pm. Ck-out 11 am. Cr cds: A, DS, MC, V.

Bryson City (B-2)

Pop: 1,145 **Elev:** 1,736 ft **Area code:** 704 **Zip:** 28713

At the confluence of the Little Tennessee and Tuckasegee rivers, Bryson City is also at the entrance to Great Smoky Mountains National Park. Fontana Lake, part of the TVA system, is nearby. Industries include textiles.

What to See and Do

1. **Whitewater Rafting. Rolling Thunder River Co.** 10 mi W on US 19S/74W, at Nantahala Gorge. Guided raft, canoe, kayak trips through Smoky Mountains; day and overnight. (Apr-Oct) Reservations suggested. For information, fees contact Rolling Thunder River Co, Box 88, Almond 28702; 488-2030 or 800/344-5838. ¢¢¢¢¢
2. **Great Smoky Mountains National Park** (see). 8 mi N on US 19.
3. **Fontana Dam** (see). 35 mi SW on US 19 and NC 28.

(For further information contact the Chamber of Commerce, PO Box 509; 488-3681.)

(See Cherokee, Franklin, Waynesville)

Inns

★ **FOLKESTONE.** 101 Folkestone Rd. 704/488-2730; FAX 704/488-8689. 9 rms, 3 story. No A/C. No rm phones. S $53-$73; D $59-$79; each addl $20; family, weekly rates. Complimentary full bkfst. Ck-out 11 am, ck-in 3 pm. Lawn games. Some balconies. Picnic tables.

Built 1926; restored country farmhouse. Totally nonsmoking. No cr cds accepted.

★ ★ **HEMLOCK.** *Drawer EE, 3 mi NE, 1 mi N of US 19.* *704/488-2885.* 25 rms, 4 kit. units (1-3-bedrm). No A/C. MAP, mid-Apr-Oct: D $121-$165; each addl $20-$39; kit. cottage for 2, $144-$165. Closed rest of yr. Dining rm (public by res) 8:30 am & 6 pm sittings; Sun 8:30 am & 12:30 pm sittings. Ck-out 11 am, ck-in 1 pm. Game rm. Lawn games. Early Amer decor; mountain view. No cr cds accepted.

Cottage Colony

★ ★ **NANTAHALA VILLAGE.** *9400 US 19W, 9 mi W on US 19/74.* *704/488-2826; res: 800/438-1507 (exc NC).* 14 rms in lodge, 43 kit. cottages (1-5-bedrm). A/C in some cottages. May-Oct: S, D $70; each addl $5; cottages for 2-12, $80-$200; lower rates rest of yr. Crib $5. TV. Pool. Dining rm 7 am-9 pm. Box lunches. Ck-out 10 am, ck-in 2 pm. Tennis. Rec rm. Observation tower. Fireplace in some cottages. On 200 acres in Great Smokies, near Fontana Lake and Nantahala River; whitewater rafting. Cr cds: DS, MC, V.

Restaurant

✔ ★ **RELIA'S GARDEN.** *13 mi SW on US 19S, at Nantahala Outdoor Center.* *704/488-9186.* Hrs: noon-2 pm, 5-9 pm; Sat & Sun also 8-10:30 am. Closed Nov-Mar. Res accepted. Semi-a la carte: bkfst $2.75-$3.95, lunch $3.10-$7.95, dinner $5.25-$12.95. Specializes in seafood, beef, pasta. Porch dining. Rustic decor. Cr cds: A, DS, MC, V.

Burlington (A-6)

Settled: ca 1700 **Pop:** 39,498 **Elev:** 663 ft **Area code:** 910 **Zip:** 27216

In 1837, E.M. Holt converted his father's gristmill on Alamance Creek into a textile mill. The Alamance Mill produced the first commercially dyed plaids south of the Potomac, changing the face of the textile industry in the South.

What to See and Do

1. **Alamance Battleground State Historic Site.** 6 mi SW on NC 62. On May 16, 1771, a two-hour battle was fought here between the colonial militia under Royal Governor Tryon and about 2,000 rebellious "Regulators." The latter were defeated. Restored log house; visitor center, exhibits, audiovisual presentation; picnic area. (Apr-Oct, daily; rest of yr, daily exc Mon; closed most major hols) Phone 227-4785. **Free.**

2. **Dentzel Menagerie Carousel** (ca 1910). S Main, at Church St in City Park. Rare hand-carved carousel; restored. (Apr-Oct, daily exc Mon) Phone 222-5030. ¢

3. **Lake Cammack Park and Marina.** 6 mi N on Union Ridge Rd, off NC 62. An 800-acre city reservoir. Waterskiing; fishing; boating. Picnic area, playground. (Daily exc Thurs; days vary winter) Phone 421-3872. ¢

(For further information contact the Burlington/Alamance County Convention & Visitors Bureau, PO Drawer 519; 570-1444 or 800/637-3804.)

Annual Event

Alamance Balloon Fest. Hot-air balloon race, air show, parachuting, music. Mother's Day wkend.

Seasonal Event

The Sword of Peace Summer Celebration. 18 mi SW via I-85, Liberty-49S exit, then NC 49S and NC 1005 to Snow Camp. Repertory outdoor theater (evenings) and summer arts festival; 150-year-old & 200-year-old buildings converted into museums, craft gallery & cane mill. Thurs-Sat. Contact PO Box 535, Snow Camp 27349; 376-6948 or 800/726-5115. Late June-late Aug.

(See Greensboro, High Point)

Motels

✔ ★ **DAYS INN.** *2133 W Hanford Rd (27215), I-85 exit 145.* *910/227-1270; FAX 910/227-1702.* 124 rms, 2 story. S $36; D $41; each addl $5; under 12 free. Crib avail. TV. Pool. Complimentary continental bkfst, coffee. Restaurant adj 6 am-11 pm; Fri & Sat to 1 am. Ck-out noon. Meeting rms. Valet serv. Cr cds: A, C, D, DS, ER, JCB, MC, V.

★ ★ **HAMPTON INN.** *2701 Kirkpatrick Rd (27215).* *910/584-4447; FAX 910/721-1325.* 118 rms, 4 story. S $49; D $51-$58; suites $82; under 18 free; higher rates Furniture Market (Apr & Oct). Crib free. TV; cable. Pool. Complimentary continental bkfst. Complimentary coffee in lobby. Restaurant adj 5-10 pm. Ck-out 11 am. Meeting rms. Exercise equipt; weight machine, bicycles, whirlpool, sauna. Cr cds: A, D, DS, MC, V.

✔ ★ **KIRK'S MOTOR COURT.** *1155 N Church St (27215).* *910/228-1383.* 102 rms, 1-2 story, 14 kits. S $28-$36; D $36-$42; each addl $4; kit. units $175-$210/wk; under 12 free. Crib $4. TV; cable. Pool; wading pool. Restaurant adj 11 am-9 pm. Ck-out 11 am. Meeting rms. Valet serv. Sundries. Cr cds: MC, V.

★ ★ **RAMADA INN.** *(27215).* On NC 62 at jct I-85. *910/227-5541.* 138 rms, 2 story. S $39-$42; D $45-$48; each addl $6; under 18 free; higher rates: Furniture Market, special events. Crib free. TV; cable. Pool. Restaurant 6 am-2 pm, 5-10 pm. Rm serv. Bar 5 pm-1 am, closed Sun. Ck-out noon. Meeting rms. Cr cds: A, C, D, DS, JCB, MC, V.

Burnsville (A-3)

Pop: 1,482 **Elev:** 2,814 ft **Area code:** 704 **Zip:** 28714

A Ranger District office of the Pisgah National Forest (see BREVARD) is located here.

(For further information contact the Yancey County Chamber of Commerce, 2 Town Square, Room 3; 682-7413.)

Annual Event

Mt Mitchell Crafts Fair. Town Square. 1st Fri & Sat Aug.

Seasonal Events

Music in the Mountains. Chamber music concerts. Sun late June-early Aug.

Parkway Playhouse. 1 mi NE off US 19E. Five Broadway shows, professional summer theater. Wed-Sat evenings. Phone 682-6151. July-mid-Aug.

(See Asheville, Little Switzerland)

Inn

★ ★ **NU-WRAY.** *Box 156, Town Square, on US 19E.* 704/682-2329. 32 rms, 25 baths, 3 story. No A/C. No rm phones. June-Aug, Oct: S $55; D $69; each addl $10; MAP; wkly rates; lower rates May-Sept & Nov. Closed rest of yr. TV in some rms; cable. Dining rm sittings: 8:30 am & 6:30 pm; Sun 8:30 am, 1 pm & 2:30 pm. Ck-out 11 am, ck-in after noon. Inn built in 1833. Cr cds: MC, V.

Buxton (Outer Banks) (B-10)

Pop: 3,250 **Elev:** 10 ft **Area code:** 919 **Zip:** 27920

This town is on Hatteras Island, part of the Outer Banks (see). It is surrounded by Cape Hatteras National Seashore (see).

Motels

★ **CAPE HATTERAS.** *Box 339, on NC 12.* 919/995-5611. 6 motel rms, 1-2 story, 29 kit. units. No rm phones. Mid June-Labor Day: S, D $90; each addl $3; kit. units $85-$160; lower rates rest of yr. Crib $3. TV; cable. Pool; whirlpool. Ck-out 11 am. Cr cds: A, MC, V.

★ ★ **COMFORT INN.** *PO Box 1089, on NC 12, near Cape Hatteras lighthouse.* 919/995-6100; FAX 919/995-5444. 60 rms, 2 story. Mid-June-mid-Sept: S, D $85-89; each addl $5; under 18 free; lower rates rest of yr. Crib free. TV; cable. Pool. Complimentary continental bkfst. Restaurant nearby. Ck-out 11 am. Free lndry facilities. Refrigerators. Near beach. Cr cds: A, C, D, DS, MC, V.

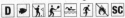

✔ ★ **FALCON.** *(NC 12, Buxton)* 919/995-5968; res: 800/635-6911. 35 rms, 5 kits. No rm phones. Memorial Day-Labor Day: S, D $50-$65; kits. $70; under 6 free; wkly rates; higher rates hols (3-day min); lower rates Labor Day-mid-Dec. Closed rest of yr. Crib free. TV; cable. Pool. Restaurant opp 6:30 am-9:30 pm. Ck-out 11 am. Refrigerators avail. Picnic tables. Near ocean. Cr cds: MC, V.

Resort

★ **CASTAWAYS OCEANFRONT RESORT.** *(PO Box 557, Avon 27915) N on NC 12.* 919/995-4444; res: 800/845-6070; FAX 919/995-4704. 68 rms, 5 story. AP, May-Sept: S, D $68-$108; each addl $5; under 18 free; wkly rates; lower rates rest of yr. Crib free. TV; cable. Pool; whirlpool, sauna, poolside serv. Supervised child's activities. Dining rm 7-10:30 am, 5-9 pm. Rm serv. Ck-out 11 am, ck-in 3 pm. Meeting rms. Tennis. 9-hole golf privileges, greens fee $20. Swimming beach. Bicycles (rentals). Lawn games. Refrigerators, wet bars. Balconies. Picnic tables, grills. Cr cds: A, MC, V.

Restaurant

✔ ★ **TIDES.** *(NC 12, Buxton)* 919/995-5988. Hrs: 6-11:30 am, 5:30-9:30 pm. Closed Jan-Mar & Dec. Wine, beer. Semi-a la carte: bkfst $2.50-$5.50, dinner $7.50-$15. Specializes in seafood, steak. Parking. Nautical decor. Cr cds: MC, V.

Cape Hatteras National Seashore (B-10)

(Enter from Cedar Island or Swan Quarter toll ferry. Reservations advised. Free ferry from Ocracoke Island to Hatteras Island.)

This thin strand stretches for 75 miles along the Outer Banks (see), threaded between the windy, pounding Atlantic and shallow Pamlico Sound. Nags Head (see) is the northern limit of the recreational area, which has three sections (separated by inlets): Bodie (pronounced *body*), Hatteras (largest of the barrier islands) and Ocracoke (see), the most picturesque. Bounded on three sides by the park, but separate from it, are the villages of Rodanthe, Waves, Salvo, Avon, Buxton, Frisco, Hatteras and Ocracoke. Although the area is noted for long expanses of sand beaches, wildflowers bloom most of the year. There are also stands of yaupon (holly), loblolly pine and live oak. Several freshwater ponds are found on Bodie and Hatteras Islands. Many migratory and nonmigratory waterfowl winter here, including gadwalls, greater snow and Canada geese, loons, grebes and herons.

There is an information station at Whalebone Junction (Memorial Day-Labor Day, daily), south of Nags Head. Near Bodie Island Lighthouse is a bird observation platform, a nature trail and a visitor center (Memorial Day-Labor Day, daily) with natural history exhibits. There are also visitor centers with history exhibits at Ocracoke (same hrs) and the Cape Hatteras Lighthouse at Buxton (daily).

(Do not drive off the highways—you are likely to get stuck.)

Sport fishing, boating, sailing, swimming (recommended only at protected beaches); picnicking and camping (fee), also waterfowl hunting in season under regulation.

For further information contact the Superintendent, Rte 1, Box 675, Manteo 27954, or phone 919/473-2111.

(For accommodations see Buxton, Hatteras, Kill Devil Hills, Nags Head, Ocracoke)

Cashiers (B-2)

Pop: 1,200 **Elev:** 3,486 ft **Area code:** 704 **Zip:** 28717

High in the Blue Ridge Mountains, this well-known summer resort area offers scenic drives on twisting mountain roads, hiking trails, views, waterfalls, lake sports, fishing and other recreational activities.

What to See and Do

1. **Fairfield Sapphire Valley Ski Area.** 3 mi E on US 64. Chairlift, 1 rope tow; patrol, school, snowmaking. Longest run 2,400 ft; vertical drop 425 ft. (Mid-Dec-mid-Mar, daily, nightly exc Sun) Evening, half-day rates. Other seasons: swimming, fishing, boating; hiking, horseback riding; golf, tennis; recreation center. Restaurants, inn (see RESORTS). Phone 743-3441. ¢¢¢¢

2. **Lake Thorpe.** 5 mi N on NC 107. Fishing, swimming, waterskiing. Boats may be rented at Glenville (on lake) or launched from here.

(For further information contact the Cashiers Area Chamber of Commerce, PO Box 238; 743-5191.)

(See Franklin, Highlands)

Motel

★ **OAKMONT LODGE.** *On NC 107, 1/2 mi N of jct US 64.* 704/743-2298. 20 rms. No A/C. June-Oct: S, D $54; each addl $5; kit. cottages $95 & $385/wk. Crib free. TV; cable. Restaurant 8 am-9 pm. Ck-out 11 am. Downhill ski 2 mi. Cr cds: MC, V.

Inn

★ ★ ★ **GREYSTONE.** *(Greystone Lane, Lake Toxaway 28747) 8 mi E on US 64.* 704/966-4700; res: 800/824-5766 (exc NC); FAX 704/862-5689. 33 rms, 3 story, 17 A/C. May-Dec: S $200-$280; D $240-$320; each addl $70; family, wkly rates; higher rates wkends (2-night min); lower rates Apr. Closed rest of yr. Crib free. TV; cable. Pool. Supervised child's activities (May-Aug). Complimentary full bkfst. Complimentary tea/sherry, coffee. Restaurant adj 8-10 am, 6:30-9:30 pm. Ck-out noon, ck-in 3 pm. Concierge. Bellhops. Tennis, pro. 18-hole golf, greens fee $35-$45, putting green, driving range. Refrigerators, minibars. Balconies. Picnic tables. On swimming beach. Cr cds: A, MC, V.

Resorts

★ ★ ★ **FAIRFIELD SAPPHIRE VALLEY.** *(4000 US 64W, Sapphire 28774) 3 mi E.* 704/743-3441; FAX 704/743-2641. 210 villas (summer), 160 villas (winter), 1-2 story. S, D $85; kit. villas $85-$225; wkly, monthly rates, ski, golf, tennis package plans. Crib $3. TV; cable. Indoor/outdoor pool. Playground. Supervised child's activities (June-mid-Aug). Dining rm 11 am-10 pm. Ck-out 10 am, ck-in 4 pm. Sports dir. Lighted tennis, pro. 18-hole golf, greens fee $40, driving range. Private beach; boats (no motors). Downhill ski 1 mi. Miniature golf. Lawn games. Soc dir; entertainment. Exercise rm; instructor, weights, bicycles, whirlpool, sauna, steam rm. Refrigerators, fireplaces. Whirlpool in some villas. Rms vary. 5,700 acres in mountain setting; on lake. Gardens, extensive lawns. Cr cds: A, DS, MC, V.

★ ★ ★ **HIGH HAMPTON INN & COUNTRY CLUB.** *PO Box 338, 2 mi S on NC 107.* 704/743-2411; res: 800/334-2551; FAX 704/743-5991. 34 rms in 3-story inn, 15 cottages, 29 golf villas. No A/C. AP, July, Aug & Oct: S $78-$90; D $136-$172; each addl $52; golf villas $169-$252; wkly rates; golf, tennis package plans; lower rates Apr-June, Sept & Nov. Closed rest of yr. Crib free. Pet accepted, some restrictions. TV rm; cable. Supervised child's activities (June-Labor Day). Free afternoon tea. Dining rm 7-9:30 am, noon-2:15 pm, 6:30-8:15 pm. Box lunches, buffets. Setups. Ck-out 1 pm, ck-in 3 pm. Coin lndry. Valet serv. Gift shop. Airport transportation. Sports dir. Tennis. 18-hole golf, greens fee $20, pro, 2 putting greens, driving range. Swimming. Boats, dockage. Archery. Trail guides. Bicycle rentals. Outdoor, indoor games. Soc dir; entertainment, movies. Rec rm, library. Lawn games. Kennels. 1,400-acre mountain estate, 2 lakes. Rustic resort; established 1924. Former hunting lodge of a Civil War general. Cr cds: A, MC, V.

Cedar Island (C-9)

Pop: 333 (est) **Elev:** 7 ft **Area code:** 919 **Zip:** 28520

There is daily ferry service from Cedar Island to Ocracoke (see).

Motel

✔ ★ **DRIFTWOOD.** *Cedar Island Beach, on NC 12 N at Cedar Island-Ocracoke ferry terminal.* 919/225-4861. 37 rms. May-mid-Oct: S $40; D $50; each addl $4; under 12 free; lower rates rest of yr. Crib free. TV; cable. Coffee in rms. Restaurant 6-8:30 pm. Ck-out noon. Sundries. On ocean. Cr cds: MC, V.

Chapel Hill (B-6)

Founded: 1793 **Pop:** 38,719 **Elev:** 487 ft **Area code:** 919

The community of Chapel Hill is centered around the University of North Carolina, the oldest state university in the US. This school has been a leader in American education for more than 170 years and is now part of a "research triangle," together with Duke University at Durham and North Carolina State University at Raleigh. Despite heavy losses of faculty and students to the Civil War, the school remained open until the years of Reconstruction, 1870-1875. During the next decade the university was reborn.

What to See and Do

1. **University of North Carolina at Chapel Hill** (1795). (Approx 24,000 students) This institution, the first state university in the country, is on a 720-acre campus and has more than 200 buildings. On campus are

   Old Well. Cameron Ave in center of campus. Long the unofficial symbol of the University, this well was the only source of water here for nearly a century. The present "Greek temple" structure dates from 1897.

   South (Main) Building. Opposite Old Well. Cornerstone laid in 1798 but building not completed until 1814, during which time the boys lived inside the roofless walls in little huts. Future President James K. Polk lived here from 1814-1818.

   Old East. E of Old Well. Oldest state university building in the country; cornerstone laid in 1793. Matched by Old West (1823). Still being used as a residence hall.

   Davie Poplar. N of Old Well. Ancient ivy-covered tree named for the "father of the university," William Richardson Davie; more than 200 years old.

   Memorial Hall (1930). Opposite New West. White columns front this structure dedicated to war dead, honored alumni and university benefactors. James K. Polk, class of 1818, has a commemorative tablet here. He graduated first in his class and became the 11th President of the US.

   Coker Arboretum. Cameron Ave & Raleigh St. Covers 5 acres. Extensive collection of ornamental plants and shrubs.

   Morehead-Patterson Memorial Bell Tower (1930). A 172-foot Italian Renaissance campanile; concert chimes. The 12 bells range in weight from 300 pounds to almost 2 tons. Popular tunes are rung daily.

   Kenan Stadium (1927). Behind Bell Tower. Seats 52,000; in wooded natural bowl.

   Louis Round Wilson Library. Houses special collections. Includes North Carolina Collection Gallery; historic rooms, texts and artifacts. Also here is the Southern Historical Collection, featuring manuscripts, rare books and photographs.

   Morehead Planetarium. E Franklin St. Offers indoor star-gazing, art gallery with permanent and changing exhibits, scientific exhibits; rare Zeiss instrument. Shows (daily; closed Dec 24, 25). Rose garden has mammoth sundial showing time around the world. Sr citizen rate. Phone 549-6863. Shows **¢¢**

Playmakers Theater (1851). Greek-revival temple was designed as a combination library and ballroom.

Paul Green Theater (1978). PlayMakers Repertory Company. Named for one of the first dramatic arts students at the University. Green is known as the father of American outdoor drama. (Sept-May)

(For further information on the University phone Visitor Services at 962-1630.)

2. **North Carolina Botanical Garden.** Old Mason Farm Rd & US 15/501 Bypass. Approx 600 acres; variety of trees and plants of southeastern US; wildflower areas, herb gardens. Nature trails (daily). (Mid-Mar-mid-Nov, daily; rest of yr, Mon-Fri) Phone 962-0522. **Free.**

3. **Chapel of the Cross** (1842-48). 304 E Franklin St, adj to Morehead Planetarium. Antebellum Gothic-revival Episcopal church. (Daily) Phone 929-2193.

(For further information contact the Chapel Hill-Carrboro Chamber of Commerce, PO Box 2897, 27515; 967-7075.)

(See Durham, Raleigh)

Motels

★ ★ **BEST WESTERN UNIVERSITY INN.** *Box 2118 (27515), Raleigh Rd, 2 mi E on NC 54, 1/4 mi E of US 15/501 Bypass. 919/932-3000; FAX 919/968-6513.* 84 rms, 1-2 story. S $45-$74; D $55-$85; each addl $5; suites $152-$168; studio rms $76-$84; under 13 free. Crib $5. TV; cable. Pool. Coffee in rms. Continental bkfst. Restaurant 5:30-10:30 pm. Bar 4:30-11 pm. Ck-out noon. Bellhops. Sundries. Tennis privileges. Golf privileges adj, greens fee $15. Health club privileges. 1 mi from UNC campus. Cr cds: A, C, D, DS, MC, V.

★ ★ **CAROLINA INN.** *211 Pittsboro St (27516). 919/933-2001; res: 800/962-8519.* 140 rms, 3 story. S $45-$85; D $65-$94; suites $99-$199. Crib free. TV; cable. Restaurant 6-9:30 am, 11:30 am-10 pm. Bar 5-10 pm. Ck-out noon. Meeting rms. Colonial decor. Owned and operated by university; on campus. Cr cds: A, C, D, DS, MC, V.

✔ ★ ★ **HAMPTON INN.** *1740 US 15/501 (27514). 919/968-3000; FAX 919/929-0322.* 122 rms, 2 story. S $46-$58; D $50-$60; under 18 free. Crib free. Pet accepted. TV; cable. Pool. Complimentary continental bkfst. Restaurant adj 11 am-10 pm. Ck-out noon. Meeting rms. Health club privileges. Cr cds: A, C, D, DS, MC, V.

★ ★ **HOLIDAY INN.** *1301 N Fordham Blvd (27514), 2 mi S of I-40 exit 270, at Eastgate Shopping Center. 919/929-2171; FAX 919/929-5736.* 135 rms, 2 story. S, D $59-$64; each addl $5; higher rates: football season (2-day min), graduation (3-day min). Crib free. TV; cable. Pool. Restaurant 7-11 am, 5:30-10 pm. Rm serv. Bar 5-11 pm. Ck-out noon. Meeting rms. Exercise equipt; weight machine, bicycles. Cr cds: A, C, D, DS, JCB, MC, V.

Hotel

★ ★ **OMNI EUROPA.** *1 Europa Dr (27514). 919/968-4900; FAX 919/968-3520.* 172 rms, 4 story. S $118; D $128; each addl $10; suites $175-$280; under 16 free. Crib free. TV; cable. Pool. Restaurant 6:30 am-2 pm, 6-10 pm. Rm serv 6:30 am-11 pm. Bar 2 pm-1 am; entertainment, dancing wkends. Meeting rms. Concierge. Gift shop. Lighted tennis. Health club privileges. Private patios, balconies. Cr cds: A, C, D, DS, MC, V.

Inn

★ ★ ★ ★ **FEARRINGTON HOUSE.** *(2000 Fearrington Village Center, Pittsboro 27312) 8 mi S on US 15/501. 919/542-2121; FAX 919/542-4202.* 24 rms, 2 story. S, D $150-$200; suites $200-$250. TV; cable. Pool; whirlpool. Complimentary continental bkfst, refreshments. Dining rm (see FEARRINGTON HOUSE). Rm serv 24 hrs. Beer, wine. Ck-out noon, ck-in 3 pm. Meeting rms. Tennis. Lawn games. Country pine furniture; original art. Courtyard; fountain. Totally nonsmoking. Cr cds: MC, V.

Restaurants

★ ★ **AURORA.** *(200 Greensboro St, Carrboro 27510) Carr Mill Shopping Center. 919/942-2400.* Hrs: 11:30 am-2 pm, 6-10 pm; Sat & Sun from 6 pm. Closed some major hols. Res accepted. Northern Italian menu. Bar. Semi-a la carte: lunch $3.95-$7.95, dinner $8.95-$17.95. Child's meals. Specialties: grilled lamb with garlic, linguine Caterina. Parking. In renovated textile mill. Cr cds: A, MC, V.

★ **CRACOVIA.** *220 W Rosemary. 919/929-9162.* Hrs: 5:30-10 pm; Fri, Sat from 6 pm. Closed major hols. Res accepted. Continental menu. Bar. A la carte entrees: dinner $9.95-$17.95. Specialties: Wienerschnitzel, lamb tenderloin kebob, seafood. Parking. Outdoor dining. Intimate dining in 1920 house; tapestries, fireplaces; original fixtures. Cr cds: A, D, DS, MC, V.

✔ ★ **DRAGON GARDENS.** *407 W Franklin St. 919/929-8143.* Hrs: 11 am-2 pm, 5-9:30 pm; Fri, Sat to 10:30 pm. Closed July 4, Thanksgiving, Dec 25. Res accepted. Chinese menu. Wine, beer. A la carte entrees: lunch $4.10-$4.75, dinner $5.75-$13.95. Specializes in seafood, beef. Parking. Chinese decor. Cr cds: DS, MC, V.

★ ★ ★ **FEARRINGTON HOUSE.** *(See Fearrington House Inn) 919/542-2121.* Hrs: 6-9 pm; Sun to 8 pm. Closed Mon. Res required. Wine list. Complete meals: dinner $48. Specialties: lamb loin, Carolina crab cakes. Own baking. Parking. Colonial decor. Totally nonsmoking. Cr cds: MC, V.

★ ★ **LA REZ.** *202 W Rosemary. 919/967-2506.* Hrs: 6-9:30 pm; Sun to 8:30 pm. Closed Mon; July 4, Dec 24-25. Res accepted. French, Amer menu. Bar. A la carte entrees: dinner $9.95-$18.95. Specializes in local seafood, North Carolina duckling, wild game. Outdoor dining. Cr cds: A, C, D, MC, V.

✔ ★ **SQUID'S.** *1201 US 15/501 Bypass. 919/942-8757.* Hrs: 5-9:30 pm; Fri & Sat to 10 pm; Sun to 9 pm. Closed Jan 1, Dec 24, 25. Bar. Semi-a la carte: dinner $10-$13. Child's meals. Specializes in fresh seafood. Oyster bar. Parking. Nautical decor. Cr cds: A, MC, V.

Charlotte (B-5)

Settled: 1748 **Pop:** 395,934 **Elev:** 700 ft **Area code:** 704

The Carolinas' largest metropolis, Charlotte grew quickly as a regional retail, financial and distribution center and became the nation's leader in the textile industry. General Cornwallis occupied the town for a short time in 1780 but met such determined resistance that he called it a "hornet's nest," a name that has been applied with pride on the city seal and by several local groups. Gold was discovered here in 1799, and the region around Charlotte was the nation's major gold producer until the California gold rush in 1848. There was a US Mint here between 1837-1861. The last Confederate Cabinet meeting was held here in 1865.

Chiefly agricultural and dependent on slave labor in antebellum days, the region took eagerly to industry after Appomattox. Abundant water power for electricity from the Catawba River has been a principal reason for its rapid growth. Today, Charlotte is among the largest banking centers in the country.

Transportation

Charlotte/Douglas Intl Airport: Information 359-4013; lost and found 359-4012; weather 359-8284; club lounges, USAir Clubs (US Air), Concourses B, C, and D.

Car Rental Agencies: See toll-free numbers under Introduction.

Public Transportation: Buses (Charlotte Transit System), phone 336-3366.

Rail Passenger Service: Amtrak 800/872-7245.

What to See and Do

1. **Mint Museum of Art.** 2730 Randolph Rd. First Branch US Mint operated here 1837-1861 and 1867-1913, and in 1933 it was chartered as an art museum. Collections include European and American art from Renaissance to contemporary; fine pottery and porcelain collection; maps; period costumes; survey collection of pre-Columbian and African artifacts; exhibition of coins. (Daily exc Mon; closed Jan 1, Thanksgiving, Dec 25) Phone 337-2000. ¢¢

2. **The Charlotte Museum of History and Hezekiah Alexander Homesite.** 3500 Shamrock Dr. Includes Hezekiah Alexander House (1774), oldest dwelling still standing in Mecklenburg County; 2-story springhouse; working log kitchen. Tours (fee). (Tues-Fri, also Sat & Sun afternoons; closed major hols) Phone 568-1774. **Free.**

3. **Nature Museum.** 1658 Sterling Rd. Live Animal Room, nature trail, puppet theater; earth science hall. (Daily; closed Thanksgiving, Dec 25) Phone 372-6261. ¢

4. **Discovery Place.** 301 N Tryon St. Hands-on science museum features aquarium; also science circus, life center, rain forest, collections gallery; Omnimax theater; Space Voyager Planetarium; major traveling exhibits. (Daily; closed Thanksgiving, Dec 25) Sr citizen rate. Phone 372-6261 or 800/935-0553. ¢¢

5. **Latta Plantation Park.** 12 mi NW via I-77, exit 16B (Sunset Rd W), right at Beattie's Ford Rd 5 mi, then left at Sample Rd. Approx 1,000-acre nature preserve on Mt Island Lake. Interpretive Center, Carolina Raptor Center, Audubon Sanctuary, Equestrian Center, bridle paths, hiking trails, fishing, picnicking, canoe access. (Daily) Phone 875-1391. **Free.** Also here is

   Latta Place (ca 1800). Restored Federal-style plantation house, original storehouse, log slave house replica; barns, farm animals; kitchen garden, cotton field. (Tues-Sun, daily exc Mon; closed most major hols) Phone 875-2312. ¢

6. **Ovens Auditorium.** 2700 E Independence Blvd, 5 mi E on US 74. Shows by touring Broadway companies (fall-late spring); musicals; symphony. Phone 372-3600 for schedule.

7. **Charlotte Coliseum.** 100 Paul Buck Blvd. This 23,000-seat arena hosts various sports events as well as family shows and concerts. For schedule information phone 357-4700.

8. **Spirit Square Center for the Arts.** 345 N College St. Exhibitions by well-known contemporary artists; studio art classes (fee); performances (fee). Parking fee. Phone 372-9664 or 372-SHOW (box office).

9. **University of North Carolina at Charlotte** (1946). NE off I-85. (15,000 students) Beautiful landscaping and blooming plants (Mar-Nov); rhododendron garden (blooms Apr-May); ornamental garden, public greenhouse with rainforest and orchid collection. Sculpture garden. Rare Book Room and panoramic view of campus, 10th floor of library (Mon-Fri; closed hols). Walking-tour guide and map. Phone 547-4286.

10. **Paramount's Carowinds.** 10 mi S off I-77. An 83-acre family entertainment complex with 10 theme areas, 3 for children; over 30 rides include skytower, monorail, 5 roller coasters, sternwheeler, whitewater rapids ride, log flume; 6-acre water area, wave pool; restaurants and musical shows. (Mid-June-late-Aug, daily; mid-Mar-May & mid-Aug-mid-Oct, Sat & Sun only) Admission includes all rides, shows and water area. Sr citizen rate. Phone 800/888-4FUN. ¢¢¢¢

11. **James K. Polk Memorial State Historic Site.** 12 mi S on US 521, in Pineville. Replica of log cabin and outbuildings at birthsite of 11th President of the United States. Visitor center with exhibits, film. Guided tour. (Apr-Oct, Mon-Sat, also Sun afternoons; rest of yr, Tues-Sat, also Sun afternoons; closed major hols) Phone 889-7145. **Free.**

(For further information contact the Charlotte Convention & Visitors Bureau, 122 E Stonewall St, 28202; 331-2700 or 800/231-4636.)

Annual Events

Springfest. 3-day festival in uptown, offers food, live entertainment. Phone 332-0126. Last wkend Apr.

Festival in the Park. Freedom Park. Arts & crafts, entertainment. Phone 338-1060. 6 days mid-Sept.

Seasonal Events

Symphony. Charlotte Symphony Orchestra, Inc. Phone 332-6136. Performs year-round.

Theatre Charlotte. 501 Queens Rd. Classic and Broadway plays. Features 6 productions a year on alternate months beginning in Sept. Thurs-Sat evenings. Phone 376-3777.

Opera. Opera Carolina. Phone 332-7177. Oct-Apr.

Auto racing. Charlotte Motor Speedway. 12 mi N on US 29 or off I-85 exit W.T. Harris Blvd. Coca-Cola 600 Winston Cup stock car race (Memorial Day wkend); Mello Yello 500 Winston Cup stock car race (early Oct); Spring AutoFair car show & flea market (mid-Apr); Fall Autofair (mid-Sept). Phone 455-3200.

(See Gastonia; also see Rock Hill, SC)

Motels

✔ ★ **COMFORT INN AIRPORT.** 4040 I-85 S (28208), exit 32 (Little Rock Rd), near Douglas Intl Airport. 704/394-4111. 117, 2 story. S $41.95; D $46.95; each addl $5; under 18 free; higher rates stock car races. Crib $5. TV; cable. Pool. Complimentary continental bkfst. Restaurant adj 7 am-10 pm. Bar 5-11 pm. Ck-out 11 am. Meeting rms. Free airport transportation. Exercise equipt; stair machine, rowers. Refrigerators avail. Cr cds: A, C, D, DS, JCB, MC, V.

D ⊠ ⌘ ✈ ⤢ ⋙ SC

✔ ★ **COMFORT INN-SUGAR CREEK.** 5111 N Sugar Creek Rd (28269). 704/598-0007; FAX 704/598-0007, ext. 302. 87 rms, 2 story. S $37.95; D $41-$53; each addl $6; under 18 free; higher rates special events. Crib free. Pet accepted, some restrictions. TV; cable. Pool. Complimentary continental bkfst, coffee. Restaurant nearby. Ck-out 11 am. Meeting rms. Valet serv. Exercise equipt; weight machine, bicycles, whirlpool. Cr cds: A, C, D, DS, ER, JCB, MC, V.

D ⌫ ⊠ ⌘ ⋙ SC

★ ★ **COURTYARD BY MARRIOTT.** 800 E Arrowwood Rd (28217), I-77 exit 3. 704/527-5055; FAX 704/525-5848. 146 rms, 3 story. S $62.95; D $72.95; under 6 free; wkend rates. Crib free. TV; cable. Pool. Bkfst avail. Bar 5-9 pm. Ck-out noon. Meeting rms. Coin

Indry. Valet serv. Exercise equipt; weights, bicycles, whirlpool. Some refrigerators. Private patios, balconies. Cr cds: A, C, D, DS, MC, V.

⊡ ≋ 🏃 ⛵ 🔥 SC

★★★ **COURTYARD BY MARRIOTT-UNIVERSITY.** *333 W Harris Blvd (28262).* 704/549-4888; FAX 704/549-4946. 152 rms, 4 story. S, D $57; suites $69.95-$72.95; under 12 free; wkend rates; higher rates special events. Crib free. TV; cable. Pool. Complimentary coffee in rms. Bkfst avail. Bar. Ck-out noon. Coin Indry. Meeting rms. Exercise equipt; weight machine, bicycles, whirlpool. Refrigerator in suites. Near University of NC at Charlotte. Cr cds: A, C, D, DS, MC, V.

⊡ ≋ 🏃 ⛵ 🔥 SC

★ **CRICKET INN.** *1200 W Sugar Creek Rd (28213).* 704/597-8500; res: 800/274-2538; FAX 704/598-1815. 132 rms, 2 story. S $36; D $41; suites $42-$49; under 18 free; higher rates special events. Crib free. TV; cable. Pool. Complimentary coffee in lobby. Restaurant opp open 24 hrs. Ck-out 11 am. Refrigerator in suites. Cr cds: A, C, D, DS, MC, V.

⊡ ≋ ⛵ 🔥 SC

✔ ★★ **FAIRFIELD INN BY MARRIOTT.** *5415 N I-85 Sevice Rd (28262),* I-85 exit 41. 704/596-2999; FAX 704/596-2999, ext. 709. 133 rms, 3 story. S $34-$40; D $43-$46; under 18 free; higher rates special events. Crib free. TV; cable. Pool. Complimentary continental bkfst in lobby. Restaurant nearby. Ck-out noon. Meeting rm. Cr cds: A, C, D, DS, MC, V.

⊡ ≋ ⛵ 🔥 SC

★★ **HAMPTON INN.** *440 Griffith Rd (28217),* approx 6 mi S via I-77, Tyvola Rd exit 5. 704/525-0747; FAX 704/522-0968. 161 rms, 4 story. S $51-$58; D $57-$64; under 18 free. Crib free. TV; cable. Pool. Complimentary continental bkfst. Ck-out noon. Meeting rms. Valet serv. Airport transportation. Exercise equipt; weights, bicycles, sauna. Cr cds: A, C, D, DS, MC, V.

⊡ ≋ 🏃 ⛵ 🔥 SC

✔ ★ **INNKEEPER.** *305 Archdale Drive (28217).* 704/525-3033; res: 800/822-9899. 70 rms, 2 story. S $32.95-$36.95; D $39.95-$42.95; each addl $5; under 16 free; higher rates special events. Crib free. TV; cable. Pool. Complimentary continental bkfst, coffee. Restaurant nearby. Ck-out 11 am. Cr cds: A, C, D, DS, MC, V.

⊡ ≋ ⛵ 🔥 SC

★★ **LA QUINTA-SOUTH.** *7900 Nations Ford Rd (28217),* S via I-77 to exit 4 (Nations Ford Rd). 704/522-7110; FAX 704/521-9778. 118 rms, 3 story. S, D $43-$51; each addl $6; under 18 free; higher rates auto race wkends. Crib free. Pet accepted, some restrictions. TV; cable. Heated pool. Continental bkfst. Restaurant adj open 24 hrs. Ck-out noon. Valet serv. Cr cds: A, C, D, DS, MC, V.

⊡ 🐾 ≋ ⛵ 🔥 SC

✔ ★ **RED ROOF INN-COLISEUM.** *131 Red Roof Dr (28217),* I-77 S to exit 4 (Nations Ford Rd). 704/529-1020; FAX 704/529-1020, ext. 444. 116 rms, 3 story. S $27-$31; D $34.99-$42.99; up to 5, $44.99; under 18 free. Crib free. Pet accepted, some restrictions. TV; cable. Complimentary coffee in lobby. Ck-out noon. Cr cds: A, C, D, DS, MC, V.

⊡ 🐾 ⛵ 🔥

★★ **RESIDENCE INN BY MARRIOTT.** *5800 Westpark Dr (28217),* off I-77S at Tyvola Rd exit 5. 704/527-8110; FAX 704/521-8282. 80 kit. suites, 1-2 story. S, D $99-$119. Crib free. Pet accepted; $50 deposit and $5 per day. TV; cable. Heated pool; whirlpool. Complimentary continental bkfst. Restaurant adj 7 am-10 pm. Coin Indry. Ck-out noon. Valet serv. Health club privileges. Lawn games. Private patios, balconies. Cr cds: A, C, D, DS, MC, V.

⊡ 🐾 ≋ ⛵ 🔥 SC

✔ ★ **RODEWAY INN.** *1416 W Sugar Creek Rd (28213).* 704/597-5074. 56 rms, 2 story. S $35.95; D $40.95; each addl $2;

under 12 free. Crib free. TV; cable. Pool. Complimentary continental bkfst. Restaurant adj open 24 hrs. Ck-out 11 am. Cr cds: A, C, D, DS, MC, V.

⊡ ≋ ⛵ 🔥 SC

Motor Hotels

★★ **HOLIDAY INN-WOODLAWN.** *212 Woodlawn Rd (28217),* at I-77S exit 6A. 704/525-8350; FAX 704/522-0671. 425 rms, 4 story. S, D $60-$84; each addl $8; suites $120-$150; under 12 free; wkend rates; higher rates special events. Crib free. TV; cable. Pool. Restaurant 6 am-10 pm. Rm serv. Bar 4 pm-1 am; entertainment, dancing exc Sun. Ck-out noon. Meeting rms. Bellhops. Valet serv. Sundries. Airport transportation. Exercise equipt; weight machine, bicycle, whirlpool. Refrigerator in suites. Cr cds: A, C, D, DS, JCB, MC, V.

⊡ ≋ 🏃 ⛵ 🔥 SC

★★ **HOMEWOOD SUITES.** *4920 S Tryon St (28217).* 704/525-2600; FAX 704/521-9932. 144 suites, 5 story. S $95; D $95-$149. Crib free. Pet accepted; $8 per day. TV; cable, in-rm movies. Heated pool. Complimentary continental bkfst. Restaurant adj 8 am-10 pm. Ck-out noon. Coin Indry. Meeting rms. Bellhops. Sundries. Free airport transportation. Exercise equipt; weights, bicycles, whirlpool. Refrigerators. Cr cds: A, C, D, DS, JCB, MC, V.

⊡ 🐾 ≋ 🏃 ⛵ 🔥 SC

★★★ **SHERATON AIRPORT PLAZA.** *3315 S I-85 (28208),* at Billy Graham Pkwy, near Douglas Intl Airport, I-85 exit 33. 704/392-1200; FAX 704/393-2207. 225 rms, 8 story. S $87-$115; D $97-$125; each addl $10; suites $150-$175; under 16 free; wkend rates. Crib free. Pet accepted. TV; cable. Indoor/outdoor pool; poolside serv. Complimentary continental bkfst. Coffee in rms. Restaurant 6:30 am-10:30 pm. Rm serv. Bar 11-2 am; entertainment Wed, dancing exc Sun. Ck-out noon. Meeting rms. Bellhops. Valet serv. Gift shop. Free airport transportation. Exercise equipt; weights, bicycles, whirlpool, sauna. Bathrm phones. Cr cds: A, C, D, DS, MC, V.

⊡ 🐾 ≋ 🏃 🍴 ⛵ 🔥 SC

★★★ **WYNDHAM GARDEN HOTEL.** *2600 Yorkmont Rd (28208),* off Billy Graham Pkwy at Tyvola Rd & Coliseum exit. 704/357-9100; FAX 704/357-9159. 173 rms, 3 story. S $99; D $109; each addl $10; suites $109-$119; under 12 free; wkend rates; higher rates special events. Crib free. Pet accepted, some restrictions; $50. TV; cable. Heated pool. Complimentary coffee in rms. Restaurant 6:30 am-2:30 pm, 5-10 pm. Rm serv from 5 pm. Bar 4 pm-midnight. Ck-out noon. Meeting rms. Bellhops. Valet serv. Free airport transportation. Exercise equipt; weight machine, bicycles, whirlpool. Refrigerator in some suites. Situated on well-landscaped grounds. Cr cds: A, C, D, DS, ER, MC, V.

⊡ 🐾 ≋ 🏃 ⛵ 🔥 SC

Hotels

★★★ **ADAM'S MARK.** *555 S McDowell St (28204),* at jct US 74. 704/372-4100; FAX 704/846-4645. 598 rms, 18 story, 37 suites. S $79-$109; D $89-$119; each addl $15; suites $275-$350; under 18 free; wkend rates. Crib free. TV; cable. Heated pools, 1 indoor. Restaurant 6 am-midnight. Bars 11-1 am; entertainment, dancing. Ck-out noon. Convention facilities. Concierge. Gift shop. Exercise equipt; weights, bicycles, whirlpool, sauna. Some refrigerators. Wet bar in some suites. Opp park. Cr cds: A, C, D, DS, ER, MC, V.

⊡ ≋ 🏃 ⛵ 🔥 SC

★★★ **DOUBLETREE CLUB.** *895 W Trade St (28202).* 704/347-0070; FAX 704/347-0267. 187 rms, 8 story. S $109-$119; D $119-$129; each addl $10; under 12 free; wkend rates; higher rates auto races (May & Oct). TV; cable. Pool. Complimentary continental bkfst, coffee. Restaurant 6-9 am, 5-10 pm. Bar 5 pm-1 am. Ck-out 1 pm. Meeting rms. Covered parking. Free downtown transportation. Exercise equipt; weight machine, bicycles, whirlpool, sauna. Cr cds: A, C, D, DS, ER, JCB, MC, V.

[D] [≈] [✕] [⊠] [🔥] [SC]

★ ★ ★ **DUNHILL.** 237 N Tryon St (28202). 704/332-4141; res: 800/354-4141; FAX 704/376-4117. 60 rms, 10 story. S $99; D $109; each addl $10; under 16 free; wkend rates; higher rates special events. Crib free. TV; cable. Restaurant 6:30 am-10:30 pm. Bar; pianist Mon-Thurs. Ck-out noon. Meeting rms. Concierge. Free garage parking. Free airport transportation. Exercise equipt; stair machine, treadmill. Health club privileges. Refrigerators. European-style hotel built circa 1920; 18th-century furnishings, original artwork. Cr cds: A, C, D, DS, MC, V.

[D] [≈] [⊠] [🔥] [SC]

★ ★ ★ **EMBASSY SUITES.** 4800 S Tryon St (28217). 704/527-8400; FAX 704/527-7035. 274 units, 8 story. Suites $124-$160; each addl $20; under 12 free; wkend rates; higher rates special events. Crib free. TV; cable. Indoor pool; poolside serv. Complimentary full bkfst. Complimentary coffee in rms. Restaurant 11 am-10 pm. Bar 10-2 am; entertainment, dancing. Ck-out noon. Coin lndry. Meeting rms. Gift shop. Covered parking. Free airport transportation. Tennis privileges. Exercise equipt; treadmill, bicycles, whirlpool, sauna. Refrigerators, wet bars; some bathrm phones. Cr cds: A, C, D, DS, MC, V.

[D] [🏃] [≈] [✕] [⊠] [🔥] [SC]

★ ★ ★ **HILTON AT UNIVERSITY PLACE.** 8629 J M Keynes Dr (28262), off I-85, exit 45A (Harris Blvd). 704/547-7444; FAX 704/548-1081. 243 rms, 12 story. S $75-$135; D $85-$135; each addl $10; family, wkend rates. Crib free. TV; cable. Heated pool; poolside serv. Restaurant 6:30 am-10 pm. Bar 11:30-1 am; entertainment, dancing (May-Sept). Ck-out noon. Convention facilities. Exercise equipt; weights, bicycles. Cr cds: A, C, D, DS, MC, V.

[D] [≈] [✕] [⊠] [🔥] [SC]

★ ★ ★ **HYATT.** 5501 Carnegie Blvd (28209), opp South Park Mall. 704/554-1234; FAX 704/554-8319. 262 rms, 7 story. S $125-$150; D $150-$175; suites $350-$750; under 18 free. Crib free. Free valet parking. Pet accepted, some restrictions. TV; cable. Indoor pool; poolside serv. Restaurant 6 am-10:30 pm. Rm serv 24 hrs. Bar 11-1 am. Ck-out noon. Convention facilities. Gift shop. Free airport transportation. Exercise equipt; weights, bicycles, whirlpool, sauna. Some bathrm phones, refrigerators. Some balconies. **LUXURY LEVEL :** 41 rms. Suites $550-$650. Private lounge. Complimentary continental bkfst. Cr cds: A, C, D, DS, ER, JCB, MC, V.

[D] [🏄] [≈] [✕] [🏃] [⊠] [🔥] [SC]

★ ★ ★ **MARRIOTT-CITY CENTER.** 100 W Trade St (28202). 704/333-9000; FAX 704/342-3419. 431 rms, 19 story. S $130; D $140; suites $200-$350; under 12 free. Crib free; wkend rates. Covered parking, valet $10. TV; cable. Heated pool; poolside serv. Restaurant 6:30 am-10 pm. Bar 11:30-1 am. Ck-out noon. Coin lndry. Convention facilities. Concierge. Gift shop. Airport transportation. Exercise equipt; weights, bicycles, whirlpool. Refrigerators. Shopping adj. **LUXURY LEVEL : CONCIERGE LEVEL.** 67 rms, 4 suites, 2 floors. S $119; D $145; suites $300-$350. Private lounge, honor bar. Complimentary continental bkfst, refreshments. Cr cds: A, C, D, DS, ER, JCB, MC, V.

[D] [≈] [✕] [🏃] [⊠] [🔥] [SC]

★ ★ ★ **OMNI.** 222 E Third St (28202). 704/377-6664; FAX 704/377-4143. 410 rms, 22 story. S $109-$149; D $124-$164; each addl $10; suites $189; under 18 free. Crib free. Garage parking; valet $10. Pool privileges adj. Restaurant 6 am-11 pm; wkends from 7 am. Bar 11-1:30 am. Ck-out noon. Convention facilities. Concierge. Shopping arcade. Airport transportation. Tennis privileges. 18-hole golf privileges. Health club privileges. Minibars; some bathrm phones. Refrigerators avail. Wet bar in suites. Elegant hotel in heart of city's financial center. Cr cds: A, C, D, DS, JCB, MC, V.

[D] [🏃] [🏃] [⊠] [🔥] [SC]

★ ★ ★ ★ **THE PARK HOTEL.** 2200 Rexford Rd (28211). 704/364-8220; res: 800/334-0331; FAX 704/365-4712. 194 rms, 6 story. S $115-$135; D $125-$145; each addl $10; suites $325-$625; under 18 free; wkend rates. Crib free. TV; cable. Heated pool; poolside serv. Restaurant (see MORROCROFTS). Rm serv 24 hrs. Bars 11-2 am; entertainment, dancing. Ck-out noon. Meeting rms. Concierge. Free valet parking. Airport, RR station, bus depot transportation. Tennis & golf privileges. Exercise equipt; weight machines, bicycles, whirlpool, steam rm. Some refrigerators. Elegant decor. Cr cds: A, C, D, DS, JCB, MC, V.

[D] [🏃] [🏄] [≈] [✕] [🏃] [⊠] [🔥] [SC]

★ ★ ★ **RADISSON EXECUTIVE PARK.** 5624 Westpark Dr (28217), I-77 exit 5. 704/527-8000; FAX 704/527-4278. 178 rms, 7 story, 34 suites. S $100; D $110; each addl $10; suites $120; under 18 free. Crib free. Pet accepted; $50 ($30 refundable). TV; cable. Heated pool. Complimentary full bkfst. Restaurant 6:30 am-2 pm, 5-10 pm. Bar 2 pm-midnight. Ck-out noon. Meeting rms. Free airport, RR station transportation. Exercise equipt; weight machine, treadmill, whirlpool. Refrigerator in suites. Cr cds: A, C, D, DS, MC, V.

[D] [🏄] [≈] [✕] [⊠] [🔥] [SC]

★ ★ ★ **RADISSON PLAZA.** 5624 Westpark Dr (28217), at jct Trade & Tryon Sts. 704/377-0400; FAX 704/347-0649. 365 rms, 15 story. S, D $109; each addl $10; suites $119-$325; under 18 free; wkend rates. Crib free. TV; cable. Heated pool; poolside serv. Restaurant 6:30 am-10:30 pm. Bar 6:30 am-midnight. Ck-out noon. Convention facilities. Concierge. Shopping arcade. Barber, beauty shop. Covered parking. Exercise equipt; weights, stair machine, sauna. Health club privileges. Refrigerator, wet bar in suites. **LUXURY LEVEL : PLAZA CLUB.** 69 rms. S, D $119; suite $325. Private lounge. Complimentary bkfst, refreshments, newspaper. Cr cds: A, C, D, DS, ER, MC, V.

[D] [≈] [✕] [⊠] [🔥] [SC]

★ ★ ★ **SOUTHPARK.** 6300 Morrison Blvd (28211), near South Park Mall. 704/364-2400; res: 800/647-8483; FAX 704/362-0203. 208 kit. suites, 3-6 story. S $95-$125; D $105-$250; under 18 free; wkend rates. Crib avail. TV; cable. Pool; poolside serv. Restaurant 6:30 am-11 pm. Bar 4 pm-midnight. Ck-out noon. Lndry facilities avail. Meeting rms. Gift shop. Airport transportation. Exercise equipt; weights, bicycles, whirlpool, sauna. Private patios, balconies. Cr cds: A, C, D, DS, MC, V.

[D] [≈] [✕] [⊠] [🔥] [SC]

Restaurants

★ ★ ★ **EPICUREAN.** 1324 East Blvd. 704/377-4529. Hrs: 6-10 pm. Closed Sun; major hols; also 1st 2 wks July. Res accepted. Continental menu. Serv bar. Wine list. Semi-a la carte: dinner $11.50-$19.95. Child's meals. Specializes in prime beef, fresh seafood, lamb. Own baking. Parking. Family-owned. Cr cds: A, C, D, MC, V.

[D]

★ ★ **THE FISHMARKET.** 6631 Morrison Blvd. 704/365-0883. Hrs: 11:30 am-2 pm, 6-10 pm; Sat, Sun from 6 pm. Closed major hols. Res accepted. Bar 4 pm-1 am. Semi-a la carte: lunch $6.25-$10.95, dinner $13.95-$28.95. Specializes in seafood, pasta, desserts. Cr cds: A, D, MC, V.

★ ★ **HEREFORD BARN STEAK HOUSE.** 4320 N I-85, on service road between Sugar Creek Rd & Graham St. 704/596-0854. Hrs: 5-10 pm; Fri & Sat to 11 pm. Closed Sun; major hols. Serv bar. Semi-a la carte: dinner $9.95-$33.95. Child's meals. Specializes in steak, prime rib, chicken. Parking. Country-barn decor; farm implements; fireplace. Family-owned. Cr cds: A, C, D, DS, MC, V.

[SC]

★ ★ ★ **LA BIBLIOTHEQUE.** 1901 Roxborough Rd (28211), in Morrison office bldg. 704/365-5000. Hrs: 11:30 am-2:30 pm, 5:30-10:30 pm. Closed Sun; Jan 1, Dec 25. Res required. French menu. Serv bar. A la carte entrees: lunch $7.50-$8.95, dinner $19-$26. Specializes in seafood, beef, veal. Parking. Terrace dining. Traditional decor; oil paintings. Jacket (dinner). Cr cds: A, C, D, DS, MC, V.

★ ★ ★ **LAMP LIGHTER.** *1065 E Morehead St.* *704/372-5343.* Hrs: 5:30-10 pm; Fri, Sat to 10:30 pm. Closed Jan 1, Thanksgiving, Dec 25. Res accepted. Bar. Extensive wine list. Semi-a la carte: dinner $14.50-$26.95. Specializes in fresh seafood, wild game, Maine lobster. Own baking. Valet parking. In Spanish-colonial house built 1926. Jacket. Cr cds: A, C, D, MC, V.

D

★ ★ ★ **MORROCROFTS.** *(See The Park Hotel)* *704/364-8220.* Hrs: 6:30 am-11 pm; early-bird dinner 5-6:30 pm; Sun brunch 9:30 am-2 pm. Res accepted. Bar. Wine list. Semi-a la carte: bkfst $2.50-$6.95, lunch $5-$8, dinner $12.95-$21.95. Sun brunch $11.95. Child's meals. Specializes in fresh seafood, regional cuisine. Own baking. Pianist. Valet parking. Outdoor dining. English club decor. Cr cds: A, C, D, DS, JCB, MC, V.

D

✔ ★ **OLD SPAGHETTI FACTORY.** *911 E Morehead St.* *704/375-0083.* Hrs: 11:30 am-2 pm, 5-9:30 pm; Fri to 10:30 pm; Sat 5-10:30 pm; Sun noon-9 pm. Closed Dec 25. Italian menu. Bar. Semi-a la carte: lunch $2.95-$5.35, dinner $4.10-$9.25. Child's meals. Specializes in lasagne, chicken Mediterranean-style. Parking. In former skating rink. Cr cds: DS, MC, V.

D

★ **RANCH HOUSE.** *5614 Wilkinson Blvd (28208).* *704/399-5411.* Hrs: 5-11 pm. Closed Sun; major hols. Serv bar. Semi-a la carte: dinner: $9.50-$19.50. Child's meals. Specializes in steak, seafood, chicken. Parking. Western decor. Family-owned. Cr cds: A, D, DS, MC, V.

★ ★ ★ **TOWNHOUSE.** *1011 Providence Rd.* *704/335-1546.* Hrs: 6-10 pm. Closed Sun; some major hols. Res accepted. Bar from 5 pm. Wine list. Semi-a la carte: dinner $12.95-$29.95. Specializes in fowl, seafood, prime beef. Own baking, pasta. Parking. 18th-century English decor. Cr cds: A, C, D, MC, V.

D

Cherokee (B-2)

Pop: 8,519 **Elev:** 1,991 ft **Area code:** 704 **Zip:** 28719

This is the capital of the Eastern Band of the Cherokee, who live on the Qualla Reservation at the edge of Great Smoky Mountains National Park (see) and the Blue Ridge Parkway. The reservation is the largest east of the Mississippi. These descendants of members of the tribe who avoided being driven to Oklahoma over the "Trail of Tears" are progressive in their ideas, yet determined to maintain their ancient traditions.

What to See and Do

1. **Oconaluftee Indian Village.** 1/2 mi N on US 441, adj to Mountain-side Theater. Replica of Native American village of more than 250 years ago. Includes seven-sided council house; lectures; herb garden; craft demonstrations. Guided tours (Mid-May-late Oct, daily). Phone 497-2111. ¢¢¢

2. **Museum of the Cherokee Indian.** On US 441 at Drama Rd, on Cherokee Reservation. Arts and crafts, audiovisual displays, portraits, prehistoric artifacts. (Daily; closed Jan 1, Thanksgiving, Dec 25) Phone 497-3481. ¢¢

3. **Cherokee Heritage Museum and Gallery.** On US 441 & Big Cove Rd, in Saunooke's Village. Interpretive center features Cherokee culture and history. Gift shop. (Daily; closed 3 wks late Dec-early Jan) Phone 497-3211. ¢

4. **Santa's Land.** 3 mi E on US 19N. Christmas theme park featuring Santa Claus and helpers; rides; zoo; entertainment, including magic show; lake with pedal boats; primitive crafts; snack shops, picnic area, play areas; gardens. (Early May-late Oct, daily) Phone 497-9191. ¢¢¢¢

(For further information contact Cherokee Travel and Promotion, PO Box 460; 497-9195 or 800/438-1601.)

Seasonal Event

Unto These Hills. Mountainside Theater. On US 441, 1/2 mi from jct US 19. Kermit Hunter drama re-creating the history of Cherokee Nation from 1540-1838; in natural amphitheater. Nightly exc Sun. Phone 497-2111. Mid-June-late Aug.

(See Bryson City, Maggie Valley, Waynesville)

Motels

★ ★ **BEST WESTERN-GREAT SMOKIES INN.** *Box 1809, 1 mi N on US 441N, at Acquoni Rd.* *704/497-2020; FAX 704/497-3903.* 152 rms, 2 story. June-Oct: S $55; D $72; each addl $6; under 12 free; lower rates Apr, May, Nov. Closed rest of yr. Crib free. TV; cable. Pool; wading pool. Restaurant 7 am-9 pm (May-Oct). Rm serv. Ck-out 11 am. Coin lndry. Meeting rms. Sundries. Cr cds: A, C, D, DS, MC, V.

D ⚿ ⚒ 🐾 **SC**

✔ ★ **COOL WATERS.** *Box 950, 1 1/2 mi E on US 19.* *704/497-3855; FAX 704/497-3855.* 50 rms. Mid-June-Oct: S, D $42-$65; lower rates Apr-mid-June, after Labor Day-Sept. Closed rest of yr. Crib $3. TV; cable. Pool; wading pool. Restaurant opp 6:30 am-9 pm. Ck-out 11 am. Tennis. Some patios. Picnic tables, grills. On stream; trout pond nearby. Cr cds: C, D, MC, V.

🐾 👟 ⚿ 🐾

★ **CRAIG'S.** *PO Box 1047, 1 mi E on US 19.* *704/497-3821.* 30 rms. S, D $49-$63; each addl $4; higher rates: hols, wkends, fall foliage season. Closed Nov-Apr. Crib $4. TV; cable. Pool. Playground. Restaurant 7 am-10 pm. Ck-out 11 am. On stream; picnic tables nearby. Cr cds: A, MC, V.

🐾 ⚿ ⚒ 🐾 **SC**

★ ★ **DAYS INN.** *On US 19.* *704/497-9171.* 58 rms, 1-2 story. Mid-June-Labor Day, Oct: S, D $60-$75; each addl $3; lower rates Apr-mid June, after Labor Day-Sept. Closed rest of yr. Crib free. TV; cable. 2 pools; wading pool. Playground. Restaurant adj 7 am-noon, 5-9 pm. Ck-out 11 am. Cr cds: A, C, D, DS, JCB, MC, V.

⚿ ⚒ 🐾 **SC**

★ ★ ★ **HOLIDAY INN.** *Box 1929, 1 mi W on US 19.* *704/497-9181; FAX 704/497-5973.* 154 rms, 2 story. Mid-June-Oct: S, D $66-$76; each addl $6; under 19 free; lower rates rest of yr. Crib free. TV; cable. 2 pools, 1 indoor; wading pool, whirlpool, sauna. Playground. Restaurant 7 am-9 pm. Rm serv. Ck-out 11 am. Coin lndry. Meeting rm. Sundries. Gift shop. Game rm. Cr cds: A, C, D, DS, JCB, MC, V.

D ⚿ ⚒ 🐾 **SC**

Cherryville (B-4)

Founded: 1881 **Pop:** 4,756 **Elev:** 960 ft **Area code:** 704 **Zip:** 28021

Customs of Cherryville's original German settlers still live on in two celebrations held each year in this town nestled in the rolling hills of the Piedmont.

(For further information contact the Chamber of Commerce, 301 E Main St, PO Box 305; 435-3451 or -4200.)

Annual Events

Shooting in the New Year. Old rite to bring fertility to fruit trees in the coming year. Men chant blessings and fire black powder muzzle-loaders as they go from home to home New Year's Eve until midnight, Jan 1.

Easter Egg Fighters. Centuries-old custom on Sugar Hill. Opponents test durability of their dyed, hard-boiled eggs by tapping them against others. Morning of Easter Sun.

(For accommodations see Gastonia, Shelby)

Concord (Cabarrus Co) (B-5)

Pop: 27,347 **Elev:** 704 ft **Area code:** 704 **Zip:** 28026

Concord was founded by Scottish-Irish and German-Dutch settlers and received its name when the two factions settled a dispute regarding the location of the county seat. An early textile area in the South, Concord continues to lead in dyeing, finishing and weaving of hosiery and knitted textiles.

What to See and Do

1. **Reed Gold Mine State Historic Site.** 10 mi SE on US 601 and NC 200 to Georgeville, then 2 mi S on NC 1100. First documented discovery of gold in the United States (1799) occurred here. Panning area (Apr-Oct, daily; fee); underground mine tours, history trail; working machinery, demonstrations, exhibits, visitor center; film; picnicking. (Apr-Oct, Mon-Sat, also Sun afternoons; rest of yr, Tues-Sat, also Sun afternoons) Phone 786-8337. **Free.**

2. **Industrial tour. Fieldcrest Cannon, Inc.** Cannon Village Visitor Center, 200 West Ave, 10 mi N on US 29A, in Kannapolis. Approx one-hour guided tours take visitors through manufacturing process of sheeting material. Reservations advised. No cameras allowed on tours. Children under 16 yrs not admitted. (Mon-Fri; closed hols) Phone 938-3200. **Free.**

(For further information contact the Chamber of Commerce, 23 Union St N, PO Box 1029; 782-4111.)

(See Albemarle, Charlotte)

Motels

★ **COLONIAL INN.** (28025). ³/₄ mi NW on US 29/601 Concord exit. 704/782-2146. 65 rms. S $40; D $50. Crib $4.25. TV; cable. Pool. Complimentary morning coffee. Restaurant adj 6 am-midnight. Ck-out 11 am. Meeting rms. Lawn games. Cr cds: A, C, D, DS, MC, V.

[≈] [🖼] [SC]

✔ ★ ★ **COMFORT INN.** 5171 S Cannon Blvd (28025). 704/786-3100; FAX 704/784-3114. 71 rms, 2 story. S $44.95-$49.95; D $49.95-$54.95; each addl $5; suites $52.95-$58.95; under 18 free; higher rates: auto races, horse shows. Crib $5. TV; cable. Pool. Complimentary bkfst. Complimentary coffee in rms. Restaurant adj 11 am-11 pm. Ck-out 11 am. Coin lndry. Many refrigerators. Cr cds: A, C, D, DS, ER, JCB, MC, V.

[D] [≈] [🖼] [🔥] [SC]

Unrated Dining Spot

K & W CAFETERIA. On US 29N (28025). ¹/₂ mi E of I-85 Concord-Kamapolis exit, in Carolina Mall. 704/786-6151. Hrs: 11 am-2:30 pm, 4-8:30 pm; Sat 11 am-8:30 pm; Sun 11 am-8 pm. Closed Dec 25. Avg ck: lunch $3.50, dinner $3.75. Specializes in fried chicken, pot pies, chicken & dumplings. Family-owned. No cr cds accepted.

Cornelius (B-4)

Founded: 1893 **Pop:** 2,581 **Elev:** 831 ft **Area code:** 704 **Zip:** 28031

A dispute between two cotton companies in Davidson during the late 1800s led to one of the firms relocating south of the city limits and establishing a new town. Originally called Liverpool, the community changed its name to Cornelius in honor of an investor.

What to See and Do

Lake Norman. NW of town. The state's largest freshwater lake (32,510 acres); created by Cowans Ford Dam, a Duke Power project on the Catawba River. Eight public access areas. Phone 382-8587.

(For further information contact North Mecklenburg Chamber of Commerce, PO Box 760; 892-1922.)

(See Charlotte, Statesville)

Motels

★ ★ **BEST WESTERN LAKE NORMAN.** 19608 Liverpool Pkwy. 704/896-0660; FAX 704/896-8633. 77 rms, 4 story, 10 suites. S $44.95; D $51.95; each addl $7; suites $69.95-$76.95; under 15 free; higher rates special events. Crib free. Pet accepted. TV; cable. Pool. Supervised child's activities. Complimentary continental bkfst. Complimentary coffee in lobby. Restaurant nearby. Ck-out 11 am. Meeting rms. Exercise equipt; weight machine, bicycles. Refrigerators. Cr cds: A, C, D, DS, MC, V.

[D] [🖼] [≈] [🏋] [🔥] [SC]

★ ★ **COMFORT INN.** (20740 Torrence Chapel Rd, Davidson 28036) 1 mi W on I-77, exit 28. 704/892-3500; FAX 704/892-6473. 90 rms, 2-3 story, 12 suites. Apr-Sept: S $44.95-$55.95; D $50.95-$60.95; each addl $5; suites $63.95-$90; under 18 free; wknd, hol, wkly rates; golf plans; higher rates special events; lower rates rest of yr. Crib $5. TV; cable. Pool. Complimentary continental bkfst. Complimentary coffee in rms. Restaurant adj 11:30 am-10:30 pm. Ck-out 11 am. Coin lndry. Meeting rms. Bellhops. Tennis privileges. Golf privileges. Health club privileges. Refrigerators. Cr cds: A, C, D, DS, ER, JCB, MC, V.

[D] [🏋] [🛴] [≈] [🖼] [🔥] [SC]

✔ ★ ★ **HAMPTON INN.** PO Box 1349, 19501 Statesville Rd. 704/892-9900; FAX 704/892-9900, ext. 605. 118 rms, 5 story. S $43-$47; D $47-$51; under 18 free; higher rates special events. Crib free. TV; cable. Pool. Complimentary continental bkfst. Complimentary coffee in lobby. Restaurant adj 11 am-10 pm. Ck-out 11 am. Meeting rms. Some refrigerators. Cr cds: A, C, D, DS, MC, V.

[D] [≈] [🖼] [🔥] [SC]

★ ★ **HOLIDAY INN.** PO Box 1278, Jct NC 73 & I-77 exit 28. 704/892-9120; FAX 704/892-9120, ext. 326. 120 rms, 2 story. S $54; D $60; each addl $6; suite $85; under 18 free; higher rates special events. Crib free. Pet accepted. TV; cable. Pool. Complimentary coffee in rms. Restaurant 6 am-2 pm, 5-10 pm. Rm serv. Bar 4 pm-1 am. Ck-out 11 am. Coin lndry. Meeting rms. Bellhops. Some refrigerators. Cr cds: A, C, D, DS, JCB, MC, V.

[D] [🖼] [≈] [🖼] [🔥] [SC]

Restaurants

★ ★ **KOBE JAPANESE HOUSE OF STEAK & SEAFOOD.** 20465 Chartwell Center Dr. 704/896-7778. Hrs: 11:30 am-2 pm, 5-10 pm; Sat 5-11 pm; Sun 5-10 pm; early-bird dinner Sun-Thurs 5-6:30 pm.

Closed Thanksgiving, Dec 25. Res accepted. Japanese menu. Bar. Semi-a la carte: lunch $5.95-$14.95, dinner $8.95-$19.95. Serv charge 15%. Child's meals. Specializes in teppanyaki preparation, Kobe beef & seafood. Sushi bar (dinner). Parking. Japanese decor. Cr cds: A, C, D, DS, MC, V.

D **SC**

✔ ★ **KP'S PLACE.** *20208 Knox Rd. 704/896-0085.* Hrs: 11:30 am-10 pm; Fri & Sat to 11 pm; Sun brunch 10:30 am-3 pm. Closed Thanksgiving, Dec 25. Res accepted. Mediterranean menu. Bar. Semi-a la carte: lunch $4.25-$6.95, dinner $6.95-$16.95. Child's meals. Specializes in rotisserie chicken, fresh seafood, pizza. Entertainemnt Fri & Sat evenings. Parking. Outdoor dining. Mediterranean atmosphere. Cr cds: A, C, D, DS, MC, V.

D

Dunn (B-7)

Pop: 8,336 **Elev:** 213 ft **Area code:** 910 **Zip:** 28334

What to See and Do

Bentonville Battleground State Historic Site. 15 mi E via NC 55 to Newton Grove, 3 mi N via US 701 to NC 1008, then 3 mi E. Biggest battle on North Carolina soil, March 19-21, 1865. It was the last organized attempt to stop General William Tecumseh Sherman after he left Atlanta. A month later, the rebel cause was lost; Lee surrendered at Appomattox April 9; Lincoln was shot April 14; and Johnston surrendered April 26. The restored Harper House was used as a hospital to treat wounded of both sides. Reconstructed and original trenches; history trail with exhibits. Picnic area. Visitor center, audiovisual show. (Apr-Oct, daily; rest of yr, daily exc Mon; closed Thanksgiving, Dec 24-25) Phone 594-0789. **Free.**

(See Fayetteville, Goldsboro)

Motels

✔ ★ **BEST WESTERN.** *Rte 1, Box 1000, I-95, exit 72. 910/892-2162.* 146 rms, 2 story. S, D $29.95-$49.95; each addl $5; family rates. Crib $5. TV; cable. Pool; wading pool. Restaurant 6-10 am, 6-9 pm. Ck-out 11 am. Cr cds: A, C, D, DS, MC, V.

D 🏊 ✈ 🔥 **SC**

★ **COMFORT INN.** *1125 E Broad St. 910/892-1293; FAX 910/891-1038.* 105 units, 2 story. S $39.95-$54.95; D $44.95-$59.95; each addl $5; under 18 free; wkly rates. Crib free. TV; cable, in-rm movies. Pool. Complimentary continental bkfst. Restaurant 11:30 am-10 pm. Bar. Ck-out 11 am. Coin lndry. Meeting rms. Game rm. Cr cds: A, C, D, DS, MC, V.

D 🏊 ✈ 🔥 **SC**

★ **RAMADA INN.** *PO Box 729, 1011 E Cumberland St. 910/892-8101; FAX 910/892-2836.* 100 rms, 2 story. S $39-$59; D $49-$69; each addl $6; under 18 free. Crib free. TV; cable. Pool. Restaurant 6:30 am-2 pm, 5-9 pm. Rm serv. Ck-out noon. Meeting rms. Valet serv. Cr cds: A, C, D, DS, JCB, MC, V.

D 🏊 ✈ 🔥 **SC**

Durham (A-7)

Founded: 1853 **Pop:** 136,611 **Elev:** 406 ft **Area code:** 919

Durham's sparkle has brought it near-top national ranking in numerous livability studies. Known for excellence in medicine, education, re-search and industry, Durham is also a recreational and cultural center in the rolling Piedmont region.

In 1924, an endowment from James B. Duke, head of the American Tobacco Company, helped establish Duke University as a leader among the nation's institutions of higher learning. North Carolina Central University makes its home here. In the 1950s, Durham County was chosen as the site of Research Triangle Park, a planned scientific research center that includes the Environmental Protection Agency, the National Institute for Environmental Health Sciences, IBM Corporation, the Burroughs Wellcome Company and others. Duke University Medical Center, Durham County General Hospital and several other outstanding medical institutions here have earned Durham the title "city of medicine."

What to See and Do

1. **Duke University** (1838). (10,000 students) Two campuses, East and West, on 8,000 acres. Includes original Trinity College. The West Campus, occupied since 1930, is the showplace of the university. On campus are

   Duke Chapel. Chapel Dr to main quadrangle. Beautiful Gothic-style chapel with a carillon of 50 bells in its 210-foot tower; 5,000-pipe Flentrop organ. (Daily) Phone 684-2572.

   Duke Medical Center. Research and teaching complex. Treats more than one-half million patients annually. Phone 684-8111 for information.

   Duke Libraries. Most comprehensive in the South, with more than 4 million volumes and more than 7 million manuscripts. Large Confederate imprint collection; Walt Whitman manuscripts. Phone 684-3009.

   Art Museum. East Campus, off W Main St. (Daily exc Mon; closed hols) Phone 684-5135. **Free.**

   Duke's Wallace Wade Stadium (33,941 capacity) and the 8,564-seat Cameron Indoor Stadium. Home of the Duke Blue Devils.

   Sarah P. Duke Gardens. Main entrance on Anderson St. 55 acres of landscaped gardens, pine forest. Continuous display. (Daily) Phone 684-3698. **Free.**

2. **North Carolina Museum of Life and Science.** 433 Murray Ave. North Carolina wildlife; hands-on science exhibits; aerospace, weather and geology collections; train ride; farmyard; science park; discovery rooms. Picnic area. (Daily; closed Jan 1, Thanksgiving, Dec 25) Sr citizen rate. Phone 220-5429. ¢¢

3. **Duke Homestead State Historic Site** (1852). 2828 Duke Homestead Rd, ½ mi N of jct I-85, Guess Rd. Ancestral home of Duke family; first Duke tobacco factory; curing barn; outbuildings; farm crops. Tobacco Museum, exhibits, film; furnishings of period. Tours. (Apr-Oct, daily; rest of yr, daily exc Mon; closed major hols) Phone 477-5498. **Free.**

4. **Bennett Place State Historic Site.** Just SW of jct I-85 exit 172 & US 70. Site of signing (April 26, 1865) of surrender of Confederate General Johnston to Union General Sherman, one of the last and most significant of the Confederate surrenders. Reconstructed Bennett homestead. Picnicking. Visitor Center, exhibits, audiovisual show. (Apr-Oct, daily; rest of yr, daily exc Mon; closed major hols) Phone 383-4345. **Free.**

5. **Stagville Preservation Center.** 7 mi NE via Roxboro Rd and Old Oxford Hwy. State-owned historic property, once part of the Bennehan-Cameron plantation; several historic 18th- and 19th-century plantation buildings on 71 acres of land. (Mon-Fri; closed hols) Phone 620-0120. **Free.**

6. **West Point on the Eno.** I-85, Duke St exit then 3½ mi N. A 371-acre park along the scenic Eno River; restored farmhouse (1850); working gristmill; museum of photography; blacksmith shop. Picnicking; fishing, hiking, boating; environmental programs (fee). Park (daily). Mill, farmhouse, museum (Mar-Dec, Sat & Sun). Phone 471-1623. **Free.**

(For further information contact the Convention & Visitors Bureau, 101 E Morgan St, 27701; 800/772-2855.)

Annual Event

CenterFest. Downtown. 2-day event with over 250 artists and craftsmen; musicians, jugglers and clowns; continuous entertainment from 3 stages. Phone 560-2722. Sept.

Seasonal Event

American Dance Festival. Page Auditorium and Reynolds Industries Theater, Duke University, West Campus. Six-weeks of performances by the finest of both major and emerging modern dance companies from the US and abroad. Contact the Festival at PO Box 6097, College Station 22708; 684-6402. June-July.

(See Chapel Hill, Raleigh)

Motels

(Rates may be higher for graduation, football wkends)

★ **BEST WESTERN SKYLAND.** *Rte 2, Box 560 (27705), Jct I-85 exit 170 & US 70W.* 919/383-2508; FAX 919/383-7316. 31 rms. Apr-Oct: S $38; D $48; each addl $6; under 12 free; lower rates rest of yr. Crib $3. Pet accepted. TV; cable. Pool. Playground. Complimentary coffee, newspaper in rms. Complimentary continental bkfst. Ck-out noon. Refrigerators. Picnic tables, grills. Situated atop hill. Duke University, Medical Center, VA Hospital 4 mi. Cr cds: A, C, D, DS, ER, JCB, MC, V.

[D] [⚓] [≈] [⛄] [🔥] [SC]

★ ★ **COMFORT INN-UNIVERSITY.** *3508 Mount Moriah Rd (27707).* 919/490-4949; FAX 919/419-0535. 138 rms, 4 story, 18 suites. S $52; D $58; each addl $6; suites $91-$116; under 18 free; higher rates special events. Crib free. TV; cable. Pool. Complimentary continental bkfst. Complimentary coffee in lobby. Restaurant nearby. Ck-out noon. Coin lndry. Meeting rms. Exercise equipt; weight machine, bicycles, whirlpool. Cr cds: A, C, D, DS, ER, JCB, MC, V.

[D] [≈] [🏃] [⛄] [🔥] [SC]

★ **DAYS INN.** *I-85 & Redwood Rd (27704).* 919/688-4338; FAX 919/688-3118. 119 rms, 2 story. S $29-$36; D $35-$42; each addl $5. Crib free. Pet accepted. TV; cable. Pool. Playground. Restaurant open 24 hrs. Ck-out noon. Coin lndry. Many refrigerators. Cr cds: A, D, DS, MC, V.

[⚓] [≈] [⛄] [🔥] [SC]

✔ ★ **FAIRFIELD INN BY MARRIOTT.** *3710 Hillsborough Rd (27705).* 919/382-3388. 135 rms, 3 story. S $34.95; D $40.95; each addl $3. Crib free. TV; cable. Pool. Complimentary continental bkfst. Ck-out noon. Cr cds: A, C, D, DS, MC, V.

[D] [≈] [⛄] [🔥] [SC]

★ ★ **HAMPTON INN.** *1816 Hillandale Rd (27705), 1/2 blk N of I-85.* 919/471-6100; FAX 919/479-7026. 136 units, 5 story. S, D $42-$62; each addl $6; suites $80; under 18 free. Crib free. Pet accepted, some restrictions; $6. TV; cable. Pool. Continental bkfst. Complimentary coffee. Restaurant nearby. Ck-out noon. Meeting rms. Free airport, medical center transportation. Exercise equipt; weights, bicycles, sauna. Some refrigerators. Cr cds: A, C, D, DS, MC, V.

[D] [⚓] [≈] [🏃] [⛄] [🔥] [SC]

★ **HOLIDAY INN WEST.** *3460 Hillsborough Rd (27705).* 919/383-1551. 100 rms, 2 story. S $50; D $58; under 12 free. Crib free. TV; cable. Pool. Complimentary continental bkfst. Restaurant 6:30 am-2 pm, 5:30-10 pm. Rm serv. Bar 4:30 pm-midnight. Ck-out noon. Coin lndry. Meeting rms. Health club privileges. Cr cds: A, C, D, DS, JCB, MC, V.

[D] [≈] [⛄] [🔥] [SC]

✔ ★ **RED ROOF INN.** *2000 I-85 Service Rd (27705).* 919/471-9882; FAX 919/477-0512. 120 rms, 3 story. S $32.99-$39.99; D $39.99-$47.99. Crib free. Pet accepted, some restrictions. TV. Complimentary coffee in lobby. Restaurant nearby. Ck-out noon. Cr cds: A, C, D, DS, MC, V.

[D] [⚓] [⛄] [🔥] [SC]

Motor Hotels

★ ★ **MEREDITH SUITES AT THE PARK.** *300 Meredith Dr (27713), I-40 exit 278.* 919/361-1234; res: 800/866-4787; FAX 919/361-1213. 97 kit. suites, 2-3 story. S, D $99; 2-bedrm suites $130. Crib $10. TV; cable. Pool. Complimentary full bkfst Mon-Fri; continental bkfst Sat & Sun. Bar 5-9 pm Mon-Thurs. Ck-out 11 am. Meeting rms. Bellhops. Free airport transportation. Private patios. Cr cds: A, C, D, MC, V.

[D] [≈] [🔥]

★ ★ **SHERATON INN UNIVERSITY CENTER.** *2800 Middleton Ave (27705).* 919/383-8575; res: 800/633-5379; FAX 919/383-8495. 322 rms, 4 story. S $85-$105; D $95-$115; each addl $10; suites $175-$375; under 18 free. Crib free. Pet accepted, some restrictions; $50. TV. Heated pool; poolside serv. Restaurant 6:30 am-2 pm, 5-10:30 pm. Rm serv 6:30 am-11 pm. Bar 11:30 am-midnight. Ck-out noon. Meeting rms. Bellhops. Concierge. Free airport transportation. Exercise equipt; weight machine, stair machine, whirlpool. Refrigerator in suites. *LUXURY LEVEL : CHANCELLOR'S QUARTERS.* 72 units. S $95; D $105; suites $275-$375. Ck-out 2 pm. Wet bar, in-rm whirlpool in some suites. Complimentary full bkfst, refreshments. Cr cds: A, C, D, DS, MC, V.

[D] [⚓] [≈] [🏃] [⛄] [🔥] [SC]

Hotels

★ ★ **BEST WESTERN CROWN PARK.** *(4620 S Miami Blvd, Morrisville 27560) 10 mi SE on I-40, exit 281, near Research Triangle Park.* 919/941-6066; FAX 919/941-6363. 177 rms, 7 story. S $89; D $99; each addl $10; suites $175; under 16 free; wknd rates. Crib free. TV; cable. Pool. Complimentary coffee in rms. Restaurant 6:30-10 am, 11 am-1:30 pm, 5-10 pm. Bar. Ck-out noon. Meeting rms. Free airport transportation. Exercise equipt; weight machine, bicycles, whirlpool, sauna. Some refrigerators. Cr cds: A, C, D, DS, MC, V.

[D] [≈] [🏃] [⛄] [🔥] [SC]

★ ★ ★ **GUEST QUARTERS.** *Box 14067 (27713), 2515 Meridian Pkwy, 1 blk N of I-40 exit 278, near Research Triangle Park.* 919/361-4660; FAX 919/361-2256. 203 suites, 7 story. Suites $130-$150; under 18 free; wkend rates. Crib free. TV; cable. 2 heated pools, 1 indoor; poolside serv. Complimentary coffee in rms. Restaurant 6:30 am-10 pm. Bar 11 am-midnight. Ck-out noon. Coin lndry. Meeting rms. Free airport transportation. Lighted tennis. Exercise equipt; weight machine, bicycles, whirlpool, sauna. Refrigerators. Private patios, balconies. Small lake adj; paddleboat rentals. Cr cds: A, C, D, DS, ER, JCB, MC, V.

[D] [🏃‍♂️] [≈] [🏃] [⛷️] [⛄] [🔥] [SC]

★ ★ ★ **HILTON.** *3800 Hillsborough Rd (27705).* 919/383-8033; FAX 919/383-4287. 154 rms, 6 story. S $91-$101; D $101-$111; each addl $10; suites $135-$270; family rates. Crib free. TV; cable. Pool. Restaurant 7 am-10 pm. Bar 2 pm-1 am, Sun to 11 pm; dancing. Ck-out noon. Meeting rms. Exercise equipt; weights, bicycles, whirlpool, sauna. Bathrm phones. Cr cds: A, C, D, DS, ER, MC, V.

[D] [≈] [🏃] [⛄] [🔥] [SC]

★ ★ ★ **OMNI.** *Box 2172 (27701), 201 Foster St.* 919/683-6664; FAX 919/683-2046. 188 rms, 10 story. S $86-$100; D $96-$116; each addl $10; suites $150-$225. Crib free. TV; cable. Restaurant 6:30 am-2 pm, 5-10 pm. Rm serv. Bar 3 pm-1 am. Ck-out noon. Meeting rms. Gift shop. Health club privileges. Cr cds: A, C, D, DS, MC, V.

[D] [⛄] [🔥] [SC]

★ ★ ★ **SHERATON IMPERIAL HOTEL & CONVENTION CEN-TER.** *(4700 Emperor Blvd, Research Triangle Park 27709) 1 blk S of I-40 exit 282.* 919/941-5050; FAX 919/941-5156. 333 rms, 10 story, 21 suites. S, D $90-$101; each addl $10; suites $150-$170; under 18 free; wkend packages. TV; cable. 2 heated pools, 1 indoor; poolside serv. Coffee in rms. Restaurant 6:30 am-10 pm. Bar 4 pm-1 am; entertainment. Ck-out noon. Convention facilities. Concierge. Gift shop. Free valet parking. Free airport transportation. Lighted tennis. Golf privileges. Exercise equipt; weight machines, bicycles, whirlpool, sauna, steam rm. Game rm. Some bathrm phones. Refrigerator in suites. *LUXURY LEVEL :* TOWERS. 107 rms, 3 floors. S $108-$123; D $125-$135; each addl $20; suites $160-$400. Concierge. Private lounge. Wet bar. In-rm movies. Complimentary continental bkfst, refreshments. Cr cds: A, C, D, DS, JCB, MC, V.

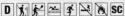

★ ★ ★ **WASHINGTON DUKE INN & GOLF CLUB.** *3001 Cameron Blvd (27706).* 919/490-0999; res: 800/443-3853; FAX 919/688-0105. 171 rms, 5 story. S, D $125-$155; each addl $10; suites $285-$485; under 18 free; golf plans. Crib free. TV; cable, in-rm movies avail. Heated pool. Complimentary coffee in lobby. Restaurant 7 am-10 pm. Bar 11:30 am-midnight; Sun from 1 pm. Ck-out noon. Meeting rms. Concierge. Gift shop. Airport transportation. Lighted tennis, pro. 18-hole golf, greens fee $30-$45, pro, putting green, driving range. Health club privileges. Refrigerators avail. Antiques and memorabilia from the Duke family, founders of the American Tobacco Company and benefactors of Duke University. On university campus. Cr cds: A, C, D, DS, MC, V.

Inn

★ **ARROWHEAD.** *106 Mason Rd (27712).* 919/477-8430; res: 800/528-2207. 8 rms, 2 story, 2 suites. S, D $70-$90; each addl $10; suites $125-$150. Crib free. TV in some rms. Complimentary full bkfst, tea. Ck-out 11 am, ck-in 3 pm. Game rm. Lawn games. Picnic tables. In colonial house (1775) and converted carriage house; on 4 acres. Cr cds: A, D, DS, MC, V.

Restaurants

★ ★ **BAK'S BISTRO.** *1821 Hillandale Rd, in Loehmann's Plaza at Croasdaile.* 919/383-8502. Hrs: 5:30-10 pm; Fri & Sat to 11 pm. Closed Sun & Mon; Dec 25. Res accepted. French, Thai menu. Bar. Semi-a la carte: dinner $8.95-$16.95. Own baking. Parking. Cr cds: A, MC, V.

✔ ★ **BULLOCK'S BBQ.** *3330 Wortham St.* 919/383-3211. Hrs: 11:30 am-8 pm. Closed Sun, Mon; Jan 1, Dec 24 & 25. Res accepted. Semi-a la carte: lunch, dinner $3.50-$9. Child's meals. Specializes in barbecued pork, seafood, chicken. Parking. Family-owned. No cr cds accepted.

★ ★ **MAGNOLIA GRILL.** *1002 9th St.* 919/286-3609. Hrs: 6-9:30 pm; Fri, Sat to 10 pm. Closed Sun; major hols. Res accepted. Bar from 5:30 pm. A la carte entrees: dinner $12-$20. Specialties: grilled yellow fin tuna on warm green lentils with Mediterranean salsa & red pepper vinaigrette, pan-seared sea scallops on fennel polenta with lobster bordelaise, grilled Black Angus strip steak with mushroom ragout. Parking. Local artwork on display. Cr cds: MC, V.

✔ ★ **SHANGHAI.** *3433 Hillsborough Rd.* 919/383-7581. Hrs: 11:30 am-2:30 pm, 5-9:30 pm; Sun from 5 pm. Closed Thanksgiving, Dec 25. Res accepted. Chinese menu. Bar. Semi-a la carte: lunch

$4-$5.25, dinner $5-$13.95. Specializes in seafood, chicken, pork, kan shih fish. Parking. Oriental decor. Cr cds: A, C, D, DS, MC, V.

Edenton (A-9)

Settled: 1658 **Pop:** 5,268 **Elev:** 16 ft **Area code:** 919 **Zip:** 27932

This is one of the oldest communities in North Carolina and was the capital of the colony for more than 22 years. The women of Edenton staged their own Revolutionary tea party on October 25, 1774, signing a resolution protesting British injustice. A bronze teapot, at the west side of the Courthouse Green, commemorates the event.

The seat of Chowan County, Edenton is now an important industrial town and marketing place. It is a charming town with the graciousness of the Old South and many houses and buildings that date back to the 1700s. Joseph Hewes, a signer of the Declaration of Independence, lived here.

What to See and Do

1. **Historic Edenton.** Tour of historic properties, which may be seen individually or as a group; allow 2¹/₂ to 3 hours for complete tour. (Apr-Dec, daily; rest of yr, daily exc Mon; closed some major hols; also day after Thanksgiving, 3 days at Christmas) Phone 482-2637. ¢¢¢

   Historic Edenton Visitor Center. 108 N Broad St. Audiovisual program (free), exhibits, visitor information, gift shop, tickets for guided tours of Historic Edenton.

   Chowan County Courthouse (1767). E King & Court Sts. A fine example of Georgian architecture, in continuous use since built.

   St Paul's Episcopal Church (1736). W Church & Broad Sts. A charming church with many old gravestones in its yard; three colonial governors are buried here.

   James Iredell House (1773). E Church St. Home of early attorney general of North Carolina who was appointed by George Washington to first US Supreme Court.

   Cupola House (1758). W Water and S Broad Sts. Considered an outstanding example of Jacobean architecture. Formal garden restored from 1769 map of Edenton.

2. **Newbold-White House** (1680s). 15 mi N on US 17 Bypass to Hertford, SE on SR 1336. Oldest house in state, this brick structure was a meeting place for the proprietary government of North Carolina. (Mar-Dec, daily exc Sun) Phone 426-7567. ¢

3. **Other historic buildings** are shown in a guidebook published by the Edenton Woman's Club and sold at Historic Edenton Visitor Center ($4). Since most houses are not open to the public, we suggest calling the Historic Edenton Visitor Center for further information. Phone 482-2637.

4. **Somerset Place State Historic Site.** 18 mi SE via NC 32, US 64 to Creswell, then 7 mi S; on Lake Phelps in Pettigrew State Park. Original plantation, one of the largest in North Carolina, encompassed more than 100,000 acres. First primary crop was rice, which gave way to corn. Mansion and outbuildings built ca 1830. (Apr-Oct, daily; rest of yr, daily exc Mon; closed Jan 1, Thanksgiving, Dec 24-25) Phone 797-4560. **Free.**

5. **Merchant's Millpond State Park.** 25 mi N on NC 32, 5 mi N of Gatesville on SR 1403. This 2,900-acre swamp forest is dominated by massive gum and cypress trees. Pond fishing, canoeing (rentals). Nature trails. Picnicking. Developed & primitive camping. Interpretive program. Standard fees. Contact Superintendent, Rte 1, Box 141-A, Gatesville 27938; 357-1191.

(For further information contact the Chamber of Commerce, 116 E King St, PO Box 245; 482-3400.)

Inns

 GOVERNOR EDEN. *304 N Broad St. 919/482-2072.* 4 rms, 2 story. No rm phones. S $55; D $70; each addl $15. TV; cable. Complimentary full bkfst. Ck-out 11 am, ck-in 2 pm. Free airport transportation. Antiques. Built 1906. Neoclassical design; Ionic columns, oval portals. Cr cds: MC, V.

★ ★ **LORDS PROPRIETORS'.** *300 N Broad St. 919/482-3641; FAX 919/482-2432.* 20 rms in 3 buildings, 2 story. S, D $140-$180; each addl $20. TV; cable, in-rm movies. Private pool privileges. Bkfst, dinner by res. Ck-out 11 am, ck-in 1 pm. Meeting rms. Gift shop. Library. Three adj restored homes furnished with antiques. No cr cds accepted.

★ **TRESTLE HOUSE.** *Soundside Rd, 4 mi S on NC 32, turn right on Soundside Rd. 919/482-2282.* 4 rms, 2 story. No rm phones. S $55; D $70; each addl $15; wkly rates. Crib free. TV; cable. Complimentary full bkfst. Complimentary refreshments in sitting rm. Ck-out noon. Tennis privileges. 18-hole golf privileges. Exercise equipt; bicycle, rowing machine. Minibars. Picnic tables. Private lake fed by Albermarle Sound. Some antiques. Totally nonsmoking. Cr cds: A, MC, V.

Elizabeth City (A-9)

Settled: ca 1665 **Pop:** 14,292 **Elev:** 18 ft **Area code:** 919 **Zip:** 27909

A town with a freshwater harbor on the Pasquotank River and access to the ocean, Elizabeth City has seen seafaring activity since 1666, when men from Bermuda built ships nearby. Trade with the West Indies was stimulated by the digging, in 1790, of the Dismal Swamp Canal. Before the Civil War, the docks were crowded with ships trading rum, sugar, fruit and materials for shingles and barrel staves. Some of the many private homes built in the early 19th century can still be seen. Now the town has substantial traffic from the Intracoastal Waterway and is a base for sport fishing and hunting as well as for the shipping of local crops. It also serves as a gateway to Nags Head and Cape Hatteras National Seashore (see). Wood and textiles are the main industrial products.

What to See and Do

1. **Museum of the Albemarle.** 3 mi SW on US 17. Regional historical displays; Indian exhibits; local artifacts, including decoys, fire engines; changing exhibits. (Daily exc Mon; closed state hols) Phone 335-1453. **Free.**
2. **Historic District.** A 30-block area in the city center, contains largest number of antebellum commercial buildings in the state.

(For further information contact the Chamber of Commerce, 502 E Ehringhaus St, PO Box 426; 335-4365.)

Annual Events

RiverSpree. Water events, arts, crafts, live entertainment. Memorial Day wkend.

Albemarle Craftsman's Fair. Late Oct.

Mistletoe Show. Crafts, wood carvings. 2nd wkend Nov.

Motels

★ ★ **COMFORT INN.** *306 S Hughes Blvd. 919/338-8900; FAX 919/338-6420.* 80 rms, 5 story, 28 suites. S, D $49-$57; each addl $6; suites $59-$67; under 18 free; higher rates hol wkends. Crib $6. TV;

cable. Heated pool. Complimentary continental bkfst. Restaurant nearby. Ck-out 11 am. Refrigerator in suites. Cr cds: A, C, D, MC, V.

★ ★ **HOLIDAY INN.** *522 S Hughes Blvd. 919/338-3951; FAX 919/338-6225.* 158 rms, 2 story. S $56-$66; D $61-$71; each addl $5; under 19 free. Crib free. TV; cable. Pool. Restaurant 6:30 am-2 pm, 5:30-10 pm. Rm serv. Bar 4 pm-1 am. Ck-out noon. Coin lndry. Meeting rms. Cr cds: A, C, D, DS, JCB, MC, V.

Restaurant

 ★ **MARINA.** *Camden Causeway, 1/2 mi E on US 158. 919/335-7307.* Hrs: 11 am-9 pm; Sat from 5 pm. Closed Mon; Jan 1, Thanksgiving, Dec 25. Serv bar. Semi-a la carte: lunch, dinner $3-$12.95. Child's meals. Specializes in steak, seafood. Parking. Overlooks Pasquotank River. Cr cds: MC, V.

Fayetteville (C-7)

Founded: 1739 **Pop:** 75,695 **Elev:** 102 ft **Area code:** 910

Originally known as Cross Creek City, Fayetteville was renamed in 1783 for the Marquis de Lafayette and was the first US city to thus honor him. It was the site of North Carolina's Constitutional Convention in 1787 and the capital of the state from 1789-93. By 1831 it had become a busy commercial city.

Fayetteville is the state's farthest inland port, at the head of navigation on the Cape Fear River, with an 8-foot-deep channel connecting it to the Intracoastal Waterway. Fayetteville State University (1867) and Methodist College (1956) are located here. In 1985 Fayetteville received the All-America City Award. Today, it's a a center for retail, manufacturing and conventions.

What to See and Do

1. **Museum of the Cape Fear.** 801 Arsenal Ave. Retraces the regional cultural history from prehistoric Indian artifacts through 20th century. A branch of the North Carolina Museum of History. (Daily exc Mon; closed hols) Phone 486-1330. **Free.**
2. **Barge's Tavern.** 515 Ramsey St. Built in 1790s, this is one of the city's earliest taverns and the site of many early conventions and celebrations. This is the second oldest building in Fayetteville. It is now home for the Convention and Visitors Bureau (Mon-Fri; closed major hols). **Free.**
3. **Fort Bragg & Pope AFB.** 10 mi NW on NC 87. Here are

   82nd Airborne Div War Memorial Museum. Ardennes & Gela Sts, Bldg C-6841. Weapons, relics of the First & Second World Wars, Vietnam; library; gift shop. (Daily exc Mon; closed Jan 1, Dec 25) Phone 432-5307. **Free.**

   John F. Kennedy Special Warfare Museum. Ardennes St & Reilly Rd, in Smoke Bomb Hill area. Guerrilla warfare weapons. (Daily exc Mon; closed some major hols). Phone 432-1533. **Free.**

   Parachute Jumps. For schedule infomation phone 396-6366.

   (For further information, contact the Public Affairs Office, Fort Bragg & XVIII Airborne Corps, Fort Bragg 28307-5000; 396-5620.)
4. **First Presbyterian Church.** Bow & Ann Sts. Classic colonial-style architecture, handmade locks and woodwork; crystal chandeliers and silver communion service. Among contributors to the original building (destroyed by fire in 1831) were James Monroe and John Quincy Adams. Tours (by appt only). Phone 483-0121.

(For further information and walking tours of historic areas, contact the Convention & Visitors Bureau, 515 Ramsey St, 28301; 483-5311 or 800/255-8217.)

Annual Event

Dogwood Festival. Early Apr.

(See Goldsboro)

Motels

★★ **COMFORT INN CROSS CREEK.** *1922 Skibo Rd (28314), off US 401 Bypass.* 910/867-1777; FAX 910/867-0325. 176 rms, 4 story. S, D $45-$57; each addl $6; suites $65-$90; under 16 free. Crib free. TV; cable. Pool. Complimentary continental bkfst. Restaurant nearby. Ck-out noon. Exercise equipt; stair climber, bicycles. Bathrm phone, refrigerator in suites. Cr cds: A, C, D, DS, ER, MC, V.

D ≋ 🏃 🚭 🔥 SC

✔ ★ **DAYS INN.** *2065 Cedar Creek Rd (28302).* 910/483-6191; FAX 910/483-4113. 122 rms, 2 story. S $34-$44; D $39-$47; each addl $6; under 12 free. Crib free. TV; cable. Pool. Complimentary full bkfst. Restaurant 6:30 am-2 pm, 5-10 pm. Rm serv. Bar. Ck-out noon. Meeting rms. Bellhops. Valet serv. Free airport, RR station, bus depot transportation. Game rm. Cr cds: A, C, D, DS, MC, V.

D ≋ 🚭 🔥 SC

★ **ECONO LODGE.** *PO Box 65177 (28306), Jct NC 210 & US 53; I-95 exit 49.* 910/433-2100; FAX 910/433-2009. 150 rms, 2 story. S $41.95-$46.95; D $44.95-$49.95; each addl $5; under 18 free. Crib free. TV; cable. Pool. Complimentary continental bkfst. Restaurant nearby. Ck-out noon. Cr cds: A, C, D, DS, ER, JCB, MC, V.

D ≋ 🚭 🔥 SC

✔ ★ **FAIRFIELD INN BY MARRIOTT.** *562 Cross Creek Mall (28301).* 910/487-1400; FAX 910/487-1400, ext. 709. 135 rms, 3 story. S $35.95-$45.95; D $41.95-$53.95; each addl 6; under 18 free. Crib free. TV; cable. Pool. Complimentary coffee in lobby. Restaurant nearby. Ck-out noon. Meeting rms. Valet serv. Cr cds: A, C, D, DS, MC, V.

D ≋ 🚭 🔥 SC

★★ **HAMPTON INN.** *1922 Cedar Creek Rd (28301), at I-95 exit 49.* 910/323-0011; FAX 910/323-8764. 122 rms, 2 story. S $46; D $51; under 18 free. Crib free. TV; cable, in-rm movies. Pool. Complimentary continental bkfst, coffee. Restaurant nearby. Ck-out noon. Valet serv. Cr cds: A, C, D, DS, MC, V.

D ≋ 🚭 🔥 SC

★★ **HOLIDAY INN.** *I-95 exit 49 (28302).* 910/323-1600; FAX 910/323-0691. 200 rms, 2 story. Mar-Nov: S, D $55-$95; each addl $5; kits. $79-$99; under 12 free; lower rates rest of yr. Crib free. TV; cable. Indoor pool. Complimentary coffee in rms. Restaurant 6:30 am-2 pm, 5:30-10 pm. Rm serv. Bar; entertainment Wed-Sat. Ck-out noon. Coin lndry. Meeting rms. Bellhops. Free airport transportation. Exercise equipt; weights, bicycles, whirlpool. Game rm. Cr cds: A, C, D, DS, ER, JCB, MC, V.

D ≋ 🏃 🚭 🔥 SC

✔ ★ **HORNE'S MOTOR LODGE.** *PO Box 466 (28301), 220 Eastern Blvd.* 910/483-1113; res: 800/682-1919; FAX 910/483-3366. 134 units, 2 story, 12 kits. S, D $32.95-36.95; kit. units $168/wk; wkly rates. TV; cable. Pool. Complimentary coffee. Restaurant 6 am-9 pm. Ck-out noon. Bathrm phones. Cr cds: A, C, D, MC, V.

≋ 🚭 🔥 SC

★★ **QUALITY INN AMBASSADOR.** *Box 64166 (28306), Jct I-95 Business, US 301S.* 910/485-8135. 62 rms. S $38; D $52; each addl $6; under 18 free; golf packages avail. Crib $6. TV; cable. Pool.

Playground. Restaurant 6 am-9 pm. Ck-out noon. Meeting rms. Picnic tables. Cr cds: A, D, DS, JCB, MC, V.

≋ 🚭 🔥 SC

Motor Hotels

★★★ **HOLIDAY INN BORDEAUX.** *1707 Owen Dr (28304).* 910/323-0111; FAX 910/484-9444. 290 units, 6 story. S $60-$70; D $66-$76; each addl $6; suites $150-$225; under 18 free. Crib free. TV; cable. Pool. Restaurant 6 am-2 pm, 5-11 pm; Fri & Sat open 24 hrs. Bar 4 pm-1 am; entertainment, dancing. Ck-out noon. Convention facilities. Some covered parking. Free airport transportation. Exercise equipt; weights, treadmill. Private patios, balconies. *LUXURY LEVEL :* LUXURY LEVEL. 30 rms. S, D $150. Concierge. Private lounge. Complimentary continental bkfst, refreshments. Cr cds: A, C, D, DS, JCB, MC, V.

D ≋ 🏃 🚭 🔥 SC

★★★ **HOWARD JOHNSON.** *Box 2086 (28302), I-95 exit 49.* 910/323-8282; FAX 910/323-3484. 168 rms, 4 story. S $48.95-$60; D $51-$64; each addl $6; suites $73-$77; under 18 free; golf plans. Crib free. TV; cable. Indoor pool. Restaurant 6 am-2 pm, 5-10 pm. Rm serv 7 am-10 pm. Bar; dancing. Ck-out noon. Meeting rms. Bellhops. Free airport transportation. Exercise equipt; weights, bicycles, whirlpool, sauna, steam rm. Some private patios. *LUXURY LEVEL :* EXECUTIVE LEVEL. 34 rms, 8 suites. S, D $62-$66. Concierge. Private lounge. Full wet bar. Complimentary continental bkfst, refreshments. Cr cds: A, C, D, DS, ER, MC, V.

D ≋ 🏃 🚭 🔥 SC

Restaurants

✔ ★ **CANTON STATION.** *301 N McPherson Church Rd.* 910/864-5555. Hrs: 11 am-2:30 pm, 5-10 pm; Sat from noon; Sun noon-9 pm. Res accepted. Cantonese menu. Bar. Semi-a la carte: lunch $3.50-$4.50, dinner $6.95-$14.95. Buffet: lunch $4.50, dinner $6.95. Specializes in seafood, pork, chicken. Parking. Chinese decor. Cr cds: A, MC, V.

D SC

★★ **DE LAFAYETTE.** *6112 Cliffdale Rd.* 910/868-4600. Hrs: 5 pm-midnight. Closed Sun, Mon; some major hols. Res accepted. Continental menu. Bar. A la carte entrees: dinner $10.50-$22. Specializes in French & Creole cooking. Piano, jazz quartet Fri. Parking. Formal dining rms with views of lake. Cr cds: A, C, D, DS, MC, V.

D

★★ **JOHNATHON'S.** *525 Grove St.* 910/483-8620. Hrs: 11 am-10 pm; Sat from 5 pm. Closed Sun; Jan 1. Res accepted. Bar. Semi-a la carte: lunch $3-$13, dinner $9-$21. Child's meals. Specializes in beef, seafood, chicken. Salad bar. Parking. English pub atmosphere. Cr cds: A, D, MC, V.

D

★★ **LOBSTER HOUSE.** *448 Person St.* 910/485-8866. Hrs: 11 am-2 pm, 5:30-10 pm; Fri to 11 pm; Sat 5:30-11 pm. Closed Sun; some major holidays. Res accepted. Bar. Semi-a la carte: lunch $2.95-$9.95, dinner $12.90-$53.90. Specializes in lobster, steak. Intimate dining in formal atmosphere. Cr cds: A, MC, V.

D

★★ **SEA.** *201 S McPherson Church Rd.* 910/868-2287. Hrs: 11 am-2 pm, 5-10 pm; Fri, Sat to 10:30 pm. Closed Jan 1, Thanksgiving, Dec 25. Bar. A la carte entrees: dinner $8.50-$35. Buffet (Thai cuisine only): lunch $5-$7. Specializes in mesquite-grilled seafood. Parking. Cr cds: A, C, D, MC, V.

Fontana Dam (B-1)

Founded: 1947 **Pop:** 130 (est) **Elev:** 2,900 ft **Area code:** 704 **Zip:** 28733

At the southwest corner of Great Smoky Mountains National Park, this village was originally built for the construction crew that worked on the Fontana Dam project. The 480-foot dam is crossed by the Appalachian Trail. The region is now a resort area, with swimming, fishing, boating, hiking and horseback riding centering around Fontana Lake, 30 miles long.

(See Bryson City)

Fort Raleigh National Historic Site (A-10)

(Off US 64, 3 mi N of Manteo)

The first English colony in America was attempted here on Roanoke Island in 1585. Virginia Dare, born here August 18, 1587, was the first child of English parents born in what is now the United States.

Governor John White left the island for England a few days after Virginia's birth, intending to return shortly with supplies. He was detained by the war with Spain and did not get back until August, 1590. The colony had disappeared, leaving behind only the mysterious word "CROATOAN" cut into a tree or post.

What happened to the colonists is unknown, though some believe that the present-day Lumbee Indians of Robeson County descend from them. Fort Raleigh has been excavated and the fort built by the colonists reconstructed. The Lindsay Warren Visitor Center has relics, an audiovisual program and exhibits. Park and Visitor Center (daily; closed Dec 25). For further information, contact Fort Raleigh National Historic Site, Rte 1, Box 675, Manteo 27954; 919/473-5772. **Free.**

Seasonal Event

The Lost Colony Outdoor Drama. Waterside Theater, 3 mi NW of Manteo on US 64/264. Outdoor drama by Pulitzer prize winner Paul Green about the first English colony established in the New World, whose curious disappearance remains a mystery to this day. Nightly exc Sun. Reservations advised. Contact Box 40, Manteo 27954; 919/473-3414 or 800/488-5012. Mid-June-late Aug.

(For accommodations see Kill Devil Hills, Nags Head, also see Cape Hatteras National Seashore, Outer Banks)

Franklin (Macon Co) (B-2)

Pop: 2,873 **Elev:** 2,133 ft **Area code:** 704 **Zip:** 28734

Home of the Cowee Valley ruby mines, Franklin attracts rockhounds who often find interesting gems in surface mines. Franklin is surrounded by waterfalls, mountain lakes and streams that offer excellent fishing for trout and bass, or boating, tubing and swimming. Around the county are 420,000 acres of the Nantahala National Forest, which offers hiking trails, camping and fishing. A Ranger District office is located here. The Appalachian Trail bisects the western part of the county through Standing Indian Wildlife Management area and over Wayah Bald Mountain.

What to See and Do

1. **Nantahala National Forest.** W of town. Nantahala, a Native American name meaning Land of the Noonday Sun, refers to Nantahala Gorge, so deep and narrow that the sun reaches the bottom only at noonday. Scenic drives through the Southern Appalachians, sparkling waterfalls, including the Whitewater Falls—a series of cascades dropping 411 feet within a distance of 500 feet—and the 17,013-acre Joyce Kilmer-Slickrock Wilderness (see ROBBINSVILLE), with more than 100 species of trees native to the region are part of this 518,560-acre forest. Hiking; swimming; fishing for bass and trout; hunting for deer, wild boar, turkey and ruffed grouse; boating; camping (fee). For further information contact the District Ranger, 100 Otis St, PO Box 2750, Asheville 28802; 524-6441.

2. **Gem mines.** There are more than a dozen mines in the area, most offering assistance and equipment for beginners. For a complete list of mines contact the Chamber of Commerce.

3. **Franklin Gem & Mineral Museum.** 2 W Main St, in the Old Jail. Gems & minerals; Native American artifacts, fossils; fluorescent mineral display. (May-Oct, daily) Phone 369-7831. **Free.**

4. **Macon County Historical Museum.** 6 W Main St. Artifacts, documents depicting early history of Macon County; genealogical material. (Apr-Oct, Mon-Fri, also Sat mornings) Phone 524-9758. **Free.**

5. **Perry's Water Garden.** 8 mi NW on NC 28 to Cowee Creek Rd, then E 2 mi to Leatherman Gap Rd. Water park with 4½-acre sunken garden, waterfall, hundreds of water lilies and other flowers, wishing well, trails, picnicking. (Mid-May-Labor Day, daily) Phone 524-3264. **Free.**

(For further information contact the Chamber of Commerce, 180 Porter St; 524-3161.)

Annual Events

Macon County Gemboree. Jewelry and gem exhibits, ruby mining, field trips. Late July.

Macon County Fair. Mid-Sept.

Leaf Lookers Bluegrass & Clogging Show. Championship cloggers from throughout the US. Mid-Oct.

(See Cashiers, Highlands)

Motels

✔ ★ **COUNTRY INN TOWN.** PO Box 529, 277 E Main St. 704/524-4451; res: 800/233-7555. 46 rms. S $35-$40; D $37-$44; each addl $4; under 16 free; higher rates fall foliage season. Crib $4. TV; cable. Pool. Restaurant opp 6 am-9 pm. Ck-out 11 am. Sundries. On Little Tennessee River. Cr cds: A, C, D, DS, MC, V.

[D] [≈] [✕] [🔥] [SC]

★ **DAYS INN.** PO Box 997, US 441/23N, 1 mi N. 704/524-6491. 41 rms. May-Sept: S, D $49-$59; each addl $5; higher rates: Gemboree, Labor Day wkend, Oct; lower rates rest of yr. TV; cable. Pool. Restaurant opp 7 am-11 pm. Scenic view of mountains. Cr cds: A, C, D, DS, MC, V.

[≈] [✕] [🔥] [SC]

Restaurant

✔ ★ **THE SUMMIT INN.** 125 E Rogers St. 704/524-2006. Hrs: 5-9 pm. Bar; entertainment Fri, Sat. Semi-a la carte: dinner $9.50-$13.95. Specializes in seafood, trout, steak. Salad bar. Parking. Renovated farm house (1898); Victorian furnishings, antiques. Gift shop. Guest rms avail. Cr cds: MC, V.

Gastonia (B-4)

Pop: 54,732 **Elev:** 816 ft **Area code:** 704

This is an industrial town in the Piedmont, turning out textiles, textile machinery and supplies. In addition, Gastonia produces chain saws, plastics, oil seals, lithium, automotive parts, trucks and truck parts.

What to See and Do

1. **Gaston County Museum of Art & History.** 6 mi N via US 321, Dallas exit. Sculpture, paintings, Gaston County artifacts and documents, carriage and sleigh collection, textile history exhibit. 19th-century parlors; walking tour of historic district by appt. Located in Hoffman Hotel (1852) and Dallas Depot (1901). (Daily exc Mon; closed hols) Phone 922-7681. **Free.**

2. **Schiele Museum of Natural History and Planetarium.** 1500 E Garrison Blvd. Habitat settings showcasing more than 75,000 mounted birds, mammals, reptiles, fish; rocks and minerals, Native American arts & crafts, forestry exhibits; 28-acre nature park. Major exhibits on the Southeast and North Carolina; special exhibits and events, films. Restored mid-1700s pioneer farm with living history programs. Hall of Natural History, Hall of Earth and Man. Also here is Catawba Indian Village, with re-created dwellings from 1500s to 1900s. Planetarium programs & Cinema 360 Wide-Screen science films (fee). (Daily exc Mon; closed hols and Christmas wk) Special gallery for the visually impaired. Phone 866-6900. **Free.**

3. **Lake Wylie.** S on NC 274. Artificial lake formed by Duke Power Co development; fishing, swimming, waterskiing; marina. Phone 803/831-2101.

(For further information contact Gaston County Travel and Tourism, 2551 Pembroke, PO Box 2339, 28053; 867-2170 or 800/849-9994.)

(See Charlotte)

Motel

★★ **HAMPTON INN.** *1859 Remount Rd (28054), I-85 exit New Hope Rd.* 704/866-9090. 108 rms, 5 story. S $50; D $55; under 12 free. Crib free. TV; cable. Pool. Complimentary continental bkfst, coffee. Restaurant adj 6 am-11 pm. Ck-out noon. Meeting rm. Valet serv. Cr cds: A, C, D, DS, MC, V.

Unrated Dining Spot

MORRISON'S CAFETERIA. *At I-85N & New Hope Rd.* 704/867-0244. Hrs: 11 am-8 pm; Fri, Sat to 8:30 pm; Sun to 7 pm. Avg ck: lunch $4.50, dinner $5. Specializes in roast beef, seafood, custard pie. Cr cds: A, D, MC, V.

Goldsboro (B-8)

Established: 1847 **Pop:** 40,709 **Elev:** 121 ft **Area code:** 919

Center of the bright-leaf tobacco belt, Goldsboro is also the seat of Wayne County and home of Seymour Johnson Air Force Base. Poultry production and tobacco warehousing and processing are important industries. There are also many food, wood product and textile plants here.

What to See and Do

1. **Cliffs of the Neuse State Park.** 14 mi SE, off NC 111. Approx 700 acres on Neuse River. Swimming, bathhouse; fishing; boating (rowboat rentals). Nature trails. Picnicking. Tent & trailer sites (mid-Mar-Nov; fee). Museum, interpretive center. Standard fees. Contact Superintendent, Rte 2, Box 50, Seven Springs 28578; 778-6234.

2. **Governor Charles B. Aycock Birthplace State Historic Site.** 12 mi N, off US 117 just S of Fremont. Mid-1800s farmhouse and outbuildings; audiovisual presentation in one-room school (1893); exhibits in visitor center portray life of the "educational governor." Picnicking. (Apr-Oct, daily; rest of yr, daily exc Mon; closed most major hols) Phone 242-5581. **Free.**

(For further information contact the Wayne County Chamber of Commerce, PO Box 1107, 27533-1107; 734-2241.)

Motels

★★ **COMFORT INN.** *909 Spence Ave (27534).* 919/751-1999; FAX 919/751-1506. 122 rms, 5 story. S $50-$70; D $54-$90; each addl $6; suites $85-$95; under 17 free. TV; cable. Pool. Complimentary continental bkfst, coffee. Restaurant adj. Bar 5 pm-2 am, closed Sun; entertainment, dancing. Ck-out noon. Sundries. Cr cds: A, C, D, DS, ER, MC, V.

✔ ★ **DAYS INN.** *2000 Wayne Memorial Dr (27534).* 919/734-9471; FAX 919/736-2623. 120 rms, 2 story. S $38-$40; D $42-$44; each addl $4. Crib free. TV; cable. Pool. Playground. Restaurant 6 am-9 pm; Sun to 2 pm. Ck-out noon. Meeting rms. Sundries. Exercise equipt; weight machine, bicycles. Some refrigerators. Cr cds: A, C, D, DS, MC, V.

★★ **HOLIDAY INN.** *Box 1973 (27530), 1 1/2 mi NE on US 13, 70 Bypass.* 919/735-7901; FAX 919/734-2946. 120 rms, 2 story. S $49; D $52; each addl $5; suites $85; under 16 free. Pet accepted. TV; cable. Pool. Restaurant 6:30 am-2 pm, 5:30-10 pm. Rm serv. Ck-out 11 am. Meeting rms. Cr cds: A, C, D, DS, JCB, MC, V.

✔ ★ **RAMADA INN.** *808 W Grantham St (27530), jct US 70 & US 117S.* 919/736-4590; FAX 919/735-3218. 128 rms, 2 story. S $36-$55; D $41-$60; suites from $75; under 18 free; wkly rates. Crib free. TV; cable. Pool. Restaurant 5:30 am-10 pm. Rm serv. Bar 5:30 pm-2 am; entertainment Thurs-Sat. Ck-out noon. Coin lndry. Meeting rms. Valet serv. Sundries. Game rm. Some refrigerators. Picnic tables, grills. Cr cds: A, C, D, DS, JCB, MC, V.

Restaurant

★ **CAPTAIN BOB'S SEAFOOD.** *430 N Berkeley Blvd, in Eastgate Shopping Center.* 919/778-8332. Hrs: 11 am-9 pm; Fri to 9:30 pm; Sat 4-9:30 pm; Sun 11 am-8 pm. Closed Mon; Thanksgiving, Dec 25. Res accepted Tues-Fri. Semi-a la carte: lunch $2.99-$3.65, dinner $5.50-$8.50. Child's meals. Specializes in seafood, beef, steak. Salad bar. Nautical decor. Cr cds: MC, V.

Great Smoky Mountains National Park (B-1 - B-2)

(50 mi W of Asheville off US 19)

The Appalachian Mountains, product of a slow upthrusting of ancient sediments, which took place more than 200 million years ago, stand tall and regal in this 800-square-mile area. Red spruce, basswood, eastern hemlock, yellow birch, white ash, cucumber trees, silverbells, Fraser fir, tulip poplar, red maple and Fraser magnolias tower above hundreds of other species of flowering plants. Perhaps the most spectacular of these are the purple rhododendron, mountain laurel and flame azalea, in bloom from early June to mid-July.

The moist climate has helped make this a rich wilderness. From early spring to late fall the "coves" (as the open valleys surrounded by peaks are called) and forest floors are covered with a succession of flowers with colorful variety. Summer brings heavy showers, days that are warm (although 15° to 20° cooler than in the valleys below) and cool nights. Autumn is breathtaking as the deciduous trees change color. Winter brings snow, occasionally heavy, and fog over the mountains. Winter is a very good time to visit the park; but be aware of temporary road closures.

Half in North Carolina and half in Tennessee, with the Appalachian Trail following the state line along the ridge for 70 miles, this is a place to hike. Nearby are the cabins, barns and mills of the mountain people whose ancestors came years ago from England and Scotland. It is also a place to see the descendants of the once-mighty Cherokee Nation, whose ancestors hid in the mountains from the soldiers in the winter of 1838-39 to avoid being driven over the "Trail of Tears" to Oklahoma. This is the tribe of Sequoyah, the brilliant chief who invented a written alphabet for the Cherokee people.

Stop first at one of the three visitor centers: Oconaluftee Center in North Carolina, 2 miles north of Cherokee on Newfound Gap Road, designated US 441 outside of park (daily; closed Dec 25; phone 704/497-9146); Sugarlands, in Tennessee, 2 miles southwest of Gatlinburg (daily; closed Dec 25; phone 615/436-1200); or Cades Cove, 8 miles SW of Townsend, TN (mid-Mar-Nov; Dec, wkends; phone 615/436-1200). All three have exhibits and information about the park. There are hundreds of miles of foot trails and bridle paths. Camping is popular; ask at any visitor center for locations and regulations. There are developed campgrounds (fee). For reservations at Elkmont, Cades Cove or Smokemont phone 800/365-CAMP; reservations are not taken for other sites.

The views from Newfound Gap and the observation tower at Clingman's Dome (closed in winter), about 7 miles southwest, are spectacular. Cades Cove is an outdoor museum reflecting the life of the original mountain people, about 25 miles west of Sugarlands. It has log cabins and barns. Park naturalists conduct campfire programs and hikes during the spring and summer. There are also self-guided nature trails. LeConte Lodge, reached only by foot or horseback, is an accommodation within the park; phone 615/436-1200 (late Mar-mid-Nov).

Fishing is permitted with a state license. Obtain list of regulations at visitor centers and campgrounds. The park is a wildlife sanctuary; any disturbance of plant or animal life is forbidden. Dogs and cats are not permitted on trails but may be brought in if kept on leash or other physical restrictive controls. Never feed, tease or frighten bears; always give them a wide berth, as they can inflict serious injury. Watch bears from car with the windows closed. Park (daily). For the disabled, there is a special asphalt trail (1¼ mi) leading to falls and an accessibility guide at visitor centers.   **Free.**

CCInc Auto Tape Tours offer a mile-by-mile self-guided tour (90-min cassette) of the park. Written in cooperation with the National Park Service, it provides information on history, points of interest and flora and fauna of the park. Available in Cherokee at Qualla Gift Shop on Main St, and Log Cabin Trading Post, across from the cinema; or in Gatlinburg, TN at various gift shops. Tapes also may be purchased directly from CCInc, PO Box 227, 2 Elbrook Dr, Allendale, NJ 07401; 201/236-1666. **¢¢¢¢**

For information contact the Superintendent, Great Smoky Mountains National Park, 107 Park Headquarters Rd, Gatlinburg, TN 37738; 615/436-1200.

(For accommodations see Bryson City, Cherokee, Maggie Valley, also see Fontana Dam)

Greensboro (A-6)

Founded: 1808 **Pop:** 183,521 **Elev:** 841 ft **Area code:** 910

William Sydney Porter (O. Henry) was born and raised near Greensboro, a diversified Piedmont industrial city whose products are typical of North Carolina: textiles, cigarettes, machinery and electronic components. It was settled by Quakers, Germans and the Scottish-Irish with a zeal for political, religious and economic freedom. Men from this region fought in the Revolution and the War of 1812, and turned to the Confederacy in 1861. It was in Greensboro, the rebel supply depot, that Jefferson Davis met General Johnston after Richmond fell in 1865 and agreed on surrender terms. Today it is an educational, manufacturing and distribution center.

What to See and Do

1. **Guilford Courthouse National Military Park.** 6 mi NW and ¼ mi E off US 220 on New Garden Rd. On March 15, 1781, Lord Cornwallis won a costly victory that was one link in a series of events that led to his surrender at Yorktown in October of the same year. After destroying a quarter of the enemy troops, General Nathanael Greene (for whom the city is named) made a successful retreat and then severely hampered the British plan of subduing the Southern colonies. The 220-acre park, established in 1917, has monuments marking important locations and honoring those who fought here; two signers of the Declaration of Independence, John Penn and William Hooper, are also buried here. Self-guided auto tour; walking trails. The visitor center has a museum housing Revolutionary War weapons, other items; 20-minute film. (Daily; closed Jan 1, Dec 25) For additional information contact the Superintendent, PO Box 9806, 27429-0806; 288-1776. **Free.**

2. **Greensboro Historical Museum.** 130 Summit Ave. Housed in 19th-century church; exhibits on First Lady Dolley Madison, author O. Henry; military history, including Revolutionary Battle of Guilford Courthouse; 1960s lunch counter sit-ins; decorative arts; vintage autos; period furnishings. (Daily exc Mon; closed most hols) Phone 373-2043. **Free.**

3. **Charlotte Hawkins Brown Memorial State Historic Site.** 10 mi E on I-85 to exit 135, then ½ mi W on US 70. North Carolina's first state historic site, honoring the achievements of African-American education in the state. In 1902, C.H. Brown, granddaughter of former slaves, founded Palmer Memorial Institute, which became one of the finest preparatory schools for blacks in the nation. Guided tours of historic campus (several buildings being restored), visitor center, audiovisual program. Picnicking. (Apr-Oct, daily; rest of yr, daily exc Mon; closed some hols) Phone 449-4846. **Free.**

4. **University of North Carolina at Greensboro** (1891). (12,100 students) 1000 Spring Garden St. Phone 334-5243. On campus is

    Weatherspoon Art Gallery. Anne and Benjamin Cone Bldg. Permanent collection of over 4,000 contemporary paintings, graphic arts, sculpture. (Daily exc Mon; closed school hols) Phone 334-5770. **Free.**

5. **Guilford College** (1837). (1,200 students) 5800 W Friendly Ave, 2 mi N of I-40. Oldest coed college in the South. Beautiful wooded

300-acre campus with Georgian-style buildings and a unique solar-energy fieldhouse. Quaker archives dating from 1680 (Tues-Fri, by appt; closed some hols). Official home of Eastern Music Festival (July-Aug). Phone 316-2000 or -2264 (archives).

6. **Natural Science Center of Greensboro, Inc.** 4301 Lawndale Dr, 5¹/₂ mi N. Natural science museum with zoo, trails & indoor exhibits including geology, paleontology and science & technology. Kid's Alley, an exploratorium for young children. Planetarium shows; inquire for schedule. Some fees. (Daily; closed major hols) Sr citizen rate. Phone 288-3769. ¢¢

7. **Hagan-Stone Park.** 6 mi S on US 421, then 2 mi W on Hagan-Stone Park Rd. Swimming; fishing. Hiking. Picnicking, playground. Camping (hookups, dump station). Park (all yr). Some fees. Pets on leash only. Phone 674-0472.

(For further information contact the Greensboro Area Convention & Visitors Bureau, 317 S Greene St, 27401; 274-2282 or 800/344-2282.)

Annual Event

Greater Greensboro Open Golf Tournament. Top golfers compete for more than $1,500,000; on PGA circuit. Mid-late Apr.

(See Burlington, High Point)

Motels

(Rates are generally higher during Furniture Market)

★ **COMFORT INN.** 2001 Veasley St (27407). 910/294-6220; FAX 910/294-6220, ext. 199. 124 rms, 2 story. S $47; D $52; each addl $5; under 16 free; higher rates special events. Crib free. TV; cable. Pool. Complimentary continental bkfst. Ck-out noon. Meeting rm. Cr cds: A, C, D, DS, ER, JCB, MC, V.

✔ ★ ★ **DAYS INN.** I-85 & S Elm (27406), SW of jct US 29, 70, 421, I-85. 910/275-9571. 122 rms, 2 story. S $29-$52; D $36-$58; each addl $6; family rates. Crib free. TV; cable. Pool; wading pool. Playground. Complimentary continental bkfst. Ck-out 11 am. Cr cds: A, C, D, DS, MC, V.

★ ★ **FAIRFIELD INN BY MARRIOTT.** 2003 Athena Ct (27407). 910/294-9922; FAX 910/294-9922, ext. 709. 135 rms, 3 story. S $45.95; D $51.95; 3rd addl $3; under 18 free. Crib avail. TV; cable. Pool. Complimentary continental bkfst. Complimentary coffee in lobby. Restaurant nearby. Ck-out noon. Meeting rms. Valet serv (Tues-Sat). Cr cds: A, D, DS, MC, V.

★ ★ **HAMPTON INN.** 2004 Veasley St (27407). 910/854-8600; FAX 910/854-8741. 121 rms, 2 story. S $40-$48; D $52-$54; under 18 free. Crib free. Pet accepted, some restrictions. TV. Pool. Complimentary continental bkfst. Meeting rm. Cr cds: A, C, D, DS, JCB, MC, V.

★ ★ **RAMADA INN AIRPORT.** 7067 Albert Pick Rd (27409), near Piedmont Triad Airport. 910/668-3900; FAX 910/668-7012. 170 rms, 2 story. S, D $58-$68; each addl $5; suites $110; higher rates special events. Crib free. Pet accepted, some restrictions. TV; cable. Pool; sauna, poolside serv. Restaurant 7-10 am, 11:30 am-2 pm, 5-10 pm; Sat 7-10 am, 5-10 pm; Sun 7-10 am, 11:30 am-2 pm. Rm serv. Bar 4 pm-midnight. Ck-out noon. Meeting rms. Bellhops. Valet serv. Free airport transportation. Some in-rm steam baths. Cr cds: A, C, D, DS, JCB, MC, V.

✔ ★ **TRAVELODGE.** 2112 W Meadowview Rd (27403). 910/292-2020; FAX 910/852-3476. 107 rms, 2 story. S, D $35-$50; each addl $5; under 17 free; higher rates: Furniture Market, golf tourna-

ment. Crib free. TV; cable. Heated pool. Complimentary coffee in rms. Restaurant adj 11 am-10 pm. Ck-out noon. Meeting rms. Health club privileges. Cr cds: A, D, DS, MC, V.

Motor Hotels

★ ★ ★ **HOLIDAY INN-FOUR SEASONS.** 3121 High Point Rd (27407), I-40 exit 217A in Four Seasons Mall. 910/292-9161; FAX 910/292-9161, ext. 181. 524 rms, 17 story. S $109-$118; D $120-$129; each addl $10; under 18 free; higher rates special events. Crib free. TV; cable. Indoor/outdoor pool; wading pool; poolside serv. Restaurant 6 am-midnight. Rm serv to 10 pm. Bar 11-1 am, Sun from 1 pm; entertainment, dancing. Ck-out noon. Meeting rms. Bellhops. Valet serv. Sundries. Gift shop. Free airport transportation. Exercise equipt; weight machine, bicycles, whirlpool. Some rms with balcony. Cr cds: A, C, D, DS, JCB, MC, V.

★ ★ **HOWARD JOHNSON-COLISEUM.** 3030 High Point Rd (27403), at I-40 exit 217B. 910/294-4920; FAX 910/299-0503. 175 rms, 12 story. S $45-$65; D $49-$65; each addl $5; suites $59-$75; under 18 free; higher rates special events. Crib free. TV; cable. Heated pool; wading pool. Bar 5-11 pm. Ck-out noon. Meeting rms. Valet serv. Airport transportation. Tennis. Exercise equipt; weights, bicycles, sauna. Some bathrm phones. Cr cds: A, C, D, DS, JCB, MC, V.

★ ★ **PARK LANE HOTEL/FOUR SEASONS.** 3005 High Point Rd (27403). 910/294-4565; FAX 910/294-0572. 161 rms, 4 story. S $55-$65; D $60-$70; each addl $5; suites $125; under 16 free. Crib free. TV; cable. Pool. Complimentary continental bkfst. Restaurant 6-10 am, 5-9:30 pm; wkends 7-11 am. Rm serv. Bar 4:30-10 pm. Ck-out noon. Coin lndry. Meeting rms. Sundries. Airport transportation. Exercise equipt; weights, bicycles, sauna. Some in-rm whirlpools; refrigerator, wet bar in suites. Cr cds: A, C, D, DS, ER, JCB, MC, V.

Hotels

★ ★ ★ **BILTMORE GREENSBORO HOTEL.** 111 W Washington St (27401). 910/272-3474; res: 800/332-0303; FAX 910/275-2523. 25 rms. S, D $75-$110; under 18 free. Crib free. TV; cable. Complimentary continental bkfst; evening refreshments. Ck-out noon. Meeting rm. Concierge. Refrigerators, wet bars. Rich appointments, period furnishings. Built 1895. Cr cds: A, C, D, DS, MC, V.

★ ★ ★ **EMBASSY SUITES.** 204 Centreport Dr (27409), near Piedmont Triad Airport. 910/668-4535; FAX 910/668-3901. 215 suites, 7 story. Suites $84-$175; under 16 free; higher rates golf tournament (Apr). Crib free. TV; cable. Indoor pool. Complimentary full bkfst. Restaurant 6 am-10 pm. Bar 4 pm-midnight; entertainment. Ck-out noon. Coin lndry. Meeting rms. Gift shop. Free airport transportation. Exercise equipt; weight machine, bicycles, whirlpool, sauna. Game rm. Refrigerators, wet bars. Balconies. Atrium lobby; glass elevators. Cr cds: A, C, D, DS, JCB, MC, V.

★ ★ ★ **MARRIOTT.** 1 Marriott Dr (27409), I-40 exit 210, at Piedmont Triad Airport. 910/852-6450; FAX 910/665-0900. 299 rms. S $99-$109; D $109-$119; each addl $10; suites $150-$200; under 16 free. Crib free. TV; cable. Indoor/outdoor pool; poolside serv. Restaurant 6 am-11 pm. Bar 11:30-2 am; dancing. Ck-out noon. Coin lndry. Convention facilities. Gift shop. Free airport transportation. Lighted tennis. Exercise equipt; weight machines, bicycles, whirlpool. Game rm. Lawn games. *LUXURY LEVEL : CONCIERGE LEVEL.* 52 rms. S,

D $116. Concierge. Private lounge, honor bar. Complimentary continental bkfst, refreshments. Cr cds: A, C, D, DS, JCB, MC, V.

★ ★ ★ **SHERATON.** *303 N Elm St (27401). 910/379-8000; FAX 910/275-2810.* 283 rms, 11 story. S, D $89-$105; each addl $10; suites $150-$385; under 17 free; wkend rates. Crib free. TV; cable. Indoor pool. Restaurant 6:30 am-10 pm. Bar 11-1 am. Ck-out noon. Convention facilities. Free covered parking. Exercise rm; instructor, weight machines, bicycles, whirlpool, sauna. Refrigerators. Cr cds: A, C, D, DS, ER, MC, V.

Greenville (B-8)

Founded: 1786 **Pop:** 44,972 **Elev:** 55 ft **Area code:** 919

An educational, cultural, commercial and medical center, Greenville is one of the towns named for General Nathanael Greene, a hero of the American Revolutionary War.

What to See and Do

1. **Greenville Museum of Art.** 802 Evans St. Collections emphasize North Carolina contemporary fine arts and drawings, also paintings and prints of the period 1900-45. (Tues-Fri, also Sun afternoons; closed major hols) Donation. Phone 758-1946.

2. **East Carolina University** (1907). (17,600 students) E side of town. Jenkins Fine Arts Center, ECU Music School and Museum of Art offer many cultural events to the public. Medical Center campus, W side of town. Phone 757-6131 for information.

3. **River Park North Science & Nature Center.** 5 mi N on Mumford Rd. A 309-acre park with 4 lakes and 1.2 miles of Tar River water frontage. Science center near park entrance offers hands-on exhibits. Fishing, boating (boat ramp; no gas motors), pedal boats. Picknicking. (Daily exc Mon; closed most major hols) Phone 830-4561. ¢

4. **East Carolina Village of Yesteryear.** 2 mi N via US 264. Restoration and preservation of small town life (1840-1940) within Pitt County and eastern North Carolina. The area contains a general store, railroad depot, museum, farmhouse, chicken house and schoolhouse. Open by appt. Phone 758-6385. ¢

(For further information contact the Greenville-Pitt County Convention and Visitors Bureau, 525 S Evans St, PO Box 8027, 27835-8027; 752-8044.)

(See Washington, Williamston)

Motels

✔ ★ **CRICKET INN.** *821 S Memorial Dr (27834). 919/758-5544; res: 800/274-2538; FAX 919/758-1416.* 115 rms, 2 story. S $33.88-$39.88; D, suites $39.88-$45.88; each addl $6; under 16 free. Crib free. TV; cable. Pool. Complimentary continental bkfst. Restaurant adj open 24 hrs. Valet serv. Free airport, hospital transportation. Cr cds: A, C, D, DS, MC, V.

★ ★ **HAMPTON INN.** *3439 S Memorial Dr (27834). 919/355-2521; FAX 919/355-2521, ext. 509.* 121 rms, 2 story. S $41-$47; D $47-$53; under 18 free. Crib free. TV; cable. Pool. Complimentary continental bkfst, coffee. Restaurant nearby. Ck-out noon. Meeting rms. Cr cds: A, C, D, DS, MC, V.

★ **HOLIDAY INN MEDICAL CENTER.** *702 S Memorial Dr (27835). 919/758-3401; FAX 919/758-6403.* 145 rms, 2 story. S, D $48-$65; each addl $3; suites $150; under 19 free; wkly rates; higher rates ECU events. Crib free. Pet accepted, some restrictions. TV; cable. Indoor pool; whirlpool, poolside serv. Complimentary continental bkfst. Restaurant 6 am-2 pm, 5-10 pm. Rm serv. Bar. Ck-out noon. Meeting rms. Bellhops. Sundries. Valet serv. Holidome. Health club privileges. Rec rm. Refrigerators avail. Near airport. Cr cds: A, C, D, DS, JCB, MC, V.

✔ ★ **SUPER 8.** *1004 S Memorial Dr (27834). 919/758-8888; FAX 919/758-0523.* 52 rms, 2 story. S $31.99; D $36.99; each addl $5; under 12 free. Crib free. TV; cable. Complimentary coffee in lobby. Ck-out 11 am. Cr cds: A, C, D, DS, MC, V.

Hotels

★ ★ ★ **HILTON.** *207 SW Greenville Blvd (27834). 919/355-5000; FAX 919/355-5099.* 140 rms, 6 story. S, D $79-$94; each addl $10; suites $150-$225; under 18 free. Crib free. TV; cable. Pool; poolside serv. Restaurant 6:30 am-10:30 pm. Bar 11 am-1 am; dancing Wed-Sat. Ck-out noon. Meeting rms. Airport transportation. Exercise equipt; weights, bicycles, whirlpool. Refrigerator in suites. Cr cds: A, C, D, DS, MC, V.

★ ★ **RAMADA.** *203 W Greenville Blvd (27834), at jct US 264, NC 43, 11 on US 264 Bypass. 919/355-8300; FAX 919/756-3553.* 192 rms, 4 story. S $44-$61; D $48-$65; each addl $6; suites $70-$100; under 12 free. Crib free. TV; cable. Pool. Restaurant 6:30 am-10 pm. Rm serv. Bar 5 pm-2 am; entertainment, dancing. Ck-out noon. Meeting rms. Exercise equipt; bicycles, weights. Cr cds: A, C, D, DS, JCB, MC, V.

Restaurants

★ ★ **BEEF BARN.** *400 St Andrews Dr. 919/756-1161.* Hrs: 11:30 am-2 pm, 6-10 pm; Sat, Sun from 6 pm. Closed some major hols. Res accepted. Bar. Semi-a la carte: lunch $3.95-$6.95, dinner $8.95-$25.95. Child's meals. Specializes in beef, steak, seafood. Salad bar. Parking. Antiques. Family-owned. Cr cds: A, DS, MC, V.

✔ ★ **PARKER'S BAR-B-QUE.** *3109 Memorial Dr (27834). 919/756-2388.* Hrs: 9 am-9 pm. Closed Thanksgiving, Dec 24 & 25; also 1 wk mid-June. Res accepted. Semi-a la carte: lunch, dinner $4.40-$5.20. Child's meals. Specializes in pork barbecue, fried chicken. Parking. Outdoor dining. Family-owned. No cr cds accepted.

Hatteras (Outer Banks) (B-10)

Pop: 1,660 **Elev:** 2 ft **Area code:** 919 **Zip:** 27943

This Hatteras Island fishing village on the Outer Banks (see) was settled, it is said, by shipwrecked sailors from Devon, England. The Devon accent is indeed heard here and on the islands of Ocracoke and Manteo. There are ferries south to Ocracoke (see).

Motels

★ **HATTERAS MARLIN.** *PO Box 250, on NC 12.* 919/986-2141; FAX 919/986-2436. 32 rms, 2 story, 5 kits. Memorial Day-Labor Day: S, D $50; each addl $5; kit. units for 1-4, $55-$60; under 6 free; lower rates rest of yr. Crib free. TV; cable. Pool. Restaurant nearby. Ck-out 11 am. Sun deck. Picnic tables. Cr cds: MC, V.

★ **SEA GULL.** *PO Box 280, on NC 12.* 919/986-2550. 45 rms, 1-2 story, 10 kits. No rm phones. Mar-Dec: S, D $45-$70; each addl $5; kit. units $60-$90; under 5 free. Closed rest of yr. Crib $5. TV; cable. Pool; wading pool. Restaurant opp 6 am-9 pm. Ck-out 11 am. Picnic table. Beach adj. Cr cds: MC, V.

Restaurant

★ ★ **CHANNEL BASS.** *NC 12, 8 mi S of lighthouse, 1 mi N of ferry docks.* 919/986-2250. Hrs: 5:30-9:30 pm; Sun from 5 pm. Closed Dec-Mar. Res accepted. Semi-a la carte: dinner $8.95-$24.50. Child's meals. Specializes in seafood, pies. Parking. On channel; nautical decor. Family-owned. Cr cds: MC, V.

Henderson (A-7)

Founded: 1840 **Pop:** 15,655 **Elev:** 509 ft **Area code:** 919 **Zip:** 27536

Tobacco has historically been the major crop in Vance County, of which Henderson is the seat. In recent years, dairy farming and the raising of livestock and feed have increased. Manufacture and processing of textiles, hosiery, furniture, food, tobacco, mobile homes and glass containers are local industries.

What to See and Do

Kerr Reservoir. 6 mi N off I-85. Part of the development of the Roanoke River Basin by the US Army Corps of Engineers. Approx 800 mi of shoreline and 50,000 acres of water. Swimming, water-skiing; fishing; boating, several private marinas. Picnicking. Camping (fee). Seven state recreation areas around lake, some open only Apr-Oct. (Daily) State camping areas (water & electric hookups in all exc Bullocksville; standard fees); for 7-14-day reservations phone 438-7791.

(For further information contact the Chamber of Commerce, 414 S Garnett St, PO Box 1302; 438-8414.)

Annual Event

Governor's Cup Regatta. Kerr Lake. 2 days mid-June.

Seasonal Event

Tobacco auctions. Held at 7 warehouses. Inquire Chamber of Commerce. Sept-Nov.

Motels

★ ★ **HOLIDAY INN.** *Box 845, 1¼ mi N on US 1, 158 at jct I-85 exit 215.* 919/492-1126; FAX 919/492-2575. 156 rms, 2 story. S $47-$60; D $48-$63; each addl $6; under 19 free. Crib free. TV; cable. Pool; wading pool. Restaurant 6:30 am-2 pm, 5-10 pm. Rm serv. Bar

5-11 pm. Ck-out noon. Meeting rms. Sundries. Cr cds: A, C, D, DS, JCB, MC, V.

★ ★ **HOWARD JOHNSON.** *Drawer F, Parham Rd at jct US 1, 158 & I-85.* 919/492-7001; FAX 919/438-2389. 100 rms, 2 story. S $40-$52; D $44-$57; each addl $6; under 18 free. Crib free. TV; cable. Pool. Restaurant 6 am-10 pm. Ck-out noon. Meeting rms. Sundries. Balconies; some private patios. Cr cds: A, C, D, DS, JCB, MC, V.

Hendersonville (B-3)

Pop: 7,284 **Elev:** 2,146 ft **Area code:** 704

The county seat of Henderson County, Hendersonville is well-known as a summer resort colony and popular retirement community. Year-round industries produce clothing, paper products, metalwork, office furniture, hosiery, lighting fixtures and other products.

What to See and Do

1. **Carl Sandburg Home National Historic Site** (Connemara). 1928 Little River Rd, 3 mi S on US 25, in Flat Rock. The famous poet's 264-acre farm residence is maintained as it was when Sandburg and his family lived here from 1945 until his death in 1967. On grounds are house and buildings for animals as well as a visitor center. (Daily; closed Dec 25) For further information contact the Superintendent, Flat Rock 28731; 693-4178. ¢

2. **Holmes State Forest.** SW on Crab Creek Rd. Managed forest designed to facilitate better understanding of the value of forests in our lives. Features "talking trees" with recorded narration about site and forest history. Picnicking. Camping (reservations required). (Mid-Mar-Nov, daily exc Mon) For reservations or information contact Rte 4, Box 308; phone 692-0100. **Free.**

3. **Jump-Off Rock.** 5th Ave, 6 mi W. Panoramic view from atop Jump-Off Mountain.

(For further information contact the Chamber of Commerce, 330 N King St, 28792; 692-1413.)

Annual Event

North Carolina Apple Festival. Labor Day wkend.

Seasonal Event

Flat Rock Playhouse. 3½ mi S on US 25 in Flat Rock. Outstanding professional theater since 1939; State Theater of North Carolina since 1961. Vagabond Players offer eight Broadway and London productions in 15 weeks. Wed-Sat evenings; Thurs, Sat, Sun matinees. For reservations phone 693-0731. Late May-early Sept.

(See Asheville, Brevard)

Motels

★ **COMFORT INN.** *206 Mitchell Dr (28792).* 704/693-8800. 85 rms, 2 story. June-Oct: S $55.95; D $60.95; each addl $6; under 18 free; higher rates wkends; lower rates rest of yr. Crib free. Pet accepted. TV; cable, in-rm movies. Pool; whirlpool. Complimentary continental bkfst, coffee. Restaurant nearby. Ck-out 11 am. Meeting rm. Cr cds: A, C, D, DS, JCB, MC, V.

★ ★ **HAMPTON INN.** *155 Sugarloaf Rd (28792).* 704/697-2333; FAX 704/693-5280. 119 rms, 4 story. June-Oct: S $53-$60; D $58-$69; under 18 free; higher rates wkends in July, Aug & Oct; lower rates rest of yr. Crib free. TV; cable. Pool. Continental bkfst. Ck-out noon. Cr cds: A, C, D, DS, MC, V.

 ⊠ ⊠ ⊠ SC

★ ★ **HOLIDAY INN.** *201 Sugarloaf Rd (28792), at jct I-26 & US 64. 704/692-7231; FAX 704/693-9905.* 150 rms, 2 story. June-Oct: S $62-$75; D $72-$85; each addl $6; under 18 free; lower rates rest of yr. Crib $5. TV; cable. Heated pool; whirlpool, sauna. Playground. Restaurant 6:30-10:30 am, 5:30-9:30 pm. Rm serv. Ck-out 11 am. Meeting rms. Valet serv. Sundries. Rec rm. Some refrigerators. Cr cds: A, C, D, DS, JCB, MC, V.

D ⊠ ⊠ ⊠ SC

Inns

★ ★ **ECHO MOUNTAIN.** *2849 Laurel Park Hwy (28739). 704/693-9626.* 33 units, 2 story, 7 kits. Memorial Day-Labor Day, Oct & late Dec: S, D $42-$125; kit. suites $90-$135; each addl $10; lower rates rest of yr. Crib free. TV; cable. Pool. Complimentary continental bkfst. Restaurant (see ECHO MOUNTAIN). Ck-out 11 am, ck-in 2:30 pm. On mountain top. Built 1896; stone & frame structure. Totally nonsmoking. Cr cds: A, D, DS, MC, V.

 ⊠ ⊠ ⊠ SC

★ ★ **WAVERLY INN.** *783 N Main St (28792). 704/693-9193; res: 800/537-8195.* 15 rms, 3 story. S $70; D $79-$109; each addl $15; under 12 free; wkly rates. Crib free. TV; cable. Complimentary full bkfst, coffee, tea, refreshments. Restaurant nearby. Ck-out 11 am, ck-in after 1 pm. Golf privileges. Game rm. Restored guest house (1898); Victorian decor, upstairs sun porch. Cr cds: A, DS, MC, V.

⊠ ⊠

★ ★ **WOODFIELD INN.** *(US 25, Flat Rock 28731) 3 mi S on US 25. 704/693-6016; res: 800/533-6016.* 18 rms, 9 with bath, 3 story. No A/C. May-Oct: S $55-$90; D $65-$100; lower rates rest of yr. Complimentary continental bkfst. Ck-out noon. Antiques. Nature trail. Built 1852. Cr cds: MC, V.

⊠

Restaurants

★ ★ **ECHO MOUNTAIN.** *(See Echo Mountain) 704/693-9626.* Hrs: 11:30 am-2 pm, 5-9 pm. Closed Mon & Tues; also Jan. Res accepted. Bar. Semi-a la carte: lunch $5.95-$9.95, dinner $9.95-$19.95. Specializes in fresh seafood, beef. Parking. Dining rm of inn built 1896. Cr cds: A, DS, MC, V.

★ ★ ★ **EXPRESSIONS.** *114 N Main St. 704/693-8516.* Hrs: 6-9 pm. Closed Sun; most major hols; also mid-Jan-mid-Feb. Res accepted. Creative Amer menu. Bar. Wine cellar. Semi-a la carte: dinner $13.50-$22.50. Child's meals. Specializes in veal, pork, fish. Fine dining in subdued atmosphere. Cr cds: D, MC, V.

D

Hickory (B-4)

Pop: 28,301 **Elev:** 1,163 ft **Area code:** 704 **Zip:** 28601

Nationally known brands of furniture and hosiery are produced here, as are ceramics and electronic equipment.

What to See and Do

1. **Arts Center of Catawba Valley.** 243 3rd Ave NE. Here are

 Hickory Museum of Art. American realist 19th- & 20th-century art, including works by Gilbert Stuart; Hudson River School, Thos.

Cole to Homer Martin; American Impressionists; European, Oriental and pre-Columbian pieces; changing exhibits quarterly. (Daily exc Mon; closed Easter, Dec 25) Phone 327-8576. **Free.**

 Catawba Science Center. Interactive exhibits feature life, earth, medical and physical sciences. Also changing exhibits. (Daily exc Mon; closed hols) Phone 322-8169. **Free.**

2. **Lenoir-Rhyne College** (1891). (Approx 1,500 students) 8th St & 7th Ave NE. Observatory (Sept-Apr, evenings, weather permitting). Concerts, athletic contests, dramatic productions, art exhibits, convocation programs and other special events throughout the academic year. Phone 328-1741.

3. **Lake Hickory.** 4 mi N. A 4,100-acre lake with 105-mi shoreline; created by the Oxford Dam on the Catawba River. Boating, fishing, swimming, marinas.

4. **Catawba County Museum of History.** 3 mi S via US 321, in Newton. Exhibits include a fire engine (1919), country doctor's office (1920), Waugh Cabin (1839), Barringer Cabin (1759), blacksmith shop (1870), and an agriculture exhibit. (Daily exc Mon; closed major hols) Phone 465-0383. **Free.**

5. **Bunker Hill Covered Bridge.** On US 70, approx 10 mi N. One of only two remaining covered bridges in state. Built in 1895, it spans Lyle's Creek. Nature trail, picnicking. Phone 465-0383.

6. **Murray's Mill** (1890). 10 mi E via I-40, in Catawba. Overshot waterwheel; working machinery; milling museum and demonstrations. Country store (1890), folk art gallery (1880) (Thurs-Sun; closed major hols). Mill (Thurs-Sun; also by appt; closed major hols). Sr citizen rate. Phone 465-0383. ¢

(For further information contact the Catawba Co Chamber of Commerce, 470 US 70 SW, PO Box 1828, 28603; 328-6111.)

Seasonal Event

 Auto racing. Hickory Motor Speedway. 4 mi E on US 70. Stock car racing. For schedule, prices phone 464-3655. Mid-Mar-early Oct.

(See Statesville)

Motels

(Rates are generally higher during Furniture Market)

★ ★ **COMFORT SUITES.** *Box 3062 (28603), 1125 13th Ave Dr SE, off I-40 exit 125. 704/323-1211; FAX 704/322-4395.* 114 suites, 2 story, 12 kits. S $60-$100; D $65-$100; each addl $6; under 18 free. Crib free. TV; cable. Pool. Complimentary full bkfst. Coffee in rms. Restaurant adj 6:30 am-11 pm. Ck-out 11 am. Coin lndry. Meeting rms. Exercise equipt; weights, bicycles. Refrigerators, minibars. Cr cds: A, C, D, DS, ER, JCB, MC, V.

D ⊠ ⊠ ⊠ ⊠ SC

★ ★ **HAMPTON INN.** *1520 13th Ave Dr SE. 704/323-1150; FAX 704/324-8979.* 119 air-cooled rms, 2 story. S $50-$54; D $57-$61; under 18 free. Crib free. TV; cable. Pool. Complimentary continental bkfst. Restaurant adj 6 am-8 pm. Ck-out noon. Meeting rm. Cr cds: A, C, D, DS, MC, V.

D ⊠ ⊠ ⊠ SC

✔ ★ **HICKORY MOTOR LODGE.** *484 US 70 SW. 704/322-1740; FAX 704/322-6824.* 86 rms, 1-2 story. S $24-$28; D $28-$33; each addl $4. Crib $4. TV; cable. Complimentary coffee in lobby. Restaurant adj 6 am-8 pm. Ck-out 11 am. Coin lndry. Lawn games. Cr cds: A, DS, MC, V.

★ ★ **HOLIDAY INN.** *1385 Lenoir Rhyne Blvd SE, I-40 exit 125. 704/323-1000; FAX 704/322-4275.* 201 rms, 2 story. S $60-$75; D $66-$81; each addl $6; under 19 free. Crib free. TV; cable, in-rm movies. Indoor pool; whirlpool, sauna. Complimentary coffee in rms. Restaurant 6 am-2 pm, 5-10 pm. Rm serv. Bar 4:30 pm-1 am, Sun to midnight. Ck-out noon. Coin lndry. Meeting rms. Valet serv. Sundries. Some refrigerators. Balconies. Cr cds: A, C, D, DS, JCB, MC, V.

✔ ★ **RED ROOF INN.** *1184 Lenoir Rhyne Blvd.* *704/323-1500; FAX 704/323-1509.* 108 rms, 2 story. S $29.99-$40.99; D $36.99-$47.99; each addl $7; under 18 free. Crib free. Pet accepted, some restrictions. TV; cable. Complimentary coffee in lobby. Restaurant adj. Ck-out noon. Cr cds: A, C, D, DS, MC, V.

✔ ★ **SLEEP INN.** *1179 13th Avenue Dr SE.* *704/323-1140; res: 800/354-7150; FAX 704/324-6203.* 100 rms, shower only, 3 story. S $37-$50; D $42-$60; each addl $5; under 18 free. Crib free. TV; cable, in-rm movies. Swimming privileges. Complimentary continental bkfst, coffee. Restaurant adj open 24 hrs. Ck-out noon. Valet serv. Cr cds: A, C, D, DS, ER, JCB, MC, V.

Inn

★ ★ **HICKORY BED & BREAKFAST.** *464 7th St SW.* *704/324-0548; res: 800/654-2961.* 4 rms, 2 story. Phones avail. S, D $70-$80. Children over 12 yrs only. TV in sitting rm. Pool. Complimentary full bkfst; coffee & iced tea. Ck-out 11 am, ck-in 3 pm. Built 1908; Georgian-style architecture, antiques. Totally nonsmoking. No cr cds accepted.

Restaurant

★ ★ **1859 CAFE.** *433 2nd Ave SW.* *704/322-1859.* Hrs: 5-10 pm. Closed Sun; some major hols. Res accepted. Bar. Semi-a la carte: dinner $13.95-$19.50. Specializes in fresh seafood, prime beef. Entertainment Fri & Sat. Outdoor dining. 3 dining rms in converted house. Cr cds: A, C, D, MC, V.

Highlands (C-2)

Pop: 948 **Elev:** 3,835 ft **Area code:** 704 **Zip:** 28741

Highlands is a summer resort near the Georgia state line. Many unusual plants are part of the primeval rain forest preserve. Completely encircled by Nantahala National Forest (see FRANKLIN), the area surrounding the town is called "land of the waterfalls." A Ranger District office is located here.

What to See and Do

1. **Bridal Veil Falls, Dry Falls.** NW of town on US 64, NC 28. Behind Dry Falls the visitor may stand and look through to the Cullasaja River without getting wet. Also Lower Cullasaja Falls. The road here was cut from vertical cliffs and overlooks the river 250 ft below.

2. **Highlands Nature Center.** E Main St (Horse Cove Rd), 1/2 mi E of jct US 64, NC 28, on grounds of Highlands Biological Station. Cherokee artifacts, minerals of North Carolina; local flora and fauna, botanical garden; nature trail, hikes, lectures, movies. (Late May-Labor Day, daily exc Sun) Phone 526-2623.   **Free.**

3. **Scaly Mountain Ski Area.** 7 mi S on NC 106. Chairlift, rope tow; patrol, school, rentals; snowmaking; cafeteria. Longest run 2,200 ft; vertical drop 225 ft. (Mid-Dec-early Mar, daily) Half-day rates. Phone 526-3737.   ¢¢¢¢¢

(For further information contact the Chamber of Commerce, PO Box 404; 526-2112.)

(See Cashiers, Franklin)

Motels

★ ★ **HIGHLANDS SUITE HOTEL.** *200 Main St.* *704/526-4502; FAX 704/526-4840.* 28 suites, 2 story. Late June-early Sept & Oct-early Nov: S, D $109-$169; under 17 free; higher rates wkends, hols (2-night min); lower rates rest of yr. Crib free. TV; cable, in-rm movies. Complimentary continental bkfst. Complimentary coffee in rms. Restaurant opp 7 am-9 pm. Ck-out noon. Meeting rms. Bellhops. Minibars, fireplaces. Balconies. Cr cds: A, MC, V.

★ ★ **MOUNTAIN HIGH.** *Box 939, Main St.* *704/526-2790; res: 800/445-7293 (exc NC).* 55 rms, 1-2 story. July-Labor Day, Oct: S, D $78-$128; under 18 free; higher rates: wkends, hols; lower rates rest of yr. Crib $5. Pet accepted. TV; cable. Complimentary continental bkfst. Complimentary coffee in rms. Restaurant opp 7:15 am-9:30 pm. Ck-out noon. Meeting rms. 18-hole golf privileges. Downhill ski 7 mi. Some bathrm phones, in-rm whirlpools, refrigerators, fireplaces. Balconies. Picnic tables. Cr cds: MC, V.

Inn

★ ★ **HIGHLANDS INN.** *Box 1030, Main St near 4th St.* *704/526-9380.* 30 rms, 3 story. Apr-Nov: S, D $79-$99; suites $89; wkly rates. Closed rest of yr. TV in suites. Complimentary continental bkfst. Ck-out 11 am, ck-in 4 pm. Balconies. Built 1880. Antiques. Cr cds: A, MC, V.

Restaurants

★ ★ **FROG AND OWL CAFE.** *3 mi E on US 64 to Buck Creek Rd.* *704/526-5500.* Hrs: 5:30-9:30 pm; Sun 5-9 pm. Closed Nov-Apr. Res required. French menu. Semi-a la carte: dinner $18.95-$27.95. Specialties: trout bleu, Roquefort duck. Parking. Renovated gristmill (ca 1880); operating waterwheel. Intimate dining. Family-owned. Totally nonsmoking. Cr cds: MC, V.

★ ★ **NICK'S.** *NC 28 at Satulah Rd, 4 blks S on NC 28.* *704/526-2706.* Hrs: 11 am-3 pm, 5:30-10 pm. Closed Jan-Feb. Res accepted. Continental menu. Semi-a la carte: lunch $4.95-$10.95, dinner $9.95-$22.95. Child's meals. Specializes in veal, prime rib, seafood, steak. Parking. Cr cds: MC, V.

★ ★ **ON THE VERANDAH.** *2 mi N on US 64W, at Sequoyah Lake.* *704/526-2338.* Hrs: 6-10 pm; Sun brunch noon-2:30 pm. Closed Jan-Mar. Res accepted. No A/C. Setups. Semi-a la carte: dinner $11-$22. Sun brunch $14.50. Specializes in pasta, seafood. Pianist. Valet parking. Verandah dining. Vaulted ceiling; contemporary rustic decor. Cr cds: MC, V.

High Point (A-5)

Founded: 1859 **Pop:** 69,496 **Elev:** 939 ft **Area code:** 910

Furniture and hosiery are the products that make High Point prosperous. The city rests on the highest point along the North Carolina and Midland Railroad, which the state built in 1853. The plank road (finished in 1854), stretching 130 miles from Salem to Fayetteville, made it a center of trade; mileposts on this road had carved numbers instead of painted ones so travelers could feel their way at night.

What to See and Do

1. **High Point Museum.** 1805 E Lexington Ave, at McGuinn Ave. Furniture; materials reflecting the area's military, industrial, social and civic history. (Daily exc Mon; closed major hols) John Haley House (1786) contains 18th- & 19th-century furnishings; blacksmith shop (demonstrations some wkends), weaving house. Phone 885-6859. **Free.**

2. **Giant Bureau.** 508 N Hamilton St. Building designed to look like a chest of drawers, symbolizes city's position as a furniture center. Built in 1926.

3. **Peterson Doll and Miniature Museum.** Main & Green Sts. Collection of more than 1,500 dolls and related artifacts from around the world, some dating back to the 15th century. (Daily exc Mon; closed hols) Phone 885-3655 or 887-3876. ¢¢

(For further information contact the Convention and Visitors Bureau, 300 S Main St, PO Box 2273, 27261; 884-5255.)

Annual Event

Gas Boat Drag Championships. One of several World Series Championship races; on Oak Hollow Lake. 4th wkend July.

Seasonal Event

North Carolina Shakespeare Festival. 220 E Commerce Ave, High Point Theater. Season includes 4 productions and *A Christmas Carol.* Phone 841-6273 or -2273. Late July-Oct & Dec.

(See Burlington, Greensboro, Lexington)

Motor Hotel

★★ HOLIDAY INN-MARKET SQUARE. *236 S Main St (27260).* 910/886-7011; FAX 910/886-5595. 165 rms, 2-6 story. S $50-$53; D $60-$63; each addl $10 suites $95-$110; under 18 free; higher rates Furniture Market. Crib free. TV; cable. Pool. Restaurant 7 am-2 pm, 5-9 pm. Rm serv. Bar 5 pm-midnight. Ck-out noon. Coin lndry. Meeting rms. Barber. Many poolside rms with balcony. Cr cds: A, C, D, DS, MC, V.

Hotel

★★ RADISSON. *135 S Main (27260).* 910/889-8888; FAX 910/889-8888, ext. 7988. 249 rms, 8 story. S $89; D $99; each addl $10; under 18 free. Crib free. TV; cable. Indoor pool. Restaurant 6:30 am-10 pm. Bar 11-2 am. Meeting rms. Concierge. Free airport transportation. Exercise equipt; weights, bicycle, whirlpool, sauna. *LUXURY LEVEL :* BUSINESS CLASS. 36 rms. S $99; D $109; suite $179-$249. Complimentary full bkfst, refreshments. Cr cds: A, C, D, DS, ER, JCB, MC, V.

Restaurant

★★ J. BASUL NOBLE. *114 S Main St.* 910/889-3354. Hrs: 6-11 pm. Closed Sun; major hols. Res accepted. French, Amer menu. Bar to 1 am. A la carte entrees: dinner $12.95-$24.95. Child's meals. Specializes in beef, veal, seafood. Jazz combo Thurs-Sat. Cr cds: A, D, MC, V.

Jacksonville (C-8)

Pop: 30,013 **Elev:** 15 ft **Area code:** 910

This town is on the edge of the New River Marine Base (Camp Lejeune). There is excellent fishing nearby.

Motel

★★ HAMPTON INN. *474 Western Blvd (28546).* 910/347-6500; FAX 910/347-6858. 120 rms, 2 story. S, D $50-$60; each addl $5; under 18 free. Crib free. TV; cable. Pool. Complimentary continental bkfst, coffee. Restaurant adj 11-1 am. Ck-out noon. Meeting rms. Sundries. Health club privileges. Cr cds: A, C, D, DS, MC, V.

Motor Hotels

★★ HOLIDAY INN. *2115 US 17N (28546).* 910/347-1900; FAX 910/347-7593. 118 rms, 4 story. S $50; D $55; each addl $5; under 19 free. Crib free. TV; cable. Pool. Restaurant 6-10 am, 5-10 pm. Rm serv. Bar from 5 pm. Ck-out noon. Bellhops. Valet serv. Some refrigerators. Cr cds: A, C, D, DS, MC, V.

✔ ★★ ONSLOW INN. *201 Marine Blvd (28540),* on US 17, NC 24. 910/347-3151; res: 800/763-3151; FAX 910/346-4000. 92 rms, 2 story. S $37-$42; D $42-$50; each addl $4; under 12 free. Crib free. Pet accepted. TV; cable. Pool; wading pool. Complimentary coffee. Restaurant 6 am-9 pm; Sun 7 am-8 pm. Rm serv. Ck-out noon. Meeting rms. Lawn games. Some private patios, balconies. Picnic tables, grills. Cr cds: A, C, D, DS, MC, V.

Jefferson (A-4)

Founded: 1800 **Pop:** 1,300 **Elev:** 2,960 ft **Area code:** 910 **Zip:** 28640

What to See and Do

1. **Mt Jefferson State Park.** 1 mi S off US 221, at summit of Mt Jefferson. National natural landmark; excellent view of Blue Ridge Mountains. Approx 500 acres. Hiking, nature trails. Picnicking. No camping available. Phone 246-9653.

2. **Industrial tour. Ashe County Cheese Factory.** 2 mi S on NC 194, in West Jefferson. North Carolina's only cheese factory. Viewing of cheese production; samples. (Daily exc Sun; closed some major hols, also Dec 26) Phone 246-2501 or 800/445-1378. **Free.**

(For further information contact the Ashe County Chamber of Commerce, PO Box 31, West Jefferson 28694; 246-9550.)

(See Boone)

Motel

★★ BEST WESTERN ELDRETH. *Box 12, US 221 & NC 88.* 910/246-8845; res: 800/221-8802. 48 rms, 1-2 story. Mid-May-Dec: S, D $51-$62; each addl $5; higher rates wkends mid-May-late Oct; lower rates rest of yr. Crib free. TV; cable. Restaurant 6 am-9 pm. Rm serv. Ck-out 11 am. Meeting rms. Exercise rm; sauna. Cr cds: A, C, D, DS, MC, V.

Kill Devil Hills (Outer Banks) (A-10)

Pop: 4,238.**Elev:** 20 ft **Area code:** 919 **Zip:** 27948

Although the name Kitty Hawk is usually associated with the Wright Brothers, their early flying experiments took place on and near these dunes on the Outer Banks (see).

What to See and Do

Wright Brothers National Memorial. Off US 158, between mileposts 7 & 8. Field where first powered flight took place, Dec 17, 1903, is marked showing takeoff point and landing places. The living quarters and hangar buildings used by the Wrights during their experiments have been reconstructed. The visitor center has reproductions of 1902 glider and 1903 flyer with exhibits on story of their invention. 3,000-ft airstrip. (Daily; closed Dec 25) Sr citizen rate. Phone 441-7430. ¢

(See Manteo, Nags Head)

Motels

✔ ★ BEACH HAVEN. *(4104 Virginia Dare Trail, Kitty Hawk 27949) NC 12 milepost 4.* 919/261-4785. 5 rms. Early July-Labor Day: S, D $59-$89; each addl $5; wkly, wkend rates; higher rates hols (3-day min); lower rates Apr-June & Sept-Oct. Closed rest of yr. Crib free. TV; cable. Complimentary coffee in rms. Restaurant nearby. Ck-out 10 am. Coin lndry. Refrigerators. Swimming beach. Cr cds: MC, V.

★ ★ COMFORT INN. *PO Box 3427, 401 Virginia Dare Trail, NC 12 milepost 8.* 919/480-2600; FAX 919/480-2873. 120 rms, 3 story. Memorial Day-Labor Day: S, D $89-$150; each addl $5; under 18 free; lower rates rest of yr. Crib free. TV; cable. Pool. Complimentary continental bkfst. Complimentary coffee in rms. Ck-out 11 am. Coin lndry. Meeting rms. Some refrigerators. Balconies. On ocean; swimming beach. Cr cds: A, C, D, DS, ER, JCB, MC, V.

★ DAYS INN-OCEAN FRONT. *PO Box 3189, 101 N Virginia Dare Trail, NC 12 milepost 8.5.* 919/441-7211; FAX 919/441-8080. 52 units, 2 story, 15 kits. Mid-June-early Sept: S, D $85-$100; each addl $5; kit. units $120-$145; wkly rates; higher rates: hols, wkends; lower rates mid-Jan-mid-June, early Sept-mid-Dec. Closed rest of yr. Crib free. TV; cable. Pool. Complimentary continental bkfst, coffee. Ck-out 11 am. On swimming beach. Cr cds: A, D, DS, MC, V.

★ ★ RAMADA INN. *PO Box 2716, 1701 S Virginia Dare Trail, milepost 9.5, NC 12.* 919/441-2151; res: 800/635-1824; FAX 919/441-1830. 172 rms, 5 story. Memorial Day-Labor Day: D $119-$149; each addl $10; under 18 free; hol plans; lower rates rest of yr. Crib free. Pet accepted. TV; cable. Indoor pool; whirlpool. Restaurant 7-11:30 am, 5-9 pm; summer 7 am-2 pm, 5-9 pm. Rm serv. Bar 7:30-11:30 am, 5-11 pm; entertainment wkends (in season). Ck-out 11 am. Meeting rms. Bellhops. Sundries. Refrigerators. Private balconies. Lawn games. Cr cds: A, C, D, DS, JCB, MC, V.

Motor Hotels

★ ★ BEST WESTERN OCEAN REEF SUITES. *Box 1440, 107 Virginia Dare Trail.* 919/441-1611; FAX 919/441-1482. 70 kit. suites, 5 story. Apr-Oct: kit. suites (up to 6) $143-$180; each addl $10; under 17 free; lower rates rest of yr. Crib $10. TV; cable, in-rm movies

avail. Heated pool. Complimentary coffee. Restaurant 11 am-11 pm. Ck-out 11 am. Exercise equipt; weight machines, bicycles, whirlpool, sauna, steam rm. Private patios, balconies. Cr cds: A, C, D, DS, JCB, MC, V.

★ ★ HAMPTON INN. *PO Box 1349, 804 N Virginia Dare Trail.* 919/441-0411; FAX 919/441-7811. 96 rms, 4 story. Mid-June-early Sept: S, D $78-$98; under 18 free; higher rates hol wkends; lower rates rest of yr. Crib free. TV; cable. Pool. Complimentary continental bkfst, coffee. Ck-out 11 am. Refrigerators. Many balconies. Cr cds: A, C, D, DS, MC, V.

★ ★ HOLIDAY INN. *1601 Virginia Dare Trail, on US 158 Business between mileposts 9 & 10.* 919/441-6333; FAX 919/441-7779. 105 rms, 4 story. May-Sept: S, D $110-$155; each addl $10; under 19 free; lower rates rest of yr. Crib free. TV; cable. Pool; whirlpool, wading pool. Restaurant 7 am-noon, 5-9 pm. Rm serv. Bar 5:30 pm-1:30 am; entertainment, dancing. Ck-out 11 am. Coin lndry. Meeting rms. Private patios, balconies. Oceanfront deck. On beach; many oceanfront rms. Cr cds: A, C, D, DS, JCB, MC, V.

Inn

✔ ★ CHEROKEE INN. *500 N Virginia Dare Trail, on NC 12, milepost 8.* 919/441-6127; res: 800/554-2764; FAX 919/441-1077. 6 rms, 2 story. No rm phones. June-Aug: S, D $60-$90; lower rates Apr-May & Sept-Nov. Closed rest of yr. Children over 12 yrs only. TV; cable. Complimentary continental bkfst. Ck-out 11 am, ck-in 3-6 pm. Sitting rm. Near swimming beach. Totally nonsmoking. Cr cds: A, MC, V.

Restaurants

★ JOLLY ROGER. *Virginia Dare Trail, just off NC 12 between mileposts 6.5 & 7.* 919/441-6530. Hrs: 6 am-10 pm; Sun from 7 am. Bar. Semi-a la carte: bkfst $1.50-$5.95, lunch $3.95-$6.95, dinner $7.95-$16.95. Specializes in seafood, pasta, beef. Parking. Cr cds: A, D, DS, MC, V.

★ ★ PORT O' CALL. *504 Virginia Dare Trail.* 919/441-7484. Hrs: 5-10 pm; Sun buffet 9:30 am-1:30 pm. Closed Jan-Feb. Res accepted. Bar. Semi-a la carte: dinner $9.95-$16.95. Buffet: lunch (Sun) $9.95. Child's meals. Specializes in seafood, veal, pasta. Entertainment Tues-Sun. Parking. Turn-of-the-century Victorian decor. Cr cds: A, MC, V.

Kinston (B-8)

Pop: 25,295 **Elev:** 44 ft **Area code:** 919 **Zip:** 28501

What to See and Do

CSS *Neuse* State Historic Site. 1 mi W on US 70A. Remains of Confederate ironclad gunboat sunk by her crew in 1865 and not raised until 1963. Visitor center relates story of the *Neuse* through an audio show, artifacts recovered from the gunboat; photographs; memorial has exhibits on life of Caswell, first elected governor of the state of North Carolina. Picnicking. (Apr-Oct, daily; rest of yr, daily exc Mon; closed major hols) Phone 522-2091. **Free.**

Motel

★ ★ **HOLIDAY INN.** Box 130, 3/4 mi S on US 70, NC 58 at jct US 258. 919/527-4155; FAX 919/527-2900. 100 rms, 2 story. S $51-$63; D $53-$68; each addl $4. Crib free. TV; cable. Pool; wading pool. Restaurant 6:30 am-2 pm, 5:30-9 pm. Rm serv. Bar 5 pm-1 am. Ck-out noon. Meeting rms. Cr cds: A, C, D, DS, JCB, MC, V.

Motor Hotel

★ ★ **SHERATON.** 1403 Richlands Rd. 919/523-1400; FAX 919/523-1326. 124 rms, 4 story. June-late Sept: S $70; D $80; each addl $10; under 17 free; wkly, wkend rates; lower rates rest of yr. Crib free. TV; cable. Pool. Restaurant 6:30 am-2 pm, 5-10 pm. Rm serv. Bar 5 pm-1 am; entertainment, dancing. Ck-out noon. Meeting rms. Some refrigerators. Cr cds: A, C, D, DS, MC, V.

Kitty Hawk (Outer Banks) (A-10)

(see Kill Devil Hills)

Laurinburg (C-6)

Settled: (ca 1700) **Pop:** 11,643 **Elev:** 227 ft **Area code:** 910 **Zip:** 28352

Laurinburg is the seat of Scotland County, named for its early Highland Scottish settlers. Industrial development has expanded this agricultural center's economy.

What to See and Do

St Andrews Presbyterian College (1958). (800 students) S city limits. Contemporary-style buildings on an 800-acre campus around a 70-acre lake. Mosaic tile wall depicts story of mankind. Phone 277-5000. On campus are

Vardell Art Gallery. Vardell Bldg. (Mid-Sept-May, Mon-Fri; closed school hols) Phone 277-5000, ext 5023. **Free.**

Science Center. Features interdisciplinary laboratory, guides. (Sept-May & summer session, Mon-Fri; other times by appt) **Free.**

(For further information contact the Laurinburg-Scotland County Area Chamber of Commerce, PO Box 1025, 28353; 276-7420.)

(See Pinehurst, Southern Pines)

Motels

✔ ★ ★ **COMFORT INN.** 1705 US 401 S, 1 mi S of US 74 on US 15/401. 910/277-7788; FAX 910/277-7229. 80 rms, 3 story. S $45-$85; D $45-$95; each addl $6; suites $75; under 18 free; family rates; higher rates Rockingham Races. Crib free. TV; cable. Pool. Complimentary continental bkfst, coffee. Restaurant adj 5:30-9:30 pm. Ck-out noon. Meeting rms. Valet serv. Sundries. Exercise equipt; weights, bicycles. Some in-rm saunas, refrigerators. Cr cds: A, C, D, DS, ER, JCB, MC, V.

★ ★ **HAMPTON INN.** 115 Hampton Circle. 910/277-1516; FAX 910/277-1514. 50 rms, 3 story. S $49-$56; D $56-$62; under 18 free; higher rates race wkends (2-day min). Crib avail. TV; cable. Pool.

Complimentary continental bkfst. Restaurant nearby. Meeting rms. Cr cds: A, C, D, DS, MC, V.

★ ★ **HOLIDAY INN.** Box 1688, 1 1/2 mi SW on US 15, 401 Bypass. 910/276-6555; FAX 910/277-0138. 120 rms, 2 story. S $48-$58; D $54-$64; each addl $6. Crib free. TV; cable. Pool. Restaurant 6 am-2 pm, 5-10 pm. Rm serv 7 am-9 pm. Bar 5 pm-1 am; dancing. Ck-out noon. Meeting rms. Cr cds: A, C, D, DS, JCB, MC, V.

✔ ★ **PINE ACRES LODGE.** Rte 5, Box 135A, US 15, 401 S Bypass. 910/276-1531; res: 800/348-8242; FAX 910/277-1481. 74 rms. S, D $22-$35; each addl $6. TV; cable. Pool; wading pool. Complimentary continental bkfst. Restaurant nearby. Ck-out 11 am. Refrigerators. Cr cds: A, D, MC, V.

Lenoir (A-4)

Pop: 14,192 **Elev:** 1,182 ft **Area code:** 704 **Zip:** 28645

(See Blowing Rock)

Motel

★ ★ **HOLIDAY INN EXPRESS.** 142 Wilkesboro Blvd SE. 704/758-4403. 100 rms, 2 story. S $42-$57; D $52-$57; each addl $5; under 12 free. Crib free. TV. Pool. Complimentary continental bkfst. Ck-out 11 am. Meeting rms. Cr cds: A, C, D, DS, MC, V.

Lexington (B-5)

Settled: 1750 **Pop:** 16,581 **Elev:** 809 ft **Area code:** 704 **Zip:** 27292

In 1775, settlers learned of the battle of Lexington in Massachusetts and decided to name this town for it. Local industry is diversified and includes furniture making, textiles and clothing, food processing, electronics, ceramics, machinery and fiberglass. Native to the area is traditional pork barbecue, which can be found in many local restaurants.

What to See and Do

1. **High Rock Lake.** 10 mi SW on US 70 or S on NC 8. Its 300-mile shoreline is a center for water sports in the piedmont.
2. **Old Davidson County Courthouse** (1858). Center of city. Greek-revival building facing the town square; old courtroom houses museum of local history. (Tues-Fri, also Sun afternoons; closed hols) Phone 242-2035. **Free.**

(For further information contact the Lexington Chamber of Commerce, 235 E Center St, Box C, 27293; 246-5929.)

(For accommodations see Asheboro, High Point, Winston-Salem)

Linville (A-3)

Pop: 244 (est) **Elev:** 3,669 ft **Area code:** 704 **Zip:** 28646

Linville is in the heart of a ruggedly beautiful resort area. Several miles to the south, just off the Blue Ridge Parkway, is scenic Linville Falls, cascading down the steep Linville Gorge, designated a national wilderness. Visible from vantage points in this area are the mysterious Brown Mountain lights.

What to See and Do

Grandfather Mountain (5,964 ft). 2 mi NE via US 221, 1 mi S of intersection of Blue Ridge Pkwy & US 221. Highest peak in the Blue Ridge, with spectacular views, rugged rock formations; mile-high swinging bridge; bald eagles, deer, cougars and black bears and bear cubs in natural habitats. Hiking trails, picnic areas. Museum with exhibits on local animals, birds, flowers, geology; restaurant; gift shop. (Daily; winter, open weather permitting; closed Thanksgiving, Dec 25) Phone 733-4337. ¢¢¢

Annual Events

Grandfather Mountain Nature Photography Weekend. Grandfather Mountain. Nationally known photographers give illustrated lectures; nature photography contest; picnic dinner. Pre-registration required. Early June.

"Singing On The Mountain." On the slopes of Grandfather Mountain. All-day program of modern & traditional gospel music featuring top groups and nationally known speakers. Concessions or bring your own food. 4th Sun June.

Grandfather Mountain Highland Games. MacRae Meadows, on US 221 at Grandfather Mountain. Gathering of members of over 100 Scottish clans and societies to view or participate in traditional Scottish sports, track & field events, mountain marathon; highland dancing, piping and drumming; ceremonies & pageantry. 2nd full wkend July.

(See Banner Elk, Blowing Rock, Boone)

Motel

 ★ **PIXIE MOTOR INN.** Box 277, 1 blk N on NC 181, at jct US 221 & NC 105. 704/733-2597. 25 rms. S $28-$32; D $30-$36; each addl $2. Crib $2. TV; cable. Restaurant adj 7 am-10 pm. Ck-out noon. Beauty shop. Downhill ski 7 mi. No cr cds accepted.

Lodge

★ ★ ★ **ESEEOLA LODGE.** PO Box 99, On US 221, NC 105, 181, 2 mi W of Blue Ridge Pkwy. 704/733-4311; res: 800/742-6717; FAX 704/733-3227. 29 rms, 2 story. No A/C. MAP, Mid-May-mid-Oct: S $130-$220; D $215-$260; each addl $50. Closed rest of yr. Crib free. TV; cable. Pool; wading pool, lifeguard. Supervised child's activities (mid-June-mid Aug). Coffee in rms. Dining rm (public by res) 7:30-9:30 am, 11:30 am-2:30 pm, 7-9 pm (jacket, tie at dinner). Rm serv. Box lunches. Bar. Ck-out noon. Grocery 2 blks. Tennis $10/day. 18-hole golf, greens fee $30, putting green. Croquet court. Rec rm. Soc dir. Free morning newspaper. Rustic architecture; on Lake Kawana; boating, trout fishing. Cr cds: MC, V.

Little Switzerland (B-3)

Founded: 1910 **Pop:** 200 (est) **Elev:** 3,500 ft **Area code:** 704 **Zip:** 28749

A restful summer resort amid the high mountains of western North Carolina, Little Switzerland is bisected by the Blue Ridge Parkway.

What to See and Do

1. **Emerald Village.** NW on County 1100 (McKinney Mine Rd), at Blue Ridge Pkwy milepost 334. Historical area includes mines; North Carolina Mining Museum; Main Street 1920s Mining Community Museum; Gemstone Mine, where visitors can prospect for gems under shaded flumes (fee; equipment furnished); Mechanical Music Maker Museum; waterfall and scenic overlook; shops and deli. (Daily; closed some major hols) Sr citizen rate. Phone 765-6463. ¢¢

2. **Museum of North Carolina Minerals.** At jct Blue Ridge Pkwy, NC 226. Mineral exhibits of the state. (Daily; closed Jan 1, Thanksgiving, Dec 25) Phone 765-2761. **Free.**

3. **Mt Mitchell State Park.** 20 mi S on Blue Ridge Pkwy, then N on NC 128. Adj Pisgah National Forest; natural national landmark. Road leads to summit (6,684 ft; highest point east of the Mississippi River) for incomparable views. Trails. Picnicking, restaurant, refreshment stands. Small tent camping area. Observation tower, museum. Standard fees. Phone 675-4611.

(For further information contact the Mitchell County Chamber of Commerce, Rte 1, Box 796, Spruce Pine 28777; 765-9483.)

(See Burnsville, Linville, Morganton)

Motel

★ ★ **BIG LYNN LODGE.** Box 459, 1½ mi W on NC 226A. 704/765-4257; res: 800/654-5232. 26 motel rms, 2 story, 12 cottages. No A/C. MAP, Mid-Apr-early Nov: S $68-$105; D $77-$105; each addl $23; wkly rates; lower rates (EP) rest of yr. TV lounge. Complimentary full bkfst & dinner. Restaurant 7:30-9 am, 6-7:30 pm. Ck-out 11 am. Coin lndry. Bellhops. Sundries. Rec rm; player piano. Lawn games. Hiking trails. Library. Cr cds: DS, MC, V.

Lodge

★ ★ ★ **SWITZERLAND INN.** Box 399, Blue Ridge Pkwy at milepost 334. 704/765-2153; res: 800/654-4026. 60 units, 8 with A/C, 2 story. May-Oct: S, D $75-$100; each addl $15; suites $90; family rates. Closed rest of yr. TV. Pool. Dining rm 7 am-2 pm, 5:30-9:30 pm. Ck-out 11 am. Meeting rms. Sundries. Tennis. Balconies. Picnic tables. Mountain view. Cr cds: A, MC, V.

Lumberton (C-7)

Founded: 1787 **Pop:** 18,601 **Elev:** 137 ft **Area code:** 910 **Zip:** 28358

Lumberton is the county seat of Robeson County and the home of many industries, including one of the largest tobacco marketing centers in the state. Hunting for quail, duck, dove and rabbit is excellent in the area. Pembroke, to the northwest, is the population center for some 30,000 Lumbee Indians, believed by some historians to include descendants of the "lost colonists" (see FORT RALEIGH NATIONAL HISTORIC SITE).

What to See and Do

1. **One-room schoolhouse.** Restored early American furnished classroom. (Mon-Fri; closed hols) **Free.**

2. **Jones Lake State Park.** 25 mi E on NC 41 to Elizabethtown, then 4 mi N on NC 242. More than 2,200 acres with swimming; fishing; boating. Interpretive trails. Picnicking. Primitive camping (mid-Mar-Nov). Standard fees. Phone 588-4550.

(For further information contact the Chamber of Commerce, PO Box 1008, 28359; 739-4750.)

Seasonal Event

Strike at the Wind. 13 mi W of I-95, at Lakeside Amphitheater on grounds of North Carolina Indian Cultural Center. Outdoor drama about folk hero Henry Berry Lowrie & the Lumbee Indians of Robeson County, NC. Thurs-Sat. Phone 521-3112. Early July-early Sept.

Motels

★ ★ **COMFORT SUITES.** *215 Wintergreen Dr.* 910/739-8800; FAX 910/739-0027. 93 suites, 4 story. Suites $55-$75; each addl $5; under 18 free; wkly rates. Crib free. TV; cable. Pool. Complimentary continental bkfst. Restaurant nearby. Ck-out 11 am. Coin lndry. Meeting rms. Exercise equipt; weights, bicycles, whirlpool, sauna. Health club privileges. Refrigerators. Cr cds: A, C, D, DS, ER, JCB, MC, V.

[D] [≈] [✕] [⊠] [火] [SC]

★ ★ **HOLIDAY INN.** *5201 Fayetteville Rd.* 910/671-1166; FAX 910/671-1166, ext. 314. 108 rms, 2 story. S $55; D $61.50; each addl $6; under 18 free. Crib free. TV; cable. Pool. Restaurant. Rm serv. Ck-out noon. Meeting rms. Bellhops. Valet serv. Airport transportation. Health club privileges. Cr cds: A, C, D, DS, ER, JCB, MC, V.

[D] [≈] [⊠] [火] [SC]

✔ ★ **RAMADA INN.** *3608 Kahn Dr.* 910/738-8261; FAX 910/671-9075. 119 rms, 2 story. Late May-mid-Sept: S $45-$51; D $51-$57; each addl $6; suites $65-$71; under 17 free; higher rates Rice University special events; lower rates rest of yr. Crib free. TV; cable. Pool; sauna. Restaurant 6-10 am, 11:30 am-2 pm, 5:30-9:30 pm. Rm serv. Bar 5 pm-2 am. Ck-out noon. Meeting rms. Health club privileges. Some refrigerators. Cr cds: A, C, D, DS, ER, MC, V.

[D] [≈] [⊠] [火] [SC]

Restaurant

★ ★ **JOHN'S.** *4880 Kahn Dr.* 910/738-4709. Hrs: 5:30-10 pm. Closed Sun; major hols. Res accepted. Continental menu. Wine, beer. Semi-a la carte: dinner $8.95-$22.95. Specializes in beef, seafood, prime rib. Parking. Cr cds: A, C, D, DS, MC, V.

Maggie Valley (B-2)

Pop: 185 **Elev:** 3,020 ft **Area code:** 704 **Zip:** 28751

In 1909 Henry Setzer decided the expanding community of Plott needed a post office. He submitted the names of his three daughters to the Postmaster General, who selected Maggie, then age 14. Lying in the shadow of the Great Smoky Mountains National Park (see), the town is 4 miles from the Soco Gap entrance to the Blue Ridge Parkway and has become a year-round resort area.

What to See and Do

1. **Ghost Town in the Sky.** On US 19. Chairlift, incline railway or shuttle to top of mountain; shows, rides, gun fights, shops; food. (Early May-late Oct, daily) Phone 926-1140. ¢¢¢¢

2. **Soco Gardens Zoo.** On US 19. A 2½-acre zoo with more than 25 different species of animals, including exotic birds, alligators, bears, snow leopards, monkeys, jaguar and wallabies. Reptile house; poisonous and nonpoisonous snake shows. Guided tours. Gift shop. (Memorial Day-Labor Day, daily; early May-Memorial Day & Labor Day-late Oct, daily exc Thurs) Sr citizen rate. Phone 926-1746. ¢¢

3. **Stompin Ground.** US 19. Bluegrass and country music; clogging; exhibition dancers; square dancing (audience participation). (May-Oct, nightly) Phone 926-1288. ¢¢¢

4. **Cataloochee Ski Area.** 4 mi N via US 19 to Fie Top Rd. Double chairlift, T-bar, rope tow; patrol, school, rentals; snowmaking; half-day and twilight rates; cafeteria, bar. Longest run 5,300 ft; vertical drop 740 ft. (Dec-mid-Mar, daily) Phone 926-0285 or 800/768-0285. ¢¢¢¢

(For further information contact the Chamber of Commerce, PO Box 87; 926-1686.)

Annual Event

International Folk Festival. Dance, music and specialty acts; representatives from over ten countries. Phone 452-2997. Last wkend July-1st wkend Aug.

(See Asheville, Cherokee, Waynesville)

Motels

★ ★ **COMFORT INN.** *848 Soco Rd, on US 19.* 704/926-9106. 68 rms, 2 story. June-Oct: S $45-$59; D $57-$80; each addl $8; under 18 free; lower rates rest of yr. Crib free. TV; cable. Pool. Continental bkfst. Complimentary coffee. Restaurant opp 7 am-10 pm. Ck-out 11 am. Meeting rms. Whirlpool in some suites. Cr cds: A, C, D, DS, ER, JCB, MC, V.

[D] [≈] [⊠] [火] [SC]

★ **JOHNATHAN CREEK INN.** *1314 Soco Rd, on US 19.* 704/926-1232. 42 rms, 2 story. June-early Sept, Oct: S, D $59-$89; each addl $5; under 16 free; higher rates: Memorial Day, July 4, Labor Day; lower rates May, rest of Sept. Closed rest of yr. Crib free. TV; cable. Heated pool. Complimentary morning coffee. Restaurant opp 7 am-noon. Ck-out 11 am. Some in-rm whirlpools, refrigerators. Some balconies. Cr cds: A, DS, MC, V.

[D] [⊵] [≈] [⊠] [火] [SC]

✔ ★ **RIVERLET.** *1210 Soco Rd (US 19), ½ mi W on US 19.* 704/926-1900; res: 800/691-9952. 21 rms. July-Labor Day & Oct: S, D $35-$85; lower rates rest of yr. Crib free. TV; cable. Pool. Bkfst avail 7-11 am. Ck-out 11 am. Overlooks 2 streams. Cr cds: DS, MC, V.

[⊵] [≈] [火] [SC]

★ **ROCKY WATERS.** *Rte 1, Box 515, 1½ mi W on US 19, 3 mi E of Blue Ridge Pkwy Soco exit.* 704/926-1585. 32 rms, 2 kits. Mid-June-Labor Day, Oct: S $50; D $65; kit. units $75; lower rates May-mid-June, after Labor Day-Sept. Closed rest of yr. Crib free. TV; cable. Heated pool; wading pool. Playground. Complimentary coffee. Restaurant nearby. Ck-out 11 am. Lawn games. Picnic tables, grill. Rear porches overlook mountain brook. Cr cds: A, DS, MC, V.

[⊵] [≈] [火] [SC]

Resort

★ ★ ★ **MAGGIE VALLEY RESORT COUNTRY CLUB.** *PO Box 99, 2 mi E on US 19.* 704/926-1616; res: 800/438-3861; FAX 704/926-2906. 64 motel rms, 2 story. MAP, Apr-Oct: S $109-$119; D $99-$109/person; each addl $50; under 14 free; wknd rates; lower rates rest of yr. Crib free. TV; cable. Heated pool. Dining rm 7 am-9:30 pm. Box lunches, snack bar, picnics. Bar. Ck-out noon, ck-in 3 pm. Meeting rms. Airport transportation. Tennis. 18-hole golf, greens fee $30, pro, driving range, putting green. Downhill ski 2 mi. Balconies. Cr cds: A, MC, V.

Guest Ranch

★ ★ ★ **CATALOOCHEE RANCH.** *Rte 1, Box 500, 3 mi NE of US 19. 704/926-1401; res: 800/868-1401.* 15 rms in two 2-story lodges, 7 cabins, 2 suites. No A/C. MAP, July, Aug, Oct: S $90-$100; D $120-$180; each addl $55-$60; suites, kit. cottages $175-$210; lower rates mid-Dec-mid-Mar, May, June, Sept. Closed rest of yr. Crib $5. Serv charge 15% in lieu of tipping. Box lunches, cookouts. Beer, wine, setups. Ck-out 11 am, ck-in 3 pm. Tennis. Whirlpool. Downhill ski 1 mi. Lawn games. Card rm. Mountain music entertainment. Fireplace in lobby, cottages, some rms. 5,000-ft elevation. 1,000-acre working ranch; Appalachian stone barn (1870) remodeled to ranch house. Cr cds: A, MC, V.

Restaurant

★ ★ **J ARTHUR'S.** *801 Soco Rd, on US 19 S. 704/926-1817.* Hrs: 5-9:30 pm. Closed Thanksgiving, Dec 25. Bar. Semi-a la carte: dinner $8.75-$21.95. Child's meals. Specializes in gorgonzola cheese salad, steak, fresh seafood. Own desserts. Parking. Loft dining area. Cr cds: A, D, MC, V.

Manteo (A-10)

Pop: 991 **Elev:** 5 ft **Area code:** 919 **Zip:** 27954

Fishing in the waters off Manteo is excellent. A large sport fishing fleet is available for booking at Oregon Inlet as well as on Roanoke Island.

What to See and Do

1. **Fort Raleigh National Historic Site** (see). 3 mi N via US 64.
2. **Elizabethan Gardens.** 3 mi N on US 64/264, on Roanoke Island. 10½ acres include Great Lawn, Sunken Garden, Queen's Rose Garden, herb garden, 16th-century gazebo with thatched roof, ancient garden statuary. Plants bloom all year: spring peak (mid-Apr); summer peak (mid-July); fall peak (mid-Oct); and winter peak (mid-Feb). Gate House Reception Center displays period furniture, English portraits, coat of arms. (Mar-Nov, daily; rest of yr, Mon-Fri; closed Jan 1, Dec 25) Phone 473-3234. ¢¢
3. **North Carolina Aquarium on Roanoke Island.** 3 mi N via US 64/264, Airport Rd exit. Aquarium and marine-oriented educational and research facility. Public aquaria and exhibits, films and educational programs. (Daily; closed Jan 1, Thanksgiving, Dec 25) Phone 473-3493. **Free.**
4. *Elizabeth II* **State Historic Site.** Manteo waterfront. Representative 16th-century sailing vessel similiar to those that brought the first English colonists to the New World more than 400 years ago. Living history interpretation (summer). Visitor center with exhibits and audiovisual program. (Apr-Oct, daily; rest of yr, daily exc Mon; closed some major hols) Sr citizen rate. Phone 473-1144. ¢¢

(For further information contact the Dare County Tourist Bureau, PO Box 399; 473-2138 or 800/446-6262.)

Seasonal Event

The Lost Colony. Drama by Paul Green (see FORT RALEIGH NATIONAL HISTORIC SITE).

(See Kill Devil Hills, Nags Head)

Inn

★ ★ **TRANQUIL HOUSE.** *PO Box 2045, Queen Elizabeth St. 919/473-1404; res: 800/458-7069; FAX 919/473-1526.* 25 rms, 3 story. Memorial Day-Labor Day: S, D $109-$149; suites $149; wkly rates; lower rates rest of yr. Crib $10. TV; cable. Complimentary continental bkfst, coffee. Restaurant 7:30-10:30 am, 5-9:30 pm. Ck-out 11 am, ck-in 3 pm. Bellhops. Airport transportation. Picnic tables. Library. Built in style of a 19th-century Outer Banks inn; cypress woodwork, beveled glass doors, observation tower. On bay; overlooks marina. Cr cds: A, DS, MC, V.

Restaurants

✔ ★ **CLARA'S SEAFOOD GRILL.** *Sir Walter Raleigh St, on the waterfront. 919/473-1727.* Hrs: 11:30 am-9:30 pm; Sun brunch to 2 pm. Closed Thanksgiving, Dec 25; also Jan & Feb. Bar. Semi-a la carte: lunch, dinner $4.95-$15.95. Sun brunch $7.95. Child's meals. Specializes in fresh seafood, beef. Parking. Outdoor dining. 3 dining rms with view of bay. Marine decor. Cr cds: A, DS, MC, V.

★ ★ **QUEEN ANNE'S REVENGE.** *(PO Box 427, Wanchese 27981) S on NC 345. 919/473-5466.* Hrs: 5-9 pm; Fri, Sat to 9:30 pm. Closed Tues; Jan 1, Thanksgiving, Dec 24-25. Wine, beer. Semi-a la carte: dinner $13-$25. Child's meals. Specialty: bouillabaisse. Parking. Artwork. Cr cds: A, DS, MC, V.

Marion (B-3)

Founded: 1843 **Pop:** 4,765 **Elev:** 1,395 ft **Area code:** 704 **Zip:** 28752

Permits for the Linville Gorge Wilderness of the Pisgah National Forest (see BREVARD) can be obtained at the Grandfather Ranger District Office (PO Box 519; 652-2144), located here.

What to See and Do

Linville Caverns. 17 mi N on US 221. Beneath Humpback Mountain. ½-hr guided tours. Gift shop. (Mar-Nov, daily; rest of yr, wkends only) Phone 756-4171. ¢¢

(For accommodations see Little Switzerland, Morganton)

Morehead City (C-9)

Founded: 1857 **Pop:** 6,046 **Elev:** 16 ft **Area code:** 919 **Zip:** 28557

Just across the Intracoastal Waterway from Beaufort, Morehead City is the largest town in Carteret County and a year-round resort town. It is involved in both sport and commercial fishing. The port accommodates oceangoing vessels and charter boats and is one of the world's largest tobacco export terminals. There is also a large summer cottage colony here.

What to See and Do

1. **Town of Atlantic Beach.** 3 mi S on Bogue Banks by causeway & bridge. Swimming, fishing, boating; boardwalk.
2. **Fishing.** Onshore and offshore; charter boats available. Gulfstream fishing (Apr-Nov) for marlin, amberjack, dolphin, mackerel, bluefish.

3. Fort Macon State Park. 2 mi E of Atlantic Beach, on Bogue Banks. This restored fort, built in 1836, was originally used as a harbor defense. Beach (lifeguards in summer), bath house (fee); surf fishing; hiking, nature trails. Museum; interpretive program (summer); battle reenactments. Snack bar. Phone 726-3775. **Free.**

(For further information contact the Carteret County Tourism Development Bureau, PO Box 1406; 726-8148.)

Annual Events

Big Rock Blue Marlin Tournament. Largest tournament of its kind on the East Coast. Fishing for blue marlin; cash awards; registration required. Phone 247-3575. Six days beginning 2nd Mon June.

Atlantic Beach King Mackerel Tournament. Phone 247-2334. Mid-Sept.

North Carolina Seafood Festival. Seafood, arts & crafts, music. Phone 726-NCSF. First wkend Oct.

(See Beaufort)

Motels

★ ★ **BEST WESTERN BUCCANEER.** *2806 Arendell St. 919/726-3115; res: 800/682-4982; FAX 919/726-3864.* 91 rms, 2 story. June-Aug: S, D $59-$75; each addl $5; under 18 free; lower rates rest of yr. Crib $5. TV; cable. Pool. Complimentary full bkfst, coffee. Restaurant adj 6 am-2:30 pm, 5-11 pm. Ck-out noon. Meeting rms. In-rm whirlpools. Cr cds: A, C, D, DS, MC, V.

★ **DAYS INN.** *(602 W Fort Macon Rd, Atlantic Beach 28512)* S on Atlantic Beach Bridge, then 1/2 mi W on Fort Macon Rd (NC 58). *919/247-6400; FAX 919/247-2264.* 90 rms, 2 story. May-Sept: S, D $70-$99; under 12 free; fishing plans; lower rates rest of yr. Crib free. TV; cable. Pool. Complimentary continental bkfst. Restaurant nearby. Ck-out noon. Coin lndry. Refrigerators. Balconies. Picnic tables. Ocean nearby. Cr cds: A, C, D, DS, MC, V.

✔ ★ ★ **ECONO LODGE CRYSTAL COAST.** *PO Box 1229, 3410 Bridges St, 1 blk off US 70. 919/247-2940; FAX 919/247-0746.* 56 rms, 2 story. June-Aug: S, D $48-$79; each addl $5; under 19 free; wkly rates; lower rates rest of yr. Crib free. TV; cable. Pool; wading pool. Complimentary continental bkfst, coffee. Restaurant nearby. Ck-out 11 am. Meeting rms. Cr cds: A, C, D, DS, MC, V.

★ ★ **HAMPTON INN.** *4035 Arendell St. 919/240-2300; FAX 919/240-2311.* 120 rms, 4 story. Memorial Day-Labor Day: S $60-$68; D $66-$74; suites $84-$90; under 18 free; higher rates wkends; lower rates rest of yr. Crib free. TV; cable. Pool. Complimentary continental bkfst. Restaurant nearby. Ck-out 11 am. Meeting rms. Exercise equipt; bicycles, rowing machines. Cr cds: A, C, D, DS, MC, V.

✔ ★ **HOLLOWELL'S.** *(108 E Fort Macon Rd, Atlantic Beach 28512)* S on US 70, then W on NC 58. *919/726-5227.* 29 rms, 1-2 story, 18 kits. June-Aug: S, D $40-$60; kit. cottages $85; under 19 free; lower rates Apr-June & Sept-Oct. Closed rest of yr. Crib free. TV; cable. Pool. Restaurant adj 6 am-10 pm. Ck-out noon. On ocean, swimming beach. Cr cds: D, MC, V.

★ **SEAHAWK MOTOR LODGE.** *(Hwy 58N, Atlantic Beach 28512)* S on US 70, then W on NC 58. *919/726-4146; res: 800/682-6898.* 38 rms, 2 story. June-Labor Day: S, D $80-$90; kit. cottages $1,200/wk; under 12 free; 2-day min wkends; lower rates rest of yr. TV; cable. Restaurant (Apr-Oct) 7 am-2:30 pm. Rm serv. Ck-out noon.

Refrigerators. Many balconies, patios. On ocean, swimming beach. Cr cds: MC, V.

★ ★ **WINDJAMMER INN.** *(PO Box 2906, Atlantic Beach 28512)* S on US 70, then W on NC 58. *919/247-7123; res: 800/233-6466; FAX 919/247-0133.* 45 rms, 5 story. May-Sept: S, D $80-$105; under 12 free; wkly rates; lower rates rest of yr. Crib free. TV; cable. Pool. Complimentary coffee in lobby. Restaurant nearby. Ck-out 11 am. Meeting rms. Bathrm phones, refrigerators. Balconies. On beach. Cr cds: A, MC, V.

Motor Hotel

★ ★ **HOLIDAY INN.** *(Box 280, Salter Path Rd, Atlantic Beach 28512)* 3 mi W on NC 58. *919/726-2544; FAX 919/726-6570.* 114 rms, 5 story. Late Mar-early Sept: S, D $89-$135; each addl $10; under 18 free; golf plans; lower rates rest of yr. Crib free. TV; cable. Pool; wading pool. Restaurant 7 am-1 pm, 5:30-9 pm. Rm serv. Bar 5-10 pm. Ck-out 11 am. Meeting rms. Tennis, golf privileges. Private patios, balconies. Picnic tables. On beach. Cr cds: A, C, D, DS, JCB, MC, V.

Hotel

★ ★ ★ **SHERATON RESORT & CONFERENCE CENTER.** *(PO Box 3040, Atlantic Beach 28512)* 3 mi W on NC 58 to Salter Path Rd. *919/240-1155; FAX 919/240-1452.* 200 rms, 9 story, 16 suites. Mid-May-Labor Day: S, D $104-$154; each addl $15; suites $189; under 18 free; lower rates rest of yr. Crib free. TV; cable. Indoor/outdoor pool; poolside serv. Supervised child's activities (Memorial Day-Labor Day). Complimentary coffee in rms. Restaurant 7 am-10 pm. Bar noon-2 am; entertainment, dancing. Ck-out noon. Meeting rms. Concierge. Gift shop. Exercise equipt; weight machine, bicycles, whirlpool. Refrigerators. Balconies. On ocean. Cr cds: A, C, D, DS, MC, V.

Restaurants

★ ★ **ANCHOR INN.** *N 28th St. 919/726-2156.* Hrs: 6 am-noon, 5-10 pm; Fri, Sat to 11 pm. Closed Dec 24-25. Res accepted. Bar 5-11 pm; Fri, Sat to midnight. Semi-a la carte: bkfst $2-$6, dinner $8.95-$17.95. Child's meals. Specializes in Black Angus beef, fresh local seafood, chicken. Parking. Rattan furniture, ceiling fans, paintings. Cr cds: DS, MC, V.

★ **CAPTAIN BILL'S WATERFRONT.** *701 Evans St. 919/726-2166.* Hrs: 11 am-9 pm; Fri, Sat to 10 pm. Semi-a la carte: lunch $3.95-$17.95, dinner $5.95-$17.95. Child's meals. Specializes in seafood, lemon pie. Parking. Gift shop. On Bogue Sound; overlooks fishing fleet. Cr cds: DS, MC, V.

★ **CHARTER.** *405 Evans St. 919/726-9036.* Hrs: 11 am-10 pm; winter hrs vary. Closed Thanksgiving, Dec 25. Serv bar. A la carte entrees: lunch $3.95-$7.95, dinner $8.95-$26. Child's meals. Specializes in crab cakes, stuffed flounder, shrimp scampi. Salad bar. Parking. Nautical decor. View of waterfront. Cr cds: D, MC, V.

★ **MRS WILLIS.** *3114 Bridges St. 919/726-3741.* Hrs: 11:30 am-9:30 pm; Fri & Sat to 10 pm. Closed Dec 24 & 25. Res accepted. Bar 5 pm-2 am. Semi-a la carte: lunch $3-$5, dinner $5-$20. Child's meals. Specializes in fresh seafood, beef. Parking. Three dining rms. Family-owned. Cr cds: DS, MC, V.

★ **REX.** *4251 Arendell St. 919/726-5561.* Hrs: 5-11 pm. Closed Thanksgiving, Dec 25. Italian, Amer menu. Serv bar. Semi-a la carte: dinner $5-$30. Child's meals. Specialties: live lobster, veal scaloppini. Parking. Own desserts. Cr cds: A, C, D, MC, V.

D | SC

★ **SANITARY FISH MARKET & RESTAURANT.** *501 Evans St. 919/247-3111.* Hrs: 11 am-8:30 pm; June-Aug to 9 pm. Closed Dec-Jan. Semi-a la carte: lunch $3.95-$19.95, dinner $6.95-$19.95. Child's meals. Specializes in fresh seafood. Parking. Overlooks water, fishing fleet, state port. Family-owned. Cr cds: DS, MC, V.

SC

Morganton (B-3)

Pop: 15,085 **Elev:** 1,182 ft **Area code:** 704 **Zip:** 28655

This is the seat of Burke County and a manufacturing town producing furniture, textiles, shoes, chemicals, electronics, clothing and other products. In 1893, the county became a haven for the Waldenses, a religious group from the French-Italian Alps that was seeking freedom and space to expand outside their Alpine homeland.

What to See and Do

Boating, fishing, swimming. Lake James. 8 mi W on NC 126. **Lake Rhodhiss.** 10 mi E off US 70.

(For further information contact the Burke County Chamber of Commerce, PO Box 751, 28680-0751; 437-3021.)

Annual Events

Waldensian Celebration of the Glorious Return. On I-40, exit 112 in Valdese. Commemoration of the end of persecution during the reign of Louis XIV; ethnic games, arts and crafts, dances, food. Phone 879-2129. Mid-Aug.

Historic Morganton Festival. Downtown. Arts, crafts, ethnic foods, band concert. First full wkend Sept.

Seasonal Event

From This Day Forward. Church St, Valdese. Outdoor historical drama depicting hardships of the Waldenses and their struggle for religious freedom. Phone 874-0176. Thurs-Sun evenings. Late July-mid-Aug.

(See Little Switzerland, Marion)

Motels

★ ★ **HOLIDAY INN.** *2400 South Sterling St, 1 mi SE on NC 18, at I-40. 704/437-0171; FAX 704/437-0171, ext. 297.* 135 rms, 2 story. S $44-$49; D $47-$54; each addl $5; under 19 free. Crib free. TV; cable. Pool. Restaurant 6 am-2 pm, 5-10 pm. Rm serv. Bar 5 pm-midnight, Sun from 6 pm. Ck-out noon. Meeting rms. Valet serv. Cr cds: A, C, D, DS, JCB, MC, V.

D | ≋ | ✕ | 🔥 | SC

✔ ★ **SLEEP INN.** *2400 A South Sterling St. 704/433-9000; FAX 704/433-9000, ext. 310.* 61 rms, shower only, 2 story. S $34; D $35-$37; each addl $4; under 19 free; higher rates wkends. Crib free. TV; cable. Swimming privileges. Complimentary coffee in lobby. Restaurant adj 6 am-10 pm. Ck-out noon. Valet serv. Refrigerators avail. Cr cds: A, C, D, DS, JCB, MC, V.

D | ✕ | 🔥 | SC

Nags Head (Outer Banks) (A-10)

Pop: 1,838 **Elev:** 10 ft **Area code:** 919 **Zip:** 27959

This is a year-round fishing and beachcombing town on the Outer Banks (see), just south of Kill Devil Hills. There are fishing piers and boats for rent. Swimming is good in summer. A museum is located at Jockey's Ridge State Park, which boasts one of the largest sand dunes on the East Coast.

The soft sand dunes and Atlantic breezes make this a popular area for hang gliding. Offshore, partly buried in the drifting sand, are many wrecks of both old sailing ships and more modern vessels.

Cape Hatteras National Seashore (see) is south of Nags Head.

Annual Events

Gliding Spectacular. Hang gliding competition, novice through advanced. Spectacular flying and fun events. Phone 441-4124. 2nd wkend May.

Rogallo Kite Festival. Competition for homebuilt kites; stunt kite performances, demonstrations; kite auction. Phone 441-4124. 1st wkend June.

(See Kill Devil Hills, Manteo)

Motels

✔ ★ **BEACON MOTOR LODGE.** *Box 729, 2617 S Virginia Dare Trail, on the oceanfront at milepost 11. 919/441-5501; res: 800/441-4804; FAX 919/441-2178.* 47 rms, 1-2 story, 20 kits. Late May-early Sept: S, D $75-$95; each addl $5; suites $665-$750/wk; kit. units $600/wk; kit. cottages $675-$775/wk; higher rates hols, wkends; lower rates mid-Mar-late May, early Sept-late Oct. Closed rest of yr. Crib $3. TV; cable. Pool; 2 wading pools. Playground. Restaurant nearby. Ck-out 11 am. Coin lndry. Refrigerators. Picnic tables, grill. Sun deck. Beach. Cr cds: A, D, DS, MC, V.

✎ | ≋ | ✕ | 🔥 | 🖌

★ **BLUE HERON.** *6811 Virginia Dare Trail. 919/441-7447.* 30 rms, 3 story, 11 kits. No elvtr. June-Labor Day: D $80-$86; each addl $5; kit. units $89; varied lower rates rest of yr. Crib $2. TV; cable. 2 pools, 1 indoor; whirlpool. Complimentary coffee in rms. Restaurant nearby. Ck-out 11 am. Refrigerators. Porches overlook private beach. Cr cds: MC, V.

D | ✎ | ≋ | 🔥 | 🖌

★ **COMFORT INN.** *(8031 Old Oregon Inlet Rd, Nags Head) 919/441-6315.* 105 rms, 7 story. S, D $95-$145; each addl $10; under 17 free; higher rates hols (3-day min). Crib free. TV; cable. Pool; wading pool. Complimentary continental bkfst. Restaurant nearby. Bar. Ck-out 11 am. Meeting rms. Some refrigerators. Balconies. Swimming beach. Cr cds: A, C, D, DS, MC, V.

D | ✎ | ≋ | ✕ | 🖌 | SC

✔ ★ ★ **ISLANDER.** *PO Box 605, 7001 Virginia Dare Trail, on US 158 Business, near milepost 16. 919/441-6229.* 24 rms, 3 story, 6 kits. No elvtr. Mid-June-early Sept: D, kit. units $95; each addl $7; lower rates Apr-mid-June, early Sept-Oct. Closed rest of yr. TV; cable. Pool. Restaurant nearby. Ck-out 11 am. Coin lndry. Refrigerators. Private patios, balconies. Picnic table, grill. On beach. Cr cds: A, MC, V.

✎ | ≋ | 🔥 | 🖌

★ ★ **QUALITY INN SEA OATEL.** *Box 489, 3¹/₂ mi S on US 158 Business at milepost 16.5. 919/441-7191; FAX 919/441-1961.* 111 rms, 1-3 story. Memorial Day-Labor Day: S, D $90-$125; each addl $8; lower rates rest of yr. Crib free. TV; cable, in-rm movies. Pool; wading pool. Ck-out 11 am. Most rms with balcony overlook ocean. Some rms across street. Cr cds: A, C, D, DS, ER, JCB, MC, V.

★ ★ **SEA FOAM.** *7111 S Virginia Dare Trail. 919/441-7320; FAX 919/441-7324.* 51 rms, 2 story, 18 kits., two 2-bedrm kit. cottages, 1 apt. Late May-early Sept: D $71-$86; each addl $5; kit. units $485-$575/wk; kit. cottages $660/wk; apt. $630/wk; under 12 free; lower rates Mar-late May, early Sept-mid-Dec. Closed rest of yr. Crib $5. TV; cable. Pool. Playground. Restaurant adj 5:30 am-10 pm. Ck-out 11 am. Lawn games. Refrigerators. Some private patios, balconies. Beach. Cr cds: A, MC, V.

★ ★ **SURF SIDE.** *PO Box 400, 6701 S Virginia Dare Trail. 919/441-2105; res: 800/552-7873; FAX 919/441-2456.* 76 rms, 5 story, 14 suites. Mid-June-early Sept: S, D $92-$102; each addl $5; suites, kit. units $159-$169; under 12 free; higher rates hol wkends; lower rates rest of yr. Crib $5. TV; cable. 2 pools, 1 indoor; whirlpool. Complimentary continental bkfst. Restaurant nearby. Ck-out 11 am. Coin lndry. Meeting rms. Rec rm. Refrigerators. Balconies. On beach. Cr cds: A, DS, MC, V.

Motor Hotel

★ ★ **NAGS HEAD INN.** *PO Box 1599, 4701 S Virginia Dare Trail. 919/441-0454; res: 800/327-8881; FAX 919/441-0454.* 100 rms, 5 story. Late May-Labor Day: S, D $95-$145; each addl $10; suites $195; wkly rates; lower rates rest of yr. Crib $5. TV; cable. Indoor/outdoor pool; whirlpool. Complimentary coffee in lobby. Restaurant nearby. Ck-out 11 am. Refrigerators. Balconies. On ocean, swimming beach. Cr cds: A, DS, MC, V.

Inn

★ ★ **FIRST COLONY.** *6720 S Virginia Dare Trail. 919/441-2343; res: 800/368-9390; FAX 919/441-9234.* 26 rms, 3 story, 4 kits. Memorial Day-Labor Day: S, D $125-$200; each addl $30; kit. units $130-$200; lower rates rest of yr. Crib free. TV; cable. in-rm movies avail. Pool. Complimentary continental bkfst, tea. Complimentary coffee in rms. Restaurant nearby. Ck-out 11 am, ck-in 3 pm. Picnic tables, grills. Two-story veranda; overlooks ocean. On 5 acres of landscaped grounds. Cr cds: A, DS, MC, V.

Restaurants

★ ★ **KELLY'S.** *(2316 S Croatan Hwy, Nags Head) 919/441-4116.* Hrs: 5-10 pm. Closed Dec 24 & 25. Bar to 2 am. Semi-a la carte: dinner $10-$20. Child's meals. Specializes in seafood, prime rib, sweet potato biscuits. Parking. Several distinct dining areas. Nautical decor. Cr cds: A, C, D, DS, MC, V.

D

★ ★ **OWENS'.** *7114 S Virginia Dare Trail. 919/441-7309.* Hrs: 5-10 pm. Closed Jan 1, also Dec-Feb. Bar to midnight. Semi-a la carte: dinner $12.95-$16.95. Child's meals. Specializes in crab cakes, grilled fish, lobster bisque. Parking. Historic artifacts of US Lifesaving Service (forerunner of US Coast Guard) on display; uniforms, log books, photographs. Family-owned. Cr cds: A, DS, MC, V.

D

★ ★ **PENGUIN ISLE.** *6708 S Croatan Hwy (US 158), milepost 16. 919/441-2637.* Hrs: 5-10 pm; early-bird dinner to 6 pm. Closed Dec 24-25. Bar 5 pm-midnight. Semi-a la carte: dinner $9.95-$19.95. Child's meals. Specializes in fresh pasta, shrimp Aristotle, mesquite-

grilled tuna steak. Entertainment Fri, Sat. Parking. Nautical decor. View of sound. Cr cds: A, DS, MC, V.

D

✔ ★ ★ **SWEETWATERS.** *2407 S Croatan Hwy (US 158). 919/441-3427.* Hrs: 7 am-10 pm. Closed Nov-Feb. Bar. Semi-a la carte: bkfst $1.95-$5.95, lunch $3.95-$15.95, dinner $8.95-$15.95. Child's meals. Specializes in prime rib, seafood. Parking. Cr cds: A, MC, V.

★ ★ **WINDMILL POINT.** *US 158. 919/441-1535.* Hrs: 4:30-10 pm. Res accepted. Bar. Semi-a la carte: dinner $12.95-$17.95. Child's meals. Specializes in seafood, beef, pasta. Parking. Features memorabilia of SS United States. Cr cds: A, D, MC, V.

D

New Bern (B-9)

Settled: 1710 **Pop:** 17,363 **Elev:** 15 ft **Area code:** 919

The first settlers in this, one of North Carolina's earliest towns, were Germans and Swiss seeking political and religious freedom in the New World. The name Bern came from the city in Switzerland. Many Georgian and Federal-style buildings give New Bern an architectural ambiance unique in North Carolina. Many of these homes can be visited during April and October.

Swimming, boating and freshwater and saltwater fishing can be enjoyed on the Neuse and Trent rivers. A Ranger District office of the Croatan National Forest is located here.

What to See and Do

1. **Tryon Palace Historic Sites & Gardens.** 610 Pollock St, S end of George St, 1 blk S of US 17, 70 Business, NC 55. Built in 1767-70 by the Royal Governor, William Tryon, this "most beautiful building in the colonial Americas" burned by accident in 1798 and lay in ruins until rebuilt between 1952-59. It served as the colonial and first state capitol. Reconstruction, furnishings and 18th-century English gardens are beautiful and authentic. Dramas performed daily during summer. Docent-guided tours (daily; closed Jan 1, Thanksgiving, Dec 24-26). Also self-guided garden tours. Phone 638-1560. Combination ticket includes admission to all historic sites and gardens that are part of the Tryon Palace. Combination ticket ¢¢¢¢ On grounds is

   Dixon-Stevenson House (ca 1830). Early Federal architecture reflects maritime history of the area in its interior woodwork and widow's walk. Furnished in Federal and Empire antiques.

   John Wright Stanly House (ca 1780). Georgian-style house, furnished with 18th-century American antiques. Elegant interior woodwork. Formal gardens typical of the period.

   New Bern Academy (ca 1810). 4 blks from Tryon Palace complex, in the historic residential district. Major surviving landmark of an educational institution founded in the 1760s, the Academy is restored as a self-guided museum of New Bern Civil War history, early education and local architecture. Phone 638-1560.

2. **Attmore-Oliver House** (ca 1790). 510 Pollock St. This house, headquarters for the New Bern Historical Society, exhibits 18th- and 19th-century furnishings and historical objects, including Civil War artifacts, doll collection. (Early Apr-mid-Dec, Tues-Sat; also by appt; closed July 4, Thanksgiving, Dec 25) Phone 638-8558. **Free.**

3. **New Bern Firemen's Museum.** 410 Hancock St, off US 17, 70 Business. Antique firefighting equipment, relics and pictures, 1917 double-size ladder trucks & engines, 1913 pumper. (Daily; closed some major hols) Phone 636-4020 or -4087. ¢

4. **Croatan National Forest.** SE via US 17, 70. A unique coastal forest (157,724 acres), with many estuaries and waterways; north-

ernmost habitat of the alligator. Pocosins (Indian for "swamp on a hill") have many unusual dwarfed and insect-eating plants. Swimming, boating and fishing in Neuse River; hunting for deer, bear, turkey, quail and migratory waterfowl; picnicking; camping (fee). For further information contact the Forest Supervisor, 100 Otis St, PO Box 2750, Asheville 28802, phone 704/257-4200; or the District Ranger, 141 E Fisher Ave, 28560, phone 638-5628.

(For further information contact the Visitor Information Center, 219 Pollock St, PO Box 1413, 28560; 637-9400 or 800/437-5767.)

(See Kinston)

Motel

✔ ★ ★ **HAMPTON INN.** *200 Hotel Dr (28562). 919/637-2111; res: 800/448-8288; FAX 919/637-2000.* 101 rms, 4 story. S $54-$61; D $59-$64; under 18 free; higher rates wknds. Crib free. TV; cable. Pool. Complimentary continental bkfst. Restaurant nearby. Ck-out noon. Meeting rms. Exercise equipt; rowers, stair machine. Cr cds: A, C, D, DS, MC, V.

Motor Hotel

★ ★ **RAMADA WATERFRONT INN & MARINA.** *101 Howell Rd (28562). 919/636-3637; FAX 919/637-5028.* 116 rms, 4 story. S $69; D $74; each addl $5; suites $100; under 16 free; wkly rates. Crib free. TV; cable. Pool. Restaurant hrs vary. Rm serv. Bar 4:30 pm-2 am; entertainment. Ck-out noon. Bellhops. Valet serv. Bathrm phones. Refrigerator, whirlpool in suites. Sun deck overlooking marina. Cr cds: A, C, D, DS, ER, JCB, MC, V.

Hotel

★ ★ ★ **SHERATON GRAND.** *Box 130 (28563), One Bicentennial Park. 919/638-3585; FAX 919/638-8112.* 172 rms, 5 story. S $75-$104; each addl $10; suites $150; under 17 free. Crib free. TV; cable. Pool. Restaurant 6:30 am-2 pm, 5-10 pm. Bar 12:30 pm-2 am; entertainment Fri & Sat, dancing. Ck-out noon. Meeting rms. Free airport transportation. Exercise equipt; weight machine, bicycle. Balconies. On river; marina facilities. Cr cds: A, C, D, DS, MC, V.

Inns

★ ★ **AERIE.** *509 Pollock St (28562). 919/636-5553; res: 800/849-5553.* 7 rms, 2 story. S $54-64; D $79-89; each addl $15; under 6 free. TV; cable. Complimentary full bkfst. Ck-out 11 am, ck-in 3 pm. Victorian house built 1882; antiques. One block E of Tryon Palace. Cr cds: A, MC, V.

★ ★ **HARMONY HOUSE.** *215 Pollock St (28560). 919/636-3810.* 9 rms, 2 story. Rm phones avail. S $55; D $85; each addl $20. TV; cable. Complimentary full bkfst, refreshments. Ck-out 11 am, ck-in 3 pm. Greek-revival house built 1850; antiques, artwork. Cr cds: A, MC, V.

★ ★ **KINGS ARMS.** *212 Pollock St (28560). 919/638-4409; res: 800/872-9306.* 10 rms, 3 story. S, D $65-$85; each addl $10. TV; cable. Complimentary continental bkfst. Rm serv. Ck-out 11 am, ck-in 3 pm. Valet serv. Airport transportation. Tennis; golf privileges. In restored house built ca 1848; antiques, canopied beds. Cr cds: A, MC, V.

★ **NEW BERNE HOUSE.** *709 Broad St (28560). 919/636-2250; res: 800/842-7688.* 7 rms, 3 story. S $60; D $80. Children over 12 yrs only. TV in sitting rm; cable. Full bkfst, tea. Restaurant nearby. Ck-out 11 am, ck-in 2 pm. Free airport transportation. Colonial-revival house (1923); porch. Totally nonsmoking. Cr cds: A, MC, V.

Restaurants

✔ ★ **FRED & CLAIRE'S.** *247 Craven St. 919/638-5426.* Hrs: 11 am-7 pm; Sat to 3 pm. Closed Sun; some major hols. Res accepted. Wine, beer. Semi-a la carte: lunch $1.50-$5.50, dinner $4.95-$7.95. Specializes in casserole dishes, quiche. Housed in historic building (1870). Casual dining. No cr cds accepted.

★ ★ ★ **HARVEY MANSION.** *221 Tryon Palace Dr. 919/638-3205.* Hrs: 11:45 am-2:30 pm, 5:30-10 pm. Closed Sun, Mon; 1st wk of Jan & Dec 25. Res accepted. International menu. Bar. Semi-a la carte: lunch $3.95-$7.50, dinner $11.95-$23.95. Dinner buffet: $8.75. Specializes in seafood, beef, veal. Parking. In 18th-century mansion near confluence of Trent & Neuse rivers. Cr cds: A, C, D, DS, MC, V.

★ ★ **HENDERSON HOUSE.** *216 Pollock St. 919/637-4784.* Hrs: 11:30 am-2 pm, 6-9 pm. Closed Sun-Tues; some hols. Res accepted. Semi-a la carte: lunch $10-$15, dinner $17.95-$26.95. Specializes in veal, Angus beef, seafood, lamb, plum duckling. Parking. In restored historic house built 1790; art gallery on premises. Totally nonsmoking. Cr cds: A, MC, V.

★ **SCALZO'S.** *415 Broad St (28560). 919/633-9898.* Hrs: 5-10 pm. Closed Sun; Dec 25. Res accepted. Italian menu. Wine, beer. Semi-a la carte: dinner $7.95-$14.95. Child's meals. Specializes in chicken, veal, beef. Parking. Three dining areas. Prints, murals of Italian scenes. Cr cds: A, MC, V.

Ocracoke (Outer Banks) (B-10)

Pop: 658 (est) **Elev:** 6 ft **Area code:** 919 **Zip:** 27960

Settled in the 17th century, Ocracoke was, according to legend, once used as headquarters by the pirate Blackbeard. On the Outer Banks (see), Ocracoke offers excellent fishing and hunting for wildfowl. The lighthouse, built in 1823, is still in use.

One of the visitor centers for Cape Hatteras National Seashore (see) is here.

What to See and Do

1. **Cedar Island to Ocracoke Ferry Service.** (Winter & summer, daily) **Swan Quarter to Ocracoke.** (All yr, daily) Ferries are crowded; there may be a wait. Reservations are recommended; they may be made up to 30 days in advance by phone or in person at the ferry terminal: Ocracoke 928-3841; Cedar Island 225-3551; Swan Quarter 926-1111. Reservations are void if vehicle is not in loading lane at least 30 minutes before departure.

2. **Ocracoke to Hatteras Ferry.** Northward across Hatteras Inlet.

(For a complete list of ferry schedules and rates, contact the Ferry Division, Department of Transportation, 113 Arendell St, Morehead City 28557; 726-6446.)

(See Buxton)

Motels

★ ★ **ANCHORAGE INN.** *PO Box 130, Front St.* 919/928-1101. 41 rms, 4 story. May-Oct: S, D $59-$99; higher rates special events; lower rates rest of yr. Crib $5. TV; cable. Pool. Complimentary continental bkfst. Restaurant adj 7 am-9:30 pm. Ck-out 11 am. Local airport transportation. Refrigerator in suites. Balconies. Marina. Cr cds: DS, MC, V.

★ ★ **BLUFF SHOAL.** *Box 217, on NC 12.* 919/928-4301. 7 rms. Memorial Day-Labor Day: S, D $65; each addl $8; under 12, $5; lower rates rest of yr. Crib free. TV; cable. Restaurant opp 6:30 am-9 pm. Ck-out 11 am. Refrigerators. On Silver Lake. Cr cds: DS, MC, V.

★ **BOYETTE HOUSE.** *Box 39, on NC 12, 1 1/2 blks from harbor in village.* 919/928-4261. 12 rms, 2 story. Memorial Day-Labor Day: S $55-$70; D $60-$95; each addl $5; lower rates rest of yr. Crib free. TV. Restaurant adj 7 am-9 pm. Ck-out 11 am. Near beach; swimming. Cr cds: MC, V.

✔ ★ **ISLAND INN.** *PO Box 9, on NC 12.* 919/928-4351. 35 rms, 2-3 story. No elvtr. Late May-early Sept: D $30-$90; each addl $5; cottages $500/wk; lower rates rest of yr. Crib free. TV; cable. Heated pool. Restaurant 7 am-2 pm, 5-9 pm. Ck-out 11 am. Free local airport transportation. Private patios. Near beach. Built 1901; antiques. Cr cds: DS, MC, V.

★ **PONY ISLAND.** *Box 309, 1/2 mi E on NC 12.* 919/928-4411. 39 rms, 9 kits. Memorial Day-Labor Day: S $57; D $67; each addl $5; kit. units $75; cottages $600-$650/wk; lower rates Apr-Memorial Day & after Labor Day-Nov. Closed rest of yr. TV; cable. Restaurant adj 7-11 am, 5-9 pm. Pool. Ck-out 11 am. Sundries. Bicycle rentals. Cr cds: MC, V.

Inn

★ **BERKLEY CENTER COUNTRY INN.** *PO Box 220, on NC 12, near south ferry docks.* 919/928-5911. 9 rms in 2 bldgs, 2 story. No rm phones. S, D $65-$85; each addl $10; under 18 free. Closed Nov-Mar. Crib avail. TV in sitting rm; cable. Complimentary continental bkfst. Restaurant nearby. Ck-out 11 am, ck-in 2 pm. Antiques. Library/sitting rm. No cr cds accepted.

Restaurants

★ ★ **BACK PORCH.** *On NC 12.* 919/928-6401. Hrs: 5-9:30 pm. Closed early Sept-late May. Wine, beer. Semi-a la carte: dinner $10.95-$16.95. Child's meals. Specializes in crab cakes, fresh fish. Parking. Porch dining. Cr cds: MC, V.

✔ ★ **ISLAND INN.** *NC 12.* 919/928-7821. Hrs: 7 am-2 pm, 5-9 pm. Closed Dec-Feb. Semi-a la carte: bkfst $1.95-$5.95, lunch $1.95-$7.95, dinner $7.95-$15.95. Child's meals. Specialties: clam chowder, crab cakes, prime rib. Parking. Nautical decor. Cr cds: MC, V.

Outer Banks (A-10 - B-10)

The Outer Banks are a chain of narrow, sandy islands stretching 175 miles from Cape Lookout to Back Bay, Virginia. Parts of the chain are 30 miles from the mainland. Cape Hatteras is about 75 miles from the southern end. The islands may be reached by bridge from Point Harbor and Manteo or by ferry from Cedar Island and Swan Quarter to Ocracoke (see).

The following Outer Banks areas are included in the *Mobil Travel Guide.* For information on any one of them, see the individual alphabetical listing: Buxton, Cape Hatteras National Seashore, Hatteras, Kill Devil Hills, Nags Head, Ocracoke.

(For further information on the Outer Banks contact the Chamber of Commerce, PO Box 1757, Kill Devil Hills 27948; 919/441-8144.)

Pilot Mountain (A-5)

Pop: 1,181 **Elev:** 1,152 ft **Area code:** 910 **Zip:** 27041

What to See and Do

Pilot Mountain State Park. 5 mi S on US 52. More than 3,700 acres; hard-surfaced road up mountain to parking. Foot trail to base of rocky knob; extensive view. Canoeing & rafting on the Yadkin River. Nature & riding trails. Picnicking. Camping. Standard fees. Phone 325-2355.

Motel

✔ ★ **HOLIDAY INN EXPRESS.** *Box 668, 1 mi W on US 52 at jct NC 268.* 910/368-2237. 68 rms, 2 story. S $39.95; D $46.95; each addl $5; under 12 free. Crib free. TV; cable. Pool. Complimentary continental bkfst. Restaurant 6 am-2 pm, 5-10 pm. Rm serv. Ck-out 11 am. Meeting rms. Valet serv. Sundries. View of mountain. Cr cds: A, C, D, DS, MC, V.

Inn

★ ★ ★ **PINE RIDGE INN.** *(2893 W Pine St, Mt Airy 27030) NW on US 52 then W on NC 89.* 910/789-5034. 6 rms, 2 story. S, D $60-$100; each addl $10. Crib $10. TV; cable. Pool. Complimentary continental bkfst, tea, wine. Dining rm 7:30-9:30 am. Ck-out 11 am, ck-in 2 pm. Bus depot transportation. Tennis privileges 10 mi. Lawn games. Picnic tables, grills. English manor (1949); antique furnishings. Cr cds: A, MC, V.

Pinehurst (B-6)

Founded: 1895 **Pop:** 5,103 **Elev:** 529 ft **Area code:** 910 **Zip:** 28374

A famous year-round resort village, Pinehurst preserves an era steeped both in tradition and golfing excellence. Its New England style was designed over 90 years ago by the firm of Frederick Law Olmsted, which also designed New York's Central Park and landscaped Asheville's Biltmore Estate. Handsome estates and other residences, mostly styled in Georgian colonial, dot the village. The Pinehurst Resort and Country Club (see RESORT) has seven 18-hole golf courses, a

200-acre lake, 28 tennis courts, a gun club and other recreational facilities that are open to members as well as to guests staying there.

What to See and Do

PGA World Golf Hall of Fame. PGA Blvd. Memorabilia, photographs and displays of famous golfers and tournaments; displays depict the history of golf, associations involved in golf and inductees into the Hall of Fame. Also research library. (Mar-Nov, daily; closed Thanksgiving) Sr citizen rate. Phone 295-6651. ¢¢

(For further information contact the Pinehurst Area Convention & Visitors Bureau, PO Box 2270, Southern Pines 28388; 692-3330 or 800/346-5362.)

(See Southern Pines)

Inns

★ ★ ★ **HOLLY INN.** *PO Box 2300, Cherokee Rd.* 910/295-2300; res: 800/682-6901; FAX 910/295-0988. 76 units, 5 story. S, D $119; each addl $20; suites $144; under 10 free. Crib free. TV; cable. Pool. Dining rm 7-10 am, noon-2 pm, 6-9:30 pm; Fri, Sat to 10 pm. Bar 5 pm-midnight; entertainment, pianist Fri-Sat. Ck-out noon, ck-in 3 pm. Tennis, golf privileges. Bicycles avail. Antique furnishings. Built in 1895. Cr cds: A, D, MC, V.

★ ★ **MAGNOLIA.** *PO Box 818, Jct Magnolia & Chinquapin Rds.* 910/295-6900; res: 800/526-5562. 12 rms, 3 story. No rm phones. Mar-May, Oct-Nov: S $85-$100; D $110-$150; family, wkly rates; golf plan; higher rates PGA tour championship; lower rates rest of yr. Crib free. TV; cable. Pool. Complimentary full bkfst. Dining rm 11:30 am-2 pm, 6-9:30 pm. Ck-out noon, ck-in 2 pm. Golf privileges. Restored, turn-of-the-century inn; Victorian decor, antiques, veranda. Cr cds: A, MC, V.

★ **PINE CREST.** *Box 879, Dogwood Rd.* 910/295-6121. 40 rms, 3 story. MAP, Mar-May & early Sept-Nov: S $85-$105; D $140-$180; under 12 free; lower rates rest of yr. Crib free. TV; cable. Dining rm 7-9 am, 7-9 pm. Ck-out noon, ck-in 2 pm. Tennis privileges. 18-hole golf privileges. Golf decor and artifacts in lobby. Cr cds: A, C, D, DS, MC, V.

Resort

★ ★ ★ **PINEHURST RESORT AND COUNTRY CLUB.** *Box 4000, 1/4 mi W on NC 5, 11/2 mi W of US 15, 501.* 910/295-6811; res: 800/487-4653. 270 rms in 4-story lodge, 140 villas (1-3 bedrm), 46 golf, tennis lodges. MAP, mid-Mar-mid-June & early Sept-mid-Nov: D $153/person; villas: D $176/person; tennis, golf, recreational & special hol package plans; under 5 free; varied lower rates rest of yr. Serv charge 15%. Crib free. TV; cable. 5 pools. 5 pools; poolside serv, lifeguard in summer. Dining rm 6:30-10 am, noon-2 pm, 6:30-9:30 pm. Rm serv 6:30 am-11 pm. Box lunches, snack bar. Bar noon-1 am. Ck-out noon, ck-in 4 pm. Concierge. 28 tennis courts, 8 lighted, pro. Seven golf courses, pro; greens fee $70, cart fee $19/person, driving range. Sailing. Bicycles. Skeet, trap shooting, gun club. Soc dir; dancing; entertainment. Rec rm. Exercise equipt; weights, bicycles. Spacious, landscaped grounds. Carriage rides avail. Cr cds: A, C, D, DS, MC, V.

Restaurant

★ **COVES.** *At Market Square, across from Holly Inn.* 910/295-3400. Hrs: 11:30 am-10:30 pm. Res accepted. Continental menu. Bar 11:30-2 am. Semi-a la carte: lunch $2.95-$9, dinner $2.95-

---

$20. Specializes in seafood, pasta, veal. Entertainment Thurs-Sat. Nautical decor. Cr cds: A, MC, V.

Raleigh (B-7)

Founded: 1792 **Pop:** 207,951 **Elev:** 363 ft **Area code:** 919

Though the capital of North Carolina, Raleigh is also known as a center of education and high-technology research. It still retains the flavor of a relaxed residential town with two centuries of history. Fine residences coexist with apartment houses and modern shopping centers; rural areas with meadows and plowed fields can be found within a few miles.

Named for Sir Walter Raleigh, the town was laid out in 1792, following a resolution by the North Carolina General Assembly that an "unalterable seat of government" should be established within 10 miles of Isaac Hunter's tavern. The founders were able to find a site just four miles from the tavern. The site was laid off in a square. Lots within and just outside the city were sold as residences, which helped finance the capitol building and the governor's residence. Both structures were subsequently destroyed (the capitol by fire in 1831, the governor's residence by Union troops during the Civil War). Their replacements remain standing today. Fortunately, many of the lovely homes and gardens of the antebellum period have survived.

Like much of North Carolina, Raleigh was sprinkled with Union sympathizers until Fort Sumter was fired upon. Lincoln's call for volunteers was regarded as an insult, and North Carolina joined the Confederacy. Raleigh surrendered quietly to General Sherman in April, 1865. During Reconstruction, carpetbaggers and scalawags controlled the Assembly, voted themselves exorbitant salaries, set up a bar in the capitol and left permanent nicks in the capitol steps from the whiskey barrels rolled up for the thirsty legislators.

Located within 15 miles of Raleigh is the Research Triangle Park, a 6,000-acre research and development center with more than 50 companies. Complementing these facilities are the resources of three major universities that form the triangle region—North Carolina State University, Duke University in Durham and the University of North Carolina at Chapel Hill.

What to See and Do

1. **State Capitol** (1840). Capitol Square. A simple, stately Greek-revival style building. Statues of honored sons and daughters decorate the grounds. The old legislative chambers, in use until 1963, have been restored to their 1840s appearance, as have the old state library room and the state geologist's office. (Daily; closed Jan 1, Thanksgiving, late Dec) Phone 733-4994 or -3456. **Free.**

2. **State Legislative Building.** Corner of Salisbury and Jones Sts. First building constructed to house a state general assembly (1963); designed by Edward Durell Stone in a blend of modern and classical styles. Tours of chambers may include view of legislators at work. (Daily; closed Jan 1, Thanksgiving, Dec 25) Phone 733-7928. **Free.**

3. **Capital Area Visitor Center.** 301 N Blount St. Information and rest center; brochures. Tours may be scheduled to the State Capitol, the Governor's Executive Mansion, the State Legislative building, museums, historic sites and other attractions. (Daily; closed Jan 1, Thanksgiving, Dec 25 & 26) Phone 733-3456. **Free.**

4. **State Museum of Natural Sciences.** 102 N Salisbury St, N of Capitol Sq. Exhibits depict natural resources of state; Fossil Hall; Marine Mammal Hall. (Daily; closed hols) Phone 733-7450. ¢

5. **North Carolina Museum of Art.** 2110 Blue Ridge Rd. European and American painting and sculpture; Egyptian, Greek, Roman, African and pre-Columbian objects; Judaica collection; changing exhibits. Restaurant. (Daily exc Mon; closed some hols) Braille guides available on request. Phone 833-1935. **Free.**

6. Mordecai Historic Park. Mimosa St and Wake Forest Rd. Preserved plantation home (1785 & 1826) with many original furnishings, noted for its neoclassical architecture; early Raleigh office building, St Mark's chapel, Badger-Iredell Law Office, 1830s herb garden. Also house in which Andrew Johnson, 17th President of the United States, was born. Guided tours. (Daily; closed hols) Phone 834-4844. ¢¢

7. William B. Umstead State Park. Crabtree Creek Section, 10 mi NW on US 70. On 5,377 acres with a 55-acre lake. Fishing; boating. Hiking, riding. Picnicking. Camping (Apr-mid-Dec, Thurs-Sun). Nature study. **Reedy Creek Section,** 10 mi NW off I-40. Approx 1,800 acres. Fishing. Hiking, riding. Picnicking. Nature study. Phone 787-3033 or 677-0062 (Reedy Creek). Gates open from dawn to dusk. Standard hrs, fees.

8. Falls Lake. 12 mi N via NC 50. Man-made lake built as a reservoir and for flood control. Approx 38,000 acres of land and water offer swimming beach, waterskiing; fishing; boating (ramps). Hiking. Picnicking (shelters), playground. Three state recreation areas in vicinity. Phone 676-1027. Per vehicle ¢¢

(For further information contact the Greater Raleigh Convention & Visitors Bureau, 225 Hillsborough St, Suite 400, PO Box 1879, 27602-1879; 834-5900.)

Annual Events

Great Raleigh Festival. 500 Fayetteville St Mall, at Raleigh Civic and Convention Center. Carnival rides & games; arts & crafts; food. Phone 831-6011. Late Apr-Early May.

Artsplosure. Moore Square & City Market. City-wide arts festival. Showcase for regional dance, music, theater performances by nationally known artists; outdoor arts and crafts show. For further information phone 832-8699. Mid-May.

State Fair. State Fairgrounds. 5 mi W on US 1, then 1 mi W on NC 54. For further information contact 1025 Blue Ridge Blvd, 27607; 733-2145 or 821-7400. Oct 13-22.

(See Chapel Hill, Durham)

Motels

★ ★ COMFORT INN. *2910 Capitol Blvd (27604).* 919/878-9550; FAX 919/876-5457. 149 rms, 2-4 story. S $50; D $58; each addl $5; kit. suite $93; family rates; higher rates state fair. Crib free. TV; cable. Pool. Complimentary continental bkfst, coffee. Restaurant nearby. Ck-out noon. Coin lndry. Meeting rms. Exercise equipt; weights, rowers. Some refrigerators. Cr cds: A, C, D, DS, ER, JCB, MC, V.

D 🌊 🏋 ⊠ 🔥 SC

★ ★ COURTYARD BY MARRIOTT. *1041 Wake Towne Dr (27609).* 919/821-3400; FAX 919/821-1209. 153 rms, 4 story, 13 suites. S $65; D $75; suites $75-$85; under 12 free; wkend rates. Crib free. TV; cable. Pool. Complimentary coffee in rms. Restaurant 6:30-10 am; Sat & Sun 7 am-noon. Bar 4-11 pm. Ck-out noon. Coin lndry. Meeting rms. Valet serv. Exercise equipt; weights, bicycles, whirlpool. Refrigerator in suites. Balconies. Cr cds: A, C, D, DS, MC, V.

D 🌊 🏋 ⊠ 🔥 SC

✔ ★ CRICKET INN. *3201 Old Wake Forest Rd (27609).* 919/878-9310; FAX 919/790-1451. 147 rms, 2 story. S, D $39; under 18 free. Crib free. Pet accepted; $100. TV; cable. Pool. Complimentary continental bkfst. Restaurant adj open 24 hrs. Ck-out 11 am. Valet serv. Cr cds: A, C, D, DS, MC, V.

D 🐾 🌊 ⊠ 🔥 SC

★ ★ DAYS INN-SOUTH INN. *3901 S Wilmington (27603).* 919/772-8900; FAX 919/772-1536. 103 rms, 3 story. S $40; D $44; each addl $5; under 12 free. Crib free. TV; cable. Pool. Complimentary continental bkfst. Restaurant adj open 24 hrs. Ck-out 11 am. Cr cds: A, C, D, DS, MC, V.

D 🌊 ⊠ 🔥 SC

✔ ★ ★ FAIRFIELD INN BY MARRIOTT. *2641 Appliance Ct (27604).* 919/856-9800; FAX 919/856-9800, ext. 709. 132 rms, 3 story. S $37; D $40-$42.95; each addl $6; under 18 free. TV; cable. Pool. Complimentary continental bkfst in lobby. Restaurant nearby. Ck-out noon. Meeting rms. Valet serv. Cr cds: A, C, D, DS, MC, V.

D 🌊 ⊠ 🔥 SC

★ ★ HAMPTON INN. *1001 Wake Towne Dr (27609).* 919/828-1813; FAX 919/834-2672. 131 rms, 5 story. S $48-$58; D $54-$62; under 18 free; wkend rates. Crib free. TV; cable. Pool. Complimentary continental bkfst, coffee. Restaurant nearby. Ck-out noon. Meeting rms. Valet serv. Sundries. Health club privileges. Cr cds: A, C, D, DS, MC, V.

D 🌊 ⊠ 🔥 SC

★ ★ THE PLANTATION INN RESORT. *Box 11333 (27604),* 6401 N Capitol Blvd, 9 mi NE on US 1. 919/876-1411; res: 800/992-9662 (exc NC), 800/521-1932 (NC); FAX 919/790-7093. 98 rms, 2 story. S, D $42-$49; suites $55-$70; each addl $5; under 16 free. Crib free. Pet accepted; $25. TV; cable. Pool; wading pool, poolside serv. Playground. Restaurant 7 am-2:30 pm; Sat to 10:30 am. Dining rm 5:30-10:30 pm. Rm serv. Ck-out noon. Meeting rms. Bellhops. Sundries. Putting green. Some refrigerators. Greek-revival detailing. Spacious grounds; attractive landsdcaping. Cr cds: A, C, D, MC, V.

🐾 🛥 🌊 🏃 ⊠ 🔥 SC

✔ ★ RED ROOF INN. *3520 Maitland Dr (27610).* 919/231-0200; FAX 919/231-0228. 115 rms, 3 story. S $30.99-$36.99; D $35.99-$42.99; each addl $5; under 18 free. Crib free. TV; cable. Complimentary coffee in lobby. Restaurant adj 6 am-10 pm. Ck-out noon. Free airport, RR station, bus depot transportation. Cr cds: A, C, D, DS, MC, V.

D ⊠ 🔥

★ ★ RESIDENCE INN BY MARRIOTT. *1000 Navaho Dr (27609).* 919/878-6100; FAX 919/876-4117. 144 kit. suites, 1-2 story. S, D $95-$125; wkly, monthly rates. Crib free. Pet accepted, some restrictions; $100. TV; cable. Heated pool; whirlpool. Complimentary continental bkfst, coffee. Ck-out noon. Coin lndry. Valet serv. Health club privileges. Some bathrm phones. Private patios, balconies. Picnic tables, grills. Cr cds: A, C, D, DS, JCB, MC, V.

D 🐾 🌊 ⊠ 🔥 SC

Motor Hotels

★ ★ COMFORT SUITES-CRABTREE HOTEL. *3908 Arrow Dr (27612).* 919/782-6868; FAX 919/881-9340. 88 suites, 4 story. Suites $70-$100; wkend rates. Crib free. TV; cable. Pool. Complimentary full bkfst Mon-Fri; continental bkfst Sat & Sun. Restaurant nearby. Ck-out noon. Meeting rms. Free airport, RR station, bus depot transportation. Health club privileges. Refrigerators, wet bars. Cr cds: A, C, D, DS, ER, JCB, MC, V.

D 🌊 ⊠ 🔥 SC

★ ★ MEREDITH GUEST HOUSE. *2603 Village Court (27607),* I-440 exit 5, adj to Lake Boone Shopping Center. 919/787-2800; res: 800/237-9363; FAX 919/783-0514. 54 kit. units, 3 story. S, D $65-$105; monthly rates. Crib free. TV; cable. Pool. Playground. Complimentary continental bkfst. Restaurant opp 6 am-10 pm. Ck-out 11 am. Coin lndry. Meeting rms. Free airport transportation. Health club privileges. Picnic tables. Cr cds: A, D, DS, MC, V.

🌊 🔥 SC

★ ★ QUALITY SUITES. *4400 Capital Blvd (27604).* 919/876-2211. 114 suites, 3 story. S, D $105; under 18 free; wkend rates. Crib free. TV; cable, in-rm movies. Pool. Complimentary full bkfst. Complimentary coffee in rms. Restaurant adj 11 am-11 pm. Ck-out noon. Meeting rms. Bellhops. Valet serv. Free airport transportation. Exercise equipt; weight machine, bicycles. Bathrm phones, refrigerators, minibars. Grills. Cr cds: A, C, D, DS, ER, JCB, MC, V.

★ ★ ★ **VELVET CLOAK INN.** *1505 Hillsborough St (27605), in university area, west of downtown.* 919/828-0333; res: 800/334-4372 (exc NC), 800/662-8829 (NC); FAX 919/828-2656. 171 rms, 5 story. S, D $59-$101; each addl $10; suites $95-$285; under 12 free; wkend rates. Crib free. Pet accepted. TV; cable. Indoor/outdoor pool. Complimentary afternoon tea. Restaurant (see CHARTER ROOM). Rm serv. Bar 4:30 pm-1 am. Ck-out noon. Meeting rms. Bellhops. Concierge. Sundries. Airport transportation. Health club privileges. Bathrm phones. Complimentary newspaper. Cr cds: A, C, D, DS, ER, JCB, MC, V.

Hotels

★ ★ **BROWNESTONE.** *1707 Hillsborough St (27605).* 919/828-0811; res: 800/237-0772 (exc NC), 800/331-7919 (NC); FAX 919/834-0904. 192 rms, 9 story. S $70; D $77-$95; each addl $4. Crib free. TV; cable. Pool. Restaurant 6:30 am-10 pm; Sat, Sun from 7 am. Bar 5 pm-midnight. Ck-out 1 pm. Meeting rms. Airport transportation. Balconies. Cr cds: A, C, D, DS, ER, MC, V.

★ ★ **EMBASSY SUITES.** *4700 Creedmoor Rd (27612).* 919/881-0000; FAX 919/782-7225. 225 kit. suites, 9 story. Suites $114-$134; under 12 free; wkend rates. Crib free. TV; cable. Indoor pool. Complimentary full bkfst. Restaurant 11 am-11 pm. Bar to 1 am. Ck-out noon. Meeting rms. Gift shop. Free covered parking. Airport transportation. Exercise equipt; weight machines, stair machine, whirlpool, sauna. Cr cds: A, C, D, DS, JCB, MC, V.

★ ★ ★ **HILTON-NORTH.** *3415 Wake Forest Rd (27609).* 919/872-2323; FAX 919/876-0890. 340 units, 6 story. S $99-$120; D $120-$130; each addl $10; suites $135-$450; wkend rates. Crib free. TV; cable. Indoor pool. Restaurant 6:30 am-10 pm. Bars 11-2 am; entertainment, dancing. Ck-out noon. Convention facilities. Gift shop. Free airport transportation. Exercise equipt; weight machines, bicycles, whirlpool. *LUXURY LEVEL :* **EXECUTIVE TOWERS.** 74 rms. S, D $130; suite $275-$450. Concierge. Private lounge. Full wet bars. Complimentary continental bkfst, refreshments. Cr cds: A, C, D, DS, ER, MC, V.

★ ★ **HOLIDAY INN DOWNTOWN-STATE CAPITAL.** *320 Hillsborough St (27603).* 919/832-0501; FAX 919/833-1631. 202 rms, 20 story. S, D $69-$79; each addl $8; suites $99-$139; under 19 free; wkend rates. Crib free. TV; cable. Pool. Restaurant 6:30 am-2 pm, 5:30-10 pm; Sat 7 am-1 pm, Sun 6:30 am-2 pm. Bar 4 pm-1 am. Ck-out noon. Meeting rms. Free garage parking. Balconies. Cr cds: A, C, D, DS, ER, JCB, MC, V.

★ ★ **HOLIDAY INN-CRABTREE.** *4100 Glenwood Ave (27612).* 919/782-8600; FAX 919/782-8600, ext. 1329. 174 rms, 12 story. S $58-$68; D $62-$74; each addl $6; under 12 free. Crib free. Pet accepted; $6. TV; cable. Indoor pool. Restaurant 6:30 am-10 pm. Bar 5 pm-1 am. Ck-out noon. Meeting rms. Free airport, RR station, bus depot transportation. Exercise equipt; weight machine, treadmill. Some bathrm phones. Cr cds: A, D, DS, JCB, MC, V.

★ ★ ★ **MARRIOTT CRABTREE.** *4500 Marriott Dr (27612), on US 70W opp Crabtree Valley Mall.* 919/781-7000; FAX 919/781-3059. 375 rms, 6 story. S, D $98; wkend plans. Crib free. TV; cable. In-

door/outdoor pool; poolside serv. Complimentary morning coffee. Restaurant 6:30 am-2:30 pm, 5-11 pm; Sat, Sun 7 am-2:30 pm, 5-10 pm. Bar; entertainment, dancing. Ck-out 1 pm. Convention facilities. Gift shop. Free airport transportation. Golf privileges. Exercise equipt; weight machines, bicycles, whirlpool. Balconies. *LUXURY LEVEL :* **CONCIERGE LEVEL.** 68 rms, 5 suites. S, D $105-$123; suites $175-$250. Concierge. Private lounge. Wet bar in suites. Complimentary bkfst, refreshments. Cr cds: A, C, D, DS, ER, JCB, MC, V.

★ ★ ★ **RADISSON PLAZA.** *421 S Salisbury St (27601), in Downtown Mall.* 919/834-9900; FAX 919/833-1217. 362 rms, 17 story. S, D $80-$110; each addl $10; suites (1-2 bedrm) $150-$240; under 18 free; wkend rates. Crib free. TV; cable. Indoor pool. Restaurant 6:30 am-10 pm. Bar 4 pm-1 am. Ck-out noon. Exercise equipt; weights, bicycles, whirlpool, sauna. Cr cds: A, C, D, DS, ER, JCB, MC, V.

★ ★ **SHERATON INN AT CRABTREE VALLEY.** *4501 Creedmore Rd (27612).* 919/787-7111; FAX 919/783-0024. 318 rms, 4-10 story. S $69-$102; D $95-$102; each addl $15; suites $110-$140; under 18 free; wkend rates. Crib free. TV; cable. Indoor pool. Restaurant 6:30 am-10 pm; Sat & Sun 7-10 pm. Bar 4 pm-midnight. Ck-out noon. Meeting rms. Concierge. Gift shop. Free airport, RR station, bus depot transportation. Exercise equipt; weights, bicycles. *LUXURY LEVEL :* **VIP LEVEL.** 24 rms, 2 floors. S $99; D $109. Private lounge, honor bar. Complimentary continental bkfst, refreshments, newspaper. Cr cds: A, C, D, DS, JCB, MC, V.

Inn

★ ★ **THE OAKWOOD INN.** *411 N Bloodworth St (27604).* 919/832-9712; res: 800/267-9712; FAX 919/836-9263. 6 rms, 2 story. S $65-$90; D $75-$110. TV avail. Complimentary full bkfst, tea, sherry. Ck-out 11:30 am, ck-in 3 pm. Historic district; built 1871. Cr cds: A, D, DS, MC, V.

Restaurants

★ ★ **42nd STREET OYSTER BAR.** *508 W Jones St.* 919/831-2811. Hrs: 11:30 am-11 pm; Sat from 5 pm; Sun 5-10 pm. Closed Jan 1, Thanksgiving, Dec 24 & 25. Res accepted. Bar. Semi-a la carte: lunch $4.95-$9.95, dinner $10.95-$34.95. Child's meals. Specializes in seafood, fresh fish, beef, chicken. Jazz, rhythm & blues band Thurs-Sat. Oyster bar. Parking. Nautical decor. Cr cds: A, C, D, MC, V.

★ ★ ★ **ANGUS BARN, LTD.** *Durham Hwy, 12 1/2 mi NW on US 70.* 919/787-3505. Hrs: 5-11 pm; Sun to 10 pm. Closed Jan 1, Thanksgiving, Dec 24-25. Res accepted Sun-Fri. Bar 4 pm-midnight. Wine list. Semi-a la carte: dinner $13.95-$39.95. Child's meals. Specializes in prime ribs of beef, charcoal-broiled steak, seafood. Own baking. Valet parking. Farm decor; fireplaces; Colt revolver display. Family-owned. Cr cds: A, D, MC, V.

★ ★ ★ **CHARTER ROOM.** *(See Velvet Cloak Inn Motor Hotel)* 919/828-0333. Hrs: 6:30 am-10 pm; Sun to 10:30 pm. Res accepted. French, Amer menu. Bar 4:30 pm-1 am. Wine list. Semi-a la carte: bkfst $2-$10, lunch $6.95-$13.95, dinner $7.95-$27.95. Sun brunch $10.95. Child's meals. Own baking, desserts. Valet parking. Cr cds: A, C, D, DS, ER, JCB, MC, V.

✔ ★ **COURTNEY'S.** *407 Six Forks Rd. 919/834-3613.* Hrs: 7 am-2:30 pm. Closed Thanksgiving, Dec 25. Semi-a la carte: bkst, lunch $4-$8. Child's meals. Specializes in omelettes. Parking. Cr cds: MC, V.

D

✔ ★ **IRREGARDLESS CAFE.** *901 W Morgan. 919/833-8898.* Hrs: 11:30 am-2:15 pm, 5:30-9:30 pm; Fri to 10 pm; Sat 5:30-10 pm; Sun 10 am-2 pm. Bar. Semi-a la carte: lunch $3-$6, dinner $10-$13. Specializes in chicken, natural foods, seafood, vegetarian dishes. Jazz, folk & classical musician. Totally nonsmoking. Cr cds: A, MC, V.

D SC

★ **JACQUELINE'S.** *6401 Capital Blvd. 919/876-1411.* Hrs: 7 am-2:30 pm, 5:30-10:30 pm; Sat 7-10:30 am, 5:30-10:30 pm; Sun 7 am-3 pm; Sun brunch 11:30 am-3 pm. Closed Jan 1. Res accepted. Bar. Buffet: bkfst $2.95-$4.50, lunch $5.75-$8.95. Semi-a la carte: lunch $3.95-$6.95, dinner $6.95-$13.95. Sun brunch $8.95. Child's meals. Salad bar. Parking. Cr cds: A, MC, V.

D

✔ ★ **PEKING GARDEN.** *126 Millbrook Rd, in Colony Shopping Ctr. 919/848-4663.* Hrs: 11:30 am-2:30 pm, 5-10 pm. Chinese menu. Bar. Buffet: lunch $4.95, dinner $7.95. Parking. Modern decor with Chinese accents. Cr cds: A, DS, MC, V.

D

★ ★ **WINSTON'S GRILLE.** *6401 Falls of Neuse Rd, in Sutton Square Shopping Center. 919/790-0700.* Hrs: 11 am-10 pm; Fri to 11 pm; Sat 4:30-11 pm; Sun 10:30 am-9:30 pm. Closed most major hols. Res accepted. Bar. A la carte entrees: lunch $4.95-$9.95, dinner $4.95-$17.95. Sun brunch $4.95-$8.95. Child's meals. Specializes in beef, seafood, pasta. Parking. Outdoor dining. Cr cds: A, D, DS, MC, V.

D

Unrated Dining Spots

K & W CAFETERIA. *North Hills Mall, 5¹/₂ mi N off US 1/64 Bypass. 919/782-0353.* Hrs: 11 am-8:30 pm. Closed Dec 25. Avg ck: lunch $3.25-$4, dinner $3.25-$5. Specializes in fried chicken, chicken stew, roast beef. No cr cds accepted.

D

MORRISON'S CAFETERIA. *4011 Capitol Blvd. 919/850-9643.* Hrs: 10:45 am-2:30 pm, 4-8:30 pm; Sat, Sun 10:45 am-8:30 pm. Closed Dec 25. Avg ck: lunch, dinner $3.85. Salad bar. Parking. Cr cds: A, DS, MC, V.

D

Roanoke Rapids (A-8)

Pop: 15,722 **Elev:** 170 ft **Area code:** 919 **Zip:** 27870

What to See and Do

1. **Historic Halifax State Historic Site.** 9 mi SE off US 301 or S on I-95 exit 168. The Halifax Resolves, first formal sanction of American independence, were adopted here April 12, 1776. Buildings include Owens House (1760), Burgess Law Office, Eagle Tavern (1790), Sally-Billy House, clerk's office, jail, Montfort Archaeology Exhibit Center. Other features are Magazine Spring, garden and churchyard. Visitor center; audiovisual programs, exhibits. (Apr-Oct, daily; rest of yr, daily exc Mon; closed some hols) Historical dramas presented in summer (fee). Phone 583-7191. **Free.**

2. **Roanoke Rapids Lake.** NW edge of town. Covers 5,000 acres. Launching facilities.

3. **Lake Gaston.** 10 mi W via US 158 & NC 1214. A 34-mi-long, 20,300-acre lake has fishing, boating (ramps); picnicking.

(For further information contact the Chamber of Commerce, PO Box 519; 537-3513.)

Motels

✔ ★ **COMFORT INN.** *PO Box 716, At I-95 exit 176. 919/537-1011; FAX 919/537-9258.* 100 rms, 2 story. S $38-$50; D $39-$50; each addl $5; under 18 free. Crib free. TV; cable. Indoor pool. Restaurant 6:30 am-10 pm. Ck-out 11 am. Gift shop. Exercise equipt; weight machine, bicycles, whirlpool. Cr cds: A, C, D, DS, MC, V.

D ≈ ✕ ⊠ 🔥 SC

★ ★ **HAMPTON INN.** *1914 Weldon Rd, I-95 exit 173. 919/537-7555; FAX 919/537-9852.* 124 rms, 2 story. S $49-$70; D $54-$70; under 18 free. Crib free. TV; cable. Pool. Complimentary continental bkfst. Restaurant adj 6 am-10 pm. Ck-out noon. Meeting rms. Health club privileges. Cr cds: A, C, D, DS, MC, V.

D ≈ ⊠ 🔥 SC

★ ★ ★ **HOLIDAY INN.** *100 Holiday Dr, jct US 158, I-95. 919/537-1031; FAX 919/537-7848.* 140 rms, 2 story. S $50-$68; D $56-$75; each addl $6; under 19 free. Crib free. TV; cable. Pool. Playground. Restaurant 6 am-2 pm, 5-10 pm. Rm serv. Beer, wine 5 pm-midnight. Ck-out noon. Coin lndry. Meeting rms. Sundries. Health club privileges. Private patios. Cr cds: A, C, D, DS, ER, JCB, MC, V.

D ≈ ⊠ 🔥 SC

Robbinsville (B-1)

Pop: 709 **Elev:** 2,064 ft **Area code:** 704 **Zip:** 28771

A Ranger District office of the Nantahala National Forest (see FRANKLIN) is located here.

What to See and Do

Joyce Kilmer-Slickrock Wilderness. 13 mi NW via US 129, SR 1116 & 1127. A 17,013-acre area within Nantahala National Forest (see FRANKLIN). More than 100 species of trees native to region; trails through forest to view prime specimens. Located within the area is the Joyce Kilmer Memorial Forest, a 3,840-acre stand of virgin timber dedicated to the author of the poem "Trees"; and a National Recreation Trail. Inquire at District Ranger Office (mid-Apr-Oct, wkends & hols), N off US 129; phone 479-6431. **Free.**

(See Bryson City, Fontana Dam)

Motels

★ **SAN-RAN.** *PO Box 75, ¹/₄ mi E on US 129 Bypass. 704/479-3256.* 10 rms. S $30; D $35; each addl $2. TV; cable. Restaurant nearby. Ck-out 10 am. Cr cds: MC, V.

★ ★ **SNOWBIRD MOUNTAIN LODGE.** *275 Santeetlah Rd, 12 mi NW, off US 129. 704/479-3433.* 21 rms, 2 story. No A/C. No rm phones. AP, mid-Apr-early Nov: D $119-$125. Closed rest of yr. Children over 12 yrs only. Dining rm (by res only) 7:45-8:30 am, 1-1:30 pm, 6:15-7 pm. Setups. Ck-out 10 am, ck-in noon. Hiking trails. Lawn games. Rec rm. 100 acres atop mountain; stone lodge with great room; adj to Joyce Kilmer Memorial Forest. Cr cds: MC, V.

D 🔥

Rocky Mount (A-8)

Settled: 1840 **Pop:** 48,997 **Elev:** 120 ft **Area code:** 919

This is one of the country's largest bright-leaf tobacco marts. Cotton products in the form of yarn, bolts of fabric and ready-to-wear clothing flow from the mills. The factories produce fertilizer, furniture, chemicals, metal products, lumber and pharmaceuticals. Rocky Mount is also the home of Hardee's Food Systems.

What to See and Do

Children's Museum. 1610 Gay St, Sunset Park, off US 64, 301 Bypass. Includes touch tank, greenhouse; live animal collection, exhibits. (Easter-mid-Oct, daily; rest of year, Mon-Fri; closed Thanksgiving, Dec 25) Phone 972-1167 or -1168. **Free.**

(For further information contact the Chamber of Commerce, 437 Falls Rd, PO Box 352, 27802; 442-5111.)

Seasonal Event

Tobacco auctions. Numerous warehouses. Inquire locally. Aug-mid-Nov.

(See Wilson)

Motels

✔ ★ **BEST WESTERN.** *1921 N Wesleyan Blvd (27408). 919/442-8101; FAX 919/442-1048.* 72 rms, 2 story. S $37-$42; D $42-$47; each addl $5; under 12 free; higher rates Easter, July 4. Crib free. TV; cable. Pool. Complimentary continental bkfst; full bkfst avail. Ck-out 11 am. Meeting rms. Cr cds: A, C, D, DS, MC, V.

★ **CARLETON HOUSE.** *Box 1246 (27804), 215 N Church. 919/977-0410; FAX 919/985-2115.* 42 rms, 2 story. S $38; D $45; suites $65; under 16 free. Crib free. TV; cable. Pool. Coffee in rms. Restaurant 6:30 am-9 pm; Sat 7 am-10 pm; Sun 7:30 am-8 pm. Ck-out noon. Meeting rms. Sundries. Health club privileges. Cr cds: A, C, D, MC, V.

✔ ★ ★ **FAIRFIELD INN BY MARRIOTT.** *1200 Benvenue Rd (27804). 919/972-9400; FAX 919/972-9400, ext. 709.* 104 rms, 3 story. S $36.95-$45.95; D $40.95-$49.95; each addl $6; under 18 free. Crib free. TV; cable. Pool. Complimentary continental bkfst, coffee in lobby. Ck-out noon. Valet serv. Cr cds: A, C, D, DS, MC, V.

★ **HOLIDAY INN EXPRESS.** *I-95 exit 145 (27809). 919/985-1450; FAX 919/985-2236.* 81 rms, 2 story. S $48; D $52; each addl $4; under 19 free. Crib free. TV; cable. Pool. Complimentary continental bkfst. Restaurant adj open 24 hrs. Ck-out 11 am. Meeting rm. Cr cds: A, C, D, DS, JCB, MC, V.

★ **RAMADA INN.** *Rte 1, Box 160 (27809), 10 mi N at jct US 301 Connector, NC 48, I-95. 919/446-2041.* 121 rms, 2 story. S $44-$59; D $49-$69; each addl $4; under 18 free. Crib free. TV; cable. Pool. Playground. Restaurant 6 am-10 pm. Rm serv 7 am-9 pm. Wine, beer. Ck-out noon. Meeting rms. Sundries. Cr cds: A, C, D, DS, JCB, MC, V.

Motor Hotels

★ ★ **COMFORT INN.** *PO Box 8093 (27804), 200 Gateway Blvd. 919/937-7765; FAX 919/937-7765, ext. 603.* 125 rms, 5 story. S,
D $58-$64; each addl $5; suites $90; under 18 free. Crib free. TV; cable. Pool. Complimentary continental bkfst, coffee. Restaurant adj 6 am-10 pm. Ck-out 11 am. Valet serv. Exercise equipt; weight machine, bicycles. Refrigerator avail, wet bar in suites. Cr cds: A, C, D, DS, ER, JCB, MC, V.

★ ★ ★ **HOLIDAY INN.** *PO Box 7577 (27804), 651 Winstead Ave, 1 mi E of I-95, exit 138. 919/937-6888; FAX 919/937-6888, ext. 194.* 171 rms, 4 story. S, D $75-$81; each addl $6; suites $95-$170; under 12 free. Crib free. TV; cable. Pool. Restaurant 6:30 am-10 pm. Rm serv. Bar. Ck-out noon. Meeting rms. Bellhops. Valet serv. Refrigerator in suites. Cr cds: A, C, D, DS, ER, JCB, MC, V.

Salisbury (B-5)

Founded: 1753 **Pop:** 23,087 **Elev:** 746 ft **Area code:** 704 **Zip:** 28144

A trading, cultural and judicial center since 1753, it is here that Daniel Boone spent his youth and Andrew Jackson studied law. Salisbury's wide, shady streets were twice taken over by military troops. The first time was by Lord Cornwallis during the Revolutionary War, and the Civil War brought General Stoneman. During the Civil War, Salisbury was the site of a Confederate prison for Union soldiers where 5,000 died; they are buried here in the National Cemetery. Among the dead was Robert Livingstone, Union soldier and son of African missionary David Livingstone. Livingstone College was named for the father. Catawba College and Rowan-Cabarrus Community College complete Salisbury's triad of higher learning.

What to See and Do

1. **Dr. Josephus Hall House** (1820). 226 S Jackson. Large antebellum house set amid giant oaks and century-old boxwoods; contains most of its original Federal and Victorian furnishings. House was used as Union commander's headquarters following Civil War. (Sat & Sun afternoons) Phone 636-0103. ¢¢

2. **Rowan Museum.** 116 S Jackson St. In Maxwell Chambers house (1819). Period rooms, authentic regional furniture; material on history of the county; 19th-century garden. (Thurs-Sun, afternoons; closed legal hols, Dec 24) Phone 633-5946. ¢

3. **Old Stone House** (1766). 4 mi SE, off US 52 in Granite Quarry. Built of hand-laid granite with walls two feet thick. Restored (1966); authentically furnished; family burial ground opp. (Apr-Nov, Sat & Sun afternoons) Phone 633-5946. ¢

4. **Waterworks Visual Arts Center.** 1 Water St. Adaptive restoration of former Salisbury Waterworks into arts center. Changing exhibits; studios, classes; courtyard; sensory garden. Guided tours. (Daily exc Mon; closed legal hols). Phone 636-1882. **Free.**

5. **N.C. Transportation Museum.** 2 mi NE via I-85, in Spencer. Transportation museum, railroad yards and shops. Back shop and 37-stall roundhouse. Rolling stock includes six engines (steam and diesel); restored luxury private cars; freight cars, trolley, passenger coaches. Train ride (seasonal; fee). Visitor Center, two exhibit buildings, audiovisual show. (Apr-Oct, daily; rest of yr, daily exc Mon; closed Jan 1, Thanksgiving, Dec 24-25) Phone 636-2889. **Free.**

6. **Poets & Dreamers Garden.** On campus of Livingstone College. Formal, Biblical and Shakespearean gardens; fountain, sundial. Tomb of founder Joseph Charles Price in garden.

7. **Dan Nicholas Park.** 8 mi N on I-85, exit 79. This 330-acre park has lake with fishing; paddle boats (fee). Hiking, nature trail; tennis, miniature golf (fee). Picnicking. Camping hookups (fee). Outdoor theater; two nature museums; petting zoo. Park (all yr). Phone 636-0154 or -2089. **Free.**

(For further information write the Rowan County Convention & Visitors Bureau, PO Box 4044, 28145; 638-3100 or 800/332-2343 or visit the Visitor Information Center at 215 Depot St for brochures, maps and audio tape tours.)

(See Concord, Lexington, Statesville)

Motels

★ ★ **HAMPTON INN.** *1001 Klumac Rd, I-85 exit 75.* 704/637-8000; FAX 704/639-9995. 121 rms, 4 story. S $43; D $49; suites $70; under 18 free; higher rates: Furniture Market, auto racing events. Crib free. Pet accepted, some restrictions. TV; cable. Pool. Complimentary continental bkfst. Complimentary coffee in lobby. Restaurant adj 11 am-11 pm. Ck-out noon. Meeting rms. Health club privileges. Refrigerator in suites. Cr cds: A, C, D, DS, MC, V.

★ ★ ★ **HOLIDAY INN.** *Jake Alexander Blvd S, I-85 exit 75.* 704/637-3100; FAX 704/637-9152. 124 rms, 2 story. S $57-$88; D $60-$88; each addl $6; suites $95-$125; under 18 free; higher rates special events. Crib free. Pet accepted, some restrictions. TV; cable. Indoor/outdoor pool. Restaurant 6:30 am-2 pm, 5:30-10 pm. Rm serv. Bar 4 pm-1 am, Sat from 6 pm; entertainment, dancing Fri, Sat. Ck-out noon. Bellhops. Valet serv. Local airport transportation. Some in-rm steam baths. Refrigerator avail in suites. Cr cds: A, C, D, DS, JCB, MC, V.

Sanford (B-6)

Pop: 14,475 **Elev:** 375 ft **Area code:** 919 **Zip:** 27330

What to See and Do

1. **Raven Rock State Park.** 18 mi S on US 421. A 2,990-acre park characterized by 152-foot outcrop of rock jutting over Cape Fear River. Fishing. Nature trails, interpretive programs. Picnicking. Primitive camping. Standard hrs, fees. Phone 893-4888.

2. **House in the Horseshoe State Historic Site.** 12 mi W on NC 42 to Carbonton, then 5 mi S on SR 1644. House (ca 1770) was the residence of North Carolina Governor Benjamin Williams; site of a Revolutionary War skirmish. (Apr-Oct, daily; rest of yr, daily exc Mon; closed some major hols) Phone 947-2051. **Free.**

Motels

★ ★ **HAMPTON INN.** *1904 S Horner Blvd.* 919/775-2000; FAX 919/775-2005. 50 rms, 3 story. S $42-$50; D $48-$55; under 18 free. Crib free. TV; cable. Pool. Complimentary continental bkfst. Restaurant opp open 24 hrs. Ck-out noon. Meeting rms. Cr cds: A, C, D, DS, MC, V.

✔ ★ **PALOMINO.** *Box 777 (27331), 2¹/₂ mi on US 1, US 15/501 Bypass.* 919/776-7531; res: 800/641-6060; FAX 919/776-9670. 92 rms. S $30-$35; D $35-$40; each addl $2. Crib free. TV; cable. Pool. Playground. Restaurant 6 am-10 pm. Ck-out noon. Meeting rms. Golf privileges. Exercise equipt; weight machines, bicycles, whirlpool, sauna. Picnic tables, grill. Cr cds: A, C, D, DS, MC, V.

Shelby (B-4)

Pop: 14,669 **Elev:** 853 ft **Area code:** 704 **Zip:** 28150

Seat of Cleveland County, this town in the Piedmont boasts of diversified industry and agriculture. It is named for Colonel Isaac Shelby, hero of the Battle of Kings Mountain in the Revolutionary War. (See KINGS MOUNTAIN NATIONAL MILITARY PARK, SC)

(For further information contact the Cleveland County Chamber, PO Box 879, 28151-0879; 487-8521.)

(See Gastonia)

Motel

★ ★ **DAYS INN.** *PO Box 1940, Dixon Blvd & Weisler St.* 704/482-6721; FAX 704/480-1423. 97 rms, 2 story. S $42; D $46; each addl $5; under 18 free. Crib free. TV; cable. Pool. Restaurant 6 am-2 pm, 5-10 pm; Sun 6-10:30 am, 2-11:30 pm. Rm serv. Ck-out noon. Meeting rms. Cr cds: A, D, DS, MC, V.

Inn

★ ★ ★ **INN AT WEBBLEY.** *403 S Washington St (28151).* 704/481-1403; FAX 704/487-0619. 5 rms, 3 story. S, D $95-$150; children over 16 yrs only. TV; cable. Complimentary full bkfst, afternoon tea/sherry. Restaurant nearby. Ck-out 11 am, ck-in 3 pm. Baby grand piano in sitting rm. Colonial-revival house built 1852; antiques. Landscaped grounds with gardens. Cr cds: DS, MC, V.

Smithfield (B-7)

Pop: 7,540 **Elev:** 153 ft **Area code:** 919 **Zip:** 27577

(See Dunn, Goldsboro, Raleigh)

Motels

★ ★ **HOWARD JOHNSON.** *PO Box 1454, 1¹/₂ mi E at jct US 70 & I-95.* 919/934-7176. 60 rms, 2 story. S $40-$45; D $50-$55; each addl $5; under 18 free. Crib free. TV; cable. Pool. Playground. Restaurant 6 am-10 pm. Rm serv. Ck-out noon. Lawn games. Private patios, balconies. Cr cds: A, C, D, DS, ER, JCB, MC, V.

✔ ★ **MASTERS ECONOMY INN.** *Box 529, Jct US 70A & I-95.* 919/965-3771. 119 rms, 2 story. S, D $26; each addl $6; under 18 free. Crib $6. TV; cable. Pool. Ck-out noon. Meeting rms. Cr cds: A, C, D, DS, ER, JCB, MC, V.

South Brunswick Islands (D-7)

The South Brunswick Islands offer wide, gently sloping beaches and beautiful scenery. Located just 50 miles from the Gulf Stream, the region has a subtropical climate and mild temperatures. Resort activities are plentiful and include fishing, swimming, tennis and golf. Shallotte is the hub of the area that includes Holden, Ocean Isle and Sunset beaches. The islands are reached by bridges across the Intracoastal Waterway.

(For further information contact the Chamber of Commerce, PO Box 1380, Shallotte 28459; 910/754-6644 or 800/426-6644.)

Annual Event

North Carolina Oyster Festival. 3rd wkend Oct.

(See Southport; also see Myrtle Beach, SC)

Hotel

★ **CLARION INN-THE WINDS OCEAN FRONT.** *(310 E First St, Ocean Isle Beach 28469)* 1¹/₂ mi N of jct NC 904 & E First St. 910/579-6275; FAX 910/579-2884. 73 units, 3 story, 45 suites, 58 kit. units, 5 houses (1-4 bedrm). No elvtr. Early June-late Aug: S, D $95-$174; each addl $15; suites, kits. $138-$212; houses $389-$439; under 19 free; lower rates rest of yr. Crib $5. TV; cable. Indoor/outdoor pool. Complimentary continental bkfst. Complimentary coffee in rms. No rm serv. Ck-out 11 am. Coin lndry. Meeting rms. No bellhops. Airport transportation. Tennis privileges. 18-hole golf privileges, pro, putting green, driving range. Exercise equipt; weights, bicycles, whirlpool, sauna. Rec rm. Lawn games. Refrigerators, wet bars. Balconies. Picnic tables, grills. On beach. Cr cds: A, C, D, DS, ER, JCB, MC, V.

Southern Pines (B-6)

Pop: 9,129 **Elev:** 512 ft **Area code:** 910 **Zip:** 28387

The Sandhills, among fine longleaf and loblolly pines, are famed for golf and horses. Known as "sand country," it first gained popularity as a resort in the 1880s, but the enthusiasm for golf in the 1920s fueled Southern Pines' growth as a recreational and resort area. The area is still steeped in tradition and history, with golf and equestrian activities as popular as ever.

What to See and Do

1. **Shaw House.** SW Broad St & Morganton Rd. Antebellum house of simple and sturdy style is lightened by unusual mantels of carved cypress. Guided tours (mid-Jan-June & Sept-mid-Dec, Wed-Sun afternoons). Also on premises are Britt Sanders Cabin and Garner House. Phone 692-2051. **Free.**

2. **Weymouth Woods-Sandhills Nature Preserve.** 400 N Ft Bragg, 3 mi SE on Indiana Ave, then N on Ft Bragg Rd. Excellent examples of Sandhills ecology. Hiking trails along pine-covered "sandridges." Natural history museum. (Daily; closed Dec 25) Phone 692-2167. **Free.**

(For further information contact the Pinehurst Area Convention & Visitors Bureau, PO Box 2270, 28388; 800/346-5362.)

Annual Events

Stoneybrook Steeplechase Races. Phone 692-8000. 2nd Sat Apr.

House & Garden Tour. Conducted by Southern Pines Garden Club. Mid-Apr.

(See Pinehurst)

Motels

★ ★ **HAMPTON INN.** *1675 US 1S.* 910/692-9266; FAX 910/692-9298. 126 rms, 2 story. Mar-May, Sept-Nov: S, D $52-$58; each addl $5; under 18 free; golf plan; higher rates: NASCAR races, PGA tournament, Stoneybrook Steeplechase races; lower rates rest of yr. Crib free. TV; cable. Pool. Complimentary continental bkfst, coffee. Restaurant nearby. Ck-out noon. Coin lndry. Meeting rms. Valet serv. Tennis, golf privileges. Health club privileges. Cr cds: A, C, D, DS, MC, V.

★ ★ ★ **HOLIDAY INN.** *Box 1467, On US 1 at Morganton Rd.* 910/692-8585; res: 800/262-5737; FAX 910/692-5213. 158 rms, 2 story. Mar-Oct: S $49-$68; D $59-$78; each addl $6; suites $85-$160; studio rms $49-$75; under 18 free; lower rates rest of yr. Crib free. TV; cable. Pool. Restaurant 6:30 am-9:30 pm. Rm serv. Bar 4 pm-midnight. Ck-out noon. Meeting rms. Valet serv. Tennis. Golf privileges. Exercise equipt; weights, bicycles. Game rm. Cr cds: A, C, D, DS, ER, JCB, MC, V.

Resorts

★ ★ ★ **MID PINES GOLF CLUB.** *1010 Midland Rd, W via US 1, NC 2.* 910/692-2114; res: 800/323-2114; FAX 910/692-4615. 118 rms in 3-story hotel, 7 golf cottages, 10 lakeside villas. Mar-May, Sept-Nov: S $84-$99; D $88-$118; each addl $10; villas S, D $59-$99; under 12 free; MAP avail; golf, tennis package plans; lower rates rest of yr. TV; cable. Pool. Dining rm (public by res) 6:30-9 am, 11:30 am-2 pm, 7-8:30 pm. Box lunches; snack bar. Rm serv in hotel. Bar 11:30 am-11 pm. Ck-out 11 am, ck-in 2 pm. Meeting rms. Airport transportation. Lighted tennis. 18-hole golf, greens fee $35-$65, pro lessons, putting green. Lawn games. Rec rm. Some refrigerators. Cr cds: A, D, MC, V.

★ ★ **PINE NEEDLES.** *PO Box 88, On NC 2, 1 mi W of jct US 1.* 910/692-7111; res: 800/747-7272; FAX 910/692-5349. 71 rms in 10 lodges, 2 story. AP, mid-Mar-mid-June & mid-Sept-mid-Nov: S, D $102-$122/person; under 4 free; wkly rates; golf plans; lower rates rest of yr. Crib free. TV; cable. Heated pool; whirlpool, sauna, poolside serv. Complimentary coffee in rms. Dining rm 7 am-10 pm. Box lunches. Snack bar. Picnics. Rm serv. Bar 2-11 pm. Ck-out 11 am, ck-in 2 pm. Meeting rms. Bellhops. Valet serv. Gift shop. Lighted tennis. 18-hole golf, greens fee $40-$60, pro, putting green, driving range. Bicycles (rentals). Lawn games. Rec rm. Game rm. Some refrigerators. Balconies. Family-owned golf resort with course designed in 1927 by renowned golf course architect Donald Ross. Cr cds: A, MC, V.

Restaurants

★ **LA TERRACE.** *270 Southwest Broad St.* 910/692-5622. Hrs: 11:30 am-2 pm, 6-10 pm. Closed Sun, Mon; Jan 1, Dec 25. Res accepted. Continental menu. Serv bar. A la carte entrees: lunch $7.50-$8.50, dinner $13.50-$18.50. Child's meals. Specializes in seafood, lamb, stuffed Dover sole. Parking. Outdoor dining. Intimate dining in formal atmosphere. Cr cds: MC, V.

★ **THE SQUIRE'S PUB.** *1720 US 1, S on US 1.* 910/695-1161. Hrs: 11 am-10 pm; Fri & Sat to 11 pm. Closed Sun; Thanksgiving, Dec 24 & 25. British menu. Bar. Semi-a la carte: lunch $3.95-$8.49, dinner $3.95-$16.95. Child's meals. Specializes in traditional pub fare, steak, seafood. Parking. 5 dining areas. English decor. Cr cds: MC, V.

✔ ★ **VITO'S.** *311 SE Broad St, off US 1.* 910/692-7815. Hrs: 5-9:30 pm; Sun to 9 pm. Closed Mon; major hols. Italian menu. Semi-a la carte: dinner $5-$13. Child's meals. Specializes in veal, chicken. Parking. Italian decor. No cr cds accepted.

Southport (D-8)

Founded: 1792 **Pop:** 2,369 **Elev:** 22 ft **Area code:** 910 **Zip:** 28461

Saltwater and freshwater fishing is very good in the vicinity of Cape Fear. Deep-sea charter boats are available at Southport, Long Beach and Shallotte Point. There is a good yacht harbor facility for small boats and yachts, a municipal pier, three ocean piers, as well as several beaches and golf courses nearby.

Fort Johnston (1764) was the first fort built in North Carolina. With Fort Fisher and Fort Caswell (1825), it guarded the mouth of the Cape Fear River during the Civil War, making it possible for blockade runners to reach Wilmington. Fort Johnston (restored) is the residence of the Commanding Officer of the Sunny Point Military Ocean Terminal.

What to See and Do

1. **Fort Fisher State Historic Site.** 6 mi E via US 421, ferry. The largest earthworks fort in the Confederacy; until the last few months of the Civil War, it kept Wilmington open to blockade runners. Some of the heaviest naval bombardment of land fortifications took place here on Dec 24-25, 1864 and Jan 13-15, 1865. Tours. Visitor Center has exhibits, audiovisual shows. Reconstructed gun emplacement. Picnic area. (Apr-Oct, daily; rest of yr, daily exc Mon; closed some major hols) Phone 458-5538. **Free.**

2. **Brunswick Town-Fort Anderson State Historic Site.** 14 mi N on NC 133, then 5 mi S on Plantation Road. Brunswick, founded in 1726, thrived as a major port exporting tar and lumber. Fearing a British attack, its citizens fled when the Revolution began; in 1776 the town was burned by British sailors. Twenty-three foundations have been excavated. Built across part of the town are the Civil War earthworks of Fort Anderson, which held out for 30 days after the fall of Fort Fisher in 1865. Visitor Center, exhibits, audiovisual show; marked historical trailside exhibits; nature trail, picnic area. (Apr-Oct, daily; rest of yr, daily exc Mon; closed some major hols) Phone 371-6613. **Free.**

3. **Carolina Power & Light Company Visitors Center.** 2 mi N on NC 87. Audiovisual presentations show history of energy & its use; nuclear reactor model. Picnic area. (June-Aug, daily exc Sat; rest of yr, Mon-Fri; closed hols exc July 4) Phone 457-6041. **Free.**

4. **Ferry Service. Southport to Fort Fisher.** Approx 30 min crossing. For schedule and fee information phone 457-6942 (local service) or 800/293-3779 (NC Dept of Transportation).

5. **Long Beach Scenic Walkway.** E at 20th St SE & 19th Place, across Davis Canal in Long Beach. Crosses several important wetland communities; viewing of maritime forests, wetland birds, marsh animals and seacoast fowl. Phone 278-5518.

(For further information contact the Southport-Oak Island Chamber of Commerce, 4841 Long Beach Rd SE; 457-6964.)

Annual Events

Robert Ruark Chili Cook Off. Easter wkend.

US Open King Mackerel Tournament. 1st wkend Oct.

(See South Brunswick Islands, Wilmington)

Motel

✔ ★ **PORT.** 4821 Long Beach Rd. 910/457-4800. 32 units, 8 kits. Mar-Oct: S, D $33-$43; each addl $3; kit. units $375-$450/month; wknd, wkly rates; lower rates rest of yr. TV; cable. Pool. Restaurant

nearby. Ck-out 11 am. Refrigerators. Beach 1 mi. Cr cds: D, DS, MC, V.

Restaurants

★ ★ **THE PHARMACY.** 110 E Moore St. 910/457-5779. Hrs: 11 am-2:30 pm, 5-9 pm; Sat 5-11 pm. Closed Sun; Jan 1, Thanksgiving, Dec 25. Bar. Semi-a la carte: lunch, dinner $3.75-$24.95. Child's meals. Specializes in prime rib, gourmet sandwiches. 1900s nautical atmosphere. Built 1887, former pharmacy. Cr cds: D, MC, V.

✔ ★ **SAND FIDDLER.** On NC 211, near jct NC 87. 910/457-6588. Hrs: 11 am-2 pm, 5-9 pm; Sat from 5 pm; Sun brunch 11:30 am-2 pm. Closed some major hols. Semi-a la carte: lunch $3-$7, dinner $6-$12. Sun brunch $6.95. Child's meals. Specializes in seafood, prime rib. Parking. Nautical decor. Cr cds: MC, V.

Statesville (B-4)

Founded: 1789 **Pop:** 17,567 **Elev:** 923 ft **Area code:** 704 **Zip:** 28677

Statesville is a community of many small, diversified industries, including furniture, apparel, metalworking and textiles. Iredell County, of which Statesville is the seat, is known for its dairy and beef cattle.

What to See and Do

1. **Duke Power State Park.** 10 mi S via I-77, US 21. On Lake Norman (see CORNELIUS); 1,500 acres. Swimming; fishing; boating (ramp, rentals). Nature trails. Picnicking. Tent & trailer sites. Standard fees. Phone 528-6350.

2. **Fort Dobbs State Historic Site.** N via I-40, US 21, State Rd 1930, then 1 1/2 mi W. Named for Royal Governor Arthur Dobbs, the now-vanished fort was built during the French and Indian War to protect settlers. Exhibits, nature trails, excavations. (Apr-Oct, daily; rest of yr, daily exc Mon; closed some major hols, also wkends Dec-Feb) Phone 873-5866. **Free.**

(For further information contact the Greater Statesville Chamber of Commerce, 115 E Front St, PO Box 1064, 28687; 873-2892.)

Annual Events

Carolina Dogwood Festival. Apr.

Tar Heel Classic Horse Show. Early May.

Iredell County Fair. 1 wk beginning Labor Day.

National Balloon Rally. Van Hoy Campground. 3rd wkend Sept.

(See Cornelius, Hickory, Salisbury)

Motels

★ **FAIRFIELD INN BY MARRIOTT.** 1503 E Broad St. 704/878-2091; FAX 704/873-1368. 118 rms, 2 story. S $40-$46; D $48-$52; each addl $5; under 17 free. Crib free. TV; cable. Pool. Complimentary continental bkfst. Restaurant nearby. Ck-out noon. Cr cds: A, C, D, DS, MC, V.

✔ ★ ★ **HAMPTON INN.** 715 Sullivan Rd. 704/878-2721; FAX 704/873-6694. 122 rms, 2 story. S $38-$44; D $40-$50; under 18 free. Crib free. TV; cable. Pool. Complimentary continental bkfst. Ck-out 11 am. Meeting rm. Cr cds: A, C, D, DS, MC, V.

★ ★ **HOWARD JOHNSON.** *1215 Garner Bagnal Blvd.* *704/878-9691; FAX 704/873-6927.* 136 rms, 2 story. S, D $54-$59; each addl $8; under 18 free. Crib free. TV; cable. Pool; wading pool. Coffee in rms. Restaurant 6:30 am-2 pm, 5-9 pm. Rm serv. Bar 5 pm-midnight. Ck-out noon. Meeting rms. Sundries. Cr cds: A, C, D, DS, ER, JCB, MC, V.

D ≈ ⊠ 🔥 SC

✔ ★ **RED ROOF INN.** *1508 E Broad St.* *704/878-2051; FAX 704/878-2051, ext. 444.* 116 rms, 3 story. S $29.99-$39.99; D $38.99-$49.99; each addl $5; under 18 free. Crib free. TV; cable. Complimentary morning coffee. Restaurant nearby. Ck-out noon. Cr cds: A, C, D, DS, MC, V.

D ⊠ 🔥 SC

Tryon (B-3)

Pop: 1,680 **Elev:** 1,085 ft **Area code:** 704 **Zip:** 28782

On the southern slope of the Blue Ridge Mountains in the "thermal belt," almost at the South Carolina border, Tryon was named for Royal Governor William Tryon, who held office during the Revolution. The Fine Arts Center is the focal point for much of the cultural life of the community.

What to See and Do

White Oak Mountain. Scenic drive around the mountain. Turn off onto Houston Rd at Columbus and take dirt road, which winds around mountain.

(For further information contact the Chamber of Commerce, 401 N Trade St; 859-6236.)

(See Hendersonville)

Inn

★ ★ ★ **PINE CREST.** *200 Pine Crest Lane.* *704/859-9135; res: 800/633-3001.* 4 rms in main building, 25 rms in 9 cottages, 1-2 story, 10 suites. S, D $125-$150; each addl $35; cottage rms $100-$165; suites $140-$435; under 12 free. Crib free. TV; cable. Swimming privileges. Complimentary continental bkfst, sherry. Restaurant (see PINE CREST INN). Rm serv. Ck-out 11 am, ck-in 3 pm. Tennis, golf privileges. Lawn games. Situated on 3 acres in the foothills of the Blue Ridge Mountains; library, stone fireplaces; some rms with equestrian, hunt club theme. Cr cds: A, DS, MC, V.

🎿 🚶 ⊠ 🔥

Restaurant

★ ★ ★ **PINE CREST INN.** *(See Pine Crest Inn)* *704/859-9135.* Hrs: 8-9:30 am, 6-9 pm. Closed Sun. Res accepted. Continental menu. Serv bar. Wine cellar. Semi-a la carte: bkfst $5-$8, dinner $17-$25. Specializes in crab cakes, rack of lamb, crème brulée. Parking. Outdoor dining. Elegant, rustic decor; heavy pine tables, beamed ceiling, stone fireplace. Cr cds: A, DS, MC, V.

Warsaw (C-7)

Pop: 2,859 **Elev:** 160 ft **Area code:** 910 **Zip:** 28398

What to See and Do

Duplin Wine Cellars. 2 mi S via US 117; off I-40 exit 380. Largest winery in state. Videotape, tour, wine-tasting, retail outlet. (Daily exc Sun; closed most hols) Phone 289-3888. **Free.**

Motel

★ ★ **SQUIRE'S VINTAGE INN.** *Rte 2, Box 130 R, On NC 24/50, 5 mi E.* *910/296-1831.* 12 rms. S $49-$56; D $56-$61; each addl $15; under 12 free. TV. Complimentary continental bkfst. Restaurant 11:30 am-2 pm, 5:30-10 pm; Sat, Sun from 5:30 pm. Ck-out 11 am. Golf privileges. Nature trail. English gardens; gazebos. Cr cds: A, D, MC, V.

🎿 🚶 🔥

Restaurant

★ ★ **COUNTRY SQUIRE.** *748 NC 24 & 50.* *910/296-1831.* Hrs: 11:30 am-2 pm, 5:30-10 pm; Sat 5:30-11 pm; Sun noon-2 pm, 5:30-10 pm. Closed Thanksgiving, Dec 24 & 25. Res accepted. Bar. Semi-a la carte: lunch $2.25-$11.25, dinner $8.95-$30.95. Child's meals. Specializes in beef, poultry. Parking. Five dining rms with historical themes. Gardens. Cr cds: A, C, D, MC, V.

D

Washington (B-9)

Founded: 1776 **Pop:** 9,075 **Elev:** 14 ft **Area code:** 919 **Zip:** 27889

First American village named for the first president, Washington was rebuilt on the ashes left by evacuating Union troops in April, 1864. The rebels lost the town in March, 1862, and, because it was an important saltwater port, tried to retake it for two years. Evidence of the shelling and burning can be seen in the stone foundations on Water St. Water sports, including sailing, yachting, fishing and swimming, are popular.

What to See and Do

Bath State Historic Site. 14 mi E on US 264 & NC 92. Oldest incorporated town in state (1705). Buildings include Bonner House (ca 1820), Van Der Veer House (ca 1790) and Palmer-Marsh House (ca 1745). (Apr-Oct, daily; rest of yr, daily exc Mon; closed some major hols) St Thomas Episcopal Church (ca 1735) (daily; free). Visitor Center, film. Picnic area. Phone 923-3971. ¢

(For further information contact the Chamber of Commerce, PO Box 665; 946-9168.)

Annual Event

Washington Summer Festival. Beach music street dance, ski show, arts & crafts, children's rides, more. 3 days last full wknd July.

(See Greenville)

Motels

✔ ★ **COMFORT INN.** *1636 Carolina Ave, US 17N.* *919/946-4444; FAX 919/946-2563.* 55 rms, 2 story. May-early Sept: S $46-$49;

D $51-$55; each addl $5; under 18 free; lower rates rest of yr. Crib free. TV; cable. Pool. Complimentary continental bkfst. Restaurant adj 6 am-10 pm. Ck-out noon. Meeting rm. Exercise equipt; weight machine, stair machine. Refrigerator avail. Cr cds: A, C, D, DS, JCB, MC, V.

⊡ ⩳ 🏃 ⤫ 🔥 SC

★ ★ **HOLIDAY INN.** *916 Carolina Ave.* 919/946-6141; FAX 919/946-6167. 76 rms, 2 story. S $49-$54; D $50-$55; each addl $4; under 18 free. Crib free. TV; cable. Pool. Restaurant 6:30 am-2 pm, 5:30-10 pm. Rm serv. Ck-out noon. Meeting rms. Cr cds: A, C, D, DS, JCB, MC, V.

⊡ ⩳ ⤫ 🔥 SC

Inns

★ **PAMLICO HOUSE.** *400 E Main St.* 919/946-7184. 4 rms, 2 story. S $55-$65; D $65-$75; each addl $10. Children over 6 yrs only. TV; cable. Complimentary full bkfst, coffee, tea. Ck-out 11 am, ck-in 3 pm. Former rector's house (1906); antiques; library. Cr cds: A, DS, MC, V.

⤫ 🔥

✔ ★ ★ **RIVER FOREST MANOR.** *(600 E Main St, Belhaven 27810) Approx 30 mi E on US 264 at marina on Intracoastal Waterway.* 919/943-2151; res: 800/346-2151; FAX 919/943-6628. 12 rms, 2 story. S, D $50-$85. TV; cable. Pool; whirlpool. Complimentary continental bkfst, coffee. Restaurant (see RIVER FOREST MANOR). Ck-out 11 am, ck-in 2 pm. Gift shop. Tennis. View of river. 1899 building, antique furnishings. Golf carts avail for touring town. Cr cds: A, MC, V.

⊡ 🎣 🏌 ⩳ ⤫ 🔥

Restaurant

★ ★ **RIVER FOREST MANOR.** *(See River Forest Manor Inn)* 919/943-2151. Hrs: 6-8:30 pm; Sun brunch 11 am-2 pm. Bar. Dinner buffet $12.95-$15.95. Sun brunch $6.95. Specialties: crabmeat casserole, pickled sausages, oyster fritters. Salad bar. Parking. Classical Revival house built 1899. Cr cds: A, MC, V.

⊡

Waynesville (B-2)

Pop: 6,758 **Elev:** 2,644 ft **Area code:** 704 **Zip:** 28786

Popular with tourists, this area offers mountain trails for riding and hiking, superb scenery, golf and fishing in cool mountain streams. Waynesville is 26 miles from the Cherokee Indian Reservation (see CHEROKEE) and Great Smoky Mountains National Park (see). Maggie Valley (see), about 6 miles northwest, is in a particularly attractive area.

(For information about this area, contact Visitor & Lodging Information, PO Drawer 600, 28786-0600; 800/334-9036.)

(See Asheville, Cherokee, Maggie Valley)

Motels

★ **ECONO LODGE.** *1202 Russ Ave.* 704/452-0353; FAX 704/452-3329. 40 rms, 2 story. June-Oct: S $40; D $54; each addl $5; under 18 free; lower rates rest of yr. Crib free. TV; cable. Pool. Complimentary continental bkfst. Restaurant nearby. Ck-out 11 am. Cr cds: A, C, D, DS, MC, V.

⊡ ⩳ ⤫ 🔥 SC

✔ ★ **PARKWAY INN.** *2506 Dellwood Rd W.* 704/926-1841. 30 rms. June-Labor Day: S, D $30-$48; higher rates Oct, lower rates Apr-May, Sept. Crib $2. TV; cable. Complimentary coffee. Restaurant

nearby. Ck-out 11 am. Refrigerators avail. Picnic tables. Cr cds: A, DS, MC, V.

SC

Inns

★ ★ **BALSAM MOUNTAIN INN.** *PO Box 40 (28707), 7 mi W on US 74W Balsam exit.* 704/456-9498; FAX 704/456-9298. 34 rms, 19 with shower only, 2 story, 3 suites. No A/C. No rm phones. June-Oct & winter wkends: S $80; D $85; each addl $15; suites $115-$130; wkend, hol rates (2-night min); lower rates rest of yr. Crib free. Complimentary coffee in library. Dining rm 8-9:30 am, 11:30 am-1:30 pm, 6-7:30 pm; wkend hrs vary. Ck-out 11 am, ck-in 2 pm. Gift shop. Restored, turn-of-the-century inn nestled on scenic mountainside. Near Great Smoky Mountain Scenic Railway. Cr cds: DS, MC, V.

⊡ ⤫ 🔥 SC

★ **GRANDVIEW LODGE.** *809 Valley View Circle Rd.* 704/456-5212; res: 800/255-7826. 11 rms, 6 with shower only, 1 A/C, 1-2 story, 2 kit. suites. No rm phones. MAP: S $78; D $95-$100; each addl $25; kit. suites $115; family, wkly rates. TV; cable. Dining rm, sittings: 8 am & 6 pm; also 1 pm Sun. Ck-out 10 am, ck-in 1 pm. 27-hole golf privileges. Game rm. Lawn games. Some refrigerators. Picnic tables. Built 1890; restored mountain guest lodge. Totally nonsmoking. No cr cds accepted.

🏌 ⤫ 🔥

★ ★ **HEATH LODGE.** *900 Dolan Rd.* 704/456-3333; res: 800/432-8499. 22 rms, 1-2 story. No A/C. No rm phones. S $40-$80; D $55-$95; MAP avail. TV; cable. Dining rm 8-9 am, 6-7:30 pm. Ck-out 10 am, ck-in 3 pm. Whirlpool. Porches. Cr cds: DS, MC, V.

⤫ 🔥

★ ★ ★ **THE SWAG.** *Rte 2, Box 280A, W on US 19, then 2.3 mi N on US 276 to Hemphill Rd, then left for 4 mi, follow sign up private driveway.* 704/926-0430; FAX 704/926-2036. 15 rms, 1-2 story. AP, Late May-Oct: S $125-$240; D $150-$325; each addl $60; higher rates: 2-night wkends, hols (3-night min), fall foliage. Closed rest of yr. Children over 7 yrs only. Coffee & tea in rms. Dining rm (public by res), 2 sittings: 12:30 & 7 pm. Rm serv. Ck-out 11 am, ck-in 3 pm. Gift shop. Underground raquetball court. Badminton, croquet court. Sauna. Fireplaces. Balconies. Library. Assembled from 6 authentic log structures (including old church) moved to mountaintop. Early American furniture and crafts. Library, video collection. Swimming pond with swinging bridge. 250 wooded acres with walking trails. Cr cds: MC, V.

⊡ 🎣 ⩳ 🏃 ⤫ 🔥

★ ★ ★ **WINDSONG.** *(120 Ferguson Ridge, Clyde 28721) W on I-40, exit 24, then 3 mi N on NC 209, then 2½ mi W on Riverside Dr, then 1 mi N on Ferguson Cove Loop.* 704/627-6111; FAX 704/627-8080. 5 rms, 2 story. No A/C. Rm phones avail. S $81-$85.50; D $90-$95; guest house $120-$140; each addl $20; wkly rates. Closed mid-Dec-mid-Feb. Children over 8 yrs only. Heated pool. Complimentary full bkfst. Ck-out 11 am, ck-in 3 pm. Tennis. Game rm. Balconies. Grills. Contemporary log house on mountainside; fireplace and special theme decor in rms. Totally nonsmoking. Cr cds: MC, V.

🏃 ⩳ ⤫ 🔥

Resort

★ ★ ★ **WAYNESVILLE COUNTRY CLUB INN.** *PO Box 390, 1½ mi W on US 23/19A Bypass off I-40.* 704/456-3551; FAX 704/456-3555. 92 rms, eight 1-bedrm cottages, 1-2 story. MAP, mid-Apr-Oct: S $105-$126; D $134-$168; cottages $150-$200; each addl $50; lower rates rest of yr. TV; cable. Pool. Dining rm 7-9:15 am, 10 am-4 pm, 7-8:30 pm. Bar 4-10 pm; entertainment Wed, Fri & Sat. Ck-out noon. Meeting rms. Bellhops. Airport transportation. Tennis. 27-hole golf, greens fee $20-$25, pro. Downhill ski 20 mi. Balconies. Cr cds: MC, V.

Wilkesboro (A-4)

Settled: 1779 **Pop:** 2,573 **Elev:** 1,042 ft **Area code:** 910 **Zip:** 28697

What to See and Do

Stone Mountain State Park. 25 mi NE on NC 18, SR 1002, John P. Frank Pkwy. A 13,378-acre natural landmark with waterfalls and wooded areas. The mountain, in the center of the park, is a 600-foot dome-shaped granite mass measuring 6 miles in circumference. The park is popular for mountain climbing. There are 17 miles of designated trout streams. Extensive nature, hiking trails. Picnicking, concession. Developed and primitive camping (dump station). Interpretive program in summer. Standard fees. Phone 957-8185.

(See Jefferson)

Motels

★★ **ADDISON.** *Box 410, 2 mi N on US 421. 910/838-1000; res: 800/672-7218; FAX 910/667-7548.* 114 rms, 2 story. S $40.99-$42.99; D $45.99-$47.99; each addl $5; under 18 free. Crib free. TV; cable. Pool. Complimentary continental bkfst. Restaurant adj 6 am-11 pm; Fri, Sat to 1 am. Ck-out 11 am. Meeting rm. Some refrigerators. Cr cds: A, C, D, DS, MC, V.

✔★ **QUALITY INN.** *Jct US 421 & NC 268 Bypass. 910/667-2176; FAX 910/838-9103.* 100 rms, 2 story. S $38.95; D $43.95; each addl $5. Crib free. TV; cable. Pool. Complimentary continental bkfst. Restaurant 11 am-9:30 pm. Ck-out noon. Meeting rms. Valet serv. Cr cds: A, C, D, DS, JCB, MC, V.

Williamston (B-9)

Pop: 5,503 **Elev:** 80 ft **Area code:** 919 **Zip:** 27892

What to See and Do

Hope Plantation. US 13 to Windsor, then 4 mi W on NC 308. One-hour guided tour of Georgian plantation house (ca 1800) built by Governor David Stone. Period furnishings; outbuildings; gardens. (Mar-Dec 22, Mon-Sat, also Sun afternoons) Phone 794-3140. ¢¢   Included in admission is

King-Bazemore House (1763). Tour of this unique colonial-style house with gambrel roof, dormer windows and solid brick ends. Period furnishings; outbuildings; gardens.

(See Washington)

Motels

✔★ **COMFORT INN.** *PO Box 663, Jct US 17 & US 13/64. 919/792-8400; FAX 919/792-9003.* 59 rms, 2 story. S $43; D $47; each addl $6; suites $46-$51; under 18 free. Crib free. TV; cable. Complimentary continental bkfst. Restaurant nearby. Ck-out noon. Exercise equipt; weight machine, bicycles. Cr cds: A, C, D, DS, ER, JCB, MC, V.

★★ **HOLIDAY INN.** *PO Box 711, 1 mi S on US 17. 919/792-3184; FAX 919/792-9003.* 100 rms, 2 story. S $43-$48; D $49-$54; each addl $4; under 18 free. Crib free. TV; cable, in-rm movies. Pool.

Restaurant 6 am-9:30 pm. Rm serv. Bar 5 pm-midnight. Ck-out noon. Meeting rms. Cr cds: A, C, D, DS, JCB, MC, V.

Wilmington (D-8)

Settled: 1732 **Pop:** 55,530 **Elev:** 25 ft **Area code:** 910

Chief port of North Carolina, Wilmington is the region's major trade and retail center. Manufacturing, tourism and port-oriented business lead the area's growth.

Patriots who defied the Crown in the Revolution were led by William Hooper, signer of the Declaration of Independence. In 1765, eight years before the Boston Tea Party, the citizens of Wilmington kept the British from unloading their stamps for the Stamp Act. Cornwallis held the town for almost a year in 1781 as his main base of operation. After the battle of Guilford Courthouse, the Lord General came back to Wilmington before heading for Yorktown and defeat.

During the Civil War, blockade runners brought fortunes in goods past Federal ships lying off Cape Fear, making Wilmington the Confederacy's chief port until January, 1865, when it fell. Wilmington was North Carolina's biggest town until 1910, when railroad-fed industries of the inland Piedmont area outgrew the limited facilities of the harbor. The channel, harbor and expanded port facilities bring goods from throughout the world to the area.

What to See and Do

1. **Burgwin-Wright House** (1770). 224 Market St, at 3rd St. Restored colonial town house built on foundation of abandoned town jail. British General Cornwallis had his headquarters here during April, 1781. 18th-century furnishings and garden. Tours. (Tues-Sat; closed some major hols; also Sat in Jan & wk of Dec 25) Phone 762-0570.   ¢¢

2. **Cape Fear Museum.** 814 Market St. Interprets social and natural history of Lower Cape Fear. Changing exhibits. (Daily exc Mon; closed major national holidays) Sr citizen rate. Phone 341-7413. ¢

3. **Cotton Exchange.** N Front St. Specialty shops & restaurants in historic buildings on Cape Fear River. (Daily exc Sun; closed some major hols) Phone 343-9896.

4. **St John's Museum of Art.** 114 Orange St. Collection of Mary Cassatt prints; paintings and works on paper, Jugtown Pottery, sculpture. Changing exhibits; lectures; educational programs. (Daily exc Mon; closed hols) Phone 763-0281.   ¢

5. **Greenfield Gardens.** 2½ mi S on US 421. A 150-acre municipal park with 130-acre lake, 5-mi scenic drive; canoe and paddleboat rentals (Apr-Oct); bike path; fragrance garden; amphitheater; picnicking; nature trail. (Daily) Phone 341-7855.   **Free.**

6. **Moores Creek National Battlefield.** 17 mi N on US 421, then 3 mi W on NC 210. In 1776 the loosely knit colonists took sides against each other—patriots versus loyalists. Colonels Moore, Lillington and Caswell, with the blessing of the Continental Congress, broke up the loyalist forces, captured the leaders and seized gold and quantities of weapons. The action defeated British hopes of an early invasion through the South and encouraged North Carolina to be the first colony to instruct its delegates to vote for independence in Philadelphia. The 86-acre park has a visitor center near entrance to explain the battle. Picnic area. (Daily; closed Jan 1, Dec 25) Phone 283-5591.   **Free.**

7. **Orton Plantation Gardens.** 18 mi S on NC 133. 20 acres. Formerly a rice plantation, now beautiful gardens with ancient oaks, magnolias, ornamental plants, lawn and water scenes; rice fields now a waterfowl refuge. Antebellum Orton House (not open), begun in 1730, can be seen from garden paths. Overlooks Cape Fear River. (Mar-Nov, daily) Phone 371-6851.   ¢¢¢

8. **Poplar Grove Plantation** (ca 1850). 9 mi NE on US 17. Restored Greek-revival plantation; manor house, smokehouse, tenant house, blacksmith, weaver; also restaurant, country store. Guided tours (daily; closed Easter, Thanksgiving, also day after Thanksgiving & late Dec-Jan). Sr citizen rate. Phone 686-9989 or -4868. ¢¢¢

9. **Battleship *North Carolina*.** Jct of US 74/76, 17 & 421. World War II vessel moored on west bank of Cape Fear River. Tour of museum, gun turrets, galley, bridge, sick bay, engine room, wheelhouse. (Daily) (See SEASONAL EVENT) Phone 251-5797.   ¢¢¢

10. **North Carolina Aquarium/Fort Fisher.** S on US 421, near Kure Beach. Fifteen aquariums of North Carolina native sea life; marine exhibits, films, workshops, programs; nature trails. (Daily; closed Jan 1, Thanksgiving, Dec 25) Phone 458-8257.   **Free.**

11. **Wilmington Railroad Museum.** 501 Nutt St. Exhibits on railroading past and present, centering on the Atlantic Coast Line and other Southeastern rail lines. HO scale regional history exhibit on 2nd floor; outside are ACL steam locomotive and caboose for on-board viewing. (Mar-Oct, daily; rest of yr, schedule varies; closed Jan 1, Thanksgiving, Dec 25) Phone 763-2634.   ¢¢

12. **Carolina Beach State Park.** 15 mi S off US 421. This 1,773-acre park is a naturalist's delight; the rare Venus' flytrap as well as 5 other species of insect-eating plants grow here. Fishing; boating (ramps, marina). Picnicking, concession. Nature, hiking trails. Camping (dump station). Naturalist program. Standard fees. Phone 458-8206.

13. **Sightseeing cruises.**

Captain J.N. Maffitt River Cruises. Located at the foot of Market St. Five-mile narrated sightseeing cruise covering Wilmington's harbor life and points of interest. Also "river taxi" service (addl fee) from USS *North Carolina* (see #9). (May-Sept, daily) Phone 343-1611 or 800/676-0162.   ¢¢

Henrietta II Paddlewheel Riverboat Cruises. Downtown, at riverfront. One-and-one-half-hour narrated sightseeing cruise down Cape Fear River to North Carolina State Port. (June-Aug, 2 cruises daily exc Mon; Apr-May, Sept-Oct, 1 cruise daily exc Mon) Dinner cruises (Apr-Dec, Fri & Sat; June-Aug, Wed-Sat). For reservations phone 343-1611 or 800/676-0162.   ¢¢¢

(For further information contact the Cape Fear Coast Convention & Visitors Bureau, 24 N 3rd St, 28401; 341-4030 or 800/222-4757; 800/457-8912 in Canada)

Annual Events

North Carolina Azalea Festival. Garden tours, horse show, pageants, parades, more. Early Apr.

Riverfest. Arts and crafts, music, dancing and entertainment; boat rides; raft regatta. Phone 452-6862. 1st full wkend Oct.

Seasonal Event

The Immortal Showboat. Battleship *North Carolina* (see #9). Sound and light show about the battleship *North Carolina*. Seventy-minute show, nightly (weather permitting). Phone 251-5797. 1st Fri June-Labor Day.

(See Southport, Wrightsville Beach)

Motels

✔ ★ **DAYS INN.** 5040 Market St (28405). 910/799-6300; FAX 910/791-7414. 122 rms, 2 story. S $32-$70; D $38-$70; each addl $6; family rates; higher rates: Azalea Festival, summer hol wkends. Crib free. TV; cable. Pool. Restaurant 6 am-9 pm. Ck-out 11 am. Sundries. Cr cds: A, C, D, DS, MC, V.

D 🏊 ⚊ 🔥 SC

★ ★ **FAIRFIELD INN BY MARRIOTT.** 306 S College Rd (28403). 910/392-6767; FAX 910/392-6767, ext. 709. 134 rms, 3 story. Apr-Sept: S $41.95-$49.95; D $50.95-$64.95; each addl $8; under 18 free; lower rates rest of yr. Crib free. TV; cable. Pool. Complimentary continental bkfst in lobby. Restaurant nearby. Ck-out noon. Meeting rms. Cr cds: A, C, D, DS, MC, V.

D 🏊 ⚊ 🔥 SC

★ **FAIRFIELD INN BY MARRIOTT MARKET STREET.** 4926 Market St (28403). 910/791-8850; FAX 910/791-8858. 119 rms, 2 story. Apr-Sept: S, D $48-$58; each addl $6; under 18 free; lower rates rest of yr. Crib free. TV; cable. Pool. Complimentary continental bkfst, coffee. Restaurant nearby. Ck-out noon. Cr cds: A, C, D, DS, MC, V.

D 🏊 ⚊ 🔥 SC

★ ★ **HAMPTON INN.** 5107 Market St (28403). 910/395-5045; FAX 910/799-1974. 118 rms, 2 story. Apr-Sept: S $60; D $68; under 18 free; lower rates rest of yr. Crib free. TV; cable. Pool. Complimentary continental bkfst, coffee. Restaurant nearby. Ck-out noon. Meeting rms. Cr cds: A, C, D, DS, MC, V.

D 🏊 ⚊ 🔥 SC

★ **HoJo INN.** 3901 Market St (28403). 910/343-1727. 79 rms. Apr-Labor Day: S, D $65; each addl $5; under 16 free; lower rates rest of yr. Crib free. TV; cable. Complimentary coffee in lobby. Restaurant nearby. Ck-out 11 am. Meeting rms. Cr cds: A, C, D, DS, MC, V.

D ⚊ 🔥 SC

★ ★ **HOLIDAY INN.** 4903 Market St (28405). 910/799-1440; FAX 910/799-2683. 230 rms, 2 story. Apr-Sept: S $65-$85; D $75-$110; each addl $6; under 12 free; wkly plans; lower rates rest of yr. Crib free. TV; cable. Pool; poolside serv. Restaurant 6 am-1 pm, 5-10 pm. Rm serv. Bar 11-2 am. Ck-out noon. Coin lndry. Meeting rms. Bellhops. Valet serv. Sundries. Free airport transportation. Cr cds: A, DS, ER, MC, V.

D 🏊 ⚊ 🔥 SC

★ ★ **RAMADA INN CONFERENCE CENTER.** 5001 Market St (28405). 910/799-1730; FAX 910/799-1730, ext. 375. 100 rms, 2 story. Apr-Sept: S, D $44-$79; under 18 free; wkly rates; golf plans; higher rates: Azalea Festival, summer & hol wkends; lower rates rest of yr. Crib free. TV; cable. Pool. Playground. Complimentary bkfst. Restaurant 6 am-2 pm, 5-10 pm. Rm serv. Bar 5 pm-2 am; entertainment, dancing. Ck-out noon. Meeting rms. Valet serv. Free airport transportation. Cr cds: A, C, D, DS, JCB, MC, V.

D 🏊 ⚊ 🔥 SC

✔ ★ **SUPER 8.** 3604 Market St (28403). 910/343-9778. 62 rms, 3 story. S $35.88-$45.88; D $40.88-$47.88; each addl $5; suites $50.88; under 12 free. Crib free. TV; cable. Complimentary coffee in lobby. Restaurant opp 11 am-10:30 pm. Ck-out 11 am. Cr cds: A, C, D, DS, MC, V.

D ⚊ 🔥 SC

Motor Hotels

★ ★ **COMFORT INN-EXECUTIVE CENTER.** 151 S College Rd (28403). 910/791-4841; FAX 910/791-4841, ext. 125. 146 rms, 6 story. S, D $48-$79; each addl $6; suites $85; under 18 free; golf package. Crib free. TV; cable. Pool. Complimentary continental bkfst. Restaurant nearby. Ck-out noon. Meeting rms. Valet serv. Free airport transportation. Exercise equipt; weight machines, bicycles. Cr cds: A, C, D, DS, ER, MC, V.

D 🏊 🏋 ⚊ 🔥 SC

★ ★ **HOWARD JOHNSON PLAZA.** 5032 Market St (28405). 910/392-1101. 124 rms, 5 story. S, D $69-$89; each addl $10; suites $95-$225; under 18 free; higher rates: Azalea Festival, Memorial Day, July 4, Labor Day. Crib free. TV; cable. Indoor pool. Restaurant 6 am-2 pm, 4-10 pm. Rm serv. Bar to 11 pm. Ck-out noon. Meeting rms.

Bellhops. Airport transportation. Exercise equipt; weights, bicycles, whirlpool, sauna. Refrigerator in suites. Cr cds: A, C, D, DS, MC, V.

Hotel

★ ★ ★ **HILTON.** *301 N Water St (28401). 910/763-5900; FAX 910/763-0038.* 178 rms, 9 story. S, D $95-$145; each addl $10; suites $100-$275; golf package. Crib free. TV; cable. Pool; whirlpool. Restaurant 6:30 am-10:30 pm. Bar 4 pm-1 am. Ck-out noon. Meeting rms. Gift shop. Free airport transporation. Boat dock. *LUXURY LEVEL .* 24 rms, 2 suites. S, D $105-$155; suites $150-$250. Concierge. Private lounge. Complimentary continental bkfst, refreshments. Cr cds: A, C, D, DS, JCB, MC, V.

Inns

★ ★ **INN AT ST THOMAS COURT.** *101 S 2nd St (28401). 910/343-1800; res: 800/525-0909; FAX 910/251-1149.* 36 suites, 1-3 story. S, D $88-$98; 2-bedrm suites $169; under 12 free; golf plan. Crib free. TV; cable, in-rm movies avail. Complimentary continental bkfst. Complimentary coffee in rms. Restaurant nearby. Taproom (wine, beer) open 24 hrs. Ck-out 11 am, ck-in 3 pm. Meeting rm. Bellhops. Valet serv. Concierge. Kit. Suites avail. Balconies. Renovated commercial building (1906) in historic district; entrance court, library, antiques. Cr cds: A, D, MC, V.

★ **MARKET STREET BED & BREAKFAST.** *1704 Market St (28403). 910/763-5442; res: 800/242-5442.* 4 rms (2 share bath), 3 story. No rm phones. S $65; D $80-$90; each addl $15. Children over 10 yrs only. TV in parlor; cable. Complimentary full bkfst. Ck-out 11 am. Built 1917; antiques. Totally nonsmoking. Cr cds: MC, V.

★ **TAYLOR HOUSE.** *14 N 7th St (28401). 910/763-7581; res: 800/382-9982.* 3 rms, 2 story, 1 suite. S, D $75; suite $90; wkly rates; higher rates wkends & hols (2-day min). Children over 12 yrs only. Complimentary full bkfst. Complimentary coffee, tea, sherry in library. Ck-out 11 am, ck-in 4-7 pm. Built 1908; many fireplaces, antiques. Totally nonsmoking. Cr cds: A, MC, V.

Restaurants

★ ★ **BEACHES.** *2025 Eastwood Rd (28403). 910/256-4622.* Hrs: 5:30-10 pm; Fri & Sat to 10:30 pm. Closed Thanksgiving, Dec 24 & 25. Res accepted. Bar. Semi-a la carte: dinner $8.95-$16.95. Child's meals. Specializes in steak, seafood. Parking. 2 dining rms. Maritime theme. Cr cds: A, C, D, DS, MC, V.

✔ ★ **EDDIE ROMANELLI'S.** *5400 Oleander Dr (28403). 910/799-7000.* Hrs: 11:30 am-11 pm. Closed some major hols. Res accepted. Italian, Amer menu. Bar. Semi-a la carte: lunch $3.95-$7.95, dinner $8.95-$15.95. Child's meals. Specializes in marinated steak, pasta, salads. Parking. Beamed ceiling with skylight. Cr cds: A, MC, V.

★ ★ **ELIJAH'S.** *2 Ann St. 910/343-1448.* Hrs: 11:30 am-3 pm, 5-10 pm; Fri, Sat 5-11 pm. Sun brunch to 3 pm. Closed Mon; Jan 1, Thanksgiving, Dec 25. Bar 11:30 am-midnight. Semi-a la carte: lunch $4.95-$7.95, dinner $9.95-$22.95. Sun brunch $4.95-$7.95. Child's meals. Specializes in chowder, hot crab dip, sandwiches. Pianist. Sun brunch. Parking. View of river. Outdoor dining. Nautical decor; former maritime museum. Cr cds: A, DS, MC, V.

★ **FRAZIER'S.** *4126 Oleander Dr. 910/392-7300.* Hrs: 5-10 pm; Sun 11:30 am-2:30 pm, 5-10 pm. Closed Dec 24, 25. Bar. Semi-a la carte: lunch, dinner $6.95-$18.95. Child's meals. Specializes in seafood, steak. Parking. Nautical decor. Cr cds: A, D, MC, V.

★ ★ **GIUSEPPE'S.** *1924 A Eastwood Rd. 910/256-9600.* Hrs: 5:30-10 pm. Closed Jan 1, Easter, Thanksgiving, Dec 24-25. Italian, Amer menu. Bar to 2 am. Semi-a la carte: dinner $8-$25. Specializes in grilled shrimp, veal. Entertainment. Venetian decor; artwork. Cr cds: A, D, MC, V.

✔ ★ ★ **HIERONYMUS SEAFOOD.** *5035 Market St. 910/392-6318.* Hrs: 11 am-10 pm; Fri, Sat to 11 pm; early-bird dinner 5-6:30 pm. Closed Jan 1, Thanksgiving, Dec 24, 25. Res accepted. Bar to 2 am. Semi-a la carte: lunch $3.95-$7.95, dinner $4.95-$14.95. Child's meals. Specializes in seafood, prime rib. Entertainment, pianist. Parking. Outdoor dining. Oyster bar in lounge. Nautical decor. Cr cds: A, C, D, DS, MC, V.

✔ ★ **MARKET STREET CASUAL DINING.** *6309 Market St. 910/395-2488.* Hrs: 5-11 pm. Closed Thanksgiving, Dec 25. Bar to 1 am. Semi-a la carte: dinner $4.95-$13.95. Specializes in grilled seafood & steak. Parking. Cr cds: A, MC, V.

✔ ★ **OH! BRIAN'S.** *4311 Oleander Dr (28403). 910/791-1477.* Hrs: 11 am-11 pm; Sun to 10 pm. Closed Thanksgiving, Dec 25. Res accepted Mon-Fri. Bar to 2 am. Semi-a la carte: lunch $3.95-$6.95, dinner $4.95-$14.95. Child's meals. Specializes in barbecue ribs, chicken, salads. Parking. Atrium. Cr cds: A, D, MC, V.

★ **OUTBACK STEAKHOUSE.** *302 S College Rd (28403). 910/791-5335.* Hrs: 4-10:30 pm; Fri to 11:30 pm; Sat 3-11:30 pm; Sun 3-10 pm. Closed Thanksgiving, Dec 25. Bar. Semi-a la carte: dinner $7.95-$17.95. Child's meals. Specializes in steak, Australian fare. Parking. Australian artifacts. Cr cds: A, D, DS, MC, V.

★ ★ **PILOT HOUSE.** *2 Ann St, Chandler's Wharf on waterfront. 910/343-0200.* Hrs: 11:30 am-3 pm, 5-10 pm; Fri, Sat to 11 pm; Sun brunch 11:30 am-3 pm. Closed major hols. Res accepted. A la carte entrees: lunch $2.95-$8.95, dinner $8.95-$22. Child's meals. Specialties: crab melt sandwich, fresh fish, Caribbean fudge pie. Own bread. Parking. Located in restored area of waterfront; built 1870. Cr cds: A, DS, MC, V.

Unrated Dining Spots

K & W CAFETERIA. *3501 Oleander Dr. 910/762-7011.* Hrs: 6:30 am-8:30 pm. Closed Dec 25. Avg ck: bkfst $3, lunch $4, dinner $4.50. Specializes in fresh vegetables. No cr cds accepted.

SAM'S. *1401 Floral Pkwy. 910/799-1237.* Hrs: 7 am-9 pm; Sat to 4 pm. Closed Sun; most major hols. Semi-a la carte: lunch $2.10-$5.25, dinner $2.10-$6. Specializes in sandwiches, chicken salad. Ice cream specialties. Cr cds: MC, V.

Wilson (B-8)

Pop: 36,930 **Elev:** 145 ft **Area code:** 919 **Zip:** 27893

Located just off I-95, midway between New York and Florida, Wilson is a convenient rest stop for road-weary travelers. It is one of the Southeast's leading antique markets and is said to have one of the nation's largest tobacco markets.

(See Rocky Mount)

Motels

★ ★ **HAMPTON INN.** *PO Box 1329, 1801 S Tarboro St, 6 mi E of I-95, exit 121.* 919/291-2323; FAX 919/291-7696. 100 rms, 2 story. S $45-$50; D $48-$53; under 18 free. Crib free. TV; cable. Pool. Complimentary continental bkfst, coffee. Restaurant nearby. Ck-out 11 am. Meeting rm. Cr cds: A, C, D, DS, MC, V.

✔ ★ **HEART OF WILSON.** *501 W Nash St.* 919/237-3124. 72 rms, 2 story, 8 condos. S $35-$41; D $41; suites $45; condos $101; under 18 free. Crib free. TV; cable. Pool. Restaurant 7 am-9:30 pm. Rm serv. Bar 5 pm-1 am. Ck-out 11 am. Meeting rms. Refrigerator in suites. Cr cds: A, C, D, DS, MC, V.

★ **HOLIDAY INN.** *1815 US 301 S.* 919/243-5111; FAX 919/291-9697. 100 rms, 2 story. S $57-$60; D $62-$65; each addl $5; under 12 free. Crib free. TV; cable. Pool. Restaurant 6 am-2 pm, 5-10 pm. Rm serv. Bar. Ck-out noon. Meeting rms. Cr cds: A, C, D, DS, MC, V.

Inn

★ **MISS BETTY'S.** *600 W Nash St.* 919/243-4447; res: 800/258-2058. 10 rms (3 with shower only), 2 story, 3 suites. S $50-$60; D $60-$75. Adults only. TV; cable. Complimentary full bkfst. Restaurant opp 6 am-10 pm. Ck-out 11 am, ck-in 3 pm. Two restored houses (1859 & 1900). Many antiques. Totally nonsmoking. Cr cds: A, C, D, DS, MC, V.

Winston-Salem (A-5)

Founded: Salem: 1766; Winston: 1849; combined as Winston-Salem: 1913 **Pop:** 143,485 **Elev:** 912 ft **Area code:** 910

First in industry in the Carolinas and one of the South's chief cities, Winston-Salem is a combination of two communities. Salem, with the traditions of its Moravian founders and Winston, an industrial center, matured together. Tobacco markets, large banks and arts & crafts galleries contribute to this thriving community.

What to See and Do

1. **Reynolda House, Museum of American Art.** Approx 2 mi N on University Pkwy, then 1/2 mi E on Coliseum Dr then N on Reynolda Rd. On estate of the late R.J. Reynolds of the tobacco dynasty. American paintings, original furniture, art objects, costume collection. Adj is Reynolda Gardens, 125 acres of open fields and naturalized woodlands; formal gardens, greenhouses. (Daily exc Mon; closed Jan 1, Thanksgiving, Dec 25) Sr citizen rate. Phone 725-5325. ¢¢¢

2. **Historic Bethabara Park.** 2147 Bethabara Rd. Site of first Moravian settlement in North Carolina (1753); restored buildings include Gemeinhaus (1788), Potter's House (1782), Buttner House (1803); reconstructed palisade fort (1756-63); stabilized archaeololgical foundations of original settlement and God's Acre (graveyard); reconstructed community gardens (1759). Visitor center; exhibits, slide show. Nature trails. Picnicking. (See #3) (Apr-Nov, daily; walking tour all yr) Phone 924-8191. **Free.**

3. **Historic Old Salem** (1766). S of business district on Old Salem Rd. Restoration of a planned community which Moravians, with their Old World skills, made the 18th-century trade and cultural center of North Carolina's Piedmont. (See #2) Many of the sturdy structures built for practical living have been restored and furnished with original or period pieces. Early crafts are demonstrated throughout the town. Here also is an original Tannenberg organ in working condition. A number of houses are privately occupied. Nine houses plus outbuildings are open to the public. Tours (self-guided and guided) start at Visitor Center on Old Salem Rd. (Daily; no tours Thanksgiving, Dec 24 & 25) Phone 721-7300. Ticket to all buildings (exc museum) ¢¢¢ Special events are held during the yr. In the old village are

   Salem Academy and College (1772). (850 women) Church St, on Salem Sq in Old Salem. When founded by the Moravians, it was the only school of its kind for women in the South. The Fine Arts Center offers art exhibits, lectures, films, concerts and plays (mid-Sept-mid-May, daily; evenings during special events; some fees). Campus tours on request; phone 721-2702.

   Museum of Early Southern Decorative Arts. 924 S Main St. Nineteen period rooms and six galleries (1690-1820), with decorative arts of Maryland, Virginia, Georgia, Kentucky, Tennessee and the Carolinas. (Daily; closed Thanksgiving, Dec 24 & 25) Phone 721-7360. Museum ¢¢; Combination ticket including Old Salem ¢¢¢¢

4. **Southeastern Center for Contemporary Art.** 750 Marguerite Dr. Exhibits by contemporary artists from across the country with accompanying educational programs. (Daily exc Mon; closed hols) Sr citizen rate. Phone 725-1904. ¢¢

5. **Wake Forest University** (1834). (5,600 students) 3 mi NW off Reynolda Rd. On campus are Fine Arts Center, Museum of Anthropology; also Reynolda Village, a complex of shops, offices & restaurants. Bowman Gray School of Medicine is on Medical Center Boulevard. Phone 759-5000.

6. **Tanglewood Park.** 12 mi SW off I-40, in Clemmons. Swimming, water slide; fishing; boating (paddleboats, canoes); horseback riding; golf, miniature golf, tennis; nature trail. Picnicking, playgrounds, restaurant. Camping (fee); accommodations. Deer park. Steeplechase (early May). (Daily) Phone 766-0591. Entrance fee/vehicle ¢

7. **SciWorks.** 400 Hanes Mill Rd. Hands-on exhibits of physical & natural sciences; planetarium; 31-acre outdoor animal park. (Daily; closed Jan 1, Thanksgiving, Dec 25) Phone 767-6730. ¢¢

8. **Hanging Rock State Park.** 32 mi N, between NC 66 & 89 near Danbury. Approx 6,200 acres in Sauratown Mts. Lake swimming, bathhouse; fishing; boating (rentals). Nature trails. Picnicking, concession. Tent & trailer sites, six family cabins (Mar-Nov, by reservation only). Observation tower. Standard fees. Phone 593-8480.

9. **Industrial tours.**

   R.J. Reynolds Tobacco Company, Whitaker Park Cigarette Plant. 1100 Reynolds Blvd. Guided tours (Mon-Fri; closed hols) Phone 741-5718. **Free.**

   Stroh Brewery Co. US 52 at S Main St. Thirty-minute guided tour (Mon-Fri; closed hols). Phone 650-8102. **Free.**

(For further information contact the Convention and Visitors Bureau, PO Box 1408, 27102; 777-3796 or 800/331-7018.)

(See Greensboro, High Point, Lexington)

Motels

(Rates are generally higher during Furniture Market)

✔ ★ **COURTYARD BY MARRIOT.** *3111 University Pkwy (27105).* 910/727-1277; FAX 910/722-8219. 123 rms, 2 story. S $49; D $54; each addl $6; suite $100; under 18 free; higher rates: Furniture Market (Apr & Oct), graduation (May). Crib free. TV; cable. Pool. Complimentary continental bkfst. Complimentary coffee in lobby. Restaurant nearby. Ck-out 11 am. Coin lndry. Meeting rm. Cr cds: A, C, D, DS, MC, V.

`D` `≋` `⊠` `⚒` `SC`

★ **DAYS INN.** *3330 Silas Creek Pkwy S (27103), I-40 Wake Forest exit.* 910/760-4770; FAX 910/760-1085. 135 rms, 5 story. S $50-$52; D $55-$58; each addl $5; under 17 free. Crib free. TV; cable. Pool; whirlpool. Complimentary continental bkfst, coffee. Ck-out noon. Meeting rms. Health club privileges. Cr cds: A, D, MC, V.

`D` `≋` `⊠` `⚒` `SC`

✔ ★ ★ **HAMPTON INN.** *5719 University Pkwy, (27105).* 910/767-9009; FAX 910/661-0448. 117 rms, 2 story. S $49-$50; D $54-$57; under 18 free. Crib free. TV; cable. Pool. Complimentary continental bkfst, coffee. Restaurant adj 6 am-10 pm. Ck-out 11 am. Meeting rms. Cr cds: A, C, D, DS, MC, V.

`D` `≋` `⊠` `⚒` `SC`

★ ★ **RESIDENCE INN BY MARRIOTT.** *7835 N Point Blvd (27106).* 910/759-0777; FAX 910/759-9671. 88 kit. suites, 2 story. S, D $86-$106; children free; wkly rates. Crib free. Pet accepted; $75 nonrefundable. TV; cable. Heated pool; whirlpool. Continental bkfst. Complimentary coffee in rms. Ck-out noon. Coin lndry. Valet serv. Health club privileges. Refrigerators. Picnic tables, grills. Cr cds: A, C, D, DS, JCB, MC, V.

`D` `🐾` `≋` `⊠` `⚒` `SC`

Hotels

★ ★ ★ **ADAM'S MARK AT WINSTON PLAZA.** *425 N Cherry St (27101).* 910/725-3500; FAX 910/722-6475. 315 rms, 17 story. S $133-$153; D $153-$173; each addl $20; suites $275-$550; under 18 free; wkend plans. Crib free. Garage $4.50. TV; cable. Indoor pool; sauna, poolside serv. Outdoor sun deck. Restaurants 6:30 am-11 pm. Rm serv 24 hrs. Bar 11:30-1 am; piano bar, entertainment Fri-Sat. Ck-out 1 pm. Convention facilities. Concierge. Gift shop. Airport transportation. Tennis, golf privileges. Exercise equipt; weight machine, bicycles. Game rm. Refrigerator in suites. Local art displayed throughout hotel. **LUXURY LEVEL : CLUB LEVEL.** 60 rms, 4 suites, 3 floors. S $158-$178; D $178-$198. Wet bar in suites. Complimentary continental bkfst, refreshments. Cr cds: A, C, D, DS, MC, V.

`D` `🏋` `🏃` `≋` `🎿` `⚒` `SC`

★ ★ ★ **THE MARQUE OF WINSTON-SALEM.** *460 N Cherry St (27101).* 910/725-1234; res: 800/527-2341; FAX 910/722-9182. 293 rms, 9 story. S $110; D $125; each addl $20; 1-3 bedrm suites $195-$400; under 18 free; wkend rates. Crib free. Garage $5. TV; cable. Heated pool. Restaurant 6:30 am-10 pm. Bar noon-1 am, Sun to 11 pm. Ck-out noon. Convention facilities. Gift shop. Tennis, golf privileges. Exercise equipt; weights, bicycles, whirlpool. Health club privileges. Built around 9-story atrium; glass-enclosed elvtrs. **LUXURY LEVEL : CLUB LEVEL.** 100 rms, 3 floors. S $125; D $145. Concierge. Private lounge. Complimentary continental bkfst, refreshments. Cr cds: A, C, D, DS, MC, V.

`D` `🏋` `🏃` `≋` `🎿` `⊠` `SC`

★ ★ **SHERATON.** *5790 University Pkwy (27105).* 910/767-9595; FAX 910/744-1888. 150 rms, 6 story. S $60-$80; D $65-$85; each addl $10; suites $110; under 18 free; wkend rates; higher rates Furniture Market (Apr & Oct). Crib free. TV; cable. Pool. Restaurant 6:30 am-2 pm, 5:30-10 pm. Bar; entertainment. Ck-out noon. Meeting rms.

Exercise equipt; weight machine, bicycles. Some refrigerators, minibars. Cr cds: A, C, D, DS, MC, V.

`D` `≋` `🏋` `🏃` `🎿` `⚒` `SC`

Inns

★ ★ ★ **BROOKSTOWN INN.** *200 Brookstown Ave (27101).* 910/725-1120; res: 800/845-4262; FAX 910/773-0147. 71 units, 4 story. S $90-$115; D, suites $105-$125; each addl $15; under 12 free. Crib free. TV; cable. Complimentary continental bkfst 7-10 am. Complimentary wine, cheese. Rm serv for bkfst. Ck-out noon, ck-in 2 pm. Restored brick cotton mill (1837); antiques, handmade quilts. Cr cds: A, D, ER, MC, V.

`D` `⊠` `⚒` `SC`

★ ★ **COLONEL LUDLOW.** *Summit & W Fifth Sts (27101).* 910/777-1887; FAX 910/777-1890. 10 rms, 2 story, 1 suite. S $62-$149; D, suite $72-$149; higher rates special events. TV; cable, in rm movies. Complimentary full bkfst. Complimentary coffee & tea in rms. Restaurant adj 11:30 am-2 pm, 5-10 pm. Ck-out noon, ck-in 4:30 pm. Concierge. Valet serv. Health club privileges. Refrigerators. Balconies. In-rm whirlpools. Victorian home built in 1887; restored and converted. Cr cds: A, DS, MC, V.

`⚒`

✔ ★ ★ **MANOR HOUSE BED & BREAKFAST.** *(Box 1040, Clemmons 27012) 12 mi SW on US 158, I-40 exit 182, in Tanglewood Park.* 910/766-0591; FAX 910/766-8723. 18 rms in lodge, 10 rms in manor house, 2 story. S $35-$95; D $45-$107. Crib $3. TV. Pool; wading pool, lifeguard. Continental bkfst (manor house guests only). Ck-out noon, ck-in 2 pm. Meeting rms. Tennis. Golf. Bicycle rentals. Facilities of Tanglewood Park avail. Cr cds: A, C, D, MC, V.

`🐾` `🏃` `🏋` `🎿` `≋` `🎿` `SC`

Restaurants

★ ★ **OLD SALEM TAVERN.** *736 S Main St.* 910/748-8585. Hrs: 11:30 am-2 pm, 5-9 pm; Fri, Sat to 9:30 pm; Sun to 2 pm. Closed Jan 1, Dec 25. Res accepted. Serv bar. Semi-a la carte: lunch $4.75-$7.50, dinner $11.75-$23. Child's meals. Specialties: roast duck, fresh seafood, rack of lamb. Parking. Outdoor dining. Cr cds: A, MC, V.

★ ★ **RYAN'S.** *719 Coliseum Dr.* 910/724-6132. Hrs: 5:30-10 pm; Fri to 10:30 pm; Sat 5:30-10:30 pm. Closed Sun; Jan 1, Thanksgiving, Dec 24, 25. Res accepted. Continental menu. Bar 4:30-11:45 pm. Semi-a la carte: dinner $14.95-$27.95. Own soup, some desserts. Specializes in beef, seafood. Valet parking. Wooded setting. Cr cds: A, C, D, MC, V.

`D`

★ ★ **STALEY'S CHARCOAL STEAK HOUSE.** *2000 Reynolda Rd.* 910/723-8631. Hrs: 5-10 pm; Fri & Sat 5-11 pm. Closed Sun; major hols. Res accepted. Serv bar. Semi-a la carte: dinner $11.95-$39.95. Child's meals. Specializes in steak, prime rib, shish kebab. Parking. Fountain at entrance. Cr cds: A, MC, V.

★ ★ **ZEVELY HOUSE.** *901 W 4th St.* 910/725-6666. Hrs: 11:30 am-1:30 pm, 5:30-9 pm; Sat from 5:30 pm; Sun brunch 11 am-2 pm. Closed some major hols. Res accepted. Bar. Semi-a la carte: lunch $5.95-$10.95, dinner $12.95-$24. Sun brunch $6.95-$9.50. Child's meals. Specialties: potato cakes with smoked salmon & caviar, chicken pie, mixed grill with lamb chop, venison & beef filet. Parking. Outdoor dining. Antiques, fireplace in older brick house. Cr cds: A, D, MC, V.

Wrightsville Beach (D-8)

Pop: 2,937 **Elev:** 7 ft **Area code:** 910 **Zip:** 28480

A very pleasant family-oriented resort town, Wrightsville Beach offers swimming, surfing, fishing and boating. The public park has facilities for tennis, basketball, soccer, softball, volleyball, shuffleboard and other sports.

(See Wilmington)

Motels

★ **ONE SOUTH LUMINA.** *1 S Lumina Ave. 910/256-9100; res: 800/421-3255.* 21 kit. suites, 3 story. Memorial Day-Labor Day: S, D $125-$145; each addl $10; wkly rates; lower rates rest of yr. Crib $3. TV; cable. Pool. Complimentary coffee in rms. Restaurant nearby. Ck-out 11 am. Lndry facilities avail. Balconies. On swimming beach. Cr cds: A, MC, V.

★★ **SILVER GULL.** *PO Box 658, 20 E Salisbury St, adj to fishing pier. 910/256-3728; res: 800/842-8894.* 32 kit. units, 3 story. June-Labor Day: S, D $95-$175; each addl $7; lower rates rest of yr. Crib $7. TV; cable. Ck-out 11 am. Coin lndry. Balconies. On ocean. Cr cds: A, C, D, DS, MC, V.

★ **SURF MOTEL SUITES.** *711 S Lumina Ave. 910/256-2275.* 45 kit. suites, 4 story. Late May-early Sept: S, D $120-$130; each addl $10; wkly rates; wkend rates (2-day min); lower rates rest of yr. Crib $5. TV; cable. Pool. Complimentary coffee in lobby. Restaurant adj 11 am-10 pm. Ck-out 11:30 am. Coin lndry. Balconies. Swimming beach. Cr cds: A, C, D, MC, V.

★ **WATERWAY LODGE.** *7246 Wrightsville Ave. 910/256-3771; FAX 910/256-6916.* 42 units, 3 story. May-Sept: S, D $60-$75; each addl $5; kits. $75-$90; under 15 free; wkly rates; golf plans; higher rates wkends (2-day min); lower rates rest of yr. Pet accepted; $10. TV; cable. Pool. Complimentary coffee in lobby. Restaurant opp 11 am-10 pm. Ck-out 11:30 am. Refrigerators. Near beach. Cr cds: A, DS, MC, V.

Motor Hotels

★★★ **BLOCKADE RUNNER.** *Box 555, ¼ mi S on US 76. 910/256-2251; res: 800/541-1161.* 150 rms, 7 story. May-mid-Sept: S, D $155-$225; suites $300-$350; each addl $15; under 12 free; lower rates rest of yr. Crib free. TV; cable. Heated pool; lifeguard. Supervised child's activities (June-Labor Day). Restaurant (see OCEAN TERRACE). Rm serv 24 hrs. Bar; entertainment, dancing. Ck-out 11:30 am. Meeting rms. Free airport transportation. Golf, tennis privileges. Exercise rm; instructor, bicycles, whirlpool, sauna, steam rm. Sailboat rentals. Private patios, balconies. On ocean. Cr cds: A, C, D, DS, MC, V.

★★ **DUNERIDGE RESORT.** *PO Box 526, 2400 N Limina Ave. 910/256-3101; res: 800/822-4588; FAX 910/256-3015.* 55 kit. suites, 4 story. Mid-May-mid-Sept: suites $1,000-$1,500/wk; lower rates rest of yr. Crib $45/wk. TV; cable. Pool. Ck-out 10 am. Maid serv wkly. Tennis. Balconies. On swimming beach. Cr cds: MC, V.

★★ **HOLIDAY INN.** *1706 N Lumina Ave, at end of US 74. 910/256-2231; FAX 910/256-9208.* 147 rms, 4 story. Mid-May-mid-Sept: S, D $120-$150; each addl $10; under 17 free; lower rates rest of yr. Crib free. TV; cable. Pool. Supervised child's activities (in season). Restaurant 6:30 am-10 pm. Rm serv. Bar 5 pm-1 am. Ck-out 11 am. Meeting rms. Gift shop. Bellhops. Private balconies. Cr cds: A, C, D, DS, ER, JCB, MC, V.

Restaurants

★★ **BRIDGE TENDER.** *1414 Airle Rd, at Wrightsville Beach Bridge. 910/256-4519.* Hrs: 11:30 am-2 pm, 5:30-10 pm; Sat 5:30-11 pm. Closed Jan 1, Thanksgiving, Dec 25. Bar. Semi-a la carte: lunch $3.25-$7.95, dinner $13.95-$21.95. Specializes in seafood, Angus beef. Parking. View of waterway, marina. Cr cds: A, D, DS, MC, V.

★★ **CAROLINE'S.** *1610 Pavilion Place, adj to Plaza East Shopping Center. 910/256-5008.* Hrs: 11:30 am-3 pm, 5:30-10 pm. Closed some major hols. Res accepted. Continental menu. Bar. Semi-a la carte: lunch $4.25-$5.95, dinner $12.95-$17.95. Specializes in pasta, beef, seafood. Parking. Cr cds: A, MC, V.

✔ ★ **DOCKSIDE.** *1308 Airlie Rd. 910/256-2752.* Hrs: 11 am-9:30 pm; wkends to 10 pm. Closed Thanksgiving, Dec 24-25. Bar. Semi-a la carte: lunch $1.50-$6.95, dinner $7.95-$15.95. Specializes in grilled grouper, hamburgers. Parking. Outdoor dining. Casual dining. Overlooks dock, waterway; docking facilities. Cr cds: A, MC, V.

★★ **KING NEPTUNE.** *11 N Lumina Ave on US 76. 910/256-2525.* Hrs: 5-10:30 pm; Sun 5:30-9:30 pm. Closed Thanksgiving, Dec 25. Bar to 2 am. Semi-a la carte: dinner $5.25-$17.75. Child's meals. Specializes in prime rib, seafood. Parking. Nautical decor. Cr cds: A, MC, V.

★ **MEDITERRANEO.** *22 N Lumina Ave. 910/256-3840.* Hrs: 5-11 pm. Closed Thanksgiving, Dec 24-25. Italian, Amer menu. Res accepted. Bar 5 pm-1 am. Semi-a la carte: dinner $6.75-$15.75. Specialty: seafood linguine. Parking. Intimate dining; artwork on display. Cr cds: A, C, D, DS, MC, V.

★★ **OCEAN TERRACE.** *(See Blockade Runner) 910/256-2251.* Hrs: 6:30 am-midnight; Sun brunch 11:30 am-2 pm. Closed wk of Dec 25. Res accepted. Bar. Semi-a la carte: bkfst $5.95-$8, lunch $5.95-$8, dinner $11.95-$19.95. Sun brunch $12.95. Child's meals. Specializes in seafood, pasta, beef. Comedy club Fri & Sat; jazz Sun. Parking. Oceanfront outdoor dining. Cr cds: A, D, DS, MC, V.

★★ **OCEANIC.** *703 S Lumina Ave. 910/256-5551.* Hrs: Sun-Fri 11 am-11 pm; Sat 11 am-midnight, Sun brunch 10 am-4 pm. Closed Jan 1, Dec 25. Bar. Semi-a la carte: lunch $2.95-$6.95, dinner $7.95-$27.95. Sat, Sun brunch $4.75-$7.95. Child's meals. Specializes in seafood. Oyster bar. Parking. Outdoor dining. Panoramic view of ocean. Cr cds: A, MC, V.

✓ ★ **WRIGHTSVILLE CAFE.** *530 Causeway Dr, in The Landing Shopping Center. 910/256-2777.* Hrs: 11:30 am-3 pm, 5-10 pm. Closed Thanksgiving, Dec 24-25. Bar. Semi-a la carte: lunch $3.50-$6.95, dinner $6.95-$13.95. Child's meals. Specialty: seafood chowder. Outdoor dining. Gift shop. Beach decor. Cr cds: A, MC, V.

Pennsylvania

Population: 11,881,643

Land area: 44,892 square miles

Elevation: 0-3,213 feet

Highest point: Mt Davis (Somerset County)

Entered Union: Second of original 13 states (December 12, 1787)

Capital: Harrisburg

Motto: Virtue, Liberty and Independence

Nickname: Keystone State

State flower: Mountain laurel

State bird: Ruffed grouse

State tree: Eastern hemlock

State fair: (Pennsylvania Farm Show), January 7-12, 1995, in Harrisburg

Time zone: Eastern

From its easternmost tip near Bordentown, New Jersey, to its straight western boundary with Ohio and West Virginia, Pennsylvania's 300-mile giant stride across the country covers a mountain-and-farm, river-and-stream, mine-and-mill topography. Its cities, people and resources are just as diverse. Philadelphia is a great city in the eastern part of the state, a treasure house of tradition and historical shrines; Pittsburgh is a great city in the western part, a mighty arsenal of industry. In this state are the Pennsylvania Dutch, their barns painted with vivid hex signs; here also are steel mills. Pennsylvania miners dig nearly all the anthracite coal in the US and still work some of the oldest iron mines in the country. Oil men work more than 19,000 producing wells, and 55,000 farm families make up 20 percent of the Pennsylvania work force.

Pennsylvania, the keystone of the original 13 states, remains one of the keystones in modern America. A leader in steel and coal production, the state also is a leader in cigar leaf tobacco, apples, grapes, ice cream, chocolate products, mushrooms (nearly half of the US total) and soft drinks, plus factory and farm machinery, electronics equipment, scientific instruments, watches, textile machines, railroad cars, ships, assorted metal products and electrical machinery. This fifth most populous state is also a major factor in national politics.

Pennsylvania has been a keystone of culture. The first serious music in the colonies was heard in Bethlehem; today, it resounds throughout the state—Pittsburgh has its own symphony, as does Philadelphia. There are 140 institutions of higher learning (including the oldest medical school in the US at the University of Pennsylvania), celebrated art galleries and hundreds of museums.

Despite its size, all of Pennsylvania is within the motorist's grasp. Its 44,000 miles of state highways, including the 470-mile Pennsylvania Turnpike (pioneer of superhighways), plus 69,363 miles of other roads make up one of the largest road networks in the nation.

Swedes made the first settlement on this fertile land at Tinicum Island in the Delaware River in 1643. The territory became Dutch in 1655 and British in 1664. After Charles II granted William Penn a charter that made him proprietor of "Pennsilvania," this Quaker statesman landed here in 1682 and invested the land with his money, leadership and fellow Quakers. The Swedes, Finns and Dutch already in the new land were granted citizenship; soon came Welsh, Germans, Scots, Irish and French Huguenots. Of these, the Germans left the strongest imprint on the state's personality. Commercial, agricultural and industrial growth came quickly, and all these resources were contributed to the Revolution. In Pennsylvania, Washington camped at Valley Forge, the Declaration of Independence was signed and the Constitution drafted.

With Philadelphia the capital of the new nation, tides of pioneers pushed west and north to develop far corners of the state. The Civil War brought fresh industrial development, and for the past century Pennsylvania has continued to develop at an ever-quickening industrial pace. Today the Keystone State is an empire of industry and a storehouse of historic traditions.

National Park Service Areas

The National Park Service administers Delaware Water Gap National Recreation Area (see), Fort Necessity National Battlefield (see UNIONTOWN), Independence National Historical Park (see PHILADELPHIA, #1), Gettysburg National Military Park (see), which includes Eisenhower National Historic Site, and Hopewell Furnace National Historic Site (see), Johnstown Flood National Memorial (see JOHNSTOWN), Thaddeus Kosciuszko National Memorial (see PHILADELPHIA), Allegheny Portage Railroad National Historic Site (see EBENSBURG), Edgar Allan Poe National Historic Site (see PHILADELPHIA), Friendship Hill National Historic Site, Steamtown National Historic Site (see SCRANTON), Delaware National Scenic River, Upper Delaware Scenic and Recreational River, Potomac Heritage National Scenic Trail and Valley Forge National Historical Park (see).

National Forest

Allegheny National Forest (see WARREN): Forest Supervisor in Warren; Ranger offices in Bradford, Marienville*, Ridgway*, Sheffield*.

*Not described in text

State Recreation Areas

The following towns list state recreation areas in their vicinity under What to See and Do; refer to the individual town for directions and park information.

Listed under **Altoona:** see Canoe Creek and Prince Gallitzin state parks.

Listed under **Ambridge:** see Raccoon Creek State Park.

Listed under **Bedford:** see Blue Knob and Shawnee state parks.

Listed under **Bellefonte:** see Black Moshannon State Park.

Listed under **Brookville:** see Clear Creek State Park.

Listed under **Butler:** see Moraine State Park.

Listed under **Carlisle:** see Pine Grove Furnace State Park.

Listed under **Chambersburg:** see Caledonia State Park.

Listed under **Clarion:** see Cook Forest State Park.

Listed under **Clearfield:** see Parker Dam and S.B. Elliott state parks.

Listed under **Conneaut Lake:** see Pymatuning State Park.

Listed under **Erie:** see Presque Isle State Park.

Listed under **Fort Washington:** see Fort Washington State Park.

Listed under **Galeton:** see Ole Bull State Park.

Listed under **Hanover:** see Codorus State Park.

Listed under **Hawley:** see Promised Land State Park.

Listed under **Indiana:** see Yellow Creek State Park.

Listed under **Kane:** see Bendigo and Kinzua Bridge state parks.

Listed under **Lewistown:** see Greenwood Furnace and Reeds Gap state parks.

Listed under **Lock Haven:** see Bald Eagle and Kettle Creek state parks.

Listed under **Mansfield:** see Hills Creek State Park.

Listed under **Media:** see Ridley Creek State Park.

Listed under **Mount Pocono:** see Gouldsboro and Tobyhanna state parks.

Listed under **New Castle:** see McConnell's Mill State Park.

Listed under **Port Allegany:** see Sizerville State Park.

Listed under **Pottstown:** see French Creek State Park.

Listed under **Somerset:** see Kooser and Laurel Hill state parks.

Listed under **State College:** see Whipple Dam State Park.

Listed under **Uniontown:** see Ohiopyle State Park.

Listed under **Warren:** see Chapman State Park.

Listed under **White Haven:** see Hickory Run State Park.

Listed under **Williamsport:** see Little Pine State Park.

Listed under **York:** see Gifford Pinchot State Park.

Water-related activities, hiking, riding, various other sports, picnicking and visitor centers, as well as camping, are available in many of these areas. More than 110 state parks and four environmental centers are scattered throughout the commonwealth. 55 campgrounds offer family camping. 21 are open all year; 9 are open from 2nd Fri Apr-3rd Sun Oct; 25 are open from 2nd Fri Apr-mid-Dec. Occupancy is limited to two consecutive weeks; $7 resident, $9 non-resident/night (primitive areas); $9 resident, $11 non-resident/night (modern areas). Cabins (daily and weekly rentals spring, fall & winter; 1 wk only, Sat after Memorial Day-Sat before Labor Day). Boat launching $5 resident, $6 non-resident. No pets allowed. Write to Department of Commerce, Office of Travel Marketing, 453 Forum Building, Harrisburg 17120, or Bureau of State Parks, PO Box 8551, Harrisburg 17105-8551, for detailed information. Cabin reservations are made by calling the park directly. For other state park information, phone 800/63-PARKS.

Fishing

Pennsylvania is one of the country's leading states in the amount of waters open to public and private fishing. There are nearly 5,000 miles of trout streams stocked annually and many thousands of miles of warmwater streams plus thousands of acres of lakes with walleye, panfish, muskellunge, and bass. Nonresident fishing license $25.50; 5-day tourist license $20.50. A $5.50 trout/salmon stamp also is required. Write to Pennsylvania Fish and Boat Commission, PO Box 67000, Harrisburg 17106-7000 for the annual "Summary of Fishing Regulations and Laws."

Hunting

A license is required to hunt, take, trap or kill any wild bird or animal in the state. Nonresident hunting license $80.75; children 12-16, $40.75. The license tag must be displayed on the back of outer garment, between the shoulders, at all times. For big-game hunting and small game & turkey hunting in the fall, 250 square inches of fluorescent orange must be worn on the head, chest and back combined. For the "Official Digest, Pennsylvania Hunting and Trapping Regulations," contact the Pennsylvania Game Commission, 2001 Elmerton Ave, Harrisburg 17110-9797; phone 717/787-6286.

Skiing

The following towns list ski areas in their vicinity under What to See and Do; refer to the individual town for directions and information.

Listed under **Allentown:** see Blue Mountain and Doe Mountain ski areas.

Listed under **Bedford:** see Blue Knob Ski Area.

Listed under **Carbondale:** see Elk Mt and Mount Tone† ski areas.

Listed under **Donegal:** see Seven Springs Mountain Ski Area.

Listed under **Edinboro:** see Edinboro Ski Area.

Listed under **Galeton:** see Ski Denton/Denton Hill Ski Area†.

Listed under **Gettysburg:** see Ski Liberty Ski Area.

Listed under **Hawley:** see Tanglwood Ski Area.

Listed under **Limerick:** see Spring Mountain Ski Area.

Listed under **Mount Pocono:** see Mount Airy Lodge Ski Area†.

Listed under **Pittsburgh:** see Boyce Park Ski Area.

Listed under **Scranton:** see Montage Ski Area.

Listed under **Shawnee on Delaware:** see Shawnee Mountain Ski Area.

Listed under **Somerset:** see Hidden Valley Ski Area†.

Listed under **Stroudsburg:** see Alpine Mountain Ski Area.

Listed under **Tannersville:** see Camelback Ski Area.

Listed under **Wellsboro:** see Ski Sawmill Resort.

Listed under **White Haven:** see Big Boulder and Jack Frost ski areas.

Listed under **York:** see Ski Roundtop Ski Area.

†Also cross-country trails

Safety Belt Information

Safety belts are mandatory for all persons in front seat of vehicle. Children under 4 years must be in an approved passenger restraint anywhere in vehicle; age 4 and older may use a regulation safety belt; ages 1-3 may use a regulation safety belt in back seat only. Children under 4 years must use an approved safety seat in front seat; under age 1 must use an approved safety seat anywhere in the vehicle. For further information phone 717/787-6853.

Interstate Highway System

The following alphabetical listing of Pennsylvania towns in *Mobil Travel Guide* shows that these cities are within 10 miles of the indicated Interstate highways. A highway map should, however, be checked for the nearest exit.

INTERSTATE 70: Bedford, Breezewood, Donegal, Greensburg, New Stanton, Somerset, Washington.

INTERSTATE 78: Allentown, Bethlehem, Easton, Hamburg, Kutztown, Lebanon, Shartlesville.

INTERSTATE 79: Conneaut Lake, Edinboro, Erie, Harmony, Meadville, Mercer, Pittsburgh, Washington.

INTERSTATE 80: Bellefonte, Bloomsburg, Brookville, Clarion, Clearfield, Danville, Du Bois, Hazleton, Lewisburg, Lock Haven, Mercer, Mount Pocono, Sharon, Shawnee on Delaware, Stroudsburg, Tannersville, White Haven.

INTERSTATE 81: Ashland, Carlisle, Chambersburg, Harrisburg, Hazleton, Scranton, Wilkes-Barre.

INTERSTATE 83: Harrisburg, York.

INTERSTATE 84: Milford, Scranton.

INTERSTATE 90: Erie, North East.

INTERSTATE 95: Bristol, Philadelphia.

Weather

Despite its close proximity to the Atlantic Ocean, Pennsylvania has a continental climate because the prevailing winds are from the west. This makes for extreme heat and cold, although not as marked as in the central states. There are only minor variations throughout the state caused by altitude and geographical features. The frost-free period is longest in southeastern Pennsylvania, the Ohio and Monongahela river valleys, and the region bordering Lake Erie. The higher lands have only three to five months free from frost. The rainfall is usually adequate for temperate zone crops.

Additional Visitor Information

A free Visitors Guide and numerous pamphlets on Pennsylvania vacationing, historical tours, skiing, campgrounds and resorts are available by calling 800/VISIT-PA, at the Pennsylvania Office of Travel Marketing, Department of Commerce, PO Box 61, Warrendale 15086.

There are eleven state-run traveler information centers in Pennsylvania; visitors who stop by will find information and brochures most helpful in planning stops at points of interest. Their locations are as follows: I-79 Edinboro (southbound), 1 mile south of the Edinboro exit; I-81 Greencastle (northbound), 1 mile north of the Pennsylvania/Maryland border; I-95 Linwood (northbound), 1/2 mile north of the Pennsylvania/Delaware border; I-70 Warfordsburg (westbound), 1 mile from the Pennsylvania/Maryland border; I-80 West Middlesex (eastbound), 1/2 mile east of the Pennsylvania/Ohio border; Neshaminy Welcome Center, Mile Marker 351 (westbound) on the Pennsylvania Turnpike, 7 miles west of the Pennsylvania/New Jersey border, located inside the plaza building; I-78 Easton (westbound), 1 mile west of the Pennsylvania/New Jersey border; Sideling Hill Welcome Center, Mile Marker 172 (eastbound and westbound) on the Pennsylvania Turnpike, 10 miles east of the Breezewood exit, located inside the plaza building; I-81 Lenox (southbound), 4 miles south of the Lenox exit 64; I-83 Shrewsbury (northbound), 1/2 mile north of the Pennsylvania/Maryland border; Zelienople Welcome Center, Mile Marker 21 (eastbound), 21 miles east of the Pennsylvania/Ohio border, located inside the plaza building. Centers are open (May-Sept, daily 8 am-6 pm; rest of yr to 5 pm; also most holidays).

Ride With Me-Pennsylvania, Interstate 81 is a 90-minute audio cassette tape that provides information on points of interest along I-81, from New York to Maryland. Topics such as the history of the Pennsylvania Dutch, notable battlegrounds and areas related to the Civil War and anthracite coal miners are discussed. Contact RWM Associates, PO Box 1324, Bethesda, MD 20817; 301/299-7817.

Allentown (D-9)

Founded: 1762 **Pop:** 105,090 **Elev:** 364 ft **Area code:** 610

Allentown, situated in the heart of Pennsylvania Dutch country, is conveniently accessible via a network of major highways. Allentown was originally incorporated as Northamptontown. The city later took the name of its founder, William Allen, a Chief Justice of Pennsylvania. Allentown was greatly influenced by the Pennsylvania Germans who settled the surrounding countryside and helped the city become the business hub for a rich agricultural community.

What to See and Do

1. **Liberty Bell Shrine.** 622 Hamilton, at Church St. Reconstructed Zion's church has shrine in basement area where Liberty Bell was hidden in 1777; contains a full-size replica of the original bell; a 46-foot mural depicts the journey of the bell; other historical exhibits, art collection. (Mon-Sat afternoons; closed Jan 1, Easter, Thanksgiving, Dec 25) Phone 435-4232. **Free.**

2. **Trout Hall** (1770). 414 Walnut St. Oldest house in city, Georgian colonial; restored. Period rooms, museum. Guided tours (Apr-Nov, Tues-Sun afternoons; other times by appt; closed most major hols) Phone 435-4664. **Free.**

3. **Lehigh County Museum.** Old Courthouse, 5th & Hamilton Sts. Exhibits illustrate economic, social and cultural history of the county. (Mon-Sat, mid-morning-mid-afternoon & Sun afternoons; closed hols) Phone 435-4664. **Free.**

4. **Frank Buchman House.** 117 N 11th St. Constructed in 1892, this 3-story row house, typical of Allentown's inner city, is an example of Victorian architecture; period rooms. (Sat & Sun afternoons; also by appt) Phone 435-4664. **Free.**

5. **Muhlenberg College** (1848). (1,600 students) Chew & 24th Sts. Founded by the Lutheran Church to honor patriarch of Lutheranism in America. On campus is the Gideon F. Egner Memorial Chapel, an example of Gothic architecture. Also here is the Center for the Arts, a dramatic building designed by renowned architect Philip Johnson, which houses the Muhlenberg Theater Association. Campus tours. Phone 821-3230.

6. **Cedar Crest College** (1867). (1,400 women) 100 College Dr. An 84-acre campus that includes nationally-recognized William F. Curtis Arboretum (tours); chapel with stained-glass windows portraying outstanding women in history; College Center houses art gallery and theater. Campus tours. Phone 437-4471.

7. **Trexler-Lehigh County Game Preserve.** 4 mi W on US 22, then 6 mi N on US 309, near Schnecksville. Herds of bison, elk, deer; palomino horses; many other native and exotic animals on 1,700 acres; 25-acre children's zoo; picnic grounds. (Memorial Day-Labor Day, daily; May-Memorial Day & after Labor Day-Oct, Sun only) Sr citizen rate. Phone 799-4171. **¢¢**

8. **Trexler Memorial Park.** Cedar Crest Blvd. Spring outdoor bulb display (Apr-May.) **Gross Memorial Rose Garden** (at peak 2nd wk June) and **Old-Fashioned Garden** Cedar Pkwy (June-Aug). **Trout Nursery** and Fish-for-Fun stream, Lehigh Pkwy; picnic areas. **West Park.** 16th and Turner. Band concerts (June-Aug). Phone 437-7628. **Free.**

9. **George Taylor House and Park** (1768). 4 mi N off US 22, at Front & Poplar Sts in Catasauqua. House of a signer of the Declaration of Independence; 18th-century restoration period rooms; mu-

seum; walled garden. Guided tours. (June-Oct, Sat & Sun afternoons; other times by appt) Phone 435-4664. **Free.**

10. **Dorney Park & Wildwater Kingdom.** 3830 Dorney Park Rd. Theme park/water park featuring more than 100 rides and attractions, three world-class roller coasters, 12 water slides; midway games and entertainment; more than 20 picnic groves. **Wildwater Kingdom** is considered to be one of the top seasonal water parks in the country. Dorney Park (May-Sept). Water park (mid-May-Sept). Operating hrs may vary. Phone 395-3724. ¢¢¢¢¢

11. **Troxell-Steckel House and Farm Museum** (1756). 6 mi N on PA 145, then 1 mi W on PA 329, at 4229 Reliance St in Egypt. Stone house is an example of German medieval architecture. Period rooms; museum. Swiss-style bank barn adj has exhibits of farm implements, carriages and sleighs. Guided tours. (June-Oct, Sat & Sun afternoons; other times by appt) Phone 435-4664. **Free.**

12. **Lock Ridge Furnace Museum.** 6 mi SW via US 222 in Alburtis. Exhibits on the development of the US iron and steel industry; emphasis on the anthracite coal-heated iron industry. Located in a reconstructed 19th-century iron furnace. (May-Sept, Sat & Sun afternoons; also hols and by appt) Phone 435-4664. **Free.**

13. **Haines Mill Museum** (ca 1760). 3 mi W via Hamilton St, at 3600 Dorney Park Rd (Cetronia). Operating gristmill (reconstructed 1909); exhibits portray the development and importance of the gristmill in rural America. (May-Sept, Sat & Sun afternoons; also hols and by appt) Phone 435-4664. **Free.**

14. **Saylor Park Cement Industry Museum.** 4 mi NE via MacArthur Rd, on N 2nd St in Coplay. Exhibits on the historical development of the cement industry and its role in modern society. Located in rebuilt cement kilns. (May-Sept, Sat & Sun afternoons; also hols and by appt) Phone 435-4664. **Free.**

15. **Skiing.**

Doe Mountain. 12 mi SW, 4½ mi off PA 100, just N of Hereford. Four chairlifts, T-bar, 2 rope tows; 12 slopes; patrol, school, rentals; snowmaking; restaurant, cafeteria, bar; nursery. Longest run 4,700 ft; vertical drop 500 ft. (Dec-mid-Mar, daily) Phone 682-7109 or (in PA) 800/282-7107 (snow report). ¢¢¢¢¢

Blue Mountain. 17 mi N via PA 145, Treichlers exit, at "Y" turn right to Cherryville, and on to Danielsville, to top of Blue Mountain. Six chairlifts, T-bar; school, rentals; snowmaking; cafeteria, bar, lodge. Vertical drop 1,053 ft. Also 19 trails with day and night skiing. (Dec-Mar, daily) Phone 826-7700; ski reports 800/235-2226 (PA). ¢¢¢¢¢

(For further information contact the Lehigh Valley Convention & Visitors Bureau, PO Box 20785, Lehigh Valley 18002; 882-9200.)

Annual Events

Mayfair. Allentown parks. Visual and performing arts festival with music, crafts and food. Phone 437-6900. Thurs-Mon, Memorial Day wkend.

Das Awkscht Fescht. Macungie Memorial Park. 2,500 antique and special interest autos; arts and crafts; antique toy show, fireworks. Phone 967-2317. 1st wkend Aug.

Drum Corps International-Eastern Regional Championship. J. Birney Crum Stadium. Phone 966-5344. Early Aug.

Great Allentown Fair. Fairgrounds. 17th & Chew Sts. Farm and industrial exhibits, stock car races, children's rides, food, entertainment. Phone 435-SHOW. Late Aug-early Sept.

Super Sunday. Hamilton Street Mall. Arts & crafts, food, entertainment. Phone 437-7616. Mid-Sept.

(See Bethlehem, Easton, Kutztown, Quakertown)

Motels

★ **ALLENWOOD.** 1058 Hausman Rd (18104), E on US 22 to PA 309S to Hausman Rd. 610/395-3707. 21 rms. S, D, studio rms $40; each addl $3. Crib free. Pet accepted. TV; cable. Restaurant nearby. Ck-out 11 am. Cr cds: A, DS, MC, V.

★★ **COMFORT SUITES.** 3712 Hamilton Blvd (18103). 610/437-9100; FAX 610/437-0221. 122 suites, 4 story. Suites $79-$99; each addl $10; under 18 free. Crib free. TV; cable, in-rm movies. Complimentary continental bkfst. Restaurant 7-2 am. Rm serv. Bar; entertainment Thurs-Sat. Ck-out noon. Meeting rms. Sundries. Free airport, RR station, bus depot transportation. Exercise equipt; weights, bicycles. Refrigerators. Cr cds: A, C, D, DS, ER, JCB, MC, V.

D ✕ ⊠ 🔥 SC

✔ ★★ **DAYS INN CONFERENCE CENTER.** 1151 Bulldog Dr (18104). 610/395-3731; FAX 610/395-9899. 281 rms, 2 story. May-Oct: S $49-$59; D $55-$65; each addl $6; suites $90; under 18 free; wkly rates; ski, golf, Dorney Park plans; higher rates: US Open, local festivals; lower rates rest of yr. Crib free. TV; cable. Pool; poolside serv; lifeguard. Playground. Restaurant 6:30 am-10 pm. Rm serv. Bar 11-1 am. Ck-out noon. Coin lndry. Convention facilities. Sundries. Free airport, bus depot transportation. 18-hole golf privileges. Downhill ski 15 mi. Game rm. Lawn games. Some refrigerators. Some balconies. Cr cds: A, C, D, DS, MC, V.

D ⊠ ✕ 🎿 ≋ ⊠ 🔥 SC

★★ **HAMPTON INN.** 7471 Keebler Way (18106), I-78 exit 14A, S on PA 100. 610/391-1500; FAX 610/391-0386. 127 rms, 5 story. S $55-$65; D $61-$71; under 18 free. Crib free. TV; cable. Complimentary continental bkfst. Restaurant nearby. Ck-out noon. Meeting rms. Free airport transportation. Exercise equipt; weight machine, bicycle, sauna. Cr cds: A, C, D, DS, MC, V.

D ✕ ⊠ ⊠ 🔥 SC

✔ ★ **HOLIDAY INN EXPRESS.** 15th St & US 22 (18103). 610/435-7880; FAX 610/432-2555. 84 rms, 4 story. S $35-$40; D $50-$55; each addl $4; under 18 free. Crib free. Pet accepted. TV; cable. Complimentary continental bkfst. Restaurant nearby. Ck-out 11 am. Cr cds: A, C, D, DS, MC, V.

⊠ ⊠ 🔥 SC

Hotel

★★★ **HILTON.** 904 Hamilton Mall (18101), at Hamilton & 9th Sts, in center of town. 610/433-2221; FAX 610/433-6455. 224 rms, 9 story. S $80-$104; D $90-$114; each addl $10; suites $140-$195; children free; wkend rates. Crib free. TV; cable, in-rm movies. Heated pool; lifeguard. Restaurant 6:30 am-10 pm. Bar 11-2 am. Ck-out 11 am. Meeting rms. Free airport, bus depot transportation. Exercise equipt; weights, bicycle, sauna. Cr cds: A, C, D, DS, ER, MC, V.

D ≋ ✕ ⊠ 🔥 SC

Inn

★★★ **GLASBERN.** (2141 Pack House Rd, Fogelsville 18051) Approx 10 mi W on I-78, exit PA 100 N, W on Main St, N on Church St to Pack House Rd. 610/285-4723; FAX 610/285-2862. 23 rms, 2 story, 13 suites. S $85-$105; D $100-$250; each addl $15; suites $115-$250; 2-night min special wkends, hols. Crib $15. TV; cable, in-rm movies avail. Heated pool. Complimentary full bkfst. Dining rm (public by res) 6-8 pm. Ck-out noon, ck-in 4 pm. Meeting rm. Many whirlpools, fireplaces. Farmhouse, barn, gate house and carriage house built in late 1800s; antiques. Cr cds: MC, V.

Restaurants

★★★ **APPENNINO.** 3079 Willow St, at Cedar Crest Blvd. 610/799-2727. Hrs: 11:30 am-2:30 pm, 5:30-10 pm; Sat from 5:30 pm;

Sun 4-9 pm. Closed major hols. Res accepted. Northern Italian menu. Bar. Wine list. A la carte entrees: lunch $7.75-$9.50, dinner $10-$24. Specialities: veal Valdostana, filet of sole in green sauce with shrimp. Own desserts. Parking. Restored hotel (1800s); imported Italian lamps, chandeliers and tapestry on chairs. Jacket. Cr cds: A, D, DS, MC, V.

D

★ ★ ★ **BALLIETSVILLE INN.** *(2700 Balliet St, Ballietsville)* Approx 6 mi N on 15th St/Mauch Chunk Rd, then left at sign, just S of jct PA 329. 610/799-2435. Hrs: 5:30-10 pm. Closed Sun; Jan 1, Memorial Day, July 4, Thanksgiving, Dec 24 & 25. Res accepted. Country French menu. Bar. A la carte entrees: dinner $12.50-$27.50. Specialties: Dover sole meunière, roast rack of lamb, game. Parking. Gracious, old country inn atmosphere. Cr cds: A, C, D, MC, V.

Altoona (E-4)

Founded: 1849 **Pop:** 51,881 **Elev:** 1,170 ft **Area code:** 814

The rough, high Alleghenies ring this city, which was founded by the Pennsylvania Railroad. Altoona expanded rapidly after 1852, when the difficult task of spanning the Alleghenies with track, linking Philadelphia and Pittsburgh, was completed. The railroad shops still offer substantial employment for residents of the city and Blair County, but new and diversified industries now provide the economic base.

What to See and Do

1. **Baker Mansion Museum** (1844-48). 3500 Oak Lane. Stone Greek-revival house of early ironmaster; now occupied by Blair County Historical Society. Hand-carved Belgian furniture of the period; transportation exhibits, gun collection, clothing, housewares. (Memorial Day-Labor Day, daily exc Mon; mid-Apr-Memorial Day & Labor Day-Oct, Sat & Sun) Sr citizen rate. Phone 942-3916. ¢¢

2. **Railroader's Memorial Museum.** 1300 9th Ave. Exhibits feature railroad artifacts, art and theme displays. Railroad rolling stock, steam and electric locomotive collections. (May-Oct, daily; rest of yr, daily exc Mon; closed Jan 1, Thanksgiving, Dec 25) Sr citizen rate. Phone 946-0834. ¢¢

3. **Horseshoe Curve Visitors Center.** 5 mi W via well-marked, un-numbered road. World-famous engineering feat, carrying main-line Conrail and Amtrak trains around western grade of 91 feet per mile. Curve is 2,375 feet long and has a central angle of 220 degrees. Incline plane runs between interpretive center and observation area. Gift shop. (May-Oct, daily; rest of yr, daily exc Mon) Phone 941-7960. Incline, tours ¢

4. **Wopsononock Mt.** 6 mi NW on Juniata Gap Rd. Lookout provides view of 6-county area from height of 2,580 feet; offers one of the best views in the state.

5. **Bland's Park.** 10 mi N, on US 220 in Tipton. More than 24 rides and attractions including antique carousel, miniature golf and pony rides. Also here are arcade games, picnic pavilions and restaurant. (Memorial Day-Labor Day, daily exc Mon; May & Sept, wkends) Phone 684-3538. All-day ride pass ¢¢¢

6. **Forest Zoo.** Approx 8 mi W, 3 mi off US 22 Gallitzin exit on Gallitzin-Coupon Rd in Gallitzin. Large collection of wild animals; contact area; picnicking, concession. Phone 944-4811. ¢

7. **Fort Roberdeau.** 8 mi NE via US 220, Kettle St exit onto PA 1013. Reconstructed Revolutionary War horizontal log fort contains lead smelter, blacksmith shop, lead miners' hut, barracks, storehouse, officers' quarters, powder magazine. Costumed guides; wkend reenactments. Visitor's center. Picnicking, nature trails. (Mid-May-early Oct, daily exc Mon) Phone 946-0048. ¢¢

8. **Lakemont Park.** 700 Park Ave, junction Frankstown Rd & US 220. An amusement park with more than 30 rides and attractions; home of the nation's oldest roller coaster; water park, entertain-

ment. (Memorial Day-Labor Day, daily) Phone 949-7275. All-day ride pass ¢¢-¢¢¢

9. **Prince Gallitzin State Park.** 8 mi NW on PA 36, then 1 1/4 mi NW off PA 53, then W on SR 1026. Approx 6,200 acres; 26 miles of shoreline on 1,600-acre lake. Swimming beach; fishing; boating (rentals, mooring, launching, marina). Hiking trails, horseback riding. Cross-country skiing, snowmobiling, ice-skating, ice fishing. Picnicking, snack bar, store, laundry facilities. Tent & trailer sites, cabins. Nature center; interpretive program. Standard fees. Phone 674-1000 or -1007 for reservations.

10. **Canoe Creek State Park.** 12 mi E via US 22. Approx 950-acre park features 155-acre lake. Swimming beach; fishing; boating (launches, rentals). Hiking. Picnicking (reservations for pavilion). Cross-country skiing, sledding, ice boating, ice-skating. Cabins. Standard fees. Phone 695-6807.

(For further information contact the Blair County Convention & Visitors Bureau, 1231 11th Ave, 16601; 943-4183 or 800/84-ALTOONA.)

Annual Events

Blair County Arts Festival. Downtown. Arts, crafts, hobbies on display. Mid-May.

Keystone Country Festival. Lakemont Park (see #8). Arts & crafts, continuous music; food. Contact Convention & Visitors Bureau for details. Wkend after Labor Day.

(See Ebensburg)

Motor Hotel

★ ★ ★ **RAMADA.** 1 Sheraton Dr (16601), 5 mi S on US 220. 814/946-1631; FAX 814/946-0785. 219 rms, 2-3 story. Jan-May: S $60-$65; D $64-$70; each addl $5; suites $120-$140; studio rms $65; under 18 free; some wkend rates; higher rates: football games, ski season; lower rates rest of yr. Crib $5. Pet accepted. TV; cable. Indoor pool; wading pool, lifeguard. Restaurant 6:30 am-2:30 pm, 5:30-10 pm; Sat to 11 pm. Rm serv. Bar 11-2 am; entertainment, dancing exc Sun. Ck-out noon. Meeting rms. Bellhops. Valet serv. Sundries. Airport transportation. 18-hole golf privileges. Downhill ski 20 mi. Exercise rm; instructor, weights, bicycles, whirlpool, sauna. Rec rm. Cr cds: A, C, D, DS, JCB, MC, V.

Restaurants

★ ★ ★ **ALLEGRO.** 3926 Broad Ave. 814/946-5216. Hrs: 4-9:30 pm; Sat to 10 pm. Closed Sun; major hols. Res accepted. Italian, Amer menu. Bar. Wine list. Semi-a la carte: dinner $9.95-$32.95. Child's meals. Specializes in veal, seafood. Own baking, sauces, pasta. Cr cds: A, C, D, DS, MC, V.

D

✔ ★ **HOUSE OF CHANG.** 601 Logan Blvd. 814/942-3322. Hrs: 11:30 am-10 pm; Sat from noon; Sun noon-9 pm. Closed Thanksgiving, Dec 25. Chinese menu. Bar. Semi-a la carte: lunch $4.25-$5.95, dinner $6.50-$14.95. Buffet: lunch (Sun) $6.75. Child's meals. Specialties: Peking shrimp, subgum wonton. Parking. Oriental decor. Cr cds: A, MC, V.

Ambridge (D-1)

Founded: 1901 **Pop:** 8,133 **Elev:** 751 ft **Area code:** 412 **Zip:** 15003

Founded by and taking its name from the American Bridge Co, this city rests on part of the site of Old Economy Village. In 1825, under the leadership of George Rapp, the Harmony Society established a communal pietistic colony that for many decades was important in the industrial life and development of western Pennsylvania. Despite its spiritual emphasis, Old Economy Village enjoyed a great material prosperity; farms were productive, craft shops were busy and factories made textiles widely acclaimed for their quality. Surplus funds financed railroads and industrial enterprises throughout the upper Ohio Valley. After celibacy was adopted and unwise investments were made, the community's productivity decreased. Officially dissolved in 1905, the remains of the community were taken over by the Commonwealth of Pennsylvania in 1916.

What to See and Do

1. **Old Economy Village.** 14th & Church Sts. Seventeen original Harmony Society buildings located on six acres, restored and filled with furnishings of the community. Included are the communal leader's 32-room Great House, the Feast Hall, the Grotto in the Gardens, wine cellars, a 5-story granary, shops, dwellings and community kitchens. Cobblestone streets link the buildings. Special festivals and events. (Daily exc Mon; closed hols) Sr citizen rate. Phone 266-4500. **¢¢**

2. **Raccoon Creek State Park.** 9 mi W on PA 151, then 7 mi S on PA 18, near Frankfort Springs. Approx 7,300 acres. Swimming beach; fishing, hunting; boating (rentals, mooring, launching). Hiking, horseback riding. Cross-country skiing, sledding, snowmobiling, ice-skating, ice fishing. Snack bar. Tent & trailer sites. Nature and historical centers. Standard fees. Phone 899-2200.

(For further information contact the Beaver County Tourist Promotion Agency, 215B Ninth St, Monaca 15061-2028; 728-0212 or 800/342-8192 outside 412 area code.)

Annual Event

Nationality Days. Ethnic cultural displays, foods; native music, dancing. Mid-May.

(For accommodations see Beaver Falls, Pittsburgh)

Ashland (D-8)

Pop: 3,859 **Elev:** 1,000 ft **Area code:** 717 **Zip:** 17921

What to See and Do

1. **Pioneer Tunnel Coal Mine and Steam Lokie Ride.** 19th & Oak Sts. Tour and explanation of mining in original coal mine tunnel; indoor temperature 52°F. Narrow-gauge steam train ride; picnic park. (Memorial Day-Labor Day, daily; May & Sept-Oct, wkends) Phone 875-3850 or -3301. Mine tour **¢¢**; Train ride **¢¢**

2. **Museum of Anthracite Mining.** Pine & 17th Sts. Museum on geology and technology of mining "hard" coal. (May-Oct, Mon-Sat, also Sun afternoons; rest of yr, Tues-Sat, also Sun afternoons; closed hols) Phone 875-4708. **¢¢**

(For further information contact the Schuylkill County Visitors Bureau, 91 S Progress Ave, Pottsville 17901-0237; 622-7700.)

(For accommodations see Hazleton)

Beaver Falls (D-1)

Founded: 1806 **Pop:** 10,687 **Elev:** 800 ft **Area code:** 412 **Zip:** 15010

Founded as Brighton, the town changed its name for the falls in the Beaver River. The plates from which US currency is printed are made in Beaver Falls. Geneva College (1848) is located here.

(For information about this area contact the Beaver County Tourist Promotion Agency, 215B Ninth St, Monaca 15061-2028; 728-0212 or 800/342-8192 outside 412 area code.)

(See Ambridge, Harmony)

Motels

✔ ★ **BEAVER VALLEY.** 7257 Big Beaver Blvd, on PA 18, 1/2 mi N of PA Tpke exit 2. 412/843-0630; res: 800/400-8312; FAX 412/843-1610. 27 rms. S $33-$40; D $43-$64; each addl $8; kit. units $44-$52; under 18 free; wkly rates. Crib free. TV; cable. Complimentary coffee in lobby. Ck-out 11 am. Cr cds: A, C, D, DS, MC, V.

★ **BEST WESTERN CONLEY'S MOTOR INN.** Big Beaver Blvd, on PA 18, 1/4 mi S of PA Tpke exit 2. 412/843-9300; res: 800/345-6819. 54 rms, 4 kits. S $49; D $59; each addl $8; under 12 free; wkly, monthly rates. TV; cable. Restaurant 7 am-10 pm. Bar. Ck-out noon. Meeting rms. Refrigerators. Cr cds: C, D, DS, MC, V.

Motor Hotel

★ ★ ★ **HOLIDAY INN.** Box 696, PA 18N at PA Tpke exit 2. 412/846-3700; FAX 412/846-3700, ext. 290. 156 rms, 3 story. S $69-$72; D $77-$80; each addl $8; under 18 free; wkend rates. Crib free. Pet accepted. TV. Indoor pool; whirlpool, sauna, poolside serv, lifeguard. Restaurant 6 am-10 pm. Rm serv. Bar 11-2 am. Ck-out noon. Meeting rms. Valet serv. Miniature golf. Game rm. Cr cds: A, C, D, DS, JCB, MC, V.

Restaurant

★ ★ ★ **WOODEN ANGEL.** (Leopard Lane, Beaver 15009) From jct PA 51 & 68, 1/2 mi N on PA 51, 1/4 mi W on Leopard Lane. 412/774-7880. Hrs: 11:30 am-11 pm. Closed Sun, Mon; major hols exc Mother's Day. Res accepted. Bar. Extensive wine cellar. Semi-a la carte: lunch $5.75-$10.75, dinner $13.50-$28. Specializes in rack of lamb, fresh seafood. Own baking. Parking. Cr cds: A, C, D, MC, V.

Bedford (F-4)

Settled: 1751 **Pop:** 3,137 **Elev:** 1,106 ft **Area code:** 814 **Zip:** 15522

Fort Bedford was a major frontier outpost in pre-Revolutionary War days. After the war it became an important stopover along the route of western migration and has remained so up until the present. Garrett Pendergrass, the second settler here, built Pendergrass's Tavern, which figures in a number of novels by Hervey Allen.

What to See and Do

1. **Bedford County Courthouse.** S Juliana St. Federal-style building constructed in 1828 has unique hanging spiral staircase. (Mon-Fri; closed hols) Phone 623-4807. **Free.**

2. **Fort Bedford Park and Museum.** Ft Bedford Dr, N end of Juliana St, park along Raystown River. Log blockhouse, erected during Bedford's bicentennial. Contains large-scale replica of original fort, displays of colonial antiques and relics, Indian artifacts. (May-late Oct, daily) Phone 623-8891. **¢¢**

3. **Old Bedford Village.** 1 mi N on US Business 220N. More than 40 authentic log and frame structures (1750-1851) house historical

exhibits; crafts demonstrations; operating pioneer farm. (1st Sat May-last Sun Oct, daily; also open evenings first 2 wkends Dec) Many special events throughout the yr. Sr citizen rate. Phone 623-1156. ¢¢¢

4. State parks.

Shawnee. 8 mi W on US 30. Approx 450-acre lake surrounded by 3,840 acres. Swimming beach; fishing, hunting; boating (rentals, mooring, launching). Cross-country skiing, snowmobiling, sledding, ice-skating, ice fishing. Picnicking, playfield, snack bar. Camping; tent and trailer sites. Standard fees. Phone 733-4218.

Blue Knob. 10 mi N on US 220, then 8 mi NW on PA 869. Approx 6,000 acres. Swimming pool; fishing, hunting. Hiking. Cross-country skiing, snowmobiling, sledding. Picnicking, playfield. Camping (mid-Apr-mid-Oct). Standard fees. Phone 276-3576. In park is

5. Blue Knob Ski Area. Two triple and 2 double chairlifts, 3 platter pulls; patrol, school, rentals; snowmaking; bar, cafeteria; nursery. Longest run approx 2 mi; vertical drop 1,072 ft. (Dec-Mar, daily) Half-day rates avail. Phone 239-5111 or (in PA) 800/458-3403 for snow conditions. ¢¢¢¢¢

(For further information contact the Bedford County Tourist Promotion Agency, 137 E Pitt St; 623-1771.)

Annual Events

Old Bedford Village Folk Festival. Juried arts and craft demonstrations and sales; variety of foods; village tours (see #3), children's activities, continuous entertainment. Phone 623-1156 or 800/622-8005. Late June.

Civil War Reenactment. Old Bedford Village (see #3). Early Sept.

Motels

 ★★ **BEST WESTERN HOSS'S INN.** *RD 2, Box 33B, 2 mi N via US 220 Business, PA Tpke exit 11.* 814/623-9006; FAX 814/623-7120. 107 rms, 2 story. Apr-Oct: S $38-$46; D $48-$56; each addl $8; under 12 free; lower rates rest of yr. Crib free. Pet accepted, some restrictions; $50. TV; cable. Pool; lifeguard. Restaurant 6:30-11 am, 5-10 pm; Sat & Sun 6:30 am-10 pm. Bar 5 pm-midnight. Ck-out noon. Meeting rms. Gift shop. Exercise equipt; weight machine, treadmill, sauna. Game rm. Cr cds: A, C, D, DS, MC, V.

D ⚓ 🏊 🏋 ⛷ 🔥 SC

★★ **QUALITY INN.** *RD 2, Box 171, 2 mi N on US 220 Business, 1 blk N of PA Tpke exit 11.* 814/623-5188; FAX 814/623-7296. 66 rms. May-Nov: S $54-$60; D $60-$66; each addl $6; under 18 free; lower rates rest of yr. Crib $4. Pet accepted, some restrictions. TV; cable. Pool. Restaurant 7 am-10 pm. Bar 11 am-11 pm. Ck-out 11 am. Meeting rms. Downhill ski 20 mi. Cr cds: A, C, D, DS, ER, JCB, MC, V.

D ⚓ 🏊 ⛷ 🔥 SC

Restaurant

 ★★ **ED'S STEAK HOUSE.** *2 mi N on US 220 Business, 1/4 mi N of PA Tpke exit 11.* 814/623-8894. Hrs: 7 am-10 pm; Sun to 9 pm. Closed Dec 25. Res accepted. Bar. Semi-a la carte: bkfst $1.99-$4.99, lunch $2.99-$5.99, dinner $5.95-$22.50. Child's meals. Specializes in steak, seafood. Parking. Family-owned. Cr cds: A, MC, V.

D

Bellefonte (D-5)

Settled: 1770 **Pop:** 6,358 **Elev:** 809 ft **Area code:** 814 **Zip:** 16823

When the exiled French minister Talleyrand saw the Big Spring here in 1794, his exclamation—"beautiful fountain"—gave the town its name. Bellefonte is perched on seven hills at the southeast base of Bald Eagle Mountain.

What to See and Do

1. Centre County Library and Historical Museum. 203 N Allegheny St. Local historical museum includes central Pennsylvania historical and genealogical books, records. (Daily exc Sun; closed hols) Phone 355-1516. **Free.**

2. Curtin Village. 2 mi N on PA 150 at I-80 exit 23. Mansion, built in 1831 by Roland Curtin; iron furnace (1848), worker's cabin, herb garden. Restored by the Pennsylvania Historical and Museum Commission. (Memorial Day-Labor Day, Wed-Sun; Labor Day-mid-Oct, wkends only) Phone 355-1982 for tours. Tours ¢¢

3. Black Moshannon State Park. N via PA 144/150, SW via US 220, then approx 12 mi W on PA 504. Approx 3,450 acres. Swimming beach; fishing, hunting; boating (rentals, mooring, launching). Hiking. Cross-country skiing, snowmobiling, ice-skating, ice fishing, ice boating. Picnicking, snack bar. Tent & trailer sites, cabins. Interpretive program. Standard fees. Phone 342-5960.

(For further information contact the Bellefonte Area Chamber of Commerce, Train Station; 355-2917.)

(For accommodations see State College)

Restaurant

★★ **GAMBLE MILL TAVERN.** *160 Dunlap St, at Lamb St Bridge.* 814/355-7764. Hrs: 11:30 am-2 pm, 5-8 pm. Closed Sun; Thanksgiving, Dec 25. Res accepted. Continental menu. Bar. A la carte entrees: lunch $6-$10, dinner $10-$20. Specializes in fresh seafood, veal, duck. Own desserts. Parking. Restored mill (1786); rustic early American decor. Cr cds: MC, V.

Bethlehem (D-9)

Founded: 1741 **Pop:** 71,428 **Elev:** 340 ft **Area code:** 610

The city is famous throughout the world for Bethlehem Steel products and is also well-known for its Bach Festival, for Lehigh University (1865), Moravian College (1807), Musikfest, its historic district and as "America's Christmas city."

Moravians, members of a very old Protestant sect that came here to the banks of the Lehigh River, assembled on Christmas Eve, 1741, in the only building, a log house that was part stable. Singing a hymn that praised Bethlehem, they found a name for their village. The musical heritage, too, dates from this moment; string quartets and symphonies were heard here before any other place in the colonies.

The opening of the Lehigh Canal in 1829 started industrialization of the area and development of the borough of South Bethlehem (1865), which was incorporated into the city of Bethlehem in 1917.

What to See and Do

1. Kemerer Museum of Decorative Arts. 427 N New St. Exhibits include art, Bohemian glass, china; regional folk art from 1750-1900; Federal furniture; period room settings. (Daily exc Mon; closed hols) Phone 868-6868. ¢¢

2. **Moravian Museum (Gemein Haus)** (1741). 66 W Church St. This five-story log building is the oldest structure in the city; docents interpret the history and culture of early Bethelehem and the Moravians. 2 tours avail: 45-min tour of museum only; a 2-hr walking tour of the community includes the museum, Old Chapel, Central Moravian Church, God's Acre and a walk down historic Church St. (Tues-Sat; closed Good Friday, Holy Saturday, most major hols & Jan) Phone 867-0173. Museum ¢¢; Walking tour ¢¢¢

3. **Apothecary Museum.** 424 Main St, in rear; entry gate next to book shop. Original fireplace (1752), where prescriptions were compounded; collection of artifacts including retorts, grinders, mortars and pestles, scales, blown glass bottles, labels and a set of Delft jars (1743); herb and flower garden. (By appt only) Phone 867-0173. ¢

4. **Brethren's House** (1748). Church and Main Sts. Early residence and shop area for single men of the Moravian Community. Used as a general hospital by the Continental Army during the Revolutionary War. Now serves Moravian College as its Center for Music and Art. Phone 861-3916.

5. **Old Chapel** (1751). Heckewelder Place, adjoining Moravian Museum. Once called the "Indian chapel" because so many natives attended the services, this stone structure, the second church for the Moravian congregation, is still used frequently. May be toured only in combination with Moravian Museum community walking tour (see #2).

6. **Central Moravian Church** (1806). Main & W Church Sts. Federal-style with hand-carved detail, considered foremost Moravian church in the US. Noted for its music, including a trombone choir in existence since 1754. May be toured only in combination with Moravian Museum community walking tour (see #2).

7. **God's Acre** (1742-1910). Market St. Old Moravian cemetery following Moravian tradition that all gravestones are laid flat, indicating that all are equal in the sight of God. May be toured only in combination with Moravian Museum community walking tour (see #2).

8. **Hill-to-Hill Bridge.** Main St, PA 378 over Lehigh River. Joins old and new parts of the city and provides excellent view of historic area, river and Bethlehem Steel plant.

9. **Historic Bethlehem Inc's 18th-Century Industrial Quarter.** Ohio Rd & Main St (pedestrian entrance); Old York Rd & Union Blvd (parking lot entrance). Guided tours (Tues-Sun afternoons). (See ANNUAL EVENTS) Phone 691-5300. Tours ¢¢ Tour of area includes

   Springhouse (1764). Reconstruction on site of original spring that served Moravian community as a water source from the time of settlement in 1741 until 1912.

   Waterworks (1762) with reconstructed 18-ft wooden waterwheel and pumping mechanisms.

   Tannery (1761). Exhibits Moravian crafts, trades and industries. Includes a working model of the original oil mill.

   Luckenbach Mill (1869). Restored gristmill contains contemporary craft gallery and museum shop; also the offices of Bethlehem Area Chamber of Commerce and Historic Bethlehem Inc. Interpretive display here is included in guided tour.

   Goundie House (1810). 501 Main St. Restored Federal-style brick house has period-furnished rooms and interpretive exhibits.

10. **Lost River Caverns.** Durham St, 3 mi SE via PA 412 in Hellertown. Stalagmites, stalactites, other formations. Picnic area; Gilman Museum with rocks and minerals, ancient and modern armor; also jungle garden (free). 30-min guided tours. (Daily; closed Jan 1, Thanksgiving, Dec 25) Phone 838-8767. Tours ¢¢¢

(For further information contact the Bethlehem Tourism Authority, 509 Main St, 18018; 868-1513.)

Annual Events

Shad Festival. Historic Bethlehem Inc's 18th-century Industrial Quarter (see #9). Old-fashioned planked shad bake (reservations required for dinner), exhibits, demonstrations. Phone 691-5300. 1st Sun May.

Bach Festival. Packer Church, Lehigh University campus. One of the country's outstanding musical events. Famous artists and the Bach Choir of Bethlehem participate. Phone 866-4382. Mid-late May.

Moravian College Alumni Association Antiques Show. Johnston Hall, Moravian College Campus. Phone 861-1366. Early June.

Musikfest. 9-day festival celebrating Bethlehem's rich musical and ethnic heritage. More than 600 performances (most free) of all types of music including folk, big-band, jazz, Bach, country-western, chamber, classical, gospel, rock, swing; held at 9 different sites in downtown historic area. Also children's activities. Phone 861-0678. Late Aug.

Christmas. Bethlehem continues more than two centuries of Christmas tradition with candlelight, music and a number of special events. Moravians sing their own Christmas songs intermingled with Mozart and Handel. A huge "Star of Bethlehem" shines from the top of South Mountain and the Hill-to-Hill Bridge has special lighting. The community "Putzes," a Moravian version of nativity scenes, are open to the public daily. Thousands of people post their Christmas cards from Bethlehem. Night Light Tours of city's Christmas displays and historical areas are offered (Dec) by the Bethlehem Tourism Authority. Reservations suggested. Phone 868-1513. 1st Sun of Advent-Jan 3.

Live Bethlehem Christmas Pageant. Scores of volunteers, garbed in Biblical costumes; live animals (including camels, horses, donkey and sheep) join together to re-create the Nativity story; narrated. Phone 867-2893. 2nd wkend Dec.

(See Allentown, Easton, Quakertown)

Motels

★ **COMFORT INN.** *3191 Highfield Dr (18017), US 22 exit 191.* 610/865-6300; FAX 610/865-6300, ext. 333. 116 rms. S $51-$65; D $61-$75; each addl $6; under 18 free; ski plan. Crib free. Pet accepted. TV; cable, in-rm movies. Complimentary continental bkfst. Restaurant adj. Bar noon-2 am; entertainment Wed, Fri & Sat. Ck-out noon. Valet serv. Cr cds: A, C, D, DS, ER, JCB, MC, V.

✔ ★ **ECONO LODGE.** *US 22 (18018), near Allentown-Bethlehem-Easton Airport.* 610/867-8681; FAX 610/867-6426. 119 rms. S $38.95-$43.95; D $45.95-$48.95; each addl $5; under 18 free. Crib free. TV; cable. Pool; lifeguard. Restaurant 11:30 am-2 pm. Ck-out noon. Meeting rm. Free airport transportation. Tennis. Some in-rm whirlpools. Cr cds: A, C, D, DS, ER, JCB, MC, V.

★ ★ **HOLIDAY INN.** *US 22 & PA 512 (18017).* 610/866-5800; FAX 610/867-9120. 192 rms, 2 story. S $73-$85; D $79-$91; each addl $10; under 18 free; golf plan. Crib free. TV; cable. Pool; wading pool, lifeguard. Restaurant 6:30 am-10 pm. Rm serv. Bar 11-2 am; dancing exc Sun. Ck-out noon. Meeting rms. Valet serv. Gift shop. Free airport, bus depot transportation. Exercise equipt; bicycle, stair machine. Cr cds: A, C, D, DS, JCB, MC, V.

Hotel

★ ★ **BETHLEHEM.** *437 Main St (18018).* 610/867-3711; res: 800/545-5158; FAX 610/867-0598. 126 rms, 9 story. S $70; D $82; each addl $10; suites $95-$152; studio rms $47; under 13 free. Crib free. TV; cable. Restaurant 6:30 am-11 pm. Bar 11:30-2 am. Ck-out 11 am. Meeting rms. Shopping arcade. Beauty shop. Free garage parking.

Free airport, bus depot transportation. Many refrigerators. Cr cds: A, C, D, DS, ER, MC, V.

Bird-in-Hand (F-8)

Pop: 700 (est) **Elev:** 358 ft **Area code:** 717 **Zip:** 17505

This Pennsylvania Dutch farming village got its name from the signboard of an early inn.

What to See and Do

1. **Folk Craft Center & Museum.** 1½ mi W on PA 340, then N on Mt Sidney Rd, in Witmer. Early 18th-century buildings display tools, household implements, stoneware pottery, toys, Stiegel glass, quilts, coverlets and early Pennsylvania Dutch memorabilia; log cabin loom house (1762); herb and ornamental gardens; turn-of-the-century woodworking and print shops; audiovisual presentation. (Apr-Nov, daily) Sr citizen rate. Phone 397-3609. ¢¢

2. **Amish Village.** 1 mi W on PA 340, then 3 mi S on PA 896. Reconstructed and original buildings include blacksmith shop, schoolhouse, operating smokehouse; livestock. Guided tours of Amish farmhouse. (Mid-Mar-Dec, daily; closed wk of Thanksgiving) Phone 687-8511. ¢¢¢

3. **Weavertown One-Room Schoolhouse.** 1 mi E via PA 340. Life-size animated re-creation of activities at a one-room schoolhouse. (Good Friday-Thanksgiving, daily) Phone 768-3976 or 291-1888 (winter). ¢

4. **Bird-in-Hand Farmers' Market.** On PA 340 & Maple Ave. Indoor market with a wide variety of Pennsylvania Dutch foods and gifts. (July-Oct, Wed-Sat; Apr-June & Nov, Wed, Fri & Sat; rest of yr, Fri & Sat; closed Thanksgiving, Dec 25) Phone 393-9674.

5. **The People's Place.** 5 mi E on PA 340, on Main St in Intercourse. Arts and heritage center features three-screen documentary on the Amish; interpretive museum with hands-on exhibits; Amish quilt museum; Mennonite feature film (June-Aug). Also bookstore, craft shop. (Daily exc Sun; closed Jan 1, Thanksgiving, Dec 25) Phone 768-7171. ¢¢-¢¢¢

(For further information contact the Pennsylvania Dutch Convention and Visitors Bureau, 501 Greenfield Rd, Lancaster 17601; 299-8901 or 800/735-2629.)

(See Ephrata, Lancaster)

Motel

★ ★ **BIRD-IN-HAND FAMILY INN.** Box 402, 2740 Old Philadelphia Pike. 717/768-8271; res: 800/537-2535. 100 rms, 1-2 story. May-Nov: S $55-$77; D $63-$79; each addl $8; under 16 free; lower rates rest of yr. Crib $6. TV; cable. 2 pools, 1 indoor; lifeguard. Playground. Complimentary coffee in rms. Restaurant 6 am-8 pm. Ck-out 11 am. Coin lndry. Meeting rms. Sundries. Lighted tennis. Game rm. Picnic tables. Cr cds: A, D, DS, MC, V.

Inn

★ ★ ★ **VILLAGE.** Box 253, 2695 Old Philadelphia Pike. 717/293-8369. 11 units, 3 story, 4 suites. Mid-June-Nov 1: S, D $75-$89; each addl $10; suites $95-$139; under 6 free; lower rates rest of yr. Closed mid-Dec-Dec 26 & Jan 1-mid-Jan. Crib free. TV; cable. Pool privileges. Complimentary continental bkfst, tea. Restaurant nearby. Ck-out noon, ck-in 3 pm. Tennis privileges. Built in 1734 to serve as inn

on Old Philadelphia Pike. Interior Victorian in ambience. Cr cds: A, DS, MC, V.

Restaurants

✔ ★ ★ **AMISH BARN.** 1½ mi E on PA 340. 717/768-8886. Hrs: 8 am-7 pm; summer 7 am-9 pm. Res accepted exc hols. Pennsylvania Dutch menu. A la carte entrees: bkfst $3-$5.25, lunch $3.95-$6, dinner $7.50-$12.95. Child's meals. Specialties: apple dumplings, shoofly pie. Parking. Courtyard patio dining. Rustic Amish decor. Braille menu. Family-owned. Cr cds: A, DS, MC, V.

★ **PLAIN & FANCY FARM.** 2 mi E on PA 340. 717/768-8281. Hrs: 8-10 am, 11:30 am-8 pm; early Sept-Apr from 11:30 am. Res accepted. Pennsylvania Dutch cuisine. Closed Dec 25. Prix fixe: bkfst $5.95, lunch, dinner $12.95. Child's meals. Family-style food service. Parking. Authentic Amish farmhouse. Buggy rides avail 8 am-dusk. Variety of specialty shops. Family-owned. Cr cds: A, C, D, DS, MC, V.

Bloomsburg (D-7)

Settled: 1802 **Pop:** 12,439 **Elev:** 530 ft **Area code:** 717 **Zip:** 17815

Situated on the north bank of the Susquehanna River, Bloomsburg is the seat of Columbia County. The town was a center of mining, transportation and industry during the 19th and early 20th centuries. Although manufacturing continues to be the largest employer here, Bloomsburg retains the relaxed atmosphere of earlier days with its lovely scenery and many covered bridges. In nearby Orangeville, 9 miles west on PA 93, Fishing Creek offers trout, bass and pickerel.

The only incorporated town in the state (all the others are boroughs or cities), Bloomsburg has silk and rayon manufacturers; it also produces architectural aluminum, processed foods and electronic products. During the Civil War, Union troops came here to crush the "Fishing Creek Confederacy," a group of alleged draft dodgers who were reportedly building fortifications; no fort was found, and the men were released. One of the "Molly Maguire" murder trials was held here. (The Molly Maguires was a miners' society seeking improved conditions through force and violence.)

What to See and Do

1. **Historic District.** Center of town. More than 650 structures spanning architectural styles ranging from Georgian to art deco. Phone 784-7703.

2. **Columbia County Historical Society.** 8 mi N on PA 487; Main St, in Orangeville. Museum and Edwin M. Barton Library with local history exhibits, pioneer items. (Apr-Oct, Tues-Thurs; closed major hols) Phone 683-6011. Museum tour **free;** Library research ¢ /hr.

3. **Bloomsburg University of Pennsylvania** (1839). (6,600 students) E 2nd St. On campus are Carver Hall (1867); the Harvey A. Andruss Library (1966); Haas Center for the Arts (1967) with 2,000-seat auditorium and art gallery; McCormick Center for Human Services (1985); Redman Stadium and Nelson Field House. Tours daily (academic yr). Phone 389-4316.

4. **Twin covered bridges.** 10 mi N on PA 487. Believed to be only twin covered bridges in US. More than 20 other covered bridges are in the area.

(For further information contact the Columbia-Montour Tourist Promotion Agency, 121 Papermill Rd; 784-8279.)

Annual Events

Bloomsburg Fair. Fairgrounds, W side of town. Fair held since 1854. Agricultural and industrial exhibits; harness racing. 7 days late Sept.

Covered Bridge & Arts Festival. I-80, exit 35. Tours of covered bridges; apple butter boil, weaving, quilting; old-fashioned arts & crafts. 2nd wkend Oct.

Seasonal Event

Bloomsburg Theatre Ensemble. Alvina Krause Theatre, 226 Center St. Three to four weeks of performances for each of five plays. For information contact BTE, Box 66; 784-8181. Main stage Oct-May.

(See Danville)

Motels

✔ ★ **BUDGET HOST PATRIOT INN.** *6305 New Berwick Hwy (US 11).* 717/387-1776; FAX 717/387-9611. 30 rms. S $41.50-$45; D $43.50-$55; each addl $5; under 18 free. Crib free. TV; cable, in-rm movies avail. Restaurant adj 6 am-10 pm. Bar from 4 pm. Ck-out noon. Meeting rms. Health club privileges. Some refrigerators. Cr cds: A, C, D, DS, MC, V.

D ⊠ 🕭 SC

★ ★ **QUALITY INN-BUCKHORN PLAZA.** *1 Buckhorn Rd, I-80 at Buckhorn exit 34.* 717/784-5300; FAX 717/387-0367. 120 rms, 2 story. S $44.90-$64.90; D $49.90-$69.90; each addl $5; under 18 free. Crib $5. Pet accepted. TV; cable. Coffee in lobby. Restaurant adj 6 am-10 pm. Bar 7-2 am, Sun from 11 am. Ck-out noon. Sundries. Balconies. Cr cds: A, C, D, DS, ER, JCB, MC, V.

🕭 ⊠ 🕭 SC

Inns

★ ★ ★ **INN AT TURKEY HILL.** *991 Central Rd, at I-80 exit 35.* 717/387-1500. 18 rms, 2 story. S $72-$130; D $84-$90; each addl $15; suites $100-$170; under 12 free. Pet accepted. TV; cable. Complimentary continental bkfst. Dining rm 5-9 pm. Rm serv. Bar. Ck-out noon, ck-in 2 pm. Airport, bus depot transportation. Fireplace in some rms. Down comforters; elegant antiques. Old homestead (1839); guest rooms overlook beautifully landscaped courtyard; gazebo, lily pond. Cr cds: A, C, D, DS, MC, V.

D 🕭 ⊠ 🕭 SC

★ ★ **MAGEE'S MAIN STREET.** *20 W Main St.* 717/784-3200; *res:* 800/331-9815; FAX 717/784-5517. 45 rms, 3 story. S $50-$75; D $58-$83; each addl $3.95-$7.95; under 6 free. TV; cable. Complimentary full bkfst. Dining rm 7 am-midnight. Bar 11-1 am, Sun to 11 pm. Ck-out noon. Meeting rms. Cr cds: A, C, D; DS, MC, V.

🕭 ⊠ 🕭 SC

Bradford (B-4)

Settled: 1827 **Pop:** 9,625 **Elev:** 1,442 ft **Area code:** 814 **Zip:** 16701

When oil was discovered here the price of land jumped from about 6¢ to $1,000 an acre; wells appeared on front lawns, backyards, even in a cemetery. An oil exchange was established in 1877, two years after the first producing well was brought in. Diversified industry now provides the city's economic base. A Ranger District office of the Allegheny National Forest (see WARREN) is located here.

What to See and Do

1. **Penn-Brad Oil Museum.** 3 mi S on US 219. 1890-style wooden oil well drilling rig in operation; oil country display. (Memorial Day-Labor Day, daily) Sr citizen rate. Phone 362-5984. ¢¢

2. **Bradford Landmark Society.** 45 E Corydon St. Headquartered in restored bakery; local history exhibits, period rooms. (Mon, Wed & Fri; closed hols) Phone 362-3906. **Free.**

3. **Crook Farm** (1848). On Seaward Ave extension near the Tuna Crossroad. Original home of Erastus and Betsy Crook; being restored to the 1870s period. (May-Sept, Tues-Fri afternoons, also Sat by appt; closed hols) (See ANNUAL EVENT) Phone 368-5981 or 362-3906. ¢ Includes

    Old One-Room School #8 (1880). Authentic structure where classes are still held occasionally.

    Old Barn (ca 1870). Identical to the original; moved to Crook Farm in 1981 and rebuilt on the site of the original barn.

    Carpenter Shop (ca 1870). Reconstruction of original; old hand tools.

(For further information contact the Bradford Area Chamber of Commerce, 10 Main St, PO Box 135; 368-7115.)

Annual Event

Crook Farm Country Fair. Crook Farm (see #3). Arts & crafts, exhibits, entertainment, food. Last wkend Aug.

(See Kane, Warren)

Motels

✔ ★ ★ **DE SOTO HOLIDAY HOUSE.** *515 South Ave.* 814/362-4511. 70 rms, 2-3 story. No elvtr. S $37-$48; D $45-$52; each addl $4. Crib free. TV; cable. Heated pool; whirlpool, sauna. Playground. Restaurant 7 am-10 pm; Sun to 8 pm. Bar 11-2 am; entertainment, dancing Fri & Sat. Ck-out noon. Meeting rms. Sundries. Rec rm. Driving range, miniature golf. Cr cds: A, C, D, DS, MC, V.

≈ ⊠ 🕭

★ ★ **HOWARD JOHNSON.** *100 S Davis St, US 219 exits Elm & Forman Sts.* 814/362-4501; FAX 814/362-2709. 120 rms, 3 story. S $66-$76; D $71-$82; each addl $10; under 12 free. Crib free. TV. Heated pool; lifeguard. Restaurant 7 am-2 pm, 5-10 pm. Bar 3 pm-1 am. Ck-out noon. Meeting rms. Valet serv. Cr cds: A, C, D, DS, JCB, MC, V.

D ≈ ⊠ 🕭 SC

Breezewood (F-4)

Pop: 180 (est) **Elev:** 1,356 ft **Area code:** 814 **Zip:** 15533

(See Bedford, Chambersburg)

Motels

★ ★ **BEST WESTERN PLAZA MOTOR LODGE.** *On US 30 at jct I-70, 1 blk W of PA Tpke exit 12.* 814/735-4352. 89 rms, 2 story. S $41; D $52; each addl $7; golf packages. Crib $7. TV; cable. Pool; lifeguard. Restaurant 7 am-11 pm. Ck-out 11 am. Meeting rm. Sundries. 18-hole golf privileges. Cr cds: A, C, D, DS, JCB, MC, V.

★ ★ **QUALITY INN BREEZE MANOR.** *Rte 1, Box 36, E on US 30, 1 blk E of I-70 & PA Tpke exit 12.* 814/735-4311. 50 rms, 1-2 story. May-Nov: S $41-$54; D $46-$54; each addl $5; family rates;

lower rates rest of yr. Crib $5. TV; cable. Heated pool; wading pool, lifeguard. Playground. Restaurant opp open 24 hrs. Ck-out noon. Coin Indry. Sundries. Cr cds: A, C, D, DS, ER, JCB, MC, V.

Bristle (Bucks Co) (E-10)

Settled: 1697 **Pop:** 10,405 **Elev:** 20 ft **Area code:** 215 **Zip:** 19007

Since the first forge was erected here in 1753, Bristol has been an industrial center; today it manufactures chemical products, aircraft parts, textiles and paper. An early port of call for Delaware River traffic and later for canal traffic, Bristol has been an important boat building center since 1785.

What to See and Do

1. **Sesame Place.** Approx 7 mi N, near Oxford Valley Mall (Langhorne), just N of Philadelphia off I-95 between Philadelphia and Trenton, NJ. Family theme park combines fun with learning. More than 50 outdoor physical play activities develop skills and coordination with kid-powered units. The indoor computer and science galleries offer games to challenge the mind. Sesame Food Factory: visible kitchen-in-the-round serves wholesome favorites. Mr. Hooper's Emporium: complete shop for all Sesame Street items. Sesame Island area with Caribbean theme; water activities include Big Bird's Rambling River and Ernie's Waterworks. Musical revue with Sesame Street characters. (May-Labor Day, daily; after Labor Day-mid-Oct, wkends only) Phone 752-7070. ¢¢¢¢¢

2. **Historic Fallsington.** 4 Yardley Ave, Fallsington, 5 mi N of PA Tpke, off PA 13. Restored 17th-, 18th- & 19th-century buildings. Self-guided walking tour of 17th-century log house, 18th-century schoolmaster's house, Burges-Lippincott house, tavern. Also museum store. (See ANNUAL EVENT) Guided tours by appt (mid-May-Oct, daily; closed some hols). Phone 295-6567. ¢¢

3. **Pennsbury Manor.** 5 mi NE on Pennsbury Memorial Rd, off Bordentown Rd. Reconstruction of William Penn's 17th-century country manor; formal and kitchen gardens; livestock. Craft demonstrations; hands-on workshops. (Daily exc Mon; closed some hols) Sr citizen rate. Phone 946-0400. ¢¢

4. **Grave of Captain John Green.** St James Protestant Episcopal Church Burial Ground. Cedar & Walnut Sts. Grave of US Navy captain who piloted the *Columbia* around the world in 1787-89 on first such voyage by vessel flying American flag.

(For further information contact the Bucks County Tourist Commission, PO Box 912, Dept 68, Doylestown 18901; 345-4552 or 800/836-BUCKS.)

Annual Event

Fallsington Day. In Fallsington (see #2). Outdoor fair; restored buildings open; colonial craft demonstrations; entertainment. 2nd Sat Oct.

(See Philadelphia)

Motel

★ **COMFORT INN.** (6401 Bristol Pk, Levittown 19057) N on US 13. 215/547-5000; FAX 215/547-9698. 75 rms, 2 story. S $50; D $60; each addl $10; under 18 free. Crib free. Pet accepted, some restrictions. TV; cable. Complimentary continental bkfst, coffee. Restaurant nearby. Ck-out 11 am. Meeting rms. Exercise equipt; weight machine, bicycles. Some in-rm whirlpools. Cr cds: A, C, D, DS, ER, JCB, MC, V.

Brookville (C-3)

Settled: 1801 **Pop:** 4,184 **Elev:** 1,269 ft **Area code:** 814 **Zip:** 15825

What to See and Do

Clear Creek State Park. 8 mi N on PA 36, then 4 mi NE on PA 949. Approx 1,200 acres. Swimming beach; fishing; canoeing. Hiking trails. Cross-country skiing. Picnicking, playing field, concession. Camping, cabins (dump station). Nature center; interpretive activities. Standard fees. For information contact Park Manager, RD 1, Box 82, Sigel 15860; 752-2368.

(For further information contact the Brookville Area Chamber of Commerce, 233 Main St; 849-8448.)

Annual Event

Western Pennsylvania Laurel Festival. June.

(See Clarion)

Motels

★ ★ **DAYS INN.** PA 36 & I-80, exit 13. 814/849-8001; FAX 814/849-8943. 134 rms, 3 story. S $40-$60; D $45-$85; each addl $5; under 18 free; higher rates hunting season. Crib free. TV; cable. Heated pool; wading pool, poolside serv, lifeguard. Restaurant 6-10 am, 4:30-10 pm; winter from 7 am. Rm serv. Bar 5 pm-2 am, Sun to 7 pm. Ck-out noon. Coin Indry. X-country ski 17 mi. Game rm. Cr cds: A, D, DS, MC, V.

✔ ★ **RAMADA LIMITED.** RD 5, Box 151, 235 Allegheny Blvd. 814/849-8381; FAX 814/849-8386. 69 rms, 3 story. S $37-$70; D $42-$90; each addl $5; under 12 free; higher rates hunting season. Crib free. TV; cable. Pool; lifeguard. Restaurant adj 11 am-11 pm. Ck-out noon. Coin Indry. Meeting rm. Sundries. X-country ski 16 mi. Private patios, balconies. Cr cds: A, C, D, DS, MC, V.

Restaurant

✔ ★ ★ **MEETING PLACE.** 209 Main St. 814/849-2557. Hrs: 8 am-9 pm; Fri to 10 pm; Sat 9 am-10 pm; Sun 10 am-3 pm; early-bird dinner Mon-Sat 4-5:30 pm. Closed some major hols. Res accepted. Bar. Semi-a la carte: bkfst $2-$5, lunch $2.75-$7, dinner $4.50-$10. Child's meals. Specializes in salads, chicken, shrimp scramble. Restored Victorian building (1872); casual dining. Cr cds: A, DS, MC, V.

Ⓓ

Bucks County (E-9 - E-10)

Bucks County's great natural resources, location and waterway transportation were known to the Leni-Lenape Indians centuries ago. Dutch explorers, followed by Swedes, English Quakers and Germans, began to take possession of the area in the 1600s. William Penn established his country estate in this area in the seventeenth century.

The county's historic importance is highlighted in the central section—it was here that General George Washington crossed the Delaware River with the Continental Army during the Revolution. More recently, artists and writers have settled in and around New Hope, giving rise to the village's fame as an art center.

Bucks County's scenic beauty and rich history make it a popular tourist spot. The Bucks County Tourist Commission, PO Box 912, Dept 68, Doylestown 18901, phone 215/345-4552 or 800/836-BUCKS, can provide information on the area.

Following are the places in Bucks County included in the *Mobil Travel Guide*. For full information on any one of them, see the individual alphabetical listing. Bristol, Doylestown, New Hope, Quakertown, Washington Crossing Historical Park.

Bushkill (C-10)

Pop: 900 (est) **Elev:** 365 ft **Area code:** 717 **Zip:** 18324

What to See and Do

1. **Bushkill Falls.** 2 mi N off US 209 on local road. Largest series of falls in Pocono Mts. Main falls have 100-foot drop. Scenic gorge. Fishing; boating. Picnicking. Wildlife exhibit of mounted animals and birds of Pennsylvania. (Apr-mid-Nov, daily) Phone 588-6682. ¢¢¢

2. **Pocono Indian Museum.** 3 mi S on US 209. Traces history of the Delaware Indians through displays of artifacts, weapons and tools. Gift shop. (Daily; closed Dec 25) Phone 588-9338 or -9164. ¢¢

3. **Delaware Water Gap** (see). 15 mi W on US 209.

(For further information contact the Pocono Mts Vacation Bureau, 1004 Main St, Stroudsburg 18360, phone 424-6050; for free brochures phone 800/POCONOS.)

(For accommodations see Milford)

Butler (D-2)

Settled: 1793 **Pop:** 15,714 **Elev:** 1,077 ft **Area code:** 412 **Zip:** 16003

This is a manufacturing city nestled amid rolling hills, which were owned by Robert Morris of Philadelphia, financier of the American Revolution. The city and county are named for General Richard Butler, who died in the St Clair Indian Expedition. During the 1930s, the Butler-based American Austin Company—later called American Bantam Company—pioneered the development of small, lightweight cars in America and invented the prototype of the jeep.

What to See and Do

1. **Moraine State Park.** 12 mi NW on US 422. A 3,225-acre lake in a 16,180-acre park. Swimming beaches; fishing, hunting; boating (rentals, mooring, launching, marina). Hiking, horseback riding. Cross-country skiing, sledding, ice-skating, ice fishing, ice boating. Picnicking, playground, snack bar, restaurant. Cabin rentals. Waterfowl observation area; interpretive programs. Standard fees. Phone 368-8811.

2. **Jennings Environmental Education Center.** 12 mi N, at jct PA 8, 528, 173. Blazing Star, a relict prairie wild flower, blooms profusely here in late July-early Aug. Trails, guided walks, interpretive center; picnicking. (Memorial Day-Labor Day, daily; rest of yr, Mon-Fri, some Sun) Phone 794-6011. **Free.**

(For further information contact the Butler County Visitors Bureau, 100 N Main St, PO Box 1082; 283-2222.)

(See Harmony, Pittsburgh)

Motels

★ ★ **CONLEY'S RESORT INN.** *740 Pittsburgh Rd (PA 8) (16001).* 412/586-7711. 56 rms, 2-3 story, 10 kits. No elvtr. S $62-$65; D $84-$99; each addl $10; under 18 free; golf plans. Crib free. TV. Indoor pool; whirlpool, sauna, lifeguard. Restaurant 7 am-10 pm. Rm serv. Bar 11-2 am, Sun to midnight. Ck-out 1 pm. Meeting rms. Sundries. Rec rm. Tennis. 18-hole golf, greens fee $17-$25, putting green. X-country ski on site. Game rm. 150-ft indoor water slide. Cr cds: A, C, D, DS, MC, V.

★ ★ **DAYS INN.** *139 Pittsburgh Rd (PA 8) (16001).* 412/287-6761; FAX 412/287-4307. 139 rms, 2 story. S $56-$72; D $62-$77; each addl $6; family rates; golf package plan. Crib free. TV; cable. Indoor pool; whirlpool, lifeguard. Restaurant 6 am-10 pm. Rm serv. Bar 3 pm-2 am, Sun 1 pm-midnight; entertainment, dancing. Ck-out noon. Meeting rms. Valet serv. Sundries. Game rm. Cr cds: A, D, DS, MC, V.

✔ ★ **McKEE'S.** *930 Newcastle Rd (US 422) (16001).* 412/865-2272. 23 rms. S $29.68-$33.92; D $32.86-$37.10; kit. units $47.70; under 5 free; wkly rates. Crib $4. TV; cable. Ck-out 11 am. Cr cds: A, DS, MC, V.

Inn

★ ★ ★ **APPLEBUTTER.** *(152 Applewood Lane, Slippery Rock 16057) 15 mi N on US 8 to US 173, N to Slippery Rock.* 412/794-1844. 12 rms, 2 story. S $55-$81; D $69-$115; each addl $10-$15; golf plan. Adults preferred. TV. Complimentary full bkfst, tea. Restaurant adj 11 am-9 pm; wkends 8 am-11 pm; closed Mon. Ck-out 11 am, ck-in 3-10 pm. Sitting rm. Restored brick farmhouse (1844) furnished with antiques; addition added 1988. Totally nonsmoking. Cr cds: MC, V.

Canadensis (C-9)

Pop: 1,200 (est) **Area code:** 717 **Zip:** 18325

What to See and Do

Industrial tour. Holley Ross Pottery. S on PA 390, NW on PA 447, in La Anna. 20-min guided tours with demonstration of pottery-making. Swinging bridge, park, sawdust trails. (May-mid-Dec, Mon-Fri) Phone 676-3248. **Free.**

Inns

★ ★ ★ **CRESCENT LODGE.** *(Paradise Valley, Cresco 18326) S on PA 191 to PA 447.* 717/595-7486; res: 800/392-9400. 12 lodge rms, 4 motel rms, 9 suites, 6 cottages (some with kit.). Mid-June-mid-Sept: S, D $80-$175; suites $165-$260; kit. cottages $950-$1,100/wk; EP, MAP, wkly rates; ski plans; lower rates rest of yr. Crib $15. TV; cable. Heated pool. Complimentary continental bkfst (exc summer). Restaurant (see CRESCENT LODGE). Bar. Ck-out 11 am, ck-in 2 pm. Free bus depot transportation. Gift shop. Tennis. Golf nearby. Downhill/x-country ski 5 mi. Fitness trail. Lawn games. Whirlpool in suites; some refrigerators. Varied accommodations. Private patios. Picnic tables. Same owners more than 40 yrs. Cr cds: A, D, DS, MC, V.

★★ **OVERLOOK.** *Box 680, Dutch Hill Rd. 717/595-7519; res: 800/441-0177; FAX 717/223-7304.* 20 rms, 3 story. MAP: D $150; higher rates some hols (2-day min). TV in sitting rm; cable. Pool. Afternoon tea. Restaurant (see OVERLOOK INN). Bar. Ck-out noon, ck-in 3 pm. Downhill ski 5 mi; x-country ski on site. Lawn games. Country farmhouse; built 1880. Antiques. Cr cds: A, MC, V.

★★ **PINE KNOB.** *PA 447. 717/595-2532.* 27 units, 18 baths. No rm phones. MAP: S $69-$80; D $74-$83 (per person); wkly rates. Children over 12 yrs only. TV in lounge; cable. Pool. Dining rm 6-9 pm. Bar 5-10 pm. Ck-out 11 am, ck-in 2 pm. Tennis. Downhill/x-country ski 5 mi. Lawn games. Pre-Civil War period inn (1847); antiques. Art gallery. Cr cds: MC, V.

★★ **PUMP HOUSE.** *PO Box 430, Skytop Rd. 717/595-7501.* 8 rms, 2 story. S, D $65-$100; each addl $5; suites $85-$100. Complimentary continental bkfst. Restaurant (see PUMP HOUSE INN). Ck-out 11 am, ck-in 2 pm. Built as stagecoach stop in 1842; furnished in country decor with antiques throughout. Cr cds: C, D, MC, V.

Restaurants

★★ **CRESCENT LODGE.** *(See Crescent Lodge Inn)* 717/595-7486. Hrs: 5:30-9 pm; Sun 3-8 pm. Closed Dec 25; also Mon-Wed from Jan-May. Res accepted. Continental menu. Bar 4 pm-midnight. A la carte entrees: dinner $16.95-$28.95. Specializes in seafood, veal, chicken. Pianist Sat. Parking. Family-owned. Cr cds: A, D, DS, MC, V.

★★ **OVERLOOK INN.** *(See Overlook Inn)* 717/595-7519. Hrs: 8-9:30 am, 6-9 pm; Sun 5-8:30 pm. Res accepted. Continental menu. Bar 11 am-midnight. Semi-a la carte: bkfst $8, dinner $8.50-$22. Specializes in baby rack of lamb, fresh seafood, medallions of filet mignon. Parking. Built 1880. Cr cds: A, MC, V.

SC

★★★ **PUMP HOUSE INN.** *(See Pump House Inn)* 717/595-7501. Hrs: 5-9 pm; Sun 2:30-8:30 pm. Closed Mon; Dec 25. Res accepted. French, Amer menu. Bar. Wine list. Semi-a la carte: dinner $13.95-$24.45. Specializes in roast rack of lamb, shrimp in beer batter, chocolate mousse. Own breads. Parking. Country inn (1842). Cr cds: C, D, MC, V.

Carbondale (C-9)

Founded: 1822 **Pop:** 10,664 **Elev:** 1,070 ft **Area code:** 717 **Zip:** 18407

Carbondale, located in the heart of the northeast Pocono area, has excellent sports facilities. There are 33 lakes within an 8-mile radius and 201 more lakes within 25 miles. One of the first railroad lines in the country was built to haul coal from Carbondale.

What to See and Do

1. **Skiing.**

    Elk Mt Ski Center. NW on PA 106, E on PA 374. At an elevation of 2,693 ft, this is eastern Pennsylvania's highest mountain. Five double chairlifts; patrol, school, rentals; cafeteria, restaurant, bar. Longest run, 2 mi; vertical drop, 1,000 ft. (Early Dec-late Mar, daily) Half-day rate. Phone 679-2611; for snow conditions, 800/233-4131 (East Coast states). ¢¢¢¢¢

    Mount Tone Ski Resort. N via PA 171, E via PA 370 to Lakewood, then S on PA 247 to Lake Como, follow signs. Triple chairlift, T-bar, double rope tow, mighty mite; school, rentals;

snowmaking; cafeteria; lodge. Vertical drop 450 ft. (Late Dec-1st or 2nd wkend Mar) Two mountains, eleven trails; also night skiing, cross-country trails. Phone 798-2707. ¢¢¢¢¢

2. **Merli-Sarnoski Park.** 1/2 mi off PA 106. Covers 825 acres of woodlands with 40-acre lake. Swimming beach (lifeguards); fishing (seasonal); boating (launch). Hiking trails. Winter activities include cross-country skiing, ice-skating, ice fishing. Picnicking. (Daily)

(For further information contact the Scranton/Lacawanna County Visitors and Convention Bureau, 222 Mulberry St, Scranton 18501; 342-7711.)

(For accommodations see Hawley, Scranton)

Carlisle (E-6)

Settled: 1720 **Pop:** 18,419 **Elev:** 478 ft **Area code:** 717 **Zip:** 17013

In the historically strategic Cumberland Valley, Carlisle was a vital point for Indian fighting during the Revolutionary and the Civil wars.

Carlisle Barracks (see #1) is one of the oldest military posts in America. Soldiers mounted guard here as early as 1750 to protect the frontier. From here began British campaigns that drove the French from the Ohio Valley and, in 1763, the march to relieve Fort Pitt. In 1794 President Washington reviewed troops assembled to march against the "Whiskey Rebels." Troops went from the Barracks to the Mexican and Civil wars. The famous Carlisle Indian School, first nonreservation school, was here until 1918. The Barracks was reopened in 1920 as the Medical Field Service School. It is now the home of the US Army War College.

George Ross, James Wilson and James Smith, all signers of the Declaration of Independence, lived in Carlisle, as did Molly Pitcher.

What to See and Do

1. **Carlisle Barracks.** 1 mi N on US 11. Army War College, senior school in US Army's educational system. Includes the US Army Military History Institute and Hessian Powder Magazine Museum (1777), built by prisoners captured at the Battle of Trenton. The Carlisle Indian Industrial School (1879-1918) was one of first institutions of higher learning for Native Americans. Also includes the Omar Bradley Museum, containing a collection of personal and military memorabilia of the five-star general. Jim Thorpe and other famous Native American athletes studied here. Hessian Powder Magazine Museum (May-Sept, Sat & Sun afternoons); Military History Institute and the Omar Bradley Museum (Mon-Fri). Post/grounds (daily; closed federal hols). Phone 245-3611. **Free.**

2. **Cumberland County Historical Society and Hamilton Library Association.** 21 N Pitt St. Woodcarvings, furniture, silver, tools, redware, ironware, tall-case clocks, coverlets, paintings by local artisans; mementos of the Carlisle Indian School; special exhibits and programs. Library contains books, tax lists, early photographs, genealogical material. (Daily exc Sun; closed hols) Phone 249-7610. Museum **free;** Library (non-members) ¢

3. **Dickinson College** (1773). (1,900 students) W High St (US 11). Tenth college chartered in US; President James Buchanan was a graduate. On campus is "Old West" (1804), a building registered as a National Historic Landmark that was designed by Benjamin Henry Latrobe, one of the designers of the Capitol in Washington. Tours of campus. Phone 243-5121. Also here is

    The Trout Gallery. Emil R. Weiss Center for the Arts. Permanent and temporary exhibits. (Sept-mid-June, Tues-Sat) Phone 245-1711. **Free.**

4. **Grave of "Molly Pitcher"** (Mary Ludwig Hays McCauley). In Old Graveyard, E South St. Soldiers in the Battle of Monmouth (June, 1778) gave Molly her nickname because of her devotion to her

husband and others who were fighting by bringing them pitchers of water. When her husband was wounded, Molly took his place at a cannon and continued fighting for him.

5. **Pine Grove Furnace State Park.** 10 mi SW on I-81, exit 11, then 8 mi S on PA 233. Pre-Revolutionary iron, slate and brick works were in this area. Approx 696 acres. Swimming beaches; fishing, hunting; boating (rentals, mooring, launching). Hiking, bicycling (rentals). Cross-country skiing, ice-skating, ice fishing. Picnicking, snack bar, store. Tent & trailer sites. Visitor center. Lodging avail (phone 486-7575). Standard fees. Park office phone 486-7174.

6. **Huntsdale Fish Hatchery.** 10 mi SW in Huntsdale. Springs and mountain stream fill tanks and ponds of brown, rainbow and palomino trout, muskellunge and walleye; visitor center. (Daily) Phone 486-3419. **Free.**

(For further information contact the Greater Area Chamber of Commerce, 212 N Hanover St, Box 572; 243-4515.)

Annual Event

Art Festival & Octoberfest. Oct.

(See Harrisburg)

Motels

★ **ALLENBERRY.** *(PO Box 7, Boiling Springs 17007)* 6 mi SE on PA 174. 717/258-3211; FAX 717/258-1464. 54 rms in lodges, 1 cottage (3 bedrm). S $75; D $89; each addl $12; cottage $260; under 17 free; bkfst, lunch, dinner, theater package plan. Crib free. TV. Pool; wading pool, lifeguard. Dining rm 8-10:30 am, 11 am-2 pm, 5-9 pm (also see CARRIAGE ROOM). Bar 11 am-midnight. Ck-out noon. Meeting rms. Airport transportation. Lighted tennis. Professional theater. On 57 wooded acres, 200-yr-old trees; several remodeled limestone buildings date from 1785, 1812. On Yellow Breeches Creek. Cr cds: A, DS, MC, V.

✔ ★ ★ **APPALACHIAN TRAIL INN.** *1825 Harrisburg Pike (US 11), off I-81S exit 17E.* 717/245-2242; res: 800/445-6715; FAX 717/258-4881. 200 rms, 2 story. Apr-Oct: S $42-$52; D $47-$57; each addl $5; suites $85-$125; under 12 free; higher rates car shows; lower rates rest of yr. Crib free. TV; cable. Restaurant 5-1 am. Rm serv. Ck-out noon. Downhill ski 16 mi. Picnic tables. Cr cds: A, C, D, DS, ER, MC, V.

★ ★ **BEST WESTERN INN OF THE BUTTERFLY.** *1245 Harrisburg Pike (US 11).* 717/243-5411; FAX 717/243-07787008. 132 rms, 2 story. S $46.50-$64.50; D $63.50-$77.50; each addl $7; suites $68.50-$140; under 18 free. Crib free. TV; cable. Pool; lifeguard. Restaurant 6:30 am-9 pm. Bar 11-1 am. Ck-out noon. Meeting rms. Valet serv. Sundries. Airport, bus depot transportation. Cr cds: A, C, D, DS, ER, MC, V.

★ ★ **DAYS INN.** *101 Alexander Spring Rd, I-81 exit 13.* 717/258-4147; FAX 717/258-4147, ext. 510. 95 rms, 2 story. S $47-$50; D $52-$55; each addl $5; under 18 free; higher rates special events. Crib free. TV; cable, in-rm movies avail. Pool; lifeguard. Complimentary continental bkfst, coffee. Restaurant nearby. Ck-out noon. Meeting rm. Sundries. Airport transportation. Game rm. Some refrigerators. Cr cds: A, D, DS, MC, V.

★ ★ **EMBERS INN & CONVENTION CENTER.** *1700 Harrisburg Pike (US 11), I-81 exit 17, I-76 exit 16.* 717/243-1717; res: 800/692-7315; FAX /7171/243. 270 rms. S $53-$55; D $58-$60; each addl $5; suites $110-$173; under 18 free. Crib $5. Pet accepted. TV; cable. Indoor pool; wading pool, whirlpool, sauna, poolside serv, lifeguard. Restaurant 7 am-9 pm; Sat to 9:30 am. Rm serv. Bar 11-2 am.

Ck-out 11 am. Meeting rms. Bellhops. Sundries. Gift shop. Tennis. Putting green. Lawn games. Refrigerators. Cr cds: A, C, D, DS, ER, MC, V.

Restaurants

★ ★ **BOILING SPRINGS TAVERN.** *(Front & First Sts, Boiling Springs 17007)* 6 mi SE on PA 174, on town square. 717/258-3614. Hrs: 11:30 am-10 pm. Closed Sun, Mon; major hols. Res accepted. Continental menu. Bar. Semi-a la carte: lunch $3.50-$8.50, dinner $8.50-$20.95. Child's meals. Specializes in fresh seafood, aged Western steak. Parking. Old stone structure (1832), originally an inn. Colonial decor. Cr cds: A, MC, V.

★ ★ **CALIFORNIA CAFE.** 52 W Pomfret St. 717/249-2028. Hrs: 11 am-2 pm, 5-9 pm. Closed Sun-Mon; major hols. Res accepted; required wkends. French, California menu. Serv bar. Semi-a la carte: lunch $3.95-$6.95. Complete meals: dinner $13.95-$17.95. Specialties: escalope de veau aux artichauts, poulet grillé chasseur. Revolutionary War era building; French and Florentine artwork, mural, fireplace. Cr cds: A, C, D, DS, MC, V.

★ ★ **CARRIAGE ROOM.** *(See Allenberry Inn)* 717/258-3211. Hrs: 5-9 pm; Wed-Sat to 10 pm. Closed mid-Nov-Mar. Res accepted. Continental menu. Bar to midnight. Semi-a la carte: dinner $14-$25. Specializes in seafood, prime rib. Salad bar. Pianist, guitarist Thurs-Sat. Colonial decor. Cr cds: A, DS, MC, V.

Chambersburg (F-5)

Settled: 1730 **Pop:** 16,647 **Elev:** 621 ft **Area code:** 717 **Zip:** 17201

Named for Colonel Benjamin Chambers, a Scottish-Irish pioneer, this is an industrial county seat amid peach and apple orchards. John Brown had his headquarters here. During the Civil War, Confederate cavalry burned down the town, destroying 537 buildings after the citizens refused to pay an indemnity of $100,000.

What to See and Do

1. **The Old Jail.** 175 E King St. Jail complex (1818) restored and renovated for use as the Kittochtinny Historical Society's Museum and Library. An 1880 cell block houses community cultural activities, art and historical exhibits; other events. Also on grounds are Colonial, Fragrance and Japanese gardens; 19th-century barn; agricultural museum. Cultural programs (May-Oct). Tours (May-Nov, Thurs-Sat). Phone 264-1667. **Free.**

2. **Caledonia State Park.** 10 mi E on US 30. Confederate General Jubal A. Early came through here during the Civil War and destroyed an iron furnace, which had been producing arms for the Union armies. Approx 1,100 acres. Swimming pool (fee); fishing. Nature, hiking trails; bicycling, 18-hole golf course. Cross-country skiing. Picnicking, playground, snack bar. Tent & trailer sites. Standard fees. (See SEASONAL EVENT) Phone 352-2161.

(For further information contact the Chamber of Commerce, 75 S Second St; 264-7101. Information is also available at the Visitors Station, 1235 Lincoln Way E; 261-1200.)

Annual Event

Franklin County Fair. Arts & crafts displays, needlework, home and dairy products, state turkey calling contest, tractor pull, agricultural and livestock exhibits, entertainment. Phone 369-4100. 3rd full wk Aug.

Seasonal Event

Totem Pole Playhouse. Caledonia State Park (see #2). Resident professional theater company performs dramas, comedies and musicals in 453-seat proscenium theatre. Tues-Sun evenings; matinees Wed, Sat-Sun. Phone 352-2164. June-Aug.

Motels

✔ ★ **DAYS INN.** 30 Falling Spring Rd, I-81 exit 6. 717/263-1288; FAX 717/263-6514. 107 rms, 3 story. Apr-Oct: S $49-$65; D $57-$65; each addl $8; suites $67-$75; under 17 free; lower rates rest of yr. Crib free. TV; cable, in-rm movies avail. Complimentary continental bkfst. Restaurant 6 am-11 pm. Ck-out 11 am. Meeting rms. Downhill ski 20 mi. Cr cds: A, C, D, DS, MC, V.

D ✖ ☒ 🔥 SC

★ ★ **HAMPTON INN.** 955 Lesher Rd, ¼ mi off I-81 exit 5. 717/261-9185; FAX 717/261-1984. 84 rms, 3 story. May-Oct: S $53-$58; D $61-$67; under 18 free; monthly plans; higher rates special events; lower rates rest of yr. Crib free. TV; cable, in-rm movies avail. Complimentary continental bkfst. Restaurant adj 6 am-11 pm. Ck-out noon. Meeting rms. Sundries. Exercise equipt; weight machine, bicycles. Refrigerators. Cr cds: A, C, D, DS, MC, V.

D ✖ ☒ 🔥 SC

★ ★ **HOWARD JOHNSON LODGE.** 1123 Lincoln Way E (US 30), I-81 exit 6. 717/263-9191; FAX 717/263-4752. 132 rms, 3 story. S $55-$68; D $62-$78; each addl $7; under 18 free. Crib free. TV; cable. Indoor pool; sauna. Complimentary coffee in rms. Restaurant 6 am-11 pm; Fri, Sat to midnight. Bar 11 am-midnight, closed Sun. Ck-out noon. Meeting rms. Valet serv. Sundries. Downhill ski 20 mi. Refrigerators. Private patios, balconies. Cr cds: A, C, D, DS, MC, V.

✖ ☒ 🔥 SC

✔ ★ **TRAVELODGE.** 565 Lincoln Way E (US 30), I-81 exit 6. 717/264-4187; FAX 717/264-2446. 51 rms, 3 story. S $46-$51; D $51-$67; each addl $7; under 18 free. Crib free. Pet accepted, some restrictions. TV; cable. Coffee in rms. Restaurant 6:30 am-2 pm, 4:30-9:30 pm. Rm serv. Bar 11 am-2 pm, 4:30-10:30 pm. Ck-out noon. Meeting rm. Health club privileges. Refrigerators avail. Some balconies. Cr cds: A, C, D, DS, ER, JCB, MC, V.

D ☒ 🔥 SC

Inn

★ ★ **MERCERSBURG INN.** (405 S Main St, Mercersburg 17236) 13 mi S on I-81, then 11 mi W on PA 16. 717/328-5231; FAX 717/328-3403. 15 rms, 3 story. S, D $110-$180; each addl $25. TV in sitting rm. Complimentary continental bkfst. Restaurant (see MOREL). Rm serv. Ck-out 11 am, ck-in 3 pm. Some fireplaces. Some balconies. Brick Georgian-revival mansion (1910) with double staircase in hall, mahogany paneling and beams, original lighting fixtures; period & antique furnishings. Views of Blue Ridge Mts. Totally nonsmoking. Cr cds: DS, MC, V.

☒

Restaurants

★ ★ **COPPER KETTLE.** 1049 Lincoln Way E (US 30), 2 blks W of I-81 exit 6. 717/264-3109. Hrs: 5-9:30 pm; Fri, Sat to 10 pm. Closed Sun; major hols. Res accepted; required Fri, Sat. Bar 5 pm-midnight. Semi-a la carte: dinner $7-$19. Child's menu. Specializes in seafood, steak, ribs. Parking. Early Amer decor; antiques. Cr cds: A, C, D, MC, V.

★ ★ ★ **MOREL.** (See Mercersburg Inn) 717/328-5231. Sitting: 8 pm. Closed Mon-Wed; Thanksgiving. Res required. Bar. Complete meals: 6-course dinner $45. Specialties: grilled salmon with mango

chutney, baron of rabbit with morels, cognac and black and white pasta. Parking. Casual elegance; view of grounds. Cr cds: DS, MC, V.

Chester (F-9)

Settled: 1643 **Pop:** 41,856 **Elev:** 20 ft **Area code:** 610

The oldest settlement in the state, Chester was established by the Swedish Trading Company as Upland. William Penn came to Upland in 1682 to begin colonization of the land granted to him by King Charles II. He renamed the settlement in honor of Chester, a Quaker center in Cheshire, England. The first Assembly here adopted Penn's Framework of Government, enacted the first laws and organized the county of Chester—from which Delaware County broke off in 1789. On the Delaware River, 15 miles southwest of Philadelphia, Chester is a busy port and home of shipyards where every type of vessel has been built for the navy and merchant marine.

What to See and Do

1. **Penn Memorial Landing Stone.** Front & Penn Sts. Marks spot where William Penn first landed Oct 28, 1682.

2. **Morton Homestead** (ca 1655). 4 mi NE on US 13, then SW on PA 420, at 100 Lincoln Ave in Prospect Park. Two-part log house built by ancestors of John Morton, signer of Declaration of Independence. Contemporary outdoor exhibits on Pennsylvania's Swedish Period, log-house construction, Morton family. Sr citizen rate. (Daily) Phone 583-7221. ¢¢

3. **Caleb Pusey Home, Landingford Plantation** (1683). 15 Race St, in Upland, 2 mi W. Built for manager and agent of Penn's mill; only remaining house in state visited by William Penn. Period furniture. Also on 27 acres of original plantation are a log house (1790), stone schoolhouse-museum (1849), and herb garden. (May-Sept, Sat & Sun afternoons; also by appt; closed hols) Phone 874-5665. ¢

4. **Widener University** (1821). (8,700 students) 14th & Chestnut Sts. On campus are Old Main, a national historic landmark, and the University Art Museum, with a permanent collection of 19th- & 20th-century American Impressionist and European academic art as well as contemporary exhibits (Sept-May, Tues-Sat; June & Aug, Mon-Thurs; closed July). Also here is Wolfgram Memorial Library. Campus tours. Phone 499-4000.

5. **Swarthmore College** (1864). (1,320 students) 4 mi N on PA 320, in Swarthmore. Coeducational; on wooded 330-acre campus are Friends Historical Library and Peace Collection; an art gallery; concert hall; performing arts center; observatory; grassy, terraced amphitheater; Friends Meeting House; Scott Arboretum, a collection of trees, shrubs and herbaceous plants throughout campus. Symposia, exhibits, music and dance programs are open to the public. Phone 328-8000.

(For further information contact the Delaware County Convention & Tourist Bureau, 200 E State St, Suite 100, Media 19063; 800/343-3983.)

(See Kennett Square, King of Prussia, Media, Philadelphia, West Chester)

Motor Hotel

★ ★ **HOWARD JOHNSON.** 1300 Providence Rd (19013), I-95 exit 6. 610/876-7211; FAX 610/874-5210. 117 rms, 7 story. S $50-$72; D $60-$77; each addl $6; under 18 free. Crib free. TV; cable. Indoor pool. Restaurant 6 am-11 pm, wkends from 7 am. Bar from 11 am. Ck-out noon. Free airport, RR station transportation. Exercise equipt; weights, bicycles, steam rm. Cr cds: A, C, D, DS, ER, JCB, MC, V.

 ☒ ✖ ☒ 🔥 SC

Clarion (C-3)

Founded: 1839 **Pop:** 6,457 **Elev:** 1,491 ft **Area code:** 814 **Zip:** 16214

Once the forests were so thick and tall here that, according to tradition, the wind in the treetops sounded like a distant clarion. That's how the town, county and river got their names. Today many campers and sports and outdoors enthusiasts enjoy the beauty and recreation the Clarion area offers.

What to See and Do

1. **Clarion County Historical Society.** 18 Grant St. Museum housed in mid-19th century Sutton-Ditz house. Contains exhibits on county industry and business; Victorian bedroom and parlor; genealogical & historical library (researchers may call ahead for appt other than regular hrs); changing exhibits. (Apr-Dec, Tues, Thurs & Fri afternoons; closed hols) Phone 226-4450. **Free.**

2. **Cook Forest State Park.** 11 mi NE on Clarion to Cook Forest Rd, then 3 mi S on PA 36. Approx 6,700 acres. Swimming pool (fee); fishing, hunting. Hiking, bicycling, horseback riding. Cross-country skiing (rentals), snowmobiling, sledding, ice-skating. Picnicking. Tent & trailer sites, cabins (rentals). Nature & historical center. Standard fees. Phone 744-8407. **Tionesta Reservoir.** 5 mi NW on US 322, then 20 mi NW on PA 66, in Allegheny National Forest (see WARREN).

(For further information contact the Clarion Area Chamber of Commerce, 41 S Fifth Ave; 226-9161.)

Annual Events

Clarion River Country Days. Cook Forest State Park (see #2). Canoe float. Square dancing, crafts. June.

Autumn Leaf Festival. Parade, carnival, autorama, walking tours, flea market, craft shows. Late Sept-early Oct.

Motels

★ ★ **DAYS INN.** *PA 68 & I-80, exit 9N. 814/226-8682; FAX 814/226-8372.* 150 rms, 2 story. S $48-$56; D $53-$61; each addl $5; under 18 free; tennis, golf, ski plans; higher rates: Autumn Leaf Festival, hunting season. Crib free. TV; cable, in-rm movies avail. Heated pool; lifeguard. Restaurant 6 am-2 pm, 5-10 pm. Rm serv. Bar 4 pm-2 am; entertainment, dancing. Ck-out noon. Coin lndry. Meeting rms. Sundries. Tennis, golf privileges. Health club privileges. Cr cds: A, C, D, DS, MC, V.

D 🏃 🛐 🏊 🏄 🔥 SC

★ ★ **HOLIDAY INN.** *I-80 at PA 68 exit 9. 814/226-8850; FAX 814/226-8850, ext. 250.* 122 rms, 2 story. S, D $66-$82; suites $116; under 20 free. Crib free. TV; cable. Indoor pool; sauna, lifeguard. Restaurant 7 am-10 pm. Rm serv. Bar 4 pm-1 am. Ck-out noon. Meeting rms. 18-hole golf privileges, greens fee $22, putting green. Game rm. Indoor balconies. Courtyard with pool. Cr cds: A, C, D, DS, JCB, MC, V.

D 🛐 🏊 🏄 SC

✔ ★ **KNIGHTS INN.** *RD 3, I-80 exit 9. 814/226-4550.* 99 rms, 9 kits. S $35.95-$39.95; D $40.95-$44.95; each addl $5; kit. units $42.95-$52.95; wkly, monthly rates (winter); under 18 free. Crib free. TV; cable. Pool; lifeguard. Restaurant adj 6 am-10 pm. Ck-out noon. Meeting rm. Cr cds: A, C, D, DS, ER, MC, V.

🏊 🏄 🔥 SC

Restaurant

✔ ★ ★ **CLARION CLIPPER.** *On PA 68 N, 1/2 mi N of I-80 exit 9. 814/226-7950.* Hrs: 6:30 am-10 pm. Closed Thanksgiving, Dec 25. Bar noon-midnight. Semi-a la carte: bkfst $2.50-$4.75, lunch $3.50-$5.25, dinner $5.50-$11.95. Child's meals. Specializes in steak, seafood. Salad bar. Parking. Exterior modeled after steamboats that operated on the Allegheny and Ohio Rivers in 1848. Cr cds: A, C, D, DS, MC, V.

D SC

Clearfield (Clearfield Co) (D-4)

Settled: 1805 **Pop:** 6,633 **Elev:** 1,109 ft **Area code:** 814 **Zip:** 16830

The old and important Indian town of Chinklacamoose occupied this site until it was burned in 1757. Coal and clay mining and more than 20 diversified plants producing school supplies, firebrick, fur products, precision instruments, electronic products and sportswear now occupy what used to be cleared fields. Easy access to other parts of the state and rich river bottom land led to the establishment of the county seat here.

What to See and Do

State parks.

S.B. Elliott. 9 mi N, off PA 153, just N of I-80 exit 18. Approx 300 acres in the heart of the Moshannon State Forest; entirely wooded; display of mountain laurel in season. Fishing in small mountain streams surrounding the park. Hiking. Snowmobile trails. Tent & trailer sites, cabins. Standard fees. Phone 765-7271 or -0630.

Parker Dam. 14 mi NW on PA 153, 6 mi off I-80 exit 18, then 2 mi E on unnumbered road. Approx 950 acres in Moshannon State Forest. Swimming beach; fishing; boating (launch, rentals). Hiking. Cross-country skiing, snowmobiling, sledding, ice-skating, ice fishing. Snack bar. Tent & trailer sites (electric hookups), cabins. Nature center. Standard fees. Phone 765-0630

(For further information contact the Clearfield Chamber of Commerce, 125 E Market St, PO Box 250; 765-7560.)

Annual Events

Laurel Tour. Late June-early July.

Clearfield County Fair. Late July-early Aug.

Motel

★ ★ **DAYS INN.** *Box 966, PA 879 & I-80 exit 19. 814/765-5381; FAX 814/765-7885.* 121 rms, 2 story. S $48-$52; D $52-$57; each addl $6; under 18 free. Crib free. TV. Pool; lifeguard. Restaurant 6 am-10 pm. Rm serv. Bar 4 pm-2 am. Ck-out noon. Meeting rms. Cr cds: A, C, D, DS, MC, V.

D 🏊 🏄 🔥 SC

Conneaut Lake (B-1)

Pop: 699 **Elev:** 1,100 ft **Area code:** 814 **Zip:** 16316

Located on the largest natural lake in Pennsylvania (929 acres), this resort town has swimming, boating and excellent fishing for perch, muskellunge, walleye, bass and crappie.

What to See and Do

1. **Conneaut Cellars Winery.** Jct US 6, 322. Tours and tastings. (May-Dec, daily; rest of yr, daily exc Mon; closed Jan 1, Easter, Thanksgiving, Dec 25) Phone 382-3999. **Free.**

2. **Pymatuning State Park.** SW via US 322, 1 mi N of Jamestown. Approx 21,100 acres with 17-mi lake. Swimming beach; fishing, hunting; boating (rentals, mooring, launching, marina). Hiking. Cross-country skiing, snowmobiling, sledding, ice-skating. Picnicking, playground, snack bar. Tent & trailer areas along shore. Cabins. Waterfowl museum and refuge; fish hatchery. Standard fees. Phone 412/932-3141.

3. **Pymatuning Spillway.** NW via US 6 on N end of reservoir. Part of Pymatuning State Park (see #2). When fish are fed bread, they flock so thickly that ducks walk on them. Phone 412/932-3141. **Free.**

4. **Conneaut Lake Park.** Off I-79. Lakeside resort and amusement park; More than 30 rides, including roller coaster, water slide. Concerts, festivals. Campground. (Memorial Day-early Sept, daily exc Mon; also Mon hols) Phone 800/828-9619. ¢¢¢

5. **Pymatuning Visitors Center.** 9 mi W on US 285, then N on Hartstown-Linesville Rd. Part of Pennsylvania Game Commission; birds and animals indigenous to Pymatuning Reservoir area; bald eagle's nest visible from museum. Educational and interpretive programs. (Mar-Oct, daily) Phone 683-5545. **Free.**

(For further information contact the Crawford County Tourist Association, 969 Park Ave, Meadville 16335; 333-1258.)

(For accommodations see Edinboro, Meadville)

Connellsville (F-2)

Pop: 9,229 **Elev:** 885 ft **Area code:** 412 **Zip:** 15425

Located in an area visited by George Washington and where he owned land, the region has many references to him in place names. The restored Crawford Cabin near the river was the home of Colonel William Crawford, surveyor of these properties and Washington's surveying pupil.

Northwest of town in Perryopolis are many historic restorations. The town square is named for Washington, who some believe planned the design of the town.

What to See and Do

1. **Fallingwater (Kaufmann Conservation on Bear Run).** 8 mi E on PA 711, then 8 mi S on PA 381, near Mill Run. One of the most famous structures of the 20th century, Fallingwater, designed by Frank Lloyd Wright in 1936, is cantilevered on three levels over a waterfall; interior features Wright-designed furniture, textiles, lighting, as well as sculpture by modern masters; extensive grounds are heavily wooded and planted with rhododendron, which blooms in early July. Visitor center with self-guided orientation program; concession; gift shop. Guided tours (Apr-mid-Nov, daily exc Mon; winter, Sat-Sun). No children under 10; child care center. No pets. Res required. Phone 329-8501. ¢¢¢

2. **Linden Hall** (1913). 4 mi W on PA 201, then 1 mi N in Dawson. Conference and convention center in mountaintop mansion, situated in picturesque Laurel Highlands. Golf, tennis. Guided tours of mansion (Mar-Dec, daily). Phone 529-7543, -2882 or 461-2424. ¢¢¢

(For further information contact the Greater Connellsville Chamber of Commerce, 319 N Pittsburgh St; 628-5500.)

(For accommodations see New Stanton, Uniontown)

Coraopolis (E-1)

(see Pittsburgh Intl Airport Area)

Cornwall (E-8)

Settled: 1732 **Pop:** 3,231 **Elev:** 680 ft **Area code:** 717 **Zip:** 17016

The Cornwall Ore Banks were a major source of magnetic iron ore for nearly 250 years.

What to See and Do

1. **Cornwall Iron Furnace.** Rexmont Rd at Boyd St. In operation 1742-1883. Open pit mine; 19th-century Miners Village still occupied. Furnace building houses "great wheel" and 19th-century steam engine. Visitor center, exhibits, book store. (Daily exc Mon; closed most hols) Sr citizen rate. Phone 272-9711. ¢¢

2. **Historic Schaefferstown.** 6 mi SE of Lebanon at jct PA 419, 501, 897. An 18th-century farm established by Swiss-German settlers. Village square with authentic log and stone and half-timber buildings; site of first waterworks in US (1758), still in operation. Schaeffer Farm Museum has Swiss Bank House and Barn (1737); early farm tools; colonial farm garden. The museum N of the Square has antiques and artifacts of settlers. (See ANNUAL EVENTS) House and museum (both open during festivals; otherwise June-Sept, by appt). Phone 949-3235 or -2374. ¢¢

(For further information contact the Lebanon Valley Tourist & Visitors Bureau, 625 Quentin Rd, PO Box 329, Lebanon 17042; 272-8555.)

Annual Events

Historic Schaefferstown Events (see #2). Events during the yr include **Cherry Fair,** 4th Sat June; **Folk Festival,** mid-July; **Harvest Fair & Horse Plowing Contest,** 2nd wkend Sept.

(For accommodations see Ephrata, Hershey, Lancaster, Lebanon, also see Manheim)

Danville (D-7)

Pop: 5,165 **Elev:** 490 ft **Area code:** 717 **Zip:** 17821

What to See and Do

1. **Joseph Priestley House** (1794). SW via US 11 in Northumberland at 472 Priestley Ave. American house of the 18th-century Englishman and Unitarian theologian who, in 1774, was first to isolate the element oxygen. Sr citizen rate. For appointment phone 473-9474. ¢¢

2. **PP & L Montour Preserve.** From I-80 exit 33, then PA 54W to Washingtonville, and NE on local roads. Fishing; boating (no gasoline motors) on 165-acre Lake Chillisquaque. Hiking and nature

trails. Picnicking. Birds of prey exhibit in visitors center; scheduled programs (fee for some). Phone 437-3131. **Free.**

(For further information contact the Chamber of Commerce, 14 W Market St; 275-5200.)

(See Bloomsburg, Lewisburg)

Motel

 ★ ★ **HOWARD JOHNSON.** *15 Valley West Rd, I-80 exit 33.* 717/275-5100; FAX 717/275-1886. 77 rms, 2 story. Apr-Oct: S $40-$55; D $45-$65; each addl $5; under 18 free; lower rates rest of yr. Crib free. Pet accepted. TV; cable. Pool. Restaurant adj 6 am-8 pm. Ck-out noon. Coin lndry. Meeting rms. Game rm. Cr cds: A, C, D, DS, ER, JCB, MC, V.

Inn

★ ★ **PINE BARN.** *1 Pine Barn Place.* 717/275-2071; *res:* 800/627-2276; FAX 717/275-3248. 69 rms in inn, motel, 1-2 story. S $39-$55; D $44-$68; each addl $2; under 16 free. Crib $1. TV; cable. Restaurant (see PINE BARN INN). Rm serv. Bar 11 am-midnight, Sun 1-8 pm. Ck-out 1 pm. Meeting rms. Valet serv. Gift shop. Geisinger Medical Center adj. Cr cds: A, C, D, DS, MC, V.

Restaurant

★ ★ **PINE BARN INN.** *(See Pine Barn Inn)* 717/275-2071. Hrs: 7 am-10 pm; Sun 8 am-8 pm; Sun brunch 11 am-2 pm. Closed major hols. Res accepted. Bar 11 am-midnight; Sun 1-8 pm. Semi-a la carte: bkfst $2.50-$5.50, lunch $4.50-$9.50, dinner $11-$26. Sun brunch $5-$13. Child's meals. Specializes in New England seafood, steak. Salad bar. Parking. Outdoor dining. Converted 19th-century barn. Fireplace. Family-owned. Cr cds: A, C, D, DS, MC, V.

Delaware Water Gap (C-10)

It is difficult to believe that the quiet Delaware River could carve a path through the Kittatinny Mountains, which are nearly a quarter of a mile high at this point. Conflicting geological theories account for this natural phenomenon, which is part of a national recreation area. The prevailing theory is that the mountains were formed after the advent of the river, rising up from the earth so slowly that the course of the Delaware was never altered.

Despite the speculation about the origin of the gap, there is no doubt about the area's recreational value. A relatively unspoiled area along the river boundary between Pennsylvania and New Jersey, stretching approximately 35 miles from Matamoras to area just south of I-80, the site of the Delaware Water Gap is managed by the National Park Service.

Trails and overlooks (yr round) offer scenic views. Also here are canoeing and boating, hunting and fishing; camping is nearby at the Dingmans Campground within the recreation area. Swimming and picnicking at Smithfield and Milford beaches. Dingmans Falls and Silver Thread Falls, 2 of the highest waterfalls in the Poconos, are near here (see MILFORD). Several 19th-century buildings are in the area: Slateford Farm (farmhouse open June-Sept) on the Pennsylvania side, Millbrook Village (several buildings open May-Oct) and Peters Valley (see BRANCHVILLE, NJ). Interpretive programs and guided walks. There are two visitor centers, one is located off I-80 in New Jersey, at Kittatinny Point (Apr-Nov, daily; rest of yr, Sat & Sun only; closed Jan 1, Dec 25), phone 908/496-4458; the other is located near Dingmans

Falls, 1 mi W of PA 209 (Apr-Nov, daily). Park headquarters is in Bushkill, PA. Phone 717/588-2435.

(For accommodations see Milford, Stroudsburg, also see Pocono Mountains)

Denver/Adamstown (E-8)

Pop: Denver 2,861; Adamstown 1,108 **Elev:** Denver 380 ft; Adamstown 500 ft **Area code:** 717 **Zip:** Denver 17517; Adamstown 19501

Located near a Pennsylvania Turnpike exit, Denver and Adamstown are in the center of an active antique marketing area, which preserves its Pennsylvania German heritage.

What to See and Do

Stoudt's Black Angus. Along PA 272 from PA Turnpike exit 21 to just beyond Adamstown. More than 350 dealers display quality antiques for sale. (Sun) Phone 484-4385.

(For further information contact the Pennsylvania Dutch Convention and Visitors Bureau, 501 Greenfield Rd, Lancaster 17601; 299-8901 or 800/735-2629.)

Seasonal Event

Bavarian Summer Festival. SW via PA 272 in Adamstown at Black Angus Bier Garten. Oom-pah bands, schuhplattler dance groups; Oktoberfest atmosphere. Includes special events, German folklore, German food, displays, shops. Fri-Sun. Phone 484-4385 (wkends). Mid-July-early Sept.

(See Ephrata, Lancaster, Reading)

Motels

★ ★ ★ **BLACK HORSE LODGE.** *PO Box 343 (Denver), 2180 N Reading Rd, jct PA Tpke exit 21 & US 272.* 717/336-7563; FAX 717/336-1110. 74 rms, 2 story. Mid-Apr-mid-Nov: S $55-$129; D $62-$139; under 18 free; suites $100-$250; wkly, monthly rates; lower rates rest of yr. Crib free. Pet accepted, some restrictions. TV; cable. Pool. Complimentary full bkfst 7-10 am. Complimentary coffee in rms. Restaurant 11:30 am-2:15 pm, 4:30-9:30 pm. Bar to 11 pm. Ck-out noon. Coin lndry. Golf privileges. Many refrigerators, some bathrm phones. Private patios, balconies. Picnic tables, grills. Cr cds: A, C, D, DS, MC, V.

★ ★ ★ **HOLIDAY INN.** *PO Box 129 (Denver), US 272 & PA Tpke exit 21.* 717/336-7541; FAX 717/336-0515. 110 rms, 2 story. June-Oct: S $72-$97; D $80-$105; each addl $8; suites $84-$107; under 18 free; golf packages; higher rates special events; lower rates rest of yr. Crib free. Pet accepted. TV; cable, in-rm movies avail. Pool; poolside serv, lifeguard. Restaurant 6:30 am-2 pm, 5-10 pm. Rm serv. Bar 5 pm-midnight; Fri & Sat to 2 am. Ck-out noon. Coin lndry. Meeting rms. Valet serv. Golf privileges. Cr cds: A, C, D, DS, JCB, MC, V.

Donegal (E-3)

Pop: 212 **Elev:** 1,814 ft **Area code:** 412 **Zip:** 15628

What to See and Do

Seven Springs Mountain Resort Ski Area. 12 mi SE of PA Tpke exit 9 on Champion-Trent Rd. Two quad chairlifts, 7 triple chairlifts, 2 double chairlifts, 7 rope tows; patrol, school, rentals; snowmaking; cafeteria, restaurant, bar; lodge. Longest run 1¼ mi; vertical drop 750 ft. Night skiing. (Dec-Mar, daily) Alpine slide (May-Sept, daily). Hotel and conference center; summer activities include 18-hole golf, tennis, swimming. Phone 814/352-7777. Lift ¢¢¢¢

(See Connellsville, Greensburg, Ligonier, Somerset)

Resort

★ ★ ★ **SEVEN SPRINGS.** *(RD 1, Champion 15622)* On County Line Rd, 12 mi SE of PA Tpke exit 9. 814/352-7777; res: 800/452-2223; FAX 814/352-7911. 385 rms in 10 story lodge; 20 kit. chalets & cabins, 1-3 bedrm, 2 story. Lodge: S $160; D $170; each addl $30; under 16 free; suites $420; kit. chalets $490; ski, golf, tennis, honeymoon package plans; cabins for 6-25, $495-$805/wk; also daily rates (2-day min); wkend rates. Crib free. Maid serv avail in chalets, cabins $5/bed. TV. Heated indoor/outdoor pools (open to public); wading pool, poolside serv, lifeguard. Playground. Free supervised child's activities. Dining rm 7 am-10 pm. Snack bar; box lunches. Bar 11-2 am. Ck-out noon, ck-in 5 pm. Coin lndry. Convention facilities. Bellhops. Shopping arcade. Barber, beauty shop. Airport transportation. Sports dir. Tennis. Golf, greens fee $50-$60, pro, putting green, driving range. Miniature golf. Outdoor games. Hay rides. Mountain bikes avail. Soc dir; dancing, entertainment. Rec rm. Bowling. Indoor roller skating. Exercise equipt; weight machine, bicycles, whirlpool, sauna, steam rm. Wet bar in suites. Many private patios, balconies. Cr cds: DS, MC, V.

Restaurant

★ ★ ★ **NINO BARSOTTI'S.** *Mt Pleasant, 3 mi E on PA 31.* 412/547-2900. Hrs: 11 am-3 pm, 5-10 pm; Sat to 11 pm; Sun to 9 pm; Sun brunch 11:30 am-2 pm. Closed Mon; Jan 1, Thanksgiving, Dec 24 & 25. Res required Fri, Sat. Italian, Amer menu. Bar. Semi-a la carte: lunch $4.25-$9.45, dinner $7.45-$23.45. Buffet (Tues): dinner $7.95. Sun brunch $7.50. Child's meals. Specializes in fresh seafood, steak, homemade desserts. Salad bar. Own pasta. Valet parking. Family-owned. Cr cds: A, D, DS, MC, V.

D

Downingtown (F-9)

Settled: 1702 **Pop:** 7,749 **Elev:** 244 ft **Area code:** 610 **Zip:** 19335

Settled by emigrants from Birmingham, England, Downingtown honors Thomas Downing, who erected a log cabin here in 1702. The borough was first called Milltown, after the mill built here by Roger Hunt in 1765. The town, with its many historically interesting homes, retains much of its colonial charm. Jacob Eichholtz, a leading early American portrait artist, was born here.

What to See and Do

1. **Hibernia County Park.** From US 30 Bypass take PA 82 approx 2 mi N to Cedar Knoll Rd, then left 1¼ mi to park entrance on left.

Once the center of an iron works community, it is now the largest of the county parks, encompassing 800 acres of woodlands and meadows. The west branch of the Brandywine Creek, Birch Run and a pond are stocked with trout; hiking trails; picnicking; tent & trailer camping (dump station). Park features Hibernia Mansion; portions of house date from 1798, period furnishings. Tours of mansion (Memorial Day-Labor Day, Sun; fee) Phone 384-0290. **Free.**

2. **Historic Yellow Springs.** 10 mi NE via PA 113, NW on Yellow Springs Rd. From its beginnings as a fashionable spa, this historic village has been everything from a Revolutionary hospital to an art school. Countryside covers 145 acres with buildings, medicinal herb garden and mineral springs. Events and educational programs throughout the yr (some fees). Self-guided tour. Office (Mon-Fri). Phone 827-7414.

3. **Fox Meadow Farm & Vineyards.** 10 mi NE via PA 113, E on Clover Mill Rd, near Chester Springs. Visit the farm and vineyards; winery operates in historic barn (ca 1820). Tasting room. (Apr-Jan, Sat & Sun; also by appt) Phone 827-9731. **Free.**

4. **Valley Forge National Historical Park** (see). 10 mi E on I-76.

(For further information contact the Chester County Tourist Bureau, 601 Westtown Rd, Ste 170, West Chester 19382; 344-6365.)

Annual Events

Old Fiddlers' Picnic. Hibernia County Park (see #1). 2nd Sat Aug.

Hibernia Mansion Christmas Tours. Hibernia County Park (see #1). 1st wk Dec.

(See King of Prussia, West Chester)

Motor Hotel

★ ★ **HOLIDAY INN.** *(815 N Pottstown Pike, Exton 19341)* N on PA 113 to PA 100, 1 mi S of PA Tpke exit 23. 610/363-1100; FAX 610/524-2329. 213 rms, 4 story. S $89; D $97; under 18 free. Crib free. Pet accepted. TV; cable. 2 pools, 1 indoor; poolside serv, lifeguard. Complimentary continental bkfst. Coffee in rms. Restaurant 6:30 am-10 pm; Sat from 7 am; Sun 7 am-2 pm. Rm serv. Bar 2 pm-2 am; entertainment ex Sun. Ck-out noon. Coin lndry. Meeting rms. Valet serv. Airport transportation. Health club privileges. Picnic tables. Cr cds: A, C, D, DS, JCB, MC, V.

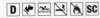

Restaurant

★ ★ **VICKERS.** *(192 Welsh Pool Rd, Lionville)* ½ mi W on PA 100, 1 mi S of PA Tpke exit 23 on Gordon Dr. 610/363-7998. Hrs: 11:30 am-2 pm, 5:30-11 pm. Closed Sun (exc Easter & Mother's Day). Res accepted; required Sat. French, continental menu. Bar. Semi-a la carte: lunch $6.50-$12.50, dinner $16-$26. Specialties: beef Wellington, Dover sole, rack of lamb. Parking. Own desserts. Pianist Wed, Fri & Sat. Authentic farmhouse, built 1823. Cr cds: A, D, MC, V.

D

Doylestown (Bucks Co) (E-10)

Settled: 1735 **Pop:** 8,575 **Elev:** 340 ft **Area code:** 215 **Zip:** 18901

Doylestown is the county seat of historic and colorful Bucks County.

What to See and Do

1. **Mercer Mile.** Three reinforced-concrete structures built between 1910-1916 within a one-mile radius by Dr. Henry Chapman Mercer, archaeologist, historian, world traveler and tile-maker. They include

   Mercer Museum of the Bucks County Historical Society. 84 S Pine St. Collection of over 50,000 early American artifacts and tools. Changing exhibits gallery. (Daily; closed Jan 1, Thanksgiving, Dec 25) Phone 345-0210. ¢¢

   Fonthill Museum. E Court St at PA 313. Concrete castle of Henry Chapman Mercer (1856-1930) displays his collection of tiles and prints from around the world. Guided tours (times vary; phone ahead). (Daily; closed Jan 1, Thanksgiving, Dec 25) Phone 348-9461. ¢¢

   Moravian Pottery and Tile Works. E Court St & Swamp Rd. Restored and established as a living history museum; tiles are handcrafted on premises. Slide show and self-guided tour explain ceramic process and history of Mercer's work, which appears in buildings all over the country. (Daily; closed some hols) Sr citizen rate. Phone 345-6722. ¢¢

2. **James A. Michener Art Museum.** 138 S Pine St. Changing exhibitions of 20th century American art, contemporary crafts and sculpture garden. Located in restored old Bucks County jail. (Daily exc Mon; closed major hols) Phone 340-9800. ¢¢

3. **Pearl S. Buck House** (1835). 520 Dublin Rd, 8 mi NW via PA 611, 313 in Hilltown Township. House of Pulitzer and Nobel Prize winning author, Pearl S. Buck. Original furnishings include desk at which *The Good Earth* was written; memorabilia, Chinese artifacts. Picnicking on grounds. Gift shop. One-hour guided tours (Mar-Dec, daily exc Mon; closed most major hols) Sr citizen rate. Phone 249-0100. ¢¢

4. **Covered bridges.** Descriptive list, map of 11 bridges in Bucks County may be obtained at Bucks County Tourist Commission.

(For information contact Bucks County Tourist Commission, PO Box 912, Dept 68; 345-4552 or 800/836-BUCKS.)

(See Philadelphia, Quakertown)

Motel

★★ **COMFORT INN.** *(678 Bethlehem Pike/PA 309, Montgomeryville 18936)* S on US 202. 215/361-3600; FAX 215/361-7949. 84 rms, 3 story. S $70.95-$100.95; D $75.95-$82.95; each addl $5; suites $100.95-$110.95; under 18 free. Crib free. TV; cable, in-rm movies avail. Complimentary continental bkfst. Restaurant nearby. Ck-out noon. Coin lndry. Meeting rm. Valet serv. Health club privileges. Refrigerator, wet bar in suites. Cr cds: A, C, D, DS, ER, MC, V.

[D] [⊠] [🐾] [SC]

Restaurants

★★★ **CAFÉ ARIELLE.** 100 S Main St. 215/345-5930. Hrs: noon-2:30 pm, 6-9 pm; Sat 6-9:30 pm. Closed Sun & Mon; Jan 1, Easter, Dec 25. Res required Fri, Sat. French menu. Bar. A la carte entrees: lunch $6-$12, dinner $18.50-$24. Specializes in duck, seafood. Own baking. Parking. Restored livery (1800s); original artwork. Open kitchen. Cr cds: A, D, MC, V.

[D]

★★★ **CONTI INN.** PA 313, at jct Old PA 611. 215/348-9600. Hrs: 11:30 am-10 pm; Sat from 10 pm. Closed Sun; hols. Res accepted. Bar. Semi-a la carte: lunch $10-$12, dinner $15-$19.50. Child's meals. Specialties: beef Wellington, fresh seafood. Parking. Colonial atmosphere. Inn since 1758. Family-owned. Cr cds: A, C, D, DS, MC, V.

[D]

Du Bois (C-4)

Settled: 1865 **Pop:** 8,286 **Elev:** 1,420 ft **Area code:** 814 **Zip:** 15801

At the entrance to the lowest pass of the Allegheny Range, Du Bois is a transportation center—once the apex of huge lumbering operations. Destroyed by fire in 1888, the town was rebuilt on the ashes of the old community and today ranks as one of the 12 major trading centers in the state.

(For further information contact the Brookville Area Chamber of Commerce, 233 Main St, Brookville 15825; 849-8448.)

(See Clearfield)

Motels

✔ ★★ **BEST WESTERN-PENN ROSE MOTOR INN.** *82 N Park Place.* 814/371-6200; FAX 814/371-4608. 60 rms, 3 story. S $43-$47; D $49-$57; each addl $6; under 12 free. Crib free. TV; cable. Playground. Complimentary continental bkfst in lobby. Restaurant nearby. Ck-out 11 am. Sundries. Golf privileges. Picnic tables. Cr cds: A, C, D, DS, MC, V.

[D] [🌲] [🐾] [SC]

★★ **HOLIDAY INN.** US 219 & I-80 exit 16. 814/371-5100; FAX 814/375-0230. 161 rms, 2 story. S $55-$64; D $61-$72; each addl $6; studio rms $75; under 18 free. TV; cable. Pool; wading, poolside serv, lifeguard. Restaurant 7 am-2 pm, 5-10 pm. Rm serv. Bar 5 pm-1 am. Ck-out noon. Coin lndry. Meeting rms. Bellhops. Free airport transportation. Cr cds: A, C, D, DS, JCB, MC, V.

[D] [≈] [⊠] [🐾] [SC]

★★ **RAMADA.** Jct I-80 exit 17 & PA 255. 814/371-7070; FAX 814/371-1055. 96 rms, 2-3 story. No elvtr. S $53-$65; D $59-$75; each addl $10; suites $80-$150; under 18 free. Crib free. TV; cable. Indoor pool; sauna, poolside serv. Restaurant 6:30 am-2 pm, 5-10 pm. Rm serv. Bar 4 pm-2 am; entertainment exc Sun, dancing. Ck-out noon. Meeting rms. Airport transportation. Golf privileges, pro. Cr cds: A, C, D, DS, JCB, MC, V.

[D] [🌲] [≈] [⊠] [🐾] [SC]

★★ **TOWNE HOUSE INN.** *(138 Center St, St Mary's 15857)* 27 mi NE on PA 255. 814/781-1556; FAX 814/834-4449. 42 rms (3 with shower only), 3 story. S $48-$85; D $53-$85; each addl $5. Crib $5. TV; cable. Complimentary coffee in rms. Restaurant Mon-Fri 7 am-1:30 pm. Rm serv. Ck-out 11 am. Meeting rms. Exercise equipt; weight machine, treadmill. Picnic tables. Cr cds: A, D, DS, MC, V.

[🌲] [⊠] [🐾]

Easton (D-9)

Founded: 1752 **Pop:** 26,276 **Elev:** 300 ft **Area code:** 610 **Zip:** 18042

Named by Thomas Penn, one of the proprietors, for the English birthplace of his bride, Easton today is the gateway to the great industrial Lehigh Valley. Lafayette College, with its beautiful campus, and the historic Great Square are of interest. Easton, the seat of Northampton County, is part of a larger metropolitan area, the Lehigh Valley, which also includes Allentown and Bethlehem.

What to See and Do

1. **"The Great Square."** Center of business district. Now called Center Square. Dominated by Soldiers' and Sailors' Monument. Bronze marker shows replica of Old Courthouse, which stood until 1862 on land rented from the Penns for one red rose a year. From

Old Courthouse steps, the Declaration of Independence was read on July 8, 1776, when the Easton Flag, the first stars and stripes of the united colonies, was unfurled here.

2. **Northampton County Historical Society.** 101 S 4th St, diagonally opp Parsons-Taylor House. Changing exhibits; library (Thurs & Fri); museum (Thurs-Sun; closed hols). Phone 253-1222. Museum ¢

3. **Hugh Moore Park.** S 25th St, 2 mi S of US 22. Restored Lehigh Canal, locks and locktender's house; mule-drawn canal boat rides (Memorial Day-Labor Day; days may vary, phone for schedule). Also hiking, picnicking; boat and bicycle rentals in park. Park (daily). Phone 250-6700. Boat rides ¢¢

4. **Canal Museum.** PA 611, 1 mi S of US 22. Exhibits include photographs, models, documents and artifacts from the era of mule-drawn canal boats in the 1800s; electronic map and audiovisual programs. (Daily; closed Jan 1, Thanksgiving, Dec 25) Phone 250-6700. ¢

5. **Lafayette College** (1826). (2,000 students) N side of town. Bronze statue of Lafayette by Daniel Chester French in front of college chapel; American historical portrait collection in Kirby Hall of Civil Rights. Tour of campus. Phone 250-5000.

(For further information contact the Two Rivers Area Chamber of Commerce, 157 S 4th St, PO Box 637, 18044; 253-4211.)

(See Allentown, Bethlehem)

Restaurant

★ ★ **MANDARIN TANG.** *25th St Shopping Center. 610/258-5697.* Hrs: 11:30 am-10 pm; Fri, Sat to 11 pm. Closed Thanksgiving. Res accepted Fri-Sun. Chinese menu. Semi-a la carte: lunch $3.95-$5.50, dinner $5-$16.95. Specialties: mandarin orange beef, General Tso's chicken. Chinese decor. Authentic Chinese dishes. Cr cds: A, D, MC, V.

Ebensburg (E-4)

Pop: 3,872 **Elev:** 2,140 ft **Area code:** 814 **Zip:** 15931

What to See and Do

Allegheny Portage Railroad National Historic Site. 12 mi E on US 22. Remains of railroad built 1831-34 to link east and west divisions of the Pennsylvania Mainline Canal. Cars were pulled up 10 inclined planes by ropes powered by steam engines. Horses or locomotives pulled the cars over the level stretches of the 36-mile route across the Alleghenies from Hollidaysburg to Johnstown. The Skew Arch Bridge, an engine house exhibit, and the Lemon House, an historic tavern, help tell the story of the Allegheny Portage Railroad. A visitor center (daily; closed Dec 25) has exhibits and a 20-minute film. There are ranger-led programs (summer, daily) and costumed demonstrations (summer, wkends); picnic area (daily). Phone 886-6150. **Free.**

(For accommodations see Altoona, Johnstown)

Edinboro (B-2)

Pop: 7,736 **Elev:** 1,210 ft **Area code:** 814 **Zip:** 16412

This is a resort town on Edinboro Lake and the home of Edinboro State College.

What to See and Do

Edinboro Ski Area. 4 mi E on US 6N, then 3 mi S on PA 86, in Cambridge Springs. Two T-bars, Pomalift; patrol, school, rentals; snowmaking; cafeteria. Longest run 2,800 ft; vertical drop 350 ft. (Dec-Mar, daily) Half-day & evening rates. Phone 734-1641. ¢¢¢¢

(See Erie, Meadville)

Motel

★ ★ ★ **EDINBORO RESORT CONFERENCE CENTER.** *US 6, off I-79 exit 38. 814/734-5650; res: 800/352-3182; FAX 814/734-7532.* 105 rms, 2 story. S $60-$72; D $76-$84; each addl $5; wkend, ski, golf plans. Crib free. TV; in-rm movies. Indoor pool; sauna, lifeguard. Restaurant 7 am-9 pm. Rm serv. Bars 11:30-2 am; entertainment, dancing Fri, Sat. Ck-out noon. Coin lndry. Meeting rms. Bellhops. 18-hole golf adj, greens fee $18-$22, putting green. Downhill ski 7 mi. Cr cds: A, C, D, DS, MC, V.

Inn

★ ★ **RIVERSIDE.** *(1 Fountain Ave, Cambridge Springs 16403) At US 6/19 & PA 99. 814/398-4645; res: 800/964-5173.* 74 rms, 10 share bath, 3 story. S $40-$60; D $55-$75; each addl $10-$20; suites $90; under 3 free. Closed Jan-Mar. TV in suites & sitting rm. Pool. Complimentary full bkfst. Dining rm 11:30 am-2 pm, 5:30-8:30 pm; Fri, Sat to 10 pm; Sun 10:30 am-2 pm, 5-8:30 pm. Ck-out 11 am, ck-in 3 pm. Private parking. Tennis, golf privileges. Lawn games. Victorian inn (1885) overlooking French Creek. Cr cds: DS, MC, V.

Ephrata (E-8)

Settled: 1732 **Pop:** 12,133 **Elev:** 380 ft **Area code:** 717 **Zip:** 17522

What to See and Do

1. **Ephrata Cloister.** 632 W Main St. Buildings stand as a monument to an unusual religious experiment. In 1732 Conrad Beissel, a German Seventh-Day Baptist, began to lead a hermit's life here; within a few years he established a religious community of recluses, with a Brotherhood, a Sisterhood and a group of married "householders." The members of the solitary order dressed in concealing white habits; the buildings (1735-49) were without adornment, the halls were narrow, the doorways were low and board benches served as beds and wooden blocks as pillows. Their religious zeal and charity, however, proved to be their undoing. After the Battle of Brandywine, the cloistered community nursed the Revolutionary sick and wounded, but contracted typhus, which decimated their numbers. Celibacy also contributed to the decline of the community, but the Society was not formally dissolved until 1934. Surviving and restored buildings include the Sisters' House, Chapel, Almonry and eight others. (Daily; closed some hols) Craft demonstrations (summer). Sr citizen rate. Phone 733-6600. ¢¢

2. **Museum and Library of the Historical Society of Cocalico Valley.** 249 W Main St. Italianate Victorian mansion contains period displays; historical exhibits; genealogical and historical research library on Cocalico Valley area and residents. (Tues-Fri) Phone 733-1616. **Free.**

(For further information contact the Chamber of Commerce, 23 Washington Ave; 738-9010.)

Annual Event

Street Fair. One of largest in state. Last full wk Sept.

(See Bird-in-Hand, Denver/Adamstown, Lancaster, Lebanon, Reading)

Inns

★ ★ ★ **1777 HOUSE.** *301 W Main St. 717/738-9502; FAX 717/738-9552.* 12 rms, 3 story, 2 carriage house suites. S $61-$81; D $69-$89; each addl $10; suites $119-$175; extended stay packages. Crib $8. TV; cable in sitting rm. Complimentary continental bkfst. Restaurant nearby. Ck-out 11 am, ck-in 3 pm. Health club privileges. Restored clockmaker's house (1777). Antiques. Hand-cut stenciling. Cr cds: A, C, D, DS, MC, V.

✔ ★ ★ ★ **DONECKERS GUEST HOUSE.** *318-324 N State St. 717/738-9502; FAX 717/738-9552.* 19 rms, 2 story. S $51-$81; D $59-$89; each addl $10; suites $139-$149. Crib $8. Complimentary continental bkfst. Restaurant (see DONECKERS). Ck-out 11 am, ck-in 3 pm. Health club privileges. Some balconies. Mansion furnished with antiques. Cr cds: A, C, D, DS, MC, V.

★ ★ **SMITHTON COUNTRY.** *900 W Main St, at Academy Dr. 717/733-6094.* 8 rms, 2 story. S $55-$125; D $65-$135; each addl $20-$35; suites $140-$170. Crib free. Complimentary full bkfst, coffee & tea. Restaurant nearby. Ck-out noon, ck-in 3:30 pm. Concierge. Classic stone inn (1763); fireplaces, antiques. Totally nonsmoking. Cr cds: A, MC, V.

Restaurant

★ ★ ★ **DONECKERS.** *(See Doneckers Guest House Inn) 717/738-9501.* Hrs: 11 am-10 pm; Sun brunch 11:30 am-3 pm. Closed Wed; major hols. Res accepted. Serv bar. Wine list. French, Amer menu. A la carte entrees: lunch $3.75-$12.95, dinner $7.50-$24.95. Sun brunch $12.95. Child's meals. Specialties: Dover sole with strawberry sauce, steak au poivre. Own baking. Elegant French decor. Cr cds: A, C, D, DS, MC, V.

Erie (A-2)

Settled: 1753 **Pop:** 108,718 **Elev:** 744 ft **Area code:** 814

Third largest city in the state and only Great Lakes port in Pennsylvania, Erie has a fine natural harbor on Lake Erie, which is protected and bounded by Presque Isle peninsula, the site of many historic events. Greater Erie is also one of the nation's mighty industrial centers, with more than 750 highly diversified manufacturing firms and several large industrial parks. The lake and city take their name from the Eriez Indians, who were killed by the Seneca about 1654.

On the south shore of Presque Isle Bay, Commodore Oliver Hazard Perry built his fleet, floated the ships across the sandbars and fought the British in the Battle of Lake Erie (1813). Fort Presque Isle, built by the French in 1753 and destroyed by them in 1759, was rebuilt by the English, burned by the Indians and rebuilt again in 1794 by the Americans.

What to See and Do

1. **Erie Historical Museum & Planetarium.** 356 W 6th St. Housed in 1890s Victorian mansion. Museum features regional history and decorative arts exhibits; multimedia presentations on regional maritime history; restored period rooms; changing exhibits (June-Aug, daily exc Mon; rest of yr, Tues-Sun afternoons; closed most hols). Also planetarium with shows (July-Aug, Thurs-Sun afternoons; rest of yr, wkend afternoons). Phone 871-5790. Museum ¢; planetarium ¢

2. **Wayne Memorial Blockhouse.** On grounds of State Soldiers' and Sailors' Home, 560 E 3rd St. Replica of blockhouse in which General Anthony Wayne died Dec 15, 1796, after becoming ill on a voyage from Detroit. He was buried at the foot of the flagpole; later, his son had the body disinterred and the remains moved to Radnor. (Memorial Day-Labor Day, daily) Phone 871-4531. **Free.**

3. **Gridley's Grave.** Lakeside Cemetery, 1718 E Lake Rd. Final resting place of Captain Charles Vernon Gridley, to whom, at the battle of Manila Bay in 1898, Admiral Dewey said, "You may fire when ready, Gridley." Gridley died in Japan; his body was returned here for burial. Four old Spanish cannons from Manila Harbor, built in 1777, guard the grave. Offers view of peninsula, Lake Erie and entrance to Erie Harbor from cliff by Gridley Circle. Phone 459-8200.

4. **Firefighters Historical Museum.** 428 Chestnut St. More than 1,300 items of firefighting memorabilia are displayed in the old #4 Firehouse. Exhibits include fire apparatus dating from 1823, alarm systems, uniforms, badges, ribbons, helmets, nozzles, fire marks and fire extinguishers; fire safety films are shown in the Hay Loft Theater. (May-Oct, Sat & Sun) Sr citizen rate. Phone 456-5969. ¢

5. **Erie Art Museum.** 411 State St. Temporary art exhibits in a variety of media; regional artwork and lectures in the restored Greek-revival Old Customs House (1839). Art classes, concerts, lectures and workshops are also offered. (Tues-Sat, also Sun afternoons; closed major hols) Phone 459-5477. ¢

6. **Land Lighthouse** (1866). Foot of Dunn Blvd. The first lighthouse on the Great Lakes was constructed on this site in 1813.

7. **Waldameer Park & Water World.** 220 Peninsula Drive, at entrance to Presque Isle State Park (see #11). Rides, midway, kiddieland, water park, picnic area, food, dance pavilion. (Memorial Day-Labor Day, daily exc Mon; open Mon hols) Fee for some activities. Phone 838-3591.

8. **Erie Zoo.** 3 mi N of I-90 State St exit 7. Zoo houses more than 300 animals, including gorillas, polar bears and giraffes; children's zoo (May-Sept); one-mile tour of grounds on Safariland Express Train (fee). Indoor ice rink (Oct-Mar, phone 868-3652). Zoo (daily). Sr citizen rate. Phone 864-6272. Zoo ¢¢

9. **Presque Isle State Park.** N off PA 832. Peninsula stretches seven miles into Lake Erie and curves back toward city. Approx 3,200 acres of recreation and conservation areas. Swimming; fishing; boating (rentals, mooring, launching, marina). Hiking, birding, trails. Cross-country skiing, ice-skating, ice fishing, ice boating. Picnicking, concessions. Visitor Center, environmental education and interpretive programs. Phone 871-4251.

10. **Misery Bay.** NE corner of Presque Isle Bay. State monument to Perry; named after Perry defeated British and the fleet suffered cold and privations of a bitter winter.

(For further information contact the Erie Area Chamber of Commerce, 1006 State St, 16501; 454-7191.)

(See North East)

Motels

★ ★ **COMFORT INN.** *8051 Peach St (16509), I-90E exit 6. 814/866-6666; FAX 814/866-6666, ext. 309.* 110 rms, 2 story, 50 suites. Mid-May-Sept: S $79; D $89; each addl $10; suites $89-$119; under 18 free; higher rates hol wkends; lower rates rest of yr. Crib free. TV; cable, in-rm movies. Heated pool; lifeguard. Complimentary continental bkfst, coffee. Restaurant adj 6 am-midnight. Ck-out noon. Meeting rm. Exercise equipt; bicycles, rowers, whirlpool. Refrigerator, wet bar in suites. Some balconies. Cr cds: A, C, D, DS, JCB, MC, V.

★ ★ **ECONO LODGE.** *8050 Peach St (16509), I-90E exit 6. 814/866-5544.* 97 rms, 3 story. Late May-Oct: S $69.95-$79.95; D $89.95-$109.95; each addl $6; higher rates special events; lower rates rest of yr. Crib free. TV; cable, in-rm movies. Indoor pool; lifeguard. Complimentary continental bkfst. Restaurant adj 7-2 am. Ck-out noon. Meeting rms. Sundries. Free airport transportation. Exercise equipt; weight machine, bicycles, whirlpool, sauna. Some refrigerators, wet bars. Cr cds: A, C, D, DS, JCB, MC, V.

✔ ★ ★ **GLASS HOUSE INN.** *3202 W 26th St (16506). 814/833-7751; FAX 814/833-4222.* 30 rms. June-Labor Day: S, D $45-$79; each addl $7; family rates; lower rates rest of yr. Crib $4. TV; cable. Heated pool; sauna. Complimentary continental bkfst. Restaurant nearby. Ck-out 11 am. Sundries. Gift shop. Downhill/x-country ski 20 mi. Cr cds: A, C, D, DS, MC, V.

★ **HOWARD JOHNSON.** *7575 Peach St (16509), jct I-90 & US 19, exit 6. 814/864-4811.* 111 rms, 1-2 story. Late May-Sept: S $59-$65; D $69-$74; each addl $10; under 18 free. Crib free. TV; cable. Indoor pool; wading pool, sauna, lifeguard. Complimentary continental bkfst. Restaurant nearby. Ck-out noon. Coin lndry. Valet serv. Private patios, balconies. Cr cds: A, C, D, DS, ER, JCB, MC, V.

✔ ★ **KNIGHTS INN.** *7455 Schultz Rd (16509), on PA 97 at I-90 exit 7. 814/868-0879.* 105 rms. S $38.95-$44.95; D $44.95-$51.95; each addl $4; under 18 free. Crib free. Pool. TV; cable. Complimentary coffee. Restaurant adj 6:30 am-11:30 pm. Ck-out noon. Meeting rm. Refrigerators. Cr cds: A, C, D, DS, ER, MC, V.

★ ★ **RAMADA INN.** *6101 Wattsburg Rd (16509). 814/825-3100; FAX 814/825-0857.* 122 rms, 2 story. July-Sept: S $65; D $75; each addl $8; suites $65-$95; under 16 free; ski, wkend plans; lower rates rest of yr. Crib free. TV; cable, in-rm movies avail. Heated pool; wading pool, lifeguard. Restaurant 6:30 am-10 pm. Rm serv. Bar 5 pm-midnight. Ck-out noon. Meeting rms. Sundries. Downhill ski 15 mi. Game rm. Cr cds: A, C, D, DS, MC, V.

✔ ★ **SCOTT'S.** *2930 W 6th St (PA 832) (16505). 814/838-1961.* 58 rms, 1-2 story, 14 kits. (no equipt). June-Labor Day: S, D $48-$79; each addl $5; kit. units $75-$90; lower rates rest of yr. Crib $5. TV; cable. Playground. Heated pool; wading pool, lifeguard. Ck-out 11 am. Downhill/x-country ski 20 mi. Lawn games. Cr cds: A, C, D, DS, MC, V.

Motor Hotels

★ ★ ★ **BEL AIRE.** *2800 W 8th St (16505). 814/833-1116; res: 800/888-8781; FAX 814/838-3242.* 151 rms, 3 story. Mid-June-mid-Sept: S, D $95-$100; each addl $10; suites $125-$200; under 19 free; lower rates rest of yr. Crib $10. TV; cable. Indoor pool; lifeguard. Restaurant 6 am-11 pm. Bar 11-2 am, Sun to midnight. Ck-out noon. Meeting rms. Sundries. Exercise equipt; weights, bicycles, whirlpool, sauna. Private patios, balconies. Cr cds: A, C, D, DS, MC, V.

★ ★ **HOLIDAY INN DOWNTOWN.** *18 W 18th St (16501). 814/456-2961; FAX 814/456-7067.* 134 rms, 4 story. Memorial Day-Labor Day S, D $69-$89; each addl $6; under 19 free; lower rates rest of year. Crib free. TV. Heated pool; poolside serv, lifeguard. Restaurant 6:30 am-10 pm. Rm serv. Bar 11:30-2 am; entertainment, dancing. Ck-out noon. Lndry facilities. Meeting rms. Bellhops. Valet serv. Free

airport transportation. Health club privileges. Cr cds: A, C, D, DS, JCB, MC, V.

★ ★ **HOLIDAY INN SOUTH.** *8040 Perry Hwy (PA 97), I-90 exit 7 (16509). 814/864-4911; FAX 814/864-3743.* 216 rms, 2-4 story. S $65-$74; D $69-$74; each addl $6; suites $75-$85; under 18 free. Crib free. TV; cable. Heated pool; poolside serv, lifeguard. Restaurant 6:30 am-10 pm. Rm serv. Bar 11-1 am; entertainment, dancing Fri & Sat. Ck-out noon. Meeting rms. Bellhops. Valet serv. Free airport, RR station transportation. Health club privileges. Cr cds: A, C, D, DS, JCB, MC, V.

Restaurant

★ ★ **PUFFERBELLY.** *414 French St. 814/454-1557.* Hrs: 11 am-10 pm; Fri, Sat to midnight; Sun to 8 pm; Sun brunch to 2:30 pm. Closed major hols. Res accepted. Bar. Semi-a la carte: lunch $3.95-$6, dinner $8.95-$14.25. Sun brunch $8.95. Specializes in regional cuisine, steak, seafood. Combo, vocalist Fri. Outdoor dining. Restored firehouse (1907). Cr cds: A, DS, MC, V.

Fort Washington (E-9)

Pop: 3,699 **Elev:** 250 ft **Area code:** 215 **Zip:** 19034

What to See and Do

1. **Hope Lodge** (ca 1745). 1 mi S, Old Bethlehem Pike. Colonial Georgian mansion; headquarters for General John Cochran after Battle of Germantown. Historic furnishings, paintings, ceramics. (Daily exc Mon; closed most hols) Sr citizen rate. Phone 646-1595. ¢¢

2. **The Highlands** (1796). 7001 Sheaff Lane. Late Georgian mansion on 43 acres built by Anthony Morris, active in both state and federal government. Formal gardens and crenelated walls built ca 1845. Tours (by appt). (Mon-Fri) Phone 641-2687. ¢

3. **Fort Washington State Park.** 500 Bethlehem Pike. Commemorates the site of Washington's northern defense line against the British in 1777. Fishing. Hiking, ball fields. Picnicking. Phone 646-2942.

(For further information contact the Valley Forge Convention & Visitors Bureau, 600 W Germantown Pike, Suite 130, Plymouth Meeting, 19462; 610/834-1550.)

Hotel

★ **DAYS HOTEL.** *530 Pennsylvania Ave. 215/643-1111; FAX 215/643-2459.* 135 rms, 5 story. S, D $69; each addl $6; under 12 free; wkend rates. Crib free. Pet accepted, some restrictions. TV; cable. Pool; wading pool, lifeguard. Complimentary coffee in rms. Restaurant 6 am-10 pm; Sat & Sun from 7 am. Bar 5 pm-2 am; entertainment, dancing Fri, Sat. Ck-out noon. Meeting rms. Health club privileges. Game rm. Some in-rm whirlpools. Cr cds: A, C, D, DS, MC, V.

Franklin (Venango Co) (C-2)

Settled: 1787 **Pop:** 7,329 **Elev:** 1,020 ft **Area code:** 814 **Zip:** 16323

A series of French and British forts was erected in this area. The last one, Fort Franklin, was razed by local settlers who used the stone and timber in their own buildings. Old Garrison took its place in 1796 and later served as the Venango County Jail. In 1856 Billy Smith, a blacksmith, dug a well to find water and instead loosed a gusher of oil and an oil boom. Today oil dominates the industries of the area, but Franklin boasts many diversified manufacturers.

What to See and Do

1. **Venango County Court House** (1868). 12th and Liberty Sts. Unique styling; contains display of Indian artifacts. (Mon-Fri; closed hols) Phone 432-9500. **Free.**
2. **Hoge-Osmer House** (ca 1865). Corner of South Park and Elk Sts. Museum owned by Venango County Historical Society; houses displays of materials and artifacts relating to Venango County history; period furnishings, research library. House open (May-Dec, Tues-Thurs & Sat, mid-morning-early afternoon; rest of yr, Sat; closed major hols). Inquire for genealogy library hrs. Phone 437-2275. **Free.**
3. **Antique Music Museum.** 1675 Pittsburgh Rd. Features nickelodeons, band organs, calliopes, German organs, a variety of music boxes, many other items. Unique "see and hear" concept allows visitors to hear music played on the antique instruments. Guided tours. (Late Apr-late Oct, daily) Phone 432-5823. ¢¢
4. **Pioneer Cemetery** (1795-1879). Otter & 15th Sts.

(For further information and a walking tour map, contact the Franklin Area Chamber of Commerce, 1256 Liberty St, Suite 2; 432-5823.)

Annual Event

Rocky Grove Fair. July.

Seasonal Event

Franklin Silver Cornet Band Concerts. City Park. Thurs, mid-June-Aug.

(See Meadville, Oil City, Titusville)

Motel

★ ★ **INN AT FRANKLIN.** *1411 Liberty St.* 814/437-3031; res: 800/535-4052; FAX 814/432-7481. 85 rms, 6 story. Apr-Sept: S $65; D $70; each addl $5; under 18 free; wkly, monthly rates; lower rates rest of yr. TV; cable. Complimentary continental bkfst. Restaurant 6 am-2 pm, 5-10 pm; Sun 7 am-8 pm. Bar. Ck-out 11 am. Valet serv. Barber, beauty shop. Free airport, bus depot transportation. Cr cds: A, C, D, DS, MC, V.

Inn

★ ★ **QUO VADIS.** *1501 Liberty St, near Chess-Lamberton Airport.* 814/432-4208. 6 rms, 3 story. S, D $60-$80; each addl $10; wkly rates. TV in sitting rm. Complimentary full bkfst, coffee & tea. Restaurant nearby. Ck-out 11 am, ck-in 4-9 pm. Victorian mansion (1867); detailed woodwork, heirloom antiques. Totally nonsmoking. Cr cds: A, MC, V.

Galeton (B-6)

Pop: 1,370 **Elev:** 1,325 ft **Area code:** 814 **Zip:** 16922

What to See and Do

1. **Pennsylvania Lumber Museum.** 10 mi W on US 6. Exhibits on lumbering and its techniques, forest industries and products; reconstructed lumber camp and sawmill; restored locomotive and log-loader; nature trails, picnicking. Slide show in visitor center. (Daily; closed hols) (See ANNUAL EVENTS) Sr citizen rate. Phone 435-2652. ¢¢
2. **Ole Bull State Park.** 18 mi SW off PA 144. At upper reaches of the Kettle Creek. Site of unsuccessful effort by the famous Norwegian violinist, Ole Bornemann Bull, to establish a colony called "New Norway." Approx 100 acres. Swimming beach; fishing, hunting. Hiking. Cross-country skiing, snowmobiling. Tent & trailer sites (electric hookups). Interpretive program. Standard fees. Phone 435-2169.
3. **Ski Denton/Denton Hill.** 10 mi W on US 6. One triple, 1 double chairlift, 2 Pomalifts; patrol, school, rentals; snowmaking; cafeteria, restaurant; lodge, cabins. Longest run 1 mi; vertical drop 650 ft. (Dec-Mar, daily) 100 miles of cross-country trails; night skiing; camping. (See ANNUAL EVENTS) Phone 435-2115. ¢¢¢¢¢

(For further information contact Potter County Recreation, PO Box 245, Coudersport 16915; 435-2290 or -8230.)

Annual Events

Bark Peeler's Convention. On grounds of Pennsylvania Lumber Museum (see #1). Re-creation of old-time festival held by lumber camp workers celebrating the end of the work year. Features many demonstrations, including cross-cut sawing, hewing, bark peeling; entertainment; period music; exhibits. Phone 435-2652. Wkend early July.

Woodsmen's Carnival. Horse-pulling and woodcutting competitions; food; displays. Phone 435-2907. Early Aug.

Germania Old Home Day. 7 mi SE via PA 144 in Germania. Food, dancing, events, games, entertainment. Phone 435-8881. Early Sept.

Bowhunter's Festival. Denton Hill (see #3). Wkend mid-Sept.

(See Wellsboro)

Motel

✔ ★ **OX YOKE INN.** *W Main St (US 6).* 814/435-6522. 40 rms. No rm phones. S $28-$32; D $36-$40; each addl $4; under 7 free; higher rates hunting season. Crib $4. Pet accepted. TV; cable. Playground. Restaurant 6 am-9 pm. Ck-out 11 am. Meeting rms. Gift shop. Downhill/x-country ski 10 mi. Picnic tables, grill. Cr cds: DS, MC, V.

Gettysburg (F-6)

Founded: 1798 **Pop:** 7,025 **Elev:** 560 ft **Area code:** 717 **Zip:** 17325

Because of the historical nature of this area and the many attractions in this town, visitors may want to stop in at the Gettysburg Travel Council Office and Information Center for complete information about bus tours, guide service (including a tape-recorded and self-guided tour) and help in planning your visit here.

What to See and Do

1. **Gettysburg National Military Park** (see).

2. **Eisenhower National Historic Site** (see Gettysburg National Military Park).

3. **Lincoln Room Museum.** 12 Lincoln Square. Preserved bedroom in Wills House; collection of Lincoln items; huge plaque inscribed with Gettysburg address, audiovisual display. (Daily) Sr citizen rate. Phone 334-8188. ¢¢

4. **Gettysburg Railroad.** Washington St. A 16-mile round trip to Biglerville on steam train. Also charter trips and special runs. (July-Aug, daily; May-June & Sept-Oct, Thurs-Sun; Apr, Sat & Sun) Phone 334-6932. ¢¢¢

5. **Gettysburg College** (1832). (2,000 students) 3 blks NW of Lincoln Square off US 15 Business. Liberal arts; oldest Lutheran-affiliated college in US. Pennsylvania Hall was used as Civil War hospital; Eisenhower House and statue on grounds. Tour of campus. Phone 337-6000.

6. **Lutheran Theological Seminary** (1826). (250 students) Confederate Ave, 1 mi W of Lincoln Square on US 30. Oldest Lutheran seminary in US; cupola on campus used as Confederate lookout during battle. Old Dorm, now home of Adams County Historical Society, served as hospital for both Union and Confederate soldiers. Phone 334-6286.

7. **General Lee's Headquarters.** 401 Buford Ave. Robert E. Lee planned Confederate strategy for the Gettysburg battle in this house; contains collection of historical items from the battle. (Mid-Mar-mid-Nov, daily) Phone 334-3141. **Free.**

8. **Land of Little Horses.** 5 mi W off US 30, on Knoxlyn Rd to Glenwood Dr; follow signs. A variety of performing horses—all in miniature. Continuous entertainment; indoor arena; exotic animal races. Saddle and wagon rides. Picnic area, snack bar, gift shop. (Easter wkend -Oct, daily) Phone 334-7259. ¢¢¢

9. **Soldiers' National Museum.** 777 Baltimore St, at Gettysburg Tour Center. Dioramas of major battles, with sound; Civil War collection. (Mar-Nov, daily; schedule may vary, phone ahead) Phone 334-4890. ¢¢

10. **Hall of Presidents and First Ladies.** 789 Baltimore St, adj National Cemetery. Costumed life-size wax figures of all the presidents; reproductions of their wives' inaugural gowns; "The Eisenhowers at Gettysburg" exhibit. (Mid-Mar-Nov, daily) Phone 334-5717. ¢¢

11. **National Civil War Wax Museum.** 297 Steinwehr Ave. Highlights Civil War era and Battle of Gettysburg. (Mar-Nov, daily; rest of yr, Sat & Sun; closed Jan 1, Thanksgiving, Dec 25) Phone 334-6245. ¢¢ Available here are

    CCInc Auto Tape Tours. This 90-minute cassette offers a mile-by-mile self-guided tour and narration of the three-day Battle of Gettysburg. Written with the park service, it provides information on history, points of interest. Includes tape & player rental. Available at the National Civil War Wax Museum; phone 334-6245. ¢¢¢¢ Tapes may also be purchased directly from CCInc, PO Box 227, Allendale, NJ 07401, phone 201/236-1666.

12. **The Lincoln Train Museum.** 1/2 mi S via US 15 on Steinwehr Ave. Museum features more than 1,000 model trains and railroad memorabilia; Lincoln Train Ride—simulated trip of 20 miles. (Mar-Nov, daily) Sr citizen rate. Phone 334-5678. ¢¢

13. **"The Conflict."** 213 Steinwehr Ave. A triple-screen program depicts the Civil War and battle at Gettysburg in 7 different 50-min programs. Multiple projectors blend camera, artwork of the period and modern panoramic photography with narration. Military bookshop. Abraham Lincoln performances (mid-June-Labor Day, Mon-Fri evenings). (Daily; closed Thanksgiving, Dec 25) Phone 334-8003. The Conflict ¢¢; Lincoln performance ¢¢¢

14. **A. Lincoln's Place.** 213 Steinwehr Ave. Live portrayal of the 16th president; 45 min. (Mid-June-Labor Day, Mon-Fri) For reservations phone 334-6049 or 334-8003. ¢¢¢

15. **Gettysburg Battle Theatre.** 571 Steinwehr Ave. Miniature battlefield with 25,000 figures; 30-min multimedia program showing battle strategy. (Mar-Nov, daily) Phone 334-6100. ¢¢

16. **National Tower.** 1 mi S via US 97. Four observation decks (two enclosed) on 300-foot-high tower permit 360° view of battlefield; 12-min sight-and-sound program, displays; landscaped grounds, picnicking. (Apr-Oct, daily; Nov, wkends only; Mar, inquire for date) Braille and text for visually or hearing impaired; also nine translations. Phone 334-6754. ¢¢

17. **Ski Liberty.** 9 mi W on PA 116, in Carroll Valley. Two quad, 3 double chairlifts, J-bar, handle tow; patrol, school, rentals; snowmaking; cafeteria, restaurant, bar; nursery, lodge. Longest run approx 1 mi; vertical drop 600 ft. (Dec-Mar, daily) Phone 642-8282. ¢¢¢¢

(For further information contact the Gettysburg Travel Council, Inc, 35 Carlisle St; 334-6274.)

Annual Events

Apple Blossom Weekend. South Mountain Fairgrounds, 8 mi NW. 1st wkend May.

Civil War Heritage Days. Lectures by historians; Civil War collectors show; entertainment; Civil War book show; firefighters' festival; fireworks; parade. Late June-early July.

Apple Harvest Festival. Fairgrounds. Demonstrations; arts and crafts; guided tours of orchard, mountain areas. 1st & 2nd wkends Oct.

(See Hanover, York)

Motels

✔ ★ **BLUE SKY.** *2585 Biglerville Rd. 717/677-7736; res: 800/745-8194; FAX 717/677-6794.* 16 rms. S, D $29-$55; each addl $4; higher rates special events. Crib $4. TV; cable. Pool. Playground. Complimentary morning coffee. Ck-out 11 am. Downhill ski 8 mi. Exercise equipt; bicycle, treadmill. Lawn games. Picnic table. Cr cds: A, C, D, DS, MC, V.

≋ ≋ 🎋 🔥 **SC**

★ ★ **COLLEGE.** *345 Carlisle St, opp Gettysburg College. 717/334-6731; res: 800/367-6731.* 21 rms. Mid-June-Labor Day: S, D $56-$60; each addl $5; higher rates: graduation, parents' wkend; lower rates rest of yr. TV; cable. Pool; lifeguard. Restaurant nearby. Ck-out 11 am. Cr cds: A, MC, V.

≋ 🔥 **SC**

★ ★ **COMFORT INN.** *871 York Rd. 717/337-2400; FAX 717/337-1400, ext. 301.* 81 rms, 2 story. June-Aug: S $60-$70; D $75-$85; each addl $5; under 18 free; higher rates: antique car show, college events; lower rates rest of yr. Crib free. TV; cable. Indoor pool; whirlpool, lifeguard. Free coffee in lobby. Cafe adj open 24 hrs. Ck-out 11 am. Refrigerator in suites; some in-rm whirlpools. Cr cds: A, C, D, DS, ER, JCB, MC, V.

D ≋ ≋ 🔥 **SC**

★ ★ **CROSS KEYS.** *(PO Box 428, 6110 York Rd, New Oxford 17350) At jct US 30 & PA 94. 717/624-7778; FAX 717/624-7941.* 64 rms, 4 story. Apr-Sept: S $42-$47; D $48-$55; each addl $5; suites $75; under 16 free; wkly rates; higher rates special events; lower rates rest of yr. Crib free. TV; cable. Complimentary full bkfst Dec-Apr. Restaurants 5 am-10 pm; Sat open 24 hrs. Rm serv. Bar 4 pm-2 am. Ck-out 11 am. Meeting rms. Gift shop. Golf privileges. Downhill ski 15 mi. Cr cds: A, DS, MC, V.

≋ 🎋 ≋ 🔥 **SC**

✔ ★ ★ **HOWARD JOHNSON LODGE.** *301 Steinwehr Ave.* 717/334-1188. 77 rms, 2 story. June-Oct: S $46-$66; D $52-$72; each addl $6; under 18 free; lower rates rest of yr. Crib free. Pet accepted, some restrictions. TV; cable. Pool; lifeguard. Complimentary coffee in lobby. Restaurant adj 6:30 am-11 pm. Bar 4 pm-1 am, closed Sun. Ck-out noon. Sundries. Free bus depot transportation. Downhill ski 9 mi; x-country ski adj. Private patios. Sun deck. Cr cds: A, C, D, DS, MC, V.

⬛ 🐾 🏊 ≋ ⛷ 🔥 SC

✔ ★ **PERFECT REST.** *2450 Emmitsburg Rd, 4 mi S on US 15 Business, at edge of National Military Park.* 717/334-1345; res: 800/336-1345. 25 rms. Apr-early Nov: S, D $30-$63; suites $58-$85; higher rates: spring & fall wkends, college & area events; lower rates rest of yr. Crib $4. TV; cable. Pool. Complimentary coffee. Restaurant nearby. Ck-out 11 am. Picnic tables, grills. Cr cds: MC, V.

🏊 ≋ 🔥 SC

★ ★ **QUALITY INN.** *380 Steinwehr Ave.* 717/334-1103; FAX 717/334-1103, ext. 325. 104 rms, 2 story. Memorial Day-Oct: S $52-$71; D $58-$77; each addl $6; suite $63-$96; under 16 free; lower rates rest of yr. Crib free. Pet accepted, some restrictions. TV; cable. Pool; lifeguard. Complimentary coffee in lobby. Restaurant opp 6 am-11 pm. Bar 6 pm-1 am. Ck-out noon. Coin lndry. Meeting rm. Gift shop. Free bus depot transportation. Downhill/x-country ski 8 mi. Exercise equipt; weight machines, ski machine, sauna. Balconies. Cr cds: A, C, D, DS, MC, V.

⬛ 🐾 🏊 ≋ 🎿 ⛷ 🔥 SC

★ ★ **QUALITY INN LARSON'S.** *401 Buford Ave.* 717/334-3141. 41 rms. June-early Sept: S $54-$74; D $64-$74; each addl $5; under 17 free; lower rates rest of yr. Crib $2. TV. Pool. Restaurant 7 am-9 pm. Bar from noon. Ck-out noon. Putting green. Downhill ski 6 mi. General Lee's Headquarters (museum) adj. Cr cds: A, C, D, DS, ER, JCB, MC, V.

🏊 ≋ ⛷ 🔥 SC

Motor Hotel

★ ★ **DAYS INN.** *865 York Rd.* 717/334-0030. 113 rms, 5 story. Mid-June-Aug: S $59-$75; D $69-$85; each addl $5; under 18 free; ski plans; higher rates special events; lower rates rest of yr. Crib free. TV; cable, in-rm movies avail. Pool; lifeguard. Complimentary coffee in lobby. Restaurant adj open 24 hrs. Ck-out noon. Coin lndry. Meeting rms. Valet serv. Sundries. Free bus depot transportation. Downhill ski 10 mi. Exercise equipt; weight machines, stair machine. Game rm. Cr cds: A, D, DS, MC, V.

⬛ 🏊 ≋ 🎿 ⛷ 🔥

Hotel

★ ★ ★ **BEST WESTERN GETTYSBURG HOTEL.** *1 Lincoln Square, US 15 & 30.* 717/337-2000; FAX 717/337-2075. 83 rms, 6 story, 23 suites. Mid-June-mid-Sept: S $79-$119; D $89-$120; each addl $5; suites $119-$139; under 16 free; ski & golf plans; higher rates: graduation, homecoming; lower rates rest of yr. Crib free. TV; cable. Pool; whirlpool, poolside serv, lifeguard. Complimentary coffee, tea. Restaurant 7:15-10:30 am, 5-9 pm. Bar from 5 pm. Ck-out 11 am. Meeting rms. Free garage parking. Airport, RR station, bus depot transportation. Tennis privileges. Downhill ski 8 mi. Some refrigerators. Established 1797. Cr cds: A, C, D, DS, ER, MC, V.

⬛ 🏊 🏌 ≋ ⛷ 🔥 SC

Inns

★ ★ **BALADERRY INN.** *40 Hospital Rd, at edge of battlefield.* 717/337-1342. 5 rms, 3 with shower only, 2 story. No rm phones. S, D $68-$98; each addl $15; higher rates hols (2-night min). Children over

8 yrs only. Complimentary full bkfst, coffee, tea. Ck-out 11 am, ck-in 2 pm. Tennis. Downhill ski 10 mi; x-country ski adj. Built 1812; used as a field hospital during the Civil War battle of Gettysburg. Restored; furnished with antiques and reproductions. Extensive grounds. Cr cds: A, C, D, MC, V.

🏌 ⚡ 🎿 ≋ 🐾 SC

★ ★ **BRAFFERTON.** *44 York St.* 717/337-3423. 10 rms, 2 story, 1 suite. No rm phones. S, D $75-$110; each addl $10; suite $120. TV in suite. Complimentary full bkfst. Restaurant nearby. Ck-out 11 am, ck-in 2 pm. First house built in town (1786); antiques. Cr cds: MC, V.

≋ 🔥

★ ★ **FARNSWORTH HOUSE INN.** *401 Baltimore St, at corner of South St.* 717/334-8838. 4 rms, 2 story. No rm phones. Apr-Oct: S $65-$75; D $75-$85; each addl $10; under 5 free; wkly rates; higher rates hols (min stay); lower rates rest of yr. TV; cable in sitting rm. Complimentary full bkfst. Restaurant (see FARNSWORTH HOUSE). Ck-out 11 am, ck-in 3 pm. Concierge. Bellman. Downhill ski 7 mi; x-country ski ¼ mi. Historic house (1810), restored to its 1863 appearance. Authentic 19th-century furnishings; Victorian-style decor. House was used as a Union headquarters during the Civil War. The uppermost level of the inn was once used by Confederate sharpshooters; more than 100 bullet holes still remain in the south wall of the inn. Daily tours of the house and garret museum are given by a guide dressed in Civil War uniform. Cr cds: A, DS, MC, V.

🐾 ≋ 🔥

★ ★ **GETTYSTOWN INN.** *89 Steinwehr Ave.* 717/334-2100; FAX 717/334-6905. 5 rms, 2 story, 1 suite. No rm phones. Apr-Oct: S, D $75-$95; each addl $6; suite $95; under 12 free; wkly rates; higher rates: hols (2-night min), special events; lower rates rest of yr. TV in some rms; cable, also in sitting rm. Complimentary full bkfst; tea and coffee in parlor. Restaurant (see DOBBIN HOUSE). Rm serv. Ck-out 10 am, ck-in 2 pm. Downhill ski 7 mi; x-country ski 1 mi. Refrigerators. Renovated 1860s home, furnished with antiques. Overlooks site of Abraham Lincoln's Gettysburg Address. Totally nonsmoking. Cr cds: A, MC, V.

🏊 ≋ 🔥 SC

Restaurants

★ ★ ★ **DOBBIN HOUSE.** *(See Gettystown Inn)* 717/334-2100. Hrs: 11:30 am-midnight. Closed Jan 1, Thanksgiving, Dec 25. Res accepted. Continental menu. Bar 11:30 am-midnight. Semi-a la carte: lunch $4.25-$13.25, dinner $14.95-$29.95. Child's meals. Specializes in 1700s recipes, fresh seafood, large selection of meats. Own baking. Parking. Oldest building in Gettysburg; built 1776. Cr cds: A, MC, V.

⬛ SC

★ ★ **FARNSWORTH HOUSE.** *(See Farnsworth House Inn)* 717/334-8838. Hrs: 5-10 pm. Closed Thanksgiving, Dec 25. Res accepted. Bar to midnight. Semi-a la carte: dinner $11.95-$18. Child's meals. Specializes in peanut soup, game pie, pumpkin fritters. Parking. Outdoor dining. House built in 1810; tour avail. Cr cds: A, DS, MC, V.

✔ ★ ★ **STONEHENGE.** *985 Baltimore Pike.* 717/334-9227. Hrs: 11:30 am-8 pm; Fri & Sat to 10 pm; Sun 4-8 pm; Sun brunch 11 am-4 pm. Closed Jan 1, Dec 24, 25. Res accepted. Continental menu. Bar to 2 am. Semi-a la carte: lunch $3.95-$6.95, dinner $7.95-$19.95. Buffet: lunch (Mon-Fri) $2.99, dinner (Fri & Sat) $14.95. Sun brunch $7.95. Child's meals. Specialties: Cajun prime rib, crab cakes, veal Marsala, pasta. Salad bar. Parking. Intimate dining; oil lamps. Cr cds: A, MC, V.

Gettysburg National Military Park (F-6)

The hallowed battlefield of Gettysburg, scene of one of the most decisive battles of the Civil War and immortalized by Lincoln's Gettysburg address, is preserved by the National Park Service. The town itself is still a college community, as it was more than a hundred years ago on July 1, 2 and 3, 1863, when General Robert E. Lee led his Confederate Army in its greatest invasion of the North. The defending Northerners under Union General George Meade repulsed the Southern assault after 3 days of fierce fighting, which left 51,000 men dead, wounded or missing.

The Gettysburg National Military Park has more than 35 miles of roads through 5,700 acres of the battlefield area. There are more than 1,300 monuments, markers and tablets of granite and bronze; 400 cannons are also located on the field.

Visitors may wish to tour the battlefield with a Battlefield Guide, licensed by the National Park Service (two-hour tour; fee). The guides escort visitors to all points of interest and sketch the movement of troops and details of the battle. Or, visitors may wish to first orient themselves at the Visitor Center-Electric Map (see #1) and Cyclorama (see #3); then using the park folder, the battlefield can be toured without a guide.

The late President Dwight D. Eisenhower's retirement farm, a National Historic Site, adjoins the battlefield. It is open to the public on a limited-tour basis. All visitors must obtain tour tickets at the tour information center, located at the rear of the Visitor Center-Electric Map building. Transportation to the farm is by shuttle (fee). For further information contact visitor services; 717/334-1124.

What to See and Do

1. **Visitor Center-Electric Map-Gettysburg Museum of the Civil War.** On PA 134. Visits to the park should begin here. Park information, including a self-guided auto tour, and guides may be obtained at the center. Story of battle told on 750-sq-ft electric map surrounded by 525 seats (every 45 min; fee). Gettysburg Museum of the Civil War has an extensive collection of Civil War relics (free). (Daily; closed Jan 1, Thanksgiving, Dec 25) Electric map ¢ Obtain tickets here for

2. **Eisenhower National Historic Site.** Farm house of the 34th President of the United States and his wife, Mamie. Self-guided tour (1.5 hrs) of the home and grounds. Access to site only by shuttle bus from the tour information center (rear of Visitor Center-Electric Map bldg). Tour tickets dispensed individually on a first-come, first-served basis for the next tour. Limited number of tours per day. (Apr-Oct, daily; rest of yr, Wed-Sun; closed Thanksgiving, Dec 25, also Jan) Make special arrangements at tour center for wheelchairs. Phone 717/334-1124. Tour and shuttle bus ¢¢

3. **Cyclorama Center.** Adj to visitor center. Instructive film and exhibits: Lincoln's original Gettysburg Address (Easter-Labor Day); 356-ft Cyclorama painting of Pickett's Charge. (Daily) Cyclorama ¢

4. **Whitworth Guns on Oak Hill.** Only breech-loading cannon used here.

5. **East Cemetery Hill.** Rallying point for Union forces on 1st day of battle. Scene of fierce fighting on evening of 2nd day.

6. **The Gettysburg National Cemetery.** Site of Lincoln's Gettysburg Address.

7. **The Angle.** Spot where Pickett's Charge was repulsed on July 3rd, referred to as "high water mark of the Confederacy."

8. **Little Round Top.** Key Union position during 2nd and 3rd days of battle.

9. **Devil's Den.** Stronghold of Confederate sharpshooters following its capture during action on the 2nd day.

10. **The Wheatfield and Peach Orchard.** Scene of heavy Union and Confederate losses on the second day of fighting.

11. **The Eternal Light Peace Memorial.** On Oak Ridge. Erected in 1938 and dedicated by President Roosevelt to "peace eternal in a nation united."

12. **Seminary Ridge.** Main Confederate battle line.

13. **Memorials to State Units.** Includes Pennsylvania State Monument, with names of more than 34,500 Pennsylvanian soldiers who participated in the battle.

(For accommodations see Gettysburg, Hanover)

Gibsonia (D-2)

(see Pittsburgh)

Greensburg (E-2)

Founded: 1785 **Pop:** 16,318 **Elev:** 1,099 ft **Area code:** 412 **Zip:** 15601

Greensburg was named for Revolutionary General Nathanael Greene.

What to See and Do

1. **Westmoreland Museum of Art.** 221 N Main St. 18th, 19th and early 20th-century American paintings, sculpture, furniture and decorative arts. 19th and early 20th-century southwestern Pennsylvania paintings. Extensive toy collection. Lectures, guided tours. (Tues-Sat, also Sun afternoons; closed hols) Phone 837-1500. **Free.**

2. **Bushy Run Battlefield.** NW on PA 993. Here Colonel Henry Bouquet defeated united Indian forces during Pontiac's War on Aug 5 & 6, 1763. The battle lifted the siege of Fort Pitt and was the turning point of the war. Picnicking, park (free); hiking trails. Visitor center exhibits depict battle (daily exc Mon; closed most hols). Sr citizen rate. Phone 527-5584. ¢¢

3. **Westmoreland County Courthouse.** Main & Pittsburgh Sts. Building in style of Italian Renaissance; restored in 1982. (Mon-Fri; closed hols) Phone 830-3000. **Free.**

4. **Historic Hanna's Town.** 3 mi NE via US 119. Costumed tour guide tells story of Hanna's Town, site of first court west of Alleghenies. Includes reconstructed courthouse, tavern, jail and stockaded fort; picnic area. (June-Aug, daily exc Mon; May, Sept & Oct, wkends only) Phone 836-1800. ¢

(For further information contact Laurel Highlands Tourist Promotion Agency, Town Hall Bldg, 120 E Main St, Ligonier 15658; 238-5661.)

(See Connellsville, Donegal, Ligonier, New Stanton)

Motels

✔ ★ **KNIGHTS INN.** 1215 S Main St, at jct US 119 & US 30. 412/836-7100; res: 800/843-5644; FAX 412/837-5390. 110 rms, 10 suites, 11 kits. May-Oct: S $39.95-$49.95; D $41.95-$55.95; each addl $6; suites $43.95-$59.95; kit. units $46.95-$64.95; under 18 free; lower rates rest of yr. Crib free. TV; cable, in-rm movies avail. Pool. Complimentary coffee in lobby. Restaurant adj 6 am-11 pm. Ck-out noon. Meeting rm. Lndry facilities. Refrigerators avail. Cr cds: A, C, D, DS, MC, V.

⊘ ⊠ ⊗ ⊗ SC

★ ★ ★ **SHERATON INN.** 100 Sheraton Dr. 412/836-6060; FAX 412/834-5640. 146 rms, 2 story. S $68-$80; D $70-$91; each addl $10;

suites $105-$250; under 17 free; golf, wkend package plans. Crib free. TV. Indoor pool; sauna, lifeguard. Restaurant 6:30 am-2 pm, 5-10 pm. Bar 11-2 am; entertainment, dancing. Ck-out noon. Meeting rms. Bellhops. Valet serv. Sundries. Free local airport, RR station, bus depot transportation. 9-hole golf course, greens fee, pro shop, putting green. Game rm. Some refrigerators. Shopping mall opp. Cr cds: A, C, D, DS, JCB, MC, V.

Motor Hotels

★★ **COMFORT INN.** *1129 E Pittsburgh St, PA Tpke exit 8, E on PA 30.* 412/832-2600; FAX 412/834-3442. 78 rms, 3 story. May-Sept: S $64-$89; D $69-$94; each addl $5; suites $79-$135; under 18 free; higher rates special events; lower rates rest of yr. Crib free. TV; cable, in-rm movies avail. Heated pool. Complimentary continental bkfst. Complimentary coffee in lobby. Restaurant nearby. Ck-out 11 am. Meeting rms. Valet serv. Some refrigerators, wet bars, in-rm whirlpools. Cr cds: A, C, D, DS, ER, JCB, MC, V.

★★★ **MOUNTAIN VIEW INN.** *5 mi E on US 30, 11 mi NE of PA Tpke exit 8.* 412/834-5300. 56 rms. S $50-$92; D $58-$100; each addl $8; suites $85-$92; ski package. TV; cable, in-rm movies avail. Pool. Restaurant 7 am-2 pm, 5-9 pm; wkend hrs vary. Rm serv 7:30 am-11 pm. Bar 11 am-midnight, Fri, Sat to 1 am, Sun 1-8 pm; entertainment Fri-Sat. Ck-out noon. Meeting rms. Sundries. Antique decor; English and herb gardens; gazebo. Cr cds: A, C, D, MC, V.

Restaurant

★★ **CARBONE'S.** *(Main St, Crabtree) 6 mi N on US 119.* 412/834-3430. Hrs: 4:30-10 pm; Fri, Sat to 11 pm. Closed Sun; major hols. Res accepted. Italian, Amer menu. Bar to midnight. Semi-a la carte: dinner $5.95-$14.95. Child's meals. Specializes in angel pie, antipasto, braciole. Parking. Mediterranean decor. Family-owned. Cr cds: A, C, D, MC, V.

Hamburg (E-8)

Founded: 1779 **Pop:** 3,987 **Elev:** 373 ft **Area code:** 610 **Zip:** 19526

Situated on the banks of the Schuylkill River, Hamburg is a center for one of the finest farming sections in Pennsylvania. The town's industries include the manufacture of brooms, iron and steel castings, knitwear and soft-drink products.

What to See and Do

1. **Hawk Mountain Sanctuary.** 11 mi N via PA 61 & 895, follow signs. Hawk, eagle flights visible with binoculars from lookouts mid-Aug-Nov; museum, bookstore. (Daily; closed Jan 1, Thanksgiving, Dec 25) Phone 756-6961. ¢¢

2. **Blue Rocks.** 5 mi E on I-78 to Lenhartsville, then 2 mi N on PA 143. Covers 90 acres; pool; fishing (stocked pond); picnicking, two pavilions; hiking, Appalachian Trail; camping, trailer facilities (fee; hookups addl). Game room. Phone 756-6366. Park (day use) per person ¢

3. **Pennsylvania Dutch Folk Culture Center.** 5 mi E, in Lenhartsville; US 22 & I-89, exit 143 S. Five buildings with displays of art, customs, folkways; Baver Memorial Library with genealogy, folklore, local history. (June-Aug, daily; Apr-May & Sept-Oct, Sat & Sun) Phone 562-4803 or 682-7432. ¢¢

4. **Wanamaker, Kempton & Southern, Inc.** 5 mi E on I-78 to Lenhartsville exit, then 5 mi N on PA 143 to Kempton. A six-mile, 40-min round trip on steam train or Berksy trolley along the Ontelaunee Creek at the foot of Hawk Mountain. Model railroad (Sun), antique shop. Snack bar, picnic area. Steam train (June-Aug, Sat & Sun afternoons; May & Sept-Oct, Sun afternoons). Trolley (May & Sept-Oct, Sat afternoons). Phone 756-6469. ¢¢

(For further information contact the Reading/Berks County Visitors Bureau, VF Factory Outlet Complex, Park Rd & Hill Ave, PO Box 6677, Reading 19610; 375-4085 or 800/443-6610.)

(For accommodations see Reading, also see Kutztown, Shartlesville)

Hanover (F-7)

Founded: 1763 **Pop:** 14,399 **Elev:** 609 ft **Area code:** 717 **Zip:** 17331

Known in early days as "McAllisterstown" (for founder Colonel Richard McAllister) and "Rogue's Harbor" (for lack of law enforcement), Hanover is in the rich Conewago Valley. Here, on June 30, 1863, Confederate General J.E.B. Stuart's cavalry tangled with Union forces under Generals Kilpatrick and Custer. The battle prevented Stuart from reaching Gettysburg in time to function as "the eyes of Lee's army."

Among the products of the town's diversified industry are shoes, books, wirecloth, yarns, furniture, industrial machinery, textiles and foods, including snack foods.

What to See and Do

1. **Neas House Museum.** 113 W Chestnut St. Neas House (ca 1783), restored Georgian home, serves as local history museum. (May-Nov, Tues-Fri) Special events (spring, summer, late Dec). Phone 632-3207. **Free.**

2. **Conewago Chapel** (1741). 30 Basilica Dr, 2 mi W on PA 116, then 2 mi N. Designated Sacred Heart Basilica in 1962. Cemetery dates from 1752. (Daily) Phone 637-2721.

3. **Codorus State Park.** 4 mi E on PA 216. Approx 3,300 acres. Swimming pool; fishing in 1,275-acre Lake Marburg, hunting; boating (rentals, mooring, launching, marina). Hiking, bridle trails. Cross-country skiing, snowmobiling, sledding, ice-skating, ice boating, ice fishing. Picnicking, playground, snack bar. Tent & trailer sites. Standard fees. Phone 637-2816.

4. **Industrial tour.** Utz Quality Foods, Inc. 900 High St. Producers of potato chips and snack foods. Glass-enclosed tour gallery overlooks production area; push-to-talk audio program & closed-circuit TV monitors. (Mon-Thurs; closed major hols) Phone 637-6644. **Free.**

(For further information contact the Hanover Area Chamber of Commerce, 146 Broadway; 637-6130.)

(See Gettysburg, York)

Inn

★★★ **BEECHMONT.** *315 Broadway.* 717/632-3013; res: 800/553-7009. 7 rms, 2 story, 3 suites. S, D $80-$95; suites $115-$135. Children over 12 yrs preferred. Complimentary full bkfst. Restaurant nearby. Ck-out 11 am, ck-in 3 pm. Federal period house (1834); landscaped courtyard. Cr cds: A, MC, V.

Harmony (D-1)

Founded: 1804 **Pop:** 1,054 **Elev:** 925 ft **Area code:** 412 **Zip:** 16037

First settlement of George Rapp's Harmony Society, Harmony served the colony only until 1814. More than 100 of the original group are buried in Harmonists Cemetery, southeast of town. Several of the Rappite Society's sturdy brick houses still stand in the village.

What to See and Do

Harmony Museum (1809). 218 Mercer St. Exhibits depict early life under Harmonists and Mennonites; regional history. The Harmony Society was one of America's most successful experiments in communal living. Harmony was the society's first home (1804). Tour. (June-Sept, Tues-Sun afternoons; rest of yr, Mon, Wed, Fri & also Sun afternoons) Phone 452-7341. ¢¢

(For further information contact the Butler County Visitors Bureau, 100 N Main St, PO Box 1082, Butler 16003; 283-2222.)

Annual Events

Dankfest. Pioneer craft festival held on grounds of Harmony Museum (see). Crafts, entertainment, tours, refreshments. Contact museum for schedule. Late Aug.

Christmas Open House. Candlelight tour of Harmony Museum, Wagner House and Ziegler log house. Entertainment, refreshments. Contact museum for schedule. Early Dec.

(For accommodations see Butler, Pittsburgh)

Harrisburg (E-7)

Settled: 1718 **Pop:** 52,376 **Elev:** 360 ft **Area code:** 717

This midstate metropolis is graced by what many consider the finest capitol building in the nation. Its riverside park (known as City Island), Italian Lake, unique museum and beautiful Forum are the showplaces; commerce, industry and politics keep the city going.

The site was viewed in 1615 by Etienne Brulé on a trip down the Susquehanna, but more than a century passed before John Harris, the first settler, opened his trading post here. His son established the town in 1785. It became the seat of state government in 1812; the cornerstone of the first capitol building was laid in 1819.

What to See and Do

1. **Capitol Hill buildings.** N 3rd & Walnut Sts. Phone 787-6810. Clustered in a 45-acre complex, the major buildings are

   The Capitol (dedicated 1906). Main entrance, 3rd & State Sts. Italian Renaissance building covers two acres, has 651 rooms; 26,000-ton, 272-foot dome, imitating that of St Peter's in Rome, dominates city skyline. Includes murals by Abbey and Okley. Tours (daily; closed Dec 25). **Free.**

   North Office Building. Map inscribed on main lobby floor shows state highways, seals of Pennsylvania cities.

   South Office Building. Colorful murals by Edward Trumbull depict *Penn's Treaty with the Indians* and *The Industries of Pittsburgh.*

   Forum Building. Includes auditorium below constellation-bedecked ceiling; walls review man's progress through time. Main lobby boasts a Maragliotti ceiling. General and Law libraries.

   Finance Building. Ceiling murals by Maragliotti, Eugene Savage; mural in south vestibule illustrates *The Collection of Taxes.* (Mon-Fri)

   The State Museum of Pennsylvania. N of Capitol Building, 3rd & North Sts. A six-story circular building housing four stories of galleries, authentic early country store, Indian life exhibit, technological and industrial exhibits, collection of antique autos and period carriages; planetarium; natural history and geology exhibits and one of world's largest framed paintings, Rothermel's *The Battle of Gettysburg.* Planetarium has public shows (Sat & Sun; fee). (Daily exc Mon; closed most hols) Phone 787-4978. **Free.**

2. **Museum of Scientific Discovery.** 3rd & Walnut Sts, 1st level, Strawberry Square. Hands-on exhibits demonstrating various scientific and math principles; daily programs. (Daily exc Mon; closed most major hols) Phone 233-7969. ¢¢

3. **John Harris Mansion.** 219 S Front St. Home of city's founder, now Historical Society of Dauphin County headquarters. Stone house has 19th-century furnishings, library (Mon-Thurs; fee), collection of county artifacts. Tours (Mon-Fri & 2nd Sun each month). Phone 233-3462. ¢¢

4. **Dauphin County Courthouse.** Front & Market Sts. Seven imposing courtrooms; outline map on floor of main foyer pictures borough and township boundaries. (Mon-Fri; closed hols) Phone 255-2741.

5. **Fort Hunter Park.** 6 mi N on North Front St. Historic 37-acre property; site of British-built fort erected in 1754 to combat mounting threats prior to the French and Indian War. In 1787 the land was purchased and became a farm that eventually grew into a self-sufficient village. The Pennsylvania Canal runs through the park; on the grounds are historic buttonwood trees dating from William Penn's time; a 19th-century boxwood garden; herb gardens; paths along the banks of the Susquehanna River; picnic area. Also here are an ice house, springhouse (ca 1800), Centennial barn (1876), and corncrib (1880). Also on the grounds, but not open to the public because of restoration, are the old tavern (1800), blacksmith shop (1890) and stone stable. Outstanding feature of park is

   Fort Hunter Mansion. 5300 N Front St, in park. Federal-style stone mansion, built in three sections. Front stone portions were built in 1786 and 1814; rear wooden portion built in 1870. Spacious mansion displays period furnishings, clothing, toys and other artifacts. Guided tours. (May-Dec, daily exc Mon) Sr citizen rate. Phone 599-5751. ¢¢

6. **Riverfront Park.** 4 mi along Susquehanna River, with park promenade flanking Front St, concrete walk along river.

7. **Italian Lake.** N 3rd & Division Sts. Bordered with flowers, shrubs and shade trees in summer.

8. **Reservoir Park.** Walnut & N 19th Sts. View of E end of city, five nearby counties.

9. **Rockville Bridge** (1902). 4 mi N on US 22. A 3,810-foot stone arch bridge; 48 spans carry four tracks of Penn Central Railroad main line.

10. **Indian Echo Caverns.** 10 mi E on US 322, 422, in Hummelstown. Stalagmite and stalactite formations. Picnicking, playground. (Daily, inquire for hrs; closed Jan 1, Dec 25) Phone 566-8131. ¢¢¢

(For further information contact the Capital Region Chamber of Commerce, 114 Walnut St, PO Box 969, 17108-0969, phone 232-4121; or the Harrisburg-Hershey-Carlisle Tourism & Convention Bureau, phone 232-1377.)

Annual Events

Kipona. Boating & water-related activites. Labor Day wknd.

(All of the following events are held in State Farm Show Building, 11th & Maclay Sts.)

Pennsylvania State Farm Show (state fair). Mid-Jan.

Eastern Sports & Outdoor Show. Early-mid-Feb.

All American Dairy Show and Country Craft Market. 5 days late Sept.

Pennsylvania National Horse Show. 10 days mid-Oct.

Pennsylvania Livestock Exposition. 8 days early Nov.

(See Carlisle, Hershey, York)

Motels

★ ★ **BEST WESTERN.** *300 N Mountain Rd (17112), I-81 exit 26.* 717/652-7180. 49 rms, 2 story. S $49-$79; D $49-$82; each addl $3; under 13 free. Crib $5. Pet accepted. TV; cable. Restaurant 6:30 am-9 pm. Bar 11 am-11 pm. Ck-out 11 am. Sundries. Airport, RR station, bus depot transportation. Cr cds: A, C, D, DS, MC, V.

★ **BUDGETEL INN.** *200 N Mountain Rd (17112), I-81 exit 26.* 717/540-9339; FAX 717/540-9486. 66 rms, 3 story, 8 suites. Apr-Oct: S $49.95-$54.95; D $56.95-$63.95; suites $60.95-$67.95; under 19 free; lower rates rest of yr. Crib free. Pet accepted. TV; cable. Complimentary continental bkfst. Complimentary coffee in rms. Restaurant nearby. Ck-out noon. Coin lndry. Meeting rms. Sundries. Refrigerator in suites. Cr cds: A, C, D, DS, MC, V.

★ **COMFORT INN.** *4021 Peifers Lane (17109).* 717/561-8100; FAX 717/561-1357. 117 rms, 5 story. June-Oct: S $62; D $72; each addl $7; suites $138-$145; under 18 free; higher rates car shows; lower rates rest of yr. Crib free. Pet accepted; $20. TV; cable, in-rm movies avail. Heated pool; lifeguard. Complimentary continental bkfst, coffee. Restaurant adj 6 am-10 pm. Ck-out noon. Coin lndry. Meeting rms. Free airport transportation. Exercise equipt; weight machine, bicycles. Refrigerator in suite. Cr cds: A, C, D, DS, ER, JCB, MC, V.

✔ ★ **DAYS INN.** *3919 N Front St (17110).* 717/233-3100; FAX 717/233-6415. 116 rms, 3 story. S $43-$60; D $49-$65; each addl $5; under 12 free; higher rates: car shows, farm show. Crib free. TV; cable. Pool; lifeguard. Playground. Complimentary continental bkfst. Restaurant nearby. Ck-out noon. Coin lndry. Refrigerators avail. Picnic tables. Cr cds: A, D, DS, MC, V.

★ ★ **HOWARD JOHNSON.** *473 Eisenhower Blvd (17111), I-283 exit 1.* 717/564-4730; FAX 717/564-6300. 176 rms, 2 story. S $55-$75; D $62-$85; each addl $8; under 17 free; higher rates Hershey Antique Auto Show. Crib free. TV; cable. Pool; wading pool, lifeguard. Restaurant 5 am-midnight; Fri, Sat to 1 am. Bar from 11 am. Ck-out noon. Meeting rms. Valet serv. Sundries. Free airport, RR station transportation. Health club privileges. Private patios, balconies. Cr cds: A, C, D, DS, ER, MC, V.

★ ★ **PENN HARRIS INN.** *(1150 Camp Hill Bypass, Camp Hill 17011) S on US 15, Camp Hill Bypass; 6 mi N of PA Turnpike exit 17.* 717/763-7117; res: 800/345-7366; FAX 717/763-4518. 257 rms, 2-3 story. No elvtr. S $62-$82; D $70-$90; each addl $8; suites $125-$250; under 18 free. Crib free. Pet accepted. TV; cable. Pool; poolside serv, lifeguard. Restaurant 6:30 am-10 pm. Rm serv. Bar 3 pm-2 am. Ck-out noon. Convention facilities. Valet serv. Bellhops. Gift shop. Cr cds: A, C, D, DS, MC, V.

✔ ★ **RED ROOF INN.** *400 Corporate Circle (17110), I-81 exit 24.* 717/657-1445; FAX 717/657-2775. 110 rms, 2 story. S $39.99-$46.99; D $42.99-$52.99; under 18 free. Crib free. TV; cable. Complimentary coffee in lobby Mon-Fri. Restaurant nearby. Ck-out noon. Cr cds: A, D, DS, MC, V.

Motor Hotels

★ ★ ★ **HOLIDAY INN EAST.** *4751 Lindle Rd (17111), jct I-283 & PA 441 exit 1.* 717/939-7841; FAX 717/939-9317. 300 rms, 4 story. S $99-$129; D $111-$132; each addl $12; under 18 free. Crib free. TV; cable, in-rm movies. 2 pools, 1 indoor; poolside serv, lifeguard. Restaurant 7 am-2 pm, 5-10 pm. Rm serv 7 am-10 pm. Bar 11-2 am; dancing. Ck-out noon. Valet serv. Convention facilities. Airport transportation. Lighted tennis. Putting green. Exercise equipt; bicycles, treadmill, whirlpool, sauna. Game rm. Private patios, balconies. Cr cds: A, C, D, DS, JCB, MC, V.

★ ★ ★ **MARRIOTT.** *4650 Lindle Rd (17111), jct I-283 & PA 441.* 717/564-5511; FAX 717/564-6173. 348 rms, 10 story. S $89-$135; D $89-$149; each addl $14; suites $265; under 18 free. Crib free. TV; cable. Indoor/outdoor pool; poolside serv, lifeguard. Restaurant 6:30 am-11 pm. Rm serv. Bar 11-2 am; entertainment, dancing. Ck-out noon. Meeting rms. Bellhops. Valet serv. Sundries. Gift shop. Airport transportation. Exercise equipt; weights, bicycles, whirlpool, sauna. Game rm. Balconies. *LUXURY LEVEL :* 33 rms, 1 suite, 2 floors. S $129; D $148; suite $295. Concierge. Private lounge, honor bar. Complimentary continental bkfst, refreshments, newspaper. Cr cds: A, C, D, DS, ER, MC, V.

★ ★ ★ **SHERATON HARRISBURG EAST.** *800 East Park Dr (17111), I-83 exit 29.* 717/561-2800; FAX 717/561-8398. 172 rms, 3 story. S $86-$105; D $96-$115; each addl $10; suites $135-$155; under 18 free. Crib free. Pet accepted, some restrictions. TV; cable. Heated pool; lifeguard. Restaurant 6:30 am-10:30 pm. Rm serv. Bar 11-2 am; entertainment, dancing Tues-Sat. Ck-out noon. Convention facilities. Bellhops. Valet serv. Shopping arcade. Airport transportation. Golf privileges. Exercise rm; instructor, weights, bicycles, whirlpool, sauna. Game rm. Cr cds: A, C, D, DS, MC, V.

Hotels

★ ★ **BEST WESTERN CROWN PARK.** *765 Eisenhower Blvd (17111).* 717/558-9500; FAX 717/558-8956. 167 rms, 6 story. May-Oct: S $69-$89; D $79-$99; each addl $10; suites $150; under 19 free; ski plans; wkend rates; Hershey Park packages; higher rates car shows; lower rates rest of yr. Crib free. Pet accepted. TV; cable, in-rm movies avail. Heated pool; lifeguard. Complimentary bkfst. Coffee in rms. Restaurant 6 am-10 pm. Bar 5 pm-2 am. Ck-out noon. Meeting rms. Concierge. Free airport, RR station, bus depot transportation. Downhill ski 20 mi. Exercise equipt; weight machine, bicycles. Refrigerator, wet bar in suites. Cr cds: A, C, D, DS, ER, MC, V.

★ ★ **HARRISBURG HOTEL-ON MARKET SQUARE.** *23 S 2nd St (17101).* 717/234-5021; res: 800/222-8733; FAX 717/234-5079. 261 rms, 10 story. S $75-$95; D $85-$105; each addl $10; studio rms $78-$90; suites $145; under 19 free. TV; cable. Indoor pool; lifeguard. Restaurant 6:30 am-2 pm, 5-10 pm. Bar 11:30-1 am. Ck-out noon. Meeting rms. Gift shop. Free garage parking. Rooftop patio. Cr cds: A, C, D, DS, ER, JCB, MC, V.

★ ★ **HILTON AND TOWERS.** *1 N 2nd St (17101).* 717/233-6000; FAX 717/233-6271. 341 rms, 15 story. S, D $99-$129; each addl $10; suites $190; wkend rates. Crib avail. TV. Indoor pool. Restaurant 6:30 am-11 pm. Bar 11-1 am; entertainment. Ck-out noon. Convention facilities. Concierge. Shopping arcade connected to Strawberry Square Mall. Valet parking. Free airport transportation. Exercise equipt; weight machine, bicycles. Minibars; refrigerator in suites. *LUXURY LEVEL :* **THE TOWERS.** 38 rms, 2 floors, 5 suites. S, D $154-$164;

suites $190-$300. Private lounge, honor bar. Minibars. Complimentary continental bkfst, newspaper. Cr cds: A, C, D, DS, ER, MC, V.

Restaurants

★ ★ ★ **ALFRED'S VICTORIAN RESTAURANT.** *(38 N Union St, Middletown)* E on I-83, then S on I-283, then SE on PA 230 to PA 441. 717/944-5373. Hrs: 11:30 am-2 pm, 5-10 pm; Sat from 5 pm; Sun 3-9 pm. Closed some major hols. Res accepted. Italian, continental menu. Bar. Wine list. Semi-a la carte: lunch $5-$12.50, dinner $9.95-$27.95. Specialties: homemade pastas, crepes fruits de mar, seafood. Own baking. Tableside cooking. Patio dining. Victorian mansion; antique chandeliers, furnishings; floor-to-ceiling windows; fireplaces. Family-owned. Cr cds: A, C, D, DS, MC, V.

SC

✔ ★ ★ **BERKLEY'S-THE PLACE.** *3745 N 6th St.* 717/232-4131. Hrs: 11 am-3 pm, 4:30-10 pm; Sun 4:30-9 pm. Closed major hols. Res accepted. Bar to 11 pm. Semi-a la carte: lunch $2.95-$7.50, dinner $7.95-$15.95. Child's meals. Specializes in fresh seafood, veal, steak. Parking. Cr cds: A, MC, V.

D

★ ★ **MANADA HILL INN.** *128 N Hershey Rd.* 717/652-0400. Hrs: 4-9 pm; Fri-Sat to 10 pm; Sun 11 am-8 pm; Sun brunch to 2:30 pm. Closed Dec 25. Res accepted. Continental menu. Bar to 11 pm. Semi-a la carte: dinner $7.95-$19.95. Sun brunch $11.50. Child's meals. Specializes in fresh seafood, prime rib. Parking. Restored house; artwork, antique brass chandeliers. 3 dining rms. Cr cds: A, DS, MC, V.

D

Hawley *(C-9)*

Settled: 1827 **Pop:** 1,244 **Elev:** 920 ft **Area code:** 717 **Zip:** 18428

A major attraction in this Pocono resort area is man-made Lake Wallenpaupack, offering summer recreation on the lake as well as winter recreation nearby.

What to See and Do

1. **Gravity Coach.** W of town on US 6. Car used on Pennsylvania Gravity Railroad (22 inclined planes between Hawley and Scranton, 1850-85).

2. **Lake Wallenpaupack.** One of the largest man-made lakes in state (5,600 acres), formed by damming of Wallenpaupack Creek. Swimming, fishing, boating, water sports; ice fishing; camping. Information center, 1/2 mi NW on US 6 at PA 507 (daily; closed Easter, Thanksgiving, Dec 25). Phone 226-2141. **Free.**

3. **Promised Land State Park.** 12 mi S on PA 390. Approx 2,950 acres. Swimming beach; fishing; boating (rentals, mooring, launch). Hiking. Cross-country skiing, snowmobiling, ice-skating, ice fishing. Picnicking, snack bar. Tent & trailer sites, cabins. Nature center, interpretive program. Phone 676-3428. Camping ¢¢¢-¢¢¢¢

4. **Skiing. Tanglwood.** 4 mi S via PA 390, off I-84 in Tafton. Two double chairlifts, 2 T-bars, rope tow, beginner lift; patrol, school, rentals; snowmaking; cafeteria, bar; nursery. Longest run 1 mi; vertical drop 415 ft. Night skiing. (Early Dec-late Mar, daily) Half-day rates. Phone 226-9500. ¢¢¢¢

5. **Pennsylvania Power & Light Co.** Approx 1 1/2 mi E on US 6. Hydroelectric facilities, dam; recreation area. Visitor center near lake has exhibits. Superintendent's office has information on region; observation point. (Daily) **Free.**

6. **Claws 'N Paws Wild Animal Park.** 12 mi W via PA 590, near Lake Wallenpaupack (see #2). A zoo-in-the-woods with more than 100 species of exotic animals. Petting zoo with tame deer, lambs and goats. Farmyard area. Three animal shows (spring & summer). Picnicking, snack bar. (May-Oct, daily) Sr citizen rate. Phone 698-6154. ¢¢¢

(For further information contact the Pocono Mts Vacation Bureau, 1004 Main St, Stroudsburg 18360, phone 424-6050; for brochures phone 800/POCONOS.)

(See Milford, Scranton)

Motel

✔ ★ **GRESHAM'S LAKEVIEW.** *HC 6, Box 6150, 2 mi E on US 6.* 717/226-4621. 21 rms, 2 story. S, D $55-$60; each addl $5; under 5 free; wkly rates; ski plans; lower rates off-season. Crib free. TV; cable. Complimentary coffee in lobby. Restaurant nearby. Ck-out 11 am. Downhill/x-country ski 2 1/2 mi. Balconies. Overlooks Lake Wallenpaupack. Cr cds: A, DS, MC, V.

D

Inn

★ ★ **THE SETTLERS.** *4 Main Ave.* 717/226-2993; res: 800/833-8527. 18 rms, 2 story, 5 suites. S $50-$75; D $70-$110; each addl $15; suites $110-$125; under 12 free. Crib $10. Complimentary full bkfst. Restaurant (see THE SETTLERS INN). Ck-out noon, ck-in 1 pm. Airport transportation. Downhill ski 8 mi; x-country ski 1 mi. Golf course nearby. Bingham Park opp. Tudor-revival manor (1927); stone fireplace, sitting rooms with many antiques. Totally nonsmoking. Cr cds: A, MC, V.

 SC

Resort

★ ★ **CAESARS COVE HAVEN.** *Lakeville (18438), 8 mi W on PA 590.* 717/226-4506; res: 800/233-4141; FAX 717/226-4697. 282 units, 3 story. Couples only; MAP: D $180-$320; wkly rates. TV. Indoor/outdoor pools; poolside serv. Bars 11:30-1:30 am; entertainment, dancing. Ck-out 11 am. Coin lndry. Gift shop. Free bus depot transportation. Indoor tennis; racquetball. Driving range, indoor miniature golf. Boats, waterskiing. Snowmobiling. Soc dir. Indoor ice skating and roller skating. Rec rm. Game rm. Exercise equipt; bicycles, rowers, whirlpools, saunas. Refrigerators, some balconies. On lake. Cr cds: A, D, DS, MC, V.

 SC

Restaurants

★ **EHRHARDT'S LAKESIDE.** *On PA 507, 1 mi S of US 6.* 717/226-2124. Hrs: 11 am-10 pm; Sun from 9 am; Sun brunch 9 am-12:30 pm. Closed Thanksgiving, Dec 25. Res accepted. Bar. Semi-a la carte: lunch $2.50-$10, dinner $9-$20. Sun brunch $7.95. Child's meals. Specializes in steak, seafood. Parking. Tri-level dining area; overlooks lake. Cr cds: A, DS, MC, V.

D

✔ ★ **PERNA'S.** *1 mi SW on PA 590.* 717/226-3108. Hrs: 4:30-11 pm; Sun to 10 pm. Closed Mon, Tues, Dec-late Mar. Italian, Amer menu. Bar. Semi-a la carte: dinner $2.50-$14.95. Specializes in homemade pasta, braciole. Parking. Fireplace. Family-owned. No cr cds accepted.

D

★ ★ ★ **THE SETTLERS INN.** *(See The Settlers Inn)* 717/226-2993. Hrs: 11:30 am-2 pm, 5-9 pm; Sun brunch to 2 pm. Closed Dec 23-25. Res accepted wkends and July-Aug. Bar. A la carte entrees:

lunch $5-$9, dinner $13-$20. Sun brunch $5.95-$10.95. Child's meals. Specializes in pheasant, seafood, trout. Pianist Fri, Sat. Parking. Dining rm of Tudor-style hotel constructed in 1920s. Cr cds: A, MC, V.

Hazleton (D-8)

Settled: 1809 **Pop:** 24,730 **Elev:** 1,660 ft **Area code:** 717 **Zip:** 18201

On top of Spring Mountain, Hazleton calls itself the highest city in Pennsylvania. Surrounded by rich agricultural land, its early and rapid economic growth was spurred by the rich anthracite coal reserves found in the area. Although coal dominated the town's economy during the 19th century, today there are many diversified industries located here, producing building materials, textiles, office furniture, business forms, foods and food containers, boxes, heavy fabricated steel, plastics, electronic parts and other products.

What to See and Do

1. **National Shrine of the Sacred Heart.** 1½ mi NE on US 309, PA 940, in Harleigh section of Hazleton. Large outdoor shrine includes stations of the cross and crucifixion scene; picnic area. (Mar-Oct, daily) Phone 455-1162. **Free.**
2. **Eckley Miners' Village** (Pennsylvania Anthracite Museum Complex). 10 mi NE off PA 940, near Freeland. Mining coal patch town (1850s) portrays life in the anthracite region until about 1940. Walking tour (Memorial Day-Labor Day). (Daily exc Mon; closed some hols) Sr citizen rate. Phone 636-2070. ¢¢

(For further information contact the Greater Hazleton Chamber of Commerce, 1 S Church St; 455-1508.)

(See Ashland, Bloomsburg, Jim Thorpe, Wilkes-Barre)

Motels

★ ★ **BEST WESTERN GENETTI MOTOR LODGE.** *Box 250, 2 mi N on PA 309.* 717/454-2494; FAX 717/455-7793. 89 rms, 3 story. June-Oct: S $49-$60; D $59-$76; each addl $7; suites $95-$120; under 12 free; higher rates special events; lower rates rest of yr. Crib free. TV; cable. Heated pool; lifeguard. Playground. Complimentary continental bkfst. Ck-out 11 am. Coin lndry. Valet serv. Sundries. Bus depot transportation. Cr cds: A, C, D, DS, MC, V.

★ ★ **HOLIDAY INN.** *1½ mi N on PA 309.* 717/455-2061; FAX 717/455-9387. 107 rms, 2 story. S, D, studio rms $69; under 18 free. Crib free. Pet accepted. TV; cable. Pool; wading pool, lifeguard. Restaurant 6 am-10 pm. Rm serv. Bar 4 pm-2 am; entertainment Sat & Sun. Ck-out noon. Meeting rms. Bellhops. Sundries. Cr cds: A, C, D, DS, ER, JCB, MC, V.

Restaurant

★ ★ ★ **SCATTON'S.** *22nd & N Vine Sts.* 717/455-6630. Hrs: 5-10 pm; Thurs 11:30 am-2 pm, 5-10 pm. Closed Sun; Jan 1, Thanksgiving, Dec 25. Northern Italian menu. Bar. Semi-a la carte: lunch $3.50-$11.25, dinner $10.50-$24.75. Specializes in fresh seafood, veal, pasta. Parking. Casual; collection of antique prints. Cr cds: A, C, D, MC, V.

D SC

Hershey (E-7)

Founded: 1903 **Pop:** 11,860 **Elev:** 420 ft **Area code:** 717 **Zip:** 17033

One of America's most fascinating success stories, this planned community takes its name from founder M.S. Hershey, who established his world-famous chocolate factory here in 1903, then built a town around it. The streets have names like Chocolate and Cocoa, and streetlights are shaped like chocolate kisses. But there's more than chocolate here. Today, Hershey is known as one of the most diverse entertainment and resort areas in the eastern US. Hershey is also known as the "golf capital of Pennsylvania," and has a number of well-known golf courses.

What to See and Do

1. **Hershey Gardens.** Hotel Rd. From mid-June to first frost, 8,000 rose plants bloom on 23 acres. Tulip garden has more than 22,000 blooms (mid-Apr-mid-May). Also chrysanthemums and annuals; 6 theme gardens. (Mid-Apr-Oct, daily) Phone 534-3492. ¢¢
2. **Hersheypark.** Entrance on Hersheypark Dr (PA 39). Theme areas include Rhine Land, Tudor Square, Dutch crafts barn; more than 50 rides; Tower Plaza; live family shows. (Mid-May-Labor Day, daily; selected wkends May & Sept) For further information phone 800/HERSHEY. ¢¢¢¢¢ Also here is

   ZooAmerica. An 11-acre environmental zoo depicting 5 climatic regions of North America. (Daily; closed some major hols) Combination admission with Hersheypark avail. Phone 534-3860. Separate admission ¢¢
3. **Hershey Museum.** Near entrance to Hersheypark. Pennsylvania German, Native American, Eskimo collections; displays of Stiegel glass; "Apostolic Clock" depicting life of Christ; Milton Hershey history. (Daily; closed Jan 1, Thanksgiving, Dec 25) Phone 534-3439. ¢¢ Adj is

   Hersheypark Arena. Capacity 10,000; professional hockey, basketball, ice-skating, variety shows, concerts. Phone 534-3911.
4. **Hersheypark Stadium.** Seats 17,000; sports and entertainment events. Phone 534-3911.
5. **Founders Hall.** Campus center of Milton Hershey School, noted for its striking rotunda. (Daily; closed Jan 1, Thanksgiving, Dec 25) Phone 534-3500.
6. **Hershey's Chocolate World.** Entrance adj to Hersheypark visitor information. Tour via automated conveyance; simulates steps of chocolate production from cacao bean plantations through chocolate-making in Hershey. Also tropical gardens, shopping village. (Daily; closed Jan 1, Easter, Thanksgiving, Dec 25) Phone 534-4900. **Free.**
7. **Industrial tour.** Seltzer's Lebanon Bologna Co. 230 N College St, 3 blks N of US 422, in Palmyra. Outdoor wooden smokehouses since 1902. 15-min and 7-min guided tours (Mon-Fri; closed hols). Phone 838-6336. **Free.**

(For further information contact Hershey Information & Reservations, 300 Park Blvd; 800/HERSHEY.)

Annual Events

Chocolate Lovers' Extravaganza. Feb.

Antique Automobile Club. National fall rally. 2nd wkend Oct.

Christmas in Hershey. Mid-Nov-Dec.

(See Cornwall, Harrisburg, Lebanon)

Motels

★ ★ **BEST WESTERN INN.** *Box 364, jct US 422 & Sipe Ave.* 717/533-5665; FAX 717/533-5675. 123 rms, 3 story. No elvtr. May-

Aug: S, D $95-$125; each addl $10; under 17 free; wkly rates; higher rates special events; lower rates rest of yr. Crib $2. TV; cable, in-rm movies avail. Pool; wading pool, lifeguard. Complimentary continental bkfst. Restaurant nearby. Ck-out noon. Coin lndry. Meeting rms. Valet serv. Health club privileges. Game rm. Refrigerators. Cr cds: A, D, DS, ER, MC, V.

✔ ★ **DAYS INN.** *350 W Chocolate Ave. 717/534-2162; FAX 717/533-6409.* 75 rms, 4 story. Late June-Aug: S $55-$99; D $79-$108; each addl $5; under 18 free; higher rates antique car shows; lower rates rest of yr. Crib free. TV; cable, in-rm movies avail. Pool privileges. Complimentary continental bkfst, coffee. Restaurant opp 11:30 am-10 pm. Ck-out noon. Valet serv. Free airport, RR station, bus depot transportation. Health club privileges. Some refrigerators. Cr cds: A, C, D, DS, MC, V.

★ ★ **FRIENDSHIP INN.** *43 W Areba. 717/533-7054; FAX 717/533-3405.* 24 rms, 2 story, 10 kits. Mid-June-early Sept: S $70; D $85; each addl $5; kits. $105-$150; under 18 free; wkly rates; lower rates rest of yr. Crib free. TV; cable. Complimentary coffee in lobby. Restaurant nearby. Ck-out 11 am. Some refrigerators. Cr cds: A, C, D, DS, MC, V.

★ ★ **HERSHEY LODGE.** *PO Box 446, W Chocolate Ave at University Dr. 717/533-3311; res: 800/437-7439; FAX 717/533-9642.* 457 rms, 1-2 story. May-Labor Day: S $96-$118; D $104-$128; each addl $15; suites $200-$425; studio rms $240; under 18 free; packages avail; lower rates rest of yr. Crib free. TV; cable. 2 pools, 1 indoor; wading pool, poolside serv, lifeguard. Free supervised child's activities (May-early Sept, late Nov-Jan 1). Complimentary coffee & tea in rms. Restaurant 7 am-10 pm; also dining rm. Bar 11-2 am; entertainment, dancing. Ck-out noon. Convention facilities. Valet serv. Sundries. Gift shop. Free airport transportation. Lighted tennis. 18-hole golf privileges, greens fee $15-$60, pitch & putt, putting green. Exercise equipt; weights, bicycles, whirlpool, sauna. Rec rm. Cinema. Cr cds: A, C, D, DS, MC, V.

✔ ★ ★ **MILTON MOTEL.** *1733 E Chocolate Ave. 717/533-4533; FAX 717/533-0369.* 31 rms, 2 story. Mid-May-Labor Day: S $45-$46; D $56-$79; each addl $5; wkly rates Sept-May; higher rates hol wknds; lower rates rest of yr. Crib $6. TV; cable. Heated pool. Restaurant adj 11 am-2 pm. Ck-out 11 am. Game rm. Refrigerators avail. Cr cds: A, D, DS, MC, V.

✔ ★ **SIMMONS.** *355 W Chocolate Ave, 2½ blks W of town square. 717/533-9177; FAX 717/533-3605.* 32 rms, 4 with shower only, 2 story. Many rm phones. June-Oct: S $55-$65; D $65-$90; each addl $5; apt (1-2 bedrm) $110-$175; kit. units $85-$105; wkly, family rates; higher rates antique car show; lower rates rest of yr. Crib free. TV; cable. Complimentary coffee in lobby. Restaurant nearby. Ck-out 11 am. Many refrigerators. Picnic tables, grills. Cr cds: A, D, DS, MC, V.

★ ★ **WHITE ROSE.** *1060 E Chocolate Ave. 717/533-9876; FAX 717/533-6923.* 24 rms, 2 story. July-Aug: S, D $85-$95; each addl $5; lower rates rest of yr. Crib $5. TV; cable. Heated pool; lifeguard. Complimentary coffee. Restaurant nearby. Ck-out 11 am. Gift shop. Private patios, balconies. Picnic tables. Cr cds: A, D, MC, V.

Motor Hotel

★ ★ ★ **HOLIDAY INN HARRISBURG-GRANTVILLE.** *(I-81 at exit 28, Grantville 17028) N on PA 743 to I-81. 717/469-0661; FAX 717/469-7755.* 195 rms, 4 story. Memorial Day-mid-Oct: S $98-$133;

D $105-$160; each addl $10; suites $150-$225; under 19 free; lower rates rest of yr. Crib free. Pet accepted. TV; cable. 2 pools, 1 indoor; wading pool. Restaurant 7 am-10 pm. Rm serv. Bar 11-2 am; entertainment, dancing. Ck-out noon. Coin lndry. Meeting rms. Bellhops. Valet serv. Shopping arcade. Airport, RR station, bus depot transportation. Exercise equipt; weight machine, bicycles, sauna. Lawn games. Balconies. Cr cds: A, C, D, DS, ER, JCB, MC, V.

Resort

★ ★ ★ **HOTEL HERSHEY.** *PO Box 400, off US 322/422. 717/533-2171; res: 800/533-3131; FAX 717/534-8887.* 241 rms, 5 story. MAP, Apr-Oct: S, D $275-$525; each addl $55; under 3 free; AP avail; package plans; lower rates rest of yr. Crib $10. TV; cable. 2 pools, 1 indoor; wading pool, lifeguard. Supervised child's activities. Restaurants 7 am-11 pm. Rm serv 24 hrs. Bar 4 pm-1 am; entertainment. Ck-out noon, ck-in after 4 pm. Package store 1 mi. Convention facilities. Bellhops. Valet serv. Daily maid, linen serv avail. Gift shop. Airport, RR station, bus depot transportation. 4 tennis courts. 9-hole golf, greens fee $14-$16, putting green. Championship 18-hole golf privileges. X-country ski on site. Bicycle rentals. Lawn bowling, outdoor games. Carriage rides. Exercise equipt; bicycles, rowing machine, whirlpool, sauna. Extensive gardens, landscaping; scenic hilltop location. Cr cds: A, C, D, DS, MC, V.

Restaurant

★ ★ **DIMITRI'S.** *1311 E Chocolate Ave. 717/533-3403.* Hrs: 11 am-11 pm. Closed Jan 1, Dec 25. Res accepted. Greek, continental menu. Bar to 2 am. Semi-a la carte: lunch $2.95-$7.95, dinner $6.95-$21.95. Child's meals. Specializes in seafood, steak. Parking. Cr cds: MC, V.

Honesdale (C-9)

Founded: 1826 **Pop:** 4,972 **Elev:** 980 ft **Area code:** 717 **Zip:** 18431

Named in honor of Philip Hone, a mayor of New York City and first president of the Delaware & Hudson Canal Co, Honesdale was for many years the world's largest coal storage center, transshipping millions of tons of anthracite. A gravity railroad brought coal here in winter; in spring it was reshipped by canal boats to tidewater. The *Stourbridge Lion,* first steam locomotive to operate in the US (1829), was used by the Delaware & Hudson Canal Co, but when the rail bed proved too weak, mule power replaced the steam engine. Today Honesdale manufactures textile products, business forms and furniture, and is surrounded by dairy farms in the beautiful rolling countryside.

What to See and Do

1. **Replica of the *Stourbridge Lion*** (original is in Smithsonian Institution). Main St. First steam locomotive to operate in the US (1829).

2. **Wayne County Historical Society Museum.** 810 Main St. Dorflinger glass collection. (Apr-Dec, daily; rest of yr, Tues, Thurs & Sat; closed Jan 1, Good Friday, Thanksgiving, Dec 25) Phone 253-3240. ¢

3. **Stourbridge Rail Excursions.** Scenic rail excursions from Honesdale to Lackawaxen, centering on the change of seasons, with entertainment and activities. Contact the Chamber of Commerce for schedule, fees.

(For further information contact the Wayne County Chamber of Commerce, 742 Main St; 253-1960.)

Annual Event

Wayne County Fair. Exhibits, livestock, horse racing. 1st full wk Aug.

(See Hawley, Scranton)

Inn

★ ★ ★ **BEACH LAKE HOTEL.** *(Box 144, Main & Church Sts, Beach Lake 18405) E on US 6, 5 mi E on PA 652, left at fire station, 3 blks.* 717/729-8239; res: 800/382-3897. 6 rms, 3 story. No rm phones. S, D $95. Adults only. Complimentary full bkfst; tea/sherry. Complimentary coffee in rms. Dining rm 5-9 pm (public by res). Ck-out 11 am, ck-in 1 pm. At Beach Lake. Built in 1830 as country inn; also served as general store and post office. Victorian antiques. Cr cds: A, MC, V.

Hopewell Furnace National Historic Site (E-8)

(15 mi SE of Reading via US 422, PA 82 to Birdsboro, then SE on Birdsboro-Warwick Rd/PA 345; 10 mi NE of Tpke Morgantown Interchange)

Hopewell, an early industrial community, was built around a charcoal-burning cold-blast furnace, which made pig iron and many other iron products from 1771 to 1883. Nearby mines and forests supplied ore and charcoal for the furnace. The National Park Service has restored the buildings, and interpretive programs emphasize the community's role in the history of American industry. Hopewell is surrounded by the approximately 7,330-acre French Creek State Park (see POTTSTOWN).

The Visitor Center has a museum and audiovisual program on ironmaking and community life. Self-guided tour includes: charcoal house, where fuel for furnace was stored; anthracite furnace ruin; waterwheel and blast machinery; casting house, where 16 moulders produced up to 5,000 stoves annually; cold-blast charcoal-burning furnace; blacksmith shop; tenant houses; barn for horses and mules transporting charcoal, ore, iron products to market; office store, which was source of staples, clothing and house furnishings; springhouse, which supplied "refrigeration"; ironmaster's house, home of proprietor or manager. Stove moulding and casting demonstrations (July-Labor Day). (Daily; closed Jan 1, Thanksgiving, Dec 25) Captioned slide program for the hearing impaired; Braille map and large print pamphlets for the visually impaired; wheelchair access. Sr citizens **free.** For further information contact the Superintendent, 2 Mark Bird Lane, Elverson 19520; 610/582-8773 or -2093 (TDD). Admission **free** Dec-Feb; rest of yr ¢

(For accommodations see Pottstown, Reading)

Huntingdon (E-5)

Founded: 1767 **Pop:** 6,843 **Elev:** 643 ft **Area code:** 814 **Zip:** 16652

Founded on the site of an Oneida Indian village in the Juniata Valley, Huntingdon was first called Standing Stone—for a 14-foot etched stone pillar venerated by the Indians.

What to See and Do

1. **Standing Stone Monument** (1896). Penn & 3nd Sts. Erected to replace Indian Stone. Phone 643-1110.
2. **Swigart Auto Museum.** 4 mi E on US 22. Changing exhibits of American steam, gas, electric autos. Large collection of nameplates, license plates and auto memorabilia; picnic area. (July-Labor Day, daily; June & after Labor Day-Oct, wkends) Sr citizen rate. Phone 643-0885. ¢¢
3. **Lincoln Caverns.** 3 mi W on US 22. The one-hour tour of two caves includes Frozen Niagara, Diamond Cascade; visitors' center & gift shop. (Mar-Dec, schedule varies) Sr citizen rate. Phone 643-0268. ¢¢¢
4. **Raystown Dam and Lake.** 7 mi S on PA 26, follow signs to Hesston. Earthfill dam has created 8,300-acre, 30-mile-long lake for flood control and recreation. Swimming; fishing, hunting; boating (seven launches & two marinas). Hiking. Picnicking, restaurant. Camping. Observation area. Fee for some activities. Phone 658-3405.
5. **Indian Caverns.** 7 mi NW via US 22, PA 45 in Spruce Creek. A one-mile guided tour; extensive scenic beauty and authentic Native American history; relic room contains artifacts, tablet of picture writing; picnic area. (Apr-Nov, daily; rest of yr, wkends) Phone 632-7578 or -8333. ¢¢¢

(For further information contact the Huntingdon County Tourist Promotion Agency, 241 Mifflin St; 643-3577.)

Annual Event

Hartslog Day. 7 mi NW via US 22, in Alexandria. Heritage festival includes more than 100 craftsmen; food, music, games. 2nd Sat Oct.

(See Altoona, Orbisonia)

Motels

★ ★ **DAYS INN.** *RD 1, Box 353, 4th St at US 22.* 814/643-3934; FAX 814/643-3005. 76 rms, 3 story. S $38-$47; D $45-$54; each addl $5; under 13 free. Crib free. Pet accepted; $5. TV; cable. Restaurant 6 am-11 pm; Fri, Sat to midnight. Bar 4:30 pm-2 am. Ck-out 11 am. Meeting rms. Valet serv. Sundries. X-country ski 10 mi. Cr cds: A, C, D, DS, MC, V.

✔ ★ ★ **HUNTINGDON MOTOR INN.** *Box 356, US 22 & PA 26.* 814/643-1133. 48 rms, 2 story. S $35-$38; D $44-$52; each addl $4. Crib $3. Pet accepted, some restrictions. TV; cable. Restaurant 7 am-9 pm. Rm serv. Bar 4:30-11 pm. Ck-out noon. Meeting rms. Balconies. Cr cds: A, C, D, DS, MC, V.

Indiana (D-3)

Founded: 1805 **Pop:** 15,174 **Elev:** 1,310 ft **Area code:** 412 **Zip:** 15701

Named after the Indian population in the area, this borough was established on 250 acres donated for a county seat by George Clymer of Philadelphia, a signer of the Declaration of Independence. Indiana University of Pennsylvania (1875) is located here. This is also the birthplace of actor Jimmy Stewart.

What to See and Do

1. **County parks. Blue Spruce.** 6 mi N off PA 110. Covers 420 acres. Fishing for bass, perch, catfish and crappie; boating (rowboat, canoe rentals). Winter sports area. Picnicking, grills, playground.

(Daily) **Pine Ridge.** SW via US 22 near Blairsville. Covers 630 acres. Trout fishing. Hiking, nature study. Picnicking. (Daily) **Hemlock Lake.** W on PA 286 near Rossiter. Covers 200 acres. Fishing, small game hunting. Hiking. Ice-skating. Nature study, photography. (Daily) For general information phone 463-8636 (park commission).

2. **Yellow Creek State Park.** 12 mi E via US 422. Approx 2,900 acres. Swimming beach; fishing, hunting; boating (rentals, launching). Hiking. Cross-country skiing, snowmobiling, sledding, ice-skating, ice fishing, ice boating. Picnicking, playground, snack bar. Standard fees. Phone 463-3850.

(For further information contact the Indiana County Chamber of Commerce, 1019 Philadelphia St, PO Box 727; 465-2511.)

(See Johnstown)

Motels

★ ★ **BEST WESTERN UNIVERSITY INN.** *1545 Wayne Ave.* 412/349-9620; FAX 412/349-2620. 108 rms, 2 story. S $55-$65; D $60-$70; each addl $5; under 12 free; higher rates special university events. Crib free. TV; cable. Heated pool. Coffee in rms. Restaurant 6:30 am-1:30 pm, 5-9 pm; Sun 8 am-1:30 pm. Rm serv. Bar 4 pm-midnight. Ck-out noon. Meeting rms. Cr cds: A, C, D, DS, MC, V.

★ ★ ★ **HOLIDAY INN.** *1395 Wayne Ave.* 412/463-3561; FAX 412/463-8006. 159 rms, 2 story. S $69-$74; D $79-$82; each addl $8; suites $125; family, wkend rates; golf plans; higher rates university events. Crib free. TV; cable. Indoor pool; whirlpool, sauna, poolside serv, lifeguard. Restaurant 6:30 am-10 pm; Sat, Sun from 7 am. Rm serv. Bar 11-2 am; entertainment, dancing. Ck-out noon. Meeting rms. Bellhops. Miniature golf. Game rm. Cr cds: A, C, D, DS, ER, JCB, MC, V.

Jenkintown (F-10)

Pop: 4,574 **Elev:** 250 ft **Area code:** 215 **Zip:** 19046

What to See and Do

Beth Sholom Synagogue. Old York & Foxcroft Rds, 1 mi S, in Elkins Park. The only synagogue designed by Frank Lloyd Wright. (By appt only) Phone 887-1342. **Free.**

(For further information contact the Valley Forge Convention & Visitors Bureau, 600 W Germantown Pike, Suite 130, Plymouth Meeting, 19462; 610/834-1550.)

(For accommodations see Fort Washington, Philadelphia, Willow Grove)

Restaurants

★ **CAFE PREEYA.** *(2651 Huntingdon Pike, Huntingdon Valley 19009)* E on Meeting House Rd to Huntingdon Pike. 215/947-6195. Hrs: 4-10 pm; Sat 5-11 pm; Sun 4-9 pm. Closed Mon; Thanksgiving. Res accepted. Continental, Thai menu. Setups. A la carte entrees: dinner $10.95-$22.95. Specialties: whole red snapper, shrimp Siam, veal medallion. Parking. Slanted thatched roof covers part of dining area. Totally nonsmoking. Cr cds: MC, V.

★ ★ **JOHNNY MOTT'S.** *(Cedarbrook Hill Apts, bldg #1, Wyncote 19095-2695)* W on US 309. 215/887-1263. Hrs: 11:30 am-2 pm, 4:30-10 pm. Closed Jan 1, Dec 25. Res accepted. Continental menu. Bar. Semi-a la carte: lunch $4.95-$7.50, dinner $12.95-$19.95. Speci-

alities: seafood pescatore, lobster diablo, trout with basil and crabmeat. Valet parking. Cr cds: A, C, D, MC, V.

✔ ★ **STAZI MILANO.** *Township Line 8 & Greenwood Ave.* 215/885-9000. Hrs: 11:30 am-3 pm, 4-10:30 pm; Sat 5 pm-midnight; Sun 1-9 pm; early-bird dinner Sun-Thurs 4-6 pm. Italian menu. Bar to midnight, Fri, Sat to 2 am. Semi-a la carte: lunch $2.75-$15.45, dinner $3.50-$15.45. Specializes in pasta, pizza, veal. Parking. In 1931 RR station; mahogany railings. Cr cds: A, MC, V.

★ ★ **YORKTOWN INN.** *(Church & Old York Rds, Elkins Park)* 2 mi S on York Rd (PA 611). 215/887-0600. Hrs: 11:30 am-3 pm, 4:30-9 pm; Fri & Sat 4:30-10 pm; Sun brunch 11 am-2 pm; early-bird dinner Mon-Fri 4:30-6 pm. Closed Dec 25. Res accepted. Continental menu. Bar. Semi-a la carte: lunch $4.75-$8.75, dinner $11.75-$18.75. Sun brunch $5.75-$9.75. Specializes in Maine lobster, rack of lamb, Dover sole. Parking. Originally built in late 19th century; rebuilt after fire. Atmosphere of colonial Williamsburg. Traditional English pub. Family-owned. Cr cds: A, D, DS, MC, V.

Jim Thorpe (D-9)

Settled: 1815 **Pop:** 5,048 **Elev:** 600 ft **Area code:** 717 **Zip:** 18229

The twin towns, Mauch Chunk (Bear Mountain) and East Mauch Chunk, built on the sides of a narrow gorge of the Lehigh River, merged in 1954 and adopted the name of Jim Thorpe, the great Native American athlete. This, together with a "nickel-a-week" plan whereby each man, woman, and child paid five cents to promote the community and attract industry, gave the area (formerly dependent on coal mining) a new lease on economic life. Little has changed in appearance after more than a century; a walking tour will reveal 19th-century architecture.

What to See and Do

1. **Stone Row.** Race St, downtown. Sixteen town houses built by Asa Packer (see #3) for the engineers on his railroad; reminiscent of Philadelphia's Elfreth's Alley. Some are stores open to the public. Also here is

    St Mark's Church. Has Tiffany windows and copy of reredos from Windsor Castle. (June-Oct, daily; Apr-May, wkends) ¢¢

2. **Jim Thorpe Memorial.** 1 mi E on PA 903. A 20-ton granite mausoleum built in memory of the 1912 Olympic champion.

3. **Asa Packer Mansion.** Packer Hill. Former showplace home of founder of Lehigh Valley Railroad and Lehigh University, one of state's wealthiest men. Packer's house, treasures and money were left to the borough. (June-Oct, daily; Apr-May, wkends) Phone 325-3229. ¢¢ Adj is

4. **Whitewater rafting.** On upper and lower gorges of Lehigh River.

    Pocono Whitewater Adventures. 8 mi NE of Jim Thorpe Bridge on PA 903. Also bike tours. (Mar-Nov, daily) For information, reservations phone 325-3655. ¢¢¢¢¢

    Jim Thorpe River Adventures, Inc. Coalport Rd, NE via PA 903. (Mar-Nov, daily) For information, reservations phone 325-2570 or -4960. ¢¢¢¢¢

(For further information contact the Carbon County Tourist Promotion Agency Information Center, Box 90; 325-3673.)

Annual Events

Laurel Blossom Festival. Arts & crafts, entertainment, food, steam train rides. Early or mid-June.

Fall Foliage Festival. Sat & Sun, Columbus Day wkend.

(See Hazleton)

Inn

★ ★ ★ **INN AT JIM THORPE.** *24 Broadway. 717/325-2599; res: 800/329-2599; FAX 717/325-9145.* 22 rms, 4 story. S $65-$80; D $65-$100; each addl $10. Crib free. TV; cable. Complimentary continental bkfst. Dining rm 11:30 am-9 pm. Bar 11:30-2 am; entertainment Sat. Ck-out 11 am, ck-in 2 pm. Victorian-era hotel (1864), with ornamental-iron galleries, hosted Buffalo Bill, Thomas Edison, John D. Rockefeller, and Presidents Grant & Taft. Restored with period furnishings. Cr cds: A, D, DS, MC, V.

Johnstown (E-3)

Settled: 1800 **Pop:** 28,134 **Elev:** 1,180 ft **Area code:** 814

On May 31, 1889, a break in the South Fork Dam that impounded an old reservoir 10 miles east of the city, poured a wall of water onto the city in the disastrous "Johnstown Flood." The death toll rose to 2,209, and property damage totaled $17,000,000. The city has been flooded 22 times since 1850, most recently in 1977.

Founded by a Swiss Mennonite, Joseph Johns, the city today is the center of Cambria County's iron and steel industry, producing iron and steel bars, railroad cars, parts and railroad supplies.

What to See and Do

1. **Johnstown Flood Museum.** 304 Washington St. Museum depicts history of Johnstown, with permanent exhibits on 1889 Johnstown Flood; Academy award-winning film, photographs, artifacts, memorabilia. (Daily; closed some hols) Sr citizen rate. Phone 539-1889. ¢¢

2. **Inclined Plane Railway.** Vine St & Roosevelt Blvd. Joins Johnstown and Westmont. Ride is on steep (72% grade) passenger incline 500-foot ascent. Counterbalanced cable cars take 50 passengers and 2 automobiles each. (Daily; closed Jan 1, Dec 25) Sr citizens free. Phone 536-1816. ¢

3. **Grandview Cemetery.** 1 mi W on PA 271, in Westmont. 777 unidentified victims of the 1889 flood are buried under blank headstones in the "Unknown Plot."

4. **Johnstown Flood National Memorial.** Jct US 219, PA 869. Commemorates 1889 Johnstown Flood; preserved remnants of the South Fork Dam. Visitor center with exhibits, 30-min movie (daily; closed Dec 25). Phone 495-4643. **Free.**

5. **Conemaugh Gap.** Located at the W end of the city. Gorge, 7 miles long and 1,700 feet deep, cuts between Laurel Hill Ridge and Chestnut Ridge.

(For further information contact the Cambria County Tourist Council, 111 Market St, 15901; 536-7993 or 800/237-8590.)

(See Ebensburg, Ligonier)

Motel

✔ ★ ★ **COMFORT INN.** *455 Theatre Dr (15904). 814/266-3678; FAX 814/266-9783.* 117 rms, 5 story, 27 suites. S $49-$54; D $55-$60; each addl $6; suites $79-$89; kit. units $85-$95; under 18 free; monthly rates; higher rates special events. Crib free. Pet accepted. TV; cable. in-rm movies avail. Indoor pool; lifeguard. Complimentary continental bkfst, coffee. Restaurant nearby. Ck-out noon. Coin lndry. Meeting rms. Sundries. Free airport transportation. Exercise equipt; weights, bicycles, whirlpool. Game rm. Refrigerator, wet bar in suites. Picnic table, grill. Cr cds: A, C, D, DS, ER, JCB, MC, V.

Hotel

★ ★ **HOLIDAY INN-DOWNTOWN.** *250 Market St (15901). 814/535-7777; FAX 814/535-7777, ext. 123.* 164 rms, 6 story. S $59-$79; D $59-$89; suites $238-$290; under 19 free. Crib free. Pet accepted, some restrictions. TV; cable. Indoor pool; whirlpool, sauna, poolside serv, lifeguard. Restaurant 7 am-10 pm. Bar 4 pm-midnight. Ck-out noon. Meeting rms. Cr cds: A, C, D, DS, JCB, MC, V.

Restaurant

★ ★ **SURF N'TURF.** *100 Valley Pike. 814/536-9250.* Hrs: 4-10 pm; Sun 11 am-8 pm. Closed Dec 25. Bar. Semi-a la carte: dinner $7.95-$32.95. Child's meals. Specializes in seafood, steak. Salad bar. Parking. Cr cds: A, C, D, DS, MC, V.

Kane (B-4)

Settled: 1864 **Pop:** 4,590 **Elev:** 2,000 ft **Area code:** 814 **Zip:** 16735

Situated on a lofty plateau, Kane offers hunting, fishing and abundant winter sports. Summers are cool and winters are bracing. Allegheny National Forest is to the north, west and south; there are scenic drives through 4,000 acres of virgin timber. General Thomas L. Kane of "Mormon War" fame settled here and laid out the community, which prospered as a lumber and railroad town. General Ulysses Grant was once arrested here for fishing without a license.

What to See and Do

1. **Thomas L. Kane Memorial Chapel** (1878). 30 Chestnut St. Built as a chapel for the new town under the direction of General Kane, a Civil War hero and humanitarian who championed the persecuted Mormons. Visitor center includes film of General Kane's life; small museum. (Daily exc Mon) Phone 837-9729. **Free.**

2. **Twin Lakes.** 8 mi S of E Kane on PA 321, then 2 mi N on Forest Rd 191, in Allegheny National Forest. Swimming; fishing. Hiking. Picnicking. Camping. Phone 723-5150.

3. **Bendigo State Park.** 9 mi SE on PA 321, then 7 mi S on US 219, then 3 mi NE on unnumbered road. Approx 100 acres. Swimming pool; fishing. Sledding. Standard fees. Phone 965-2646.

4. **Kinzua Bridge State Park.** 12 mi E via US 6 in Mt Jewett. An approx 300-acre park surrounds Kinzua Bridge. When built in 1882, the bridge was the highest railroad bridge in the world, taking its 2,053 foot span 301 feet above the Kinzua Creek. Overlooks, picnicking. (Daily) Phone 965-2646. **Free.**

(For further information contact the Seneca Highlands Tourist Association, PO Box 698, Mt Jewett 16740; 368-9370.)

(For accommodations see Clarion, Warren)

Kempton (D-8)

(see Hamburg)

Kennett Square (F-9)

Settled: 1705 **Pop:** 5,218 **Elev:** 370 ft **Area code:** 610 **Zip:** 19348

What to See and Do

1. **Longwood Gardens.** 3 mi NE on US 1. Longwood was the estate of Pierre S. du Pont, chairman of the board of both Du Pont Chemicals and General Motors, who designed the 1,050 acres of gardens around Peirce's Park, a grove of trees planted in 1798. Estate includes the original grove; the Peirce-du Pont House (1730); a variety of exterior gardens, including the rose, peony, wisteria, idea, hillside, heath, waterlily and topiary gardens; the Italian Water Garden, Open Air Theatre and Main Fountain Garden, which together feature more than 1,700 water jets; and the neo-classical Conservatories, nearly 4 acres under glass, housing indoor gardens that are among the most spectacular in the world. Display of color-illuminated fountains (Memorial Day wkend-Sept, Tues, Thurs & Sat evenings). Organ concerts, orchestral concerts, plays, holiday displays, horticultural lectures (schedules at visitor center). Restaurant; picnic areas; museum shop. (Daily) Phone 388-6741. ¢¢¢; Adult admission lower on Tues.

2. **Phillips Mushroom Place.** 2 mi NE on US 1. Museum explains history, lore and mystique of mushrooms through motion picture, diorama, slides and exhibits. Gift shop. (Daily; closed some major hols) Sr citizen rate. Phone 388-6082. ¢

3. **Brandywine River Museum.** 7 mi NE on US 1, in Chadds Ford. Converted 19th-century gristmill houses largest collection of paintings by Andrew Wyeth and other Wyeth family members; also collections of American illustration, still life and landscape painting. Nature trail; wildflower gardens; restaurant, museum shop, guided tours. (Daily; closed Dec 25) Sr citizen rate. Tours ¢¢ Phone 388-2700. **Free.**

4. **Brandywine Battlefield.** 2 mi W of jct US 1, 202, near Chadds Ford. Includes Lafayette's quarters and Washington's headquarters. Here, and around Chadds Ford, the Battle of the Brandywine (1777) took place—a decisive battle for Washington. Visitor center with exhibits; tours of historic buildings; museum shop. Picnicking. (Daily exc Mon; closed some hols) Sr citizen rate. Tours ¢¢ Phone 459-3342. **Free.**

5. **John Chads House.** 7 mi NE via US 1, then 1/4 mi N on PA 100, in Chadds Ford. Stone building (ca 1725) is fine example of early 18th-century Pennsylvania architecture; authentically restored and furnished as a house museum. Narrated tours by guides in colonial costume; baking demonstrations in beehive oven. (May-Sept, Sat-Sun; also by appt) Sr citizen rate. Phone 388-7376. ¢

6. **Barns-Brinton House** (1714). 5 1/2 mi NE on US 1, in Chadds Ford. Authentically restored 18th-century tavern, now a house museum furnished in the period. Guides in colonial costume offer interpretive tours; domestic art demonstrations. (June-Aug, Sat-Sun; also by appt) Sr citizen rate. Phone 388-7376. ¢

7. **Chaddsford Winery.** 5 mi NE on US 1, in Chadds Ford. Tours of boutique winery, housed in renovated old barn; view of production process; tasting room. Tours (Sat-Sun; also by appt); tastings (daily exc Mon, free). Phone 388-6221. ¢¢

(For further information contact the Chester County Tourist Bureau, 601 Westtown Rd, Ste 170, West Chester 19382, phone 344-6365; or the Southeastern Chester County Chamber of Commerce, 206 E State St, PO Box 395, phone 444-0774.)

(See West Chester; also see Wilmington, DE)

Motel

★ **LONGWOOD INN.** *815 E Baltimore Pike. 610/444-3515; FAX 610/444-4285.* 28 rms. S $69; D $75; each addl $6; under 12 free. Crib free. TV. Complimentary continental bkfst. Restaurant (see LONG-

WOOD INN). Rm serv. Ck-out noon. Airport, RR station transportation. Cr cds: A, D, DS, MC, V.

Motor Hotel

★ ★ ★ **MENDENHALL HOTEL & CONFERENCE CENTER.** *(Box 606, PA 52/Kennett Pike, Mendenhall 19357) 3 mi E on US 1. 610/388-2100; FAX 610/388-1184.* 70 rms, 3 story. S $81; D $91; each addl $15; suites $130-$160; under 12 free. Crib free. TV. Complimentary continental bkfst. Rm serv. Bar from 11:30 am. Ck-out noon. Meeting rms. Bellhops. Valet serv. Concierge. Airport transportation. Exercise equipt; weights, bicycles. Bathrm phones. Cr cds: A, C, D, DS, MC, V.

Inns

★ ★ ★ **BRANDYWINE RIVER HOTEL.** *(Box 1058, US 1 & PA 100, Chadds Ford 19317) Approx 10 mi E on US 1. 610/388-1200.* 40 rms, 2 story, 10 suites. S $99; D $109; each addl $10; suites $130. Crib free. TV. Complimentary continental bkfst & afternoon tea. Restaurant adj 11:30 am-10 pm. Ck-out 11 am, ck-in 2 pm. Meeting rms. Valet serv. Airport, RR station, bus depot transportation. Bathrm phones; refrigerator in suites. Specialty shops on site. Cr cds: A, C, D, DS, MC, V.

★ ★ ★ **FAIRVILLE.** *(PO Box 219, PA 52, Mendenhall 19357) 3 mi E on US 1. 610/388-5900; FAX 610/388-5902.* 15 rms, 2 story. S, D $100-$180; each addl $10. Adults preferred. TV; cable. Complimentary bkfst & afternoon tea. Ck-out 11 am, ck-in after 3 pm. Fireplaces. Private patios, balconies. Built 1826; antiques, period decor. View of surrounding countryside. Totally nonsmoking. Cr cds: A, DS, MC, V.

★ ★ **SCARLETT HOUSE.** *503 W State St. 610/444-9592.* 4 rms, 2 with bath, 2 story, 1 suite. No rm phones. S, D $65-$85; suite $95-$105. Children over 12 yrs only. Complimentary full bkfst, coffee, tea. Restaurant nearby. Ck-out 11 am, ck-in 2 pm. Street parking. American Foursquare house built in 1910; Victorian decor. 3 sitting rms. Totally nonsmoking. No cr cds accepted.

Restaurants

★ **KENNETT SQUARE INN.** *201 E State St. 610/444-5687.* Hrs: 11:30 am-2:30 pm, 5:30-10 pm; Mon & Tues to 9 pm. Closed Sun; Jan 1, Dec 25. Res accepted. Bar 11:30-2 am. Semi-a la carte: lunch $4.50-$8.25, dinner $10.95-$20.95. Specializes in fresh mushroom dishes. Entertainment Wed, Thurs. Restored country inn; built 1835. Cr cds: A, C, D, MC, V.

★ ★ **LONGWOOD INN.** *(See Longwood Inn Motel) 610/444-3515.* Hrs: 7:30-10:30 am, 4-9 pm; Fri, Sat to 10 pm; Sun brunch 10:30 am-2:30 pm. Closed Jan 1, Dec 25. Res accepted. Bar from 4 pm. Semi-a la carte: bkfst $2.95, dinner $8.95-$21.95. Sun brunch $8.95-$13.50. Child's meals. Specializes in mushroom dishes, fresh seafood. Parking. Prints of area artists. Guest rms avail. Cr cds: A, C, D, DS, MC, V.

★ ★ ★ **MENDENHALL INN.** *(PA 52, Mendenhall) 3 mi E on US 1 to PA 52. 610/388-1181.* Hrs: 11:30 am-2:30 pm, 5-10 pm; Sun 10 am-8 pm; Sun brunch to 2 pm. Closed Dec 25. Res required. Continental menu. Bar. Wine cellar. Semi-a la carte: lunch $6-$12, dinner $17-$31.95. Child's meals. Specializes in veal, seafood, wild game.

Pianist, harpist. Valet parking. Country inn; colonial decor. Cr cds: A, C, D, DS, MC, V.

D

✔ ★ ★ **THE TERRACE.** *Longwood Gardens. 610/388-6771.* Hrs: 11 am-3 pm; dinner hrs same as Longwood Gardens; wkend hrs vary; Dec to 7:30 pm. Cafeteria 10 am-4 pm; wkend hrs vary; Jan & Feb 11 am-3 pm; Dec 10 am-8 pm. Dining rm closed Jan-Mar. Res accepted. Bar. Semi-a la carte: lunch $6.95-$13.95, dinner $10.95-$16.95. Child's meals. Specialties: crab cakes, mushroom strudel, snapper soup. Cafeteria avg ck: lunch, dinner $7. Outdoor dining. Admission to Longwood Gardens required. Cr cds: A, MC, V.

D

King of Prussia (F-9)

Settled: early 1700s **Pop:** 18,406 **Elev:** 200 ft **Area code:** 610 **Zip:** 19406

Originally named Reeseville for the Welsh family who owned the land, the town changed its name to that of the local inn, which is still standing. The area around the town is full of historic interest.

What to See and Do

1. **Mill Grove** (1762). 5 mi NW via US 422 & Audubon Rd, N of Valley Forge National Historic Park, on Pawlings Rd, in Audubon. Includes 175-acre wildlife sanctuary, developed around the first American home of ornithologist John James Audubon, now a museum. Prints, including complete elephant folio. Hiking trails. (Tues-Sat, also Sun afternoons; closed Jan 1, Thanksgiving, Dec 25) Phone 666-5593. **Free.**

2. **Harriton House** (1704). 6 mi SE via Old Gulph Rd to Harriton Rd. Early American domestic architecture of the Philadelphia area. Originally 700-acre estate, now 16½ acres. House of Charles Thomson, Secretary of the Continental Congresses; restored to early 18th-century period. Nature park. (Wed-Sat; Sun by appt; closed hols) Sr citizen rate. Phone 525-0201. ¢

3. **Valley Forge National Historical Park** (see). Just W of town.

4. **Swiss Pines.** 6 mi SW via PA 202, Great Valley exit, on Charlestown Rd in Malvern. Japanese gardens featuring azalea and rhododendron collection; ponds, waterfalls, winding pathway; herb and groundcover garden. Children under 12 yrs not permitted. (Mid-Apr-Nov, Mon-Fri, also Sat mornings; closed hols & inclement weather) Phone 933-6916. **Free.**

(For further information contact the Valley Forge Convention & Visitors Bureau, 600 W Germantown Pike, Suite 130, Plymouth Meeting, 19462; 834-1550.)

(See Norristown, Philadelphia, West Chester)

Motels

★ ★ ★ **COURTYARD BY MARRIOTT.** *(1100 Drummers Lane, Wayne 19087) S on US 202, Warner Rd exit. 610/687-6700; FAX 610/687-1149.* 150 rms, 2 story. S, D $68-$95; each addl $10; suites $88-$120; under 16 free; wkly, wkend rates. TV; cable. Indoor pool. Complimentary coffee in rms. Restaurant 6:30-11 am, 5-10 pm. Bar 4-11 pm. Ck-out noon. Coin lndry. Meeting rms. Valet serv. Sundries. Airport transportation. Exercise equipt; weight machine, bicycles, whirlpool. Refrigerator. Many balconies. Cr cds: A, D, DS, MC, V.

D ≈ ✗ 🐾 SC

★ ★ **HOWARD JOHNSON LODGE.** *US 202N & S Gulph Rd. 610/265-4500; FAX 610/337-0672.* 168 units, 2 story. S $59.50-$87.50; each addl $10; suites $99-$120; under 18 free; wkend rates. Crib free. TV; cable. Pool; wading pool, lifeguard. Complimentary con-

tinental bkfst in lobby. Restaurant adj. Ck-out noon. Coin lndry. Valet serv. Airport transportation. Some bathrm phones. Private patios, balconies. Cr cds: A, C, D, DS, MC, V.

≈ ✗ 🐾 SC

✔ ★ **McINTOSH INN.** *260 N Gulph Rd. 610/768-9500; FAX 610/768-0225.* 212 rms, 7 story. S $48.95; D $53.95-$58.95; each addl $3. Crib free. TV. Complimentary coffee. Restaurant adj open 24 hrs. Ck-out 11 am. Valet serv Mon-Fri. Cr cds: A, C, D, MC, V.

D ≈ 🐾 SC

Motor Hotels

✔ ★ ★ **COMFORT INN-VALLEY FORGE.** *550 W DeKalb (US 202N). 610/962-0700; res: 800/222-0222; FAX 610/962-0218.* 121 rms, 5 story. S, D $49-$95; under 18 free. Crib free. Pet accepted, some restrictions. TV; cable, in-rm movies avail. Complimentary continental bkfst. Restaurant open 24 hrs. Ck-out noon. Coin lndry. Meeting rm. Concierge. Airport transportation. Exercise equipt; weights, bicycle, treadmill. Bathrm phones, refrigerators, minibars. Cr cds: A, C, D, DS, ER, JCB, MC, V.

D 🐾 ✗ ≈ 🐾 SC

★ ★ **HOLIDAY INN-KING OF PRUSSIA.** *260 Mall Blvd. 610/265-7500; FAX 610/265-4076.* 305 rms, 5 story. S, D $95-$114; each addl $10; under 18 free. Crib free. Pet accepted, some restrictions; $10. TV. Indoor pool; lifeguard. Restaurant 6:30 am-10 pm. Rm serv. Bar 11-2 am. Ck-out noon. Meeting rms. Bellhops. Valet serv. Gift shop. Barber, beauty shop. Exercise rm; instructor, weights, bicycles, whirlpool, sauna, steam rm. Cr cds: A, C, D, DS, MC, V.

D 🐾 ≈ ✗ 🐾 ≈ 🐾 SC

Hotels

★ ★ ★ **GUEST QUARTERS.** *(888 Chesterbrook Blvd, Wayne 19087) I-76 exit 26B to US 202S, at Chesterbrook exit; adj to Valley Forge Historical Park. 610/647-6700; FAX 610/889-9420.* 229 suites, 5 story. Suites $130-$150; each addl $20; under 18 free; wkend rates. Crib free. TV; cable. Indoor pool; whirlpool, sauna, poolside serv, lifeguard. Coffee in rms. Restaurant 6:30-9:30 am, 11:30 am-2:30 pm, 5:30-10 pm; Fri, Sat to 11 pm; Sun 7 am-2 pm, 5:30-9 pm. Bar 11:30 am-11 pm, wkends to 1 am; entertainment Wed-Sat. Ck-out noon. Meeting rms. Gift shop. Airport, RR station, bus depot transportation. Tennis privileges. Exercise equipt; weights, bicycles, whirlpool, sauna. Refrigerators, wet bars, bathrm phones. Cr cds: A, C, D, DS, JCB, MC, V.

D 🐾 ≈ ✗ ≈ 🐾

★ ★ **HILTON VALLEY FORGE.** *251 W DeKalb Pike. 610/337-1200; FAX 610/337-2224.* 340 rms, 9 story. S, D $89-$99; each addl $10; suites $130-$475; under 16 free; wkend rates. Crib free. TV; cable. Indoor/outdoor pool; lifeguard. Restaurants 6:30 am-11 pm. Bars 11:30-2 am; entertainment Tues-Sat. Ck-out noon. Meeting rms. Concierge. Gift shop. Garage parking. Airport, bus depot transportation. Exercise equipt; weights, bicycles, whirlpool, sauna. ***LUXURY LEVEL*** . 36 rms, 6 suites. S $114-$134; D $134; suites $250-$475. Concierge. Private lounge, honor bar. Wet bars. Bathrm phones. In-rm whirlpool. Complimentary continental bkfst, refreshments. Cr cds: A, C, D, DS, ER, JCB, MC, V.

D ≈ ✗ ✗ 🐾 SC

★ ★ **SHERATON PLAZA.** *1200 First Avenue. 610/265-1500; FAX 610/768-3290.* 160 rms, 6 story, 70 suites. S, D $118-$128; each addl $10; suites $135-$145; wkend rates. Crib free. TV; cable. Heated pool; wading pool, poolside serv, lifeguard. Restaurant 6:30 am-10:30 pm. Bar 11-1 am; entertainment Tue-Sat. Ck-out noon. Meeting rms. Concierge. Gift shop. Airport transportation. Lighted tennis. Exercise rm; instructor, weights, bicycles, whirlpool, sauna, steam rm. Bathrm phones, minibars; wet bars in suites. Connected to Sheraton-Valley

Forge Hotel by convention center. Cr cds: A, C, D, DS, ER, JCB, MC, V.

★★ **SHERATON-VALLEY FORGE.** *1150 First Ave.* 610/337-2000; FAX 610/768-3222. 326 rms, 15 story. S $107; D $113; each addl $12; suites $150-$175; under 18 free. Crib $5. TV; cable. Heated pool; wading pool, poolside serv, lifeguard. Restaurant 6:30 am-11 pm; wkends to midnight. Bars 11-2 am; Las Vegas revues, dancing Tues-Sat. Ck-out noon. Meeting rms. Barber, beauty shop. Airport, RR station, bus depot transportation. Tennis. Exercise rm; instructor, weights, bicycles, whirlpool, sauna, steam rm. Minibars. Connected to Sheraton Plaza Hotel by convention center. Cr cds: A, C, D, DS, ER, JCB, MC, V.

★★ **STOUFFER'S VALLEY FORGE.** *480 N Gulph Rd.* 610/337-1800; FAX 610/337-4506. 288 rms, 6 story. S, D $125-$165; suites $295-$495; under 18 free; wkend packages. Crib free. TV; cable. Pool; poolside serv, lifeguard. Complimentary morning coffee. Restaurant 6:30 am-10 pm; also dining rm. Rm serv 24 hrs. Bar 3 pm-1 am. Ck-out 1 pm. Convention facilities. Gift shop. Airport, RR station, bus depot transportation. Lighted tennis. Exercise equipt; weights, bicycles. Minibars. Private patios, balconies. Many rms overlook pool. Mall and Valley Forge Park adj. *LUXURY LEVEL : THE CLUB.* 20 rms. S, D $145-$165. Private lounge, honor bar. Complimentary continental bkfst, refreshments, newspaper. Cr cds: A, C, D, DS, ER, JCB, MC, V.

★★ **WAYNE.** *(139 E Lancaster Ave, Wayne 19087) S on US 202, S on PA 252 to US 30; from Blue Rte (I-476), exit 5 to US 30W.* 610/687-5000; FAX 610/687-8387. 35 rms, 6 story. S $105-$120; D $115-$130; each addl $10; suites $150; under 12 free; wkly rates. Crib free. TV; cable. Complimentary continental bkfst. Restaurant (see TAQUET). Bar 11:30 am-midnight. Ck-out noon. Meeting rms. Concierge. Airport, RR station transportation. Restored Victorian building (1906) with ornate furnishings, antiques. Cr cds: A, D, MC, V.

Restaurants

★★★ **A.T. SAMUELS.** *(503 W Lancaster Ave, Wayne) S on US 202, S on PA 252, E on US 30.* 610/687-2840. Hrs: 11:30 am-2:30 pm, 5-10 pm. Closed Jan 1, Dec 25. Res required. Contemporary Amer menu. Bar. Wine list. A la carte entrees: lunch $8-$14, dinner $17-$24. Specializes in seafood, fowl. Own desserts. Pianist, jazz. Parking. Outdoor dining. French country decor. Cr cds: A, C, D, DS, MC, V.

★★★ **KENNEDY-SUPPLEE MANSION.** *1100 W Valley Forge Rd, opp main entrance to Valley Forge National Historical Park.* 610/337-3777. Hrs: 11:30 am-2 pm, 5:30-10 pm; Mon from 5:30 pm; Sat 5:30-10:30 pm. Closed Sun; Dec 25. Res accepted. Continental menu. Bar. Semi-a la carte: lunch $7-$15, dinner $18-$26. French & Northern Italian cuisine. Own baking. Valet parking. 8 dining rooms in mansion (1850s). Crystal chandeliers, original artwork. Jacket (dinner). Cr cds: A, MC, V.

★★ **LA FOURCHETTE.** *(110 N Wayne Ave, Wayne) S on US 202, S on PA 252, E on US 30.* 610/687-8333. Hrs: 6-10 pm; Sat from 5:30 pm; Sun brunch 11 am-2:30 pm. Closed major hols. Res accepted. Classical seasonal French menu. Bar 6 pm-midnight. Wine cellar. A la carte entrees: dinner $18-$28. Sun brunch $11.75-$18.75. Specializes in seafood, lamb, game. Own pastries. Formal atmosphere. Jacket. Cr cds: A, C, D, MC, V.

★★ **TAQUET.** *(See Wayne Hotel)* 610/687-5005. Hrs: 11:30 am-2:30 pm, 5:30-10 pm; Fri & Sat to 10:30 pm; Sun 5-9 pm; Sun brunch 11 am-2 pm. Closed Jan 1, Dec 25. Res accepted. French menu. Bar. Semi-a la carte: lunch $8-$16.50, dinner $15-$19.75. Sun brunch $15-$27.50. Specializes in venison, seasonal fish, roasted Cornish hen, crème brulée. Parking. Outdoor dining. Victorian decor. Totally nonsmoking. Cr cds: A, C, D, MC, V.

★★★ **VILLA STRAFFORD.** *(115 Strafford Ave, Wayne) S on US 202, S on PA 252, E on US 30.* 610/964-1116. Hrs: 11:30 am-2:30 pm, 5:30-10 pm. Closed Sun; Jan 1, Dec 25. Res accepted. Continental menu. Bar. A la carte entrees: lunch $9-$14, dinner $13.95-$24.95. Specialties: rack of lamb, lobster Française. Own pasta, pastries, desserts. Jazz Fri-Sat. Parking. Mansion built 1909. Cr cds: A, D, MC, V.

Kulpsville (E-9)

Pop: 1,200 (est) **Elev:** 290 ft **Area code:** 215 **Zip:** 19443

What to See and Do

Morgan Log House (1695). E on PA 63, then N on Troxel Rd, E on Snyder Rd and N on Weikel Rd; house is on Weikel Rd, between Snyder & Allentown Rds. Built by the grandfather of General Daniel Morgan and Daniel Boone, this is the oldest and finest surviving medieval-style log house in the country. Partially restored; authentic early 18th-century furnishings. Guided tours (late Apr-Nov, wkends; other times by appt). Phone 368-2480. ¢¢

(For further information contact the Valley Forge Country Convention & Visitors Bureau, 600 W Germantown Pike, Suite 130, Plymouth Meeting, 19462; 610/834-1550.)

(See Norristown, Philadelphia)

Motor Hotel

★★ **HOLIDAY INN.** *1750 Sumneytown Pike, at exit 31 of PA Tpke NE extension.* 215/368-3800; FAX 215/368-7824. 185 rms, 4 story. S $76-$81; D $81-$86; each addl $6; suites $95-$100. Crib free. TV; cable. Pool; poolside serv, lifeguard. Restaurant 7 am-2 pm, 5:30-10 pm. Rm serv. Bar 4 pm-2 am; entertainment, dancing Wed-Sat. Ck-out noon. Meeting rms. Valet serv. Airport transportation. Exercise equipt; weights, treadmill. Cr cds: A, C, D, DS, JCB, MC, V.

Kutztown (E-9)

Founded: 1771 **Pop:** 4,704 **Elev:** 417 ft **Area code:** 610 **Zip:** 19530

Home of a popular folk festival, Kutztown is named for its founder, George Kutz. The town's population includes many descendants of the Pennsylvania Germans.

What to See and Do

Crystal Cave Park. 3 mi NW off US 222. Discovered in 1871; crystal formations, stalactites, stalagmites, natural bridges—all enhanced by indirect lighting. Also museum; nature trail; miniature golf (fee); theater. Cafe, rock shop, gift shop. Tours (Mar-Nov, daily). Phone 683-6765. ¢¢¢

Annual Event

Folk Festival. Festival grounds. Celebration of Pennsylvania Dutch folk culture; quilts, music, dancing and food of Plain and Fancy Dutch. Craftspeople make baskets, brooms, rugs, toleware and other handcrafts. Phone 683-8707. Late June-early July.

(For accommodations see Allentown, Reading, also see Hamburg, Pennsylvania Dutch Area)

Lancaster (F-8)

Settled: 1721 **Pop:** 55,551 **Elev:** 380 ft **Area code:** 717

Lancaster blends the industrial modern, the colonial past, and the Pennsylvania Dutch present. It is the heart of the Pennsylvania Dutch Area, one of the East's most colorful tourist attractions. To fully appreciate the area visitors should leave the main highways and travel on country roads, which Amish buggies share with automobiles. Lancaster was an important provisioning area for the armies of the French and Indian War and the Revolution. Its craftsmen turned out fine guns, which brought the city fame as the "arsenal of the Colonies." When Congress, fleeing from Philadelphia, paused here, September 27, 1777, the city was the national capital for one day. It was the state capital from 1799-1812.

What to See and Do

1. **Fulton Opera House** (1852). 12 N Prince St. One of the oldest American theaters, many legendary people have performed here. It is believed that more than one ghost haunts the theater's Victorian interior. Professional regional theatre; home of community theatre, opera and symphony organizations. Phone 397-7425.

2. **Wheatland** (1828). 1120 Marietta Ave, 1¹/₂ mi W on PA 23. Residence of President James Buchanan from 1848-68; restored Federal mansion with period rooms containing American Empire and Victorian furniture and decorative arts. Tours by costumed guides (Apr-Nov, daily). Christmas candlelight tours (early Dec). Sr citizen rate. Phone 392-8721. ¢¢

3. **Landis Valley Museum.** 2451 Kissel Hill Rd, 2¹/₂ mi N, off PA 272. Interprets Pennsylvania German rural life. Largest collection of Pennsylvania German objects in US; craft and living history demonstrations (May-Oct; see ANNUAL EVENTS); farmsteads, tavern, country store among other exhibit buildings. (Daily exc Mon; closed most hols) Sr citizen rate. Phone 569-0401. ¢¢¢

4. **Amish Farm and House.** 4¹/₂ mi E via US 30. Typical Amish farm in operation. Lecture on the Amish and tour through early 19th-century stone buildings furnished and decorated as old-order Amish household; waterwheels, windmill, hand-dug well, carriages, spring wagon, sleighs. (Daily; closed Dec 25) Phone 394-6185. ¢¢

5. **Hans Herr House** (1719). 1849 Hans Herr Dr, in Willow Street. Example of medieval Germanic architecture; served as an early Mennonite meetinghouse and colonial residence of the Herr family. Mennonite rural life exhibit; blacksmith shop. House tours. (Apr-Dec, daily exc Sun; closed major hols) Phone 464-4438. ¢¢

6. **Heritage Center of Lancaster County** (1795). Penn Square. Houses examples of early Lancaster County arts and crafts. Furniture, tall clocks, quilts, needlework, silver, pewter, fraktur, rifles. (May-mid-Nov, Tues-Sat; mid-Nov-mid-Dec, Fri-Sun) Sr citizen rate. Phone 299-6440. **Free.**

7. **Franklin and Marshall College** (1787). (1,810 students) College Ave. Liberal arts college. Rothman Gallery showcases Pennsylvania-German artifacts: quilts, Fraktur and stoneware. More than 200 varieties of trees, plants and shrubs on grounds. Tours of campus. Phone 291-3981. Also here are

   North Museum. General science and natural history; planetarium shows (Sat & Sun); children's Discovery Room; film series;

monthly art exhibits. (Sept-Dec, Feb-June, Wed-Sun; July-Aug, Sat & Sun) Phone 291-3942. Planetarium shows ¢

Joseph R. Grundy Observatory. An 11-inch refractor and 16-inch reflecting telescope demonstrations. Phone 394-3544. **Free.**

8. **Historic Rock Ford** (1794). 3 mi S on Rock Ford Rd, off S Duke St at Lancaster County Park. Preserved home of General Edward Hand, Revolutionary War commander, member of Continental Congress. (Apr-Oct, daily exc Mon) Phone 392-7223. ¢¢ Fee includes

   Kauffman Museum. Collection of folk art & crafts; antique pewter, rifles, copper and tinware collections housed in restored 18th-century barn. (Apr-Oct, daily exc Mon)

9. **Strasburg Rail Road.** 8 mi SE via US 30, PA 896, 741, in Strasburg. Railroad runs 4¹/₂ mi to Paradise. Picnic stop. This 160-year-old line uses late 19th-century coaches, various steam locomotives. (Mid-Mar-Nov, daily; winter, wkends) Phone 687-7522. ¢¢¢ Adj is

   Railroad Museum of Pennsylvania. More than 50 locomotives, freight and passenger cars dating from 1825; audiovisual exhibits; railroading memorabilia. Picnicking. (Mar-Oct, daily; rest of yr, daily exc Mon; closed some hols) Sr citizen rate. Phone 687-8628. ¢¢¢

10. **Sturgis Pretzel House.** 9 mi N via PA 501, 772 at 219 E Main St, in Lititz. First US commercial pretzel bakery (1861), restored as museum. Early equipment (also modern plant); pretzel-making demonstrations, visitors may try twisting pretzels; outlet store. (Daily exc Sun; closed Jan 1, Thanksgiving, Dec 25) Phone 626-4354 or 800/227-9342. ¢

11. **Candy Americana Museum.** 5 mi N via PA 501 at Wilbur Chocolate Co, 48 N Broad St, in Lititz. Antique candy production equipment, confectionery molds, unusual candy containers; outlet store. (Daily exc Sun; closed Labor Day, Thanksgiving, Dec 25 & 26) Phone 626-0967. **Free.**

12. **Mennonite Information Center.** E on US 30, 2209 Millstream Rd. Tourist information; interpretation of Mennonite and Amish origins, beliefs. Free video. Guided tours arranged (fee). (Daily exc Sun; closed Jan 1, Thanksgiving, Dec 25) Phone 299-0954. **Free.** Also here is

   Hebrew Tabernacle Reproduction. Tours (daily exc Sun; closed Jan 1, Thanksgiving, Dec 25). ¢¢

13. **Muddy Run Recreation Park of Philadelphia Electric Co.** 11 mi S on PA 272, then 3¹/₂ mi SW on PA 372. Covers 700 acres with 100-acre lake for boating (no power boats), rentals; fishing; picnicking, playgrounds, snack bar, concession; camping. Park (Apr-late Nov). Phone 284-4325. Camping per day ¢¢¢¢ Also here is

   Muddy Run Information Center of Philadelphia Electric Co. Energy and environmental center; exhibits and movies; illustrated talks periodically. (Apr-Nov, Wed-Sun; rest of yr, Tues-Sat) Phone 284-2538. **Free.**

14. **Mill Bridge Village.** S Ronks Rd, 4 mi E of jct US 30E, PA 462 in Strasburg. Restored historic colonial mill village with operating water-powered gristmill (1738); covered bridge; country crafts including broommaking, quilting, candlemaking, blacksmithing; quilt log cabin; Amish kitchen exhibit; music boxes and nickelodeons; horse-drawn hay & carriage rides; 1890s playground; picnicking. Amish house and schoolhouse tour avail. Oktoberfest (Sept & Oct wkends). Camp resort (daily; fee). Village (early Apr-Oct, daily; Nov-Dec, wkends only). Sr citizen rate. Phone 687-6521 or -8181 (camping reservations). ¢¢¢

15. **Dutch Wonderland.** 4 mi E via US 30. Family fun park with rides, botanical gardens, diving shows, shops. (Memorial Day-Labor Day, daily; Easter-Memorial Day & after Labor Day-Oct, Sat & Sun) Phone 291-1888. ¢¢¢¢-¢¢¢¢¢ Adj is

   National Wax Museum of Lancaster County Heritage. Figures re-create Lancaster County's history from the 1700s to present. (Daily; closed Dec 25) Sr citizen rate. Phone 393-3679. ¢¢

16. **Choo-Choo Barn, Traintown, USA.** E via US 30, then SE on PA 741, in Strasburg. A 1,700-square-foot layout of Lancaster County in miniature, featuring 14 operating trains and more than 130 animated and automated figures and vehicles. Gift shop. Picnicking. (Apr-Dec, daily) Phone 687-7911. ¢¢

17. **Toy Train Museum.** E via US 30, PA 896, 741, to Paradise Lane, in Strasburg. Trains from the 1880s to present; 5 operating layouts; movies; rare, unusual and specialty trains. (May-Oct, daily; Apr & Nov-mid-Dec, Sat & Sun) Sr citizen rate. Phone 687-8976. ¢¢

18. **The Watch and Clock Museum** of the National Association of Watch and Clock Collectors. 12 mi W via US 30, at 514 Poplar St in Columbia. Living museum of timepieces and related tools and memorabilia. Over 8,000 items representing the 1600s to the present. Extensive research library. Special exhibitions. (Tues-Sat; May-Sept, also Sun afternoons; closed major hols) Sr citizen rate. Phone 684-8261. ¢¢

19. **Robert Fulton Birthplace.** 14 mi S via PA 222. Robert Fulton, a great inventor and accomplished artist, is best known for having built the steamboat *Clermont*, which, in 1807, successfully made a trip up the Hudson River against winds and strong current. This little stone house, where Fulton was born, was nearly destroyed by fire about 1822; now refurbished. (Memorial Day-Labor Day, Sat & Sun) Phone 548-2679. ¢

20. **Bube's Brewery.** 102 N Market St, in Mount Joy. Historic brewery, built before the Civil War, is the only brewery left in the country that has remained intact since the mid-1800s; now operates as a restaurant (see THE CATACOMBS-ALOIS'S-THE BOTTLING WORKS). Guided tours take visitors 43 ft below the street into the brewery's aging vaults and passages, which were built from a cave and were part of what became known as the underground railroad; narrator tells about the history of the brewery and explains methods of producing beer in a Victorian-age brewery. Historic tours (Memorial Day-Labor Day, Sat & Sun). Restaurants are open all yr (free tour included with reservations for the Catacombs restaurant). Phone 653-2056. Historic tours (Memorial Day-Labor Day) ¢¢

21. **Gast Classic Motorcars Museum.** 5 mi SE via US 30, in Strasburg. Collection of 50 favorite antique, classic, sports and celebrity cars in changing display. Self-guided tours. (Daily; closed Jan 1, Dec 24 & 25) Phone 687-9500. ¢¢¢

22. **Twin Brook Winery.** 17 mi E via US 30, S on PA 41, E on Strasburg Rd, located in Gap at 5697 Strasburg Rd. Estate winery housed in a restored 19th-century barn offers wine tasting, tours of wine making facilities, visits to the vineyard; picnic areas. Outdoor concerts (late June-mid-Sept, Sat evenings); special events throughout the yr. (Apr-Dec, Mon-Sat, also Sun afternoons; rest of yr, Tues-Sat, also Sun afternoons) Phone 442-4915.

23. **Sightseeing tours.**

Historic Lancaster Walking Tour. 100 S Queen St. A 90-min tour of historic downtown area. Costumed guide narrates 50 points of architectural or historic interest covering 6 square blocks. (Apr-Oct, 2 tours daily, 1 in the morning and 1 in the afternoon; rest of yr, by appt only) Sr citizen rate. Phone 392-1776. ¢¢

Amish Country Tours. Tours of Pennsylvania Dutch country, Hershey and Philadelphia. Phone 392-8622. ¢¢¢¢-¢¢¢¢¢

Brunswick Tours. 2249 Lincoln Hwy E, at National Wax Museum (see #15). Private guide and auto tape tours. Phone 397-7541. ¢¢-¢¢¢¢¢

Abe's Buggy Rides. 6 mi E on PA 340, at 2596 Old Philadelphia Pike, Bird-in-Hand. A tour through Amish country in an Amish family carriage. (Daily) Contact PA Dutch Convention and Visitors Bureau for more information.

24. **CCInc Auto Tape Tours.** This 90-minute cassette offers a mile-by-mile self-guided tour of the Lancaster area. Written by experts, it describes the train museum at Strasburg and other points of interest; explains history and legends of the Mennonite, Amish and Dunker sects. Obtain at Dutch Wonderland (see #15); Old Mill

Stream Camping Manor, US 30; National Wax Museum, US 30; and Holiday Inn East, US 30 Bypass. Includes tape & player rental. Tape may also be purchased directly from CCInc, PO Box 227, 2 Elbrook Dr, Allendale, NJ 07401; 201/236-1666. ¢¢¢¢

(For information on walking, auto or historic tours and other general information, contact the Pennsylvania Dutch Convention & Visitors Bureau, 501 Greenfield Rd, 17601; 299-8901 or 800/735-2629.)

Annual Events

Sheep Shearing. Amish Farm and House (see #4). Phone 394-6185. Last Thurs & Fri Apr.

Victorian Circus and Fair. Takes place at Wheatland (see #2). Festivities include crafts and 19th-century activities. Phone 392-8721. Mid-May.

Landis Valley Fair. Landis Valley Museum (see #3). Living history; pie-eating contests, craft demonstrations. Phone 569-0401. 1st wkend June.

Harvest Days. Landis Valley Museum (see #3). Demonstrations of more than 75 traditional craft and harvest time activities. Phone 569-0401. Columbus Day wkend.

Victorian Christmas Week. On grounds of Wheatland (see #2). Phone 392-8721. Early Dec.

Seasonal Event

Music at Gretna. 15 mi N via PA 72, in Mt Gretna. Chamber music and jazz; well-known artists. Phone 964-3836. Mid-June-early Sept.

(See Bird-in-Hand, Cornwall, Ephrata, Lebanon, Reading, Wrightsville, York)

Motels

★ **1722 MOTOR LODGE.** *1722 Old Philadelphia Pike (17602).* 717/397-4791. 21 rms. Late June-Labor Day: S, D $48-$59; each addl $5; varied lower rates rest of yr. Crib $4. TV; cable. Playground. Complimentary continental bkfst. Restaurant nearby. Ck-out 11 am. Coin lndry. Sundries. Lawn games. Picnic tables. Cr cds: A, MC, V.

🏊 🔥

✔ ★ ★ **COUNTRY LIVING.** *2406 Old Philadelphia Pike (17602).* 717/295-7295. 34 rms, 2 story. Early June-Oct: S, D $41-$78; each addl $5; suites $85-$125; higher rates hol wkends; lower rates rest of yr. Crib free. TV; cable. Complimentary continental bkfst (May-Oct wkends), coffee. Restaurant nearby. Ck-out noon. Whirlpool. Cr cds: MC, V.

🏊 🔥

★ ★ **DAYS INN.** *30 Keller Ave (17601).* 717/299-5700; FAX 717/295-1907. 193 rms, 2-3 story. S $60-$85; D $70-$95; each addl $10; under 12 free. Crib free. Pet accepted, some restrictions; $10. TV; cable. 2 pools, 1 indoor; wading pool, poolside serv, lifeguard. Playground. Restaurant 7-11 am, 5-9 pm. Bar 11 am-midnight. Ck-out noon. Coin lndry. Meeting rms. Tennis. Game rm. Some refrigerators. Balconies. Cr cds: A, C, D, DS, MC, V.

🏌 ⛷ 🏊 ✈ 🏊 🔥 SC

✔ ★ **GARDEN SPOT.** *2291 US 30E (17602).* 717/394-4736. 18 rms. S $29-$49; D $32-$58; each addl $4; under 5 free; higher rates hols. Closed Dec-Feb. Crib $4. TV; cable. Restaurant 7:30-11 am. Ck-out 11:30 am. Gift shop. Cr cds: A, DS, MC, V.

🏊 🔥

★ ★ **HOWARD JOHNSON.** *2100 Lincoln Hwy E (17602).* 717/397-7781; FAX 717/397-6340. 112 rms, 2 story. Mid-June-early Sept: S $48-$75; D $68-$88; each addl $7; higher rates major hols; lower rates rest of yr. Crib free. TV; cable, in-rm movies avail. Indoor pool; wading pool, lifeguard. Restaurant 6 am-midnight. Bar from 11 am. Ck-out 11 am. Meeting rms. Sundries. Shopping arcade. Game rm. Private patios, balconies. Cr cds: A, C, D, DS, ER, JCB, MC, V.

★ ★ ★ **LANCASTER-HILTON GARDEN INN.** *101 Granite Run (17601).* 717/560-0880; FAX 717/560-5400. 155 rms, 2 story. May-Oct: S $84-$120; D $89-$130; suites $200; family rates; lower rates rest of yr. TV. Indoor pool; lifeguard. Complimentary continental bkfst. Complimentary coffee in rms. Restaurant 6:30 am-2 pm, 5-10 pm. Bar 11:30 am-midnight. Coin lndry. Meeting rms. Sundries. Exercise equipt; weights, bicycles, whirlpool. Cr cds: A, C, D, DS, MC, V.

★ ★ **RAMADA-LANCASTER.** *2250 Lincoln Hwy E (17602).* 717/393-5499; FAX 717/293-1014. 166 rms, 5 story. Mid-June-Oct: S, D $72-$109; each addl $10; under 18 free; lower rates rest of yr. Crib free. Pet accepted, some restrictions. TV; cable. 2 pools, 1 indoor; sauna. Playground. Ck-out 11 am. Coin lndry. Meeting rms. Tennis. 27-hole golf privileges, pro, putting green, driving range. Game rm. Lawn games. Refrigerators; many bathrm phones. Balconies. Picnic tables. Cr cds: A, C, D, DS, MC, V.

★ ★ **ROCKVALE VILLAGE INN.** *24 S Willowdale Dr (17602).* 717/293-9500; res: 800/524-3817; FAX 717/293-8558. 113 rms, 2 story. Late June-Oct: S $69-$79; D $79-$89; each addl $5; under 18 free; lower rates rest of yr. Crib free. TV; cable. Pool; poolside serv, lifeguard. Restaurant 7 am-9 pm. Bar noon-midnight. Ck-out 11 am. Meeting rm. Cr cds: A, C, D, DS, MC, V.

✔ ★ ★ **WESTFIELD INN.** *2929 Hempland Rd (17601), US 30W exit Centerville Rd.* 717/397-9300; res: 800/547-1395; FAX 717/295-9240. 84 rms, 2 story. July-Oct: S, D $49-$79; each addl $5; suites $59-$89; under 18 free; lower rates rest of yr. Crib free. TV; cable. Pool; lifeguard. Complimentary coffee in lobby. Restaurant nearby. Ck-out 11 am. Coin lndry. Some refrigerators. Cr cds: A, C, D, DS, MC, V.

★ ★ ★ **WILLOW VALLEY FAMILY RESORT & CONFERENCE CENTER.** *2416 Willow St Pike (17602).* 717/464-2711; res: 800/444-1714; FAX 717/464-4784. 353 rms, 5 story. Mid-June-early Sept, hol wkends: S, D $97-$121; each addl $8; ages 6-11, $4; under 6 free; lower rates rest of yr. Crib free. TV; cable, in-rm movies avail. 3 pools, 2 indoor; lifeguard. Playground. Restaurants 6 am-9 pm. Ck-out noon. Free lndry facilities. Meeting rms. Shopping arcade. Free airport, RR station, bus depot transportation. Lighted tennis. 9-hole golf, putting green. Exercise equipt; weight machine, bicycles, whirlpool, sauna, steam rm. Game rm. Some private patios, balconies. Country view; large landscaped grounds. Cr cds: MC, V.

Motor Hotels

★ ★ ★ **BEST WESTERN EDEN RESORT INN.** *222 Eden Rd (17601).* 717/569-6444; FAX 717/569-4208. 275 rms, 3 story. July-Sept: S, D $79-$119; each addl $10; suites $165; under 18 free; varied lower rates rest of yr. Crib free. TV; cable. 2 pools, 1 indoor; poolside serv, lifeguard. Restaurant 6:30 am-11 pm; wkends to midnight. Rm serv. Bar 11-2 am; entertainment, dancing. Ck-out noon. Meeting rms. Valet serv. Gift shop. Lighted tennis. Exercise equipt; weights, bicycles, whirlpool, saunas. Lawn games. Some balconies. Cr cds: A, C, D, DS, MC, V.

★ ★ **HOLIDAY INN EAST.** *521 Greenfield Rd (17601), opp Tourist Bureau.* 717/299-2551; FAX 717/397-0220. 189 rms, 4 story. Early May-Nov: S $69-$79; D $79-$99; under 18 free; lower rates rest of yr. Crib free. TV; cable. 2 pools, 1 indoor. Restaurant 6:30 am-2 pm,

5-10 pm. Rm serv. Bar 4 pm-2 am; dancing. Ck-out noon. Meeting rms. Valet serv. Sundries. Tennis. Cr cds: A, C, D, DS, ER, JCB, MC, V.

Hotel

✔ ★ **HOTEL BRUNSWICK.** *PO Box 749 (17603), at jct Chestnut & Queen Sts.* 717/397-4801; res: 800/233-0182; FAX 717/397-4991. 222 rms, 7 story. S $50-$78; D $60-$88; each addl $6; under 18 free; monthly, wkly, wkend rates; golf plan; lower rates Dec-Mar. Crib free. Pet accepted; $100. TV; cable. Indoor pool; lifeguard. Restaurant 7 am-1:30 pm, 5-9 pm. Bar; entertainment. Ck-out noon. Coin lndry. Meeting rms. Free garage parking. Exercise equipt; weights, bicycles. Some refrigerators avail. Cr cds: A, C, D, DS, MC, V.

Inns

★ ★ ★ **CAMERON ESTATE.** *(1895 Donegal Springs Rd, Mount Joy 17552) 15 mi W on PA 283, Rheems exit, Colebrook Rd to Donegal Springs Rd.* 717/653-1773; FAX 717/653-9432. 18 rms, 2 share bath, 3 story. No rm phones. Apr-Nov: S, D $65-$110; lower rates rest of yr. Children over 12 yrs only. TV in sitting rm. Pool privileges. Complimentary continental bkfst & tea. Restaurant (see CAMERON ESTATE INN). Ck-out 11 am, ck-in 1 pm. Tennis privileges. Brick Federal structure (1805), on 15-acre estate, was acquired as a country house, then rebuilt and expanded, by Simon Cameron, political kingmaker, US Senator and Abraham Lincoln's first secretary of war. Three generations of the Cameron family lived on the estate. Interior features many antiques and Oriental rugs. Cr cds: A, D, DS, MC, V.

★ ★ ★ **GENERAL SUTTER.** *(14 E Main St, Lititz 17543) 6 mi N via PA 501, on the Square.* 717/626-2115. 12 rms, 3 story. S, D $70-90. Crib $4. TV; cable. Dining rm 7 am-9 pm; Sun 8 am-8 pm. Bar 11 am-11 pm. Ck-out noon, ck-in 2 pm. Spacious brick-lined patio. Built 1764; antique country and Victorian furniture. Fireplace in parlor. Cr cds: A, DS, MC, V.

★ ★ **HISTORIC STRASBURG.** *(PA 896, Strasburg 17579) 8 mi SE via US 30, PA 896.* 717/687-7691; res: 800/872-0201; FAX 717/687-6098. 101 rms in 5 buildings, 2 story. Apr-Nov: S $75-$85; D $85-$95; each addl $10; suites $110-$120; under 13 free; lower rates rest of yr. Crib $5. Pet accepted; $30. TV; cable. Pool. Playground. Restaurant (see WASHINGTON HOUSE). Bar 11:30 am-11 pm. Ck-out noon. Meeting rms. Sundries. Gift shop. Lawn games. Balconies. On 58 acres. Cr cds: A, C, D, DS, MC, V.

★ ★ ★ **KING'S COTTAGE.** *1049 E King St (17602).* 717/397-1017; res: 800/747-8717. 8 rms. Rm phones avail. S, D $80-$135. Children over 12 yrs only. TV; cable in library. Complimentary full bkfst, tea/sherry. Restaurant nearby. Ck-out 11 am, ck-in 4 pm. Restored Spanish/mission-style house (1913); library, antiques, fireplaces. Totally nonsmoking. Cr cds: DS, MC, V.

Restaurants

★ ★ **CAMERON ESTATE INN.** *(See Cameron Estate Inn)* 717/653-1773. Hrs: 6-10 pm; Sun champagne brunch 10:30 am-1:45 pm. Closed Dec 25. Res required. Continental menu. Bar. Semi-a la carte: dinner $15.95-$31.95. Sun brunch $5.95-$9.95. Specialties: chicken and shrimp Versailles, veal Cameron, filet mignon stuffed with smoked oysters. Parking. In mansion, dating from 1805, that was owned and rebuilt by Simon Cameron, Abraham Lincoln's first secretary of war; fireplace, sun porch. Cr cds: A, C, D, DS, MC, V.

★★ THE CATACOMBS-ALOIS'S-THE BOTTLING WORKS. *(102 N Market St, Mount Joy) W on PA 283, exit Mount Joy, 2 mi W on PA 230, turn right at third light.* 717/653-2056. Hrs: 11 am-2 pm, 5:30-9 pm; Fri & Sat to 10 pm; Sun 4:30-9 pm. Closed some major hols. Res required. Continental menu. Bar. Semi-a la carte: lunch $2.95-$7.45. Complete meals: dinner $15.95-$26.95. Specializes in shrimp, roast duck. Entertainment Fri, Sat. Parking. In old Victorian hotel brewery (1876); dining areas are located in original bottling plant, original dining rms of the hotel portion (Victorian decor) and below ground, in the cellars (medieval atmosphere, costumes, entertainment). Guided tours. Cr cds: A, DS, MC, V.

★★ CENTER CITY GRILLE. *10 S Prince St, in Stevens Courtyard.* 717/299-3456. Hrs: 4 pm-2 am. Res accepted. Bar to 1 am; Fri & Sat to 2 am. Semi-a la carte: dinner $8.95-$24.95. Specializes in seafood, beef, chicken, pasta. Entertainment Fri & Sat. Cr cds: A, C, D, DS, MC, V.

★★ GROFF'S FARM. *(650 Pinkerton Rd, Mount Joy) 11 mi SW via US 30, PA 283 (1st Mt Joy exit) and PA 772 to Pinkerton Rd, 1 mi S.* 717/653-2048. Hrs: 11:30 am-1:30 pm, sittings 5 & 7:30 pm; Sat 11:30 am-1:30 pm, sittings 5 & 8 pm. Closed Sun, Mon; Dec 24-26; also wkdays in Jan. Res required. Serv bar. Wine list. A la carte entrees: lunch $2.50-$7.50, dinner $12.50-$25. Complete meals: dinner $13-$25. Child's meals. Specialties: chicken Stoltzfus, home-cured ham, fresh seafood, prime rib. Own pastries. Parking. Located in family farmhouse built in 1756. Family-owned. Cr cds: A, C, D, DS, MC, V.

★★★ HAYDN ZUG'S. *(1987 State St, East Petersburg) N on PA 72.* 717/569-5746. Hrs: 11:30 am-2 pm, 5-9 pm; Sat from 5 pm. Closed Sun; most major hols. Res accepted. Bar 5-9 pm. A la carte entrees: lunch $4.25-$6.95, dinner $10.75-$22.50. Specialties: cheesy chowder, grilled lamb tenderloin, crab cakes. Own pastries. Parking. Colonial setting. Family-operated. Cr cds: A, MC, V.

★★★ LOG CABIN. *(11 Lehoy Forest Dr, Leola) 6 mi NW on PA 272.* 717/626-1181. Hrs: 5-10 pm; Sun 4-9 pm. Closed major hols. Res accepted. Bar. Wine cellar. Semi-a la carte: dinner $14.50-$28. Child's meals. Specializes in charcoal-broiled steak, fresh seafood. Own baking. Parking. Log cabin in woods; paintings, fireplace. Entry through covered "kissing" bridge. Cr cds: A, MC, V.

★★ WASHINGTON HOUSE. *(See Historic Strasburg Inn)* 717/687-9211. Hrs: 7 am-2 pm, 5-9 pm; Sun 7 am-9 pm. Res accepted. Continental menu. Bar 11:30 am-9 pm. A la carte entrees: bkfst $2.25-$5.45, lunch $5.25-$12.50, dinner $10.95-$22.95. Sun buffet: dinner $12.95. Child's meals. Specializes in seafood, prime rib. Parking. Colonial decor. Cr cds: A, C, D, DS, MC, V.

SC

✔ ★★★ WINDOWS ON STEINMAN PARK. *16-18 W King St, adj to Steinman Park.* 717/295-1316. Hrs: 11:30 am-2 pm, 5-9 pm; Fri to 10 pm; Sat 5-10 pm; Sun brunch to 2 pm. Closed major hols. Res accepted. French menu. Bar. Wine cellar. A la carte entrees: lunch $4.50-$9.75, dinner $18-$27. Sun brunch $17.95. Specialties: Caesar salad for 2, Dover sole, roast rack of lamb. Own pastries. Pianist. Parking. 3 dining levels; overlooks park. Cr cds: A, C, D, MC, V.

Lebanon (E-7)

Founded: 1756 **Pop:** 24,800 **Elev:** 460 ft **Area code:** 717 **Zip:** 17042

This industrial city, steeped in German traditions, is the marketplace for colorful Lebanon County. Many Hessians were confined here after the Battle of Trenton. Today Lebanon bologna factories and food processing are important to the city's economy. Master planning for redevelopment of city and county combines with the traditional atmosphere to make this a charming community.

What to See and Do

1. **Stoy Museum of the Lebanon County Historical Society.** 924 Cumberland St. Local historical museum containing 30 permanent room and shop displays on 3 floors of house built in 1773 and used as 1st county courthouse; research library. Tours. (Daily exc Sat; closed Sun & Mon of hol wkends) Sr citizen rate. Phone 272-1473. ¢¢

2. **Coleman Memorial Park.** 2 mi N on PA 72, W Maple St. This 100-acre former estate has swimming pool (Memorial Day-Labor Day, daily; fee), tennis courts, athletic fields, picnic facilities. Fee for some activities. Park (yr round, daily). Phone 228-4470. **Free.**

3. **Stoevers Dam Recreational Area.** 2 mi N on PA 343, Miller St. A 153-acre park with 52-acre lake for fishing; boating (electric motors only), canoeing. A 1.5-mile trail for jogging, hiking, bicycling. Primitive camping (permit only; fee). Nature trails; nature barn (Apr-Oct, daily exc Mon; winter by appt); community park (all yr, daily). Phone 228-4470. **Free.**

4. **Fort Zeller.** 11 mi E on US 422, then S on PA 419, in Newmanstown. One of state's oldest existing forts; originally built of logs, rebuilt of stone in 1745; has 12-ft wide Queen Anne fireplace in kitchen. (By appt) Donation. Phone 610/589-4301 or 717/272-0662.

5. **Middlecreek Wildlife Management Area.** 11 mi SE on PA 897 to Kleinfeltersville, then 1 mi S. A 5,144-acre tract provides refuge for waterfowl, forest and farmland wildlife. Permit and open hunting areas, inquire at Visitor Center for regulations. Fishing; boating (mid-May-mid-Sept). Hiking. Picnicking. Visitor Center (Mar-Nov, daily exc Mon). Braille trail for the visually impaired. Phone 733-1512. **Free.**

6. **Industrial tour. The Daniel Weaver Company.** 15th Ave & Weavertown Rd. Manufacturers, since 1885, of Weaver's Famous Lebanon Bologna and other wood-smoked gourmet meats; smoked in 100-year-old outdoor smokehouses. Samples. (Daily exc Sun) Phone 274-6100 or 800/WEAVERS. **Free.**

(For further information contact the Lebanon Valley Tourist & Visitors Bureau, 625 Quentin Rd, PO Box 329; 272-8555.)

Annual Event

Bologna Fest. Festival features Lebanon bologna, Pennsylvania Dutch food, arts & crafts, entertainment. Fri-Sun, usually 2nd wkend Aug.

(See Cornwall, Ephrata, Hershey, Lancaster, Pennsylvania Dutch Area)

Motel

★★★ LANTERN LODGE. *(411 N College St, Myerstown 17067) 7 mi E on PA 501 at US 422.* 717/866-6536; res: 800/262-5564; FAX 717/866-6536, ext. 112. 79 rms, 2 story. S $55-$75; D $70-$85; each addl $10; suites $100-$225; cottage $125-$165. Crib free. TV. Playground. Complimentary coffee in rms. Restaurant 7 am-10 pm. Rm serv. Ck-out 11 am. Meeting rms. Bellhops. Barber, beauty shop. Valet serv. Sundries. Tennis. Early Amer decor. Cr cds: A, C, D, MC, V.

Motor Hotel

★ ★ ★ **QUALITY INN OF LEBANON VALLEY.** *625 Quentin Rd, on PA 72.* 717/273-6771; FAX 717/273-4882. 56 hotel rms, 74 motel rms, 5 story. Late May-Oct: S $76-$82; D $82-$100; each addl $7; under 18 free; lower rates rest of yr. Crib $5. TV; cable. Pool; lifeguard. Restaurant 7 am-9 pm. Rm serv. Bar 11-2 am; entertainment, dancing Fri & Sat. Ck-out noon. Meeting rms. Sundries. Barber. Game rm. Cr cds: A, C, D, DS, ER, JCB, MC, V.

Lewisburg (D-7)

Settled: 1785 **Pop:** 5,785 **Elev:** 460 ft **Area code:** 717 **Zip:** 17837

Home of Bucknell University (1846), this college community also has light industry. The Native American village of Old Muncy Town was located nearby before the region was opened by Ludwig (Lewis) Doerr.

What to See and Do

1. **Fort Augusta** (1757). 9 mi SE on PA 147, in Sunbury, at 1150 N Front St. Museum collection of Northumberland County Historical Society. (Mon, Wed, Fri & Sat) Phone 286-4083. ¢

2. **Packwood House Museum.** 15 N Water St. A 3-story, 27-room log and frame building begun in the late 18th century. Former hostelry houses a wide-ranging collection of Americana, period furnishings, textiles and decorative arts. Changing exhibits; museum shop. Tours. (Daily exc Mon; closed hols) Sr citizen rate. Phone 524-0323. ¢¢

3. **Slifer House Museum.** 1 mi N, on grounds of Lewisburg United Methodist Homes. Elaborate 3-story, 20-room Victorian mansion. First and second floors have been restored, complete with Victorian parlor, dining room, library, 5 bedrooms and the summer kitchen exhibit room. (Apr-Dec, daily exc Mon; rest of yr, Tues-Fri afternoons and by appt) Phone 524-2271, ext 124. ¢¢

(For further information contact the Union County Chamber of Commerce, 418 Market St; 524-2815.)

(See Danville, Williamsport)

Motels

★ ★ **BEST WESTERN COUNTRY CUPBOARD INN.** *Box 46, I-80 exit 30A, 5 mi S on US 15.* 717/524-5500; FAX 717/524-4291. 105 rms, 3 story. S $65-$93; D $71-$99; each addl $6; suites $99-$149; under 18 free; higher rates university events. Crib free. TV; cable. Heated pool; lifeguard. Complimentary continental bkfst. Restaurant adj 7 am-9 pm. Ck-out 11 am. Coin lndry. Meeting rms. Exercise equipt; weight machine, bicycle. Game rm. Refrigerator in suites. 5 blks to river. Cr cds: A, C, D, DS, MC, V.

★ ★ **DAYS INN-UNIVERSITY.** *PO Box 253, on US 15, 1 blk S of jct PA 192.* 717/523-1171; FAX 717/524-4667. 108 rms, 2 story. S $47.70-$60.30; D $52.50-$60.30; each addl $6; under 16 free. Crib free. TV; cable. Pool; lifeguard. Restaurant adj open 24 hrs. Ck-out noon. Exercise equipt; weight machine, bicycles. Cr cds: A, C, D, DS, MC, V.

Restaurant

✔ ★ ★ **COUNTRY CUPBOARD.** *Hafer Rd (US 15), 4 mi S of I-80 exit 30A.* 717/523-3211. Hrs: 7 am-9 pm. Closed Dec 25. Res accepted Mon-Fri. Semi-a la carte: bkfst $2.25-$5.50, lunch, dinner $4.99-$10.99. Buffet: bkfst (Sat, Sun), lunch (Mon-Sat) $5.49, dinner $8.49-$10.49. Child's meals. Specializes in poultry, ham. Country dining. Part of complex, with shops. Totally nonsmoking. Cr cds: DS, MC, V.

Lewistown (E-6)

Settled: 1754 **Pop:** 9,341 **Elev:** 520 ft **Area code:** 717

Surrounded by rich farmland and beautiful forested mountain ranges, Lewistown lies in the scenic Juniata River Valley, in the heart of central Pennsylvania. Lewistown retains the charm of its rustic surroundings, which yearly attract thousands of sportsmen and outdoor enthusiasts to the area's fine hunting, fishing and camping facilities. A large Amish population, which thrives on the farmland of the Kishacoquillas Valley, has contributed greatly to the area's culture and heritage.

What to See and Do

1. **Greenwood Furnace State Park.** 5 mi N on US 322, then 9 mi W on PA 655, then NW on PA 305. Remains of Greenwood Works, last iron furnace to operate in area (ca 1833-1904); restored stack. Approx 400 acres. Swimming beach; fishing. Hiking. Snowmobiling, ice-skating, ice fishing. Picnicking, playground, snack bar, store. Tent & trailer sites. Visitor center, interpretive program. Standard fees. Phone 814/667-3808.

2. **Reeds Gap State Park.** 8 mi N off US 322 & unnumbered road. Approx 200 acres. Swimming pool; fishing. Hiking. Picnicking, snack bar, store. Tent sites only. Phone 667-3622. Camping ¢¢¢-¢¢¢¢

3. **Brookmere Farm Vineyards.** Approx 5 mi N via US 322 then SW on PA 655, near Belleville. In 19th-century stone & wood barn. Winery tour, wine tasting; picnicking. (Mar-Dec, Mon-Sat, also Sun afternoons; rest of yr, daily exc Sun; closed hols) Phone 935-5380. **Free.**

(For further information contact the Juniata Valley Area Chamber of Commerce, 19 S Wayne St, 17044; 248-6713.)

Motel

✔ ★ ★ ★ **HOLIDAY INN.** *(US 322, Burnham 17009) just off US 322 at Burnham exit.* 717/248-4961; FAX 717/242-3013. 122 rms, 2 story. S $39-$55; D $44-$60; each addl $5; under 18 free. Crib free. Pet accepted. TV; cable. Pool; poolside serv, lifeguard. Restaurant 6 am-2 pm, 5-10 pm. Rm serv. Bar 4 pm-2 am. Ck-out noon. Meeting rms. Valet serv. Cr cds: A, C, D, DS, JCB, MC, V.

Ligonier (E-3)

Founded: 1816 **Pop:** 1,638 **Elev:** 1,200 ft **Area code:** 412 **Zip:** 15658

Fort Ligonier, built in 1758 by the British, was the scene of one of the key battles of the French and Indian War. It also served as a supply base during Pontiac's War in 1763. The town is now a center of dairying, farms, woodlands and summer and winter sports.

What to See and Do

1. **Fort Ligonier.** S Market St, on US 30, PA 711. Reconstructed 18th-century British fort; includes buildings with period furnishings. Museum houses outstanding French and Indian War collec-

tion, 18th-century artifacts; introductory film. (May-Oct, daily) (See ANNUAL EVENTS) Sr citizen rate. Phone 238-9701. ¢¢

2. **Forbes Road Gun Museum.** 4 mi N on PA 711. Collection of firearms from 1450 to the present, including Revolutionary and Civil War rifles, muskets. Picnic area; trailer facilities. (Daily) Sr citizen rate. Phone 238-9544. ¢

3. **Compass Inn Museum.** 3 mi E on US 30, in Laughlintown. A 1799 stagecoach stop; original log and stone inn authentically restored and furnished; log barn houses Conestoga wagon and stagecoach; cookhouse with beehive oven and fireplace; blacksmith shop contains working forge. (May-Oct, daily exc Mon) Phone 238-4983. ¢¢

4. **Idlewild Park.** 2 mi W on US 30. Amusement rides; entertainment; picnicking; children's play area; water park. (Memorial Day-late Aug, daily exc Mon) (See ANNUAL EVENTS) Phone 238-3666. ¢¢¢¢ Adj is

   Story Book Forest. Children's park with animals, people and buildings portraying nursery rhymes. (Memorial Day-late Aug, daily exc Mon) Phone 238-3666. Admission included with Idlewild Park.

5. **St Vincent Archabbey and College** (1846). (1,000 students) 8 mi W on US 30, in Latrobe. Includes Benedictine monastery, seminary and coeducational liberal arts college. St Vincent Theatre has performances at theater-in-the-round; for schedule phone 537-8900. Free self-guided tape tours. Phone 537-4560.

(For further information contact the Ligonier Valley Chamber of Commerce, Town Hall, 120 E Main St; 238-4200.)

Annual Events

Ligonier Highland Games & Gathering of the Clans of Scotland. Idlewild Park (see #4). Sports; massed pipe bands; Highland dancing competitions, Scottish fiddling; sheep dog, wool spinning & weaving demonstrations; genealogy booth, Scottish fair. Phone 238-3666 (Tues-Sun). 1st Sat after Labor Day.

Fort Ligonier Days (see #1). Living history program of the French and Indian War. Parade, pioneer craft demonstrations, food and special events. Usually 2nd wkend Oct.

Seasonal Event

Mountain Playhouse. 11 mi SE on US 30, then ½ mi N on US 985, in Jennerstown. Broadway shows in restored gristmill (1805). Matinees and evening performances. Phone 814/629-9201. Mid-May-mid-Oct.

(See Donegal, Greensburg, Johnstown)

Motels

✔ ★ **FORT LIGONIER MOTOR LODGE.** *US 30 E, 2 blks S on US 30, jct PA 711. 412/238-6677.* 35 rms, 2 story. May-Oct: S, D $49-$57; each addl $6; higher rates: wkends, special events; lower rates rest of yr. Crib $4. TV; cable. Pool. Complimentary coffee. Restaurant nearby. Ck-out 11 am. Sundries. Downhill/x-country ski 7 mi. Picnic tables. Trout stream. Cr cds: A, MC, V.

★★ **RAMADA INN-HISTORIC LIGONIER.** *216 W Loyalhanna St. 412/238-9545; FAX 412/238-9803.* 66 rms, 3 story. S, D $65-$95; each addl $6; suites $95-$150; under 19 free; ski plans. Crib free. TV; cable. Pool. Restaurant 6:30 am-10 pm. Rm serv. Bar 4 pm-2 am. Ck-out 11 am. Meeting rms. Cr cds: A, D, DS, MC, V.

Inn

★★ **GRANT HOUSE.** *244 W Church St. 412/238-5135.* 3 rms, some share bath. S, D $70-$75; each addl $20. TV in sitting rm. Complimentary bkfst. Ck-out 11 am, ck-in 2 pm. Airport transportation. Tennis. 18-hole golf privileges, pro, putting green. Picnic tables, grills. Antique furnished. Victorian mansion built 1888. No cr cds accepted.

Limerick (E-9)

Pop: 800 (est) **Elev:** 302 ft **Area code:** 610 **Zip:** 19468

What to See and Do

Spring Mountain Ski Area. 6 mi N, off PA 29 near Schwenksville. Triple, 3 double chairlifts, 2 rope tows; patrol, school, rentals; snowmaking; cafeteria. Longest run ½ mi; vertical drop 450 ft. (Mid-Dec-mid-Mar, daily) Also camping avail (fee; hookups). Phone 287-7900. ¢¢¢¢

(For further information contact the Valley Forge Convention & Visitors Bureau, 600 W Germantown Pike, Suite 130, Plymouth Meeting, 19462; 834-1550.)

(For accommodations see Pottstown, Reading, also see Norristown)

Lock Haven (C-6)

Founded: 1833 **Pop:** 9,230 **Elev:** 564 ft **Area code:** 717 **Zip:** 17745

Founded on the site of pre-Revolutionary Fort Reed, the community takes its name from two sources. The lock of the Pennsylvania Canal once crossed the West Branch of the Susquehanna River here, and the town was once a "haven" for the rafts and lumberjacks of nearby logging camps. Near the geographic center of the state, the town today is a center of commerce and small industry.

What to See and Do

1. **The Heisey Museum.** 362 E Water St. Victorian house-museum; early 1800s kitchen; ice house containing logging, farming and canal artifacts. (Tues-Fri; some Sun by appt) Phone 748-7254. ¢

2. **Fin, Fur & Feather Wildlife Museum.** 18 mi N via PA 664. Personal collection of animals from across the globe. More than 500 animals are mounted on display. (Mid-Apr-late Dec, daily; rest of yr, Fri-Sun; closed Dec 25) Phone 769-6620 or -6482. ¢¢

3. **Bull Run School House** (1899). 12 mi S via I-80, PA 880, exit 27. Only remaining one-room schoolhouse in county; fully restored with all of its original equipment, including double desks, schoolmaster's and recitation desks, Waterbury clock, bell. (May-Oct, Sat & Sun; rest of yr, by appt) Phone 893-4037. **Free.**

4. **Bucktail Natural Area.** Scenic area extends from mountain rim to mountain rim for 75 miles from Lock Haven N to Renovo and W to Emporium. Connecting the three towns and weaving through the park is PA 120, an outstanding drive through mountain scenery. Historic site W of Renovo commemorates Bucktail Trail, which served pioneers and Civil War volunteers. Fishing.

5. **Hyner View.** 22 mi NW on PA 120. At 2,000 feet, "Laurel Drive to the top of the world" provides panoramic view of valley, river, highway and forest. Site of state and national hang gliding competitions.

6. State parks.

Kettle Creek. 35 mi NW on PA 120 to Westport, then 7 mi N on SR 4001. Approx 1,600 acres. Winds through beautiful valley developed as tourist area. Swimming beach; fishing, hunting; boating (rentals, mooring, launching). Hiking. Snowmobiling, sledding, ice-skating. Picnicking, playground, snack bar, store. Tent & trailer sites (electric hookups). Standard fees. Phone 923-0206.

Bald Eagle. 13 mi SW off PA 150. A 1,730-acre lake on approx 5,900 acres. Swimming beach; fishing, hunting; boating (rentals, mooring, launching, marina). Hiking. Snowmobiling, sledding, ice-skating, ice boating. Picnicking, playground, snack bar, store. Tent & trailer sites. Standard fees. Phone 814/625-2775.

(For further information contact the Clinton County Tourist Promotion Agency, Court House Annex, 151 Susquehanna Ave; 893-4037.)

Annual Events

Beech Creek Bean Soup Festival. 10 mi W via PA 150, in Beech Creek. Flea market, crafts; features bean soup cooked in huge iron kettles. Phone 893-4037. Early Oct.

Flaming Foliage Festival. 29 mi NW on PA 120, in Renovo. Includes parade, craft show and contest for festival queen. Phone 923-2411. 2nd wkend Oct.

(For accommodations see Williamsport)

Manheim (E-8)

Founded: 1762 **Pop:** 5,011 **Elev:** 400 ft **Area code:** 7.17 **Zip:** 17545

Baron Henry William Stiegel founded Manheim and started manufacturing the flint glassware that bore his name. In 1770 he owned the town; by 1774 he was in debtor's prison, the victim of his own generosity and his poor choice of business associates. After his imprisonment, he made a meager living teaching here.

What to See and Do

1. **Zion Lutheran Church** (1891). 2 S Hazel St, 1 blk E of PA 72. Victorian-Gothic structure built on site of original church; Stiegel donated the ground (1772) in exchange for one red rose from the congregation every year. (Mon-Fri) Phone 665-5880. (See ANNUAL EVENT)

2. **Mt Hope Estate & Winery.** 1/2 mi S of exit 20 at jct PA 72 & PA Tpke. Restored sandstone mansion was originally built in the Federal style (ca 1800), then increased its size to 32 rooms from an extension built in 1895, which changed the house's style to Victorian. Turrets, winding walnut staircase, hand-painted 18-ft ceilings, Egyptian marble fireplaces, grand ballroom, crystal chandeliers; greenhouse, solarium, gardens. Vineyards on grounds; wine-tasting in billiards room. (Daily; closed Jan 1, Thanksgiving, Dec 25) (See SEASONAL EVENT) Phone 665-7021. ¢¢

(For further information contact the Chamber of Commerce, 210 S Charlotte St; 665-6330.)

Annual Event

Rose Festival. Celebration during which Stiegel decendant accepts annual rent of one red rose for church grounds (see #1). 2nd Sun June.

Seasonal Event

Pennsylvania Renaissance Faire. Mt Hope Estate & Winery (see #2). A 16th-century village is created in the acres of gardens surrounding the mansion. Eleven stages include a jousting arena with capacity of 6,000. Highlights include medieval jousting tournament, trial & dunk-

ing, human chess match, knighthood ceremonies. 16 wkends July-mid-Oct.

(For accommodations see Lancaster, Lebanon, also see Cornwall)

Mansfield (B-6)

Pop: 3,538 **Elev:** 1,120 ft **Area code:** 717 **Zip:** 16933

What to See and Do

1. **Hills Creek State Park.** 6 mi W, then N on unnumbered road. Approx 400 acres. Swimming beach; fishing for muskellunge, largemouth bass, walleye in Hills Creek Lake; boating (rentals, mooring, launching). Hiking. Sledding, ice-skating, ice fishing. Picnicking, playground, snack bar, store. Tent & trailer sites, cabins. Interpretive program. Standard fees. Phone 724-4246.

2. **Tioga-Hammond Lakes.** 10 mi N on US 15, then 7 mi SW on PA 287. Twin lakes and dams for flood control and recreation. Swimming; fishing, hunting; boating. Trails. Picnicking. Camping (fee; some sites free). (Late Apr-Dec) Phone 835-5281.

3. **Cowanesque Lake.** 15 mi N on US 15 to Lawrenceville, then 3 1/2 mi W on Bliss Rd. Same facilities as Tioga-Hammond Lakes. (May-Sept) Phone 835-5281.

(For further information contact the Wellsboro Area Chamber of Commerce, PO Box 733, Wellsboro 16901; 724-1926.)

(See Wellsboro)

Motels

★★ **COMFORT INN.** 300 Gateway Dr. 717/662-3000; FAX 717/662-2551. 100 rms, 2 story. S $49-$75; D $59-$75; each addl $6; under 18 free; golf plans; higher rates seasonal events. Crib avail. Pet accepted. TV; cable. Complimentary continental bkfst, coffee. Ck-out noon. Meeting rms. Exercise equipt; stair machines, bicycles. Cr cds: A, C, D, DS, ER, JCB, MC, V.

✔ ★ **WEST'S DELUXE.** RD 1, Box 97, 3 mi S on US 15. 717/659-5141; res: 800/995-9378. 20 rms. S $32-$36; D $40-$55; each addl $5. Crib $5. Pet accepted. TV; cable. Pool. Restaurant 3-9:30 pm. Bar to 2 am. Ck-out 11 am. Picnic tables, grills. Cr cds: A, DS, MC, V.

Meadville (B-2)

Settled: 1788 **Pop:** 14,318 **Elev:** 1,100 ft **Area code:** 814 **Zip:** 16335

David Mead—Revolutionary War ensign, tavernkeeper and major-general in the War of 1812—and his brothers established Mead's Settlement in 1788. Colonel Lewis Walker started manufacture of hookless slide fasteners here; since 1923 these fasteners (also known as "zippers") have been the leading local industry. The city is also a major producer of yarn and thread and is home to many tool and die manufacturers.

What to See and Do

1. **Baldwin-Reynolds House Museum** (1841-43). 639 Terrace St. Restored mansion of Henry Baldwin, congressman and US Supreme Court justice. First and second floors refurbished in period; ground-level and third floors house interpretive museum with medical, dental, textile arts, military, Indian and other historical exhibits. Also on grounds is 1890 doctor's office. Elaborate land-

scaping. Tours (Memorial Day-Labor Day, Wed, Sat & Sun). Phone 724-6080. ¢

2. **Allegheny College** (1815). (1,750 students) N Main St. Bentley Hall (1820) is a fine example of Federalist architecture. Also on campus are Bowman, Penelec & Megahan Art Galleries (Jan-May & Sept-Dec, daily exc Mon; phone 332-4365). Library has colonial, Ida Tarbell and Lincoln collections. Tours of campus. Phone 332-3100.

3. **Erie National Wildlife Refuge.** 10 mi E on PA 27. Over 250 species of birds, as well as woodchuck, white-tailed deer, fox, beaver and muskrat are found on this 8,750-acre refuge. Fishing and hunting permitted; regulations at refuge office. Nature and ski trails; overlook; photo blind. Office, 1 mi E of Guys Mills on PA 198 (Mon-Fri). Phone 789-3585. **Free.**

4. **Colonel Crawford Park.** 6 mi NE via PA 86, PA 198. Within park is Woodcock Creek Lake. Swimming (fee); fishing, hunting; boating. Nature trail. Picnicking. Camping (fee). Park (Memorial Day-Labor Day, daily). Swimming; boating. Trails. Picnicking. Camping. Phone 724-6879. Camping per night ¢¢¢

(For further information contact the Crawford County Tourist Assn, 969 Park Ave; 333-1258.)

Annual Event

Crawford County Fair. 3rd wk Aug.

(See Conneaut Lake, Franklin)

Motels

★ ★ **DAVID MEAD INN.** *Box 395, 455 Chestnut St, off I-79 exit 36A. 814/336-1692.* 67 rms, 2 story. S $51-$56; D $56-$61; each addl $5; suites $106-$120; under 18 free. Crib free. TV; cable. Heated pool; wading pool, poolside serv, lifeguard. Restaurant 7 am-2 pm, 5:30-9 pm; Sun 8 am-8 pm. Rm serv. Bar 4:30 pm-1 am, Fri & Sat to 2 am. Ck-out noon. Meeting rms. Cr cds: A, C, D, DS, MC, V.

★ ★ **DAYS INN.** *240 Conneaut Lake Rd, I-79 exit 36A. 814/337-4264; FAX 814/337-7304.* 163 rms, 2 story. S $65-$85; D $70-$85; each addl $6; under 18 free; higher rates special events. Crib free. TV; cable. Indoor pool; whirlpool, lifeguard. Restaurant 6 am-2 pm, 5-10 pm; Sat from 7 am; Sun 7 am-2 pm. Bar 3 pm-2 am. Ck-out 11 am. Coin lndry. Meeting rms. Cr cds: A, D, DS, MC, V.

Media (F-9)

Pop: 5,957 **Elev:** 300 ft **Area code:** 610

What to See and Do

1. **Franklin Mint Museum.** 4 mi SW on US 1. Houses original works by Andrew Wyeth and Norman Rockwell; collectibles are on display, including books, dolls, jewelry, furniture; artworks in porcelain, bronze, pewter, crystal and precious metals; one of the world's largest private mints. (Daily exc Mon; closed major hols) Phone 459-6168. **Free.**

2. **Ridley Creek State Park.** S on US 1, then N on PA 352. Approx 2,600 acres of woodlands and meadows. Fishing. Hiking, bicycling. Sledding. Picnicking, playground. Phone 566-4800. Within park is

Colonial Pennsylvania Plantation. A 200-year-old farm is a living history museum that re-creates the life of a typical farm family of the late 1700s. Period tools and methods are used to

perform seasonal and daily chores. Tours (Tues-Sat, by appt). Visitors may participate in some activities. (Mid-Apr-Nov, Sat & Sun) Sr citizen rate. Phone 566-1725. ¢¢

3. **Tyler Arboretum.** Off PA 352 via Forge & Painter Rds, adj to Ridley Creek State Park. 650 acres of ornamental and native plants. Outdoor "living museum" with a 20-mile system of trails; special fragrant garden and bird garden; notable trees planted in the 1800s; bookstore. Guided walks and educational programs each wk; phone for information. (Daily) Phone 566-5431. ¢¢

4. **Newlin Mill Park.** 7 mi SW via US 1, in Glen Mills. Park with operating stone gristmill (1704), furnished miller's house (1739), springhouse, blacksmith shop; milling exhibit. Tours, picnicking, fishing, nature trails. (Daily) Phone 459-2359. ¢

(For further information contact the Delaware County Convention & Visitors Bureau, 200 E State St, Suite 100, 19063; 800/343-3983.)

(For accommodations see Chester, Kennett Square, King of Prussia, Philadelphia, West Chester)

Mercer (C-1)

Settled: 1795 **Pop:** 2,444 **Elev:** 1,270 ft **Area code:** 412 **Zip:** 16137

What to See and Do

1. **Magoffin House Museum** (1821). 119 S Pitt St. Houses collection of Native American artifacts, pioneer tools, furniture, children's toys, clothing; military items. Some original furnishings; memorabilia. Special collection of artifacts from John Goodsell's trip to the North Pole with Peary in 1908-1909, as well as early maps, historic records; restored print shop. Office of Mercer County Historical Society is located here. (Tues-Sat; closed hols) Phone 662-3490. **Free.**

2. **Industrial tour. Wendell August Forge, Inc.** 10 mi SE on PA 58, in Grove City at 620 Madison Ave. Creators of hand-hammered aluminum, bronze, copper, pewter, sterling silver and glass and crystal items hand-cut on stone wheel lathe; also limited edition collectors' items. Gift shop. Self-guided tours (15-30 min). (Mid-Apr-late Dec, daily exc Sun; rest of yr, Mon-Fri; closed hols) Phone 458-8360. **Free.**

(For further information contact the Mercer Area Chamber of Commerce, PO Box 473; 662-4185.)

(See Franklin)

Motel

★ ★ ★ **HOWARD JOHNSON.** *835 Perry Hwy, US 19 S, just off I-80 exit 2. 412/748-3030; FAX 412/748-3484.* 102 rms, 2 story. S $62; D $66-$69; each addl $6; suites $79-$106; under 18 free; higher rates special events. Crib free. TV; cable. Heated pool; lifeguard. Playground. Restaurant 6 am-11 pm; Fri, Sat open 24 hrs. Rm serv. Bar. Ck-out noon. Coin lndry. Meeting rms. Bellhops. Bus depot transportation. Exercise equipt; weights, bicycles, sauna. Game rm. Private patios, balconies. Amish craft shop in lobby. Cr cds: A, C, D, DS, JCB, MC, V.

Restaurant

✔ ★ ★ **TIMBERS.** *103 Timber Village Center, on US 19. 412/662-4533.* Hrs: 11:30 am-10 pm; Fri & Sat to 11 pm; Sun to 8 pm. Closed major hols. Bar. Complete meals: dinner $6.45-$16.95. Child's meals. Specializes in seafood, prime rib. Parking. Rustic atmosphere; in converted barn (1872). Cr cds: A, DS, MC, V.

Milford (C-10)

Settled: 1733 **Pop:** 1,064 **Elev:** 503 ft **Area code:** 717 **Zip:** 18337

The borough of Milford was settled by Thomas Quick, a Hollander. Governor Gifford Pinchot, noted forester and conservationist, lived here. His house, Grey Towers (see #3), is near the town.

What to See and Do

1. **Dingmans Falls & Silver Thread Falls.** 8 mi S and W on US 209 near Dingmans Ferry. Part of Delaware Water Gap National Recreation Area (see). Two of the highest waterfalls in the Pocono Mountains; many rhododendrons bloom in July. Visitor center has audiovisual program, nature exhibits. (Apr-Nov, daily) Phone 828-7802. **Free.**

2. **Canoeing, rafting, kayaking and tubing. Kittatinny Canoes.** S to Dingman's Ferry via US 209, then 1/2 mi E via PA 739 S, at Dingman's Ferry toll bridge. Trips travel down the Delaware River. Camping. (Mid-Apr-Oct, daily) Phone 828-2338 or 800/FLOAT-KC. ¢¢¢¢

3. **Grey Towers** (1886). On US 6, 1/2 mi W via PA 206, 2 mi E of I-84 exit 10. A 100-acre estate originally built as summer house for philanthropist James W. Pinchot; became residence of his son, Gifford Pinchot, "father of American conservation," governor of Pennsylvania and first chief of USDA Forest Service. Now site of Pinchot Institute for Conservation Studies. Tours. (Memorial Day wkend-Labor Day wkend, daily; after Labor Day-Veterans Day, Fri-Mon afternoons; rest of yr, by appt; occasionally closed for conferences, call ahead) Phone 296-6401. **Free.**

(For further information contact the Pocono Mts Vacation Bureau, 1004 Main St, Stroudsburg 18360, phone 424-6050; for free brochures phone 800/POCONOS.)

(See Bushkill, Delaware Water Gap)

Motels

★ ★ **BEST WESTERN INN AT HUNTS LANDING.** *(900 US 6 & US 209, Matamoras 18336) 6 mi E on I-84, exit 11. 717/491-2400; FAX 717/491-2422.* 108 rms, 4 story. May-Oct: S $60-$68; D $70-$78; each addl $6; suites $100; under 12 free; lower rates rest of yr. Crib free. Pet accepted. TV; cable, in-rm movies avail. Indoor pool; sauna. lifeguard. Playground. Restaurant 6:30 am-9 pm; Fri & Sat to 10 pm; Sun from 7 am. Bar 11-2 am; entertainment, dancing Fri & Sat. Ck-out 11 am. Coin lndry. Meeting rms. Sundries. Gift shop. Game rm. Lawn games. Cr cds: A, C, D, DS, MC, V.

✔ ★ **MYER.** *RD 4, Box 8030, 1/4 mi E on US 6, PA 209. 717/296-7223; res: 800/764-6322; res: 800/866-9870.* 19 cottages, 1 kit. S $40-$50; D $45-$70; each addl $5; kit. unit $90. Crib free. Pet accepted, some restrictions. TV; cable. Restaurant nearby. Ck-out 11 am. Lawn games. Refrigerators. Picnic tables, grills. Cr cds: A, C, D, DS, MC, V.

Inns

★ **BLACK WALNUT.** *RD 2, Box 9285, Firetower Rd, 2 mi W off US 6, I-84 exit 10, 1 mi, follow signs. 717/296-6322; res: 800/866-9870.* 12 rms, 8 with bathrm, 2 story. No A/C. D $60-$100; hols 2 day min stay. TV in sitting rm; movies. Dining rm 8:30-10 am, 5:30-8 pm; Fri to 9 pm; Sat to 10 pm; closed Mon. Ck-out 11 am, ck-in 3 pm. Rec rm. Tudor-style stone house; marble fireplace; some antiques. 160-acre estate on the bank of a 5-acre stocked pond; paddleboats, rowboats. Cr cds: A, MC, V.

★ ★ ★ **CLIFF PARK.** *RR 4, Box 7200, 1 1/2 mi W of PA 6, on 6th St. 717/296-6491; res: 800/225-6535; FAX 717/296-3982.* 18 rms, 1-3 story. S $75-$125; D $95-$205; EP, MAP avail; wkend plans. Dining rm 8-10 am, noon-3 pm, 6-9 pm. 9-hole golf, greens fee $6-$22, pro, putting green, rentals. X-country ski 7 mi, rentals. Hiking trails. Near Delaware River. Classic country inn; originally a farmhouse built 1820. Some fireplaces. Screened porches. Cr cds: A, C, D, DS, MC, V.

★ ★ **PINE HILL FARM.** *PO Box 1001, 2 1/2 mi N on US 6, PA 209 (Broad St); left on Cummins Hill Rd; turn at the first Pine Hill Farm sign and continue on a 1-mi climb on a public access road; drive cautiously as deer frequently congregate there. 717/296-7395.* 3 rms in main house, 2 story, 2 suites in adj cottage. No rm phones. S $75-$95; D $80-$85; each addl $25; suites $95-$105; higher rates hols (2-night min). Adults only. TV in some rms and sitting rm. Complimentary full bkfst. Ck-out 11 am, ck-in 3 pm. Bellman. X-country ski on site. Main house was the original farmhouse (ca 1870); fireplace, many antique furnishings. Located atop a hill, overlooking the Delaware River. Includes 268 acres of fields and forests, with 5 mi of 1800s logging trails for walking, birdwatching. Cr cds: D, MC, V.

Monroeville (E-2)

(see Pittsburgh)

Mount Pocono (C-9)

Pop: 1,795 **Elev:** 1,840 ft **Area code:** 717 **Zip:** 18344

One of the many thriving resort communities in the heart of the Pocono Mountains, Mount Pocono offers recreation year round in nearby parks, lakes and ski areas.

What to See and Do

1. **Pocono Knob.** 1 1/2 mi E on Knob Rd. Excellent view of surrounding countryside.

2. **Pennsylvania Dutch Farm, Inc.** Grange Rd. Amish exhibit home; buggies, wagons, farm machinery; animals; horse-drawn rides. (Apr-Nov, daily) Phone 839-7680. ¢¢

3. **Memorytown, USA.** 2 mi E via PA 940. Old-time village includes hex shop, country store, Indian Museum (fee), Print Shop Museum; ice cream parlor; paddle boats, mini-raceway; fishing; entertainment; lodging, picnic area, restaurant and tavern. Summer festivals. Fee for some activities. (June-Sept, daily; Mar-May, Fri-Sun) Phone 839-1680. **Free.**

4. **Mount Airy Lodge Ski Area.** Just E of town via PA 940. Two double chairlifts; patrol, school, rentals; snowmaking; cafeteria, restaurant, bar; nursery, lodge. Longest run 1,800 ft; vertical drop 240 ft. Also cross-country trails. (Mid-Dec-late Mar) Phone 839-8811. ¢¢¢¢¢

5. **Tobyhanna State Park.** 5 mi N on PA 611, then NE on PA 423. Approx 5,400 acres with 170-acre lake. Swimming beach; fishing, hunting; boating (rentals, mooring, launching). Hiking, biking. Cross-country skiing. Snowmobiling, ice-skating, ice fishing. Store. Tent & trailer sites. Standard fees. Phone 894-8336.

6. **Gouldsboro State Park.** 10 mi N on PA 611 & I-380, then NE on PA 507. Approx 3,000 acres; 250-acre lake. Swimming beach; fishing, hunting; boating (rentals, mooring, launching). Hiking. Ice-skating, ice fishing. Standard fees. Phone 894-8336.

(For further information contact the Pocono Mts Vacation Bureau, 1004 Main St, Stroudsburg 18360, phone 424-6050; for brochures phone 800/POCONOS.)

(See Pocono Mountains)

Motels

✔ ★ **HAMPTON COURT INN.** *MCR 1, Box 4, 1/2 mi E on PA 940.* 717/839-2119. 14 rms. No rm phones. S $40-$45; D $50-$65; each addl $8. TV; cable. Pool. Complimentary continental bkfst. Restaurant 5-10 pm; wkends to 11 pm; closed Tues. Ck-out 11 am. Cr cds: A, C, D, MC, V.

★ ★ **POCONO FOUNTAIN.** *HCR 1, Box 115, 1 1/2 mi S on PA 611.* 717/839-7728. 37 rms, 2 kits. May-Sept: S $50-$125; D $53-$125; each addl $5; kit. unit $67-$75; lower rates rest of yr. Crib $5. TV; cable. Pool; whirlpool. Playground. Restaurant 6 am-10 pm. Ck-out 11 am. Sundries. Downhill ski 5 mi. Private patios, picnic tables. Cr cds: A, C, D, DS, MC, V.

Inns

★ ★ ★ **FRENCH MANOR.** *(PO Box 39, South Sterling 18460) N on PA 196, E on PA 423, then continue N on PA 191, left on Huckleberry Rd.* 717/676-3244; res: 800/523-8200. 8 rms, 3 story, 3 story. No rm phones. MAP: D $190-$240. Adults only. TV in sitting rm. Indoor pool privileges. Dining rm (public by res; jacket required) 8:30-10 am, noon-2 pm, 6-9 pm. Rm serv. Ck-out 11 am, ck-in 2 pm. Airport, bus depot transportation. X-country ski on premises. French chateau-style summer home built by Joseph Hirschorn (1932-1937); Spanish slate roof; patio surrounding house offers spectacular view of area; 38-ft high dining rm with beamed ceilings; Great Hall has 2 floor-to-ceiling fireplaces. Antiques throughout. Cr cds: A, DS, MC, V.

★ ★ ★ **STERLING.** *(PA 191, South Sterling 18460) N on PA 196, E on PA 423, N on PA 191.* 717/676-3311; res: 800/523-8200; FAX 717/676-9786. 56 units, 3 story, 12 suites, 4 cottages. No rm phones. MAP: S $65-$95, D $130-$160; suites, cottages $160-$220; family, wkly rates; ski, golf plans; lower rates mid-wk. Crib $10. TV in some rms; cable. Indoor pool; whirlpool. Dining rm 8-10 am, noon-1:30 pm, 6-8:30 pm. Ck-out 11 am, ck-in 2 pm. Airport, bus depot transportation. Tennis. Downhill ski 10 mi, x-country ski on site, rentals. Sleigh rides. Rec rm. Lawn games. On lake. Built in 1850s; country and Victorian suites. Some fireplaces. Cr cds: A, DS, MC, V.

Resorts

★ ★ **CAESARS PARADISE STREAM.** *3 mi E on PA 940.* 717/839-8881; res: 800/233-4141. 171 rms. Couples only. MAP: D $185-$330; wkly rates. TV; cable, in-rm movies avail. 2 pools, 1 indoor; poolside serv, lifeguard. Rm serv limited hrs. Snack bar. Bar noon-2 am. Ck-out 11 am, ck-in 3 pm. Grocery, package store. Sundries. Bus depot transportation. Tennis. Miniature golf. Bicycles. Boats, paddleboats. Snowmobiles available. Lawn games. Soc dir; entertainment, dancing, movies. Game rm. Exercise equipt; weights, bicycles, whirlpool, sauna. Hiking trails. Archery. Fireplace, pool, sauna in some rms. Cr cds: A, C, D, DS, MC, V.

★ ★ **POCONO GARDENS LODGE.** *PA 940 & PA 390.* 717/595-7431; res: 800/441-4410 (exc PA). 153 rms, 8 cottages. Couples only, AP, July-Sept: D, suites $125-$270; cottages $140; lower rates rest of yr. TV; cable. Indoor/outdoor pool; poolside serv, lifeguard. Dining rm 8:30-10:30 am, 6-8 pm. Snack bar. Picnics. Rm serv noon-5 pm, 9-midnight. Bar 11-2 am; entertainment, dancing. Ck-out 11 am, ck-in 2 pm. Grocery 1 mi. Coin lndry, package store 2 mi. Bellhops. Valet serv. Gift shop. Free bus depot transportation. Sports dir. Lighted tennis. Golf privileges. Swimming beach, boats. Downhill

ski 2 mi. Snowmobiles. Hiking. Bicycles. Lawn games. Soc dir. Rec rm. Game rm. Refrigerators. Balconies. Picnic tables. Cr cds: A, C, D, DS, MC, V.

★ ★ **POCONO MANOR.** *Pocono Manor (18349), on PA 314, 2 mi W of PA 611 in Pocono Manor.* 717/839-7111; res: 800/233-8150; FAX 717/839-0708. 190 rms in inn, 65 in 2 lodges. MAP: S $90-$120; D $160-$200; each addl $50; under 8 free; higher rates special events. Crib $7. Serv charge. TV. Indoor/outdoor pool; poolside serv, lifeguard. Free supervised child's activities. Dining rm (public by res) 7:30-9 am, noon-1 pm, 6:30-8:30 pm. Rm serv. Box lunches, snacks. Bar 11-2 am. Ck-out 11 am, ck-in 4 pm. Bellhops. Grocery, package store 2 mi. Free local airport, bus depot transportation. Sports dir. Tennis, pro. 36-hole golf, pro, putting green, driving range. Trapshooting. Artificial ice rink, sleigh rides. Indoor, outdoor games. Bicycles. Soc dir. Dancing, movies, entertainment. Rec rm; library. Exercise equipt; weights, bicycles, sauna. Extra fee for some activities. On 3,100-acre mountain estate. Cr cds: A, C, D, MC, V.

Restaurants

★ **BAILEYS.** *604 Pocono Blvd.* 717/839-9678. Hrs: 11:30 am-10 pm; wkends to midnight; early-bird dinner 4-6 pm. Closed Thanksgiving, Dec 25. Bar to midnight; Fri, Sat to 2 am. Semi-a la carte: lunch $3.95-$7.95, dinner $6.95-$21.95. Child's meals. Specializes in steak, hickory smoked ribs. Salad bar. Parking. Cr cds: A, DS, MC, V.

✔ ★ ★ **OLD HEIDELBERG.** *Swiftwater (18370), 3/4 mi S on PA 611, 2 mi N of I-80 exit 44 in Swiftwater.* 717/839-9954. Hrs: 11:30 am-9 pm; Sun 11 am-8 pm. Closed Mon & Tues. Continental menu. Bar. Semi-a la carte: lunch $3.50-$5.25, dinner $9.50-$15. Specializes in sauerbraten, schnitzel, turkey. Parking. Cr cds: A, MC, V.

New Castle (D-1)

Settled: 1798 **Pop:** 28,334 **Elev:** 860 ft **Area code:** 412

At the junction of the Shenango, Mahoning and Beaver rivers, this was long an important Native American trading center; the Delawares used it as their capital. Today, the fireworks and plastics industries have become an integral part of the community.

What to See and Do

1. **Hoyt Institute of Fine Arts.** 124 E Leasure Ave. Cultural arts center housed in two early 20th-century mansions on four acres of landscaped grounds; permanent art collection, changing exhibits, period rooms, performing arts programs, classes. (Tues-Sat; closed major hols) Donation. Phone 652-2882.

2. **Scottish Rite Cathedral.** Highland & Lincoln Aves. On hillside, dominating city's skyline. Large auditorium; local Masonic headquarters. Phone 654-6683.

3. **Greer House.** 408 N Jefferson. Turn-of-the-century restored mansion houses the Lawrence County Historical Society. Museum has extensive Shenango and Castleton China collection, Sports Hall of Fame, fireworks rm. Archives; workshops and speakers. (Wed & Sun; also by appt) Donation. Phone 658-4022.

4. **McConnell's Mill State Park.** 12 mi E via US 422. Approx 2,500 acres. Century-old mill surrounded by beautiful landscape and scenery. Fishing, hunting, whitewater boating. Hiking. Picnicking, store. Historical center, interpretive program. Standard fees. Phone 368-8091 or -8811.

(For further information contact the Lawrence County Tourist Promotion Agency, 138 W Washington St, 16101; 654-5593.)

(For accommodations see Beaver Falls, also see Harmony)

New Hope (Bucks Co) (E-10)

Founded: 1681 **Pop:** 1,400 **Elev:** 76 ft **Area code:** 215 **Zip:** 18938

The river village of New Hope was originally the largest part of a 1,000-acre land grant from William Penn to Thomas Woolrich of Shalford, England. In the 20th century, the area gained fame as the home of artists, literary and theatrical personalities.

What to See and Do

1. **Parry Mansion Museum.** (1784). S Main & Ferry Sts. Restored stone house built by Benjamin Parry, prosperous merchant and mill owner. Eleven rooms on view, restored and furnished to depict period styles from late 18th to early 20th centuries. (May-Oct, Fri-Sun; also by appt) Sr citizen rate. Phone 862-5652 or -5148. ¢¢

2. **Parry Barn** (1784). S Main St, opp Mansion. Owned by New Hope Historical Society; operated as commercial art gallery. **Free.**

3. **New Hope & Ivyland Rail Road.** West Bridge St, adj to Delaware Canal. A 9-mile, 50-minute narrated train ride through Bucks County. Reading Railroad passenger coaches from the 1920s depart from restored 1890 New Hope Station. Gift shop. (Early Apr-Nov, daily; Dec, special Santa Train Fri-Sun; rest of yr, wkends) Phone 862-2332. ¢¢¢

4. **Washington Crossing Historical Park** (see). 7 mi S on PA 32.

5. **Canoe and raft trips** on the Delaware River. Two- to four-hour canoeing, rafting and tubing trips. (Apr-Oct) Contact Point Pleasant Canoe & Tube, Inc, PO Box 6, Point Pleasant 18950; 297-8823. ¢¢¢¢-¢¢¢¢¢

(For further information contact the Information Center, 1 W Mechanic St; 862-5880.)

(See Doylestown; also see Lambertville & Trenton, NJ)

Inns

★ ★ ★ **1740 HOUSE.** *(River Rd, Lumberville 18933) 7 mi N on PA 32.* 215/297-5661. 24 rms. Wkends (Sat 2-night min), hols (3-4-day min): D $110; lower rates wkdays. Pool. Complimentary buffet bkfst 8:30-10 am; dinner Fri & Sat 6-8 pm. Ck-out, ck-in noon. Meeting rms. Private patios, balconies. Overlooks Delaware River. No cr cds accepted.

★ ★ **AARON BURR HOUSE.** *80 W Bridge St.* 215/862-2343. 6 rms, 2 story, 2 suites. S, D $75-$140; each addl $20; suite $140-$180; wkly rates; lower rates mid-wk. Crib free. TV in sitting rm; cable. Complimentary full bkfst, coffee & tea/sherry. Restaurant nearby. Ck-out 11 am, ck-in 2 pm. Concierge. Free bus depot transportation. Downhill ski 2 mi; x-country ski adj. Lawn games. Fireplace in suites. Built 1854, some antiques. Screened flagstone patio. Totally nonsmoking. Cr cds: A, MC, V.

★ ★ **BARLEY SHEAF FARM.** *(Rte 202, Box 10, 5281 York Rd, Holicong 18928) Approx 7 mi S on US 202.* 215/794-5104; FAX 215/794-5565. 10 rms, 3 story, 2 suites. Rm phones avail. July-Oct, wkends: D $116-$145; each addl $17; suites $130-$175; lower rates rest of yr. Closed wk of Dec 25. Children over 8 yrs only. TV in sitting

rm; cable. Pool. Complimentary full bkfst. Ck-out 11 am, ck-in 2 pm. Meeting rm. Lawn games. Thirty-acre farm; house built 1740. Cr cds: A, C, MC, V.

★ ★ **CENTRE BRIDGE.** *Star Rte, Box 74, PA 32 & PA 263.* 215/862-9139. 9 rms, 2 story. No rm phones. D $60-$135; each addl $15. TV in some rms; cable. Complimentary continental bkfst. Restaurant (see CENTRE BRIDGE). Bar. Ck-out noon, ck-in 2 pm. Sitting rm and terrace overlook river. Fireplace, antiques. Cr cds: A, MC, V.

★ ★ ★ **GOLDEN PLOUGH.** *(Box 218, US 202 & Street Rd, Lahaska 18931) 6 mi S on US 202, in Peddler's Village, Bucks County.* 215/794-4004; FAX 215/794-4008. 60 units in 6 buildings, 2-3 story, 7 suites, 4 kit. units. S, D $95-$150; each addl $15; suites $175-$300; kit. units $150. Crib free. TV. Complimentary continental bkfst. Complimentary coffee & tea in rms. Restaurant (see SPOTTED HOG). Ck-out 11 am, ck-in 3 pm. Some balconies. Country decor, antiques. Cr cds: A, C, D, DS, MC, V.

★ ★ **HOLLILEIF.** *(677 Durham Rd/PA 413, Wrightstown 18940) S on PA 232, approx 1/2 mi S on PA 413.* 215/598-3100. 5 rms, 3 story. No rm phones. Apr-Dec: D $80-$125; each addl $20; lower rates rest of yr. TV in sitting rm. Complimentary full bkfst, tea/sherry. Ck-out 11:30 am, ck-in 3 pm. Lawn games. 18th-century house; antiques, fireplace. Totally nonsmoking. Cr cds: A, DS, MC, V.

★ ★ **HOTEL DU VILLAGE.** *N River Rd (PA 32) & Phillips Mill Rd.* 215/862-5164. 20 rms, 2 story. No rm phones. S, D $85-$100; each addl $5; wkly rates. Pool. Complimentary continental bkfst. Dining rm 5:30-9 pm; Fri & Sat to 10:30 pm; Sun 3-9 pm; closed Mon & Tues. Bar. Ck-out 11 am, ck-in after 2 pm. Tennis. Small Tudor-style country inn on spacious grounds; former estate. Cr cds: A, D.

★ **INN AT PHILLIPS MILL.** *2590 N River Rd, (PA 32).* 215/862-2984. 5 rms, 3 story, 1 suite. D $75; suite $85. Closed Jan. Adults only. Pool. Dining rm 5:30-9:30 pm. Rm serv. Ck-out 1 pm, ck-in 2 pm. Built 1750 as stone barn; antiques. No cr cds accepted.

★ ★ **TATTERSALL.** *(PO Box 569, 16 Cafferty Rd, Point Pleasant 18950) 8 mi N on PA 32.* 215/297-8233. 6 rms, 2 story, 1 suite. No rm phones. S $75-$84; D $85-$94; each addl $15; suite $99-$109. TV in sitting rm. Complimentary continental bkfst in rms. Complimentary coffee & tea. Restaurant nearby. Ck-out noon, ck-in 2 pm. Lawn games. House (1740) with porches, marble fireplace, antiques. Smoking in sitting rm only. Cr cds: A, DS, MC, V.

★ ★ **WEDGWOOD.** *111 W Bridge St.* 215/862-2570. 12 rms, 2 story. Some rm phones. S $65-$110; D $70-$140; each addl $20; suites $150-$190. Pet accepted. Complimentary bfkst (8:30-10 am), afternoon tea. Ck-out 11 am, ck-in 2 pm. Concierge. Free bus depot transportation. Meeting rm. Picnic tables, grills. Built 1870; antiques, some fireplaces. Totally nonsmoking. Cr cds: A, MC, V.

Restaurants

★ ★ **BLACK BASS HOTEL.** *Lumberville (18933), 8 mi N on PA 32.* 215/297-5770. Hrs: noon-3 pm, 5:30-9 pm; Fri to 10 pm; Sat 5:30-10 pm; Sun 4:30-8:30 pm; Sun brunch 11 am-2:30 pm. Closed Dec 24, 25. Res accepted. Bar 6 pm-midnight; wkends from 1 pm. A la carte entrees: lunch $6.95-$12.95, dinner $17.95-$24.95. Sun brunch $26.50. Specializes in fresh fish, duckling. Pianist Sat. Parking. Built in

1740s. Dining on veranda overlooking Delaware River, hills and footbridge. Cr cds: A, D, DS, MC, V.

★ ★ **CENTRE BRIDGE.** *(See Centre Bridge Inn)* 215/862-9139. Hrs: 5:30-9:30 pm; Fri, Sat to 10 pm; Sun 3-9 pm. Closed Dec 25. Res accepted Fri-Sun. French, continental menu. Bar. Semi-a la carte: dinner $14.95-$30.95. Specializes in rack of lamb, seafood. Parking. Outdoor dining. Stone fireplace. Patio overlooks canal. Cr cds: A, MC, V.

✔ ★ ★ **COCK 'N BULL.** *(PO Box 218, Lahaska 18931)* S on US 202, in Peddler's Village. 215/794-4000. Hrs: 11 am-3 pm, 5-9 pm; Fri to 10 pm; Sat 4-10 pm; Sun 4-8 pm; Sun brunch 10 am-3 pm. Closed Jan 1, Dec 25. Res accepted. Bar. Semi-a la carte: lunch $4.95-$8.50, dinner $10.95-$18.25. Sun brunch $12.95. Specialties: country chicken pie, beef Burgundy. Salad bar. Parking. Family-owned. Cr cds: A, D, DS, MC, V.

★ ★ **CUTTALOSSA INN.** *(3498 River Rd/PA 32, Lumberville)* N on PA 32. 215/297-5082. Hrs: 11 am-2 pm, 5:30-9 pm; Fri, Sat 5:30-10 pm. Closed Sun; Jan 1, Dec 24, 25. Bar. Complete meals: lunch $6-$15, dinner $18-$28. Specialties: crab imperial, seafood. Entertainment exc Mon. Parking. Outdoor dining along Delaware River. Built 1750; overlooks waterfall and wooden bridge. Cr cds: A, MC, V.

★ ★ **GOLDEN PHEASANT INN.** *(763 River Rd/PA 32, Erwinna)* 13 mi N on PA 32. 610/294-9595. Hrs: 5:30-10 pm; Sun 11 am-3 pm, 5:30-9 pm. Closed Mon. Res accepted. French menu. Bar. A la carte entrees: dinner $21.95-$26.95. Sun brunch $18.95. Specializes in roast lamb, crabmeat Brittany, steak au poivre. Own baking. Parking. Restored 1857 inn; dining rm in solarium. Guest rms avail. Cr cds: C, MC, V.

★ ★ **HOTEL DU VILLAGE.** *2535 N River Rd (PA 32), jct Phillips Mill Rd.* 215/862-9911. Hrs: 5:30-9 pm; Fri, Sat to 10:30 pm; Sun 3-9 pm. Closed Mon, Tues; Dec 25; also Jan. Res accepted. French menu. Bar. A la carte entrees: dinner $13.95-$19.95. Specialties: filet of beef Béarnaise, sweet breads. Parking. Outdoor dining. English manor house; elegant dining. Cr cds: A, D.

★ ★ ★ **JEAN PIERRE'S.** *(101 S State St, Newtown)* State St & Centre Ave. 215/968-6201. Hrs: 11:30 am-2 pm, 5:30-9 pm; Sat 5:30-9:30 pm; Sun 4:30-8 pm. Closed Mon; Jan 1, Dec 25. Res accepted. French menu. Wine cellar. Prix fixe: lunch $17.50. A la carte entrees: dinner $22-$29. Specializes in imported fish, rack of lamb, fresh game. Own pastries. In home built 1747. Fireplace. Cr cds: A, C, D, DS, MC, V.

★ ★ **JENNY'S.** *(Jct US 202 & Street Rd, Lahaska)* 6 mi S on US 202, in Peddler's Village. 215/794-4021. Hrs: 11 am-9 pm; Mon to 3 pm; wkend hrs vary; early-bird dinner Tues-Fri 4-6 pm. Closed Dec 25. Res accepted. Continental menu. Bar. A la carte entrees: lunch $4.95-$9.95, dinner $12.95-$22.95. Specialties: lobster crab sauté, filet Chesterfield, mushrooms Pennsylvania. Jazz Fri, Sat; Dixieland trio Sun. Parking. Cr cds: A, C, D, DS, MC, V.

★ **SPOTTED HOG.** *(See Golden Plough Inn)* 215/794-4040. Hrs: 7 am-11 pm; Sun to 9 pm. Closed Jan 1, Dec 25. Bar to midnight; Sun to 9 pm. A la carte entrees: bkfst $2.95-$7.25, lunch, dinner $4.25-$19.95. Child's meals. Specializes in steak sandwiches. Musicians Thurs-Sat. Parking. Cr cds: A, C, D, DS, MC, V.

New Stanton (E-2)

Pop: 2,081 **Elev:** 980 ft **Area code:** 412 **Zip:** 15672

What to See and Do

Industrial tour. L.E. Smith Glass Co. 6 mi SE via US 119, PA 31, in Mt Pleasant, 1900 Liberty St. Reproductions of several styles of antique handcrafted glass. Children under 6 yrs not admitted. No open-toe shoes. (Mon-Fri; closed 1st 2 wks July) Phone 547-3544 for tour schedule. **Free.**

(For further information contact the Laurel Highlands Tourist Promotion Agency, Town Hall, 120 E Main St, Ligonier 15658; 238-5661.)

(See Connellsville, Greensburg)

Motels

★ ★ **DAYS INN.** *Box J, 127 W Byers Ave.* 412/925-3591. 142 rms, 3 story. S $47-$50; D $49-$56; each addl $5; under 18 free. Crib free. TV. Pool; lifeguard. Restaurant 4-10 pm; closed Sun. Rm serv. Bar 4 pm-midnight; entertainment, dancing Sat & Sun. Ck-out 11 am. Coin lndry. Meeting rms. Sundries. Beauty shop. Exercise equipt; bicycles, treadmill. Cr cds: A, C, D, DS, MC, V.

✔ ★ ★ **HOWARD JOHNSON.** *Box 214, 1 blk S off US 119, ¹/₄ mi SW of PA Tpke exit 8.* 412/925-3511; FAX 412/925-3511. 87 rms, 2 story. Mid-May-Sept: S $38-$69; D $45-$71; each addl $5; under 18 free; lower rates rest of yr. Crib free. Pet accepted. TV; cable, in-rm movies. Heated pool. Playground. Complimentary continental bkfst. Restaurant adj open 24 hrs. Ck-out noon. Valet serv. Refrigerators avail. Cr cds: A, C, D, DS, JCB, MC, V.

Norristown (E-9)

Founded: 1704 **Pop:** 30,749 **Elev:** 130 ft **Area code:** 610

William Penn, Jr, owner of the 7,600-acre tract around Norristown, sold it to Isaac Norris and William Trent for 50¢ an acre in 1704. It became a crossroads for colonial merchants and soldiers; Washington's army camped nearby. Dutch, German, Swedish, Welsh and English immigrants left their mark on the city. Today Norristown, still a transportation hub, houses many industries and serves as a county government center.

What to See and Do

1. **Peter Wentz Farmstead.** 10 mi NW via US 202, W via PA 73 on Shearer Rd, in Worcester. Restored and furnished mid-18th-century country mansion, twice used by Washington during the Pennsylvania campaign. More than 70 acres with demonstration field and orchard crops of the period. Slide presentation; costumed interpreters; reconstructed 1744 barn with farm animals. (Daily exc Mon; closed Jan 1, Thanksgiving, Dec 25; also 2nd wk Sept) Phone 584-5104. **Free.**

2. **Valley Forge National Historical Park** (see). NW on US 422 to Trooper, then S.

3. **Elmwood Park Zoo.** Harding Blvd, off US 202. Features extensive North American waterfowl area; cougars, bobcats, bison, elk; outdoor aviary; birds of prey; children's zoo barn; museum with exhibit on animal senses. (Daily; closed Jan 1, Thanksgiving, Dec 25) Phone 277-3825. **¢**

(For further information contact the Valley Forge Convention and Visitors Bureau, 600 W Germantown Pike, Suite 130, Plymouth Meeting 19462; 610/834-1500.)

(For accommodations see King of Prussia, Kulpsville, Philadelphia)

Restaurants

★ ★ **JOHAN'S.** *(8 Garfield Ave, West Point 19486)* PA Tpke exit 31, 3 mi E on Sumneytown Pike to West Point Pike, S to Garfield Ave. 215/699-5150. Hrs: 11:30 am-11 pm; Sat from 4 pm. Closed Sun. Res accepted. Continental menu. Bar. A la carte entrees: lunch $6.50-$12. Semi-a la carte: dinner $15-$30. Specialties: lobster Johan's, veal Zelande, medallion of lamb. Parking. Intimate dining in multiple dining rms. Tiffany-style windows; paintings. Cr cds: A, C, D, MC, V.

D

★ ★ **TIFFANY DINING PLACE AND GAZEBO.** *(799 DeKalb Pike, Centre Square)* 9 mi N on US 202, in Centre Square. 610/272-1888. Hrs: 5-10 pm; Fri to 11 pm; Sat 4:15-11 pm; Sun 3:30-10 pm; early-bird dinner Mon-Fri 5-6:30 pm, Sat 4:15-5:30 pm; Sun brunch 10:30 am-2 pm. Closed Dec 25. Bar. Semi-a la carte: dinner $8.95-$18.95. Sun brunch $12.95. Child's meals. Specializes in New York sirloin, teriyaki steak, seafood. Salad bar. Parking. Victorian decor. Also gazebo dining area. Cr cds: A, D, DS, MC, V.

D **SC**

★ ★ **TROLLEY STOP.** *(PA 73, Skippack)* 9 mi N on US 202 to PA 73W. 610/584-4849. Hrs: 11:30 am-11 pm; early-bird dinner Mon-Fri 3-6 pm, Sat, Sun 2-5 pm. Closed Jan 1, Dec 25. Res accepted. Bar. Semi-a la carte: lunch $4.95-$9.95, dinner $6.95-$29.95. Sun brunch $6.95-$15.95. Child's meals. Specializes in seafood, veal. Pianist Wed-Sat. Parking. Dining rm in 1900s trolley. Cr cds: A, D, DS, MC, V.

D **SC**

★ ★ ★ **WILLIAM PENN INN.** *(US 202 & Sunneytown Rd, Gwynedd)* 11 mi N on US 202. 215/699-9272. Hrs: 11:30 am-3 pm, 5-10 pm; Fri, Sat to 11 pm; Sun 2-8 pm; early-bird dinner Mon-Fri 5-6:30 pm; Sun brunch 10:30 am-2 pm. Closed Dec 25. Res accepted. Continental menu. Bar. Semi-a la carte: lunch $4.25-$15, dinner $15-$30. Sun brunch $14.95. Specializes in seafood, rack of lamb. Salad bar. Own pastries. Harpist, pianist Tues-Sat. Parking. Originally a tavern (1714); antiques. Guest rms avail. Cr cds: A, C, D, DS, MC, V.

D

North East (A-2)

Settled: 1801 **Pop:** 4,617 **Elev:** 801 ft **Area code:** 814 **Zip:** 16428

In 1792, when Pennsylvania bought from the federal government the tract containing North East, the state gained 46 miles of Lake Erie frontage, a fine harbor, and some of the best Concord grape country in the nation.

What to See and Do

Winery tours.

Penn-Shore Vineyards and Winery. 10225 East Lake Rd. Guided tours; wine tastings. (Daily; closed some hols) Phone 725-8688. **Free.**

Heritage Wine Cellars. 12162 E Main Rd. Guided tours; wine tastings. (Daily; closed some hols) Phone 725-8015. **Free.**

(For further information contact North East Chamber of Commerce, 17 S Lake St, PO Box 466; 725-4262.)

Annual Events

Cherry Festival. Concessions, rides, games, parade. Mid-July.

Wine Country Harvest Festival. Arts & crafts, bands, buses to wineries, food. Last wkend Sept.

(For accommodations see Erie)

Oil City (C-2)

Pop: 11,949 **Elev:** 1,000 ft **Area code:** 814 **Zip:** 16301

Spreading on both sides of Oil Creek and the Allegheny River, Oil City was born of the oil boom. Oil refining and the manufacture of oil machinery are its major occupations today. Nearby are natural gas fields. Seven miles northwest stood the famous oil-boom town of Pithole. In 1865 it expanded from a single farmhouse to a population of more than 10,000 in 5 months, as its first oil well brought in 250 barrels a day.

(See Franklin, Titusville)

Motor Hotel

★ ★ **HOLIDAY INN.** 1 Seneca St, at State St Bridge. 814/677-1221; FAX 814/677-0492. 103 rms, 5 story. S $59; D $69; each addl $5; suites $75-$85; family rates. Crib free. TV; cable. Heated pool; lifeguard. Restaurant 6:30 am-2 pm, 5-10 pm. Rm serv. Bar 11-2 am, Sun from 1 pm; dancing. Ck-out noon. Meeting rms. Bellhops. Valet serv. X-country ski 2 mi. Cr cds: A, C, D, DS, JCB, MC, V.

D 🏊 🏊 🎿 🔥 **SC**

Orbisonia (E-5)

Pop: 447 **Elev:** 640 ft **Area code:** 814 **Zip:** 17243

What to See and Do

East Broad Top Railroad. On US 522. The oldest surviving narrow gauge railroad east of the Rockies. Train ride (50 min); fascinating old equipment, buildings. Picnic area. (June-Oct, wkends only; Mon-Fri by res only) Phone 447-3011. **¢¢¢** Opp is

Rockhill Trolley Museum. 1/2 mi W off US 522, on PA 994, in Rockhill Furnace. Old-time trolleys; car barn and restoration shop tours. A 2-mile ride on Shade Gap Electric Railway. Gift shop. (Memorial Day-Oct, wkends) Phone 447-9576. **¢¢**

(For accommodations see Chambersburg, Huntingdon)

Pennsylvania Dutch Area (E-8 - F-8)

From the Rhineland and Palatinate of Germany came great migrations of settlers to Pennsylvania in the 18th century, first near Philadelphia, and then moving west. Because they retained their customs and speech and developed beautiful and bountiful farms, the Pennsylvania Dutch (corruption of the German, *Deutsch*) country is one of the state's greatest tourist attractions. There are all degrees of conservatism among these descendants of German immigrants, ranging from the Amish to the Brethren, but all share tremendous vigor, family devotion, love of the Bible and belief in thrift and hard work.

Many of the "plain people"—the Amish, Old Order Mennonites and Brethren (Dunkards)—live today much as they did a century ago. Married men wear beards, black coats and low-crowned black hats; women wear bonnets and long, simple dresses. They drive horses and buggies instead of cars, work long hours in the fields, shun the use of modern farm machinery and turn to the Bible for guidance. Despite their refusal to use machinery they are master farmers. (They were among the first to rotate crops and practice modern fertilization methods.) Their harvests are consistently among the best in the country.

Many of the Amish regard photographs as "graven images"; visitors should not take pictures of individuals without their permission.

(For further information contact the Pennsylvania Dutch Convention & Visitors Bureau, 501 Greenfield Rd, Lancaster 17601; 717/299-8901 or 800/735-2629. There is also a downtown visitor center, at 100 S Queen St in the Lancaster Chamber of Commerce & Industry Building, which provides brochures, maps and other general information; also another on US 272 near PA Tpke exit 21.)

(For accommodations see Allentown, Bird-in-Hand, Ephrata, Lancaster, Lebanon, Reading, also see Kutztown, Manheim)

Philadelphia (F-10)

Founded: 1682 **Pop:** 1,585,577 **Elev:** 45 ft **Area code:** 215

The nation's first capital has experienced a rebirth in the past few decades. Philadelphia has successfully blended its historic past with an electricity of modern times, all the while keeping an eye on the future. In the mid-18th century it was the second largest city in the English-speaking world. Now, nearing the end of the 20th century, Philadelphia is the second-largest city on the East Coast and the fifth-largest in the country. Here, in William Penn's City of Brotherly Love, the Declaration of Independence was written and adopted, the Constitution was molded and signed, the Liberty Bell was rung, Betsy Ross was said to have sewn her flag and Washington served most of his years as president.

This is the city of "firsts," including the first American hospital, medical college, women's medical college, bank, paper mill, steamboat, zoo, sugar refinery, daily newspaper, US Mint, and public school for black children (1750).

The first Quakers, who came here in 1681, lived in caves dug into the banks of the Delaware River. During the first year, 80 houses were raised; by the following year, William Penn's "greene countrie towne" was a city of 600 buildings. The Quakers prospered in trade and commerce, and Philadelphia became the leading port in the colonies. Its leading citizen for many years was Benjamin Franklin—statesman, scientist, diplomat, writer, inventor and publisher.

The fires of colonial indignation burned hot and early in Philadelphia. Soon after the Boston tea party, a protest rally of 8,000 Philadelphians frightened off a British tea ship. In May, 1774, when Paul Revere rode from Boston to Philadelphia to report that Boston's harbor had been closed, all of Philadelphia went into mourning. The first and second Continental Congresses convened here, and Philadelphia became the headquarters of the Revolution. After the Declaration of Independence was composed and accepted by Congress, the city gave its men, factories and shipyards to the cause. But British General Howe and 18,000 soldiers poured in on September 26, 1777, to spend a comfortable and social winter here while Washington's troops endured the bitter winter at Valley Forge. When the British evacuated the city, Congress returned. Philadelphia continued as the seat of government until 1800, except for a short period when New York City held the honor. The Constitution of the United States was written here and President George Washington graced the city's halls and streets.

Since those historic days, Philadelphia has figured importantly in the politics, economy and culture of the country. Here national conventions have nominated presidents. During four wars the city has served as an arsenal and shipyard. More than 1,400 churches and synagogues grace the city. There are over 25 colleges, universities and professional schools in Philadelphia as well. Fine restaurants are in abundance, along with an exciting night life to top off an evening. Entertainment is offered by the world-renowned Philadelphia Orchestra, theaters, college and professional sports, outstanding parks, recreation centers and playgrounds. Shoppers may browse major department stores, hundreds of specialty shops and antique shopping areas (see #8).

Between the Delaware River and 9th Street for 10 blocks lies a history-rich part of Philadelphia. Here are the shrines of American liberty; Independence Hall, the Liberty Bell Pavilion and many other historical sites in and around Independence National Historical Park.

Transportation

Car Rental Agencies: See toll-free numbers under Introduction.

Public Transportation: Subway and elevated trains, commuter trains, buses, trolleys (SEPTA), phone 580-7800.

Rail Passenger Service: Amtrak 800/872-7245.

Airport Information

Philadelphia Intl Airport: Information 492-3181; lost and found 937-6888; weather 936-1212; Crown Room (Delta), Terminal Unit E; Red Carpet Club (United), between Terminal Unit C and Terminal Unit D; USAir Club (US Air), between Terminal Unit A and Terminal Unit B.

What to See and Do

1. **Independence National Historical Park** has been called "America's most historic square mile." The Visitor Center at 3rd & Chestnut Sts has a tour map, information on all park activities and attractions and a 30-minute film entitled *Independence.* An exhibit to mark the 200th anniversary of the United States Constitution, "Promise of Permanency," is composed of an interactive computer system with 16 touch-sensitive monitors that will inform visitors of the meaning of the Federal Constitution, how it has endured for 2 centuries and its relevance to modern America. For information phone 597-8974. Unless otherwise indicated, all historic sites and museums in the park are open daily and are free. They include

Independence Square (known as State House Yard in colonial times). Bounded by Chestnut, Walnut, 5th & 6th Sts. Contains Independence Hall, Congress Hall, Old City Hall, and Philosophical Hall.

Independence Mall extends 3 blks N of the Square. The tree-lined walks add to the ambience while viewing the Square's Georgian structures. On the mall is a glass pavilion housing the Liberty Bell.

Declaration House. 701 Market St. Reconstructed house on site of writing of Declaration of Independence by Thomas Jefferson; two rooms Jefferson rented have been reproduced. Short orientation and movie about Jefferson, his philosophy on the common man and the history of the house.

Liberty Bell Pavilion. The Liberty Bell, created to commemorate the 50th anniversary of the Charter of Privileges granted by William Penn to his colony in 1701, bears the inscription, "Proclaim liberty throughout all the land unto all the inhabitants thereof" (Leviticus, Chapter 25). It was rung at public occasions thereafter, including the first reading of the Declaration of Independence on July 8, 1776, and was last rung formally on Washington's Birthday in 1846. The bell got its name from 19th-century antislavery groups who adopted it as a symbol of their cause. At 12:01 am on Jan 1, 1976, it was moved across the street from its original home in Independence Hall to its own glass structure. The Liberty Bell faces

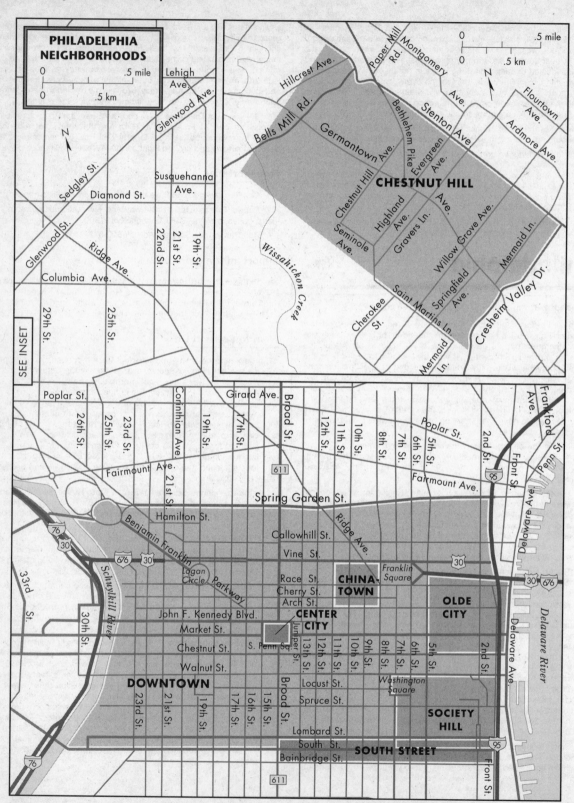

PHILADELPHIA NEIGHBORHOODS

0   .5 mile

0   .5 km

N

Lehigh Ave.

Glenwood Ave.

Sedgley St.

Diamond St.

Susquehanna Ave.

19th St.

21st St.

22nd St.

Glenwood St.

Ridge Ave.

Columbia Ave.

29th St.

25th St.

SEE INSET

0   .5 mile

0   .5 km

N

Hillcrest Ave.

Paper Mill Rd.

Montgomery Ave.

Flourtown Ave.

Ardmore Ave.

Bells Mill Rd.

Germantown Ave.

Stenton Ave.

Bethlehem Pike

Evergreen Ave.

CHESTNUT HILL

Chestnut Hill Ave.

Highland Ave.

Gravers Ln.

Willow Grove Ave.

Mermaid Ln.

Seminole Ave.

Springfield Ave.

Cresheim Valley Dr.

Wissahickon Creek

Cherokee St.

Saint Martins Ln.

Mermaid Ln.

Poplar St.

Girard Ave.

26th St.

25th St.

23rd St.

Corinthian Ave.

19th St.

17th St.

Broad St.

12th St.

11th St.

10th St.

8th St.

7th St.

6th St.

5th St.

Poplar St.

2nd St.

Frankford Ave.

Penn St.

Fairmount Ave.

21st St.

611

Fairmount Ave.

95

Front St.

Spring Garden St.

Ridge Ave.

Delaware Ave.

Hamilton St.

Benjamin Franklin Parkway

76

30

Callowhill St.

30

30

676

676

33rd St.

Schuylkill River

676

30

Vine St.

Logan Circle

Race St.

Cherry St.

Arch St.

CHINA-TOWN

Franklin Square

OLDE CITY

Delaware River

30th St.

John F. Kennedy Blvd.

Market St.

CENTER CITY

S. Penn Sq.

Juniper St.

13th St.

12th St.

11th St.

10th St.

9th St.

8th St.

7th St.

6th St.

5th St.

2nd St.

Chestnut St.

Walnut St.

DOWNTOWN

23rd St.

21st St.

19th St.

17th St.

16th St.

15th St.

Broad St.

Locust St.

Spruce St.

Washington Square

SOCIETY HILL

Lombard St.

South St.

Bainbridge St.

SOUTH STREET

95

76

611

Front St.

Independence Hall (1732). Chestnut St between 5th & 6th Sts. Site of the adoption of the Declaration of Independence. First used as the Pennsylvania State House, it housed the Second Continental Congress 1775-83 and the Constitutional Convention in 1787—when the Constitution of the United States was written. Admission by tour only. Beside Independence Hall is

Congress Hall. 6th & Chestnut Sts. Congress met here during the last decade of the 18th century. House of Representatives and Senate chambers are restored. On the other side of Independence Hall is

Old City Hall (1789). Chestnut & 5th Sts. Built as City Hall, but was also home of first US Supreme Court, 1791-1800. Exterior restored. Interior depicts the judicial phase of the building. Nearby is

Philosophical Hall. (1785-89). 5th St side of Square. Home of the American Philosophical Society, oldest learned society in America (1743), founded by Benjamin Franklin. Not open to public. Across 5th St is

Library Hall. 5th & Library Sts. Reconstruction of Library Company of Philadelphia (1789-90) building is occupied by library of American Philosophical Society. Open to scholars. (Mon-Fri). To the E is

The Second Bank of the United States (1824-41). 420 Chestnut St, between 4th & 5th Sts. Was also used as US Custom House (1845-1934). Now houses Independence National Historical Park's Portrait Gallery. One blk NE is

Franklin Court. Between Market and Chestnut Sts, in block bounded by 3rd & 4th Sts. The site of Benjamin Franklin's house has been developed as a tribute to him; area includes working printing office and bindery, underground museum with multimedia exhibits, an archaeological exhibit and the B. Free Franklin Post Office. One-half blk S is

Carpenters' Hall (1770). 320 Chestnut St. Constructed as guild hall; meeting site of first Continental Congress (1774). Historical museum since 1857; still operated by Carpenters Co. Contains original chairs; exhibits of early tools. (Daily exc Mon) Adj is

New Hall. 4th & Chestnut Sts, in Carpenters' Court. This reconstruction houses the US Marine Corps Memorial Museum, featuring exhibits on the early history of the Marines. Also in Carpenters' Court is

Pemberton House. Reconstruction of Quaker merchant's house; now Army-Navy Museum with exhibits depicting the early years of the Army and Navy. Nearby is

The First Bank of the United States (1797-1811). 3rd St between Walnut & Chestnut Sts. Organized by Alexander Hamilton; country's oldest bank building; exterior restored. Closed to public. Walk approx one-half blk S to

Bishop White House (1786-87). 309 Walnut St. House of Bishop William White, first Episcopal Bishop of Pennsylvania. Restored and furnished. Tours. Free tickets at park's Visitor Center. One blk W is

Todd House (1775). 4th & Walnut Sts. House of Dolley Payne Todd, who later married James Madison and became First Lady; 18th-century furnishings depict middle-class Quaker family life. Tours. Free tickets at park's Visitor Center. Retrace steps one blk to

The Merchant's Exchange. 3rd & Walnut Sts. Designed by William Strickland, one of the East's finest examples of Greek-revival architecture. Exterior restored; now houses regional offices of the National Park Service. Closed to public. Proceed E on Dock St.

Thaddeus Kosciuszko National Memorial. 3rd and Pine Sts. House of Polish patriot during his second visit to US (1797-98). He was one of the 18th century's greatest champions of American and Polish freedom and one of the first volunteers to come to the aid of the American Revolutionary Army. Exterior and 2nd floor bedroom have been restored. (Daily)

For further information about the park contact Visitor Center, 3rd and Chestnut Sts, 19106; 597-8974 (voice), 597-1785 (TDD) or 627-1776 (recording).

2. City Hall. Broad & Market Sts. (Mon-Fri; closed hols)

3. Edgar Allan Poe National Historic Site. 532 N 7th, at Spring Garden St. Where Poe lived before his move to New York in 1844. The site is the nation's memorial to the literary genius of Edgar Allan Poe. Exhibits, slide show, tours and special programs. (Daily; closed Jan 1, Dec 25) Phone 597-8780. **Free.**

4. Betsy Ross House. 239 Arch St. Where the famous seamstress is said to have made the first American Flag. Upholsterer's shop, memorabilia. Flag Day ceremonies, June 14. (Daily exc Mon; closed Jan 1, Thanksgiving, Dec 25) Phone 627-5343. **Free.**

5. Elfreth's Alley. Off 2nd St between Arch and Race Sts. Oldest continuously residential street in America, with 30 houses dating from 1728-1836 (see ANNUAL EVENTS). At #126 is the mid-18th-century **Museum House;** period furnishings, historical exhibit. (Daily) Phone 574-0560. Museum ¢

6. Society Hill Area. Area bounded approx by Front, Walnut, 7th, and Lombard Sts. This historic area, the name of which is derived from the Free Society of Traders, was created by William Penn as the city's original land company and has undergone extensive renewal of its historic buildings. (See SEASONAL EVENTS) In this area are

"A Man Full of Trouble" Tavern Museum (1759). 127-129 Spruce St. Former 18th-century tavern; now houses private collection of 17th- & 18th-century furnishings, pewter, homespun linens, English delftware and more. Costumed guides. (2nd Sun afternoon every month) Phone 922-1759. ¢

Powel House (1765). 244 S 3rd St. Georgian town house of Samuel Powel, last colonial mayor of Philadelphia and first mayor under the new republic. Period furnishings, silver and porcelain; garden. Tours (daily exc Mon; closed most hols). For tour schedule phone 627-0364. ¢¢

Physick House (1786). 321 S 4th St. House of Dr. Philip Sung Physick, "father of American surgery," from 1815-1837. Restored Federal-style house with period furnishings; garden. (Daily exc Mon) For tour schedule phone 925-7866. ¢¢

Athenaeum of Philadelphia. 219 S 6th St. Landmark example of Italian Renaissance architecture (1845-47); restored building has American neoclassical-style decorative arts, paintings, sculpture; research library; furniture and art from the collection of Joseph Bonaparte, King of Spain and older brother of Napoleon; changing exhibits of architectural drawings, photos and rare books. (Mon-Fri; closed hols) Phone 925-2688. **Free.**

7. Germantown.

Deshler-Morris House (1772-73). 5442 Germantown Ave. Residence of President Washington in the summers of 1793, 1794; period furnishings, garden. (Apr-Nov, daily exc Mon; rest of yr, by appt; closed most hols) Phone 596-1748. ¢

Stenton House (1723-30). 18th St between Courtland St & Windrim Ave. Mansion built by James Logan, secretary to William Penn. Excellent example of Pennsylvania colonial architecture, furnished with 18th- and 19th-century antiques. General Washington spent Aug 13, 1777, here and General Sir William Howe headquartered here for the Battle of Germantown. Colonial barn, gardens, kitchen. (Apr-Dec, Tues-Sat afternoons; rest of yr, by appt only; closed hols) Phone 329-7312. ¢¢

Cliveden (1767). 6401 Germantown Ave, between Johnson & Cliveden Sts. A two-and-a-half-story stone Georgian house of individual design built as summer home by Benjamin Chew, Chief Justice of colonial Pennsylvania. On Oct 4, 1777, British soldiers used house as a fortress to repulse Washington's attempt to recapture Philadelphia. Used as Chew family residence for 200 years; many original furnishings. A National Trust for Historic Preservation property. (Apr-Dec, daily exc Mon; closed Easter, Thanksgiving, Dec 25) Phone 848-1777. ¢¢¢

8. **Shopping.**

Italian Market. 9th St between Christian and Wharton Sts. Historical outdoor food mall sells fresh foods, cookware and clothing. Also here are restaurants and South Philly cheesesteaks. (Daily)

Jeweler's Row. 7th & Sansom Sts. Largest jewelry district in the country other than New York City. More than 300 shops, including wholesalers and diamond cutters.

Antique Row. From 9th to 13th Sts along Pine St. Dozens of antique, third world craft and curio shops.

Gallery. 10th & Market Sts. Concentration of 250 shops and restaurants in four-level mall with glass elevators, trees, fountains and benches. Phone 925-7162.

The Bourse (1893-95). 5th St, across from Liberty Bell Pavilion (see #1). Restored Victorian building houses shops and restaurants.

The Shops at the Bellevue. Broad St at Walnut. Beaux-arts architecture of the former Bellevue Stratford Hotel has been preserved and transformed; it now contains offices, a hotel and a four-level shopping area centered around an atrium court. (Daily exc Sun) Phone 875-8350.

9. **Balch Institute for Ethnic Studies.** 18 S 7th St. A multicultural library, archive, museum and education center that promotes intergroup understanding using education. 300 years of US immigration are documented here. Features "Peopling of Pennsylvania," as well as changing exhibits. (Mon-Fri; closed hols) Donation. Phone 925-8090.

10. **Free Library.** Logan Sq, 19th & Vine Sts. Large central library with over 9 million indexed items in all fields. Rare books, maps, theater scripts and orchestral scores; automobile reference collections; changing exhibits. (Memorial Day-Labor Day, daily exc Sun; rest of yr, daily; closed hols) Phone 686-5322. **Free.**

11. **Washington Square.** Walnut St from 6th St, where hundreds of Revolutionary War soldiers and victims of the yellow fever epidemic are buried. Life-size statue of Washington has tomb of Revolutionary War's Unknown Soldier at its feet. Across the street is

Philadelphia Savings Fund Society building (1816). Walnut & 8th Sts. Site of oldest savings bank in US. Not open to public.

12. **Academy of Music** (1857). Broad & Locust Sts. City's opera house, concert hall; home of Philadelphia Orchestra, Philly Pops, Opera Company of Philadelphia and Pennsylvania Ballet. (See SEASONAL EVENTS) Phone 893-1935.

13. **Walnut Street Theatre** (1809). Ninth & Walnut Sts. America's oldest theater. The Walnut Mainstage offers musicals, classical and contemporary plays. The two studio theaters provide a forum for new and avant-garde works. Phone 574-3550.

14. **US Mint.** On Independence Mall at 5th & Arch Sts. Produces coins of all denominations. Gallery affords visitors an elevated view of the coinage operations. Medal-making may also be observed. Audio-visual, self-guided tours. Rittenhouse Room on the mezzanine contains historic coins, medals and other exhibits. (July-Aug, daily; rest of yr, Mon-Fri; closed Jan 1, Thanksgiving, Dec 25) Phone 597-7350. **Free.**

15. **Pennsylvania Hospital** (1751). 8th & Spruce Sts. First in country, founded by Benjamin Franklin.

16. **Fort Mifflin.** From the airport, follow Island Ave toward the Delaware River, follow brown and white signs. Site of a seven-week siege during the Revolutionary War. Served as a military installation until 1959. Guided tours (Apr-Nov, Wed-Sun). Phone 492-1881. ¢¢

17. **Sightseeing tours.**

Centipede Tours. 1315 Walnut St. Candlelight strolls (1½ hrs) through historic Philadelphia and Society Hill areas led by guides in 18th-century dress; begins and ends at City Tavern (see #1).

(Mid-May-mid-Oct, Thurs-Sat) Reservations preferred. Sr citizen rate. Phone 735-3123. ¢¢

Philadelphia Carriage Company. 500 N 13th St. Guided tours via horse-drawn carriage covering Society Hill and other historic areas; begin and end in front of Independence Hall & Liberty Bell Pavilion (see #1). (Daily, weather permitting; closed Dec 25) Phone 922-6840. ¢¢¢¢-¢¢¢¢¢

AudioWalk & Tour/Historic Philadelphia. Office in the Norman Rockwell museum (see #22). Recorded walking tour of the historic area with music, little-known facts, stories; rental of cassette and tape player (accommodates up to 5 people); easy to follow map. (Daily) Phone 922-4345. ¢¢¢¢¢

Gray Line bus tours. For information, reservations, contact PO Box 5985, 3101 E Orthodox St, 19137; 569-3666 or 800/220-3133.

MUSEUMS

18. **Philadelphia Maritime Museum.** 321 Chestnut St. *Scheduled to move to Penn's Landing (see #40) as part of the Port of History Museum in spring of 1995 and undergo major renovation.* Ship models, figureheads, whaling equipment, paintings. Exhibits illustrate maritime history of Delaware Bay and River, life of a sailor; special exhibits. Waterfront facility at Penn's Landing houses boat building workshop and small gallery. (Daily exc Mon; closed hols) Phone 925-5439. ¢¢

19. **New Year Shooters & Mummer's Museum.** 2nd St & Washington Ave. Participatory exhibits and displays highlighting the history and tradition of the Mummers Parade (see ANNUAL EVENTS). Costumes and videotapes of past parades. Free outdoor string band concerts (May-Sept, Tues evenings, weather permitting); 20 string bands, different every week. (Sept-June, Mon-Sat, also Sun afternoons; rest of yr, daily exc Sun; closed major hols) Sr citizen rate. Phone 336-3050. ¢¢

20. **National Museum of American Jewish History.** Independence Mall East, 55 N 5th St. Exhibit portrays the American Jewish experience from 1654 to the present; changing exhibits; art, artifacts; audio-visual display. (Daily exc Sat; limited hrs Fri & Sun; closed Jan 1, Thanksgiving, Jewish hols) Sr citizen rate. Phone 923-3811. ¢¢

21. **Norman Rockwell Museum.** 6th & Sansom Sts, opp Independence Hall. Drawings, canvases, lithographs, prints and sketches covering 60 years of the artist's career; replica of Rockwell studio; video presentation. Gift shop. (Daily, mid-morning-mid-afternoon; closed Jan 1, Easter, Thanksgiving, Dec 25) Sr citizen rate. Phone 922-4345. ¢

22. **Afro-American Historical and Cultural Museum.** 7th & Arch Sts. Built to house and interpret African American culture. Changing exhibits; public events including lectures, workshops, films and concerts. (Daily exc Mon; closed Jan 1, Thanksgiving, Dec 25) Accessible to wheelchairs. Phone 574-0380. ¢¢

23. **Atwater Kent Museum—The History Museum of Philadelphia.** 15 S 7th St. Hundreds of fascinating artifacts, toys and miniatures, maps, prints, paintings and photographs reflecting the city's social and cultural history. (Tues-Sat; closed hols) Phone 922-3031. **Free.**

24. **American Swedish Historical Museum.** 1900 Pattison Ave. From tapestries to technology, the museum celebrates Swedish influence on American life. Special exhibits on the New Sweden Colony. Research library, collections. (Daily exc Mon; closed hols) Phone 389-1776. ¢

25. **Historical Society of Pennsylvania.** 1300 Locust St. Museum exhibit features first draft of Constitution, 500 artifacts and manuscripts plus video tours of turn-of-the-century urban and suburban neighborhoods. Research library and archives house historical and genealogical collections. (Tues-Sat; closed hols). Phone 732-6201. ¢¢

26. **Civil War Library and Museum.** 1805 Pine St. Four-story brick 19th-century town house filled with 18,000 books and periodicals

dealing with events leading up to the American Civil War, the war itself and early Reconstruction. Unique collection of arms, uniforms, flags of the period, memorabilia and artifacts begun in 1888 by former officers of the Union Army. Exhibits on Lincoln, Grant and Meade; also the Navy Room and the Armory. (Daily exc Sun; closed hols) Phone 735-8196. ¢¢

27. **Academy of Natural Sciences Museum** (1812). 19th St & Benjamin Franklin Pkwy. Dinosaurs, Egyptian mummies, animal displays in natural habitats, live animal programs, hands-on children's museum. (Daily; closed Jan 1, Thanksgiving, Dec 25) Sr citizen rate. Phone 299-1000. ¢¢¢

28. **Wagner Free Institute of Science.** Montgomery & 17th Sts. Victorian science museum with more than 50,000 specimens illustrating the various branches of the natural sciences. Dinosaur bones, fossils, reptiles and rare species are all mounted in the Victorian style. Reference library and research archives. (Tues-Fri, by appt) Phone 763-6529. **Free.**

29. **Please Touch Museum for Children.** 210 N 21st St. Unique museum, designed especially for children 7 years old and younger. Hands-on exhibits, including "Move It," "Studio PTM," "Foodtastic Journey" and "Step Into Art." (Daily; closed Jan 1, Thanksgiving, Dec 25) Phone 963-0667. ¢¢¢

30. **Mütter Museum.** 19 S 22nd St. In the College of Physicians of Philadelphia. Medical antiques and memorabilia; anatomical and pathological specimens and models. (Tues-Fri; closed hols) Donation. Phone 563-3737.

31. **Franklin Institute Science Museum.** 20th St & Ben Franklin Pkwy. **Science Center** includes exhibits on trains, shipmaking, astronomy, bioscience, communications, aviation and electricity; highlights include a Baldwin #60000 locomotive and a giant walk-through heart. **Mandell Futures Center** is dedicated to the science and technology shaping the 21st century; it explores such areas as space, earth, health and computers. Also here are **Benjamin Franklin National Memorial, Fels Planetarium** and the four-story screen of the **Tuttleman Omniverse Theater** (30-40-min films). (Daily; closed major hols) Sr citizen rate. Phone 448-1200. ¢¢¢

32. **Rodin Museum.** 22nd St & Franklin Pkwy. Largest collection of Rodin sculpture outside Paris. (Tues-Sun; closed legal hols) Donation. Phone 684-7788.

33. **Philadelphia Museum of Art.** 26th St & Benjamin Franklin Pkwy. Over 200 galleries with collections of paintings, graphics, sculpture; period rooms, medieval cloister, Indian temple, Chinese palace hall, Japanese teahouse; armor collection. American wing includes rural Pennsylvania Dutch crafts, Shaker furniture and paintings of early American artists, such as Gilbert Stuart and Thomas Eakins. Free guided tours. (Tues-Sun, also Wed evenings; closed legal hols) Sr citizen rate. Free admission Sun mornings. Phone 763-8100. ¢¢¢

34. **Rosenbach Museum.** 2010 DeLancey Pl. This 19th-century town house has permanent and changing exhibits of fine and decorative arts; collection includes 18th- and 19th-century English and French prints, 18th-century American silver, historical manuscripts and American and British literature collection, including a *Canterbury Tales* manuscript. (Daily exc Mon; closed hols, also Aug) Phone 732-1600. Tours ¢¢

35. **University Museum of Archaeology and Anthropology.** University of Pennsylvania (see #50), 33rd & Spruce Sts. World-famous archaeological and ethnographic collections developed from the museum's own expeditions, gifts and purchases; features Chinese, Near Eastern, Greek, ancient Egyptian, African, Pacific, and North, Middle & South American materials; library. Restaurant, shops. (Daily exc Mon; closed hols, also Sun in summer) Phone 898-4000. ¢¢

36. **Fireman's Hall Museum.** 149 N 2nd St. Collection of antique firefighting equipment; displays and exhibits of fire department history since its beginning in 1736; library. (Tues-Sat; closed hols) Donation. Phone 923-1438.

37. **Pennsylvania Academy of the Fine Arts.** 118 N Broad St. Oldest art museum and school in US; housed in restored Victorian building by architect Frank Furness. Outstanding permanent collection of three centuries of American art; rotating exhibits. Guided tours (daily exc Mon; closed major hols). Sr citizen rate. Phone 972-7600. ¢¢¢

38. **Penn's Landing.** Columbus Blvd & Spruce St. Here are

   USS *Olympia*. Commodore Dewey's flagship during Spanish-American War; restored. Naval museum has weapons, uniforms, ship models, naval relics of all periods. Also here is World War II submarine, **USS *Becuna*.** (Daily; closed Jan 1, Dec 25) Sr citizen rate. Phone 922-1898. *Olympia* and *Becuna* ¢¢

   Gazela of Philadelphia (1883). Columbus Blvd & Chestnut St. Portuguese square-rigger, tall ship. (June-Sept, Sat & Sun) Donation. Phone 923-9030.

HISTORIC CHURCHES AND CEMETERIES

39. **Gloria Dei Church National Historic Site ("Old Swedes")** (1700). Columbus Blvd & Christian St, 8 blks S of Chestnut. State's oldest church. Memorial to John Hanson, President of the United States under Articles of Confederation. (Daily) Phone 389-1513.

40. **St George's United Methodist Church** (1769). 235 N 4th St. Oldest Methodist Church in continuous service in US. Colonial architecture; collection of Methodist memorabilia; has only Bishop Asbury Bible and John Wesley Chalice Cup in America. (Daily) Phone 925-7788.

41. **Burial Ground of the Congregation Mikveh Israel** (1738). Spruce & 8th Sts. Graves of Haym Salomon, Revolutionary War financier, and Rebecca Gratz, probable model for "Rebecca" of Sir Walter Scott's *Ivanhoe*.

42. **Old Pine St Presbyterian Church** (1768). 412 Pine St, at 4th St. Colonial Church and graveyard, renovated in 1850s in Greek-revival style. Phone 925-8051.

43. **St Peter's Church** (Episcopal) (1761). 3rd & Pine Sts. Georgian colonial architecture; numerous famous people buried in churchyard. (Most Sat mornings) Phone 925-5968 for appt.

44. **Old St Mary's Church** (1763). 252 S 4th St, between Locust & Spruce Sts. Commodore John Barry, "father of the US Navy," is interred in graveyard behind the city's first Catholic cathedral. (Daily) Phone 923-7930.

45. **Christ Church** (Episcopal). 2nd St between Market and Arch Sts. Patriots, loyalists and heroes have worshiped here since 1695. Sit in pews once occupied by Washington, Franklin and Betsy Ross. (Mar-Dec, daily; rest of yr, Wed-Sun; closed Jan 1, Thanksgiving, Dec 25) Phone 922-1695.

46. **Christ Church Burial Ground.** 5th & Arch Sts. Resting place of Benjamin Franklin, his wife, Deborah and four other signers of the Declaration of Independence. (Mid-Apr-mid-Oct, daily) Phone 922-1695.

47. **Arch Street Friends Meetinghouse** (1804). 4th & Arch Sts. Perhaps the largest Friends meetinghouse in the world. Exhibits, slide show, tours. (Daily exc Sun; closed Jan 1, Thanksgiving, Dec 25) Donation. Phone 627-2667.

EDUCATIONAL CENTERS

48. **University of Pennsylvania** (1740). (23,000 students) Chestnut to Pine Sts & 32nd to 40th Sts. On campus are the newly restored Fisher Fine Arts Library (phone 898-4401), Annenberg Center for performing arts (phone 898-6791); University Museum of Archaeology and Anthropology (see #36) and Institute of Contemporary Art, located at 36th and Sansom Sts (daily exc Mon; phone 898-7108; fee). For information phone 898-1000.

49. **Temple University** (1884). (33,000 students) Cecil B. Moore Ave & Broad St. Undergraduate, professional and research school. Walking tours of campus. Phone 204-8551.

50. **Haverford College** (1833). (1,100 students) 10 mi W on US 30, in Haverford. Founded by members of the Society of Friends. The 216-acre campus includes Founders Hall; James P. Magill Library; Arboretum; Morris Cricket Library and Collection (by appt only; phone 610/896-1162). Tours of arboretum and campus. Phone 610/896-1000.

PARKS AND RECREATIONAL FACILITIES

51. **Fairmount Park.** Begins at Philadelphia Museum of Art, extends NW on both sides of Wissahickon Creek and Schuylkill River. Covers 8,700 acres. Phone 685-0000. In park are

    Colonial Mansions. Handsome 18th-century dwellings in varying architectural styles, authentically preserved and furnished, include Mount Pleasant (1761) (daily exc Mon); Cedar Grove (1756) (daily exc Mon); Strawberry Mansion (1797) (daily exc Mon); Sweetbriar (1797) (daily exc Tues); Lemon Hill (1799) (Wed-Sun); Woodford (1756) (daily exc Mon); Laurel Hill (1760) (Wed-Sun). Further details and guided tours from Park Houses office at Philadelphia Museum of Art (see #34). Phone 684-7922. Each house ¢

    Boat House Row. On E bank of river. Used by collegiate and club oarsmen. Schuylkill River is scene of many nationally important crew competitions; crews practice all spring and summer during early morning and afternoon. Phone 978-6919 for rowing, regatta schedules.

    Japanese Exhibition House. Fairmount Park Horticulture Center. Re-creates a bit of Japan, complete with garden, pond, bridge. (May-Oct) Phone 878-5097. ¢

    Robin Hood Dell East. (See SEASONAL EVENTS)

    Philadelphia Zoological Garden. 3400 W Girard Ave. America's first zoo. More than 1,700 animals, many in natural surroundings; World of Primates; TREEHOUSE (fee); waterfowl collection; bear country; five-acre African plains exhibit; reptile house; bird house; carnivore kingdom; children's zoo. Picnic areas; cafe. Guided tours by appt. Main zoo (daily; closed Jan 1, Thanksgiving, Dec 24, 25, 31). Sr citizen rate. Phone 243-1100. ¢¢¢

52. **Schuylkill Center for Environmental Education.** 9 mi NW, at 8480 Hagy's Mill Rd. A 500-acre natural area with more than 7 miles of trails; discovery room; gift shop/bookstore. (Daily; closed hols) Sr citizen rate. Phone 482-7300. ¢¢

53. **Historic Bartram's Garden.** 54th St & Lindbergh Blvd. Pre-revolutionary home of John Bartram, the royal botanist to the colonies under George III, naturalist and plant explorer. The 18th-century stone farmhouse (fee), barn, stable and cider mill overlook the Schuylkill River. Museum shop. (May-Oct, Wed-Sun afternoons; rest of yr, Wed-Fri afternoons; closed hols) Phone 729-5281. House tour ¢; Combination house & garden tour ¢¢

54. **Morris Arboretum of the University of Pennsylvania** (1887). Approx 12 mi NW in Chestnut Hill; entrance on Northwestern Ave. Public garden with more than 1,600 types of native and exotic trees and shrubs on 166 acres; special garden areas such as Swan Pond, Rose Garden and Japanese gardens. (Daily; closed Dec 24-Jan 1) Tours (Sat & Sun afternoon; one departure each day). Sr citizen rate. Phone 247-5777. ¢¢

55. **John Heinz National Wildlife Refuge at Tinicum.** S via I-95, W PA 291 exit, right on Bartram Ave, left on 84th St, left on Lindbergh Blvd, at 86th & Lindbergh Blvd. Largest remaining freshwater tidal wetland in the state, protecting more than 1,000 acres of wildlife habitat. Area was first diked by Swedish farmers in 1643; Dutch farmers and the colonial government added dikes during the Revolutionary War. More than 280 species of birds and 13 resident mammal species. Hiking, bicycling, nature observation, canoeing on Darby Creek, fishing. (Daily) Phone 365-3118 or 610/521-0662. **Free.**

56. **Sesame Place.** 20 mi NE via I-95 to Levittown exit (25E). Follow signs for the Oxford Valley Mall on the US 1 Bypass. (See BRISTOL)

Annual Events

Mummers Parade. An 8-hour spectacle along Broad St. Jan 1.

Presidential Jazz Weekend. Jazz concerts around the city. 4 days mid-Feb.

Philadelphia Open House. House and garden tours in different neighborhoods; distinguished selection of over 150 private homes, gardens, historic sites. Many tours include lunches, candlelight dinners or high teas. Phone 928-1188. Late Apr-mid-May.

Devon Horse Show. Approx 20 mi NW via US 30, at Horse Show Grounds, in Devon. One of America's leading equestrian events. More than 1,200 horses compete; country fair; antique carriage drive. Phone 610/964-0550. 9 days beginning Memorial Day wknd.

Elfreth's Alley Fete Day (see #5). Homes open to public, costumed guides, demonstrations of colonial crafts; food, entertainment. 1st wknd June.

Freedom Festival. Re-creation of historic and patriotic events; tours of historic areas; parade, fireworks. Early July.

Thanksgiving Day Parade. Giant floats; celebrities.

Army-Navy Football Game. John F. Kennedy Memorial Stadium or Veterans Stadium. 1st Sat Dec.

Fairmount Park Historical Christmas Tours. Period decorations in 18th-century mansions. Phone 684-7922. Early Dec.

Seasonal Events

American Music Theater Festival. Repertory includes new opera, musical comedy, cabaret-style shows, revues and experimental works. Phone 567-0670. Main stage productions Mar-June.

Head House Open Air Craft Market. Pine & 2nd Sts, in Society Hill area in Head House Square (see #6). Crafts demonstrations, children's workshops. Sat & Sun, June-Aug.

Mann Music Center. 52nd St & Parkside Ave, West Fairmount Park. Philadelphia Orchestra performs Mon, Wed & Thurs; outdoor amphitheater seats 13,243. Also popular attractions. Phone 567-0707. Late June-late July.

Robin Hood Dell East. 33rd & Dauphin Sts, in Fairmount Park (see #51). Top stars in outdoor popular music concerts. Phone 477-8810. July-Aug.

Performing arts.

Philadelphia Orchestra. Academy of Music (see #12). Phone 893-1900. Sept-May. Also Mann Music Center (see above), late June-late July.

Philadelphia Company. Plays and Players Theatre, 1714 Delancy St. Five contemporary American plays per season. Phone 592-8333. Oct-Mar.

The Opera Company of Philadelphia. Academy of Music (see #12). Phone 928-2100. Oct-Apr.

Philadelphia Drama Guild. Zellerbach Theatre in Annenberg Center, 3680 Walnut St (see #48). Daily exc Mon; matinees Wed, Sat, Sun. Five mainstage plays; interpreted performances for the hearing impaired throughout season. Hot line 563-7529; box office 898-6791. Oct-May.

Pennsylvania Ballet. Performs at Merriam Theatre and at Academy of Music (see #12). Phone 551-7000.

Professional sports. Phillies (baseball), 463-1000; Eagles (football), 463-2500; Philadelphia Veterans Stadium, Broad St & Pattison Ave. '76ers (basketball), 339-7600; Flyers (hockey), 465-4500; Spectrum Sports Arena, Broad St & Pattison Ave.

Horse racing. Flat racing at Philadelphia Park, Richlieu & Street Rds in Bensalem. For schedule phone 639-9000.

Additional Visitor Information

The Visitors Center of the Philadelphia Convention and Visitors Bureau, 1525 John F. Kennedy Blvd, 19102, has tourist information and maps (daily; closed Thanksgiving, Dec 25). Phone 636-1666 or 800/537-7676.

There is also a visitor center (see #1) at 3rd & Chestnut Sts, operated by the National Park Service. (Daily) Phone 597-8975 or -8974 for information on park attractions.

Philadelphia Area Suburbs

The following suburbs in the Philadelphia area are included in the *Mobil Travel Guide.* For information on any one of them, see the individual alphabetical listing. Bristol, Chester, Fort Washington, Jenkintown, Kennett Square, King of Prussia, Media, Norristown, West Chester, Willow Grove; also see Wilmington, DE and Camden, NJ.

City Neighborhoods

Many of the restaurants, unrated dining establishments and some lodgings listed under Philadelphia include neighborhoods as well as exact street addresses. A map showing these neighborhoods can be found immediately following the airport map. Geographic descriptions of these areas are given, followed by a table of restaurants arranged by neighborhood.

Center City: Area of Downtown around city hall; south of Kennedy Blvd, west of Juniper St, north of S Penn Square and east of 15th St.

Chestnut Hill: South of Stenton Ave, west and north of Cresheim Valley Dr and east of Fairmount Park; along Germantown Ave.

Chinatown: North central area of Downtown; south of Vine St, west of 8th St, north of Arch St and east of 11th St.

Downtown: South of Spring Garden St, west of I-95, north of South St and east of the Schuylkill River. **North of Downtown:** North of Spring Garden St. **South of Downtown:** South of South St. **West of Downtown:** West of Schuylkill River.

Olde City: Area of Downtown south of I-676, west of the Delaware River, north of Chestnut St and east of Independence Mall.

Society Hill: Southeast side of Downtown; south of Walnut St, west of Front St, north of Lombard St and east of 7th St.

South Street: Downtown area; South St between Broad St on the west and the Delaware River on the east; also north to Pine St and south to Bainbridge St.

PHILADELPHIA RESTAURANTS
BY NEIGHBORHOOD AREAS

(For full description, see alphabetical listings under Restaurants)

CENTER CITY

Bookbinder's Seafood House. 215 S 15th St
Di Lullo Centro. 1407 Locust St

CHESTNUT HILL

Flying Fish. 8142 Germantown Ave
Roller's. 8705 Germantown Ave
Under the Blue Moon. 8042 Germantown Ave

CHINATOWN

Ho Sai Gai. 1000 Race St
Van's Garden. 121 N 11th St

DOWNTOWN

Baci Bistro. 211 S Broad St
Ciboulette. 200 S Broad St
Cutters Grand Cafe. 2005 Market St
Deux Cheminées. 1221 Locust St
The Dining Room (The Ritz-Carlton, Philadelphia Hotel). 17th and Chestnut Sts
Dock Street Brewery & Restaurant. 2 Logan Square
Fountain (Four Seasons Hotel Philadelphia). 1 Logan Square
The Garden. 1617 Spruce St
Harry's Bar & Grill. 22 S 18th St
Jack's Firehouse. 2130 Fairmount Ave
Le Bar Lyonnais. 1523 Walnut St
Le Bec-Fin. 1523 Walnut St
London Grill. 2301 Fairmount Ave
Mango Bay. 264 S 16th St
Marabella's. 1420 Locust St
The Palm. 200 S Broad St
Restaurant 210 (The Rittenhouse Hotel). 210 W Rittenhouse Square
Sfuzzi. 1650 Market St
Suzanna Foo. 1512 Walnut St
Swann Lounge (Four Seasons Hotel Philadelphia). 1 Logan Square
White Dog Cafe. 3420 Sansom St

NORTH OF DOWNTOWN

Dilullo Oggi. 7955 Oxford Ave
Fisher's Seafood. 7312 Castor Ave
Napoleon Cafe. 2652 E Somerset St

SOUTH OF DOWNTOWN

D'Medici. 824 S 8th St
Famous 4th St Delicatessen. 700 S 4th St
Felicia's. 1148 S 11th St
Osteria Romana. 935 Ellsworth St

WEST OF DOWNTOWN

The Restaurant School. 4207 Walnut St
Zocalo. 3600 Lancaster Ave

OLDE CITY

Cafe Einstein. 208 Race St
Dinardo's. 312 Race St
La Famiglia. 8 S Front St
La Truffe. 10 S Front St
Los Amigos. 50 S 2nd St
Meiji-En. Pier 19 North
Middle East. 126 Chestnut St
Sassafras. 48 S 2nd St
Serrano. 20 S 2nd St
Spirit of Philadelphia. Pier 3

SOCIETY HILL

Dickens Inn. Head House Square
Old Original Bookbinder's. 125 Walnut St

SOUTH STREET AREA

Alouette. 334 Bainbridge St

Bridget Foy's South Street Grill. 200 South St

Cafe Nola. 328 South St

Knave of Hearts. 230 South St

Monte Carlo Living Room. 2nd & South Sts

South Street Diner. 140 South St

Note: When a listing is located in a town that does not have its own city heading, it will appear under the city nearest to its location. In these cases, the address and town appear in parenthesis immediately following the name of the establishment.

Motels

★ ★ **BEST WESTERN HOTEL PHILADELPHIA NORTH-EAST.** 11580 Roosevelt Blvd (19116), north of downtown. 215/464-9500; FAX 215/464-8511. 100 rms, 2 story. S, D $80-$125; under 18 free; wkly, wkend rates. Crib free. TV. Pool; lifeguard. Complimentary continental bkfst. Bar from 4 pm. Ck-out 11 am. Coin lndry. Meeting rms. Exercise equipt; weight machine, bicycles. Lawn games. Some bathrm phones, refrigerators, minibars. Many balconies. Picnic tables. Cr cds: A, C, D, DS, ER, JCB, MC, V.

D ⚡ 🏊 ⚓ ⛷ 🔥 SC

✔ ★ **COMFORT INN.** (3660 Street Rd, Bensalem 19020) N on I-95 to Street Rd W exit, 3 mi W. 215/245-0100; FAX 215/245-0100, ext. 451. 141 units, 3 story. S $60-$95; D $70-$95; each addl $10; suites $99-$109; family rates. Crib free. Pet accepted, some restrictions. TV; cable, in-rm movies avail. Complimentary continental bkfst. Restaurant nearby. Bar 4 pm-1 am; entertainment. Ck-out noon. Meeting rms. Gift shop. Exercise equipt; weights, bicycles. Game rm. Some in-rm whirlpools. Cr cds: A, C, D, DS, ER, JCB, MC, V.

D ⚡ ⛷ ⚓ 🔥 SC

Motor Hotels

✔ ★ ★ **DAYS INN-AIRPORT.** 4101 Island Ave (19153), near Intl Airport, south of downtown. 215/492-0400; FAX 215/365-6035. 177 rms, 5 story. S $99; D $109; each addl $15; under 18 free. Crib free. TV. Pool; lifeguard. Restaurant 6 am-2 pm, 5-11 pm; Sat, Sun to noon. Rm serv. Bar 4 pm-midnight. Ck-out noon. Coin lndry. Meeting rms. Valet serv. Free airport transportation. Cr cds: A, C, D, DS, MC, V.

D 🏊 ⛷ ✈ ⚓ 🔥 SC

★ **HOLIDAY INN EXPRESS MIDTOWN.** 1305 Walnut St (19107). 215/735-9300; FAX 215/732-2682. 164 rms, 20 story. S $105-$125; D $115-$135; each addl $10; under 19 free. Crib free. Garage $9.75. TV; cable. Pool; lifeguard. Restaurant nearby. Ck-out 1 pm. Meeting rms. Bellhops. Concierge. Airport transportation. Cr cds: A, C, D, DS, JCB, MC, V.

D 🏊 🔥 SC

★ ★ **HOLIDAY INN-INDEPENDENCE MALL.** 400 Arch St (19106), downtown. 215/923-8660; FAX 215/923-4633. 364 rms, 8 story. S, D $85-$150; each addl $10; suites $250-$300; under 19 free; wkend rates. Garage $12. Crib free. TV; cable. Rooftop pool; lifeguard. Restaurant 6:30 am-10:30 pm; dining rm 11:30 am-2 pm, 5:30-10:30 pm. Rm serv. Bar 11-1 am, Sun from noon. Ck-out 11 am. Coin lndry. Meeting rms. Bellhops. Valet serv. Sundries. Gift shop. Cr cds: A, C, D, DS, JCB, MC, V.

D 🏊 ⚓ 🔥 SC

★ ★ **MARRIOTT-PHILADELPHIA AIRPORT.** 4509 Island Ave (19153), at Intl Airport, south of downtown. 215/365-4150; FAX 215/365-3875. 331 rms, 9 story. S $132; D $145; suites $350; studio rms $150; under 18 free; wkend rates. Crib free. Pet accepted, some restrictions. TV; cable. Indoor pool. Restaurant 6 am-11 pm. Rm serv.

Bar 11-2 am; dancing. Ck-out 1 pm. Meeting rms. Bellhops. Valet serv. Gift shop. Free airport transportation. Exercise equipt; weights, bicycles, whirlpool, sauna. Game rm. **LUXURY LEVEL .** 38 rms, 2 suites. S $139; D $155. Concierge. Private lounge, honor bar. Complimentary continental bkfst, refreshments, newspaper. Cr cds: A, C, D, DS, ER, MC, V.

D ⚡ 🏊 ⛷ ✈ ⚓ 🔥 SC

★ ★ **SHERATON INN-PHILADELPHIA, NORTHEAST.** 9461 Roosevelt Blvd (19114), north of downtown. 215/671-9600; FAX 215/464-7759. 188 rms, 6 story. S $99; D $109; each addl $10; suites $175; under 17 free; wkend rates. Crib free. TV; cable. Indoor/outdoor pool; poolside serv. Restaurant 6:30 am-10 pm. Rm serv. Bar 2 pm-midnight. Ck-out 11 am. Coin lndry. Meeting rms. Valet serv. Sundries. Gift shop. Exercise equipt; weights, bicycles. Health club privileges. Some refrigerators. Cr cds: A, C, D, DS, MC, V.

D 🏊 ⛷ ⚓ 🔥 SC

Hotels

★ ★ ★ **ADAM'S MARK.** City Ave & Monument Rd (19131), west of downtown. 215/581-5000; res: 800/444-2326; FAX 215/581-5069. 515 rms, 23 story. S $145-$157; D $144-$164; each addl $12; suites $150-$600; under 18 free; wkend, wkly rates. Crib free. TV; cable. Indoor/outdoor pool; poolside serv, lifeguard. Restaurant 6 am-11 pm. 3 bars; entertainment, dancing. Ck-out noon. Convention facilities. Concierge. Shopping arcade. Barber, beauty shop. Airport, RR station, bus depot transportation. Exercise rm; instructor, weights, bicycles, whirlpool, sauna, steam rm. Refrigerators. Cr cds: A, C, D, DS, MC, V.

D 🏊 ⛷ ⚓ 🔥 SC

★ ★ **BARCLAY.** 237 S 18th St (19103), on Rittenhouse Square, downtown. 215/545-0300; res: 800/421-6662; FAX 215/545-2896. 240 rms, 22 story. S $145-$185; D $155-$195; each addl $10; suites, kit. suites $200-$400; under 18 free; wkend rates. Crib free. Pet accepted; $50. Valet parking $15.75. TV; cable. Complimentary continental bkfst. Restaurant 7 am-11 pm. Bar to 2 am; entertainment Fri & Sat. Ck-out 1 pm. Meeting rms. Concierge. Airport, RR station, bus depot transportation. Bathrm phones. Cr cds: A, C, D, DS, ER, MC, V.

⚡ ⚓ 🔥 SC

★ ★ ★ **BEST WESTERN INDEPENDENCE PARK INN.** 235 Chestnut St (19106), in Society Hill. 215/922-4443; FAX 215/922-4487. 36 rms, 5 story. S, D $99-$155; each addl $10. Crib free. TV; cable. Complimentary continental bkfst, afternoon tea. Ck-out noon. Meeting rms. Restored historic building (1856); ornate furnishings. Cr cds: A, C, D, DS, ER, JCB, MC, V.

D ⚓ 🔥 SC

✔ ★ ★ **BEST WESTERN RADNOR.** (591 E Lancaster, St Davids 19087) 17 mi W on US 30, 1/4 mi W of Blue Rte (I-476) exit 5. 610/688-5800; res: 800/537-3000; FAX 610/341-3299. 168 rms, 4 story. S $69-$110; D $79-$120; each addl $10; suites $162-$180; under 16 free. Crib free. TV; cable. Pool; wading pool, lifeguard. Restaurant 6:30 am-10 pm. Rm serv 24 hrs. Bar 11-2 am; entertainment. Ck-out noon. Meeting rms. Airport transportation. Exercise equipt; weight machine, rowing machine. Game rm. **LUXURY LEVEL .** 45 rms, 7 suites. S, D $99-$120. Private lounge. Complimentary continental bkfst, refreshments, newspaper. Cr cds: A, C, D, DS, ER, JCB, MC, V.

D 🏊 ⛷ ⚓ 🔥 SC

★ ★ **CHESTNUT HILL.** 8229 Germantown Ave (19118), I-76 exit Lincoln Dr to Allen's Lane, in Chestnut Hill. 215/242-5905; res: 800/628-9744; FAX 215/242-8778. 28 rms, 4 story, 3 bldgs, 3 suites. S, D $80-$120; each addl $10; suites $120; under 12 free; package plans. Crib free. TV. Complimentary continental bkfst. Restaurants 11:30 am-10 pm. Bar to midnight. Ck-out 11 am. Meeting rms. Airport transportation. Cr cds: A, C, D, MC, V.

D 🔥 SC

✔ ★ **COMFORT INN.** *100 N Christopher Columbus Blvd (19106), downtown.* 215/627-7900; FAX 215/238-0809. 185 rms, 10 story. S, D $75-$125; each addl $10; suites $160; under 18 free; higher rates some hols. Crib free. TV; cable. Complimentary continental bkfst, coffee. Coffee in rms. Restaurant nearby. Bar 5 pm-2 am. Ck-out noon. Meeting rms. Valet serv. Airport, RR station, bus depot transportation. Overlooking Delaware River. Cr cds: A, C, D, DS, ER, JCB, MC, V.

D ⊠ 🏃 🐾 SC

★ ★ ★ **DOUBLETREE.** *Broad St at Locust (19107), downtown.* 215/893-1600; FAX 215/893-1663. 428 rms, 25 story. S $155-$170; D $165-$180; each addl $15; suites $250-$500; under 18 free; wkend rates; higher rates New Year's hols. Crib free. Garage $13, valet $17. TV; cable. Indoor pool; poolside serv, lifeguard. Restaurant 6:30 am-11 pm; Fri, Sat to midnight. Bar to 1:30 am. Ck-out noon. Convention facilities. Concierge. Gift shop. Airport transportation. Exercise rm; instructor, weights, bicycles, whirlpool, sauna, steam rm. **LUXURY LEVEL :** 40 rms. S, D $190-$225. Private lounge. Cr cds: A, C, D, DS, ER, MC, V.

D ≈ 🏃 🏃 ⊠ 🐾 SC

★ ★ ★ ★ **FOUR SEASONS HOTEL PHILADELPHIA.** *1 Logan Square (19103), on Logan Circle, downtown.* 215/963-1500; FAX 215/963-9506. 371 rms, 8 story. S $220-$295; D $250-$325; each addl $30; suites $525-$1,275; under 18 free; wkend rates. Garage $12-$21. Pet accepted. TV; cable. Indoor pool; poolside serv, lifeguard. Restaurant 6:30-1 am; Sat, Sun from 7 am (also see FOUNTAIN; and see SWANN LOUNGE, Unrated Dining). Rm serv 24 hrs. Bar 11-2 am; pianist. Ck-out 1 pm. Convention facilities. Concierge. Beauty shop. Complimentary downtown transportation (as available). Exercise rm; instructor, weights, bicycles, whirlpool, sauna. Massage. Minibars. Some balconies. Cr cds: A, C, D, ER, JCB, MC, V.

D 🤿 ≈ 🏃 ⊠ 🐾 SC

★ ★ ★ **GUEST QUARTERS.** *4101 Island Rd (19153), at I-95 Island Ave exit, near Intl Airport, south of downtown.* 215/365-6600; FAX 215/492-8421. 251 suites, 8 story. S, D $119-$155; each addl $15; under 18 free; wkend rates. Crib free. TV; cable. Indoor pool; lifeguard. Complimentary continental bkfst (wkends). Restaurant 6 am-11 pm. Bar noon-2 am. Ck-out noon. Meeting rms. Gift shop. Free airport transportation. Exercise equipt; weights, bicycles, whirlpool, sauna, steam rm. Bathrm phones, refrigerators, minibars. Cr cds: A, C, D, DS, JCB, MC, V.

D ≈ 🏃 🏃 ✈ ⊠ SC

★ ★ ★ **GUEST QUARTERS.** *(640 W Germantown Pike, Plymouth Meeting 19462) W on I-76, exit I-476N to Germantown Pike West exit, right on Hickory Rd.* 610/834-8300; FAX 610/834-7813. 252 suites, 7 story. S, D $150-$170; family, wkend rates. Crib free. TV; cable. Indoor pool; wading pool, poolside serv, lifeguard. Restaurant 6:30 am-10 pm. Bar. Ck-out noon. Coin lndry. Meeting rms. Shopping arcade. Airport, RR station, bus depot transportation. Exercise equipt; weights, bicycles, whirlpool, sauna. Bathrm phones, refrigerators, minibars. Some private patios, balconies. Cr cds: A, C, D, DS, MC, V.

D ≈ 🏃 ⊠ 🐾 SC

★ ★ ★ **HOLIDAY INN-CITY CENTRE.** *1800 Market St (19103), in Center City.* 215/561-7500; FAX 215/561-4484. 445 rms, 25 story. S, D $118-$140; each addl $10; suites $200-$350; under 18 free; wkend rates. Crib free. Garage fee. TV; cable. Pool; lifeguard. Restaurant 6:30 am-11 pm. Bar 11 am-midnight. Ck-out noon. Coin lndry. Convention facilities. Gift shop. Airport transportation. Exercise equipt; weights, bicycles. **LUXURY LEVEL :** 53 rms, 6 suites, 2 floors. S $140; D $150. Private lounge. Complimentary continental bkfst. Cr cds: A, C, D, DS, JCB, MC, V.

D ≈ 🏃 ✈ ⊠ 🐾 SC

★ ★ ★ **HOTEL ATOP THE BELLEVUE.** *1415 Chancellor Court (19102), downtown.* 215/893-1776; res: 800/221-0833; FAX 215/893-9868. 170 rms, 7 story. S $210-$260; D $230-$290; suites $350-$1,300; under 18 free; special packages. Crib free. Garage $13, valet $18.50. TV; cable, in-rm movies. Indoor pool privileges; whirlpool,

sauna, lifeguard. Restaurants 7 am-11 pm. Dinner/dancing Fri & Sat. Rm serv 24 hrs. Bar 11-1 am. Ck-out 1 pm. Meeting rms. Concierge. Shopping arcade. Barber, beauty shop. Airport, RR station, bus depot transportation. Health club privileges. Bathrm phones, minibars. Some balconies. Turn-of-the-century decor. European-style service and amenities. Hotel is located atop French Renaissance-style, restored landmark building and features a sunlit 7-story atrium. State-of-the-art athletic club is connected by skywalk. Cr cds: A, C, D, DS, ER, JCB, MC, V.

D ≈ 🏃 🏃 ⊠ 🐾

✔ ★ ★ ★ **KORMAN SUITES.** *2001 Hamilton St (19130), just off the Pkwy, downtown.* 215/569-7000. 99 suites, 27 story. Suites $109-$159; under 18 free; wkend rates. Crib free. TV; cable, in-rm movies. Pool; poolside serv, lifeguard. Complimentary continental bkfst. Restaurant 6:30 am-2:30 pm, 5:30-9:30 pm. Bar; entertainment. Ck-out 11 am. Convention facilities. Gift shop. Barber, beauty shop. Lighted tennis. Exercise rm; instructor, weight machine, bicycles, whirlpool. Complete fitness center. Three original art installations: Neon for Buttonwood," a roofline neon sculpture; Spirit Dance,"a glass wall with carved, etched and painted designs; and a landscaped Japanese sculpture garden. Cr cds: A, D, MC, V.

D 🏃 ≈ 🏃 ⊠ 🐾 SC

★ ★ ★ **MARRIOTT PHILADELPHIA WEST.** *(111 Crawford Ave, West Conshohocken 19428) 11 W on I-76, exit 29.* 215/482-5600. 288 rms, 17 story. S $134-$154; D $149-$169; each addl $15; suites $295-$375; under 18 free; wkend, hol rates. Crib free. Valet parking $8. TV; cable. Indoor pool; poolside serv, lifeguard. Restaurant 6 am-11 pm. Bar. Ck-out 3 pm. Convention facilities. Concierge. Shopping arcade. Free airport, RR station transportation. Exercise equipt; weight machine, stair machine, whirlpool, sauna. 1 blk from Schuylkill River. **LUXURY LEVEL :** 52 rms, 3 story, 1 suite. S $139-$159; D $154-$174; suite $295-$350. Concierge. Private lounge. Honor bar. Complimentary newspaper. Cr cds: A, C, D, DS, MC, V.

D ≈ 🏃 ✈ ⊠ 🐾 SC

★ ★ ★ ★ **OMNI HOTEL AT INDEPENDENCE PARK.** *4th & Chestnut Sts (19106), on Independence Park, adj to Independence Hall, in Olde City.* 215/925-0000; FAX 215/925-1263. 150 rms, 14 story, 10 suites. S $195; D $225; each addl $25; suites from $350; under 18 free; wkend rates. Crib free. Garage (fee). TV; cable, in-rm movies. Indoor pool. Restaurant 7 am-2:30 pm, 5:30-10 pm. Rm serv 24 hrs. Bar 3-11 pm; entertainment Tues-Sat. Ck-out noon. Meeting rms. Concierge. Airport transportation. Exercise equipt; weight machine, bicycles, whirlpool, sauna. Bathrm phones, minibars. Complimentary newspaper. Every room has a view of Independence Park. Cr cds: A, C, D, DS, ER, JCB, MC, V.

D ≈ 🏃 ⊠ 🐾 SC

★ ★ ★ **RADISSON.** *500 Stevens Dr (19113), near Intl Airport, south of downtown.* 610/521-5900; FAX 610/521-4362. 353 rms, 12 story. S $119; D $129; each addl $10; suites $275; under 18 free; wkend packages. Crib free. TV; cable. Indoor pool; poolside serv. Restaurant 6:30 am-2:30 pm, 5-11 pm. Bars 2 pm-midnight. Ck-out noon. Meeting rms. Gift shop. Free airport transportation. Exercise equipt; weight machine, bicycle, whirlpool. Game rm. Wet bars. Balconies. Cr cds: A, C, D, DS, ER, MC, V.

D ≈ 🏃 ✈ ⊠ 🐾 SC

★ ★ ★ ★ **THE RITTENHOUSE.** *210 W Rittenhouse Square (19103), downtown.* 215/546-9000; res: 800/635-1042; FAX 215/732-3364. 133 rms, 9 story, 11 suites. S $225-$250; D $250-$275; suites $350-$1,000; wkend rates. Crib free. Garage; valet parking $21. Pet accepted. TV; cable, in-rm movies. Indoor pool; poolside serv. Restaurant 6:30 am-10:30 pm (also see RESTAURANT 210). Rm serv 24 hrs. Bar; entertainment. Ck-out 1 pm. Meeting rms. Concierge. Shopping arcade. Barber, beauty shop. Airport transportation. Exercise rm; instructor, weight machine, bicycles, sauna, steam rm. Massage. Health club privileges. Bathrm phones, minibars. Complimentary newspaper.

Luxury hotel with expansive views of Rittenhouse Square and the city panorama. Cr cds: A, C, D, DS, MC, V.

★ ★ ★ ★ **THE RITZ-CARLTON, PHILADELPHIA.** *17th and Chestnut Sts (19103), at Liberty Place, downtown.* 215/563-1600; FAX 215/567-2822. 290 rms, 15 story, 17 suites. S, D $175-$245; suites $350-$950; wkend rates. Crib free. Garage fee. TV; cable. Swimming privileges. Restaurant (see THE DINING ROOM). Rm serv 24 hrs. Bar 11-1 am; pianist. Ck-out noon. Meeting rms. Concierge. Gift shop. Airport, RR station transportation. Town car transportation within city. Exercise rm; instructor, weight machine, bicycles, sauna. Masseuse. Bathrm phones, minibars. *LUXURY LEVEL : THE RITZ-CARLTON CLUB.* 30 rms, 8 suites, 2 floors. S, D $245; suites $410-$950. Concierge. Private lounge. Complimentary continental bkfst, refreshments. Cr cds: A, C, D, DS, ER, JCB, MC, V.

★ ★ ★ **SHERATON SOCIETY HILL.** *1 Dock St (19106), in Society Hill.* 215/238-6000; FAX 215/922-2709. 365 units, 4 story. S, D $145-$215; suites $300-$1,000; under 17 free; wkend rates. Crib free. Covered parking fee. TV; cable. Indoor pool; wading pool, poolside serv, lifeguard. Coffee in rms. Restaurant 6:30 am-2 pm, 5-10 pm. Rm serv 24 hrs. Bar noon-2 am. Ck-out noon. Convention facilities. Concierge. Shopping arcade. Transportation to business district (Mon-Fri). Exercise rm; instructor, weights, bicycles, whirlpool, sauna. Minibars; some refrigerators. Complimentary newspaper. Cr cds: A, C, D, DS, ER, JCB, MC, V.

★ ★ ★ **THE WARWICK.** *1701 Locust St (19103), downtown.* 215/735-6000; res: 800/523-4210 (exc PA); FAX 215/790-7766. 180 rms, 20 story, 20 kits. S $145-$185; D $195-$200; each addl $15; suites $180-$380; studio rms $185; apt $195; under 12 free; wkend plans. Crib free. Garage (fee). TV; cable. Restaurant 6:30 am-midnight. Bar 11-2 am. Ck-out noon. Meeting rms. Concierge. Barber, beauty shop. Health club privileges. Complimentary newspaper. Cr cds: A, C, D, DS, MC, V.

★ ★ ★ **WYNDHAM FRANKLIN PLAZA.** *2 Franklin Plaza (19103), jct 17th & Vine Sts, downtown.* 215/448-2000; FAX 215/448-2864. 758 rms, 26 story. S $145-$185; D $165-$195; each addl $20; suites $300-$1,000; under 18 free. Crib free. Garage $13. TV; cable. Indoor pool; poolside serv. Complimentary coffee in rms. Restaurant 6:30 am-11:30 pm. Bars 11-1 am. Ck-out noon. Convention facilities. Drugstore. Barber, beauty shop. Airport transportation avail. Tennis. Exercise rm; instructor, weights, bicycles, whirlpool, sauna, steam rm. Masseuse. Refrigerators. Cr cds: A, C, D, DS, ER, JCB, MC, V.

Inns

★ ★ ★ **PENN'S VIEW.** *14 N Front St (19106), in Olde City.* 215/922-7600; res: 800/331-7634; FAX 215/922-7642. 27 rms, 5 story. S, D $100-$150; under 12 free; wkend rates. Crib free. TV; cable. Complimentary continental bkfst. Dining rm noon-2:30 pm, 5:30-10 pm; Fri, Sat 5:30-11 pm. Ck-out noon, ck-in 3 pm. Bellhops. Concierge. Airport, RR station, bus depot transportation. Overlooks Delaware River. Built 1828; Old World elegance, antiques, some fireplaces in rms. Cr cds: A, D, MC, V.

✔ ★ **SOCIETY HILL HOTEL.** *301 Chestnut St (19106), in Society Hill.* 215/925-1919. 12 rms, 4 story. S, D $95-$135. TV. Complimentary continental bkfst in rms. Restaurant 11 am-11 pm. Bar; jazz pianist Tues-Sat. Ck-out noon, ck-in 3 pm. Historic building (1832); pension ambience. Cr cds: A, C, D, MC, V.

✔ ★ ★ **THE THOMAS BOND HOUSE.** *129 S 2nd St (19106), in Olde City.* 215/923-8523; res: 800/845-2663. 12 rms, 4 story, 2 suites. No elvtr. S, D $80-$150; each addl $15; suites $150. Parking $9. TV. Complimentary continental bkfst (full bkfst wkends), tea/sherry. Restaurant nearby. Ck-out noon, ck-in 3-9 pm. Valet serv. Airport transportation. Library/sitting rm; antiques. Restored guest house (1769) built by Dr Thomas Bond, founder of the country's first public hospital. Individually decorated rms. Cr cds: A, D, MC, V.

Restaurants

★ ★ **ALOUETTE.** *334 Bainbridge St, in South Street Area.* 215/629-1126. Hrs: 11:30 am-2:30 pm, 5:30-9:30 pm; Fri to 10:30 pm; Sat 5:30-10:30 pm; Sun brunch 11:30 am-2:30 pm. Closed Tues; Dec 25. Res accepted wkends. French, Asian menu. Bar. Semi-a la carte: lunch $10-$15, dinner $17-$24. Sun brunch $8.95-$15.75. Specialties: escargot in puff pastry, Thai chicken curry. Courtyard dining. 1890s decor includes brass railings, tin ceiling, etched glass. Cr cds: A, D, MC, V.

★ ★ **BACI BISTRO.** *211 S Broad St, downtown.* 215/731-0700. Hrs: 11:30 am-11 pm; wkends 12:30 pm-midnight. Closed Dec 25. Res accepted. Italian menu. Bar. A la carte entrees: lunch $5-$12, dinner $9-$25. Specialties: capellini brivido, pollo al girarrosto, mezze lune con mascarpone. Own pasta, desserts. Cr cds: A, D, MC, V.

★ ★ **BOOKBINDER'S SEAFOOD HOUSE.** *215 S 15th St, in Center City.* 215/545-1137. Hrs: 11:30 am-10 pm; Sat 4-11 pm; Sun 3-10 pm. Closed Thanksgiving, Dec 25. Res accepted. Bar. Semi-a la carte: lunch $6-$13.50, dinner $14.95-$23.95. Child's meals. Specializes in seafood, steak. Own pastries. Family-owned since 1893. Cr cds: A, C, D, MC, V.

✔ ★ ★ **BRIDGET FOY'S SOUTH STREET GRILL.** *200 South St, near Head House Square, in South Street Area.* 215/922-1813. Hrs: 11:30 am-10:30 pm; Fri & Sat to midnight. Closed Thanksgiving, Dec 25. Res accepted. Bar. A la carte entrees: lunch $5.95-$8.95, dinner $10.95-$15.95. Specializes in grilled fish & meat. Outdoor dining. Cr cds: A, C, D, DS, MC, V.

✔ ★ **CAFE EINSTEIN.** *208 Race St, in Olde City.* 215/625-0904. Hrs: 5-11 pm; Fri, Sat to midnight; Sun brunch 11:30 am-2:30 pm. Closed most major hols. Res accepted. Bar to 1 am. Semi-a la carte: dinner $9.95-$18.95. Sun brunch $3.95-$9.95. Specializes in crab cakes, Caesar salad. Jazz Sun. Parking. Informal bistro-type cafe. Cr cds: A, MC, V.

★ ★ **CAFE NOLA.** *328 South St, in South Street Area.* 215/627-2590. Hrs: noon-2:45 pm, 5-11 pm; Mon from 5 pm; Fri & Sat to 10:45 pm; Sun brunch 10:30 am-2:45 pm. Res required Fri, Sat. Bar. A la carte entrees: lunch $8-$12, dinner $15-$26. Sun brunch $11.95-$16.95. Specializes in Creole and Cajun dishes. Parking. Colorful New Orleans decor. Cr cds: A, C, D, DS, MC, V.

★ ★ ★ **CIBOULETTE.** *200 S Broad St, downtown.* 215/790-1210. Hrs: noon-2 pm, 5:30-10:30 pm; Mon & Sat from 5:30 pm. Closed Sun; most major hols. Res accepted; required Sat. French Provençal menu. Bar. Wine cellar. Complete meals: lunch $21-$29, dinner $45 (4-course) & $60 (5-course). A la carte entrees: dinner $18-$35. Specialties: roasted Maine lobster, black sea bass, loin of veal. Own desserts. Valet parking. French Renaissance-style architecture; tapestry wall hangings, many paintings; original mosaic tile floor; one rm with ceiling mural. Cr cds: A, MC, V.

★ ★ **CUTTERS GRAND CAFE.** *2005 Market St, at Commerce Square, downtown.* 215/851-6262. Hrs: 11:30 am-midnight; Fri to 1 am; Sat 5 pm-1 am; Sun 5-11 pm. Closed July 4, Dec 25. Res accepted. Bar. A la carte entrees: lunch $3.95-$13.95, dinner $9.95-$23.95. Specializes in fresh seafood, pasta, salads. Parking (evenings). Outdoor dining. Contemporary decor, murals. Cr cds: A, C, D, DS, MC, V.
D

★ ★ **D'MEDICI.** *824 S 8th St (19147), south of downtown.* 215/922-3986. Hrs: 5-11 pm; Sun 3-10 pm. Closed Mon; some major hols. Res accepted. Italian menu. Bar. A la carte entrees: dinner $7.95-$32.95. Child's meals. Specialties: veal Luisa, shrimp d'Medici, stuffed sirloin. Valet parking. Exposed brick & stucco walls; statuary in alcoves. Bronze & glass chandeliers. Cr cds: A, MC, V.
D

★ ★ ★ **DEUX CHEMINÉES.** *1221 Locust St, downtown.* 215/790-0200. Hrs: 5:30-8:30 pm; Sat to 9 pm. Closed Sun & Mon; major hols. Res accepted. French menu. Serv bar. Wine cellar. Prix fixe: dinner $65. Specializes in rack of lamb, crab soup. Menu changes daily. Own baking, desserts. 3 dining areas in Frank Furness-designed mansion (1880); antique furnishings; 5 fireplaces. Chef-owned. Cr cds: A, C, D, DS, MC, V.

★ ★ ★ **DI LULLO CENTRO.** *1407 Locust St, opp Academy of Music, in Center City.* 215/546-2000. Hrs: 5:30-9 pm; Fri also 11:45 am-2 pm; Sat 5:30-10 pm; Sun 4-8 pm. Closed most major hols. Res accepted. Northern Italian menu. Bar. Wine cellar. A la carte entrees: lunch $8-$13, dinner $8-$27. Prix fixe: dinner $27. Specializes in seafood, homemade pasta, rack of lamb. Own pastries. In Old Locust St Theatre; elegant decor, hand-painted murals. Cr cds: A, C, D, MC, V.
D

★ ★ ★ **DICKENS INN.** *Head House Square, on 2nd St, in Society Hill.* 215/928-9307. Hrs: 11:30 am-3 pm, 5:30-10 pm; Sat to 10:30 pm; Sun 4:30-9 pm; Sun brunch 11:30 am-3 pm. Closed Dec 25. Res accepted. Continental menu. Bar. A la carte entrees: lunch $4.75-$10.75, dinner $7.50-$21.50. Sun brunch $14.75. Child's meals. Specializes in roast beef with Yorkshire pudding, beef Wellington, seafood. In historic Harper House (1788); Victorian decor; artwork imported from England. Cr cds: A, D, DS, MC, V.
D

✔ ★ ★ ★ **DILULLO OGGI.** *7955 Oxford Ave, north of downtown.* 215/725-6000. Hrs: 5:30-9 pm; Sat to 10 pm; Sun 5-8 pm. Closed Dec 25. Italian menu. Wine cellar. Semi-a la carte: dinner $12-$19. Specializes in homemade pasta, veal dishes, fish. Own pastries. Parking. Cr cds: A, C, D, MC, V.
D

★ ★ **DINARDO'S.** *312 Race St, in Olde City.* 215/925-5115. Hrs: 11 am-10 pm; Fri & Sat to 11 pm; Sun 3-9 pm. Closed major hols. Bar. Semi-a la carte: lunch $4-$9, dinner $7-$20. Specializes in steamed hard shell crab, seafood. Family-owned. Cr cds: A, C, D, MC, V.
D

★ ★ ★ **THE DINING ROOM.** *(See The Ritz-Carlton, Philadelphia Hotel)* 215/563-1600. Hrs: 6:30 am-2:30 pm, 6-10 pm; Mon to 11:30 am; Sun brunch 10:30 am-2:30 pm. Res accepted. Bar 11-1 am. Wine list. A la carte entrees: bkfst $7-$15, lunch $15-$21, dinner $22-$50. Sun brunch $32. Child's meals. Specialities: fresh Maine scallops with seaweed salad, baby rack of lamb with eggplant. Pianist. Valet parking. Formal dining; antique china displayed, chandeliers. Jacket. Cr cds: A, C, D, DS, ER, JCB, MC, V.
D

✔ ★ ★ **DOCK STREET BREWERY & RESTAURANT.** *2 Logan Square, at 18th & Cherry Sts, downtown.* 215/496-0413. Hrs: 11:30 am-midnight; Fri to 2 am; Sat noon-2 am; Sun noon-11 pm. Closed Labor Day, Dec 25. Res accepted. Bar (beer). Setups. A la carte

entrees: lunch $5-$9.95, dinner $5-$14.95. Specializes in freshly brewed beer, homemade breads, desserts. Entertainment Fri & Sat. Brewery tanks; beer brewed on premises, tours avail Sat. Billiard tables and English dart board. Cr cds: A, C, D, DS, MC, V.
D

★ ★ **FELICIA'S.** *1148 S 11th St, south of downtown.* 215/755-9656. Hrs: 11:30 am-2:30 pm, 5-10:30 pm; Fri to 11 pm; Sat 5-11 pm; Sun 4-9:30 pm. Closed Mon; most major hols. Res accepted; required Sat, Sun. Italian menu. Bar. Semi-a la carte: lunch $6.95-$12.50, dinner $10.95-$18.50. Specialties: ricotta gnocchi, ricotta cheesecake, veal chop. Own desserts. Valet parking. Cr cds: A, C, D, MC, V.
D

✔ ★ **FISHER'S SEAFOOD.** *7312 Castor Ave, north of downtown.* 215/725-6201. Hrs: 11 am-9 pm; Fri & Sat to 10 pm; Sun noon-9 pm. Closed Mon; Labor Day, Dec 25. Bar. Semi-a la carte: lunch $3.25-$6.95, dinner $6.25-$12.95. Complete meals: lunch $6-$9.20, dinner $9.25-$15.95. Child's meals. Specializes in seafood, stir-fried dishes. Parking. Six large dining areas, individually decorated. Family-owned. Cr cds: A, MC, V.
D

★ ★ **FLYING FISH.** *8142 Germantown Ave, in Chestnut Hill.* 215/247-0707. Hrs: 11:30 am-2:30 pm, 5:30-9 pm; Mon from 5:30 pm; Sat noon-2:30 pm, 5:30-10 pm. Closed Sun; some major hols. Bar. A la carte entrees: lunch $6.50-$8, dinner $12-$18. Child's meals. Specializes in seafood, clam bake (summer). Own pasta, pastries, ice cream. Totally nonsmoking. No cr cds accepted.
D

★ ★ ★ **FOUNTAIN.** *(See Four Seasons Hotel Philadelphia)* 215/963-1500. Hrs: 6:30 am-2:30 pm, 6-10:30 pm; Fri, Sat to 11 pm; Sun brunch 11 am-2:30 pm. Res accepted. Continental menu. Bar to 2 am. Wine cellar. A la carte entrees: bkfst $10-$15, lunch $22-$25, dinner $29-$38. Prix fixe: dinner $49. Sun brunch $16-$32. Child's meals. Specialties: vegetable lasagne, whole-roasted snapper, sautéed venison medallion. Own baking, desserts. Entertainment exc Sun. Valet parking. Overlooks Logan Square and fountain. Jacket (dinner). Cr cds: A, C, D, ER, JCB, MC, V.
D

★ ★ ★ **THE GARDEN.** *1617 Spruce St, downtown.* 215/546-4455. Hrs: 11:30 am-1:45 pm, 5:30-9:30 pm; Sat 5:30-10 pm. Closed Sun; major hols. Res accepted. Continental menu. Bar. Extensive wine list. A la carte entrees: lunch $9.95-$24.95, dinner $15.95-$24.95. Specializes in fresh seafood, aged prime beef. Valet parking. Spacious outdoor dining. Cr cds: A, C, D, MC, V.

★ ★ **GENERAL WAYNE INN.** *(625 Montgomery Ave, Merion)* 7 mi W on I-76, exit City Line Ave. 610/667-3330. Hrs: 11:30 am-11 pm; Sun 11:30 am-10 pm. Closed Mon. Res accepted. Continental menu. Bar. Semi-a la carte: lunch $4.95-$10.95, dinner $11.50-$19.95. Sun brunch $15.95. Specializes in prime beef, seafood. Own desserts. Valet parking. Established as inn in 1704. Family-owned. Cr cds: A, D, MC, V.
D

★ ★ ★ **HARRY'S BAR & GRILL.** *22 S 18th St, downtown.* 215/561-5757. Hrs: 11:30 am-1:45 pm, 5:30-9 pm. Closed Sat, Sun; major hols. Res accepted. Italian, Amer menu. Bar 11:30 am-9:30 pm. Wine cellar. A la carte entrees: lunch $9.95-$23.95, dinner $14.95-$23.95. Specializes in fresh seafood, homemade pasta, aged prime steak. Own pastries. Parking. English club atmosphere. Jacket. Cr cds: A, C, D, MC, V.
D

✔ ★ **HO SAI GAI.** *1000 Race St, in Chinatown.* 215/922-5883. Hrs: 11:30-4 am; Fri & Sat to 5 am. Closed Thanksgiving. Res accepted. Chinese menu. Serv bar. Semi-a la carte: lunch $4.95-$8.95, dinner $9-$15.95. Specializes in Mandarin & Hunan cuisine. Cr cds: A, C, D, MC, V.

★ ★ **JACK'S FIREHOUSE.** *2130 Fairmount Ave, downtown.* 215/232-9000. Hrs: 11 am-2:30 pm, 5-10:30 pm; Sat & Sun from 5 pm; Sun brunch 11 am-3 pm. Closed some major hols. Res accepted. Bar 4:30 pm-1 am. A la carte entrees: lunch $5-$13, dinner $15-$22.95. Sun brunch $14.95. Specialties: bison with Jack Daniel's sauce, venison with beech nut sauce. Guitarist Thur-Sat; jazz trio Sun brunch. Outdoor dining. Red brick firehouse (ca 1860); original wood-paneled walls and brass pole, local artwork. Cr cds: A, C, D, MC, V.

D

★ **KNAVE OF HEARTS.** *230 South St, in South Street Area.* 215/922-3956. Hrs: noon-4 pm, 5:30-11 pm; Fri, Sat to 11:30 pm; Sun 5-10 pm; Sun brunch 11 am-4 pm. Closed Dec 25. Res accepted. Bar. A la carte entrees: lunch $5-$9, dinner $12-$20. Sun brunch $12.50-$13.50. Specialties: rack of lamb, roast duckling, cajun salmon. Intimate dining. Cr cds: A, C, D, MC, V.

★ ★ **LA COLLINA.** *(37-41 Ashland Ave, Bala Cynwyd) W on I-76, exit 31, left at exit, right on Jefferson St, 1st bldg on the right.* 610/668-1780. Hrs: 11:30 am-2:30 pm, 5:30-10 pm; Fri & Sat to 11 pm. Closed Sun; major hols. Res accepted. Italian menu. Bar. Wine cellar. A la carte entrees: lunch $8.95-$13.95, dinner $13.95-$24.95. Specializes in grilled fish, rack of veal, soft shell crab in season. Entertainment Wed, Fri & Sat. Valet parking. Atop a hill overlooking the city; brick fireplace; intimate atmosphere. Cr cds: A, C, D, MC, V.

D

★ ★ **LA FAMIGLIA.** *8 S Front St, in Olde City.* 215/922-2803. Hrs: noon-2 pm, 5:30-9:30 pm; Sat 5:30-10 pm; Sun 4:30-9 pm. Closed Mon; major hols; also last wk Aug. Res accepted. Italian menu. Bar. Wine cellar. A la carte entrees: lunch $12.95-$19.95, dinner $19.95-$32. Specializes in veal, fresh fish. Own desserts, pasta. Built in 1878 in one of city's first blocks of buildings. Jacket. Cr cds: A, C, D, MC, V.

D

★ ★ **LA TRUFFE.** *10 S Front St, in Olde City.* 215/925-5062. Hrs: noon-2 pm, 5:30-11 pm; Mon, Sat from 5:30 pm. Closed Sun; major hols. Res accepted. Bar. Wine list. A la carte entrees: lunch $9.50-$14.95, dinner $22-$35. Specialties: rack of lamb with thyme, Dover sole meunière, sea bass with white pepper corn sauce. Own pastries. Singer Fri. Elegant French Provincial decor; former coffeehouse built in 1783. Cr cds: A, MC, V.

★ ★ ★ **LE BAR LYONNAIS.** *1523 Walnut St (19102), downstairs at Le Bec Fin, downtown.* 215/567-1000. Hrs: 11:30-1 am; Sat from 6 pm. Closed Sun; major hols. French bistro menu. Bar. A la carte entrees: lunch, dinner $6-$18. Specialties: escargots au champagne, galette de crabe, thon au poivres. Valet parking (dinner). Elegant bistro atmosphere; original art. Cr cds: A, C, D, DS, MC, V.

★ ★ ★ ★ ★ **LE BEC-FIN.** *1523 Walnut St, downtown.* 215/567-1000. Sittings: lunch 11:30 am & 1:30 pm, dinner 6 pm & 9 pm, Fri & Sat 9:30 pm. Closed Sun; major hols. Res required. French menu. Bar to 1 am. Wine cellar. Prix fixe: lunch $32, dinner $94. Specializes in seasonal dishes. Own baking. Valet parking. Elegant dining. Louis XVI furnishings and decor. Chef-owned. Jacket. Cr cds: A, C, D, DS, MC, V.

D

★ ★ **LONDON GRILL.** *2301 Fairmount Ave (19130), downtown.* 215/978-4545. Hrs: 11:30 am-3 pm, 5:30-10:30 pm; Sat 5:30 pm-midnight; Sun 11:30 am-9 pm. Closed Jan 1, Thanksgiving, Dec 25. Res accepted; required Sun brunch. Continental menu. Bar to 2 am. A la carte entrees: lunch $5.95-$9, dinner $14-$20. Sun brunch $4-$10. Child's meals. Specialties: Szechuan duck, salmon with horseradish crust, rack of lamb. Parking. Eclectic decor. Atrium. Cr cds: A, D, DS, MC, V.

✔ ★ **LOS AMIGOS.** *50 S 2nd St, in Olde City.* 215/922-7061. Hrs: 11:30 am-11:30 pm; Fri & Sat to 1:30 am; Sun 11 am-11:30 pm; Sun brunch to 2 pm. Closed some major hols. Mexican menu. Bar.

Semi-a la carte: lunch $3.95-$11.95, dinner $6.75-$12.95. Sun brunch $9.95. Own desserts. Cr cds: A, C, D, MC, V.

D

✔ ★ ★ **MARABELLA'S.** *1420 Locust St, downtown.* 215/545-1845. Hrs: 11:30 am-11 pm; Fri & Sat to midnight; Sun 3-10 pm. Closed Dec 25. Italian menu. Bar. Semi-a la carte: lunch $5.50-$9.75, dinner $7-$14.50. Child's meals. Specializes in pizza, pasta with fresh seafood, oven-baked manicotti. Cr cds: A, D, DS, MC, V.

★ ★ **MEIJI-EN.** *Pier 19 North, Delaware Ave at Callowhill St, Penn's Landing, in Olde City.* 215/592-7100. Hrs: 5-9 pm; Fri & Sat to 11 pm; Sun brunch 10:30 am-2:30 pm. Closed Thanksgiving, Dec 24, 25. Res accepted; required Sun. Japanese menu. Bar; wkends to 1 am. A la carte entrees: dinner $18.95. Specialties: sukiyaki, sushi, tempura, teppanyaki-grilled items. Jazz trio Fri-Sun. Valet parking. Exotic bird display. Overlooks Delaware River. Cr cds: A, C, D, DS, MC, V.

D

★ ★ **MIDDLE EAST.** *126 Chestnut St, in Olde City.* 215/922-1003. Hrs: 5 pm-midnight; Fri, Sat to 2 am; Sun from 3 pm. Closed Thanksgiving, Dec 24 & 25. Res accepted. Middle Eastern, Amer menu. Bar. Semi-a la carte: dinner $14.50-$21.50. Specializes in shish kebab, moussaka, seafood. Middle Eastern band Fri-Sun, belly dancing. Middle Eastern decor. Cr cds: A, C, D, DS, MC, V.

D

★ ★ ★ **MONTE CARLO LIVING ROOM.** *2nd & South Sts, in South Street Area.* 215/925-2220. Hrs: 6-10:30 pm; Fri, Sat 5:30-11 pm; Sun 5-9 pm. Closed major hols. Res accepted. Northern Italian menu. Bar; closed Sun, Mon. Wine cellar. A la carte entrees: dinner $24-$30. Degustation dinner $65. Specializes in fresh imported & domestic fish, veal, beef. Own pastries. Mediterranean decor. Jacket. Cr cds: A, C, D, MC, V.

★ ★ **NAPOLEON CAFE.** *2652 E Somerset St, Port Richmond area, north of downtown.* 215/739-6979. Hrs: 11:30 am-2:30 pm, 5-8:30 pm; Fri & Sat to 10:30 pm; Sun 5-8 pm. Closed Mon & Tues; major hols. Res accepted; required Sat. Continental menu. Serv bar. A la carte entrees: lunch $6-$9.50, dinner $12.50-$18.50. Specialties: tagliolini vongole, rosemary & lemon roasted chicken. Outdoor dining. 4 dining rms on 2nd floor; 2 rms on 1st floor lunch/coffee house. Each dining area individually decorated. Totally nonsmoking. Cr cds: A, D, DS, MC, V.

★ ★ **OLD ORIGINAL BOOKBINDER'S.** *125 Walnut St, in Society Hill.* 215/925-7027. Hrs: 11:45 am-10 pm; Sun 3-9 pm; Sat, Sun hrs vary July-Aug. Closed Thanksgiving, Dec 25. Res accepted. Bars. A la carte entrees: lunch $7.95-$14.95, dinner $16.95-$35. Child's meals. Specializes in seafood, steak. Own pastries. Valet parking. Established 1865; in historic bldg. Family-owned. Cr cds: A, C, D, DS, MC, V.

D

★ ★ **OSTERIA ROMANA.** *935 Ellsworth St, south of downtown.* 215/271-9191. Hrs: 5:30-10:30 pm. Closed Mon; most major hols. Res accepted wkends. Italian menu. Bar. A la carte entrees: dinner $14.50-$26.50. Specialties: pappardelle verdi ai porcini, angel hair pasta with salmon caviar, pescatora capricciosa. Parking. Intimate dining. Cr cds: A, D, MC, V.

★ ★ **THE PALM.** *200 S Broad St (19102), downtown.* 215/546-7256. Hrs: 11:30 am-11 pm; Sat from 5 pm; Sun 4:30-9:30 pm. Closed most major hols. Res accepted. Continental menu. Bar. A la carte entrees: lunch $7.50-$25, dinner $12.50-$40. Specializes in fresh seafood, prime aged beef, lamb chops. Valet parking. Counterpart of famous New York restaurant. Caricatures of celebrities. Cr cds: A, C, D, MC, V.

D

★ ★ ★ **RESTAURANT 210.** *(See The Rittenhouse Hotel)* 215/790-2534. Hrs: 11:30 am-2:30 pm, 6-10 pm; Sat 6-10:30 pm.

Closed Sun. Res accepted. Continental cuisine with regional American influences. Bar 11:30-2 am. Wine list. Semi-a la carte: lunch, $23-$30, dinner $21.50-$35. Specializes in seafood, steak, veal. Seasonal menu. Own pastries. Valet parking. Formal decor. Overlooks park. Cr cds: A, C, D, DS, MC, V.

D

★ ★ **RISTORANTE ALBERTO.** (1415 City Line Ave, Wynnewood) I-76 W to City Line Ave. 215/896-0275. Hrs: 5-10 pm; Fri, Sat 5-11 pm; Sun 4-10 pm. Closed Jan 1, Thanksgiving, Dec 25; also month of Aug. Res accepted; required Fri & Sat. Italian menu. Bar. A la carte entrees: dinner $12.95-$24.95. Specializes in grilled Dover sole, double veal chop, fresh fish. Guitarist wkends. Valet parking. Display of wine bottles; original art. Cr cds: A, D, MC, V.

D

✔ ★ **SERRANO.** 20 S 2nd St, in Olde City. 215/928-0770. Hrs: 11:30 am-2:30 pm, 5:30-10 pm; Fri & Sat to 11 pm. Closed Sun; major hols. Res accepted. International menu. Bar. Semi-a la carte: lunch $5.50-$7.50, dinner $6.95-$15.95. Child's meals. Specialties: chicken Hungarian, Malaysian pork chops, filet mignon. Own desserts. Entertainment Wed-Sat. Cr cds: A, D, DS, MC, V.

D

★ **SFUZZI.** 1650 Market St, downtown. 215/851-8888. Hrs: 11:30 am-3 pm, 5:30-10 pm; Thurs-Sat to 11 pm; Sun 5-9 pm; Sun brunch 11:30 am-3 pm. Closed Thanksgiving, Dec 25. Res accepted. Italian menu. Bar. A la carte entrees: lunch $10.50-$17.50, dinner $11.50-$17.50. Sun brunch $14.50. Specializes in calamari, pasta, vegetable lasagne. Outdoor dining. Cr cds: A, D, MC, V.

D

✔ ★ **SOUTH STREET DINER.** 140 South St, in South Street Area. 215/627-5258. Open 24 hrs. Semi-a la carte: bkfst $1.95-$7.95, lunch, dinner $1.50-$13.95. Specializes in seafood, Greek and Italian specialties. Cr cds: A, C, D, DS, MC, V.

★ ★ ★ **SUZANNA FOO.** 1512 Walnut St (19102), downtown. 215/545-2666. Hrs: 11:30 am-2:30 pm, 5:30-10 pm; Fri & Sat to 11 pm; Sun to 9 pm. Closed some major hols. Res accepted. Chinese, French menu. Bar. Wine cellar. A la carte: lunch $9-$16, dinner $11-$24. Specialties: crispy duck, soft-shell crabs, hundred corner crab cake. Valet parking. Chinese art and artifacts. Dim Sum bar on second level. Jacket. Cr cds: A, C, D, MC, V.

D

★ ★ **UNDER THE BLUE MOON.** 8042 Germantown Ave, in Chestnut Hill. 215/247-1100. Hrs: 6-9 pm; Fri, Sat to 10 pm. Closed Sun, Mon, major hols. Continental menu. Bar. A la carte entrees: dinner $10-$18. Specializes in seafood, chicken, duck. Unique modern decor. Cr cds: MC, V.

✔ ★ **VAN'S GARDEN.** 121 N 11th St, in Chinatown. 215/923-2438. Hrs: 10 am-10 pm. Closed Thanksgiving. Vietnamese menu. Semi-a la carte: lunch, dinner $2.95-$6.95. Specialties: lobster salad, barbecued beef on rice noodles, sautéed chicken with lemon grass. Adj to convention center. No cr cds accepted.

★ ★ **WHITE DOG CAFE.** 3420 Sansom St, downtown. 215/386-9224. Hrs: 11:30 am-2:30 pm, 5:30-10 pm; Fri-Sat 5:30-11 pm; Sun 5-10 pm; Sat, Sun brunch 11 am-2:30 pm. Closed Thanksgiving & Dec 25. Res accepted. Bar. Semi-a la carte: lunch $6.50-$10, dinner $14-$19. Sat, Sun brunch $6-$10. Child's meals. Specializes in seafood, roasted quail, spring trout. Own desserts. Former house (ca 1870) of author Madame Blavatsky, founder of the Theosophical Society. Cr cds: A, D, DS, MC, V.

✔ ★ ★ **ZOCALO.** 3600 Lancaster Ave, west of downtown. 215/895-0139. Hrs: noon-2:30 pm, 5:30-10 pm; Fri & Sat 5:30-11 pm; Sun 5-9:30 pm. Closed major hols. Res accepted. Mexican menu. Bar. Semi-a la carte: lunch $6-$10, dinner $10-$18. Prix fixe: dinner $13.95 & $15. Specializes in spicy shrimp, swordfish tacos. Parking. Outdoor dining. Cr cds: A, D, DS, MC, V.

Unrated Dining Spots

FAMOUS 4TH ST DELICATESSEN. 700 S 4th St, south of downtown. 215/922-3274. Hrs: 7 am-6 pm; Sun to 4 pm. Closed Rosh Hashana, Yom Kippur. Delicatessen fare. Beer. A la carte: bkfst $2-$6, lunch $3.50-$10. Specializes in chocolate chip cookies, fresh roasted turkey, corned beef. Antique telephones. Family-owned more than 70 yrs. Cr cds: A.

MANGO BAY. 264 S 16th St, downtown. 215/735-3316. Hrs: noon-midnight; Mon to 11 pm; Sun noon-3 pm, 4:30-11 pm. Closed Dec 25; also lunch most major hols. Bar to 2 am. A la carte entrees: lunch, dinner $6.50-$15. Specializes in Caribbean cuisine, seafood, pasta. Island atmosphere. Cr cds: A, D, MC, V.

THE RESTAURANT SCHOOL. 4207 Walnut St, near University of Pennsylvania, west of downtown. 215/222-4200. Hrs: 5:30-10 pm. Closed Sun, Mon; also during student breaks. Res accepted. Bar. Complete meals: dinner $13.50. Seasonal menu; occasionally an extraordinary and elaborate theme dinner is offered. Own baking. Valet parking. Bakery shop on premises. Unique dining experience in a "restaurant school." Consists of 2 buildings; a restored 1856 mansion is linked by a large atrium dining area to a new building housing the kitchen and classrooms. Cr cds: A, C, D, DS, MC, V.

D

ROLLER'S. 8705 Germantown Ave, in Top-of-the-Hill Plaza, in Chestnut Hill. 215/242-1771. Hrs: 11:30 am-2:30 pm, 5:30-9 pm; Fri to 10 pm; Sat noon-2:30 pm, 5:30-10 pm; Sun 5-9 pm; Sun brunch 11 am-2:30 pm. Closed Mon; most major hols. Bar. Semi-a la carte: lunch $6-$11, dinner $16-$24. Sun brunch $6-$10. Specializes in fresh fish, veal, duck. Parking. Outdoor dining. Modern cafe atmosphere. No cr cds accepted.

SASSAFRAS. 48 S 2nd St, in Olde City. 215/925-2317. Hrs: noon-midnight; Fri, Sat to 1 am. Closed Sun; major hols. Bar. A la carte entrees: dinner $4-$15. Specializes in salads, omelettes, Béarnaise burgers, grilled fish. Cr cds: A, D, MC, V.

SPIRIT OF PHILADELPHIA. Pier 3, on Delaware Ave, in Olde City. 215/923-1419. Hrs: lunch cruise noon-2 pm, dinner cruise 7-10 pm; Sun brunch cruise 1-3 pm. Closed Dec 25. Res required. Bar. Buffet: lunch $16.95 (adults), $9.50 (children), dinner $28.95-$32.95 (adults), $15.95 (children). Sun brunch $18.95 (adults), $9.50 (children). Musical revue, bands, dancing. Parking. Dining and sightseeing aboard Spirit cruise liner. Cr cds: A, MC, V.

D

SWANN LOUNGE. (See Four Seasons Hotel Philadelphia) 215/963-1500. Hrs: 7-10 am, 11:30 am-2:30 pm; tea 3-5 pm; Sun brunch 11 am-2:30 pm; Viennese buffet Fri, Sat 9 pm-1 am. Closed Mon. Res accepted. Bar 11:30-1 am; Fri, Sat to 2 am. Buffet: bkfst $9.75-$14, lunch $12-$21. Afternoon tea $12. Sun brunch $24. Viennese buffet $11. Specializes in English tea service with sandwiches & cakes. Valet parking. Outdoor dining (lunch). Elegant atmosphere. Cr cds: A, C, D, ER, JCB, MC, V.

D

Pittsburgh (E-2)

Settled: 1758 **Pop:** 369,879 **Elev:** 760 ft **Area code:** 412

Pittsburgh has had a remarkable renaissance, to become one of the most spectacular civic redevelopments in America, with modern buildings, clean parks and community pride. In fact, it has been named "all-America city" by the National Civic League. The new Pittsburgh is a result of a rare combination of capital-labor cooperation, public-private support, enlightened political leadership and imaginative, venturesome community planning. Its $1 billion international airport was designed to be the most user-friendly in the country.

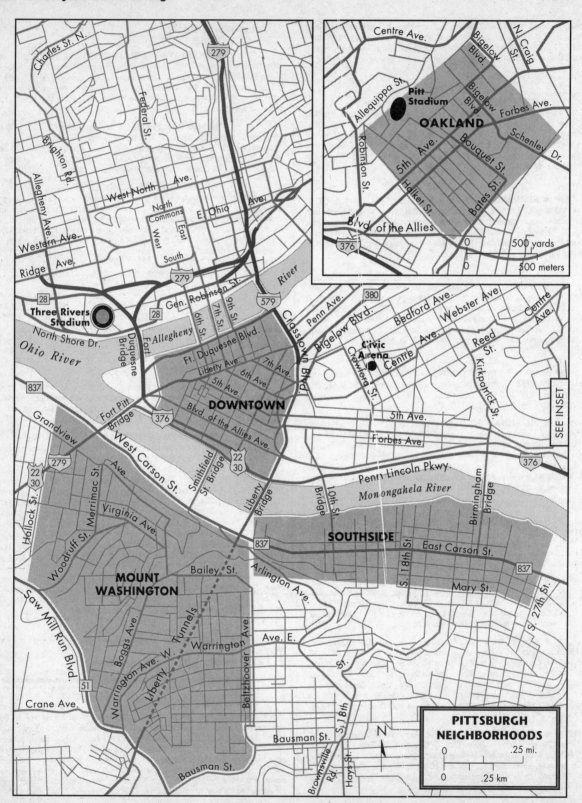

PITTSBURGH
NEIGHBORHOODS

| 0 | | .25 mi. |
| 0 | | .25 km |

After massive war production, Pittsburgh labored to eliminate the 1930s image of an unsophisticated mill town. During the 1950s and 1960s, Renaissance I began, a $500 million program to clean the city's air and develop new structures, such as Gateway Center, the Civic Arena and Point State Park. The late 1970s and early 1980s ushered in Renaissance II, a $3 billion expansion program reflecting the movement away from industry and toward high technology.

Today, Pittsburgh has completed this dramatic shift from industry to a diversified base, including high technology, health care and education, and continues its transition to a services-oriented city.

Pittsburgh's cultural personality is expressed by the Pittsburgh Symphony Orchestra, Pittsburgh Opera, Pittsburgh Ballet, Phipps Conservatory and The Carnegie, which includes the Museum of Natural History and Museum of Art. The city has 25 parks, 45 "parklets," 60 recreation centers and 27 swimming pools.

Born of frontier warfare in the shadow of Fort Pitt, the city is named after the elder William Pitt, the great British statesman. Its militarily strategic position was an important commercial asset and Pittsburgh soon became a busy river port and transit point for the western flow of pioneers.

Industry grew out of the West's needs for manufactured goods; foundries and rolling mills were soon producing nails, axes, frying pans and shovels. The Civil War added tremendous impetus to industry, and by the end of the war Pittsburgh was producing half the steel and one-third of the glass made in the country. Such captains of industry and finance as Thomas Mellon, Andrew Carnegie and Henry Clay Frick built their industrial empires in Pittsburgh. The American Federation of Labor was born here (1881); the city has been the scene of historic clashes between labor and management.

World War I brought a fresh boom to the city, as well as changes in its industrial character. It was a vast arsenal for the Allies during World War II.

Transportation

Airport. See PITTSBURGH INTL AIRPORT AREA.

Car Rental Agencies: See toll-free numbers under Introduction.

Public Transportation: Subway and surface trains, buses (Port Authority of Allegheny County), phone 442-2000.

Rail Passenger Service: Amtrak 800/872-7245.

What to See and Do

1. **Civic Arena.** In Golden Triangle. This $22 million all-weather amphitheater accommodates 17,500 people. Retractable roof can fold up within two-and-a-half minutes.

2. **Inclines** (hill-climbing trolleys). Travel to top of Mount Washington for excellent view of Golden Triangle, where the Allegheny and Monongahela rivers join to form the Ohio River.

   Monongahela Incline. Station on W Carson St near Station Square & Smithfield St Bridge. Panoramic views from observation deck. (Daily) Phone 231-5707. ¢

   Duquesne Incline. Lower station, W Carson St, opposite the fountain, SW of Fort Pitt Bridge; upper station, 1220 Grandview Ave, in restaurant area. Built 1877; restored and run by community effort; observation deck. (Daily) Free parking at lower station. Phone 381-1665. ¢

3. **Point State Park.** Foot of Ft Duquesne & Ft Pitt Blvds. "Point" where the Allegheny and Monongahela rivers meet to form the Ohio; 36 acres. Giant fountain symbolizes joining of rivers. There are military drills with fifes and drums, muskets and cannon (May-Labor Day; some Sun afternoons). Phone 471-0235. In the park are

   Fort Pitt Museum. 101 Commonwealth Place. Built on part of original fort. Exhibits on early Pittsburgh and Fort Pitt; military struggles between France and Britain for western Pennsylvania

and the Old Northwest Territory. (Daily exc Mon; closed some hols) Sr citizen rate. Phone 281-9284. ¢¢

   Block House of Fort Pitt. Last remaining building of original fort (1764). (Daily exc Mon) **Free.**

4. **Gateway Center.** Covers 23 acres adj to Point State Park (see #3). Complex includes four skyscrapers of Equitable Life Assurance Society. Equitable Plaza, a 2-acre open-air garden over underground parking garage, has lovely walks, 3 fountains, more than 90 types of trees and 100 varieties of shrubs and seasonal flowers. (Mon-Fri; closed major hols) Phone 392-6000.

5. **Benedum Center.** Penn and 7th Aves, at 719 Liberty Ave. Expansion and restoration of the Stanley Theater, a movie palace based upon Versailles, built in 1928. Gilded plasterwork, 500,000-piece crystal chandelier and a 9-story addition to backstage area make this an exceptional auditorium. The center is home to Pittsburgh Ballet Theatre, the Pittsburgh Dance Council, the Pittsburgh Opera and Civic Light Opera. Free guided tours (by appt only). For program information, schedule phone 456-6666.

6. **Alcoa Building.** 425 6th Ave. Pioneer in aluminum for skyscraper construction, exterior work was done from inside; no scaffolding was required. Draped in aluminum waffle, 30 stories high; it is considered to be one of the country's most daring experiments in skyscraper design.

7. **USX Tower.** Grant St and Seventh Ave. Once known as the US Steel Building, it is 64 stories high and the tallest building in Pittsburgh. Ten exposed triangular columns and an exterior paneling of steel make up its construction.

8. **PPG Place.** Market Sq. Designed by Philip Johnson, this is Pittsburgh's most popular Renaissance II building. PPG Place consists of six separate buildings designed in a post-modern, Gothic skyscraper style. Shopping and a food court can be found in Two PPG Place.

9. **Two Mellon Bank Center.** 5th Ave & Grant St. Formerly the Union Trust Building, its Flemish-Gothic style was modeled after a library in Louvain, Belgium. Interior has a glass rotunda.

10. **Allegheny County Courthouse.** Grant St & 5th Ave. One of the country's outstanding Romanesque-style buildings, the two square-city block structure was designed by Henry Hobson Richardson in 1884. (Mon-Fri; closed hols) Phone 355-5313. **Free.**

11. **Children's Museum.** 1 Landmarks Square. Hands-on exhibits. Hands-on silkscreen studio; storytelling; regularly scheduled puppet shows; live performances; 2-story climber. (Tues-Sat, also Sun afternoons) Phone 322-5058. Sr citizen rate. Tues, Wed & Fri-Sun ¢¢; Thurs ¢

12. **Station Square.** Along Monongahela River across from downtown, via Smithfield St Bridge. This 45-acre area features shopping, dining and entertainment in and among the historic buildings of the P & LE Railroad (see RESTAURANTS). Shopping in warehouses that once held loaded railroad boxcars. (Daily; closed some hols) Phone 261-9911.

13. **University of Pittsburgh** (1787). (34,000 students) 5th Ave & Bigelow Blvd. Tours of Nationality Rooms in Cathedral of Learning (wkends; fee). Campus of 70 buildings on 125 acres. Phone 624-4141. Buildings include

   Cathedral of Learning (1935). Unique skyscraper of classrooms, stretching its Gothic-moderne architecture 42 floors high (535 ft); vantage point on 36th floor. Surrounding a 3-story Gothic commons room are an Early American Room and 23 Nationality Rooms, each reflecting the distinctive culture of the ethnic group that created and furnished it. Tours (daily; closed Jan 1, Dec 24, 25, 31). Sr citizen rate. Phone 624-6000. Tours ¢

   Heinz Chapel. E of Cathedral of Learning. Tall stained-glass windows; French Gothic architecture. (Daily exc Sat; closed hols) Phone 624-4157. **Free.**

   Stephen Foster Memorial. Auditorium/theater. Collection of the Pittsburgh-born composer's music and memorabilia. Said to be one of the most elaborate memorials ever built to a musician. (Mon-Sat, also Sun afternoons; closed hols) Phone 624-4100.

Henry Clay Frick Fine Arts Building. Schenley Plaza. Glass-enclosed cloister; changing exhibits; art reference library. (Sept-mid-June, daily; rest of yr, Mon-Fri; closed univ hols, Dec 24-Jan 2) Phone 648-2400. **Free.**

14. **The Carnegie.** 4400 Forbes Ave. Public complex built by industrialist Andrew Carnegie. (Daily exc Mon; closed hols) Sr citizen rate. Phone 622-3131. **¢¢** Includes

Musuem of Natural History. Houses one of the most complete collections of dinosaur fossils. Exhibits include Dinosaur Hall, Polar World, Hillman Hall of Minerals and Gems, the Walton Hall of Ancient Egypt; changing exhibits.

Museum of Art. Possibly America's first modern art museum, as Carnegie urged the gallery to exhibit works dated after 1896. Collection of Impressionist and Post-Impressionist paintings; Hall of Sculpture; Hall of Architecture; films, videos.

Music Hall. Home to the Mendelssohn Choir, the Pittsburgh Chamber Music Society and the River City Brass Band. Elaborate gilt and marble foyer; walls of French eschallion, 24 pillars made of green stone and a gold baroque ceiling.

Library of Pittsburgh. Central branch contains more than 4$\frac{1}{2}$ million books. Houses first department of science and technology established in a US public library.

15. **Carnegie Mellon University** (1900). (7,900 students) Adj to Schenley Park (see #16). Founded by Andrew Carnegie. Composed of seven colleges. Tours of campus. Phone 268-2000 or -5052.

16. **Schenley Park.** Forbes Ave, adj Carnegie-Mellon University. Covers 456 acres; picnic areas; 18-hole golf course, lighted tennis courts; swimming pool; ice-skating (winter); softball fields, running track; nature trails; bandstand (summer; free). Fee for some activities. Park (daily). **Free.** Also in park is

Phipps Conservatory. Constantly changing array of flowers; tropical gardens; outstanding orchid collection. Seasonal flower shows (see SEASONAL EVENTS). (Daily) Sr citizen rate. Phone 622-6914. **¢¢**

17. **Riverview Park.** 2 mi N on US 19. Covers 251 acres. Swimming pool (mid-June-Labor Day, daily, fee); tennis courts (Apr-Nov, daily); picnic shelter (May-Sept, permit required). Also playgrounds, parklet; nature, jogging trail. Fee for some activities. **Free.**

Allegheny Observatory. Center of park, entrance on Riverview Ave off US 19. Slides, tour of building. Maintained by University of Pittsburgh. (Apr-Oct, Thurs-Fri; closed hols) Children under 12 yrs only with adult. Reservation required. Phone 321-2400. **Free.**

18. **The Carnegie Science Center.** One Allegheny Ave, adj to Three Rivers Stadium on Ohio River. Learning and entertainment complex has over 40,000 square feet of exhibit galleries that demonstrate how human activities are affected by science and technology. USS *Requin*, moored in front of the center, is a World War II diesel-electric submarine; tours (40 min) demonstrate the electronic, visual and voice communication devices on board. Henry Buhl, Jr Planetarium and Observatory is a technologically sophisticated interactive planetarium with control panels at every seat. Also here are 350-seat Omnimax Theater and Health Sciences Amphitheater. Restaurant, gift shop. (Daily; closed Dec 25) For combination ticket prices and information phone 237-3400. Submarine **¢¢**; Exhibits and planetarium **¢¢¢**; Omnimax Theater **¢¢¢**

19. **The Pittsburgh Zoo.** NE on Highland Ave in Highland Park area. Over 70 acres containing over 6,000 animals, children's farm (late May-Oct), reptile house, tropical and Asian forests, African savanna and aqua zoo. Merry-go-round and train rides (fee). Highland Park covers 75 acres and has tennis courts, picnic grounds, shelters (some require permit), twin reservoirs, swimming pool (fee). (Daily; closed Dec 25) Sr citizen rate. Phone 665-3640 or -3639. **¢¢¢**

20. **The Aviary.** Allegheny Commons West, approx 1 mi W of downtown. The Aviary is home to one of the world's premier bird collections and is the only indoor bird facility independent of a larger zoo in North America. A veritable jungle of colorful, amusing and exotic birds. (Daily; closed Jan 1, Thanksgiving, Dec 25) Sr citizen rate. Phone 323-7235. **¢¢**

21. **Sandcastle Water Park.** Approx 5 mi SE of downtown via I-376 & PA 837. The city's down-by-the-riverside water park has 15 slides, adult & kiddie pools; boardwalk; food. (1st Sat June-Labor Day, daily; closed hols) Sr citizen rate. Phone 462-6666. All day slide pass **¢¢¢¢**

22. **Frick Park.** Beechwood Blvd & English Lane. Covers 476 acres, largely in natural state; nature trails wind through ravines and over hills; also nature center (2005 Beechwood Blvd), tennis courts, picnic areas, playgrounds. Park (daily). **Free.**

23. **Rodef Shalom Biblical Botanical Garden.** 4905 5th Ave. The natural world of ancient Israel is re-created here in settings that specialize in plants of the Bible. A waterfall, desert and stream all help simulate the areas of the Jordan, Lake Kineret and the Dead Sea. Tours (by appt). Special programs and exhibits. (June-mid-Sept, daily exc Fri; Sat hrs limited) Phone 621-6566. **Free.**

24. **Historical Society of Western Pennsylvania.** 4338 Bigelow Blvd. Museum contains local history exhibits; collection of decorative arts; library, archives; gift shop. (Tues-Sat) Phone 681-5533. **¢**

25. **Soldiers and Sailors Memorial Hall and Military History Museum.** 5th Ave & Bigelow Blvd. Auditorium has Lincoln's Gettysburg Address inscribed above stage; flags, weapons, uniforms, memorabilia from US wars. (Mon-Fri, also Sat & Sun afternoons; closed Jan 1, Labor Day, Thanksgiving, Dec 25) Phone 621-4253. **Free.**

26. **James L. Kelso Bible Lands Museum.** 616 N Highland, on grounds of Pittsburgh Theological Seminary. Artifacts and displays from the ancient Near East, especially Palestine. (Sept-May, Wed; also by appt) Phone 362-5610. **Free.**

27. **Kennywood Park.** 8 mi SE on PA 837, 4800 Kennywood Blvd, in W Mifflin. Four roller coasters, 30 rides, gardens, picnic groves. (Mid-May-Labor Day, daily) Sr citizen rate. Phone 461-0500. **¢¢¢¢¢**

28. **County parks.** South Park, 12 mi S on PA 88. **North Park,** 14 mi N on PA 19. **Boyce Park,** 14 mi E on I-376, US 22. **Settler's Cabin Park,** 9 mi W on I-279, US 22. Swimming; fishing; boating. Bicycling (rentals), ball fields; golf, tennis. Cross-country skiing, ice-skating (winter, daily). Picnicking. Parks open daily. Fees for activities. Attractions for each park vary; phone 392-8455 (permits) or 355-7275 (general information).

29. **The Frick Art and Historical Center.** Between Reynolds St and Penn Ave, along S Homewood Ave. Museum complex built on grounds of estate once belonging to industrialist Henry Clay Frick; gardens, carriage house museum, greenhouse and restored children's playhouse that now serves as a visitor's center. (Daily exc Mon; closed some major hols) For tour schedule and information, phone 371-0606. **Free.** Also on grounds are

Clayton, the Henry Clay Frick Home. 7227 Reynolds St. A restored 4-story Victorian mansion with 23 rooms; only remaining house of area in East End once known as "millionaire's row." Some original decor and personal mementos of the Fricks. Tours; reservation recommended. **¢¢**

The Frick Art Musuem. 7227 Reynolds St. Collection of Helen Clay Frick, daughter of Henry Clay Frick, includes Italian Renaissance, Flemish and French 18th-century paintings and decorative arts. Italian and French furniture, Renaissance bronzes, tapestries, Chinese porcelains. Also changing exhibits; concerts, lectures. Phone 371-0600. **Free.**

30. **Sightseeing tours.**

Small van tours. Offered through the Pittsburgh History and Landmarks Foundation. For information and reservations phone 471-5808. **¢¢¢**

Gray Line bus tours. For information and reservations contact 110 Lenzner Ct, Sewickley 15143; 741-2720, 761-7000 or 800/342-2349.

31. **Hartwood** (1929). 12 mi N via PA 8, at 215 Saxonburg Blvd. A 629-acre re-creation of English country estate; Tudor mansion with many antiques; formal gardens, stables. Tours (daily exc Mon; closed hols & 1 wk late Nov). Also music and theater events during summer. Sr citizen rate. For information and tour reservations, phone 767-9200. ¢¢

32. **Fallingwater.** 27 mi S on PA 51, 10 mi E on PA 201 to Connellsville, 8 mi E on PA 711, then 8 mi S on PA 381, near Mill Run. (See CONNELLSVILLE)

33. **Boyce Park Ski Area.** 18 mi E on I-376 to Plum exit (#16B); follow signs to park. Beginner-intermediate slopes; 2 double chairlifts; 2 Pomalifts; patrol, school, rentals; snowmaking; cafeteria. Longest run, 1/4 mi; vertical drop, 175 ft. (Dec-Feb, daily) Phone 733-4656; snow conditions 733-4665 (24-hr recording). ¢¢¢¢

34. **Tour-Ed Mine.** 20 mi NW via PA 28 (Allegheny Valley Expy) to Tarentum, then 1/4 mi W via Red Belt West. Complete underground coal mining operation; sawmill; furnished log house (1789); old company store; historical mine museum; shelters; playground. (May-Labor Day wk, daily) Phone 224-4720. ¢¢¢

Annual Events

Folk Festival. Pittsburgh Expo Mart, Monroeville. Foods of many nations; arts & crafts; folk music, dancing. Phone 373-0123. Memorial Day wkend.

Three Rivers Arts Festival. Point State Park, Gateway Center, USX Tower, PPG Place. Juried, original works of local and national artists: paintings, photography, sculpture, crafts and videos; artists' market in outdoor plazas. Ongoing performances include music, dance, and performance art. Special art projects; film festival; food; children's activities. Phone 481-7040. Early-mid-June.

Regatta. Point State Park (see #3). Water, land and air events; water shows and speedboat races. 1st wkend Aug.

Pittsburgh Irish Festival. Irish foods, dances and entertainment. Phone 422-5642. Early or mid-Sept.

Seasonal Events

Phipps Conservatory Flower Shows. Schenley Park (see #16). Phone 622-6914. Spring, summer, fall & holidays.

Concerts. Pittsburgh Symphony Orchestra. Heinz Hall for the Performing Arts, 600 Penn Ave. Phone 392-4900. Sept-May.

Pittsburgh Public Theater. Allegheny Square, North Side. City's largest resident professional company. Phone 321-9800. Sept-June.

Professional sports. Pirates (baseball), Steelers (football), Three Rivers Stadium, 400 Stadium Circle; Penguins (hockey), Civic Arena (see #1).

Additional Visitor Information

For additional information about Pittsburgh, contact the Pittsburgh Convention and Visitors Bureau, 4 Gateway Center, 15222 (Mon-Fri); 281-7711 or 800/366-0093. A Visitor Information Center is along Liberty Ave, adj to 4 Gateway center (Mar-Nov, daily; rest of yr, daily exc Sun); 281-9222. Other centers can be found in the Carnegie Library's Grandview Ave branch, 381-5134 and on the University of Pittsburgh's campus, Log Cabin, Forbes Ave, 624-4660. For a schedule of events in Pittsburgh, 24-hr visitor information, phone 391-6840.

Pittsburgh Area Towns

The following towns in the Pittsburgh area are included in the *Mobil Travel Guide.* For information on any one of them, see the individual alphabetical listing. Ambridge, Beaver Falls, Connelsville, New Stanton, Washington.

Pittsburgh Intl Airport Area

For additional accommodations, see PITTSBURGH INTL AIRPORT AREA, which follows PITTSBURGH.

City Neighborhoods

Many of the restaurants, unrated dining establishments and some lodgings listed under Pittsburgh include neighborhoods as well as exact street addresses. A map showing these neighborhoods can be found immediately following the city map. Geographic descriptions of these areas are given, followed by a table of restaurants arranged by neighborhood.

Downtown: South of the Allegheny River, west of I-579, north of the Monongahela River and east of Point State Park. **North of Downtown:** North of Allegheny River. **South of Downtown:** South of Monongahela River. **East of Downtown:** East of US 579.

Mount Washington: Across the Monongahela River south of Downtown; north of Saw Mill Run Blvd, south of West Carson St, east of Hallock and west of Beltzhoover.

Oakland: East of Downtown; centered on and around 5th Ave between Bellefield St on the north and Halket St on the south.

South Side: Across the Monongahela River south of Downtown; Station Square area east of the Liberty Bridge, west of S 27th St and north of Mary St.

PITTSBURGH RESTAURANTS BY NEIGHBORHOOD AREAS

(For full description, see alphabetical listings under Restaurants)

DOWNTOWN

1902 Landmark Tavern. 24 Market St
British Bicycle Club. 923 Penn Ave
Carlton. 1 Mellon Bank Center
Common Plea. 308 Ross St
Jake's Above the Square. 430 Market St
Palm Court (Westin William Penn Hotel). 530 Wm Penn Place

NORTH OF DOWNTOWN

Max's Allegheny Tavern. Middle & Suisman Sts
Rico's. 1 Rico Lane

SOUTH OF DOWNTOWN

Colony. Greentree & Cochran Rds
Piccolo Mondo. 661 Anderson Dr
Samurai Japanese Steak House. 2100 Greentree Rd
Tambellini's. PA 51

EAST OF DOWNTOWN

Bentley's. 5608 Wilkens Ave
D'Imperio's. 3412 Wm Penn Hwy
Jimmy Tsang's. 5700 Centre Ave
Pasta Piatto. 738 Bellefonte St
Poli's. 2607 Murray Ave
Thai Place. 809 Bellefonte St

MOUNT WASHINGTON

Christopher's. 1411 Grandview Ave

Cliffside. 1208 Grandview Ave

Le Mont. 1114 Grandview Ave

OAKLAND

Dave And Andy's Ice Cream Parlor. 207 Atwood St

Per Favore. 3955 Bigelow Blvd

SOUTH SIDE

Cafe Allegro. 51 S 12th St

Grand Concourse. 1 Station Square

Le Pommier. 2104 E Carson St

Station Square Cheese Cellar. #25 Freight House Shops

Note: When a listing is located in a town that does not have its own city heading, it will appear under the city nearest to its location. In these cases, the address and town appear in parenthesis immediately following the name of the establishment.

Motels

★ ★ **CLUBHOUSE INN.** 5311 Campbells Run Rd (15205), jct I-279 & PA 60, west of downtown. 412/788-8400; FAX 412/788-2577. 150 rms, 3 story, 26 suites. S $73-$86; D $83-$96; each addl $10; suites $86-$96; under 10 free; lower rates Fri, Sat. Crib free. TV; cable. Heated pool. Complimentary full buffet bkfst, coffee. Restaurant adj 11 am-11 pm. Ck-out noon. Coin lndry. Meeting rms. Free airport transportation. Exercise equipt; treadmill, stair machine, whirlpool. Refrigerator in suites. Cr cds: A, D, DS, MC, V.

🔲 🏊 🏋 ⏫ 🔥

✔ ★ ★ **HAMPTON INN.** 555 Trumbull Dr (15205), across river, west of downtown. 412/922-0100; FAX 412/922-0100, ext. 109. 135 rms, 6 story. June-Nov: S $65-$70; D $68-$73; under 18 free; wkend rates; lower rates rest of yr. Crib free. Pet accepted. TV; cable. Complimentary continental bkfst, coffee. Restaurant nearby. Ck-out noon. Meeting rms. Valet serv. Free airport transportation. Picnic tables. Cr cds: A, C, D, DS, ER, MC, V.

🔲 🤚 ⏫ 🔥 SC

★ ★ **HAWTHORN SUITES.** 700 Mansfield Ave (15205), at Noblestown Rd, south of downtown. 412/279-6300; FAX 412/279-4993. 152 suites, 2 story. S $82-$116; D $103-$146; wkly, monthly rates. Crib free. Pet accepted, some restrictions; $50 and $6 per day. TV; cable. Pool; whirlpool, lifeguard. Complimentary continental bkfst. Ck-out noon. Meeting rms. Airport, RR station, bus depot transportation. Health club privileges. Sport court. Refrigerators, fireplaces. Private patios, balconies. Picnic tables, grills. Chalet-style buildings. Cr cds: A, C, D, DS, MC, V.

🔲 🤚 🏊 ⏫ 🔥 SC

★ ★ **HOLIDAY INN ALLEGHENY VALLEY.** 180 Gamma Dr (15238), PA 28 exit 10. 412/963-0600; FAX 412/963-7852. 225 rms, 2 story. S $90; D $100; each addl $10; suites $150-$175; under 18 free. TV; cable. Heated pool; pooside serv, lifeguard. Restaurant 6 am-10 pm; Sat, Sun from 7 am. Rm serv. Bar 11-2 am; Sun 1 pm-1 am. Ck-out 11 am. Meeting rms. Bellhops. Valet serv. Free airport transportation. Refrigerators in suites. Cr cds: A, C, D, DS, MC.

🔲 🏊 ⏫ 🔥 SC

★ ★ ★ **HOLIDAY INN GREENTREE-CENTRAL.** 401 Holiday Dr (15220), south of downtown. 412/922-8100; FAX 412/922-6511. 201 rms, 4 story. S $99-$107; D $99-$124; each addl $10; under 18 free. Crib free. Pet accepted. TV; cable. Heated pool; poolside serv, lifeguard. Restaurant 6:30 am-10 pm; Fri, Sat to 11 pm. Rm serv. Bar 11-2 am, Sun from 1 pm; entertainment. Ck-out noon. Meeting rms. Valet

serv. Sundries. Free airport transportation. Tennis privileges. Exercise equipt; weight machine, bicycles. Private patios. Cr cds: A, C, D, DS, ER, JCB, MC, V.

🔲 🤚 🏃 🏊 🏃 ⏫ 🔥 SC

★ ★ **HOWARD JOHNSON-SOUTH.** 5300 Clairton Blvd (PA 51) (15236), south of downtown. 412/884-6000; FAX 412/884-6009. 95 rms, 3 story. No elvtr. S $67-$79; D $77-$89; each addl $10; under 18 free. Crib free. TV. Pool; lifeguard. Complimentary bkfst. Restaurant nearby. Ck-out noon. Meeting rms. Valet serv. Near Allegheny County Airport. Cr cds: A, C, D, DS, ER, JCB, MC, V.

🔲 🏊 ⏫ 🔥 SC

✔ ★ **RED ROOF INN.** 6404 Steubenville Pike (PA 60) (15205), south of downtown. 412/787-7870; FAX 412/787-8392. 120 rms, 2 story. S $38-$43; D $45-$53; under 18 free. Crib free. Pet accepted, some restrictions. TV; cable. Complimentary morning coffee. Restaurant adj open 24 hrs. Ck-out noon. Cr cds: A, C, D, DS, MC, V.

🤚 ⏫ 🔥

✔ ★ ★ **REDWOOD INN.** 2898 Banksville Rd (US 19) (15216), south of downtown. 412/343-3000; res: 800/334-0060; FAX 412/341-4611. 95 rms, 4 story. S $55-$62; D $61-$66; each addl $5; under 12 free; some wkend rates. Crib free. Pet accepted, some restrictions. TV; cable. Pool; lifeguard. Restaurant 6:30-10:30 am, 5-9 pm; Sat 6 am-noon; Sun 6:30 am-1 pm. Rm serv. Bar 3 pm-2 am. Ck-out 11 am. Meeting rms. Bellhops. Cr cds: A, C, D, DS, MC, V.

🤚 🏊 ⏫ 🔥 SC

Motor Hotels

✔ ★ ★ ★ **BEST WESTERN-PARKWAY CENTER INN.** 875 Greentree Rd (15220), adj Parkway Center Mall, west of downtown. 412/922-7070; FAX 412/922-4949. 138 rms, 6 story, 44 kits. S $55-$101; D $61-$107; each addl $9; kit. units $93-$107; under 12 free; wkly (14-day min), wkend rates. Crib free. Pet accepted; $25. TV; cable. Indoor pool; sauna, lifeguard. Complimentary bkfst. Ck-out noon. Coin lndry. Meeting rms. Bellhops. Valet serv. Sundries. Barber, beauty shop. Free airport transportation. Rec rm. Cr cds: A, C, D, DS, ER, MC, V.

🔲 🤚 🏊 ⏫ 🔥 SC

★ ★ **HARLEY.** 699 Rodi Rd (15235), at jct PA 791 & I-376, east of downtown. 412/244-1600; FAX 412/829-2334. 152 rms, 3 story. No elvtr. S $92-$99; D $100-$109; each addl $8; under 18 free; wkend plan. Crib free. TV; cable. 2 heated pools, 1 indoor; whirlpool, sauna, poolside serv, lifeguard. Restaurant 6:30 am-10 pm; Fri, Sat 7 am-11 pm. Rm serv 7 am-11 pm. Bar 4:30 pm-midnight, Fri to 1:30 am, Sat noon-1:30 am, Sun 4:30-11 pm; entertainment, dancing Fri & Sat. Ck-out 1 pm. Meeting rms. Bellhops. Valet serv. Sundries. Airport transportation. Lighted tennis. Private patios, balconies. Cr cds: A, C, D, DS, MC, V.

🔲 🏃 🏊 ⏫ 🔥 SC

★ ★ ★ **HOLIDAY INN.** 164 Fort Couch Rd (15241), south of downtown. 412/343-4600; FAX 412/831-8539. 210 rms, 8 story. S $64; D $74; each addl $10; suites $120-$130; under 18 free; wkend rates. Crib free. Pet accepted, some restrictions. TV; in-rm movies avail. Pool; poolside serv, lifeguard. Restaurant 6:30 am-11 pm; Sat, Sun from 7 am. Rm serv. Bar 11-2 am; entertainment, dancing Tues-Sat. Ck-out noon. Meeting rms. Bellhops. Valet serv. Shopping arcade. Airport transportation. Health club privileges. Game rm. Balconies. Cr cds: A, C, D, DS, ER, JCB, MC, V.

🔲 🤚 🏊 ⏫ 🔥 SC

★ ★ ★ **MARRIOTT GREENTREE.** 101 Marriott Dr (15205), across river, west of downtown. 412/922-8400; FAX 412/922-8981. 467 rms, 7 story. S $99-$125; D $115-$135; each addl $15; suites $175-185; studio rms $99; under 18 free; wkend, honeymoon rates. Crib free. Pet accepted. TV. 3 pools, 1 indoor; poolside serv, lifeguard.

Restaurant 6:30 am-midnight. Rm serv. Bar 11-2 am; entertainment, dancing. Ck-out noon. Meeting rms. Bellhops. Valet serv. Sundries. Gift shop. Barber, beauty shop. Free airport transportation. Lighted tennis. Indoor tennis privileges. Exercise equipt; weight machines, bicycles, whirlpool, sauna, steam rm. Rec rm. Many minibars. *LUXURY LEVEL:* CONCIERGE LEVEL. 41 rms, 2 suites. S $135; D $150. Private lounge, honor bar. Complimentary continental bkfst, refreshments. Cr cds: A, C, D, DS, ER, MC, V.

D ⛵ 🏃 ≋ ✕ ⊠ 🔥 SC

Hotels

★ ★ ★ **HILTON.** *Gateway Center (15222), at Point State Park, downtown.* 412/391-4600; FAX 412/391-0927 or 594-5161. 712 rms, 24 story. S $129-$189; D $149-$199; each addl $20; suites $325; studio rms $100; children free; wkend plans. Crib free. Pet accepted, some restrictions. TV; cable. Restaurant 6:30 am-11:30 pm. 2 bars 11-2 am; entertainment. Ck-out noon. Meeting rms. Concierge. Drugstore. Barber, beauty shop. Garage avail; valet parking. Airport transportation. Exercise equipt; weights, treadmill. Minibars; some bathrm phones, refrigerators. *LUXURY LEVEL:* TOWERS. 118 rms, 4 floors. S $165-$185; D $185-205; suites $350-$1,200. Private lounge, honor bar. In-rm movies. Full wet bar & kitchen area in suites. Bathrm phones. Complimentary continental bkfst, refreshments, newspaper. Cr cds: A, C, D, DS, ER, JCB, MC, V.

D ⛵ ✕ ⊠ 🔥 SC

★ ★ ★ **HYATT REGENCY-CHATHAM CENTER.** *112 Washington Place (15219), downtown.* 412/471-1234; FAX 412/355-0315. 400 rms, 21 story. S $115-$145; D $131-$170; each addl $15; suites $220-$500; under 18 free; wkend rates. Crib free. Garage $5-$10. TV; cable. Pool. Restaurants 6:30 am-11 pm. Bars 11-1 am; entertainment. Ck-out noon. Meeting rms. Airport, RR station, bus depot transportation. Exercise equipt; weights, bicycles, whirlpool, sauna, steam rm. Cr cds: A, C, D, DS, ER, JCB, MC, V.

D ≋ ✕ ⊠ 🔥 SC

★ ★ ★ **SHERATON.** *7 Station Square (15219), on South Side.* 412/261-2000; FAX 412/261-2932. 293 rms, 15 story. S $141-$156; D $156-$181; each addl $15; suites $210-$600; under 18 free; wkend rates. Crib free. TV; cable. In-rm movies avail. Pool; lifeguard. Coffee in rms. Restaurant 6 am-midnight. Bar 11-2 am; entertainment. Ck-out noon. Meeting rms. Shopping arcade. RR station, bus depot transportation. Exercise equipt; weights, bicycles, whirlpool. Game rm. On riverfront. *LUXURY LEVEL:* EXECUTIVE FLOOR. 18 rms, 3 suites. Private lounge. Complimentary continental bkfst, refreshments. Cr cds: A, C, D, DS, ER, JCB, MC, V.

D ≋ ✕ ⊠ 🔥 SC

★ ★ ★ **VISTA INTERNATIONAL.** *1000 Penn Ave (15222), downtown.* 412/281-3700; FAX 412/227-4500. 616 rms, 26 story. S $160-$200; D $180-$215; each addl $20; suites $245-$1,550; family rates; wkend packages. Crib free. TV; cable. Indoor pool. Restaurants 6:30 am-10:30 pm. Rm serv 24 hrs. Bar 11-2 am. Ck-out noon. Lndry facilities. Convention facilities. Concierge. Shopping arcade. Courtesy limo downtown. Exercise rm; instructor, weights, bicycles, whirlpool, sauna, steam rm. Refrigerators; many bathrm phones. Private patios. Cr cds: A, C, D, DS, ER, JCB, MC, V.

D ≋ ✕ ⊠ 🔥 SC

★ ★ ★ **WESTIN WILLIAM PENN.** *530 Wm Penn Place (15219), on Mellon Square, downtown.* 412/281-7100; FAX 412/553-5252. 595 rms, 24 story. S $99-$140; D $120-$150; each addl $20; suites $275-$1,115; under 18 free; wkend rates. Crib free. Pet accepted. Valet parking $15.75. TV; cable. Restaurant 6:30 am-11 pm (also see PALM COURT, Unrated Dining). Rm serv 24 hrs. Bar 11-2 am; entertainment. Ck-out 1 pm. Convention facilities. Gift shop. Barber shop. Airport, RR station, bus depot transportation. Exercise equipt; bicycles, treadmill.

Bathrm phones. Historic, landmark hotel. Cr cds: A, C, D, DS, ER, JCB, MC, V.

D ⛵ ✕ ≋ ⊠ 🔥 SC

Inn

★ ★ ★ **THE PRIORY.** *614 Pressley St (15212), north of downtown.* 412/231-3338; FAX 412/231-4838. 24 rms, 3 story. S $68-$98; D $103-$120; each addl $10; suites $110-$143; under 7 free; lower rates wkends. TV; cable. Complimentary continental bkfst, evening refreshments. Ck-out 11 am, wkends noon, ck-in 3 pm. Meeting rms. Previously a haven for Benedictine monks (1888); European-style inn with fountain and floral arrangements in courtyard. Cr cds: A, C, D, DS, MC, V.

D ⊠ 🔥 SC

Restaurants

★ ★ **1902 LANDMARK TAVERN.** *24 Market St, downtown.* 412/471-1902. Hrs: 11:30 am-11 pm; Fri & Sat to midnight. Closed Sun; major hols. Res accepted. Continental menu. Bar to 1 am. Semi-a la carte: lunch $5.25-$11.50, dinner $10.95-$22. Specialties: veal Marengo, prime rib, pasta. Restored tavern (1902); ornate tin ceiling, original tiles. Cr cds: A, D, DS, MC, V.

✔ ★ ★ **BENTLEY'S.** *5608 Wilkens Ave, east of downtown.* 412/421-4880. Hrs: 11:30 am-10 pm; Fri & Sat to 11 pm; extended hrs summer; early-bird dinner Mon-Sat 4-6 pm. Closed Thanksgiving, Dec 25. Res accepted. Continental menu. Bar. Complete meals: lunch $5.95-$6.95, dinner $8.95-$14.95. Child's meals. Specializes in seafood, veal, pasta. Parking. Outdoor dining. Cr cds: A, D, DS, MC, V.

✔ ★ **BRITISH BICYCLE CLUB.** *923 Penn Ave, downtown.* 412/391-9623. Hrs: 10 am-10 pm. Closed Sat & Sun; major hols. Res accepted. Bar. Semi-a la carte: lunch $3.25-$8.75, dinner $3.25-$14.95. Specializes in prime rib, sandwiches, steak salad. English pub atmosphere. Cr cds: A, C, D, DS, MC, V.

★ ★ **CAFE ALLEGRO.** *51 S 12th St, on South Side.* 412/481-7788. Hrs: 5-11 pm. Closed major hols. Res accepted. Bar. Semi-a la carte: dinner $17-$23. Child's meals. Specialties: pasta del sole, grilled seafood, seafood arrabbiata, grilled veal chop. Parking. Ambience of Riviera cafe; artwork. Cr cds: D, MC, V.

D

★ ★ ★ **CARLTON.** *1 Mellon Bank Center, on grounds of Mellon Bank Center Commercial Bldg, at Grant St, downtown.* 412/391-4099. Hrs: 11:30 am-2:30 pm, 5-10 pm; Fri to 11 pm; Sat 5-11 pm. Closed Sun; major hols. Res accepted. Continental menu. Bar. Semi-a la carte: lunch $7.95-$13.95, dinner $13.95-$24.95. Child's meals. Specializes in charcoal-grilled seafood, prime steak, veal. Own pastries. Parking. Cr cds: A, C, D, DS, MC, V.

D

★ ★ ★ **CHRISTOPHER'S.** *1411 Grandview Ave, on Mount Washington.* 412/381-4500. Hrs: 5-10 pm; Fri & Sat to 11 pm. Closed Sun; major hols. Res accepted. American menu. Bar 5 pm-midnight. Wine list. Semi-a la carte: dinner $15-$33. Child's meals. Specializes in seafood, lamb, flaming desserts. Own baking. Pianist (dinner). Valet parking. View of the Golden Triangle. Braille menu. Jacket. Cr cds: A, C, D, DS, MC, V.

D

★ ★ ★ **CLIFFSIDE.** *1208 Grandview Ave, on Mount Washington.* 412/431-6996. Hrs: 5-10 pm; Fri & Sat to 11 pm. Closed major hols. Res accepted. Continental menu. Bar. Semi-a la carte: dinner $15.25-$24. Child's meals. Specializes in fresh seafood, chicken, veal. Pianist. Contemporary decor in older building (1897). Cr cds: A, C, D, DS, MC, V.

★ ★ ★ **COLONY.** *Greentree & Cochran Rds, south of downtown.* 412/561-2060. Hrs: 5-10:30 pm; Sun 4-9 pm. Res accepted. Continental menu. Bar 4 pm-1 am. Wine list. Complete meals: dinner $20.50-$29.95. Specializes in swordfish, sirloin, grilled veal steak. Own baking. Pianist exc Mon, vocalist Fri, Sat. Valet parking. Family-owned. Jacket. Cr cds: A, C, D, DS, MC, V.

★ ★ ★ **COMMON PLEA.** *308 Ross St, downtown.* 412/281-5140. Hrs: 11:30 am-2:30 pm, 5-10:30 pm; Sat 5-10 pm. Closed Sun; major hols. Res accepted. Bar. Complete meals: lunch $6.50-$10.75, dinner $15.50-$26.95. Child's meals. Specializes in seafood, veal, chicken. Own baking. Valet parking (dinner). Family-owned. Cr cds: A, D, MC, V.

★ ★ ★ **D'IMPERIO'S.** *3412 Wm Penn Hwy, east of downtown.* 412/823-4800. Hrs: noon-3 pm, 5-11 pm; Sat & Sun from 5 pm. Closed major hols. Res accepted; required wkends. Italian, Amer menu. Bar. Semi-a la carte: dinner $13.50-$28. Child's meals. Specialties: shrimp Sorrento, lobster sausage, veal Genovese. Own bread. Pianist. Parking. Cr cds: A, C, D, DS, MC, V.
D

★ ★ ★ **GRAND CONCOURSE.** *1 Station Square, jct Carson & Smithfield Sts, on South Side.* 412/261-1717. Hrs: 11:30 am-2:30 pm, 4:30-10 pm; Fri to 11 pm; Sat 4:30-11 pm; Sun 4:30-9 pm; early-bird dinner 4:30-6 pm; Sun brunch 10 am-2:30 pm. Closed Dec 25. Res accepted. Continental menu. Bar 11:30-2 am; Sun 11 am-10 pm. Wine list. Semi-a la carte: lunch $6-$12, dinner $10-$20. Sun brunch $15.95. Child's meals. Specializes in seafood, steak, pasta. Own baking, pasta. Pianist. Parking. Converted railroad station. Braille menu. Cr cds: A, C, D, DS, MC, V.
D

★ ★ ★ **JAKE'S ABOVE THE SQUARE.** *430 Market St, downtown.* 412/338-0900. Hrs: 11 am-11 pm; Fri to midnight; Sat 5 pm-midnight; Sun 4-10 pm. Closed most major hols. Res accepted. Continental menu. Bar. Wine cellar. Semi-a la carte: lunch $4.50-$11.50, dinner $17.50-$29.50. Child's meals. Specialties: Dover sole, soft shell crabs, homemade dessert and pastries. Valet parking. Casual elegance in atrium setting. View of historic Market Square. Cr cds: A, C, D, DS, MC, V.

✔ ★ ★ **JIMMY TSANG'S.** *5700 Centre Ave, at Negley, in Kennilworth Bldg, east of downtown.* 412/661-4226. Hrs: 11:30 am-10 pm; Fri & Sat to 11 pm; Sun 3:30-9 pm; early-bird dinner Mon-Sat 3-6 pm. Closed July 4, Thanksgiving. Chinese menu. Bar. A la carte: lunch $4.95-$5.75, dinner $7.95-$9.95. Specializes in Peking duck, honey chicken, Mongolian Beef. Parking. Oriental decor, artwork. Cr cds: A, C, D, MC, V.
D

★ ★ ★ **LE MONT.** *1114 Grandview Ave, on Mount Washington.* 412/431-3100. Hrs: 5-11:30 pm; Sun 4-10 pm. Closed major hols. Res accepted. American menu. Bar to midnight. Wine list. Semi-a la carte: dinner $11-$35. Specialties: rack of lamb Persille, variety of wild game dishes, flaming desserts. Own baking. Pianist Fri & Sat. Valet parking. Atop Mt Washington; panoramic view of city. Cr cds: A, C, D, DS, MC, V.
D

★ ★ ★ **LE POMMIER.** *2104 E Carson St, on South Side.* 412/431-1901. Hrs: 5:30-9 pm; Sat to 10:30 pm. Closed Sun; some major hols. Res accepted. French menu. Bar. Wine cellar. A la carte entrees: dinner $18-$30. Specialties: couscous, veal chops with fresh herbs, bouillabaisse. Own baking. Located in oldest storefront in area (1863). Country French decor. Cr cds: A, C, D, DS, MC, V.
D

✔ ★ **MAX'S ALLEGHENY TAVERN.** *Middle & Suisman Sts, north of downtown.* 412/231-1899. Hrs: 11 am-11 pm; Fri & Sat to midnight; Sun to 8:30 pm. Closed most major hols. German menu. Bar. A la carte entrees: lunch $4.25-$7.95, dinner $5.95-$13.95. Specialties: jägerschnitzel, käse spätzle, sauerbraten. Entertainment Fri, Sat. Tavern with German memorabilia and collection of photographs. Cr cds: A, D, DS, MC, V.

★ ★ **PASTA PIATTO.** *738 Bellefonte St, in Shadyside, east of downtown.* 412/621-5547. Hrs: 11:30 am-3 pm, 4:30-10 pm; Wed & Thurs to 10:30 pm; Fri & Sat to 11 pm; Sun 3-9 pm. Closed major hols. Northern Italian menu. Bar. Semi-a la carte: lunch $3.50-$8.95, dinner $8.50-$19.95. Child's meals. Specializes in homemade pasta, veal, seafood. Cr cds: A, MC, V.

★ ★ ★ **PER FAVORE.** *3955 Bigelow Blvd, in Oakland.* 412/681-9080. Hrs: 11 am-10 pm; Fri to 11 pm; Sat 4-11 pm. Closed Sun; major hols. Res accepted. Continental menu. Bar. Semi-a la carte: lunch $6.95-$8.95, dinner $12.95-$21.95. Child's meals. Specialties: veal piccata, angel hair Favore, salmon with lump crab meat. Entertainment Fri, Sat. Valet parking. Roman garden setting. Italian paintings. Cr cds: A, C, D, DS, MC, V.
D

★ ★ ★ **PICCOLO MONDO.** *661 Anderson Dr, Bldg 7, Foster Plaza, Green Tree, south of downtown.* 412/922-0920. Hrs: 11:30 am-4 pm, 5-10 pm; Sat 5-11 pm. Closed Sun exc Mother's Day; some hols. Res accepted. Northern Italian menu. Bar. Wine list. Semi-a la carte: lunch $5.50-$13, dinner $13-$23. Child's meals. Specializes in fresh fish, veal. Own desserts. Parking. Jacket. Cr cds: A, C, D, DS, MC, V.
D

★ ★ ★ **POLI'S.** *2607 Murray Ave, east of downtown.* 412/521-6400. Hrs: 11:30 am-11 pm; Sun 11 am-9:30 pm; early-bird dinner Tues-Fri 3-5 pm. Closed Mon; Thanksgiving, Dec 25. Italian menu. Bar. Semi-a la carte: lunch $5.95-$9.95, dinner $10.25-$21.95. Child's meals. Specializes in fresh seafood, veal, pasta. Own baking. Valet parking. Family-owned. Cr cds: A, C, D, MC, V.
D

★ ★ ★ **RICO'S.** *1 Rico Lane, off of Evergreen Rd in North Hills, north of downtown.* 412/931-0556. Hrs: 11:30 am-3 pm, 4-10:30 pm; Fri & Sat 4-11:30 pm. Closed Sun; major hols. Italian, Amer menu. Bar to midnight. Wine cellar. Semi-a la carte: lunch $6.50-$11.50, dinner $14-$30. Specializes in fresh seafood, veal. Valet parking. Old World atmosphere; Italian lithographs. Jacket. Cr cds: A, D, DS, MC, V.
D

★ ★ **SAMURAI JAPANESE STEAK HOUSE.** *2100 Greentree Rd, south of downtown.* 412/276-2100. Hrs: 11:30 am-2 pm, 5:30-10 pm; Fri to 11 pm; Sat 5-11:30 pm; Sun 4:30-9 pm. Closed Thanksgiving, Dec 25. Res accepted. Japanese menu. Bar. Semi-a la carte: lunch $5.50-$8.50, dinner $10.50-$28. Child's meals. Specializes in steak, seafood. Parking. Japanese garden. Cr cds: A, C, D, DS, MC, V.
D

✔ ★ ★ **STATION SQUARE CHEESE CELLAR.** *#25 Freight House Shops, Station Square (Smithfield & Carson Sts), on South Side.* 412/471-3355. Hrs: 11:30-1 am; Sun 10:30 am-11 pm. Closed Dec 25. Res accepted Sun-Thurs. Continental menu. Bar to 2 am. Semi-a la carte: bkfst $5.95-$6.50, lunch, dinner $4.95-$9.95. Child's meals. Specializes in fondues, imported cheese, pasta. Outdoor dining. Rustic decor. Cr cds: A, C, D, DS, MC, V.
D

★ ★ **TAMBELLINI'S.** *PA 51, 2 mi south of downtown.* 412/481-1118. Hrs: 11:30 am-10 pm. Closed Sun; Jan 1, Thanksgiving, Dec 25. Res accepted. Continental menu. Bar. Semi-a la carte: lunch $7.50-$7.95, dinner $11.95-$27.50. Complete meals: dinner $21.95. Child's meals. Specializes in seafood, pasta, steak. Valet parking. Modern decor. Cr cds: A, D, MC, V.
D

✔ ★ ★ **THAI PLACE.** *809 Bellefonte St, in Shadyside, east of downtown.* 412/687-8586. Hrs: 11:30 am-10 pm; Fri to 11 pm; Sat noon-11 pm; Sun noon-9:30 pm; Mon from 4:30 pm. Thai menu. Bar. A la carte entrees: lunch $5.50-$7.50, dinner $7.50-$14.95. Specializes in authentic Thai cuisine. Outdoor dining. Oriental art. Cr cds: A, D, DS, MC, V.

Unrated Dining Spots

DAVE AND ANDY'S ICE CREAM PARLOR. *207 Atwood St, in Oakland.* 412/681-9906. Hrs: 11:30 am-10 pm; Fri to 11 pm; Sat 1 pm-11 pm; Sun 1-11 pm. Closed major hols. Specialties: homemade ice cream (fresh daily), homemade cones. 1930s look; no tables, some counters. No cr cds accepted.

PALM COURT. *(See Westin William Penn Hotel)* 412/281-7100. Hrs: tea time 2:30-4:30 pm. English custom tea serv. Bar. Complete tea: $7.25. A la carte items also avail. Specializes in tea, finger sandwiches, pastries. Pianist. Parking avail opp. Lobby room; Georgian decor; elaborate floral arrangements. Cr cds: A, C, D, DS, ER, JCB, MC, V.

[D]

PIZZERIA UNO. *(333 Penn Center Blvd, Monroeville 15146)* 15 mi E on US 376, Penn Center Blvd exit. 412/824-8667. Hrs: 11 am-11 pm; Fri & Sat to 12:30 am; Sun noon-10 pm. Closed Thanksgiving, Dec 25. Italian, Amer menu. Bar. Semi-a la carte: lunch $3.95-$8.95, dinner $4.95-$10.95. Specialties: deep-dish pizza, pasta, salad. Parking. Casual dining. Cr cds: A, DS, MC, V.

[D]

SEASON'S HARVEST. *(Box 115, Valencia 16059)* 15 mi N of PA Turnpike exit 4, on PA 8. 412/898-3030. Hrs: 4:30-8:30 pm; Sun from 11:30 am. Closed Mon; Dec 24 evening, Dec 25. Buffet: dinner $7.95-$9.95. Specializes in roast beef, baked chicken, french fried mushrooms. Salad bar. Own soups. Parking. Two dining levels. Art exhibits. Cr cds: MC, V.

[SC]

Pittsburgh Intl Airport Area (E-1)

Services and Information

Information: 412/472-3525 or -5525.

Lost and Found: 412/472-3500.

Weather: 412/644-2882.

Cash Machines: Landside Terminal, entrance; Airside Terminal, throughout concourses in Passenger Service Centers.

Club Lounges *(All airline clubs are located in the Airside Terminal on the concourse level):* British Airways Lounge (British Airways), Concourse C; Crown Room (Delta), Concourse D; USAir Club A (USAir) in Concourse A, Club B in Concourse B and Club C in Airside Core.

(For information on this area contact Pittsburgh Airport Area Chamber of Commerce, 986 Brodhead Rd, Coraopolis 15108; 412/264-6270.)

(See Pittsburgh)

Motels

★ ★ **HAMPTON INN-NORTHWEST.** *(1420 Beers School Rd, Coraopolis 15108)* N on PA 60. 412/264-0020; FAX 412/264-0020, ext. 185. 128 rms, 5 story. S $57-$63; D $62-$68; under 18 free. Crib free. Pet accepted, some restrictions. TV. Complimentary continental bkfst. Restaurant adj 6 am-10 pm. Ck-out noon. Meeting rms. Valet serv. Airport transportation. Cr cds: A, C, D, DS, ER, MC, V.

★ ★ **LA QUINTA.** *(1433 Beers School Rd, Coraopolis 15108)* N on PA 60. 412/269-0400; FAX 412/269-9258. 129 rms, 3 story. S $56-$61; D $63-$71; each addl $7; under 18 free. Crib free. Pet accepted. TV; cable. Heated pool; lifeguard. Complimentary continental bkfst, coffee. Restaurant adj 6 am-11 pm. Ck-out noon. Meeting rms. Valet serv. Sundries. Free airport transportation. Cr cds: A, C, D, DS, MC, V.

[D] [symbols] [SC]

✔ ★ ★ **PITTSBURGH PLAZA.** *(1500 Beers School Rd, Coraopolis 15108)* I-79 Bus 60 exit. 412/264-7900; res: 800/542-8111; FAX 412/262-3229. 185 rms, 2 story. S, D $39.99; suites $59.99; under 18 free. Crib free. Pet accepted; $50 refundable. TV; cable. Complimentary continental bkfst 5-9 am in lobby. Restaurant open 24 hrs. Ck-out noon. Meeting rms. Valet serv. Sundries. Free airport transportation. Exercise equipt; weights, bicycles, sauna. Some refrigerators. Some balconies. Cr cds: A, C, D, DS, MC, V.

[symbols] [SC]

✔ ★ **RED ROOF INN.** *(1454 Beers School Rd, Coraopolis 15108)* N on PA 60. 412/264-5678; FAX 412/264-8034. 119 rms, 3 story. S $39.99-$45.95; D $46.99-$52.99; each addl $4; under 18 free. Crib free. TV. Coffee in lobby 6-10 am. Restaurant opp 6 am-10 pm. Ck-out noon. Coin lndry. Meeting rm. Valet serv. Free airport transportation. Cr cds: A, C, D, DS, MC, V.

[D] [symbols]

Motor Hotels

★ ★ **BEST WESTERN AIRPORT INN.** *(PA 60 at Montaur Run Rd, Pittsburgh 15231)* 412/262-3800; FAX 412/695-1068. 140 rms, 4 story. S $75-$90; D $85-$100; each addl $10; suites $175-$215; studio rms $85-$100; family rates; wkend plan. Crib free. Pet accepted. TV. Heated pool; lifeguard. Restaurant 6:30 am-10 pm; Sat, Sun from 7 am. Rm serv. Bar 11-2 am; entertainment exc Sun. Ck-out noon. Meeting rms. Bellhops. Valet serv. Gift shop. Free airport transportation. Exercise equipt; weights, bicycles. Cr cds: A, C, D, DS, ER, MC, V.

[D] [symbols]

★ ★ **RAMADA INN AIRPORT.** *(1412 Beers School Rd, Coraopolis 15108)* N on PA 60. 412/264-8950; FAX 412/262-5598. 135 rms, 6 story. S $65-$75; D $75-$80; each addl $10; suites $125; under 18 free; wkend rates. Crib free. Pet accepted, some restrictions; $10. TV. Pool; poolside serv, lifeguard. Restaurant 6 am-2 pm, 5-11 pm; Sun to 3 pm, 5-11 pm. Rm serv. Bar 4 pm-2 am; entertainment Wed, Fri-Sat, dancing exc Sun. Ck-out noon. Meeting rms. Free airport transportation. Cr cds: A, C, D, DS, JCB, MC, V.

[symbols] [SC]

Hotels

★ ★ ★ **MARRIOTT.** *(100 Aten Rd, Coraopolis 15108)* S on PA 60, exit Montaur Run Rd. 412/788-8800; FAX 412/788-6299. 314 rms, 14 story. S, D $99-$159; each addl $15; suites $175-$425; family, wkly rates. Crib free. Pet accepted. TV; cable, in-rm movies avail. 2 pools, 1 indoor; poolside serv, lifeguard. Restaurant 6:30 am-11 pm. Bar 11-2 am; entertainment, dancing. Ck-out noon. Convention facilities. Concierge. Shopping arcade. Free airport, bus depot transportation. Exercise equipt; weights, bicycles, whirlpool, sauna. Some refrigerators. **LUXURY LEVEL : CONCIERGE LEVEL.** 21 rms, 1 floor, 1 suite. S, D $137-$180. Private lounge, honor bar. Complimentary continental bkfst, refreshments. Cr cds: A, C, D, DS, ER, JCB, MC, V.

[D] [symbols] [SC]

★ ★ ★ **ROYCE.** *(1160 Thorn Run Rd Extension, Coraopolis 15108)* S on PA 60, exit Thorn Run Rd. 412/262-2400; FAX 412/262-9373. 198 rms, 9 story. S $59-$119; D $59-$129; each addl $10; suites $79-$139; under 18 free; wkend rates. Crib free. TV; cable. Pool; lifeguard. Restaurant 6 am-2 pm, 5-11 pm; Sat, Sun 7 am-11 pm. Bar

11-2 am; entertainment, dancing Thurs-Sat. Ck-out noon. Meeting rms. Free airport transportation. Exercise equipt; weight machines, bicycles. Cr cds: A, C, D, DS, MC, V.

 D ≈ 🏃 ✈ 🚭 🔥 SC

Restaurant

★ ★ ★ **HYEHOLDE.** (190 Hyeholde Dr, Coraopolis) PA 60 to Beers School Rd, right on Beaver Grade Rd, left on Coraopolis Heights Rd. 412/264-3116. Hrs: 11:30 am-2 pm, 5-10 pm; Sat from 5 pm. Closed Sun exc Mother's Day; major hols. Res accepted. Continental menu. Serv bar. Wine list. Complete meals: lunch $8.50-$13.50, dinner $19-$32. Specialties: rack of lamb, baked Virginia spots fish (in season). Own baking, desserts. Valet parking. Patio dining. Herb garden. English Tudor decor; fireplaces; estate grounds. Cr cds: A, C, D, DS, MC, V.

D SC

Pocono Mountains (C-9)

(Northeast Pennsylvania resort area)

The Pocono Mountains area in northeast Pennsylvania extends north from Wind Gap and Delaware Water Gap into Pike, Carbon, Monroe and Wayne counties. Within its 2,400 square miles almost any form of recreation can be found.

This scenic country with more than 200 lakes, including Lake Wallenpaupack (see HAWLEY), has hundreds of accommodations and is a well-established resort area. Visitors, many of whom return year after year, take advantage of the large plush resorts, smaller family-run resorts, housekeeping cottage resorts, camping resorts and country and bed & breakfast inns. There is primitive, forested country for those who wish to rough it. For the hunter there are deer, bear, wildcat and fox. For the freshwater angler there are black bass, trout, pickerel and walleye.

Summer offers boating, swimming, hiking, horseback riding, golf, theaters and a host of other diversions. In the autumn there is a magnificent display of foliage as well as heritage festivals and country fairs. The first snowfall brings skiing, ice-skating, sleigh rides, tobogganing and snowmobiling.

The name "pocono" was probably taken from the Indian "pocohanne," meaning a stream between the mountains. Settled in the mid-1700s, the Poconos yielded iron, and later, coal. The lakes and forest still retain their charm. The "land between the mountains" is as inviting as it always has been.

(For further information contact the Pocono Mts Vacation Bureau, 1004 Main St, Stroudsburg 18360, phone 717/424-6050; for free brochures phone 800/POCONOS.)

(For accommodations see Canadensis, Hawley, Milford, Mount Pocono, Shawnee on Delaware, also see Bushkill)

Port Allegany (B-4)

Settled: 1816 **Pop:** 2,391 **Elev:** 1,481 ft **Area code:** 814 **Zip:** 16743

Native Americans called this spot "canoe place" because here on the portage route between the Allegheny and Susquehanna headwaters they paused to build canoes. Early settlers followed their route. Soon after the town was established, lumbering operations reached their peak; later industrial expansion included coal mining and tanning. In the late 1890s the borough became the center of a boom resulting from the discovery of natural gas and glass sand.

What to See and Do

Sizerville State Park. 19 mi S on PA 155, in Sizerville. Approx 385 acres. Swimming pool; fishing, hunting. Cross-country skiing, snowmobiling. Picnicking, playground, snack bar. Tent & trailer sites. Standard fees. Phone 486-5605.

(For further information contact the Chamber of Commerce, PO Box 434; 642-2181.)

(See Bradford)

Motel

★ **MID-TOWN.** 111 Main St (PA 155). 814/642-2575. 25 rms, 2 story. S, D $38-$46; each addl $5. Crib $5. TV; cable, in-rm movies. Restaurant opp 6 am-11 pm. Ck-out 11 am. Cr cds: A, D, DS, MC, V.

🔥

Pottstown (E-9)

Settled: 1701 **Pop:** 21,831 **Elev:** 160 ft **Area code:** 610 **Zip:** 19464

An iron forge operating in 1714 at Manatawny Creek, about three miles north of Pottstown, was the first industrial establishment in the state. The borough was established by John Potts, an ironmaster, on land William Penn had earlier deeded to his son, John. Today the community is the commercial and cultural hub for an area with a population of 130,000. Nearly 200 modern industries are located here.

What to See and Do

1. **Pottsgrove Manor** (1752). W King St & PA 100. Newly restored house of John Potts, 18th-century ironmaster and founder of Pottstown; outstanding example of early Georgian architecture and furniture. Includes recently discovered slave quarters and Potts' office. Slide orientation. Museum shop. (Daily exc Mon; closed major hols) Phone 326-4014. **Free.**

2. **French Creek State Park.** 9 mi W on PA 724, then 4 mi S on PA 345. Approx 7,330 acres, two lakes. Boating (rentals, mooring, launching), fishing. Swimming pool. Hiking. Ice fishing. Picnicking. Tent & trailer sites, cabins. Standard fees. Phone 582-9680. Also here is

    Hopewell Furnace National Historic Site (see).

3. **Ringing Rocks Park.** 3 mi N off PA 663. Roller-skating (Fri-Sun; phone 323-6560; fee); nature trails, picnicking, interesting rock formations. (Daily) Phone 323-6560 for park information. **Free.**

4. **Boyertown Museum of Historic Vehicles.** 7 mi N via PA 100, 73, in Boyertown, on Warwick St. Collection of over 100 antique autos, trucks, sleighs, buggies and bicycles. Also includes the Hill, which was among the first gasoline-powered cars. (Daily exc Mon) Phone 367-2090. ¢¢

5. **Merritt's Museum of Childhood.** 1 mi W on US 422, in Douglassville. Antique toys, costumed figures, furnishings; Indian relics; gift shop in lobby. (Daily; closed major hols) Phone 385-3408. ¢¢ Admission includes

    Mary Merritt Doll Museum. Antique dolls and toys dating from 1725 to 1900. (Daily; closed major hols) Phone 385-3809.

(For further information contact the Tri-County Area Chamber of Commerce, 238 High St; 326-2900.)

Annual Event

Duryea Day Antique & Classic Auto Meet. Boyertown Community Park. Antique autos, trucks and other vehicles; displays, arts &

crafts, flea market with automotive memorabilia, activities, Pennsylvania Dutch food. Sat of Labor Day wkend.

(See Limerick, Norristown, Reading)

Motel

★ ★ **COMFORT INN.** *PA 100 & Shoemaker Rd. 610/326-5000; FAX 610/970-7230.* 121 rms, 4 story, 20 suites. May-Oct:: S $53-$74; D $56-$84; each addl $7; suites $59-$87; under 18 free; golf plans; wkend rates; lower rates rest of yr. Crib free. TV; cable. Heated pool; lifeguard. Complimentary continental bkfst, coffee. Restaurant adj 6 am-10 pm. Ck-out noon. Coin lndry. Meeting rms. Free bus depot transportation. Exercise equipt; weights, bicycles. Refrigerator in suites. Cr cds: A, C, D, DS, ER, JCB, MC, V.

Restaurant

★ ★ ★ **COVENTRY FORGE INN.** *3360 Coventryville Rd, 5 mi S on PA 100, 1¹/₂ mi W on PA 23 in Coventryville. 610/469-6222.* Hrs: 5:30-9 pm; Sat 5-10 pm. Res accepted. Closed Sun, Mon; Dec 25. French menu. Bar. Wine cellar. A la carte entrees: dinner $16.95-$25.95. Prix fixe: (Sat) dinner $38.50. Specialties: carre d'agneau Provençal, escalopes de veau. Own baking. Inn built in 1717; antiques on display. Cr cds: A, C, D, MC, V.

Quakertown (Bucks Co) (E-9)

Founded: 1715 **Pop:** 8,982 **Elev:** 500 ft **Area code:** 215 **Zip:** 18951

Once a station on the "underground railroad," Quakertown today still retains some of its colonial appearance. In 1798, angered by what they considered an unfair Federal tax and incited by one John Fries, Quakertown housewives started greeting tax assessors with pans of hot water. The "hot water" rebellion cooled down when Federal troops arrived, but the town switched political parties (from Federalist to Jeffersonian) almost en masse.

What to See and Do

The MeetingHouse. 4 mi S of PA 309 on PA 113, in Harleysville, 565 Yoder Rd. An interpretive video and exhibits including quilts, Pennsylvania German fraktur, furniture, books, deeds and clothing show the history of local Mennonites through three centuries. (Daily exc Mon) Phone 256-3020. **Free.**

(For further information contact the Upper Bucks County Chamber of Commerce, 303 W Broad St, PO Box 484; 536-3211.)

(For accommodations see Allentown, Bethlehem, Doylestown, Pottstown)

Restaurant

★ ★ ★ **SIGN OF THE SORREL HORSE.** *243 Old Bethlehem Rd. 215/536-4651.* Hrs: 5:30-9:30 pm. Closed Mon, Tues; Dec 25; also 2 wks Mar. Res required. French, continental menu. Bar. A la carte entrees: dinner $20-$28. Specialties: Swedish elk, pheasant, game dishes. Parking. Outdoor dining. Stone house (1749) built as stagecoach stop; herb gardens, glass aviary. Guest rms avail. Jacket. Totally nonsmoking. Cr cds: A, C, D, MC, V.

Reading (E-8)

Founded: 1748 **Pop:** 78,380 **Elev:** 260 ft **Area code:** 610

A city of railroads and industry famous for its superb pretzels, Reading (RED-ing) was the second community in the United States to vote a socialist government into office; however, the city has not had such a government for many years. Love of music and the thrift and vigor of the "Dutch" are reflected in the character of this unofficial capital of Pennsylvania Dutch Land.

William Penn purchased the land now occupied by Reading from the Lenni-Lenape Indians and settled his two sons, Thomas and Richard, on it. They named it Reading (fern meadow) for their home in England. During the Revolution, the citizens of Reading mustered troops for the Continental army, forged cannon and provided a depot for military supplies and a prison for Hessians and British. The hundreds of skilled German craftspeople, plus canal and railroad transportation, ignited Reading's industrial development. Today 594 factories, some the largest of their kind in the world, are located here.

What to See and Do

1. **Penn's Common.** 11th & Penn Sts. A 50-acre park deeded as a free public commons by the Penns. Formerly site of public hangings; now has playgrounds, flowerbeds, monuments.

2. **Reading Public Museum and Art Gallery.** 500 Museum Rd. In 25-acre Museum Park with stream. Exhibits of art and science. (Wed-Sun; closed most major hols) Phone 371-5850. ¢¢ Adj is

   Planetarium. For schedule and information, phone 371-5854. ¢¢

3. **Historical Society of Berks County.** 940 Centre Ave. Local history exhibits; decorative arts, antiques, transportation displays. (Tues-Sat; closed most hols) Phone 375-4375. ¢¢

4. **Mid-Atlantic Air Museum.** Reading Regional Airport, at PA 183 and Van Reed Rd. Aviation museum dedicated to the preservation of vintage aircraft; planes are restored to flying condition by volunteers. Collection of 40 airplanes and helicopters; 20 on public display, including Martin 4-0-4 airliners, B-25 bomber and others. (Daily; closed Jan 1, Thanksgiving, Dec 25) Phone 372-7333. ¢¢

5. **Berks County Heritage Center.** 4 mi N via PA 183, then W onto Red Bridge Rd, in Bern Twp. Historical interpretive complex. Here are the Gruber Wagon Works (1882), where finely crafted wagons were produced for farm and industry; Wertz's Red Bridge (1867), the longest single-span covered bridge in the state; Deppen Cemetery, with graves of Irish workers who died of "swamp fever" while building the Union Canal; C. Howard Hiester Canal Center, with its collection of canal artifacts. Tours of wagon works and canal center, orientation slide program. (May-Oct, daily exc Mon) Sr citizen rate. Phone 374-8839 or 372-8939. ¢¢

6. **Daniel Boone Homestead.** 7 mi E on US 422 to Baumstown, then N on Boone Rd. Birthplace of Daniel Boone in 1734. Approx 570 acres; includes Boone House, barn, blacksmith shop and sawmill. Picnicking. Nature trails. Youth camping. Visitor's center. (Daily exc Mon; closed some hols) Sr citizen rate. Phone 582-4900. ¢¢

7. **Koziar's Christmas Village.** NW via PA 183, in Bernville. Valley set aglow with over 500,000 Christmas lights; Wishing Well Lane; two barns filled with handmade items, decorations; theme exhibits, Santa's Post Office. (Thanksgiving Day-Dec) Phone 488-1110. ¢¢

8. **Conrad Weiser Homestead** (1729). 14 mi W via US 422. Restored and furnished house of colonial "ambassador" to the Iroquois Indian nation; springhouse; gravesite; visitor center; picnicking in 26-acre park. (Wed-Sun; closed most hols) Grounds **free.** Sr citizen rate. Phone 589-2934. Homestead ¢¢

(For further information contact the Reading/Berks County Visitors Bureau, VF Factory Outlet Complex, Park Rd & Hill Ave, PO Box 6677, Wyomissing 19610; 375-4085 or 800/443-6610.)

(See Denver/Adamstown, Hamburg, Kutztown, Lancaster, Pottstown)

Motels

✔ ★ **COMFORT INN.** *2200 Stacy Dr (5th St Hwy) (19605).* 610/371-0500; FAX 610/478-9421. 60 rms, 2 story. Apr-Oct: S $50-$65; D $50-$70; each addl $5; under 18 free; wkly rates; higher rates: car shows, antique shows; lower rates rest of yr. Crib free. TV; cable. Complimentary continental bkfst, coffee & tea. Restaurant nearby. Ck-out 11 am. Meeting rms. Valet serv. Free airport transportation. Exercise equipt; weight machine, bicycles. Some refrigerators. Cr cds: A, C, D, DS, ER, JCB, MC, V.

★ ★ **DUTCH COLONY INN.** *4635 Perkiomen Ave (19606).* 610/779-2345; res: 800/828-2830; FAX 610/779-8348. 77 rms, 2 story. May-Nov: S $55; D $59; each addl $5; lower rates rest of yr. Crib free. Pet accepted, some restrictions; $4. TV; cable. Pool; lifeguard. Restaurant (see ANTIQUE AIRPLANE). Rm serv. Bar 11-2 am. Ck-out noon. Coin lndry. Meeting rms. Valet serv. Sundries. Exercise equipt; weight machine, bicycles. Lawn games. Balconies. Cr cds: A, C, D, DS, ER, MC, V.

★ ★ **HOLIDAY INN-NORTH.** *N 5th St Hwy (19605), at Warren St Bypass.* 610/929-4741; FAX 610/929-5237. 140 rms, 2 story. S $60-$129; D $60-$139; each addl $10; under 19 free; some wkend rates. Crib free. Pet accepted. TV; cable. Pool; wading pool, lifeguard. Restaurant 6:30 am-10 pm. Rm serv. Bar 3 pm-1:30 am, Sun to 11 pm; dancing exc Sun. Ck-out noon. Meeting rms. Bellhops. Valet serv. Sundries. Cr cds: A, C, D, DS, ER, JCB, MC, V.

★ ★ ★ **INN AT READING.** *(1040 Park Rd, Wyomissing 19610) 3 mi W, just off US 422 at Warren St Bypass.* 610/372-7811; res: 800/383-9713; FAX 610/372-4545. 250 rms, 1-2 story. S $79-$99; D $89-$109; suites $99-$129; each addl $7; under 18 free; some wkend rates. Crib free. Pet accepted, some restrictions. TV; cable, in-rm movies avail. Pool; poolside serv, lifeguard. Playground. Restaurant 6:30 am-10 pm. Rm serv. Bar 11-1 am; entertainment, dancing Fri, Sat. Ck-out 11 am. Meeting rms. Bellhops. Valet serv. Sundries. Gift shop. Free airport, bus depot transportation. Tennis, golf privileges. Picnic tables. Cr cds: A, C, D, DS, MC, V.

Motor Hotels

★ ★ ★ **HOLIDAY INN.** *Morgantown (19543), PA Tpke exit 22.* 610/286-3000; FAX 610/286-0520. 197 rms, 4 story. S $73-$93; D $83-$103; each addl $10; under 18 free. Crib free. Pet accepted, some restrictions. TV; cable. Indoor pool. Free supervised child's activities (Sat). Restaurant 6:30-11:30 am, 5-10 pm; Sat, Sun 5-11 pm. Rm serv. Bar 5 pm-1 am. Ck-out noon. Meeting rms. Sundries. Exercise equipt; weight machine, bicycles, whirlpool. Some refrigerators. Cr cds: A, C, D, DS, MC, V.

★ ★ **SHERATON BERKSHIRE.** *US 422 W (19610), Paper Mill Rd exit, adj to Berkshire Mall.* 610/376-3811; FAX 610/375-7562. 256 rms, 5 story. S, D $59-$95; each addl $10; suites $135-$155; studio rms $100-$110; under 18 free; some wkend rates. Crib free. Pet accepted; $50. TV; cable. Indoor pool; wading pool, poolside serv, lifeguard. Restaurant 6:30 am-10:30 pm. Rm serv. Bar 11:30-2 am; entertainment, dancing. Ck-out noon. Meeting rms. Bellhops. Valet serv. Gift shop. Airport, bus depot transportation. Putting green. Exercise equipt; weights, bicycles, sauna. Some bathrm phones. Cr cds: A, C, D, DS, MC, V.

Restaurants

✔ ★ ★ **ALPENHOF BAVARIAN.** *1¹/4 mi S of jct US 222, Morgantown Rd.* 610/373-1624. Hrs: 11:30 am-2 pm, 5-8:30 pm; Mon to 2 pm; Sat to 9 pm; Sun 11:30 am-7 pm. Closed Jan 1, Dec 25. Res accepted. German menu. Bar. Semi-a la carte: lunch $2.95-$5.25, dinner $6.75-$17.95. Specializes in schnitzel, sauerbraten. Parking. Bavarian Gasthaus with authentic decor. Family-owned. Cr cds: A, MC, V.

★ ★ **ANTIQUE AIRPLANE.** *(See Dutch Colony Inn)* 610/779-2345. Hrs: 7 am-3 pm, 5-10 pm; Sun to 1 pm. Closed Jan 1, Dec 25. Res accepted. Bar. Semi-a la carte: bkfst $2.25-$3.95, lunch $2.95-$5.95, dinner $6.95-$17.95. Child's meals. Specializes in seafood, steak. Salad bar. Parking. Casual elegance among aviation theme. Cr cds: A, C, D, DS, ER, MC, V.

★ ★ ★ **GREEN HILLS INN.** *2444 Morgantown Rd.* 610/777-9611. Hrs: 11:30 am-1:30 pm, 5:30-9 pm; Sat 5:30-10 pm. Closed Sun. Res accepted. French menu. Wine cellar. A la carte entrees: lunch $6.95-$10.95, dinner $16.95-$23.95. Specialties: quenelle de brochet, boneless squab with honey ginger glaze, grilled veal chop with wild mushrooms. Parking. Family-owned. Cr cds: A, C, D, MC, V.

★ ★ ★ **MOSELEM SPRINGS INN.** *(RD 4, Box 4035, Fleetwood 19522) 12 mi N on US 222.* 610/944-8213. Hrs: 11:30 am-9 pm; Fri & Sat to 10 pm; Sun, hols to 8 pm. Closed Dec 24, 25. Res accepted. Pennsylvania Dutch menu. Bar. Semi-a la carte: lunch $5-$11, dinner $10-$18. Child's meals. Specializes in filet mignon, smoked meats, fresh seafood. Parking. Built in 1852; six distinct dining areas with individual decor, including the elegant Presidential Room. Cr cds: A, C, D, MC, V.

Scranton (C-9)

Settled: 1771 **Pop:** 81,805 **Elev:** 754 ft **Area code:** 717

The first settlers here found a Monsey Indian Village on the site. In 1840 George and Seldon Scranton built five iron furnaces using the revolutionary method of firing with anthracite coal instead of charcoal. Manufacture of iron and steel remained an important industry until 1901, when the mills moved to Lake Erie to ease transportation problems.

After World War II, Scranton thoroughly revamped its economy when faced with depletion of the anthracite coal mines, which for more than a century had fired its forges. Scranton's redevelopment drew nationwide attention and served as a model for problem cities elsewhere. Today, Scranton is the home of electronic and printing industries and is host to several major trucking firm terminals.

What to See and Do

1. **Nay Aug Park.** Arthur Ave & Mulberry St in E Scranton. More than 35 acres with memorials to pioneer days. Picnicking, swimming pool (fee), walking trail, refreshment stands and the "Pioneer," a gravity railroad car dating back to 1850; wkend concerts (summer). (Daily) Phone 348-4186. In park is

Everhart Museum. Permanent collections include 19th- and 20th-century American art; Dorflinger glass; Native American, Oriental and primitive art; natural history displays, including Dinosaur Hall. Gift shop. (Daily exc Mon; closed some hols) Donation. Phone 346-8370 or -7186.

Pennsylvania Anthracite Heritage Museum. History and culture of anthracite region. Other affiliated parts of the complex are the Iron Furnaces (see #3); Museum of Anthracite Mining (see ASHLAND), with emphasis on the technology of the industry, and the 19th-century miners' village of Eckley, near Hazleton (see). (Daily exc Mon; closed some hols) Sr citizen rate. Phone 963-4804. ¢¢

Lackawanna Coal Mine Tour. Underground coal mine 300 feet below ground shows world of anthracite miners. Conditions are authentic (damp, dark, slippery and cold); dress appropriately. Above-ground facilities include a "shifting shanty" exhibit room with photo-mural graphic displays, mine artifacts and video presentations; gift shop; restaurant. (May-Nov, daily) Sr citizen rate. Phone 963-MINE or 800/238-7245. ¢¢

2. **Scranton Iron Furnaces.** 159 Cedar Ave. Partially restored site of four anthracite-fired iron furnaces built 1848-1854 and used until 1902. Visitor center, outdoor exhibits. (Daily) Phone 963-3208. ¢¢

3. **Catlin House** (1912). 232 Monroe Ave. Headquarters of Lackawanna Historical Society; period furnishings (colonial-1900s), historic exhibits, antiques; research library. (Tues-Fri; closed hols) Phone 344-3841. **Free.**

4. **Steamtown National Historic Site.** 150 S Washington Ave. Site with large collection of steam locomotives and other memorabilia located in an authentic freight yard. Steam train ride through yard (Memorial Day-Oct; daily). 25-mi train excursion (July-Oct, Sat & Sun) Phone 961-2033 for information or -2035 for tickets. Excursion ¢¢¢

5. **Lackawanna County Stadium.** Exit 51 off I-81, Montage Mountain Rd. Open-air stadium/civic arena seats 11,000. Home of AAA baseball, high school and college football and marching band competitions. (Apr-Nov) For schedule phone 969-2255. ¢¢

6. **Montage Ski Area.** S on I-81, exit 51, follow signs. Quad, double, 3 triple chairlifts; school, rentals; snowmaking; bar, restaurant; lodge. Vertical drop 1,000 ft. Night skiing. More than 130 acres of trails set in 400 acres of mountainside. (Early Dec-late Mar, daily) Summer activities include alpine slides, water slides and scenic chairlift rides (late June-Labor Day). Phone 969-7669. ¢¢¢¢

(For further information contact the Scranton/Lackawanna County Visitors & Convention Bureau, Chamber of Commerce, 222 Mulberry St, PO Box 431, 18501; 342-7711.)

(See Carbondale, Pocono Mountains, Wilkes-Barre)

Motels

 ★ ★ **BEST WESTERN UNIVERSITY INN.** *Franklin & Mulberry Sts (18503). 717/346-7061; FAX 717/347-4667.* 98 rms, 2 story. May-Oct: S $45-$60; D $55-$85; each addl $5; under 12 free; higher rates: St Ubaldo Day, Pocono 500 wkends, college graduation; lower rates rest of yr. Crib $10. Pet accepted. TV; cable. Pool; whirlpool, lifeguard. Restaurant 7 am-11 pm. Bar 11-2 am; entertainment, dancing Fri, Sat. Ck-out 11 am. Meeting rms. Free airport, RR station, bus depot transportation. Cr cds: A, C, D, DS, ER, MC, V.

⊟ ≋ ⊠ ⌧ SC

★ ★ ★ **HOLIDAY INN-EAST.** *(200 Tique St, Dunmore 18512)* I-380 exit 1, just E of I-81. 717/343-4771; FAX 717/343-5171. 139 rms, 2-3 story. S $79-$89; D $89-$99; each addl $10; under 18 free; some wkend rates; ski plan. Crib free. TV; cable. Pool. Restaurant 6:30 am-10 pm. Rm serv. Bar noon-2 am. Ck-out noon. Meeting rms. Valet serv. Cr cds: A, C, D, DS, JCB, MC, V.

D ⊷ ≋ ⊠ ⌧ SC

★ ★ ★ **INN AT NICHOLS VILLAGE.** *(1101 Northern Blvd, Clarks Summit 18411) 3 mi N on I-81, exit 58. 717/587-1135; res: 800/642-2215; FAX 717/586-7140.* 135 rms, 4 story. S $78-$100; D $88-$110; each addl $10; under 18 free. Crib free. TV; cable. Indoor pool; lifeguard. Restaurant 6 am-10 pm. Rm serv. Bar 5-11 pm. Ck-out

noon. Meeting rms. Sundries. Free airport transportation. Exercise equipt; weights, bicycles, sauna. Rec rm. 12 acres include over 1,000 rhododendrons, forestland. Cr cds: A, C, D, DS, MC, V.

⊟ ≋ ⌧ ⊠ ⌧ SC

Hotel

★ ★ **LACKAWANNA STATION.** *700 Lackawanna Ave (18503), I-81 exit 53. 717/342-8300; res: 800/347-6888; FAX 717/342-0380.* 145 rms, 6 story. S $99; D $109; each addl $10; suites $119-$300; studio rms $115; wkend package plans. Crib free. TV; cable. Indoor pool. Restaurant 7 am-10 pm. Bar 11-2 am. Ck-out noon. Meeting rms. Gift shop. Free airport, bus depot transportation. Exercise equipt; weights, bicycles, whirlpool, sauna, steam rm. Downhill/x-country ski 4 mi. Some refrigerators, in-rm whirlpools. Located in historic Lakawanna RR station building. Cr cds: A, C, D, DS, JCB, MC, V.

⊟ ⊠ ≋ ⌧ ⊠ ⌧ SC

Restaurants

★ **COOPER'S SEAFOOD HOUSE.** *701 N Washington Ave. 717/346-6883.* Hrs: 11 am-midnight. Closed major hols. Bar 4 pm-1 am; Sun to 11 pm. Complete meals: lunch $3.99-$6.99, dinner $9.99-$21.99. Child's meals. Specializes in seafood. Pianist, vocalist exc Mon. Parking. Nautical decor. Cr cds: DS, MC, V.

D

★ **FIREPLACE.** *(US 6, Tunkhannock) 15 mi N on US 11, W on US 6. 717/836-9662.* Hrs: 11 am-10 pm; Fri, Sat to 11 pm. Closed Dec 25. Bar. A la carte entrees: lunch, dinner $2-$18.95. Child's meals. Parking. Cr cds: A, D, MC, V.

 ★ **TINK'S CAFE.** *519 Linden St. 717/346-8465.* Hrs: 11:30-2 am. Closed Sun; some major hols. Res accepted. Bar. A la carte entrees: lunch $3.95-$6.95, dinner $9.95-$17.95. Specializes in barbecued chicken and ribs. Salad bar. Entertainment Wed & Fri evenings. Outdoor dining. Cr cds: A, C, D, DS, MC, V.

D

Shamokin Dam (D-7)

Settled: 1790 **Pop:** 1,690 **Elev:** 500 ft **Area code:** 717 **Zip:** 17876

Motel

★ ★ **DAYS INN.** *On US 15, 11. 717/743-1111; FAX 717/743-1190.* 151 rms, 2 story. S $42-$56; D $50-$60; each addl $5; under 18 free. Crib free. Pet accepted. TV; cable. Pool; lifeguard. Restaurant 6:30-10 am, 5-9 pm. Rm serv. Bar from 5 pm; entertainment Fri, Sat. Ck-out noon. Meeting rms. Valet serv. Sundries. Cr cds: A, C, D, DS, JCB, MC, V.

D ⊷ ≋ ⊠ ⌧ SC

Sharon (C-1)

Settled: 1802 **Pop:** 17,493 **Elev:** 998 ft **Area code:** 412 **Zip:** 16146

In the heart of the rich Shenango Valley, Sharon is a busy industrial city that started with a lonely mill on the banks of the Shenango River. Steel, fabrication of steel products and manufacture of electric transformers are a major part of the economic base. The Shenango Dam and its reservoir is northeast of town, near Sharpsville, and offers many recreational activities.

What to See and Do

Shenango Lake. 6 mi N of I-80, PA 18. Swimming, waterskiing; fishing, hunting; boating (ramps). Picnicking. More than 300 tent & trailer sites (mid-May-Labor Day; rest of Sept, reduced number of sites; electric hookups addl). Phone 646-1115 (camping); 962-7746 (general information). Inquire about facilities for the disabled. Camping per night ¢¢¢-¢¢¢¢

(For further information contact the Mercer County Tourist Promotion Agency, 1 W State St; 981-5880 or 800/637-2370.)

Annual Event

The Small Ships Review. Downtown. Parade of ships, entertainment, fireworks, food. Phone 981-3123. July.

(See Mercer)

Inn

★ ★ ★ ★ **TARA-A COUNTRY INN.** *(Box 475, 3665 Valley View Rd, Clark 16113)* I-80 exit 1N, 7 mi on PA 18N exit PA 258. 412/962-3535; res: 800/782-2803; FAX 412/962-3250. 27 rms, 2 story. MAP: S, D $180-$355; wkly rates; package plans; higher rates Sat. Adults preferred. TV; cable, in-rm movies. 2 pools, 1 indoor. Dining: Stonewall's Tavern 11 am-3 pm, 5-8 pm; wkend hrs vary. Ashley's Gourmet Dining 11 am-2:30 pm, 6-8 pm. Ck-out noon, ck-in 2 pm. Meeting rm. Exercise equipt; ski machine, treadmill, whirlpool. Croquet court. Antebellum mansion (1854); antique furnishings; in-rm whirlpools; library. Formal gardens overlooking Schenago Lake. Cr cds: A, DS, MC, V.

Restaurants

★ **QUAKER STEAK & LUBE.** 101 Connelly Blvd. 412/981-7221. Hrs: 11-2 am; Sun from noon. Bar. Semi-a la carte: lunch $3.99-$12, dinner $5.50-$18. Child's meals. Specializes in chicken wings, steak, hamburgers. Salad bar. Parking. Outdoor dining. Former gas station; vintage automobiles, license plates, memorabilia. Casual dining. Cr cds: A, D, DS, MC, V.

✔ ★ ★ **SEAFOOD EXPRESS AND TULLY'S GRILLE ROOM.** 110 Connelly Blvd. 412/981-3123. Hrs: 4 pm-2 am; Sun noon-7 pm. Closed Mon; Dec 25. Res accepted. Bar. Semi-a la carte: dinner $8.99-$15.99. Sun buffet: roast beef & seafood $16.99. Child's meals. Specializes in fresh seafood, char-grilled steak, live lobster. Casual dining in Grille Room; specializes in fajitas, wings, stir-fry. Salad bar. Entertainment Wed-Sun (nightly in Sharky's Lounge). Parking. Outdoor dining. 2 dining rooms in a converted, restored railroad depot. Family-owned. Cr cds: A, C, D, DS, MC, V.

Shartlesville (E-8)

Pop: 300 (est) **Elev:** 560 ft **Area code:** 610 **Zip:** 19554

What to See and Do

Roadside America. Just off US 22, Shartlesville exit at I-78. This miniature "village" consists of O-gauge trains, villages and scenes, with 66 miniature displays re-creating 200 years of life in rural America. Started in 1903, displays now cover 6,000 square feet. (Daily; closed Dec 25) Phone 488-6241. ¢¢

(For accommodations see Reading, also see Hamburg)

Restaurant

✔ ★ **SHARTLESVILLE HOTEL.** *Main St, 1 blk S of PA 22, I-78 exit 8.* 610/488-1918. Hrs: 11 am-7 pm. Res accepted wkends; required some hols. Pennsylvania Dutch menu. Bar to 8 pm. Semi-a la carte: lunch, dinner $4.50-$5.50. Complete meals: dinner $11.95. Child's meals. Parking. Family-style serv. Bar and lobby built ca 1745. No cr cds accepted.

Shawnee on Delaware (D-10)

Pop: 400 (est) **Elev:** 320 ft **Area code:** 717 **Zip:** 18356

What to See and Do

1. **Delaware Water Gap** (see). 6 mi E along Delaware River.
2. **Shawnee Mountain Ski Area.** 6 mi N of I-80, exit 52, follow signs. Nine chairlifts; patrol, school, rentals; snowmaking; cafeteria, bar; nursery. 23 slopes and trails; longest run 1 mi; vertical drop 700 ft. (Dec-Mar, daily) Night skiing. Half-day rates. Phone 421-7231; ski report 800/233-4218. ¢¢¢¢¢

(For further information contact the Pocono Mts Vacation Bureau, 1004 Main St, Stroudsburg 18360, phone 424-6050; for free brochures phone 800/POCONOS.)

(See Bushkill, Stroudsburg)

Resort

★ ★ **SHAWNEE INN.** *Shawnee-on-Delaware, E on I-80, exit 52.* 717/421-1500; res: 800/742-9633; FAX 717/424-9168. 103 rms, 3 story. MAP, May-Oct: S $70-$100; D $77.50-$95; suites $50 addl; kit. units (Nov-Apr) $55-$90; EP: S, D $65-$85; under 16 free; some wkly, wkend rates; higher rates Christmas hols; lower rates rest of yr. Crib free. Serv charge 10%. TV; cable. 4 pools, 1 indoor; wading pool; lifeguard. Playground. Supervised child's activities. Dining rm 7 am-9 pm. Snack bar. Picnics. Bar hrs vary. Ck-out noon, ck-in 4 pm. Coin lndry. Grocery, package store 4 mi. Meeting rms. Airport transportation. Lighted tennis, pro (summer). 27-hole golf, pro, putting green, driving range, miniature golf. Boats, rowboats. Downhill/x-country ski 3 mi. Sleighing, tobogganing. Lawn games. Soc dir; entertainment, dancing, movies. Rec rm. Game rm. Exercise rm; instructor, weights, bicycles. Cr cds: A, C, D, DS, MC, V.

Somerset (F-3)

Settled: 1783 **Pop:** 6,454 **Elev:** 2,190 ft **Area code:** 814 **Zip:** 15501

Somerset, a county seat, is also the marketing place for farms, lumber mills and coal mines in the area. James Whitcomb Riley described the countryside in his poem *'Mongst the Hills of Somerset.* Nearby lakes offer fishing and boating.

What to See and Do

1. **Somerset Historical Center.** 5 mi N on PA 985. Museum exhibits on rural life; outdoor display includes log house, log barn, covered bridge, sugarhouse. (Daily exc Mon; closed most hols) (See ANNUAL EVENTS) Sr citizen rate. Phone 445-6077. ¢¢

2. **State parks.**

   Laurel Hill. 8 mi W on PA 31, then SW on unnumbered road. Approx 3,900 acres. Swimming beach, snack bar; hunting; boating (mooring, launching). Hiking. Snowmobiling, ice fishing. Picnicking. Tent & trailer sites. Standard fees. Phone 445-7725.

   Kooser. 9 mi NW on PA 31. Approx 250 acres. Cross-country skiing, sledding. Picnicking. Tent & trailer sites, cabins. Standard fees. Phone 445-8673.

3. **Mt Davis.** 26 mi S on US 219 to Salisbury, then W on unnumbered road. Highest point in state (3,213 ft). Phone 412/238-9533.

4. **Hidden Valley Ski Area.** 12 mi W of PA Tpke Somerset exit 10; 8 mi E of PA Tpke Donegal exit 9, on PA 31. Eight lifts; patrol, school, rentals; snowmaking; cafeteria, restaurant, bars; nursery. Longest run 5,280 ft; vertical drop 610 ft. 16 slopes. (Dec-Mar, daily) 30 miles of cross-country trails (rentals). Shuttle service. Conference center, lodging. Year-round facilities, activities. Phone 443-2600. ¢¢¢¢¢

(For further information contact the Information Center, 829 N Center Ave; 445-6431.)

Annual Events

Maple Festival. Festival Park in Meyersdale. Phone 634-0213. Late Mar-early Apr.

Somerfest. Laurel Arts/Phillip Dressler Center for the Arts. German festival: dancing, competitions, entertainment, food, tours. Phone 443-2433. Mid-July.

Mountain Craft Days. Somerset Historical Center (see #1). More than 125 traditional craft demonstrations; antique exhibits; entertainment. Early Sept.

Farmers' and Threshermen's Jubilee. 9 mi SW via PA 281, in New Centerville. Equipment demonstrations; tractor-pulling, horseshoe-pitching, tobacco-spitting contests; antique car show and flea market; food. Early Sept.

Springs Folk Festival. On PA 669, in Springs. Crafts demonstrations include bread baking, wheat weaving, basket and broom making, candle dipping, quilt stitching; entertainment featuring banjo & fiddle music; pioneer exhibits on forest trail; maple sugaring, apple butter boiling, log hewing; museum adj with antique tools, furnishings, historical artifacts. Phone 662-4158 or 662-4298. Early Oct.

(See Johnstown, Ligonier)

Motels

★ **ECONOMY INN.** *RD 2, Box 5, PA Tpke exit 10. 814/445-4144.* 19 rms, 15 with shower only. S $35-$45; D $35-$50; each addl $5; under 12 free; higher rates special events. TV; cable. Restaurant nearby. Ck-out 11 am. Coin lndry. Game rm. Refrigerators. Cr cds: A, DS, MC, V.

✕ ✕ SC

✔ ★ **HIGHLANDER.** *799 N Center Ave. 814/445-7988.* 28 rms, 2 story. S $32-$35; D $34-$42; each addl $4. Crib $4. TV. Complimentary coffee in lobby. Restaurant nearby. Ck-out 11 am. Downhill ski 10 mi; x-country ski 13 mi. Cr cds: A, C, D, DS, MC, V.

✕ ✕ SC

✔ ★ **KNIGHTS INN.** *PA Tpke entrance, exit 10 off I-70/76. 814/445-8933; res: 800/843-5644.* 113 rms, 10 kit. units. S $37.95-$43.95; D $44.95-$50.95; each addl $6; kit. units $49.95-$56.95; under 18 free; wkly rates; higher rates Dec-Mar wkends. Crib free. Pet ac-

cepted. TV; cable. Pool. Complimentary coffee in lobby. Restaurant nearby. Ck-out noon. Meeting rms. Downhill ski 15 mi. Cr cds: A, C, D, DS, ER, MC, V.

D ✕ ✕ ✕ ✕ SC

Motor Hotel

★ ★ ★ **RAMADA INN.** *Box 511, at PA Tpke exit 10. 814/443-4646.* 152 rms, 2 story. S $56-$70; D $66-$80; each addl $10; suites $95-$125; under 18 free; some wkend rates. Crib free. Pet accepted. TV. Indoor pool; whirlpool, sauna, poolside serv, lifeguard. Restaurant 6:30 am-2 pm, 5-10 pm; Sun 7-11 am. Rm serv. Bar 11-2 am; Sun to 9 pm; entertainment, dancing Tues-Sat. Ck-out noon. Meeting rms. Bellhops. Valet serv. Sundries. Downhill/x-country ski 12 mi. Game rm. Cr cds: A, C, D, DS, JCB, MC, V.

D ✕ ✕ ✕ ✕ SC

Resort

★ ★ ★ **HIDDEN VALLEY.** *(1 Craighead Dr, Hidden Valley 15502) PA Tpke exit 9, (then 8 mi E on PA 31) or exit 10 (then 12 mi W on PA 31). 814/443-6454; res: 800/458-0175; FAX 814/443-1907.* 213 units, some A/C, 2-3 story. Mid-Dec-mid-Mar: S $120-$180; D $150-$210; each addl $30; under 13 free; ski, golf packages; MAP avail; lower rates rest of yr. Crib free. TV; cable. 4 pools, 1 indoor; lifeguard. Playground. Supervised child's activities (June-Sept). Dining rms 6:30 am-midnight. Bars 11-1 am; entertainment. Ck-out noon, ck-in 4 pm. Grocery. Coin lndry. Package store. Convention facilities. Bellhops. Valet serv. Gift shop. Airport transportation. Sports dir. Lighted tennis, pro. 18-hole golf, greens fee $43-$53, pro, putting green, driving range. Boats. Downhill/x-country ski on site. Hiking. Soc dir. Exercise equipt; weight machine, bicycles, whirlpool, sauna. Fireplaces. Balconies. Picnic tables. Located in scenic Laurel Highlands mountain area. Cr cds: C, D, DS, MC, V.

D ✕ ✕ ✕ ✕ ✕ ✕ ✕ ✕ SC

Restaurant

✔ ★ ★ **OAKHURST TEA ROOM.** *6 mi W on PA 31. 814/443-2897.* Hrs: 11 am-10 pm; Sun to 8 pm. Closed Mon; Dec 24, 25. Bar. Semi-a la carte: lunch $3-$7. Complete meals: lunch, dinner $9.95-$26. Buffet (Tues-Sat): lunch $6.50, dinner $9.95, seafood dinner (Fri) $19.95. Sun brunch $7.95. Child's meals. Specializes in waffles, own noodles in chicken broth. Salad bar. Entertainment Sat-Sun. Parking. Outdoor dining. Early Amer decor. Fireplace. Family-owned. Cr cds: DS, MC, V.

D SC

State College  (D-5)

Settled: 1859 **Pop:** 38,923 **Elev:** 1,154 ft **Area code:** 814

The home of Pennsylvania State University, and principally concerned with services to this institution, this borough is near the geographic center of the state. In the beautiful Nittany Valley, State College is surrounded by farmland famous for its production of oats and swine. Iron ore was discovered just east of town, in 1790, and many iron furnaces later sprang up.

What to See and Do

1. **Pennsylvania State University** (1855). (39,000 students) On US 322 in University Park. Approximately 290 major buildings on a 5,005-acre campus; it is the land-grant institution of Pennsylvania. Phone 865-4700. On campus are

Old Main (1929). E of Mall near Pollock Rd. Present building, on site of original Old Main (1863), uses many of the original stones; topped by lofty bell tower. Here are Henry Varnum Poor's land-grant frescoes. (Mon-Fri; closed major hols) Phone 865-2501. **Free.**

Earth and Mineral Sciences Museum. Steidle Building on Pollock Rd. Exhibitions of ores, gems and fossils; automated displays; art gallery. (Mon-Fri; closed major hols) Phone 865-6427. **Free.**

"Ag Hill," The College of Agriculture. Showplace for state's dairy industry includes the dairy center, off Park Rd near stadium, with five herds of cows, automatic milking equipment (daily). The creamery, Curtain Rd, has retail salesroom for cheeses, milk, cream, ice cream (daily; closed major hols). Also test flower gardens off Park Rd near East Halls (July-Sept). **Free.**

2. **Columbus Chapel—Boal Mansion Museum.** 4 mi E on US 322, in Boalsburg. The mansion has been the Boal family home since 1789 and includes original furnishings, china, tools and weapons. Colonel Theodore Davis Boal, who outfitted his own troop for World War I, lived here. The 16th-century chapel belonged to the family of Christopher Columbus in Spain and was brought here in 1909 by Boal relatives. It contains religious items and Renaissance and baroque art, as well as an admiral's desk and explorer's cross that belonged to Columbus himself. (Daily exc Tues) Summer concerts on grounds. Phone 466-6210. Mansion **¢¢**

3. **Pennsylvania Military Museum.** 4 mi E on US 322, in Boalsburg. On grounds of 28th Division Shrine; dioramas; battle exhibits and equipment from the Revolutionary War to the present. Audiovisual program; military bookstore. (Daily exc Mon; closed some hols) Sr citizen rate. Phone 466-6263. **¢¢**

4. **Whipple Dam State Park.** 10 mi S on PA 26, then 1 mi E on unnumbered road. Approx 250 acres. Swimming beach; fishing, hunting; boating (launching, mooring). Hiking. Snowmobiling, ice-skating, ice fishing. Picnicking, snack bar. Standard fees. Phone 667-3808.

5. **Penn's Cave.** NE on PA 26, SE on PA 144, then 5 mi E of Centre Hall on PA 192. A one-hour, one-mile boat trip through cavern; stalactites, stalagmites; plus walk-through wildlife sanctuary. Picnic area; airplane rides; visitor center; gift shop, restaurant. (Mid-Feb-Nov, daily) Sr citizen rate. Phone 364-1664. **¢¢¢**

(For further information contact the Center County, Lion Country Visitor & Convention Bureau, 1402 S Atherton St, 16801; 231-1400.)

Annual Events

Central Pennsylvania Festival of the Arts. Open-air display of visual and performing arts; indoor exhibits; demonstrations of arts and crafts; food booths. Phone 237-3682. Mid-July.

Centre County Grange Fair. PA 144S, at Grange Park in Centre Hall. Exhibits, livestock show, rides, concessions, entertainment. Phone 364-9674. Last wk Aug.

(See Bellefonte)

Motels

(Rates higher football, art festival & special wkends; may be 2-day min)

★ ★ ★ **AUTOPORT.** 1405 S Atherton St (US 322 Business) (16801). 814/237-7666; res: 800/932-7678; FAX 814/237-7456. 86 rms, 3 story, 12 kit. units. S $45-$60; D $55-$70; each addl $5; suites $60-$85; under 16 free; wkly, wkend rates. Crib free. Pet accepted; $25. TV; cable. Heated pool; lifeguard. Restaurant 6 am-11 pm; dining rm 11:30 am-2 pm, 5-10 pm. Bar 11-2 am; Sun to midnight; entertainment exc Sun. Ck-out noon. Coin lndry. Meeting rms. Sundries. Downhill ski 4 mi. Rms vary. Cr cds: A, C, D, DS, MC, V.

★ ★ **DAYS INN-PENN STATE.** 240 S Pugh St (16801). 814/238-8454; FAX 814/234-3377. 184 rms, 6 story. S $50-$75; D $60-$75; each addl $7; suites $150; under 18 free; some wkend rates; higher rates special events. Crib free. Pet accepted, some restrictions; $7. TV; cable. Indoor pool; lifeguard. Complimentary continental bkfst Mon-Fri. Restaurant 6:30 am-midnight; Sun bkfst from 8 am. Rm serv. Bar 11-2 am; entertainment. Ck-out noon. Meeting rms. Bellhops. Valet serv. Sundries. Free airport transportation. Exercise rm; instructor, weight machine, bicycles, sauna. Rec rm. Game rm. Refrigerators avail. Cr cds: A, C, D, DS, MC, V.

✔ ★ **FRIENDSHIP INN.** 1040 N Atherton St (US 322) (16803). 814/238-6783; FAX 814/238-4519. 29 rms, 3 with shower only, 2 story. S $36-$41; D $41-$56; each addl $5; under 16 free; wkly rates. Crib $6. TV; cable. Complimentary coffee in lobby. Restaurant nearby. Ck-out 11:30 am. Some refrigerators. Cr cds: A, C, D, DS, JCB, MC, V.

★ ★ **HAMPTON INN.** 1101 E College Ave (16801). 814/231-1590; FAX 814/238-7320. 121 rms, 3 story. S $49-$56; D $60-$67; suites $68-$75; under 18 free; ski, golf plans. Crib free. Pet accepted. TV; cable. Heated pool; lifeguard. Complimentary continental bkfst. Restaurant adj. Meeting rm. Valet serv. Sundries. Airport transportation. Downhill/x-country ski 5 mi. Picnic tables. Cr cds: A, C, D, DS, ER, MC, V.

★ ★ **HOLIDAY INN-PENN STATE.** 1450 S Atherton St (US 322 Business) (16801). 814/238-3001; FAX 814/237-1345. 288 rms, 2 story. S $50-$60; D $57-$67; each addl $7; suites $75; under 19 free. Crib free. Pet accepted, some restrictions. TV; cable. 2 pools; wading pool, lifeguard. Restaurant 7 am-2 pm, 5-10 pm. Rm serv. Bar 11-2 am. Ck-out noon. Coin lndry. Meeting rms. Lighted tennis. Health club privileges. Game rm. Cr cds: A, C, D, DS, JCB, MC, V.

✔ ★ **IMPERIAL MOTOR INN.** 118 S Atherton St (US 322 Business) (16801), at PA 26. 814/237-7686; res: 800/782-0716. 37 rms, 2 story. S $43-$95; D $50-$135 each addl $5; under 16 free. Crib free. TV; cable. Pool; lifeguard. Complimentary morning coffee. Restaurant nearby. Ck-out noon. Airport transportation. Downhill ski 6 mi. Cr cds: A, C, D, DS, JCB, MC, V.

★ **NITTANY BUDGET.** 1274 N Atherton St (US 322) (16803). 814/237-7638; res: 800/248-8494. 47 rms, 16 with shower only, 10 kit. units. S $29.93; D $37.93-$39.93; each addl $7; kits. $28.57; under 18 free; wkly, monthly rates. Crib free. TV; cable. Restaurant adj 10 am-11 pm. Ck-out noon. Some refrigerators. Cr cds: A, C, D, DS, MC, V.

Hotel

★ ★ ★ **HILTON ATHERTON.** 125 S Atherton St (US 322 Business) (16801). 814/231-2100; FAX 814/231-2100, ext. 187. 150 rms, 6 story. S $75-$95; D $85-$105; each addl $10; under 18 free. Crib free. TV; cable. Restaurant 6:30 am-10 pm. Bar 11:30-2 am; entertainment Wed-Sat. Ck-out noon. Meeting rms. Free garage parking. Free airport, bus depot transportation. Tennis privileges. Golf privileges. Downhill ski 6 mi. Health club privileges. Refrigerators in suites. Cr cds: A, C, D, DS, ER, MC, V.

Inn

★ ★ ★ **NITTANY LION.** 200 W Park Ave (US 322 Business) (16803), on Penn State campus. 814/231-7500; FAX 814/231-7510. 262 rms, 3 story. S $65-$85; D $75-$95; each addl $12-$15; suites $160-$190; under 12 free; golf package. Crib free. TV; cable. Heated pool privileges. Dining rm 6:45 am-9 pm, Sun to 8 pm. Bar 11:30-1 am. Ck-out noon, ck-in 4 pm. Meeting rms. Valet serv. Airport transportation. Lighted tennis privileges. Golf privileges, greens fee $18, putting green, driving range. Exercise equipt; weight machines, stair machines. Cr cds: A, C, D, DS, MC, V.

Resort

★ ★ ★ **TOFTREES.** *1 Country Club Lane (16803). 814/234-8000; res: 800/458-3602 (exc PA), 800/252-3551 (PA); FAX 814/238-4404.* 110 units, 3 story, 22 suites. May-mid-Oct: S $95; D $110; each addl $15; suites $105-$250; AP, MAP avail; golf plans; some wkend rates; lower rates rest of yr. Crib avail. TV; cable. Heated pool; lifeguard. Dining rms 6:30 am-10 pm. Bar from 11 am; entertainment. Ck-out noon, ck-in 3 pm. Free airport, campus transportation. Tennis, pro. 18-hole golf, pro, putting green, driving range. X-country ski on site. Exercise rm; instructor, bicycles, treadmill. Refrigerators. Balconies. Mediterranean decor. Cr cds: A, C, D, DS, MC, V.

Restaurants

✔ ★ ★ **TAVERN RESTAURANT.** *220 E College Ave. 814/238-6116.* Hrs: 5-10:30 pm; Sun to 8:30 pm. Closed major hols. Res accepted Sun-Thurs. Bar 4 pm-12:30 am. Semi-a la carte: dinner $5.95-$14.95. Child's meals. Specializes in fresh veal dishes, fresh seafood, prime rib. Classical music. Colonial decor; large collection of original Pennsylvania prints. Cr cds: A, C, D, DS, MC, V.

★ ★ ★ **VICTORIAN MANOR.** *(901 Pike St, Lemont) 1³/₄ mi E on US 322, then 2 mi NE via East Branch Rd. 814/238-5534.* Hrs: 5:30-9 pm. Closed Jan 1, Memorial Day, Labor Day, Dec 25. Res accepted; required wkends. Continental menu. Wine list. Semi-a la carte: dinner $11.95-$28.45. Prix fixe: 3 course dinner $14.50. Specializes in rack of lamb, filet of salmon, veal. Own pastries. Parking. Historic building (1891). Victorian decor. Totally nonsmoking. Cr cds: A, C, D, DS, MC, V.

Stroudsburg (D-9)

Settled: 1769 **Pop:** 5,312 **Elev:** 430 ft **Area code:** 717 **Zip:** 18360

This is a center for the Pocono Mountains resort area and the surrounding rural community. It is the Monroe County seat.

What to See and Do

1. **Delaware Water Gap** (see). 3¹/₂ mi E on PA 611, I-80.

2. **Stroud Mansion** (18th century). 9th & Main Sts. Built by founder of city; houses Historical Society of Monroe County. Historical artifacts, genealogical records. Tours. (Tues-Fri, also Sun afternoons; closed major hols) Phone 421-7703. ¢

3. **Quiet Valley Living Historical Farm.** 3¹/₂ mi SW on US 209 Business, then 1¹/₂ mi S (follow signs). A log house (1765) with kitchen and parlor added 1892; 12 other original or reconstructed buildings. Demonstrations of seasonal farm activities. Guided tours with costumed guides. 1¹/₂ hrs. (June 20-Labor Day, daily) Phone 992-6161. ¢¢

4. **Canoeing.** Canoe trips on the Delaware River; equipment provided; also transportation to and from the river. (May-Oct) Contact Chamberlain Canoes, 1527 Spruce St; 421-0180. ¢¢¢¢-¢¢¢¢¢

5. **Alpine Mountain Ski Area.** 6 mi N via PA 191, 447N, just outside Analomink. Double, 2 quad chairlifts; patrol, school, rentals; snowmaking; restaurant, bar; child care center. Vertical drop 500 ft. (Dec-Mar, daily) 18 trails & slopes. Phone 595-2150 or 800/233-8240. ¢¢¢¢

(For further information contact the Pocono Mts Vacation Bureau, 1004 Main St, phone 424-6050; for free brochures phone 800/POCONOS.)

(See Easton, Pocono Mountains)

Motels

★ ★ **BEST WESTERN POCONO INN.** *700 Main St. 717/421-2200; FAX 717/421-5561.* 90 rms, 4 story. S $64-$89; D $64-$89; each addl $10; higher rates special events. Crib free. TV; cable, in-rm movies avail. Indoor pool; whirlpools. Restaurant 6 am-10 pm; wkends to 11 pm. Rm serv. Bar 11:30-2 am; entertainment, dancing. Ck-out 11 am. Meeting rms. Game rm. Cr cds: A, C, D, DS, ER, JCB, MC, V.

✔ ★ **BUDGET.** *(Box 216, E Stroudsburg 18301) E on I-80, exit 51. 717/424-5451; res: 800/233-8144.* 115 rms, 2-3 story. No elvtr. S $31; D $37-$55; each addl $3; higher rates: special events, hols, some wkends. Crib free. TV; cable. Restaurant 7-11 am, 5-10 pm. Bar 4 pm-midnight. Ck-out 11 am. Game rm. Cr cds: A, C, D, DS, MC, V.

★ ★ **SHERATON POCONO INN.** *1220 W Main St, I-80 exit 48. 717/424-1930; FAX 717/424-5909.* 133 rms, 2 story. S $76-$99; D $86-$109; each addl $10; suites $125-$160; under 18 free; some wkend rates. Crib free. TV; cable. Pool; sauna, poolside serv, lifeguard. Restaurant 7 am-10 pm. Rm serv. Bars 11-2 am; entertainment, dancing Tues-Sat. Ck-out 11 am. Meeting rms. Bellhops. Sundries. Game rm. Balconies. Cr cds: A, D, DS, ER, MC, V.

Inn

★ ★ **INN AT MEADOWBROOK.** *(RD 7, Box 7651, Cherry Lane Rd, East Stroudsburg 18301) I-80 exit 45 Tannersville, N on PA 715, turn right on PA 611, turn left on Cherry Lane Rd. 717/629-0296; res: 800/441-7619.* 16 rms, many air-cooled, some A/C, 2 story. No rm phones. S, D $50-$85. Children over 12 yrs only. TV in sitting rm; cable. Pool; lifeguard. Complimentary full bkfst. Dining rm 5-10 pm; closed Mon, Tues. Ck-out noon, ck-in 2 pm. Bus depot transportation. 2 tennis courts. Downhill ski 4 mi; x-country ski 2 mi. Game rm. Rec rm. Lawn games. On lake. Consists of Manor House (1842) and Mill House (1924); antiques. Equestrian Center adj. Cr cds: A, MC, V.

Resort

★ ★ **CAESAR'S POCONO PALACE.** *Marshalls Creek (18335), 6 mi N on US 209. 717/588-6692; res: 800/233-4141.* 169 units, 155 suites. D, suites $180-$320; wkly rates; couples only. TV; cable, in-rm movies avail. 2 pools, 1 indoor. Complimentary full bkfst & dinner. Dining rm 10-2 am. Bar from 11:30 am; entertainment, dancing. Ck-out 11 am, ck-in 10 am-3 pm. Gift shop. Lighted tennis. 9-hole golf course, pro, putting green, driving range. Marina; paddle boats, waterskiing. Downhill ski 3 mi; x-country on site. Snowmobiles, ice skating. Softball field. Volleyball. Archery. Lawn games. Rec rm. Game rm. Exercise equipt; weight machine, bicycles, whirlpool, sauna. Refrigerator in suites. Some balconies. On lake. Cr cds: A, C, D, DS, MC, V.

Restaurants

✔ ★ **ARLINGTON DINER.** *834 N 9th St. 717/421-2329.* Hrs: 6 am-10 pm; Fri, Sat to 11 pm; Sun 7 am-10 pm. Closed Jan 1, Thanksgiving, Dec 25. Semi-a la carte: bkfst 90¢-$4, lunch $3.50-$5, dinner $4.25-$10.95. Child's meals. Specializes in bread & rice pudding. Parking. No cr cds accepted.

★ **BEAVER HOUSE.** *1001 N 9th St. 717/424-1020.* Hrs: 11:30 am-9 pm; Fri to 9:30 pm; Sat to 10:30 pm; Sun 1-9 pm. Closed Dec 25. Res accepted. Bar. Complete meals: lunch $4.95-$8.95, dinner $11.25-$28.95. Specializes in seafood, Western prime rib. Parking. Many antiques; Tiffany lamps, trophies, bottles, stained glass, clocks. Family-owned. Cr cds: A, C, D, DS, MC, V.

[D]

✔ ★ **LEE'S.** *(PA 611, Bartonsville) 6 mi SE on PA 715. 717/421-1212.* Hrs: noon-10 pm; Sat 1:30-11 pm; Sun 11:30-10 pm; Sun brunch to 3 pm. Closed Thanksgiving. Res required Fri-Sun. Chinese, Japanese menu. Bar. A la carte entrees: lunch, dinner $5.25-$12.95. Lunch buffet $6.95. Specializes in steak dishes. Salad bar. Sushi bar. Parking. Oriental decor. Cr cds: A, D, MC, V.

[D]

Unrated Dining Spot

THE DANSBURY DEPOT. *(50 Crystal St, East Stroudsburg) E on I-80, exit 51. 717/476-0500.* Hrs: 11 am-10 pm; Fri & Sat to 11 pm; Sun to 9 pm. Closed Thanksgiving, Dec 25. Continental menu. Bar. Semi-a la carte: lunch $4-$6, dinner $8-$14. Child's meals. Specializes in steak, seafood. Parking. Converted railroad station depot and freight house, built 1864. Display of railroad memorabilia. Small trains move around the room, overhead on the walls. Cr cds: A, C, D, DS, MC, V.

[D]

Tannersville (D-9)

Pop: 1,200 (est) **Elev:** 890 ft **Area code:** 717 **Zip:** 18372

What to See and Do

Camelback Ski Area. 3½ mi W off I-80, exit 45, in Big Pocono State Park. Quad, 2 triple, 8 double chairlifts; patrol, school, rentals; snowmaking; cafeteria, restaurant, bar; nursery. Longest run 1 mi; vertical drop 800 ft. (Mid-Dec-late Mar, daily) 27 trails. Alpine slide, water slide, swimming pool, bumper boats, entertainment (July-Aug, daily; mid-May-June, Sept-Oct, wkends only; single & combination tickets avail). Phone 629-1661; ski report 800/233-8100 (mid-Atlantic states). ¢¢¢¢¢

(For further information contact the Pocono Mts Vacation Bureau, 1004 Main St, Stroudsburg 18360, phone 424-6050; for free brochures phone 800/POCONOS.)

(See Pocono Mountains, Stroudsburg)

Resort

★ ★ **SUMMIT.** *1 mi S on PA 715; I-80 exit 45. 717/629-0203; res: 800/233-8250; FAX 717/629-0203, ext. 343.* 184 rms, 100 suites. Couples only. AP: D $140-$222.50; wkly plans; some wkend rates. Serv charge 15%. TV. Indoor/outdoor pool; lifeguard. Dining rm 8:30-10 am, noon-1 pm, 6:30-7:30 pm. Snack bar. Bar noon-1 am. Ck-out 11:30 am, ck-in 3 pm. Sports dir. Indoor/outdoor tennis. Miniature golf. Downhill ski 5 mi. Paddleboats. Ice-skating, roller skating (summer), tobogganing, snowmobiles. Archery; rifle range. Riding. Bicycles. Indoor, outdoor games. Lawn games. Soc dir; dancing, entertainment. Exercise equipt; weight machines, bicycles, whirlpool, sauna. Some fireplaces. Private terraces, balconies. Golf course nearby. On 100 acres; private lake. Cr cds: MC, V.

Titusville (B-2)

Settled: 1796 **Pop:** 6,434 **Elev:** 1,199 ft **Area code:** 814 **Zip:** 16354

Titusville spreads from the banks of Oil Creek, so-called because of the oil that appeared on its surface. Edwin L. Drake drilled the first successful oil well in the world on August 27, 1859. Overnight, Titusville became the center of the worldwide oil industry.

What to See and Do

Drake Well Museum. 1 mi SE of PA 8. Site of world's first oil well; operating replica of Drake derrick and engine house; picnic area. Museum contains dioramas, working models, life-size exhibits depicting history of oil. (Daily; closed most hols) Sr citizen rate. Phone 827-2797. ¢¢

(For further information contact the Titusville Area Chamber of Commerce, 116 W Central Ave; 827-2941.)

(See Franklin, Meadville, Oil City)

Resort

★ ★ **CROSS CREEK.** *Box 432, 4½ mi S on PA 8. 814/827-9611; FAX 814/827-2062.* 94 rms, 1-2 story. May-Oct: S $85-$95; D $95-$110; each addl $10; suites $105-$115; under 12 free; golf plan; lower rates rest of yr. Crib free. TV; cable. Heated pool; lifeguard. Restaurant 6:30 am-2 pm, 6-10 pm. Bar 11-2 am; entertainment, dancing (in season). Ck-out 2 pm. Meeting rms. Gift shop. Tennis. 27-hole golf, greens fee $28, putting green. Some private patios, balconies. Cr cds: A, C, D, DS, MC, V.

Towanda (B-7)

Settled: 1794 **Pop:** 3,242 **Elev:** 737 ft **Area code:** 717 **Zip:** 18848

On the north branch of the Susquehanna River, Towanda is a native word meaning "where we bury the dead."

In 1793 the Asylum Company purchased a million acres of these wild valleys as a refuge for Marie Antoinette of France, should she escape to America. "La Grande Maison," a queenly house, was built. French noblemen settled here, and a thriving community (called Azilum) was planned (see #3). The colony was unsuccessful, however, and most of its founders returned to France. Many of their descendants, however, still live in Bradford County.

What to See and Do

1. **Tioga Point Museum.** 15 mi N off US 220, on PA 199, Spalding Memorial Building, 724 S Main St in Athens. Mementos of French Azilum; Civil War, Stephen Foster and Native American exhibits; historical displays of early canals and steam railroad. (Mon, Thurs & Sat afternoons; closed major hols) Donation. Phone 888-7225.
2. **Valley Railroad Museum.** 15 mi N off US 220, in Sayre on S Lehigh Ave. Century-old Lehigh Valley passenger station houses museum with displays of railroad memorabilia and railroad exhibit of

Lehigh Valley in miniature; gift shop. (Daily exc Mon; closed major hols) Sr citizen rate. Phone 888-1881. ¢¢

3. French Azilum. 10 mi SE via US 6, PA 187. Site of colony for refugees from the French Revolution (1793-1803). Five cabins with crafts, tool exhibits; log cabin museum (1793); Laporte House (1836), built by son of one of colony's founders, reflects elegant French influence. Special events. Guided tours. (June-Aug, Wed-Sun; May, Sept-Oct, Sat & Sun) Sr citizen rate. Phone 265-3376. ¢¢

4. David Wilmot's burial place. Riverside Cemetery, William St between Chestnut & Walnut Sts. Congressman (1845-51), senator (1861-63), leader of the Free-Soil Party, Wilmot introduced the Wilmot Proviso in congress, which would have required the US to outlaw slavery in any lands purchased from Mexico. This was an important factor in the dissension between North and South that led to the Civil War.

(For further information contact the Endless Mountains Visitors Bureau, RR #6 Box 132A, Tunkhannock 18657-9232; 836-5431)

(See Mansfield, Scranton)

Motel

✔ ★ **TOWANDA.** *383 York Ave (US 6).* 717/265-2178. 48 rms. S $39-$65; D $43-$70; each addl $5; under 12 free. Crib $3.50. Pet accepted. TV; cable. Pool. Restaurant 6 am-9:30 pm; Sat, Sun from 7 am. Bar 2:30 pm-2 am. Ck-out 1 pm. Meeting rms. Sundries. Cr cds: A, C, D, DS, MC, V.

Motor Hotel

★ ★ ★ **GUTHRIE INN & CONFERENCE CENTER.** *(255 Spring St, Sayre 18840) Approx 15 mi N on US 220, E on NY 17, exit 61, S on PA 199.* 717/888-7711; res: 800/627-7972. 100 rms, 4 story. S $71-$74; D $75-$78; each addl $4; suites $154; under 12 free; wkend package. Crib free. TV; cable. Indoor pool; lifeguard. Complimentary coffee in rms. Restaurant 6:30 am-9 pm; Fri, Sat to 10 pm. Rm serv. Bar; entertainment, dancing Fri, Sat. Ck-out noon. Meeting rms. Sundries. Limited airport transportation. Free Guthrie Medical Center transportation. Lighted tennis. 18-hole golf privileges. Exercise rm; instructor, weights, bicycles, whirlpool, sauna, steam rm. Balconies. Cr cds: A, C, D, DS, MC, V.

Uniontown (F-2)

Settled: 1768 **Pop:** 12,034 **Elev:** 999 ft **Area code:** 412 **Zip:** 15401

Coal and its byproducts made Uniontown prosperous, but with the decline in coal mining the city has developed a more diversified economic base. First known as Union, this city has been the Fayette County seat since 1784. General Lafayette and his son, George Washington de Lafayette, came on a visit after the Revolutionary War and were welcomed by Albert Gallatin, one-time senator and Secretary of the Treasury. Uniontown was a hotbed of the Whiskey Rebellion, and Federal troops were sent here in 1794.

What to See and Do

1. Fort Necessity National Battlefield (1754). 11 mi SE on US 40. The site of Washington's first major battle and the opening battle of the French and Indian War (1754). This land was known as the Great Meadows. A portion was later purchased by Washington, who owned it until his death. A replica of the original fort was built on the site following an archaeological survey in 1953. Picnic area

(mid-spring-late fall). Sr citizen rate. Phone 329-5512. ¢ Nearby and included in the admission fee are

Visitor Center. Exhibits on battle at Great Meadows; audiovisual program. (Daily; closed Dec 25) Overlooking Fort Necessity is

Mt Washington Tavern. Restored as historic stagecoach inn; furnishings, exhibits of 1827-55. (Daily; closed Dec 25) 1 mi W on US 40 is

2. Braddock's Grave. Granite monument marks burial place of British General Edward Braddock, who was wounded in battle with French and Indians July 9, 1755, and died four days later. Also nearby is

3. Jumonville Glen. 7 mi from Ft Necessity, 2½ mi N of US 40 on Summit Rd. This is the site of the skirmish between British and French forces that led to the battle at Fort Necessity. (Mid-Apr-mid-Oct)

4. Friendship Hill National Historic Site. 15 mi S on US 119 to PA 166. Preserves the restored home of Albert Gallatin, a Swiss immigrant who served his adopted country, in public and private life, for nearly seven decades. Gallatin made significant contributions to our young republic in the fields of finance, politics, diplomacy, and scholarship. He is best known as the Treasury Secretary under Jefferson and Madison. Exhibits, audiovisual program, and audio tour provide information on Albert Gallatin. (Daily; closed Dec 25) Phone 329-5512. **Free.**

5. Laurel Caverns. 5 mi SE on US 40, then 5 mi S on marked road. Colored lighting; unusual formations. Indoor miniature golf. Guided tours. Exploring trips; campgrounds. (May-Oct, daily) Phone 438-3003. Tours ¢¢¢

6. Ohiopyle State Park. 10 mi SE on US 40, then 6 mi NE off PA 381. Approx 18,800 acres of overlooks, waterfalls. Fishing, hunting; white-water boating. Hiking, bicycling. Cross-country skiing, snowmobiling, sledding. Picnicking, playground, snack bar. Tent & trailer sites. Nature center, interpretive program. Standard fees. Phone 329-8591.

7. River tours. Whitewater rafting on the Youghiogheny River; some of the wildest and most scenic in the eastern US. Cost includes equipment and professional guides. Age limits are imposed because of level of difficulty.

White Water Adventurers. For information contact Director, PO Box 31, Ohiopyle 15470; 800/WWA-RAFT. ¢¢¢¢

Laurel Highlands River Tours. For information contact PO Box 107, Dept PM, Ohiopyle 15470; 329-8531 or 800/472-3846. ¢¢¢¢

Mountain Streams & Trails Outfitters. Also on the Gauley, Big Sandy, Cheat and Tygart's Valley rivers. For information contact Manager, PO Box 106, Ohiopyle 15470; 329-8810. Also rentals of whitewater rafts, canoes, trail bikes; for information contact Ohiopyle Recreational Rentals, PO Box 4, Ohiopyle 15470; 800/245-4090. ¢¢¢¢

(For further information contact Laurel Highlands Inc, 120 E Main St, Ligonier 15658; 800/925-7669.)

(See Connellsville)

Motels

★ ★ **HOLIDAY INN.** *700 W Main St (US 40).* 412/437-2816; FAX 412/437-2816, ext. 100. 184 rms, 2 story. S $75-$97; D $77-$97; each addl $7; suites $145-$175; under 18 free; ski, wkend plan in winter; higher rates Labor Day wkend. Crib free. Pet accepted, some restrictions. TV; cable. Indoor pool; whirlpool, sauna, poolside serv; lifeguard. Restaurant 6:30 am-10 pm. Rm serv from 7 am. Bar 11-2 am; entertainment, dancing. Ck-out 11 am. Meeting rms. Valet serv. Sundries. Lighted tennis. Miniature golf. Rec rm. Game rm. Lawn games. Some balconies. Cr cds: A, C, D, DS, JCB, MC, V.

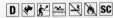

✔ ★ **LODGE AT CHALK HILL.** *(Box 240, US 40E, Chalk Hill 15421)* 9 mi E on US 40. 412/438-8880; res: 800/833-4283; FAX 412/438-1685. 60 units, 6 suites, 6 kit. units. May-Nov: S $48.95-$60.95; D $59.95-$69.95; each addl $10; suites $118.95-$142.95; kit. units $64.95-$80.95; under 14 free; higher rates: July 4, Memorial Day, Labor Day, Dec 31; lower rates rest of yr. Crib free. Pet accepted, some restrictions; $5. TV; cable. Complimentary continental bkfst, coffee. Restaurant opp 7 am-11 pm. Ck-out noon. Meeting rms. Balconies. Picnic tables. On Lake Lenore. Cr cds: A, DS, MC, V.

[icons]

Resorts

★ ★ ★ **MOUNT SUMMIT INN.** *(Box 2, Skyline Dr, Farmington 15437)* 6 mi E on US 40. 412/438-8594. 100 rms, 3 story. No elvtr. July-Labor Day: S $51-$85; D $61-$95; suites $110-$150; family rates; golf package plan, MAP avail (2 night min); some wkend rates; lower rates mid-Apr-June, after Labor Day-early Nov. Closed rest of yr. Crib $10. Pet accepted, some restrictions; $5 per day. TV. Indoor/outdoor pool; lifeguard. Playground. Dining rm (public by res) 8-11 am, noon-2 pm, 6-8:30 pm. Rm serv. Box lunches, snacks, cookouts. Bar 11-1 am. Ck-out noon, ck-in 4 pm. Grocery, package store 3 mi. Gift shop. Free bus depot transportation. Tennis. 9-hole golf, greens fee $8, pro, putting green. Exercise equipt; weight machine, treadmill, whirlpool. Scenic boat cruises. Rec rm. Soc dir; entertainment, dancing. Picnic tables, grills. Built 1907. Beautiful view; atop Mt Summit. Cr cds: DS, MC, V.

[icons] SC

★ ★ ★ **NEMACOLIN WOODLANDS.** *(PO Box 188, Farmington 15437)* 12 mi E on US 40. 412/329-8555; res: 800/422-2736; FAX 412/329-6198. 96 rms in main bldg, 4 & 5 story, 58 condo units (1-2 bedrm). May-Oct: S, D $195-$230; each addl $15; suites $240-$395; kit. condos $185; under 18 free (in condos only); AP, MAP avail; wkly rates; golf, spa plans; lower rates Dec-mid-Apr. Crib free. TV; cable, in-rm movies avail. 4 pools, 1 indoor; poolside serv, lifeguard (outdoor pools). Playground. Supervised child's activities. Dining rms. Box lunches. Snack bar. Picnics. Rm serv 24 hrs. Bar noon-2 am; entertainment, dancing (Fri & Sat). Ck-out 11 am, ck-in 3 pm. Grocery 2½ mi. Lndry facilities in condos. Package store 3 blks. Convention facilities. Bellhops. Valet serv. Concierge. Gift shop. Airport, RR station, bus depot transportation. Sports dir. Lighted tennis, pro. 18-hole golf, greens fee $55-$65 (incl cart), pro, 2 putting greens, driving range. Boats. X-country ski on premises. Equipment rentals. Sleighing, tobogganing. Equestrian center; surrey rides all yr. Hiking. Bicycle rentals. Miniature golf. Lawn games. Social dir. Rec rm. Game rm. Exercise rm; instructor, weight machine, bicycles, 3 whirlpools, 2 saunas. Massage. World-class spa facilities. Minibars; many bathrm phones, refrigerators; some wet bars. Balconies. Private collection of art and antiques from around the world. Luxurious first-class resort. Situated on 800 acres with 7 lakes; landing strip. Cr cds: A, C, D, MC, V.

[icons]

Restaurants

★ ★ **COAL BARON.** R.D. 6, 6 mi W on US 40. 412/439-0111. Hrs: 4-11 pm; Sun noon-8 pm. Closed Mon; Dec 24-25. Res accepted; required wkends. Continental menu. Bar. Wine list. Complete meals: dinner $13-$19. Child's meals. Specialties: veal saltimbocca, entrecôte maître d'hôtel. Own baking. Valet parking. Jacket. Cr cds: A, D, MC, V.

[D]

✔ ★ ★ **SUN PORCH.** *(PO Box 214, Hopwood 15445)* US 40E. 412/439-5734. Hrs: 11 am-8 pm; Sat 4-9 pm. Closed Mon; Dec 24, 25. Res accepted. Semi-a la carte: lunch $3-$7, dinner $7-$12. Buffet: dinner $7.75 (wkdays), $9.95 (Fri-Sun). Child's meals. Specializes in fresh seafood, beef, poultry, soup. Salad bar. Parking. Many plants; atmosphere of a country garden. Cr cds: D, DS, MC, V.

[D]

★ ★ **WATERING TROUGH.** *(PO Box 91, Hopwood 15445)* US 40E, 3 mi E on Summit Mt. 412/438-9716. Hrs: 4-10 pm; Fri & Sat to 11 pm. Closed some major hols. Italian, Amer menu. Bar to midnight. Semi-a la carte: dinner $5.95-$15.95. Child's meals. Specializes in fresh seafood, steak, northern Italian dishes. Parking. Country French decor. Cr cds: DS, MC, V.

[D]

Valley Forge National Historical Park (E-9)

(3 mi N of PA Tpke Interchange 24)

From December 19, 1777, to June 19, 1778—some of the darkest days of the American Revolution—the poorly supplied troops of Washington's army were camped here. Of those 12,000 to 20,000 soldiers of the Continental Army, more than 2,000 died from illness and disease brought on by weather conditions, lack of supplies and poor sanitation. The national park is a 3,600-acre memorial to their trial and success. The park itself is scenic any time of the year. A marked tour route offers the visitor a chance to see the primary encampment facilities; other roads provide a beautiful drive and a chance to view other historical features. (Daily; closed Dec 25)

What to See and Do

1. **Visitor Center.** Jct PA 23 & N Gulph Rd, just inside park. Information, exhibits, audio-visual program, tour maps. Bus tours depart from here (see #7).

2. **Soldier Life Program.** Muhlenberg Brigade. Interpreters present programs detailing camp life. (Summer, daily; rest of yr, wkends only)

3. **National Memorial Arch.** Built in 1917 to commemorate Washington's Army. Inscribed in the arch is "Naked and starving as they are, we cannot enough admire the incomparable patience and fidelity of the soldiery."

4. **Washington Headquarters.** Park staff will provide information about the house where Washington lived for six months and which served as military headquarters for the Continental Army during that time. (Daily) ¢

5. **General Varnum's Quarters.** Farmhouse of David and Elizabeth Stephens that quartered Brigadier General James Varnum of Rhode Island. This building exemplifies the architecture of small farmhouses constructed during the early 18th century; colonial furnishings. (Wkends)

6. **Washington Memorial Chapel.** On PA 23. Private property within park boundaries. Stained-glass windows depict the story of the New World, its discovery and development; hand-carved oak choir stalls, Pews of the Patriots, and Roof of the Republic bearing the State Seal of all the states. Also part of the chapel is the 58 cast-bell Washington Memorial National Carillon, with bells honoring states and territories. Phone 610/783-0120. Adj is

   Museum of the Valley Forge Historical Society. Relics of the winter at Valley Forge. (Daily; closed Easter, Thanksgiving, Dec 25) Phone 610/783-0535. ¢

7. **Tours.**

   Auto Tape Tour. Self-guided tour dramatizes Washington's winter encampment. Obtain at visitor center (May-Oct, daily); includes player rental and tape. Phone 610/783-5788. 2-hr rental ¢¢¢

   Bus Tour. Narrated tour (approx 90 min) includes stops at historic sites. Tours leave visitor center three times daily (mid-Apr-

May, early Sept-Oct). Shuttle service departures every half-hour (June-Labor Day). Phone 610/783-5788. Tours ¢¢¢

(For further information, contact the Superintendent, PO Box 953, Valley Forge 19481; 610/783-1077.)

(For accommodations see King of Prussia, Philadelphia)

Restaurants

★ ★ **COLUMBIA HOTEL.** *(148 Bridge St, Phoenixville) 6 mi NW off PA 23.* 610/933-9973. Hrs: 11:30 am-2:30 pm, 5-10 pm. Closed most major hols. Res accepted. Bar to 10 pm. A la carte entrees: lunch $5.95-$12.95, dinner $13.95-$24.95. Child's meals. Specializes in fresh Maine & Florida fish, Angus beef. Own desserts. Parking. Built in 1892. Cr cds: A, C, D, MC, V.

★ ★ **KIMBERTON INN.** *(Kimberton Rd, Kimberton) PA 23W to PA 113S.* 610/933-8148. Hrs: 11:45 am-2 pm, 5:30-9:30 pm; Mon & Sat from 5:30 pm; Sun 5:30-8:30 pm; Sun brunch 11 am-2 pm. Res accepted. Bar. Wine list. Semi-a la carte: lunch $7.95-$9.95, dinner $16.95-$22.95. Sun brunch $16.95. Specializes in veal, beef, fresh seafood. Own desserts. Harpist or pianist. Parking. Tavern (1796); colonial decor. Cr cds: A, C, D, DS, MC, V.

D

★ ★ **SEVEN STARS INN.** *(PA 23 & Hoffecker Rd, Phoenixville) 10 mi W on PA 23.* 610/495-5205. Hrs: 4:30-10 pm; wkends to 11 pm; Sun 3-7 pm. Closed Mon; most major hols. Res accepted. Bar. Complete meals: dinner $17.95-$41.95. Child's meals. Specializes in prime rib, seafood, veal. Parking. Colonial inn; large fireplace. Cr cds: A, C, D, MC, V.

D **SC**

Warren (B-3)

Founded: 1795 **Pop:** 11,122 **Elev:** 1,200 ft **Area code:** 814 **Zip:** 16365

At the junction of the Allegheny and Conewango rivers, Warren is the headquarters and gateway of the famous Allegheny National Forest. Named for General Joseph Warren, American patriot killed in the Battle of Bunker Hill, the town was once the point where great flotillas of logs were formed for the journey to Pittsburgh or Cincinnati.

What to See and Do

1. **Allegheny National Forest.** More than 510,000 acres S & E on US 6, 62, located in Warren, Forest, McKean and Elk counties. Black bear, whitetail deer and wild turkey, a diversity of small birds and mammals; streams and reservoirs with trout, walleye, muskellunge, northern pike and bass; rugged hills, quiet valleys, open meadows, dense forest. These lures, plus swimming, boating, hiking, camping and picnicking facilities draw more than 2 million visitors a year. Hundreds of campsites; fees are charged at some recreation sites. For information contact Supervisor, US Forest Service, PO Box 847, phone 723-5150; or Reservoir Area Office/Bradford District, phone 362-4613, 726-2710 (TTY). In forest are

   Buckaloons Recreation Area. 6 mi W on US 6. Site of former Indian village on the banks of the Allegheny River. Boat launching. Picnicking. Camping (fee). Seneca Interpretive Trail. Phone 968-3232, 726-2710 (TTY).

   Kinzua Dam and Allegheny Reservoir. 3 mi SE on US 6, then 6 mi E on PA 59. *(It is possible that the PA 59 bridge, 1¹/₂ miles E of Kinzua Dam will be closed; phone ahead for information.)* Dam (179 ft high, 1,897 ft long) with 27-mile-long lake. Swimming; fishing; boating (ramps, rentals; fees). Picnicking, overlooks. Camping (fee). Kinzua Dam visitor center has displays. Kinzua Point Information Center, 4 mi NE of dam, phone 726-1291. Some

fees. Phone 726-0661 or 362-4613; fishing hotline (24 hrs), 726-0164.

2. **Chapman State Park.** 7 mi SE on US 6, then W at light in Clarendon. Approx 800 acres. Lake and creek stocked with trout and bass. Swimming beach; fishing, hunting; boating (rentals, mooring, launching). Hiking. Cross-country skiing, snowmobiling, sledding, ice-skating, ice fishing. Picnicking, snack bar. Tent & trailer sites available (some with electric). Interpretive program. Phone 723-5030. Camping ¢¢¢

(For further information contact the Warren County Chamber of Commerce, 315 2nd Ave, PO Box 942, phone 723-3050; or Travel Northern Alleghenies, 315 Second St, at the point, PO Box 804, phone 726-1222 or 800/624-7802.)

Restaurant

★ ★ **JEFFERSON HOUSE & PUB.** *119 Market St.* 814/723-2268. Hrs: 11:30 am-2 pm, 5:30-9 pm. Closed Sun, Mon; major hols. Res accepted. Bar 5 pm-midnight; Fri 4 pm-2 am; Sat 5 pm-2 am. Semi-a la carte: lunch $4.95-$7.95, dinner $6.95-$17.95. Child's meals. Specialties: mesquite-grilled seafood, steak, baby back ribs. Victorian mansion (1890); antiques, artwork by local artist. Cr cds: MC, V.

Washington (E-1)

Founded: 1781 **Pop:** 15,864 **Elev:** 1,120 ft **Area code:** 412 **Zip:** 15301

Originally a Native American village known as Catfish Camp, the village of Bassettown became Washington during the Revolution. During the Whiskey Rebellion the town was a center of protest against the new Federal government's tax; arrival of Federal troops quieted the rebellious farmers. Washington and Jefferson College (1781) is located here.

What to See and Do

1. **LeMoyne House.** 49 E Maiden St. Abolitionist's home, built 1812 by LeMoyne family. was a stop on the underground railroad; period furnishings, paintings, library; gardens; museum shop. Administered by Washington County Historical Society. (1st Wed Feb-Dec, Wed-Fri & Sun afternoons) Phone 225-6740. ¢¢

2. **David Bradford House** (1788). 175 S Main St. Restored frontier home of a leader of the Whiskey Rebellion. (May-late Dec, Wed-Sat, limited hrs, also Sun afternoons) For fee information phone 222-3604.

3. **Pennsylvania Trolley Museum.** I-79 N, exit 8 (Meadowlands), follow signs. Museum displays include more than 35 trolley cars dating from 1894. Trolley rides. Shop where craftsmen rebuild and restore the relics. Picnic area; gift shop. (July-Aug, daily; May-June & Sept-Oct, wkends, hols) Sr citizen rate. Phone 228-9256. ¢¢

4. **Meadowcroft Village.** 19 mi NW via PA 18, 50, in Avella. Many wooden structures (late 1700s-1900), relocated and reconstructed, including general store, carriage barn, log houses, one-room schoohouse, blacksmith shop; all have permanent exhibits. (May-Oct, Wed-Sun) Phone 587-3412. ¢¢¢

5. **The Meadows.** 4 mi N on US 19. Harness racing. Parimutuel betting. (Tues & Thurs-Sun evenings) Phone 225-9300.

(For further information contact the Washington County Tourism Office, 59 N Main St, PO Box 4213; 222-8130.)

(See Pittsburgh)

Motels

★ **KNIGHTS INN.** *125 Knights Inn Dr, I-70 at US 19, exit 7A. 412/223-8040; res: 800/843-5644.* 102 rms, 12 kit. units. S $35.95; D $41.95; each addl $6; kit. units $45.95-$51.95; under 18 free. Crib free. Pet accepted. TV; cable. Pool. Complimentary coffee in lobby. Restaurant adj open 24 hrs. Ck-out noon. Meeting rm. Cr cds: A, C, D, DS, ER, MC, V.

D ⊁ ≈ ⋈ ⋀ SC

✔ ★ **RED ROOF INN.** *1399 W Chestnut St. 412/228-5750; FAX 412/228-5865.* 111 rms, 2 story. May-Oct: S $33.99-$40.99; D $36.99-$47.99; each addl $6; under 18 free; lower rates rest of yr. Crib free. Pet accepted, some restrictions. TV. Complimentary morning coffee. Restaurant adj open 24 hrs. Ck-out noon. Cr cds: A, C, D, DS, MC, V.

⊁ ⋈ ⋀ SC

Motor Hotel

★ ★ ★ **HOLIDAY INN-MEADOWLANDS WASHINGTON.** *340 Race Track Rd, I-79 exit 8B. 412/222-6200; FAX 412/222-6200, ext. 590.* 138 rms, 7 story. S $70-$80; D $75-$85; each addl $6; under 18 free. Crib free. Pet accepted, some restrictions. TV; cable. Pool; poolside serv, lifeguard. Restaurant 6:30 am-11 pm. Rm serv. Bars 11-2 am; entertainment, dancing. Ck-out noon. Meeting rms. Exercise equipt; weight machines, bicycles, whirlpool, sauna. Private patios. Meadows Racetrack adj. Cr cds: A, C, D, DS, ER, JCB, MC, V.

D ⊁ ≈ ⫫ ⋈ ⋀ SC

Washington Crossing Historical Park (Bucks Co) (E-10)

(Two sections: Bowman's Hill, 2 mi S of New Hope on PA 32 and Washington Crossing, 7 mi S of New Hope on PA 32)

In a blinding snowstorm on Christmas night, 1776, George Washington and 2,400 soldiers crossed the Delaware River from the Pennsylvania shore and marched to Trenton, surprising the celebrating Hessian mercenaries and capturing the city. Washington's feat was a turning point of the Revolutionary War. Park (daily; closed most hols). Sr citizen rate. Phone 215/493-4076. ¢¢

What to See and Do

Bowman's Hill

1. **Memorial Flagstaff.** Marks graves of unknown Continentals who died during encampment.
2. **Wildflower Preserve.** Adj park; two miles of native wildflower trails. (Daily) Phone 215/862-2924.

Washington Crossing

3. **Area of Embarkation.** Marked by tall granite shaft supporting Washington's statue.
4. **Concentration Valley.** Where Washington assembled troops for raid on Trenton.
5. **Memorial Building.** Near Point of Embarkation. Houses copy of Emanuel Leutze's painting, *Washington Crossing the Delaware.* Library of the American Revolution, West Wing, has books, manuscripts. Phone 215/493-4076.

6. **McConkey Ferry Inn** (1752). At Washington Crossing; restored as historic house.

Annual Event

"The Crossing." Reenactment of Washington's crossing of the Delaware River, Christmas night in 1776. Dec 25.

(For accommodations see Doylestown, New Hope, Philadelphia, PA & Trenton, NJ)

Wellsboro (B-6)

Settled: 1799 **Pop:** 3,430 **Elev:** 1,311 ft **Area code:** 717 **Zip:** 16901

Wellsboro is the gateway to Pennsylvania's "canyon country." Settled largely by New Englanders, it is sustained by an assortment of industries. The area yields coal, natural gas, hardwoods, maple syrup and farm products.

What to See and Do

1. **Robinson House Museum** (ca 1820). 120 Main St. Houses turn-of-the-century artifacts; genealogical library. (Apr-Dec, Mon-Fri afternoons) Contact Tioga County Historical Society, PO Box 724; 724-6116. **Free.**
2. **Ski Sawmill Resort.** Oregon Hill Rd, 16 mi S via PA 287. Chairlift, 3 T-bars; patrol, school, rentals; snowmaking; cafeteria, restaurant, bar. Longest run 3,250 ft; vertical drop 515 ft. (Dec-Mar, daily) Yr-round activities. Phone 800/532-SNOW. ¢¢¢-¢¢¢¢¢
3. **Auto tours.** There are more than a million acres of forests, mountains and streams to be explored. The Wellsboro Area Chamber of Commerce has published a map of three tours.

Red Arrow Tour follows PA 660 SW 10 miles from Wellsboro to Leonard Harrison State Park. Lookout Point, near the parking area, has large picnic area nearby. Path winds one mile from park to bottom of gorge, through shady glens, past waterfalls.

Yellow Arrow Tour leads from Leonard Harrison State Park, back on PA 660, NW on PA 362, then 1/4 mile W on US 6 to Colton Point Rd for views of the canyon and Four Mile Run Country. At Colton Point State Park (observation points, picnic shelters, fireplaces) the arrows follow Pine Creek S on old lumbering railroad tracks, converted into roadways called the "Switchbacks," to Bradley Wales Park overlooking Tiadaghton, the next lookout point on Pine Creek. From here continue S on W Rim Rd to Blackwell. From Blackwell, NE on PA 414 to Morris, then N on PA 287 to Wellsboro—a circle of 65 miles.

White Arrow Tour leads from the Switchbacks (1 1/2 miles W of Bradley Wales Park), 3 miles S to Leetonia, once a prosperous lumber village, now occupied by State Forest Rangers; then W & N to Cushman View, Wilson Point Rd, Lee Fire Tower, Cedar Run Mountain Rd, and US 6; approx 75 miles.

(For further information contact the Wellsboro Area Chamber of Commerce, PO Box 733; 724-1926.)

Annual Event

Pennsylvania State Laurel Festival. Wk-long event includes parade of floats, marching musical and precision units, antique cars, laurel queen contestants; crowning of the queen; arts & crafts; children's pet and hobby parade, exhibits and displays. Mid-June.

(See Galeton, Mansfield)

Motels

 ★ **CANYON.** *18 East Ave. 717/724-1681; res: 800/255-2718.* 27 rms. S $28-$45; D $32-$48; each addl $5; under 12 free; golf, ski package plans. Crib $5. Pet accepted. TV; cable. Heated pool; lifeguard. Playground. Complimentary continental bkfst. Restaurant nearby. Ck-out 11 am. Downhill/x-country ski 20 mi. Refrigerators. Picnic tables, grills. Cr cds: A, C, D, DS, MC, V.

★ ★ **PENN-WELLS LODGE.** *PO Box 158, 4 Main St. 717/724-3463; res: 800/545-2446.* 55 rms, 2 story. S $46-$57; D $52-$65; each addl $5; under 18 free. Crib $5. TV; cable. Indoor pool; lifeguard. Playground. Restaurant nearby. Ck-out noon. Downhill/x-country ski 17 mi. Exercise rm; instructor, weights, bicycles, whirlpool, sauna. Community-owned. Cr cds: A, C, D, DS, MC, V.

★ **SHERWOOD.** *2 Main St. 717/724-3424; res: 800/626-5802.* 32 rms, 1-2 story. S $30-$37; D $35-$48; each addl $5; under 10 free; golf, ski package plans. Crib $5. Pet accepted. TV; cable. Heated pool; lifeguard. Playground. Complimentary coffee. Restaurant nearby. Ck-out 11 am. Downhill/x-country ski 17 mi. Refrigerators. Cr cds: A, C, D, DS, MC, V.

Hotel

★ ★ **PENN-WELLS.** *PO Box 158, 62 Main St. 717/724-2111; res: 800/545-2446.* 74 rms. Late May-Oct, hunting season: S $30-$40; D $40-$49; each addl $5; suites $55-$60; under 18 free; golf plans; lower rates rest of yr. Crib $5. TV; cable. Indoor pool. Playground. Restaurant 7 am-1:30 pm, 5-10 pm. Bar 11:30-1 am; entertainment Fri, Sat. Ck-out noon. Meeting rms. Downhill/x-country ski 17 mi. Exercise rm; instructor, weights, bicycles, whirlpool, sauna. Built 1869; high ceilings, oak & cherry woodwork, antiques, early Americana. Community-owned. Cr cds: A, C, D, DS, MC, V.

West Chester (F-9)

Founded: 1788 **Pop:** 18,041 **Elev:** 459 ft **Area code:** 610

In the heart of three Pennsylvania Revolutionary War historic sites—Brandywine, Paoli and Valley Forge—West Chester today is a university and residential community, with fine examples of Greek-revival and Victorian architecture.

What to See and Do

Brinton 1704 House. 5 mi S just off US 202, Oakland Rd, in Dilworthtown. Stone house built by Quaker farmer William Brinton, authentically restored and furnished. (May-Oct, Sat, Sun; other times, by appt) Phone 302/478-2853. ¢

(For further information contact the Chester County Tourist Bureau, 601 Westtown Rd, Ste 170, 19382; 344-6365.)

(See Chester, Kennett Square, King of Prussia, Media, Philadelphia)

Motels

✔ ★ **ABBEY GREEN MOTOR LODGE.** *1036 Wilmington Pike. 610/692-3310.* 18 rms. S $39-$45; D $45-$55; each addl $5; cottages with kit. $40-$43; under 6 free; wkend rates. Crib free. Pet accepted. TV; cable. Restaurant nearby. Ck-out 11 am. Gift shop. RR

station, bus depot transportation. Refrigerators; some fireplaces. Picnic tables, grill. Cr cds: A, C, D, DS, MC, V.

★ ★ **WEST CHESTER INN.** *943 S High St. 610/692-1900; FAX 610/436-0159.* 143 rms, 3 story. S $72-$78; D $78-$84; each addl $10; suites $90-$100; kit. suites $100-$120; under 16 free. Crib free. TV; cable, in-rm movies. Pool; lifeguard. Restaurant 7 am-10 pm. Rm Serv. Bar 11:30-2 am; entertainment wkends. Ck-out noon. Meeting rms. Valet serv. Airport transportation. Exercise equipt; weight machines, bicycles. Health club privileges. Cr cds: A, C, D, DS, MC, V.

Inn

★ ★ ★ **DULING-KURTZ HOUSE & COUNTRY INN.** *(146 S Whitford Rd, Exton 19341) N on PA 100, 1/2 mi W on US 30. 610/524-1830; FAX 610/524-6258.* 15 rms, 3 story, 5 suites. S, D $55-$120; each addl $15; suites $79-$120; higher rates Fri, Sat & hols. Children over 2 yrs only. TV. Complimentary continental bkfst. Restaurant (see DULING-KURTZ HOUSE). Rm serv. Ck-out 11 am, ck-in 3 pm. Built in 1783; period furniture, antiques, sitting rm. Cr cds: A, C, D, DS, MC, V.

Restaurants

★ ★ ★ **DULING-KURTZ HOUSE.** *(See Duling-Kurtz House Inn)* *610/524-1830.* Hrs: 11:30 am-10 pm; Sat from 5 pm; Sun 3-9 pm. Res accepted. French, continental menu. Bar. Wine list. A la carte entrees: lunch $5.95-$13.95, dinner $13.95-$29.75. Specialties: veal tenderloin chapeau, sirloin steak au poivre (flambé), crab cakes. Valet parking (Fri & Sat). Formal dining in 7 dining rms. Country inn atmosphere. Fireplaces. Cr cds: A, C, D, DS, MC, V.

★ **MAGNOLIA GRILL.** *971 Paoli Pike, in Chester County Book Co, in West Goshen Shopping Center. 610/696-1661.* Hrs: 8 am-9 pm; Fri & Sat to 9:30 pm; Sun to 5 pm. Closed Dec 25. Semi-a la carte: bkfst $1.99-$5.95, lunch $3.95-$7.95, dinner $3.95-$14.95. Child's meals. Specializes in seafood, omelettes, Poor Boy sandwiches. Turn-of-the-century New Orleans decor. Original artwork. Cr cds: A, C, D, DS, MC, V.

West Middlesex (C-1)

Pop: 982 **Elev:** 840 ft **Area code:** 412 **Zip:** 16159

Motels

★ ★ **HOLIDAY INN.** *(3200 S Hermitage Rd, Hermitage) N on PA 60, at jct I-80 exit 1N. 412/981-1530; FAX 412/981-1518.* 180 rms, 3 story. S $62; D $68; each addl $6; under 18 free; golf packages avail. Crib free. TV; cable, in-rm movies. Heated pool; poolside serv, lifeguard. Playground. Restaurant 6:30 am-10 pm; Dec-Mar 6:30 am-2 pm, 5-10 pm. Rm serv. Bar 11-2 am; entertainment, dancing. Ck-out 11 am. Coin lndry. Meeting rms. Valet serv. Sundries. Game rm. Cr cds: A, C, D, DS, ER, JCB, MC, V.

★ ★ **RADISSON SHARON.** *Box 596, on PA 18 at I-80 exit 1N. 412/528-2501; FAX 412/528-2306.* 153 rms, 3 story. S $76-$98; D $80-$104; each addl $9; suites $95-$225; under 12 free; golf, wkend rates. Crib free. TV; cable. Indoor pool; whirlpool, sauna, poolside serv, lifeguard. Restaurant 6:30 am-10 pm. Rm serv. Bar 11-2 am. Ck-out noon. Coin lndry. Meeting rms. Bellhops. Valet serv. Sundries. Game rm. In-rm whirlpools; refrigerators in suites. Cr cds: A, C, D, DS, MC, V.

Restaurant

★ ★ **THE TAVERN.** (108 N Market St, New Wilmington) 3 mi S on PA 60, 5 mi E on PA 208. 412/946-2020. Hrs: 11:30 am-2 pm, 5-8 pm; Fri, Sat 5-9 pm; Sun noon-7 pm. Closed Tues; July 4, Thanksgiving, Dec 25. Res required. Complete meals: lunch $9-$12, dinner $11-$18. Specializes in stuffed pork chops, creamed chicken & biscuits, baked chicken. Parking. Country decor, built in 1840. No cr cds accepted.

White Haven (D-9)

Pop: 1,132 **Elev:** 1,221 ft **Area code:** 717 **Zip:** 18661

What to See and Do

1. **Hickory Run State Park.** 6 mi S on PA 534 off I-80 exit 41. Approx 15,500 acres of scenic area. Swimming beach; fishing, hunting. Hiking. Cross-country skiing, snowmobiling, sledding, ice-skating, ice fishing. Picnicking, playground, snack bar, store. Tent & trailer sites. Standard fees. Phone 443-9991.

2. **Skiing.**

   Jack Frost. 6 mi E on PA 940. Two triple, 5 double chairlifts; patrol, school, rentals; snowmaking; cafeteria, restaurant, bar; nursery. Longest run approx 1/2 mi; vertical drop 600 ft. (Dec-Mar, daily) Half-day rate. Phone 443-8425. ¢¢¢¢¢

   Big Boulder. 1 mi E off PA 903 in Lake Harmony. Five double, 2 triple chairlifts; patrol, school, rentals; snowmaking; cafeteria, bar; nursery, lodge. Night skiing. Longest run approx 3/4 mi; vertical drop 475 ft. (Dec-Mar, daily) Phone 722-0100. ¢¢¢¢¢

(For further information contact the Pocono Mts Vacation Bureau, 1004 Main St, Stroudsburg 18360, phone 424-6050; for free brochures phone 800/POCONOS.)

(See Hazleton, Jim Thorpe, Pocono Mountains, Wilkes-Barre)

Motel

★ **POCONO MOUNTAIN LODGE.** Box 141, jct PA 940 & I-80. 717/443-8461; res: 800/443-4049. 123 rms, 6 story. S $50-$60; D $58-$68; each addl $8; under 18 free; ski plans. Crib free. TV; cable. Pool. Restaurant adj 6 am-midnight. Bar 11-2 am. Ck-out noon. Meeting rms. Downhill/x-country ski 4 mi. Hiking trails. Game rm. Cr cds: A, C, D, DS, MC, V.

Resort

★ ★ **MOUNTAIN LAUREL.** Box 126, 4 mi E on PA 940 at jct PA Tpke exit 35 & I-80 exit 42. 717/443-8411; res: 800/458-5921; FAX 717/443-9741. 250 rms, 3 story. MAP: S $65-$126; D $65-$98/person; each addl $10; suites $75-$200; under 18 free; golf plan; some wkend rates; higher rates hols. Crib free. TV; cable. 2 pools, 1 indoor; poolside serv, lifeguard. Playground. Free supervised child's activities. Dining rm 6-9 pm. Box lunches, snacks, picnics. Bar 11-2 am; entertainment, dancing. Ck-out 1 pm, ck-in 4 pm. Coin lndry. Meeting rms. Valet serv. Airport, RR station, bus depot transportation. Sports dir. 4 lighted tennis courts. 18-hole golf, greens fee from $37 (incl cart), driving range, putting green, miniature golf. Archery. Downhill ski 5 mi. Soc dir; entertainment, dancing. Nursery. Movies. Game rm. Exercise rm; in-

structor, weight machine, bicycles, whirlpool, sauna. Picnic tables. Cr cds: A, C, D, DS, MC, V.

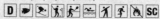

Wilkes-Barre (C-8)

Founded: 1769 **Pop:** 47,523 **Elev:** 550 ft **Area code:** 717

Named in honor of two members of the British Parliament who championed individual rights and supported the colonies, Wilkes-Barre (WILKS-berry) and the Wyoming Valley were settled by pioneers from Connecticut. Pennsylvania and Connecticut waged the Pennamite-Yankee War, the first phase ending in 1771 with Connecticut in control of the valley. It was later resumed until Connecticut relinquished its claims in 1800. Wilkes-Barre was burned by the Indians and Tories during the Revolution and again by Connecticut settlers protesting the Decree of Trenton (1782), in which Congress favored Pennsylvania's claim to the territory. Discovery of anthracite coal in the valley sparked the town's growth after Judge Jesse Fell demonstrated that anthracite could be burned in a grate without forced draft.

(For information about this area contact the Tourist Promotion Agency, 201 Hangar Rd, Avoca 18641; 457-1320.)

(See Hazleton, Pocono Mountains, Scranton, White Haven)

Motels

★ ★ **HAMPTON INN.** 1063 PA 315 (18702). 717/825-3838; FAX 717/825-8775. 123 rms, 5 story. May-Oct: S $46-$61; D $48-$67; under 18 free; ski plans; higher rates: car races, Dec 31; lower rates rest of yr. Crib free. Pet accepted. TV; cable. Complimentary continental bkfst, coffee. Restaurant adj 7 am-11 pm. Ck-out noon. Meeting rm. Valet serv Mon-Fri. Downhill ski 10 mi. Cr cds: A, C, D, DS, ER, MC, V.

★ ★ ★ **HOLIDAY INN.** 800 Kidder St (18702), at PA 309. 717/824-8901; FAX 717/824-9310. 180 rms, 2 story. S $49-$79; D $59-$89; each addl $10; studio rms $75; family plan; ski packages. TV; cable. Pool; wading pool, poolside serv, lifeguard. Restaurant 6 am-10 pm; Sat, Sun from 7 am. Rm serv. Bar noon-2 am. Ck-out noon. Meeting rms. Bellhops. Sundries. Free airport transportation. Downhill ski 10 mi. Cr cds: A, C, D, DS, ER, JCB, MC, V.

✔ ★ ★ **INN AT MARKET STREET SQUARE.** 33 Wilkes-Barre Blvd (18702). 717/829-0000; FAX 717/825-2892. 45 rms. S, D $39-$54; each addl $6; under 16 free. TV; cable. Dining rm. Entertainment, dancing. Ck-out noon. Meeting rms. Downhill ski 12 mi. Originally a railroad depot (1868); all rail cars converted into staterooms. Victorian decor. Cr cds: A, C, D, DS, MC, V.

Motor Hotel

★ ★ ★ **WOODLANDS INN & RESORT.** 1073 PA 315 (18702). 717/824-9831; res: 800/556-2222 (exc PA), 800/762-2222 (PA); FAX 717/824-8865. 179 rms, 9 story, 25 apts. S $62-$90; D $72-$110; each addl $10; package plans; wkend rates. Crib $5. TV; cable. 2 pools, 1 indoor; poolside serv, lifeguard. Restaurant 7 am-11 pm. Rm serv. Bar 11-2 am; entertainment, dancing. Ck-out noon. Meeting rms. Bellhops. Sundries. Barber, beauty shop. Free airport transportation. Lighted tennis. Exercise rm; instructor, weights, bicycles, whirlpool, sauna. Game rm. Rec rm. Lawn games. Private patios, balconies. Cr cds: A, D, MC, V.

Hotel

★ ★ ★ **BEST WESTERN-EAST MOUNTAIN INN.** *2400 E End Blvd (PA 115) (18702),* I-81 exit 47A. 717/822-1011; FAX 717/822-6072. 156 rms, 7 story, 24 suites. S $72-$84; D $77-$90; each addl $5; suites $99-$119; under 13 free; ski, golf plans; higher rates special events. Crib free. TV; cable, in-rm movies. Indoor pool; poolside serv, lifeguard. Restaurant 6 am-11 pm. Bar 11-1 am; entertainment Fri-Sun. Ck-out noon. Coin lndry. Meeting rms. Free airport, RR station, bus depot transportation. Tennis privileges. Downhill ski 10 mi. Exercise equipt; weight machine, bicycles, whirlpool, sauna. Game rm. Refrigerator, wet bar in suites. Balconies. Cr cds: A, C, D, DS, ER, MC, V.

⌐D⌐ ⌐ ⌐ ⌐ ⌐ ⌐ ⌐ SC

Williamsport (C-7)

Settled: 1795 **Pop:** 31,933 **Elev:** 528 ft **Area code:** 717 **Zip:** 17701

Now famous as the birthplace of Little League baseball, Williamsport once was known as the "lumber capital of the world." In 1870 a log boom extended 7 miles up the Susquehanna River; 300 million feet of sawed lumber were produced each year. When the timber was exhausted the city developed diversified industry and remained prosperous. The historic district of Williamsport includes homes of former lumber barons.

What to See and Do

1. **Lycoming County Historical Museum.** 858 W 4th St. Exhibits on regional history from 10,000 B.C. to present. Exhibits include Native American, frontier era; canals; steam fire engine & hose cart; military history; general store; blacksmith shop; woodworker's shop; gristmill; crafts & industry; Victorian parlor and furnished period rooms; wildlife; sports & Little League; lumber business. (May-Oct, daily; rest of yr, daily exc Sun) Sr citizen rate. Phone 326-3326. ¢¢ Within museum is

   Shempp Toy Train Collection. Extensive toy train collection. More than 350 train sets on display, including the entire Lionel collection. Two detailed running displays allow visitors to start trains, blow whistles. Twelve unique trains include an American Flyer #3117 and Lionel "Super #381."

2. **Little League Baseball International Headquarters.** 1 mi S on US 15. Summer baseball camp and Little League World Series Stadium are here. (Mon-Fri; closed hols) Phone 326-1921. **Free.** Adj is

   Little League Baseball Museum. 1 mi S on US 15. (Daily; closed Jan 1, Thanksgiving, Dec 25) Sr citizen rate. Phone 326-3607. ¢¢

3. *Hiawatha.* I-180 Reach Rd exit, in Susquehanna State Park. Sightseeing trips down Susquehanna River aboard replica of an old-fashioned paddle-wheel riverboat. Public cruises (May-Oct, daily exc Mon). Sr citizen rate. For schedule and fee information, phone 800/358-9900.

4. **Little Pine State Park.** 15 mi SW via US 220, then 13 mi N via PA 44 & Legislative Route 4001. Approx 2,000 acres. Swimming beach; fishing, hunting; boating (ramps, mooring). Cross-country skiing, snowmobiling, sledding, ice-skating, ice fishing. Picnicking, playground, store. Tent & trailer sites. Nature center, interpretive program. Phone 753-8209. Camping ¢¢¢

(For further information contact the Lycoming County Tourist Promotion Agency, 848 W 4th St; 800/358-9900.)

Annual Events

Slowpitch Softball Tournament. Teams from around the country participate. Cash prizes. Early July.

Lycoming County Fair. 20 mi SE via US 220, at Hughesville Fairgrounds. More than 50 acres of amusements, commercial displays, livestock judging, demolition derbies, grandstand entertainment, food. Mid-July.

All Breed Dog Show & National Obedience Trials. Sportsman Memorial Grounds, in Loyalsock. More than 1,100 entries include more than 100 different show quality breeds from 23 states and Canada. Phone 368-1215. Late July.

Little League World Series. Teams from all over the world compete. 3rd wk Aug.

(See Lewisburg, Lock Haven)

Motels

✔ ★ **CITY VIEW.** *RD 4, Box 550,* 2 mi S on US 15. 717/326-2601. 36 rms, 2 story. S $42; D $46-$48; each addl $5. Crib free. Pet accepted. TV; cable. Playground. Restaurant 6:30 am-9 pm. Ck-out noon. Sundries. Balconies. Picnic table. Overlooks city, Little League World Series Ball Park. Cr cds: A, C, D, DS, MC, V.

⌐D⌐ ⌐ ⌐ ⌐ SC

★ ★ **DAYS INN.** *1840 E 3rd St (US 220).* 717/326-1981; FAX 717/323-9590. 170 rms, 2 story. S $39-$57; D $58-$65; each addl $5; under 18 free; higher rates Little League World Series. Crib free. TV; cable. Pool; lifeguard. Restaurant 6:30 am-2 pm, 5-9 pm. Rm serv. Bar 4 pm-midnight. Ck-out noon. Coin lndry. Meeting rms. Cr cds: A, C, D, DS, JCB, MC, V.

⌐D⌐ ⌐ ⌐ ⌐ ⌐ SC

★ ★ **QUALITY INN.** *234 Montgomery Pike (US 15).* 717/323-9801; FAX 717/322-5231. 115 rms, 3 story. No elvtr. S $49; D $56; each addl $7; suites $85-$90; under 18 free. Crib $4. TV; cable. Pool; poolside serv, lifeguard. Restaurant 6:30 am-1:30 pm, 5-10 pm. Rm serv. Bar 4:30 pm-2 am; entertainment Wed, Fri & Sat. Ck-out noon. Valet serv. Sundries. Airport, bus depot transportation. Downhill/x-country ski 10 mi. Game rm. Cr cds: A, C, D, DS, ER, JCB, MC, V.

⌐D⌐ ⌐ ⌐ ⌐ ⌐ SC

Motor Hotel

★ ★ ★ **SHERATON INN.** *100 Pine St,* at jct PA 220 & US 15. 717/327-8231; FAX 717/322-2957. 148 rms, 5 story. S $80-$86; D $90-$96; suites $150; under 18 free. Crib free. TV; cable. Indoor pool. Restaurant 6:30 am-10 pm. Rm serv. Bar 11:30-2 am; DJ, dancing Tues-Sat. Ck-out noon. Meeting rms. Bellhops. Free airport transportation. Downhill/x-country ski 18 mi. Some refrigerators. Whirlpool in suites. 1 blk to river. Cr cds: A, C, D, DS, MC, V.

⌐D⌐ ⌐ ⌐ ⌐ ⌐ SC

Inn

★ ★ ★ **REIGHARD HOUSE.** *1323 E 3rd St (US 220).* 717/326-3593; res: 800/326-8335; FAX 717/323-4734. 6 rms, 2 story. S $48-$68; D $58-$78; each addl $10. Closed Dec 20-Jan 1. Crib $5. TV; cable. Pool privileges. Complimentary full bkfst, sherry. Complimentary coffee in rms. Restaurant nearby. Free airport, bus depot transportation. X-country ski 8 mi. Health club privileges. Brick and stone mansion (1905); music rm, library; oak & cherry millwork, paneling. Once used as state police barracks. Cr cds: A, C, D, MC, V.

 ⌐ ⌐ ⌐

Willow Grove (F-10)

Pop: 35 (est) **Elev:** 310 ft **Area code:** 215 **Zip:** 19090

What to See and Do

1. **Bryn Athyn Cathedral.** 3 mi N of PA Tpke, exit 27 on PA 611N, then 4 mi E on County Line Rd to PA 232, in Bryn Athyn. Outstanding example of Gothic architecture. Free guided tours (Apr-Nov, daily). Phone 947-0266. On grounds adj is

   Glencairn Museum. 1001 Cathedral Rd, at PA 232. Romanesque-style building features medieval sculpture and one of the largest privately-owned collections of stained glass in the world; also Egyptian, Greek, Roman, ancient Near East and Native American collections. (Mon-Fri by appt) Phone 938-2600. ¢¢

2. **Graeme Park** (1722). 5 mi N on PA 611. A fine example of Georgian architecture; stone house built by Sir William Keith, colonial governor of colony from 1717-26. (Wed-Sun; closed some hols) Sr citizen rate. Phone 343-0965. ¢¢

(See Philadelphia)

Motels

★ ★ ★ **COURTYARD BY MARRIOTT.** *2350 Easton Rd.* 215/830-0550; FAX 215/830-0572. 149 rms, 3 story. S $94; D $104; suites $107-$117; wkly, wkend rates. Crib free. TV; cable. Indoor pool. Complimentary coffee in rms. Restaurant 6:30 am-2 pm; Sat, Sun 7 am. Bar 4-11 pm. Ck-out noon. Coin lndry. Valet serv. Airport transportation. Exercise equipt; weights, bicycles, whirlpool. Refrigerators. Cr cds: A, C, D, DS, MC, V.

D ≈ ✈ ✗ 🔥 SC

★ ★ **HAMPTON INN.** *1500 Easton Rd.* 215/659-3535; FAX 215/659-4040. 150 rms, 5 story. S $76; D $85; under 18 free; wkend rates. Crib free. TV; cable. Complimentary continental bkfst, coffee. Restaurant nearby. Ck-out noon. Meeting rms. Valet serv. Sundries. Exercise equipt; bicycles, treadmill, sauna. Some refrigerators. Cr cds: A, C, D, DS, MC, V.

D ✗ ✈ ✗ 🔥 SC

Inn

★ ★ ★ **JOSEPH AMBLER.** *(1005 Horsham Rd, Montgomeryville 18936) 2 mi N on Easton Rd, 5 mi W on Horsham Rd.* 215/362-7500; FAX 215/361-5924. 28 rms, 2-3 story. S $85-$130; D $95-$140; each addl $15. TV. Complimentary full bkfst. Restaurant (see JOSEPH AMBLER INN). Ck-out 11 am, ck-in 3 pm. Private parking. Three buildings built 1734-1820; antiques. Cr cds: A, D, DS, MC, V.

D 🔥 ⚑

Restaurants

★ ★ **JOSEPH AMBLER INN.** *(See Joseph Ambler Inn)* 215/362-7500. Hrs: 6-10 pm; Sat from 5 pm; Sun 5-9 pm. Res accepted; required Sat. Continental menu. Bar 5-11:30 pm. Semi-a la carte: dinner $17.95-$24.95. Specialties: rack of lamb, grilled tournedos. Parking. In 1820s stone barn. Cr cds: A, D, DS, MC, V.

D

★ **OTTO'S BRAUHAUS.** *(233 Easton Rd, Horsham) PA Tpke exit 27,* 1/2 *mi N on PA 611.* 215/675-1864. Hrs: 7 am-10 pm; early-bird dinner 3-5:30 pm. Closed Jan 1, Dec 25. Res accepted. German, Amer menu. Bar 11 am-midnight. Semi-a la carte: bkfst $2.50-$8, lunch $3-$11, dinner $9-$20. Child's meals. Specialties:

sauerbraten, Wienerschnitzel. Own desserts. Parking. Outdoor dining. Large German beer selection. Cr cds: A, D, DS, MC, V.

D SC

✔ ★ **PASTA & COMPANY.** *(544 York Rd, Warminster 18974) N on York Rd.* 215/672-3300. Hrs: 11 am-10 pm; Fri & Sat to 11 pm; early-bird dinner 3-6 pm Mon-Fri; Sun brunch 9 am-2 pm. Bar. Buffet bkfst $5.95. Semi-a la carte: lunch $4.50-$7.95, dinner $6.95-$13.95. Sun brunch $8.95. Child's meals. Specialties: chicken Dijon, rigatoni primavera, vegetarian lasagne. Parking. 3 dining rms. Smoking at bar only. Cr cds: A, C, D, DS, MC, V.

D

Wrightsville (York Co) (F-7)

Pop: 2,396 **Elev:** 306 ft **Area code:** 717 **Zip:** 17368

What to See and Do

Donegal Mills Plantation & Inn (1800). 5 mi N via US 30, PA 441, 772, in Mt Joy (Lancaster Co). Historic village and resort dating from 1736. Mansion, bake house, gardens; restaurant and lodging (yr round). Plantation tours (Mar-Dec, Sat & Sun afternoons). Phone 653-2168. Tours ¢¢

(For further information contact the York County Visitors Information Center, 2958 Whiteford Rd, York 17402; 755-9638.)

(For accommodations see Bird-in-Hand, Lancaster, York, also see Pennsylvania Dutch Area)

Restaurant

★ ★ ★ **ACCOMAC INN.** *Accomac Rd.* 717/252-1521. Hrs: 5:30-9:30 pm; Sun 4-8:30 pm; Sun brunch 11 am-2:30 pm. Closed Dec 25. Res accepted; required wkends. Continental, French menu. Bar. Wine list. Semi-a la carte: dinner $16-$32. Sun brunch $17.95. Specialties: roast duckling, fresh seafood, steak Diane. Own pastries. Entertainment Sat. Reconstructed historic building (1775). Cr cds: A, DS, MC, V.

D

York (F-7)

Founded: 1741 **Pop:** 42,192 **Elev:** 400 ft **Area code:** 717

York claims to be the first capital of the United States. The Continental Congress met here in 1777 and adopted the Articles of Confederation, using the phrase "United States of America" for the first time. The first Pennsylvania town founded west of the Susquehanna River, York was and is still based on an agricultural and industrial economy. The city is dotted with 17 historical markers and 35 brass or bronze tablets marking historical events or places. There are 13 recreation areas nearby.

What to See and Do

1. **Historical Society of York County.** 250 E Market St. Includes library with genealogical records (daily exc Sun; fee for nonmembers). Museum features exhibits on the history of York County. (Daily; closed most major hols). Combination ticket for all historic sites maintained by the society. Sr citizen rate. Phone 848-1587. Museum ¢; Combination ticket ¢¢¢ Sites include

   General Gates' House (ca 1750). 157 W Market St (enter on N Pershing Ave). It was here that Lafayette gave a toast to Washington, marking the end of a movement to replace him. Also here are **Golden Plough Tavern** (ca 1740), one of the earliest buildings in York, which reflects the Germanic background of many of the settlers in its furnishings and half-timber architecture, and the **Bobb Log House** (ca 1810), furnished with painted and grained furniture. (Daily; closed most major hols) Sr citizen rate. **¢¢**

Bonham House (ca 1875). 152 E Market St. Historic house reflects life in late 19th century. (By appt; closed most hols) Sr citizen rate. Phone 848-1587. **¢**

2. **Friends Meeting House** (1766). 135 W Philadelphia St. Original virgin pine paneling; restored. Regular meetings are still held here. (Open by appt) Phone 843-2285. **Free.**

3. **York County Colonial Court House.** W Market & Pershing Ave. Replica of 1754 original. Exhibits include multimedia presentation of Continental Congress' adoption of the Articles of Confederation, audiovisual story of 1777-78 historic events; original printer's copy of Articles of Confederation, historic documents and artifacts. Tours. (Daily) Phone 846-1977 or 755-4067. **¢**

4. **Fire Museum of York County.** 757 W Market St. Turn-of-the-century firehouse preserves two centuries of firefighting history; from leather bucket brigades to hand-drawn hose carts and pumps, horse drawn equipment and finally to motorized equipment; artifacts & memorabilia; fire chief's office and firefighter's sleeping quarters are re-created, complete with brass slide pole. (Apr-Oct, Sat & 2nd Sun every month; also by appt; closed hols) Phone 843-0464. **Free.**

5. **Bob Hoffman Weightlifting Hall of Fame.** 4 mi N via I-83, exit 11; at York Barbell Co corporate headquarters. Weightlifting section honors Olympic weightlifters, powerlifters, bodybuilders and strongmen; displays include samples of Iron Game artifacts, memorabilia and photos. (Daily exc Sun, mid-morning-early afternoon; closed hols) Phone 767-6481. **Free.**

6. **Industrial tour. Harley-Davidson, Inc.** 1425 Eden Rd, 2 mi E on US 30. Guided tour through the motorcycle assembly plant and the Rodney Gott Antique Motorcycle Museum. Children under 12 and cameras not permitted on plant tour. Plant & museum combination tour (Mon-Fri); museum tour (Sat). Schedule may vary; phone 848-1177. **Free.**

7. **Ski Roundtop.** 12 mi NW on PA 74, then 1/2 mi N on PA 177 to Mt Airy Rd, then to Roundtop Rd, follow signs. Triple, 5 double chairlifts, 2 J-bars, 2 pony lifts; patrol, school, rentals; snowmaking; cafeteria; nursery. Longest run 4,100 ft; vertical drop 600 ft. (Mid-Nov-mid-Mar, daily) Phone 432-9631 or 800/767-4766 (snow report). **¢¢¢¢¢**

8. **Gifford Pinchot State Park.** 14 mi NW on PA 74 to Rossville, then NE on PA 177. Approx 2,300 acres; 340-acre lake. Fishing, hunting; boating (rentals, mooring, launching). Hiking. Cross-country skiing, sledding, ice-skating, ice fishing, ice boating. Picnicking, store. Tent & trailer sites, cabins. Nature center, interpretive center. Standard fees. Phone 432-5011.

9. **Warrington Friends Meeting House** (1769; expanded in 1782). 14 mi NW on PA 74. Fine example of early Quaker meetinghouse.

(For further information and a list of additional industrial tours, contact the York Convention and Visitors Bureau, 1 Market Way East, PO Box 1229, 17405, phone 800/673-2429; or the Visitors Information Center, 2958 Whiteford Rd, 17402, phone 755-9638.)

Annual Event

River Walk Art Festival. Along Codorus Creek at York County Colonial Court House (see #3). Late Aug.

(See Hanover, Harrisburg, Lancaster, Pennsylvania Dutch Area, Wrightsville)

Motels

★ **BEST WESTERN.** *1415 Kenneth Rd (17404). 717/767-6931; FAX 717/767-6938.* 105 rms, 3 story. S $55-$69; D $66-$75; each addl $5; suites, kit. units $115; under 18 free. Crib free. Pet accepted, some restrictions; $25. TV; cable. Restaurant adj 11 am-8 pm; Sat & Sun 7 am-9 pm. Ck-out noon. Meeting rms. Some refrigerators. Cr cds: A, C, D, DS, MC, V.

D ✦ ⊠ ☒ ☒ SC

★★ **HOLIDAY INN.** *2600 E Market St (17402). 717/755-1966; FAX 717/755-1966, ext. 178.* 120 rms, 2 story. S, D, studio rms $69-$79; each addl $10; under 18 free; higher rates: train collectors events, hol wkends. Crib free. TV; cable. Pool; wading pool, poolside serv, lifeguard. Restaurant 6 am-1 pm, 5:30-10 pm. Rm serv 7:30 am-9:30 pm. Bar 4 pm-midnight. Ck-out noon. Bellhops. Valet serv. Sundries. Airport transportation. Health club privileges. Refrigerators avail. Cr cds: A, C, D, DS, JCB, MC, V.

D ⊠ ☒ ☒ ☒ SC

★★ **HOLIDAY INN.** *334 Arsenal Rd (US 30) (17402), at Toronita St. 717/845-5671; FAX 717/845-1898.* 100 rms, 2 story. S, D $69-$79; each addl $10; under 18 free. Crib free. TV; cable. Pool. Restaurant 6:30 am-1:30 pm, 5-10 pm. Rm serv. Bar 4 pm-midnight. Ck-out noon. Meeting rms. Valet serv. Sundries. Cr cds: A, C, D, DS, ER, JCB, MC, V.

D ⊠ ☒ ☒ ☒ SC

✔ ★ **SPIRIT OF 76.** *RD 3 (17402), 1162 Haines Rd, I-83 exit 7. 717/755-1068.* 40 rms, 1-2 story. S $32-$36; D $35-$45; each addl $4; under 12 free. Crib $2. TV; cable. Restaurant adj open 24 hrs. Ck-out 11 am. Some refrigerators. Cr cds: A, DS, MC, V.

☒ ☒

Hotel

★★★ **YORKTOWNE.** *Box 1106 (17405), E Market & Duke Sts (17405). 717/848-1111; FAX 717/854-7678.* 150 rms, 8 story. S $52-$82; D $57-$89; each addl $7; suites $90-$175. Crib free. TV; cable. Restaurants 6:30-2 am. Bar from 11 am. Ck-out noon. Meeting rms. Gift shop. Barber. Free valet parking. Airport transportation. Exercise equipt; weight machines, stair machine. Cr cds: A, D, DS, MC, V.

D ☒ ☒ ☒ SC

Restaurants

✓ ★ **MOSER'S.** *1251 W King St. 717/854-0359.* Hrs: 5:30 am-9 pm; Sun to 8 pm. Closed major hols. Res accepted. Semi-a la carte: bkfst $2.35-$5.75, lunch, dinner $2.95-$13.95. Child's meals. Specializes in broiled seafood. Own soups. Parking. Cr cds: MC, V.

D SC

★★ **SAN CARLO'S.** *333 Arsenal Rd (US 30), I-83 exit 9E. 717/854-2028.* Hrs: 4-9:30 pm; Fri to 10 pm; Sat to 10:30 pm. Closed Jan 1. Res accepted. Continental menu. Bar. Semi-a la carte: dinner $6.95-$17.95. Child's meals. Specializes in fresh seafood, prime rib, veal. Entertainment exc Mon. Parking. Renovated 150-yr-old barn; original fieldstone walls; many hand-hewn beams; pegged ceilings. Cr cds: A, C, D, MC, V.

South Carolina

Population: 3,497,800

Land area: 30,207 square miles

Elevation: 0-3,560 feet

Highest point: Sassafras Mountain (Pickens County)

Entered Union: Eighth of original 13 states (May 23, 1788)

Capital: Columbia

Mottos: Prepared in mind and resources; While I breathe, I hope

Nickname: Palmetto State

State flower: Carolina yellow jessamine

State bird: Carolina wren

State tree: Palmetto

State fair: October 5-15, 1995, in Columbia

Time zone: Eastern

In South Carolina the modern age has neither masked the romance of the Old South nor overshadowed the powerful events of colonial and Confederate times. This state's turbulent and romantic history tells a story that remains deeply ingrained in the history of the United States.

Spanish explorers made the first attempt to settle in present-day South Carolina in 1526, less than 35 years after the Europeans discovered America. A severe winter, hostile natives and disease proved too much for the Spanish to overcome, and the settlement was abandoned. A group of French Huguenots, led by Jean Ribaut, landed near the site of present-day Parris Island Marine Corps Base in 1562. The French colony might have been a success, had not Ribaut's return to the colony from France on business been delayed. The remaining colonists, fearing they had been abandoned, built a craft and sailed for home. Light winds stranded their boat at sea, and they faced the danger of starvation until a passing English ship rescued them.

The task of settlement eventually fell to the English, whose challenge to Spanish control of the New World eventually met with success. A land grant from England's King Charles II gave the Carolinas to eight English noblemen (still known today as the "Lords Proprietors"). In 1670, the English arrived at Albemarle point and established Charles Towne, the first successful European settlement in the Carolinas.

During the Revolutionary War, 137 engagements were fought in South Carolina. The first overt act of revolution occured at Fort Charlotte on July 12, 1775; this was the first British property seized by American Revolutionary forces. On December 20, 1860, South Carolina became the first state to secede from the Union. The initial clash of the Civil War also occured on South Carolina soil; the bombardment of Fort Sumter in 1861 resulted in its seizure by Confederate forces, which maintained possession until the evacuation of Charleston in 1865. Bloodied, impoverished and blackened by the fires of General Sherman's march to the sea, South Carolina emerged from the difficult Reconstruction days and was readmitted to the Union in 1868.

For most of the period since the Civil War, South Carolina has had economic problems, but in recent years these have eased as industry has been attracted by hospitable communities and favorable tax rates. From town to town, throughout the state, diversified industries have brought with them greater prosperity. Power projects have been created by damming the Santee, Saluda, Savannah and other rivers. Four atomic energy plants provide commercial energy. Tourism, the state's second-largest industry, continues to grow.

A temperate climate makes South Carolina an attractive all-year resort. The cool upland western area merges into a subtropical seacoast. South Carolina is a major producer of tobacco, cotton, pine lumber, corn, oats, sweet potatoes, soybeans, peanuts, peaches, melons, beef cattle and hogs.

National Park Service Areas

Areas maintained by the National Park Service are Kings Mountain National Military Park (see), Cowpens National Battlefield (see GAFFNEY), Fort Sumter National Monument (see), Congaree Swamp National Monument (see COLUMBIA), and Ninety Six National Historic Site (see GREENWOOD).

National Forests

The following is an alphabetical listing of National Forests and towns they are listed under.

Francis Marion National Forest (see CHARLESTON): Forest Supervisor in Columbia; Ranger offices in McClellanville*, Moncks Corner*.

Sumter National Forest (see GREENWOOD): Forest Supervisor in Columbia; Ranger offices in Edgefield*, Greenwood, Union*, Walhalla*, Whitmire*.

*Not described in text

State Recreation Areas

The following towns list state recreation areas in their vicinity under What to See and Do; refer to the individual town for directions and park information.

Listed under **Aiken:** see Aiken State Park.

Listed under **Allendale:** see Barnwell and Rivers Bridge state parks.

Listed under **Anderson:** see Lake Hartwell and Sadlers Creek state parks.

Listed under **Beaufort:** see Hunting Island State Park.

Listed under **Camden:** see Lake Wateree and N.R. Goodale state parks.

Listed under **Charleston:** see Edisto Beach and Old Dorchester state parks.

Listed under **Cheraw:** see Cheraw State Park.

Listed under **Chester:** see Chester State Park.

Listed under **Clemson:** see Oconee State Park.

Listed under **Columbia:** see Sesquicentennial State Park.

Listed under **Dillon:** see Little Pee Dee State Park.

Listed under **Florence:** see Lynches River and Woods Bay state parks.

Listed under **Georgetown:** see Huntington Beach State Park.

Listed under **Greenville:** see Caesar's Head, Paris Mountain and Table Rock state parks.

Listed under **Greenwood:** see Baker Creek, Lake Greenwood and Hickory Knob Resort state parks.

Listed under **Hartsville:** see Lee State Park.

Listed under **Kings Mountain National Military Park:** see Kings Mountain State Park.

Listed under **Myrtle Beach:** see Myrtle Beach State Park.

Listed under **Newberry:** see Dreher Island State Park.

Listed under **Rock Hill:** see Andrew Jackson and Landsford Canal state parks.

Listed under **Santee:** see Santee State Park.

Listed under **Spartanburg:** see Croft State Park.

Listed under **Sumter:** see Poinsett State Park.

Listed under **Walterboro:** see Colleton State Park.

Water-related activities, hiking, various other sports, picnicking and visitor centers, as well as camping, are available in many of these areas. Cabins are located at Barnwell, Cheraw, Devils Fork, Edisto Beach, Givhans Ferry, Hickory Knob Resort, Hunting Island, Keowee-Toxaway, Myrtle Beach, Oconee, Poinsett, Santee and Table Rock. No pets in cabins. Cabin reservations made at individual parks. Camping: 14-day maximum; no advance reservations; $9-$15/night; pets on leash only. Not all state parks are open every day; hours of operation also vary. Contact Columbia office or individual park before making final trip plans. Daily parking fee at major coastal parks in summer, $3. Swimming fee at inland parks with supervised areas & bathhouses (early June-late Aug), $2; under 13, $1.50; ocean swimming free. Fees subject to change. For cabin rates and further information contact Dept of Parks, Recreation & Tourism, Edgar A. Brown Bldg, 1205 Pendleton St, Columbia 29201; 803/734-0156.

Fishing & Hunting

There is no closed fishing season; well-stocked lakes and rivers are close at hand in all parts of the state. Surf casting and deep-sea fishing can be enjoyed all along the Atlantic shore. Mountain streams offer trout fishing. Nonresident freshwater license: $35; seven-day nonresident license: $11. Saltwater stamp: $5.50. No license or permit required of children under 16. Fees subject to change.

Quail, dove, wild turkey, white-tailed deer, rabbit, squirrel and fox are all legal quarry. Nonresident annual license: $75; ten-day (consecutive) license: $50; three-day (consecutive) license: $25; wildlife management area permit: $76. Nonresident big game permit for deer, turkey and bear: $80. State duck stamp: $5.50. Fees subject to change. For further hunting and fishing information contact Wildlife and Marine Resources Department, PO Box 167, Columbia 29202; 803/734-3888.

Safety Belt Information

Safety belts are mandatory for all persons anywhere in vehicle. Children must be in an approved safety seat or wear a safety belt. For further information phone 803/343-0734.

Interstate Highway System

The following alphabetical listing of South Carolina towns in *Mobil Travel Guide* shows that these cities are within 10 miles of the indicated Interstate highways. A highway map should, however, be checked for the nearest exit.

INTERSTATE 20: Aiken, Camden, Columbia, Darlington, Florence.

INTERSTATE 26: Charleston, Clinton, Columbia, Newberry, Orangeburg, Spartanburg.

INTERSTATE 77: Columbia, Rock Hill.

INTERSTATE 85: Anderson, Clemson, Gaffney, Greenville, Spartanburg.

INTERSTATE 95: Darlington, Dillon, Florence, Hardeeville, Santee, Walterboro.

Additional Visitor Information

For additional information on South Carolina contact the Department of Parks, Recreation & Tourism, 1205 Pendleton St, Columbia 29201; 803/734-0122.

There are ten travel information centers in South Carolina; visitors will find the information provided at these stops useful for planning travel and making lodging reservations in the state. Their locations are: at the eastern end of the state, on I-95 on the SC/NC border; in the eastern coastal region on US 17 on SC/NC border; in the southern section on US 301 on the SC/GA border, and on I-95 on the SC/GA border; in midstate center on the southbound side of I-95 near Santee; on the southwestern side on I-20 on the SC/GA border; in the western part of the state on I-85 on the SC/GA border; located in the northwestern part of the state are centers on I-85 on the SC/NC border and on I-26 on the SC/NC border; in the northern part of the state on I-77 on the SC/NC border, and also at the State House Tour and Information Center located in Columbia.

Aiken (D-31)

Founded: 1834 **Pop:** 19,872 **Elev:** 476 ft **Area code:** 803

Aiken is a popular social and sports center in the winter months, providing flat racing training, harness racing, polo, fox hunts, drag hunts, tennis and golf. The University of South Carolina-Aiken is located here.

What to See and Do

1. **Aiken State Park.** 16 mi E, on unnumbered road between US 78 & SC 4. Approx 1,000 acres on the South Edisto River. Swimming; fishing; boating (rentals). Nature trail. Picnicking (shelters), playground. Camping (hookups, dump station). Standard fees. Phone 649-2857.

2. **Redcliffe.** 15 mi SE off US 278, near Beech Island. On 350 acres. Built in 1850s by James Henry Hammond. Greek-revival mansion furnished with family pieces, Southern antiques, art collection, historic documents and books. Picnic area. (Thurs-Mon) Phone 827-1473. Mansion ¢

3. **Hopeland Gardens.** Whiskey Rd & Dupre Place. A 14-acre public garden on former estate; terraces, reflecting pools, continuous blooms; sculptures. (Daily) Garden trail for the visually impaired. Summer concert series (May-Aug, Mon evenings). Phone 642-7630. **Free.** Also here is

   Thoroughbred Racing Hall of Fame. Enshrinement of champion horses trained and wintered in Aiken. (Oct-May, daily exc Mon) Phone 642-7630. **Free.**

4. **County Museum.** 433 Newberry St SW. Period room settings and displays in late-1800s home. Log cabin (1808) and one-room schoolhouse (1890) on grounds. Special features include an archaeology exhibit and a 1950s drug store. (Tues-Fri & Sun; closed hols) Donation. Phone 642-2015.

(For further information contact the Greater Aiken Chamber of Commerce, 400 Laurens St NW, PO Box 892, 29802; 649-3161.)

Annual Events

Triple Crown. 3 events: trials (Aiken Training Track), steeplechase (Clark Field), harness race (Aiken Mile Track). 3 consecutive Sats in Mar.

St Thaddeus Tour of Homes. Seasonal tour of houses and gardens. Phone 648-5497. Apr.

Seasonal Event

Polo games. Whitney Field. Sun afternoons. Feb-July, Sept-Nov.

(See Allendale, Orangeburg)

Motel

✔ ★ **RAMADA INN.** *Box 2166 (29802), At jct SC 19, I-20 exit 18. 803/648-4272; FAX 803/648-4272, ext. 2420.* 110 units, 2 story. S $39-$85; D $45-$91; each addl $6; suite $80-$110; under 18 free; higher rates Masters Golf Tournament. Crib free. Pet accepted, some restrictions; $10 refundable. TV; cable. Pool; wading pool. Complimentary bkfst. Restaurant 6 am-2 pm, 5:30-10 pm; Sat from 7 am. Rm serv. Bar 5-10 pm. Ck-out noon. Meeting rms. Valet serv. Refrigerators avail. Cr cds: A, C, D, DS, ER, JCB, MC, V.

Inn

★ ★ ★ **WILLCOX.** *100 Colleton Ave (29801). 803/649-1377; res: 800/368-1047; FAX 803/643-0971.* 24 rms, 3 story, 6 suites. S $105; D $120; suites $125-$140; golf, honeymoon plans; higher rates Masters Golf Tournament. TV; cable. Restaurant 6:30-10 am; Sat & Sun from 8 am. Rm serv. Bar; entertainment Fri, Sat. Ck-out noon, ck-in 3 pm. Meeting rm. Golf privileges. Refrigerators. English country decor. Built 1898; antique furnishings. Cr cds: A, D, MC, V.

Allendale (E-4)

Pop: 4,410 **Elev:** 191 ft **Area code:** 803 **Zip:** 29810

Moved six miles in 1872 to its present site to be on the old Port Royal railroad line, Allendale is an agricultural town with access to the lush hunting and fishing areas of the Savannah River Valley. More than 130

commercial farms with an average size in excess of 1,000 acres—the largest in the state—surround the town.

What to See and Do

1. **Rivers Bridge State Park.** 15 mi E off US 641. Approx 400 acres on site of Civil War skirmish. Swimming pool; river fishing. Nature trails. Picnicking (shelters); playground, recreation building. Camping (hookups, dump station). Standard fees. Phone 267-3675 or -3621.

2. **Barnwell State Park.** 17 mi N on US 278 to Barnwell, then 7 mi N on SC 3. Approx 300 acres preserved in natural state with an abundance of trees, flowers. Lake swimming (wkends only); boating (rentals); fishing. Nature trails. Picnicking (shelters), barbecue pit, playground. Camping, cabins. Standard fees. Phone 284-2212.

(For further information contact the Allendale Downtown Development Association, 512 N Main St, PO Box 171; 584-7473.)

(For accommodations see Aiken, Orangeburg, Walterboro)

Anderson (C-3)

Founded: 1826 **Pop:** 26,184 **Elev:** 770 ft **Area code:** 803

Textile mills and fiberglass plants lead an array of diversified industries that team with the products of the surrounding farmland to make Anderson a lively business center. The town was created as the seat of Anderson County; both were named for General Robert Anderson, who fought in the Revolutionary War.

What to See and Do

1. **"The Old Reformer."** In front of courthouse, Main & Whitner Sts. Cannon used by both British and Americans during Revolution; was fired in 1860, when Ordinance of Secession was signed.

2. **Pendleton Historic District.** 7 mi NW of I-85 off US 76. Settled in 1790, this town was the seat of what is now Anderson, Oconee and Pickens counties. There are self-guided tours (free), 2½-hour guided group tours (by appt, fee) or auto/walking tape tours (cassette, also in French; fee) of 45 historic homes and buildings. The Pendleton District Historical and Recreational Commission, 125 E Queen St, phone 646-3782, has tour information (Mon-Fri; closed hols). Research library, Hunter's Store (ca 1850) across from village green; arts and crafts shop; visitor center (Mon-Fri; closed hols). On Pendleton Town Square are

   Pendleton Farmers' Society Building (1826). Begun as the courthouse, bought and completed by Farmers' Society. Believed to be oldest Farmers' Society building in continuous use in America.

   Agricultural Museum. On US 76. Antique farming equipment, tools, pre-Eli Whitney cotton gin. (By appt) Phone 646-3782. **Free.**

   Historic Homes. Two of the many beautiful homes in the area are Ashtabula and Woodburn. (Apr-Oct, Sun; or by appt) Phone 646-3782. Per house ¢¢

3. **Hartwell Dam and Lake.** W and S of town, via US 29. This is a 56,000-acre reservoir with a 962-mile shoreline created by a dam on the Savannah River. Swimming, waterskiing; boating (81 ramps, 5 marinas); fishing. Picnicking (shelters). Camping (Mar-Nov; some all yr; hookups, dump station). Fee for some activities. Phone 225-3832 or 706/376-4788. On lake are

   Lake Hartwell State Park. S on I-85 exit 1. Located on 680 acres along Lake Hartwell. Swimming; fishing; boating (ramps). Nature trail. Picnicking (shelter), playground, store. Camping (hookups, dump station), laundry. (Daily) Standard fees. Phone 972-3352.

Sadlers Creek State Park. 13 mi SW off I-85 & SC 187. 395 acres. Lake fishing; boating (ramps). Nature trails. Picnicking (shelters), playground. Camping (hookups, dump station). Standard fees. (Daily) Phone 226-8950.

(For further information contact the Anderson Area Chamber of Commerce, 706 E Greenville St, PO Box 1568, 29622; 226-3454.)

Annual Event

Anderson Fair. Mid-Sept.

(See Clemson, Greenville, Greenwood)

Motels

★ ★ **HOLIDAY INN.** *3025 N Main St (29621), I-85 exit 19A, on US 76. 803/226-6051.* 130 rms, 2 story. S $54-$68; D $60-$72; each addl $6; under 18 free; higher rates Clemson Univ football games. Crib free. Pet accepted, some restrictions. TV; cable. Pool. Complimentary coffee in rms. Restaurant 6:30 am-10 pm. Rm serv. Bar 4:30 pm-2 am; entertainment Fri & Sat. Ck-out noon. Coin lndry. Meeting rms. Valet serv. Health club privileges. Refrigerators avail. Cr cds: A, C, D, DS, JCB, MC, V.

✔ ★ ★ **PARK INN INTERNATIONAL.** *3430 N Main St (29621). 803/225-3721; FAX 803/225-1607.* 100 rms, 2 story. S $35; D $40; each addl $6; studio rms $35-$40; under 12 free. Crib free. TV; cable. Pool; wading pool. Complimentary full bkfst (Mon-Fri). Restaurant 6:30-11 am. Rm serv. Ck-out 11 am. Meeting rms. Cr cds: A, C, D, DS, JCB, MC, V.

★ **SUPER 8.** *3302 Cinema Ave (29621). 803/225-8384.* 62 rms, 3 story. No elvtr. S $34.88; D $40.88-$48.88; each addl after 3, $4; under 12 free; higher rates: Clemson football wknds, special events. TV. Complimentary coffee. Restaurant nearby. Ck-out 11 am. Meeting rm. Cr cds: A, C, D, DS, JCB, MC, V.

Restaurant

✔ ★ ★ **PASTA HOUSE.** *4126 Clemson Blvd. 803/231-8811.* Hrs: 11:30 am-2:30 pm, 5-10 pm; Sat from noon; Sun noon-8 pm. Closed some major hols. Res accepted. Italian menu. Semi-a la carte: lunch $3.95-$6.95, dinner $5.95-$12.95. Specialties: veal spiedini, seafood fettucine primavera, New York-style cheesecake. Parking. Sports bar upstairs. Cr cds: A, JCB, MC, V.

D

Beaufort (F-5)

Founded: 1710 **Pop:** 9,576 **Elev:** 11 ft **Area code:** 803 **Zip:** 29902

The atmosphere of antebellum days is preserved in this old town's gracious houses and churches. Second-oldest town in the state, Beaufort (BEW-fort) looks to the sea from Port Royal Island, one of 64 islands that comprise the county. Tourism and the military are major sources of income in this community.

Spanish explorers first noted the harbor in 1514-15. In 1526, colonists from Spain made an unsuccessful attempt to settle the area. In 1562, a group of Frenchmen established the first Protestant colony on the continent, which also failed. English and Scottish attempts followed, with success finally coming when the present city was laid out and named for the Duke of Beaufort. The town was almost completely destroyed by Indians in 1715, captured by the British in the

Revolution and menaced by British cannon in 1812. Nearly the entire population evacuated Beaufort when it was captured by Northern troops during the Civil War.

What to See and Do

1. **National Cemetery** (1863). Boundary St. More than 11,000 interments, including Confederate and Union soldiers.

2. **Beaufort Museum.** 713 Craven St, in the Beaufort Arsenal (1795). Collections of antique guns, fossils, paintings, arrowheads, Civil War relics. (Mon-Fri, also Sat mornings; closed major hols) Phone 525-7077. ¢

3. **John Mark Verdier House Museum** (ca 1790). 801 Bay St. Federal period house once known as the Lafayette Building; the Marquis de Lafayette is said to have spoken here from the piazza in 1825. (Feb-mid-Dec, Tues-Sat; closed hols) Phone 524-6334. ¢¢

4. **George P. Elliott House Museum** (1844). Bay & Charles Sts. Greek-revival house was used as a hospital by Northern forces during Civil War; period furniture. (Mon-Fri; wkends by appt; closed hols) Phone 524-8450. ¢¢

5. **St Helena's Episcopal Church** (1712). 507 Newcastle St, at North St. Still in use; tombstones from surrounding burial ground became operating tables when church was used as hospital during Civil War. Silver Communion set in church was donated in 1734 by Capt John Bull in memory of his wife, who was captured by Indians. (Daily exc Sun) Phone 522-1712.

6. **Parris Island.** 10 mi S. Famous US Marine Corps Recruit Depot. Visitor Center in Building 283; Museum in War Memorial Building. Ribaut Monument is memorial to Jean Ribaut, French Huguenot founder of Charlesfort (1562); Iwo Jima monument; monument to Spanish settlement of Santa Elena (1521). Historic driving & bus tours depart from Visitor Center (driving tours, daily; bus tours, Thurs). (Daily) Phone 525-3650. **Free.**

7. **Marine Corps Air Station.** 6 mi NW on US 21. Home of Marine Aircraft Groups MACS-5, MWSS-273, MALS-31 and CSSD-23. Windshield tours avail by checking in at main gate. Phone 522-7201 or -7203. **Free.**

8. **US Naval Hospital.** 4 mi S on SC 802, between Beaufort & Port Royal, an early French settlement. On grounds are ruins of Fort Frederick (1731), one of largest "tabby" (cement & oyster shell) forts in US.

9. **Hunting Island State Park.** 16 mi SE on US 21. A 5,000-acre barrier island in a semitropical setting; beaches, forest, marshes; lighthouse. Swimming, ocean fishing. Nature trails. Picnicking (shelters), playground, boardwalk; concession. Camping (hookups, dump station), cabins. Recreation & nature programs. Standard fees (higher rates Apr-Aug). Phone 838-2011.

(For further information contact the Greater Beaufort Chamber of Commerce, 1006 Bay St, Box 910, 29901-0910; 524-3163.)

Annual Events

Beaufort Water Festival. Along waterfront at harbor. Includes parade, water show, boat races, concerts, dance. Phone 524-0600. Mid-July.

Fall Tour of Homes and Gardens. Contact Historic Beaufort Foundation, Box 11, 29901; 524-6334. Early Oct.

(See Charleston, Hardeeville, Hilton Head Island, Kiawah Island, Walterboro)

Motel

★ ★ **BEST WESTERN SEA ISLAND INN.** *1015 Bay St, in historic district. 803/522-2090; FAX 803/521-4858.* 43 rms, 2 Mid-Feb-Nov: S $69; D $79; each addl $6; under 12 free; hig Tour of Homes, Water Festival; lower rates rest of yr. Crib cable. Pool. Complimentary coffee in lobby. Restaurant nearby. Ck-out 11 am. Meeting rms. Bicycle rentals. Opp bay. Cr cds: A, C, D, DS, MC, V.

Motor Hotel

✔ ★ ★ **HOLIDAY INN.** US 21 at Lovejoy St, 1/2 mi W. 803/524-2144; FAX 803/524-2144, ext. 104. 153 rms, 4 story. S $45; D $52; each addl $8; under 19 free. Crib free. TV; cable. Heated pool. Restaurant 6 am-2 pm, 5-10 pm. Rm serv. Bar 5 pm-2 am, Sat to midnight; entertainment, dancing. Meeting rms. Valet serv. Golf privileges. Cr cds: A, C, D, DS, JCB, MC, V.

Inns

★ ★ ★ **RHETT HOUSE.** 1009 Craven St. 803/524-9030. 10 rms, 3 story. D $95-$200; each addl $20. Children over 5 yrs only. TV. Swimming privileges. Complimentary full bkfst; avail in rms. Dining rm (public by res) Wed-Sat evenings, 1 sitting 7:30 pm. Afternoon tea & cookies, evening refreshments. Ck-out 11 am, ck-in 3 pm. Gift shop. Tennis privileges, pro. 18-hole golf privileges. Rec rm. Some fireplaces. Antebellum (1820) galleried town house; antique furnishings, Oriental rugs. Gardens. Cr cds: MC, V.

★ ★ **TWOSUNS.** 1705 Bay St, in historic district. 803/522-1122; res: 800/532-4244. 5 rms, 2 story. S $99-$110; D $110-$122; each addl $20. Children over 12 yrs only. TV avail. Complimentary full bkfst, tea/sherry. Restaurant nearby. Ck-out noon, ck-in 2 pm. Neoclassic-revival house (1917); former private residence was once "teacherage" run by board of education for teachers. Veranda overlooks bay. Totally nonsmoking. Cr cds: A, MC, V.

Restaurant

★ **GADSBY'S TAVERN.** 822 Bay St. 803/525-1800. Hrs: 11:30 am-11 pm; Fri to 1 am. Closed Jan 1, Thanksgiving, Dec 25. Res accepted. Bar. Semi-a la carte: lunch $3.95-$7.95, dinner $7.95-$18. Specializes in shrimp, crab cakes, seafood pasta. Guitarist Fri, Sat. Outdoor dining. Tavern decor. Overlooks bay. Local artwork on display. Cr cds: A, MC, V.

Bennettsville (C-6)

Founded: 1819 **Pop:** 9,345 **Elev:** 150 ft **Area code:** 803 **Zip:** 29512

Near the geographic center of the Carolinas, Bennettsville radiates highway spokes in every direction. Founded by Welsh settlers, and now the seat of Marlboro County, it has diversified industry including paper and electrical products, textiles and farm equipment. Agriculture is still important; cotton is the leading crop.

What to See and Do

1. **Jennings-Brown House Restoration** (1826). 121 S Marlboro St. Served as headquarters for Union troops when Bennettsville was captured in 1865. The restored house is furnished with antiques pre-dating 1860. (Mon-Fri, or by appt; closed hols) Phone 479-5624. ¢

2. **Lake Wallace.** At N edge of city, off Country Club Dr. A 500-acre lake with separate sections for swimming (June-Labor Day), waterskiing; fishing; boating. Waterfowl refuge. Phone 479-3941.

(For further information contact the Marlboro County Chamber of Commerce, 300 W Main St, PO Box 458; 479-3941.)

(For accommodations see Florence, also see Cheraw, Darlington, Dillon, Hartsville)

Camden (D-5)

Settled: 1732 **Pop:** 6,696 **Elev:** 213 ft **Area code:** 803 **Zip:** 29020

The oldest inland town in the state, Camden was named after Lord Camden, defender of colonial rights. During the Revolution, General Cornwallis occupied Camden and made it the principal British garrison in the state and the interior command post for the South. Although several battles were fought in and near the town, including the Battle of Camden, the town was never recaptured by the Americans. Instead, it was evacuated and burned by the British in 1781. Camden contributed six generals to the Confederate cause and served as a storehouse, a hospital for the wounded and a haven of refuge until captured by General Sherman in 1865.

Today Camden is famous for its equestrian sports—horseback riding, horse shows, hunt meets, polo and steeplechase races. There are 200 miles of bridle paths in the area and three race tracks; Springdale Course is an extremely difficult and exciting steeplechase run.

What to See and Do

1. **Historic Camden.** S Broad St (US 521 S). Archaeological site of South Carolina's oldest inland town. Visitor area includes two early 19th-century log cabins and a restored 18th-century town house. Trails lead to the reconstructed foundation of a pre-Revolutionary War powder magazine, Kershaw-Cornwallis House and two reconstructed British fortifications. Picnicking, nature trail, historical film. Self-guided tours. (Daily exc Mon; closed some major hols) Phone 432-9841. ¢¢

2. **Bethesda Presbyterian Church** (1820). On US 1; 502 DeKalb St. Called House of Five Porches; steeple in rear. Designed by the architect of the Washington Monument, Robert Mills; church is considered a masterpiece. (Daily exc Sun) In front of church is

   DeKalb Monument. German-born hero of Battle of Camden is buried here; monument consists of modest shaft with a base of 24 granite blocks, one for each state in the Union at that time. General Lafayette laid the cornerstone on March 9, 1825.

3. **Quaker Cemetery.** Broad & Meeting Sts, SW edge of town. Buried here are: Richard Kirkland, who gained fame in the Battle of Marye's Hill by risking death to take water to dying Union troops; two of the three residents of the county who won Congressional Medals of Honor prior to World War II; and Dr. George Todd, brother-in-law of Abraham Lincoln.

4. **Rectory Square.** Chesnut & Lyttleton Sts. Pantheon; six columns serve as memorial to Camden's six generals of the Confederacy.

5. **Hampton Park.** Lyttleton St near US 1. Named for Confederate general who later became governor. Flagstones used in crosswalks were once part of the sidewalks of old Camden and are said to have been brought over as ballast in British ships.

6. **N.R. Goodale State Park.** 2 mi NW off US 1 on Old Wire Rd. Approx 700 acres. Lake swimming; boating (rentals); fishing. 9-hole golf course. Picnicking (shelters); recreation building. Standard fees. Phone 432-2772.

7. **Lake Wateree State Park.** S on US 1, E on SC 34 then N on US 21 to SC 41, continue W. Approx 200 acres. Fishing; boating (ramp), bait shop. Nature trail. Picnicking, store. Camping (hookups, dump station). Standard fees. Phone 482-6401.

(For further information, or to purchase a booklet with auto tour map of 63 historic sites, contact the Kershaw County Chamber of Commerce, 724 S Broad St, PO Box 605; 432-2525.)

Annual Event

Horse racing. Springdale Race Course. 200 Knights Hill Rd. Phone 432-6513. Carolina Cup Steeplechase, late Mar. Colonial Cup International Steeplechase, mid-Nov.

(See Columbia, Sumter)

Motels

✔ ★ ★ **COLONY INN.** *Box 131, 2020 W DeKalb St. 803/432-5508; res: 800/356-9801 (exc SC).* 53 rms, 2 story. S $32-$35; D $39-$43; each addl $3. Crib free. TV; cable. Pool. Restaurant 5:30-11 am. Ck-out 11 am. Valet serv. Cr cds: A, C, D, DS, MC, V.

★ ★ **HOLIDAY INN.** *(Box 96, Lugoff 29078) 3 mi S on US 1/601. 803/438-9441; FAX 803/438-9441, ext. 158.* 120 rms, 2 story. S $39.95-$65; D $43-$70; each addl $3; under 18 free; higher rates special events. Crib free. TV; cable. Pool; wading pool. Coffee in rms. Restaurant 6:30 am-2 pm, 5:30-10 pm. Rm serv. Bar 4 pm-midnight. Ck-out noon. Meeting rms. Valet serv. Health club privileges. Some in-rm whirlpools. Cr cds: A, C, D, DS, JCB, MC, V.

★ **SHONEY'S INN.** *928 US 1S. 803/438-4961.* 84 rms, 2 story. S $41; D $46; each addl $5; under 18 free. Crib free. TV; cable. Pool. Complimentary full bkfst, coffee. Restaurant adj 6 am-11 pm; Fri, Sat to 1 am. Ck-out noon. Meeting rm. Cr cds: A, C, D, DS, MC, V.

Inn

★ ★ **GREENLEAF.** *1310 Broad St. 803/425-1806; res: 800/437-5874.* 11 rms, 2 story. S $50-$65; D $55-$75; each addl $10; suite $70-$75; under 16 free. Crib free. Complimentary continental bkfst. Ck-out 11 am, ck-in varies. Built 1810. Cr cds: A, DS, MC, V.

Restaurant

★ ★ ★ **LILFRED'S.** *11 Main St. 803/432-7063.* Hrs: 6-10 pm. Closed Sun, Mon; some major hols. Res accepted. Wine cellar. Semi-a la carte: dinner $10.50-$18.95. Specializes in soft-shell crayfish, crab cakes, salmon, prime beef. Parking. Rustic decor. Cr cds: MC, V.

Charleston (E-5)

Founded: 1670 **Pop:** 80,414 **Elev:** 9 ft **Area code:** 803

This aristocratic and storied old American city lives up to its reputation for cultivated manners. Charleston's homes, historic shrines, old churches, lovely gardens, winding streets and intricate iron lace gateways exude charm and dignity.

Charleston enjoys international and coastal commerce in the fine harbor formed, according to local opinion, where the "Ashley and Cooper rivers unite to form the Atlantic Ocean." The strategic harbor, inlets and sea islands, provide recreational retreats.

The Charleston of today is the survivor of siege, flood, hurricane and epidemic. Capital of the province until 1786, its history and that of South Carolina are almost the same. Charleston received colonists from the Old World and sent them into the wilderness. The city served as the personification of Europe's luxury and culture in the New World.

The first permanent settlement in the Carolinas, Charles Towne, as it was first called, was established as a tiny colony westward across the Ashley River, by Anthony Ashley Cooper, Earl of Shaftesbury. At the same time, he established the only American nobility in history, with barons, landgraves (dukes) and caciques (earls), each owning great plantations.

This nobility lasted less than 50 years, but it was the foundation for an aristocratic tradition that still exists, even though the rice and indigo that made the early Charleston people rich are gone. Colonists from Barbados, England and Ireland came to enlarge the settlement in 1670, and by 1680 the colony moved across the river to become a city-state. Although many of the colonists went on to the Carolina Lowcountry and established grand plantations, every year on the traditional date of May 10, the planters and their families moved back to Charleston to escape the mosquitoes and malarial heat. From spring to frost, these planters created a season of dancing, sport, musicales, theater and socials. Commerce and plantations provided the prosperity on which the city's cosmopolitan graces were based. Charleston founded the first playhouse designed solely for presentation of drama, the first museum, the first public school in the colony, the first municipal college in America, and the first fire insurance company on the continent. (It was a victim the next year of a fire that destroyed half the city.) The city became famous throughout the world as "a flourishing capital of wealth and ease."

The First Provincial Congress of South Carolina met in Charleston in 1775 and prepared the city to repulse a British attack on June 28, 1776. But in 1780 the city was captured and for two and a half years was occupied by the enemy. Charleston was almost the last point in the state to be cleared of British troops. With peace came great prosperity, but rivalry between the small farmers of the interior and the merchants and plantation owners of the Lowlands resulted in removal of the capital to Columbia.

The convention that authored the Ordinance of Secession came to Charleston to pass that declaration; the Civil War then began with the bombardment of Fort Sumter by Fort Johnson. A long siege followed, including the gallant defense of Fort Sumter (1863-65), blockade running, the first submarine warfare, evacuation after Sherman had demolished Columbia and, finally, bombardment of the city by the Union Army.

What to See and Do

1. Walking tour of Old Charleston.

White Point Gardens. Murray Blvd & E Battery, at foot of peninsula. View of harbor, city, Fort Sumter National Monument (see) and Fort Moultrie. Walk N on E Battery 1/2 blk to

Edmondston-Alston House (ca 1825). 21 E Battery. Built by wealthy merchant and wharf owner, remodeled by next owner, an important rice planter, beginning in 1838; Greek-revival style. Uninterrupted view across harbor. Documents, engravings, portraits, original furnishings, elaborate woodwork. Guided tours (daily; closed Jan 1, Thanksgiving, Dec 25). Phone 722-7171 or 556-6020. Combination ticket includes Nathaniel Russell House (see) ¢¢¢ Continue N on E Battery (which becomes E Bay St) 8 blks, past Rainbow Row (14 houses dating from the mid-18th century, each painted a different color) to Broad St and the

Old Exchange & Provost Dungeon (1771). 122 E Bay St. Built by the British with material brought from England, this was the last building constructed by them on Colonial soil in Charleston prior to the Revolutionary War; served as an exchange and a customs house. Used as a prison during the Revolutionary War. Original seawall of Charleston preserved in dungeon; site of many important historical events. Phone 727-2165. ¢¢ Follow Broad St to Church St and turn S; walk past Catfish Row (made famous by *Porgy and Bess*) to

Heyward-Washington House (1772). 87 Church St. Once owned by Thomas Heyward, Jr., signer of Declaration of Independence and host to George Washington during his visit in 1791. Period pieces of exquisite design and craftsmanship; Charleston-made furniture; house is a classic example of a Georgian town house. Garden laid out with shrubs, plants that grew in city in Washington's time; carriage house, kitchen. (Daily; closed most hols) Phone 722-0354. ¢¢¢ Combination ticket (addl fee) includes The Charleston Museum (see #7), Joseph Manigault House (see #8) and Aiken-Rhett House (see #9). Walk N on Church St to

Huguenot Church (1845). 110 Church St, at Queen St. Third building on this site; rebuilt on site of earlier structure burned in 1796. Congregation founded 1681. Only church in US using Calvinist Huguenot liturgy; services were in French until 1928. Phone 722-4385. Continue N to

St Philip's Church (Episcopal) (1838). 142 Church St. Lofty steeple held mariner's light, was target for Union guns. Late Georgian architecture. Third building used by St Philip's parish. First Anglican parish (1670) south of Virginia. John C. Calhoun and other notables buried in churchyard. From here walk N to Cumberland St then W to

The Powder Magazine (ca 1710). 79 Cumberland St. Part of city's original fortifications, oldest public building remaining. Used in Revolutionary War. Walls of this 8-gabled structure are 32 inches thick. Now houses historic colonial museum. (Mon-Fri; closed Jan 1, Thanksgiving, Dec 25) Phone 723-1623. ¢ Walk W to Meeting St, then 1 blk S to

Gibbes Museum of Art. 135 Meeting St. Permanent collection of American paintings, miniatures, Japanese wood block prints; changing exhibits. (Tues-Sat, also Sun & Mon afternoons; closed hols) Sr citizen rate. Phone 722-2706. ¢¢ Walk S to

City Hall Art Gallery (1801). 80 Broad St, at Meeting St. On the site of colonial marketplace, first housed Bank of United States; became City Hall in 1818. Superb picture gallery on 2nd floor resulted from custom of commissioning artists to paint famous visitors; includes portrait of Washington by John Trumbull, considered one of the best of the general in his later years; painting of President Monroe by Samuel F.B. Morse. Tours. (Mon-Fri; closed hols) Phone 724-3799. **Free.** On next blk is

St Michael's Church (1752). Meeting & Broad Sts. Steeple rises 186 feet; tower has four-faced clock in operation since 1764. Steeple bells were captured by the British, returned after the Revolution, sent to Columbia during the Civil War and partly destroyed by the fire there. Later they were sent back to England, recast in the original molds, and returned in 1867. (Mon-Fri; closed hols and periodically for maintenance) Phone 723-0603. 2 blks S is

Nathaniel Russell House (1808). 51 Meeting St. Home of wealthy merchant; example of Adam-style architecture; free-flying staircase, oval drawing rooms, period furnishings. (Daily; closed Dec 25) Phone 724-8483. Combination ticket includes Edmondston-Alston House (see) ¢¢¢ Nearby are

Sword Gates. 32 Legare (la-GREE) St. Gates represent one of the best examples of wrought-iron art, with two spears joining at center of broadsword to form cross. (Private)

2. **Chamber of Commerce.** 81 Mary St. Building was once the South Carolina Railway Warehouse, home of one of the nation's first steam locomotives. Organized in 1773, the Chamber of Commerce (phone 577-2510) is one of the oldest city commercial organizations in the country. Also houses the Charleston Trident Convention & Visitors Bureau.

3. **St Mary's Church** (1838). 93 Hasell St, between King & Meeting Sts. Mother church for Catholic dioceses of Carolinas and Georgia. Congregation established in 1789. Stained-glass windows, paintings. (Daily) Phone 722-7696.

4. **Kahal Kadosh Beth Elohim** (1840). 90 Hasell St. Founded in 1749; first Reform Jewish congregation in America (1824). Museum. Gift shop. (Mon-Fri mornings; closed all Jewish hols) Donation. Phone 723-1090.

5. **Unitarian Church** (1772). 4 Archdale St. Second-oldest church in the city; under restoration. Fan tracery ceiling; interior modeled after Henry VII Chapel, Westminster Abbey. Phone 723-4617.

6. **St John's Lutheran Church** (1817). Archdale & Clifford Sts. Congregation established in 1742. Steeple, wrought-iron gates, churchyard fence, graves of interest. Interior restored. Pastor John Bachman (1815-74), who co-authored *Quadrupeds of America* with Audubon, is buried beneath the altar in the church nave. (Mon-Fri; also Sun worship) Phone 723-2426.

7. **The Charleston Museum** (1773). 360 Meeting St, at John St. Oldest museum in US. Cultural, historical, natural history collections; children's "Discovery Me" room; decorative arts exhibits. (Daily; closed some hols) Phone 722-2996. ¢¢¢ Combination ticket (addl fee) includes Heyward-Washington House (see #1), Joseph Manigault House (see #9) and Aiken-Rhett House (see #10).

8. **Joseph Manigault House** (1803). 350 Meeting St. Outstanding example of Adam-style architecture. Features Charleston antiques, silver; curving staircase. (Daily; closed most hols) Phone 723-2926. ¢¢¢ Combination ticket (addl fee) includes Heyward-Washington House (see #1), The Charleston Museum (see #7) and Aiken-Rhett House (see #9).

9. **Aiken-Rhett House** (1817). 48 Elizabeth St, corner of Judith St. Home of Governor William Aiken (1833-1887). Enlarged in Greek-revival style (1833-1836); subsequent additions (1858) created some of the finest rooms in Charleston, including a Rococo-revival art gallery. Many original furnishings from 1833. (Daily; closed most hols) Phone 723-1159. ¢¢¢ Combination ticket (addl fee) includes Heyward-Washington House (see #1), The Charleston Museum (see #7) and Joseph Manigault House (see #8).

10. **Charles Towne Landing.** 1500 Old Town Rd, on SC 171. Unusual 664-acre park on site of state's first permanent English settlement (1670). Reconstructed fortifications in original settlement area; replica of *Adventure*, 17th-century trading vessel; 1670 experimental crop garden; formal gardens; nature trails; Colonial Village; 20-acre animal forest. Also featured is a 30-minute movie, *Carolina.* Tram tours and bicycle rentals. Picnicking, playground; restaurant. (Daily; closed Dec 24, 25) Some fees. Sr citizen rate. Phone 852-4200. ¢¢

11. **Hampton Park.** Rutledge Ave & Cleveland St. Historic park with camellias and azaleas in spring, roses in summer; 1-mile nature trail; Charleston's mounted horse patrol stables. Phone 724-7321. **Free.**

12. **The Citadel, Military College of South Carolina** (1842). (2,000 uniformed cadets) Moultrie & Rutledge Aves, near Hampton Park. Originally located near city's pre-Revolutionary War rampart, the college moved to its present site in 1922. Dress parades (academic yr, Fri). Phone 953-5006. On campus is

The Citadel Museum. Exhibits depict history of the South Carolina Corps of Cadets at The Citadel. (Academic year, afternoons) Phone 953-6846. **Free.**

13. **Medical University of South Carolina** (1824). (2,200 students) 171 Ashley Ave. Oldest medical school in the South. Phone 792-3621. On campus is

Waring Historical Medical Library & Macaulay Museum of Dental History. (Mon-Fri; closed hols) Phone 792-2288. **Free.**

14. **Boone Hall Plantation** (1681). 8 mi N off US 17 on Long Point Rd in Mt Pleasant. A 738-acre estate with nine original slave houses and ginhouse (ca 1750), pecan grove, 1/2-mile "Avenue of Oaks." Several rooms in the house are open to the public. (Daily; closed Thanksgiving, Dec 25) Phone 884-4371. ¢¢¢

15. **Drayton Hall.** 9 mi NW via SC 61 (Old Ashley River Rd). One of the oldest surviving pre-Revolutionary War plantation houses (1738) in the area, this Georgian Palladian house is surrounded by live oaks and is located on the Ashley River. Held in the Drayton family for seven generations, the mansion has been maintained in virtually its original condition. A National Trust for Historic Preservation property. Tours (hrly). (Daily; closed Jan 1, Thanksgiving, Dec 25) Phone 766-0188. ¢¢¢

16. Magnolia Plantation and Gardens. 10 mi NW on SC 61. Internationally famous gardens are America's oldest (ca 1680); now covering 50 acres with camellias, azaleas, magnolias and hundreds of other flowering species. Azaleas best mid-Mar-Apr; camellias best mid-Nov-Mar. Also on grounds is a 125-acre waterfowl refuge; tri-level observation tower, 16th-century maze, 18th-century herb garden; Biblical gardens; topiary; nature trails; petting zoo; canoe and bicycle rentals; picnicking. Gift shop, snack shop; orientation theater. Plantation home and local art gallery (addl fee). (Daily) Sr citizen rate. Phone 571-1266. ¢¢-¢¢¢¢

Audubon Swamp Garden. Enter at Magnolia Plantation. Boardwalks, bridges and dikes make this 60-acre blackwater cypress and tupelo swamp accessible to visitors. Home to all local species of wildlife, this colorful area is planted with hundreds of varieties of local and exotic flowering shrubs. (Daily) Phone 571-1266. ¢¢

17. Middleton Place Gardens, House & Stableyards. 14 mi NW on SC 61. Once home of Arthur Middleton, signer of the Declaration of Independence, Middleton Place encompasses America's oldest landscaped Gardens, the Plantation Stableyards, and the restored House Museum. The Gardens, laid out in 1741, highlight ornamental butterfly lakes, sweeping terraces, and a wide variety of flora and fauna. The Stableyards feature numerous craftspeople demonstrating skills necessary for a self-sufficient 18th-century plantation. (Daily) House (addl fee). Guided tours (addl fee). Special events include Spoleto Finale (mid-June), Plantation Days (Nov) and Plantation Christmas (Dec). Phone 556-6020. ¢¢¢¢

18. Cypress Gardens. 24 mi N off US 52, between Goose Creek and Moncks Corner. Consists of 163 acres with giant cypresses, blackwater swamp, azaleas and camellias, dogwoods, daffodils. Boat trips. Picnic area. Free parking. Gift shop. (Daily) Sr citizen rate. Phone 553-0515. ¢

19. Palmetto Islands County Park. N on US 17, 1/2 mi past Snee Farm, then left on Long Point Rd. Nature-oriented park in tropical setting. Bicycle paths, marsh boardwalks, picnicking and grills throughout park. Two-acre pond. Canoe trails. Pedal boat, canoe & bicycle rentals. BigToy Playground. Fifty-foot observation tower with play area. Interpretive trails. Natural swimming facility with sand bottom. Fishing supplies; concession. (Daily; closed Jan 1, Thanksgiving, Dec 24-25) Phone 762-2172. ¢

20. Folly Beach County Park. S via SC 171 on W end of Folly Island. Approx 4,000 feet of ocean frontage and 2,000 feet of river frontage. There is a 600-foot section of beach for swimming (Apr-Sept); lifeguards. Dressing areas, outdoor showers; picnic areas; concessions; shelter. (Daily) Per vehicle ¢¢

21. Old Dorchester State Park. 19 mi NW on SC 642. Congregationalists from Massachusetts established a village in 1696 at the head of the Ashley River. It grew as a trading center until 1752, when there was a general exodus of Congregationalists to Georgia in a search for plentiful land and a better climate. By 1780 the once thriving town was occupied by the British and had only 40 houses and a church. In late 1781, Col. Wade Hampton advanced against Dorchester. The British did not wait for the attack but instead destroyed the town and retreated to Charleston. Remains of the church tower and Fort Dorchester may be seen; 97-acre area has been partially excavated. Fishing. Picknicking. Drawings, artifacts in interpretive building. (Thurs-Mon) Phone 873-1740. **Free.**

22. Edisto Beach State Park. 21 mi W on US 17, then 29 mi S on SC 174. Approx 1,200 acres. Two miles of beach; shell collecting is very good here. Ocean swimming, fishing. Nature trail. Picnic area (shelters), gift shop. Camping (higher fees Apr-Labor Day); cabins. Standard fees. Phone 869-2756 or -2156.

23. Francis Beidler Forest. Four Holes Swamp. 40 mi NW via I-26W to exit 187, then S on SC 27 to US 78, then W to US 178, follow signs. National Audubon Society Sanctuary. Boardwalk (1.5 mi) into the center of a beautiful blackwater swamp; close-up view of one of the largest stands of old-growth bald cypress and tupelo gum forest in the world. Self-guided tour. Visitor center, slide show. Canoe trips, night walks (in season, by res only; fee). (Daily exc Mon; closed Jan 1, Thanksgiving, Dec 24-25, 31) No pets, food facilities or camping. Phone 462-2150. ¢

24. Francis Marion National Forest. NE via US 17 & 17A, SC 41. Early colonial settlements, plantations; lakes, moss-hung oaks, flowering trees and shrubs on 250,000 acres. Camping, picnicking, boating, fishing, hiking, horseback riding, motorcycling, rifle ranges, hunting. Fees may be charged at recreation sites. Headquarters are in Columbia. HQ (Mon-Fri); forest (daily). Phone 765-5222.

25. Boat trips.

Fort Sumter Tours. Municipal Marina, Lockwood Blvd and Patriots Point, Mt Pleasant. Tour (2½ hrs) through Charleston harbor to Ft Sumter (see). (Daily; closed Dec 25) Also two-hour Charleston harbor tour of Navy base, three-hour *Spirit of Charleston* dinner cruise. Phone 722-1691. ¢¢¢; Dinner cruise ¢¢¢¢

Gray Line Water Tours. City Municipal Marina, Lockwood Blvd. Tours (approx 2 hrs) of harbor, US Naval Base, view of forts, other points of interest. For information, reservations contact PO Box 861, 29402-0861; 722-1112 or 723-5858. ¢¢¢

26. Sightseeing tours.

Charleston Carriage Co. 96 N Market St. Offers narrated, horse-drawn carriage tours of Old Charleston (1 hr). Free shuttle service from visitor center and downtown hotels. (Daily; closed Thanksgiving, Dec 25) For information phone 577-0042. ¢¢¢¢

Carolina Lowcountry Tours. Variety of semiprivate tours through Charleston and neighboring plantations; includes the town tour, which travels through historic Charleston and the early suburbs. Auto-van or bus by reservation only. (Daily; closed Jan 1, Thanksgiving, Dec 25) Phone 797-1045 or 800/489-4293. ¢¢¢¢

Palmetto Carriage Tours. 40 N Market St. One-hour tour through Old Charleston by horse- & mule-drawn carriages. Tours originate at Rainbow Market. Shuttle van from visitor center (free). (Daily; closed Dec 25) Sr citizen rate. Phone 723-8145. ¢¢¢¢

Gray Line bus tours. For information, reservations contact PO Box 219, 29402-0219; 722-4444.

27. Fort Sumter National Monument (see).

Annual Events

Southeastern Wildlife Exposition. 18 downtown historical locations. More than 500 exhibitors display wildlife art, carvings, antique collections and crafts for sale. Phone 723-1748. Mid-Feb.

Festival of Houses & Gardens. Many of the city's finest private residences (ca 1710-1850) and gardens are open to visitors. Afternoon and candlelight tours; reservations recommended. Phone 722-3405. Mid-Mar-mid-Apr.

Spoleto Festival USA. Internationally acclaimed counterpart to the arts festival in Spoleto, Italy, founded by Gian Carlo Menotti; includes opera, ballet, dance, visual arts, theater, chamber music, jazz, symphonic and choral performances and much more. Piccolo Spoleto, running concurrent with the main festival, has performances by local and regional artists. Phone 722-2764. Late May-early June.

Fall House & Garden Candlelight Tours. Evening tours of privately owned houses and gardens in the Historic District (fee). Phone 722-4630. Late Sept-late Oct.

Additional Visitor Information

The Charleston Visitor Reception and Transportation Center, 375 Meeting St, has information on other points of interest, tours, campsites, fishing trips, cultural, special and annual events, maps and self-guided walking tour of the city. (Daily; closed Jan 1, Thanksgiving, Dec 25) Contact PO Box 975, 29402; 853-8000. For city bus service information phone SCE & G at 747-0922; for DASH, Downtown Area Shuttle, phone 577-6970, ext 500.

Forever Charleston, a multimedia presentation about the city, is shown every 1/2-hr at the Visitor Center.

(See Beaufort, Kiawah Island, Walterboro)

Motels

★ **BEST WESTERN KING CHARLES INN.** *237 Meeting St (29401). 803/723-7451; FAX 803/723-2041.* 91 rms, 3 story. Mar-May: S $89-$149; D $99-$149; each addl $10; under 18 free; lower rates rest of yr. Crib free. TV; cable. Pool. Bkfst avail. Restaurant nearby. Ck-out noon. Bellhops. Valet serv. Cr cds: A, C, D, DS, MC, V.

⊠ ⊠ ⊠ 🔥 SC

★ **DAYS INN-AIRPORT.** *2998 W Montague Ave (29418), near Intl Airport. 803/747-4101; FAX 803/566-0378.* 148 rms, 2 story. S $42-$50; D $47-$55; each addl $5; under 12 free; 12-17, $3. Crib free. Pet accepted; $5. TV; cable. Pool. Playground. Restaurant 6 am-9 pm. Ck-out noon. Coin lndry. Free airport transportation. Cr cds: A, D, DS, ER, MC, V.

D 🐾 ⊠ ✈ ⊠ 🔥 SC

✔ ★ **HAMPTON INN.** *11 Ashley Pointe Dr (29407). 803/556-5200; FAX 803/556-5200, ext. 177.* 177 rms, 4 story. S $43-$67; D $45-$77; higher rates wkends & special events; under 18 free; higher rates Wildlife Exposition. Crib free. TV; cable. Pool. Complimentary continental bkfst, coffee. Restaurant adj 10 am-11 pm. Ck-out noon. Meeting rms. Valet serv. Tennis, golf privileges. Opp Ashley River; marina. Cr cds: A, C, D, DS, MC, V.

D 🧍 🤽 ⊠ ⊠ 🔥 ⊠

✔ ★ **KNIGHTS INN.** *2355 Aviation Ave (29418). 803/744-4900; res: 800/845-1927; FAX 803/745-0668.* 211 rms, 2 story, 31 kits. S $25.50-$31; D $36-$38; each addl $4; suites $55-$60; kit. units $45-$50. Crib $2. TV; cable. 2 pools. Complimentary coffee in lobby. Ck-out noon. Coin lndry. Airport transportation. Some refrigerators. Lawn games. Cr cds: A, C, D, MC, V.

D ⊠ ⊠

★ **LA QUINTA.** *209 Ashley Phosphate Rd (29420), at I-26N. 803/797-8181; FAX 803/569-1608.* 122 rms, 2 story. S $45-$52; D $53-$60; each addl $8, higher rates wkends; under 18 free. Crib free. Pet accepted. TV; cable. Heated pool. Complimentary coffee, continental bkfst. Restaurant adj 6 am-11 pm. Rm serv. Ck-out noon. Meeting rms. Valet serv. Picnic tables, grill. Cr cds: A, C, D, DS, MC, V.

D 🐾 ⊠ ⊠ 🔥 SC

✔ ★ **MASTERS INN.** *(300 Wingo Way, Mt Pleasant 29464) 3 mi E on US 17. 803/884-2814; res: 800/633-3434; FAX 803/884-2958.* 120 units, 2 story, 26 kits. S $33.95-$37.95; D $49.95-$54.95; each addl $6; kit. units $48.95-$57.95; under 18 free. Pet accepted, some restrictions; $6. TV; cable. Pool. Continental bkfst. Complimentary coffee. Restaurant nearby. Ck-out noon. Coin lndry. Meeting rm. Cr cds: A, C, D, DS, MC, V.

D 🐾 ⊠ ⊠ 🔥 SC

★ ★ **RAMADA INN.** *W Montague Ave (29418), 7 mi NW at I-26. 803/744-8281; FAX 803/744-6230.* 155 rms, 2 story. Mid-Mar-Oct: S $49-$69; D $59-$79; each addl $10; under 18 free; lower rates rest of yr. TV; cable. Pool. Restaurant 6-10 am, 5:30-10 pm; Sat & Sun 7-11 am, 5:30-10 pm. Rm serv. Bar 4 pm-1:30 am; entertainment,

dancing. Ck-out noon. Meeting rms. Valet serv. Free airport transportation. Some refrigerators. Cr cds: A, C, D, DS, MC, V.

D ⊠ ⊠ 🔥 SC

✔ ★ **RED ROOF INN.** *7480 Northwoods Blvd (29406), I-26 to exit 209. 803/572-9100; FAX 803/572-9100, ext. 444.* 109 rms, 2 story. S $32.99-$40.99; D $38.99-$46.99; each addl $6; under 18 free. Crib free. Pet accepted, some restrictions. TV; cable. Complimentary coffee in lobby. Restaurant nearby. Ck-out noon. Cr cds: A, C, D, DS, MC, V.

D 🐾 ⊠ ⊠ SC

★ ★ **TOWN AND COUNTRY INN.** *2008 Savannah Hwy (US 17) (29407). 803/571-1000; res: 800/334-6660; FAX 803/766-9444.* 130 rms, 2 story. 20 kits. Mar-Nov: S $69; D $89; each addl $7; suites $95-$175; kit. units $7 addl; under 18 free; lower rates rest of yr. Crib free. TV; cable. 2 pools, 1 indoor. Restaurant 6:30 am-10 pm. Bar 3 pm-midnight. Ck-out noon. Coin lndry. Meeting rms. Valet serv. Golf privileges, pro. Exercise equipt; weight machine, bicycles, whirlpool. Some refrigerators. Cr cds: A, C, D, DS, MC, V.

D 🧍 ⊠ 🏃 ⊠ 🔥 ⊠ SC

Motor Hotels

★ ★ **BEST WESTERN NORTHWOODS ATRIUM INN.** *(7401 Northwoods Blvd, North Charleston 29406) NW on I-26. 803/572-2200; FAX 803/863-8316.* 197 rms, 4 story. S $62-$72; D $69-$79; each addl $6; suites $125-$175; under 18 free. Crib free. TV; cable, in-rm movies. 2 pools, 1 indoor; poolside serv. Complimentary continental bkfst. Restaurant 6:30 am-2 pm, 5-10:30 pm. Rm serv. Bar 4 pm-1 am, closed Sun. Ck-out 11 am. Meeting rms. Bellhops. Valet serv. Free airport, RR station, bus depot transportation. Exercise equipt; bicycles, rowing machine, whirlpool, sauna. Game rm. Rec rm. Lawn games. Refrigerators avail. Cr cds: A, C, D, DS, ER, JCB, MC, V.

D ⊠ 🏃 ⊠ 🔥 SC

★ ★ **HAMPTON INN-HISTORIC DISTRICT.** *345 Meeting St (29403). 803/723-4000; FAX 803/722-3725.* 171 rms, 5 story, 5 suites. Mid-Mar-early Nov: S $75; D $83; each addl $6; suites $125; under 18 free; higher rates wkends; lower rates rest of yr. Crib free. Garage $7. TV; cable. Pool. Complimentary continental bkfst. Complimentary coffee in lobby. Restaurant nearby. Ck-out noon. Meeting rms. Bellhops. Concierge. Valet serv. Some refrigerators. Cr cds: A, DS, MC, V.

D ⊠ ⊠ 🔥 SC

★ ★ **HAWTHORN SUITES.** *181 Church St (29401). 803/577-2644; FAX 803/577-2697.* 165 kit. suites, 5 story. Mar-mid-June: S, D $110-$155; each addl $15; under 18 free; wkly rates; lower rates rest of yr. Crib free. TV; cable, in-rm movies. Complimentary full bkfst. Complimentary coffee in rms. Restaurant adj 7 am-11 pm. Ck-out noon. Coin lndry. Meeting rms. Bellhops. Valet serv. Concierge. Sundries. Gift shop. Exercise equipt; weight machine, bicycles. Some wet bars. In historic market area. Cr cds: A, C, D, DS, JCB, MC, V.

D 🧍 ⊠ ⊠ SC

★ ★ **HOLIDAY INN-RIVERVIEW.** *301 Savannah Hwy (US 17) (29407). 803/556-7100; FAX 803/556-6176.* 181 rms, 14 story. S $49-$99; D $49-$114; under 19 free. Crib free. TV; cable. Pool. Restaurant 6:30 am-2 pm, 5-10 pm. Rm serv. Bar 1 pm-2 am; dancing. Ck-out noon. Coin lndry. Bellhops. Valet serv. Free historic area transportation. Exercise equipt; stair machine, treadmill. Balconies. On river. Cr cds: A, C, D, DS, JCB, MC, V.

D ⊠ 🏃 ⊠ 🔥 SC

★ ★ **QUALITY SUITES.** *5225 N Arco Lane (29418). 803/747-7300; FAX 803/747-6324.* 168 suites, 5 story. Mar-mid-June: S $80-$210; D $90-$210; each addl $10; under 18 free; lower rates rest of yr. Crib free. TV; cable, in-rm movies. Pool. Complimentary full bkfst. Coffee in rms. Restaurant nearby. Ck-out noon. Coin lndry. Meeting rms. Free airport transportation. Exercise equipt; weights, bicycles.

Refrigerators, wet bars; some bathrm phones. Some balconies. Cr cds: A, C, D, DS, ER, JCB, MC, V.

★★ **RADISSON INN AIRPORT.** *5991 Rivers Ave (29406), jct Aviation Ave & I-26.* 803/744-2501; FAX 803/744-2501, ext. 11. 158 rms, 8 story. S $70-$79; D $89-$99; each addl $10; under 17 free. Crib free. TV; cable. Pool. Restaurant 6:30 am-10:30 pm. Rm serv. Bar 11-2 am, Sun 5 pm-midnight; entertainment, dancing. Ck-out noon. Meeting rms. Bellhops. Valet serv. Airport transportation. Exercise equipt; weights, bicycles, whirlpool, sauna. Cr cds: A, C, D, DS, ER, JCB, MC, V.

Hotels

★★★ **MARRIOTT.** *4770 Marriott Dr (29418), 7 mi W on I-26 exit Montague Ave.* 803/747-1900; FAX 803/744-2530. 295 rms, 8 story. S $115; D $135; suites $200; under 18 free; wkend rates. Crib free. TV; cable. Indoor/outdoor pool; poolside serv. Restaurant 6:30 am-10:30 pm. Bar; entertainment, dancing. Ck-out noon. Meeting rms. Gift shop. Free airport transportation. Tennis; golf privileges. Exercise equipt; weights, bicycles, whirlpool. Game rm. Landscaped grounds. Cr cds: A, C, D, DS, ER, JCB, MC, V.

★★★ **MILLS HOUSE.** *115 Meeting St (29401), at Queen St.* 803/577-2400; res: 800/874-9600; FAX 803/722-2112. 214 rms, 7 story. Mid-Mar-mid-June, mid-Sept-mid-Nov: S $150; D $170; each addl $20; under 20 free; lower rates rest of yr. Crib free. Garage $8.50. Pet accepted. TV. Elevated pool. Restaurant (see BARBADOES ROOM). Bar 11-2 am. Ck-out 11 am. Meeting rms. Concierge. Reproductions of antebellum furnishings; many antiques. Carriage for sightseeing. Cr cds: A, C, D, DS, JCB, MC, V.

★★★★ **OMNI HOTEL AT CHARLESTON PLACE.** *130 Market St (29401).* 803/722-4900; FAX 803/722-0728. 440 rms, 8 story. S $210; D $230; each addl $20; suites $250-$1,200; under 17 free. Crib free. Garage $7, valet parking $11. TV; cable, in-rm movies avail. Indoor/outdoor pool; poolside serv. Restaurant 6:30 am-9 pm (also see LOUIS'S CHARLESTON GRILL). Rm serv 24 hrs. Bar 11:30-1 am; entertainment. Ck-out noon. Convention facilities. Concierge. Shopping arcade. Tennis & golf privileges. Exercise rm; instructor, weights, bicycles, whirlpool, sauna, steam rm. Massage. Some balconies. Located in historic district. Pool area has retractable roof for fair weather. *LUXURY LEVEL : CLUB FLOOR.* 67 rms, 2 floors. S $240; D $260. Private lounge. Complimentary continental bkfst, high tea, refreshments, newspaper. Cr cds: A, C, D, DS, MC, V.

Inns

★★★ **ANCHORAGE.** *26 Vendue Range, in historic district.* 803/723-8300; res: 800/421-2952; FAX 803/723-9543. 19 rms, 2 story, 2 suites. Mid-Mar-mid-June, Sept-Nov: S $134-$184; suites $229; lower rates rest of yr. Garage parking $4.50/day. Complimentary continental bkfst. Complimentary coffee, tea/sherry. Restaurant nearby. Ck-out noon, ck-in 3 pm. Bellhops. Concierge. Antiques. Library/sitting rm. Renovated antebellum warehouse adj to harbor & Waterfront Park; individually decorated rms. Cr cds: A, MC, V.

★★ **ASHLEY.** *201 Ashley Ave (29403).* 803/723-1848; FAX 803/723-9080. 6 rms (5 with shower only), 1 suite, 3 story. No rm phones. Early Mar-Nov: S, D $95-$105; suite $125; lower rates rest of yr. Children over 12 yrs only. TV; cable. Complimentary full bkfst; afternoon tea/sherry. Ck-out 10 am, ck-in 3 pm. Guest bicycles. Built

1832; antiques. Garden with fish pond, fountain. Totally nonsmoking. Cr cds: A, DS, MC, V.

★★★ **BARKSDALE HOUSE.** *27 George St (29401), in historic district.* 803/577-4800. 13 rms, 3 story. Mar-Oct: S, D $85-$160; each addl $10; lower rates rest of yr. Children over 10 yrs only. TV; cable. Complimentary continental bkfst, tea/sherry. Restaurant nearby. Ck-out 11 am, ck-in 3 pm. Bellhops. Town house built in 1778; porches, courtyard in rear. Cr cds: MC, V.

★★★ **BATTERY CARRIAGE HOUSE.** *20 S Battery (29401).* 803/727-3100; res: 800/775-5575; FAX 803/727-3130. 11 rms (4 with shower only), 2 story. Mar-mid-June & mid-Sept-mid-Nov: S, D $149-$189; each addl $15; higher rates wkends (2-day min); lower rates rest of yr. Closed Dec 23-25. Crib avail. TV; cable. Complimentary coffee in rms. Complimentary continental bkfst. Ck-out noon, ck-in 3 pm. Concierge. Street parking. Picnic tables. Greek-revival mansion built 1843. Near Battery Park, harbor. Cr cds: A, D, MC, V.

★ **CANNONBORO.** *184 Ashley Ave (29403).* 803/723-8572; FAX 803/723-9080. 5 rms (4 with shower only), 2 story, 1 suite. No rm phones. Early Mar-Nov: S, D $95-$105; each addl $20; suite $135; lower rates rest of yr. Children over 12 yrs only. TV. Complimentary full bkfst; afternoon tea/sherry. Restaurant nearby. Ck-out 10 am, ck-in 3 pm. Guest bicycles. Second story porch. Some Victorian furnishings; antiques. Totally nonsmoking. Cr cds: A, DS, MC, V.

★★ **CHURCH STREET.** *177 Church St (29401).* 803/722-3420; res: 800/552-3777. 31 kit. suites, 2 story. 1-bedrm $125-$145; 2-bedrm $185; each addl (after 2nd person) $10; family rates. Crib free. Municipal garage parking $5. TV; cable. Complimentary bkfst, coffee. Restaurant adj 7 am-10 pm. Bar 5-10 pm. Ck-out noon, ck-in 3 pm. Bellhops. Valet serv. Some balconies. Antique reproductions. Courtyard. In historic market area. Cr cds: A, MC, V.

★★★ **INDIGO.** *1 Maiden Lane (29401).* 803/577-5900; res: 800/845-7639; FAX 803/577-0378. 40 rms, 3 story, 6 suites. Mar-June, Sept-Nov: S $120; D $135; each addl $10; under 12 free; lower rates rest of yr. Crib free. TV; cable. Complimentary continental bkfst. Complimentary coffee in rms. Restaurant opp 6-1 am. Ck-out noon, ck-in 3 pm. Bellhops. Valet serv. Built 1850; antique furnishings; courtyard. Cr cds: A, DS, MC, V.

★★★★ **JOHN RUTLEDGE HOUSE.** *116 Broad St (29401).* 803/723-7999; res: 800/476-9741; FAX 803/720-2615. 19 rms, 2-3 story, 3 suites. Mid-Mar-mid-June, mid-Sept-Oct: S $165-$190; D $180-$210; each addl $15; suites $285; under 12 free; lower rates rest of yr. Crib free. TV; cable. Complimentary continental bkfst, afternoon tea, wine. Restaurant nearby. Ck-out noon, ck-in 3 pm. Bellhops. Valet serv. Concierge. Stocked refrigerators. Fireplaces. Historic home built 1763; antique furnishings; library. Cr cds: A, MC, V.

★★★ **KINGS COURTYARD.** *198 King St (29401).* 803/723-7000; res: 800/845-6119; FAX 803/720-2608. 44 rms, 3 story. Mid-Mar-early June, mid-Sept-Oct: S $115-$135; D $130-$170; each addl $15; suites $200; under 12 free; 3-day package plans off-season; lower rates rest of yr. Crib free. TV; cable. Complimentary continental bkfst. Dining rm 7-10 am; Sat, Sun to 11 am. Rm serv. Serv bar. Ck-out noon, ck-in 3 pm. Meeting rms. Bellhops. Concierge. Whirlpool. Fireplaces. Built 1853; 2 inner courtyards. Cr cds: A, MC, V.

★★★ **LODGE ALLEY.** *195 E Bay St (29401).* 803/722-1611; res: 800/845-1004 (exc SC), 800/821-2791 (SC); FAX 803/722-1611. 94 rms, 4 story, 50 kit. units. Mid-Mar-early June & early Sept-early Nov:

S, D $139-$180; each addl $15; kit. suites $145-$295; under 12 free; honeymoon plans; lower rates rest of yr. Crib free. TV; cable. Complimentary morning coffee in sitting rm, sherry. Dining rm 7-10:30 am, 11:30 am-2:30 pm, 6-10 pm. Rm serv to 10:30 am. Bar 11:30 am-midnight, closed Sun; entertainment spring, fall. Ck-out noon, ck-in 4 pm. Bellhops. Valet serv. Tennis, golf privileges. Honor bar, refrigerators. Some balconies. Built 1773; some fireplaces, antiques. Courtyard gardens with fountain. Cr cds: A, MC, V.

★ ★ **MAISON DU PRE.** *317 E Bay St (29401). 803/723-8691; res: 800/844-INNS.* 15 rms, 1-3 story, 1 kit. Early Feb-mid-June, Sept-mid-Nov: S, D $98-$145; suites $160-$200; carriage house with kit. $160; lower rates rest of yr. Crib free. TV. Complimentary continental bkfst, tea/wine. Ck-out noon, ck-in 2 pm. Built 1804. Composed of 3 single Charleston houses & 2 carriage houses with enclosed porches. 3 fountains. Cr cds: A, MC, V.

★ ★ **MEETING STREET.** *173 Meeting St (29401), in heart of downtown historic district. 803/723-1882; res: 800/842-8022; FAX 803/577-0851.* 56 rms, 4 story. Mid-Mar-early June & mid-Sept-Oct: S, D $109-$149; each addl $10; under 13 free; lower rates rest of yr. Crib free. Parking $5. TV. Complimentary continental bkfst, wine & cheese (afternoons). Bar noon-2 am, closed Sun. Ck-out noon, ck-in 3 pm. Bellhops. Whirlpool. Walking tours. Courtyard with fountain. Opp Old City Market. Cr cds: A, D, MC, V.

★ ★ **MIDDLETON.** *SC 61 (29414), Ashley River Rd (29414), 14 mi W. 803/556-0500; res: 800/543-4774.* 55 rms, 2-3 story. S, D $99-$169; each addl $20; under 12 free. Crib $10. TV. Pool. Complimentary bkfst. Meeting rms. Tennis. Fireplaces. On 7,000 acres overlooking river & former rice fields; free admission to nearby Middleton Place Gardens. Cr cds: A, MC, V.

★ ★ **PLANTERS.** *112 N Market St (29401). 803/722-2345; res: 800/845-7082; FAX 803/577-2125.* 41 rms, 4 story. S, D $115-$140; suites $160-$175. Crib free. TV. Complimentary continental bkfst in rms. Ck-out noon, ck-in 3 pm. Meeting rm. Bellhops. Many antiques. Located in scenic, historic area. Cr cds: A, C, D, MC, V.

★ ★ **VENDUE.** *19 Vendue Range (29401). 803/577-7970; res: 800/845-7900 (exc SC), 800/922-7900 (SC).* 33 rms, 3 story, 7 suites. Mid-Mar-mid-June, mid-Sept-Nov: S $105-$135; D $130-$150; each addl $15; suites $160-$225; lower rates rest of yr. TV. Complimentary continental bkfst (full bkfst in suites), afternoon refreshments. Restaurant 6-9:30 pm. Bar 4 pm-midnight. Ck-out noon, ck-in 3 pm. Bellhops. Valet serv. Concierge. Fireplace in suites. Located in 1824 structure. Rooftop terrace overlooking harbor. Cr cds: A, DS, MC, V.

★ ★ **VICTORIA HOUSE.** *208 King St (29401). 803/720-2944; res: 800/933-5464; FAX 803/720-2930.* 18 rms, 3 story, 4 suites. Mar-mid-June, Sept-Oct: S $135; D $150; each addl $15; suites $190; under 12 free; lower rates rest of yr. Crib free. TV; cable. Complimentary continental bkfst, wine/sherry. Restaurant adj 8 am-3 pm. Ck-out noon, ck-in 3 pm. Bellhops. Valet serv. Concierge. Health club privileges. Refrigerators. Romanesque period-style building (1889). Cr cds: MC, V.

Resorts

★ ★ **SEABROOK ISLAND.** *(1002 Landfall Way, John's Island 29455) 23 mi SE off US 17. 803/768-1000; res: 800/845-2475; FAX 803/768-4922.* 165 kit. villas, 1-2 story. Mid-Mar-late Oct: 1-bedrm $130-$180; 2-bedrm $155-$240; 3-bedrm $175-$350; wkly, tennis, golf, honeymoon, family plans; lower rates rest of yr. Crib $5. TV; cable. 7 pools; wading pool, lifeguard. Supervised child's activities (Memorial Day-Labor Day). Dining rm 7 am-9 pm. Bar from 11 am. Ck-out 11 am, ck-in 4 pm. Grocery. Convention facilities. Tennis, pro. 36-hole golf, greens fee $65, pro, putting green, driving range. Private beach. Sailboat, windsurfer rentals. Deep sea fishing. Bicycles. Health club privileges. Entertainment. Game rm. Refrigerators; some fireplaces. Private patios, balconies. Sunset cruises avail. Cr cds: A, DS, MC, V.

★ ★ **WILD DUNES.** *Box 20575 (29413), E on US 17, N on SC 703. 803/886-6000; res: 800/845-8880; FAX 803/886-2916.* 280 kit. villas, 1-5 story, 24 cottages. June-Sept: kit. villas, cottages $125-$375; wkly rates; golf plans; lower rates rest of yr. Crib $10. TV; cable. Pools; wading pool, whirlpool, poolside serv, lifeguard. Playground. Free supervised child's activities (June-mid-Sept). Teen club. Dining rm 7 am-midnight. Box lunches, snack bar, picnics. Bar 7 am-midnight; entertainment Tue-Sat. Ck-out 11 am, ck-in 4 pm. Grocery. Package store. Convention facilities. Valet serv. Beauty shop. Gift shop. Sports dir. Lighted tennis, pro. 36-hole golf course, greens fee $29-$90, pro, putting green, driving range. Swimming beach, boats. Bicycles (rentals). Lawn games. Soc dir. Fishing guides. Balconies, lndry facilities. Picnic tables, grills. On beach. Cr cds: A, DS, MC, V.

Restaurants

★ ★ **82 QUEEN.** *82 Queen St. 803/723-7591.* Hrs: 11:30 am-3:30 pm, 6-10 pm; Fri & Sat to 10:30 pm. Res accepted. Bar to 2 am. Semi-a la carte: lunch $4.95-$10, dinner 9.95-$19.95. Specializes in seafood, regional Lowcountry dishes. Outdoor dining. Located in 1800s bldg. Cr cds: A, D, MC, V.

★ ★ **ANSON.** *12 Anson St. 803/577-0551.* Hrs: 5:30-11 pm; Fri & Sat to midnight. Closed Dec 25. Res accepted. Lowcountry menu. Bar. Wine list. A la carte entrees: dinner $12.95-$21.75. Child's meals. Specializes in cashew-crusted grouper, osso buco, crème brulée. Bi-level dining. Decor reminiscent of classical Rome. Cr cds: A, C, D, DS, MC, V.

★ ★ **BARBADOES ROOM.** *(See Mills House Hotel) 803/577-2400.* Hrs: 6:30 am-2 pm, 5:30-10 pm; Sun brunch 11 am-2 pm. Res accepted. Continental menu. Bar 11-2 am. Wine list. Semi-a la carte: bkfst $3-$7.75, lunch $4.95-$7.95, dinner $10.95-$15.95. Prix fixe: dinner $19.95. Sun brunch 14.95. Specializes in she crab soup, seafood, Kahlua mud pie. Own baking. Pianist evenings. Valet parking. Cr cds: A, C, D, DS, JCB, MC, V.

★ ★ **CAROLINA'S.** *10 Exchange St. 803/724-3800.* Hrs: 5:30-11 pm; Thurs-Sat to 12:30 am; Sun 5-10 pm. Res accepted. Bar from 3:30 pm. A la carte entrees: dinner $5.25-$22.95. Specializes in grilled seafood, pasta, regional cuisine. Cr cds: A, MC, V.

★ ★ **CATCH 'N COW.** *(508 Mill St, Mount Pleasant 29464) 3 mi E on US 17. 803/884-8103.* Hrs: 5-10:30 pm; Fri & Sat to 11 pm. Closed Thanksgiving, Dec 25. Res accepted. Bar. Semi-a la carte: dinner $14.95-$29.95. Specializes in seafood, prime beef. Parking. Two levels, overlooking creek and marshes. Cr cds: A, D, DS, MC, V.

★ ★ **GARIBALDI'S.** *49 S Market St. 803/723-7153.* Hrs: 6-11 pm. Closed Dec 25. Italian menu. Serv bar. Semi-a la carte: dinner $7.50-$18.95. Specializes in fresh seafood, pasta, veal. Own desserts. Outdoor dining. Bistro atmosphere; in center of historic Charleston Market. Cr cds: A, MC, V.

✔ ★ ★ **LE MIDI.** *337 King St. 803/577-5571.* Hrs: 11:30 am-2 pm, 6-10 pm; Sat from 6 pm. Closed Sun; Jan 1, Dec 25. French menu. Wine list. Semi-a la carte: lunch $4.95-$8, dinner $12.50-$15.50. Specializes in seafood, rabbit, chicken. Small, brick dining rm. Cr cds: A, D, MC, V.

★ ★ ★ **LOUIS'S CHARLESTON GRILL.** *(See Omni Hotel At Charleston Place)* 803/577-4522. Hrs: 6-11 pm. Res accepted. Bar 4 pm-midnight. Wine cellar. A la carte entrees: dinner $14.50-$22.50. Specializes in crabmeat & lobster cakes, beef, veal, fresh local seafood. Own baking, soups. Jazz trio. Club atmosphere; mahogany-paneled walls, marble floors, courtyard with fountain. Cr cds: A, C, D, MC, V.
D

★ ★ **MAGNOLIA.** *185 E Bay St.* 803/577-7771. Hrs: 11:30 am-11 pm; Fri & Sat to midnight; Sun noon-11 pm. Closed some hols. Res accepted. Bar. Semi-a la carte: lunch, dinner $4.75-$22.50. Specialties: pan-fried chicken livers, skillet grits cake, veal meatloaf. Contemporary decor within historic structure; overlooks Lodge Alley. Cr cds: A, MC, V.

★ ★ **MARIANNE.** *235 Meeting St.* 803/722-7196. Hrs: 6 pm-midnight; Fri & Sat to 1 am; Sun 5-11 pm. Closed Jan 1, Dec 24-25. Res accepted. French menu. Bar. A la carte entrees: dinner $11.95-$22.50. Complete meals: dinner $25.50. Specializes in beef, lamb, seafood. Pianist. French bistro decor. Tableside cooking. Cr cds: A, D, DS, MC, V.

★ ★ ★ **McCRADY'S.** *2 Unity Alley (29401).* 803/853-8484. Hrs: 11:30 am-10:30 pm; Fri to 11 pm; Sat 5:30-11 pm. Closed Sun; July 4, Dec 24 & 25. Bar to midnight. A la carte entrees: lunch, dinner $3.50-$19. Child's meals. Specializes in beef, seafood, veal. Tavern atmosphere in restored building (1788). Wood floors, iron chandeliers, fireplaces. Cr cds: A, D, MC, V.

★ **ONE EYED PARROT.** *(1130 Ocean Blvd, Isle Of Palms 29451)* E on US 17B to SC 703, then S. 803/886-4360. Hrs: 5-10:30 pm; Fri & Sat to 11 pm. Closed Thanksgiving, Dec 25. Bar. Semi-a la carte: dinner $6.95-$24.95. Child's meals. Specializes in seafood, beef, paella. Second floor dining rm overlooking ocean. Cr cds: A, DS, MC, V.

✔ ★ ★ **PAPILLON.** *32 Market St.* 803/723-6510. Hrs: 11 am-11 pm; Fri, Sat to midnight. Northern Italian menu. Semi-a la carte: lunch $4.95-$6.95, dinner $4.95-$14.95. Specializes in grilled seafood, meat pie, pizza baked in wood-burning oven. Own pastries. Trattoria atmosphere. Cr cds: A, C, D, DS, MC, V.

✔ ★ **PIER 61 LTD.** *652 St Andrews Blvd.* 503/571-7533. Hrs: 11:30 am-2:30 pm, 5:30-9 pm; Fri & Sat 5:30-9:30 pm. Closed Sun, Mon; some major hols. Wine, beer. A la carte entrees: lunch $5.50-$8.95, dinner $8.95-$15.95. Specializes in seafood, prime rib. Parking. Nautical decor. Cr cds: MC, V.
D

★ ★ **POOGAN'S PORCH.** *72 Queen St, in historic district.* 803/577-2337. Hrs: 11:30 am-2:30 pm, 5:30-10 pm; Fri, Sat to 10:30 pm. Res accepted. Regional Lowcountry cuisine. Bar. Semi-a la carte: lunch $4.95-$6.95, dinner $10.95-$19.95. Specialties: Cajun shrimp, bread pudding, shrimp creole. Outdoor dining. Restored house (1888); fireplace, garden rm. Intimate dining. Cr cds: A, MC, V.

★ ★ **RESTAURANT MILLION.** *2 Unity Alley.* 803/577-7472. Hrs: 6:30-10 pm. Closed Sun; July 4, Dec 25; also 1st 2 wks Jan. Res required. French, nouvelle cuisine. Bar. Wine cellar. A la carte entrees: dinner $22-$26. Complete meals: dinner $45-$70. Specialties: warm slices of goose liver, fricassée of Maine lobster, desserts. Own baking. Historic 1788 tavern; fireplaces. Classic French decor; antiques, original artwork. Cr cds: A, D, MC, V.

★ ★ **SUPPER AT STACKS.** *(See Guilds Inn)* 803/884-7009. Hrs: 6-10 pm. Closed Sun, Mon; some major hols. Res required. Regional Amer menu. Serv bar. Complete meals: dinner $29. Specializes in roast duck with strawberry/honey sauce, marinated salmon, beef tenderloin. Menu changes daily. Formal dining rm reminiscent of 18th-century Williamsburg, VA. Cr cds: A, MC, V.

★ ★ **VILLAGE CAFE.** *(415 Mill St, Mt Pleasant)* N on US 17. 803/884-8095. Hrs: 11 am-3 pm, 5:30-10 pm; Fri, Sat to 10:30 pm. Closed Thanksgiving, Dec 25. Res accepted. Bar. Wine list. A la carte entrees: lunch $4-$6.75, dinner $9-$21. Child's meals. Specializes in fresh seafood, crabcakes, beef. Own baking. Parking. New England-style wood frame building. Cr cds: A, D, DS, MC, V.

Unrated Dining Spots

PICCADILLY CAFETERIA. *2401 Mall Dr, at Charlestowne Square Mall.* 803/747-5813. Hrs: 11 am-8:30 pm. Closed Dec 25. Avg check: lunch, dinner $4.95. Child's meals. Specializes in seafood, chicken, beef. Cr cds: A, C, D, DS, MC, V.

REUBEN'S DELICATESSEN. *251 Meeting St, at Wentworth St.* 803/722-6883. Hrs: 8 am-4 pm. Closed Jan 1, Easter, Thanksgiving, Dec 25. Wine, beer. A la carte entrees: bkfst, lunch $1.95-$4.95. Specializes in homemade soup, salad, Reuben sandwiches. Cafeteria-style deli located in old building (1880s). No cr cds accepted.
D

Cheraw (C-6)

Settled: 1740 **Pop:** 5,505 **Elev:** 150 ft **Area code:** 803 **Zip:** 29520

Profiting in commerce from both Carolinas, Cheraw grew rapidly when the Pee Dee River was opened for traffic. It is said that the town owes its many trees to an ordinance that required every person seen intoxicated in public to go out into the woods and fetch a tree for planting within the town.

What to See and Do

1. **Historic District.** Comprises 214 acres downtown and contains more than 50 antebellum homes and public buildings, plus structures dating from later periods. The Town Green (ca 1765) is the site of the small Lyceum Museum (ca 1820). Other notable buildings are Town Hall (ca 1855), Market Hall (ca 1835) and the Inglis-McIver Law Office (ca 1810). Free brochures on the district are available at the Chamber office on the Green and at some local shops. Picnicking. Self-guided tours. Phone 537-7681.

2. **Old St David's Episcopal Church** (1768). Front & Church Sts. Restored to the 1820s period; last Anglican parish established in the state prior to the Revolutionary War. Used as a hospital by British during Revolution, later by Union Army during Civil War; about 50 British soldiers are buried in the churchyard. Tours (by appt). Phone 537-8425. **Free.**

3. **Cheraw State Park.** 4 mi SW on US 52. Located on 7,361 acres of gently rolling green sandhills. Lake swimming; boating (rentals); fishing. Nature trails; 18-hole golf. Picnicking (shelters); playground; recreation building. Camping; cabins (hookups, dump station). Standard fees. Unusually cool in hot weather periods. Phone 537-2215.

4. **Cheraw State Fish Hatchery.** 6 mi S via US 1. Propagation of largemouth and smallmouth bass, channel catfish and others. Public aquarium and picnic area. (Daily) Phone 537-7628. **Free.**

(For further information contact the Visitors Bureau, 221 Market St; 537-8425 or -7681.)

Annual Event

Spring Festival. Great Pee Dee Family Fun Run; tours; arts & crafts shows; entertainment, wagon rides, car show. Phone 537-8420. Early Apr.

(For accommodations see Camden, Florence, also see Bennettsville, Darlington, Hartsville)

Chester (C-4)

Settled: 1755 **Pop:** 7,158 **Elev:** 485 ft **Area code:** 803 **Zip:** 29706

Seat of Chester County, this town was named by settlers from Pennsylvania. Aaron Burr, guarded here in 1807 while under arrest for treason, broke away and climbed a high rock. After haranguing a surprised crowd, he was recaptured.

What to See and Do

Chester State Park. 3 mi SW on SC 72. Approx 500 acres. Lake fishing; boating. Nature trail. Picnicking (shelters); recreation building. Camping (hookups, dump station). Equestrian show ring. Standard fees. Phone 385-2680.

(For further information contact the Chester County Chamber of Commerce, 109 Gadsden St, PO Box 489; 581-4142.)

(For accommodations see Rock Hill)

Clemson (C-2)

Founded: 1889 **Pop:** 11,096 **Elev:** 850 ft **Area code:** 803 **Zip:** 29631

Home of Clemson University, this community also hosts vacationers attracted to the huge lake, which the Hartwell Dam has formed on the Savannah River.

What to See and Do

1. **Clemson University** (1889). (17,000 students) 11 mi NW of I-85 at jct US 76, SC 93. Named for Thomas G. Clemson, son-in-law of John C. Calhoun, who bequeathed the bulk of his estate, Fort Hill, for establishment of a scientific college. Phone 656-3311 or -2061. On this 1,400-acre campus are

   Fort Hill (1803). Mansion on 1,100 acres acquired by Calhoun during his first term as Vice-President. House has many original furnishings belonging to Calhoun, Clemson. (Daily; closed some major hols) Sr citizen rate. Phone 656-2475. ¢¢

   Hanover House (1716). This French Huguenot house was moved here from its original site near Pinopolis to prevent submersion by Lake Moultrie. (Wkends) Sr citizen rate. Phone 656-2241. ¢¢

   Botanical Gardens. E side of campus. This 250-acre area includes Azalea and Camelia trails, ornamental plantings, large collection of shrubs; Dwarf Conifer Flower and Turf Display gardens; Wildflower Pioneer and Bog garden is labeled in Braille. (Daily) Phone 656-3405. **Free.**

2. **World of Energy.** 12 mi NW on SC 130, 123. Three-dimensional displays on the "Story of Energy," with exhibits on hydro, coal and nuclear production of electricity; also displays on radiation and supplemental energy sources. Computer games; films. Overlooks Lake Keowee and one of the world's largest nuclear generating plants. Tour of the control room training simulator. Picnic area and boat dock adj. (Daily; closed Jan 1, Thanksgiving, Dec 24-25) Phone 885-4600 or 800/777-1004. **Free.**

3. **Raft trips.** 34 mi NW on US 76 in Long Creek. Guided whitewater rafting trips on the Chattooga National Wild & Scenic River. (Mar-Oct, daily) Reservations required. Also canoe & kayak clinics and overnight trips. Phone 800/451-9972.

4. **Oconee State Park.** 20 mi NW of town, 12 mi NW of Walhalla on SC 107. Approx 1,100 acres of park nestled in the foothills of the Blue Ridge and surrounded by Sumter National Forest (see GREENWOOD). Lake swimming, lifeguard (summer); boating (rentals); fishing. Nature, hiking trails; recreation building; recreation &

nature programs (summer); carpet golf. Picnicking (shelters), playground, concession, restaurant. Camping (hookups, dump station), cabins. Standard fees. Phone 638-5353.

5. **Stumphouse Tunnel Park.** Approx 22 mi NW via US 123 & SC 28, 6 mi N of Walhalla, adj to Sumter National Forest (see GREENWOOD) in the Blue Ridge Mts. Unfinished railroad tunnel, which was being cut in the 1850s, was interrupted by the Civil War. Temperature is always 50°F and the humidity 90%. It rains daily in the #1 shaft, regardless of outdoor weather. Issaqueena Falls, picnicking, shelter. Hiking along old roadbed. Park (daily). Phone 646-3782 or -2506. **Free.**

(For further information contact the Clemson Area Chamber of Commerce, PO Box 202, 29633; 654-1200.)

(See Anderson, Greenville)

Motels

✔ ★ **COMFORT INN.** Box 1496, 1305 Tiger Blvd. 803/653-3600; FAX 803/654-3123. 122 rms, 4 story. S, D $42-$70; each addl $5; suites $73-$125; under 18 free. Crib free. TV; cable. Pool. Complimentary continental bkfst. Restaurant nearby. Ck-out noon. Valet serv. Exercise equipt; weight machine, bicycle, whirlpool, sauna. Cr cds: A, C, D, DS, MC, V.

| D | ⊠ | ✕ | ≋ | ➔ | ⌂ | SC |

★ ★ **HOLIDAY INN.** Box 512 (29633), 1½ mi E on US 123. 803/654-4450; FAX 803/654-8451. 220 rms, 2 story. S $46-$49; D $51-$54; each addl $5; suites $109; under 19 free; higher rates football wkends. Crib free. Pet accepted. TV; cable. Pool. Coffee in rms. Restaurant 6 am-2 pm, 5-10 pm. Bar 4 pm-midnight, closed Sun. Ck-out noon. Coin lndry. Meeting rms. Valet serv. Golf privileges. On lake. Cr cds: A, C, D, DS, JCB, MC, V.

| D | ➤ | ✕ | ≋ | ➔ | ⌂ | SC |

★ ★ **RAMADA INN.** Box 1706 (29633), SC 76 & US 123. 803/654-7501; FAX 803/654-7301. 149 rms, 4 story. S $47-$58; D $54-$65; suites $125-$150; under 18 free; wkend rates; higher rates football wkends. Crib free. TV; cable. Indoor pool; whirlpool, sauna, poolside serv. Restaurant 6:30 am-2 pm, 5-10 pm. Rm serv. Bar exc Sun. Ck-out 1 pm. Meeting rms. Valet serv. Golf privileges. Some refrigerators. Cr cds: A, C, D, DS, MC, V.

| D | ✕ | ✕ | ≋ | ➔ | ⌂ | SC |

Clinton (C-3)

Pop: 7,987 **Elev:** 680 ft **Area code:** 803 **Zip:** 29325

In 1865, Clinton was "a mudhole surrounded by barrooms," according to the young Reverend William Jacobs, who not only rid the town of barrooms but founded a library, orphanage, high school and Presbyterian College (1880). A young attorney by the name of Henry Clinton Young was hired by the townspeople to help lay out the streets, hence the town came to be named for his middle name.

What to See and Do

Rose Hill (ca 1825). 15 mi E on SC 72, 2 mi N on SC 176, then W on Sardis Rd. 44 acres. Located in Rose Hill State Park, this restored cotton plantation was the home of William H. Gist, known as South Carolina's secession governor. Federal-style house with 1860 furnishings sits on a gently rising knoll amid boxwoods and roses. House (Sat & Sun; also by appt). Grounds (Thurs-Mon). Picnic area, nature trail. Phone 427-5966, -9759. Museum ¢; Grounds **free.**

(For further information contact the Laurens County Chamber of Commerce, PO Box 248, Laurens 29360; 833-2716.)

(See Greenville, Greenwood, Newberry, Spartanburg)

Motels

✔ ★ **DAYS INN.** *Jct I-26 & SC 56, exit 52. 803/833-6600; FAX 803/833-6600, ext. 242.* 58 rms, 2 story. S $32-$37; D $43-$45; each addl $5; suites $65; under 12 free. Crib free. Pet accepted. TV; cable. Pool. Complimentary continental bkfst, coffee. Restaurant adj 6:30 am-10 pm. Ck-out 11 am. Coin lndry. Meeting rms. Exercise equipt; weight machine, bicycles. Some refrigerators. Cr cds: A, C, D, DS, MC, V.

★ ★ **HOLIDAY INN.** *Jct SC 56 & I-26, exit 52. 803/833-4900; FAX 803/833-4916.* 101 rms, 2 story. S $52; D $57; each addl $5; under 19 free. TV. Pool. Restaurant 6:30 am-2 pm, 5-9 pm. Rm serv. Bar 5 pm-midnight. Ck-out noon. Coin lndry. Meeting rms. Sundries. Exericise equipt; weight machine, bicycle. Cr cds: A, C, D, DS, MC, V.

Columbia (D-4)

Founded: 1786 **Pop:** 98,052 **Elev:** 213 ft **Area code:** 803

The broad-boulevarded capital of South Carolina is not only the state's political and governmental capital, but also its wholesale and retail trade center. Located within 3 miles of the geographic center of the state, Columbia was laid out as the capital as a compromise between the contending Up Country and Low Country farmers. The city rarely departs from a checkerboard pattern; the streets are sometimes 150 feet wide, planned that way originally to discourage malaria.

The General Assembly met for the first time in the State House in Columbia on January 4, 1790. George Washington was a guest here during his Southern tour the next year. On December 17, 1860, a convention assembled in Columbia's First Baptist Church and drew up the Ordinance of Secession, setting off a chain of events that terminated, for the city, on February 17, 1865, when General William T. Sherman's troops occupied Columbia and reduced it to ashes. An area of 84 blocks and 1,386 buildings was destroyed; on Main St only the unfinished new State House and the home of the French consul were spared. From these ashes, a city of stately buildings has risen.

The economy of the city is based on trade, industry, finance and government.

Since 1801, when the South Carolina College, now the University of South Carolina, was established here, the city has been an educational center; today it is the site of nine schools of higher education.

Columbia is the headquarters for the Francis Marion National Forest (see CHARLESTON) and the Sumter National Forest (see GREENWOOD).

What to See and Do

1. **State House** (begun in 1855). Main & Gervais Sts. Considered one of the most beautiful state capitols. On the front and back porticos are some of the largest monolithic columns in the world, made of blue granite; dome departs from architect's plans, which were destroyed in burning of Columbia. Building was under construction with only the outer walls completed when Sherman shelled the city; metal stars on west and southwest walls mark places struck by shells fired by Union artillery. Memorials, monuments dot landscaped grounds, with additional statues, tablets and portraits inside. (Mon-Fri) Phone 734-2430. **Free.**

2. **Trinity Cathedral** (Episcopal) (1846). 1100 Sumter St, at Senate St, opp Statehouse. Reproduction of Yorkminster, England; the oldest church building in Columbia and one of the largest Episcopal congregations in the US. Hiram Powers baptismal font, box pews, English stained glass. Three Wade Hamptons (a politically prominent South Carolina family) are buried in the churchyard; graves of seven governors and six bishops are also here. In 1977 it became the Cathedral Parish of the Episcopal Diocese of Upper South Carolina. (Spring & fall, Mon-Fri, limited hrs) Phone 771-7300. **Free.**

3. **Town Theatre.** 1012 Sumter St. One of the oldest (since 1919) community theater groups in the US. Broadway plays and musicals. Tours (by appt). Performances (late Sept-late May; also summer show). For tour schedule, ticket information phone 799-2510.

4. **University of South Carolina** (1801). (25,000 students) Located downtown. For campus tour information phone 777-7700 (exc SC) or 800/922-9755 (SC). Points of interest include the Thomas Cooper Library and

   The Horseshoe. Original campus area off Sumter St. Ten of the 11 buildings on the quadrangle date back to the 19th century and are listed in the National Register of Historic Places. Monument erected in 1827 was designed by Robert Mills.

   McKissick Museum. At the head of the Horseshoe. Houses Bernard M. Baruch Silver Gallery with antique European silver, J. Harry Howard gemstone collection, Laurence L. Smith Mineral Library, Catawba Indian pottery collection, Southern Folk Art, historical collections, Art Gallery, Education Museum, Broadcasting Archives. (Daily; closed most major hols, also Dec 24) Phone 777-7251. **Free.**

   Carolina Coliseum. Assembly & Blossom Sts. Houses Gamecock Basketball and other sports events, concerts, exhibitions, trade shows, circuses and other entertainment.

   Koger Center for the Arts. Assembly & Greene Sts. Contemporary structure houses center for the performing arts. Diverse musical, theatrical and dance programs.

5. **South Carolina State Museum.** 301 Gervais St. Located in world's first fully electric textile mill (1894); exhibits on art, natural history, cultural history and science & technology with emphasis on contributions by South Carolinians; numerous hands-on exhibits; dioramas. Included is a center dedicated to Nobel prize-winner Charles Townes, who helped develop the laser. Gift shop. (Mon-Sat, also Sun afternoons; closed Thanksgiving, Dec 25, also morning of Jan 1) Phone 737-4921. **¢¢**

6. **Columbia Museum of Art.** Senate & Bull Sts. Galleries house Renaissance paintings from the collection of Samuel H. Kress; 19th and 20th-century American, emphasizing the Southeast, and European paintings; changing exhibitions drawn from permanent collection and from objects on loan. Concerts, films, lectures and special events accenting exhibitions. (Daily exc Mon; closed Jan 1, Dec 25) Phone 799-2810. **Free.**

   Gibbes Planetarium. Changing shows dealing with various topics; tickets available on day of presentation (Sat & Sun). Phone 254-7827 or 799-2810. **¢¢**

7. **South Carolina Archives Building.** 1430 Senate St. Historical and genealogical research facility with documents dating from 1671; changing exhibits. Research room (Tues-Sat, also Sun afternoons; closed state hols). Tours (by appt). Phone 734-8577. **Free.**

8. **First Presbyterian Church** (1853). 1324 Marion St, at Lady St. First congregation organized in Columbia (1795); President Woodrow Wilson's parents are buried in churchyard. (Daily) Phone 799-9062.

9. **First Baptist Church** (1859). 1306 Hampton St. First Secession Convention, which marked the beginning of the Civil War, met here Dec 17, 1860. (Daily exc Sat; closed hols) Phone 256-4251.

10. **Governor's Mansion** (1855). 800 Richland St. Built as officers' quarters for Arsenal Academy. Tours (Tues-Thurs). Reservations necessary. Phone 737-1710. **Free.**

11. **Woodrow Wilson Boyhood Home** (1872). 1705 Hampton St. Built by Wilson's father; items associated with Wilson's family and

career. (Daily exc Mon; closed most major hols; also 2 wks late Dec) Phone 252-1770. ¢¢

12. **Hampton-Preston Mansion** (1818). 1615 Blanding St. Purchased by Wade Hampton I; occupied by the Hamptons and the family of his daughter, Mrs. John Preston. In February, 1865, it served as headquarters for Union General J.A. Logan. Many Hampton family furnishings and decorative arts of the antebellum period. (Same days as Woodrow Wilson Home) ¢¢

13. **Robert Mills Historic House** (1823) **& Park.** 1616 Blanding St. One of a few residences designed by Robert Mills, Federal architect and designer of the Washington Monument; mantels, art, furnishings of Regency period. (Same days as Woodrow Wilson Home) ¢¢

14. **Riverbanks Zoological Park & Botanical Garden.** 500 Wildlife Pkwy. Exhibits of animals in nonrestrictive natural habitat areas; aquarium-reptile complex with diving demonstrations; birdhouse with daily rainstorm; demonstrations at Riverbanks Farm; penguin and sea lion feedings. (Daily; closed Thanksgiving, Dec 25) Phone 779-8730 (recording) or -8717. ¢¢

15. **Sherman's Battery.** 321 Moffatt Dr, across Congaree River off US 378. Small boulder marks location of guns that shelled present State House and depot.

16. **Lake Murray.** 15 mi NW via I-26, Irmo exit. Lake is 41 miles long, with 520-mile shoreline; impounded by Saluda Dam for hydroelectric purposes. Swimming, waterskiing; boating, fishing; picnicking; camping (fee). Marina in White Rock, 17 mi NW, phone 749-1554. For further information phone 781-5940.

17. **Fort Jackson.** E edge of city, between I-20 & US 76. The most active entry training center for US Army, with 16,000 soldiers assigned. Museum on Jackson Blvd has displays on history of fort and of today's Army. (Tues-Fri, also Sat & Sun afternoons; closed hols) Phone 751-7419 or -7355. **Free.**

18. **Lexington County Museum Complex.** 10 mi W via US 378 at Fox St in Lexington. Historic restoration from mid-1800s; depicts life of area farmer. Period country furnishings, textiles, decorative arts. Spinning and weaving demonstrations. (Daily exc Mon; closed hols) Phone 359-8369. ¢

19. **Sesquicentennial State Park.** 13 mi NE on US 1. 1,445 acres. Log house (1756). Interpretive center. Lake swimming, bathhouse; boating (rentals), fishing. Nature, exercise trails. Picnicking (shelters), playground. Recreation building. Camping (hookups, dump station). Standard fees. Phone 788-2706.

20. **Congaree Swamp National Monument.** 20 mi SE off SC 48. Old-growth, bottomland-hardwood forest, approximately 22,200 acres. Trees and waters teem with wildlife. Fishing, canoeing; hiking trails, boardwalks; public contact station; guided tour (Sat); primitive camping (by permit). (Daily; closed Dec 25) Phone 776-4396. **Free.**

(For further information contact the Greater Columbia Convention & Visitors Bureau, PO Box 15, 29202-0015; 254-0479 or 800/264-4884.)

Annual Event

South Carolina State Fair. Fairgrounds, 1200 Rosewood Dr. Agricultural, floral, home, craft, livestock and commercial exhibits. Entertainment, shows, carnival. Phone 799-3387. Oct 5-15.

(See Camden, Newberry, Orangeburg, Sumter)

Motels

✔ ★ **BUDGETEL INN.** *911 Bush River Rd (29210). 803/798-3222; FAX 803/731-5554.* 102 rms, 3 story. S $34.95-$37.95; D $41.95-$43.95; suites $41.95-$50.95; under 18 free. Crib free. TV; cable. Pool. Complimentary continental bkfst, coffee. Coffee in rms. Restaurant nearby. Ck-out noon. Meeting rms. Valet serv. Cr cds: A, C, D, DS, V.

D ≈ ⋈ 🔥 SC

✔ ★ **BUDGETEL INN.** *1538 Horseshoe Dr (29223), exit 74 to Horseshoe Dr.* 803/736-6400; FAX 803/788-7875. 102 rms, 3 story. S $30.95-$39.95; D $37.95-$46.95. Crib free. TV; cable. Pool. Complimentary continental bkfst. Coffee in rms. Restaurant adj open 24 hrs. Ck-out noon. Coin lndry. Meeting rm. Valet serv. Cr cds: A, C, D, DS, MC, V.

D ≈ ⋈ 🔥 SC

★ ★ ★ **COURTYARD BY MARRIOTT.** *347 Zimalcrest Dr (29210).* 803/731-2300; FAX 803/772-6965. 149 units, 3 story. S $72; up to 4, $82; suites $89; under 12 free; wkend rates. Crib free. TV; cable. Pool. Complimentary coffee in rms. Restaurant 6:30 am-1 pm; wkends 7 am-noon. Bar 4-10 pm. Ck-out noon. Coin lndry. Meeting rms. Valet serv. Exercise equipt; weight machines, bicycles, whirlpool. Refrigerators avail. Cr cds: A, C, D, DS, MC, V.

D ≈ 🏃 ⋈ 🔥 SC

★ ★ **HAMPTON INN WEST.** *I-26 & US 378 (29169).* 803/791-8940; FAX 803/739-2291. 121 rms, 4 story. S $42-$49; D $48-$55; suites $50-$65; under 18 free. Crib free. TV; cable. Pool. Complimentary continental bkfst. Cr cds: A, C, D, DS, MC, V.

D ≈ ⋈ 🔥 SC

★ ★ ★ **HOLIDAY INN-NORTHEAST.** *7510 Two Notch Rd (29223), at I-20.* 803/736-3000; FAX 803/736-6399. 253 rms, 2 story. S, D $49-$75; under 18 free; wkend rates. Crib free. Indoor/outdoor pool; whirlpool, sauna, poolside serv. Restaurant 6:30 am-2 pm, 5-10:30 pm. Rm serv. Bar noon-midnight. Ck-out noon. Coin lndry. Meeting rms. Bellhops. Holidome. Game rm. Courtyard. Cr cds: A, C, D, DS, MC, V.

D ≈ ⋈ 🔥 SC

★ ★ **LA QUINTA.** *1335 Garner Lane (29210).* 803/798-9590; FAX 803/731-5574. 120 rms, 2 story. S $42; D $48; each addl $6; under 18 free. Crib free. TV; cable. Pool. Complimentary continental bkfst. Restaurant adj 11 am-11 pm. Ck-out noon. Meeting rms. Valet serv. Cr cds: A, C, D, DS, MC, V.

D ≈ ⋈ 🔥 SC

✔ ★ ★ **RAMADA INN WEST.** *I-26 & US 378 (29169).* 803/796-2700; FAX 803/796-0166. 99 rms, 2 story. S $29.95-$79; D $35-$79; each addl $8; suite $125; under 18 free. Crib free. TV; cable. Pool; wading pool. Restaurant 7 am-9:30 pm. Rm serv. Bar 5 pm-midnight. Ck-out 11 am. Coin lndry. Meeting rms. Free airport transportation. Exercise equipt; weight machine, treadmill, whirlpool. Cr cds: A, C, D, DS, JCB, MC, V.

D ≈ 🏃 ⋈ 🔥 SC

✔ ★ **RED ROOF INN.** *7580 Two Notch Rd (29223), at I-20 Two Notch Rd exit.* 803/736-0850; FAX 803/736-4270. 109 rms, 2 story. S $30.99-$37.99; D $32.99-$43.99; 3 or more $42.99-$48.99; under 19 free. Crib free. TV. Complimentary coffee in lobby. Restaurant adj 6 am-10 pm. Cr cds: A, C, D, DS, MC, V.

D ⋈ 🔥

★ ★ **RESIDENCE INN BY MARRIOTT.** *150 Stoneridge Dr (29210), off I-126 Greystone Blvd exit.* 803/779-7000; FAX 803/779-7000, ext. 402. 128 kit. suites, 2 story. S $82-$92; D $102-$112; family rates; wkly rates. Crib free. Pet accepted; deposit. TV; cable. Pool; whirlpool. Complimentary continental bkfst. Complimentary coffee in rms. Ck-out noon. Coin lndry. Meeting rms. Valet serv. Health club privileges. Some fireplaces. Some grills. Cr cds: A, C, D, DS, JCB, MC, V.

D 🐾 ≈ ⋈ 🔥 SC

★ **TRAVELODGE COLUMBIA WEST.** *2210 Bush River Rd (29210), at I-20.* 803/798-9665; FAX 803/798-4876. 108 rms, 3 story. S $40; D $45; each addl $5; under 18 free; wkend rates. Crib free. TV; cable. Heated pool. Coffee in rms. Restaurant opp 6 am-10 pm. Ck-out

11 am. Meeting rms. Valet serv. Refrigerators avail. Cr cds: A, C, D, DS, ER, JCB, MC, V.

D ≈ ⊁ ⚒ SC

Motor Hotels

✔ ★ ★ **BEST WESTERN BRADBURY SUITES.** 7525 Two Notch Rd (29223), at I-20. 803/736-6666; FAX 803/788-6011. 112 suites, 6 story. S $39-$69; D $49-$71; each addl $5; under 16 free; wkend rates. Crib free. TV; cable. Pool; whirlpool. Complimentary full bkfst. Restaurant nearby. Ck-out noon. Meeting rms. Valet serv. Refrigerators. Cr cds: A, C, D, DS, JCB, MC, V.

D ≈ ⊁ ⚒ SC

★ ★ ★ **RAMADA HOTEL.** 8105 Two Notch Rd (29223), at I-77. 803/736-5600. 188 units, 6 story. S $62-$66; D $62-$72; suites $90-$220; under 12 free; wkend rates; golf plan. Crib $7. TV; cable. Pool. Restaurant 6:30 am-10:30 pm. Rm serv. Bar 4:30 pm-2 am; dancing. Ck-out noon. Convention facilities. Bellhops. Valet serv. Airport, RR station transportation. Tennis privileges. 18-hole golf privileges. Exercise equipt; weights, bicycles, whirlpool, sauna. Refrigerators in suites. Cr cds: A, C, D, DS, ER, JCB, MC, V.

D ⨉ ⚸ ≈ ⊁ ⚒ SC

★ ★ ★ **THE WHITNEY.** 700 Woodrow St (29205). 803/252-0845; res: 800/637-4008; FAX 803/771-0495. 74 kit. suites, 7 story. 1-bedrm $105; 2-bedrm $125; monthly rates. TV; cable. Pool. Complimentary continental bkfst. Restaurant nearby. Ck-out noon. Meeting rms. Valet serv. Free airport transportation. Exercise equipt; weights, bicycles. Balconies. In residential area. Cr cds: A, C, D, DS, MC, V.

≈ ⊁ ⚒

Hotels

★ ★ ★ **ADAM'S MARK.** 1200 Hampton St (29201). 803/771-7000; FAX 803/254-8307. 300 rms, 13 story. S $99; D $114; each addl $15; suites $195-$395; under 18 free; wkend rates. Crib free. Pet accepted. TV; cable. Indoor pool. Restaurants 6 am-11 pm. Bar 11:30-1 am. Ck-out noon. Convention facilities. Airport transportation. Exercise equipt; weights, bicycles, whirlpool, sauna. Game rm. Some refrigerators. Some balconies. **LUXURY LEVEL : CONCIERGE LEVEL.** 45 rms. S, D $119. Private lounge. Concierge. Complimentary continental bkfst; refreshments 5-9 pm. Cr cds: A, C, D, DS, ER, JCB, MC, V.

D ⚡ ⚶ ≈ ⊁ ⚒ SC

★ ★ ★ **EMBASSY SUITES.** 200 Stoneridge Dr (29210), on I-126 at Greystone Blvd exit. 803/252-8700; FAX 803/256-8749. 214 suites, 7 story. S $104-$124; D $114-$124; each addl $10; under 13 free; wkend rates. Crib free. TV; cable. Indoor pool. Complimentary full bkfst. Complimentary coffee in rms. Restaurant 11 am-10 pm. Bar to 2 am; DJ, dancing Tues-Sat. Ck-out noon. Coin lndry. Meeting rms. Gift shop. Free airport transportation. Exercise equipt; weight machines, bicycles, whirlpool, sauna. Health club privileges. Refrigerators. Atrium lobby; glass-enclosed elvtr. Cr cds: A, C, D, DS, MC, V.

D ≈ ⊁ ⚒ SC

★ ★ ★ **SHERATON HOTEL & CONFERENCE CENTER.** 2100 Bush River Rd (29210). 803/731-0300; FAX 803/731-2839. 238 rms, 5 story. S, D $79-$84; each addl $10; suites $119-$300; under 17 free. Crib free. TV. 2 pools, 1 indoor; whirlpool, sauna. Coffee in rms. Restaurant 6:30 am-10:30 pm. Bars; entertainment. Meeting rms. Gift shop. Airport transportation. Some refrigerators; bathrm phone in suites. Some balconies. Cr cds: A, C, D, DS, ER, MC, V.

D ⚡ ⚶ ≈ ⊁ ⚒ SC

Inns

★ ★ **CLAUSSEN'S.** 2003 Greene St (29205). 803/765-0440; res: 800/622-3382; FAX 803/799-7924. 29 units, 2 story. S $85-$88; D $95-$110; each addl $10; suites $100-$110; under 12 free. Crib free. TV; cable. Complimentary continental bkfst, wine/sherry. Ck-out noon, ck-in 3 pm. Meeting rms. Whirlpool. Refrigerators avail. Private patios. In renovated bakery (1928). Cr cds: A, MC, V.

D ⚶ ⚒ SC

★ ★ **RICHLAND STREET B & B.** 1425 Richland St (29201). 803/779-7001. 7 rms, 2 story, 1 suite. S $69-$99; D $79-$99; each addl $10; suite $120. Children over 12 yrs only. TV; cable. Complimentary continental bkfst. Complimentary tea, coffee in library. Restaurant nearby. Ck-out 11 am, ck-in 3-4 pm. Modern building (1992) in Victorian style. Totally nonsmoking. Cr cds: A, MC, V.

D ⚶ ⚒ SC

Restaurants

★ ★ **AL'S UPSTAIRS.** (304 Meeting St, West Columbia) 1 mi W on US 1. 803/794-7404. Hrs: 5-10 pm. Closed Sun; some major hols. Res accepted. Italian menu. Bar. Semi-a la carte: dinner $11.95-$16.95. Specializes in veal, lemon sole, seafood, fettucine, Italian cream cheesecake. Parking. Overlooks river. Views of Columbia's skyline. Cr cds: A, D, MC, V.

★ ★ **GARIBALDI'S.** 2013 Greene St. 803/771-8888. Hrs: 5:30-10:30 pm; Fri, Sat to 11 pm. Res accepted. Italian menu. Bar. A la carte entrees: dinner $5.95-$21. Specializes in fish, veal, steak, pasta. Parking. Art deco furnishings. Cr cds: A, MC, V.

★ ★ ★ **HENNESSY'S.** 1649 Main St. 803/799-8280. Hrs: 11:30 am-2:30 pm, 6-10 pm; Fri to 11 pm; Sat 6-11 pm. Closed Sun; hols. Res accepted. Continental menu. Bar. Semi-a la carte: lunch $4.95-$9.95, dinner $9.95-$23.95. Specializes in steak, prime rib, fresh seafood. Converted hardware store. Cr cds: A, C, D, MC, V.

D

★ ★ ★ **LE PETIT CHATEAU.** 4423 Devine St (US 76), at Beltline Blvd. 803/782-7231. Hrs: 6-11 pm. Closed Sun, Mon; Thanksgiving, Dec 24, 25; also wk of July 4. Res accepted. French menu. Serv bar. Semi-a la carte: dinner $10.95-$18.95. Specializes in roast duckling, seafood, veal. Cr cds: A, C, D, MC, V.

Unrated Dining Spot

MORRISON'S CAFETERIA. Bush River Rd, in Dutch Square Shopping Center. 803/772-9000. Hrs: 11 am-8:30 pm. Avg ck: lunch $4.75, dinner $5.05. Cr cds: MC, V.

Darlington (D-6)

Founded: 1798 **Pop:** 7,311 **Elev:** 157 ft **Area code:** 803 **Zip:** 29532

Darlington is situated in one of the most fertile sections of the state. Along with its agricultural economy, the area has diversified industry. Darlington was a pioneer in the culture and marketing of tobacco as a cash crop and has a large tobacco market. It is the home of what is said to be the nation's largest automobile auction market and is a stock car racing center.

What to See and Do

NMPA Stock Car Hall of Fame/Joe Weatherly Stock Car Museum. 1 mi W on SC 34 at Darlington International Raceway, the second-oldest major speedway in the country. Museum said to house largest collection of race cars in the world. Major automotive companies have displays tracing the evolution of the racing stock car and accessories from 1950 to present; cars, engines & trophies of famous drivers. (Daily; closed Dec 25) Phone 393-2103. ¢

(For further information contact the Darlington County Chamber of Commerce, Box 274; 393-2641.)

Annual Events

"**TransSouth Financial 500.**" Darlington Raceway. Late-model stock car race. Late Mar.

"**Southern 500.**" Darlington Raceway. 500-mi stock car classic; also beauty pageant, "Southern 500" Festival parade; golf tournament. Preceded by 2 days of trials. Labor Day wknd.

(For accommodations see Florence, also see Bennettsville, Cheraw, Hartsville)

Dillon (C-6)

Settled: 1887 **Pop:** 6,829 **Elev:** 115 ft **Area code:** 803 **Zip:** 29536

Industrial growth and diversification characterize this town. The county seat, Dillon also serves as a shipping center for farm produce.

What to See and Do

Little Pee Dee State Park. 11 mi SE between SC 9 & 57, near I-95. Approx 800 acres on Little Pee Dee River. Swimming; boating (rentals); fishing (bream). Nature trails. Picnicking (shelters); playground. Camping (hookups, dump station). Standard fees. Phone 774-8872.

(For accommodations see Florence, also see Bennettsville, Darlington)

Florence (D-6)

Settled: 1890 **Pop:** 29,813 **Elev:** 149 ft **Area code:** 803

Since extensive railroad shops and yards were established here by the Atlantic Coast Line, this community has grown from a sparsely settled crossroads into a major retail and wholesale distribution center. The economy is no longer dependent on agriculture; a balance of farm and industry has been attained. Florence is also the home of Francis Marion College and Florence-Darlington Technical College.

What to See and Do

1. **Florence Museum.** 558 Spruce St, at Graham St. Art, history and science exhibits. Southwest Native American pottery; Oriental & African collections; Catawba pottery; furniture gallery of mixed periods; South Carolina Hall of History. (Daily exc Mon; closed major hols) Phone 662-3351. **Free.**

2. **Timrod Park.** Timrod Park Dr & S Coit St. One-room schoolhouse in which Henry Timrod, Poet Laureate of the Confederacy, taught. Playgrounds, picnic areas, barbecue pits; lighted tennis courts. Azalea display in spring. Test rose gardens. Nature trails; fitness station, jogging trail. Special fitness court for the disabled. (Daily) Phone 665-3253. **Free.**

3. **Air & Missile Museum.** Airport entrance, 2 mi E on US 76/301 or from I-95 exit 170, follow signs. Display of 38 aircraft and missiles includes jets, cargo plane, Bomarc missile, Titan I missile, German V2 rocket, B-47 bomber; Alan Shepard's Apollo space suit; heat tiles from space shuttle *Columbia.* Approximately 2,000 displays in building. (Daily) Sr citizen rate. Phone 665-5118. ¢¢

4. **Beauty Trail.** Twelve-mile trail within city featuring beautiful gardens (usually best in Apr). **Free.**

5. **National Military Cemetery.** S on US 52/301 to Cherokee Rd. Burial ground for Union soldiers who died here in prison.

6. **City parks.**

Lucas Park. Santee Dr & Azalea Ln. Picnicking, playground; tennis courts. Rose gardens, camellias, azaleas, rhododendrons; lighted fountain. **Free.**

Jeffries Creek Nature Park. Deberry Blvd. Fishing. Nature trails. Picnicking, playground. **Free.**

McLeod Park. Santiago Dr. Swimming pool (fee), fishing pond. Lighted tennis; basketball courts, ball fields. Picnicking, playground.

7. **Lynches River State Park.** 15 mi S off US 52. Approx 650 acres. Located on old stagecoach route. Swimming pool (fee); fishing. Nature trail; bird-watching. Picnicking; playground, community building. Primitive camping. Phone 389-2785.

8. **Woods Bay State Park.** 24 mi SW, off US 301 and I-95. Approx 1,500 acres of unique natural area with an abundance of wildlife, including alligators, in a "Carolina Bay" (an elliptical, swampy depression mostly underwater). Lake fishing, canoe trail (rentals). Picnic area (shelter). Boardwalk for nature and wildlife observation. Phone 659-4445.

(For further information contact the Greater Florence Chamber of Commerce, 610 W Palmetto St, PO Box 948, 29503; 665-0515.)

Annual Event

Arts Alive. Francis Marion University. Arts, crafts, music, dance, theater, demonstrations, exhibits. Phone 661-1225. Apr.

(See Darlington, Dillon, Hartsville)

Motels

★ **COMFORT INN.** *Box 5688 (29502), Jct I-95 & US 52.* 803/665-4558. 165 rms, 2 story. S $35.95; D $42.95-$49.95; each addl $4; under 18 free. Crib free. TV; cable. Pool. Complimentary continental bkfst. Restaurant adj. Ck-out 11 am. Meeting rm. Valet serv. Exercise equipt; weights, bicycles, whirlpool. Some in-rm whirlpools. Cr cds: A, C, D, DS, ER, JCB, MC, V.

[D] [≈] [✗] [↑] [🔥] [SC]

✔ ★ **DAYS INN.** *2111 W Locust St (29501), jct I-95 & US 52.* 803/665-4444. 64 rms, 2 story. S $35-$50; D $38-$60; each addl $4; under 12 free; higher rates: race wkends, hols. Crib free. Pet accepted, some restrictions. TV; cable. Pool. Complimentary continental bkfst, coffee. Restaurant adj 6 am-midnight. Ck-out 11 am. Meeting rms. Exercise equipt; weights, bicycles, whirlpool, sauna. Some in-rm whirlpools, refrigerators. Cr cds: A, C, D, DS, MC, V.

[D] [✔] [≈] [✗] [↑] [🔥] [SC]

★ ★ ★ **RAMADA INN.** *2038 W Lucas (29501).* 803/669-4241; FAX 803/665-8883. 179 rms, 2 story. S, D $54-$60; each addl $6; suites $70-$115; under 18 free; higher rates special events. Crib free. TV; cable. Pool. Restaurant 6 am-2 pm, 5-10 pm. Rm serv. Bar; entertainment, dancing. Ck-out noon. Meeting rms. Bellhops. Exercise equipt; weights, bicycles, whirlpool. Cr cds: A, C, D, DS, MC, V.

[D] [≈] [✗] [↑] [🔥] [SC]

✔ ★ **RED ROOF INN.** *2690 David McLeod Blvd (29501).* 803/678-9000; FAX 803/667-1267. 112 rms, 2 story. S $29.95-$30.95; D $35.95-$36.95; each addl $6; under 18 free; higher rates special events. Crib free. Pet accepted. TV. Complimentary coffee in lobby. Restaurant adj open 24 hrs. Ck-out noon. Picnic tables. Cr cds: A, C, D, DS, MC, V.

[D] [✔] [↑] [🔥] [SC]

✔ ★ ★ **TRAVELERS INN.** Box 4540 (29502), at jct I-95 & US 52, exit 164. 803/665-2575; res: 800/847-7666. 168 rms, 2 story, 24 suites. S $28.95; D $37.95; each addl $4; suites $40.95-$49.95; under 10 free. TV; cable. Pool; whirlpool. Restaurant open 24 hrs. Bar 5 pm-2 am; entertainment, dancing exc Sun. Ck-out 11 am. Exercise equipt; weight machine, bicycle. Picnic tables. Cr cds: A, C, D, DS, MC, V.

⊵ 🏃 ⊠ 🔥 **SC**

Fort Sumter National Monument (F-6)

On an island in Charleston harbor. Accessible by private boat or by Fort Sumter Tour Boat, leaving Municipal Yacht Basin, Lockwood Blvd, Charleston (see) and from Patriots Point Naval Museum, Mt Pleasant (see CHARLESTON).

The national monument includes Fort Sumter, located 3 miles southeast of Charleston at the harbor entrance, and Fort Moultrie, located one mile east of Fort Sumter on Sullivan's Island. Fort Moultrie is reached via US 17 to SC 703; turn right and follow signs. Fort Moultrie was originally built in 1776, of sand and palmetto logs. Colonel William Moultrie's forces drove British ships from Charleston Harbor at Fort Moultrie in June, 1776. The present Fort Moultrie was completed in 1809 and was garrisoned by Union forces in late 1860, when these forces were moved to Fort Sumter.

South Carolina, first state to secede, passed its Ordinance of Secession December 20, 1860. Surrender of Fort Sumter was demanded on April 11, 1861. This demand was refused by Major Robert Anderson, in command of Union forces at the fort. At 4:30 am, April 12, Confederate firing began, and the fort was surrendered after 34 hours of intense bombardment. This attack compelled President Lincoln to call for 75,000 volunteers to put down the rebellion, thus beginning the Civil War. Fort Sumter and Fort Moultrie have been modified through the years. Both were active through World War II.

Fort Moultrie has been restored by the National Park Service; Visitor Center has an audiovisual program depicting the evolution of seacoast defense. (Daily; closed Dec 25) Self-guided tour. **Free.**

Fort Sumter's ruins have been partially excavated, and a museum has been established. (Daily; closed Dec 25) Contact the Superintendent, 1214 Middle St, Sullivan's Island 29482; 813/883-3123 or -3124. **Free.** Daily tour boat (fee).

(For accommodations see Charleston, Kiawah Island)

Gaffney (C-4)

Settled: 1803 **Pop:** 13,145 **Elev:** 779 ft **Area code:** 803 **Zip:** 29340

Once a prosperous resort town where plantation owners sought to cure malaria attacks with the supposedly therapeutic waters of the limestone springs, Gaffney is now a textile and metalworking center and the home of a variety of other industries and agricultural products, particularly peaches. On I-85, just outside of town, stands the Gaffney Peachoid (1981), an elevated tank that resembles a gigantic peach and holds a one million-gallon water supply.

What to See and Do

1. **Cowpens National Battlefield.** 11 mi NW on SC 11, 1/2 mi from jct SC 110. Scene of victory of General Daniel Morgan's American Army over superior British forces on Jan 17, 1781. The British suffered 110 men killed, 200 wounded, 550 captured, while the American losses were minimal. This victory was followed by the Battle of Guilford Courthouse, and then the forces moved on to Yorktown, where Cornwallis was forced to surrender. An 843-acre tract with exhibits, Information and Visitor Center, self-guided tour road and walking trail with audio stations and restored 1830 historic house. Slide program (fee). Picnicking (shelters). (Daily; closed Jan 1, Dec 25) Phone 461-2828. **Free.**

2. **Kings Mountain National Military Park** (see). 20 mi NE off I-85.

(For further information and a list of historic sites contact the Cherokee County Chamber of Commerce, 225 S Limestone St, Box 1119, 29342; 489-5721.)

Annual Event

South Carolina Peach Festival. Arts & crafts, sports events, entertainment. Mid-July.

(See Rock Hill, Spartanburg; also see Charlotte, NC)

Motel

✔ ★ **COMFORT INN.** I-85 & SC 11, exit 92. 803/487-4200. 83 rms, 2 story. S $42; D $47; each addl $5; under 18 free; higher rates special events. Crib $6. TV; cable. Pool. Complimentary continental bkfst, coffee. Ck-out 11 am. Meeting rms. Exercise equipt; weight machines, bicycle, whirlpool. Refrigerators. Cr cds: A, C, D, DS, MC, V.

D ⊵ 🏃 ⊠ 🔥 **SC**

Inn

★ **WHITE HOUSE INN.** (607 W Pine St, Blacksburg 29702) N on I-85 to exit 102, then 2 blks W. 803/839-3000. 4 rms (2 share bath), 3 story. Phone avail. S, D $70-$120; each addl $10. Children over 12 yrs only. TV; cable. Complimentary full bkfst, afternoon tea/sherry. Ck-out noon, ck-in 3 pm. Renovated Greek-revival house built 1926. Many antiques and collectibles. Cr cds: MC, V.

⊠ 🔥

Georgetown (E-6)

Founded: 1729 **Pop:** 9,517 **Elev:** 10 ft **Area code:** 803 **Zip:** 29440

A seaport throughout its long history, Georgetown enjoyed a resurgence of ship traffic following the deepening of the channel and the building of a new cargo dock. The shore of Winyah Bay, on which Georgetown is situated, was the site of the first European settlement on the North American mainland outside of Mexico. In 1526 a group of Spaniards settled here, only to be driven out within a year by disease and Indian attacks. Rice and indigo plantations were established along nearby rivers about 1700. Georgetown was founded by Rev. Elisha Screven, son of the first Baptists in the South; the city was finally laid out to honor King George II of England. It became increasingly important as an export center with quantities of lumber and naval stores, rice and indigo. Lafayette landed near here to join the American cause in the Revolution. The city was later occupied by British troops. Known as a sawmill city during the first three decades of this century, Georgetown presently boasts several manufacturing industries as well as a thriving tourist economy.

What to See and Do

1. **Town Clock Building** (rebuilt 1842). Front & Screven Sts. Tablet marks landing of Lafayette at North Island in 1777; Federal troops came ashore on the dock at the rear of building in an attempt to capture the town. Inside is

   Rice Museum. Maps, dioramas, artifacts and exhibits depict development and production of crop that was once the basis of

Georgetown's economy. (Daily exc Sun; closed hols) Phone 546-7423. ¢

2. **Prince George, Winyah Church** (ca 1750). Broad & Highmarket Sts. English stained-glass window behind altar was originally a part of St Mary's Chapel for Negroes at Hagley Plantation on Waccamaw. In continuous use except during Revolutionary and Civil wars. Tours. (Mon-Fri) Phone 546-4358. **Free.**

3. **Harold Kaminski House** (ca 1760). 1003 Front St. Pre-Revolutionary house furnished with antiques. Tours. (Mon-Fri; closed legal hols) Phone 546-7706. ¢¢

4. **Hopsewee Plantation** (ca 1740). 12 mi S on US 17. Preserved rice plantation house on North Santee River. Birthplace of Thomas Lynch, Jr, signer of Declaration of Independence. Grounds (daily). House (Mar-Oct, Tues-Fri; rest of yr, by appt). Phone 546-7891. ¢¢¢

5. **Brookgreen Gardens.** 18 mi N on US 17, 3 mi S of Murrells Inlet. On site of former rice and indigo plantation; more than 450 pieces of American sculpture in garden; boxwood, massive moss-hung oaks, native plants; wildlife park with native animals. Picnicking. (Daily; closed Dec 25) Phone 237-4218. ¢¢

6. **Hampton Plantation State Park.** 1950 Rutledge Rd, McClellanville; 20 mi S off US 17. Restored 18th-century mansion was centerpiece of large rice plantation; ancestral home of Rutledge family. Guided tours, special programs. (Thurs-Mon) Phone 546-9361. Mansion ¢

7. **Huntington Beach State Park.** 17 mi N on US 17, 3 mi S of Murrells Inlet. Approx 2,500 acres. Ocean swimming; surf fishing. Hiking, nature trails; marsh boardwalk. Picnicking (shelters); playground; concession. Camping. Standard fees (higher Apr-Sept). Phone 237-4440. ¢¢ (per vehicle) Also here is

   Atalaya. Former home and studio of the sculptress Anna Hyatt Huntington. (June-Labor Day; daily) Art festival (one wkend late Sept). ¢

8. **Fishing.** Charter boats from docks. Channel fishing for bass or deep-sea fishing for barracuda, amberjack, albacore, bonito, mackerel. (Apr-Nov)

9. **Captain Sandy's Tours.** Leaves from foot of Broad on Front St. One-hour trip through historic district; one stop. (Mon-Fri; closed July 4, Labor Day, Dec 25) Phone 527-4106. ¢¢¢

(For further information contact the Georgetown County Chamber of Commerce, PO Box 1776, 29442; 546-8436.)

(See Myrtle Beach)

Motel

★ ★ **CLARION CARRIAGE HOUSE-CAROLINIAN INN.** *706 Church St (US 17).* 803/546-5191; FAX 803/546-1514. 89 rms, 1-2 story. May-Aug: S $54-$59; D $59-$64; each addl $10; under 18 free; higher rates wk of July 4; lower rates rest of yr. Crib $5. TV; cable. Pool. Complimentary continental bkfst. Restaurant 5-10 pm; closed Sun. Ck-out 11 am. Meeting rms. Cr cds: A, C, D, DS, JCB, MC, V.

Inns

★ ★ ★ **1790 HOUSE.** *630 Highmarket St.* 803/546-4821. 6 rms, 4 with shower only, 3 story, 1 suite. Mar-Oct: S, D $65-$115; each addl $25; suite $95; lower rates rest of yr. TV; cable. Complimentary full bkfst. Complimentary tea/sherry. Restaurant nearby. Ck-out 11 am, ck-in 2 pm. Golf privileges. Built 1790; West Indies-style architecture. Antiques. Totally nonsmoking. Cr cds: A, DS, MC, V.

✔ ★ ★ **SHAW HOUSE INN.** *613 Cypress Court.* 803/546-9663. 3 rms, 2 story. S, D $45-$55. Crib free. TV; cable. Complimentary full bkfst. Complimentary tea/sherry, coffee in library. Ck-out 1 pm, ck-in

after 1 pm. Tennis privileges. Golf privileges. Greek-revival architecture; overlooks Willowbrook Marsh. Antiques. No cr cds accepted.

Greenville (C-3)

Founded: 1797 **Pop:** 58,282 **Elev:** 966 ft **Area code:** 803

Greenville has several hundred manufacturing plants producing clothing, nylon, chemicals, plastic film and machinery. It is best known for its numerous textile plants. Yet the town is also well named—beautiful trees line the streets, and there are many forested parks in the area. The Reedy River, passing over falls in the heart of Greenville, originally provided the city's power. Pleasant streets now border the twisting sylvan stream.

What to See and Do

1. **Bob Jones University** (1927). (5,000 students) At jct US 29, SC 291. During academic year, university offers vesper concerts (twice/month, Sun). Multimedia presentation (daily; closed hols). Tours. Phone 242-5100. On campus are

   Bob Jones University Collection of Religious Art. Houses collection of rare Biblical material and collection of sacred art, including works by Botticelli, Veronese, Rembrandt, Rubens. Under 6 years not permitted. (Daily exc Mon; closed Jan 1, July 4, Dec 20-25) **Free.**

   Mack Memorial Library. Contains Archives Room and Jerusalem Chamber, display area for the university's collection of rare Bibles.

2. **Greenville County Museum of Art.** 420 College St. Permanent collection of American art, featuring historical and contemporary works. Changing exhibits include painting, sculpture, photography. Lectures, tours. Museum (daily exc Mon; closed most hols). Phone 271-7570. **Free.**

3. **Greenville Zoo.** 1200 blk E Washington St. Picnicking, concessions. Lighted tennis courts, ball field; nature, jogging, hiking and bicycle trails; park. (Daily; closed Jan 1, Thanksgiving, Dec 25) Phone 467-4300. ¢¢

4. **State Parks.**

   Caesar's Head. 30 mi NW via US 276. Approx 7,000 acres. At 3,208 feet above sea level, the park overlooks a valley of almost impenetrable brush and dense forest. One side of the mountain resembles Caesar's head. Raven Cliff Falls. Scenic overlook. Hiking trails. Picnicking (shelter). Trailside camping, store, special programs. Standard fees. Phone 836-6115.

   Paris Mountain. 6 mi N off US 276 & SC 253. Approx 1,000 acres with 3 lakes. Thick forest setting with swiftly flowing streams. Lake swimming; fishing; pedal boats (rentals). Nature, hiking trail. Picnicking, playground. Camping (hookups, dump station). Standard fees. Phone 244-5565.

   Table Rock. 16 mi N on US 25, then 15 mi W on SC 11. Approx 3,000 acres. Extends over Table Rock Mt (elev 3,124 ft) and valleys. Lake swimming; fishing; boating, canoeing (rentals). Hiking trail; carpet golf. Picnicking, restaurant, store. Camping (hookups, dump station), cabins; recreation building. Nature center; nature & recreation programs. Standard fees. Phone 878-9813.

(For further information contact the Greater Greenville Chamber of Commerce, 24 Cleveland St, Box 10048, 29603; 242-1050.)

Annual Event

Freedom Weekend Aloft. More than 200 balloonists compete. Phone 232-3700. July 4 wkend.

(See Anderson, Clemson, Clinton, Spartanburg)

Motels

✔ ★ **COLONIAL INN.** *Box 2323 (29602), 755 Wade Hampton Blvd, 1 mi N on US 29.* 803/233-5393; FAX 803/233-6014. 109 rms, 1-2 story. S $28-$34; D $32-$40; each addl $2; under 16 free. Crib $3. TV; cable. Pool. Restaurant 7 am-2 pm, 5:30-9 pm; Sun 7 am-2 pm. Rm serv. Ck-out noon. Meeting rms. Bellhops. Valet serv. Exercise equipt; weights, bicycles. Cr cds: A, C, D, MC, V.

★ ★ ★ **COURTYARD BY MARRIOTT.** *70 Orchard Park Dr (29615).* 803/234-0300; FAX 803/234-0296. 146 rms, 3 story. S $74; D $84; suites $84-$94. Crib free. TV; cable. Heated pool. Complimentary coffee in rms. Restaurant 6:30-10:30 am, Sat & Sun 7-11 am. Coin lndry. Meeting rms. Valet serv. Exercise equipt; weights, bicycles, whirlpool. Refrigerator in suites. Cr cds: A, C, D, DS, MC, V.

✔ ★ ★ **FAIRFIELD INN BY MARRIOTT.** *60 Roper Mountain Rd (29607), I-385 exit 37.* 803/297-9996; FAX 803/297-9996, ext. 709. 132 rms, 3 story. S $37.95-$43.95; D $43.95-$49.95; each addl $3; under 18 free. Crib free. TV; cable. Pool. Complimentary coffee in lobby. Complimentary continental bkfst. Restaurant nearby. Ck-out noon. Meeting rm. Cr cds: A, D, DS, MC, V.

★ ★ **HAMPTON INN.** *246 Congaree Rd (29607), off I-385.* 803/288-1200; FAX 803/288-5667. 123 rms, 4 story. S $47-$55; D $53-$60; under 18 free. Crib free. TV. Pool. Complimentary continental bkfst. Ck-out noon. Meeting rm. Cr cds: A, C, D, DS, MC, V.

★ ★ **LA QUINTA.** *31 Old Country Road (29607).* 803/297-3500; FAX 803/458-9818. 122 rms, 2 story. S $42; D $48; under 18 free. Crib free. Pet accepted. TV; cable. Pool. Complimentary continental bkfst in lobby. Restaurant adj 6 am-10 pm. Ck-out noon. Coin lndry. Meeting rms. Valet serv. Free airport transportation. Health club privileges. Cr cds: A, C, D, DS, MC, V.

★ **QUALITY INN-HAYWOOD.** *50 Orchard Park Dr (29615).* 803/297-9000; FAX 803/297-8292. 147 rms, 2 story. S $47; D $53; each addl $6; suites $69; kit. unit $75; under 18 free; higher rates Textile Show. Crib $6. TV; cable. Pool. Complimentary continental bkfst. Complimentary coffee in rms. Ck-out noon. Meeting rms. Valet serv. Health club privileges. Cr cds: A, C, D, DS, JCB, MC, V.

★ **RESIDENCE INN BY MARRIOTT.** *48 McPrice Ct (29615).* 803/297-0099; FAX 803/288-8203. 96 kit. suites, 2 story. S, D $89-$109; wkly, monthly rates. Crib free. Pet accepted; some restrictions; $50 non-refundable. TV; whirlpool. Complimentary continental bkfst. Restaurant adj 11:30 am-11 pm. Ck-out noon. Meeting rms. Private patios, balconies. Cr cds: A, C, D, DS, MC, V.

✔ ★ **TRAVELODGE.** *831 Congaree Rd (29607).* 803/288-6221; FAX 803/288-2778. 124 rms, 5 story. S, D $43-$47; each addl $6; suites $65; under 18 free; wknd rates; higher rates special events. Crib free. TV; cable. Pool. Complimentary continental bkfst. Complimentary coffee in rms. Restaurant adj 6 am-10 pm. Ck-out 11 am. Meeting rms. Health club privileges. Cr cds: A, C, D, DS, ER, JCB, MC, V.

Motor Hotels

★ ★ **HOLIDAY INN.** *4295 Augusta Rd (29605), I-85 exit 45-A.* 803/277-8921; FAX 803/299-6066. 153 rms, 5 story. S, D $68-$75; each addl $6; suites $95; under 18 free; higher rates special events.

Crib free. TV; cable. Pool. Complimentary coffee in rms. Restaurant 7 am-2 pm, 5-10 pm. Rm serv. Bar 4 pm-midnight. Ck-out noon. Meeting rms. Bellhops. Valet serv. Free airport transportation. Health club privileges. Cr cds: A, C, D, DS, ER, JCB, MC, V.

★ ★ **RAMADA.** *1001 S Church St (29601).* 803/232-7666; FAX 803/232-7666, ext. 200. 142 rms, 6 story. S $49-$55; D $55-$61; each addl $6; suites $81-$143; under 18 free; wknd rates. Crib free. TV; cable, in-rm movies. Pool. Restaurant 6:30 am-10 pm. Bar 4 pm-midnight; dancing. Ck-out noon. Airport transportation. Exercise equipt; weights, bicycles. Cr cds: A, C, D, DS, ER, JCB, MC, V.

Hotels

★ ★ ★ **EMBASSY SUITES.** *670 Verdae Blvd (29607).* 803/676-9090; FAX 803/676-0669. 268 suites, 9 story. S $104; D $114; each addl $10; under 18 free. Crib free. TV; cable. 2 pools; 1 indoor. Complimentary coffee in rms. Complimentary full bkfst. Restaurant 11 am-10 pm. Bar 11 am-midnight. Coin lndry. Convention facilities. Gift shop. Free airport transportation. 18-hole golf privileges; pro, greens fee $44, putting green, driving range. Exercise equipt; weights, bicycles, whirlpool, sauna. Refrigerators. Cr cds: A, C, D, DS, MC, V.

★ ★ ★ **HILTON.** *45 W Orchard Park Dr (29615).* 803/232-4747; FAX 803/235-6248. 256 rms, 9 story. S, D $86-$116; suites $195-$295; family, wkend rates. Crib free. TV; cable. Indoor pool; poolside serv. Restaurant 6 am-11 pm. Bar 4:30 pm-2 am; entertainment, dancing exc Sun. Ck-out 1 pm. Convention facilities. Concierge. Gift shop. Airport, RR station, bus depot transportation. Exercise equipt; weight machines, bicycles, whirlpool, sauna. Refrigerator in suites. *LUXURY LEVEL : CONCIERGE FLOOR.* 33 rms, 3 suites. S $116; D $126; suites $225. Private lounge, honor bar. Complimentary continental bkfst, refreshments. Cr cds: A, C, D, DS, ER, MC, V.

★ ★ ★ **HOLIDAY INN-HAYWOOD AREA.** *I-385 & Roper Mountain Rd (29607).* 803/297-6300; FAX 803/234-0747. 208 rms, 6 story. S $92; D $97-$102; each addl $7; suites $119-$190; under 18 free; wkend rates. TV; cable. Indoor pool; whirlpool, poolside serv. Coffee in rms. Restaurant 6:30 am-2 pm, 5-10 pm. Bar 11-2 am, closed Sun; dancing. Ck-out noon. Meeting rms. Free airport transportation. Exercise equipt; treadmills, weight machine. Golf privileges. Some refrigerators. Cr cds: A, C, D, DS, JCB, MC, V.

★ ★ ★ **HYATT REGENCY.** *220 N Main St (29601).* 803/235-1234; FAX 803/232-7584. 327 rms, 8 story. S $105; D $135; each addl $25; suites $125-$475; under 18 free; wkend rates. Crib free. Covered parking $4. TV; cable. Pool; poolside serv. Restaurants 6:30 am-11 pm. Bar, closed Sun. Ck-out noon. Convention facilities. Shopping arcade. Free airport transportation. Indoor tennis privileges. Golf privileges. Exercise equipt; weight machine, bicycles, whirlpool. Cr cds: A, C, D, DS, JCB, MC, V.

★ ★ ★ **MARRIOTT AIRPORT.** *One Parkway East (29615), near Greenville/Spartanburg Airport.* 803/297-0300; res: 800/441-1737; FAX 803/281-0801. 204 rms, 7 story. S $109; D $119; each addl $10; under 18 free; higher rates Textile Show. Crib free. TV; cable. 2 pools, 1 indoor; poolside serv. Restaurant 6:30 am-10 pm. Bar 3:30 pm-1 am, Sat to midnight, closed Sun; entertainment, dancing. Ck-out noon. Convention facilities. Concierge. Free airport transportation. Tennis privileges. 18-hole golf privileges. Exercise equipt; weight machine, bicycles, whirlpool, sauna. *LUXURY LEVEL : CONCIERGE LEVEL.* 25 rms, 4 suites. S,D $119; suites $200-$350. Concierge. Private lounge, honor bar. Complimentary continental bkfst, refreshments. Cr cds: A, C, D, DS, ER, JCB, MC, V.

Restaurants

★ ★ **OPEN HEARTH.** *(2801 Wade Hampton Blvd, Taylors)* 5 *mi N on US 29.* 803/244-2665. Hrs: 5:30-10:30 pm. Closed Sun; major hols. Res accepted Fri, Sat. Bar. Semi-a la carte: dinner $7.95-$25.95. Child's meals. Specializes in aged steak, fresh seafood, Greek salad. Family-owned. Cr cds: A, C, D, DS, MC, V.

★ ★ ★ **SEVEN OAKS.** *104 Broadus Ave.* 803/232-1895. Hrs: 6-10 pm. Closed Sun; some major hols. Res accepted. Continental menu. Bar. Wine cellar. A la carte entrees: dinner $14.95-$25.50. Specializes in veal, fresh seafood, beef, lamb. Own baking. Parking. Outdoor dining. Beautifully restored 1895 mansion; eight fireplaces. Cr cds: A, D, MC, V.

★ ★ ★ **STAX'S PEPPERMILL.** *30 Orchard Pk Dr.* 803/288-9320. Hrs: 11:30 am-2:30 pm, 6-11 pm; Mon from 6 pm; Fri 11:30 am-2:30 pm, 6 pm-midnight; Sat 6 pm-midnight. Closed Sun; most major hols. Res accepted. Continental menu. Bar. Wine list. Semi-a la carte: lunch $7.25-$12.75, dinner $12.95-$25.95. Specializes in lamb, beef, fresh fish. Own baking. Pianist Tues-Sat. Outdoor dining. Tableside preparation. Cr cds: A, C, D, MC, V.

★ ★ **VINCES.** *1 E Antrim Dr.* 803/233-1621. Hrs: 11:30 am-2:30 pm, 5-10 pm; Fri, Sat to 11 pm. Closed Sun; major hols. Italian, Amer menu. Semi-a la carte: lunch $4.95-$7.95, dinner $8.95-$21.95. Child's meals. Specializes in fresh seafood, pasta, prime rib. Parking. Cr cds: A, MC, V.

★ ★ **YAGOTO.** *500 Congaree Rd, in Nippon Center Yagoto.* 803/288-8471. Hrs: 6-9:30 pm. Closed Sun; Jan 1, Dec 25; also wk of July 4. Res accepted. Japanese menu. Bar. Wine cellar. Complete meals: dinner $13.50-$40. Specializes in sushi, sashimi. Sushi bar. Teppanyaki cooking. Tatami rm. Housed in Japanese cultural center; tours. Jacket. Cr cds: A, D, JCB, MC, V.

Unrated Dining Spot

MORRISON'S CAFETERIA. *McAlister Sq, 4 mi SE on SC 291.* 803/235-4316. Hrs: 11 am-8:30 pm; Avg ck: lunch $4.75, dinner $5. Specializes in fried shrimp, grilled chicken, roast beef. In shopping center. Cr cds: MC, V.

Greenwood (D-3)

Settled: 1830 **Pop:** 20,807 **Elev:** 665 ft **Area code:** 803

At the junction of highways and railways, Greenwood was originally the plantation of Green Wood; it later became known as the community of Woodville and finally adopted its present name. Greenwood's Main Street is one of the widest (316 feet) in the nation. The town enjoys diversified industry. A Ranger District office of the Sumter National Forest is also located here.

What to See and Do

1. **The Museum.** 106 Main St. Features a nostalgic "street" lined with a house, shops. Displays of minerals, mounted animal heads, Native American artifacts, ethnographic materials. Art gallery with regional art, traveling exhibits. (Tues-Fri, also Sat & Sun afternoons; closed major hols) Phone 229-7093. **Free.**

2. **Ninety Six National Historic Site.** 9 mi E on SC 34 to present town of Ninety Six, then 2 mi S on SC 248. Site of old Ninety Six, an early village in South Carolina backcountry, so named because of its distance of 96 miles from the Cherokee Village of Keowee on the Cherokee Path. Site of the South's first land battle of the Revolutionary War in 1775, and of the 28-day siege of Ninety Six in 1781. The earthworks of the British-built Star Fort remain, along with reconstructed siegeworks and other fortifications of the period. Visitor center; museum, video presentation. Also here are subsurface remains of two village complexes, a trading post/plantation complex and a network of 18th-century roads. (Daily; closed Jan 1, Dec 25) Phone 543-4068. **Free.**

3. **Sumter National Forest.** In three sections: SW via US 221; NW via SC 28; and NE via SC 72. Approx 353,000 acres in the Piedmont Plateau and the Blue Ridge Mts. Miles of trails through pine & hardwood forest; canoeing, whitewater trips, swimming, trout fishing; hunting for deer, turkey, quail; picnicking, camping. Fees may be charged at recreation sites. Phone 765-5222.

4. **J. Strom Thurmond Lake.** 30 mi SW via US 221, 378. Formed by damming of Savannah River. Fishing; boating (ramps). Picnicking (shelters). Campgrounds (fees). (Daily) Phone 333-2476 or 706/722-3770. **Free.** On shores of reservoir are

5. **State Parks.**

Lake Greenwood. 13 mi E on SC 34, then N on SC 702. On 914 acres bordering Greenwood Lake, which is 20 miles long, 2 miles wide. Waterskiing; lake fishing, bait shop; boating (ramps). Nature trails. Picnicking (shelters), store. Camping (hookups, dump station). Recreation building. Standard fees. Phone 543-3535.

Baker Creek. 28 mi SW via US 221, US 378W. Approx 1,300 acres. Lake swimming, bathhouse; lake fishing; boating (ramps). Nature, bridle trails; carpet golf. Picnicking, playground. Camping (dump station). Standard fees. Phone 443-2457 or -5886.

Hickory Knob Resort. 32 mi SW via US 221, US 378W. On 1,091 acres. Waterskiing; lake fishing, supplies; boating (ramps, rentals). Nature trails; 18-hole golf course, putting green, field archery course, skeet range, field trial area. Playground, restaurant. Camping (hookups, dump station); lodge, cabins. Recreation and nature programs. Convention facilities. Standard fees. Phone 391-2450.

(For further information contact the Chamber of Commerce, PO Box 980, 29648; 223-8431.)

Annual Event

Festival of Flowers. Arts, crafts, photos, special entertainment. Phone 223-8411. Last wkend June.

(See Clinton, Newberry)

Motels

★ **COMFORT INN.** *1215 E US 72 Bypass (29649).* 803/223-2838; FAX 803/942-0119. 83 rms, 2 story. S $44-$50; D $50-$65; suites $90; under 12 free. Crib free. Pool. Complimentary continental bkfst. Complimentary coffee in rms. Restaurant nearby. Ck-out noon. Meeting rms. Valet serv. Exercise equipt; bicycles, treadmill, whirlpool. Refrigerators. Cr cds: A, C, D, DS, ER, JCB, MC, V.

✔ ★ ★ **DAYS INN.** *919 Montague Ave (29649), US 25N & SC 72 Bypass.* 803/223-3979. 100 rms, 2 story. S $35-$44; D $40-$49; each addl $5. TV; cable. Pool. Complimentary bkfst. Restaurant 11 am-10 pm. Bar 11 am-10 pm. Ck-out noon. Meeting rms. Valet serv. Cr cds: A, C, D, DS, MC, V.

★ ★ **HOLIDAY INN.** *1014 Montague Ave (US 25/178) (29649).* 803/223-4231; FAX 803/223-4231, ext. 145. 100 rms, 2 story.

S $39-$65; D $59-$71; each addl $6; under 19 free. Crib free. TV; cable. Pool. Restaurant 6 am-2 pm, 5:30-10 pm. Rm serv. Bar 4-10 pm, closed Sun. Ck-out noon. Coin lndry. Meeting rms. Valet serv. Cr cds: A, C, D, DS, MC, V.

Inns

★ ★ **BELMONT.** *(106 E Pickens St, Abbeville 29620) E on SC 72. 803/459-9625.* 25 rms, 3 story. S, D $67; each addl $5; suites $77-$87; higher rates wkends. Crib free. TV. Complimentary continental bkfst. Dining rm 11:30 am-2 pm, 6-9 pm. Bar 4:30 pm-midnight. Ck-out noon, ck-in 3 pm. Tennis, golf privileges 15 mi. Historic bldg (1903); restored. Period reproduction furnishings and accessories. Cr cds: A, DS, MC, V.

★ ★ ★ **INN ON THE SQUARE.** *104 Court St (29646), at Main St. 803/223-4488; FAX 803/223-7067.* 48 rms, 3 story. S $65.95-$75.95; D $75.95-$85.95; each addl $10; under 18 free. Crib $15. TV; cable. Pool. Complimentary refreshments. Dining rm 7 am-10 pm; Sat from 5 pm; Sun 11 am-2 pm. Rm serv. Ck-out noon, ck-in 4 pm. Bellhops. Atrium. Rms furnished with 18th-century reproductions. Cr cds: A, C, D, DS, MC, V.

Restaurant

★ ★ **BLAZER'S.** *US 221E & SC 72E, 8 mi E on SC 72. 803/223-1917.* Hrs: 5-10 pm; Fri, Sat to 11 pm. Closed Jan 1, Thanksgiving, Dec 24-25. Bar. Semi-a la carte: dinner $7.95-$16.95. Child's meals. Specializes in fresh seafood, steak. Parking. Overlooks Lake Greenwood. Cr cds: A, DS, MC, V.

[D]

Hardeeville (F-4)

Pop: 1,583 **Elev:** 80 ft **Area code:** 803 **Zip:** 29927

What to See and Do

Savannah National Wildlife Refuge. 17 mi S via US 17. Approx 25,600 acres. More than half the acreage consists of bottomland hardwoods reminiscent of the great cypress/tupelo swamps that once extended along the Carolina and Georgia Lowcountry. Argent Swamp may only be reached by boat; wild azaleas, iris, spider lilies & other flowers bloom in succession, beginning in spring. Laurel Hill Wildlife Drive, open to cars, allows viewing of wildlife, especially waterfowl (Dec-Feb). Migrating songbirds are abundant in spring and fall. Tupelo-Swamp Walk (Apr-Sept) is best for bird watchers and photographers. (Daily; some areas closed Oct-Nov for hunting; impoundments N of US 17 closed Nov-mid-Mar; Laurel Hill Drive hrs posted at gate) Phone 912/652-4415. **Free.**

(See Beaufort, Hilton Head Island)

Motels

★ **COMFORT INN.** *I-95 & US 17. 803/784-2188; FAX 803/784-2188, ext. 300.* 99 rms, 2 story. S $39.95; D $49.95; each addl $6. Crib free. TV; cable. Pool. Complimentary continental bkfst, coffee. Restaurant adj 6 am-11 pm. Ck-out 11 am. Exercise equipt; weights, bicycles, whirlpool. Picnic tables. Cr cds: A, C, D, DS, ER, JCB, MC, V.

✔ ★ ★ **HOWARD JOHNSON.** *PO Box 1107, on US 17 at jct I-95. 803/784-2271.* 128 rms, 2 story. S $37-$44; D $41-$54; each addl $5; under 18 free. Crib free. Pet accepted; $5. TV; cable. Pool; wading pool. Restaurant 6 am-10 pm. Ck-out noon. Private patios, balconies. Cr cds: A, C, D, DS, MC, V.

★ ★ **SUPER 8.** *Box 1109, 1/2 mi S on US 17, at I-95. 803/784-2151; FAX 803/784-2151.* 100 rms, 2 story. S $42; D $48; each addl $6. Crib free. TV; cable. Pool. Restaurant 6 am-10 pm. Rm serv. Bar 4:30 pm-midnight, closed Sun. Ck-out noon. Coin lndry. Meeting rms. Valet serv. Cr cds: A, C, D, DS, JCB, MC, V.

[D] [symbols] [SC]

Hartsville (C-5)

Settled: 1760 **Pop:** 8,372 **Elev:** 200 ft **Area code:** 803 **Zip:** 29550

From a crossroads store, Hartsville has become a vigorous trading center, raising crops of cotton, soybeans, tobacco and oats, and boasts fifteen major manufacturers—including makers of consumer packaging, plastic bags, fertilizer, roller bearings, boats, hosiery, brass, textiles and paper. The town developed from what was once the Hart plantation and the pioneer store established by Major James Lide Coker, a Harvard graduate who founded a series of businesses here and built a railroad to the town.

What to See and Do

1. **Kalmia Gardens of Coker College.** Approx 2 1/2 mi W on Carolina Ave. A 30-acre botanical garden. Walking trails through blackwater swamp, mountain laurel thickets, pine-oak-holly uplands and a beech bluff. Plantings of azaleas, camellias and other ornamentals complement the native plants. (Daily) Phone 383-8145. **Free.**

2. **Hartsville Museum.** 114 S 4th St. Housed in restored passenger train depot; two main galleries; changing exhibits of local history, arts & crafts. (Daily exc Sat; closed hols) Phone 383-3005. **Free.**

3. **H. B. Robinson Nuclear Information Center.** 4 mi NW at jct SC 151/23. Located at site of first commercial nuclear plant in Southeast. Exhibits explain generation of electricity, nuclear power and energy use. (Mon-Fri; closed hols) Phone 383-1238 or -1239. **Free.**

4. **Lee State Park.** 16 mi SW via US 15, 3 mi S on SC 341, then 2 mi E off I-20 exit 123. Approx 2,500 acres on Lynches River. Lake swimming; river fishing, boating (pedal boat rentals). Nature trails; horse trails, show ring, stable (no rentals). Picnicking (shelters), playground. Camping (hookups, dump station). Recreation building. Standard fees. Phone 428-3833.

(For further information contact the Chamber of Commerce, 214 N 5th St, PO Box 578, 29551; 332-6401.)

Annual Event

Hartscapades Festival. Parade, antique car show, outdoor concerts, regatta, arts & crafts, children's carnival. 3rd full wkend May.

(For accommodations see Camden, Florence, also see Bennettsville, Cheraw, Darlington)

Hilton Head Island (F-5)

Pop: 23,694 **Elev:** 15 ft **Area code:** 803

This year-round resort island, the development of which began in 1956, is reached by a bridge on US 278. The island is bordered by one of the few remaining unpolluted marine estuaries on the East Coast and is the largest sea island between New Jersey and Florida. Its growth was rapid; there are 12 miles of beaches and the climate is delightful. There are numerous golf courses and tennis courts, swimming, miles of bicycle paths, horseback riding, four nature preserves and deep-sea, sound and dockside fishing. The facilities also include nine marinas and a paved 3,700-foot airstrip with parallel taxiway. There are nearly 3,000 hotel and motel rooms, more than 6,000 homes/villas/condos on the rental market, more than 100 restaurants and 28 shopping centers. For the less athletic, there are many art galleries and numerous sporting and cultural events, including polo matches throughout spring and fall.

(For further information contact the Hilton Head Island Chamber of Commerce, PO Box 5647, 29938, phone 785-3673.)

Annual Events

Springfest. Food, wine and seafood festivals. Sports events. Concerts, shows and house tours. Phone 686-4944. Month of Mar.

Family Circle Magazine Cup Tennis Tournament. Sea Pines Racquet Club. Phone 671-2448. Early-mid-Apr.

MCI Heritage Classic. Top PGA golfers. Harbour Town Golf Links. Phone 671-2448. Mid-Apr.

St Luke's Tour of Homes. Tour of distinctive contemporary houses. Apr.

Hilton Head Island Celebrity Golf Tournament. Palmetto Dunes & Sea Pines Plantation. Phone 785-9299. Labor Day wkend.

(See Beaufort, Hardeeville)

Motels

✔ ★ ★ **FAIRFIELD INN BY MARRIOTT.** *9 Marina Side Dr (29928).* 803/842-4800; FAX 803/842-4800, ext. 709. 120 rms, 3 story, 14 suites. Apr-mid-Sept: S $54.95-$64.95; D $64.95-$74.95; each addl $7; suites $99.95-$109.95; under 18 free; golf plans; lower rates rest of yr. Crib free. TV; cable. Heated pool. Complimentary continental bkfst, coffee in lobby. Restaurant nearby. Ck-out 11 am. Golf privileges. Miniature golf adj. Refrigerator in suites. Picnic tables, grills. Cr cds: A, C, D, DS, MC, V.

[D] [symbols] [SC]

★ ★ **HAMPTON INN.** *1 Airport Rd (29926).* 803/681-7900; FAX 803/681-4330. 125 rms, 2 story, 20 suites, 12 kit. units. Mar-Aug: S $57-$62; D $62-$67; suites, kit. units $80-$85; under 18 free; lower rates rest of yr. Crib free. TV; cable. Pool. Complimentary continental bkfst. Restaurant opp 10 am-11 pm. Ck-out 11 am, Coin lndry. Meeting rms. Tennis privileges, pro. 18-hole golf privileges. Exercise equipt; rower, bicycles, whirlpool. Some refrigerators. Cr cds: A, C, D, DS, ER, JCB, MC, V.

[D] [symbols] [SC]

✔ ★ **RED ROOF INN.** *5 Regency Pkwy (29928), off US 278.* 803/686-6808; FAX 803/842-3352. 112 rms, 2 story. June-Sept: S $39.99; D $45.99-$58.99; 3 or more $62.99; suites $79.99; wkend rates; higher rates hols; lower rates rest of yr. Crib free. TV; cable. Pool. Complimentary morning coffee. Restaurant adj 7 am-10 pm. Ck-out noon. Cr cds: A, C, D, DS, MC, V.

[D] [symbols] [SC]

✔ ★ **SHONEY'S INN.** *200 Museum St (29926).* 803/681-3655; FAX 803/681-3655, ext. 369. 138 rms, 3 story. Early Mar-early Sept: S $47-$52; D $57-$65; each addl $5; under 18 free; lower rates rest of yr. Crib free. TV; cable. Pool. Restaurant 7 am-11 pm. Bar from 3 pm. Ck-out noon. Coin lndry. Meeting rms. Valet serv. Tennis, golf privileges adj. Cr cds: A, C, D, DS, MC, V.

[D] [symbols] [SC]

Motor Hotel

★ ★ **HOLIDAY INN OCEANFRONT.** *Box 5728 (29938), 1 S Forest Beach Dr.* 803/785-5126; FAX 803/785-6678. 200 rms, 5 story. Apr-Aug: S, D $149-$179; each addl $10; under 18 free; lower rates rest of yr. Crib free. TV; cable. Pool; wading pool, poolside serv. Coffee in rms. Restaurant 7 am-10 pm. Rm serv. Bar 4:30 pm-2 am; dancing. Ck-out 11 am. Coin lndry. Meeting rms. Bellhops. Tennis, golf privileges. Refrigerators avail. Patios. On beach. Cr cds: A, C, D, DS, ER, JCB, MC, V.

[D] [symbols] [SC]

Hotel

★ ★ **RADISSON SUITE RESORT.** *12 Park Lane (29928), off US 278.* 803/686-5700; FAX 803/686-3952. 156 kit. suites, 3 story. Mar-Nov: S, D $112-$150; under 18 free; family rates; golf, honeymoon packages; lower rates rest of yr. Crib free. TV; cable. Pool; whirlpool. Complimentary continental bkfst. Restaurant adj 11:30-1 am. Ck-out noon. Coin lndry. Lighted tennis. Golf privileges. Fireplaces. Private patios, balconies. Picnic tables. Cr cds: A, D, DS, MC, V.

[D] [symbols] [SC]

Resorts

★ ★ ★ **CRYSTAL SANDS, A CROWNE PLAZA RESORT.** *130 Shipyard Dr (29928), in Shipyard Plantation.* 803/842-2400; FAX 803/842-9975. 315 rms, 5 story. Early Mar-Nov: S, D $189-$229; suites $350-$450; family, golf rates; lower rates rest of yr. TV; cable. 2 pools, 1 indoor; wading pool, poolside serv. Supervised child's activities (mid-Mar-late Apr & Memorial Day-Labor Day). Coffee in rms. Dining rms 6 am-midnight. Box lunches. Snack bar. Rm serv. Bar 11-2 am. Ck-out noon, ck-in 4 pm. Convention facilities. Valet serv. Concierge. Gift shop. Lighted tennis, pro. 27-hole golf, greens fee $45-$67, pro, putting green, driving range. Boats, sailboats. Bicycle rentals. Entertainment, dancing, movies. Game rm. Exercise rm; instructor, weights, bicycles, whirlpool, sauna. Fishing guides, storage. Some refrigerators. Private patios, balconies. Cr cds: A, C, D, DS, JCB, MC, V.

[D] [symbols] [SC]

★ ★ ★ **HILTON.** *Box 6165 (29938), 23 Ocean Lane, on Palmetto Dunes Resort.* 803/842-8000; FAX 803/842-4988. 296 kit. units, 5 story, 28 suites. Apr-Aug: S, D $129-$219; each addl $15; suites $215-$350; under 18 free; golf, tennis, honeymoon plans; lower rates rest of yr. Crib free. TV; cable. 2 pools, 1 heated; wading pool, poolside serv. Playground. Supervised child's activities (Mar-Oct). Dining rm 7 am-11 pm (to 10 pm off-season). Rm serv. Bar 11-2 am; entertainment exc Mon. Ck-out noon, ck-in 4 pm. Coin lndry. Convention facilities. Valet serv. Concierge. Lighted tennis, pro. Three 18-hole golf courses, greens fee $55-$89, pro. Lawn games. Exercise rm; instructor, weights, bicycles, whirlpools, sauna. Balconies. On ocean. Poolside entertainment (Apr-Oct). Cr cds: A, C, D, DS, ER, MC, V.

[D] [symbols] [SC]

★ ★ ★ **HYATT REGENCY HILTON HEAD.** *Box 6167 (29938), On US 278, in Palmetto Dunes area.* 803/785-1234; FAX 803/842-4695. 505 rms, 10 story. Mar-mid-Nov: S, D $180-$260; each addl $25; suites $350-$700; under 18 free; golf, tennis package plans; lower rates rest of yr. Crib free. Valet parking $6.30/night. TV; cable. 2 pools, 1 indoor; wading pool, poolside serv. Supervised child's activities (Memorial Day-Labor Day). Dining rm (see HEMINGWAY'S). Rm serv 24 hrs. Bars 11:30-2 am, Sun from 1 pm; entertainment, dancing. Ck-out noon, ck-in 4 pm. Meeting rms. Bellhops. Valet serv. Gift shops. Barber, beauty shop. Tennis. Three 18-hole golf courses, putting green. Canoes, sailboats. Bicycle rentals. Exercise rm; instructor, weights, bicycles, whirlpool, sauna. Massage therapist. Private patios, balconies. *LUXURY LEVEL : REGENCY CLUB.* 26 rms, 1 suite. S, D $280; suite $675-$822. Concierge. Private lounge. Deluxe toiletry amenities. Complimentary bkfst, refreshments, newspapers. Cr cds: A, C, D, DS, JCB, MC, V.

⊡ 👤 ♨ 🎿 ⛷ 🔥 SC

★ ★ ★ **PALMETTO DUNES.** *Box 5606 (29938), 7 mi SE of Byrnes Bridge, off US 278.* 803/785-7300; res: 800/845-6130; FAX 803/842-4482. 500 villas, 1-5 story. Mar-Labor Day: S, D $100-$426; family, lower rates rest of yr. Crib avail. TV; cable. 30 pools; wading pools. Playground. Supervised child's activities (June-mid-Aug). Dining rms 7 am-10 pm. Rm serv. Bars to 2 am. Ck-out 10 am, ck-in 4 pm. Grocery. Package store 1 mi. Meeting rms. Valet serv. Airport transportation. Lighted tennis. 3 golf courses, greens fee $30-$72, putting green, driving range. Boats, rowboats, canoes, sailboats. Some fireplaces. Some private patios, balconies. Picnic tables. Private beach. 4,300-ft airstrip 4 mi. Cr cds: A, D, DS, MC, V.

👤 🎿 ♨ 🔥

★ ★ ★ **SEA PINES.** *Box 7000 (29938), 32 Greenwood Dr.* 803/785-3333; res: 800/925-4653; FAX 803/686-3325. 450 kit. suites in villas, 1-3 story, 45 houses. June-Aug: 1-4 bedrm units $120-$275; wkly rates; golf, tennis packages; lower rates rest of yr. TV; cable. 19 pools, 1 indoor/outdoor; wading pools, poolside serv. Playgrounds. Supervised child's activities. Dining rms (public by res) 7 am-10 pm. Snack bars. Cookouts. Bars. Ck-out 10 am, ck-in 4 pm. Lndry facilities. Grocery, package store. Convention facilities. Bellhops. Concierge. Free beach, area transportation. Sports dir. Lighted tennis, pro. Three 18-hole golf courses, greens fee $48-$98, putting green, driving range. Exercise equipt; weight machine, stair machine. Sailboat instruction, charter boats, motors, windsurfing. Bicycles. Entertainment, dancing. Refrigerators; some fireplaces. Screened porch in some houses and villas. On 5,000 acres; 605-acre forest, wildlife preserve. Cr cds: A, C, D, DS, MC, V.

🚣 🎿 👤 ♨ 🎿 ⛷ 🔥 SC

★ ★ ★ ★ **THE WESTIN RESORT.** *2 Grasslawn Avenue (29928).* 803/681-4000; FAX 803/681-1087. 410 rms, 5 story; 59 villas (2, 3 & 4 bedrm). S, D $205-$295; suites from $365; villas $245-$300/day, $1,785-$2,170/wk; under 18 free; tennis, golf, honeymoon, hol rates; lower rates rest of yr. Service fee $5 per day. TV; cable. 3 pools, 1 indoor; poolside serv. Supervised child's activities (Memorial Day-Labor Day). Dining rm 6:30 am-11 pm (also see BARONY GRILL). Rm serv 6-1 am. Bars 3 pm-2 am; entertainment, dancing. Ck-out noon, ck-in 3 pm. Meeting rms. Concierge. Resort wear shop. Valet parking. Tennis, pro. 54-hole golf, greens fee $47-$68 (incl cart), putting green, driving range. Lawn games. Exercise rm; instructor, weights, bicycles, whirlpool, sauna, steam rm. Massage. Hot tub. Bathrm phones, refrigerators. Private patios, balconies. On ocean. Extensive grounds; elaborate landscaping. Cr cds: A, C, D, DS, ER, JCB, MC, V.

⊡ 🚣 👤 🎿 ♨ ⛷ 🔥 SC

Restaurants

★ ★ **ALEXANDER'S.** *76 Queens Folly Rd, in Palmetto Dunes area.* 803/785-4999. Hrs: 5-10 pm; early-bird dinner 5-6 pm. Res accepted. Bar. A la carte entrees: dinner $14.95-$22.95. Child's meals. Specializes in sautéed abalone almondine, broiled mixed grill, blackened and broiled grouper. Parking. Garden rm decor. Overlooks lagoon. Cr cds: A, DS, MC, V.

⊡

★ **ANTONIO'S.** *Village at Wexford.* 803/842-5505. Hrs: 5-10 pm. Closed Thanksgiving, Dec 25. Res accepted. Italian menu. Bar. Semi-a la carte: dinner $8.95-$21. Child's meals. Specializes in pasta, veal, seafood. Parking. European cafe atmosphere. Cr cds: A, D, MC, V.

⊡

✔ ★ ★ **AZTECA.** *70 Marshland Rd.* 803/681-4743. Hrs: 6-9:30 pm. Closed Sun; also mid-Dec-mid-Feb. Res accepted. Traditional Mexican menu. Bar. Semi-a la carte: dinner $6.95-$13.95. Parking. Mexican decor; tiled walls, beamed ceiling. Cr cds: DS, MC, V.

★ ★ ★ **BARONY GRILL.** *(See The Westin Resort)* 803/681-4000. Hrs: 6-10 pm. Res accepted. Serv bar. Wine cellar. Semi-a la carte: dinner $17-$34. Specializes in fresh seafood, lamb, prime beef, veal. Own baking. Valet parking. Hunt club atmosphere. Cr cds: A, C, D, DS, ER, JCB, MC, V.

★ ★ **CAFE EUROPA.** *At the lighthouse in Harbour Town.* 803/671-3399. Hrs: 10 am-2:30 pm, 5:30-10 pm. Closed mid-Nov-mid-Feb. Res accepted. Continental menu. Serv bar. Semi-a la carte: bkfst $6-$8, lunch $6-$10, dinner $11-$20. Child's meals. Specialties: baked shrimp Daufuskie, flounder a l'orange, chicken Charleston-style. Parking. Pianist exc Tues. Outdoor dining. Views of sound, sunset, boardwalk. Cr cds: A, MC, V.

⊡

★ ★ **CARMINES' SEAFOOD AND STEAK.** *One Hudson Rd, adj to Hudson's.* 803/681-2772. Hrs: 6-9:30 pm. Closed Sun; Jan 1, Thanksgiving, Dec 24 & 25. Bar. Semi-a la carte: dinner $8.95-$19.95. Child's meals. Specializes in seafood, steak, peanut butter pie. Salad bar. Parking. View of Intracoastal Waterway. Country-Western decor. Cr cds: A, MC, V.

⊡

★ ★ **CRAZY CRAB.** *US 278, 1/2 mi SE of Graves Bridge.* 803/681-5021. Hrs: 5-10 pm. Closed Thanksgiving, Dec 24-25. Bar. Semi-a la carte: dinner $10.95-$16.95. Child's meals. Specializes in seafood. Own pies. Guitarist, vocalist Apr-Aug. Parking. Nautical decor; overlooks marsh. Cr cds: A, C, D, DS, MC, V.

✔ ★ **DAMON'S.** *Village at Wexford.* 803/785-6677. Hrs: 11:30 am-10 pm. Bar. Semi-a la carte: lunch $3.95-$13.95, dinner $6.50-$15.95. Child's meals. Specializes in barbecued ribs, onion loaf, prime rib. Parking. Outdoor dining (lunch). Casual atmosphere. Cr cds: A, DS, MC, V.

⊡

★ ★ ★ **GASLIGHT.** *303 Market Place.* 803/785-5814. Hrs: 11:30 am-2 pm, 6-10 pm; Sat from 6 pm. Closed Sun. Res accepted. French menu. Serv bar. Semi-a la carte: lunch $6.95-$8.95, dinner $16.95-$24. Specializes in quenelles of snapper, Dover sole, beef Wellington, caramel custard. Own baking. Parking. Garden setting. Cr cds: A, MC, V.

★ ★ ★ **HARBOURMASTER'S.** *At Shelter Cove Harbor.* 803/785-3030. Hrs: from 5 pm. Closed Sun; Dec 25; also Jan. Res accepted. Continental menu. Bar. Wine cellar. Semi-a la carte: dinner $15.25-$23. Specialties: almond crusted snapper, ginger grilled tuna, rack of lamb. Parking. Tableside preparation. View of yacht harbor. Jacket. Cr cds: A, D, MC, V.

⊡

★ ★ **HEMINGWAY'S.** *(See Hyatt Regency Hilton Head Resort)* 803/785-1234. Hrs: 6-11 pm; early-bird dinner 5-6:30 pm; Sun brunch 10 am-2 pm. Res accepted. Bar 4 pm-midnight; entertainment. Semi-a la carte: dinner $18.25-$23.50. Sun brunch $19.95. Specializes in fresh grilled seafood, steak, fruit cobbler, fried strawberries. Valet parking. Cr cds: A, C, D, DS, JCB, MC, V.

✔ ★ ★ **HOFBRAUHAUS.** *At Pope Ave Mall.* 803/785-3663. Hrs: 5-10 pm. Res accepted. German menu. Bar. Semi-a la carte: dinner $9.95-$14.75. Serv charge 15%. Child's meals. Specialties: roast young duckling, sauerbraten, Wienerschnitzel. German decor; stained-glass windows, stein & mug collection. Cr cds: A, MC, V.

⊡

✔ ★ **HUDSON'S ON THE DOCKS.** *1 Hudson Rd, 1 mi N off US 278.* 803/681-2772. Hrs: 11 am-10 pm. Closed Jan 1, Thanksgiving, Dec 24, 25. Bar. Semi-a la carte: lunch $4.95-$9.95, dinner $8.95-$15.95. Child's meals. Specializes in fresh seafood, live Maine lobster, mud pie. Magician, guitarist (Memorial Day-Labor Day). Parking. On Intracoastal Waterway; near boat docks. Cr cds: A, MC, V.

⊡

★ ★ ★ **LA MAISONETTE.** *Pope Ave, in the Craig Bldg.* *803/785-6000.* Hrs: 6-10 pm. Closed Dec 25. Res required. French menu. Serv bar. Wine cellar. Complete meals: dinner $25.75. Specialties: rack of lamb, shrimp Maisonette, escargots à la bourguignonne. Own desserts. Parking. Jacket. Cr cds: A, DS, MC, V.

★ ★ **LA POLA'S.** *11 New Orleans Rd.* *803/842-6400.* Hrs: 5-10 pm. Closed Jan. Res accepted. Italian, Amer menu. Bar. Semi-a la carte: dinner $9.99-$23.95. Child's meals. Specializes in fresh fish, veal, Black Angus steak. Own desserts. Parking. Lighted fountain in center of rm. Cr cds: A, DS, MC, V.

[D]

★ ★ **LITTLE VENICE.** *Shelter Cove.* *803/785-3300.* Hrs: noon-2:30 pm, 5-10 pm. Closed Dec 25; also Jan. Res accepted. Italian menu. Bar. Semi-a la carte: lunch $6.95-$7.95, dinner $12.95-$19.95. Specialties: veal chop, zuppa di pesce, chicken à la Fiorentina. Parking. Outdoor dining. Overlooks marina. Trattoria atmosphere. Cr cds: A, D, DS, MC, V.

★ **LONGHORN STEAK.** *841 US 278.* *803/686-4056.* Hrs: 11:15 am-10 pm; Fri to 10:30 pm; Sat 4-10:30 pm; Sun 4-10 pm. Closed Thanksgiving, Dec 25. Bar. Semi-a la carte: lunch $3.99-$7.95, dinner $6.95-$17.95. Child's meals. Specializes in steak, salmon, chicken. Country-Western decor. Cr cds: A, C, D, DS, MC, V.

[D]

★ ★ **OLD OYSTER FACTORY.** *101 Marshland Rd.* *803/681-6040.* Hrs: 5-10 pm. Closed Jan 1, Dec 25. Bar from 5 pm. Semi-a la carte: dinner $9.95-$17.95. Child's meals. Specializes in fresh seafood, local oysters, steak. Guitarist, vocalist Fri-Sun evenings. Parking. Overlooks creek, marshes. Cr cds: A, D, DS, MC, V.

[D]

★ ★ **PRIMO.** *At Orleans Plaza, Shipyard Center.* *803/785-2343.* Hrs: from 6 pm. Closed Thanksgiving, Dec 25; Super Bowl Sun. Res accepted. Contemporary Italian menu. Serv bar. Semi-a la carte: dinner $10.50-$22.95. Specializes in fresh pasta, char-grilled seafood, veal. Own bread, pasta, desserts. Parking. Italian cafe atmosphere. Cr cds: A, DS, MC, V.

[D]

✔ ★ **REILLEY'S.** *14 Greenwood Dr, in Gallery of Shops.* *803/842-4414.* Hrs: 11:30 am-midnight; Sat & Sun brunch 11:30 am-4 pm. Closed Dec 25. Bar to 2 am. Semi-a la carte: lunch, dinner $5.95-$12.95. Sun brunch $5.75-$8.95. Child's meals. Specialties: cottage pie, brownies with homemade ice cream, corned beef & cabbage, fish & chips. Irish pub atmosphere; sports memorabilia. Cr cds: A, MC, V.

[D] [SC]

★ **SCOTT'S.** *At Shelter Cove Harbour.* *803/785-7575.* Hrs: 4-10 pm; early-bird dinner 4-6 pm. Closed Sun; some major hols; also Jan. Bar. Semi-a la carte: dinner $10.95-$19.95. Specialties: Key West grouper, Bahamian fried lobster. Parking. Outdoor dining. Nautical decor. View of harbor. Cr cds: A, C, D, DS, MC, V.

[D]

Kiawah Island (F-5)

Pop: 718 **Area code:** 803

Kiawah Island (pronounced KEE-a-wah) is one of the richest natural environments in the middle Atlantic states. The island is a model for maintaining the ecological balance while allowing human habitation. Named for the Native Americans who once hunted and fished here, the island is separated from the mainland by the Kiawah River and a mile-wide salt marsh.

Extensive environmental study has helped to preserve nature while also providing for human needs. Separate resort areas and private residential neighborhoods have been planned to provide a minimum of automobile traffic and leave much of the island untouched. Some of the most stringent land-use restrictions in the United States are imposed here.

Access to the island is restricted to residents and guests of Kiawah Island Resort.

For further information contact Kiawah Island Resort, Box 12357, Charleston 29422; 768-2121 or 800/654-2924.

(See Beaufort, Charleston)

Resort

★ ★ ★ **KIAWAH ISLAND RESORT.** *12 Kiawah Beach Dr (29455), at W end of Kiawah Island, off Kiawah Beach Dr.* *803/768-2121;* res: *800/654-2924;* FAX *803/768-9339.* 150 rms, 3 story, 340 villas (1-4 bedrms). Mar-Nov: S, D $165-$230; villas $170-$455; under 18 free; wkly rates; golf, tennis, honeymoon plans; lower rates rest of yr. Crib free. TV; cable. 4 pools, 1 heated; wading pool, poolside serv, lifeguard. Playground. Supervised child's activities (Memorial Day-Labor Day). Coffee in rms. Dining rms 7 am-11 pm. Snack bar, picnics. Rm serv. Bar 11-1 am; entertainment, dancing (in season). Ck-out noon, ck-in 4 pm. Grocery 1 mi. Package store 3 mi. Meeting rms. Bellhops. Valet serv. Concierge. Gift shop. Lighted tennis, pro. Four 18-hole golf courses, greens fee $65-$140, pro, driving range. Swimming beach; boats. Canoe trips. Bicycle rentals. Nature walks. Lawn games. Rec rm. Game rm. Many wet bars. On ocean. Cr cds: A, C, D, DS, MC, V.

Kings Mountain National Military Park (B-4)

(20 mi NE of Gaffney off I-85, near Grover, NC)

On these 3,950 rugged acres, a fierce attack by Carolina, Georgia and Virginia mountain frontiersmen in October, 1780, broke up Britain's southern campaign. The mountain men and other patriots were faced with the invasion of their homes by advancing Tories. After traveling more than 200 miles, the Americans surrounded and attacked Cornwallis' left wing, which was encamped atop Kings Mountain spur and under the command of Major Patrick Ferguson. Although untrained in formal warfare, American patriots killed, wounded or captured Ferguson's entire force of 1,104 Tories. Twenty-eight patriots were killed and 62 were wounded. The battle led to renewed American resistance and American victory at Yorktown. Near the center of the park is the battlefield ridge, with several monuments, including the Centennial Monument, dedicated in 1880, and the US Monument, erected in 1909. The Visitor Center has exhibits and a film. Self-guided trail leads to main features of battlefield. (Daily; closed Jan 1, Thanksgiving, Dec 25) Phone 803/936-7921. **Free.**

King's Mountain State Park on SC 161, adj to S edge of national military park, has 6,141 acres of scenic drives; living history farm; two lakes. Swimming; fishing; boating. Nature, hiking, bridle trails; carpet golf. Picnicking (shelters), playground, store. Camping. Interpretive center. Standard fees. Phone 803/222-3209.

(For accommodations see Gaffney, Rock Hill, Spartanburg; also see Charlotte, NC)

Myrtle Beach (D-7)

Pop: 24,848 **Elev:** 30 ft **Area code:** 803

With the Gulf Stream only a few miles offshore and dunes to shelter miles of white sand, Myrtle Beach is one of the most popular seaside resorts on the Atlantic coast. Swimming, fishing, golf, tennis and boardwalk amusements combine to lure millions of vacationers each summer. The many myrtle trees in the area give this resort its name. Myrtle Beach Air Force Base is located here.

What to See and Do

1. **"The Grand Strand."** Sixty miles of beach from the North Carolina border south to Georgetown. Camping; fishing; golf; tennis; amusement parks.

2. **Myrtle Beach State Park.** 3 mi S on US 17 Business. Approx 300 acres. Ocean and pool swimming; surf fishing (supplies avail). Nature trail. Picnicking (shelters), playground, stores. Camping, cabins. Interpretive center. Standard fees (higher rates Apr-Sept). Phone 238-5325.

(For further information contact the Myrtle Beach Area Chamber of Commerce, 1301 N Kings Hwy, 29577; 626-7444 or 800/356-3016.)

Annual Event

Sun Fun Festival. More than 100 seaside entertainment events, including air show, parades. 1st wk June.

(See Georgetown)

Motels

★ ★ **CARIBBEAN.** 3000 N Ocean Blvd (29577), at 30th Ave N. 803/448-7181; res: 800/845-0883; FAX 803/448-3224. 95 rms, 5 story, 38 kits. Early June-late Aug: D $60-$86; each addl $6; kit. units $72-$91; wkly, golf rates; higher rates: Easter wk, Memorial Day wkend, wk of July 4, Labor Day wkend; lower rates rest of yr. Crib free. TV; cable. Heated pool; whirlpool. Coffee in lobby. Restaurant adj 6 am-10 pm. Ck-out 11 am. Tennis, golf privileges. Putting green. Lawn games. Refrigerators. Balconies. On beach. Cr cds: A, C, D, DS, MC, V.

✔ ★ **CASA MARINA.** 2703 N Kings Hwy (29577). 803/448-8511. 34 rms, 1-2 story, 2 kits. Mid-May-Labor Day: D $48-$60; each addl $5; kit. units $62-$70; lower rates rest of yr. Crib $2. TV; cable. Pool. Restaurant opp 6 am-midnight. Ck-out 11 am. Tennis, golf privileges. Some refrigerators. Cr cds: A, C, D, DS, MC, V.

★ ★ **CHESTERFIELD INN.** Box 218 (29578), 700 N Ocean Blvd. 803/448-3177; res: 800/392-3869; FAX 803/626-4736. 31 inn rms, 26 motel rms, 3 story, 6 kits. Mid-June-late Aug, MAP: S $76-$100; D $104-$128; each addl $28; kit. units for 2, $95 (no MAP); family rates; golf plans; varied lower rates Feb-mid-June, late Aug-Dec. Closed rest of yr. Crib free. TV; cable. Pool. Restaurant 7:30-9:30 am, 6-8 pm. Ck-out 11 am. Golf privileges. Some refrigerators. Balconies. On beach. Cr cds: A, DS, MC, V.

★ ★ **COMFORT INN.** 2801 S Kings Hwy (29577). 803/626-4444; FAX 803/626-0753. 152 rms, 4 story, 5 kit. suites. Mid-May-early Sept: S, D $74-$89; kit. suites $95-$115; higher rates hols; lower rates rest of yr. Crib free. TV; cable. Pool. Playground. Complimentary continental bkfst, coffee. Ck-out 11 am. Coin lndry. Meeting rms. Golf privileges. Exercise equipt; weights, bicycles. Game rm. Picnic tables, grills. Cr cds: A, C, D, DS, ER, MC, V.

★ ★ **HAMPTON INN.** Box 7138 (29577), jct US 17 & 48th Ave N. 803/449-5231. 152 rms, 4 story. Memorial Day-Labor Day: S $71; D $75; higher rates: wkends, Easter, July 4; lower rates rest of yr. Crib free. TV; cable. Indoor pool. Complimentary continental bkfst, coffee. Restaurant 5-10 pm. Bar 4 pm-midnight; entertainment, dancing. Ck-out 11 am. Meeting rms. Valet serv. Tennis & golf privileges. Miniature golf adj. 1½ blks to ocean. Cr cds: A, C, D, DS, MC, V.

★ ★ **INN AT MYRTLE BEACH.** 7300 N Ocean Blvd (29572). 803/449-3361; res: 800/845-0664; FAX 803/449-8297. 123 rms, 4 story, 45 kits. Mid-June-mid-Aug: D, kit. units $89-$109; each addl $5; under 16 free; golf plan; lower rates rest of yr. Crib free. TV; cable. Heated pool; whirlpool, poolside serv. Restaurant 7 am-2:30 pm (summer only), 5-10 pm. Rm serv. Bar from 5 pm. Ck-out 11 am. Coin lndry. Free airport, bus depot transportation. Tennis, golf privileges. Miniature golf, putting green. Lawn games. Refrigerators. Balconies. Sun decks. On ocean. Cr cds: A, C, D, MC, V.

★ **JONATHAN HARBOUR.** 2611 S Ocean Blvd (29577). 803/448-1948; res: 800/448-1948. 65 kit. units, 5 story. Late June-mid-Aug: kit. units $93-$165; family rates; higher rates hols; lower rates rest of yr. Crib free. TV; cable. Indoor/outdoor pool; wading pool. Restaurant adj 7 am-10 pm. Ck-out 11 am. Coin lndry. Golf privileges. Exercise equipt; weights, bicycles, whirlpool, steam rm, sauna. Balconies. On ocean; beach. Cr cds: A, MC, V.

✔ ★ **PALM CREST.** 701 S Ocean Blvd (29577). 803/448-7141; res: 800/487-9233. 41 units, 3 story, 38 kits. No elvtr. Early June-late Aug: S, D $51-$71; each addl $5; kit. units $71-$74; 1-2-bedrm units $81-$113; wkly rates; golf, tennis plans; lower rates rest of yr. Crib $2. TV; cable. Indoor/outdoor pool; wading pool. Restaurant adj 6:30 am-10:30 pm. Ck-out 11 am. Coin lndry. Sundries. Free airport transportation. Tennis, golf privileges. Picnic tables, grills. Cr cds: DS, MC, V.

✔ ★ **VIKING.** 1811 S Ocean Blvd (29577). 803/448-4355; res: 800/334-4876 (exc SC). 76 units, 5 story, 67 kits. June-Aug: S, D $50-$88; each addl $5; suites $65-$107; kit. units $53-$86; 2-bedrm apts. with kit. $58-$97; family, wkly rates; higher rates: wkends, Easter wk; lower rates rest of yr. Crib free. TV; cable. Pool; wading pool. Restaurant nearby. Ck-out 11 am. Coin lndry. Tennis, golf privileges. Refrigerators. Some private patios, balconies. On beach. Cr cds: MC, V.

Motor Hotels

★ ★ **CAPTAIN'S QUARTERS.** 901 S Ocean Blvd (29578). 803/448-1404; res: 800/843-3561 (US), 800/874-1923 (Canada). 211 units, 9 story, 150 kits. June-Aug: D $76-$104; each addl $4; kit. units $77-$154; under 18 free; golf package plan; varied lower rates rest of yr. Crib free. TV; cable. 2 pools, 1 indoor/outdoor; wading pools, whirlpools. Restaurant 6:30-11 am, 5:30-9:30 pm. Ck-out 11 am. Coin lndry. Golf privileges. Bowling. Game room. Lawn games. Refrigerators. Private patios, balconies. On beach. Cr cds: A, MC, V.

★ ★ **CARAVELLE RESORT & VILLAS.** 6900 N Ocean Blvd (29572). 803/449-3331; res: 800/845-0893; FAX 803/449-0643. 193 rms, 4-7 story, 180 kits; 210 villas, 1-3 bedrm. June-Aug: S, D $99-$104; suites $129; kit. units $102-$107; villas $130-$250; lower rates rest of yr. Crib $5. TV; cable. 8 pools, 2 indoor; poolside serv. Free supervised child's activities (Memorial Day-Labor Day). Restaurant 7-10 am, 6-9 pm. Rm serv. Ck-out 11 am. Coin Indry. Meeting rms. Bellhops. Free airport, bus depot transportation. Golf privileges. Exercise equipt; weights, bicycles, whirlpool, sauna. Rec rm. Refrigerators. Balconies. On beach. Cr cds: A, C, D, MC, V.

⊡⊡⊡⊡⊡⊡

★ ★ ★ **PAN AMERICAN MOTOR INN.** *Box 1887 (29578), 5300 N Ocean Blvd.* 803/449-7411; res: 800/845-4501; FAX 803/449-5275, ext. 78. 85 units, 6 story. Early June-mid-Aug: S, D $87; each addl $7; kit. units $90; 1-bedrm apts $112; golf plans; family rates; lower rates rest of yr. Crib free. TV; cable. Heated pool. Restaurant 7 am-2 pm; Sun & off season to 11 am. Rm serv. Ck-out 11 am. Bellhops. Tennis. Golf privileges. Refrigerators. Private patios, balconies. On beach. Cr cds: MC, V.

⊡⊡⊡⊡⊡

★ ★ ★ **SEA ISLAND.** *6000 N Ocean Blvd (29577).* 803/449-6406; res: 800/548-0767; FAX 803/449-4102. 112 units, 5 story, 46 kits. Early June-late Aug: S $91-$101; D $99-$109; each addl $8; kit. units $96-$104; under 12 free; MAP avail; lower rates rest of yr. Crib free. TV; cable. Heated pool; 2 wading pools. Restaurant 7:30-10 am, 6-8 pm. Rm serv. Ck-out 11 am. Meeting rms. Bellhops. Valet serv. Free airport transportation. Tennis, golf privileges. Refrigerators. Balconies. On ocean; swimming beach. Cr cds: A, MC, V.

⊡⊡⊡⊡⊡

★ ★ **ST JOHN'S INN.** *6803 N Ocean Blvd (29572).* 803/449-5251. 88 rms, 3 story, 26 kits. June-Labor Day: D $85; each addl $5; kit. units $96; suites $123; under 10 free; golf plan; varied lower rates rest of yr. Crib avail. TV; cable. Heated pool; whirlpool. Coffee shop 7-11 am. Ck-out 11 am. Meeting rm. Lawn games. Refrigerators. Private patios, balconies. Bathrm phones. Beach opp. Cr cds: A, D, DS, MC, V.

⊡⊡⊡

✔ ★ **SURF & DUNES.** *2201 S Ocean Blvd (29577).* 803/448-1755; res: 800/845-2109. 129 units, 3-7 story, 80 kits. Mid-May-late Oct: S, D $36-$93; each addl $5; kit. units $50-$99; under 14 free; monthly, wkly rates; golf plans; higher rates: Easter wk, all hol wkends in season; lower rates rest of yr. Crib $5. TV; cable. 3 pools, 1 indoor; poolside serv. Playground. Restaurant nearby. Ck-out 11 am. Coin Indry. Lighted tennis. Golf privileges. Exercise equipt; weight machine, treadmill, whirlpool. Game rm. Lawn games. Refrigerators. Some balconies. On beach. Cr cds: A, DS, MC, V.

⊡⊡⊡⊡⊡⊡

★ ★ **SWAMP FOX OCEAN RESORTS.** *Box 1307 (29578), 2311 S Ocean Blvd.* 803/448-8373; res: 800/228-9894. 377 units, 5-16 story, 296 kits. June-late Aug: S, D $85-$105; each addl $8; kit. units $95-$145; penthouses $185-$200; under 15 free; wkly rates; golf plans; lower rates rest of yr. Crib free. TV. 5 pools, 2 indoor; wading pool. Restaurant 6 am-10 pm. Ck-out 11 am. Coin Indry. Meeting rms. Bellhops. Golf privileges. Exercise equipt; weights, bicycles, whirlpool, sauna. Refrigerators. Balconies. Picnic tables, grills. On beach. Cr cds: A, D, DS, ER, JCB, MC, V.

⊡⊡⊡⊡⊡⊡

Hotels

★ ★ ★ **BEACH COLONY.** *5308 N Ocean Blvd (29577).* 803/449-4010; res: 800/222-2141; FAX 803/449-2810. 155 kit. suites, 22 story. Mid-June-mid-Aug: 1-bedrm $136; 2-bedrm $1,500/wk; 3-bedrm $1,650/wk; 4-bedrm $1,850/wk; lower rates rest of yr. Crib $5. TV; cable. 3 pools, 1 indoor; wading pool, poolside serv. Free supervised child's activities (Memorial Day-Labor Day). Restaurant 6-11 am, 5-10 pm. Bar 5 pm-1 am. Ck-out 11 am. Coin Indry. Meeting rms. Free covered parking. Free airport transportation. Tennis, golf privileges.

Exercise equipt; weight machines, bicycles, whirlpools, sauna. Balconies. On ocean, beach. Cr cds: A, C, D, DS, MC, V.

⊡⊡⊡⊡⊡⊡

★ ★ **BEACH COVE RESORT.** *(4800 S Ocean Blvd, North Myrtle Beach 29582)* 803/272-4044; res: 800/331-6533; FAX 803/272-2294. 260 kit. units, 16 story. Late May-mid-Aug: kit. units for up to 6, $90-$139; each addl $10; 2-bedrm cottage $1,225/wk; under 18 free; wkly rates; lower rates rest of yr. Crib $5. TV; cable. 4 pools, 1 indoor; 3 whirlpools, sauna, poolside serv. Supervised child's activities (Memorial Day-Labor Day). Restaurant 7-10:30 am, 5-10 pm. Bar; entertainment (in season), dancing. Ck-out 11 am. Meeting rms. Tennis, golf privileges. Game rm. Private patios, balconies. On ocean; beach. Cr cds: A, C, D, DS, MC, V.

⊡⊡⊡⊡⊡⊡⊡⊡

★ ★ ★ **THE BREAKERS.** *Box 485 (29578), 2006 N Ocean Blvd.* 803/626-5000; res: 800/845-0688; FAX 803/626-5001. 250 units, 11 & 15 story, 75 kit. suites, 181 kits. June-Aug: D $90-$110; each addl $8; 1-bedrm kit. suites $140; kit. units $98-$118; under 16 free; wkly rates; golf, tennis, honeymoon plans; lower rates rest of yr. Crib free. TV. 3 pools, 1 indoor/outdoor; wading pool. Free supervised child's activities (June-Labor Day). Restaurant 7-11 am, 5:30-9 pm. Bar 5 pm-2 am; entertainment, dancing exc Sun. Ck-out 11 am. Coin Indry. Meeting rms. Airport transportation. Tennis, golf privileges. Lawn games. Exercise equipt; weights, bicycles, whirlpool, sauna. Many refrigerators. Balconies. On beach. Cr cds: A, C, D, DS, MC, V.

⊡⊡⊡⊡⊡⊡

★ ★ ★ **THE BREAKERS NORTH TOWER.** *Box 485 (29578), 27th Ave N.* 803/626-5000; res: 800/845-0688; FAX 803/626-5001. 141 units, 18 story. Early June-mid-Aug: S, D $95-$110; each addl $8; 1-2-bedrm suites $140-$240; under 16 free; wkly rates; golf plans; lower rates rest of yr. Crib free. TV; cable. Pool; wading pool, poolside serv. Free supervised child's activities (June-Labor Day). Restaurant 7-11 am. Bar 5 pm-1 am. Ck-out 11 am. Coin Indry. Free covered parking. Tennis, golf privileges, pro. Exercise equipt; weights, bicycles, whirlpool, sauna. Many refrigerators. Private patios, balconies. On ocean. Cr cds: A, C, D, DS, MC, V.

⊡⊡⊡⊡⊡⊡

★ ★ **DUNES VILLAGE RESORT.** *5200 N Ocean Blvd (29577), at 52nd Ave.* 803/449-5275; res: 800/648-3539; FAX 803/449-5275, ext. 78. 93 rms, 8 story. Mid-June-mid-Aug: D $90-$93; each addl $7; kit. apts $112; under 14 free; wkly rates; lower rates rest of yr. Crib free. TV; cable. 2 pools, 1 indoor; whirlpool. Restaurant 7-10 am. Ck-out 11 am. Tennis privileges. Refrigerators. Balconies. On beach. Cr cds: DS, MC, V.

⊡⊡⊡⊡

★ ★ **HOLIDAY INN OCEANFRONT.** *415 S Ocean Blvd (29577).* 803/448-4481; FAX 803/448-0086. 311 rms, 8 story. Mid-May-Aug: S, D $99-$135; each addl $10; under 18 free; lower rates rest of yr. Crib free. TV; cable, in-rm movies. 2 pools, 1 indoor; poolside serv. Restaurant 6 am-10 pm. Bars noon-2 am; entertainment, dancing. Ck-out 11 am. Coin Indry. Convention facilities. Gift shop. Tennis privileges. Golf privileges. Exercise equipt; weight machine, bicycles, whirlpool, sauna. Game rm. On beach. Cr cds: A, C, D, DS, ER, JCB, MC, V.

⊡⊡⊡⊡⊡⊡⊡

★ ★ ★ **MYRTLE BEACH MARTINIQUE.** *Box 331 (29578), 7100 N Ocean Blvd.* 803/449-4441; res: 800/542-0048; FAX 803/497-3041. 203 units, 17 story, 92 kits. Mid-June-late Aug: D $119; each addl $10; suites $140-$312; kit. units $129; under 18 free; lower rates rest of yr. Crib free. TV; cable. 2 pools, 1 indoor; poolside serv. Complimentary coffee in rms. Restaurant 7 am-2 pm, 5-9 pm. Bar 4 pm-2 am; entertainment in season. Ck-out 11 am. Free Indry facilities. Meeting rms. Golf privileges. Exercise equipt; weights, bicycles, whirlpool, sauna.

Game rm. Refrigerators. Balconies. On ocean, beach. Cr cds: A, C, D, DS, MC, V.

★ ★ **OCEAN DUNES/SAND DUNES RESORT & VILLAS.** *PO Box 2035 (29578), 201 74th Ave N. 803/449-7441; res: 800/845-6701; FAX 803/449-0558.* 314 rms, 7-15 story, 9 townhouses, 45 villas (2-bedrm), 170 tower suites (1-bedrm). June-Labor Day: S, D $79-$118; villas $163-$225; advance deposit required for 1-night stay; golf plan; varied lower rates rest of yr. Crib free. TV; cable, in-rm movies. 8 pools, 2 indoor, 2 heated; poolside serv. Free supervised child's activities (Memorial Day-Labor Day). Restaurant 7-10 am, 6-10 pm. Rm serv. Bar 4 pm-1 am; entertainment, dancing. Ck-out 11 am. Coin lndry. Convention facilities. Bellhops. Valet serv. Beauty shop. Airport, bus depot transportation. Tennis, golf privileges. Exercise rm; instructor, weights, bicycle, whirlpool, steam rm. Game rm. Refrigerators. Balconies. Pizza parlor. On beach. Cr cds: A, C, D, DS, MC, V.

★ ★ **THE PALACE.** *1605 S Ocean Blvd (29577). 803/448-4300; res: 800/334-1397; FAX 803/448-6300.* 298 kit. units, 23 story. Late May-late Aug: 1-2 bedrm suites for up to 6, $115-$175; wkly rates; lower rates rest of yr. TV; cable. 2 pools, 1 indoor/outdoor. Restaurant 6:30 am-1 pm. Bar noon-2 am. Ck-out 10:30 am. Convention facilities. Lndry facilities avail. Free covered parking. Airport transportation. Golf privileges. Exercise equipt; weights, bicycles, whirlpool, sauna, steam rm. Game rm. Refrigerators. Private patios, balconies. Resort-style hotel on ocean. Dishwasher in all rms. Cr cds: A, C, D, DS, ER, MC, V.

★ ★ ★ **RADISSON RESORT AT KINGSTON PLANTATION.** *9800 Lake Dr (29572). 803/449-0006; FAX 803/497-1017.* 255 kit. suites, 20 story. Memorial Day-Labor Day: suites $179-$259; each addl $15; condos, villas $150-$290; under 18 free; lower rates rest of yr. Crib free. TV; cable, in-rm movies. 7 pools, 1 indoor; wading pool, poolside serv. Supervised child's activities (June-Aug). Restaurant 6 am-10 pm. Bar 10-1 am; entertainment Tues-Sat, dancing Fri, Sat. Ck-out noon. Convention facilities. Concierge. Gift shop. Lighted tennis, pro. Golf privileges. Exercise rm; instructor, weights, bicycles, whirlpool, sauna. Refrigerators. On ocean. Cr cds: A, C, D, DS, ER, MC, V.

★ ★ **RAMADA OCEAN FOREST RESORT.** *5523 N Ocean Blvd (29577). 803/497-0044; FAX 803/497-3051.* 190 kit. suites, 23 story. Memorial Day-Labor Day: 1-bedrm $115-$120; 2-bedrm $185-$190; under 18 free; wkly rates; golf packages; lower rates rest of yr. Crib free. TV; cable. 2 pools, 1 indoor; whirlpool, sauna, steam rm, poolside serv. Supervised child's activities (Memorial Day-Labor Day). Restaurant 7 am-10 pm. Bar 5-11 pm. Ck-out 11 am. Meeting rms. Gift shop. Airport transportation. Golf privileges. Game rm. Balconies. Opp beach. Cr cds: A, C, D, DS, ER, JCB, MC, V.

✔ ★ ★ **SEA MIST RESORT.** *Box 2548 (29577), 1200 S Ocean Blvd. 803/448-1551; res: 800/732-6478; FAX 803/448-5858.* 685 rms, 2-16 story, 552 kits. Mid-June-late Aug: S, D $63.50-$95.50; each addl $6; kit. units $66.50-$113.50; under 15 free; golf plans; lower rates rest of yr. Crib $4. TV; cable. 9 pools, 1 indoor/outdoor; wading pools. Playground. Supervised child's activities (mid-June-mid-Aug). Restaurant 7 am-noon. No rm serv. Ck-out 11 am. Coin lndry. Convention facilities. Gift shop. Lighted tennis. Golf privileges, putting green, miniature golf. Exercise equipt; bicycles, rowing machines, whirlpool, sauna, steam rm. Game rm. Rec rm. Lawn games. Children's water park. Pizza, ice cream parlors. Many refrigerators. Some private patios, balconies. Picnic tables, grills. On beach. Cr cds: A, C, D, DS, MC, V.

★ ★ **SHERATON.** *2701 S Ocean Blvd (29577). 803/448-2518; FAX 803/448-1506.* 219 rms, 16 story, 60 kits. Late May-late Aug: S, D $95-$119; suites $155-$170; kits. $115; under 18 free; golf plans; lower rates rest of yr. Crib free. TV; cable. 2 pools, 1 indoor.

Restaurant 6-10 am, 11 am-2 pm, 5:30-11 pm. Bar. Ck-out 11 am. Convention facilities. Gift shop. Free airport transportation. Tennis privileges. Golf privileges. Exercise equipt; weight machine, bicycles, sauna. Health club privileges. Game rm. Balconies. On oceanfront beach. Cr cds: A, D, DS, MC, V.

Inn

✔ ★ ★ **SERENDIPITY.** *407 71st Ave N (29572). 803/449-5268.* 14 rms, 2 story, 3 suites, 4 kits. June-Aug: S, D $67-$80; suites $92; kits. $80; lower rates rest of yr. Crib free. TV; cable. Heated pool; whirlpool. Complimentary continental bkfst, tea/sherry. Restaurant adj 6 am-2 pm, 5-10 pm. Ck-out 11 am, ck-in 2 pm. Golf privileges. Lawn games. Refrigerators. Balconies. Picnic tables, grills. Library/sitting rm; antiques. Beach nearby. Cr cds: A, DS, MC, V.

Restaurants

★ ★ **BISTRO.** *73rd Ave N & Ocean Blvd. 803/449-5125.* Hrs: noon-2:30 pm, 6 pm-midnight; Sat from 6 pm. Closed Sun; Jan 1, Thanksgiving, Dec 25. Continental menu. Serv bar. Semi-a la carte: lunch $4.50-$9.25, dinner $10.50-$22.50. Specializes in fresh fish, steak, snow pie. Parking. Outdoor dining. Cr cds: A, C, D, DS, MC, V. **SC**

★ **CAGNEY'S OLD PLACE.** *8 mi N on Kings Hwy (US 17). 803/449-3824.* Hrs: 5-11 pm. Closed Sun; also mid-Dec-2nd wk Feb. Bar to 2 am. Semi-a la carte: dinner $11.95-$18.95. Specializes in seafood, chicken, prime rib, beef, chocolate fudge pie. 1900s decor. Cr cds: A, DS, MC, V.

✔ **DAMON'S.** *(Hwy 17 S, North Myrtle Beach) Approx 15 mi N on US 17, in Barefoot Landing shopping center. 803/272-5107.* Hrs: 11 am-10 pm; wkends to 11 pm. Closed Thanksgiving, Dec 25. Bar. Semi-a la carte: lunch $3.50-$15.95, dinner $5.25-$15.95. Child's meals. Specializes in onion loaf, prime rib, steak. Porch dining. Overlooks lagoon. Cr cds: A, D, MC, V.

★ **DOCKSIDE.** *(US 17 Business, Murrells Inlet) 12 mi S on US 17. 803/651-5850.* Hrs: 4-10 pm. Closed Dec-Jan. Low country menu. Bar. Semi-a la carte: dinner $9.99-$24.99. Child's meals. Specializes in Cajun grilled grouper, grilled shrimp, prime rib. Entertainment (in season). Parking. Outdoor dining. Nautical decor. View of marsh, inlet. Cr cds: A, DS, MC, V.

✔ ★ **ITALIAN PEASANT.** *6003 N US 17 Business (Kings Hwy). 803/449-3031.* Hrs: 5-10 pm. Closed Dec 25. Res accepted. Italian menu. Serv bar. Semi-a la carte: dinner $7.95-$15.95. Child's meals. Specialties: chicken breast ripieno, veal Marsala, scallops choron. Anipasto salad bar. Parking. Walls lined with rows of wine bottles. Cr cds: A, DS, MC, V.

★ ★ **JOE'S BAR & GRILL.** *(810 Conway Ave, North Myrtle Beach) Approx 15 mi N on US 17. 803/272-4666.* Hrs: 5-10 pm. Closed Thanksgiving, Dec 25. Res accepted. Bar. Semi-a la carte: dinner $12.95-$25.95. Child's meals. Specialties: steak au poivre, veal Marsala, lobster tail. Parking. Outdoor dining. Overlooks marsh. Cr cds: A, DS, MC, V.

✔ ★ ★ **LATIF'S CAFE BAKERY.** *503 61st Ave. 803/449-1716.* Hrs: 8 am-4 pm; Fri & Sat to 10 pm; Sun to 3 pm. Continental menu. Serv bar. Semi-a la carte: lunch $5.95-$7.50, dinner $7.50-$14.95. Sun brunch $5.95-$7.50. Specialties: Chinese chicken salad, triple mocha torte. Parking. Outdoor dining. French bistro atmosphere. Cr cds: DS, MC, V.

D

★ ★ ★ **THE LIBRARY.** *1212 N Kings Hwy (US 17 Business).* *803/448-4527.* Hrs: 6 pm-closing. Closed Sun. Res accepted. Continental menu. Serv bar. A la carte entrees: dinner $19.95-$26.95. Specializes in lamb, veal, beef. Parking. Tableside preparation. Library decor. Cr cds: A, C, D, DS, MC, V.

★ **LONGHORN STEAKHOUSE.** *7604 N Kings Hwy (US 17).* *803/449-7013.* Hrs: 11 am-2 pm, 5-10 pm; Sun 5-9 pm. Closed Thanksgiving; also 2 wks during Christmas season. Serv bar. Semi-a la carte: lunch $4.95-$9.95, dinner $8.95-$27.95. Child's meals. Specializes in New York strip steak, filet of grouper, quail. Salad bar. Parking. Family-owned. Cr cds: A, C, D, DS, MC, V.

★ ★ **OAK HARBOR.** *(1407 13th Ave North, North Myrtle Beach) 16 mi N on US 17, at Vereen's Marina.* *803/249-4737.* Hrs: 5-9:30 pm; early bird dinner 5-6:30 pm. Closed Thanksgiving, Dec 25. Res accepted. Bar 4-11 pm. Semi-a la carte: dinner $9.95-$18.95. Child's meals. Specializes in prime rib, fresh seafood, veal. Parking. Outdoor dining. Overlooks marina. Cr cds: A, D, MC, V.

D SC

★ ★ **RICE PLANTERS.** *6707 N Kings Hwy (US 17).* *803/449-3456.* Hrs: 5-10 pm. Closed Dec 24, 25. Res accepted. Serv bar. Semi-a la carte: dinner $7.95-$17.95. Child's meals. Specializes in fresh seafood, chicken, steak, homemade pies. Own bread. Parking. Gift shop. Overlooks lake. Family-owned. Cr cds: A, DS, MC, V.

D

✔ ★ **ROSA LINDA'S CAFE.** *(4635 US 17N, North Myrtle Beach) Approx 6 mi N on US 17.* *803/272-6823.* Hrs: 11 am-midnight. Closed Thanksgiving, Dec 24-25. Bar. Semi-a la carte: lunch $2.95-$6.95, dinner $6.50-$13.95. Child's meals. Specialties: fajitas, pasta, pizza. Parking. Outdoor dining. Mexican cantina atmosphere. Cr cds: A, DS, MC, V.

D

★ ★ **SEA CAPTAIN'S HOUSE.** *3000 N Ocean Blvd.* *803/448-8082.* Hrs: 6-10:30 am, 11:30 am-2:30 pm, 5-10 pm. Wine, beer. Semi-a la carte: bkfst $4.20-$7.95, lunch, dinner $4.70-$27. Child's meals. Specializes in fresh seafood, steaks, homemade pies. Parking. Sea captain's house design, flowering shrubs. Ocean view. Cr cds: A, MC, V.

★ **SHENANIGAN'S.** *10131 N Kings Hwy (US 17) (10131).* *803/272-1171.* Hrs: 4-10:30 pm; Fri, Sat to 11 pm; Sun to 10 pm. Closed Dec 24-25. Bar. Semi-a la carte: dinner $7.95-$32.95. Specializes in Greek-style steak, prime rib, chicken Alfredo. Parking. Cr cds: A, C, D, DS, MC, V.

D

★ **SPAGHETTI FREDDIE'S.** *9708 N Kings Hwy (US 17N).* *803/449-4033.* Hrs: 5-10 pm. Closed mid-Dec-Jan. Bar to 2 am. Semi-a la carte: dinner $8.95-$24.95. Specializes in fresh seafood, crab. Salad bar. Parking. Nautical atmosphere. Cr cds: A, D, DS, MC, V.

D SC

★ ★ **TONY'S.** *(1407 US 17, North Myrtle Beach) 15 mi N on US 17.* *803/249-1314.* Hrs: 5-10 pm. Closed Dec-Jan; also Sun Sept-May. Italian menu. Bar. Semi-a la carte: dinner $8.95-$27. Child's meals. Specializes in pasta, pizza, fish. Parking. Contemporary Mediterranean decor. Family-owned. Cr cds: C, D, DS, MC, V.

D

Unrated Dining Spot

MORRISON'S CAFETERIA. *2501 N Kings Hwy (US 17), 1¼ mi N, in Myrtle Square Mall.* *803/448-4302.* Hrs: 11 am-9 pm;

off-season to 8 pm. Southern menu. Avg ck: lunch $3.75, dinner $4.25. Cr cds: MC, V.

Newberry (D-4)

Pop: 10,542 **Elev:** 500 ft **Area code:** 803 **Zip:** 29108

What to See and Do

1. **Sumter National Forest.** N via SC 121, US 176.
2. **Dreher Island State Park.** 20 mi SE via US 76 to Chapin, then 9 mi SW via unnumbered road. Approx 340 acres. Three islands with 12-mile shoreline. Lake swimming; fishing (supplies); boating (ramps, rental slips). Nature trail. Picnicking (shelters), playground, recreation building, store. Camping (hookups, dump station; higher fees for lakefront campsites in summer). Standard fees. Phone 364-3530 or -4152.

(See Clinton, Columbia, Greenwood)

Motels

✔ ★ **BEST WESTERN NEWBERRY INN.** *4 mi NE on SC 34, at jct I-26.* *803/276-5850.* 116 rms, 1-2 story. S $29.95; D $34.95-$37.95; each addl $6; under 12 free. Crib free. TV. Pool. Complimentary continental bkfst. Restaurant 5-9 am. Bar 6 pm-midnight; dancing exc Sun. Ck-out noon. Meeting rms. Exercise equipt; weights, bicycles. Cr cds: A, C, D, DS, MC, V.

≈ ✈ 🔥 SC

★ **COMFORT INN.** *1147 Wilson Rd.* *803/276-1600.* 48 rms, 2 story. July-Aug: S $45; D $47-$70; each addl $4; under 18 free. Crib free. TV; cable. Pool. Complimentary continental bkfst. Coffee in rms. Ck-out 11 am. Coin lndry. Meeting rms. Refrigerators. Cr cds: A, C, D, DS, ER, JCB, MC, V.

D ≈ ✈ 🔥 SC

Orangeburg (E-4)

Settled: 1730s **Pop:** 13,739 **Elev:** 245 ft **Area code:** 803 **Zip:** 29115

Named for the Prince of Orange, this community is the seat of Orangeburg County, one of the most prosperous farm areas in the state. Manufacturing plants for wood products, ball bearings, textiles, textile equipment, chemicals, hand tools and lawn mowers are all located within the county.

What to See and Do

1. **Edisto Memorial Gardens.** S on US 301, within city limits, alongside N Edisto River. City-owned 110-acre site. Seasonal flowers bloom all year; more than 3,200 rose bushes, camellias, azaleas; also many flowering trees. Gardens (daily). Wetlands boardwalk park. Tennis courts, picnic areas, shelters nearby, playground. Phone 533-6020. **Free.**
2. **National Fish Hatchery.** S on US 301 to SC 21 Bypass (Stonewall Jackson Dr). Breeds striped bass, redbreast sunfish, Atlantic sturgeon, endangered shortnose sturgeon, forage fish and others. Aquarium; picnic area. (Mon-Fri; closed hols) Phone 534-4828. **Free.**
3. **South Carolina State University** (1896). (5,000 students) 300 College St NE. Phone 536-7000. On campus is

I.P. Stanback Museum and Planetarium. Museum has changing exhibits (Sept-May, Mon-Fri; closed hols). Planetarium shows

(Sept-May, 2nd & 4th Sun; closed hols). Sr citizen rate. Phone 536-7174 for reservations. Shows ¢

(For further information contact the Orangeburg County Chamber of Commerce, 570 John C. Calhoun Dr, Box 328, 29116-0328; 534-6821.)

Annual Event

Orangeburg County Fair. Fairgrounds. 1st full wk Oct.

(See Aiken, Santee)

Motels

★ ★ **BEST WESTERN INN.** *826 Calhoun Dr (US 301/601). 803/534-7630.* 104 rms, 1-3 story. No elvtr. S $36-$39; D $42-$45; each addl $6; under 12 free; higher rates special events. TV; cable. Pool. Complimentary continental bkfst. Restaurant nearby. Ck-out 11 am. Meeting rms. Cr cds: A, C, D, DS, MC, V.

[D] [≈] [▥] [SC]

✔ ★ **DAYS INN.** *3691 St Matthews Rd, on US 601N. 803/531-2590.* 74 rms. S $30-$38; D $40-$50; each addl $5; under 12 free. Crib free. TV; cable. Pool. Complimentary continental bkfst. Ck-out 11 am. Cr cds: A, C, D, DS, MC, V.

[D] [≈] [▨] [▥] [SC]

★ ★ **HOLIDAY INN.** *415 John C. Calhoun Dr (US 301S). 803/531-4600; FAX 803/531-4600, ext. 189.* 160 rms, 2 story. S $52-$62; D $60-$70; each addl $8; under 19 free. Crib free. TV; cable. Pool. Restaurant 6:30 am-2 pm, 5:30-10 pm; Sat, Sun from 7 am. Rm serv. Bar, closed Sun; dancing. Ck-out noon. Meeting rms. Valet serv. Cr cds: A, C, D, DS, JCB, MC, V.

[D] [≈] [▥] [SC]

Restaurant

✔ ★ **ALEXANDER'S.** *840 Five Chop Rd, off US 301 Business. 803/536-5244.* Hrs: 6 am-2:30 pm. Closed Dec 24-26. Southern cooking. Semi-a la carte: bkfst $1.50-$3.75, lunch $4.25-$7.95. Specializes in fried chicken, seafood. Own breads, desserts. Parking. Colonial decor. No cr cds accepted.

Rock Hill (C-4)

Founded: 1852 **Pop:** 41,643 **Elev:** 667 ft **Area code:** 803

Both a college and an industrial town, Rock Hill takes its name from the flint rock that had to be cut through when a railroad was being built through town.

What to See and Do

1. **Winthrop University** (1886). (5,000 students) Oakland Ave. Coeducational; 100 undergraduate and graduate programs. Concerts, lectures, sports, plays; art galleries. Large lake and recreational area. Phone 323-2236.

2. **Museum of York County.** Mt Gallant Rd, 7 mi NE, off I-77 exit 82 A. Contains a large collection of mounted African hoofed mammals; large African artifacts collection. Hall of Western Hemisphere contains mounted animals from North and South America. Art galleries & planetarium. Catawba pottery sold here. Nature trail, picnic area. (Daily exc Mon; closed Jan 1, Thanksgiving, Dec 25) Sr citizen rate. Phone 329-2121.   ¢¢

3. **Glencairn Garden.** 725 Crest St. Municipally owned. 6 acres of colorful azaleas, dogwood, redbud; crepe myrtle, boxwood; pool, fountain (daily). Phone 329-5620.   **Free.**

4. **Andrew Jackson State Park.** 9 mi N on US 521. Approx 360 acres. Lake fishing; boating (rentals). Nature trail. Picnicking (shelters), playground. Camping. Recreation building. Log house museum contains documents, exhibits of Jackson lore. One-room school with exhibits. Standard fees. Phone 285-3344.

5. **Lake Wylie.** N on SC 274. Created by Duke Power Co. Dam on the Catawba River. Freshwater fishing, boating, waterskiing, swimming; 12,455 acres. Phone 704/382-8587.

6. **Landsford Canal State Park.** 15 mi S off US 21. Approx 250 acres. Site of canal built in 1820s; locks, stone bridges. Trail parallels canals. Picnicking (shelters), recreation building. (Thurs-Mon) Phone 789-5800.

(For further information contact the York County Visitor & Convention Bureau, 201 E Main St, Box 11377, 29731; 329-5200.)

Annual Event

"Come-See-Me." Art shows, tour of houses, entertainment, road race, concerts. 10 days early Apr.

(See Chester, Gaffney; also see Charlotte, NC)

Motels

★ ★ **COMFORT INN.** *(3725 Ave of the Carolinas, Fort Mill 29715)* N on I-77, exit 90. *803/548-5200; FAX 803/548-6692.* 155 rms, 4 story. S $56; D $66; suites, kit. unit $130-$150; under 18 free. Crib free. TV; cable. Pool. Complimentary continental bkfst, coffee. Restaurant adj 6 am-10 pm. Ck-out 11 am. Meeting rms. Valet serv. Sundries. Exercise equipt; weights, bicycles. Refrigerator in suites. Cr cds: A, C, D, DS, ER, JCB, MC, V.

[D] [≈] [🏋] [▨] [▥] [SC]

★ **DAYS INN.** *914 Riverview Rd (29730). 803/329-6581.* 113 rms, 3 story. S $51; D $56; each addl $5. Crib free. TV; cable. Pool. Complimentary full bkfst. Restaurant 6-10 am, 5-10 pm. Ck-out noon. Meeting rms. Cr cds: A, C, D, DS, MC, V.

[D] [≈] [▨] [▥] [SC]

★ **DAYS INN CHARLOTTE SOUTH/CAROWINDS.** *(3482 US 21, Ft Mill 29715)* Approx 5 mi N on I-77 exit 90. *803/548-8000; FAX 803/548-6058.* 119 rms, 2 story. Apr-Sept: S $49.95; D $54.95; each addl $5; higher rates special events; lower rates rest of yr. Crib free. Pet accepted. TV; cable, in-rm movies avail. Pool. Complimentary continental bkfst in lobby. Restaurant adj open 24 hrs. Ck-out 11 am. Cr cds: A, C, D, DS, MC, V.

[D] [✔] [≈] [▨] [▥] [SC]

✔ ★ **ECONO LODGE.** *962 Riverview Rd (29730), I-77 exit 82B. 803/329-3232; FAX 803/328-6288.* 106 rms, 2 story. S $31.46-$36.95; D $34.95-$40.95; each addl $5; under 18 free. Crib free. TV; cable. Complimentary coffee in lobby. Restaurant adj open 24 hrs. Ck-out 11 am. Cr cds: A, C, D, DS, ER, JCB, MC, V.

[D] [▨] [▥] [SC]

★ ★ **HOLIDAY INN.** *2640 Cherry Rd (29730), at jct I-77, US 21N. 803/329-1122; FAX 803/329-1072.* 126 rms, 2 story. S $52; D $52-$65; each addl $5; suites $95-$125; under 18 free. Crib free. Pet accepted. TV. Pool. Complimentary full bkfst. Restaurant 5:30-10 pm. Bar 3 pm-2 am, Sat to midnight. Ck-out noon. Meeting rms. Coin lndry. Cr cds: A, C, D, DS, JCB, MC, V.

[D] [✔] [≈] [▥]

✔ ★ ★ **HOWARD JOHNSON.** *2625 Cherry Rd (29730), I-77 exit 82B, jct US 21. 803/329-3121; FAX 803/366-1043.* 140 rms, 2 story. S $46-$53; D $48-$59; each addl $6; suites $125; under 12 free. Crib free. Pet accepted. TV; cable. Pool. Complimentary continental bkfst in lobby. Restaurant open 24 hrs. Rm serv 6 am-9 pm. Bar 5-10 pm, closed Sun. Ck-out noon. Meeting rm. Valet serv. Private patios, balconies. Cr cds: A, C, D, DS, JCB, MC, V.

★ ★ **RAMADA INN-CAROWINDS.** *(225 Carowinds Blvd, Ft Mill 29715)* I-77 Carowinds exit. 803/548-2400; FAX 803/548-6382. 211 rms, 11 story. S $57-$69; D $63-$75; each addl $6; under 19 free. Crib free. TV; cable. Pool. Playground. Restaurant 6:30 am-2 pm, 5-10 pm; Fri, Sat to 11 pm. Rm serv. Bar 4:30-11 pm; entertainment, dancing exc Sun. Ck-out 11 am. Coin lndry. Meeting rms. Airport transportation. Opp Carowinds. Cr cds: A, D, DS, MC, V.

Santee (E-5)

Pop: 638 **Elev:** 250 ft **Area code:** 803 **Zip:** 29142

This community serves as the gateway to the Santee-Cooper Lakes recreation area, created by the Pinopolis and Santee dams on the Santee and Cooper rivers. There are numerous marinas and campgrounds on the Santee-Cooper lakes.

What to See and Do

1. **Eutaw Springs Battlefield Site.** 12 mi SE off SC 6. Site where ragged colonials fought the British on Sept 8, 1781, in what is considered to be the last major engagement in South Carolina; both sides claimed victory. Three acres maintained by state. No facilities. **Free.**

2. **Fort Watson Battle Site & Indian Mound.** 4 mi N, 1 mi off US 15/301, on Lake Marion. A 48-foot-high mound; site of Revolutionary War battle Apr 15-23, 1781, during which Gen. Francis Marion attacked and captured a British fortification, its garrison, supplies and ammunition. Three acres maintained by state. No facilities. Observation point has view of Santee-Cooper waters. **Free.**

3. **Santee State Park.** 3 mi NW off SC 6, on shores of Lake Marion. Approx 2,500 acres. Lake swimming; fishing (supplies avail); boating (ramp, rentals, dock). Nature trails; tennis. Picnicking (shelters), playground, restaurant, groceries. Camping, cabins (higher fees for lakefront sites), primitive camping. Interpretive center, recreation building. Standard fees. Phone 854-2408.

4. **Santee National Wildlife Refuge.** 4 mi N on US 15/301 or exit 102 from I-95. Attracts many geese and ducks during winter. Observation tower, self-guided nature trail; visitor information center with exhibits (Mon-Fri; closed hols). Seasonal hunting and fishing, wildlife observation and photography. Phone 478-2217. **Free.**

(For further information contact Santee-Cooper Country, PO Drawer 40; 854-2131 or 800/227-8510 outside SC.)

(See Orangeburg)

Motels

★ ★ **BEST WESTERN.** *Box 188, I-95 exit 98 E.* 803/854-3089. 108 rms. S $42-$48; D $45-$55; under 12 free. Crib $4. TV; cable. Heated pool. Complimentary continental bkfst. Restaurant 5-9:30 pm. Ck-out 11 am. 18-hole golf privileges. Cr cds: A, C, D, DS, MC, V.

✔ ★ **DAYS INN.** *At jct I-95 & SC 6.* 803/854-2175; FAX 803/854-2835. 120 rms, 2 story. S $30-$47; D $35-$52; each addl $5; under 12 free; golf plans. Crib free. Pet accepted, some restrictions; $5. TV; cable. Pool; wading pool, whirlpool. Playground. Restaurant

6-11 am, 5-9 pm. Ck-out noon. 18-hole golf privileges. Cr cds: A, C, D, DS, MC, V.

Spartanburg (C-3)

Founded: 1785 **Pop:** 43,467 **Elev:** 816 ft **Area code:** 803

An array of highways and railroads feeds agricultural products into, and moves manufactured products out of, heavily industrialized Spartanburg. Textiles and peaches are the leading products. The Spartan Regiment of South Carolina militia, heroes of the Battle at Cowpens, gave both the county and its seat their names.

What to See and Do

1. **Regional Museum.** 501 Otis Blvd, at Pine St. Exhibits depict up-country history of state; Pardo Stone (1567), doll collections, Native American artifacts. (Daily exc Mon; closed hols) Phone 596-3501. **¢**

2. **The Arts Council of Spartanburg.** 385 S Spring St. Permanent and changing exhibits; classes in visual and performing arts. (Daily; closed most hols) Phone 583-2776. **Free.**

3. **Walnut Grove Plantation** (1765). 8 mi SE near jct I-26, US 221. Restored girlhood home of Kate Moore Barry, Revolutionary heroine; period furniture; schoolhouse, kitchen, doctor's office, other buildings; family cemetery; herb gardens with "dipping well." (Apr-Oct, daily exc Mon; rest of yr, Sun only; closed some hols) Sr citizen rate. Phone 576-6546. **¢¢**

4. **Croft State Park.** 3 mi SE on SC 56. On part of old Camp Croft military area. Approx 7,000 acres. Swimming pool (fee); lake fishing. Nature, exercise trails; bridle trail (no rentals); stable, show ring; tennis. Picnicking (shelters), playground. Camping (hookups, dump station). Standard fees. Phone 585-1283.

(For further information contact the Convention & Visitors Bureau, 105 N Pine St, Box 1636, 29304; 594-5050.)

Annual Event

Piedmont Interstate Fair. Art exhibit, livestock and flower shows, needlecraft and food displays; auto race. Phone 582-7042. 2nd full wk Oct.

(See Clinton, Gaffney, Greenville)

Motels

★ ★ **COMFORT INN-WEST.** *2070 New Cut Rd (29303).* 803/576-2992. 99 rms, 2 story. S $43.95-$45.95; D $48.95-$58.95; each addl $5; suites $125; under 18 free. Crib free. TV; cable. Pool. Complimentary continental bkfst. Ck-out 11 am. Meeting rm. Cr cds: A, C, D, DS, ER, JCB, MC, V.

★ ★ **HAMPTON INN.** *4930 College Dr (29301).* 803/576-6080; FAX 803/587-8901. 112 rms, 2 story. S $42-$48; D $48-$56; under 18 free. Crib free. TV; cable. Pool. Complimentary continental bkfst. Ck-out noon. Meeting rm. Cr cds: A, C, D, DS, MC, V.

★ ★ **HOLIDAY INN.** *200 International Dr (29301),* jct I-26 & I-85 exit 71. 803/576-5220; FAX 803/574-1243. 225 rms, 3 story. S $51-$76; D $56-$81; each addl $5; under 18 free. Crib free. TV. Indoor pool; wading pool, poolside serv. Restaurant 6:30 am-2 pm, 5:30-10:30 pm. Rm serv. Bar; entertainment, dancing exc Sun. Ck-out noon. Coin lndry. Meeting rms. Bellhops. Valet serv. Exercise equipt; weights, bicycles, whirlpool, sauna. Rec rm. Putting green. Lawn games. Cr cds: A, C, D, DS, JCB, MC, V.

★ ★ **RAMADA INN.** *1000 Hearon Circle (29303), at jct I-85 & I-585. 803/578-7170; FAX 803/578-4243.* 138 rms, 2-3 story. No elvtr. S $45-$54; D $52-$63; each addl $7. Crib free. TV. Pool; wading pool. Restaurant 6 am-10 pm. Rm serv. Bar 5 pm-2 am; entertainment, dancing exc Sun. Ck-out noon. Meeting rms. Bellhops. Valet serv. Cr cds: A, C, D, DS, JCB, MC, V.

Motor Hotel

★ ★ **QUALITY HOTEL AND CONFERENCE CENTER.** *7136 Asheville Hwy (29303). 803/578-5530; FAX 803/578-5530, ext. 566.* 143 rms, 6 story. S $45-$85; D $50-$85; each addl $5; under 18 free. Crib free. Pet accepted. TV; cable, in-rm movies. Pool; poolside serv. Restaurant 6:30 am-2 pm, 5-10 pm. Rm serv. Bar 4 pm-midnight; occasional entertainment, dancing exc Sun. Ck-out noon. Meeting rms. Valet serv. Exercise equipt; weight machine, treadmill. Refrigerators avail. Cr cds: A, C, D, DS, JCB, MC, V.

Restaurant

★ **SPICE OF LIFE.** *Wood Row & St John Sts. 803/585-3737.* Hrs: 11:30 am-2:30 pm, 5:30-9 pm. Closed Sun; some major hols. Res accepted. French, Italian menu. Bar. Semi-a la carte: lunch $4.95-$5.75, dinner $9.95-$23.95. Specialty: herb crusted salmon. Parking. Terrace dining. Gourmet gift shop. Cr cds: A, MC, V.

Sumter (D-5)

Settled: 1785 **Pop:** 36,933 **Elev:** 173 ft **Area code:** 803

Long the center of a prosperous agricultural area, Sumter has, in recent years, become an industrial center. Both the city and county are named for General Thomas Sumter, the "fighting gamecock" of the Revolutionary War. As a tourism spot, Sumter offers a unique contrast of antebellum mansions and modern facilities. Shaw Air Force Base, headquarters of the 9th Air Force and the 363rd Tactical Fighter Wing, is nearby.

What to See and Do

1. **Swan Lake Iris Gardens.** W Liberty St. Covers 150 acres; Kaempferi and Japanese iris; seasonal plantings, nature trails; ancient cypress, oak and pine trees; 45-acre lake with several species of swan. Picnicking, playground. (Daily) **Free.**

2. **Sumter Gallery of Art.** 421 N Main St. Regional artwork features paintings, drawings, sculpture, photography and pottery. (Tues-Sun afternoons; closed hols & July) Phone 775-0543. **Free.**

3. **Sumter County Museum.** 122 N Washington St. Two-story Edwardian house depicting Victorian lifestyle; period rooms, historical exhibits, war memorabilia, economic and cultural artifacts, artwork and archives (genealogical research). Museum is surrounded by formal gardens designed by Robert Marvin; several outdoor exhibits of farm implements, rural life; carriage house. (Daily exc Mon; closed hols) Donation. Phone 775-0908.

4. **Church of the Holy Cross** (1850). 10 mi W via US 76, exit at SC 261, in Stateburg. Built of *pise de terre* (rammed earth); unusual architectural design and construction. Also noted for stained-glass windows set to catch the rays of the rising sun. Many

notable South Carolinians from the 1700s are buried in the old church cemetery, including Joel R. Poinsett. Phone 494-8101.

5. **Poinsett State Park.** 18 mi SW via SC 763, 261. Approx 1,000 acres of mountains, swamps. Named for Joel Poinsett, who introduced the poinsettia (which originated in Mexico) to the US. Spanish moss, mountain laurel, rhododendron. Lake swimming; fishing; boating (rentals). Hiking, nature trails;. Picnicking (shelters), playground. Primitive & improved camping (dump station), cabins. Nature center; programs. Standard fees. Phone 494-8177.

(For further information contact the Convention & Visitors Bureau, Box 1449, 29151; 773-3371.)

Annual Events

Sumter Iris Festival. Fireworks display, parade, art show, golf & tennis tournaments, barbecue cook-off, local talent exhibition, square dance, iris gardens display. Late May.

Fall Fiesta of Arts. Swan Lake Gardens. Features visual & performing arts, concerts & choral groups. Phone 436-2258. 3rd wkend Oct.

(See Camden, Columbia)

Motels

★ **DAYS INN.** *378 Broad St (29150). 803/469-9210.* 104 rms. S $32.95; D $35.95-$40.95; each addl $5. Crib free. TV; cable. Pool. Complimentary coffee in lobby. Ck-out 11 am. Cr cds: A, C, D, DS, MC, V.

★ ★ **HOLIDAY INN.** *PO Drawer 6066 (29150), 2390 Broad St. 803/469-9001.* 124 rms, 2 story. S, D $50-$76; each addl $4; under 19 free; wkend rates. Crib free. TV; cable. Pool. Restaurant 6:30 am-2 pm, 5:30-10 pm. Rm serv. Bar 4 pm-midnight. Ck-out noon. Meeting rms. Valet serv. Tennis privileges. Cr cds: A, C, D, DS, JCB, MC, V.

★ ★ **RAMADA INN.** *226 N Washington St (29150), on US 76/378/521. 803/775-2323; FAX 803/773-9500.* 125 rms in 2 buildings, 2-3 story. S $42-$62; D $47-$67; each addl $6; under 18 free; golf plans. Crib free. TV; cable. Pool. Restaurant 6 am-2 pm, 6-10 pm. Rm serv. Bar 5 pm-midnight, closed Sun. Ck-out noon. Meeting rms. Cr cds: A, C, D, DS, ER, JCB, MC, V.

Restaurant

★ ★ **BIG JIM'S.** *451 Broad St. 803/773-3343.* Hrs: 11 am-11 pm; Sat 5-11 pm. Closed Sun; most major hols. Res accepted. Bar. Semi-a la carte: lunch $5.95-$7.95, dinner $10.95-$22.95. Child's meals. Specialties: broiled lobster dainties, seafood platter, Greek-style roasted chicken. Salad bar. Own pies. Parking. Family-owned. Cr cds: A, MC, V.

Walterboro (E-5)

Settled: 1784 **Pop:** 5,492 **Elev:** 69 ft **Area code:** 803 **Zip:** 29488

Settled in 1784 by Charleston plantation owners as a summer resort area, Walterboro has retained its charm of yesterday despite its growth. The town boasts a casual pace and rural lifestyle where people can enjoy fishing and hunting, early 19th-century architectural designs, plantations and beach and recreational facilities.

What to See and Do

1. **Colleton County Courthouse.** Hampton St & Jefferies Blvd. Building designed by Robert Mills; first public nullification meeting in state was held in 1828.
2. **Colleton State Park.** 11 mi N on US 15. On 35 acres; tree-shaded area on banks of Edisto River. Canoeing (dock); river fishing. Nature trails. Picnicking (shelters). Camping (hookups, dump station). Standard fees. Phone 538-8206.

(For further information and walking-tour maps and brochures contact the Walterboro-Colleton Chamber of Commerce, 109 Benson St, Box 426; 549-1035.)

Annual Event

Rice Festival. Entertainment, parade, arts & crafts; street dances, soap box derby. Last full wkend Apr.

(See Beaufort, Charleston)

Motels

★ **ECONO LODGE.** *I-95 & SC 63. 803/538-3830.* 100 rms, 2 story. S $24.95; D $31.95-$34.95; each addl $4; under 12 free. Crib free. TV. Restaurant opp open 6 am-11 pm. Ck-out 11 am. Cr cds: A, DS, MC, V.

★ ★ **HOLIDAY INN.** *Box 889, 3 mi SW on SC 63 at I-95. 803/538-5473; FAX 803/538-5473, ext. 192.* 172 rms, 2 story. S $42; D $53; each addl $5; under 18 free. Crib free. Pet accepted. TV. Pool; wading pool. Restaurant 6 am-2 pm, 5-10 pm. Rm serv. Bar 5 pm-midnight; dancing exc Sun. Ck-out noon. Meeting rms. Valet serv. Cr cds: A, C, D, DS, JCB, MC, V.

★ ★ **TOWN AND COUNTRY INN.** *1139 Sniders Hwy, at jct SC 63, I-95 exit 53. 803/538-5911; FAX 803/538-5911, ext. 197.* 97 rms, 2 story. S $21.95-$25.95; D $29.95; each addl $3; under 18 free. Crib free. TV; cable. Pool. Playground. Restaurant 6 am-10 pm. Rm serv. Bar from 5 pm. Ck-out 11 am. Private patios, balconies. Cr cds: A, DS, JCB, MC, V.

Virginia

Population: 6,377,000

Land area: 40,815 square miles

Elevation: 0-5,729 feet

Highest point: Mt Rogers (Between Smyth, Grayson Counties)

Entered Union: Tenth of original 13 states (June 25, 1788)

Capital: Richmond

Motto: Thus always to tyrants

Nickname: Old Dominion

State flower: American dogwood

State bird: Cardinal

State fair: September 28-October 8, 1995, in Richmond

Time zone: Eastern

Settled by Elizabethans and named for their Virgin Queen, the first of the Southern states still retains a degree of the graceful courtliness that reached its peak just before the Civil War. Evidence of strong ties with the past are apparent in the Old Dominion. More than 1,600 historical markers dot its 55,000 miles of paved roads. More than 100 historic buildings are open all year; hundreds more welcome visitors during the statewide Historic Garden Week (usually the last week in April).

Permanent English settlement of America began in Jamestown in 1607 and started a long line of Virginia "firsts": the first legislative assembly in the Western Hemisphere (1619); the first armed rebellion against royal government (Bacon's Rebellion, 1676); the first stirring debates, in Williamsburg and Richmond, which left pre-Revolutionary America echoing Patrick Henry's inflammatory "Give me liberty, or give me death!" Records show that America's first Thanksgiving was held Dec 4, 1619, on the site of what is now Berkeley Plantation.

To Virginia the nation owes its most cherished documents—Thomas Jefferson's Declaration of Independence, George Mason's Bill of Rights, James Madison's Constitution. From here came George Washington to lead the Revolution and to become the first of eight US presidents to hail from Virginia.

Ironically, the state so passionately involved in creating a new nation was very nearly the means of its destruction. Virginia was the spiritual and physical capital of the Confederacy; the Army of Northern Virginia was the Confederacy's most powerful weapon; General Robert E. Lee its greatest commander. More than half the fighting of the Civil War took place in Virginia; and here, in the quaint little village of Appomattox Court House, the war finally came to an end.

When chartered in 1609, the Virginia territory included about one-tenth of what is now the United States; the present state ranks 36th in size, but the remaining area is remarkably diverse. Tidewater Virginia—the coastal plain—is low, almost flat, arable land cut by rivers and bays into a magnificent system of natural harbors. It was vital to commerce and agriculture in the early days. Today it is still important commercially (the Hampton Roads port is one of the world's great

naval and shipbuilding bases) and a perennial lure to vacationers as well.

Inland lies the gentle rolling Piedmont, covering about half the state. Here is Virginia's leading tobacco area; it also produces apples, corn, wheat, hay and dairy products. The world's largest single-unit textile plant is in Danville; the Piedmont also manufactures shoes, furniture, paper products, clay and glass, chemicals and transportation equipment.

West of the Piedmont rise the Blue Ridge Mountains; high, rugged upland plateaus occur to the south. Further west is the Valley of Virginia, a series of fertile valleys. Best known is the Shenandoah, which contains some of the richest—and once bloodiest—land in the nation. Civil War fighting swept the valley for four years; Winchester changed hands some 70 times.

To the southwest are the Appalachian Plateaus, a rugged, forested region of coal mines. Here the splendid outdoor drama, the *Trail of the Lonesome Pine,* romanticized by the novelist John Fox, is performed.

For the vacationer today, the state offers colonial and Civil War history at every turn, seashore and mountain recreation the year round, such natural oddities as caverns in the west and the Dismal Swamp in the southeast, and the Skyline Drive (see SHENANDOAH NATIONAL PARK), one of the loveliest scenic drives in the East.

National Park Service Areas

Besides Shenandoah National Park (see), Virginia has two national battlefield parks (Manassas and Richmond, see both), Petersburg National Battlefield (see), two national monuments (Booker T. Washington and George Washington Birthplace, see both), Fredericksburg & Spotsylvania National Military Park (see), Assateague Island National Seashore (see CHINCOTEAGUE), the Blue Ridge Parkway (see) and two national historical parks (Appomattox Court House and Colonial, see both). The latter includes Cape Henry Memorial, Colonial Parkway, Jamestown (see all) and Yorktown Battlefield (see YORKTOWN). Wolf

Trap Farm Park for the Performing Arts (see FAIRFAX) is the country's only national park for the performing arts. The National Capital Parks Region maintains Arlington House, the Robert E. Lee Memorial (see ARLINGTON COUNTY) and Prince William Forest Park (see TRIANGLE). Part of the Chesapeake and Ohio Canal National Historical Park (see in MARYLAND) is also here. Virginia has 23 state parks, and also has cooperative management of Breaks Interstate Park (see).

National Forests

The following is an alphabetical listing of National Forests and the towns they are listed under.

George Washington National Forest (see HARRISONBURG): Forest Supervisor in Harrisonburg; Ranger offices in Bridgewater*, Buena Vista*, Covington, Edinburg*, Hot Springs, Staunton.

Jefferson National Forest (see MARION): Forest Supervisor in Roanoke; Ranger offices in Blacksburg, Natural Bridge, New Castle*, Wise, Wytheville.

*Not described in text

State Recreation Areas

The following towns list state recreation areas in their vicinity under What to See and Do; refer to the individual town for directions and park information.

Listed under **Abingdon:** see Grayson Highlands State Park.

Listed under **Appomattox Court House National Historical Park:** see Holliday Lake State Park.

Listed under **Big Stone Gap:** see Natural Tunnel State Park.

Listed under **Clarksville:** see Occoneechee State Park.

Listed under **Clifton Forge:** see Douthat State Park.

Listed under **Farmville:** see Bear Creek Lake State Park.

Listed under **Front Royal:** see Sky Meadows State Park.

Listed under **Keysville:** see Twin Lakes State Park.

Listed under **Marion:** see Hungry Mother State Park.

Listed under **Martinsville:** see Fairy Stone State Park.

Listed under **Montross:** see Westmoreland State Park.

Listed under **Radford:** see Claytor Lake State Park.

Listed under **Richmond:** see Pocahontas State Park.

Listed under **South Boston:** see Staunton River State Park.

Listed under **Surry:** see Chippokes Plantation State Park.

Listed under **Virginia Beach:** see Seashore State Park.

Listed under **Williamsburg:** see York River State Park.

Water-related activities, hiking, various other sports, picnicking and visitor centers, as well as camping, are available in many of these areas. State parks are open all year. Parking for noncampers, $1.50-$2.50/car/day, Memorial Day-Labor Day. Admission to State Historical Parks $1.25; children $1. Swimming, boat rentals, cafes and concessions, Memorial Day-Labor Day; fees for activities. Pets are allowed in camping and cabins, but must be kept inside at night. At all other times pets must be on a 6-ft leash. Facilities for the disabled at many parks.

Tent and trailer camping is available in 17 parks generally from Mar-Nov; maximum stay is two weeks. $8.50/site/night, $14 at Seashore (up to 6 persons, 1 vehicle); electricity and water $12/site/night where available. Reservations may be made 180 days-1 wk in advance (see below for addresses). Seven parks offer housekeeping cabins (May-Sept). Douthat (see CLIFTON FORGE) has a guest lodge for 15. Reservations for campsites are accepted beginning late March. Campsite and cabin reservations may be made in person at any state park with cabins and/or campgrounds or through Ticketmaster by contacting PO Box 62346, Virginia Beach 23466; phone 804/490-3939. Information and forms can be obtained from Ticketmaster or from the Divison of State Parks, 203 Governor St, Suite 306, Richmond 23219; phone 804/786-1712. Booklets with details on each park may be obtained from the Division of State Parks and a campground directory is available from Virginia Division of Tourism, Bell Tower on Capitol Square, 101 N 9th St, Richmond 23219; phone 804/786-4484.

Fishing & Hunting

Saltwater fishing on ocean, bay, river or creek is a major sport. Virginia is blessed with many miles of shoreline: 120 miles on the Atlantic Ocean, 300 miles on Chesapeake Bay, and 1,300 miles of tidal shores. There is no closed season for saltwater fishing. There are some species size and bag limits. No license is required to fish in ocean waters or seaside of the eastern shore, but a license is required to fish in the Chesapeake and tidal tributaries. Information concerning size limits and bag limits on saltwater game fish may be obtained from the Virginia Marine Resources Commission, PO Box 756, Newport News 23607; phone 804/247-2200. The Commonwealth of Virginia sponsors an annual Saltwater Fishing Awards Program (see VIRGINIA BEACH), open to the public without any charges or registration requirements.

Freshwater fishing is excellent in many of the state's large reservoirs and rivers for such species as largemouth and smallmouth bass, landlocked striped bass, muskie and a wide variety of pan fish. Lake Anna, Smith Mt Lake, Lake Gaston, Lake Philpott, Lake Moomaw & Buggs Island Lake are nationally known for excellent bass and landlocked striped bass fishing. Nonresident license: $30; $30 additional for license for trout in designated stocked waters. Five-day license to fish state-wide, $6; other special fees. Fishing in a national forest requires an additional fishing/hunting stamp, $3.

Hunting for upland game and migratory waterfowl in season. Nonresident license: $60; three-day license: $30; bear, deer, turkey, $60 additional; nonresident muzzle-loader license, $25; nonresident special archery license to hunt during special archery season, $25. Hunting in a national forest requires an additional fishing/hunting stamp, $3. For fishing and hunting regulations and information write Department of Game and Inland Fisheries, Box 11104, Richmond 23230 or phone 804/367-1000.

Skiing

The following towns list ski areas in their vicinity under What to See and Do; refer to the individual town for directions and information.

Listed under **Basye:** see Bryce Resort.

Listed under **Charlottesville:** see Wintergreen Resort.

Listed under **Hot Springs:** see Homestead Ski Area.

Safety Belt Information

Safety belts are mandatory for all persons in front seat of vehicle. Children under 4 years must be in an approved safety seat anywhere in vehicle. For further information phone 804/367-6400 or 800/533-1892 (VA).

Interstate Highway System

The following alphabetical listing of Virginia towns in *Mobil Travel Guide* shows that these cities are within 10 miles of the indicated Interstate highways. A highway map should, however, be checked for the nearest exit.

INTERSTATE 64: Ashland, Charlottesville, Chesapeake, Clifton Forge, Covington, Hampton, Jamestown, Lexington, Newport News, Norfolk, Portsmouth, Richmond, Staunton, Virginia Beach, Waynesboro, Williamsburg, Yorktown.

INTERSTATE 66: Alexandria, Arlington County, Fairfax, Falls Church, Front Royal, Manassas, McLean.

INTERSTATE 77: Wytheville.

INTERSTATE 81: Abingdon, Blacksburg, Bristol, Front Royal, Harrisonburg, Lexington, Marion, Natural Bridge, New Market, Radford, Roanoke, Salem, Staunton, Strasburg, Winchester, Woodstock, Wytheville.

INTERSTATE 85: Petersburg, South Hill.

INTERSTATE 95: Alexandria, Arlington County, Ashland, Emporia, Fairfax, Falls Church, Fredericksburg, Hopewell, McLean, Mount Vernon, Petersburg, Richmond, Springfield, Triangle.

Additional Visitor Information

Recreational and tourist information, including brochures, maps and list of events, is available from the Virginia Division of Tourism, Bell Tower on Capitol Square, 101 N 9th St, Richmond 23219; phone 804/786-4484. Virginia Department of Transportation, 1401 E Broad St, Richmond 23219, phone 804/786-2838, offers an official state map.

There are 10 welcome information centers in Virginia at the following locations: the northern end of the state, on I-81 in Clear Brook, and on I-66 in Manassas; at the northeastern side, on I-95 in Fredericksburg; around the bay area on the eastern side, on US 13 in New Church; around the southerly border, on I-95 in Skippers, and on I-85 in Bracey; in the southwest part of the state, on I-81 in Bristol, and I-77 in Lambsburg; and on the western side, on I-64 in Covington, and on I-77 in Rocky Gap.

Abingdon (F-3)

Settled: ca 1770 **Pop:** 7,003 **Elev:** 2,069 ft **Area code:** 703 **Zip:** 24210

Daniel Boone passed through this area in 1760 and dubbed it Wolf Hill after a pack of wolves from a nearby cave disturbed his dogs. Wolf Hill had long been a crossing for buffalo and Native Americans; Boone later used it for his own family's westward migration. Later, Black's Fort was built here, and the community adopted that name. Now known as Abingdon, this summer resort in the Virginia Highlands, just north of Tennessee, is the Washington County seat, Virginia's largest burley tobacco market and a livestock auction center.

What to See and Do

1. **Grayson Highlands State Park.** 35 mi SE on US 58. Within this 4,935-acre park are rugged peaks, some more than 5,000 feet; alpine scenery. Hiking, horse trails, picnicking, camping, visitor center, interpretive programs, pioneer life displays (June-Aug). Adj to Mount Rogers National Recreation Area (see MARION). (Daily) Standard fees. Phone 579-7092.
2. **White's Mill.** 3½ mi N via VA 692, on White's Mill Rd. Old gristmill and general store, still in operation. (Daily) Phone 676-0285. ¢

(For further information contact the Washington County Chamber of Commerce, 179 E Main St; 628-8141.)

Annual Event

Virginia Highlands Festival. Exhibits, demonstrations of rustic handicrafts; plays, musical entertainment; historical re-enactments; historic house tours, antique market. Last wk July-2nd wk Aug.

Seasonal Event

Barter Theatre. Main St, on US 11 off I-81, in former Town Hall. America's oldest, longest-running professional repertory theater. Founded during the Depression on the theory that residents would barter their abundant crops for first-rate professional entertainment. Designated State Theatre of Virginia in 1946. Phone 628-3991 or 800/368-3240. Barter Players perform nightly exc Mon, Apr-Oct. Children's theater mid-June-Aug.

(See Bristol, Marion)

Motels

★ **ALPINE.** Box 658, 882 E Main St. 703/628-3178. 19 rms. S $36; D $45; each addl $4. Crib $2. TV; cable. Playground. Restaurant nearby. Ck-out 11 am. View of mountains. Cr cds: A, DS, MC, V.

✔ ★ ★ **COMFORT INN.** Jct I-81 exit 14 & VA 140. 703/676-2222; FAX 703/676-2222, ext. 307. 80 rms, 2 story. S $38-$60; D $44-$70; each addl $6; under 18 free; higher rates special events. Crib free. TV; cable. Heated pool. Complimentary continental bkfst. Ck-out noon. Valet serv. Cr cds: A, C, D, DS, ER, JCB, MC, V.

★ ★ **EMPIRE.** 887 Empire Dr. 703/628-7131. 105 rms, 2 story. S $33-$34; D $39-$41; each addl $2; under 12 free; higher rates special events. Crib $5. Pet accepted. TV; cable. Restaurant 6:30 am-10 pm. Ck-out 11 am. Balconies. Cr cds: A, MC, V.

Inn

★ ★ ★ ★ **MARTHA WASHINGTON INN.** 150 W Main St. 703/628-3161; FAX 703/628-8885. 61 rms. S, D $95-$105; each addl $10; suites $175-$360; studio rms $120-$160; under 12 free. Crib $10. TV; cable. Pool privileges. Dining rm (see FIRST LADY'S TABLE). Afternoon tea 4-5 pm. Rm serv. Bar 4:30 pm-2 am, Sat from 11 am. Ck-out noon, ck-in 2 pm. Meeting rms. Bellhops. Tennis and golf privileges. Whirlpool. Lawn games. Bathrm phone in suites. Antique furnishings. Historic structure; built 1832 as a private home and once served as a girl's school. Cr cds: A, C, D, DS, MC, V.

Restaurant

★ ★ ★ **FIRST LADY'S TABLE.** (See Martha Washington Inn) 703/628-3161. Hrs: 7-10 am, 11:30 am-2 pm, 5-10 pm; Sun to 9 pm. Res accepted. Bar. Semi-a la carte: bkfst $2.25-$7.95, lunch $3.75-$11.95, dinner $10.50-$24.95. Buffet: dinner (Sun & Fri) $11.95-$19.95. Child's meals. Specialties: panéed mountain trout, veal Linstrom. Own baking. Parking. Cr cds: A, C, D, DS, MC, V.

D

Alexandria (C-8)

Settled: 1670 **Pop:** 111,183 **Elev:** 52 ft **Area code:** 703

A group of English and Scottish merchants established a tobacco warehouse at the junction of Hunting Creek and the "Potowmack" River in the 1740's. The little settlement prospered and 17 years later John West, Jr, surveyor, and his young assistant, George Washington, arrived and "laid off in streets and 84 half-acre lots" the town of Alexandria. Among the first buyers, on the July morning in 1749 when the lots were offered for public sale, were Lawrence Washington and his brother Augustus, William Ramsay, the Honorable William Fairfax and John Carlyle. Erecting handsome town houses, these gentlemen soon brought a lively and cosmopolitan air to Alexandria, with parties, balls and horse racing. It was also the hometown of George Mason and Robert E. Lee and home to George Washington.

In 1789, Virginia ceded Alexandria to the District of Columbia, but in 1846 the still Southern-oriented citizens asked to return to the Old Dominion, which Congress allowed.

In the Civil War, Alexandria was cut off from the Confederacy when Union troops occupied the town to protect Potomac River navigation. Safe behind Union lines, the city escaped the dreadful destruction experienced by many other Southern towns. After the war, even with seven railroads centering here for transfer of freight, Alexandria declined as a center of commerce and was in trade doldrums until about 1914, when the Alexandria shipyards were reopened and the Naval Torpedo Station was built. Today it has developed into a trade, commerce, transportation and science center. More than 180 national associations are based here.

What to See and Do

1. Walking Tour of Historic Sites.

Start at Alexandria Convention/Visitors Bureau in **Ramsay House** (ca 1725), 221 King St, at Fairfax St. Oldest house in Alexandria and later used as a tavern, grocery store and cigar factory. Here you can obtain special events information and a free self-guided walking tour brochure. You may also purchase "block tickets" here, good for reduced admission to four of the city's historic properties. Video shown with translations available in 18 languages. Guided walking tours, conducted by costumed guides, depart from here (spring-fall, weather permitting). The Bureau also issues free parking permits, tour and highway maps, hotel, dining and shopping guides. (Daily; closed Jan 1, Thanksgiving, Dec 25) Phone 838-4200. 1 blk N on Fairfax St is

Carlyle House (1753). 121 N Fairfax St. This stately stone mansion, built in Palladian style, was the site of a 1755 meeting between General Edward Braddock and five British colonial governors to plan the early campaigns of the French and Indian War. (Daily exc Mon; closed Jan 1, Thanksgiving, Dec 24, 25) Phone 549-2997. ¢¢ 1½ blks S on Fairfax St is

Stabler-Leadbeater Apothecary Museum (1792). 105 S Fairfax St. Largest collection of apothecary glass in its original setting in the country; more than 1,000 apothecary bottles. Original building is now a museum of early pharmacy; collection of old prescriptions, patent medicines, scales, other 18th-century pharmacy items. George Washington, Robert E. Lee and John Calhoun were regular customers. (Daily exc Sun; closed Jan 1, Thanksgiving, Dec 25) Phone 836-3713. ¢ 2 blks S on Fairfax St is

Old Presbyterian Meeting House (1774). 321 S Fairfax St. Tomb of the unknown soldier of the Revolution is in churchyard. Open on request (Mon-Fri). Phone 549-6670. **Free.** ½ blk N, then 3 blks W on Duke St is

Lafayette House. 301 St Asaph St. (Private) Fine example of Federal architecture. House was loaned to Lafayette for his last visit to America (1825). Walk 2 blks N to Prince St, then left on Prince St to SW corner of Prince and Washington Sts to

Lyceum. 201 S Washington St. Museum, exhibitions; Virginia travel information (limited). (Daily; closed Jan 1, Thanksgiving, Dec 25) Phone 838-4994. **Free.** Go 2 blks N on Washington St to

Christ Church (1773). 118 N Washington St. Washington and Robert E. Lee were pewholders. Fine Palladian window; interior balcony; wrought-brass and crystal chandelier brought from England. Structure is extensively restored but little changed since it was built. Exhibit, gift shop at Columbus St entrance. (Mon-Sat, also Sun afternoons; closed Jan 1, Thanksgiving, Dec 25; also for weddings, funerals) Donation. Phone 549-1450. 1 blk E on Cameron St is

Home of General Henry (Light Horse Harry) Lee. 611 Cameron St. (Private) 3 blks N, 1 blk W, then left on Washington St is

Lee-Fendall House (1785). 614 Oronoco St. Built by Phillip Richard Fendall and lived in by Lee family for 118 years. Both George Washington and Revolutionary War hero "Light Horse Harry" Lee were frequent visitors to the house. Remodeled in 1850, the house is furnished with Lee family belongings. (Daily exc Mon, wkend hrs may vary; closed major hols) Phone 548-1789. ¢¢ Proceed N, turn right on Oronoco St, ½ block E to

Boyhood Home of Robert E. Lee. 607 Oronoco St. Federal-style architecture; antique furnishings and paintings. Famous guests included Washington and Lafayette. (Feb-mid-Dec, daily) Phone 548-8454. ¢¢ 3 blks E, then 3 blks S on Royal St is

Gadsby's Tavern Museum (1770, 1792). 134 N Royal St. Famous hostelry, frequented by Washington and other patriots. Combines two 18th-century buildings; interesting architecture. (Daily exc Mon; closed major hols) (See RESTAURANTS) Phone 838-4242. ¢¢

Doorways to Old Virginia. Offers guided walking tours of historic district. Departs from Ramsay House. (Apr-Oct, daily) Phone 548-0100. ¢¢

2. Fort Ward Museum and Historic Site. 4301 W Braddock Rd. Restored Union Fort from Civil War; museum contains Civil War collection. Museum (daily exc Mon; closed Jan 1, Thanksgiving, Dec 25). Park, picnicking (daily to sunset). Phone 838-4848. **Free.**

3. George Washington Masonic National Memorial. 101 Callahan Dr, Shooter's Hill, W end of King St. American Freemasons' memorial to their most prominent member, this 333-foot high structure houses a large collection of objects that belonged to George Washington, which were collected by his family or the masonic lodge where he served as the first master. Guided tours explore a replica of Alexandria-Washington Lodge's first hall, a library, museum and an observation deck on the top floor. (Daily; closed Jan 1, Thanksgiving, Dec 25) Phone 683-2007. **Free.**

4. Alexandria Black History Resource Center. 638 N Alfred St. Photographs, letters, documents, and artifacts relate history of African-Americans in Alexandria. (Tues-Sat; closed hols) Donation. Phone 838-4356.

5. Torpedo Factory Arts Center. 105 N Union St. Renovated munitions plant houses artists' center with more than 160 professional artists of various media. Studios, cooperative galleries, school. Also home of Alexandria Archaeology offices, lab, museum. Phone 838-4399. (Daily; closed most major hols) Phone 838-4565. **Free.**

6. Sightseeing Boat Tours. Tours of Alexandria waterfront. Contact the Potomac Riverboat Company; 684-0580. Sr citizen rate. ¢¢¢

7. Mount Vernon (see). 9 mi S on Mt Vernon Memorial Hwy.

8. Gunston Hall (1755-59). 18 mi S on US 1, then 4 mi E on VA 242 in Lorton at 10709 Gunston Rd. The 550-acre estate of George Mason, framer of the Constitution, father of the Bill of Rights. Restored 18th-century mansion with period furnishings; reconstructed outbuildings; museum; boxwood gardens on grounds; nature trail; picnic area; gift shop. (Daily; closed Jan 1, Thanksgiving, Dec 25) Sr citizen rate. Phone 550-9220. ¢¢

9. Pohick Bay Regional Park. 6501 Pohick Bay Dr, in Lorton. Near Gunston Hall (see #9). Activities in this 1,000-acre park include swimming (Memorial Day-Labor Day); 18-hole golf; miniature and frisbee golf; boating (ramp, rentals; fee); camping (7-day limit; electric hookups avail; fee), picnicking. Park (all yr). Fee charged for activities. Phone 339-6104. Admission per vehicle (nonresidents only) ¢¢

10. Pohick Episcopal Church (1774). 9301 Richmond Hwy, 16 mi S on US 1 in Lorton. The colonial parish church of Mt Vernon and Gunston Hall. Built under supervision of George Mason and George Washington; original walls; interior fully restored. (Daily) Phone 550-9449. **Free.**

(For further information and a calendar of events, contact the Alexandria Convention/Visitors Bureau, 221 King St, 22314; 838-4200.)

Annual Events

George Washington Birthday Celebrations. February events include race, Revolutionary War re-enactment; climaxed by the birthday parade on federal holiday.

House tours. Fine colonial and federal-style houses are opened to the public: Cook's tour of kitchens (early Apr); Historic Garden Week (Apr); Hospital Auxiliary Tour of Historic Houses (Sept), phone; Scottish

Christmas Walk (Dec). Tickets, addl information at Alexandria Convention/Visitors Bureau (see #1).

Red Cross Waterfront Festival. Commemorates Alexandria's maritime heritage. Features "tall ships," blessing of the fleet, river cruises, races, arts & crafts, exhibits, food, variety of music; fireworks. Phone 549-8300. June.

Virginia Scottish Games. Athletic competition, Highland dance and music, antique cars, displays, food. 4th wkend July.

Christmas Walk. Parade, house tour, concerts, greens and heather sales, dinner-dance to emphasize city's Scottish origins. Phone 549-0100. 1st Sat Dec.

(See Arlington County, Fairfax, Falls Church; also see District of Columbia)

Motels

✔ ★ **COMFORT INN-MT VERNON.** *7212 Richmond Hwy (US 1) (22306).* 703/765-9000; FAX 703/765-2325. 92 rms, 2 story. S $50-$65; D $55-$75; each addl $7; under 17 free; wkly, wkend rates. Crib free. Pet accepted, some restrictions; $50 ($10 non-refundable). TV; cable. Pool. Complimentary continental bkfst, coffee. Restaurant nearby. Ck-out 11 am. Meeting rms. Valet serv. Sundries. Health club privileges. Cr cds: A, C, D, DS, ER, JCB, MC, V.

D ✔ ≈ ✕ 🔥 SC

★ **ECONO LODGE OLD TOWN.** *700 N Washington St (22314).* 703/836-5100; FAX 703/519-7015. 39 rms, 2 story. S $54.95; D $64.95; each addl $5; under 18 free. Crib free. Pet accepted; $25-$50. TV; cable. Restaurant nearby. Ck-out 11 am. Cr cds: A, C, D, DS, ER, MC, V.

✔ ✕ 🔥 SC

★★ **HAMPTON INN.** *4800 Leesburg Pike (22302).* 703/671-4800; FAX 703/671-2442. 130 rms, 4 story. S $79-$82; D $86-$89. Crib free. TV; cable. Pool. Complimentary continental bkfst, coffee. Ck-out noon. Meeting rm. Valet serv. Exercise equipt; treadmill, stair machines. Cr cds: A, C, D, DS, MC, V.

D ≈ 🏃 ✕ 🔥 SC

✔ ★ **RED ROOF INN.** *5975 Richmond Hwy (US 1) (22303).* 703/960-5200; FAX 703/960-5209. 115 rms, 3 story. S $49.99-$55.99; D $51.99-$62.99; each addl $3; under 18 free. Crib free. Pet accepted, some restrictions. TV; cable. Complimentary coffee in lobby. Restaurant nearby. Ck-out noon. Cr cds: A, C, D, DS, MC, V.

D ✔ ✕ 🔥 SC

✔ ★ **TRAVELERS.** *5916 Richmond Hwy (US 1) (22303).* 703/329-1310; res: 800/368-7378; FAX 703/960-9211. 30 rms. S $49.99-$59.99; D $56.99-$66.99; each addl $3. Crib free. TV; cable. Pool; lifeguard. Complimentary coffee. Restaurant opp 6 am-11 pm. Ck-out 11 am. Cr cds: A, C, D, DS, MC, V.

D ≈ ✕ 🔥 SC

Motor Hotels

★★★ **BEST WESTERN OLD COLONY INN.** *625 1st St (22314), in Old Town Alexandria.* 703/548-6300; FAX 703/548-8032. 332 rms, 2 & 4 story. S $89-$135; D $89-$145; each addl $10; suites $165-$205; under 18 free; wkend rates. Crib free. Pet accepted; $200 refundable and $10 per night. TV; cable. 2 pools, 1 indoor. Restaurant 6:30 am-10 pm. Rm serv. Bar 11 am-midnight; entertainment. Ck-out noon. Convention facilities. Bellhops. Gift shop. Free airport transportation. Exercise equipt; weight machines, bicycles, whirlpool, sauna. Refrigerator, wet bar in suites. Balconies. Cr cds: A, C, D, DS, MC, V.

D ✔ ≈ 🏃 ✕ 🔥 SC

★ **COMFORT INN-LANDMARK.** *6254 Duke St (22312).* 703/642-3422. 148 rms, 7 story. Mid-Mar-early Sept: S, D $49-$88.95;

under 18 free; lower rates rest of yr. Crib free. TV; cable. Pool; lifeguard. Complimentary continental bkfst. Restaurant 6-10 am, 5:30-10 pm; Sun 7 am-11 am. Bar 5-10 pm. Ck-out noon. Meeting rms. Valet serv. Sundries. Cr cds: A, C, D, DS, ER, JCB, MC, V.

D ≈ ✕ 🔥 SC

★ **COMFORT INN-VAN DORN.** *5716 S Van Dorn St (22310), I-95 exit 3.* 703/922-9200. 188 rms, 9 story. Apr-May & Sept-Oct: S $65-$75; D $75-$105; each addl $10; under 16 free; higher rates Cherry Blossom; lower rates rest of yr. Crib free. Pet accepted, some restrictions. TV; cable. Pool. Complimentary continental bkfst. Restaurant 6:30 am-1:30 pm, 4-10 pm. Bar. Ck-out 11 am. Coin lndry. Meeting rms. Gift shop. Health club privileges. Game rm. Some in-rm whirlpools. Cr cds: A, C, D, DS, MC, V.

D ✔ ≈ ✕ 🔥 SC

★★ **EXECUTIVE CLUB SUITES.** *610 Bashford Lane (22314).* 703/739-2582; res: 800/535-2582; FAX 703/548-0266. 78 kit. suites, 3 story. No elvtr. S, D $139-$159; wkend, hol rates. Crib free. Pet accepted. TV; cable. Pool; lifeguard. Complimentary continental bkfst. Complimentary coffee in rms. Restaurant nearby. Ck-out noon. Coin lndry. Meeting rms. Valet serv. Sundries. Free airport transportation. Exercise equipt; weight machine, treadmill, sauna. Picnic tables. Cr cds: A, C, D, DS, ER, MC, V.

✔ ≈ 🏃 ✕ 🔥

★★★ **HOWARD JOHNSON-OLDE TOWNE.** *5821 Richmond Hwy (US 1) (22303).* 703/329-1400; FAX 703/329-1424. 156 rms, 7 story. S $55-$91; D $65-$98; each addl $8; under 18 free. Crib free. Pet accepted, some restrictions. TV; cable. Indoor pool. Restaurant 6 am-11 pm; Fri, Sat to 3 am. Rm serv. Bar. Ck-out noon. Meeting rms. Valet serv. Gift shop. Beauty shop. Free airport, metro station transportation. Exercise equipt; weights, bicycles, sauna. Game rm. Some in-rm steam baths. Cr cds: A, C, D, DS, JCB, MC, V.

D ✔ ≈ ✕ 🔥 SC

Hotels

★★ **GUEST QUARTERS.** *100 S Reynolds St (22304).* 703/370-9600; FAX 703/370-0467. 225 kit. suites, 9 story. S $79-$140; D $89-$160; each addl $20; penthouses $200-$250; under 18 free; wkend rates. Crib free. Pet accepted; $10 per day. TV; cable. Pool; lifeguard. Complimentary continental bkfst. Restaurant 6:15-9:45 am, 5-10 pm. Bar from 5 pm. Ck-out noon. Coin lndry. Meeting rms. Health club privileges. Some balconies. Cr cds: A, C, D, DS, MC, V.

D ✔ ≈ ✕ 🔥 SC

★★★ **HOLIDAY INN OLD TOWN.** *480 King St (22314).* 703/549-6080; FAX 703/684-6508. 227 rms, 6 story. S $115-$160; D $130-$170; each addl $15; suites $195-$250; under 18 free; wkend plans. Crib free. Pet accepted, some restrictions. Garage $6. TV; cable. Indoor pool; lifeguard. Complimentary continental bkfst (Mon-Fri). Complimentary coffee in rms. Restaurant 6:30 am-10:30 pm. Bars 11-1:30 am. Ck-out noon. Coin lndry. Meeting rms. Concierge. Gift shop. Barber, beauty shop. Free airport transportation. Exercise equipt; bicycles, stair machines, sauna. Health club privileges. Refrigerators avail. Some balconies. Cr cds: A, C, D, DS, ER, JCB, MC, V.

D ✔ ≈ 🏃 ✕ 🔥 SC

★★ **HOLIDAY INN TELEGRAPH ROAD.** *2460 Eisenhower Ave (22314).* 703/960-3400; FAX 703/329-0953. 202 rms, 10 story. Mar-early July & mid-Sept-mid-Nov: S $94-$120; D $104-$130; each addl $10; under 18 free; wkend, hol rates; lower rates rest of yr. Crib free. Pet accepted, some restrictions; $30. TV; cable. Indoor pool. Restaurant 6:30 am-10 pm. Bar 11 am-midnight; entertainment. Ck-out noon. Coin lndry. Meeting rms. Gift shop. Free airport, RR station transportation. Exercise equipt; weight machine, rowers. Health club privileges. Game rm. Cr cds: A, C, D, DS, JCB, MC, V.

D ✔ ≈ 🏃 ✕ 🔥 SC

★ ★ ★ **RADISSON PLAZA AT MARK CENTER.** *5000 Seminary Rd (22311), 1 blk W of I-395 exit 4.* 703/845-1010; FAX 703/820-6425. 495 rms, 30 story. S, D $119-$149; each addl $20; suites $250-$450; under 18 free; wkly rates; wknd packages. Crib free. Covered parking $3.50, valet overnight parking $10. TV; cable. Indoor/outdoor pool. Restaurant 6 am-midnight. Rm serv 24 hrs. Bars 11 am-midnight; entertainment. Ck-out noon. Convention facilities. Concierge. Gift shop. Barber, beauty shop. Free airport transportation. Tennis. Exercise equipt; weights, bicycles, whirlpool, sauna. Game rm. Refrigerators; some bathrm phones. Whirlpool in some suites. Located on 50 wooded acres with nature preserve. *LUXURY LEVEL : PLAZA CLUB.* 39 rms, 3 suites, 3 floors. S $169; D $189; suites $350-$750. Private lounge. Wet bar in suites, some whirlpools. Complimentary bkfst, refreshments. Cr cds: A, C, D, DS, ER, JCB, MC, V.

D ⛷ ≈ ✗ ⊠ ⋒ SC

★ ★ ★ **RAMADA HOTEL-OLD TOWN.** *901 N Fairfax St (22314).* 703/683-6000; FAX 703/683-7597. 258 rms, 12 story. S, D $125-$150; each addl $10; under 18 free; wkend rates. Crib free. Pet accepted, some restrictions. TV; cable. Pool; lifeguard. Restaurant 6 am-10 pm. Bar 11-1 am; entertainment. Ck-out 1 pm. Gift shop. Free airport transportation. Cr cds: A, C, D, DS, MC, V.

D ⛷ ≈ ⊠ ⋒ SC

★ ★ ★ **SHERATON SUITES.** *801 N St Asaph St (22314).* 703/836-4700; FAX 703/548-4514. 249 suites, 10 story. Apr-May: S, D $172; under 12 free; wkend, hol rates; lower rates rest of yr. Crib free. Garage parking $7, in/out $7. TV; cable. Indoor pool; lifeguard. Complimentary coffee in rms. Complimentary full bkfst. Restaurant 6:30 am-10 pm; wkends from 7 am. Bar. Ck-out noon. Coin lndry. Meeting rms. Gift shop. Free airport transportation. Exercise equipt; weight machine, treadmill, whirlpool. Refrigerators. Cr cds: A, C, D, DS, MC, V.

D ≈ ✗ ⊠ ⋒ SC

Inn

★ ★ ★ **MORRISON HOUSE.** *116 S Alfred St (22314), downtown.* 703/838-8000; res: 800/367-0800; FAX 703/684-6283. 42 rms, 5 story. S, D $185-$240; each addl $20; suites $295-$470; wknd, honeymoon rates. Crib free. Covered parking $10. TV; cable. Dining rm 7-10:30 am, 11:30 am-2 pm, 6-10 pm; Fri & Sat to 11 pm. Afternoon English tea 3-5 pm. Rm serv 24 hrs. Bar 11:30 am-11 pm; entertainment Fri & Sat. Ck-out noon, ck-in after 3 pm. Meeting rms. Butlers. Health club privileges. Bathrm phones. European-style inn; mahogany paneled library, parlor with fireplace. Furnished in the Federal period; each rm individually decorated; fireplace & 4-poster canopy bed in many rms. Cr cds: A, C, D, MC, V.

D ⊠ ⋒

Restaurants

✔ ★ ★ **THE ALAMO.** *100 King St, in Old Town Alexandria.* 703/739-0555. Hrs: noon-2 am; Sun from 1 pm. Closed Thanksgiving, Dec 25. Res accepted; required Fri, Sat. Southwestern menu. Bar. A la carte entrees: lunch $5.95-$8.95, dinner $8.95-$13.95. Specializes in steak, chicken, enchiladas. Entertainment. In 1871 Corn Exchange Building; luxurious, gas-lighted interior with leaded-glass windows. Cr cds: A, MC, V.

D

★ ★ **BILBO BAGGINS.** *208 Queen St, in Old Town Alexandria.* 703/683-0300. Hrs: 11:30 am-10:30 pm; Sun 11 am-9:30 pm; Sun brunch 11 am-2:30 pm. Closed Dec 25. Res accepted. Continental menu. Bar. Semi-a la carte: lunch $5.95-$8.95, dinner $9.95-$17.95. Specialties: Bilbo's bread, chicken Queen Street, niçoise salad, eggs Valentine. Own bread, desserts. Upstairs in 1898 structure; stained glass, skylights. Cr cds: A, C, D, DS, MC, V.

D

★ ★ **BLUE POINT GRILL.** *600 Franklin St, in Old Town Alexandria.* 703/739-0404. Hrs: 11:30 am-10 pm; Fri & Sat to 11 pm; Sun 10:30 am-10 pm; Sun brunch to 3:30 pm. Closed Dec 25. Res accepted. A la carte entrees: lunch $5-$15, dinner $12.95-$19.95. Sun brunch $6-$12.95. Specializes in fresh seafood. Pastry. Parking. Outdoor dining. Cafe atmosphere; adj to gourmet Sutton Place Market. Cr cds: A, MC, V.

D

★ ★ **CHEZ ANDRÉE.** *10 E Glebe Rd.* 703/836-1404. Hrs: 11 am-2:30 pm, 5-9:30 pm; Sat from 5 pm. Closed Sun; major hols. Res accepted; required Fri, Sat. French menu. Serv bar. Semi-a la carte: lunch $8.95-$15.50, dinner $13.95-$23.95. Child's meals. Specialties: salmon Hollandaise, coquilles St-Jacques, duck à l'orange. Parking. French country decor. Family-owned. Cr cds: A, C, D, MC, V.

✔ ★ ★ **COPELAND'S OF NEW ORLEANS.** *4300 King St.* 703/671-7997. Hrs: 11 am-11 pm; Fri, Sat to midnight; Sun brunch to 3 pm. Closed Dec 25. Cajun, Creole menu. Bar. Semi-a la carte: lunch $5.45-$7.95, dinner $6.95-$15.75. Sun brunch $7.25-$9.95. Child's meals. Specializes in blackened redfish, shrimp. Parking. Outdoor dining. Cr cds: A, C, D, DS, MC, V.

D

✔ ★ ★ **EAST WIND.** *809 King St.* 703/836-1515. Hrs: 11:30 am-2:30 pm, 5:30-10 pm; Fri to 10:30 pm; Sat 5:30-10:30 pm; Sun 5:30-9:30 pm. Closed major hols. Res accepted. Vietnamese menu. Bar. Semi-a la carte: lunch $5.95-$7.95, dinner $7.95-$15.50. Specialties: cha gio, char-broiled shrimp & scallops, vegetarian dishes. Own desserts. Original Vietnamese paintings & panels. Cr cds: A, C, D, MC, V.

D

★ ★ **FISH MARKET.** *105 King St, at N Union St, in Old Town Alexandria.* 703/836-5676. Hrs: 11:15-2 am; Sun to midnight. Closed Thanksgiving, Dec 25. Res accepted. Bar. Semi-a la carte: lunch $3.95-$12.95, dinner $4.25-$16.25. Specializes in seafood, crab cakes, clam chowder. Ragtime singalong. Outdoor dining. In restored 18th-century warehouse built of bricks carried to New World as ballast in ship's hold; nautical decor. Cr cds: A, MC, V.

D

★ ★ **GADSBY'S TAVERN.** *138 N Royal St, across from Old City Hall.* 703/548-1288. Hrs: 11:30 am-3 pm, 5:30-9:30 pm; Sun brunch 11 am-3 pm. Closed Jan 1, Dec 24-25. Res accepted; required Fri, Sat. French menu. Serv bar. Semi-a la carte: lunch $6.50-$8.50, dinner $14.95-$21. Sun brunch $5-$8. Child's meals. Specialties: Sally Lunn bread, George Washington's favorite duck, English trifle. Strolling minstrels. Outdoor dining. Built 1792; Georgian architecture; colonial decor & costumes. Gadsby's Tavern Museum adj. Totally nonsmoking. Cr cds: C, D, DS, MC, V.

✔ ★ ★ **GERANIO.** *722 King St, in Old Town Alexandria.* 703/548-0088. Hrs: 11:30 am-2:30 pm, 6-10:30 pm; Sat from 6 pm; Sun 5:30-9:30 pm. Closed some major hols. Res accepted; required Fri, Sat. Italian menu. Serv bar. Semi-a la carte: lunch $5.95-$10.25, dinner $10-$15. Specializes in veal, seafood, pasta. Rustic Mediterranean decor. Fireplace, ceramic chandeliers. Cr cds: A, C, D, MC, V.

D

★ ★ **IL PORTO.** *121 King St, at N Lee St in Old Town Alexandria.* 703/836-8833. Hrs: 11:15 am-midnight. Closed Dec 25. Res accepted. Northern Italian menu. Bar from 6 pm. Semi-a la carte: lunch $3.25-$8.25, dinner $9-$16. Child's meals. Specialties: pasta de Venezia, chicken Angelica, seafood. Pianist Tues-Sat. Extensive dessert menu. In 18th-century building originally a marine warehouse. Cr cds: A, MC, V.

★ ★ **LA BERGERIE.** *218 N Lee St, 2nd fl of Crilley Warehouse, in Old Town Alexandria.* 703/683-1007. Hrs: 11:30 am-2:30 pm, 6-10:30 pm; Fri & Sat to 11 pm. Closed Sun; major hols. Res accepted; required Fri, Sat. French, Basque menu. Serv bar. Semi-a la carte: lunch $7-$14.25, dinner $14.95-$24. Specializes in fresh seafood, confit de canard. Own pastries. Restored 1890s warehouse. Cr cds: A, C, D, DS, MC, V.

★ ★ **LANDINI BROTHERS.** *115 King St, in Old Town Alexandria. 703/836-8404.* Hrs: 11:30 am-11 pm; Sun 3-10 pm. Closed major hols. Res accepted; required Fri, Sat. Italian menu. Bar. Semi-a la carte: lunch $9-$13. A la carte entrees: dinner $11.50-$22. Specializes in veal, pasta, fresh fish. 1790s building. Cr cds: A, C, D, MC, V.

★ ★ ★ **LE GAULOIS.** *1106 King St, in Old Town Alexandria. 703/739-9494.* Hrs: 11:30 am-10:30 pm; Fri, Sat to 11 pm. Closed Sun; major hols. Res accepted; required Fri, Sat. French menu. Bar. A la carte entrees: lunch $4.75-$8.75, dinner $4.75-$17.50. Specializes in rack of lamb, rabbit, veal. French provincial decor; fireplace. Cr cds: A, C, D, MC, V.

★ ★ **LE REFUGE.** *127 N Washington St, in Old Town Alexandria. 703/548-4661.* Hrs: 11:30 am-2:30 pm, 5:30-10 pm. Closed Sun; some major hols. Res accepted; required Fri, Sat. French menu. Serv bar. Semi-a la carte: lunch $6.95-$11.95, dinner $13.95-$19.95. Complete meals: lunch $8.95. Specialties: bouillabaisse, salmon encrôute, veal Normande, rack of lamb. Country French decor. Cr cds: A, C, D, MC, V.

✔ ★ ★ **RT'S.** *3804 Mt Vernon Ave. 703/684-6010.* Hrs: 11 am-10:30 pm; Fri, Sat to 11 pm; Sun 4-9 pm. Closed July 4, Labor Day, Dec 25. Res accepted. Bar. Semi-a la carte: lunch $5-$12.95, dinner $11.95-$17.95. Child's meals. Specializes in Jack Daniels shrimp, Acadian peppered shrimp, she-crab soup. Cr cds: A, C, D, DS, MC, V.

★ ★ **SANTA FE EAST.** *110 S Pitt St. 703/548-6900.* Hrs: 11:30 am-10 pm; Fri, Sat to 11 pm; Sun 11 am-10 pm. Closed July 4, Dec 25. Res accepted; required Fri, Sat. Southwestern menu. Bar. A la carte entrees: lunch $5.95-$6.95, dinner $10.95-$18.75. Sun brunch $5.25-$6.95. Specialties: chipotle chicken, pato y pollo combo, cheese raviolon with shrimp. Outdoor dining. American Indian art, artifacts. Fountain in courtyard. Cr cds: A, MC, V.

★ ★ **SCOTLAND YARD.** *728 King St, in Old Town Alexandria. 703/683-1742.* Hrs: 6-8 pm. Closed Mon; Thanksgiving. Res accepted; required Fri, Sat. Scottish menu. Serv bar. Semi-a la carte: dinner $12.95-$18.95. Complete meal: dinner $24.95. Specializes in steaks, lamb, venison, quail. Old Scottish inn (built 1792); tin ceiling, fireplace. Totally nonsmoking. Cr cds: A, MC, V.

★ ★ **SEAPORT INN.** *6 King St. 703/549-2341.* Hrs: 11:30 am-10 pm; Fri to 11 pm; Sat 11 am-11 pm; Sun brunch to 3 pm. Closed Thanksgiving, Dec 25. Res accepted; required Fri, Sat. Bar 11:30 am-midnight; Fri, Sat to 2 am. Semi-a la carte: lunch $5.75-$9.95, dinner $10.95-$24.95. Sun brunch $12.95. Child's meals. Specialties: shrimp & scallops in wine sauce, crab cakes, stuffed flounder. Entertainment exc Mon. Fireplaces. In 1765 warehouse originally owned by George Washington's aide-de-camp; overlooks Potomac River. Cr cds: A, C, D, MC, V.

★ ★ **TAVERNA CRETEKOU.** *818 King St. 703/548-8688.* Hrs: 11:30 am-2:30 pm, 5-10:30 pm; Sat noon-11 pm; Sun 5-9:30 pm; Sun brunch 11 am-3 pm. Closed Mon; some major hols. Res accepted; required Fri, Sat. Greek menu. Serv bar. A la carte entrees: lunch $5.95-$8.95, dinner $9.95-$17.95. Sun brunch $11.95. Specializes in seafood, lamb. Outdoor dining. Mediterranean decor; brick patio, arbor. Cr cds: A, DS, MC, V.

★ ★ **TAVOLA.** *710 King St (22314). 703/683-9070.* Hrs: 11:30 am-2:30 pm, 5:30-10:30 pm. Closed Thanksgiving, Dec 25. Res accepted. Italian menu. Bar. Semi-a la carte: lunch $9.95-$14.50. A la carte entrees: dinner $15-$20. Specializes in seafood, pasta. Menu changes daily. Modern decor. Cr cds: A, C, D, MC, V.

★ ★ ★ **TERRAZZA.** *710 King St. 703/683-6900.* Hrs: 11:30 am-2:30 pm, 6-10:30 pm; Sat 6-11 pm; Sun 6-10 pm. Closed Thanksgiving, Dec 25. Res accepted. Italian menu. Bar. Wine cellar. A la carte entrees: lunch $11.95-$13.95, dinner $15.95-$24.95. Specializes in linguine with lobster, spinach-stuffed pasta. Own pasta, desserts. Modern Italian decor. Cr cds: A, C, D, MC, V.

★ ★ **THAI HUT.** *408 S Van Dorn St. 703/823-5357.* Hrs: 11 am-10 pm; Fri to 11 pm; Sat noon-11 pm; Sun noon-9:30 pm. Closed Thanksgiving, Dec 25. Thai menu. A la carte entrees: lunch, dinner $5.95-$17.95. Complete meals (Mon-Fri): lunch $5.95. Specialties: curries, pad Thai, drunken noodles. Parking. Modern decor; Thai artwork. Cr cds: A, C, D, MC, V.

★ ★ ★ **TWO NINETEEN.** *219 King St. 703/549-1141.* Hrs: 11 am-10:30 pm; Sat 8 am-11 pm; Sun 5-10 pm; Sun brunch 10 am-5 pm. Closed Labor Day, Dec 25. Res accepted. French, Creole menu. Bar to 2 am. Wine list. A la carte entrees: lunch $5.95-$11.95, dinner $12.95-$22.95. Sun brunch $6.95-$12.95. Specializes in fresh seafood, steak. Jazz combo. Outdoor dining. Converted private residence (ca 1890) with period millwork; antique furnishings; original Victorian paintings; marble fireplaces, crystal chandeliers. Cr cds: A, C, D, DS, MC, V.

✔ ★ ★ **UNION STREET PUBLIC HOUSE.** *121 S Union St, between King & Prince Sts, in Old Town Alexandria. 703/548-1785.* Hrs: 11:30 am-10:30 pm; Fri, Sat to 11:30 pm; Sun brunch 11 am-3 pm. Closed Thanksgiving, Dec 25. Bar to 1:15 am. Semi-a la carte: lunch, dinner $4.95-$16.95. Sun brunch $4.95-$8.95. Child's meals. Specialties: apple-smoked barbecue pork ribs, linguine with lobster & smoked scallops, grilled seafood. Oyster raw bar. In sea captain's house & warehouse (ca 1870). Cr cds: A, C, D, DS, MC, V.

★ ★ ★ **VILLA D'ESTE.** *818 N St Asaph St, at Montgomery St. 703/549-9477.* Hrs: 11:30 am-2:30 pm, 5-10 pm; Fri to 11 pm; Sat 5-11 pm; Sun 5-10 pm. Closed July 4, Thanksgiving, Dec 25. Res accepted; required Fri, Sat. Northern Italian menu. Bar. Wine list. Semi-a la carte: lunch $5.75-$10.95, dinner $8.25-$18.95. Specialties: osso buco all'Imperiesa, "pansooti" della Nonna. Own pasta, breads, desserts. Elegant, modern decor. Cr cds: A, MC, V.

★ ★ **THE WHARF.** *119 King St (22314). 703/836-2834.* Hrs: 4-11 pm. Closed Dec 25. Res accepted. Bar. Semi-a la carte: dinner $12.95-$17.95. Child's meals. Specializes in lobster. Jazz. Late 18th-century building. Cr cds: A, C, D, DS, MC, V.

Unrated Dining Spot

HARD TIMES CAFE. *1404 King St. 703/683-5340.* Hrs: 11 am-10 pm; Fri, Sat to 11 pm; Sun noon-10 pm. Closed some major hols. Wine, extensive beer list. A la carte entrees: lunch, dinner $3.95-$5.75. Specializes in Texas, Cincinnati and vegetarian-style chili, onion rings, corn bread. Country & western music on juke box. Housed in former church; rustic decor; collection of state flags. Cr cds: A, MC, V.

Appomattox Court House National Historical Park (E-7)

(3 mi NE of Appomattox on VA 24)

The series of clashes between General Ulysses S. Grant and General Robert E. Lee that started with the Battle of the Wilderness (May 5, 1864) finally ended here on Palm Sunday, April 9, 1865, in the little village of Appomattox Court House.

A week earlier, Lee had evacuated besieged Petersburg and headed west in a desperate attempt to join forces with General Johnston in North Carolina. Ragged and exhausted, decimated by desertions, without supplies and beset by Union forces at every turn, the once great Army of Northern Virginia launched its last attack at dawn on April 9. By 10 am it was clear that further bloodshed was futile; after some difficulty in getting a message to Grant, the two antagonists met in the parlor of the McLean House. By 3 pm the generous surrender terms had been drafted and signed. The war was over. Three days later 28,231 Confederate soldiers received their parole here.

The 1,700-acre park includes the village of Appomattox Court House, restored and reconstructed to appear much as it did in 1865. As visitors tour the village, uniformed park rangers or interpreters in period dress answer questions about the people who lived here and the events that took place. (Daily; closed major hols Nov-Feb) Golden Eagle Passport accepted (see INTRODUCTION). Audiovisual programs, Braille guide folder, audio guide and large print folder avail for the hearing and visually impaired. For further information contact the Superintendent, PO Box 218, Appomattox 24522; or phone 804/352-8987. ¢

What to See and Do

1. **Appomattox Court House Bldg.** Reconstructed building houses visitor center, museum; audiovisual slide program (every half hr, 2nd floor). Self-guided tour of village begins here and includes

   Clover Hill Tavern and outbuildings (1819). Oldest structure in village; bookstore, restrooms.

   Confederate Cemetery.

   County Jail (1870), furnished.

   Woodson Law Office with period furnishings.

   Meek's Store and Meek's Storehouse with period furnishings.

   Kelly House.

   McLean House and outbuildings. Reconstruction of house where Generals Lee and Grant met on April 9, 1865. Walking east from house, past Court House and about 100 yards along Stage Road past county jail is

   Surrender Triangle, where on exactly the fourth anniversary of the firing on Ft Sumter, which triggered the outbreak of war, Confederate soldiers laid down their weapons.

2. **Holliday Lake State Park.** 9 mi NE of Appomattox on VA 24, then 6 mi SE via VA 626, 692. Approx 250 acres in Buckingham-Appomattox State Forest. Swimming beach, bathhouse; fishing, boating (launch, rentals) on 150-acre lake. Hiking trails. Picnicking, concession. Tent & trailer sites. Visitor center, interpretive programs. Standard fees. Park (daily); most activities, including camping (Memorial Day-Labor Day). Phone 804/248-6308.

(For accommodations see Lynchburg)

Arlington County (National Airport Area) (C-8)

Elev: 200 ft **Area code:** 703

Originally a part of the District of Columbia laid out for the capital in 1791, Arlington County, across the Potomac River from Washington, was returned to Virginia in 1846. The county is the urban center of northern Virginia.

Transportation

Car Rental Agencies: See toll-free numbers under Introduction.

Public Transportation: Subway trains & buses (Metro Transit System), phone 202/962-1234.

Rail Passenger Service: Amtrak 800/972-9245.

Airport Information

Washington National Airport: Information 419-8000; lost and found 419-8034; weather 202/936-1212; cash machines, at Main Terminal, main level near Travelers Aid, and at Interim Terminal, main level near Travelers Aid; club lounges, Admirals Club (American), Main Terminal, 2nd level; Crown Room (Delta), Interim Terminal, 3rd level; Red Carpet Room (United), Main Terminal, North Concourse; WorldClub (Northwest), Main Terminal, near Northwest Gates; USAir Club (USAir), Interim Terminal, 2nd level.

Terminals: Main Terminal: America West, American, American Eagle, Continental, Delta Shuttle, Midwest Express, Northwest, TWA, United, USAir Shuttle; Interim Terminal: Delta, Delta Connection, USAir, USAir Express

(Airlines and their terminal locations may change. Before leaving for the airport, you should phone the airline to confirm terminal location for your flight.)

What to See and Do

1. **Arlington National Cemetery.** The most famous of US national cemeteries was established in 1864. Here are interred more than 200,000 men and women who served their country, and two presidents, William Howard Taft, John F. Kennedy; also Sen. Robert F. Kennedy, Jacqueline Kennedy Onassis. Guided "tourmobiles" leave from visitor center (fare includes on/off privileges), phone 979-0690. (Daily) Tourmobiles ¢¢ Parking ¢¢ Here are

   The Tomb of the Unknowns. On November 11, 1921, the remains of an unknown American soldier of World War I were entombed here. A memorial was erected in 1932 with the inscription "Here rests in honored glory an American soldier known but to God." On Memorial Day 1958, an unknown warrior who died in World War II and another who died in the Korean conflict were laid beside him. On Memorial Day 1984, an unknown soldier from the Vietnam conflict was interred here. Sentries stand guard 24 hours a day; changing of the guard is every hour on the hour Oct-Mar, every 30 min Apr-Sept.

   Memorial Amphitheatre. This impressive white marble edifice is used for ceremonies, such as Memorial Day, Easter sunrise and Veterans Day services.

   Arlington House, The Robert E. Lee Memorial. National memorial to Robert E. Lee. Built between 1802 and 1818 by George Washington Parke Custis, Martha Washington's grandson and foster son of George Washington. In 1831, his daughter, Mary Anna Randolph Custis, married Lieutenant Robert E. Lee; six of

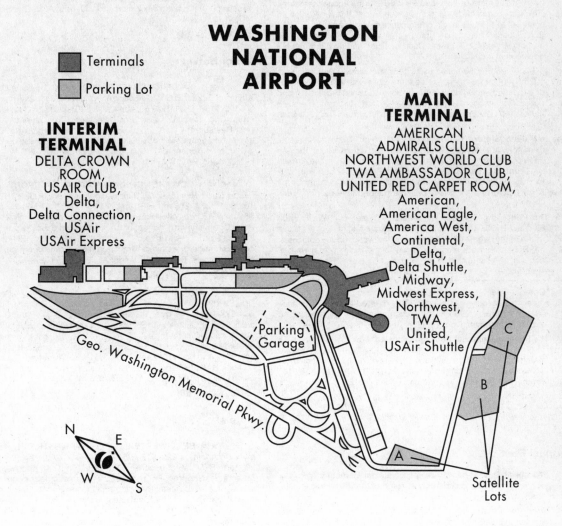

WASHINGTON NATIONAL AIRPORT

Terminals

Parking Lot

INTERIM TERMINAL
DELTA CROWN ROOM,
USAIR CLUB,
Delta,
Delta Connection,
USAir
USAir Express

MAIN TERMINAL
AMERICAN ADMIRALS CLUB,
NORTHWEST WORLD CLUB
TWA AMBASSADOR CLUB,
UNITED RED CARPET ROOM,
American,
American Eagle,
America West,
Continental,
Delta,
Delta Shuttle,
Midway,
Midwest Express,
Northwest,
TWA,
United,
USAir Shuttle

Geo. Washington Memorial Pkwy.

Parking Garage

N E W S

A

B

C

Satellite Lots

the seven Lee children were born here. As executor of Custis' estate, Lee took extended leave from the US Army and devoted his time to managing and improving the estate. It was the Lee homestead for 30 years before the Civil War.

On April 20, 1861, following the secession of Virginia, Lee made his decision to stay with Virginia. Within a month, the house was vacated. Some of the family possessions were moved for safe-keeping, but most were stolen or destroyed when Union troops occupied the house during the Civil War.

In 1864, when Mrs. Lee could not appear personally to pay property tax, the estate was confiscated by the federal government; a 200-acre section was set aside for a national cemetery. (There is some evidence that indicates that this was done to ensure that the Lee family could never again live on the estate.) G.W. Custis Lee, the general's son, later regained title to the property through a Supreme Court decision and sold it to the US government in 1883 for $150,000.

Restoration of the house to its 1861 appearance was begun in 1925. The Classic-revival house is furnished with authentic pieces of the period, including some Lee family originals. From the grand portico with its six massive, faux-marble Doric columns, there is a panoramic view of Washington, DC. (Daily; closed Jan 1, Dec 25) Phone 557-0613. **Free.**

2. **Iwo Jima Statue.** On Arlington Blvd, near Arlington National Cemetery. Marine Corps War Memorial depicts raising of the flag on Mt Suribachi, Iwo Jima, Feb 23, 1945; this is the largest sculpture ever cast in bronze. Sunset Parade concert with performances by US Marine Drum & Bugle Corps, US Marine Corps Color Guard and the Silent Drill Team (late May-late Aug, Tues evenings).

3. **The Pentagon.** Bounded by Jefferson Davis Hwy, Washington Blvd and I-395. With some six million square feet of floor area, this is one of the largest office buildings in the world; houses offices of the Department of Defense. Guided tour (1½ hr) with a walk of about 1½ miles includes movie, Hall of Heroes, Flag Corridor, Time/Life Art Collection (Mon-Fri; closed hols). Tour window located on Concourse near the Metrorail subway or by entering at Corridor One, South Parking entrance. A valid picture ID must be presented at tour registration; visitors must stay on the tour once it begins. Cameras are allowed. Accommodations for the disabled avail with 48-hour advance notice. Phone 695-1776. **Free.**

4. **The Fashion Centre at Pentagon City.** Off I-395 at jct S Hayes St & Army-Navy Dr, just S of the Pentagon. Upscale, 160-store shopping mall with restaurants, movie theaters and adjoining 360-room Ritz-Carlton hotel (see HOTELS); features 115,000-square-foot glass ceiling in atrium. Phone 415-2130.

(For further information contact the Arlington Convention & Visitors Service, 1400 N Uhle, Suite 102, 22201, phone 358-3988; or the Arlington Visitors Center, 735 S 18th St, 22202, phone 358-5720 or 800/677-6267.)

Annual Events

Memorial Day Service. Arlington National Cemetery (see #1). Presidential wreath-laying ceremony at Tomb of the Unknowns; music. Memorial Day.

Arlington County Fair. County-wide fair; arts, crafts, international foods, children's activities. Phone 358-6400. Aug.

(See Alexandria, Fairfax, Falls Church, McLean; also see District of Columbia)

Motels

✔ ★ ★ **COMFORT INN BALLSTON.** *1211 N Glebe Rd (22201), at Washington Blvd.* 703/247-3399; FAX 703/524-8739. 126 rms, 3 story. Mar-late June: S $65-$95; D $70-$100; each addl $10; suites $79-$105; under 18 free; wkend rates; lower rates rest of yr. Crib free. TV; cable. Complimentary continental bkfst. Restaurant 6:30 am-10:30

pm. Rm serv. Bar 4-11 pm. Ck-out 11 am. Meeting rms. Valet serv (Mon-Fri). Sundries. Gift shop. Garage parking. Refrigerators avail. Cr cds: A, C, D, DS, ER, JCB, MC, V.

D 🏊 🔥 SC

✔ ★ ★ **TRAVELODGE-WASHINGTON/ARLINGTON CHERRY BLOSSOM.** *3030 Columbia Pike (22204).* 703/521-5570; FAX 703/271-0081. 76 rms, 3 story, 12 kit. units. Mid-Mar-Nov: S, D $64; each addl $7; kit. units $74; under 18 free; lower rates rest of yr. Crib free. TV; cable. Pool privileges. Complimentary continental bkfst. Complimentary coffee in rms. Restaurant 11 am-midnight. Ck-out noon. Coin lndry. Valet serv. Exercise equipt; weight machine, rowers. Refrigerators. 3 mi from downtown Washington. Cr cds: A, C, D, DS, ER, JCB, MC, V.

D 🏋 🏊 🔥 SC

Motor Hotels

★ ★ **DAYS INN CRYSTAL CITY.** *(2000 Jefferson Davis Hwy, Arlington 22202)* 703/920-8600; FAX 703/920-2840. 247 rms, 8 story. S $109-$150; D $119-$160; each addl $10; under 16 free; wkend, hol rates. Crib free. TV; cable. Pool; lifeguard. Complimentary coffee in rms. Restaurant 6 am-10 pm. Rm serv. Bar 4 pm-midnight. Ck-out 11 am. Meeting rms. Bellhops. Gift shop. Valet serv. Garage parking. Free airport transportation. Cr cds: A, C, D, DS, ER, JCB, MC, V.

D 🏊 ✈ 🔥 SC

★ ★ **HOWARD JOHNSON NATIONAL AIRPORT.** *2650 Jefferson Davis Hwy (22202), near National Airport.* 703/684-7200; FAX 703/684-3217. 278 rms, 16 story. S $65-$135; D $73-$135; each addl $8; under 18 free; wkend rates. Crib free. TV; cable, in-rm movies avail. Pool. Complimentary coffee in rms. Restaurant 6 am-11 pm. Rm serv. Bar 6-11 pm. Ck-out noon. Coin lndry. Meeting rms. Bellhops. Valet serv. Gift shop. Free airport transportation. Exercise equipt; stair machine, bicycles. Balconies. Cr cds: A, C, D, DS, JCB, MC, V.

D 🏊 🏋 ✈ 🔥 SC

★ ★ **QUALITY INN-IWO JIMA.** *1501 Arlington Blvd (Fairfax Dr) (22209), ½ mi W of Iwo Jima Memorial.* 703/524-5000; FAX 703/522-5484. 141 rms, 1-3 story. Mar-June: S $75-$80; D $82-$87; each addl $7; suites $90-$97; family rates; higher rates Marine Corps Marathon; lower rates rest of yr. Crib free. TV; cable. Heated pool; poolside serv, lifeguard. Restaurant 6:30 am-10 pm; Sat, Sun from 7 am. Rm serv. Bar 11:30 am-2 pm, 5-11 pm. Ck-out noon. Coin lndry. Meeting rms. Bellhops. Sundries. Gift shop. Refrigerators avail. Some balconies. Cr cds: A, C, D, DS, ER, JCB, MC, V.

D 🏊 🔥 SC

Hotels

★ ★ **BEST WESTERN ROSSLYN WESTPARK.** *(1900 N Ft Myer Dr, Arlington 22209)* 703/527-4814; FAX 703/522-8864. 308 rms, 20 story. S, D $95-$99; suites $115-$150; under 18 free; wkly, wkend & hol rates. Crib free. Pet accepted. TV; cable. Indoor pool; whirlpool, sauna, lifeguard. Restaurant 6:30 am-11 pm. Bar 11:30 am-midnight. Ck-out noon. Coin lndry. Convention facilities. Gift shop. Garage parking. Balconies. Overlooking Potomac River. Cr cds: A, C, D, DS, ER, JCB, MC, V.

D ✔ 🏊 🔥 SC

★ ★ **COURTYARD BY MARRIOTT.** *2899 Jefferson Davis Hwy (22202), near National Airport.* 703/549-3434; FAX 703/549-7440. 272 rms, 14 story. S $129; D $144; each addl $15; suites $185-$215; under 12 free. Crib free. Garage parking $4. TV; cable. Indoor pool; lifeguard. Complimentary coffee in rms. Restaurant 6-10 am, 5-10 pm. Rm serv (dinner). Bar 4 pm-midnight. Ck-out 1 pm. Meeting rms. Valet serv. Sundries. Exercise equipt; weights, bicycles, whirlpool, steam rm. Some refrigerators, wet bars. Cr cds: A, C, D, DS, ER, JCB, MC, V.

D ✔ 🏊 🏋 🔥 SC

★ ★ **DOUBLETREE.** *300 Army/Navy Dr (22202).* *703/416-4100; FAX 703/416-4126.* 632 rms, 15 story, 265 suites. S $145-$165; D $165-$185; each addl $20; suites $165-$250; under 18 free; wkend rates. Crib free. Pet accepted. Garage $9. TV; cable. Indoor pool; sauna, lifeguard. Restaurant 6:30 am-11 pm. Bar 11-2 am; entertainment, dancing. Ck-out noon. Convention facilities. Concierge. Gift shop. Free airport transportation. Health club privileges. Many bathrm phones; some refrigerators. Some balconies. *LUXURY LEVEL* : **POTOMAC CLUB.** 20 suites. Suites $185-$270. Private lounge. Bathrm phones. Complimentary continental bkfst, refreshments. Cr cds: A, C, D, DS, ER, JCB, MC, V.

★ ★ ★ **EMBASSY SUITES-CRYSTAL CITY.** *1300 Jefferson Davis Hwy (22202),* entrance at 1402 S Eads St, near National Airport. *703/979-9799; FAX 703/920-5947.* 267 suites, 11 story. Feb-June, Sept-Nov: S $169-$199; D $179-$209; each addl $10; under 12 free; wkend rates; lower rates rest of yr. Crib free. TV; cable. Heated pool; lifeguard. Complimentary full bkfst. Complimentary coffee in rms. Restaurant 11:30 am-10 pm; Fri, Sat to 11 pm. Bar to 11 pm. Ck-out noon. Meeting rms. Gift shop. Free covered parking. Free airport transportation. Exercise equipt; weight machine, bicycles. Refrigerators. Atrium lobby. Cr cds: A, C, D, DS, JCB, MC, V.

★ ★ **HOLIDAY INN KEY BRIDGE.** *1850 N Ft Myer Dr (22209).* *703/522-0400; FAX 703/524-5275.* 177 rms, 11 story. S $106-$145; D $116-$155; each addl $10; suites $155-$165; under 18 free. Crib free. Pet accepted. TV; cable. Pool; lifeguard. Restaurant 6:30 am-10:30 pm. Ck-out noon. Meeting rms. Game rm. Refrigerator avail in suites. Cr cds: A, C, D, DS, JCB, MC, V.

★ ★ **HOLIDAY INN NATIONAL AIRPORT.** *(1489 Jefferson Davis Hwy, Arlington 22202)* *703/416-1600; FAX 703/416-1615.* 306 rms, 11 story. S $111; D $121; each addl $10; suites $140; under 20 free; wkend, hol rates. Crib free. Pet accepted. TV; cable. Pool; poolside serv. Restaurant 6:30 am-10 pm; Sat & Sun from 7 am. Bar 11 am-midnight. Ck-out noon. Meeting rms. Gift shop. Free airport transportation. Health club privileges. Game rm. Cr cds: A, C, D, DS, JCB, MC, V.

★ ★ ★ **HYATT ARLINGTON.** *1325 Wilson Blvd (22209),* near Key Bridge at Nash St. *703/525-1234; FAX 703/875-3393.* 302 rms, 16 story. S $169; D $194; each addl $25; suites $200-$500; under 12 free; wkend rates. Crib free. Pet accepted, some restrictions. Garage $6 (Sun-Thurs). TV; cable. Restaurant 6:30 am-midnight. Bars 11:30-1:30 am. Ck-out noon. Free lndry facilities. Meeting rms. Gift shop. Exercise equipt; bicycles, treadmill. Metro adj. Cr cds: A, C, D, DS, ER, JCB, MC, V.

★ ★ ★ **HYATT REGENCY-CRYSTAL CITY.** *2799 Jefferson Davis Hwy (22202),* near National Airport. *703/418-1234; FAX 703/418-1289.* 685 rms, 20 story. S $160; D $185; each addl $25; suites $225-$750; under 18 free; wkend rates. Crib free. Garage; valet $8. TV; cable. Heated pool; poolside serv, lifeguard. Restaurant 6-2 am. Bar from 3 am. Ck-out noon. Convention facilities. Concierge. Gift shop. Free airport transportation. Exercise equipt; weight machine, stair machine, whirlpool, saunas. Some refrigerators, wet bars. Some balconies. Cr cds: A, C, D, DS, ER, JCB, MC, V.

★ ★ ★ **MARRIOTT CRYSTAL CITY.** *(1999 Jefferson Davis Hwy, Arlington 22202)* *703/413-5500; FAX 703/413-0192.* 345 rms, 10 story. S $159; D $179; suites $250-$300; under 18 free; wkend rates. Crib free. Valet parking $15. TV; cable. Indoor pool; poolside serv, lifeguard. Restaurant 6:30 am-10:30 pm; Sat & Sun from 7 am. Bar 11:30 am-midnight. Ck-out 1 pm. Convention facilities. Concierge. Gift shop. Free airport transportation. Exercise equipt; weight machine, stair machines, whirlpool, sauna. Health club privileges. *LUXURY*

LEVEL : **CONCIERGE LEVEL.** 33 rms. S $179; D $199. Private lounge, honor bar. Complimentary continental bkfst, refreshments, newspaper. Cr cds: A, C, D, DS, ER, JCB, MC, V.

★ ★ ★ **MARRIOTT CRYSTAL GATEWAY.** *1700 Jefferson Davis Hwy (US 1) (22202),* entrance on S Eads St, between 15th & 17th Sts, near National Airport. *703/920-3230; FAX 703/979-6332.* 700 units, 16 story. S, D $165-$185; each addl $20; suites $175-$600; under 18 free; wkend rates. Crib free. Pet accepted, some restrictions. Garage $10; valet parking $15. TV; cable, in-rm movies avail. Indoor/outdoor pool; lifeguard. Complimentary coffee. Restaurant 6:30 am-2:30 pm, 4:30-10 pm. Bar 4 pm-2 am, Sat from 8 pm; entertainment. Ck-out 1 pm. Convention facilities. Free airport transportation. Tennis privileges. Exercise equipt; weights, bicycles, whirlpool, sauna. Original artwork. *LUXURY LEVEL* : **CONCIERGE LEVEL.** 61 rms, 4 suites. S $169; D $189; suites $195-$620. Private lounge, honor bar. Complimentary continental bkfst, refreshments. Cr cds: A, C, D, DS, ER, JCB, MC, V.

★ ★ ★ **MARRIOTT KEY BRIDGE.** *1401 Lee Hwy (22209).* *703/524-6400; FAX 703/524-8964.* 584 rms, 4-12 story. S, D $149-$184; suites $225-$325; wkend rates. Crib free. Pet accepted; $50 refundable. Garage $6. TV; cable. Indoor/outdoor pool; poolside serv, lifeguard. Restaurant 6:30 am-10:30 pm; Fri, Sat to 11 pm (also see THE VIEW). Bar 11-2 am; entertainment, dancing exc Sun. Ck-out 1 pm. Convention facilities. Concierge. Gift shop. Barber, beauty shop. Exercise equipt; weights, bicycles, whirlpool, sauna. Refrigerators. Some balconies. Overlooks Washington across Potomac River. *LUXURY LEVEL* : **CONCIERGE LEVEL.** 90 rms, 4 suites, 3 floors. S $169; D $194; suites $225-$325. Concierge. Private lounge, honor bar. Complimentary continental bkfst, refreshments. Cr cds: A, C, D, DS, ER, JCB, MC, V.

✓ ★ ★ **QUALITY HOTEL.** *1200 N Courthouse Rd (22201).* *703/524-4000; FAX 703/524-1046.* 395 rms, 1-10 story, 40 kit. suites. S $48-$101; D $54-$129; each addl $6; suites $85-$148; under 18 free; wkend rates. Crib free. TV; cable. Pool; lifeguard. Restaurant 6:30 am-2 pm, 5-10 pm. Bar 4 pm-midnight. Ck-out noon. Coin lndry. Convention facilities. Concierge. Gift shop. Exercise equipt; weight machine, rowers, sauna. Lawn games. Balconies. *LUXURY LEVEL* : **CLUB ROYALE.** 109 rms, 11 suites, 4 floors. S, D $115-$129; each addl $14; suites $125-$152. Private lounge. Complimentary continental bkfst, refreshments, newspaper. Cr cds: A, C, D, DS, ER, JCB, MC, V.

★ ★ ★ **RENAISSANCE.** *950 N Stafford St (22203),* at Fairfax Dr. *703/528-6000; FAX 703/528-4386.* 209 rms, 7 story. S $135-$165; D $150-$180; suites $195; under 18 free; wkend rates. Crib free. Pet accepted, some restrictions. TV; cable. Indoor pool; whirlpool, lifeguard. Restaurant 6:30 am-11 pm. Bar 11 am-midnight. Ck-out noon. Coin lndry. Meeting rms. Concierge. Gift shop. Barber, beauty shop. Minibars. Metro stop in building. *LUXURY LEVEL* . 40 rms, 1 suite. S $165; D $180; suite $225. Concierge. Private lounge, honor bar. Complimentary continental bkfst, refreshments. Cr cds: A, C, D, DS, ER, JCB, MC, V.

★ ★ ★ ★ **THE RITZ-CARLTON, PENTAGON CITY.** *1250 S Hayes St (22202),* in Pentagon City Fashion Centre Mall, near National Airport. *703/415-5000; FAX 703/415-5061.* 345 rms, 18 story, 41 suites. S $160-$200; D $180-$220; each addl $20; suites $300-$1,500; under 19 free; wkend plans. Crib free. Garage, valet parking $15. TV; cable. Indoor pool; lifeguard. Restaurant (see THE GRILL). Bar; entertainment. Ck-out noon. Convention facilities. Concierge. Shopping arcade. Free airport transportation. Tennis privileges. Golf privileges. Exercise rm; instructor, weight machine, bicycles, whirlpool, sauna, steam rm. Massage. Bathrm phones, minibars. Extensive collection of fine art and antiques. Panoramic view of the Capitol and Potomac River. *LUXURY LEVEL* : **RITZ-CARLTON CLUB.** 40 rms, 5 suites, 2 floors. S, D $240;

suites $400-$1,500. Concierge. Private lounge, honor bar. Complimentary continental bkfst, refreshments. Cr cds: A, C, D, DS, ER, JCB, MC, V.

★ ★ ★ **SHERATON CRYSTAL CITY.** *1800 Jefferson Davis Hwy (22202), entrance on S Eads St; 1/2 mi S of I-395 on US 1, near National Airport.* 703/486-1111; FAX 703/920-5827. 197 rms, 15 story. S $115-$150; D $125-$165; each addl $15; suites $350; under 18 free; wkend packages. Crib free. TV; cable. Rooftop pool; lifeguard, sauna. Restaurant 6:30 am-10 pm; Sat, Sun from 7 am. Bar 11 am-midnight; entertainment, pianist. Ck-out 1 pm. Convention facilities. Concierge. Gift shop. Free airport transportation. Minibars, refrigerators; some bathrm phones. *LUXURY LEVEL :* **CLUB LEVEL.** 10 rms, 2 suites. S $170; D $185; suites $350—$850. Concierge. Private lounge, bar. Complimentary continental bkfst, refreshments, newspaper. Cr cds: A, C, D, DS, MC, V.

Restaurants

★ ★ **ALPINE.** *4770 Lee Hwy.* 703/528-7600. Hrs: 11:30 am-11 pm; Sun noon-10 pm. Closed major hols. Res accepted. Italian, continental menu. Bar. Semi-a la carte: lunch $7.95-$9.50, dinner $10.50-$17.95. Child's meals. Specializes in veal, pasta dishes, seafood. Own pasta. Parking. Family-owned. Cr cds: A, C, D, MC, V.

★ ★ **BANGKOK GOURMET.** *523 S 23rd St, at S Eads.* 703/521-1305. Hrs: 11 am-3 pm, 5:30-10 pm; Mon from 5:30 pm; Sat, Sun from 5 pm. Closed Jan 1, Thanksgiving, Dec 25. Res accepted. Thai, French menu. A la carte entrees: lunch $5.95-$8.95, dinner $8.95-$17. Outdoor dining. Cr cds: C, D, DS, MC, V.

✔ ★ ★ **BISTRO BISTRO.** *(4021 S 28th St, Arlington 22206)* 703/379-0300. Hrs: 11 am-10 pm; Fri & Sat to 11 pm; early-bird dinner Mon-Thurs 5-6:30 pm; Sun brunch 10:30 am-3 pm. Closed Thanksgiving, Dec 25. Res accepted. Bar to 2 am. A la carte entrees: lunch $5.75-$10.95, dinner $6.95-$14.95. Sun brunch $6-$11. Specializes in pasta, seafood, oyster stew. Outdoor dining. Bistro atmosphere, eclectic decor. Cr cds: A, MC, V.

★ **CAFÉ DALAT.** *3143 Wilson Blvd, at N Highland St.* 703/276-0935. Hrs: 11 am-9:30 pm; Fri, Sat to 10:30 pm. Closed Chinese New Year, July 4, Thanksgiving, Dec 25. Vietnamese menu. Serv bar. Complete meals: lunch $3.95. Semi-a la carte: dinner $4.95-$7.95. Specialties: sugar cane shrimp, grilled lemon chicken. Own desserts. Totally nonsmoking. Cr cds: MC, V.

✔ ★ ★ **CARLYLE GRAND CAFE.** *(4000 S 28th St, Shirlington)* S on I-395, Shirlington exit. 703/931-0777. Hrs: 11:30 am-11 pm; Fri & Sat to 1 am; Sun brunch 10 am-2 pm. Closed Dec 25. Bar. Semi-a la carte: lunch $5.95-$9.95, dinner $5.95-$14.70. Sun brunch $4.95-$9.95. Specialties: Virginia trout, baby back ribs, smoked salmon filet. Outdoor dining. Totally nonsmoking. Cr cds: A, MC, V.

✔ ★ ★ **FUJI.** *77 N Glebe Rd.* 703/524-3666. Hrs: 11:30 am-10:30 pm; wkends from noon. Closed Jan 1. Res accepted; required Fri, Sat. Japanese, Korean menu. A la carte entrees: lunch $4.95-$8.50, dinner $8.50-$15. Complete meals: dinner $29. Buffet: lunch $6.95. Specialties: bibimbap, fried dumplings, bulgoki. Parking. Sushi bar. Modern Oriental decor. Cr cds: A, MC, V.

★ ★ ★ **THE GRILL.** *(See The Ritz-Carlton, Pentagon City Hotel)* 703/412-2760. Hrs: 6:30 am-10:30 pm; Sat & Sun 7 am-11 pm; Sun brunch 11 am-2:30 pm. Res accepted. Bar. Wine list. Semi-a la carte: bkfst $4-$10. A la carte entrees: lunch $9.50-$18, dinner $15-$24. Buffet: bkfst $8.75-$11. Sun brunch $32. High tea (3-5 pm) $11; light

tea $9. Child's meals. Specializes in beef carpaccio, rack of lamb, grilled Atlantic salmon. Pianist Fri & Sat evenings. Valet parking. English club-like decor and atmosphere. Fireplace. Cr cds: A, C, D, DS, JCB, MC, V.

✔ ★ ★ **ITALIA BELLA.** *5880 N Washington Blvd.* 703/534-7474. Hrs: 11 am-2:30 pm, 4:30-10 pm; Sat 4:30-10:30 pm; Sun 5-9 pm. Closed some major hols. Res accepted. Northern Italian menu. Serv bar. Semi-a la carte: lunch $5.50-$8.95, dinner $6.95-$11.95. Child's meals. Specialties: veal Angelica, chicken piccata, shrimp scampi. Own pasta. Parking. Outdoor dining. Italian art and ceramics. Cr cds: C, D, MC, V.

★ ★ **KABUL CARAVAN.** *1725 Wilson Blvd, in Colonial Village Shopping Ctr.* 703/522-8394. Hrs: 11:30 am-2:30 pm, 5:30-11 pm; Sat, Sun from 5:30 pm. Closed Thanksgiving, Dec 25. Res accepted. Afghan menu. Bar. Semi-a la carte: lunch $7.95-$11.95, dinner $8.95-$15.95. Specialties: sautéed pumpkin with yogurt & meat sauce, eggplant & shish kebab. Walls covered with Afghan clothing, pictures, rugs, artifacts. Cr cds: A, C, D, MC, V.

★ ★ **L'ALOUETTE.** *2045 Wilson Blvd.* 703/525-1750. Hrs: 11:30 am-2:30 pm, 6-10 pm; Fri to 10:30 pm; Sat 6-10:30 pm. Closed Sun; major hols. Res accepted. French menu. Serv bar. Semi-a la carte: lunch $7-$14.25. A la carte entrees: dinner $11.99-$20. Prix fixe: dinner $16.95. Specializes in seasonal dishes. Cr cds: A, C, D, MC, V.

✔ ★ ★ **LITTLE VIET GARDEN.** *3012 Wilson Blvd.* 703/522-9686. Hrs: 11 am-2:30 pm, 5-10 pm; Sat & Sun 11 am-10 pm. Closed Thanksgiving, Dec 25. Res accepted. Vietnamese menu. Bar. Semi-a la carte: lunch $4.95-$6.95, dinner $5.50-$8.95. Specialties: Viet Garden steak, grilled jumbo shrimp. Parking. Outdoor dining. Cr cds: A, C, D, DS, MC, V.

✔ ★ **QUEEN BEE.** *3181 Wilson Blvd.* 703/527-3444. Hrs: 11 am-10 pm. Vietnamese menu. Serv bar. Semi-a la carte: lunch $3.50-$7.50, dinner $6.50-$7.95. Specialties: spring roll, Hanoi beef noodle soup, Hanoi-style grilled pork. Totally nonsmoking. Cr cds: MC, V.

★ **RED HOT & BLUE.** *1600 Wilson Blvd.* 703/276-7427. Hrs: 11 am-10 pm; Fri to 11 pm; Sat noon-11 pm; Sun noon-9 pm. Closed Thanksgiving, Dec 25. Bar. Semi-a la carte: lunch, dinner $4.50-$16.45. Specializes in Memphis pit barbecue dishes. Parking. Memphis blues memorabilia. Cr cds: C, D, MC, V.

★ ★ ★ **RISTORANTE MICHELANGELO.** *2900 Columbia Pike, at Walter Reed Dr.* 703/920-2900. Hrs: 11:15 am-2:30 pm, 5-10:30 pm; Sat, Sun from 5 pm. Closed Jan 1, Thanksgiving, Dec 25. Res accepted. Bar. Northern Italian menu. Semi-a la carte: lunch $8-$11.95, dinner $11-$16. Child's meals. Specializes in veal, chicken, seafood. Own pasta. Parking. Renaissance-style dining rm; reproduction of works by Michelangelo. Cr cds: A, C, D, MC, V.

★ **TACHIBANA.** *4050 Lee Hwy.* 703/528-1122. Hrs: 11:30 am-2 pm, 5-10 pm; Fri & Sat to 10:30 pm. Closed Sun; some major hols. Res accepted Mon-Thurs. Japanese menu. Serv bar. Semi-a la carte: lunch $6-$10, dinner $8.95-$16. Complete meals: dinner $14.50-$21.50. Specialties: sushi, sashimi, soft shell crab tempura (in season). Parking. Circular dining rm. Cr cds: A, C, D, MC, V.

★ ★ **TOM SARRIS' ORLEANS HOUSE.** *1213 Wilson Blvd.* 703/524-2929. Hrs: 11 am-11 pm; Sat from 4 pm; Sun 4-10 pm. Res accepted. Bar. Semi-a la carte: lunch $3.95-$7.95, dinner $7.95-$16.95. Child's meals. Specializes in prime rib, NY steak, seafood.

Salad bar. Parking. New Orleans atmosphere; fountains, iron railings, Tiffany lampshades. Family-owned. Cr cds: A, C, D, DS, MC, V.

★ ★ ★ **THE VIEW.** *(See Marriott Key Bridge Hotel)* 703/243-1745. Hrs: 5-10 pm; Fri to 11 pm; Sat 6-11 pm; early-bird dinner Sun-Thurs 5-7 pm; Sun brunch 10 am-2:30 pm. Closed Jan 1. Res accepted; required July 4. Bar. Wine list. Semi-a la carte: dinner $15.95-$22.95. Sun brunch $24.95. Specializes in seafood, steak. Own pastries. Parking. Excellent view of Washington across Potomac. Cr cds: A, C, D, DS, ER, JCB, MC, V.

D **SC**

★ **VILLAGE BISTRO.** *(1723 Wilson Blvd, Arlington 22209)* 703/522-0284. Hrs: 11:30 am-2:30 pm, 5-10:30 pm; Sun 5-10 pm; early-bird dinner 5-7 pm. Closed Thanksgiving, Dec 25. Res accepted; required Fri & Sat. Continental menu. Bar. A la carte entrees: lunch $5.50-$11.95, dinner $7.95-$15.95. Specializes in seafood, pasta, vegetarian dishes. Parking. Outdoor dining. Monet prints on walls. Cr cds: A, C, D, MC, V.

D

★ ★ **WOO LAE OAK.** *1500 S Joyce St, on grounds of River House complex.* 703/521-3706. Hrs: 11:30 am-10:30 pm. Closed Jan 1. Res accepted. Korean menu. Semi-a la carte: lunch, dinner $6-$16. Specialties: barbecued dishes prepared tableside. Parking. Large, open dining rm; Korean decor. Cr cds: A, C, D, MC, V.

Ashland (E-8)

Founded: 1848 **Pop:** 5,864 **Elev:** 221 ft **Area code:** 804 **Zip:** 23005

Ashland was begun when the president of the Richmond, Fredericksburg and Potomac Railroad bought land here. He dug a well, struck mineral water and started a health resort—Slash Cottage (wilderness acres were called "slashes"). A thriving village grew up and took the name of Henry Clay's Kentucky estate. In 1866, the railroad company gave land to the Methodist church and induced the church to move Randolph-Macon College here. A section of early 1900s houses along the railroad tracks has been set aside as a historic district.

What to See and Do

1. **Randolph-Macon College** (1830). (1,100 students) 1 mi W of I-95. Coeducational, liberal arts, Methodist-affiliated college. Historic buildings include Washington-Franklin Hall, Old Chapel, and Pace Hall. Phone 752-7305. Campus tours **Free.**

2. **Patrick Henry Home "Scotchtown"** (1719). 11 mi NW via VA 54, 671, County 685. Also girlhood home of Dolley Madison; fine colonial architecture. (Apr-Oct, daily exc Mon; also by appt) Phone 227-3500 or 883-6917. **¢¢**

3. **Paramount's Kings Dominion.** 1 mi E on VA 54, then 7 mi N on I-95 in Doswell. A 400-acre family theme park consisting of 6 theme areas, including Hurricane Reef water park; Days of Thunder ride simulator; the Anaconda, a looping roller coaster that passes through underwater tunnel; also Shockwave stand-up roller coaster; 33-story likeness of the Eiffel Tower with panoramic view; monorail ride through 120-acre wildlife preserve; whitewater raft ride; live entertainment; shops. (June-Labor Day, daily; late Mar-May, after Labor Day-early Oct, wkends only) Phone 876-5000. **¢¢¢¢**

(For further information contact the Hanover Visitor Information Center, 112 N Railroad Ave; 752-6766.)

(See Richmond)

Motels

✔ ★ ★ **BEST WESTERN HANOVER HOUSE.** *Rte 6, Box 1215, 1 blk W of I-95 Atlee-Elmont exit (#86).* 804/550-2805; FAX 804/550-3843. 93 rms, 2 story. Apr-mid-Oct: S $36-$65; D $55-$65; each addl $5; under 12 free; higher rates special events; lower rates rest of yr. Crib free. TV; cable. Pool. Restaurant 5:30 am-10 pm. Bar 4 pm-2 am; entertainment Wed-Sat. Ck-out noon. Coin lndry. Meeting rms. Gift shop. Exercise equipt; bicycles, stair machine. Some balconies. Cr cds: A, C, D, DS, MC, V.

★ ★ **COMFORT INN.** *101 Cottage Green Dr.* 804/752-7777; FAX 804/798-0327. 126 rms, 2 story. S $45-$60; D $50-$65; each addl $5; suites $120; under 18 free. Crib free. TV; cable. Pool. Complimentary continental bkfst. Restaurant adj open 24 hrs. Ck-out noon. Coin lndry. Exercise equipt; weight machine, bicycles, sauna. Some refrigerators, minibars. Cr cds: A, C, D, DS, JCB, MC, V.

★ ★ **HOLIDAY INN.** *PO Box 1505, 1 blk W of I-95 exit 92, at jct VA 54.* 804/798-4231; FAX 804/798-9074. 165 rms, 2 story. S, D $45-$86; each addl $10; under 12 free; higher rates some wknds. Crib free. TV. Pool; wading pool. Restaurant 6 am-10 pm. Rm serv. Bar; entertainment. Ck-out 11 am. Coin lndry. Meeting rms. Valet serv. Exercise equipt; weights, bicycles. Private patios, balconies. Cr cds: A, C, D, DS, ER, JCB, MC, V.

Inn

★ ★ **HENRY CLAY.** *114 N Railroad Ave, adj to Amtrak station.* 804/798-3100; res: 800/343-4565; FAX 804/752-7555. 15 rms, 3 story, 1 suite. S, D $80-$90; each addl $15; suite $145; higher rates special events. Crib $15. TV; cable. Complimentary full bkfst. Dining rm 7-10 am, 11 am-2:30 pm, 6-9 pm. Ck-out 11 am, ck-in 2 pm. Health club privileges. Balconies. Authentic reproduction of Georgian-revival inn. Totally nonsmoking. Cr cds: A, MC, V.

Restaurants

★ **IRONHORSE.** *100 S Railroad Ave.* 804/752-6410. Hrs: 11:30 am-2:30 pm, 5:30-9 pm; Mon to 2:30 pm; Fri & Sat to 10 pm. Closed Sun; some major hols; also wk after Jan 1 & wk after July 4. Res accepted. Bar to midnight. Semi-a la carte: lunch $4.95-$8.95, dinner $13.95-$18.95. Specializes in Angus beef, barbecue shrimp, crabcakes. Railroad memorabilia. Cr cds: C, D, DS, MC, V.

D

★ **SMOKEY PIG.** *212 S Washington Hwy.* 804/798-4590. Hrs: 11 am-9 pm; Sun from noon. Closed Mon; major hols. Bar. Semi-a la carte: lunch $1.75-$9.95, dinner $1.75-$15.95. Child's meals. Specializes in pit-cooked meats, seafood, ribs. Parking. Cr cds: MC, V.

Basye (C-7)

Pop: 200 (est) **Elev:** 1,354 ft **Area code:** 703 **Zip:** 22810

What to See and Do

Bryce Resort. On VA 263.

Summer: Fishing, swimming, horseback riding, golf, tennis, hiking, boating, grass skiing. Fee for activities.

Winter: Skiing: 2 double chairlifts, 2 rope tows; patrol, school, rentals; snowmaking; ski shop; restaurant, cafeteria, bar. Longest run 3,500 ft; vertical drop 500 ft. (Mid-Dec-mid-Mar, daily) Phone 856-2121. ¢¢¢¢¢

(For further information contact Bryce Resort, PO Box 3; 856-2121.)

(See Luray, New Market, Woodstock)

Motel

✔ ★ ★ **BEST WESTERN-MT JACKSON.** *(Box 777, Mount Jackson 22842) At I-81 exit 273.* 703/477-2911; FAX 703/477-2392. 98 rms, 2 story. July-Oct: S $38-$42; D $44-$52; each addl $5; lower rates rest of yr. Crib free. TV; cable. Pool; wading pool. Playground. Restaurant 6 am-10 pm. Bar 5-10 pm. Ck-out 11 am. Meeting rms. Sundries. Tennis. Game rm. Cr cds: A, C, D, DS, JCB, MC, V.

Inn

★ ★ ★ **WIDOW KIP'S.** *(Rte 1, Box 117, Mt Jackson 22842) Approx 9 mi E via VA 263E, then S on VA 698.* 703/477-2400. 5 rms, 2 cottages. No rm phones. S $55-$75; D $65-$85; each addl $12. Pet accepted. TV in sitting rm, cottages; cable. Pool. Complimentary full bkfst. Picnic lunches avail. Ck-out 11:30 am, ck-in 2:30 pm. Fireplaces. Bicycles. Grill. Federal-style saltbox house (1830) on 7 acres. Victorian furnishings. Totally nonsmoking. Cr cds: MC, V.

Big Stone Gap (F-2)

Founded: 1888 **Pop:** 4,748 **Elev:** 1,488 ft **Area code:** 703 **Zip:** 24219

This rugged mountain country gave John Fox, Jr his inspiration for *Trail of the Lonesome Pine* and *Little Shepherd of Kingdom Come*. The town lies at the junction of three forks of the Powell River, which cuts a pass through Stone Mountain.

What to See and Do

1. **Southwest Virginia Museum.** W 1st St and Wood Ave. Four-story mansion contains exhibits dealing with life in southwestern Virginia during original coal boom of the 1890s; also Indians of the area and early pioneers. (Memorial Day-Labor Day, daily; Mar-late May & early Sept-Dec, daily exc Mon) Phone 523-1322. ¢

2. **Natural Tunnel State Park.** 18 mi SE, off US 23. Consists of 648 acres. Giant hole chiseled through Purchase Ridge by Stock Creek; pinnacles or "chimneys." Railroad and stream are accommodated in this vast tunnel—100 feet or more in diameter, 850 feet long. Tunnel, visitor center with exhibits. Swimming, pool; fishing. Hiking. Picnicking; concession. Camping, tent & trailer sites (Memorial Day-Labor Day). Interpretive programs. Chairlift. Park (daily); tunnel & most activities (Memorial Day-Labor Day; daily). Standard fees. Phone 940-2674.

3. **June Tolliver House.** Jerome St and Clinton Ave, jct US 23, 58A. Heroine in *Trail of the Lonesome Pine* lived here; period furnishings; now an arts and crafts center; restored 1890 house. (June-late Dec, daily exc Mon) Phone 523-1235. **Free.**

4. **John Fox, Jr House & Museum.** 117 Shawnee Ave. Occupied from 1888 by the author of *Trail of the Lonesome Pine* and *Little Shepherd of Kingdom Come*, best-selling novels of the early 1900s. Memorabilia and original furnishings. Guided tours (June-Sept, daily exc Mon; Oct, wkends). Phone 523-2747 or -1235. ¢¢

(For further information contact the Tourist Information Center, PO Box 236; 523-2060.)

Seasonal Event

Trail of the Lonesome Pine. June Tolliver Playhouse, adj to June Tolliver House (see #3). Outdoor musical drama. Thurs-Sat. For reserved seats phone 523-1235. Late June-Labor Day.

(See Breaks Interstate Park, Wise)

Blacksburg (E-5)

Settled: 1745 **Pop:** 34,590 **Elev:** 2,080 ft **Area code:** 703 **Zip:** 24060

The Jefferson National Forest, which lies to the northwest, provides a colorful backdrop: azaleas, flowering dogwood and redbud in spring and brilliant hardwoods in fall. Virginia Polytechnic Institute and State University is a source of employment for the town. The forest's Blacksburg Ranger District office is located here.

What to See and Do

1. **Smithfield Plantation** (1773). 1/4 mi W off US 460 Bypass, at VA Tech exit. Restored pre-Revolutionary house; original woodwork. Home of Colonel William Preston and three governors. Architectural link between Tidewater and Piedmont plantations of Virginia and those of the Mississippi Valley. Grounds restored by the Garden Club of Virginia. (Apr-Nov, Thurs-Sun afternoons) Phone 951-2060. ¢¢

2. **Mountain Lake.** 20 mi NW on US 460, VA 700. A resort lake, particularly inviting in late June and early July, when azaleas and rhododendron are in bloom.

(For further information contact the Greater Blacksburg Chamber of Commerce, 141 Jackson St; 552-4061.)

(See Radford, Roanoke, Salem)

Motels

★ ★ ★ **BEST WESTERN RED LION INN.** *900 Plantation Rd (VA 685).* 703/552-7770; FAX 703/552-6346. 104 rms, 1-2 story. S $46-$50; D $58-$65; each addl $6; suites $132; under 18 free; higher rates university events. Crib free. TV; cable. Pool; poolside serv. Playground. Restaurant 7 am-10 pm. Rm serv. Bar 4:30 pm-2 am; entertainment. Ck-out noon. Meeting rms. Valet serv. Sundries. Tennis. Golf privileges. X-country ski 15 mi. Lawn games. Picnic tables, grills. On 13 acres. Cr cds: A, C, D, DS, MC, V.

✔ ★ **BUDGET HOST INN.** *3333 S Main St.* 703/951-4242; FAX 703/951-4189. 46 rms, 3 story, 24 suites (2 bedrm). S $28-$38; D $34-$44; each addl $4; suites $48-$98; under 12 free; wkly rates. Crib $4. Pet accepted; $4. TV; cable. Restaurant nearby. Ck-out 11 am. Some in-rm whirlpools. Cr cds: A, C, D, DS, MC, V.

✔ ★ ★ **DAYS INN.** *(Box 768, Christiansburg 24073) 6 mi S, 1 blk NE of I-81 exit 118.* 703/382-0261; FAX 703/382-0365. 122 rms, 2 story. S $40-$60; D $44-$65; each addl $5; under 18, $2; higher rates: VPI, Radford University graduation, football games. Crib free. Pet accepted. TV; cable. Pool. Playground. Complimentary bkfst buffet. Restaurant 6 am-2 pm, 5-9 pm. Beer, wine. Ck-out noon. X-country ski 20 mi. Cr cds: A, D, DS, MC, V.

★ ★ **HAMPTON INN.** *(50 Hampton Blvd, Christiansburg 24073) S via I-81, exit 118, then E.* 703/382-2055; FAX 703/382-4515. 125 rms, 2 story. S $42; D $47; under 18 free; higher rates univ graduation, football games. Crib free. TV; cable. Pool. Restaurant opp

6 am-10 pm. Ck-out 11 am. Coin lndry. Meeting rms. Cr cds: A, D, DS, MC, V.

D ⊠ ⊠ ⊠ SC

★ ★ **HOLIDAY INN.** *3503 Holiday Lane. 703/951-1330; FAX 703/951-4847.* 98 rms, 2 story. S $48-$85; D $53-$85; each addl $5; suites $85-$100; under 12 free; higher rates univ graduation, football wkends. Crib free. TV; cable. Pool; wading pool. Restaurant 6:30 am-2 pm, 5-10 pm. Rm serv. Bar 4 pm-1 am; entertainment, dancing exc Sun. Ck-out noon. Coin lndry. Meeting rm. Valet serv. Sundries. X-country ski 20 mi. Some in-rm steam baths. Cr cds: A, C, D, DS, JCB, MC, V.

D ☞ ⊠ ⊠ ⊠ SC

★ ★ **MARRIOTT.** *900 Prices Fork Rd. 703/552-7001; FAX 703/552-0827.* 148 rms, 2 story. S $69-$89; D $69-$99; each addl $10; suites $150-$160; under 18 free. Crib free. TV; cable. 2 pools, 1 indoor; wading pool, whirlpool. Playground. Complimentary coffee. Restaurant 6:30 am-10 pm. Bar noon-2 am; entertainment, dancing. Ck-out 1 pm. Meeting rms. Bellhops. Valet serv. Sundries. Tennis. X-country ski 20 mi. Game rm. Cr cds: A, C, D, DS, ER, JCB, MC, V.

D ☞ ⊠ ⊠ ⊠ SC

Inn

★ ★ ★ **THE OAKS.** *(311 E Main St, Christiansburg 24073) S on I-81, exit 114, turn right on Main St approx 2 mi. 703/381-1500; res: 800/336-OAKS.* 6 rms, 3 story. S $75-$105; D $95-$130; lower rates Jan. Children over 14 yrs only. TV in some rms. Complimentary full bkfst, tea/sherry. Restaurant nearby. Ck-out noon, ck-in 3 pm. Valet serv. Airport transportation. Balconies. Queen Anne/Victorian residence (1889); period furnishings. Surrounded by 300-yr-old white oak trees. Totally nonsmoking. Cr cds: A, D, MC, V.

⊠ ⊠

Blue Ridge Parkway (F-4 - D-6)

Elev: 649-6,050 ft; avg, 3,000 ft

Winding 469 mountainous miles between Shenandoah and Great Smoky Mountains National Parks (about 217 miles are in Virginia), the Blue Ridge Parkway represents a different concept in highway travel. It is not an express highway (speed limit 45 MPH) but a road intended for leisurely travel. All towns are bypassed. Travelers in a hurry would be wise to take state and US routes, where speed limits are higher.

The parkway follows the Blue Ridge Mountains for about 355 miles, then winds through the Craggies, Pisgahs and Balsams to the Great Smokies. Overlooks, picnic and camp sites, visitor centers, nature trails, fishing streams and lakes, and points of interest are numerous and well marked.

Accommodations are plentiful in cities and towns along the way. The parkway itself offers lodging at four spots: Peaks of Otter (86 miles south of Waynesboro, see MOTEL), Rocky Knob Cabins (174 miles south of Waynesboro), Doughton Park (241 miles south of Waynesboro) and Pisgah Inn (409 miles south of Waynesboro). Food availability is limited on the parkway; in season, cafes are open at Whetstone Ridge, Otter Creek, Peaks of Otter, Mabry Mill, Doughton Park, Crabtree Meadows and Mt Pisgah.

The parkway is open all year, but the best time to drive it is between April and November. Some sections are closed by ice and snow for periods in winter and early spring. Fog may be present during periods of wet weather. The higher sections west of Asheville to Great Smoky Mountains National Park and north of Asheville to Mt Mitchell may be closed January through March due to hazardous driving conditions.

For maps, pamphlets and detailed information contact Superintendent, 200 BB&T Building, One Pack Square, Asheville, NC 28801;704/271-4779.

What to See and Do

(Park visitor facilities are open May-Oct. Numbered concrete posts are located at each mile of the parkway. "Milepost 0" is at Rockfish Gap; MP 469 is just above Cherokee, NC.)

1. **Visitor Centers.** Exhibits, travel information, interpretive publications. Centers (open daily during peak travel season) include

    Humpback Rocks Visitor Center. (MP 5.8) Pioneer mountain farm, park ranger.

    James River Wayside. (MP 63.6) Story of James River and Kanawha Canal, park ranger.

    Peaks of Otter Visitor Center. (MP 86) Wildlife exhibits, park ranger.

    Rocky Knob Information Station. (MP 170) Information, exhibits, park ranger.

    Mabry Mill. (MP 176) Old-time mountain industry, including tannery exhibits, picturesque mill, blacksmith shop.

    Cumberland Knob Contact Station. (MP 218) Visitor information, publications, park ranger.

    Lynn Cove Information Center. (MP 304)

    Museum of North Carolina Minerals. (MP 331) (May-Oct, daily)

    Craggy Gardens Visitor Center. (MP 364.6) 5,892-foot elevation. Natural history exhibits, naturalist. (Mid-June-Labor Day, daily; May-mid-June, early Sept-Oct, wkends)

    Folk Art Center. (MP 382) Craft Guild Headquarters, sales, parkway travel information, park ranger. (Daily)

2. **Self-guided trails.** Grades are not difficult. Walks take about 30 min. Trails on the parkway include

    Mountain Farm Trail. (MP 5.8) Typical mountain farm, reconstructed.

    Greenstone Trail. (MP 8.8) Of geological interest.

    Trail of the Trees. (MP 63.6) Leads to overlook of James River.

    Elk Run Trail. (MP 86) Forest, plant, animal community.

    Rocky Knob Trail. (MP 168) Leads to overlook of Rock Castle Gorge.

    Mabry Mill Trail. (MP 176) Old-time mountain industry.

    Cascades Trail. (MP 272) Leads to waterfall.

    Cone Park Trail. (MP 294) Manor house wild garden.

    Flat Rock Trail. (MP 308.3) Magnificent valley and mountain views.

    Linville Falls Trail. (MP 317.5) Views of falls, Linville River Gorge.

    Craggy Gardens Trail. (MP 364.6) Traverses high mountain "gardens."

    Richland Balsam Trail. (MP 431) Spruce-fir forests. Highest spot on parkway.

3. **Interpretive programs.** Outdoor talks (mid-June-Labor Day) at Otter Creek (MP 60.8), Peaks of Otter (MP 86), Rocky Knob (MP 169), Doughton Park (MP 241.1), Price Park (MP 297.1), Linville Falls (MP 316.3), Crabtree Meadows (MP 340) and Mt Pisgah (MP 408.6). Obtain schedules at Parkway Visitor Centers.

4. **Craft demonstrations and sales.**

    Northwest Trading Post. (MP 258.6) Country store sells native handicrafts.

    Parkway Craft Center. (MP 294) (See BLOWING ROCK, NC)

    Folk Art Center. (MP 382) Craft Guild Headquarters, sales, parkway travel information.

5. **Camping.** Tent and trailer sites at Otter Creek, Peaks of Otter, Roanoke Mt, Rocky Knob, Doughton Park, Julian Price Memorial Park, Linville Falls, Crabtree Meadows and Mt Pisgah. (May-Oct) 14-day limit, June-Labor Day. No electricity; pets on leash only; water is shut off with first freeze, usually late Oct. Fee/site/night. Primitive winter camping at Linville Falls when roads are passable.

6. **Fishing.** Rainbow, brook, brown trout and smallmouth bass in streams and lakes. State licenses required.

7. **Riding.** 20 mi of trails in Moses H. Cone Memorial Park (MP 292.7). Horses for hire at Blowing Rock, NC.

(See Roanoke, Waynesboro)

Motel

★ ★ ★ **PEAKS OF OTTER LODGE.** *(Box 489, Bedford 24523) On Blue Ridge Pkwy at jct VA 43 (Milepost 86). 703/586-1081; res: 800/542-5927 (VA).* 62 rms, 2 story. Mar-Nov: S $45; D $65; each addl $5; suites $75-$85; under 16 free; MAP rest of yr. Crib free. TV in lobby. Restaurant (see PEAKS OF OTTER). Bar 5-11 pm. Ck-out noon. Meeting rm. Sundries. Gift shop. Private patios, balconies. Located on a lake and surrounded by peaks. Scenic view. Cr cds: MC, V.

D ⊠ 🔥

Lodge

★ ★ ★ **DOE RUN.** *(Milepost 189, Blue Ridge Pkwy, Hillsville 24343)* 1/8 mi S of Blue Ridge Pkwy at Milepost 189. 703/398-2212; res: 800/325-6189; FAX 703/398-2833. 42 kit. suites, 1-3 story. No elvtr. Some rm phones. May-Oct: kit. suites $89-$225; each addl $15; under 12 free; wkly rates; hunting, golf plans; lower rates rest of yr. Crib free. Pet accepted; $25. TV. Heated pool; sauna, poolside serv. Complimentary coffee in rms. Restaurant (see HIGH COUNTRY). Bar; entertainment Fri, Sat. Ck-out noon. Meeting rms. Concierge. Sundries. Lighted tennis. 18-hole golf privileges, greens fee $35-$45, pro, putting green, driving range. Game rm. Rec rm. Lawn games. Balconies. Picnic tables. Cr cds: A, MC, V.

D ⊠ 🐾 ⊠ 🏃 ⛷ ⊠ ⛵ 🔥 SC

Inn

★ ★ **OSCEOLA MILL COUNTRY INN.** *Steele's Tavern (24476),* 4 mi W of Blue Ridge Pkwy Milepost 27, on VA 56. 703/377-6455; res: 800/242-7352. 12 rms, 1-2 story, 1 cottage. No rm phones. S, D $89-$109; each addl $20; cottage $139-$169; wkly rates. Pool. Playground. Complimentary full bkfst. Meals by reservation. Ck-out 11 am, ck-in 2 pm. In renovated 1849 mill, mill store and restored 1873 miller's house. Totally nonsmoking. Cr cds: MC, V.

⛵ ⊠ 🔥 SC

Restaurants

★ ★ **HIGH COUNTRY.** *(See Doe Run Lodge)* 703/398-2212. Hrs: 8 am-10 pm; Sun brunch 11 am-3 pm. Closed Dec 25. Res accepted. Bar noon-midnight; closed Sun. Complete meals: bkfst $3.95-$8.95. Semi-a la carte: lunch $4.95-$9.95, dinner $11.95-$19. Buffet (Fri): dinner $18.95-$20.95. Salad bar (Fri & Sat). Entertainment Fri & Sat. Parking. Panoramic view of countryside. Cr cds: A, MC, V.

✔ ★ ★ **PEAKS OF OTTER.** *(See Peaks Of Otter Lodge Motel)* 703/586-1081. Hrs: 7:30 am-2:30 pm, 5-8:30 pm; Sun brunch noon-8:30 pm. Bar 5-11 pm. Semi-a la carte: bkfst $2.70-$6.50, lunch $4.70-$7.95, dinner $6.75-$14.50. Sun brunch $9.50. Child's meals. Specialties: prime rib of beef au jus, barbecued "little pig" ribs, whole rainbow trout. Salad bar. Parking. Panoramic view of mountains & lake. Rustic decor. Family-owned. Cr cds: MC, V.

D

Booker T. Washington National Monument (E-5)

(Approx 18 mi S on VA 116 from Roanoke to Burnt Chimney, then continue 6 mi E on VA 122)

The 1861 property inventory of the Burroughs plantation listed, along with household goods and farm implements, the entry, "1 Negro boy (Booker)—$400." Freed in 1865, the boy and his family moved to Malden, West Virginia. There, while working at a salt furnace and in coal mines, the youngster learned the alphabet from *Webster's Blueback Spelling Book.* Later, by working at the salt furnace before school, then going to work at the mine after school, he got the rudiments of an education. When he realized that everyone else at school roll call had two names, he chose Washington for his own.

From Malden, at 16, he started the 500-mile trip to Hampton Institute, where he earned his way. He taught at Malden for 2 years, attended Wayland Seminary and returned to Hampton Institute to teach. In July, 1881, he started Tuskegee Institute in Alabama with 30 pupils, two run-down buildings and $2,000 for salaries. When Washington died in 1915 the Institute had 107 buildings, more than 2,000 acres and was assessed at more than $500,000.

The 224-acre monument includes most of the original plantation. A 1/4-mile self-guided plantation trail passes reconstructed farm buildings, a slave cabin, crops and animals of the period; there is also a 1 1/2-mile self-guided Jack-O-Lantern Branch nature trail. Costumed interpreters are on duty mid-June-Labor Day. Picnic facilities. Visitor Center has an audiovisual program, exhibits depicting his life (daily; closed Jan 1, Thanksgiving, Dec 25). Phone 703/721-2094. ¢

(See Roanoke)

Inn

★ ★ **MANOR AT TAYLOR'S STORE.** *(Rte 1, Box 533, Smith Mountain Lake 24184)* 4 mi W on VA 122S. 703/721-3951; res: 800/248-6267; FAX 703/721-5243. 7 rms, 3 story. No rm phones. S, D $80-$125. TV in sitting rm. Complimentary full bkfst. Ck-out 11 am, ck-in 4 pm. Exercise equipt; rower, ski machine, whirlpool. Rec rm. Lawn games. Some balconies. Library, sun rm. On 120 acres with pond; swimming. Historic trading post built in 1799, became a post office in 1818. Totally nonsmoking. Cr cds: MC, V.

🐾 ⛵ 🏃 ⊠ ⊠ 🔥

Breaks Interstate Park (E-3)

(8 mi N of Haysi, VA and 7 mi SE of Elkhorn City, KY on KY-VA 80)

The "Grand Canyon of the South," where the Russell Fork of the Big Sandy River plunges through the mountains, is the major attraction of this 4,600-acre park on the Virginia-Kentucky border. From the entrance, a paved road winds through an evergreen forest and then skirts the canyon rim. Overlooks provide a spectacular view of the Towers, a 1/2-mile-long, 1/3-mile-wide pyramid of rocks; the 5-mile-long, 1,600-foot-deep, 250-million-year-old gorge, odd rock formations, caves, springs and a profusion of rhododendron.

The visitor center houses natural and historical exhibits and a coal exhibit (Apr-Oct, daily). Laurel Lake is stocked with bass and bluegill. Picnicking, swimming pool, pedal boats, hiking trails and playground. Camping (Apr-Oct, fee); cottages (all yr), cafe, gift shop. Motor lodge (see). Facilities (Apr-Oct, daily); park (all yr, daily). For details contact Breaks Interstate Park, PO Box 100, Breaks, VA 24607; 703/865-4413. Memorial Day-Labor Day, per car ¢

(See Wise)

Motel

✔ ★ ★ **BREAKS MOTOR LODGE.** *(Box 100, Breaks 24607) On VA 80, 8 mi NW of Haysi, VA, 7 mi E of Elkhorn City, KY.* 703/865-4414. 34 rms, 1-2 story. No A/C. June-Aug: S $42; D $50; each addl $8; cottages $225/wk; lower rates Apr-May & Sept-Oct. Closed rest of yr (exc cottages). Crib free. TV. Pool; wading pool, lifeguard. Restaurant 7 am-9 pm. Ck-out 11 am. Meeting rm. Sundries. Gift shop. Balconies. Picnic tables, grills. Woodland setting; overlooks Breaks Canyon. Hiking trails, picnic shelters. State-owned. Cr cds: A, MC, V.

Bristol (F-3)

Founded: 1771 **Pop:** Bristol, VA: 18,426; Bristol, TN: 24,000 (est) **Elev:** 1,680 ft **Area code:** 703 (VA); 615 (TN) **Zip:** 24201 (VA); 37620 (TN)

Essentially a city in two states, Bristol is actually two cities—Bristol, TN, and Bristol, VA—sharing the same main street and the same personality. Each has its own government and city services. Together they constitute a major shopping center. Named for the English industrial center, Bristol is an important factory town in its own right. Electronics, metal goods and textiles are its major products. These carry on the pioneer tradition of an ironworks, established here about 1784, which made the first nails for use on the frontier.

What to See and Do

1. **Bristol Caverns.** 5 mi SE on US 421, off I-81. Unusual rock formations, seen from lighted, paved walkways winding through caverns and along an underground river. Guided tours every 20 min. Picnic area. (Daily; closed Thanksgiving, Dec 25) Phone 615/878-2011. ¢¢¢

2. **South Holston Dam and Lake.** 8 mi SE on US 421. One of five TVA lakes in the area. Dam on south fork of Holston River created lake with 168-mile shoreline. Fishing, boating, swimming; camping. Visitors building at dam offers free information. (Daily) Phone 615/878-2421.

3. **Steele Creek Park.** 3½ mi SW via Volunteer Pkwy and Broad St. A 1,926-acre park with a 52-acre lake. Fishing; paddleboat rental (June-mid-Sept, daily). Nine-hole golf (all-yr; fee). Picnicking. Dogs on leash only; no pets on beach. (Daily) Phone 615/968-9044. Per car ¢

4. **Rocky Mount Historic Site.** 11 mi SW on US 11E. Features the 2½-story log house (1770) that served, from 1790-1792, as capitol under William Blount, Governor of the Territory of the United States South of the River Ohio. Restored to its original simplicity; 18th-century furniture. On grounds are restored log kitchen, slave cabin, barn, blacksmith shop and smokehouse. (Daily; closed Thanksgiving, Dec 21-Jan 5; also wkends Jan, Feb) Phone 615/538-7396. ¢¢

(For further information contact the Bristol Area Chamber of Commerce, located at 20 Volunteer Pkwy, TN, or mail to PO Box 519, VA 24203; 615/989-4850.)

Seasonal Event

Bristol International Raceway. 5 mi S on US 11E. Phone 615/764-1161. Food City 500, Budweiser 250 in Apr; Budweiser 500, Food City 250 in Aug.

(See Abingdon)

Motels

(Most rates higher race weekends)

★ **BUDGET HOST.** *1209 W State St.* 703/669-5187. 24 rms. S $24-$38; D $31-$50; each addl $4; under 18 free; wkly rates. TV; cable. Restaurant nearby. Ck-out 11 am. Cr cds: A, DS, MC, V.

★ ★ **COMFORT INN.** *2368 Lee Hwy.* 703/466-3881; FAX 703/466-6544. 60 rms, 2 story. Apr-Oct: S $54-$85; D $58-$95; each addl $6; suites $85-$135; under 18 free; higher rates Highland Festival; lower rates rest of yr. Crib free. TV; cable. Pool. Complimentary continental bkfst, coffee. Restaurant nearby. Ck-out 11 am. Meeting rm. Cr cds: A, C, D, DS, ER, JCB, MC, V.

✔ ★ ★ **HoJo INN.** *15589 Lee Hwy (24202), I-81 exit 10.* 703/669-1151; res: 800/446-4656. 60 rms, 2 story. June-Oct: S $35-$74; D $38-$80; each addl $8; lower rates rest of yr. Crib free. TV; cable. Pool. Restaurant 6 am-10 pm. Ck-out noon. Cr cds: A, DS, MC, V.

★ ★ **HOLIDAY INN-WEST.** *Box 1207, W State St at Euclid Ave.* 703/669-7171; FAX 703/669-7171, ext. 300. 123 rms, 2 story. S $49-$54; D $53-$64; each addl $4; under 18 free. TV; cable. Pool. Restaurant 7 am-2 pm, 5-10 pm. Rm serv. Bar 5 pm-10 pm. Ck-out noon. Meeting rms. Sundries. Cr cds: A, C, D, DS, ER, JCB, MC, V.

★ **SUPER 8.** *2139 Lee Hwy, I-81 exit 5.* 703/466-8800. 62 rms, 3 story. S $39-$43; D $45-$49; each addl $5; under 12 free. Crib free. TV; cable. Complimentary coffee in lobby. Restaurant nearby. Ck-out 11 am. Some refrigerators. Picnic tables. Cr cds: A, C, D, DS, JCB, MC, V.

Restaurants

★ **ATHENS STEAK HOUSE.** *105 Goodson St.* 703/466-8271. Hrs: 4-10:30 pm. Closed Sun; major hols. Greek, Amer menu. Bar. Semi-a la carte: dinner $6.95-$20.45. Specializes in lobster tail, steak, Grecian dinner. Cr cds: A, D, MC, V.

★ ★ **VINYARD.** *603 Gate City Hwy.* 703/466-4244. Hrs: 7 am-10 pm; Fri, Sat to 11 pm. Closed July 4, Dec 24 (eve), 25. Res wkends. Italian, Amer menu. Bar. Semi-a la carte: bkfst $1.50-$5.95, lunch $4-$6. Complete meals: dinner $7-$22. Specializes in fresh seafood, veal. Salad bar. Cr cds: A, D, MC, V.

Brookneal (F-6)

Settled: ca 1790 **Pop:** 1,344 **Elev:** 560 ft **Area code:** 804 **Zip:** 24528

What to See and Do

Patrick Henry National Memorial (Red Hill). 3 mi E on VA 40, 2 mi on VA 600 & 619. Last home and burial place of Patrick Henry. Restoration of family cottage, cook's cabin, smokehouse, stable, kitchen. Patrick Henry's law office. Museum and gift shop on grounds. (Daily; closed Jan 1, Thanksgiving, Dec 25) Sr citizen rate. Phone 376-2044. ¢¢

(For accommodations see Lynchburg, also see South Boston)

Cape Charles (E-10)

Pop: 1,398 **Elev:** 10 ft **Area code:** 804 **Zip:** 23310

The Chesapeake Bay Bridge-Tunnel (17.6 miles long) leads from Cape Charles (12 miles south of the town) to Virginia Beach/Norfolk, VA. There is a scenic stop, gift shop, restaurant and fishing pier (bait avail). **Note:** Noncommercial vehicles entering with compressed gas containers are limited to *(a)* two nonpermanently mounted containers with a maximum individual capacity of 105 lbs water or 45 lbs LP-gas each, or one container with a maximum capacity of 60 lbs LP-gas; or *(b)* not more than 2 permanently mounted containers with a total capacity of 200 gallons water when LP-gas is used as a motor fuel. Phone 624-3511, ext 20. One-way passenger car toll ¢¢¢

(For further information contact the Chesapeake Bay Bridge & Tunnel District, Public Relations Dept, PO Box 111; 624-3511, ext 20.)

(For accommodations see Hampton, Newport News, Norfolk, Portsmouth, Virginia Beach)

Cape Henry Memorial (F-10)

(10 mi E of Norfolk on US 60)

The first English settlers of Jamestown landed here on April 26, 1607. They claimed the land for England, stayed four days, named their landing spot for Henry (then Prince of Wales and oldest son of King James I) and put up a cross.

A cross put up by the Daughters of the American Colonists in 1935 marks the approximate site of the first landing. An interpretive display describes the Battle of the Capes, a sea battle fought between England and France in 1781, a prelude to the Battle of Yorktown. Nearby is Cape Henry Lighthouse, first lighthouse in the United States authorized and built by the federal government (1791). The memorial is in Fort Story Military Reservation.

(For accommodations see Norfolk, Virginia Beach)

Charlottesville (D-7)

Founded: 1762 **Pop:** 40,341 **Elev:** 480 ft **Area code:** 804

Thomas Jefferson was born here, as was the University of Virginia, which he founded and designed. Ash Lawn-Highland, which was James Monroe's home, and Monticello are southeast of the city.

In the gently rolling terrain of Albemarle County, Charlottesville is almost at the center of Virginia; it is the trading center for a widespread area. In colonial times, tobacco was the dominant product. Today wheat, beef and dairy herds, riding and race horses, peaches, frozen foods, electronic products, light industry and mountains of native Albemarle pippin apples invigorate the economy.

The biggest Charlottesville employer, however, remains the University and its related enterprises.

What to See and Do

1. **University of Virginia** (1819). (18,100 students) W end of Main St. Founded by Thomas Jefferson and built according to his plans. Handsome red brick buildings with white trim, striking vistas, smooth lawns and ancient trees form the grounds of Jefferson's "academical village." The serpentine walls, one brick thick, which Jefferson designed for strength and beauty, are famous. Room 13, W Range, occupied by Edgar Allan Poe as a student, is displayed for the public. Walking tours start at the Rotunda (daily; closed 3 wks mid-Dec-early Jan). Phone 924-1019. Guided tours **Free.**

2. **Monticello.** 2 mi SE on VA 53. Located on a mountaintop, this is one of the most beautiful estates in Virginia and is considered a classic of American architecture. Monticello was designed by Thomas Jefferson and built over the course of 40 years, symbolizing the pleasure he found in "putting up and pulling down." Jefferson moved into the first completed outbuilding of his new home in 1771, though construction continued until 1809. Most of the interior furnishings are original. Tours of the restored orchard, vineyard and 1,000-foot-long vegetable garden; self-guided tour of Mulberry Row, once the site of plantation workshops. Jefferson died at Monticello on July 4, 1826, and was buried in the family cemetery. The Thomas Jefferson Memorial Foundation maintains the house and gardens. (Daily; closed Dec 25) Sr citizen rate. Phone 984-9822. ¢¢¢   Approx 2 mi W of here is

   Thomas Jefferson Visitor Center. On VA 20S at I-64. Personal and family memorabilia; architectural models and drawings; *Thomas Jefferson: The Pursuit of Liberty,* a 35-minute film, is shown twice daily. (Daily; closed Dec 25) Phone 984-9822. **Free.**

3. **Ash Lawn-Highland** (1799). 4¼ mi SE on County 795. Built on a site personally selected by Thomas Jefferson, this 535-acre estate was the home of President James Monroe (1799-1823). The estate is now owned by Monroe's alma mater, the College of William and Mary. This early 19th-century working plantation offers guided tours of the house with Monroe possessions, spinning and weaving demonstrations, old boxwood gardens, peacocks, picnic spots. Special events include Summer Festival (June-Aug) of operas, evening concerts, children's shows (Sat), Colonial Crafts Wkend, Spring & Christmas programs. (Daily; closed Jan 1, Thanksgiving, Dec 25) Sr citizen rate. Phone 293-9539. ¢¢¢

4. **Historic Michie Tavern** (ca 1780). 1 mi S on VA 20. Built on land granted to Patrick Henry's father and later bought by John Michie, this is one of the oldest homesteads remaining in Virginia. Museum illustrates 18th-century tavern life; 1920s preservation perspective on colonial history. Lunch buffet in converted 200-yr-old log house. (Daily; closed Jan 1, Dec 25) Phone 977-1234. Museum ¢¢

5. **Albemarle County Court House.** Court Square. N wing was used in 1820s as a "common temple," shared by Episcopalian, Methodist, Presbyterian and Baptist sects, one Sunday a month to each but with all who wished attending each Sunday. Jefferson, Monroe and Madison worshiped here.

6. **Monuments.**

   Stonewall Jackson on Little Sorrel. Adjoins courthouse. By Charles Keck.

   Robert E. Lee Monument. Jefferson St between 1st and 2nd Sts.

   Lewis and Clark Monument. Midway Park, Ridge and Main Sts. Memorial to Jefferson's secretary, Meriwether Lewis, who explored the Louisiana Territory with his friend William Clark.

   George Rogers Clark Memorial. W Main St, E of university. Brother of William Clark and soldier on the frontier, this intrepid explorer, who opened up the Northwest Territory, was an Albemarle County native son.

7. **Skiing. Wintergreen Resort.** W on US 250 to VA 151, then S to VA 664, turn right, follow signs (approx 4½ mi). Five chairlifts; patrol, school, rentals; lodge (see RESORTS); nursery. 10 runs; longest run

4,200 ft; vertical drop 1,000 ft. (1st wkend Dec-3rd wkend Mar, daily) Night skiing. Summer activities include golf, tennis, fishing and boating, horseback riding. Phone 325-2200. ¢¢¢¢¢

8. **Sightseeing tour.** The Charlottesville/Albemarle Information Center, located on VA 20S in the Thomas Jefferson Visitors Center Bldg, has information for a walking tour of historic Charlottesville.

9. **Shenandoah National Park** (see). 20 mi W on VA 250 to Afton, then N on Skyline Drive.

(For further information contact the Charlottesville/Albemarle Convention & Visitors Bureau, jct I-64 & VA 20, PO Box 161, 22902; 977-1783.)

Annual Events

Founder's Day (Jefferson's Birthday). Sunrise celebration, commemorative ceremonies. Apr 13.

Dogwood Festival. Parade, lacrosse and golf tournaments, carnival. Nine days mid-Apr.

Garden Week. Some fine private homes and gardens in the area are open. Mid-Apr.

(See Waynesboro)

Motels

★ ★ **HAMPTON INN.** *2035 India Rd (22906).* 804/978-7888; FAX 804/973-0436. 123 rms, 5 story. S $51-$53; D $60-$62; under 18 free; higher rates univ graduation. Crib free. TV; cable. Pool. Complimentary continental bkfst, coffee. Restaurant nearby. Ck-out noon. Meeting rm. Bellhops. Valet serv. Sundries. Free airport, RR station, bus depot transportation. Health club privileges. Cr cds: A, C, D, DS, MC, V.

D ≈ ⊁ ⊠ ⚒ SC

★ ★ **HOLIDAY INN.** *1600 Emmet St (22901), near jct US 29 Business & US 250 Bypass.* 804/293-9111; FAX 804/977-2780. 201 rms, 3 story. S $50-$58; D $60-$68; each addl $10; under 18 free; higher rates special univ events. Crib free. Pet accepted. TV; cable. Pool; wading pool. Restaurant 6 am-10 pm; Fri, Sat to 11 pm. Rm serv. Bar 10-1 am. Ck-out noon. Meeting rms. Bellhops. Valet serv. Free airport, RR station, bus depot transportation. Exercise equipt; bicycle, stair machine, sauna. Cr cds: A, C, D, DS, JCB, MC, V.

D ✔ ≈ ⊁ ⊠ ⚒ SC

✔ ★ **KNIGHTS INN.** *1300 Seminole Trail (22901), US 29 N.* 804/973-8133; FAX 804/973-1168. 115 units. S, D $39-$58; each addl $6; kits. $63; under 18 free; wkly rates. Crib free. Pet accepted. TV; cable. Pool. Complimentary coffee. Restaurant nearby. Ck-out noon. Meeting rm. Cr cds: A, C, D, DS, MC, V.

D ✔ ≈ ⊠ ⚒ SC

Motor Hotels

★ **BEST WESTERN CAVALIER INN.** *Box 5647 (22903), 105 Emmet St, jct US Business 29, US 250.* 804/296-8111; FAX 804/296-3523. 118 rms, 5 story. S $60-$76; D $70-$86; each addl $8; suites $125; under 18 free; 2-day packages; higher rates univ special events. Crib free. Pet accepted. TV; cable. Pool. Complimentary continental bkfst. Restaurant 11:30 am-10 pm. Rm serv. Bar to 1 am. Ck-out 1 pm. Meeting rms. Bellhops. Valet serv. Free airport, RR station, bus depot transportation. Univ of VA opp. Cr cds: A, C, D, DS, MC, V.

D ✔ ≈ ⊠ ⚒ SC

★ ★ **ENGLISH INN OF CHARLOTTESVILLE.** *2000 Morton Dr (22901).* 804/971-9900; res: 800/786-5400. 90 units, 3 story, 21 suites. S $55-$63; D $60-$68; each addl $7; suites $60-$75; under 12 free; higher rates univ graduation, sports events. Crib free. TV; cable. Indoor pool. Complimentary continental bkfst. Ck-out noon. Meeting rms. Free airport, RR station, bus depot transportation. Exercise

equipt; weights, bicycles, sauna. Refrigerator in suites. Cr cds: A, C, D, DS, MC, V.

D ≈ ⊁ ⊠ ⚒ SC

Hotels

★ ★ **OMNI CHARLOTTESVILLE.** *235 W Main St (22902).* 804/971-5500; FAX 804/979-4456. 204 rms, 7 story. S $125-$135; D $135-$150; each addl $15; under 18 free; suites $160-$230; wknd rates; higher rates univ events. Crib free. TV; cable. 2 pools, 1 indoor; poolside serv. Restaurant 6:30 am-10 pm. Bar 11-1 am. Ck-out noon. Convention facilities. Gift shop. Free covered parking. Free airport, RR station, bus depot transportation. Exercise equipt; weights, bicycles, whirlpool, sauna. Refrigerators. Ultra-modern architecture; 7-story atrium lobby. Cr cds: A, C, D, DS, MC, V.

D ≈ ⊁ ⊠ ⚒ SC

★ ★ ★ **SHERATON.** *2350 Seminole Trail (22901), near Charlottesville-Albemarle Airport.* 804/973-2121; FAX 804/978-7735. 238 units, 9 story. S, D $50-$105; each addl $10; suites $200-$289; family rates; wkend, honeymoon rates. Crib $10. TV; cable. Indoor/outdoor pool; poolside serv. Restaurant 6:30 am-10 pm. Bar 4 pm-2 am; entertainment, dancing. Ck-out noon. Convention facilities. Free airport, RR station, bus depot transportation. Tennis. Exercise equipt; weight machines, bicycles, whirlpool. Some bathrm phones, refrigerators. Cr cds: A, C, D, DS, MC, V.

D ✔ ≈ ⊁ ✈ ⊠ ⚒ SC

Inns

★ ★ **200 SOUTH STREET.** *200 South St (22902).* 804/979-0200; res: 800/964-7008. 20 units, 4 story. S, D $95-$175; each addl $20; suites $170; under 12 free. Crib free. TV in lounge. Continental bkfst 7-10:30 am. Complimentary wine, tea. Restaurant adj. Ck-out 11 am, ck-in 2 pm. Some in-rm whirlpools, fireplaces. Built 1853; antiques. Cr cds: A, MC, V.

D ⊠ ⚒ SC

★ ★ **PROSPECT HILL PLANTATION.** *(Rte 3, Box 430, Trevilians 23093)* 15 mi E on I-64, exit 136, then right to Zion Crossroads, left onto US 250 1 mi E to VA 613, turn left and proceed 3 mi. 703/967-0844; res: 800/277-0844; FAX 703/967-0102. 13 rms, 2 with shower only, 3 story, 3 suites. No rm phones. S $165-$250; D $205-$290; each addl $45; suites $250-$290; under 12 free. Closed Dec 24 eve & Dec 25. Pool. Complimentary full bkfst. Complimentary tea, sherry. Dining rm, 1 sitting: 7 pm; Fri & Sat 8 pm. Ck-out 11 am, ck-in 3 pm. Bellhop. Rec rm. Lawn games. Many refrigerators; some in-rm whirlpools. Plantation house built 1732; many antique furnishings; tree-shaded lawns, veranda, gazebo. Cr cds: MC, V.

≈ ⚒

★ ★ ★ **TRILLIUM HOUSE AT WINTERGREEN.** *(PO Box 280, Nellysford 22958)* 23¹/2 mi W on I-64 to exit 107, W on US 250, 14 mi S on VA 151, then 4¹/2 mi W on VA 664 to entry gate on grounds of Wintergreen Resort. 804/325-9126; res: 800/325-9126; FAX 804/325-1099. 12 rms, 2 story. S $85-$100; D $90-$105; each addl $35; suites $120-$150. Crib $5-$10. TV avail; cable. Pool privileges. Complimentary full bkfst. Dining rm 8-9 am; Fri, Sat 7:30 pm (prix fixe dinner). Serv bar. Ck-out noon, ck-in 3 pm. Tennis, golf privileges. Downhill ski on site. Health club privileges. Cr cds: MC, V.

≈ ⚓ ⊁ ⚒

Resorts

★ ★ ★ **BOAR'S HEAD INN & SPORTS CLUB.** *Box 5307 (22905), Ivy Rd (US 250), 2.5 mi W of jct US 29.* 804/296-2181; res: 800/476-1988; FAX 804/977-1306. 174 rms. Apr-mid-July: S $124-$155; D $134-$165; each addl $10; suites $190-$230; under 18 free;

lower rates rest of yr. Crib free. TV; cable. 3 pools; poolside serv, lifeguard. Dining rm 7 am-2 pm, 6-9:30 pm. Bar 5 pm-midnight, Thurs-Sat from 2 pm, Sun from noon; entertainment, dancing. Ck-out noon, ck-in 4 pm. Convention facilities. Valet serv Mon-Fri. Gift/wine shop. Free airport transportation. Lighted outdoor, indoor tennis, pro. Golf privileges adj, putting green, driving range. Bicycles. Horse stables nearby. Hot-air ballooning. Exercise rm; instructor, weights, bicycles, sauna. Some refrigerators. Some private patios, balconies. 2 ponds with ducks, swans & geese. Local landmark; 1834 gristmill. Flower gardens. Local winery tours. Cr cds: A, D, DS, MC, V.

★ ★ ★ **WINTERGREEN.** *Wintergreen (22958), W on US 250 to VA 151S, follow signs.* 804/325-2200; res: 800/325-2200; FAX 804/325-6760. 322 kit. units, most 2-3 story. Late Dec-mid-Mar: S, D $149-$185; family, golf, ski, tennis packages; lower rates rest of yr. Crib avail. TV; cable. 6 pools, 1 indoor; wading pool, some lifeguards. Playground. Supervised child's activities. Dining rm (dinner by res) 7-10:30 am, 11 am-2 pm, 6-10 pm. Box lunches, snack bar, picnics. Bar. Ck-out noon, ck-in 4 pm. Shopping arcade. Convention facilities. Airport, RR station transportation. Tennis, pro. 72-hole golf, greens fee $35-$55, pro, putting green, driving range. Rowboats, canoes. Downhill/x-country ski on site; equipt rentals. Bicycles. Nature programs. Soc dir; entertainment, dancing, movies. Rec rm. Game rm. Exercise equipt; bicycles, rowing machine. Fireplaces. Private patios, balconies. Picnic tables, grills. Cr cds: A, MC, V.

Restaurants

★ ★ **ABERDEEN BARN.** *2018 Holiday Dr.* 804/296-4630. Hrs: 5 pm-midnight; Sun noon-10 pm. Closed Thanksgiving, Dec 25. Res accepted. Bar. Semi-a la carte: dinner $13.95-$31.95. Child's meals. Specializes in prime rib, steak, seafood. Entertainment. Parking. Open charcoal hearth. Family-owned. Cr cds: A, D, MC, V.

★ **BLUE RIDGE BREWING CO.** *709 W Main St.* 804/977-0017. Hrs: 11:30 am-2 pm, 5-10 pm; Mon from 5 pm; Sun brunch 11:30 am-3 pm. Closed July 4, Dec 25. Res accepted. Bar 5 pm-1:30 am. Semi-a la carte: lunch $4.25-$5.25, dinner $8.95-$13.95. Specialties: Caribbean marinated chicken, marinated NY strip steak, West Indian seafood sauté. Within brewery in historic, turn-of-the-century building. Cr cds: A, D, MC, V.

★ ★ **C & O.** *515 E Water St, NW of I-64, exit VA 20 N.* 804/971-7044. Hrs: 11:30-2 am; Sat, Sun from 5 pm. Closed Thanksgiving, Dec 25. Res accepted. French, Amer nouvelle cuisine. Bar. Wine cellar. A la carte entrees: lunch $4.50-$7, dinner $9-$16 & $19-$27. Own baking. Parking. Jacket (upstairs). Cr cds: MC, V.

★ **FELLINI'S.** *200 W Market St.* 804/295-8003. Hrs: 6-10 pm. Closed Dec 25. Res accepted. Northern Italian menu. Bar. Semi-a la carte: dinner $8-$19. Specializes in pasta, seafood, veal. Intimate atmosphere. Cr cds: A, C, D, DS, MC, V.

★ ★ **IVY INN.** *2244 Old Ivy Rd.* 804/977-1222. Hrs: 5-10 pm; Sun brunch 11 am-3 pm. Res accepted. Bar. Semi-a la carte: dinner $12.95-$21.95. Sun brunch $5.50-$12.95. Specializes in regional & eclectic cuisine. Parking. Federal-era house (1804); fireplaces. Cr cds: MC, V.

★ ★ **SCHNITZELHOUSE.** *2208 Fontaine Ave.* 804/293-7185. Hrs: 5-9:30 pm. Closed Sun; major hols; also 1st wk July, 1st wk Jan. Res accepted. Swiss, German menu. Bar. Complete meals: dinner $7.95-$19.95. Child's meals. Specializes in fresh veal. Parking. Bavarian decor. Cr cds: A, MC, V.

★ ★ ★ **STARVILLE CAFE.** *320 W Main.* 804/295-4456. Hrs: 6-10 pm. Closed Sun; major hols; also 3 wks in Jan & Aug. Res accepted. French menu. Bar. A la carte entrees: dinner $20.25-$26.

Prix fixe: dinner (Mon-Thurs) $19.50. Specializes in beef Wellington, rack of lamb, veal. Own baking. Jacket. Cr cds: A, C, D, DS, MC, V.

Chesapeake (F-10)

Pop: 151,976 **Elev:** 12 ft **Area code:** 804

This city is located in the heart of the Hampton Roads area, at the northeastern boundary of the Great Dismal Swamp National Wildlife Refuge (see).

What to See and Do

Northwest River Park. 1733 Indian Creek Rd, off Battlefield Blvd (VA 168). Approx 8 miles of hiking/nature trails wind through this 763-acre city park. Fishing; boating, canoeing (ramp, rentals). Picnicking (shelters), playground, 9-hole miniature golf. Camping, tent & trailer sites (Mar-Oct, daily; fee; hookups, dump station). Shuttle tram. (Daily; closed Jan 1, Dec 25) Fragrance trail for the visually impaired. Phone 421-3145 or -7151. **Free.**

(For further information contact the Public Information Dept, PO Box 15225, 23328; 547-6241.)

Annual Event

Chesapeake Jubilee. City Park. National & regional entertainment, carnival, food booths, fireworks. 3rd wkend May.

(See Norfolk, Portsmouth, Virginia Beach)

Motels

✔ ★ **COMFORT INN.** *4433 S Military Hwy (23321).* 804/488-7900; FAX 804/488-6152. 93 rms, 2 story, 7 kit. units. May-Sept: S $41-$55; D $45-$55; each addl $5; kits. $55-$65; family rates; higher rates major summer hols; lower rates rest of yr. Crib $3. Pet accepted; $5. TV; cable. Pool. Complimentary continental bkfst, coffee. Ck-out 11 am. Meeting rm. Cr cds: A, C, D, DS, ER, JCB, MC, V.

★ ★ **DAYS INN.** *1433 N Battlefield Blvd (23320).* 804/547-9262; FAX 804/547-4334. 90 rms, 2 story. May-Sept: S, D $45-$75; each addl $5; under 12 free; wkly rates; lower rates rest of yr. TV; cable. Pool. Complimentary continental bkfst. Restaurant adj open 24 hrs. Ck-out 11 am. Some refrigerators. Cr cds: A, C, D, DS, JCB, MC, V.

✔ ★ ★ **HAMPTON INN-CHESAPEAKE.** *701A Woodlake Dr (23320).* 804/420-1550; FAX 804/424-7414. 119 rms, 4 story. Memorial Day-Labor Day: S, D $47-$59; higher rates summer wkends; lower rates rest of yr. Crib free. TV; cable. Pool. Complimentary continental bkfst. Restaurant adj 6:30 am-10 pm. Ck-out noon. Meeting rm. Cr cds: A, C, D, DS, JCB, MC, V.

Motor Hotels

★ ★ **COMFORT SUITES-GREENBRIAR.** *1550 Crossways Blvd (23320).* 804/420-1600; FAX 804/420-0099. 123 suites, 3 story. Apr-Oct: S,D $60-$90; each addl $7; under 18 free; higher rates: Labor Day, Jubilee; lower rates rest of yr. Crib $7. TV; cable, in-room movies. Heated pool; whirlpool, sauna. Complimentary continental bkfst. Ck-out 11 am. Meeting rm. Game rm. Refrigerators. Cr cds: A, C, D, DS, ER, JCB, MC, V.

★★★ **HOLIDAY INN CHESAPEAKE.** *725 Woodlake Dr (23320), I-64 exit 289A, Greenbriar N. 804/523-1500; FAX 804/523-0683.* 190 units, 7 story. S $68-$76; D $76-$84; each addl $8; suites $88; under 18 free. TV. Indoor pool. Restaurant 6:30 am-10:30 pm. Rm serv. Bar 11-midnight. Ck-out noon. Meeting rms. Bellhops. Sundries. Free airport transportation. Exercise equipt; weights, treadmill, whirlpool, sauna. Cr cds: A, C, D, DS, JCB, MC, V.

Restaurants

✔ ★ **CARA'S.** *123 N Battlefield Blvd. 804/548-0006.* Hrs: 11:30 am-2:30 pm, 4-10 pm; Fri to 11 pm; Sat 4-11 pm; Sun 10 am-9 pm; Sun brunch to 3 pm. Closed Thanksgiving, Dec 25. Res accepted. Nouvelle Amer menu. Bar. Semi-a la carte: lunch $2.25-$8.50, dinner $9-$13. Sun brunch $9.25. Child's meals. Specialties: sesame seed chicken with Cumberland sauce, crab cakes, steak Chesapeake. Tableside magician Sat. Outdoor dining overlooking wetlands. Cr cds: C, D, DS, MC, V.

D

★ **KYOTO JAPANESE STEAK HOUSE.** *1412 Greenbriar Pkwy, Suite 129. 804/420-0950.* Hrs: 11 am-2 pm, 5-10 pm; Sun 4-9 pm. Closed July 4, Thanksgiving, Dec 25. Res accepted. Japanese menu. Bar. Semi-a la carte: lunch $4.50-$13, dinner $8.95-$20.95. Child's meals. Specialties: teppanyaki, Kyoto special, sukiyaki. Sushi bar. Parking. Original Oriental art. Cr cds: A, C, D, DS, ER, JCB, MC, V.

D

★★ **LOCKS POINTE.** *136 N Battlefield Blvd. 804/547-9618.* Hrs: 11:30 am-3 pm, 5-10 pm; Sat from 5 pm; Sun 11 am-9 pm; Sun brunch to 3 pm. Closed Dec 24-25. Res accepted. Bar 4 pm-1:30 am. Semi-a la carte: lunch $4.50-$6.95, dinner $10.50-$22.50. Sun brunch $6.95-$10.95. Child's meals. Specializes in fresh seafood. Entertainment wkends. Parking. Outdoor dining. On Intracoastal Waterway; dockage. Cr cds: A, MC, V.

D

Chesapeake And Ohio Canal National Historical Park (B-7 - C-8)

(see Maryland)

Chincoteague (D-10)

Founded: 1662 **Pop:** 3,572 **Elev:** 4 ft **Area code:** 804 **Zip:** 23336

Chincoteague oysters, wild ponies and good fishing are the stock in trade of this small island, connected with Assateague Island National Seashore (see #2) by a bridge, and to the mainland by 10 miles of highway (VA 175, from US 13), causeways and bridges.

The oysters, many of them grown on the hard sand bottoms off Chincoteague from seed or small oysters brought from natural beds elsewhere, are among the best in the East. Clams and crabs are also plentiful. Commercial fishing has always been the main occupation of the islanders; but now, catering to those who fish for fun is also important economically.

Chincoteague's wild ponies are actually stunted horses; when colts no bigger than a large dog, but when full-grown somewhat larger and more graceful than Shetlands. They are thought to be descended from horses that swam ashore from a wrecked Spanish galleon, their stunted growth caused by generations of marsh-grass diet.

What to See and Do

1. **Oyster and Maritime Museum of Chincoteague.** Beach Rd. Museum contains live marine life exhibits, details the seafood industry, shows films. Also has the Wyle Maddox Library. (May-early Sept, daily; mid-Sept-Nov, Sat & Sun) Phone 336-6117. ¢

2. **Assateague Island.** Accessible by bridge from town. Includes Chincoteague National Wildlife Refuge and Virginia unit of Assateague Island National Seashore. A 37-mile barrier island, Assateague's stretches of ocean and sand dunes, forest and marshes create a natural environment unusual on the East coast. Sika deer, a variety of wildlife and countless birds, including the peregrine falcon (autumn), can be found here, but wild ponies occasionally roaming the marshes offer the most exotic sight for visitors. Nature and auto trails; boat cruises; interpretive programs. Swimming (bathhouse), lifeguards in summer; surf-fishing. Camping; hike-in and canoe-in camp sites and day use facilities. Picnicking permitted in designated areas; cars are limited to designated roads. No pets allowed. Obtain information at Toms Cove Visitor Center (spring-fall, daily) and at Chincoteague Refuge Visitor Center (daily). Access for disabled to all facilities. For further information contact the Chief of Interpretation, Assateague Island National Seashore, Rte 611, 7206 National Seashore Lane, Berlin, MD 21811; 410/641-1441 or -3030 (camping). (See OCEAN CITY, MD) Also contact Refuge Manager, Chincoteague National Wildlife Refuge, PO Box 62, 23336; 336-6122. Per car ¢¢

3. **Refuge Waterfowl Museum.** 7059 Maddox Blvd. Rotating displays of antique decoys and hunting tools. Decoy making and waterfowl art. (Daily; closed Dec 25) Phone 336-5800. ¢¢

4. **Sightseeing tours. Island Cruises, Inc.** Narrated tour (1½ hrs) through the scenic Assateague Channel on the *Osprey;* also narrated "wildlife safari" tram tour (1½ hrs) along back roads of the Chincoteague National Wildlife Refuge. Contact PO Box 83; 336-5593 or -5511. Cruise ¢¢¢ Tram tour ¢¢

(For further information contact the Chamber of Commerce, Maddox Blvd, PO Box 258; 336-6161.)

Annual Events

Easter Decoy Festival. Easter wkend.

Seafood Festival. 1st Wed May.

Pony Penning. The "wild" ponies are rounded up on Assateague Island, then swim the inlet to Chincoteague, where foals are sold at auction before the ponies swim back to Assateague. Carnival amusements. Last Wed & Thurs July.

Oyster Festival. Columbus Day wkend.

Waterfowl Week. National Wildlife Refuge open to vehicles during peak migratory waterfowl populations. Late Nov.

Motels

★ **BIRCHWOOD.** *3650 Main St. 804/336-6133; res: 800/445-5147.* 41 rms. Apr-Nov: S, D $43-$66; each addl $5; under 10 free (max 1). Closed rest of yr. Crib $4. TV; cable. Pool. Playground. Coffee in rms. Ck-out 11 am. Refrigerators. Cr cds: A, D, DS, MC, V.

✔ ★★ **COMFORT INN.** *(PO Box 205, Onley 23418) Four Corner Plaza, on US 13 at jct VA 179. 804/787-7787; FAX 804/787-4641.* 80 units, 2 story, 10 suites. S $49.50; D $56; each addl $5; suites $57-$75; under 18 free. Crib free. TV; cable. Heated pool. Complimentary continental bkfst. Restaurant adj 11 am-10:30 pm. Ck-out noon. Exercise equipt; bicycles, rowers. Refrigerators. Cr cds: A, C, D, DS, ER, JCB, MC, V.

★★ **DRIFTWOOD MOTOR LODGE.** *Box 575, 7105 Maddox Blvd. 804/336-6557; res: 800/553-6117, ext. 1.* 52 rms, 3 story. Mid-

June-early Sept: S, D $75-$85; each addl $6; under 12 free (2 max); wkend, hol rates; lower rates rest of yr. Crib $5. TV; cable. Pool. Restaurant nearby. Ck-out 11 am. Refrigerators. Private patios, balconies. Picnic tables. At entrance to Assateague Natl Seashore. Cr cds: A, D, DS, MC, V.

★★ **ISLAND MOTOR INN.** *4391 Main St. 804/336-3141; res: 800/832-2925; FAX 804/336-1483.* 48 units, 3 story, 4 suites. Mid-June-Labor Day: S, D $78-$98; suites $125; under 16 free; lower rates rest of yr. Crib $5. TV; cable. Pool. Restaurant nearby. Ck-out 11 am. Lndry facilities. Meeting rms. Sundries. Exercise equipt; weight machine, bicycles, whirlpool. Refrigerators. Bathrm phone in suites. Balconies. Picnic tables, grills. On bay. Expansive views; extensive landscaping. Cr cds: A, D, DS, MC, V.

★ **LIGHTHOUSE.** *4218 Main St. 804/336-5091.* 25 rms, 1-2 story, 3 kits. June-Aug: S, D $57-$75; each addl $5; kit. units $57-$75; min stays summer, hols, special events; lower rates Mar-May, Sept-Nov. Closed rest of yr. Crib $5. TV; cable. Pool; whirlpool. Complimentary coffee in rms. Restaurant nearby. Ck-out 11 am. Refrigerators. Picnic tables, grill. Cr cds: A, C, D, MC, V.

★★ **REFUGE MOTOR INN.** *Box 378, 7058 Maddox Blvd. 804/336-5511; res: 800/544-8469; FAX 804/336-6134.* 68 units, 2 story. June-Sept: S, D $75-$105; each addl $5-$8; under 12 free; some lower rates rest of yr. Crib $5. TV; cable. Indoor/outdoor pool. Ck-out 11 am. Coin lndry. Gift shop. Exercise equipt; weight machines, bicycles, whirlpool, sauna. Refrigerators. Picnic tables, grill. Near wildlife refuge. Chincoteague ponies on grounds. Cr cds: A, C, D, DS, MC, V.

★ **SEA HAWK.** *PO Box 618, 6250 Maddox Blvd. 804/336-6527.* 28 rms, 10 kit. units. Early June-mid-Sept: S, D $65; each addl $5; kit. units $400-$475/wk; lower rates Mar-May, mid-Sept-Dec 1. Closed rest of yr. Crib $4. TV; cable. Pool. Playground. Restaurant opp 5-9 pm. Ck-out 11 am. Lawn games. Refrigerators. Cr cds: A, DS, MC, V.

✔ ★ **SUNRISE MOTOR INN.** *Box 185, 4491 Chicken City Rd, 1/2 blk S of Maddox Blvd. 804/336-6671.* 24 units, 2 kits. Mid-June-early Sept: S $58; D $62; each addl $6; kit. units $540/wk; under 12 free (2 max); lower rates mid-Mar-mid-June, early Sept-Nov. Closed rest of yr. Crib free. TV; cable. Pool. Playground. Complimentary coffee in lobby. Restaurant nearby. Ck-out 11 am. Lawn games. Refrigerators. Picnic tables, grills. Cr cds: A, D, DS, MC, V.

★★ **WATERSIDE MOTOR INN.** *Box 347, 3761 S Main. 804/336-3434; FAX 804/336-1878.* 45 rms, 3 story. Mid-June-mid-Sept (2 day min): S, D $85-$135; each addl $5; under 12 free; lower rates rest of yr. Crib $5. TV; cable. Pool. Complimentary coffee in rms. Restaurant nearby. Ck-out 11 am. Sundries. Tennis. Exercise equipt; weight machine, bicycles, whirlpool. Refrigerators. Balconies. Picnic tables, grills. On saltwater river; marina. Cr cds: A, C, D, DS, MC, V.

Inns

★★★ **CHANNEL BASS.** *6228 Chruch St. 804/336-6148.* 10 rms, 3 story. Feb-Nov: S, D $150-$195; suites $275; wkly rates; lower rates rest of yr. Closed Dec 25. Children over 10 yrs only. Dining rm 6-9 pm (by res only). Ck-out noon, ck-in 3 pm. Built 1867; many rms furnished with antiques. Assateague Wildlife Refuge nearby. Cr cds: C, D, MC, V.

★★★ **THE GARDEN & THE SEA.** *(PO Box 275, 4188 Nelson Rd, New Church 23415) 12 mi NW via VA 175 to US 13, then N to VA 710 (Nelson Rd). 804/824-0672; res: 800/824-0672.* 5 rms in 2 bldgs. No rm phones. Apr-Oct: D $90-$150; under 5 free; wkends (2-night min); wkday rates; lower rates Apr & late Oct. Closed rest of yr. Complimentary continental bkfst, afternoon tea/sherry. Complimentary coffee in parlor. Restaurant (see THE GARDEN & THE SEA INN). Rm serv. Ck-out 11 am, ck-in 3 pm. Bellhops. Concierge. Patio and garden. Built as Bloxom's Tavern (1803) and adj farmhouse. Cr cds: A, C, D, DS, MC, V.

★ **MISS MOLLY'S.** *4141 Main St. 804/336-6686.* 7 rms, 2 share bath, 3 story. Memorial Day-Sept: S $79-$109; D $89-$135; each addl $20; lower rates mid-Feb-early May & Oct-Dec. Closed rest of yr. Children over 8 yrs only. Complimentary full bkfst, afternoon tea. Restaurant nearby. Ck-out 11 am, ck-in 2 pm. On saltwater bay. In historic building (1886); library, sitting rm; antiques. Marguerite Henry stayed here while writing Misty. No cr cds accepted.

✔ ★★ **WATSON HOUSE.** *PO Box 905, 4240 Main St. 804/336-1564; res: 800/336-6787.* 6 rms, 5 with shower only, 2 story. No rm phones. Memorial Day-Labor Day: S $65-$95 D $75-$105; each addl $15; higher rates: wkends (2-night min), holidays (3-night min); lower rates Mar-late May and early Sept-Thanksgiving. Closed rest of yr. Children over 9 yrs only. Complimentary full bkfst, tea/sherry. Restaurant nearby. Ck-out 11 am, ck-in 2 pm. Bicycles avail. Victorian residence (1874). Totally nonsmoking. Cr cds: MC, V.

Restaurants

★★ **BEACHWAY.** *6455 Maddox Blvd. 804/336-5590.* Hrs: 8 am-9 pm. Closed Dec-Feb; also Tues Sept-Nov & Mar-June. Res accepted. Continental menu. Serv bar. Semi-a la carte: bkfst $3.25-$7.95, lunch $3.95-$7.95, dinner $9.95-$24.95. Child's meals. Specializes in steak, seafood, poultry. Parking. French Provincial decor; fireplace, solarium. Cr cds: A, C, D, DS, MC, V.

★★★ **THE GARDEN & THE SEA INN.** *(See The Garden & The Sea Inn) 800/824-0672.* Hrs: 6-9 pm; Sun from 5 pm. Closed Mon & Tues; also Nov-Mar, Wed & Thurs in Apr & Wed in May. Res. French menu. Wine, beer. Extensive wine list. A la carte entrees: dinner $13.95-$22. Complete meals: dinner $27.50-$33. Specializes in cuisine of France & Mediterranean regions. Parking. Intimate dining rm in historic country inn. Cr cds: A, C, D, DS, MC, V.

★★ **NONNIE'S.** *3899 Main St. 804/336-5822.* Hrs: 6-9 pm. Closed Sun; also Nov-Easter. Italian, Amer menu. Wine, beer. Semi-a la carte: dinner $10.95-$17.95. Specializes in fresh seafood, pasta. In converted bayside cottage. Cr cds: MC, V.

✔ ★ **STEAMERS SEAFOOD.** *6251 Maddox Blvd. 804/336-5478.* Hrs: 5-9 pm. Closed Nov-Apr & May-Oct. Wine, beer. Semi-a la carte: dinner $9.95-$16.95. Child's meals. Specializes in steamed crabs & shrimp. Parking. Nautical theme. Cr cds: DS, MC, V.

Clarksville (F-7)

Pop: 1,243 **Elev:** 359 ft **Area code:** 804 **Zip:** 23927

What to See and Do

1. **Occoneechee State Park.** 1 1/2 mi E on US 58. Approx 2,700 acres under development; long shoreline on John H. Kerr Reservoir (Buggs Island Lake). Fishing; boat launching. Hiking. Picnic shel-

ters. Tent and trailer sites (hookups, season varies). Amphitheater; interpretive programs. Standard fees. (Daily) Phone 374-2210.

2. **Prestwould** (1795). 2 mi N on US 15. Manor house built by Sir Peyton Skipwith; rare French scenic wallpaper; original and period furnishings; restored gardens. (May-Sept, daily; Oct, wknds; rest of yr, by appt) Sr citizen rate. Phone 374-8672. ¢¢

(For further information contact the Chamber of Commerce, 321 Virginia Ave, PO Box 1017; 374-2436.)

(See South Boston, South Hill)

Motel

 ★ **LAKE.** *PO Box 1528, 101 Virginia Ave.* 804/374-8106; FAX 804/374-0108. 76 rms, 2 story, 3 suites. Mid-May-mid-Sept: S, D $46-$60; each addl $5; suites $65-$80; under 12 free; lower rates rest of yr. TV; cable. Pool. Restaurant adj 6 am-10 pm. Bar 5 pm-1 am. Ck-out 11 am. Meeting rms. Free airport transportation. Refrigerators avail. Picnic tables, grills. On lake; swimming. Cr cds: A, MC, V.

🛶 ⛱ 🚫 🔥 **SC**

Inn

★ **SIMPLY SOUTHERN.** *307 Commerce St.* 804/374-9040. 4 rms (2 share bath, 1 with shower only, 3 A/C), 2 story. No rm phones. S $45-$60; D $50-$65; each addl $15; under 10 free. TV in sitting rm; cable. Complimentary full bkfst. Ck-out 11 am. Buggs Island Lake 1 blk. Built 1890; antiques. No cr cds accepted.

🚫 🔥

Clifton Forge (E-5)

Settled: 1878 **Pop:** 4,679 **Elev:** 1,079 ft **Area code:** 703 **Zip:** 24422

The town, named after a tilt-hammer forge that operated profitably for almost a hundred years, is in the Warm Springs Mountain area of the Allegheny Mountains.

What to See and Do

1. **C & O Historical Society Archives.** 312 E Ridgeway St, opp terminal building. Includes C & O Railroad artifacts, old blueprints for cars and engines, conductor uniforms, telegraph keys, books, models, collection of photos. (Daily exc Sun; closed hols) Phone 862-2210. **Free.**

2. **Iron Gate Gorge.** 2 mi S on US 220. Perpendicular walls of rock rise from banks of Jackson River. James River Div of C & O Railroad and US 220 pass through gorge. Restored chimney of old forge is here.

3. **Douthat State Park.** 8 mi N on VA 629. Nearly 4,500 acres, high in the Allegheny Mountains, with 50-acre lake. Swimming beach, bathhouse; trout fishing (fee/day); boating (Memorial Day-Labor Day; rentals, launching, electric motors only). Hiking, self-guided trails. Picnicking, restaurant, concession. Camping, tent & trailer sites (Mar-Sept; no hookups); 31 cabins (all yr). Visitor center, interpretive programs. Standard fees. (Daily) Phone 862-7200. **Free.**

(For further information contact the Alleghany Highlands Chamber of Commerce, 241 W Main St, Covington 24426; 962-2178.)

(For accommodations see Covington, Lexington, Warm Springs)

Colonial National Historical Park (E-9)

Made up of four independent areas—Cape Henry Memorial, Colonial Parkway, Jamestown (see all three) and Yorktown Battlefield (see YORKTOWN)—this is where America, as we know it, began. Jamestown, Yorktown and Williamsburg (not a National Park Service area) are connected by the Colonial Parkway. Each of these areas is described in this book under its own name. Abundant in natural as well as historical wealth, the park boundaries enclose more than 9,000 acres of forest woodlands, marshes, shorelines, fields and a large variety of wildlife.

Colonial Parkway (E-9)

The Colonial Parkway is a 23-mile link between the 3 towns that formed the "cradle of the nation"—Jamestown, Williamsburg and Yorktown. It starts at the Visitor Center at Jamestown, passes through Williamsburg (the Colonial Williamsburg Information Center is near north underpass entrance) and ends at the Visitor Center in Yorktown.

At turnouts and overlooks along the route, information signs note such historic spots as Glebeland, Kingsmill, Indian Field Creek, Powhatan's Village, Fusilier's Redoubt and others. A free picnic area is provided during the summer at Ringfield Plantation, midway between Williamsburg and Yorktown.

The parkway is free to private vehicles. Commercial vehicles are not permitted. Speed limit is 45 MPH. There are no service stations.

(For accommodations see Williamsburg, Yorktown, also see Colonial National Historical Park, Jamestown)

Covington (E-5)

Founded: 1833 **Pop:** 6,991 **Elev:** 1,245 ft **Area code:** 703 **Zip:** 24426

Named for its oldest resident, Covington developed from a small village on the Jackson River. It is located in the western part of Virginia known as the Alleghany Highlands. The James River Ranger District office of the George Washington National Forest is located here.

What to See and Do

1. **Humpback Bridge.** 3 mi W just off US 60/I-64. Erected in 1835, this 100-foot-long structure was made of hand-hewn oak, held together with locust-wood pins. In use until 1929, it is now maintained as part of a 5-acre state highway wayside and is the only surviving curved-span covered bridge in the US.

2. **Fort Young.** Off I-64, exit 14. Reconstruction of original fort taken from George Washington's original plans and built near the location of the first fort.

3. **Moomaw Lake.** 13 mi N via US 220, VA 687, follow signs to Gathright Dam. The 12-mile-long lake has a rugged shoreline of more than 43 miles, set off by towering mountains. Surrounded by the Gathright Wildlife Management Area and portions of the George Washington National Forest. Boating, swimming, fishing and waterskiing. Picnicking. Camping (fee). Visitor center. (Apr-Oct, daily) Phone 962-2214. Per vehicle ¢

(For further information contact the Alleghany Highlands Chamber of Commerce, 241 W Main St; 962-2178.)

(See Clifton Forge, Hot Springs)

Motels

★ ★ **COMFORT INN.** *Rte 5, Mallow Rd, I-64 exit 16.* 703/962-2141; FAX 703/965-0964. 100 units, 2 story, 32 suites. S $53.95-$59.95; D $61.95-$67.95; each addl $8; suites $59.95-$67.95; under 18 free. Crib free. Pet accepted; $10. TV; cable, in-rm movies avail. Pool; whirlpool, sauna. Restaurant 7-10:30 am, 11:30 am-9 pm. Bar. Ck-out 11 am. Meeting rms. Lndry serv. Sundries. Some refrigerators. Cr cds: A, C, D, DS, ER, JCB, MC, V.

✔ ★ ★ **HOLIDAY INN.** *P.O. Box 920, on US 60 at jct I-64 exit 16.* 703/962-4951; FAX 703/962-4951, ext. 242. 79 rms, 2 story. S $48-$56; D $52-$64; each addl $4; under 18 free; some wkend rates. Crib free. Pet accepted. TV; cable. Pool; wading pool. Restaurant 6 am-2 pm, 5-10 pm. Rm serv. Bar 5 pm-1 am. Ck-out noon. Meeting rms. Bellhops. Valet serv. Cr cds: A, C, D, DS, ER, JCB, MC, V.

Inn

★ ★ ★ **MILTON HALL BED & BREAKFAST.** *207 Thorny Lane.* 703/965-0196. 6 rms, 2 with shower only, 2 story, 1 suite. Some rm phones. S $75; D $85; each addl $10; suite $130-$140; under 10 free; hunting, fishing plans. Crib free. Pet accepted. TV in some rms, sitting rm; cable. Complimentary full bkfst. Ck-out noon, ck-in 2 pm. Lawn games. Historic country manor house (1874) on 44 acres adj George Washington National Forest. Cr cds: MC, V.

Culpeper (D-7)

Founded: 1748 **Pop:** 8,581 **Elev:** 430 ft **Area code:** 703 **Zip:** 22701

Volunteers from Culpeper, Fauquier and Orange counties marched to Williamsburg in 1777, in answer to Governor Patrick Henry's call to arms. Their flag bore a coiled rattlesnake, with the legends, "Don't Tread on Me" and "Liberty or Death."

In the winter of 1862-63, churches, homes and vacant buildings in Culpeper were turned into hospitals for wounded from the battles of Cedar Mountain, Kelly's Ford and Brandy Station. Later, the Union Army had headquarters here.

Today, Culpeper is a light industry and trading center for a five county area, with a healthy agriculture industry.

What to See and Do

Dominion Wine Cellars. Winery Ave, 2 mi S on VA 3. Tours and tasting. (Daily; closed major hols) Phone 825-8772. **Free.**

(For further information contact the Chamber of Commerce, 133 W Davis St; 825-8628 or 800/829-8628.)

(See Orange, Warrenton)

Motels

★ **COMFORT INN.** *890 Willis Ln.* 703/825-4900; FAX 703/825-4904. 49 rms, 2 story. Apr-Oct: S $55-$59; D $62-$66; each addl $8; under 18 free. Crib free. Pet accepted; $10. TV; cable. Pool. Complimentary coffee in rms, complimentary continental bkfst. Ck-out 11 am. Refrigerators avail. Cr cds: A, C, D, DS, ER, JCB, MC, V.

✔ ★ ★ **HOLIDAY INN.** *Box 1206, 2½ mi S on US 29.* 703/825-1253; FAX 703/825-7134. 159 rms, 2 story. Apr-Oct: S $49; D $56-$62; each addl $4; under 19 free; some lower rates rest of yr. Crib free. TV;

cable. Pool; wading pool. Restaurant 6 am-2 pm, 5-10 pm. Rm serv. Bar 4 pm-12:30 am; entertainment. Ck-out noon. Coin lndry. Meeting rms. Valet serv. Sundries. Cr cds: A, C, D, DS, JCB, MC, V.

Inn

★ ★ **FOUNTAIN HALL BED & BREAKFAST.** *609 S East St.* 703/825-8200; res: 800/476-2944 (exc VA). 5 rms, 2 story, 1 suite. S $50-$75; D $65-$115; suite $115; higher rates: Oct & some hols (2-night min). Crib $10. TV in some rms; cable. Complimentary continental bkfst, refreshments. Complimentary coffee in rms. Ck-out 11 am, ck-in 2 pm. Free RR station transportation. Lawn games. Some in-rm whirlpools, fireplaces. Balconies. Picnic tables, grills. Colonial-revival house (1859). Totally nonsmoking. Cr cds: A, C, D, MC, V.

Guest Ranch

★ ★ **GRAVES' MOUNTAIN LODGE.** *(VA 670, Syria 22743)* 20 mi W via US 29, VA 609 & VA 231 to VA 670. 703/923-4231; FAX 703/923-4312. 38 rms, 9 cottages, 5 kits. AP, mid-Mar-Nov: S $85-$95/person; D $75-$85/person; kit. cottages $110-$205; higher rates Oct. Closed rest of yr. Crib free. Pet accepted. Pool; wading pool, lifeguard. Playground. Dining rm (public by res) 8:30-9:30 am, 12:30-1:30 pm, 6:30-7:30 pm. Box lunches. Ck-out 11 am, ck-in 3 pm. Coin lndry. Grocery ¼ mi. Meeting rms. Tennis. Golf privileges, greens fee $35. Lawn games. Rec rm. Some fireplaces. Picnic tables, grills. Cr cds: MC, V.

Danville (F-6)

Founded: 1792 **Pop:** 53,056 **Elev:** 500 ft **Area code:** 804

This textile and tobacco center blends the leisurely pace of the Old South with the modern tempo of industry. It is one of the nation's largest bright-leaf tobacco auction markets. Dan River, Inc houses the largest single-unit textile mill in the world. Other major industries are located here. Nancy Langhorne, Viscountess Astor, the first woman to sit in the British House of Commons, was born in Danville in 1879.

What to See and Do

1. **Tobacco auctions.** Several huge warehouses ring with the chants of tobacco auctioneers. (Aug-mid-Nov, Mon-Thurs; closed Labor Day, Columbus Day, Veterans Day) Phone 793-5422. **Free.**

2. **"Last Capitol of the Confederacy"** (Danville Museum of Fine Arts and History). 975 Main St. Home of Major W.T. Sutherlin; built 1857. President Jefferson Davis and his cabinet fled to Danville after receiving news of General Lee's retreat from Richmond. It was during this time that the Sutherlin mansion served as the last capitol of the Confederacy. Victorian restoration in historical section of house, (parlor, library and Davis bedroom). Rotating art exhibits by national and regional artists. Permanent collection includes silver, textiles, costumes. (Tues-Fri, also Sat & Sun afternoons; closed major hols, also Dec 24-Jan 2) Phone 793-5644. **Free.**

3. **"Wreck of the Old 97" Marker.** On Riverside Dr (US 58) between N Main and Locust Lane overpass. Site of celebrated train wreck (Sept 27, 1903), made famous by a folk song.

4. **Chatham.** 17 mi N via US 29. Founded in 1777, this county seat of Pittsylvania County has many historically interesting houses, schools and public buildings: Hargrave Military Academy (1909) with the Owen Cheatham Chapel and Yesteryear Hall (museum);

Chatham Hall (1894) with Renaissance Chapel, stained-glass windows of women, and St Francis mural in Commons Building; Old Clerk's Office (1813) restored as museum; Courthouse (1853) in Greek-revival style with delicate plaster ceiling frescoes and portraits; Emmanuel Episcopal Church (1844) with Gothic interior and signed Tiffany windows; Sims-Mitchell House (1860s). Also of interest are the Educational and Cultural Center with planetarium and museum; antique shops, restaurants, trolley diners and the many private houses, several of which offer overnight accommodations. Self-guided walking tour information for town and county may be obtained at the Chamber of Commerce, 38 Main St, Chatham 24531; 432-1650.

(For information on self-guided walking tours of "millionaires' row" historic district and for Civil War sites, contact the Danville Area Chamber of Commerce, 635 Main St, PO Box 1538, 24543; 793-5422.)

Annual Events

Festival in the Park. Arts, crafts, entertainment. Phone 799-5200. 3rd wkend May.

Hot Air Balloon Rally. More than a dozen hot air ballons participate; several flights. Phone 793-5422. July 4 wkend.

Danville Harvest Jubilee. Celebration of tobacco harvest season. Phone 793-5200. Mid-Oct.

Annual National Auctioneering Contest. In conjunction with Harvest Jubilee. Mid-Oct.

(See Martinsville, South Boston)

Motels

(Rates may be higher during sports car races in Martinsville)

★ **BEST WESTERN.** *2121 Riverside Dr (US 58) (24540). 804/793-4000; FAX 804/799-5516.* 98 rms, 3 story. S $44-$46; D $48-50; each addl $5; under 6 free. Crib free. TV; cable. Pool. Complimentary continental bkfst, coffee. Restaurant adj 6 am-10 pm. Ck-out 11 am. Meeting rms. Health club privileges. Bathrm phones; some refrigerators. Deck overlooking river. Cr cds: A, C, D, DS, ER, MC, V.

D ⮕ ≋ ⊁ 🔥 SC

✔ ★ **INNKEEPER MOTOR LODGE WEST.** *3020 Riverside Dr (US 58) (24541). 804/799-1202; res: 800/822-9899; FAX 804/799-9672.* 118 rms, 2 story. S $37.95-$45.95; D $45.95-$59.95; each addl $5. Crib free. TV; cable, in-rm movies avail. Pool; whirlpool. Complimentary continental bkfst. Restaurant adj 6 am-midnight. Ck-out 11 am. Valet serv. Cr cds: A, C, D, DS, MC, V.

D ≋ ⊁ 🔥 SC

✔ ★ **INNKEEPER NORTH.** *1030 Piney Forest Rd (24540). 804/836-1700.* 53 rms, 2 story. S $39.95-$42.95; D $44.95-$46.95; each addl $5; under 16 free. Crib free. TV; cable. Pool. Complimentary continental bkfst. Restaurant adj 6 am-midnight. Ck-out 11 am. Health club privileges. Cr cds: A, C, D, DS, ER, MC, V.

≋ ⊁ 🔥 SC

★ ★ **STRATFORD INN.** *2500 Riverside Dr (US 58) (24540). 804/793-2500; res: 800/326-8455; FAX 804/793-6960.* 157 rms, 2 story. S $43-$48; D $48-$55; each addl $5; suites $76-$131; under 18 free. Crib free. Pet accepted. TV; cable. Heated pool; wading pool. Complimentary full bkfst. Restaurant 6 am-10 pm. Rm serv. Bar to midnight. Ck-out noon. Coin lndry. Meeting rms. Valet serv. Sundries. Exercise equipt; treadmill, stair machine, whirlpool. Cr cds: A, C, D, DS, MC, V.

D ⮕ ≋ 🕺 ⊁ 🔥 SC

Motor Hotel

★ ★ **HOWARD JOHNSON.** *100 Tower Dr (24540), at jct US 29N & US 58, adj Piedmont Mall. 804/793-2000; FAX 804/792-4621.* 118 rms, 6 story, 20 suites. S $49-$65; D $60-$75; each addl $8; suites $65-$80; under 18 free. Crib avail. TV; cable. Pool. Restaurant 6:30 am-midnight. Rm serv. Bar from 11 am. Ck-out noon. Coin lndry. Meeting rms. Valet serv. Free local airport transportation. Health club privileges. Cr cds: A, C, D, DS, JCB, MC, V.

D ≋ ⊁ 🔥 SC

Dulles Intl Airport Area (C-8)

Services and Information

Information: 703/419-8000.

Lost and Found: 703/661-2920.

Weather: 703/260-0307.

Airport Lounges: Admirals Club (American); Red Carpet Club (United), Midfield Terminal.

Terminals

Main Terminal, Concourse A: Delta Connection, Northwest, TACA, USAir, United Express

Midfield Terminal, Concourses C and D: American, Continental, Continental Express, TWA, United

Mobile Lounge Departure Areas:

Concourses B & E (directly to aircraft): Air France, ANA, Delta, Japan Airlines, Russian Intl; Saudi Arabian Airlines

Concourses C & D (to terminal gates): British Airways, Lufthansa, Transbrasil

(Airlines and their terminal locations may change. Before leaving for the airport, you should phone the airline to confirm terminal location for your flight.)

What to See and Do

Reston Town Center. Adj Dulles Toll Rd (VA 267) at Reston Pkwy in Reston. A 20-acre urban development incorporating elements of a traditional town square. Includes more than 60 retail shops and restaurants, an 11-screen movie theater complex, office space and a 514-room Hyatt hotel. (See ANNUAL and SEASONAL EVENTS) Phone 800/368-TOWN.

Annual Events

Northern Virginia Fine Arts Festival. Reston Town Center (see). Art sale, children's activity area, barbecue. June.

Oktoberfest. Reston Town Center (see). Biergarten with authentic German music, food. Mid-Sept.

Seasonal Events

Summer Concerts. Reston Town Center (see). Alternate Sat evenings June-Aug; also Fri evenings July.

Fountain Square Ice Rink. Reston Town Center (see). Outdoor public ice rink. Mid-Nov-mid-Mar.

WASHINGTON DULLES INTERNATIONAL AIRPORT

N
W E
S

■ Terminals

▢ Parking Lot

i Information

International
Arrivals,
Customs,
Immigration

i

Currency
Exchange
& Fax

CONCOURSE A

US Air,
Delta Connection,
Northwest,
TACA,
United Express

Shuttles

CONCOURSE D

CONCOURSE C

American Airlines,
United,
Continental,
AMERICAN ADMIRALS CLUB,
BRITISH AIRWAYS CLUB

TWA,
UNITED RED
CARPET CLUB

Fountain Square Holiday Celebration. Reston Town Center (see). Choral groups, puppeteers, magicians, ice shows, dancers. Thanksgiving-Dec 24.

(See Fairfax)

Motels

★ ★ **COMFORT INN-DULLES NORTH.** *(200 Elden St, Herndon 22070) Dulles Toll Rd exit 3 then left on Baron Cameron Ave (VA 606).* 703/437-7555; FAX 703/437-7572. 103 rms, 3 story. S $67-$80; D $73-$84; each addl $6; under 19 free; wkend plans. TV; cable. Complimentary continental bkfst. Complimentary coffee in rms. Restaurant adj 11 am-10 pm. Ck-out noon. Meeting rms. Valet serv. Free airport transportation. Tennis privileges. Golf privileges. Exercise equipt; weights, bicycles. Refrigerators. Cr cds: A, C, D, DS, ER, JCB, MC, V.

D 🧍🏃✈️🏊🔥 SC

★ ★ **HOLIDAY INN EXPRESS.** *(485 Elden St, Herndon 22070) Dulles Toll Rd exit 2, then E on Elden St.* 703/478-9777; FAX 703/471-4624. 116 rms, 4 story. S, D $67-$79; each addl $6; under 12 free; wkly rates. Crib free. Pet accepted, some restrictions; $3 per day. TV; cable. Complimentary coffee in rms. Complimentary continental bkfst. Restaurant nearby. Ck-out 11 am. Meeting rms. Valet serv. Free airport transportation. Health club privileges. Refrigerators avail. Cr cds: A, C, D, DS, JCB, MC, V.

D 🐾✈️🏊🔥 SC

★ ★ **HOLIDAY INN WASHINGTON DULLES.** *(1000 Sully Rd, Sterling 20166) Dulles Toll Rd exit 1 (US 28/Sully Rd), then 1 mi N.* 703/471-7411; FAX 703/471-7411, ext. 515. 297 rms, 2 story. S $75-$115; D $85-$125; each addl $10; under 18 free; wkend rates. Crib free. TV; cable. Pool; lifeguard. Restaurant 6:30 am-10:30 pm. Rm serv. Bars 11-2 am, Sun to midnight; entertainment, dancing. Ck-out noon. Coin lndry. Meeting rms. Bellhops. Valet serv. Free airport transportation. Exercise equipt; weights, bicycles, whirlpool, sauna. Rec rm. Cr cds: A, C, D, DS, JCB, MC, V.

D 🏊✈️🏊🔥 SC

★ ★ **RESIDENCE INN BY MARRIOTT.** *(315 Elden St, Herndon 22070) Dulles Toll Rd exit Reston Pkwy N, then left on Baron Cameron Rd (VA 606).* 703/435-0044; FAX 703/437-4007. 168 kit. units, 2 story. S, D $115-$145; Wkend rates. Crib free. Pet accepted; $100 non-refundable, $6/day; TV; cable. Pool; whirlpool, lifeguard. Playground. Complimentary continental bkfst. Complimentary coffee in rms. Restaurant opp 6:30 am-10 pm. Ck-out noon. Coin lndry. Valet serv. Sundries. Lighted tennis. Health club privileges. Picnic tables. Cr cds: A, C, D, DS, JCB, MC, V.

D 🐾🏃🏊🔥 SC

Motor Hotel

✔ ★ ★ **DAYS INN DULLES AIRPORT.** *(2200 Centreville Rd, Herndon 22070) 2 mi E on Dulles Toll Rd, exit 2.* 703/471-6700; FAX 703/742-8965. 205 rms, 4 story. Apr-June, Sept-Oct: S, D $49-$129; each addl $10; under 18 free; wkend, monthly rates; lower rates rest of yr. Crib free. TV; cable. Pool; whirlpool, lifeguard. Restaurant 6 am-10 pm. Rm serv. Bar. Ck-out noon. Bellhops. Sundries. Gift shop. Free airport transportation. Tennis privileges, pro. Game rm. Cr cds: A, C, D, DS, MC, V.

D 🏃🏊✈️🏊🔥 SC

Hotels

★ ★ ★ **HYATT DULLES.** *(2300 Dulles Corner Blvd, Herndon 22071) Dulles Toll Rd exit 1 (VA 28/Sully Rd), then S, left on Frying Pan Rd, left on Horsepen Rd, then left on Dulles Corner Blvd.* 703/713-1234; FAX 703/713-3410. 317 rms, 14 story. S $125-$139; D $150-

$164; suites $450; wkly, wkend rates. Crib free. TV; cable. Indoor pool; lifeguard. Restaurant 6 am-12 am. Bar 11:30 am-midnight; pianist. Ck-out noon. Free airport transportation. Exercise equipt; weights, bicycles, whirlpool, sauna. Cr cds: A, C, D, DS, ER, JCB, MC, V.

D 🏊🧍🏃✈️🏊🔥 SC

★ ★ ★ **HYATT REGENCY-RESTON TOWN CENTER.** *(1800 President's St, Reston 22090) Dulles Toll Rd Reston Ave exit, at Reston Town Center.* 703/709-1234; FAX 703/709-2291. 514 rms, 12 story. S $150-$165; D $175-$190; each addl $25; suites $250-$500; under 18 free; wkend packages. Crib free. Garage parking; valet (fee). TV; cable. Indoor pool; poolside serv, lifeguard. Restaurant 6 am-midnight. Bar 11:30-2 am; entertainment Fri-Sun. Ck-out noon. Convention facilities. Concierge. Shopping arcade. Free airport transportation. Tennis, golf privileges. Exercise rm; instructor, weights, bicycles, whirlpool, sauna. *LUXURY LEVEL : REGENCY CLUB.* 72 rms, 6 suites, 2 floors. S, D $190-$215; suites $500-$1,000. Private lounge, honor bar. Some in-rm whirlpools. Complimentary continental bkfst, refreshments. Cr cds: A, C, D, DS, ER, JCB, MC, V.

D 🏊🧍🏃✈️🏊🔥 SC

★ ★ ★ **MARRIOTT SUITES.** *(13101 Worldgate Dr, Herndon 22070) Dulles Toll Rd exit 2, in Worldgate Center.* 703/709-0400; FAX 703/709-0434. 254 suites, 11 story. S $140; D $155; under 18 free; wkend rates. Crib free. TV; cable. Indoor/outdoor pool; lifeguard. Complimentary coffee in rms. Restaurant 6:30 am-10:30 pm. Bar to 11 pm. Ck-out 1 pm. Free lndry facilities. Meeting rms. Free garage parking. Free airport transportation. Exercise equipt; weight machine, rowers, whirlpool, sauna. Health club privileges. Refrigerators, wet bars. Cr cds: A, C, D, DS, ER, JCB, MC, V.

D 🏊✈️🏊🔥 SC

★ ★ ★ **MARRIOTT WASHINGTON DULLES AIRPORT.** *(333 W Service Rd, Chantilly 22021) Dulles Access Rd, at airport.* 703/471-9500; FAX 703/661-8714. 370 rms, 3 story. S $109; D $124; each addl $15; suites $275-$300; under 18 free; wkend plans. Crib free. TV; cable. 2 pools, 1 indoor; poolside serv. Complimentary continental bkfst. Restaurant 6 am-midnight; Sat, Sun from 6:30 am. Bar 11:30-1 am. Ck-out noon. Coin lndry. Convention facilities. Gift shop. Free airport transportation. Lighted tennis. Exercise equipt; weights, bicycles, whirlpool, sauna. Picnic area. On 21 acres with small lake; attractive landscaping. *LUXURY LEVEL : CONCIERGE LEVEL.* 23 rms. S, D $129-$144. Concierge. Private lounge, honor bar. Complimentary continental bkfst, refreshments. Cr cds: A, C, D, DS, ER, JCB, MC, V.

D 🏃🏊✈️🏊🔥 SC

✔ ★ ★ **RENAISSANCE-WASHINGTON DULLES.** *(13869 Park Center Rd, Herndon 22071) On Sully Rd (VA 28), Dulles Toll Rd exit 1, then 1 mi S to McLearen Rd.* 703/478-2900; FAX 703/478-9286. 301 rms, 5 story. S, D $89-$119; each addl $10; parlor rms $126; under 18 free; wkend rates. Crib free. Pet accepted, some restrictions. TV; cable. 2 pools, 1 indoor; poolside serv, lifeguard. Restaurant 6 am-11:30 pm. Bars 11:30-1:30 am; entertainment exc Sun, dancing. Ck-out noon. Convention facilities. Gift shop. Barber, beauty shop. Free airport transportation. Indoor tennis, pro. Exercise equipt; weight machines, bicycles. Some bathrm phones, refrigerators. 3-story atrium; glass-enclosed lobby elvtrs. *LUXURY LEVEL : RENAISSANCE CLUB.* 65 rms, 2 floors. S, D $129. Concierge. Private lounge, honor bar. Full wet bars. Complimentary continental bkfst, refreshments, newspaper. Cr cds: A, C, D, DS, ER, JCB, MC, V.

D 🐾🏃🏊🧍✈️🏊🔥 SC

✔ ★ ★ **SHERATON RESTON.** *(11810 Sunrise Valley Dr, Reston 22091) Off Dulles Toll Rd exit 3.* 703/620-9000; FAX 703/620-0696. 302 rms, 4 & 6 story. S $88-$108; D $90-$118; each addl $15; suites $150-$250; under 17 free; wkend rates. Crib free. TV; cable. Pool; lifeguard. Coffee in rms. Restaurant 6:30 am-10:30 pm. Bar 11-1 am; entertainment. Ck-out 1 pm. Convention facilities. Free airport transportation. Lighted tennis. Exercise equipt; weight machine, rower, sauna. Some minibars. Cr cds: A, C, D, DS, ER, MC, V.

D 🏃 ≋ ✈ 🏊 🔥 SC

Restaurants

★ ★ ★ **IL CIGNO.** *(1617 Washington Plaza, Reston 22090) In Lake Anne Shopping Center.* 703/471-0121. Hrs: 11:30 am-2:30 pm, 5:30-10 pm. Closed Sun (exc summer); most major hols. Res accepted; required Fri & Sat. Northern Italian menu. Bar. Semi-a la carte: lunch $4.95-$12.95, dinner $4.95-$17.95. Specializes in fish, veal, pasta. Outdoor dining overlooking Lake Anne. Split-level dining rm with original art. Cr cds: A, C, D, MC, V.

✔ ★ **TORTILLA FACTORY.** *(648 Elden St, Herndon) Off Dulles Toll Rd exit 2, Pines Shopping Center.* 703/471-1156. Hrs: 11 am-10 pm; Mon to 9 pm; Fri & Sat to 10:30 pm; Sun noon-9 pm. Closed most major hols. Res accepted. Mexican menu. Serv bar. Semi-a la carte: lunch $4.55-$6.50 dinner $5-$11.25. Child's meals. Specialties: carne machaca, chimichangas, vegetarian dishes. Own tortillas. Folk music Tues. Cr cds: A, C, D, DS, MC, V.

D SC

Emporia (F-8)

Pop: 5,306 **Elev:** 110 ft **Area code:** 804 **Zip:** 23847

Motels

★ ★ **BEST WESTERN.** *1100 W Atlantic St.* 804/634-3200; FAX 804/634-5459. 97 rms, 2 story. Feb-Sept: S $45; D $52; each addl $5; under 18 free; lower rates rest of yr. Crib free. TV; cable. Pool. Complimentary continental bkfst. Restaurant opp 6 am-10 pm. Ck-out 11 am. Meeting rms. Exercise equipt; treadmill, stair machine. Some refrigerators. Cr cds: A, C, D, DS, MC, V.

D ≋ ✈ 🏊 🔥 SC

★ **COMFORT INN.** *1411 Skipper's Rd (10960), at I-95 exit 8..* 804/348-3282; FAX 804/3483445. 96 rms, 2 story. S $42.95; D 44.95; each addl $4; family, wkend rates. Crib $2. Pet accepted. TV; cable. Heated pool. Playground. Restaurant adj. 5:30 am-11 pm. Cr cds: A, C, D, DS, ER, JCB, MC, V.

D 🏌 ≋ 🏊 🔥 SC

✔ ★ **DAYS INN.** *921 W Atlantic St.* 804/634-9481; FAX 804/348-0746. 121 rms, 2 story. S $41; D $46; each addl $5; under 12 free. Crib free. TV; cable. Pool. Complimentary bkfst. Restaurant adj open 24 hours. Ck-out noon. Cr cds: A, C, D, DS, MC, V.

≋ 🏊 🔥 SC

★ ★ **HAMPTON INN.** *1207 W Atlantic St (10960), off I-95 exit 11B..* 804/634-9200; FAX 804/6249200, ext. 100. 115 rms, 2 story. S $44-$50; D $50-58; under 18 free. Crib free. Pet accepted. TV. Pool. Complimentary continental bkfst. Restaurant nearby. Ck-out 11 am. Cr cds: A, C, D, DS, MC, V.

D 🏌 ≋ 🏊 🔥 SC

Fairfax (C-8)

Pop: 19,622 **Elev:** 447 ft **Area code:** 703

What to See and Do

1. **George Mason University** (1957). (20,000 students) 4400 University Dr. State-supported, started as branch of University of Virginia. Fenwick Library maintains the largest collection anywhere of material pertaining to the Federal Theatre Project of the 1930s. The Research Center for the Federal Theatre Project contains 7,000 scripts, including unpublished works by Arthur Miller, sets and costume designs and an oral history collection of interviews with former Federal Theatre personnel. (Mon-Fri; closed hols) Phone 993-1000.

2. **Sully** (1794). 10 mi W on US 50, then N on VA 28 (Sully Rd), near Chantilly. Restored house of Richard Bland Lee, brother of General "Light Horse Harry" Lee; some original furnishings; kitchen-washhouse, log house store, smokehouse on grounds. Guided tours. (Daily exc Tues; closed Jan 1, Thanksgiving, Dec 25) Phone 437-1794. ¢¢

3. **Regional parks.** Contact Northern Virginia Regional Park Authority, 5400 Ox Road, Fairfax Station 22039; phone 352-5900.

   Meadowlark Gardens. 9750 Meadowlark Gardens Ct, 6 mi N off VA 123. Lilac, wildflower, herb, hosta and landscapped gardens on 95 acres. Includes 3 ponds; water garden; gazebos; trails. Visitor center. (Daily) Phone 255-3631. **Free.**

   Bull Run. From Beltway I-66W, exit at Centreville, W on US 29 3 mi to park sign. Consists of 5,000 acres. Themed swimming pool (Memorial Day-Labor Day, daily; fee). Camping (1-3 persons, fee; electricity avail; res accepted, phone 631-0550). Concession; picnicking; playground; mini-golf; frisbee golf; nature trail. (Mid-Mar-Dec) Phone 631-0550. Admission per vehicle (nonresidents only) ¢¢

   Algonkian. 6 mi NE on VA 123 to VA 7, then 9 mi NW to Cascades Parkway N, then 3 mi N near Sterling. Located on the Potomac River, this 600-acre park offers swimming (Memorial Day-Labor Day, fee); fishing; boating (ramp); golf, miniature golf; picnicking; vacation cottages. Phone 450-4655. **Free.**

4. **County parks.** For additional information, contact Fairfax County Park Authority, 3701 Pender Dr, 22030; 246-5700.

   Burke Lake. 6 mi S on VA 123, in Fairfax Station. Consists of 888 acres. Fishing, boating (ramp, rentals). Picnicking, playground, concession; miniature train, carousel (summer, daily; early May & late Sept, wkends), 18-hole, par-3 golf course. Camping (May-Sept; 7-day limit; fee/night includes entrance fee). Beaver Cove Nature Trail; fitness trail. Fee for activities. (Daily; closed Dec 25) Phone 323-6601. Nonresident day-use fee/vehicle (wkends & hols) ¢¢

   Lake Fairfax. On VA 606 near Leesburg Pike in Reston. Pool; boat rentals, fishing. Picnicking, concession; miniature golf; excursion boat, carousel; miniature train (late May-Labor Day, daily). Camping (Mar-Dec; 7-day limit; fee/night includes entrance fee; electric addl). Fee for activities. (Daily; closed Dec 25) Phone 471-5415. Nonresident day-use fee/vehicle (wkends & hols) ¢¢

(For further information contact the Fairfax County Visitor Center, 7764 Armistead Rd, Suite 160, Lorton 22079; 550-2450 or 800/7-FAIRFAX.)

Annual Events

Mobil Invitational Track & Field Meet. George Mason University campus. Early Feb.

Antique Car Show. Sully (see #2). 400 antique cars, flea market and music. June.

Quilt Show. Sully (see #2). Quilts for sale, quilting demonstrations and antique quilts on display. Sept.

Seasonal Events

Wolf Trap Farm Park for the Performing Arts. In Vienna, 8 mi NE on VA 123, then W on US 7 to Towlston Rd (Trap Rd), then follow signs. Varied programs include ballet, musicals, opera, classical, jazz and folk music. Filene Center open theater seats 3,800 under cover and 3,000 on the lawn. Picnicking on grounds, all yr. Also free interpretive children's programs, July-Aug. For schedules and prices contact Wolf Trap Foundation, 1624 Trap Rd, Vienna 22182; 255-1900. Late May-Sept.

Barns of Wolf Trap Foundation. 3/4 mi S of Wolf Trap Farm Park on Trap Rd. A 350-seat theater/conference center with chamber music, recitals, mime, jazz, theater and children's programs. For schedule contact the Barns, 1635 Trap Rd, Vienna 22182; 938-2404. Late Sept-early May.

(See Alexandria, Arlington County, Falls Church, McLean; also see District of Columbia)

Motels

★ ★ ★ **COURTYARD BY MARRIOTT-FAIR OAKS.** *11220 Lee Jackson Hwy (US 50) (22030).* 703/273-6161; FAX 703/273-3505. 144 rms, 3 story. S, D $69-$79; suites $75-$100; under 13 free; wkly, wkend rates. Crib free. TV; cable. Indoor pool; lifeguard. Complimentary coffee in rms. Restaurant 6:30-11 am. Bar 4-11 pm. Ck-out 1 pm. Coin lndry. Meeting rms. Valet serv. Sundries. Exercise equipt; weights, bicycles, whirlpool. Some refrigerators. Private patios, balconies. Cr cds: A, C, D, DS, MC, V.

D ⊠ ⅋ ⊠ ⊠ SC

★ ★ **HAMPTON INN.** *10860 Lee Hwy (22030).* 703/385-2600; FAX 703/385-2742. 86 rms, 5 story. S $68-$78; D $73-$83; under 18 free. Crib free. TV; cable. Complimentary continental bkfst. Restaurant adj 7 am-11 pm. Ck-out noon. Meeting rms. Exercise equipt; treadmill, stair machine. Some refrigerators, wet bars. Cr cds: A, C, D, DS, MC, V.

D ⅋ ⊠ ⊠ SC

Motor Hotel

✔ ★ ★ **COMFORT INN-UNIVERSITY CENTER.** *11180 Main St (22030).* 703/591-5900; FAX 703/591-5900, ext. 133. 212 rms, 2-6 story, 125 kit. units. S $57-$95; D $67-$95; each addl $10; kit. units $10 addl; under 18 free; wkend rates. Crib free. Pet accepted, some restrictions; $15. TV; cable. Heated pool; poolside serv, lifeguard. Complimentary continental bkfst. Restaurant 11 am-11 pm. Rm serv. Bar. Ck-out 11 am. Coin lndry. Meeting rms. Bellhops. Valet serv. Lighted tennis. Exercise equipt; weight machine, bicycles. Game rm. Some in-rm whirlpools, wet bars. Picnic tables. Cr cds: A, C, D, DS, ER, JCB, MC, V.

D ⅋ ⅋ ⊠ ⅋ ⅋ ⊠ ⊠ SC

Hotels

★ ★ **HOLIDAY INN FAIR OAKS MALL.** *11787 Lee Jackson Hwy (22033).* 703/352-2525; FAX 703/352-4471. 245 rms, 6 story. S $97; D $103; each addl $6; under 19 free; wkend, hol rates. Crib free. Pet accepted, some restrictions. TV; cable. Indoor pool; lifeguard. Complimentary coffee in rms. Restaurant 6:30 am-10 pm. Bar; entertainment. Ck-out noon. Coin lndry. Convention facilities. Concierge. Gift shop. Free airport transportation. Exercise equipt; weight machine, bicycles, sauna. Health club privileges. Game rm. Balconies. *LUXURY LEVEL : CONCIERGE LEVEL.* 62 rms, 5 suites. S $110; D $116; suites

$150-$225. Concierge. Private lounge, honor bar. Complimentary continental bkfst, refreshments. Cr cds: A, C, D, DS, ER, JCB, MC, V.

D ⅋ ⊠ ⅋ ⅋ ⊠ ⊠ SC

★ ★ **HYATT FAIR LAKES.** *12777 Fair Lakes Circle (22033),* at I-66 exit 55. 703/818-1234; FAX 703/818-3140. 316 rms, 14 story. S $120; D $145; each addl $25; suites $120-$375; under 18 free; wkend rates. Crib free. Pet accepted, some restrictions. TV; cable. Indoor pool; lifeguard. Restaurant 6:30 am-11 pm. Bar 11:30-1 am; entertainment. Ck-out noon. Convention facilities. Free airport, RR station, transportation. Exercise equipt; weights, bicycles, whirlpool, sauna. Refrigerators avail. Cr cds: A, C, D, DS, ER, JCB, MC, V.

D ⅋ ⅋ ⊠ ⅋ ⅋ ⊠ SC

Inn

★ ★ ★ **BAILIWICK.** *4023 Chain Bridge Rd (VA 123) (22030).* 703/691-2266; res: 800/366-7666; FAX 703/934-2112. 14 rms, some rms with shower only, 4 story. No elvtr. Rm phones avail. S, D $130-$275. Complimentary full bkfst, tea. Ck-out 11 am, ck-in 2 pm. Some in-rm whirlpools, fireplaces. Restored private residence (1800); antiques. An early Civil War skirmish occured here (June, 1861). Totally nonsmoking. Cr cds: A, MC, V.

D ⊠ ⊠ SC

Restaurants

★ ★ **ARTIE'S.** *3260 Old Lee Hwy.* 703/273-7600. Hrs: 11:30-2 am; Sun from 10:30 am; Sun brunch to 3 pm. Closed Thanksgiving, Dec 25. Bar. Semi-a la carte: lunch $5.95-$8.95, dinner $5.95-$18.95. Sun brunch $5.25-$9.75. Specializes in steak, seafood, pasta. Parking. Cr cds: A, MC, V.

D

★ ★ ★ **BAILIWICK INN.** *(See Bailiwick)* 703/691-2266. Hrs: 6-9 pm. Closed Mon & Tues. Res required. Continental menu. Wine cellar. Complete meals: dinner $45; Fri & Sat $55. Specializes in seafood, poultry, beef. Parking. Patio dining overlooking English garden. In restored inn (1800). Cr cds: A, MC, V.

★ ★ **HEART-IN-HAND.** *(7145 Main St, Clifton)* S on VA 123 to Chapel Rd, then W. 703/830-4111. Hrs: 11 am-2:30 pm, 6-9:30 pm; Sun 5-8 pm; Sun brunch 11 am-2:30 pm. Closed Jan 1, July 4, Dec 25. Res accepted. Semi-a la carte: lunch $5.95-$10.95, dinner $13.95-$22.95. Sun brunch $6.95-$12.95. Child's meals. Specializes in seafood, beef Wellington, rack of lamb. Own ice cream. Parking. Outdoor dining. Converted general store (ca 1870). Antique decor; original floors, ceiling fans, antique quilts. Cr cds: A, C, D, DS, MC, V.

★ ★ ★ **HERMITAGE INN.** *(7134 Main St, Clifton)* W on US 29 to Clifton Rd (VA 645), then S. 703/266-1623. Hrs: 11:30 am-2:30 pm, 6-10 pm; Sun 11 am-3 pm, 5-9 pm. Closed Mon; Jan 1, Dec 25. Res accepted. French menu. Serv bar. Semi-a la carte: lunch $7.25-$11, dinner $14.25-$22.95. Sun brunch $17.95. Specializes in rack of lamb, Dover sole, châteaubriand. Own pastries. Parking. Outdoor dining. Located in 1869 clapboard hotel. Country French decor. Cr cds: A, C, D, DS, MC, V.

D

★ ★ **J.R.'S STEAK HOUSE.** *9401 Lee Hwy, in Circle Towers office building.* 703/591-8447. Hrs: 5:30-9:30 pm; Fri, Sat to 10:30 pm; Sun 5-9:30 pm. Closed Mon; Thanksgiving, Dec 25. Res accepted. Bar. Semi-a la carte: dinner $12.95-$22.95. Child's meals. Specializes in aged steak, grilled meat and fish. Salad bar. Parking. Patio dining. Cr cds: A, C, D, DS, MC, V.

D

✔ ★ **P.J. SKIDOO'S.** *9908 Lee Hwy.* 703/591-4516. Hrs: 11-2 am; Sun 10 am-9 pm. Closed Jan 1, Thanksgiving, Dec 25. Bar. Semi-a la carte: lunch, dinner $4.95-$12.95. Sun brunch $7.95. Child's meals. Specializes in salads, steak, fresh seafood, chicken. Entertainment Tues-Sat from 10 pm. Parking. 1890s saloon atmosphere. Cr cds: A, MC, V.

★ ★ **SHUN LEE.** *10195 Lee Hwy. 703/273-2800.* Hrs: 11:30 am-3 pm, 5-10 pm; Fri, Sat to 11 pm; Sun brunch noon-3 pm. Closed Thanksgiving, Dec 25. Chinese menu. Bar. Semi-a la carte: lunch $4.50-$5.75, dinner $5.50-$18. Lunch buffet $5.95. Sun brunch $6.95. Specializes in seafood in a bird's nest, two season lamb, sesame chicken. Parking. Outdoor dining. Cr cds: A, MC, V.

✔ ★ **TRES AMIGOS.** *10900 Lee Hwy. 703/352-9393.* Hrs: 11:30 am-11 pm. Closed Thanksgiving, Dec 25. Mexican menu. Bar to 2 am. Semi-a la carte: lunch, dinner $3.50-$11.50. Child's meals. Specializes in fajitas, enchiladas. Entertainment Thurs-Sat evenings. Outdoor dining. Parking. Cr cds: MC, V.

D SC

Unrated Dining Spot

THE ESPOSITOS/PIZZA 'N PASTA. *9917 Lee Hwy. 703/385-5912.* Hrs: 11 am-11 pm; Fri to midnight; Sat noon-midnight; Sun noon-11 pm. Closed Thanksgiving, Dec 24 evening, 25. Southern Italian menu. Wine, beer. A la carte entrees: lunch, dinner $3.50-$11.50. Semi-a la carte: lunch $5.50-$12.95, dinner $6.25-$13.95. Specialties: pollo cardinale, fettucine alla Romano. Own pasta. Parking. Pizza baked in wood-burning oven imported from Italy. Italian trattoria decor. Cr cds: A, C, D, MC, V.

D

Falls Church (C-8)

Pop: 9,578 **Elev:** 340 ft **Area code:** 703

Falls Church is a pleasant, cosmopolitan suburb of Washington, DC just over the Arlington County line, graced with many interesting old houses. This was a crossover point between the North and the South, through which pioneers, armies, adventurers and merchants passed.

What to See and Do

1. **The Falls Church** (Episcopal) (1769). 115 E Fairfax St at Washington St, on US 29. This building replaced the original wooden church built in 1732. Served as recruiting station during Revolution; abandoned until 1830; used during the Civil War as a hospital and later as a stable for cavalry horses. Restored according to original plans with gallery additions in 1959. (Daily exc Sat; closed some hols) Phone 532-7600. **Free.**

2. **Fountain of Faith.** In National Memorial Park. Also in park is a memorial dedicated to the four chaplains—two Protestant, one Jewish, one Catholic—who were aboard the USS *Dorchester* when it was torpedoed off Greenland in 1943. They gave their life jackets to four soldiers on deck who had none.

(For further information contact the Greater Falls Church Chamber of Commerce, 417 W Broad St, PO Box 491, 22040-0491; 532-1050.)

(See Alexandria, Arlington County, Fairfax, McLean; also see District of Columbia)

Motel

✔ ★ **QUALITY INN GOVERNOR.** *6650 Arlington Blvd (US 50) (22042), at I-495 exit 8A. 703/532-8900; FAX 703/532-7121.* 121 rms. Mar-Sept: S $55-$62; D $60-$68; each addl $5; suites $85-$95; under 18 free; lower rates rest of yr. Crib free. TV; cable. Pool; lifeguard.

Restaurant 6:30 am-10 pm; Sat, Sun from 7 am. Ck-out noon. Meeting rms. Some refrigerators. Cr cds: A, C, D, DS, JCB, MC, V.

D ≈ ⊠ 🔥 SC

Hotel

★ ★ ★ **MARRIOTT-FAIRVIEW PARK.** *3111 Fairview Park Dr (22042), at I-495 exit 8A. 703/849-9400; FAX 703/849-8692.* 394 rms, 15 story. S $125; D $145; suites $250-$500; under 16 free. Crib free. TV; cable. Indoor/outdoor pool; poolside serv, lifeguard. Restaurant 6:30 am-10 pm; Fri, Sat to 11 pm. Bar 11-2 am; entertainment, dancing. Ck-out noon. Coin lndry. Convention facilities. Concierge. Gift shop. Free Metro transportation. Exercise equipt; weights, bicycles, whirlpool, sauna. Some bathrm phones. Some balconies. *LUXURY LEVEL :* 57 rms. S $145-$165; D $165-$185. Private lounge, honor bar. Complimentary continental bkfst, refreshments. Cr cds: A, C, D, DS, ER, JCB, MC, V.

D ≈ 🏋 ⊠ 🔥 SC

Restaurants

✔ ★ **BANGKOK VIENTIANE.** *926A W Broad St. 703/534-0095.* Hrs: 11 am-10 pm; wkends to 11 pm. Res accepted. Thai, Laotian menu. Semi-a la carte: lunch $5-$8.95, dinner $6.50-$9.25. Buffet: lunch $6. Prix fixe: lunch $4.75. Specialties: spicy Thai beef noodle, tom yam gung, kaeng seafood combo. Parking. Asian decor. Cr cds: A, C, D, DS, MC, V.

★ ★ ★ **DUANGRAT'S.** *5878 Leesburg Pike, adj Glen Forest Shopping Center. 703/820-5775.* Hrs: 11:30 am-2:30 pm, 5-10:30 pm; Fri to 11 pm; Sat 11:30 am-11 pm; Sun 11:30 am-10:30 pm. Res accepted. Thai menu. Bar. Semi-a la carte: lunch $5.95-$7.95, dinner $8.95-$14.95. Specializes in phad Thai noodles, Thai curry, crispy fish with chili sauce. Parking. Display of Thai headdresses and masks. Dinner show (Fri & Sat) features classical Thai dance performances. Cr cds: A, C, D, MC, V.

D

✔ ★ ★ **HAANDI.** *1222 W Broad St. 703/533-3501.* Hrs: 11:30 am-2:30 pm, 5-10 pm; wkends to 10:30 pm. Closed Dec 25. Res accepted Sun-Thur. Northern Indian menu. Serv bar. Semi-a la carte: lunch $5.25-$8.95, dinner $6.95-$13.95. Specializes in barbecued meats, vegetarian dishes. Parking. Cr cds: A, C, D, MC, V.

D

★ ★ **LA GUINGUETTE.** *8111 Lee Hwy, at Merrifield Plaza. 703/560-3220.* Hrs: 11 am-11 pm; Sun 5-10 pm. French, Italian menu. Bar. Semi-a la carte: lunch $5.95-$13.95, dinner $10.50-$19.75. Entertainment Fri & Sat. Parking. Garden atmosphere. Cr cds: A, DS, MC, V.

★ ★ **MOUNTAIN JACKS.** *127 E Broad St. 703/532-6500.* Hrs: 11:30 am-2 pm, 5-10 pm; Fri, Sat 5-11 pm; Sun noon-9 pm. Res accepted. Bar. Complete meals: lunch $5-$7, dinner $12.95-$18.95. Child's meals. Specializes in prime rib, steak. Entertainment Tue-Sat. Parking. Original artwork, stained glass. Cr cds: A, C, D, DS, MC, V.

D

✔ ★ ★ **PANJSHIR.** *924 W Broad St. 703/536-4566.* Hrs: 11 am-2 pm, 5-11 pm; Sun 5-9 pm. Closed July 4, Thanksgiving, Dec 25. Afghan menu. Bar. Semi-a la carte: lunch $6.50-$7.25, dinner $9.95-$13.25. Specializes in kebab, palows, vegetarian dishes. Parking. Cr cds: A, C, D, MC, V.

★ ★ ★ **PEKING GOURMET INN.** *6029-6033 Leesburg Pike, 4 mi SE on VA 7 (Leesburg Pike). 703/671-8088.* Hrs: 11 am-10:30 pm; Fri, Sat to midnight. Closed Thanksgiving. Res accepted; required Fri, Sat. Northern Chinese menu. Serv bar. Semi-a la carte: lunch $6.25-$8.95, dinner $8.45-$21.95. Specialties: Peking duck, beef Szechwan, striped bass Peking-style. Parking. Oriental antiques and screens; 300

yr-old jade Buddha; original artwork. Favorite of Washington politicians. Cr cds: A, MC, V.

★ ★ **SECRET GARDEN BEEWON.** 6678 Arlington Blvd. 703/533-1004. Hrs: 11 am-10 pm. Closed Jan 1. Res accepted; required Fri & Sat. Korean menu. Bar. Semi-a la carte: lunch $4.95-$9.95, dinner $8.95-$18. Complete meals: lunch $5.95-$9.95. Specialties: bulgogi, heamul chongol. Sushi bar. Parking. Tableside preparation. Traditional Korean decor. Cr cds: A, C, D, DS, MC, V.

★ **SIR WALTER RALEIGH INN.** 8120 Gatehouse Rd. 703/560-6768. Hrs: 11:30 am-2 pm, 5-9 pm; Fri to 10 pm; Sat 5-10 pm; Sun 4-8:30 pm. Closed Thanksgiving, Dec 25. Bar. Semi-a la carte: lunch $5.75-$10.95, dinner $5.95-$17.95. Child's meals. Specializes in steak, seafood. Salad bar. Parking. Cr cds: A, C, D, DS, MC, V.

D

Farmville (E-7)

Pop: 6,046 **Elev:** 304 ft **Area code:** 804 **Zip:** 23901

Longwood College's Jeffersonian buildings provide architectural interest in downtown Farmville.

What to See and Do

1. **Bear Creek Lake State Park.** 20 mi NE on VA 45, then 4 1/2 mi on VA 622W. A 150-acre park in the Cumberland State Forest; 50-acre lake. Swimming, bathhouse; fishing; boating (launch, rentals, electric motors only). Hiking trails. Picnicking; concession. Camping, tent & trailer sites (electrical hookups). Standard fees. Park (daily); activities & camping (Memorial Day-Labor Day). Phone 492-4410. Parking ¢-¢¢

2. **Sailor's Creek Battlefield Historic State Park.** 9 mi E on US 460, then 7 mi NE on VA 307 and 2 mi N on VA 617. Site of last major battle of Civil War, which took place on Apr 6, 1865, preceding Lee's surrender at Appomattox by three days. Auto tour. Phone 392-3435. **Free.**

3. **Appomattox Court House National Historical Park** (see). 26 mi NW via US 460, VA 24.

(See Keysville)

Motel

✔ ★ ★ **COMFORT INN.** HC 6, Box 1740, US 15 & US 460 Bypass. 804/392-8163; FAX 804/392-1966. 50 rms, 2 story. S $38-$53; D $46-$59; each addl $6; under 18 free; higher rates special events. TV; cable. Pool. Continental bkfst avail. Ck-out noon. Gift shop. Exercise equipt; bicycle, rowing machine. Cr cds: A, C, D, DS, ER, JCB, MC, V.

D ⚊ 🏃 ⛗ 🚫 SC

Fredericksburg (D-8)

Settled: 1727 **Pop:** 19,027 **Elev:** 61 ft **Area code:** 703

One of the seeds of the American Revolution was planted here when a resolution declaring independence from Great Britain was passed on April 29, 1775. Here is where George Washington went to school, where his sister Betty lived and his mother, Mary Ball Washington, lived and died. James Monroe practiced law in town. Guns for the Revolution were manufactured here, and four of the most savage battles of the Civil War were fought nearby.

Captain John Smith visited the area in 1608 and gave glowing reports of its possibilities for settlement. In 1727, the General Assembly directed that 50 acres of "lease-land" be laid out and the town called Fredericksburg, after the Prince of Wales.

Ships from abroad sailed up the Rappahannock River to the harbor—ampler then than now—to exchange their goods for those brought from "up country" by the great road wagons and river carriers. The town prospered.

The Civil War left Fredericksburg ravaged. Situated midway between Richmond and Washington, it was recurringly an objective of both sides; the city changed hands seven times, and the casualties were high.

Even so, many buildings put up before 1775 still stand. Proudly aware of their town's place in the country's history, the townspeople keep Fredericksburg inviting with fresh paint, beautiful lawns and well-kept gardens. The city's main sources of income include dairy and beef cattle, softwood timber, men's clothing and shoes, bookbinding and concrete blocks.

What to See and Do

1. **Walking or driving tour of Fredericksburg.** Begin at

   Visitor Center. 706 Caroline St. Orientation film; information; obtain walking tour brochure and combination tickets here. 3 blks N begin at

   Hugh Mercer Apothecary Shop. 1020 Caroline St. 18th-century medical office and pharmacy offers exhibits on the medicine and methods of treatment used by Dr. Hugh Mercer before he left to join the Revolutionary War as brigadier general. Authentic herbs and period medical instruments. (Daily; closed Jan 1, Thanksgiving, Dec 24, 25, 31) Phone 373-3362. ¢¢ Follow Caroline St 3 blks N to

   Rising Sun Tavern (ca 1760). 1306 Caroline St. Washington's youngest brother, Charles, built this tavern, which became a social and political center and stagecoach stop. Restored and authentically refurnished as an 18th-century tavern; costumed tavern wenches, English and American pewter collection. (Daily; closed Jan 1, Thanksgiving, Dec 24, 25, 31) Phone 371-1494. ¢¢ W to Princess Anne St, 4 blks S is the

   Fredericksburg Area Museum (Town Hall) (1814). 907 Princess Anne St. Museum and cultural center interprets the history of Fredericksburg area from its first settlers to the 20th century. Changing exhibits. Children's events. (Daily; closed Jan 1, Thanksgiving, Dec 25) Phone 371-3037. ¢¢ Behind Town Hall to the S on Princess Anne St is

   St George's Episcopal Church and Churchyard. NE corner of Princess Anne and George Sts. St. Patrick Henry, uncle of the orator, was the first rector. Headstones in the churchyard bear the names of illustrious Virginians. (Daily) Phone 373-4133. 1 blk S to Hanover St is

   Fredericksburg Masonic Lodge #4, AF and AM. Princess Anne and Hanover Sts. Washington was initiated into this Lodge Nov 4, 1752; the building, dating from 1812, contains relics of his initiation and membership; authentic Gilbert Stuart portrait; 300-year-old Bible on which Washington took his Masonic obligation. (Mon-Sat, also Sun afternoons; closed Jan 1, Thanksgiving, Dec 25) Phone 373-5885. ¢ Across the street is the

   Presbyterian Church (1833). SW corner of Princess Anne and George Sts. Cannonballs in the front pillar and other damages inflicted in 1862 bombardment. Pews were torn loose and made into coffins for soldiers. Clara Barton, founder of the American Red Cross, is said to have nursed wounded here. A plaque to her memory is in the churchyard. Open on request (daily exc Sat). Phone 373-7057. 1 blk W on George St is

   Masonic Cemetery. George and Charles Sts. One of nation's oldest Masonic burial grounds. Just N on Charles St is

   James Monroe Museum. 908 Charles St. James Monroe, as a young lawyer, lived and worked in Fredericksburg from 1786 to

1789 and even served on Fredericksburg's City Council. Museum houses one of the nation's largest collections of Monroe memorabilia, articles and original documents. Included are the desk bought in France in 1794 during his years as ambassador and used in the White House for signing of the Monroe Doctrine; formal attire worn at Court of Napoleon; and more than 40 books from Monroe's library. Also garden. Site is a National Historic Landmark. Owned by Commonwealth of VA, and administered by Mary Washington College. (Daily; closed Jan 1, Thanksgiving, Dec 24, 25, 31) Phone 899-4559. ¢¢ Continue N on Charles St to

Old Slave Block. William and Charles Sts. Circular block of sandstone about 3 feet high, from which ladies mounted their horses, and slaves were auctioned in antebellum days. 2 blks N on Charles St is

Mary Washington House. 1200 Charles St. Bought by George for his mother in 1772. She lived here until her death in 1789. Here she was visited by General Lafayette. Some original furnishings. Boxwood garden. (Daily; closed Jan 1, Thanksgiving, Dec 24, 25, 31) Phone 373-1569. ¢¢ On Charles St is

St James House. 1300 Charles St. Frame house built in 1760s, antique furnishings, porcelain and silver collections; landscaped gardens. (Open Historic Garden Week in Apr and 1st week in Oct; other times by appt) Phone 373-1569. ¢¢ Walk back 1 blk to Lewis St and walk 2 blks W to

Kenmore (1752). 1201 Washington Ave. Considered one of the finest restorations in Virginia; former home of Col Fielding Lewis, commissioner of Fredericksburg gunnery, who married George Washington's only sister, Betty. On an original grant of 863 acres, Lewis built a magnificent home; three rooms have full decorative molded plaster ceilings. Diorama of 18th-century Fredericksburg. (Daily; closed Jan 1, Thanksgiving, Dec 24, 25, 31) Tea and gingerbread served free (with paid admission) in the colonial kitchen. Phone 373-3381. ¢¢ 2½ blks N is

Mary Washington Monument. Near "Meditation Rock," where Mrs. Washington often went to rest and pray, and where she is buried. 5 blks S on Washington is

Confederate Cemetery. Washington Ave between Amelia and William Sts. 2,640 Confederate Civil War soldiers are buried here, some in graves marked "unknown."

2. **Belmont** (The Gari Melchers Estate & Memorial Gallery). 224 Washington St. Residence from 1916 to 1932 of American-born artist Gari Melchers (1860-1932), best known for his portraits of the famous and wealthy, including Theodore Roosevelt, William Vanderbilt and Andrew Mellon, and as an important impressionist artist of the period. The artist's studio comprises the nation's largest collection of his works, housing more than 1,800 paintings and drawings. Site is a registered National and State Historic Landmark and includes 27-acre estate, frame house built in the late 18th century, and enlarged over the years, and a stone studio built by Melchers, which today houses his artwork. Owned by the State of Virginia, Belmont is administered by Mary Washington College. (Daily; closed Jan 1, Thanksgiving, Dec 24, 25, 31) Phone 899-4860. ¢¢

3. **Mary Washington College** (1908). (3,700 students) College Ave. Liberal arts and sciences including historic preservation, computer science and business administration. Coeducational. Includes 275 acres of open and wooded campus; red brick, white-pillared buildings. President of the college occupies Brompton (private), a house built in 1830 on land sold to Fielding Lewis in 1760 and expanded by a later owner, Colonel John Lawrence Marye. Campus tours. Phone 899-4681 or 800/468-5614.

4. **Fredericksburg and Spotsylvania National Military Park** (see).

(For self-guided tour information including film, map, pamphlet and special rate combination tickets, contact the Visitor Center, 706 Caroline St, 22401; 373-1776 or 800/678-4748.)

Annual Events

Historic Garden Week. Private homes open. Usually last wk Apr.

Market Square Fair. Entertainment, crafts demonstrations, food. Mid-May.

Quilt Show. Exhibits at various locations. Demonstrations and sale of old & new quilts. Sept.

Christmas Candlelight Tour. Historic homes open to the public; carriage rides; Christmas decorations and refreshments of the colonial period. 1st Sun Dec.

(See Triangle)

Motels

★ ★ **BEST WESTERN JOHNNY APPLESEED INN.** *543 Warrenton Rd (22406), I-95 exit 133, jct US 17/522.* 703/373-0000; FAX 703/373-5676. 87 rms, 2 story. May-Oct: S $40-$46; D $46-$52; each addl $7; under 18 free; lower rates rest of yr. Pet accepted. TV; cable. Pool. Playground. Restaurant 6 am-10 pm. Serv bar. Ck-out noon. Coin lndry. Meeting rms. Sundries. Cr cds: A, C, D, DS, MC, V.

D ⟆ ≋ ⊠ 🔥 SC

✔ ★ ★ **BEST WESTERN THUNDERBIRD.** *3000 Plank Rd (22401).* 703/786-7404; FAX 703/371-1753. 76 rms, 3 story. Mar-Oct: S $40.95; D $45.95-$49.95; each addl $4; under 12 free. Crib $2. Pet accepted, some restrictions. TV; cable. Complimentary continental bkfst. Restaurant nearby. Ck-out noon. Sundries. Valet serv. Refrigerators avail. Cr cds: A, C, D, DS, ER, MC, V.

D ⟆ ⊠ 🔥 SC

★ ★ **COMFORT INN NORTH.** *557 Warrenton Rd (22406), jct I-95 exit 133 & US 17N.* 703/371-8900; FAX 703/372-6958. 80 rms, 3 story, 10 kit. units. S $45.95-$85.95; D $50.95-$85.95; each addl $5; kit. units $70.95; under 18 free; family, wkly rates. Crib free. TV; cable. Indoor pool. Complimentary coffee in lobby. Restaurant adj open 24 hrs. Ck-out 11 am. Meeting rms. Exercise equipt; weight machine, step machine, whirlpool. Cr cds: A, C, D, DS, ER, JCB, MC, V.

D ≋ 🏃 ⊠ 🔥 SC

★ **COMFORT INN SOUTHPOINT.** *5422 Jefferson Davis Hwy (22407), I-95 exit 126.* 703/898-5550; FAX 703/891-2861. 125 rms, 5 story. July-Aug: S $54-$59; D $60-$65; each addl $6; under 18 free; golf plan; lower rates rest of yr. Crib free. TV; cable. Indoor pool. Complimentary continental bkfst. Restaurant adj 6 am-10 pm. Ck-out noon. Meeting rms. Sundries. Valet serv. 18-hole golf privileges; greens fee $35, pro, putting green, driving range. Exercise equipt; weight machine, bicycles, whirlpool, sauna. Cr cds: A, C, D, DS, ER, JCB, MC, V.

D 🏃 ≋ 🏃 ⊠ 🔥 SC

✔ ★ **DAYS INN-NORTH.** *14 Simpson Rd (22406), jct I-95 & US 17N.* 703/373-5340. 120 rms, 2 story. S $38-$41; D $48-$51; each addl $5 (children $2). Crib free. Pet accepted; $5. TV; cable. Pool. Complimentary continental bkfst. Restaurant 6-9 am, 5-9 pm. Ck-out noon. Cr cds: A, C, D, DS, MC, V.

⟆ ≋ ⊠ 🔥 SC

★ ★ **HAMPTON INN.** *2310 William St (22401), E of I-95 exit 130-A.* 703/371-0330; FAX 703/371-1753. 166 rms, 2 story. S $44; D $59; under 18 free; mid-wk rates. Crib free. TV; cable. Pool. Complimentary continental bkfst. Ck-out noon. Coin lndry. Meeting rms. Cr cds: A, C, D, DS, MC, V.

D ≋ ⊠ 🔥 SC

★ ★ **HOLIDAY INN-NORTH.** *564 Warrenton Rd (22405), at jct US 17, I-95 (Warrenton exit).* 703/371-5550; FAX 703/373-3641. 150 rms, 2 story. S $45; D $55; each addl $7; under 18 free. Crib free. TV; cable. Pool; wading pool. Restaurant 6 am-2 pm, 5-10 pm. Rm serv. Bar 3 pm-2 am; entertainment, dancing Fri, Sat. Ck-out noon. Coin lndry. Meeting rms. Valet serv. Sundries. Refrigerators avail. Cr cds: A, C, D, DS, JCB, MC, V.

D ⟆ ≋ ⊠ 🔥 SC

★ RAMADA INN-SPOTSYLVANIA MALL. *Box 36 (22404), jct I-95, VA 3W, exit 130-B.* 703/786-8361; FAX 703/786-8811. 130 rms, 2 story. S $40-$55; D $45-$59; each addl $5; suites $75-$100; under 18 free. Crib free. Pet accepted. TV; cable. Pool. Restaurant 6 am-10 pm. Rm serv 11 am-9 pm. Ck-out 1 pm. Meeting rms. Valet serv. Sundries. Cr cds: A, C, D, DS, ER, JCB, MC, V.

D ⚫ ⚫ ⚫ ⚫ SC

Motor Hotels

★ HOLIDAY INN SOUTH. *5324 Jefferson Davis Hwy (22408), I-95 exit 126.* 703/898-1102; FAX 703/898-2017. 195 rms, 2 story. S, D $61-$65; each addl $6; under 18 free. Crib free. Pet accepted. TV; cable. Indoor pool. Restaurant 6 am-2 pm, 5-10 pm. Rm serv. Bar 4 pm-2 am. Ck-out noon. Coin lndry. Meeting rms. Bellhops. Sundries. Valet serv. Exercise equipt; bicycles, rowers, whirlpool. Holidome. Game rm. Cr cds: A, C, D, DS, JCB, MC, V.

D ⚫ ⚫ ⚫ ⚫ ⚫ SC

★ ★ SHERATON INN. *PO Box 618 (22404), 2801 Plank Rd. I-95 exit 130-B, jct VA 3.* 703/786-8321; FAX 703/786-3957. 195 rms, 3 story. May-mid-Nov: S $60-$95; D $75-$105; each addl $10; suites $150-$275; under 18 free; lower rates rest of yr. Crib free. TV; cable. Pool; wading pool, poolside serv, lifeguard. Complimentary coffee in rms. Restaurant 6:30 am-10 pm. Rm serv. Bar 11:30-2 am; entertainment, dancing exc Sun. Ck-out noon. Meeting rms. Bellhops. Valet serv. Sundries. Gift shop. Airport transportation. Tennis. 18-hole golf, greens fee $26-$34 (incl cart), pro, putting green, driving range. Exercise equipt; weight machine, stair machine. Lawn games. Private patios, balconies. Refrigerators avail. Picnic tables. Cr cds: A, C, D, DS, ER, JCB, MC, V.

D ⚫ ⚫ ⚫ ⚫ ⚫ ⚫ SC

Inns

★ ★ FREDERICKSBURG COLONIAL. *1707 Princess Anne St (22401).* 703/371-5666; FAX 703/373-7557. 30 rms, 2 story. S, D $55; each addl $6; suites $65-$70; under 12 free. Crib free. TV; cable. Complimentary continental bkfst, coffee. Ck-out 11 am, ck-in 2 pm. Refrigerators. Built 1928; antiques. Cr cds: A, MC, V.

D ⚫ ⚫ SC

★ ★ KENMORE. *1200 Princess Anne St (22401).* 703/371-7622; res: 800/437-7622; FAX 703/371-5480. 12 rms, 2 story. S $75-$105; D $85-$105; each addl $10; suite $150. Crib free. TV in lounge; cable. Complimentary continental bkfst, coffee, tea; afternoon sherry. Dining rm 11:30 am-2:30 pm, 5:30-9:30 pm. Rm serv. Bar 11:30 am-11 pm. Ck-out noon, ck-in 2 pm. Fireplace, canopy bed in some rms. Refrigerators avail. Structure built late 1700s; in historic district. Cr cds: A, C, D, MC, V.

D ⚫ ⚫ SC

★ ★ RICHARD JOHNSTON. *711 Caroline St (22401).* 703/899-7606. 7 rms, 3 story, 2 suites. No rm phones. S, D $90-$115; suites $130. Complimentary continental bkfst. Ck-out 11 am, ck-in 2-8 pm. Built 1787; antiques. In historic district. Totally nonsmoking. Cr cds: A, D, MC, V.

⚫ ⚫

Restaurants

★ ★ LA PETIT AUBERGE. *311 William St.* 703/371-2727. Hrs: 11:30 am-2:30 pm, 5:30-10 pm; early-bird dinner Mon-Thurs 5:30-7 pm. Closed Sun; major hols. Res accepted. French, Amer menu. Bar. A la carte entrees: lunch $4.95-$11.75, dinner $8.95-$19.95. Specializes in fresh seafood, seasonal specialties. French café decor. Cr cds: A, C, D, MC, V.

★ ★ ★ OLDE MUDD TAVERN. *(PO Box 181, Thornburg 22565) 1/4 mi W of I-95 Thornburg exit 118.* 703/582-5250. Hrs: 4-9 pm; Sun noon-8 pm. Closed Mon, Tues; Jan 1, Dec 25; also 1st wk July. Res accepted. Serv bar. Semi-a la carte: dinner $12.95-$20. Child's meals. Specializes in fresh vegetables, seafood, steak. Own baking. Entertainment Sat. Parking. Early Amer decor. Civil War pictures. Cr cds: MC, V.

D SC

★ ★ ★ RISTORANTE RENATO. *422 William St.* 703/371-8228. Hrs: 11:30 am-2 pm, 4:30-10 pm; Sat, Sun from 4:30 pm. Closed most major hols. Northern Italian menu. Bar. Semi-a la carte: lunch $5.95-$9.95, dinner $9.95-$21.95. Specializes in seafood, poultry, pasta. Parking. Antique chandeliers; fireplace. Cr cds: A, MC, V.

D

Fredericksburg and Spotsylvania National Military Park (D-8)

(Visitor Center on Old US 1 in Fredericksburg)

Midway between Washington and Richmond, on a good railroad, and protected by the Rappahannock and Rapidan rivers, the Fredericksburg area represented one of the main barriers to Union invasion during the Civil War. Four major engagements—the heaviest, most concentrated fighting ever seen on this continent—were fought in and around this town between December, 1862 and May, 1864.

Union General A.E. Burnside, after a hard-won crossing of the Rappahannock, engaged in the Battle of Fredericksburg (Dec 13, 1862). Damage to the city was severe as Burnside attempted a frontal assault on Lee's Confederate forces entrenched behind a stone wall. The attempt proved suicidal. Burnside retreated across the Rappahannock River and went into winter quarters.

The Battle of Chancellorsville (Apr 27-May 6, 1863) was another victory for Lee, this time against Union General Joseph Hooker. Outmaneuvered, Hooker also retired across the Rappahannock, and Lee prepared his second invasion of the North. It was during this battle, on May 2, that Stonewall Jackson was mistakenly wounded by his own men; he died 8 days later.

The Battle of the Wilderness (May 5-6, 1864) was the first encounter between Lee and Union General Ulysses S. Grant. When bloody fighting finally reached a stalemate, Grant elected to go around Lee, toward Richmond.

Savage fighting in the ensuing Battle of Spotsylvania Court House (May 8-21, 1864) produced no clear-cut victory; again Grant sidestepped and moved on toward Richmond. The relentless attrition of these two battles and the engagements that followed finally destroyed the offensive capabilities of Lee's Army of Northern Virginia.

Some 5,900 park acres include parts of all four battlefields, as well as Fredericksburg National Cemetery, the house at Guinea Station (where Jackson died), Old Salem Church and Chatham Manor. Miles of original trenches and gun pits remain; park roads provide ready access to many of them. (Daily) **Free.**

For further information contact the Superintendent, 120 Chatham Lane, Fredericksburg 22405; 703/373-4461.

What to See and Do

1. Fredericksburg Visitor Center. Lafayette Blvd (US 1) and Sunken Rd. Information and directions for various parts of park. Tours should start here. (Daily; closed Jan 1, Dec 25) Phone 703/373-6122. Center includes

Museum. Slide program, diorama, exhibits. (Same days as Visitor Center)   **Free.**   Across Sunken Rd is

Fredericksburg National Cemetery. More than 15,000 Federal interments; almost 13,000 unknown.

2. **Chancellorsville Visitor Center.** Slide program, museum with exhibits; dioramas. (Daily; closed Jan 1, Dec 25) Phone 703/786-2880.   **Free.**

3. **Chatham Manor.** Georgian brick manor house, owned by a wealthy planter, was converted to Union headquarters during two of the battles of Fredericksburg. The house was eventually used as a hospital where Clara Barton and Walt Whitman nursed the wounded. (Daily; closed Jan 1, Dec 25) Phone 703/373-4461.   **Free.**

4. **Stonewall Jackson Shrine.** 12 mi S on I-95 to Thornburg exit, then 5 mi E on VA 606 to Guinea. Plantation office where on May 10, 1863, Confederate General Jackson, ill with pneumonia and with his shattered left arm amputated, murmured, "Let us cross over the river, and rest under the shade of the trees," and died. (Mid-June-Labor Day, daily; Apr-mid-June, after Labor Day-Oct, Fri-Tues; rest of yr, Sat-Mon) Phone 804/633-6076.   **Free.**

5. **Old Salem Church** (1844). 1 mi W of I-95 on VA 3. Scene of battle on May 3-4, 1863. Building used as a field hospital and refugee center. Grounds (daily). Interior (Memorial Day-Labor Day, wkends). Phone 703/373-4461.   **Free.**

(For accommodations see Fredericksburg)

Front Royal (C-7)

Founded: 1788 **Pop:** 11,880 **Elev:** 567 ft **Area code:** 703 **Zip:** 22630

Originally named Hell Town, for all the wild and reckless spirits it attracted, Front Royal was a frontier stop on the packhorse road north. The present name is supposed to have originated in the command, "front the royal oak," given by an English officer to his untrained mountain militia recruits.

Belle Boyd, the Confederate spy, worked here extracting military secrets from Union officers. It is said that she invited General Nathaniel Banks and his officers, whose regiment was occupying the town, to a ball once. Later, she raced on horseback to tell General Jackson what she had learned. Next morning (May 23, 1862), the Confederates attacked and captured nearly all of the Union troops.

Front Royal was a quiet little village until the entrance to the Shenandoah National Park (see) and the beginning of the Skyline Drive opened in 1935, just one mile to the south. With millions of motorists passing through every year, the town has grown rapidly. The production of automotive finishes, limestone and cement contributes to the town's economy, but the tourism industry remains one of its largest.

What to See and Do

1. **Warren Rifles Confederate Museum.** 95 Chester St. Historic relics and memorabilia of War between the States. (Mid-Apr-Oct, daily; rest of yr by appt) Phone 636-6982.   ¢

2. **Belle Boyd Cottage.** 101 Chester St, behind Ivy Lodge. Relocated to its present site, the two-story cottage has been restored to reflect life in Front Royal between 1840 and 1860. For a two-year period during the Civil War, Belle Boyd stayed in this cottage while visiting relatives and used the opportunity to spy on Union troops occupying the town. This modest dwelling was also used to house wounded soldiers of both armies. (May-Oct, daily, limited hrs Sun; rest of yr, Mon-Fri; closed hols) Phone 636-1446.   ¢

3. **Skyline Caverns.** 1 mi S on US 340. Extensive, rare, intricate flowerlike formations of calcite ("anthodites"); sound and light presentation; 37-foot waterfall; clear stream stocked with trout

(observation only). Electrically lighted; 54°F yr-round. Miniature train provides trip through surrounding wooded area (Mar-mid-Nov, daily, weather permitting). Snack bar; gift shop. Cavern tours start every few minutes. (Daily) Sr citizen rate. Phone 635-4545 or 800/296-4545.   ¢¢¢

4. **Sky Meadows State Park.** 20 mi E on US 66, 7 mi N on VA 17. A 1,800-acre park. Fishing pond. Hiking, bridle trails. Picnicking. Primitive, walk-in camping. Visitor center; programs. (Daily) Standard fees. Phone 592-3556.

(For further information contact the Chamber of Commerce of Front Royal-Warren County, 414 E Main St, PO Box 568; 635-3185.)

Annual Events

Warren County Garden Tour. Garden Club sponsors tours of historic houses and gardens. Contact Chamber of Commerce. Last wk Apr.

Virginia Mushroom Festival. Virginia shiitake mushrooms, wine & cheese, herbs. Cooking demonstrations; entertainment, parade. 3rd Sat May.

Warren County Fair. Entertainment, livestock exhibits and sale, contests. Aug.

Festival of Leaves. Arts and crafts, demonstrations; historic home and church tour. 2nd wkend Oct.

(See Winchester, Woodstock)

Motels

★ ★ **QUALITY INN.** 10 Commerce Ave, US 522 Bypass at end of Main St. 703/635-3161. 107 rms, 3 story. Apr-Oct: S $45-$60; D $45-$70; each addl $9; under 18 free; some lower rates rest of yr. Crib free. TV; cable. Pool. Complimentary continental bkfst. Restaurant 5 am-10 pm. Bar; entertainment. Ck-out 11 am. Meeting rms. Gift shop. Cr cds: A, C, D, DS, ER, MC, V.

✔ ★ **TWIN RIVERS.** 1801 Shenandoah Ave. I-66 exit 6, 1¹/₂ mi S on US 522. 703/635-4101. 20 rms. Mid-Apr-Oct: S, D $38-$45; each addl $5; some lower rates rest of yr. Crib free. TV; cable. Pool. Playground. Complimentary coffee in lobby. Restaurant nearby. Ck-out 11 am. Picnic table. Cr cds: A, MC, V.

Inn

★ ★ **CHESTER HOUSE.** 43 Chester St. 703/635-3937; res: 800/621-0441. 6 rms (2 share bath, 1 shower only), 2 story, 1 suite. S, D $65-$105; suite $110; higher rates special events (2-day min). Children over 12 yrs only. TV lounge. Complimentary full bkfst. Complimentary evening refreshments in library. Restaurant nearby. Ck-out 11 am, ck-in 3 pm. Luggage handling. Health club privileges. Lawn games. Guest refrigerator. Picnic tables. Formal gardens with fountain and statuary. Georgian-style mansion built 1905. Cr cds: A, MC, V.

Galax (F-4)

Settled: 1904 **Pop:** 6,670 **Elev:** 2,382 ft **Area code:** 703 **Zip:** 24333

Galax is named for the pretty evergreen with heart-shaped leaves that florists use in various arrangements. It grows in the mountainous regions around Galax and is gathered for sale all over the US. Nearby are three mountain passes: Fancy Gap, Low Gap and Piper's Gap. Some of the town's major industries include the production of furniture, glass & mirrors, textiles and clothing.

What to See and Do

1. **Jeff Matthews Memorial Museum.** 606 W Stuart Dr, adj to Vaughan Memorial Library. Two authentically restored log cabins (1834 & 1860s). Relocated to present site and furnished with items used in the period in which the cabins were inhabited. Also houses collection of photos of Civil War veterans, artifacts and memorabilia of the area; covered wagon; farm implements. Restored log cabin used as a blacksmith's shop. (Wed-Sun, phone for hrs; closed hols) Phone 236-7874.   **Free.**
2. **Recreation.** Swimming, boating, fishing on New River. Hunting and hiking. Canoeing & kayaking 8 mi W on VA 94 with the River Wind Outfitters, Rte 5, Box 378; phone 236-7580.
3. **Blue Ridge Parkway** (see). 7 mi S.

(For further information contact the Galax-Carroll-Grayson Chamber of Commerce, 405 N Main St; 236-2184.)

Annual Event

Old Fiddler's Convention. Felts Park. Folk songs, bands & dancing. 2nd wk Aug.

(For accommodations see Wytheville)

George Washington Birthplace National Monument (D-9)

(38 mi E of Fredericksburg on VA 3, then 2 mi E on VA 204)

George Washington, first child of Augustine and Mary Ball Washington, was born Feb 11, 1732 (celebrated Feb 22 according to the new-style calendar) at his father's estate on Popes Creek on the south shore of the Potomac. The family moved in 1735 to Little Hunting Creek Plantation, later called Mt Vernon, then in 1738 to Ferry Farm near Fredericksburg.

The 538-acre monument includes much of the old plantation land. (Daily; closed Jan 1, Dec 25)

What to See and Do

1. **Visitor Center.** Orientation film; museum exhibits. Phone 804/224-1732.   ¢
2. **Memorial House.** Original house burned (1779) and was never rebuilt. The Memorial House is not a replica of the original; it represents a composite of typical 18th-century Virginia plantation house. Bricks were handmade from nearby clay. Furnishings are typical of the times. Near house is

   Colonial farm. "Living" farm, designed to show 18th-century Virginia plantation life; livestock, colonial garden, several farm buildings, furnished colonial kitchen, household slave quarters and spinning and weaving room.
3. **Family burial ground.** 1 mi NW on Bridges Creek. Site of 1664 home of Colonel John Washington, first Washington in Virginia and great-grandfather of the first president. Washington's ancestors are buried here.
4. **Picnic area.** 1/4 mi N of house.

(For accommodations see Fredericksburg, Montross)

Gloucester (E-9)

Founded: 1769 **Pop:** 900 (est) **Elev:** 70 ft **Area code:** 804 **Zip:** 23061

In the spring, acres of daffodil blooms make this area a treat for the traveler. This elm-shaded village is the commercial center of Gloucester (GLOSS-ter) County. There are many old landmarks and estates nearby.

What to See and Do

1. **County Courthouse** (18th century). On US 17 Business. Part of Gloucester Court House Square Historic District. Portraits of native sons are in the courtroom; plaques memorializing Nathaniel Bacon, leader in the rebellion of 1676, first organized resistance to British authority, and Major Walter Reed, surgeon, conqueror of yellow fever. (Mon-Fri; closed hols)   **Free.**   Adj is Debtors Prison and opp is the pre-Revolutionary Botetourt Building. Also here is

   Historic Rosewell Ruins. The early home of the Page family. Celebrated for its architecture and brick work. (Apr-Oct, Sun; other times by appt) Contact PO Box 1456 for information and hrs. Donation. Phone 693-3992 or 642-5736.
2. **Walter Reed Birthplace.** 5 mi W at jct VA 614, 616. The physician who discovered the cause of yellow fever was born here in September, 1851. Open on request. Donation. Phone 693-7452.
3. **Virginia Institute of Marine Science, College of William and Mary.** Gloucester Point. Small marine aquarium & museum display sea turtles, local fishes and invertebrates; marine science exhibits, bookstore. (Mon-Fri; closed major hols) Phone 642-7000.   **Free.**

(For accommodations see Newport News, Yorktown, also see Williamsburg)

Restaurant

★ ★ **SEAWELL'S ORDINARY.** US 17 N of Coleman Bridge. 804/642-3635. Hrs: 11 am-3 pm, 5-9:30 pm; Sun brunch to 3 pm. Closed Dec 25. Res accepted. Bar. Semi-a la carte: lunch $3.75-$10.75, dinner $10.95-$18.95. Sun brunch $5.95-$7.95. Specializes in traditional Virginian cuisine. Parking. Outdoor dining. Built 1712; became country tavern 1757; was frequented by Washington, Jefferson, Lafayette. Cr cds: A, MC, V.

Great Dismal Swamp National Wildlife Refuge (F-9)

Harriet Beecher Stowe found Virginia's Dismal Swamp a perfect setting for her antislavery novel *Dred* (1856); modern hunters, fishermen and naturalists find the area fits their ambition just as well. From its northern edge just southwest of Norfolk, the swamp stretches almost due south like a great ribbon, 25 miles long and 11 miles wide. Centuries of decaying organic matter have created layers of peat so deep that fires sometimes smolder under the surface for weeks.

Creation of the refuge began in 1973, when the Union Camp Corporation donated 49,100 acres of land to the Nature Conservancy, which in turn conveyed it to the Department of Interior. The refuge was officially established through the Dismal Swamp Act of 1974 and is managed for the primary purpose of protecting and preserving a unique ecosystem. The refuge now consists of nearly 107,000 acres of forested wetlands that have been greatly altered by drainage and logging operations.

Near the center is Lake Drummond, 18 square miles of juniper water, which is water that combines the juices of gum, cypress and maple with a strong infusion of juniper or white cedar. The chemical mix added by the tree resins results in a water that remains sweet, or fresh, indefinitely. In the days of long sailing voyages, when ordinary water became foul after a few weeks, this "dark water" was highly valued.

The Great Dismal swamp has also been commercially exploited for its timber, particularly cypress and cedar. A company organized by George Washington and several other businessmen bought a large piece of the swamp and used slave labor to dig the Dismal Swamp Canal, which both facilitated drainage of timber land and provided a transportation route in and out of the swamp.

Animal and bird life continues to abound in this eerie setting. There are white-tailed deer and rarely-observed black bear, foxes, bobcats—and a large number of snakes, including copperheads, cottonmouths and rattlesnakes.

For further information contact Refuge Manager, PO Box 349, Suffolk 23439; 804/986-3705.

(For accommodations see Chesapeake, Portsmouth)

Hampton (F-9)

Settled: 1610 **Pop:** 133,793 **Elev:** 12 ft **Area code:** 804

Hampton is one of the the oldest continuously English-speaking communities in the US—Jamestown, settled in 1607, is a national historical park, but not a town. The settlement began at a place then called Kecoughtan, with the building of Fort Algernourne as protection against the Spanish. In the late 1600s and early 1700s the area was harassed by pirates. Finally, in 1718, the notorious brigand Blackbeard was killed by Lt. Robert Maynard, and organized piracy came to an end here.

Hampton was shelled in the Revolutionary War, sacked by the British in the War of 1812 and burned in 1861 by retreating Confederates to prevent its occupation by Union forces. Only the gutted walls of St John's Church survived the fire. The town was rebuilt after the Civil War by its citizens and soldiers. Commercial fishing and aerospace research are now big business here.

Langley Air Force Base, headquarters for the Air Combat Command, Fort Monroe, headquarters for the US Army's Training and Doctrine Command, and the NASA Langley Research Center are located here.

What to See and Do

1. **Settlers Landing Monument.** 1/2 mi S, on grounds of the Veterans Affairs Medical Center between Hampton River and Mill Creek, off I-64 exit 268. Marks approximate site of first settlers' landing near Strawberry Banks in 1607. Painting by Sidney King depicts visit to Kecoughtan by colonists en route to Jamestown. (Daily) **Free.**

2. **St John's Church** (1728) and Parish Museum. W Queen's Way and High Court Lane. Fourth site of worship of Episcopal parish established in 1610. Bible dating from 1599; Communion silver from 1618; Colonial Vestry Book; taped historical message. (Daily) Phone 722-2567. **Free.**

3. **Virginia Air and Space Center & Hampton Roads History Center.** Downtown, off I-64 exit 267. Exhibits show the historical link between Hampton Roads' seafaring past and spacefaring future. Exhibits include 12 full-sized aircraft, the Apollo 12 Command Module, a moon rock and rare NASA artifacts. Films shown in 300-seat IMAX theater (daily). Gift shop. (Daily; closed Dec 25) Phone 727-0900 or 800/296-0800. **¢¢¢**

4. **Hampton University** (1868). (5,700 students) E end of Queen St, 1/4 mi off I-64 exit 267. Founded by Union Brigadier General Samuel Chapman Armstrong, chief of the Freedman's Bureau, to prepare the youth of the South, regardless of color, for the work of organizing and instructing schools in the Southern states; many blacks and Indians came to be educated. Now Virginia's only coeducational, nondenominational, four-year private college. The Hampton choir is famous. It "sang up" a building, Virginia-Cleveland Hall, in 1870 on a trip through New England and Canada, raising close to $100,000 at concerts. Phone 727-5253. On campus are

Emancipation Oak. The Emancipation Proclamation was read here.

Museum. Academy Bldg. Collection of ethnic art; Indian & African artifacts; contemporary Afro-American works; paintings by renowned artists. (Daily; closed mid-Dec-early Jan) **Free.**

5. **Hampton Carousel** (1920). 610 Settlers Landing Rd, downtown, on waterfront. Completely restored in 1991, antique carousel is housed in its own pavilion and features 48 intricately decorated horses. (Apr-Oct, Mon-Sat, also Sun afternoons, weather permitting) Phone 727-6381 or -6347 (Parks & Rec Dept). **¢**

6. **Fort Monroe.** 3 mi SE via Mercury Blvd, Ingalls Rd. First fort here was a stockade called Fort Algernourne (1609); second, Fort George, though built of brick, was destroyed by hurricane in 1749; present fort was completed about 1834. **Free.**

Casemate Museum provides insight on heritage of the fort, Old Point Comfort and of the Army Coast Artillery Corps. Museum offers access to a series of casemates and a walking tour of the fort. Jefferson Davis casemate contains cell in which the Confederacy's president was confined on false charges of plotting against the life of Abraham Lincoln. Museum features Civil War exhibits, military uniforms and assorted artwork, including three original Remington drawings, along with audiovisual programs. Scale models of coast artillery guns and dioramas represent the role of the coast artillery from 1901-1946. (Daily; closed Jan 1, Thanksgiving, Dec 25) Phone 727-3391. **Free.**

Chapel of the Centurion (1858). This is one of the oldest churches on the Virginia peninsula. Woodrow Wilson worshiped here occasionally.

7. **Air Power Park.** 413 W Mercury Blvd, US 258. On Display are 7 jet aircraft, 13 rockets & missiles; local aviation history and model aircraft exhibits. (Wed-Sun; closed Jan 1, Thanksgiving, Dec 25) Picnicking; playground. Phone 727-1163. **Free.**

8. **Buckroe Beach.** 4 mi E on VA 351, foot of E Pembroke Ave on Chesapeake Bay. Swimming; fishing pier; public park, concerts. Fishing in bays, rivers and lakes throughout Hampton Roads area. Lifeguards (Memorial Day-Labor Day). Phone 727-6347. **Free.**

9. **Bluebird Gap Farm.** 60 Pine Chapel Rd. This 15-acre farm includes barnyard zoo; indigenous wildlife such as deer and wolves; antique and modern farm equipment and farmhouse artifacts. Picnicking; playground. (Wed-Sun; closed major hols) Phone 727-6347. **Free.**

(For further information contact the Hampton Visitor Center, 710 Settlers Landing Rd, 23669, phone 727-1102 or 800/800-2202.)

Annual Events

Hampton Jazz Festival. Hampton Coliseum. Phone 838-4203 (box office). 3 days late June.

Hampton Cup Regatta. Inboard hydro-plane races. Mid-July.

Hampton Bay Days. Arts and crafts, rides, science exhibits; entertainment. Phone 727-3200. Early Sept.

(See Newport News, Norfolk, Portsmouth, Virginia Beach)

Motels

✔ ★ **ARROW INN.** 7 Semple Farm Rd (23666), I-64 to exit 261B or 262B, N on VA 134 to Semple Farm Rd, then right. 804/865-0300; res: 800/833-2520; FAX 804/766-9367. 60 rms, 3 story, 21 kit.

units. No elvtr. Memorial Day-Labor Day: S $39.90-$45.90; D $44.90-$54.90; each addl $5; kit. units $47.90-$60.90; under 18 free; wkly rates; higher rates jazz festival; lower rates rest of yr. Crib free. Pet accepted; $5 per day. TV; cable. Complimentary coffee in lobby. Restaurant adj 6-1 am. Ck-out noon. Coin Indry. Refrigerators. Cr cds: A, C, D, DS, MC, V.

D ❧ ⌖ 🔥 SC

★ ★ ★ **COURTYARD BY MARRIOTT.** *1917 Coliseum Dr (23666). 804/838-3300; FAX 804/838-6387.* 146 rms, 3 story. June-Sept: S, D $72.95; each addl (after 4 persons) $10; suites $89.95; under 18 free; higher rates jazz festival; lower rates rest of yr. Crib avail. TV; cable. Heated pool. Complimentary coffee in rms. Restaurant 6:30-11 am, 6-10 pm; Sat, Sun from 7 am. Bar 6-10 pm. Ck-out noon. Coin Indry. Meeting rms. Valet serv. Sundries. Exercise equipt; weight machine, bicycles, whirlpool. Refrigerator avail in suites. Cr cds: A, C, D, DS, MC, V.

D ≋ ⌖ ⌖ 🔥 SC

✔ ★ **HAMPTON INN.** *1813 W Mercury Blvd (23666). 804/838-8484; FAX 804/838-8484, ext. 7777.* 132 rms, 6 story. S $38-$50; D $42-$55. Crib free. Pet accepted, some restrictions. TV; cable. Pool privileges. Complimentary continental bkfst, coffee. Restaurant adj 6 am-10 pm. Ck-out noon. Cr cds: A, C, D, DS, MC, V.

D ❧ ⌖ 🔥 SC

★ ★ ★ **HOLIDAY INN HAMPTON-COLISEUM HOTEL & CONFERENCE CENTER.** *1815 W Mercury Blvd (23666). 804/838-0200; FAX 804/838-0200, ext. 7700.* 322 rms, 2-4 story. S, D $72-$79; each addl $7; suites $125-$180; some wkend rates; higher rates jazz festival. Crib free. TV; cable. 2 pools, 1 indoor. Coffee in rms. Restaurant 6 am-10 pm. Rm serv to 11 pm. Bar 11 am-midnight. Ck-out noon. Coin Indry. Convention facilities. Bellhops. Valet serv. Gift shop. Free airport transportation. Exercise equipt; weight machine, bicycles, whirlpool, sauna. Game rm. Some refrigerators. Balconies. Cr cds: A, C, D, DS, ER, JCB, MC, V.

D ≋ ⌖ ⌖ 🔥 SC

Hotel

★ ★ **RADISSON-HAMPTON.** *700 Settlers Landing Rd (23669). 804/727-9700; FAX 804/722-4557.* 172 rms, 9 story. S, D $84-$102; each addl $10; suites $175-$410; studio rms $69-$79; under 18 free; wkend rates; higher rates special events. Crib free. TV; cable. Pool; poolside serv. Restaurant 6:30 am-10 pm. Bar 11-2 am; DJ, dancing. Ck-out noon. Meeting rms. Gift shop. Free airport, RR station, bus depot transportation. Exercise equipt; weights, bicycles, whirlpool. Some refrigerators. On Hampton River. **LUXURY LEVEL : BUSINESS CLASS FLOOR.** 18 rms. S, D $99. Private lounge. Complimentary continental bkfst, newspaper. Cr cds: A, C, D, DS, ER, JCB, MC, V.

D ≋ ⌖ 🔥 SC

Restaurant

★ ★ **FIRE AND ICE.** *2040 Coliseum Dr, in Coliseum Square Shopping Center. 804/826-6698.* Hrs: 11 am-10 pm. Closed Sun; hols. Res accepted; required Fri & Sat. Bar. A la carte entrees: lunch $2.50-$6.95, dinner $8.95-$18.95. Specialties: onion-crusted salmon, fantasy flat breads, New Orleans-style po' boy sandwiches. Large modern art murals. Cr cds: MC, V.

Harrisonburg (D-6)

Founded: 1780 **Pop:** 30,707 **Elev:** 1,352 ft **Area code:** 703 **Zip:** 22801

Originally named Rocktown due to the limestone outcroppings prevalent in the area, Harrisonburg became the county seat of Rockingham County when Thomas Harrison won a race against Mr. Keezle of Keezletown, three miles east. They had raced on horseback to Richmond to file their respective towns for the new county seat. Harrisonburg is noted for good hunting and fishing, beautiful scenery and turkeys. The annual production of more than 5 million turkeys, most of them processed and frozen, has made Rockingham County widely known. This is a college town with three 4-year colleges. The headquarters for George Washington National Forest (see #8) are here.

What to See and Do

1. **Caverns.** There are several caverns within 24 miles of Harrisonburg. They include

   Shenandoah Caverns. 24 mi N on US 11. (See NEW MARKET)

   Grand Caverns Regional Park. 12 mi S on I-81, then 6 mi E on VA 256 in Grottoes. Known for its immense underground chambers and spectacular formations. Visited by Union and Confederate troops during the Civil War. Unique shield formations. Electrically lighted; 54°F. Park facilities include swimming pool; tennis courts, miniature golf; picnic pavilions; hiking and bicycle trails. Guided tours. (Apr-Oct, daily; Mar, wkends) Sr citizen rate. Phone 249-5705. ¢¢¢

2. **Shenandoah Valley Heritage Museum.** 115 Bowman Rd. Featured is the Stonewall Jackson Electric Map that depicts his Valley Campaign of 1862. The 12-foot vertical relief map fills an entire wall and lets visitors see and hear the campaign, battle by battle. Also displays of Shenandoah Valley history, artifacts. (May-Oct, Mon-Sat, also Sun afternoons; rest of yr, Fri-Sat, also Sun afternoons; closed hols) Donation. Phone 879-2616.

3. **Lincoln Homestead.** 9 mi N on VA 42. Brick house, the rear wing of which was built by Abraham Lincoln's grandfather, and where his father was born. Main portion of the house was built about 1800 by Captain Jacob Lincoln. (Private)

4. **James Madison University** (1908). (11,000 students) S Main St. Interesting old bluestone buildings. Campus tours through Admissions Office. Phone 568-3621. On campus is

   Miller Hall Planetarium and Sawhill Art Gallery. Phone 568-3621 for schedules. **Free.**

5. **Eastern Mennonite College & Seminary** (1917). (1,100 students) 2 mi NW on VA 42. Many Mennonites live in this area. On campus is an art gallery, planetarium (shows by appt, free), natural history museum and the Menno Simons Historical Library, containing many 16th-century Mennonite volumes (school yr, daily exc Sun). Campus tours. Phone 432-4000.

6. **Natural Chimneys Regional Park.** 15 mi SW off VA 42 in Mt Solon. Seven colorful and massive rock towers rise 120 feet above the plain. Picnic facilities, camping (fee; limited Nov-Feb); bicycle, nature trails; pool; playground. Park (daily). Phone 350-2510. Per car ¢¢

7. **Shenandoah National Park** (see). 24 mi E on US 33.

8. **George Washington National Forest.** 10 mi W on US 33. Consists of more than one million acres. Hunting for deer, bear, wild turkey, small game; fishing for trout, bluegill and bass; riding trails; camping, picnicking, swimming. Scenic drives past Crabtree Falls, hardwood forests and unusual geologic features. Overlooks of Shenandoah Valley. Part of Appalachian Trail crosses forest. Fees are charged at some recreation sites. Trails for the visually impaired. For information contact Forest Supervisor, Harrison Plaza, PO Box 233; 433-2491. **Free.**

9. **Fishing. Lake Shenandoah,** 3 mi E. **Silver Lake,** 5 mi SW on VA 42 in Dayton. Good bass fishing in the Shenandoah River.

(For further information contact the Harrisonburg-Rockingham Convention and Visitors Bureau, 800 Country Club Rd, PO Box 1; 434-3862.)

Annual Events

Virginia Poultry Festival. Parade, golf tournament, tennis, dancing, reception. Phone 433-2451. 4 days mid-May.

Natural Chimneys Jousting Tournament. In Natural Chimneys Regional Park (see #6). America's oldest continuous sporting event, held annually since 1821. "Knights" armed with lances charge down an 80-yard track and attempt to spear 3 small rings suspended from posts. Each knight is allowed 3 rides at the rings, thus, a perfect score is 9 rings. Ties are run off using successively smaller rings. 3rd Sat June & Aug.

Rockingham County Fair. Mid-Aug.

(See Luray, New Market, Staunton)

Motels

✔ ★ ★ **COMFORT INN.** *1440 E Market St, off I-81 exit 247A.* 703/433-6066; FAX 703/434-0253. 60 rms, 2 story. S $43-$55; D $55-$65; each addl $5; under 18 free. Crib free. TV; cable. Pool. Complimentary continental bkfst, coffee. Ck-out noon. Cr cds: A, C, D, DS, ER, JCB, MC, V.

⊡ 🏄 ≋ 🔌 🔥 SC

★ **DAYS INN.** *1131 Forest Mill Rd, I-81 exit 245.* 703/433-9353; FAX 703/433-5809. 89 rms, 4 story. June-Oct: S $55; D $68; each addl $5; under 17 free; ski, golf plans; higher rates for special events, wkends (2-day min); lower rates rest of yr. Crib free. Pet accepted; $5 per day. TV; cable. Indoor pool; whirlpool. Complimentary continental bkfst. Restaurant 7:30 am-9:30 pm. Ck-out 11 am. Meeting rms. Sundries. Valet serv. 27-hole golf privileges; greens fee $30, pro, putting green, driving range. Downhill ski 12 mi. Health club privileges. Refrigerators avail. Cr cds: A, C, D, DS, MC, V.

⊡ 🏄 🏊 ≋ 🔌 🔥 SC

✔ ★ **ECONO LODGE.** *1703 E. Market St. (Box 1311), 1/2 mi E of I-81 exit 247A.* 703/433-2576. 88 rms, 2 story. S $39.95; D $45-$55.95; each addl $5; suites $74.95; under 18 free. Crib free. TV; cable. Pool. Complimentary continental bkfst. Restaurant adj open 24 hrs. Ck-out 11 am. Exercise equipt; weights, bicycles. Some in-rm whirlpools. Cr cds: A, C, D, DS, JCB, MC, V.

⊡ ≋ 🏊 🔌 🔥 SC

★ ★ **HAMPTON INN.** *85 University Blvd.* 703/432-1111; FAX 703/432-0748. 126 rms, 4 story. May-Oct: S $47-$54; D $52-$59; under 19 free; higher rates university events; lower rates rest of yr. Crib free. TV; cable. Pool. Complimentary continental bkfst, coffee. Restaurant nearby. Ck-out noon. Meeting rms. Valet serv. Sundries. Cr cds: A, C, D, DS, MC, V.

⊡ ≋ 🔌 🔥 SC

✔ ★ ★ **HoJo INN.** *Box 68, 1/4 mi E of I-81 exit 245 at Port Republic Rd.* 703/434-6771. 134 rms, 2 story. S $34.95-$44.95; D $39.95-$49.95; each addl $5; higher rates some univ events; lower rates Dec-Feb. Crib free. Pet accepted. TV; cable. Pool; wading pool. Restaurant 6 am-10:30 pm. Ck-out noon. Refrigerators. Private patios, balconies. Cr cds: A, C, D, DS, ER, JCB, MC, V.

⊡ 🏄 ≋ 🔌 🔥 SC

★ **SHONEY'S INN.** *45 Burgess Rd, I-81 exit 247A.* 703/433-6089; FAX 703/433-6485. 98 rms, 3 story. May-Oct: S $42; D $48-$50; each addl $4; under 18 free; ski plan; higher rates university events; lower rates rest of yr. Crib $4. TV; cable. Indoor pool. Complimentary coffee in lobby. Restaurant adj 6 am-11 pm. Ck-out noon. Meeting rms. Sundries. Valet serv. Downhill ski 12 mi. Exercise equipt;

weight machine, rowers, whirlpool, sauna. Some in-rm whirlpools. Cr cds: A, C, D, DS, ER, MC, V.

⊡ ≋ 🏃 🔌 🔥 SC

✔ ★ ★ **VILLAGE INN.** *Rte 1, Box 76, on VA 11, N of of I-81 exit 240.* 703/434-7355; res: 800/736-7355. 36 rms. S $36; D $42-$52; each addl $5; kit. units $57. Crib $2. Pet accepted. TV; cable; in-rm movies avail. Pool. Playground. Restaurant 7-10 am, 5:30-9 pm; closed Sun. Ck-out noon. Meeting rm. Sundries. Free airport transportation. Lawn games. Picnic tables. Valley setting. Cr cds: A, C, D, DS, MC, V.

⊡ 🏄 ≋ 🔌 🔥

Motor Hotel

★ ★ **SHERATON HARRISONBURG INN.** *1400 E Market St, off I-81 exit 247A.* 703/433-2521; FAX 703/434-0253. 138 rms, 1-5 story. S $59-$69; D $69-$84; each addl $10; suites $95-$275; under 18 free. Crib free. Pet accepted. TV; cable. 2 pools, 1 indoor; wading pool, whirlpool, sauna, poolside serv. Restaurant 6:30 am-2 pm, 5-10:30 pm. Rm serv. Bar 11:30-2 am; entertainment, dancing. Ck-out noon. Meeting rms. Bellhops. Valet serv. Bathrm phones. Cr cds: A, C, D, DS, ER, JCB, MC, V.

⊡ 🏄 ≋ 🔌 🔥 SC

Hopewell (E-8)

Founded: 1613 **Pop:** 23,101 **Elev:** 50 ft **Area code:** 804 **Zip:** 23860

The second permanent English settlement in America has been an important inland port since early times, having a fine channel 28 feet deep and 300 feet wide. It was the birthplace of statesman John Randolph of Roanoke. Edmund Ruffin, an early agricultural chemist who fired the first shot at Fort Sumter, was born near here.

"Cittie Point," at the junction of the James and Appomattox rivers, finally became one of Virginia's big cities during World War I when an E.I. du Pont de Nemours Company dynamite plant on Hopewell Farm supplied guncotton to the Allies.

Hopewell's industrial production includes chemicals, paper products and synthetic textiles.

What to See and Do

1. **Merchants Hope Church** (1657). 6 mi E on VA 10, then 1/2 mi S on VA 641. Given the name of a plantation that was named for a barque plying between Virginia and England. Exterior has been called the most beautiful colonial brickwork in America. Oldest operating Protestant church in the country. (Open by request) Donation. Phone 458-6197.

2. **Flowerdew Hundred.** 10 mi SE on VA 10. Outdoor museum on the site of an early English settlement on the south bank of the James River. Originally inhabited by Native Americans, settled by Governor George Yeardley in 1618. Archaeological excavations are in progress. Thousands of artifacts, dating from the prehistoric period through the present, have been found and are on exhibit in the museum. A replicated 19th-century detached kitchen and working 18th-century-style windmill are open to visitors. Exhibits, interpretive tours. Picnicking. (Apr-Nov; daily exc Mon; rest of yr by appt) Sr citizen rate. Phone 541-8897 or -8938. ¢¢

3. **City Point Unit of Petersburg National Battlefield** (see). Intersection of Cedar Lane and Pecan Ave. Grant's headquarters during the siege of Petersburg and largest Civil War supply depot. Includes Appomattox Manor, home to one family for 340 years; Grant's headquarters were on front lawn. Many other buildings. (Daily; closed Jan 1, Dec 25) Phone 458-9504. **Free.**

(For further information contact the Hopewell Area-Prince George Chamber of Commerce, 110 N 2nd Ave, PO Drawer 1297; 458-5536.)

Annual Events

Prince George County Heritage Fair. Flowerdew Hundred (see #2). Arts & crafts; educational exhibits & demonstrations; music, food, children's rides, hayrides. Last wkend Apr.

Hooray for Hopewell Festival. Downtown. Arts & crafts, food, entertainment, childrens's rides. 3rd wkend Sept.

(See Petersburg, Richmond, Surry, Williamsburg)

Motels

★ **DAYS INN.** *4911 Oaklawn Blvd, at jct I-295 & VA 36. 804/458-1500; res: 800/458-3297; FAX 804/458-9151.* 115 rms, 50 kit. suites, 2 story. S $46; D $60; each addl $5; kit. suites $45-$52; under 12 free; wkly rates. Crib $4. TV; cable. Pool. Complimentary continental bkfst, coffee. Restaurant nearby. Ck-out 11 am. Coin lndry. Exercise equipt; weight machine, bicycle, whirlpool, sauna. Game rm. Refrigerators. Cr cds: A, D, DS, MC, V.

✔ ★ **INNKEEPER.** *3952 Courthouse Rd. 804/458-2600; FAX 804/458-1915.* 104 rms, 3 story. S $39.95-$59.98; D $46.95-$59.98; each addl $5. Crib free. TV; cable. Pool. Complimentary continental bkfst, coffee. Restaurant adj 6:30 am-10 pm. Ck-out 11 am. Coin lndry. Meeting rms. Some refrigerators. Cr cds: A, C, D, DS, MC, V.

Hot Springs (D-5)

Pop: 300 (est) **Elev:** 2,238 ft **Area code:** 703 **Zip:** 24445

A Ranger District office of the George Washington National Forest is located here.

What to See and Do

Homestead Ski Area. On US 220. Double chairlift, T-bar, J-bar, baby rope tow; patrol, school, rentals; snowmaking; cafe, cafeteria, bar; nursery. (Nov-Mar, daily) Ice curling, ice-skating rink (Thanksgiving-Mar). Lower fees for Homestead guests. Phone 839-7721 (ski information), 800/336-5771 (resort). ¢¢¢¢-¢¢¢¢¢

(See Clifton Forge, Covington, Warm Springs)

Motel

✔ ★ **ROSELOE.** *Rte 2, Box 590, 3 mi N on US 220. 703/839-5373.* 14 rms, 6 kits. S $34; D $44; each addl $4; kits. $4-$7 addl; family rates. Crib free. Pet accepted; $5. TV; cable. Coffee in rms. Restaurant nearby. Ck-out noon. Downhill ski 3 mi. Refrigerators. Cr cds: A, D, MC, V.

Inns

★ **CARRIAGE COURT.** *Rte 2, Box 620, on US 220. 703/839-2345.* 4 rms, 2 story. S, D $52-$68; each addl $7; kit. unit $68; under 10 free. Crib free. Pet accepted, some restrictions. TV. Dining rm 11 am-9 pm. Ck-out 11 am, ck-in 2 pm. Golf privileges. Downhill ski 1 mi. Converted carriage house. Scenic mountain views. Cr cds: MC, V.

✔ ★ **VINE COTTAGE INN.** *PO Box 918, on US 220, at entrance to Homestead. 703/839-2422; res: 800/666-8463.* 12 rms, 3 story. S $40-$65; D $65-$90; each addl $15; dormitory rms $25/per-

son; ski, golf plans. Closed Dec 24, 25. Crib $10. TV; cable in sitting rm. Complimentary continental bkfst. Restaurant nearby. Ck-out noon, ck-in after noon. Downhill/x-country ski 1 mi. Built 1900. Cr cds: MC, V.

Resort

★ ★ ★ **THE HOMESTEAD.** *On US 220. 703/839-5500; res: 800/336-5771; FAX 703/839-7556.* 600 units, 4-12 story. Apr-Oct: S $170-$295; D $195-$320; parlor $100-$120 addl; children over 12 yrs $25; under 13 free; MAP avail; ski, golf, tennis packages; some seasonal rates; some lower rates rest of yr. Service charges: $7.50 daily housekeeping, and 16% at all dining outlets. Crib free. TV; cable. 3 pools, 1 indoor; wading pool, lifeguard. Supervised playground, playroom. Supervised child's activities. Dining rm 7-10 am, noon-2:30 pm, 7-9:30 pm. Indoor/outdoor luncheon buffets Apr-Nov. Afternoon tea. Box lunches, snack bar. Rm serv 7 am-midnight. Bar 11 am-midnight. Ck-out noon, ck-in 3 pm. Convention facilities, Valet serv. Gift shops. Airport, RR station, bus depot transportation. Sports pros. Tennis. Three 18-hole golf courses, greens fee $70-$85, cart $15/person, putting greens, driving range. Downhill/x-country ski on site. Skating. Hiking & horseback trails. Skeet & trap shooting. Archery. Lawn games. Rec rm. Movies. Bowling. Exercise rm; instructor, weights, bicycles, whirlpool, sauna, steam rm. Spa, mineral pool, medical dir. Extra fees for sports facilities. Picnic tables. 5,600-ft airstrip. Established in 1891 on 15,000-acre estate. Cr cds: A, MC, V.

Restaurant

★ **SAM SNEAD'S TAVERN.** *Main St. 703/839-7666.* Hrs: 11:30 am-4 pm, 5-10 pm. Res required. Semi-a la carte: lunch $4.25-$8.95, dinner $7.95-$15.95. Specializes in fresh mountain trout, steak. Entertainment wkends. Parking. Outdoor dining. Rustic decor. Cr cds: A, MC, V.

Irvington (E-9)

Pop: 496 **Elev:** 31 ft **Area code:** 804 **Zip:** 22480

What to See and Do

Historic Christ Church (1735). 4½ mi W, off VA 3. Built by Robert Carter, forefather of 8 governors of Virginia, 2 presidents, 3 signers of the Declaration of Independence, a chief justice and many others who served the country with distinction. Restored; original structure and furnishings, 3-decker pulpit. Built on site of earlier wooden church (1669); family tombs. (Daily; closed Dec 25) Phone 438-6855. **Free.** On the grounds is

Carter Reception Center. Narrated slide show; museum with artifacts from Corotoman, home of Robert Carter, and from the church construction; photographs of the restoration. Guides. (Apr-Thanksgiving wkend, daily) **Free.**

(See Lancaster)

Motel

★ **WHISPERING PINES.** *(Box 156, White Stone 22578)* ¼ mi N on VA 3. 804/435-1101. 29 rms. S, D $54-$59; each addl $5. Crib $5. TV. Pool; wading pool. Restaurant nearby. Ck-out 11 am. Sundries. Picnic tables. Wooded grounds. Cr cds: A, DS, MC, V.

Resort

★ ★ ★ **TIDES LODGE.** *Box 309, N on VA 200, then W on VA 646 to Christ Church, then SW on County 709, follow signs.* 804/438-6000; res: 800/248-4337; FAX 804/438-5950. 60 units. EP, mid-Mar-Dec: S $79-$139; D $99-$189; each addl $20; suites $149-$269; cottages to 4 persons $210-$260; under 18 free; AP, MAP avail; golf packages; higher rates some wkends. Closed rest of yr. Crib free. Pet accepted, some restrictions; $8. TV; cable. 2 pools, 1 saltwater, 1 heated; poolside serv. Playground. Free supervised child's activities (June-Labor Day). Coffee in rms. Dining rm 8-10 am, noon-2 pm, 6-10 pm. Rm serv 7 am-10 pm. Bar noon-11 pm; dancing Tues, Thurs, Sat. Ck-out 1 pm, ck-in after 3:30 pm. Coin lndry. Meeting rms. Bellhops. Valet serv. Gift shop. Airport transportation (res required). Lighted tennis. 45-hole golf, greens fee $38, pro, putting greens, driving range. Marina, cruises, boat rental. Bicycles. Lawn games. Game rm. Rec rm. Exercise equipt; weights, bicycles, sauna. Refrigerators. Balconies. Cr cds: A, DS, MC, V.

D ⟋ ⬩ ➤ 🧍 🏃 ⌇ 🏊 🕴 🏃 🐾 🖌

Jamestown (Colonial National Historical Park) (E-9)

Area code: 804 **Zip:** 23081

On May 13, 1607, in this unpromising setting, the first permanent English settlement in the New World was founded. From the beginning, characteristics of the early United States were established—self-government, industry, commerce and the plantation system. The 104 men and boys who landed here that day and the people who followed them forecast the varied origins of the American populace. There were English, Dutch, Germans, Africans, French, Belgians, Italians, Poles, Swiss, Irish and Welsh.

The *Susan Constant* (125 tons), the *Godspeed* (40 tons) and the *Discovery* (20 tons) brought the settlers here after a landing at Cape Henry. Thus, 20 years after the tragic failure to establish a colony at Roanoke Island and 13 years before the Pilgrims landed at Plymouth, Massachusetts, the English succeeded in settling in America.

The landing was not auspicious. Captain John Smith, ablest man in the group, was in chains; most of the others possessed a singular ineptitude for existing in a strange, hostile wilderness. Smith's ability and driving personality soon made him the acknowledged leader. For about a year he kept the bickering at a minimum, and the establishment of a colony was well under way.

The London Company, under whose patronage the colonists had set forth, continued to send "gentlemen" and adventurers to reinforce the colony. The second such shipment (September, 1608) elicited the famous "Smith's rude answer" to company demands for gold and assorted riches. He wrote in part, "I entreat you rather send but thirty carpenters, husbandmen, gardeners, fishermen, blacksmiths, masons and diggers up of trees, roots . . . than a thousand of such as we have: for except we be able both to lodge them and feed them, the most will consume with want of necessaries before they can be made good for anything."

Good for anything or not, this little band made glass in 1608, introduced the first commercial tobacco cultivation in 1612 and produced the country's first representative legislative body in 1619. Clapboards (some of which were shipped back to England) and bricks were also made here, as well as fishing nets, pottery, a variety of tools and other items needed in the colony.

The first Africans were brought to the colony in 1619 on a Dutch warship. They were indentured servants, pledged to work until their passage had been paid off. This was a common arrangement at the time.

There was not an easy day for any of the colonists for years. Crops failed, and rats ate the corn. Until John Rolfe married Pocahontas, daughter of Chief Powhatan, in 1614, the Indians were suspicious and unfriendly. Mosquitoes and disease plagued the settlers. The winter of 1609-10 was called the "starving time." The 500-person colony was reduced to about 60 emaciated, defeated survivors who decided to give up and return to England. The June, 1610 arrival of Lord De la Warre with reinforcements and supplies dissuaded them. Then the colony began to build and hope returned.

When Jamestown became a Royal Colony in 1624, feeling against personal (and often high-handed) government began to mount. By 1676 there was open revolt, led by Nathaniel Bacon, the younger. Bacon's forces finally burned the town, calling it a "stronghold of oppression." It was partially rebuilt, but decline was irrevocable, in part due to the damp, unhealthy climate of the area. The statehouse burned in 1698, and in 1699 the government moved to Middle Plantation and renamed it Williamsburg. By Revolutionary days Jamestown was no longer an active community. About the same time, the James River washed away the sandy isthmus, and the site became an island.

Nothing of the 17th-century settlement remains above ground except the Old Church Tower. Since 1934, however, archaeological exploration by the National Park Service has made the outline of the town clear. Cooperative efforts by the Park Service and the Association for the Preservation of Virginia Antiquities (which owns 22.5 acres of the island, including the Old Church Tower) have exposed foundations and restored streets, property ditches, hedgerows and fences. Markers, recorded messages, paintings and monuments are everywhere. Entrance station (daily; closed Dec 25). For further information contact the Superintendent, PO Box 210, Yorktown 23690; 898-3400. Colonial National Historical Park *free;* Jamestown Island entrance fee $8/car; Golden Eagle Passport (see INTRODUCTION).

What to See and Do

1. **Colonial National Historical Park.** Recommended as a starting point is the

   Visitor Center. Guide leaflets, introductory film and exhibits. Post office. (Daily; closed Dec 25) From here you can walk through

   "New Towne." Area where Jamestown expanded around 1620 may be toured along "Back-Streete" and other original streets. Section includes reconstructed foundations indicating sites of Country House, Governor's House, homes of Richard Kemp, builder of one of the first brick houses in America, Henry Hartwell, a founder of College of William and Mary, and Dr. John Pott and William Pierce, who led the "thrusting out" of Gov John Harvey in 1635.

   First landing site. Fixed by tradition as point in river, about 200 yards from present seawall, upriver from Old Church Tower. First fort may have been in the same area.

   Old Church Tower. Only standing ruin of the 17th-century town. Believed to be part of first brick church (1639). Has 3-ft-thick walls of handmade brick.

   Memorial Church. Built in 1907 by the National Society of the Colonial Dames of America over foundations of original church. Within are two foundations alleged to be of earlier churches, one from 1617 that housed first assembly.

   First Statehouse. Foundations of brick building have been discovered near river; recent research has suggested that the structure may *not* actually be the "first" statehouse.

   Tercentenary Monument. Located near Jamestown Visitor Center. Erected by US (1907) to commemorate 300th Jamestown anniversary. Other monuments include Captain John Smith statue (by William Couper), Pocahontas Monument (by William Ordway Partridge), House of Burgesses Monument (listing members of first representative legislative body in America).

Confederate Fort (1861). Near Old Church Tower. One of two Civil War fortifications on the island.

Trails. Five-mile auto drive provides access to entire area. Visitor center has 45-minute auto drive and townsite tape tours available.

Glasshouse. Colonists produced glass here in 1608. Demonstration exhibits, glassblowing (daily exc Dec 25).

Dale House Pottery. Pottery exhibit and demonstrations (Mar-Dec, daily exc Dec 25).

2. **Jamestown Settlement.** Adj to historic Jamestown. Living history museum re-creates the first permanent English settlement in New World. Recalls early 17th-century Jamestown with full-scale reproductions of ships which arrived in 1607 and the triangular James Fort. Powhatan Indian Village depicts Native American culture encountered by English colonists. Museum complex features orientation film, changing gallery and three exhibit galleries focusing on the history of Jamestown and the Powhatan Indians. Food service avail. (Daily; closed Jan 1, Dec 25) Combination ticket with Yorktown Victory Center (see YORKTOWN) avail. Phone 229-1607. ¢¢¢

Annual Events

Jamestown Weekend. Jamestown Island. Commemorates arrival of first settlers in 1607; special tours and activities. Early May.

First Assembly Day. Commemorates first legislative assembly in 1619. Late July or early Aug.

(For accommodations see Newport News, Williamsburg, Yorktown, also see Colonial Parkway, Surry)

Keysville (F-7)

Pop: 606 **Elev:** 642 ft **Area code:** 804 **Zip:** 23947

What to See and Do

Twin Lakes State Park. 15 mi NE on US 360, then 1¹/₂ mi NW off VA 613. More than 250 acres of state forest; two lakes. Swimming, bathhouse; fishing; boating (rentals, launching, electric motors only). Hiking, bicycle, self-guided trails. Picnicking, playground, concession. Camping, tent & trailer sites (May-Sept). Standard fees. Phone 392-3435.

Motel

✔ ★ **SHELDON'S.** *RFD 2, 1¹/₂ mi N on US 15 Business, 360. 804/736-8434; FAX 804/736-9402.* 40 rms, 1-2 story. S $31.95-$35.95; D $39.95-$46.95; each addl $6. Crib $6. TV; cable. Playground. Restaurant 6:30 am-10 pm. Ck-out noon. Some refrigerators. Cr cds: A, DS, MC, V.

D ✔ 🔥 🏊

Lancaster (E-9)

Pop: 150 (est) **Elev:** 89 ft **Area code:** 804 **Zip:** 22503

The family of Mary Ball Washington, mother of George Washington, were early settlers of this area. Washington's maternal ancestors are buried in the churchyard of St Mary's Whitechapel Church five miles west of Lancaster.

What to See and Do

1. **Lancaster County Courthouse Historic District.** Sycamore trees surround this area around the antebellum courthouse (1860). Marble obelisk is one of the first monuments erected to Confederate soldiers (1872).

2. **Mary Ball Washington Museum & Library Complex.** Contains the Old Clerk's Office (1797), the Old Jail (1819), Old Post Office (1900), blacksmith shop (1900), a Native American longhouse and Lancaster House (1800), the headquarters and main museum building. Also lending and genealogical libraries. (Apr-Nov, Tues-Sat; rest of yr, Tues-Fri) Phone 462-7280. **Free.**

3. **St Mary's Whitechapel Church** (1740-41). 5 mi W on VA 622. Church where Mary Ball and her family worshiped; many of the tombstones bear the Ball name.

(See Irvington)

Inn

★ ★ **INN AT LEVELFIELDS.** *PO Box 216, 2 mi E on VA 3, beyond the Courthouse. 804/435-6887; res: 800/238-5578.* 4 rms, 2 story. No rm phones. S $55; D $85; each addl $10. Pool. Complimentary bkfst. Bar. Ck-out 11 am, ck-in 2 pm. Lawn games. Antiques; hand-made quilts. Antebellum landmark homestead (1857) with double-tiered portico and four massive chimneys; 1,000-ft entrance drive. Located on 54 acres with 2 acres of lawn & 40 acres of timberland bounded by stream. Cr cds: MC, V.

Leesburg (C-8)

Founded: 1758 **Pop:** 16,202 **Elev:** 352 ft **Area code:** 703 **Zip:** 22075

Originally named Georgetown for King George II of England, this town was later renamed Leesburg, probably after Francis Lightfoot Lee, a signer of the Declaration of Independence and a local landowner. Leesburg is located in a scenic area of rolling hills, picturesque rural towns and Thoroughbred horse farms, where point-to-point racing and steeplechases are popular.

What to See and Do

1. **Waterford.** 3 mi NW on VA 7, ¹/₄ mi on VA 9, then 2 mi N on VA 662. Eighteenth-century Quaker village, designated a National Historic Landmark, has been restored as a residential community. An Annual Homes Tour (1st full wkend Oct) has craft demonstrations, exhibits, traditional music. Waterford Foundation has brochures outlining self-guided walking tours. ¢. Guided tours ¢¢ must be arranged in advance. Phone 882-3018. **Free.**

2. **Loudoun Museum.** 16 Loudoun St SW. Century-old restored building contains exhibits and memorabilia of the area; audiovisual presentation "A Special Look at Loudoun." Brochures, information about Loudoun County; walking tours. (Daily; closed Jan 1, Thanksgiving, Dec 25; also mid-Jan-mid-Feb) Donation. Phone 777-7427.

3. **Morven Park.** Old Waterford Rd, 1 mi N of Leesburg. Originally the residence of Thomas Swann, early Maryland governor, the estate was enlarged upon by Westmoreland Davis, governor of Virginia from 1918 to 1922. The 1,500-acre park includes a 28-room mansion; boxwood gardens; Winmill Carriage Museum with more than 100 horse-drawn vehicles; Museum of Hounds and Hunting with video presentation and artifacts depicting the history of foxhunting; and Morven Park International Equestrian Institute. (Apr-Oct, Tues-Sun afternoons, also Mon if hol). (See ANNUAL EVENTS) Sr citizen rate. Phone 777-2414. ¢¢

4. **Oatlands** (1803). 6 mi S on US 15. A 261-acre estate; classical-revival mansion, built by George Carter, was the center of a 5,000-acre plantation; the house was partially remodeled in 1827, which was when the front portico was added. Most of the building materials, including bricks and wood, came from or were made on the estate. Interior, furnished with American, English and French antiques, reflects period between 1897 and 1965, when the house was owned by Mr and Mrs William Corcoran Eustis, prominent Washingtonians. Formal garden has some of the finest boxwood in US. Farm fields provide equestrian area for races and horse shows. (Early Apr-mid-Dec, daily; closed Thanksgiving) Sr citizen rate. Phone 777-3174. ¢¢

5. **Ball's Bluff Battlefield.** N via US 15. One of the smallest national cemeteries in US, marks site of third armed engagement of Civil War. On Oct 21, 1861, four Union regiments suffered catastrophic losses while surrounded by Confederate forces; the Union commander, a US Senator and presidential confidant, was killed here along with half his troops, who were either killed, wounded, captured or drowned while attempting to recross the Potomac River. Oliver Wendell Holmes, Jr, later to become a US Supreme Court Justice, was wounded here.

6. **Vineyard and Winery Tours.** 12 mi S on US 15, then 7½ mi W on US 50 in Middleburg.

Piedmont Vineyards. W on US 50 in Middleburg to VA 626. Winery tours, tasting. (Daily exc Mon; closed Jan 1, Thanksgiving, Dec 25) Phone 687-5528. **Free.**

Meredyth Vineyards. Turn S at traffic light on US 50 in Middleburg, then 2½ mi to VA 628, then right 2½ mi. (Daily; closed Jan 1, Thanksgiving, Dec 25) Phone 687-6277. **Free.**

(For further information contact the Loudon County Conference & Visitor Bureau, 108-D South St SE; 777-0519 or 800/752-6118.)

Annual Events

Loudoun Hunt Pony Club Horse Trials. Held at Morven Park International Equestrian Institute, Morven Park (see #3). Competition in combined training: dressage, cross country and stadium jumping. Phone 777-2890. Late Mar.

Homes and Gardens Tour. Sponsored by Garden Club of Virginia. Late Apr.

Sheepdog Trials. Oatlands (see #4). May.

Wine Festival. Morven Park (see #3). Many wineries participate; includes seminar for home/commercial wine growers; grape-stomping, waiters' race, jousting tournament, music, wine tastings, awards presentations. Phone 202/537-0961. Mid-July.

August Court Days. Re-enactment of the opening of the 18th-century judicial court. Festivities resemble a country fair with craft demonstrations, games, entertainers on the street. Phone 777-0519 or 800/752-6118. 3rd wkend Aug.

Draft Horse & Mule Day. Oatlands (see #4). Sat of Labor Day wkend.

Christmas at Oatlands (see #4). Candlelight tours, 1800s decorations, refreshments. Mid-Nov-Dec.

(See Arlington County, McLean; also see District of Columbia)

Motels

★ ★ **BEST WESTERN.** 726 E Market St. 703/777-9400; FAX 703/777-5537. 99 rms, 2 story. S $55; D $60; each addl $5; suites $65-$70; under 18 free. Crib free. Pet accepted, some restrictions; $25. TV; cable. Pool; lifeguard. Restaurant 7 am-2 pm, 5-9 pm; wkend hrs vary. Rm serv to 2 pm. Bar 4 pm-1 am; entertainment, dancing Fri & Sat. Ck-out noon. Meeting rms. Valet serv. Free Dulles Airport transportation. Tennis privileges. Golf privileges. Health club privileges. Rec rm. Cr cds: A, C, D, DS, MC, V.

✔ ★ **DAYS INN.** 721 E Market St, near Prosperity Shopping Center. 703/777-6622; FAX 703/777-4119. 80 rms, 2 story. Mar-Oct: S $48; D $50; each addl $3; under 12 free; wkly, monthly rates; lower rates rest of yr. Crib free. Pet accepted, some restrictions; $6 per pet. TV; cable. Complimentary continental bkfst. Restaurant nearby. Ck-out noon. Coin lndry. Cr cds: A, C, D, DS, JCB, MC, V.

★ **RAMADA INN AT HISTORIC CARRADOC HALL.** 1500 E Market St. 703/771-9200; FAX 703/771-1575. 126 rms, 2 story. S $55; D $59; each addl $7; suites $105; under 16 free. Crib free. TV; cable. Heated pool; lifeguard. Complimentary continental bkfst. Restaurant 11 am-3 pm, 5-10 pm. Bar 11:30 am-midnight; entertainment Tues-Sat, dancing. Ck-out noon. Coin lndry. Meeting rms. Free airport transportation. Colonial mansion (1773). Cr cds: A, C, D, DS, MC, V.

Hotel

★ ★ ★ **LANSDOWNE CONFERENCE RESORT.** (44050 Woodridge Pkwy, Lansdowne) E on VA 7, left onto Lansdowne Blvd, then right onto Woodridge Pkwy. 703/729-8400; res: 800/541-4801; FAX 703/729-4111. 305 units, 9 story. S $149; D $169; suites $250-$650; under 18 free; wkend rates; golf plans. Crib free. TV; cable. 2 pools, 1 indoor; poolside serv, lifeguard. Restaurant 6 am-midnight. Bar; entertainment Fri-Sun. Ck-out noon. Convention facilities. Concierge. Gift shop. Airport transportation. Lighted tennis. 18-hole golf, pro, greens fee $75-$85, putting green, driving range. Exercise rm; instructor, weights, bicycles, whirlpool, sauna. Lawn games. Bicycle rentals. Refrigerators avail. Balconies. Picnic tables. Cr cds: A, C, D, DS, MC, V.

Inns

★ ★ **COLONIAL.** 19 S King St, above Balls Bluff Tavern. 703/777-5000; res: 800/392-1332. 10 rms, 3 story. S $58-$150; D $68-$150; under 10 yrs free. Crib free. Pet accepted, some restrictions. TV; cable. Complimentary coffee; tea/sherry in library. Dining rm 7-10 pm. Rm serv. Ck-out noon, ck-in 2 pm. Luggage handling. Free Dulles Airport transportation. Tennis, golf privileges ½ mile. Health club privileges. Picnic tables. Historic building (1759) built of same stone as Capital in DC. Fireplaces; some in-rm whirlpools. Cr cds: A, C, D, DS, MC, V.

✔ ★ **LITTLE RIVER.** (Box 116, Aldie 22001) S on VA 15, then 2 mi W on US 50. 703/327-6742. 9 units, 6 with bath, 2 story, 3 cottages. Some rm phones. S $65-$75; D $80-$90; each addl $20; cottages $115-$210. Children under 10 yrs in cottages only. Complimentary full bkfst. Pool privileges. Ck-out noon, ck-in 3 pm. Meeting rm. Private patios, balconies. Picnic tables. Built 1810; antiques. In foothills of Blue Ridge Mts. Cr cds: MC, V.

★ ★ **MIDDLEBURG.** (PO Box 2065, 209 E Washington St, Middleburg 22117) 16 mi SW on VA 50. 703/687-6082; res: 800/262-6082; FAX 703/687-5603. 8 rms, 3 story, 1 suite. MAP: S, D $95-$125; suite $225; higher rates Sat. Crib avail. TV; cable, in-rm movies. Complimentary full bkfst, coffee. Ck-out 11 am, ck-in 3 pm. Airport transportation. Lawn games. Brick residence and former Episcopal parsonage (1820 & 1858). Cr cds: A, C, D, DS, MC, V.

★ ★ **NORRIS HOUSE.** 108 Loudoun St SW. 703/777-1806; res: 800/644-1806; FAX 703/771-8051. 6 rms (shared bath), 3 story. No rm phones. S $65-$100; D $85-$120; each addl $25; higher rates wkends (2-day min), Apr-June & Sept-mid-Nov. Children wkdays only. Complimentary full bkfst; afternoon refreshments. Restaurant nearby. Ck-out noon, ck-in 3-8 pm. Lawn games. Picnic tables. Built 1806.

Veranda overlooking gardens. Antique furnishings; most rms with fireplace. Totally nonsmoking. Cr cds: A, C, D, DS, MC, V.

⊠ 🔥 **SC**

★ ★ ★ **RED FOX.** *(Box 385, 2 E Washington St, Middleburg 22117)* Approx 22 mi SW of Leesburg via US 15, 50. 703/687-6301; res: 800/223-1728; FAX 703/687-6187. 45 rms in 4 buildings, 3 story, 9 suites. S, D $135; each addl $25; suites $145-$225; under 12 free. Crib $10. TV; some with cable. Complimentary continental bkfst. Dining rm 8 am-9:30 pm; Sun to 8 pm. Bar from 11:30 am. Ck-out noon, ck-in 3 pm. Some fireplaces. Some private patios, balconies. Operated as an inn since 1728; pine floors and paneling; antique furnishings. Cr cds: A, C, D, DS, MC, V.

D ⊠ 🔥 **SC**

Restaurants

✔ ★ ★ ★ **GREEN TREE.** 15 S King St. 703/777-7246. Hrs: 11:30 am-10 pm; Sun brunch 11:30 am-3:30 pm. Res accepted. Serv bar. Semi-a la carte: lunch $4.95-$9.95, dinner $9.95-$15.95. Sun brunch $11.95. Specialties: Robert's Delight (beef dish), Jefferson's Delight (calf's liver soaked in milk). Own baking, bread pudding. Parking. Authentic 18th-century recipes. Windows open to street. Cr cds: A, C, D, DS, MC, V.

D **SC**

★ ★ **LAUREL BRIGADE INN.** 20 W Market St. 703/777-1010. Hrs: noon-2 pm, 5:30-8:30 pm; Fri, Sat to 9 pm; Sun noon-7 pm. Closed Mon. Res accepted; required hols. Serv bar. Semi-a la carte: lunch $3.75-$8.25. Complete meals: lunch $10.75-$12.50, dinner $12.50-$24. Child's meals. Specializes in fried chicken, fresh seafood. Outdoor dining. Oldest section dates from 1759; colonial decor, stone walls, fireplace. Family-owned. No cr cds accepted.

Lexington (E-6)

Founded: 1777 **Pop:** 6,959 **Elev:** 1,060 ft **Area code:** 703 **Zip:** 24450

Lexington was home to two of the greatest Confederate heroes: Robert E. Lee and Thomas J. "Stonewall" Jackson. Both are buried here. Sam Houston, Cyrus McCormick and James Gibbs (inventor of the sewing machine) were born nearby.

This town, set in rolling country between the Blue Ridge and Allegheny mountains, is the seat of Rockbridge County. Lexington is known for attractive homes, trim farms, fine old mansions and two of the leading educational institutions in the Commonwealth: Washington and Lee University and Virginia Military Institute.

What to See and Do

1. **Stonewall Jackson House.** 8 E Washington St. Only home owned by Confederate General Stonewall Jackson, restored to its appearance of 1859-61. Many of the furnishings were once owned by Jackson. Interpretive slide presentation and guided tours last 30 minutes. Restored gardens; shop. (Daily; closed Jan 1, Easter, Thanksgiving, Dec 25) Phone 463-2552. ¢¢

2. **Washington and Lee University** (1749). (1,900 students) W Washington St. Liberal arts university situated on an attractive campus with white colonnaded buildings; also includes Washington and Lee Law School. Founded as Augusta Academy in 1749; became Liberty Hall in 1776; its name was changed to Washington Academy in 1798, after receiving 200 shares of James River Canal Company stock from George Washington, and then to Washington College. General Robert E. Lee served as president from 1865-70; soon after Lee's death in 1870, it became Washington and Lee University. Phone 463-8400. Within the university grounds is

Lee Chapel. Robert E. Lee is entombed here. It also houses Lee family crypt and museum, the marble "recumbent statue" of Lee and some of the art collection of Washington and Lee families. Lee's office remains as he left it. (Daily; closed Jan 1, Thanksgiving & following Fri, Dec 24-25, 31) **Free.**

3. **Virginia Military Institute** (1839). (1,300 men) On US 11. State military, engineering, sciences and arts college. Stonewall Jackson taught here, as did Matthew Fontaine Maury, famed naval explorer and inventor. George Catlett Marshall, a General of the Army and author of the Marshall Plan, was a graduate. Mementos of these men are on display in campus museums (daily; closed Jan 1, Thanksgiving, Dec 24-31). Dress parade (Sept-May, Fri afternoons, weather permitting). Phone 464-7207. **Free.** Located on the S end of the parade ground is

George C. Marshall Museum (1964). Faces parade ground of VMI. Displays on life and career of the illustrious military figure and statesman (1880-1959); World War I, electric map and recorded narration of World War II; Marshall Plan; gold medallion awarded with his Nobel Prize for Peace (1953). (Daily; closed Jan 1, Thanksgiving, Dec 25) Phone 463-7103. **Free.**

4. **Stonewall Jackson Memorial Cemetery.** E side of S Main St. General Jackson and more than one hundred other Confederate soldiers are buried here.

5. **Goshen Pass.** 19 mi NW on VA 39. Scenic mountain gorge formed by Maury River. Memorial to Matthew Fontaine Maury is here.

(For further information and maps for self-guided walking tours contact the Visitors Bureau, 106 E Washington St; 463-3777.)

Annual Events

Garden Week in Historic Lexington. Tour of homes and gardens in the Lexington, Rockbridge County area. Phone 463-3777. Late Apr.

"Holiday in Lexington." Parade, plays, children's events. Phone 463-3777. Early Dec.

Seasonal Event

Lime Kiln Arts' Theater at Lime Kiln. 14 S Randolph St. Professional theatrical productions and concerts in outdoor theater. Phone 463-3074. Memorial Day-Labor Day.

(See Clifton Forge, Natural Bridge)

Motels

✔ ★ ★ **DAYS INN KEYDET-GENERAL.** 1 mi W on US 60. 703/463-2143. 53 rms, 10 kit. units. S $47.95-$57.95; D $55.95-$65.95; each addl $5. Crib free. Pet accepted, some restrictions. TV; cable. Cafe 6:30-10 am, 5-9 pm. Ck-out 11 am. Meeting rm. Some bathrm phones, refrigerators. Picnic tables. View of mountains. Cr cds: A, C, D, DS, ER, MC, V.

D 🐾 ⊠ 🔥 **SC**

★ ★ **HOLIDAY INN.** Box 1108, 1 mi N on US 11. 703/463-7351; FAX 703/463-7351, ext. 148. 72 rms, 2 story. S $55-$66; D $61-$72; each addl $6; studio rms $55-$66; under 18 free. Crib free. Pet accepted. TV; cable. Pool; wading pool. Restaurant 6:30 am-2 pm, 5-10 pm. Rm serv. Bar 5 pm-midnight. Ck-out noon. Meeting rms. Bellhops. Valet serv. View of mountains. Cr cds: A, C, D, DS, ER, JCB, MC, V.

D 🐾 ≈ ⊠ 🔥

Motor Hotels

★ ★ **COMFORT INN.** PO Box 905, jct US 11 S & I-64 exit 55, I-81 exit 191. 703/463-7311; FAX 703/463-4590. 80 rms, 4 story. Apr-Nov: S, D $59-$69; each addl $5; under 18 free; lower rates rest of yr. Crib free. Pet accepted. TV; cable. Indoor pool. Complimentary continental bkfst, coffee. Restaurant adj 6 am-11 pm. Ck-out 11 am. Coin lndry. Sundries. Cr cds: A, C, D, DS, ER, JCB, MC, V.

✔ ★ ★ **HOWARD JOHNSON.** *6 mi N on US 11. 703/463-9181; FAX 703/464-3448.* 100 rms, 5 story. S $39-$65; D $46-$73; each addl $7; under 18 free; higher rates special events. Crib free. Pet accepted. TV; cable. Pool. Restaurant 6 am-10 pm. Ck-out noon. Coin lndry. Meeting rm. Sundries. Gift shop. Balconies. Private patios. On hill; panoramic view of mountains. Cr cds: A, C, D, DS, ER, JCB, MC, V.

Inns

★ ★ **FASSIFERN.** *Rte 5, Box 87, 3 mi N at jct VA 39 & County Rd 750; just N of jct US 11 & I-64 exit 55. 703/463-1013.* 5 rms, 2 story. S $75; D $79-$87. Complimentary continental bkfst. Restaurant nearby. Ck-out 11 am, ck-in 4 pm. Restored 1867 house; antiques. Grounds with pond, woods. Near VA Horse Center. Totally nonsmoking. Cr cds: MC, V.

★ ★ **McCAMPBELL.** *11 N Main St. 703/463-2044; FAX 703/463-7262.* 16 units, 4 story. S $80-$120; D $95-$135; each addl $15; family rates. Crib $15. TV; cable. Pool privileges. Complimentary continental bkfst, tea, sherry. Restaurant opp 5:30-9 pm. Ck-out noon, ck-in 2 pm. Tennis privileges. Refrigerators. Private patios, balconies. Picnic tables. Built 1809; antiques. Cr cds: MC, V.

Restaurant

★ ★ ★ **WILLSON-WALKER HOUSE.** *30 N Main St. 703/463-3020.* Hrs: 11:30 am-2:30 pm, 5:30-9 pm. Closed Mon; Jan 1, Dec 24, 25; also Sat lunch Dec-Mar. Res accepted. Serv bar. Wine list. Semi-a la carte: lunch $5-$7, dinner $10-$17. Child's meals. Specializes in pasta, veal, fresh seafood. Outdoor dining. In restored Greek-revival house (1820) located in downtown historic district; period antiques. Cr cds: A, MC, V.

Luray (C-7)

Founded: 1812 **Pop:** 4,587 **Elev:** 789 ft **Area code:** 703 **Zip:** 22835

The name of this town is of French origin; its fame comes from the caverns discovered here in 1878. Luray, at the junction of US 211 and US 340, is 9 miles away from, and within sight of, Shenandoah National Park (see) and Skyline Drive. Headquarters of the park are here. There are three developed recreation areas north and west of town in George Washington National Forest.

What to See and Do

1. **Luray Caverns.** W edge of town on US 211. One of the largest caverns in the East. Huge underground rooms (one is 300 ft wide, 500 ft long, with a 140-ft ceiling) connected by natural corridors and paved walkways, are encrusted with colorful rock formations, some delicate as lace, others massive. In one chamber is the world's only "stalacpipe" organ, which produces music of symphonic quality from stone formation. Indirect lighting permits taking color photos within caverns. Temperature is 54°F. Guided tours start about every 20 min. (Daily) Sr citizen rate. Phone 743-6551. ¢¢¢¢ Fee includes

Car and Carriage Museum. Exhibits include 140 restored antique cars, carriages and coaches featuring the history of transportation dating from 1625.

2. **Luray Singing Tower.** In park adjoining caverns. Houses a 47-bell carillon; largest bell weighs 7,640 lbs. Features 45-min recitals by a celebrated carillonneur. (June-Aug, Tues, Thurs, Sat & Sun evenings; Mar-May & Sept-Oct, wkend afternoons) Phone 743-6551. **Free.**

3. **Luray Reptile Center and Dinosaur Park.** 1/2 mi W on US 211. Features large reptile collection, exotic animals and tropical birds; petting zoo; life-sized dinosaur reproductions. Gift shop. (Mid-Apr-Oct, daily) Phone 743-4113. ¢¢

4. **Massanutten One-room School.** In Lawn Park. Restored and furnished as it was in the 1800s. Period displays and pictures. (By appt) Contact Chamber of Commerce. **Free.**

5. **Shenandoah National Park** (see). 9 mi E on US 211, then S on Skyline Dr.

(For further information contact the Page County Chamber of Commerce, 46 E Main St; 743-3915.)

Annual Event

Page County Heritage Festival. Self-guided tour of churches and old homes. Arts & crafts exhibits. Columbus Day wkend.

(See Basye, Front Royal, Harrisonburg, New Market)

Motels

✔ ★ **INTOWN MOTOR INN.** *410 W Main St (US 221). 703/743-6511.* 40 rms, 2 story. Apr-Nov: S, D $32.50-$73.50; each addl $5; under 18 free; higher rates foliage season; lower rates rest of yr. Crib $4. Pet accepted; $10 per day. TV; cable. Pool. Playground. Restaurant 6 am-2 pm, 5-9 pm. Rm serv. Ck-out noon. Gift shop. Lawn games. Cr cds: A, C, D, DS, MC, V.

★ **LURAY CAVERNS MOTEL.** *Box 748, on US 211, opp caverns entrance. 703/743-6551.* 63 rms. S, D $52-$62; each addl $7; under 16 free; golf plans; higher rates: wkends, Sept & Oct. TV; cable. Pool. Restaurant nearby. Ck-out 11 am. Some balconies. Cr cds: A, DS, MC, V.

★ ★ **MIMSLYN INN.** *401 W Main St (US 221). 703/743-5105; res: 800/296-5105; FAX 703/743-2632.* 49 rms (2 with shower only), 3 story, 11 suites. Mid-June-Oct: S $53.95-$59; D $64-$69; suites $94-$109; under 18 free; lower rates rest of yr. Crib $7. Pet accepted. TV; cable. Restaurant 7-10 am, 11:30 am-2 pm, 5-9 pm. Rm serv. Ck-out noon. Bellhops. Art gallery, antique shop. Built 1930 in style of antebellum mansion. Cr cds: A, C, D, DS, MC, V.

★ ★ **RAMADA LURAY INN & CONFERENCE CENTER.** *Box 389, 1 mi E on US 211 Bypass, jct VA 656. 703/743-4521; FAX 703/743-6863.* 99 rms, 2 story. Mid-May-Oct: S $55-$125; D $60-$125; each addl $5; suites $110-$185; under 16 free; higher rates: wkends, foliage season, special events; lower rates rest of yr. Crib free. Pet accepted; $10. TV; cable; in-rm movies avail. Pool. Restaurant 6:30 am-2 pm, 5-9 pm. Rm serv. Ck-out noon. Meeting rms. Miniature golf. American Presidents Museum on premises. Cr cds: A, C, D, DS, JCB, MC, V.

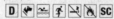

Inn

★ ★ ★ **JORDAN HOLLOW FARM INN.** *(Rte 2, Box 375, Stanley 22851)* S on US 340, then E on VA 624, N on VA 689, then E on VA 626.

703/778-2285; FAX 703/778-1759. 21 rms in 3 bldgs, 1-2 story. S $115-$155; D $140-$180; each addl $35; family rates. Crib free. TV in some rms; cable. Dining rm 8:30-10:30 am, 6-9 pm. Ck-out noon, ck-in 3 pm. Game rm. Some in-rm whirlpools. Converted 45-acre horse farm; sun deck with view of Blue Ridge Mts. Cr cds: C, D, DS, MC, V.

🛠️ 🚳 🔥

Restaurants

✔ ★ **BROOKSIDE.** *On US 211, 4¹/2 mi E.* 703/743-5698. Hrs: 7 am-8:30 pm; Fri, Sat to 9 pm. Closed mid-Dec-mid-Jan. Res accepted. Wine, beer. Semi-a la carte: bkfst $3-$6, lunch $3.50-$7.50, dinner $6.50-$13. Buffet: bkfst (Sat & Sun) $5.95, lunch $4.95, dinner $7.50-$8.50. Child's meals. Specializes in rib-eye steak, spaghetti, seafood. Salad bar. Parking. Cr cds: A, C, D, DS, MC, V.

D

★ ★ **PARKHURST.** *On US 211, 2 mi W.* 703/743-6009. Hrs: 4-10 pm; Fri, Sat to 11 pm. Closed some major hols. Res accepted. Continental menu. Bar. Semi-a la carte: dinner $9.95-$19.95. Child's meals. Specializes in steak, fowl, seafood. Parking. View of Blue Ridge Mts. Cr cds: A, C, D, DS, MC, V.

Lynchburg (E-6)

Settled: 1757 **Pop:** 66,049 **Elev:** 795 ft **Area code:** 804

Lynchburg is perched on hills overlooking the James River, which was for many years its means of growth. Today the city is home to more than 3,000 businesses and diversified industries. Colleges located here include Lynchburg College, Randolph-Macon Woman's College and Liberty University.

One of the first buildings in the town was a ferryhouse built by John Lynch. The same enterprising young man later built a tobacco warehouse, probably the first one in the country. During the Civil War Lynchburg was important as a supply base and hospital town. In June of 1864, General Jubal A. Early successfully defended the town from an attack by Union forces. More than 2,500 Confederates are buried in Old City Cemetery.

What to See and Do

1. **Randolph-Macon Woman's College** (1891). (750 women) 2500 Rivermont Ave. A 100-acre campus on historic Rivermont Ave near the James River. First college for women in the South granted a Phi Beta Kappa chapter. Campus is interesting mixture of architecture including the Vincent Kling design for the Houston Chapel. Tours on request. Phone 947-8100. On campus is

   Maier Museum of Art. Collection is representative of 19th- and 20th-century American painting. Artists include Thomas Hart Benton, Edward Hicks, Winslow Homer, James McNeil Whistler, Mary Cassatt and Georgia O'Keeffe. Changing exhibits. (Academic yr, daily exc Mon) Phone 947-8000. **Free.**

2. **Point of Honor** (1815). 112 Cabell St. Restored mansion on Daniel's Hill above the James River, built by Dr. George Cabell, Sr, physician to Patrick Henry. Federal style with octagon-bay facade and finely crafted interior woodwork; period furnishings; gardens and grounds being restored. (Daily; closed Jan 1, Thanksgiving, Dec 24, 25) Phone 847-1459. ¢¢

3. **Old Court House Museum** (1855). 901 Court St. Restored to original Greek-revival appearance. Three galleries have exhibits on early history of the area, highlighting Quaker settlement and role of tobacco; restored mid-19th-century courtroom. (Daily; closed Jan 1, Thanksgiving, Dec 24, 25) Phone 847-1459. ¢¢

4. **Anne Spencer House.** 1313 Pierce St. House of noted poet, only black woman and only Virginian to be included in *Norton Anthol-*

ogy of Modern American and British Poetry. On grounds is Spencer's writing cottage "EdanKraal." Many dignitaries have visited here. Museum with artifacts, memorabilia, period antique furnishings; formal garden. (By appt) Phone 846-0517. ¢

5. **Pest House Medical Museum.** Old City Cemetery, 4th and Taylor Sts. The 1840s white frame medical office of Quaker physician Dr. John Jay Terrell, has been joined with the Pest House quarantine hospital to typefy the standard of medicine during the late 1800s. Original medical instruments include an operating table, hypodermic needle, clinical thermometer and chloroform mask. Period furnishings on one side duplicate Dr. Terrell's office during the Civil War; the other represents the quarantine hospital for Confederate soldiers in which Dr. Terrell volunteered to assume responsibility. Window displays with audio description. Tours (by appt). (Daily) Phone 847-1811. **Free.**

6. **South River Meeting House.** 5810 Fort Ave. Completed in 1798, the stone building remained the site of Quaker worship and activity until the 1840s. John Lynch, the founder of Lynchburg, and other early leaders of the community are buried in the adj historic cemetery. (Daily; closed major hols) Phone 239-2548. **Free.**

7. **Riverside Park.** Rivermont Ave. (Daily) **Free.** In park are

   Miller-Claytor House (1791). Believed to have been the fourth house built in Lynchburg. Living history interpretation with early craft demonstrations. (May-Sept, Thurs-Mon) Phone 847-1459. **Free.**

   Packet Boat *Marshall.* Mounted on a stone base, this is the boat that carried the remains of Stonewall Jackson home to Lexington; for many years packets were the principal mode of transportation along the James River and Kanawha Canal.

8. **Fort Early.** Memorial and Fort Aves. Defense earthwork for Lynchburg's closest battle during the Civil War. Confederates under General Jubal A. Early turned back forces under General David Hunter in 1864. (Daily) **Free.**

9. **Blackwater Creek Natural Area.** In the center of the city. Ruskin Freer Nature Preserve (115 acres) includes trails with plants; athletic area; bikeway winds past wildflower area and historical sites, ending downtown; Creekside Trunk Trail, natural grass trail with typical Piedmont species of plants, moist ravines, north-facing rocky bluffs. (Daily) **Free.**

10. **Appomattox Court House Natl Historical Park** (see). 21 mi E on US 460.

11. **Jefferson's Poplar Forest.** Just SW of Lynchburg on US 221, then left on VA 811 & left again on VA 661 in Bedford County. Designed and built by Thomas Jefferson as a personal retreat; begun in 1806. Restoration in progress; house unfurnished. (Apr-Nov, Wed-Sun & major hols) Sr citizen rate. Phone 525-1806. ¢¢

(For further information contact the Visitors Information Center, 12th & Church Sts, 24504; 847-1811.)

Motels

★ ★ **DAYS INN.** *3320 Candlers Mt Rd (24502).* 804/847-8655; FAX 804/846-3297. 131 rms, 5 story. S, D $59-$79; each addl $8; under 17 free. Crib free. TV; cable. Pool. Playground. Restaurant 6 am-10 pm. Rm serv. Ck-out noon. Meeting rms. Valet serv. Sundries. Airport, RR station, bus depot transportation. Private patios, balconies. Cr cds: A, D, DS, MC, V.

D 🏊 🚳 🔥 SC

✔ ★ **ECONO LODGE.** *PO Box 2028 (24501), 2400 Stadium Rd, US 29S Expressway City-Stadium exit.* 804/847-1045. 47 rms, 2 story. S $33.95-$37.95; D $39.95-$43.95. Crib free. Pet accepted. TV; cable, in-rm movies avail. Continental bkfst. Restaurant nearby. Ck-out 11 am. Exercise equipt; weights, bicycles. Cr cds: A, C, D, DS, MC, V.

🏋️ 🚳 🔥 SC

★ ★ **HOWARD JOHNSON.** *PO Box 10729 (24506), 2 mi N on US 29.* 804/845-7041; FAX 804/845-0222. 70 rms, 2 story. S, D $46-

$63; each addl $7; under 18 free. Crib free. TV; cable. Pool; wading pool. Restaurant open 24 hrs. Rm serv 7-10 pm. Ck-out noon. Coin lndry. Meeting rm. Valet serv. Sundries. Free airport transportation. Some refrigerators. Private patios, balconies. Cr cds: A, C, D, DS, JCB, MC, V.

✔ ★ ★ **INNKEEPER.** *2901 Candler's Mountain Rd (24502). 804/237-7771; res: 800/822-9899; FAX 804/239-0659.* 104 rms, 3 story. S $41.95-$46.95; D $46-$51; each addl $5; under 16 free. Crib free. TV; cable. Pool. Complimentary continental bkfst. Restaurant nearby. Ck-out 11 am. Meeting rms. Valet serv. Cr cds: A, C, D, DS, MC, V.

Motor Hotel

★ ★ ★ **HILTON LYNCHBURG.** *2900 Candlers Mountain Rd (24502). 804/237-6333; FAX 804/237-4277.* 168 rms, 5 story. S $70-$105; D $90-$125; studio rms $92-$110; each addl $20; suites $186; family rates. Crib free. TV; cable. Indoor pool. Restaurant 6:30 am-10 pm. Rm serv. Bar 11-1:30 am; entertainment, dancing exc Sun. Ck-out 11 am. Meeting rms. Bellhops. Valet serv. Sundries. Gift shop. Free airport transportation. Exercise equipt; weights, bicycles, whirlpool, sauna. Bathrm phone in suites. Cr cds: A, C, D, ER, MC, V.

Hotel

★ ★ **HOLIDAY INN CROWNE PLAZA.** *PO Box 6136 (24504), 601 Main St. 804/528-2500; FAX 804/528-0062.* 243 units, 8 story. S $69-$79; D $79-$89; each addl $15; suites $85-$100; under 17 free. Crib free. TV; cable. Pool; poolside serv. Restaurant 6:30 am-10 pm. Bar 3 pm-1 am. Ck-out noon. Convention facilities. Free airport, RR station, bus depot transportation. Golf privileges 15 mi, greens fee $20.30. Exercise equipt; weights, bicycles. Some bathrm phones, refrigerators. Entryway has three-tiered marble fountain beneath 32-ft domed rotunda. Cr cds: A, C, D, DS, ER, MC, V.

Inn

★ ★ ★ **DULWICH MANOR.** *(Rte 5, Box 173A, Amherst 24521) Approx 17 mi N on US 29, then 1/2 mi E on US 60. 804/946-7207.* 6 rms, 4 with bath, 3 story. No rm phones. S $64-$84; D $69-$89; each addl $20; wkly rates. Complimentary full bkfst. Restaurant nearby. Ck-out 11 am, ck-in 3 pm. Whirlpool. English manor house (1912); antique furnishings. No cr cds accepted.

Restaurants

★ ★ ★ **CAFE FRANCE.** *3225 Old Forest Rd. 804/385-8989.* Hrs: 11:30 am-3 pm, 5:30-10 pm; Mon to 3 pm. Closed Sun; some major hols. Res accepted. Bar. Semi-a la carte: lunch $4-$12, dinner $6-$32. Child's meals. Specializes in fresh seafood, prime rib. Parking. Extensive wine & beer selection. Country French decor. Gourmet retail shop adj. Cr cds: A, MC, V.

★ ★ **CROWN STERLING.** *6120 Fort Ave. 804/239-7744.* Hrs: 6-10 pm; Sat from 5:30 pm. Closed Sun; major hols. Res accepted. Bar from 5 pm. Semi-a la carte: dinner $11-$20. Specializes in charcoal steak. Salad bar. Parking. Colonial decor. Cr cds: A, C, D, DS, MC, V.

★ ★ **JEANNE'S.** *8 mi E on US 460. 804/993-2475.* Hrs: 11:30 am-2:30 pm, 4:30-9 pm; wkends to 10 pm; Sun noon-9 pm; Jan-Mar noon-2 pm, 5-9 pm. Closed July 4, Thanksgiving; also late Dec. Continental menu. Bar. Semi-a la carte: lunch $3.95-$8.50, dinner $6.95-$17.95. Child's meals. Specializes in steak, seafood. Salad bar. Own desserts. Parking. Rustic, redwood structure; overlooks lake. Cr cds: A, C, MC, V.

★ ★ **LANDMARK STEAK HOUSE.** *6113 Fort Ave. 804/237-1884.* Hrs: 11:30 am-2 pm, 5:30-10 pm; Fri to 10:30 pm; Sat 5:30-10:30 pm; Sun 5:30-10 pm. Closed some hols. Bar. Semi-a la carte: lunch $3.95-$6.95, dinner $6.25-$24.95. Child's meals. Specializes in prime rib, filet mignon. Salad bar. Parking. Cr cds: A, D, MC, V.

★ ★ ★ **SACHIKO'S.** *126 Old Graves Mill Rd. 804/237-5655.* Hrs: 5:30-10 pm. Closed Sun; some hols. Res accepted. Continental menu. Bar. Wine cellar. Semi-a la carte: dinner $11.95-$25.95. Specializes in steak, veal, seafood. Own baking, desserts. Parking. Fireplace. Cr cds: A, MC, V.

✔ ★ **T.C. TROTTERS.** *2496 Rivermont Ave. 804/846-3545.* Hrs: 11:30 am-11:30 pm; Fri, Sat to midnight. Closed Thanksgiving, Dec 25. Res accepted. Bar to 2 am. Semi-a la carte: lunch $1.95-$8.50, dinner $1.95-$13.95. Child's meals. Specializes in fajitas, steak, seafood. Entertainment Thurs-Sat. Parking. Outdoor dining. Cr cds: A, MC, V.

Unrated Dining Spot

MORRISON'S CAFETERIA. *3405 Candlers Mountain Rd, at Riverridge Mall. 804/237-6549.* Hrs: 11 am-8:30 pm; Sun to 8 pm. Avg ck: lunch $5, dinner $5.40. Child's meals. Cr cds: MC, V.

Manassas (C-8)

Pop: 27,957 **Elev:** 321 ft **Area code:** 703

Though the Native Americans who had lived in this area for thousands of years were driven out under a treaty in 1722, settlement remained sparse until the coming of the railroad in 1858. The Manassas rail junction was vital to the South, and many troops were stationed along this line of communication. Control of this junction led to two major battles nearby (see MANASSAS [BULL RUN] NATIONAL BATTLEFIELD PARK).

What to See and Do

The Manassas Museum. 9101 Prince William St. Museum features collections dealing with Northern Virginia Piedmont history from prehistoric to modern times, with special emphasis on the Civil War. (Daily exc Mon; closed Jan 1, Thanksgiving, Dec 24, 25) Sr citizen rate. Phone 368-1873. ¢

(For further information contact the Prince William County Conference & Visitors Bureau, 4349 Ridgewood Center Drive, Suite 100, Prince William 22192; 792-6680 or 800/432-1792.)

Annual Events

Prince William County Fair. Carnival, entertainment, tractor pull, exhibits, contests. Phone 368-0173. Mid-Aug.

Re-enactment of the Civil War Battle of Manassas. Long Park. Phone 792-7060. Late Sept.

(See Arlington County, Fairfax, Falls Church, Triangle; also see District of Columbia)

Motels

✔ ★ **BEST WESTERN.** *8640 Mathis Ave (22110). 703/368-7070; FAX 703/368-7292.* 60 rms, 2 story. Apr-Oct: S $45-$55; D $50-$60; each addl $5; kit. units $55-$60; under 12 free; wkly, monthly rates; lower rates rest of yr. Crib free. TV; cable. Complimentary coffee in lobby & rms. Restaurant adj 4 pm-2 am. Ck-out 11 am. Coin Indry. Valet serv. Whirlpool, sauna. Some refrigerators. Cr cds: A, C, D, DS, ER, MC, V.

⊡ ✔ ⋈ 🔥 SC

★ ★ **COURTYARD BY MARRIOTT.** *10701 Battleview Pkwy (22110). 703/335-1300; FAX 703/335-9442.* 149 rms, 3 story. S, D $53-$74; each addl $5; suites $70-$90; under 19 free. Crib free. TV; cable. Indoor pool; lifeguard. Complimentary coffee in rms & lobby. Restaurant 6:30-10 am, 5-10 pm; Sat & Sun 7 am-noon. Bar. Ck-out 1 pm. Coin Indry. Meeting rms. Valet serv. Sundries. Exercise equipt; weights, bicycles. Refrigerators. Balconies. Cr cds: A, C, D, DS, MC, V.

⊡ ⋈ 🏃 ⋈ 🔥 SC

★ **DAYS INN.** *10653 Balls Ford Rd (22110). 703/368-2800; FAX 703/368-0083.* 120 rms, 2 story. S $48; D $54; each addl $5; under 18 free. Crib free. TV; cable. Pool. Complimentary continental bkfst, coffee. Ck-out 11 am. Picnic table. Cr cds: A, C, D, DS, MC, V.

⊡ ⋈ ⋈ 🔥 SC

★ ★ **RAMADA INN.** *10820 Balls Ford Rd (22110). 703/361-8000.* 121 rms, 2 story. S $54-$69; D $60-$75; each addl $6; under 18 free. Crib free. Pet accepted. TV; cable, in-rm movies. Pool. Restaurant 6 am-midnight; Thurs-Sat to 2 am. Rm serv 7 am-10 pm. Bar from 11 am; entertainment Wed, Fri, Sat, dancing. Ck-out noon. Meeting rms. Sundries. Cr cds: A, C, D, DS, ER, JCB, MC, V.

⊡ ✔ ⋈ ⋈ 🔥 SC

✔ ★ **RED ROOF INN.** *10610 Automotive Dr (22110), I-66 exit 47A. 703/335-9333; FAX 703/335-9342.* 119 rms, 3 story. S $35.99-$44.99; D $37.99-$59.99; under 18 free; wkly rates; higher rates: Cherry Blossom, hol wkends. Crib free. Pet accepted, some restrictions. TV; cable. Complimentary coffee in lobby. Restaurant adj 6-2 am. Ck-out noon. Sundries. Health club privileges. Cr cds: A, C, D, DS, MC, V.

⊡ ✔ ⋈ 🔥 SC

✔ ★ **SHONEY'S INN.** *8691 Phoenix Dr (22110). 703/369-6323; FAX 703/369-9206.* 78 rms, 3 story. S $36-$46; D $42-$50; each addl $4; under 18 free. Crib free. TV; cable. Indoor pool. Complimentary coffee in rms. Restaurant adj 6 am-11 pm. Bar 4-10 pm. Ck-out noon. Meeting rms. Exercise equipt; weights, bicycles, whirlpool, sauna. Some in-rm whirlpools. Cr cds: A, C, D, DS, ER, MC, V.

⊡ ⋈ 🏃 ⋈ 🔥 SC

Motor Hotel

★ ★ **HOLIDAY INN.** *10800 Vandor Lane (22110), I-66 exit 47A. 703/335-0000; FAX 703/361-8440.* 160 rms, 5 story. S $45-$85; D $52-$91; each addl $6; under 18 free. Crib $5. Pet accepted. TV; cable. Pool. Complimentary coffee in lobby. Restaurant 6 am-2 pm, 5-10 pm; Sun from 7 am. Rm serv. Bar 4 pm-2 am; entertainment, dancing exc Mon. Ck-out noon. Meeting rms. Valet serv. Excercise equipt: weight machines, bicycle. Near Manassas (Bull Run) Battlefield. Cr cds: A, C, D, DS, ER, MC, V.

⊡ ✔ ⋈ 🏃 ⋈ 🔥 SC

Restaurants

★ ★ **CARMELLO'S.** *9108 Center St. 703/368-5522.* Hrs: 11:30 am-2:30 pm, 5-10 pm; Sat from 5 pm, Sun 4-9 pm. Closed Jan 1, Thanksgiving, Dec 25. Res accepted. Northern Italian menu. Bar. Semi-a la carte: lunch $5-$10, dinner $7-$17. Child's meals. Specializes in fresh seafood, veal, chicken. Own pasta. Pianist Sat evenings. Located in 2-story brick storefront. Cr cds: A, C, D, DS, MC, V.

⊡

✔ ★ **RED, HOT & BLUE.** *8637 Sudley Rd. 703/330-4847.* Hrs: 11:30 am-10 pm; Fri to 11 pm; Sun noon-9 pm. Closed Thanksgiving, Dec 25. Bar. A la carte entrees: lunch, dinner $4.50-$12.75. Complete meals: lunch, dinner $10.95. Child's meals. Specializes in barbecue, beef, chicken. Cr cds: DS, MC, V.

⊡

Manassas (Bull Run) National Battlefield Park (C-8)

(26 mi SW of Washington, DC, at jct US 29, VA 234)

This 5,000-acre park was the scene of two major Civil War battles. More than 26,000 men were killed or wounded here in struggles for control of a strategically important railroad junction.

The first major land battle of the war (July 21, 1861) was fought here between poorly-trained volunteer troops from both North and South. The battle finally resolved itself into a struggle for Henry Hill, where "Stonewall" Jackson earned his nickname. With the outcome in doubt, Confederate reinforcements arrived by railroad from the Shenandoah Valley and turned the battle into a rout.

Thirteen months later (Aug 28-30, 1862), in the second battle of Manassas, Robert E. Lee outmaneuvered and defeated Union General John Pope and cleared the way for a Confederate invasion of Maryland.

For further information contact Park Superintendent, 12521 Lee Highway, Manassas 22110; or phone 703/361-1339.

Park (daily; closed Dec 25). ¢

What to See and Do

1. **Visitor Center.** On Henry Hill, just N of I-66 off VA 234. Hill affords view of much of battlefield. Information; self-guided tours start here (walking tour of First Manassas, driving tour of Second Manassas). Markers throughout park explain various aspects of battles. Ranger-conducted tours in summer. In same building is

   Battlefield Museum. Exhibits present stories of battles; audiovisual presentations of background information. (Daily; closed Dec 25)

2. **Stone Bridge.** Where Union artillery opened the battle of First Manassas; it afforded an avenue of escape for the Union troops after both First and Second Manassas.

3. **Unfinished Railroad.** Fully graded railroad bed, never completed, behind which Stonewall Jackson's men were positioned during the second battle.

4. **Chinn House Ruins.** The house served as a field hospital in both engagements and marked the left of the Confederate line at First Manassas; also the scene of Longstreet's counterattack at Second Manassas.

5. **Dogan House.** An original structure at Groveton, a village that gave its name to the second day's battle of Second Manassas.

6. **Stone House.** Originally a tavern, used as field hospital in both battles. (Summer, daily)

(For accommodations see Falls Church, Manassas)

Marion (F-3)

Founded: 1835 **Pop:** 6,630 **Elev:** 2,178 ft **Area code:** 703 **Zip:** 24354

This popular vacation spot is surrounded by Jefferson National Forest, abounding in game and birds, near a state park, and high enough to promise an invigorating climate. It was named for General Francis Marion, known during the American Revolution as the "Swamp Fox."

What to See and Do

1. **Hungry Mother State Park.** 3 mi N on VA 16. More than 2,180 acres amid the mountains with a 108-acre lake; panoramic views. Swimming beach, bathhouse; fishing; boating (rentals, launching, electric motors only). Hiking, self-guided trails; horseback riding (rentals). Picnicking, cafe, concession. Tent & trailer sites (electrical hookups, late May-Sept), cabins (mid-May-Sept). Hilltop visitor center, interpretive programs. Standard fees. Phone 783-3422. Parking ¢

2. **Jefferson National Forest.** A 705,000-acre area. Camping, fishing, hiking, mountain bike & bridle trails, picnicking and hunting are good throughout the recreation areas in the forest. Fees may be charged at recreation sites. (Daily) For information contact Supervisor, 6152 Valley Point Pkwy, Roanoke 24019; 800/446-9670. SE of town via VA 16 is the

   Mount Rogers National Recreation Area. A 117,000-acre area that includes Mount Rogers, the state's highest point (5,729 ft), mile-high open meadows known as "balds," and a great variety of animals and plants. Swimming, fishing, hunting, camping (fee at some areas), three visitor centers, approx 400 miles of hiking, bicycle & bridle trails. Mount Rogers Scenic Byway (auto); Virginia Creeper Trail (hikers, bicycles, horses) follows an abandoned railroad grade through spectacular river gorges. Adj to Grayson Highlands State Park (see ABINGDON). (Summer, daily; rest of yr, Mon-Fri) Some fees. Phone 783-5196. **Free.**

(For further information contact the Smyth County Chamber of Commerce, 124 W Main St, Box 924; 783-3161.)

Annual Event

Hungry Mother Arts and Crafts Festival. Hungry Mother State Park (see #1). Mid-July.

(See Abingdon, Wytheville)

Motel

✔ ★ ★ **HOLIDAY INN.** 1424 N Main St. 703/783-3193; FAX 703/783-3193, ext. 184. 120 rms, 1-3 story. S $46-$58; D $52-$64; each addl $4; under 18 free. Crib free. TV; cable. Pool. Restaurant 6:30 am-10 pm. Rm serv. Bar 5 pm-midnight, closed Sun. Coin lndry. Meeting rms. Bellhops. Valet serv. Cr cds: A, C, D, DS, ER, JCB, MC, V.

Inn

★ ★ **FOX HILL.** (Rte 2, Box 1-A-1, Troutdale 24378) 20 mi S via VA 16, then follow sign. 703/677-3313; res: 800/874-3313. 8 rms, 2 story. No A/C. No rm phones. S, D $65; each addl $5; under 18 free; wkly rates. Crib free. TV in sitting rm. Complimentary full bkfst, coffee. Restaurant nearby. Ck-out 10 am, ck-in 3 pm. X-country ski 5 mi.

Situated on mountain top with panoramic view. On 70 acres of woods & pasture land; wildlife, farm animals; hiking trails. Cr cds: DS, MC, V.

Martinsville (F-5)

Founded: 1793 **Pop:** 16,162 **Elev:** 1,020 ft **Area code:** 703

Martinsville was named for Joseph Martin, a pioneer who settled here in 1773. Henry County takes it name from Patrick Henry, who lived here. When Henry County Court first opened in October 1776, 640 residents pledged an oath of allegiance to the United States; 40 refused to renounce allegiance to England. Located near the beautiful Blue Ridge Mountains, this industrial community is home to Bassett Furniture, E. I. duPont de Nemours and textile plants.

What to See and Do

1. **Virginia Museum of Natural History.** 1001 Douglas Ave. State museum focuses on preservation, study and interpretation of Virginia's natural heritage. Features visual and hands-on exhibits; includes a computer-animated triceratops dinosaur and a life-size ground sloth model. Special events during the year include Earth Day (Apr) and Virginia Indian Festival (Sept). (Daily exc Mon; closed Jan 1, Thanksgiving, Dec 25) Phone 666-8600. **Free.**

2. **Blue Ridge Farm Museum.** VA 40 in Ferrum. Presents the heritage of mountain region through reconstructed farmsteads and "folklife galleries." Authentic buildings from 1800 German-heritage farm, including log house, kitchen, blacksmith shop and barn. Costumed interpreters demonstrate farm and household chores. (May-Aug, wkends; rest of yr, by appt) Phone 365-4415. ¢¢

3. **Fairy Stone State Park.** 21 mi NW via US 220/VA 57, VA 346. Consists of 4,570 acres, with a 168-acre lake (see #4) adjoining Philpott Reservoir. Nestled in the foothills of the Blue Ridge Mountains, this park is named for the "fairy stones" (staurolites) found near the southern tip of its boundary. Swimming beach, bathhouse; boating (launch, rentals, electric motors only). Hiking, bicycle trails. Picnic shelters, concession, cafe. Tent & trailer sites (dump station, electrical hookups), cabins (May-Sept). Visitor center, evening programs. Standard fees. Access for the disabled to bathhouse, lake, picnic shelter. (Daily) Phone 930-2424.

4. **Philpott Lake.** Just NE of Fairy Stone State Park. State's fourth largest lake, formed by Philpott Dam, a US Army Corps of Engineers project. Swimming, skindiving; waterskiing, boating, fishing. Hunting, hiking, picnicking; 5 camping areas (Apr-Oct; one area free). Some fees. Phone 629-2703.

(For further information contact the Martinsville-Henry County Chamber of Commerce, 115 Broad St, PO Box 709, 24114; 632-6401.)

Annual Event

Blue Ridge Folklife Festival. Held at Blue Ridge Farm Museum (see #2). Gospel, blues and string band music; traditional regional crafts; regional foods; quilt show, antique autos, steam & gas-powered farm equipment. Sports events include horse-pulling & log-skidding contests, coon dog swimming and treeing contests. Phone 365-4415. Late Oct.

Seasonal Event

Stock car races. Martinsville Speedway. 3 mi S. Phone 956-3151. "Miller Genuine Draft 500," mid-Mar. "Hanes 500," late Apr. "Goody's 500," late Sept. "Winston Classic," mid-Oct.

(See Danville)

Motels

✔ ★ ★ **BEST WESTERN.** *PO Box 1183 (24114), on US 220N.* 703/632-5611; FAX 703/632-1168. 97 rms, 2 story, 20 suites. S $38; D $44; each addl $6; suites $42-$48; under 13 free; wkly, monthly rates; higher rates Mar-Apr & Sept-Oct. Crib free. TV. Pool; wading pool. Complimentary coffee in rms. Restaurant 6 am-10 pm; Sat, Sun from 7 am; closed Sun dinner. Rm serv. Bar 4 pm-midnight. Ck-out noon. Coin lndry. Meeting rms. Valet serv. Sundries. Exercise equipt; weight machine, treadmill. Cr cds: A, C, D, DS, MC, V.

✔ ★ ★ **DUTCH INN.** *(633 Virginia Ave, Collinsville 24078) 1¼ mi N on US 220 Business.* 703/647-3721; FAX 703/647-4857. 150 rms, 2 story. S $44-$86; D $51-$92; each addl $6; suites $85-$125; studio rms $49-$67; under 16 free; higher rates race wks. Crib free. Pet accepted. TV; cable. Pool; poolside serv. Restaurant 6 am-10:30 pm. Rm serv. Bar 4 pm-midnight. Ck-out noon. Meeting rms. Valet serv. Sundries. 18-hole golf privileges. Exercise equipt; bicycle, treadmill, sauna. Many bathrm phones, refrigerators. Cr cds: A, C, D, DS, MC, V.

McLean (C-8)

Pop: 38,168 **Elev:** 300 ft **Area code:** 703

What to See and Do

1. **Claude Moore Colonial Farm** at Turkey Run. 2 mi E on VA 193 (Georgetown Pike). Demonstration of 1770s low-income working farm; costumed interpreters work with crops and animals using 18th-century techniques. (Apr-mid-Dec, Wed-Sun weather permitting; closed Thanksgiving) Phone 442-7557. ¢

2. **Colvin Run Mill Park.** 3 mi W via VA 123, then 5 mi NW via VA 7, on Colvin Run Rd in Great Falls. Tours of historical gristmill. Operating general store, miller's house exhibit, barn and grounds (free). (Mar-Dec, daily exc Tues; rest of yr, wkends; closed Jan 1, Thanksgiving, Dec 25) Phone 759-2771. Tours ¢¢

3. **Evans Farm.** Chain Bridge Rd, on VA 123, 1 mi E of I-495 McLean-VA 123N exit 11. Approx 25 acres of farmland. Colonial atmosphere; 18th-century-style building with restaurant (see). Collection of early American cooking utensils; Robert E. Lee memorabilia. Country store, handcraft and doll shop, old mill. Farm animals for children to feed. (Daily) Phone 356-8000. **Free.**

(For further information contact the Fairfax County Visitor Center, 7764 Armistead Rd, Suite 160, Lorton 22079; 550-2450 or 800/7-FAIRFAX.)

(For accommodations see Arlington County, Fairfax, Falls Church, Tysons Corner; also see District of Columbia & Rockville, MD)

Restaurants

✔ ★ **ANGKOR WAT.** *6703 Lowell Ave, at Old Dominion Dr (VA 309), in shopping center.* 703/893-6077. Hrs: 11 am-2:30 pm, 5-9:30 pm; Fri, Sat to 10 pm; Sun 5-9:30 pm. Closed some major hols. Res accepted. Far Eastern menu. Wine, beer. Semi-a la carte: lunch $5.25-$6.95, dinner $6.95-$9.95. Complete meals: dinner $12.99. Specializes in Cambodian soup, char-broiled dishes, kuong. Cr cds: A, C, D, MC, V.

★ ★ **CHARLEY'S PLACE.** *6930 Old Dominion Dr, jct VA 123 & VA 309/738.* 703/893-1034. Hrs: 11:15 am-10 pm; Fri, Sat to 10:30 pm; Sun 10:30 am-9 pm; early-bird dinner 4-6:30 pm; Sun brunch 10:30 am-2 pm. Closed Dec 25. Res accepted. Bar to 1 am. Semi-a la carte: lunch $5.95-$10.95, dinner $5.95-$18.95. Child's meals. Spe-

cialties: regional dishes. Outdoor dining. Parking. Fireplaces. Cr cds: A, C, D, DS, MC, V.

★ ★ ★ **DANTE RISTORANTE.** *(1148 Walker Rd, Great Falls)* 703/759-3131. Hrs: 11:30 am-2:30 pm, 5:30-10:30 pm; Sat from 5:30 pm; Sun 4-9 pm. Closed Jan 1, Thanksgiving, Dec 25. Res accepted; required Fri, Sat. Northern Italian menu. Bar. Wine list. A la carte entrees: lunch $8.25-$14.25, dinner $13.25-$21.95. Child's meals. Specialties: grilled Dover sole, grilled veal chops. Own pasta & bread. Parking. Patio dining. Converted country house. Cr cds: A, C, D, MC, V.

★ ★ ★ **EVANS FARM INN.** 1696 Chain Bridge Rd. 703/356-8000. Hrs: 11:30 am-2:30 pm, 5-11 pm; Sat 11:30 am-3 pm, 5-11 pm; Sun 11 am-9 pm; Sun brunch to 2 pm. Closed Dec 25. Res accepted; required Fri-Sun. Bar to 11 pm; Fri, Sat to midnight. Semi-a la carte: lunch $8.95-$10.95, dinner $12.95-$23.95. Buffet (Mon-Fri): lunch $9.95. Sun brunch $6.95-$12.25. Child's meals. Specializes in barbecued baby spare ribs, Virginia ham, fresh seafood, colonial-era cooking. Own baking. Salad bar. Parking. 18th century-style inn. Family-owned. Cr cds: A, C, D, DS, JCB, MC, V.

★ ★ ★ **FALLS LANDING.** *(774 Walker Rd, Great Falls) I-495 exit 13A, in Village Center.* 703/759-4650. Hrs: 11:30 am-2:30 pm, 5:30-10 pm; Fri to 10:30 pm; Sat 5:30-10:30 pm; Sun 4-9 pm. Closed most major hols. Res accepted. Bar. Semi-a la carte: lunch $8.95-$12.95, dinner $16.95-$24.95. Child's meals. Specializes in seafood, veal, beef. Outdoor dining. 18th-century colonial-style decor; beamed ceiling, century-old pine paneling. Cr cds: A, C, D, DS, MC, V.

★ ★ ★ ★ **L'AUBERGE CHEZ FRANCOIS.** *(332 Springvale Rd, Great Falls) 4 mi N of jct VA 7 & 674N.* 703/759-3800. Hrs: 5:30-9:30 pm; Sun 2-8 pm. Closed Mon; Jan 1, July 4, Dec 25. Res required. French menu. Serv bar. Wine cellar. Table d'hôte: dinner $30-$36. Specialties: salmon soufflé de l'Auberge, le sauté gourmandise de l'Auberge, la choucroute royale garnie comme en Alsace, Alsatian dishes. Own baking, ice cream. Outdoor dining. Chef-owned. Jacket. Cr cds: A, C, D, MC, V.

★ ★ ★ **LA MIRABELLE.** 6645 Old Dominion Dr, in McLean Square Shopping Ctr. 703/893-8484. Hrs: 11:30 am-2 pm, 5-9 pm; Sat from 5 pm; Sun 5-8 pm. Closed major hols; also Sun May-mid-Oct. French menu. Bar. A la carte entrees: lunch $8.95-$16.75, dinner $14.95-$22. Specialties vary with season: seafood, venison (Nov, Dec), goose (Christmas). Own desserts. Pianist Mon-Fri. Parking. Cr cds: A, C, D, DS, MC, V.

★ ★ ★ **SERBIAN CROWN.** *(1141 Walker Rd, Great Falls) 5 mi W on VA 7, then ½ mi N on VA 743.* 703/759-4150. Hrs: 11:30 am-2:30 pm, 5:30-10 pm; Mon from 5:30 pm; Sat 5:30-11 pm; Sun 4-9:30 pm; early-bird dinner Mon-Fri 5:30-6:45 pm. Res accepted; required Fri-Sun. Russian, Serbian, French menu. Bar. Wine list. A la carte entrees: lunch $9.50-$15.95, dinner $16.95-$26. Specialties: kulebiaka (Russian salmon), seasonal game. Extensive vodka selection. Gypsy music Wed-Sun. Parking. Intimate atmosphere; antique Russian paintings. Enclosed, heated terrace dining. Family-owned. Jacket. Cr cds: A, MC, V.

★ ★ **SITTING DUCK PUB.** 1696 Chain Bridge Rd (22102), in basement of Evans Farm Inn Restaurant. 703/356-8000. Hrs: 11:30 am-2 pm, 5-11 pm; Sat from 5 pm; Sun 11 am-2 pm. Closed Dec 25. Res accepted. Continental menu. Bar. Semi-a la carte: lunch $7.95-$10.95, dinner $13.95-$23.95. Sun brunch $7.25-$9.95. Specializes in barbecue, beef, seafood. Pianist Fri-Sun. Parking. Large stone fireplace. Colonial-era prints. Family-owned. Cr cds: A, C, D, DS, JCB, MC, V.

Monterey (D-6)

Pop: 222 **Elev:** 2,881 ft **Area code:** 703 **Zip:** 24465

What to See and Do

Maple Museum. S on US 220. Covers the history of sugar making from the most primitive to the most modern methods. (Daily) **Free.**

(For further information contact the Highland County Chamber of Commerce, PO Box 223; 468-2550.)

Annual Event

Highland Maple Festival. Tours of sugar camps; demonstrations of sugar syrup making, crafts; showing and sale of antiques; antique sugar-making equipment on display; tasting. 2nd & 3rd wkend Mar.

(See Staunton, Warm Springs)

Motel

★ **MONTVALLEE.** *Box 25, at jct US 220, 250. 703/468-2500.* 14 rms, 2 story. No A/C. S $25-$30; D $35-$40; each addl $2-$4. TV; some B/W. Restaurant nearby. Ck-out 11 am. No cr cds accepted.

D 🔥

Inn

★★ **HIGHLAND INN.** *Main St, jct of US 220, 250. 703/468-2143.* 17 rms, 2 story. No A/C. S, D $55-$75; suites $75. TV, some B/W; cable. Dining rm 6-8 pm; Sun 11 am-2 pm; closed Mon & Tues. Ck-out 11 am, ck-in after 2 pm. Meeting rm. Porches. Victorian building furnished with period antiques. Built 1904. Cr cds: MC, V.

🔀 🔥 SC

Montross (D-9)

Pop: 359 **Elev:** 149 ft **Area code:** 804 **Zip:** 22520

What to See and Do

1. **Stratford Hall Plantation.** 6 mi N on VA 3 to Lerty, then E on VA 214. Boyhood home of Richard Henry Lee and Francis Lightfoot Lee and birthplace of General Robert E. Lee. Center of restored, working plantation is monumental Georgian house, built circa 1735, famous for its uniquely grouped chimney stacks. Interiors span approximately 100-year period and feature a federal-era parlor and neo-classical paneling in the Great Hall. Flanking dependencies include, kitchen, plantation office and gardener's house. Boxwood garden; 18th- & 19th-century carriages; working mill; visitor center with museum, slide presentations. (Daily; closed Dec 25) Plantation luncheon (Apr-Oct, daily). Sr citizen rate. Phone 493-8038. ¢¢

2. **Westmoreland State Park.** 5 mi NW on VA 3, then N on VA 347. Approx 1,300 acres on Potomac River. Sand beach, swimming pool, bathhouse; fishing, boating (ramp, rentals). Hiking trails. Picnicking, playground, concession. Camping, tent & trailer sites (May-Sept; dump station, electrical hookups), cabins (May-Sept). Visitor center, evening programs. Access for the disabled to visitor center & swimming complex. Standard fees. Phone 493-8821.

Inn

★★★ **MONTROSS.** *Box 908, Courthouse Square. 804/493-9097.* 6 rms, 3 story. S, D $65-$75; each addl $10; MAP avail wkends. TV; cable. Complimentary continental bkfst, coffee, brandy. Dining rm (open to public), 5-8 pm; Fri & Sat to 9 pm; Sun noon-8 pm. Rm serv. Bar. Ck-out noon, ck-in 2 pm. Originally built 1683. Four-poster beds, original antiques, primitive and modern art. Grand piano on main floor. Balcony. Tennis adj. Cr cds: A, DS, MC, V.

Mount Vernon (C-8)

Area code: 703 **Zip:** 22121

(16 mi S of Washington, DC on Mt Vernon Memorial Hwy)

What to See and Do

1. **Mount Vernon.** George Washington brought his gracious and beautiful bride here in 1759 and, with characteristic and ingenious industry, began his plan to become the leading scientific farmer in America. He kept elaborate notes, conferred with many other farmers, tried crop rotation and other new experiments, added to the house, which became a stately Georgian-colonial mansion, and planned for the family that nature unhappily denied him. He and Mrs. Washington brought up her two children by a previous marriage and raised two of her grandchildren.

   The nucleus of the existing house was built in approximately 1735 by Augustine Washington, George's father. George acquired it in 1754, after the death of his half-brother, Lawrence.

   Family, home and farm became the focal point of Washington's life. But he was a great patriot as well as a brilliant planner, and when he was called in 1775 to lead the armies of the country he loved, he did not hesitate. When he had won freedom for his fellow Americans he returned, determined to live as he wished. But four years later he was called to preside at the Constitutional Convention in Philadelphia and in 1789 became the new nation's first president. From March, 1797, until his death on December 14, 1799, he lived again at Mount Vernon. He and Martha Washington are buried here.

   Mount Vernon has been accurately restored to its appearance in the last year of Washington's life, from the paint colors on the walls to the actual arrangement of the furnishings, many of which are original. The estate has been owned and maintained by the Mount Vernon Ladies' Association since 1858 and was, in effect, the nation's first tourist attraction of historic interest. Gift shop, restaurant nearby (see MOUNT VERNON INN RESTAURANT). (Daily) Sr citizen rate. Phone 780-2000. ¢¢¢

   Spirit of Washington offers round-trip, Potomac River cruises from Washington, DC to Mount Vernon; the stay is sufficient for a complete tour of house, gardens and tomb (mid-March-mid-Oct, 2 trips daily). For rates phone 202/554-8000.

2. **Woodlawn Plantation** (1800-1805). 3 mi W of George Washington Pkwy on US 1. In 1799 George Washington gave 2,000 acres of land as a wedding present to Eleanor Parke Custis, his foster daughter, who married his nephew, Major Lawrence Lewis. Dr. William Thornton, first architect of the US Capitol, then designed this mansion. The Lewises entertained such notables as Andrew Jackson, Henry Clay and the Marquis de Lafayette. The house was restored in the early 1900s and later became the residence of a US senator; 19th-century period rooms; many original furnishings. Formal gardens. (Feb-Dec, daily; rest of yr, wkends; closed Jan 1, Thanksgiving, Dec 25) National Trust for Historic Preservation property. Sr citizen rate. Phone 780-4000. ¢¢

Frank Lloyd Wright's Pope-Leighey House (1940). Erected in Falls Church in 1940, the house was disassembled (due to the construction of a new highway) and rebuilt at the present site in 1964. Built of cypress, brick and glass, the house is an example of Wright's "Usonian" structures, which he proposed as a prototype of affordable housing for Depression-era middle-income families; original Wright-designed furniture. (Mar-Dec, daily; rest of yr, wkends only; closed Thanksgiving, Dec 25) National Trust for Historic Preservation property. Sr citizen rate. Combination ticket for both houses available. Phone 780-4000. **¢¢**

3. **Grist Mill Historical State Park.** 3 mi W on VA 235. This mill was reconstructed in 1930 on original foundation of a mill George Washington operated on Dogue Run. Visitor center, programs. (Memorial Day-Labor Day, daily) Phone 780-3383. **¢**

(For accommodations see Alexandria, Fairfax, Springfield; also see District of Columbia)

Restaurant

★ ★ **MOUNT VERNON INN.** *On grounds of Mount Vernon, S end of George Washington Pkwy.* 703/780-0011. Hrs: 11 am-3:30 pm, 5-9 pm; Sun to 4 pm. Res accepted. Bar. A la carte entrees: lunch $4.25-$7.25, dinner $12-$17.50. Child's meals. Specializes in mesquite-grilled seafood, game dishes. Own desserts. Parking. Waiters in colonial costume. Hand-painted murals of colonial scenes. Cr cds: A, DS, MC, V.

D

Natural Bridge (E-6)

Founded: 1774 **Pop:** 200 (est) **Elev:** 1,078 ft **Area code:** 703 **Zip:** 24578

Native Americans worshipped the stone bridge that nature formed across a deep gorge; town and county were both named after it. The limestone arch, 215 feet high, 90 feet long and 150 feet wide in some places, attracted the interest of Thomas Jefferson, who purchased the bridge and 157 surrounding acres from King George III for 20 shillings, about $2.49, in 1774. Fully appreciative of this natural wonder, Jefferson built a cabin for visitors and installed caretakers. His guest book reads like a colonial "Who's Who." Surveyed by George Washington, and painted by many famous artists, the bridge easily accommodates US Highway 11. The Glenwood Ranger District of the Jefferson National Forest has its office in Natural Bridge.

What to See and Do

1. **Natural Bridge.** Jct US 11 & VA 130; I-81, exit 175 or 180. Self-guided tours (1 hr). (Daily) **¢¢¢** Ticket includes entrance to

   Drama of Creation. Musical presentation, viewed from beneath Natural Bridge, includes light show cast under and across arch. (Nightly) Combination tickets can also include

   Caverns of Natural Bridge. More than 300 feet below ground on three levels; streams, hanging gardens of formations, flowstone cascade, totem pole, colossal dome and more. One-mile guided tour (1 hr). (Mar-Nov, daily) **¢¢¢**

2. **Natural Bridge Wax Museum.** US 11 and VA 130. Wax figures depicting local history; self-guided factory tours. (Daily) Phone 291-2426. **¢¢¢**

3. **Cave Mountain Lake Recreation Area.** 7 mi S via VA 130, right on VA 759, then right on Forest Service Road 781 in Jefferson National Forest. Swimming. Picnicking. Camping **¢¢¢**. (May-Oct) Phone 291-2189 or 265-6054. **¢**

(For further information contact Natural Bridge Village, PO Box 57; 291-2121 or 800/533-1410.)

(See Lexington)

Motel

★ **WATTSTULL.** *(Rte 1, Box 21, Buchanan 24066)* 8 mi S on US 11; I-81 exit 168. 703/254-1551. 26 rms. S, D $38-$44; each addl $4. Crib $4. Pet accepted. TV. Pool; wading pool. Restaurant 6 am-10 pm. Ck-out 11 am. Panoramic view of Shenandoah Valley. Cr cds: MC, V.

Hotel

✔ ★ ★ **NATURAL BRIDGE HOTEL & STONEWALL INN.** *I-81 exits 175 & 180, at jct US 11, VA 130.* 703/291-2121; res: 800/533-1410; FAX 703/291-1551. 180 rms in hotel & inn. S, D $30-$80; under 18 free. Crib free. Pet accepted. TV; cable. Indoor pool. Restaurant 7 am-9:30 pm. Bar. Ck-out noon. Meeting rms. Tennis. Miniature golf. Game rm. Cr cds: A, D, DS, MC, V.

New Market (C-7)

Settled: 1761 **Pop:** 1,435 **Elev:** 1,060 ft **Area code:** 703 **Zip:** 22844

New Market, situated in the Shenandoah Valley, gained its niche in Virginia history on May 15, 1864, when, in desperation, Confederate General Breckinridge ordered the cadets from Lexington's Virginia Military Institute to join the battle against the forces of General Franz Sigel. The oldest was 20, but they entered the fray fearlessly, taking prisoners and capturing a battery. Their heroism inspired the Confederate defeat of Sigel's seasoned troops.

What to See and Do

1. **Shenandoah Caverns.** 4 mi N, off I-81 exit 269. Elevator lowers visitors 220 feet to large subterranean rooms, fascinating rock formations; snack bar, picnic areas. Interior a constant 56°F. (Daily; closed Dec 25) Sr citizen rate. Phone 477-3115. **¢¢¢**

2. **Endless Caverns.** Via I-81, exit 257 or 264, then approx 3 mi on US 11 to entrance. Lighted display of unusual rock formations; stalagmites and stalactites, columns, shields, flowstone and limestone pendants, presented in natural color. Temperature 55°F summer & winter. Camping. Guided tours (75 min). (Daily; closed Dec 25) Sr citizen rate. Phone 896-CAVE. **¢¢¢**

3. **New Market Battlefield Historical Park.** 1 mi N of I-81 exit 264. Site of Civil War Battle of New Market (May 15, 1864), in which 257 VMI cadets played a decisive role. Original Bushong farmhouse and outbuildings restored, period furnishings. Hall of Valor; exhibits; films. Scenic overlooks, walking tour. (Daily; closed Jan 1, Thanksgiving, Dec 25) Phone 740-3101. **¢¢** Also here is

   New Market Battlefield Military Museum. Rte 305 (Collins Dr), 1/4 mi N of I-81 exit 264. Located on actual site of Battle of New Market, the museum houses a private collection of more than 2,000 military artifacts and genuine, personal artifacts of the American soldier from 1776 to the present. Includes uniforms, weapons, battlefield diaries, medals, mementos; film (30 min). Book shop has more than 500 titles, some antique. Union & Confederate troop position markers are on museum grounds. (Mid-Mar-Nov, daily) Sr citizen rate. Phone 740-8065. **¢¢**

(For further information contact the Shenandoah Valley Travel Association, PO Box 1040; 740-3132. Information Center adj to I-81, exit 264.)

(See Basye, Harrisonburg, Luray)

Motels

✔ ★ **BATTLEFIELD.** *Rte 1, Box 127, 1 mi N on US 11; I-81 exit 264. 703/740-3105; res: 800/296-6835.* 14 rms. Mid-Apr-mid-Nov: S $24-$34; D $28-$40; each addl $3; under 12 free; higher rates special events; lower rates rest of yr. Crib $3. TV; cable. Playground. Complimentary coffee in rms. Restaurant nearby. Ck-out 11 am. Refrigerators. Picnic tables. Cr cds: A, C, D, DS, MC, V.

★ ★ **QUALITY INN SHENANDOAH VALLEY.** *PO Box 100, on VA 211 at I-81 exit 264. 703/740-3141; FAX 703/740-3250.* 101 rms, 2 story. May-Oct: S $50-$55; D $56-$71; each addl $6; lower rates rest of yr. Crib free. TV; cable. Pool; sauna. Playground. Restaurant 6:30 am-9 pm. Rm serv. Bar from 5 pm. Ck-out noon. Coin lndry. Meeting rms. Sundries. Gift shops. Golf privileges. Game rm. Miniature golf. Tennis nearby. Cr cds: A, C, D, DS, ER, MC, V.

✔ ★ ★ **SHENVALEE.** *PO Box 930, I-81 exit 264, at jct US 11. 703/740-3181; FAX 703/740-8931.* 42 rms, 1-2 story. Apr-early Nov: S $36-$50; D $44-$60; each addl $7.50; under 13 free; golf plan; lower rates rest of yr. Crib $5. TV; cable. Pool; wading pool. Restaurant 7 am-9 pm; Sun to 8 pm. Bar 4:30 pm-midnight; wkends to 2 am. Ck-out 1 pm. Meeting rms. Sundries. Tennis. Golf, greens fee $18-$20, putting green, driving range. Balconies. Picnic tables. On 200 acres. Cr cds: A, C, D, MC, V.

Newport News (F-9)

Settled: 1619 **Pop:** 170,045 **Elev:** 25 ft **Area code:** 804

One of the three cities (also see NORFOLK and PORTSMOUTH) that make up the Port of Hampton Roads, Newport News has the world's largest shipbuilding company, the Newport News Shipbuilding Company. Hampton Roads, 14 miles long and 40 feet deep, formed by the James, York, Elizabeth and Nansemond rivers as they pass into Chesapeake Bay, is one of the world's finest natural harbors. The largest ships are accommodated at Newport News docks; huge tonnages of coal, ore, tobacco and grain are shipped from the port annually. During the two world wars it was a vitally important point of embarkation and supply. The area still has many important defense establishments.

Newport News is located on the historic Virginia Peninsula, 25 miles long and 8 to 10 miles wide. The peninsula contains Hampton, Yorktown, Jamestown and Williamsburg. Some of the earliest landings in this country were here. The name of the town is said to derive from the good "news" of the arrival of Captain Christopher Newport, who brought supplies and additional colonists to the settlement at Jamestown.

What to See and Do

1. **The Mariners' Museum.** Jct US 60 & Clyde Morris Blvd; 2¹/₂ mi off I-64 exit 258-A. Exhibits and displays represent 3,000 years of nautical history; ship models, figureheads, scrimshaw, paintings, decorative arts, and small craft. Gallery highlighting life and career of illustrious British naval hero Admiral Horatio Nelson; Age of Exploration Gallery chronicles advancements in shipbuilding, ocean navigation and cartography that led to early transoceanic exploration. The Chesapeake Bay Gallery exhibits Native American artifacts, workboats, racing shells, an interactive computer game, a working steam engine, and hundreds of artifacts and photos that tell the story of this great body of water. The Crabtree Collection of Miniature Ships showcases 16 detailed miniatures that illustrate the evolution of the sailing ship. A short film, *Mariner,* introduces the visitor to maritime activities from around the world. Historical interpreters; research library; gift gallery. A 550-acre

park on the James River features the 5-mile Noland Trail, with 14 pedestrian bridges; picnic area. Special events include Festival in the Park (June) and Christmas at The Mariners' (Dec 26 & 27). Guided tours. (Daily; closed Dec 25) Sr citizen rate. Phone 595-0368. ¢¢

2. **Peninsula Fine Arts Center.** 101 Museum Dr. Changing bi-monthly exhibits ranging from national traveling exhibitions to regional artists; classes, workshops and special events. (Daily exc Mon; closed major hols) Donation. Phone 596-8175.

3. **War Memorial Museum of Virginia.** 9285 Warwick Blvd in Huntington Park, on US 60. More than 60,000 artifacts, including weapons, uniforms, vehicles, posters, insignia and accoutrements relating to every major US military involvement from the Revolution to the Vietnam War. Military history library and film collection. (Mon-Sat, also Sun afternoons; closed Jan 1, Thanksgiving, Dec 25) Sr citizen rate. Phone 247-8523. ¢

4. **Virginia Living Museum.** 524 J. Clyde Morris Blvd, I-64 to exit 258A. Exhibits on natural science; wildlife, all native to Virginia, living in natural habitats; indoor & outdoor aviaries; aquariums; planetarium with daily shows; observatory; living model of the James River. (Daily; closed Jan 1, Thanksgiving, Dec 24 & 25) Sr citizen rate. Phone 595-1900. ¢¢

5. **Harbor Cruises at Wharton's Wharf.** Located midway between Williamsburg and Virginia Beach. Narrated sightseeing cruises (2 hrs); evening dinner cruises (4 hrs); Intracoastal Waterway cruises (8 hrs). (Apr-Oct) For schedule and information phone 245-1533. ¢¢¢¢

6. **Newport News Park.** Jct VA 105, 143. Facilities of this 8,330-acre park include freshwater fishing; canoes, paddleboats, boat rentals; history, nature trails; bicycle paths (bicycle rentals); archery; arboretum; interpretive center; picnicking; two 18-hole golf courses; 188 campsites. (All yr) Some fees. Also here is a Tourist Information Center. Phone 888-3333. **Free.** Camping ¢¢¢-¢¢¢¢¢

7. **Fort Eustis.** NW end of city on Mulberry Island. Headquarters of US Army Transportation Center. Self-guided automobile tour available; brochures at front gate. Phone 878-4920. **Free.** On grounds is

Army Transportation Museum. Depicts development of army transportation from 1776 to the present; flying saucer, amphibious vehicles, trucks, helicopters, mementos. (Daily; closed major hols) Phone 878-1182. **Free.**

(For further information contact the Newport News Dept of Recreation, Parks and Public Relations, City Hall, 23607; or the Virginia Peninsula Tourism & Conference Bureau, 8 San Jose Dr, Suite 3-B, 23606, phone 873-0092 or 800/333-7787.)

(See Hampton, Norfolk, Portsmouth, Virginia Beach, Yorktown)

Motels

★ **COMFORT INN.** *12330 Jefferson Ave (23602), at Patrick Henry Mall. 804/249-0200; FAX 804/249-4736.* 125 rms, 3 story. May-Sept: S $57; D $64; each addl $7; under 18 free; lower rates rest of yr. Crib free. Pet accepted. TV; cable, in-rm movies avail. Pool. Complimentary continental bkfst. Complimentary coffee in lobby. Restaurant adj 11 am-midnight. Ck-out noon. Coin lndry. Meeting rms. Free airport transportation. Health club privileges. Some refrigerators. Cr cds: A, C, D, DS, ER, JCB, MC, V.

✔ ★ ★ **DAYS INN.** *14747 Warwick Blvd (23602). 804/874-0201; FAX 804/874-0201, ext. 281.* 117 rms, 2 story. June-Sept: S $38-$46; D $42-$52; each addl $5; kit. units $42-$52; under 18 free; lower rates rest of yr. Crib free. Pet accepted, some restrictions; $5. TV; cable. Pool. Playground. Complimentary coffee in rms. Restaurant 6 am-11 pm. Ck-out 11 am. Coin lndry. Valet serv. Refrigerators. Picnic area with grills. Cr cds: A, C, D, DS, ER, MC, V.

✔ ★ **MOTEL 6.** *797 J. Clyde Morris Blvd (23601). 804/595-6336.* 117 units. June-Sept: S $27.99; D $31.99; each addl $2; under 16 free; lower rates rest of yr. Crib free. Pet accepted, some restrictions. TV. Pool. Restaurant nearby. Ck-out noon. Cr cds: A, C, D, DS, MC, V.

D ✔ ≋ ⋈ 🔥 SC

Hotel

★ ★ ★ **OMNI.** *1000 Omni Blvd (23606). 804/873-6664; FAX 804/873-1732.* 183 rms, 9 story. S $89; D $99; each addl $10; under 18 free. Crib avail. TV; cable. Indoor pool; poolside serv. Restaurant 6:30 am-11 pm. Bar 11-2 am; entertainment Wed-Sat, dancing. Ck-out noon. Meeting rms. Gift shop. Free airport transportation. Exercise equipt; weights, bicycles, whirlpool, sauna. 3-story atrium. Cr cds: A, C, D, DS, MC, V.

D ≋ ✗ ⋈ 🔥 SC

Restaurants

✔ ★ ★ **DAS WALDCAFE.** *12529 Warwick Blvd. 804/930-1781.* Hrs: 11:30 am-2 pm, 5-10 pm; Sat from 4 pm; Sun 11:30 am-9 pm. Closed Mon; hols. Res accepted. German menu. Bar. Semi-a la carte: lunch, dinner $3.50-$11.95. Specialties: schnitzel, rouladen, hazelnut cake. Parking. Guest rms avail. Cr cds: A, C, D, MC, V.

★ ★ **HERMAN'S HARBOR HOUSE.** *663 Deep Creek Rd. 804/930-1000.* Hrs: 11:30 am-2:30 pm, 5-10 pm; Sat from 5 pm; Sun brunch 11 am-3 pm. Closed Dec 25. Res accepted. Bar. Semi-a la carte: lunch $2.75-$8.95, dinner $7.95-$23.95. Specializes in local seafood, crab cakes, steak. Parking. Nautical decor. Cr cds: A, MC, V.

D SC

★ ★ **PORT ARTHUR.** *11137 Warwick Blvd. 804/599-6474.* Hrs: 11:30 am-10 pm; Fri, Sat to 10:30 pm; Sun noon-10 pm; Sun buffet noon-3 pm, 5:30-9 pm. Closed Thanksgiving, Dec 25. Res accepted. Chinese, Amer menu. Bar. Semi-a la carte: lunch $3.50-$4.95, dinner $5-$14.50. Complete meals: dinner $17.50-$63. Buffet (Sun): lunch, dinner $7.95. Child's meals. Specializes in Phoenix nest, steak & lobster kew. Parking. Family-owned. Cr cds: A, MC, V.

D

Norfolk (F-9)

Founded: 1682 **Pop:** 261,229 **Elev:** 12 ft **Area code:** 804

This great seaport is part of the Port of Hampton Roads. It is a bustling trade center and has many historic and resort areas nearby to attract the tourist. Many harbor tours depart from Norfolk.

In 1682, the General Assembly bought from Nicholas Wise, a pioneer settler, 50 acres on the Elizabeth River for "ten thousand pounds of tobacco and caske." By 1736 the town that developed was the largest in Virginia. During the Revolutionary War, Norfolk was shelled by the British and later burned by the colonists to prevent a British takeover. The battle between the *Merrimac* and the *Monitor* in Hampton Roads in March 1862 was followed by the fall of the city to Union forces in May of that year. In 1883, the shipment of the first coal to the port by the Norfolk and Western Railway began a new era of prosperity for the city.

Norfolk and its sister city, Portsmouth, are connected by bridge tunnels and a pedestrian ferry. Norfolk houses the largest naval facility in the world, and it is the oldest naval port in the US. It is also headquarters for the Atlantic Fleet. Norfolk is a manufacturing city, with shipbuilding and ship repair companies, consumer and industrial equipment manufacturers and food-processing plants. The city ships coal, tobacco, grain, seafood and vegetables.

Old Dominion University (1930), Virginia Wesleyan College (1967) and Norfolk State University (1935) are located here. This area is also the headquarters for year-round resort activities. Within a 50-mile radius are ocean, bay, river and marsh fishing and hunting; nearby there are 25 miles of good beaches. The 17.6-mile-long Chesapeake Bay Bridge-Tunnel, between Norfolk and the Delmarva peninsula, opened in 1964; toll for passenger cars is $10, including passengers.

Transportation

Norfolk Intl Airport: Information 857-3351; lost and found 857-3344; weather 666-1212.

Car Rental Agencies: See toll-free numbers under Introduction.

Public Transportation: Buses (Tidewater Regional Transit), phone 640-6300.

Rail Passenger Service: Amtrak 800/872-7245.

What to See and Do

1. **Norfolk Naval Base and Norfolk Naval Air Station.** Hampton Blvd & I-564. The largest naval installation in the world. Tours of designated ships are available (Sat & Sun); ship visitors should check in at the Naval Base Pass Office on Hampton Blvd, opp Gate 5. Naval base tours are also offered. Tour buses from Tour & Information Office, 9809 Hampton Blvd (Apr-Oct, daily; also, bus tours from downtown at the Waterside). Sr citizen rate. Phone 444-7955. Bus ¢¢

2. **Nauticus, The National Maritime Center.** One Waterside Dr. Comprehensive marine education and research facility interprets aspects from marine biology and ecology to exploration, trade and shipbuilding. Sophisticated exhibits allow visitors to navigate a simulated ocean voyage, climb onto a replica drilling rig, design a model ship and view actual researchers at work in two working marine laboratories. Active US Navy ships and scientific research vessels will moor at Nauticus and be open to visitors. Also 350-seat, 70mm wide-screen theater; gallery of changing exhibits. (Daily; closed Jan 1, Thanksgiving, Dec 25) Sr citizen rate. Phone 664-1000. ¢¢¢ Also here is

   Hampton Roads Naval Museum. Interprets the extensive naval history of the Hampton Roads area; includes detailed ship models, period photographs, archaeological artifacts and a superior collection of naval prints and artwork. For current status phone 444-8971.

3. **Norfolk Botanical Garden.** On Azalea Garden Rd, adj to Norfolk Intl Airport. Azaleas, camellias, rhododendrons, roses (May-Oct), dogwoods and hollies on 175 acres. Japanese, Colonial, Perennial and Rose gardens; Flowering Arboretum; Hill of Nations; Fragrance Garden for the visually impaired; picnicking, restaurant and gift shop; Tropical Pavilion. Flowering displays are best from early Apr-Oct. Gardens (daily). Information center (daily; closed Jan 1, Dec 25). Narrated boat ride (30 min) & train tours (mid-Mar-Labor Day, daily; through Oct wkends, trains only.) Sr citizen rate. Phone 441-5830. ¢

4. **The Chrysler Museum.** 245 W Olney Rd, at Mowbray Arch. Art treasures representing nearly every important culture, civilization and historical period of the past 5,000 years. Photography gallery; fine collection of decorative arts and glass, including the 8,000-piece Chrysler Institute of Glass. (Daily exc Mon; closed some major hols) Donation. Phone 622-1211.

5. **Hermitage Foundation Museum.** 7637 North Shore Rd. Guided tours of fine arts museum in Tudor-style country mansion. Collections of tapestries, Chinese bronzes and jade, ancient glass. (Daily; closed Jan 1, Thanksgiving, Dec 25) Phone 423-2052. ¢¢

6. **St Paul's Episcopal Church** (1739). 201 St Paul's Blvd, at City Hall Ave. Only building to survive burning of Norfolk in 1776. (Tues-Fri, also by appt) Donation. Phone 627-4353.

7. **Moses Myers House** (1792). 323 E Freemason St, at Bank St. Excellent example of Georgian architecture; many pieces of origi-

nal furniture, silver and china. (Apr-Dec, daily exc Mon; rest of yr, Tues-Sat; closed some major hols) Phone 622-1211, ext 283 or 255. ¢

8. **Willoughby-Baylor House** (1794). 601 E Freemason St. Restored town house with period furnishings; herb and flower garden adj. (By appt; inquire at Moses Myers House) Phone 622-1211, ext 283 or 255. ¢

9. **Hunter House Victorian Museum.** 240 W Freemason St. Built in 1894 and rich in architectural details, the house contains the Hunter family's collection of Victorian furnishings and decorative pieces, including a Renaissance-revival bedchamber suite, a nursery with children's playthings, an inglenook and stained glass windows; lavish period reproduction floor and wall coverings, lighting fixtures and drapery. Also exhibited is a collection of early 20th-century medical memorabilia. Tours begin every 30 minutes. (Apr-Dec, Wed-Sat, also Sun afternoons; closed Jan 1, Thanksgiving, Dec 25) Sr citizen rate. Phone 623-9814. ¢¢

10. **General Douglas MacArthur Memorial.** City Hall Ave and Bank St. Restored former city hall (1847) where MacArthur is buried. Eleven galleries contain memorabilia of his life and military career. There are three other buildings on MacArthur Square: a theater where a film biography is shown, a gift shop and the library/archives. (Daily; closed Jan 1, Thanksgiving, Dec 25) Phone 441-2965. **Free.**

11. **Cape Henry Memorial** (see) **and Lighthouse.** 10 mi E on US 60.

12. **Virginia Zoological Park.** 33rd and Granby Sts. In park are zoo and conservatory (daily; closed Jan 1, Dec 25). Playground, tennis courts, basketball courts, boat ramp; picnic area, concession. Fee for activities. Sr citizen rate. Phone 441-2706 (recording) or -5227. ¢

13. **The Waterside.** 333 Waterside Dr. A waterfront pavilion creating a festive marketplace with more than 120 shops, restaurants. (Daily; closed Thanksgiving, Dec 25) Bordering the Waterside are the city's marina and dock areas, where harbor tour vessels take on passengers (see #14). A brick promenade, skirting the marina, connects the Waterside to

Town Point Park. Home to Norfolk Festevents, the park hosts more than 100 free outdoor concerts, parties, dances, movies and festivals each year.

14. **Sightseeing tours.**

Norfolk-Portsmouth Harbor Tours. Departs from the Waterside. Replica of 19th-century riverboat takes narrated 90-min tour of naval shipyard and inner harbor (Apr-Oct, daily); narrated 2½-hr tour of naval base (Apr-May & Sept-Oct, daily); 2½-hr sunset cruise to Hampton Roads and naval base (June-Labor Day, daily). Phone 393-4735. (Also see PORTSMOUTH) ¢¢¢¢

American Rover. Waterside Marina, Waterside Dr exit off I-264. This 135-foot, 3-masted topsail passenger schooner cruises the "smooth waters" of Hampton Roads historical harbor; spacious sun decks; below-deck lounges; concessions. Tour passes historic forts, merchant and US Navy ships. Some tours pass the naval base (inquire for tour schedule). (May-mid-Oct, 2- & 3-hr tours daily) For information, reservations phone 627-SAIL. ¢¢¢¢-¢¢¢¢¢

Spirit of Norfolk. Departs from the Waterside. Harbor cruise aboard 600-passenger cruise ship. Captain's narration highlights the harbor's famous landmarks, including Waterside Marketplace, Portsmouth Naval Hospital, Old Fort Norfolk, Blackbeard's hiding place, Norfolk Naval Base and downtown area's dynamic skyline. Luncheon Cruise (daily); Evening Dinner Cruise (daily); Moonlight Party Cruise (Fri-Sat, in season). (Apr-Oct, weather permitting) For schedule, reservations phone 627-7771. ¢¢¢¢¢

Annual Events

International Azalea Festival. Downtown & Norfolk Botanical Garden. To honor NATO. Parade, coronation ceremony, 2-day air show

(held at Norfolk Naval Air Station), events, concerts, fair, ball, entertainment. Mid-Apr.

British and Irish Festival. Tribute to England, Scotland, Wales, Northern Ireland and Republic of Ireland. Ethnic food, music, dancing, displays and wares. 4th wkend Apr.

Harborfest. Downtown waterfront. Sailboat & speedboat races, tall ships, ship tours, skydiving, waterskiing, military demonstrations, entertainment, children's activities, fireworks, seafood. 1st full wkend June.

Seasonal Events

Virginia Symphony. Chrysler Hall and other select locations. Four series: dance, Mozart, Pops and Classical. Phone 623-2310 (tickets). Sept-May.

Professional Sports. Norfolk Tides (AAA baseball), Harbor Park Stadium; 622-2222. Mid-Apr-Labor Day. Hampton Roads Admirals (hockey), Norfolk Scope; 640-1212. Oct-Mar.

Virginia Opera. Harrison Opera House and other select locations. Statewide opera company; traditional and contemporary works. Features young American artists. Wed & Fri evenings; Sun matinees. Phone 623-1223. Oct-Mar.

Virginia Stage Company, Wells Theater. Professional theater performed by nationally known artists. Phone 627-1234 (southside) or 874-1234 (peninsula). Oct-May.

Additional Visitor Information

For further information, maps and brochures on attractions, events, shopping, lodging, dining and services in Norfolk, contact the Norfolk Convention & Visitors Bureau, 236 E Plume St, 23510; 441-5266 or 800/368-3097. For information on the many free events and festivals held in Norfolk each year, phone Festevents, 627-7809.

Norfolk Area Suburbs

The following towns and suburbs in the Norfolk area are included in the *Mobil Travel Guide.* For information on any one of them, see the individual alphabetical listing. Chesapeake, Hampton, Newport News, Portsmouth, Virginia Beach.

Motels

★ **COMFORT INN.** 8051 Hampton Blvd (23505), adj to Naval Base. 804/451-0000; FAX 804/451-8394. 120 rms, 2 story. S $56-$60; D $60; each addl $5; under 18 free. Crib free. TV; cable. Indoor pool; whirlpool. Complimentary continental bkfst, coffee. Restaurant nearby. Ck-out 11 am. Coin lndry. Refrigerators. Cr cds: A, D, DS, JCB, MC, V.

D ≈ ⊠ ⚐ SC

✔ ★ **ECONO LODGE-WEST OCEAN VIEW BEACH.** 9601 4th View St (23503). 804/480-9611; FAX 804/480-1307. 70 units, 3 story, 22 kits. Mid-May-Labor Day: S $49.95; D $59.95; each addl $5; kit. units $63.95; under 18 free; wkly rates; higher rates: some hols, special events; lower rates rest of yr. Pet accepted, some restrictions; $50 refundable. TV; cable, in-rm movies avail. Complimentary continental bkfst. Restaurant nearby. Ck-out 11 am. Coin lndry. Sauna, hot tub. Ocean; fishing pier. Beach nearby. Cr cds: A, C, D, DS, ER, JCB, MC, V.

D ⚐ ⊠ ⚐ SC

★★ **HAMPTON INN-AIRPORT.** 1450 N Military Hwy (23502). 804/466-7474; FAX 804/466-7474, ext. 309. 130 units, 2 story. Late May-early Sept: S $51; D $61; under 18 free; lower rates rest of yr. Crib free. TV; cable. Pool. Continental bkfst. Restaurant opp 7 am-11 pm. Ck-out noon. Valet serv. Free airport transportation. Health club privileges. Cr cds: A, C, D, DS, MC, V.

★ **HOLIDAY SANDS.** *1330 E Ocean View Ave (23503).* 804/583-2621; res: 800/525-5156; FAX 804/587-7540. 102 units, 2-5 story, 77 kits. Memorial Day-Labor Day: S, D $45-$90; each addl $5; suites $75-$95; kit. units $65-$95; 1 child under 12 free; lower rates rest of yr. Crib free. TV; cable. Pool. Complimentary coffee. Restaurant nearby. Ck-out 11 am. Coin lndry. Airport transportation avail. Refrigerators. Private patios, balconies. On beach. Cr cds: A, C, D, MC, V.

✔ ★ **SUPER 8.** *7940 Shore Dr (23518).* 804/588-7888; FAX 804/588-7888, ext. 400. 74 units, 3 story, 10 kit. units. June-Labor Day: S, D $46.95-$51.33; suites, kit. units $72.88-$87.47; higher rates: July 4, Labor Day; lower rates rest of yr. Crib free. TV; cable. Complimentary continental bkfst. Restaurant nearby. Ck-out 11 am. Some refrigerators. Cr cds: A, D, DS, MC, V.

Hotels

★ ★ ★ **HILTON-NORFOLK AIRPORT.** *1500 N Military Hwy (23502),* at Northampton Blvd, near Norfolk Intl Airport. 804/466-8000; FAX 804/466-8000, ext. 639. 250 rms, 6 story. S $89-$129; D $99-$134; each addl $15; suites $170-$360; under 12 free; wkly rates; some wkend rates. Crib $12. TV; cable. Pool; poolside serv. Coffee in rms. Restaurant 6:30 am-midnight. Bars noon-1 am; entertainment, dancing. Ck-out 1 pm. Convention facilities. Gift shop. Free valet parking. Free airport transportation. Lighted tennis. Exercise equipt; weights, bicycles, whirlpool, sauna. Minibars. *LUXURY LEVEL : CONCIERGE TOWER.* 27 rms. S $129; D $134; suites $270-$360. Concierge. Private lounge. Complimentary continental bkfst, refreshments. Cr cds: A, C, D, DS, ER, JCB, MC, V.

★ ★ ★ **MARRIOTT-WATERSIDE.** *235 E Main St (23510).* 804/627-4200; FAX 804/628-6452. 405 rms, 24 story. S, D $104-$119; suites $250-$600. Crib free. Garage parking $8; valet $10. TV; cable. Indoor pool; poolside serv. Restaurant 6 am-2:30 pm, 5:30-11 pm. Bar 11-1 am; entertainment Tues-Thurs. Ck-out noon. Coin lndry. Convention facilities. Concierge. Gift shop. Exercise equipt; weight machine, treadmill, whirlpool, sauna. Game rm. Refrigerator, wet bar in suites. *LUXURY LEVEL :* 60 units, 1 suite, 3 floors. S, D $125; suite $600. In-rm movies. Private lounge, honor bar. Complimentary continental bkfst, refreshments. Cr cds: A, C, D, DS, ER, JCB, MC, V.

★ ★ ★ **OMNI WATERSIDE.** *777 Waterside Dr (23510),* at St Paul's Blvd and I-264. 804/622-6664; FAX 804/625-8271. 446 rms, 10 story. S, D $128-$138; each addl $15; suites $150-$350; under 17 free; wkend packages. Crib free. Valet parking $8.50. TV. Pool; poolside serv. Restaurant 6:30 am-11 pm. Bars 11-2 am; entertainment, dancing. Ck-out noon. Convention facilities. Gift shop. Health club privileges. Dockage. Some refrigerators. Balconies. Atrium-like lobby. On harbor. *LUXURY LEVEL : OMNI CLUB.* 52 rms, 5 suites. S, D $138-$148; suites $250-$650. Concierge. Private lounge. Bathrm phones, refrigerators. Full wet bar in suites. Continental bkfst. Cr cds: A, C, D, DS, JCB, MC, V.

✔ ★ ★ **RAMADA-NORFOLK.** *Box 1218 (23501),* Granby & Freemason Sts. 804/622-6682; FAX 804/623-5949. 124 units, 8 story. S $55-$85; D $65-$95; each addl $10; suites $85-$150; under 12 free; wkend rates Nov-Feb. Crib free. Pet accepted, some restrictions; $15 non-refundable. TV; cable. Restaurant 6:30 am-2:30 pm, 5-10 pm. Bar from 5 pm. Ck-out noon. Meeting rms. Health club privileges. Cr cds: A, C, D, DS, MC, V.

★ ★ **SHERATON MILITARY CIRCLE.** *880 N Military Hwy (23502).* 804/461-9192; FAX 804/461-8290. 208 rms, 14 story. S $64-$115; D $74-$123; each addl $10; suites $175; under 18 free; wkend rates. Crib free. TV. Pool. Restaurant 6:30 am-10:30 pm. Bar 11-1 am. Ck-out noon. Meeting rms. Barber, beauty shop. Free airport transportation. Private balconies. Shopping mall adj. Cr cds: A, C, D, DS, ER, JCB, MC, V.

Inn

★ ★ ★ **PAGE HOUSE.** *323 Fairfax Ave (23507).* 804/625-5033; FAX 804/623-9451. 6 rms, 1 with shower only, 3 story, 2 suites. S $70-$115; D $75-$120; suites $125-$145. Children under 12 yrs only by arrangement. TV avail; cable. Complimentary continental bkfst, tea & coffee. Restaurant nearby. Rm serv. Ck-out 11 am, ck-in 4-6 pm. Refrigerator in suites. Totally restored Georgian-revival residence (1898) in historic district. Totally nonsmoking. Cr cds: A, MC, V.

Restaurants

★ **BIENVILLE GRILL.** *723 W 21st St.* 804/625-5427. Hrs: 11:30 am-2:30 pm, 5:30-10 pm; Fri to 1 am; Sat 5:30 pm-1 am; Sun 5:30-9 pm. Closed Mon; some major hols. Bar. A la carte entrees: lunch, dinner $4.95-$17. Specializes in grilled seafood, steak, chicken. Jazz Thurs-Sat. Parking. Cr cds: A, D, DS, MC, V.

✔ ★ ★ **BISTRO 210.** *210 W York St.* 804/622-3210. Hrs: 11:30 am-2:30 pm, 5:30-11 pm; Sat & Sun from 5:30 pm. Closed major hols. Bar. Semi-a la carte: lunch $5-$10, dinner $8.95-$15. Specializes in fresh local fish, vegetables. Own pastries, pasta. Totally nonsmoking. Cr cds: MC, V.

★ **ELLIOT'S.** *1421 Colley Ave.* 804/625-0259. Hrs: 11 am-11 pm; Fri, Sat to midnight; Sun, Mon to 10 pm; Sun Brunch 11 am-2:30 pm. Closed Thanksgiving. Bar. Semi-a la carte: lunch $2.95-$6.95, dinner $2.95-$16.95. Sun brunch $5-$6.95. Child's meals. Specializes in pasta, fresh vegetables, veal. Parking. Outdoor dining. Cr cds: A, C, D, DS, MC, V.

★ ★ **FREEMASON ABBEY.** *209 W Freemason St.* 804/622-3966. Hrs: 11:30 am-10 pm; Wed & Thurs to 11 pm; Fri & Sat to midnight; Sat & Sun brunch 11:30 am-2 pm. Closed Jan 1, Thanksgiving, Dec 25. Bar. Semi-a la carte: lunch $3.95-$7.95, dinner $9.95-$17.95. Sun brunch $4.95-$7.95. Child's meals. Specializes in whole Maine lobster, prime rib. Parking. Renovated church (1873); many antiques. Cr cds: A, MC, V.

✔ ★ **IL PORTO.** *333 Waterside Dr,* at the Waterside complex. 804/625-5483. Hrs: 11 am-11 pm; Fri & Sat to midnight. Closed Thanksgiving, Dec 25. Res accepted. Italian menu. Bar to 1:30 am. A la carte entrees: lunch $3.25-$8, dinner $6.50-$15. Child's meals. Specializes in nautical pasta, veal. Own pasta. Entertainment (evenings). Outdoor dining. Overlooks river. Mediterranean cantina atmosphere; antiques, original artwork. Cr cds: A, DS, MC, V.

★ ★ **LA GALLERIA.** *120 College Place.* 804/623-3939. Hrs: 5:30-11:30 pm; Mon to 11 pm; Fri 11:30 am-2:30 pm, 5:30 pm-midnight; Sat 5:30 pm-midnight. Closed Sun; Easter, Thanksgiving, Dec 25. Res accepted. Italian menu. Bar 4:30 pm-2 am. Semi-a la carte: Fri lunch $3.95-$7.95, dinner $11.95-$21.95. Child's meals. Specialty: salmon La Galleria. Own pasta, desserts. Valet parking. Outdoor dining. Modern decor. Cr cds: A, D, MC, V.

★ **MONASTERY.** *443 Granby St.* *804/625-8193.* Hrs: 11:30 am-2:30 pm, 5-10 pm; May-Labor Day from 5 pm. Closed Mon; Easter, Thanksgiving, Dec 25. Res accepted; required Fri, Sat. Czech, eastern European menu. Bar. Semi-a la carte: lunch $2.75-$8.50, dinner $4.75-$21. Specializes in roast duck, Wienerschnitzel, goulash. Antique mirrors, original works by local artists. Cr cds: A, MC, V.

★ **PHILLIPS WATERSIDE.** *Waterside Dr, at the Waterside.* *804/627-6600.* Hrs: 11 am-10 pm; Sun brunch to 2 pm. Closed Thanksgiving, Dec 25. Bar. Semi-a la carte: lunch $4.95-$9, dinner $10-$24. Sun brunch $4.95-$8.95. Specialties: blackened alligator, crab cakes, herb-crusted tuna. Guitarist Fri & Sat evenings. Some antiques. Cr cds: A, D, DS, MC, V.

[D]

★ ★ **PIRANHA-AN EATING FRENZY.** *8180 Shore Dr, at Taylor's Landing Marina.* *804/588-0100.* Hrs: 11 am-10 pm; Fri & Sat to 11 pm; Sun brunch to 3 pm. Closed Jan 1, Dec 24 & 25. Res accepted; required wkends. Continental menu. Bar. A la carte entrees: lunch $3.95-$8.95, dinner $4.95-$16.95. Sun brunch $9.95. Child's meals. Specialties: paella for two, Trinidadian shrimp curry, cajun crawfish ettouffe. Own desserts. Parking. Outdoor dining. Overlooks marina. Cr cds: A, MC, V.

★ **REGGIE'S BRITISH PUB.** *333 Waterside Dr, at the Waterside.* *804/627-3575.* Hrs: 11:30 am-11 pm; Sun brunch noon-3 pm. Closed Thanksgiving, Dec 25. British menu. Bar. Semi-a la carte: lunch $5.95-$7.95, dinner $7.95-$17.95. Sun brunch $5.95-$6.95. Specializes in fish & chips, mixed grill, shepherd's pie. Outdoor dining. Overlooks Elizabeth River. Cr cds: A, C, D, MC, V.

[D]

★ ★ **SHIP'S CABIN.** *4110 E Ocean View Ave.* *804/362-2526.* Hrs: 5:30-10 pm; Sun 5-9 pm. Res accepted. Bar. Wine list. Semi-a la carte: dinner $12.95-$21.95. Specializes in grilled fish & meat, live Maine lobster, local seafood. Own baking. Parking. View of bay. Fireplaces. Cr cds: A, C, D, MC, V.

✔ ★ ★ **UNCLE LOUIE'S.** *132 E Little Creek Rd.* *804/480-1225.* Hrs: 8 am-11 pm; Fri & Sat to 2 am. Sun 10 am-10 pm. Closed Thanksgiving, Dec 25. Res accepted. Bar. Semi-a la carte: bkfst $3.50-$6.95, lunch, dinner $3.50-$15.95. Child's meals. Specializes in angus beef, fresh fish, specialty coffees. Parking. Cr cds: A, C, D, DS, MC, V.

[D]

Unrated Dining Spots

DOUMAR'S. *1919 Monticello Ave.* *804/627-4163.* Hrs: 8 am-11 pm. Closed Sun; major hols. A la carte entrees: bkfst, lunch, dinner 60¢-$4. Ice cream 90¢-$2.90. Specializes in sandwiches, ice cream. Hand-rolled cones. Parking. 1950s-style drive-in with addl seating inside. Abe Doumar invented the ice cream cone in 1904; his original cone making machine is on display here. Family-owned. No cr cds accepted.

GREEN GROCER TOO. *122 Bank St.* *804/625-2455.* Hrs: 7:30 am-3 pm. Closed Sat, Sun; major hols. Wine, beer. A la carte entrees: bkfst 75¢-$2.50. Semi-a la carte: lunch $3.50-$6.95. Specializes in white meat chicken salad, soups. Own baking, desserts. Cafe, wine bar and bakery. Sandwich kiosk with take-out serv, small dining area. Cr cds: MC, V.

[D]

Orange (D-7)

Founded: 1749 **Pop:** 2,582 **Elev:** 521 ft **Area code:** 703 **Zip:** 22960

This is the seat of Orange County, which was named for William, Prince of Orange, in 1734. Located in the Piedmont (foothills) of the Blue Ridge Mountains, Orange was settled by Germans under the leadership of Alexander Spotswood between 1714 and 1719.

This is riding and hunting country, drawing its livelihood from farming, livestock and light industry. There are many antebellum houses in the county.

What to See and Do

1. **James Madison Museum.** 129 Caroline St. Exhibits commemorating Madison's life and his contributions to American history; also Orange County history and Hall of Agriculture that includes an 18th-century homestead. (Mar-Nov, daily; rest of yr, Mon-Fri) Sr citizen rate. Phone 672-1776. ¢¢

2. **Montpelier.** 4 mi SW, on VA 20. Residence of James Madison, 4th president of US. Madison was the third generation of his family to live on this extensive plantation. He inherited Montpelier and enlarged it twice. After his presidency, he and Dolley Madison retired to the estate, which Mrs. Madison sold, after the president's death, to pay her son's gambling debts. In 1901, the estate was bought by William du Pont, who enlarged the house, added many outbuildings, including a private railroad station, and built greenhouses and planted gardens. Today, under the stewardship of the National Trust for Historic Preservation, a long-term research and preservation project, "The Search for James Madison," has begun. Admission includes a bus tour of the 2,700-acre estate and a guided tour of the mansion. Self-guided tours of arboretum, nature trails and formal garden. (Mid-Mar-Dec, daily; rest of yr, wkends; closed Jan 1, Thanksgiving, Dec 25; also 1st Sat Nov) Sr citizen rate. Phone 672-0006. ¢¢¢

(See Charlottesville, Culpeper)

Inns

✔ ★ ★ ★ **HIDDEN INN.** *249 Caroline St, jct US 15, VA 20.* *703/672-3625; res: 800/841-1253; FAX 703/672-5029.* 10 rms, 2 story, 4 bldgs. S $59-$79; D $79-$119; each addl $20; suites $139-$159. TV in sitting rm. Complimentary full bkfst, afternoon tea. Dining rm; dinner (guests by res). Ck-out noon, ck-in 3 pm. Some in-rm whirlpools. Balconies. Each rm individually decorated; some with canopy bed, fireplace. Late 19th-century residence; on 7½ wooded acres. Totally nonsmoking. Cr cds: MC, V.

[symbols]

★ ★ **HOLLADAY HOUSE.** *155 W Main St.* *703/672-4893; res: 800/358-4422; FAX 703/672-3028.* 6 rms, 3 story, 1 suite, 1 kit. unit. S, D $75-$115; each addl $25; suite $185; kit. unit $120; wkly rates. TV in some rms; cable. Complimentary full bkfst. Restaurant adj 7 am-6 pm. Ck-out 11 am, ck-in 4 pm. Whirlpool. Federal-style residence (ca 1830). Totally nonsmoking. Cr cds: A, MC, V.

[symbols]

Pearisburg (E-4)

Pop: 2,064 **Elev:** 1,804 ft **Area code:** 703 **Zip:** 24134

What to See and Do

1. **White Rocks Recreation Area.** 17 mi E via VA 613, 635 in Jefferson National Forest. Fishing in Big Stony Creek; hunting (in season). Hiking. Camping (fee). (May-mid-Oct) Phone 552-4641.

2. **Walnut Flats.** 11 mi S on VA 100, then 10½ mi W on VA 42 to County 606, N 1 mi to County 201, 2½ mi. Fishing in Dismal Creek; hunting (in season). Hiking. Primitive camping. Dismal Falls and Flat Top Mt are here. (May-mid-Oct) Phone 552-4641. **Free.** Approx a half-mile from Walnut Flats on County 201 is

White Pine Horse Camp. Primitive Camping. Horse trails. (May-mid-Oct) Phone 552-4641. **Free.**

(For accommodations see Blacksburg, Radford)

Pentagon City (C-8)

(See Arlington County)

Petersburg (E-8)

Settled: 1645 **Pop:** 38,386 **Elev:** 87 ft **Area code:** 804

This city, Lee's last stand before Appomattox (1864-65), got its start in 1645 when the General Assembly authorized construction of Fort Henry at the falls of the Appomattox River. In 1784, three separate towns united to become the single city of Petersburg.

British troops under Generals Benedict Arnold and William Phillips occupied the town in 1781; the same year, on May 24, Cornwallis started the journey to his surrender at Yorktown. Between the Revolution and the Civil War, the town was a popular stopping place, with a social life that, for a time, eclipsed that of Richmond.

Physically untouched (though the town sent 17 companies to the front) during the early years of the Civil War, Petersburg in 1864 was the scene of Lee's final struggle against Grant. In April 1865, when Lee's supply routes were finally cut and he was forced to evacuate the city, the Confederacy collapsed. A week later Lee surrendered at Appomattox.

The shattered city made a new start after the war, showing amazing recuperative powers; in 1870, Petersburg had 20 more industries than there had been in 1850. Today, besides being a storehouse of colonial and Civil War history, Petersburg does a thriving business in luggage, optical lenses and ballpoint pens.

What to See and Do

1. **Petersburg National Battlefield** (see).
2. **Poplar Grove (Petersburg) National Cemetery.** S off I-85. On self-guided tour of Petersburg National Battlefield (see). Of 6,315 graves, 4,110 are unidentified.
3. **Old Blandford Church** (1735) and **Cemetery** (1702). 321 S Crater Rd. Church, since 1901 a memorial to the Confederacy, has 15 Tiffany stained-glass windows. (Daily; closed Jan 1, Thanksgiving, Dec 24, 25) Phone 733-2396. ¢
4. **Siege Museum.** 15 W Bank St. Greek-revival building houses exhibits describing the 10-month Civil War Siege of Petersburg. Film *The Echoes Still Remain*, with Joseph Cotten, is shown every hour on the hour. (Daily; closed Jan 1, Thanksgiving, Dec 24, 25) Sr citizen rate. Phone 733-2404. ¢
5. **Trapezium House** (1817). Market & High Sts. Built by eccentric Irish bachelor, Charles O'Hara, in the form of a trapezium, with no right angles and no parallel sides. O'Hara is said to have believed the superstition of his West Indian servant, who thought that ghosts and evil spirits inhabited right angles. Tours depart from Siege Museum, 15 W Bank St. (Apr-Oct, daily) Phone 733-2402. ¢
6. **Farmers Bank** (1817). 19 Bollingbrook St. Banking memorabilia includes original plates and press for printing Confederate currency. Tours depart from Visitors Center, Old Market Square. (Apr-Oct, daily) Phone 733-2400. ¢
7. **St Paul's Episcopal Church** (1856). 110 N Union between W Washington and Tabb Sts. Lee worshiped here during the siege of Petersburg (1864-1865). Open on request (Mon-Thurs). Phone 733-3415.

8. **Centre Hill Mansion** (1823). Center Hill Court. Federal-style mansion visited by Presidents Tyler, Lincoln and Taft. Chandeliers, fine detail carvings; antiques, 1886 Knabe Art grand piano with holly wood inlaid on rosewood. (Daily; closed Jan 1, Thanksgiving, Dec 24, 25) Sr citizen rate. Phone 733-2401. ¢
9. **Lee Memorial Park.** S part of town, off Johnson Rd. Facilities of this 864-acre park include lake (launch fee); fishing (fee; license required); game fields & courts (fee); picnic area. (Daily; lake facilities closed mid-Oct-mid-Apr) Phone 733-2394. Also here is

   USSSA Softball Hall of Fame Museum. 3935 S Crater Rd, 1 mi off I-95. Honors outstanding persons in amateur softball. Numerous displays, exhibits, photographs; 7-min film. (Daily; closed hols) Sr citizen rate. Phone 732-4099. ¢
10. **Appomattox River Park.** W part of town, on River Rd. A 137-acre park with canal for canoeing or fishing; access to rapids; picnic area. (Mid-Apr-Oct, daily) Phone 733-2394.
11. **Fort Lee.** 3 mi NE on VA 36. Army training center in World Wars I and II. Here is

    Quartermaster Museum. Uniforms, flags, weapons, equestrian equipment from 200 years of military service. Civil War and Memorial Rooms. (Daily exc Mon; closed Jan 1, Thanksgiving, Dec 25) Phone 734-4203. **Free.**

(For further information contact the Department of Tourism, Old Market Square, 425 Cockade Alley, PO Box 2107, 23804; 733-2400 or 800/368-3595.)

(See Hopewell, Richmond)

Motels

★ ★ **DAYS INN.** *(Box 1509, 23805)* 12208 S Crater Rd, I-95 exit 45. 804/733-4400; FAX 804/861-9559. 154 rms, 2 story. S, D $44.95-$55.95; each addl $5; kit. suites $55-$59; family rates. Crib free. Pet accepted. TV; cable. Pool; wading pool. Playground. Restaurant adj 5:30 am-10 pm. Ck-out 11 am. Coin lndry. Meeting rms. Bellhops. Sundries. Putting green. Exercise equipt; weights, bicycles. Some refrigerators. Cr cds: A, C, D, DS, ER, JCB, MC, V.

D ✔ ≋ ⚓ 🏃 ⛷ ⚞ 🔥 SC

✔ ★ ★ ★ **QUALITY INN-STEVEN KENT.** *Box 1536 (23805)*, 6 mi S, I-95 exit 45. 804/733-0600; FAX 804/862-4549. 138 rms, 1-2 story. S $35.95-$47.95; D $37.95-$49.95; each addl $5; under 18 free. Crib $5. TV; cable. Pool; wading pool, sauna; poolside serv. Playground. Restaurant 5:30 am-10 pm. Bar noon-midnight; dancing. Ck-out 11 am. Coin lndry. Sundries. Lighted tennis. Game rm. Lawn games. Miniature golf. Some refrigerators. Picnic tables. Cr cds: A, C, D, DS, ER, JCB, MC, V.

D ✔ ⚓ 🏃 ≋ ⛷ ⚞ 🔥 SC

Restaurant

✔ ★ **ALEXANDER'S.** *101 W Bank St.* 804/733-7134. Hrs: 9 am-8:30 pm; Mon, Tues to 3:30 pm. Closed Sun; Jan 1, Thanksgiving, Dec 25. Italian, Greek, Amer menu. Wine, beer. Semi-a la carte: bkfst $1.50-$4, lunch $4-$5.25, dinner $5.35-$7.55. Child's meals. Specialties: veal a la Greca, souvlaki, Athenian chicken. Parking. In old town storefront. No cr cds accepted.

Petersburg National Battlefield (E-8)

The campaign that spelled doom for the Confederacy occurred in a huge 40-mile semicircle around Richmond and Petersburg, at the price of 70,000 Union and Confederate casualties.

General Grant, after his unsuccessful attempt to take Richmond by frontal assault (at Cold Harbor, June 3, 1864), withdrew and attacked Petersburg. After 4 days of fighting and failing to capture the city, Grant decided to lay siege. Petersburg was the rail center that funneled supplies to Lee and Richmond.

The siege lasted ten months, from June 15, 1864, to April 2, 1865, with the two armies in almost constant contact. When Petersburg finally fell, Lee's surrender was only a week away.

The park, more than two square miles, preserves Union and Confederate fortifications, trenches and gun pits. A second unit of the battlefield, Five Forks Unit, is located 23 miles to the west. Park (daily). There are "living history" programs daily during summer. Access for the disabled includes several paved trails and ramps to the Visitor Center. For further information contact the Superintendent, PO Box 549, Petersburg 23804; 804/732-3531. Golden Eagle, Golden Age and Golden Access Passports honored (see INTRODUCTION). Per car ¢¢

What to See and Do

1. **Visitor Center.** Off VA 36. Information, exhibits; maps for self-guided tours. (Daily; closed Jan 1, Dec 25) Self-guided tour starts near center building at

2. **Battery 5.** Strongest original Confederate position, captured on opening day of battle. From here "the Dictator," a Union mortar, shelled Petersburg, 2½ miles away. A similar mortar is nearby.

3. **Battery 8.** Confederate artillery position captured and used by Union as Fort Friend.

4. **Battery 9.** Confederate position on original line. Site of reconstructed Union camp and "living history" programs.

5. **Harrison's Creek.** First Grant (June, 1864), then Lee (March, 1865) had advances checked here.

6. **Fort Stedman.** Lee's "last grand offensive" concentrated here (March 25, 1865). The battle lasted four hours; the Confederates failed to hold their breakthrough.

7. **First Maine Monument.** Memorial to Maine dead in greatest regimental loss in a single action of the war.

8. **Colquitt's Salient.** Section of Confederate defense line.

9. **Gracie's Dam.** Site of one of several Confederate dams intended to flood area between lines.

10. **Fort Haskell.** One of the points where Union troops stopped a desperate attempt by Lee to break the siege.

11. **Spring Garden.** Heaviest Union artillery concentration during Battle of Crater was along this ridge.

12. **The Crater.** Hole remaining after Union troops tunneled beneath Confederate artillery position and exploded four tons of powder (July 30, 1864). The resulting breach in Confederate lines failed as a major breakthrough. Several special monuments in vicinity.

13. **Five Forks Unit.** (1,115 acres) Approx 6 mi SW via VA 613 (White Oak Rd), to jct Dinwiddie Courthouse Rd (VA 627) and Wheeler Pond Rd (VA 645). This road junction, beyond Lee's extreme right flank, led to the only remaining Confederate supply line, the South Side Railroad. The Battle of Five Forks (April 1, 1865) saw Union forces under General Philip H. Sheridan smash Confederates commanded by General George Pickett and gain access to the tracks beyond. On April 2, Grant ordered an all-out assault, crumbling Lee's right flank. Only a heroic stand by Confederate forces at Fort Gregg held off the Union advance while Lee evacuated Petersburg on the night of April 2. Visitor contact station (summer). Phone 804/265-8244. **Free.**

(For accommodations see Hopewell, Petersburg, Richmond)

Portsmouth (F-9)

Founded: 1752 **Pop:** 103,907 **Elev:** 15 ft **Area code:** 804

Connected to Norfolk by two bridge tunnels and a pedestrian ferry that cross the Elizabeth River, Portsmouth is part of the great Hampton Roads port, unrivaled for commercial shipping and shipbuilding activity. It is also the headquarters of the Fifth Coast Guard District.

In Gosport, long a part of Portsmouth, Andrew Sprowle, a Scot, built a marine yard in 1767, which became in turn a British naval repair station and, after the Revolution, a federal navy yard. Now called the Norfolk Naval Shipyard, it is the largest naval shipyard in the world. The *Chesapeake,* sister of the *Constitution* and one of the US Navy's first warships, was built here. So was the *Merrimac,* which was seized by the Confederates, changed into an ironclad in 1861 and rechristened the CSS *Virginia.* The oldest drydock (1831) here is still in use.

What to See and Do

1. **The Portsmouth Museums.** Located in a four block radius, the museum complex has facilities housing artistic, educational and historic exhibits. Museums (Tues-Sat; also Sun afternoons; closed Jan 1, Thanksgiving, Dec 25). Phone 393-8983. Admission pass ¢ includes

   Portsmouth Naval Shipyard Museum. 2 High St, on Elizabeth River. Thousands of items of naval equipment, plus flags, uniforms, prints, maps and models, including models of the CSS *Virginia;* the US Ship-of-the-line *Delaware,* built in Portsmouth; and the first ship drydocked in the US.

   Portsmouth Lightship Museum. London Slip and Water St. Built in 1915, commissioned in 1916 as *Lightship 101,* it served 48 years in Virginia, Delaware and Massachusetts. Retired in 1964 and renamed *Portsmouth.*

   1846 Courthouse. 601 Court St. On the first floor is the **Children's Museum,** housing hands-on displays and participatory exhibits. The upper level was renovated especially for the **Fine Arts Gallery,** a two-story gallery housing traveling exhibits. Adj is the

   Community Arts Center. Houses galleries, classrooms and labs; visual exhibits, performing arts, lectures and demonstrations; permanent and changing exhibits.

2. **Norfolk-Portsmouth Harbor Tours.** Departs from Portside, 6 Crawford Pkwy. Replica of 19th-century riverboat makes narrated tour (1½ hrs) of naval shipyard and inner harbor (Apr-Oct, daily); narrated tour (2½ hrs) of naval base and Hampton Roads (Apr-May & Sept-Oct, daily); sunset cruise (2½ hrs) to Hampton Roads and naval base (June-Labor Day, daily). Phone 393-4735 for details. (Also see NORFOLK) ¢¢¢¢

3. **Hill House.** 221 North St. Headquarters of the Portsmouth Historical Assn. Built in early 1830s, this four-story English-basement-style house (with a raised basement) contains original furnishings collected by generations of the Hill family. In near-original condition, the house has undergone only limited renovation through the years. Garden restored. (Apr-Dec, Wed, Sat & Sun) Phone 393-0241. ¢

4. **US Naval Hospital.** N end of Effingham St, on peninsula in Elizabeth River. Oldest in US (1830); on site of Fort Nelson, British headquarters during Revolutionary War.

5. **Trinity Church** (Episcopal). 500 Court St. Oldest church building (1762) and parish in Portsmouth. Legend says that the church bell cracked while ringing out news of Cornwallis' surrender. It was later recast. Confederate Memorial window. Commodore James Barron, many colonial patriots are buried here. Open on request (Mon-Fri); office behind church in parish hall. Phone 393-0431.

6. **Monumental United Church** (Methodist) (1772). Queen & Dinwiddie Sts, 1 blk N of High St. Oldest Methodist congregation in the

South; history room. Guided tour (Mon-Fri, by appt; closed hols). Phone 397-1297.

7. **Historic houses.** Portsmouth has many excellent examples of colonial, federal and antebellum houses. Among them are Commodore Richard Dale (1st Lieutenant under John Paul Jones on the *Bonhomme Richard* and 1st Naval Shipyard Commander) House (1732), 200 Swimming Point Walk; the Nivison-Ball House (ca 1730-50), 417 Middle St, where Andrew Jackson and General Lafayette were entertained. *These houses are private and may be viewed only from the exterior.* Obtain Olde Towne Portsmouth walking tour brochures with map and descriptions of old buildings from the Portside Visitor Infomation Center.

8. **Great Dismal Swamp National Wildlife Refuge** (see). S on US 17.

(For further information contact the Portsmouth Convention and Visitors Bureau, 505 Crawford St, Suite 2, 23704; 393-5111 or 800/767-8782.)

(See Chesapeake, Hampton, Newport News, Norfolk, Virginia Beach)

Motel

★ ★ **HOLIDAY INN-PORTSMOUTH WATERFRONT.** 8 Crawford Pkwy (23704), on waterfront at Elizabeth River. 804/393-2573; FAX 804/399-1248. 268 rms, 4 story. S $60-$81; D $60-$88; each addl $6; suites $130-$161; studio rms $75-$150; under 17 free; wkend rates; higher rates Harborfest. Crib free. Pet accepted. TV; cable. Pool. Restaurant 6:30 am-10 pm. Rm serv. Bar noon-2 am. Ck-out noon. Coin lndry. Meeting rms. Bellhops. Exercise equipt; weights, stair machine. Dockage, marina adj. Cr cds: A, C, D, DS, JCB, MC, V.

Restaurants

✔ ★ ★ **CAFE EUROPA.** 319 High St. 804/399-6652. Hrs: 11:30 am-2 pm, 5-9:30 pm; Fri, Sat to 10:30 pm. Closed Sun, Mon; most major hols; also mid-Aug-mid-Sept. Res accepted; required Fri, Sat. Continental menu. Bar. Semi-a la carte: lunch $2.50-$8.50, dinner $3.25-$13.95. Specialties: salmon Russian style, veal martini, veal Romanola, French & Italian cuisine. Intimate European atmosphere; Mucha prints; antique gas-era chandeliers. Cr cds: MC, V.

D

★ **CIRCLE.** 3010 High St. 804/397-8196. Hrs: 7 am-10 pm; Fri to 11 pm; wkend hrs vary. Closed Dec 25. Serv bar. Semi-a la carte: bkfst $1.25-$4.99, lunch $2.25-$8.50, dinner $4-$28.95. Sun brunch $9.95. Child's meals. Specializes in seafood, steak. Pianist Wed-Fri. Cr cds: MC, V.

★ ★ **THE MAX.** 425 Water St. 804/397-1866. Hrs: 11:30 am-10 pm. Closed Jan 1, Dec 24, 25. Res accepted. Bar. Semi-a la carte: lunch $4.50-$9.95, dinner $6.95-$16.95. Child's meals. Specializes in fresh local seafood, grilled salmon. Outdoor patio dining overlooking Elizabeth River. Cr cds: A, MC, V.

D

★ ★ **SCALE O' DE WHALE.** 3515 Shipwright St, off W Norfolk Bridge. 804/483-2772. Hrs: 11:30 am-2:30 pm, 5-10 pm; Sat from 5:30 pm; Sun 5:30-9:30 pm. Closed major hols. Res accepted. Serv bar. Semi-a la carte: lunch $4.50-$8, dinner $11.95-$25.95. Child's meals. Specializes in seafood, steak. Parking. At end of pier, dockage. Nautical decor; ship models, antiques, scrimshaw, kerosene lights. Cr cds: A, C, D, DS, MC, V.

Radford (E-4)

Settled: 1756 **Pop:** 15,940 **Elev:** 1,820 ft **Area code:** 703 **Zip:** 24141

What to See and Do

1. **Radford University** (1910). (9,500 students) On US 11, I-81 exit 109. Flossie Martin Gallery in Powell Hall houses visual arts with an emphasis on regional and contemporary; changing exhibits. The Corinna de la Burde Sculpture Court, adjacent to the gallery, is an open-air museum displaying large-scale sculpture through changing exhibitions and permanent installations. Archives in the McConnell Library contain pamphlets, campus information, local history, oral history of Appalachia and rare books. Greenhouse (daily). The Dedmon Center, a recreation-convocation complex, features an air-supported roof, arena seating 5,600; swimming pool; indoor tennis and handball courts. (Daily) Phone 831-5324.

2. **Claytor Lake State Park.** On VA 660, 6 mi SW, just S of I-81 exit 101. Consists of 472 acres in wooded hills adjacent to 5,000-acre lake. Swimming, sand beach, bathhouse; fishing; boating (ramp, rentals, marina). Hiking, bridle trails. Picnicking, concession. Tent and trailer sites (electrical hookups, Apr-Sept); cabins (mid-May-Sept). Visitor center, interpretive programs. Standard fees. Park office and visitor center is in Howe House (1876-79), built on land once settled by Dunkers (Dunkards), a religious sect that fled persecution in Germany in the 1720s. Access for the disabled to bathhouse, lake, picnic shelter. Phone 674-5492.

(For further information contact the Chamber of Commerce, 1126 Norwood St; 639-2202.)

Seasonal Event

The Long Way Home. Outdoor historical drama by Earl Hobson Smith depicts the true story of Mary Draper Ingles, survivor of the 1755 Draper's Meadow Massacre, and her heroic 850-mile flight to warn settlers of Indian attacks. Thurs-Sun, evenings. For reservations contact PO Box 711; 639-0679. Mid-June-Aug.

(See Blacksburg, Salem)

Motels

★ ★ ★ **BEST WESTERN RADFORD INN.** PO Box 1008, 1501 Tyler Ave. 703/639-3000; FAX 703/639-3000, ext. 412. 72 rms, 2 story. S $57-$62; D $62-$67; each addl $5; under 12 free; higher rates univ events. Crib free. Pet accepted. TV; cable. Indoor pool; wading pool, whirlpool, sauna. Restaurant 6:30 am-1:30 pm, 5-9 pm; wkends from 7 am. Rm serv. Bar; entertainment, dancing. Ck-out noon. Meeting rms. Sundries. Bathrm phones; some refrigerators. Cr cds: A, C, D, DS, MC, V.

✔ ★ ★ **COMFORT INN.** (Rte 1, Box 123F, Dublin 24084) Just S of I-81 exit 98 on VA 100. 703/674-1100; FAX 703/674-2644. 98 rms, 2 story. May-Oct: S $42-$54; D $48-$60; each addl $6; under 18 free; higher rates university events; lower rates rest of yr. Crib free. TV; cable. Pool. Complimentary continental bkfst, coffee. Restaurant adj 6:30 am-9 pm. Ck-out noon. Meeting rm. Valet serv. Sundries. Cr cds: A, C, D, DS, ER, JCB, MC, V.

★ **DOGWOOD LODGE.** Rte 2, 2 mi W on US 11. 703/639-9338. 15 rms. S $26; D $32-$34; each addl $3; higher rates university events. Crib free. TV; cable. Restaurant nearby. Ck-out 11 am. Cr cds: MC, V.

Reston (C-8)

(see Dulles Intl Airport Area)

Richmond (E-8)

Settled: 1607 **Pop:** 203,056 **Elev:** 150 ft **Area code:** 804

There have been few dull moments in Richmond's history. Indians and settlers fought over the ground on which it now stands. In 1775, Patrick Henry made his "liberty or death" speech in St John's Church, and in 1780 the city was named capital of the state. At that time Virginia extended all the way to the Mississippi. British soldiers plundered it brutally in the Revolution. As the capital of the Confederacy from 1861-65, it was constantly in danger. Finally, in 1865 the city was evacuated, and retreating Confederate soldiers burned the government warehouse; a portion of the rest of the city also went up in flames.

However, Richmond did survive. As Virginia's capital, it proudly exemplifies the modern South. It is a city industrially aggressive yet culturally aware, respectful of its own historical background yet receptive to new trends in architecture and modes of living. Richmond esteems both the oldest monuments and the newest skyscrapers.

Tobacco and tobacco products, paper and paper products, aluminum, chemicals, textiles, printing and publishing, and machinery contribute to the city's economy. Richmond is also an educational center; the Virginia Commonwealth University, Virginia Union University and the University of Richmond are based here.

What to See and Do

1. **Capitol Square.** Bounded by Broad, Governor, Bank and 9th Sts, downtown.

   State Capitol (1785-1788). 9th and Grace Sts, Capitol Square. Modeled after La Maison Carrée, an ancient Roman temple at Nîmes, France, the Capitol was designed by Thomas Jefferson. In this building, where America's oldest continuous English-speaking legislative bodies still meet, is the famous Houdon statue of Washington. The old Hall of the House of Delegates features the first interior dome in the US; here, Aaron Burr was tried for treason, Virginia ratified the Articles of Secession and Robert E. Lee accepted command of the forces of Virginia; the Confederate Congress also met in the building. (Apr-Nov, daily exc Sun; rest of yr, Mon-Sat, also Sun afternoons; closed Jan 1, Thanksgiving, Dec 25) Also on Capitol Square are

   Governor's Mansion (1813). E of State Capiol. This two-story Federal-style house was built after the capital was moved from Williamsburg. It is the oldest governor's mansion in the US still in use as a governor's residence. Tours (arranged by appt only). Phone 371-2642. **Free.**

   Virginia State Library and Archives. NE corner, 11th & E Broad Sts. Outstanding collection of books, maps, manuscripts. (Daily exc Sun; closed hols) Phone 786-8929. **Free.**

   Equestrian Statue of Washington. Capitol Square, 9th & Grace Sts. By Thomas Crawford; cast in Munich over an 18-year period. Base features allegorical representations of six famous Revolutionary War figures from Virginia.

2. **St Paul's Church** (Episcopal). 9th and Grace Sts, W of Capitol Sq. Established in 1843, the church survived the Civil War intact. It was here that Jefferson Davis received news of Lee's retreat from Petersburg to Appomattox. Beginning in 1890, the church added many fine stained-glass windows, including eight from the Tiffany studios. Sanctuary ceiling features decorative plasterwork, interweaving Greek, Hebrew and Christian motifs around a central panel. A Tiffany mosaic of da Vinci's *Last Supper* surmounts the altar. (Daily; closed hols) Phone 643-3589.

3. **City Hall Observation Deck.** 9th and Broad Sts, across Broad St from Capitol. Eighteenth floor observation deck offers panoramic view of the city, including Capitol grounds, James River and Revolutionary and Civil War-era buildings contrasted with modern skyscrapers. (Mon-Fri) Phone 780-7000. **Free.** Across the street is the old City Hall (1886-94), a restored Gothic-revival building featuring an elaborate central court with arcaded galleries.

4. **Monumental Church** (1812). 1226 E Broad St, N of Capitol Sq. Located on the Medical College of VA campus of Virginia Commonwealth University. Octagonal domed building designed by Robert Mills, architect of the Washington Monument. Commemorative structure was built on site where many prominent persons, including the governor, perished in a theater fire in 1811. Interior closed. Behind the church is the distinctive Egyptian Building (1845).

5. **John Marshall House** (1790). 9th & Marshall Sts, N of Capitol Square. Restored house of famous Supreme Court justice features original woodwork and paneling; family furnishings and mementos. (Daily exc Mon; closed most major hols) Combination ticket avail for Marshall House, Valentine Museum, Museum of the Confederacy, White House of the Confederacy. Sr citizen rate. Phone 648-7998. Marshall House **¢¢** Combination ticket **¢¢¢**

6. **Valentine Museum.** 1015 E Clay St, N of Capitol Sq. Traces history of Richmond. Exhibits focus on city life, decorative arts, costumes and textiles, industrial and social history; tour of restored 1812 Wickham House. Lunch served in walled garden (Apr-Oct). (Daily; closed some hols) Sr citizen rate. Phone 649-0711. **¢¢**

7. **Museum of the Confederacy.** 1201 E Clay St, N of Capitol Sq. Contains the nation's largest collection of Confederate military and civilian artifacts, including uniforms, equipment, flags, personal belongings of Jefferson Davis, Robert E. Lee and J.E.B. Stuart, documents, manuscripts and artwork. (Daily; closed Jan 1, Thanksgiving, Dec 25) Sr citizen rate. Phone 649-1861. **¢¢** Next door is

8. **White House of the Confederacy.** 12th & E Clay Sts, N of Capitol Sq. Classical-revival house (1818) used by Jefferson Davis as his official residence during period when Richmond was capital of the Confederacy. Abraham Lincoln met with troops here during the Union occupation of the city. Restored to pre-wartime appearance; original furnishings. (Daily; closed Jan 1, Thanksgiving, Dec 25) Sr citizen rate. Phone 649-1861. **¢¢**

9. **Jackson Ward.** Bounded by I-95, 7th, Broad and Belvidere Sts. Historic downtown neighborhood that was home to many famous black Richmonders, including Bill "Bojangles" Robinson. Area has numerous 19th-century, Greek-revival and Victorian buildings with ornamental ironwork that rivals the wrought iron of New Orleans. Within the ward are

   Bill "Bojangles" Robinson Statue. Corner of Leigh & Adams Sts. Memorial to the famous dancer, who was born at 915 N 3rd St.

   Maggie Walker National Historic Site. 110-A E Leigh St. Commemorates life and career of Maggie L. Walker, daughter of former slaves, who overcame great hardships to become successful in banking and insurance; early advocate for women's rights and racial equality. Two-story, red-brick house was home to her family 1904-1934. (Wed-Sun; closed Jan 1, Thanksgiving, Dec 25) Phone 780-1380. **Free.**

10. **Richmond Children's Museum.** 740 Navy Hill Dr, downtown. Exhibits on arts, nature and the world around us designed for children 2-12 years old; many hands-on exhibits. (July-Aug, daily; rest of yr, daily exc Mon; closed hols) Phone 643-5436 or 788-4949. **¢¢**

11. **Kanawha Canal Locks.** 12th & Byrd Sts, downtown. Impressive stone locks were part of nation's first canal system, planned by George Washington. Narrated audiovisual presentation explains workings of locks and canal. Picnic grounds. (Daily) Phone 281-2369. **Free.**

12. Federal Reserve Money Museum. 701 E Byrd St, downtown, on 1st floor of bank. Exhibits of currency, including rare bills; gold and silver bars; money-related artifacts. (Mon-Fri; closed hols) Phone 697-8108. **Free.**

13. Virginia War Memorial. 621 S Belvidere St, downtown at N end of Robert E. Lee Bridge. Honors Virginians who died in WW II, Korean and Vietnam wars. Mementos of battles; eternal flame; more than 12,000 names engraved on glass and marble walls. (Daily) Phone 786-2050. **Free.**

14. Church Hill Historic Area. Bounded by Broad, 29th, Main and 21st Sts, E of Capitol Square. Neighborhood of 19th-century houses, more than 70 of which predate Civil War. Publication on buildings available at Historic Richmond Foundation, 2407 E Grace St (Mon-Fri; closed hols). Phone 643-0107. Publicaton ¢¢ Some Church Hill houses are open Historic Garden Week (see ANNUAL EVENTS). In center of Church Hill is

St John's Episcopal Church (1741). 25th and Broad Sts. Where Patrick Henry delivered his stirring "liberty or death" speech. Re-enactment of Second Virginia Convention (late May-early Sept, Sun). Guided tours. (Daily; closed Jan 1, Easter, Thanksgiving, Dec 24, 25, 31) Phone 648-5015. ¢ West of Church Hill is

Edgar Allan Poe Museum. 1914 E Main St. Old Stone House portion is thought to be oldest structure in Richmond (1737). Four additional buildings house Poe mementos; James Carling illustrations of "The Raven"; scale model of Richmond of Poe's time; slide presentation of Poe's life in Richmond. Guided tours. (Daily; closed Dec 25) Sr citizen rate. Phone 648-5523. ¢¢ East of Church Hill is

Richmond National Battlefield Park (see). Headquarters, located at 3215 E Broad St, in Chimborazo Park.

15. The Fan and **Monument Avenue.** Bounded by Franklin St & Monument Ave, Boulevard, Main & Belvidere Sts. Named for the layout of streets that fan out from Monroe Park toward the western part of town. Historical neighborhood has restored antebellum and turn-of-the-century houses, museums, shops, restaurants and famed Monument Avenue. The fashionable boulevard, between Lombard and Belmont Sts, is dotted with imposing statues of Generals Lee, Stuart and Jackson, of Jefferson Davis and of Commodore Matthew Fontaine Maury, inventor of the electric torpedo. Within the area are

Virginia Museum of Fine Arts. Boulevard St and Grove Ave. America's first state-supported museum of art. Collections of paintings, prints, sculpture from major world cultures; Russian Imperial Easter eggs and jewels by Fabergè; decorative arts of the art nouveau and art deco movements; sculpture garden; changing exhibitions. Cafeteria. (Daily exc Mon; closed Jan 1, July 4, Thanksgiving, Dec 25) Phone 367-0844. ¢¢

Virginia Historical Society. Kensington & Boulevard Sts. Comprehensive collection of Virginia history housed in Museum of Virginia History, with permanent and changing exhibits, and Library of Virginia History, with historical and genealogical research facilities. (Mon-Sat, museum also Sun afternoons; closed hols) Phone 358-4901. ¢¢

Science Museum of Virginia. 2500 W Broad St, N of Monument Ave. Hands-on museum. Major exhibits include aerospace, computers, electricity, visual perception, physical phenomena and astronomy, giant analemmic sundial and Foucault pendulum. The Ethyl Universe Planetarium Space Theater features Omnimax films and planetarium shows (inquire for schedule). (Mon-Sat, also Sun afternoons; closed Thanksgiving, Dec 25) Sr citizen rate. Phone 367-1013. Museum ¢¢; Museum & planetarium ¢¢¢

16. Parks. For general information contact the Dept of Parks & Recreation; 780-5695.

William Byrd. Boulevard St and Idlewood Ave. Includes 287 acres of groves, artificial lakes, picnic areas. Tennis courts; softball fields; fitness course. Amphitheater (June-Aug). Virginia's World War I memorial, a 240-foot, pink brick carillon tower. Nearby is

Maymont. 1700 Hampton St, at Pennsylvania Ave. Dooley mansion, late Victorian in style, houses art collection and decorative arts exhibits (daily exc Mon; fee). Also here are formal Japanese and Italian gardens, an arboretum, a nature center with wildlife habitat for native species, an aviary, a children's farm and a working carriage collection. (Daily) Phone 358-7166. **Free.**

Bryan. Bellevue Ave and Hermitage Rd. A 279-acre park, 20 acres of which is an azalea garden with more than 55,000 plants (best view late Apr-mid-May). Picnic facilities, tennis courts. **Free.**

James River. W 22nd St and Riverside Dr. Five sections. Fishing, pedestrian bridges with overlook of James River, whitewater canoe and inner-tube accesses, birdwatching, wildlife sanctuary, self-guided tours, bicycle and hiking trails, visitor center with display, information station, interpretive programs. **Free.**

Lewis Ginter Botanical Garden. 1800 Lakeside Ave, in Lakeside. Victorian-era estate features the Grace Arents Garden and the Henry M. Flagler Perennial Garden; seasonal floral displays; emphasis on daffodils, daylilies, azaleas and rhododendrons. (Daily) Phone 262-9887. ¢

17. Hollywood Cemetery (1847). 412 S Cherry St, at Albemarle St. James Monroe, John Tyler, Jefferson Davis, other notables and 18,000 Confederate soldiers are buried here; audiovisual program. (Daily; audiovisual program, Mon-Fri) Phone 648-8501. **Free.**

18. Shopping.

6th Street Marketplace. 6th St between Coliseum & Grace St, downtown. Restored area of shops, restaurants, entertainment.

Shockoe Slip. E Cary St between 12th & 14th St, downtown. Restored area of historic buildings and gaslit cobblestone streets; shopping, restaurants, galleries.

Carytown. W Cary St, between Boulevard St & I-95. Eight blocks of shops, restaurants, theaters adjacent to historic Fan neighborhood.

17th Street Market. 17th St between E Main & E Market Sts. Farmers market built on site of Indian trading village. Seasonal produce, flowers, holiday greens. (Daily)

19. Virginia Aviation Museum. 5701 Huntsman Rd in Sandston, at Richmond International Airport. Exhibits and artifacts on the history of aviation, with emphasis on Virginia pioneers. (Daily; closed Dec 25) Sr citizen rate. Phone 236-3622. ¢¢

20. Virginia House. 4301 Sulgrave Rd, 1/2 mi off VA 147 (Cary St) in Windsor Farms. A Tudor building constructed of materials from Warwick Priory (built in England in 1125 and rebuilt in 1565 as a residence); moved here in 1925. West wing is modeled after Sulgrave Manor, at one time the home of Lawrence Washington. Furniture, tapestries and paintings from 15th-20th centuries. Formal gardens. Tours by appt only exc during Historic Garden Week. (Daily exc Mon; closed major hols) Phone 353-4251. ¢¢

21. Agecroft Hall. Cary St exit off I-195, turn onto N Thompson Ave, then right on Cary to Malvern, then left on Cantebury to 4305 Sulgrave Rd. Half-timbered Tudor manor built in the late 15th century near Manchester, England. Disassembled, brought here and rebuilt during the late 1920s in a spacious setting of formal gardens and grassy terraces overlooking the James River. English furnishings from 16th-17th centuries. Audiovisual presentation explains history of house. (Daily exc Mon; closed most hols) Sr citizen rate. Phone 353-4241. ¢¢

22. Wilton (1753). S Wilton Rd off Cary St, 8 mi W. Georgian mansion built by William Randolph III. Fully paneled, authentic 18th-century furnishings. Headquarters of National Society of Colonial Dames in Virginia. (Daily exc Mon; closed hols) Open during Historic Garden Week (see ANNUAL EVENTS). Sr citizen rate. Phone 282-5936. ¢¢

23. Pocahontas State Park. S on US 10, then W on VA 655. More than 7,000 acres; Swift Creek Lake. Swimming, pool, bathhouse; fishing; boating (launch, rentals, electric motors only). Hiking trails, bicycle path (rentals). Picnicking, concession. Tent and trailer sites (seasonal), group cabins. Nature center; evening interpretive programs (summer). Access for the disabled to pool, bathhouse, trails. Standard fees. (Daily) Phone 796-4255.

24. Meadow Farm Museum (General Sheppard Crump Memorial Park). 12 mi NW via I-95N, I-295W, Woodman Rd S exit, at Courtney & Mountain Rds. Living history farm museum depicting rural life in the 1860s. Orientation center, farmhouse, barn, outbuildings, crop demonstration fields, 1860s doctor's office. Also a 150-acre park with picnic shelters, playground. (Mar-Dec, daily exc Mon) ¢ during special events. Phone 672-9496 or-1367. **Free.**

25. Sightseeing.

Paddlewheeler *Annabel Lee.* Departs from Intermediate Terminal. Triple-decked, 350-passenger 19th-century-style riverboat cruises the James River. Narrated tour; entertainment. Lunch, brunch, dinner and plantation cruises. (Apr-Dec, at least one cruise daily exc Mon) Phone 222-5700 or 800/752-7093. ¢¢¢¢

Historic Richmond Tours. Offers guided van tours with pickup at Visitors Center and major hotels (daily); reservations required. Also guided walking tours (Apr-Oct, daily; fee). For details, reservations phone 780-0107. Van tours ¢¢¢¢; Walking tours ¢¢

Plantation tours. The Richmond-Petersburg-Williamsburg area has many fine old mansions and estates. Some are open most of the year; others only during Historic Garden Week (see ANNUAL EVENTS). The Metro Richmond Visitors Center has maps, information folders, suggestions. (Daily) Located at 1710 Robin Hood Rd, 23220; phone 358-5511 for details.

26. Industrial tour. Philip Morris, USA. 3601 Commerce Rd, I-95 exit 69. Guided tours of cigarette manufacturing plant (Mon-Fri; closed major hols; also wk of July 4 & late Dec-early Jan). Phone 274-3342. **Free.**

(For further information contact the Convention and Visitors Bureau, 6th Street Marketplace, 550 E Marshall St, Box C-250, 23219; 782-2777, 358-5511 or 800/365-7272.)

Annual Events

Historic Garden Week in Virginia. Many private houses and gardens of historic or artistic interest are opened for this event, which includes more than 200 houses and gardens throughout the state. Tours. Contact 12 E Franklin St, 23219; 644-7776 or 643-7141. Apr 23-May 1.

June Jubilee. Downtown. Performing and visual arts festival with ethnic foods, African folk dances, music, crafts. Phone 643-4993. June.

Virginia State Fair. Animal and 4-H contests, music, horse show, carnival. Phone 228-3200. Sept 28-Oct 8.

Richmond Newpapers Marathon. Last Sun Oct.

Christmas Open House Tour. In the historic Fan District and Church Hill. Phone 355-0892 or 649-3519. 2nd or 3rd wkend Dec.

(See Ashland, Hopewell, Petersburg)

Motels

★ ★ ★ **COURTYARD BY MARRIOTT.** 6400 W Broad St (23230). 804/282-1881; FAX 804/288-2934. 145 rms, 3 story. S $79; D $89; suites $89-$99; under 19 free; wkend rates. Crib free. TV; cable. Pool. Coffee in rms. Bkfst avail. Bar. Ck-out noon. Coin lndry. Meeting rms. Valet serv. Sundries. Exercise equipt; weight machines, bicycles, whirlpool. Some refrigerators. Cr cds: A, C, D, DS, MC, V.

D ≈ 🏃 ⚞ 🔥 SC

★ **LA QUINTA.** 6910 Midlothian Pike (US 60W) (23225), at VA 150. 804/745-7100; FAX 804/276-6660. 130 rms, 3 story. S $46; D $51; each addl $6; under 18 free. Crib free. Pet accepted, some restrictions. TV; cable. Heated pool. Complimentary continental bkfst

in lobby. Restaurant adj 6 am-11 pm. Ck-out noon. Meeting rms. Cr cds: A, C, D, DS, ER, JCB, MC, V.

D ⚞ ≈ ⚞ 🔥 SC

✔ ★ **RED ROOF INN.** 4350 Commerce Rd (23234), south of downtown. 804/271-7240; FAX 804/271-7245. 109 rms, 2 story. S $27.99-$33.99; D $32.99-$39.99; under 18 free. TV. Complimentary coffee. Restaurant nearby. Ck-out noon. Cr cds: A, C, D, DS, MC, V.

D ⚞ 🔥

★ ★ **RESIDENCE INN BY MARRIOTT.** 2121 Dickens Rd (23230). 804/285-8200; FAX 804/285-8200, ext. 498. 80 kit. suites, 2 story. S, D $109-$139; monthly, wkly, wkend rates. Crib free. Pet accepted, some restrictions; $50 non-refundable and $5 per day. TV; cable. Pool. Complimentary continental bkfst. Ck-out noon. Coin lndry. Meeting rm. Valet serv. Health club privileges. Many fireplaces. Private patios, balconies. Picnic tables, grills. Cr cds: A, C, D, DS, MC, V.

D ⚞ ≈ ⚞ 🔥 SC

Motor Hotels

✔ ★ **BEST WESTERN JAMES RIVER INN.** 8008 W Broad St (23294). 804/346-0000; FAX 804/346-4547. 177 rms, 6 story. Apr-Oct: S $43-$48; D $51-$56; each addl $5; under 16 free; lower rates rest of yr. Crib free. TV; cable. Pool. Complimentary continental bkfst. Restaurant nearby. Ck-out 11 am. Meeting rms. Game rm. Cr cds: A, C, D, DS, ER, JCB, MC, V.

D ≈ ⚞ 🔥 SC

★ ★ **HILTON AIRPORT.** (5501 Eubank Rd, Sandston 23150) Near Intl Airport. 804/226-6400; FAX 804/226-1269. 160 rms, 5 story. 122 suites. S, D $85-$135; each addl $15; family rates; wkend rates. Crib free. TV; cable. Pool; poolside serv. Restaurant 6:30 am-10 pm. Rm serv to midnight. Bar 11-2 am. Ck-out noon. Meeting rms. Bellhops. Valet serv. Sundries. Gift shop. Free airport transportation. Exercise equipt; weight machine, bicycles, whirlpool. Some balconies. Cr cds: A, C, D, DS, ER, JCB, MC, V.

D ≈ 🏃 ✈ ⚞ 🔥 SC

★ ★ **HOLIDAY INN AIRPORT.** (5203 Williamsburg Rd, Sandston 23150) Near Intl Airport. 804/222-6450; FAX 804/226-4305. 230 rms, 3-6 story. S $67-$100; D $72-$105; under 12 free. Pet accepted. TV; cable. Pool; lifeguard. Complimentary continental bkfst. Restaurant 6 am-10:30 pm. Rm serv. Bar noon-1 am; entertainment, dancing Thurs-Sat. Ck-out 1 pm. Meeting rms. Bellhops. Free airport transportation. Refrigerators, minibars avail. Cr cds: A, C, D, DS, JCB, MC, V.

D ⚞ ≈ ✈ ⚞ 🔥 SC

★ ★ ★ **HYATT.** 6624 W Broad St (23230). 804/285-1234; FAX 804/288-3961. 372 rms, 3-8 story. S, D $109-$134; suites $150-$650; under 18 free; wkend rates. Crib free. TV; cable. Indoor/outdoor pool; poolside serv. Restaurant 6-10 pm. Rm serv 6 am to midnight. Bar noon-2 am; entertainment, dancing. Ck-out noon. Meeting rms. Bellhops. Valet serv. Gift shop. Lighted tennis. Exercise equipt; weight machine, stair machine, sauna. Some private patios. *LUXURY LEVEL : BUSINESS PLAN.* 13 rms, 1 suite. S, D $159; suite $650. Complimentary continental bkfst, newspaper. Cr cds: A, C, D, DS, ER, JCB, MC, V.

D ⚞ ≈ 🏃 🏊 ⚞ 🔥 SC

✔ ★ ★ **RAMADA INN-WEST.** 1500 Parham Rd (23229), at Quioccasin Rd. 804/285-9061; FAX 804/288-0104. 87 rms, 3 story. S $41-$49; D $46-$54; each addl $5; suites $51-$64; under 13 free. Crib free. Pet accepted, some restrictions. TV; cable. Pool. Restaurant 7 am-10 pm; Sun to 11 am. Rm serv. Bar 5 pm-2 am, Sat from 5 pm, closed Sun; dancing. Ck-out noon. Coin lndry. Meeting rms. Cr cds: A, C, D, DS, JCB, MC, V.

D ⚞ ≈ ⚞ 🔥 SC

★ ★ ★ **SHERATON INN-AIRPORT.** *4700 S Laburnum Ave (23231), near International Airport.* 804/226-4300; FAX 804/226-6516. 151 rms, 4 story. S $80-$95; D $90-$105; each addl $10; suites $95-$205; under 17 free; wkend rates. Crib free. TV; cable. Indoor pool. Restaurant 6-1 am. Rm serv. Bar 11-2 am; dancing. Ck-out noon. Bellhops. Valet serv. Gift shop. Barber, beauty shop. Free airport transportation. Exercise equipt; weights, bicycles, whirlpool, sauna. Bathrm phones. Some private patios, balconies. Cr cds: A, C, D, DS, ER, JCB, MC, V.

D 🐾 ≈ 🏃 ✈ ➤ 🔥 SC

Hotels

★ ★ ★ **BERKELEY.** *1200 E Cary St (23219), in Shockoe Slip area, downtown.* 804/780-1300; FAX 804/343-1885. 55 rms, 6 story. S $115-$154; D $128-$164; each addl $10; under 12 free; wkend rates. Crib free. TV; cable. Pool privileges. Coffee in rms. Restaurant 7 am-2 pm, 6-10 pm; Fri, Sat to 11 pm; Sun to 9 pm. Bar 11:30 am-2 pm, 4:30 pm-midnight. Ck-out noon. Meeting rms. Concierge. Free valet parking. Health club privileges. Bathrm phones. Located in Shockroe Slip, city's historic business district. Cr cds: A, C, D, DS, MC, V.

D ➤ 🔥 SC

★ ★ ★ **COMMONWEALTH PARK SUITES HOTEL.** *PO Box 455 (23203), 9th & Bank Sts, opp State Capitol.* 804/343-7300; FAX 804/343-1025. 49 suites, 11 story. S $120-$195; D $130-$215; each addl $15; under 18 free; wkend rates. Crib free. Valet parking $9.75. TV; cable. Restaurant 7 am-10 pm. Rm serv 24 hrs. Bar 4:30 pm-midnight. Ck-out noon. Meeting rms. Concierge. Airport, RR station transportation. Exercise equipt; bicycles, treadmill, whirlpool, sauna. Massage avail. Bathrm phones, refrigerators, minibars. Historic hotel built 1908. Cr cds: A, C, D, DS, ER, JCB, MC, V.

D 🏃 ➤ 🔥

✔ **DAYS INN.** *2100 Dickens Rd (23230).* 804/282-3300; FAX 804/288-2145. 180 rms, 7 story. April-Sept: S, D $85-$95; each addl $5; under 13 free; wkly rates; higher rates special events; lower rates rest of yr. Crib free. Pet accepted; $5. TV; cable. Pool. Complimentary continental bkfst. Restaurant adj open 24 hrs. Ck-out noon. Meeting rms. No bellhops. Gift shop. Refrigerators. Cr cds: A, C, D, DS, ER, MC, V.

D 🐾 ≈ ➤ 🔥 SC

★ ★ ★ **EMBASSY SUITES.** *2925 Emerywood Pkwy (23294), Commerce Center.* 804/672-8585; FAX 804/672-3749. 225 suites, 8 story. Suites $89-$127; each addl $10; under 12 free. Crib free. TV; cable. Indoor pool. Complimentary full bkfst. Restaurant 11 am-10 pm. Bar to midnight. Ck-out noon. Meeting rms. Gift shop. Exercise equipt; weight machine, bicycles, whirlpool, sauna, steam rm. Game rm. Refrigerators; wet bar in suites. Cr cds: A, C, D, DS, JCB, MC, V.

D ≈ 🏃 ➤ 🔥 SC

★ ★ ★ **THE JEFFERSON.** *Franklin & Adams Sts (23220).* 804/788-8000; res: 800/424-8014; FAX 804/344-5162. 274 rms, 9 story, 26 suites. Apr-mid-June & mid-Sept-early Dec: S $135-$175; D $150-$190; each addl $15; suites $225-$825; under 18 free; special package plans; lower rates rest of yr. Crib free. Garage $3; valet parking $4.50. TV; cable. Pool privileges. Restaurant 6:30 am-midnight (also see LEMAIRE). Rm serv 24 hrs. Bar 11-2 am. Ck-out noon. Meeting rms. Concierge. Shopping arcade. Bathrm phones, refrigerators, minibars. Some balconies. Historic hotel, restored to its original turn-of-the-century elegance; famous staircase leads from 70-ft rotunda to Thomas Jefferson statue in stained glass-domed lobby. Cr cds: A, C, D, DS, ER, JCB, MC, V.

D 🏃 🔥 SC

★ ★ ★ **MARRIOTT.** *500 E Broad St (23219), downtown.* 804/643-3400; FAX 804/788-1230. 400 rms, 17 story. S $99; D $109; each addl $10; suites $200-$700; under 18 free; honeymoon, wkend packages. Crib free. Pet accepted, some restrictions. TV; cable. Indoor pool; poolside serv, lifeguard. Restaurant 6:30 am-10 pm. Bar 11-1 am.

Ck-out noon. Convention facilities. Concierge. Exercise equipt; weights, bicycles, whirlpool, sauna. Game rm. Some bathrm phones, refrigerators. *LUXURY LEVEL :* 68 rooms. S $114; D $124. Private lounge. Full wet bar, kitchen area. Complimentary continental bkfst. Cr cds: A, C, D, DS, JCB, MC, V.

D 🐾 ≈ 🏃 ➤ 🔥 SC

★ ★ ★ **OMNI.** *100 S 12th St (23219), in Shockoe Slip area, downtown.* 804/344-7000; FAX 804/648-6704. 363 units, 19 story. Mid-Apr-mid-June, mid-Sept-mid-Nov: S $129; D $149; each addl $15; suites $175-$375; under 19 free; wkly, wkend rates; lower rates rest of yr. Crib free. TV. Indoor pool; poolside serv. Restaurant 7 am-11 pm. Bar noon-1 am; entertainment. Ck-out 1 pm. Convention facilities. Concierge. Shopping arcade. Exercise rm; instructor, weights, whirlpool, steam rm, sauna. Minibars. *LUXURY LEVEL : OMNI CLUB LEVEL.* 41 rms, 4 suites, 2 floors. S $149; D $169; suites $175-$375. Private lounge. In-rm movies. Wet bar in suites. Complimentary continental bkfst, bar, refreshments. Cr cds: A, C, D, DS, ER, JCB, MC, V.

D ≈ 🏃 ➤ 🔥 SC

★ ★ ★ **RADISSON.** *555 E Canal St (23219), downtown.* 804/788-0900; FAX 804/788-0791. 299 rms, 16 story. Apr-June, Sept-Oct: S $89-$129; D $99-$139; each addl $10; suites $150-$350; under 12 free; wkend rates; lower rates rest of yr. Crib free. TV; cable. Indoor pool. Restaurant 6:30 am-11 pm. Bar 4 pm-1:30 am; dancing. Ck-out noon. Convention facilities. Concierge. Gift shop. Exercise equipt; weights, bicycles, whirlpool. Located in center of business and financial districts. Cr cds: A, C, D, DS, JCB, MC, V.

D ≈ 🏃 ➤ 🔥 SC

Inns

★ ★ **EMMANUEL HUTZLER HOUSE.** *2036 Monument Ave (23220).* 804/353-6900. 4 rms, 3 story. S $75-$115; D $85-$135; children over 6 yrs only. TV; cable. Complimentary continental bkfst (full bkfst wkends). Complimentary coffee in library. Restaurant nearby. Ck-out noon, ck-in 3 pm. Luggage handling. Built 1914; antiques. Totally nonsmoking. Cr cds: A, DS, MC, V.

➤ 🔥

★ ★ ★ **LINDEN ROW.** *100 E Franklin St (23219), entrance at 101 N 1st St, downtown.* 804/783-7000; res: 800/348-7424; FAX 804/648-7504. 70 rms, 4 story, 7 suites. S, D $89-$109; each addl $5; suites $129. TV; cable. Complimentary continental bkfst. Dining rm (public by res) 11 am-2:30 pm, 5:30-10 pm. Rm serv. Ck-out noon, ck-in 3 pm. Bellhops. Valet serv. Concierge. Health club privileges. In block of Greek-revival rowhouses (1847) and around courtyard thought to be boyhood playground of Edgar Allan Poe; antique and period furnishings and decor. Cr cds: A, C, D, ER, MC, V.

D ➤ 🔥 SC

✔ ★ ★ **WILLIAM CATLIN HOUSE.** *2304 E Broad St (23223), in Church Hill historic district.* 804/780-3746. 5 rms, 3 with bath, 3 story. No elvtr. S $72.50; D $89.50; suites $140. Complimentary full bkfst, sherry. Ck-out 11:30 am, ck-in 3 pm. Balconies. Federal-period town house (1845) furnished with antiques, family heirlooms; fireplaces. Spacious veranda overlooks courtyard. Cr cds: DS, MC, V.

🔥

Restaurants

★ **AMICI.** *3343 W Cary St.* 804/353-4700. Hrs: 5:30-10 pm; Fri & Sat to 11 pm. Closed major hols. Res accepted. Northern Italian menu. Bar. A la carte entrees: dinner $4.95-$18.95. Specializes in pasta, game, seafood. Outdoor dining. Cr cds: A, MC, V.

★ **BYRAM'S LOBSTER HOUSE.** *3215 W Broad St (23230).* 804/355-9193. Hrs: 11:30 am-10 pm; Fri & Sat to 11 pm; early-bird dinner Mon-Fri 3:30-6 pm. Closed Sun (summer months); Dec 24 & 25. Res accepted. Continental menu. Bar. Semi-a la carte:

lunch $2-$24.95, dinner $3.75-$24.95. Specializes in Maine lobster, crab imperial. Parking. Local artwork, Greek reproductions. Family-owned. Cr cds: A, DS, MC, V.

D **SC**

✔ ★ **DELANEY'S CAFE AND GRILL.** *10622 Patterson Ave. 804/740-1921.* Hrs: 11:30 am-10 pm; Sat 5-11 pm; Sun 11 am-9 pm; Sun brunch to 3 pm. Closed Thanksgiving, Dec 25. Bar. Semi-a la carte: lunch $3.95-$7.95, dinner $8.95-$15.95. Sun brunch $4.95-$9.95. Child's meals. Specializes in seasonal seafood items. Own soups, pies, potato chips. Parking. Cr cds: DS, MC, V.

D

✔ ★ **FAROUK'S HOUSE OF INDIA.** *3033 W Cary St, west of downtown. 804/355-0378.* Hrs: 11:30 am-2:30 pm, 5:30-10:30 pm; Sat & Sun from 5:30 pm. Res accepted. Indian menu. Bar. Semi-a la carte: lunch $4-$7.50, dinner $6.50-$12. Buffet lunch: $5.99. Specializes in curries, biryanies, tandoori. Cr cds: MC, V.

★ ★ **HALF WAY HOUSE.** *10301 Jefferson Davis Hwy (Petersburg Tpke), 13 mi S on US 1, approx halfway between Richmond & Petersburg. 804/275-1760.* Hrs: 11:30 am-2 pm, 5:30-9 pm; Sat, Sun from 5:30 pm. Res accepted. Bar. Wine list. Semi-a la carte: lunch $7-$15, dinner $15-$30. Specialties: lobster Von Grinegan, filet mignon, colonial chicken & beef pies. Parking. Antique-furnished manor house (1760) was stop on Petersburg stagecoach line until late 19th century; hosted Washington, Lafayette, Patrick Henry, Jefferson, among others. Used as a Union headquarters during 1864 siege of Richmond. Cr cds: A, D, DS, MC, V.

★ ★ **KABUTO STEAK HOUSE.** *8052 W Broad St. 804/747-9573.* Hrs: 11:30 am-2 pm, 5:30-10 pm; Fri to 10:30 pm; Sat 5:30-10:30 pm; Sun 5-9:30 pm. Closed Thanksgiving, Dec 25. Res accepted. Japanese menu. Bar. Complete meals: lunch $6-$10.25, dinner $11.50-$22. Child's meals. Specializes in shrimp, steak, lobster. Teppanyaki cooking. Sushi bar. Parking. Japanese-style building. Cr cds: A, C, D, DS, MC, V.

D

★ ★ **LA PETITE FRANCE.** *2108 Maywill St. 804/353-8729.* Hrs: 11:30 am-2 pm, 5:30-10 pm; Sat 5:30-11 pm. Closed Sun, Mon; major hols; also last 2 wks Aug. Res accepted. French menu. Serv bar. Wine list. A la carte entrees: lunch $7.95-$10.95, dinner $17.95-$22.50. Child's meals. Specializes in seafood, veal. Parking. Family-owned. Jacket. Cr cds: A, C, D, MC, V.

★ ★ **LEMAIRE.** *(See The Jefferson) 804/788-8000.* Hrs: 6:30 am-2 pm, 5:30-10:30 pm. Closed Memorial Day. Res accepted. Bar. A la carte entrees: bkfst $2.25-$8.95, lunch $3.50-$13.95, dinner $3.75-$25.95. Child's meals. Specializes in regional cuisine, venison, pheasant. Valet parking. Seven small dining rms. Jacket. Cr cds: A, C, D, DS, ER, JCB, MC, V.

D

★ **MATT'S BRITISH PUB.** *109 S 12th St, in Shockoe Slip area, downtown. 804/644-0848.* Hrs: 11-2 am. Closed Dec 25. Res accepted. English menu. Bar. A la carte entrees: lunch $4.25-$8. Complete meals: dinner $9.50-$16. Specialties: steak and mushroom pie, prime rib. Comedy act Fri, Sat. In former grain warehouse (1880) located in historic district. Cr cds: A, DS, MC, V.

★ **MR. PATRICK HENRY'S INN.** *2300 E Broad St, in Church Hill Historic district. 804/644-1322.* Hrs: 11:30 am-2:30 pm, 5:30-10:30 pm. Closed Sun (exc hols); Jan 1, Dec 24-25. Res accepted. Continental menu. Bar. Semi-a la carte: lunch $6-$12, dinner $17-$24. Specializes in duckling, crabcakes. Own soups. Outdoor dining. Greek-revival antebellum row house (ca 1855); many antique furnishings. Guest rms avail. Cr cds: A, D, DS, MC, V.

D

★ ★ **NIELSEN'S SEAFOOD.** *4800 Thalbro St. 804/355-2266.* Hrs: 11:30 am-3 pm, 5-9 pm. Closed Sun; major hols. Serv bar. Semi-a la carte: lunch $4.25-$10.95, dinner $5.95-$15.95. Child's meals. Spe-

cializes in fresh seafood, steak, wide selection of vegetables. Parking. Many antiques, tapestries. Family-owned. Cr cds: A, MC, V.

✔ ★ **O'TOOLE'S.** *4800 Forest Hill Ave. 804/233-1781.* Hrs: 11-2 am; Sun to midnight. Closed Dec 24-26. Bar. Semi-a la carte: lunch $3.75-$8, dinner $4.25-$12.95. Child's meals. Specializes in seafood, steak, barbecued dishes. Pianist. Parking. Irish pub decor. Family-owned. Cr cds: A, MC, V.

★ **PEKING PAVILION.** *1302 E Cary St, in Shockoe Slip historic district, downtown. 804/649-8888.* Hrs: 11:30 am-9:45 pm; Fri to 10:45 pm; Sat 5-10:45 pm; Sun brunch 11:30 am-2 pm. Closed Thanksgiving. Chinese menu. Bar. Semi-a la carte: lunch $4.25-$6.95, dinner $6.50-$22.50. Sun brunch $9.50. Specialties: Peking duck, seafood delight, chicken imperial. Oriental antiques; teakwood sculpture. Cr cds: A, MC, V.

D

★ ★ **RUTH'S CHRIS STEAKHOUSE.** *11500 Huguenot Rd (23113), at Bellgrade Plantation House. 804/378-0600.* Hrs: 5-10 pm; Fri & Sat to 11 pm; Sun to 9 pm. Closed some major hols. Res accepted. Bar. A la carte entrees: dinner $14-$26. Specializes in steak, lobster. Organist Tues-Sat. Parking. Outdoor dining. Cr cds: A, C, D, MC, V.

D

★ ★ **SAM MILLER'S WAREHOUSE.** *1210 E Cary St, in Shockoe area of downtown. 804/643-1301.* Hrs: 11 am-11 pm; Sun brunch 10 am-5 pm. Res accepted. Bar to 1:30 am. Semi-a la carte: lunch $4.95-$10.95, dinner $11-$22.95. Sun champagne brunch $6-$13.95. Child's meals. Specializes in fresh seafood, live Maine lobster, prime Western beef. Lobster tank. In historic district; display of antique mirrors. Cr cds: A, D, MC, V.

D

★ ★ **SKILLIGALEE.** *5416 Glenside Dr. 804/672-6200.* Hrs: 11:30 am-4 pm, 5-11 pm; Sat from 5 pm; Sun 5-9 pm. Closed Thanksgiving, Dec 25. Bar. A la carte entrees: lunch $5.95-$11.95, dinner $13.95-$25.95. Specializes in fresh seafood, cheese biscuits. Own salad dressing. Parking. Nautical decor. Family-owned. Cr cds: A, MC, V.

D

★ ★ **SORRENTO.** *5604 Patterson Ave. 804/282-9340.* Hrs: 5:30-10 pm; Fri & Sat to 10:30 pm; Sun to 9:30 pm. Closed Mon; major hols; also 1st 2 wks July. Res accepted. Italian menu. Bar. Semi-a la carte: dinner $7.75-$16.50. Child's meals. Specializes in veal dishes, espresso pie. Own pasta. Parking. Cr cds: A, D, DS, MC, V.

D

✔ ★ **TANGLEWOOD ORDINARY.** *(2210 River Rd W, Maidens) 16 mi W on VA 6 (Patterson Ave). 804/556-3284.* Hrs: 5:30-9 pm; Sun noon-6 pm. Closed Mon-Wed; some major hols. Res accepted. Traditional Southern menu. Bar (wine, beer). Complete meals: dinner $7.99. Specializes in fried chicken, black-eyed peas, ham. Parking. Casual dining in log cabin building. Collection of The Saturday Evening Post dating from 1913. Totally nonsmoking. No cr cds accepted.

★ ★ **TOBACCO COMPANY.** *1201 E Cary St, in Shockoe Slip area, downtown. 804/782-9431.* Hrs: 11:30 am-2:30 pm, 5:30-10:30 pm; Sat 5-11 pm; Sun 11 am-2:30 pm, 5:30-10 pm. Closed Jan 1, Dec 25. Res accepted. Bar 11:30-2 am. A la carte entrees: lunch $2.99-$7.95, dinner $12.95-$25.95. Sun brunch $4.95-$7.95. Specializes in prime rib, fresh fish. Own baking. Band exc Sun. In former tobacco warehouse (ca 1880); built around skylighted atrium with antique cage elevator; many unusual antiques. Cr cds: A, D, MC, V.

D

★ ★ **YEN CHING.** *6601 Midlothian Tpke (23225). 804/276-7430.* Hrs: 11:30 am-10 pm; Sat & Sun to 11 pm. Closed Thanksgiving. Res required. Chinese menu. Bar. Semi-a la carte: lunch $5-$22, dinner

$7-$22. Specializes in Hunan and Szechuan dishes. Parking. Chinese tapestries and art. Cr cds: A, C, D, MC, V.

D

Richmond National Battlefield Park (E-8)

A total of seven Union drives on Richmond, the symbol of secession, were made during the Civil War. Richmond National Battlefield Park, 770 acres in 10 different units, preserves sites of the 2 efforts that came close to success—McClellan's Peninsula Campaign of 1862 and Grant's attack in 1864.

Of McClellan's campaign, the park includes sites of the Seven Days' Battles at Chickahominy Bluffs, Beaver Dam Creek, Gaines' Mill (Watt House) and Malvern Hill. Grant's campaign is represented by the battlefield at Cold Harbor, where on June 3, 1864, Grant hurled his army at fortified Confederate positions, resulting in 7,000 casualties in less than one hour. Confederate Fort Harrison, Parker's Battery and Drewry's Bluff (Fort Darling) and Union-built Fort Brady are also included. Park (daily).

What to See and Do

1. **Main Visitor Center.** In Chimborazo City Park. 3215 E Broad St, on US 60E in Richmond. Information, exhibits, film, slide program. (Daily; closed Jan 1, Thanksgiving, Dec 25) Phone 804/226-1981. **Free.** From here start

   Self-guided tour. Auto drive (60 mi) with markers, maps, recorded messages providing background, detailed information for specific places. Visitors may select own route, including all or part of the drive.

2. **Other Visitor Centers.** Cold Harbor, 16 mi NE on VA 156 (daily, unstaffed) and Fort Harrison, 10 mi SE on VA 5 & Battlefield Park Rd (June-Aug, daily). **Free.**

(For accommodations see Ashland, Richmond)

Roanoke (E-5)

Settled: 1740 **Pop:** 96,397 **Elev:** 948 ft **Area code:** 703

Roanoke was incorporated in 1882, when it became a junction of the Norfolk and Western Railway and the Shenandoah Valley Railroad. Before that, the town was called Big Lick (salt marshes in the area attracted big game).

It is the cultural, industrial, commercial, convention and medical center for western Virginia. Manufactured products include railroad cars, fabricated steel, fabrics, apparel, furniture, flour, wood products, electronic equipment, plastics, cosmetics and locks.

Set in the Shenandoah Valley, between the Blue Ridge and the Allegheny Mountains, it is near the outdoor attractions of the huge Jefferson National Forest (see MARION) and the Blue Ridge Parkway (see).

What to See and Do

1. **Mill Mountain Zoological Park.** Off US 220/I-581 and Blue Ridge Pkwy. Zoo; picnic areas, magnificent views of city; miniature train. (Daily; closed Dec 25) Phone 343-3241. ¢¢

2. **Virginia Museum of Transportation.** 303 Norfolk Ave, downtown. Vehicles from the past and present. Large steam, diesel and electric locomotive collection. Aviation exhibits; model of mini-

ature traveling circus. Hands-on exhibits. (Mar-Dec, daily; rest of yr, daily exc Mon; closed major hols) Phone 342-5670. ¢¢

3. **Center in the Square.** One Market Square, downtown. A unique facility housing five independent cultural organizations under one roof; three museums, including Roanoke Museum of Fine Arts, and two professional theater companies (see SEASONAL EVENT). (Daily exc Mon; closed major hols) Phone 342-5700. Fine arts museum **free.** Also here are

   Science Museum of Western Virginia. Museum contains hands-on exhibits in the natural and physical sciences: animals of land & ocean, computers, TV weather station. Workshops, programs and classes for children & adults; special exhibits. Hopkins Planetarium shows, films. (Daily; closed hols) Sr citizen rate. Phone 342-5710 or 343-7876 (recording). ¢¢

   Roanoke Valley History Museum. Permanent exhibits deal with Roanoke history from days of Indians to present. (Daily exc Mon; closed most hols) Sr citizen rate. Phone 342-5770. ¢

4. **Jefferson National Forest** (see MARION).

5. **Blue Ridge Pkwy** (see). 6 mi E on US 460 or 3 mi S on US 220. Runs on crest of mountains both N and S of Roanoke. Narrow in parts; limited restaurants. Beautiful seasonal views from overlooks.

(For further information contact the Roanoke Valley Convention & Visitors Bureau, 114 Market St, 24011; 342-6025.)

Annual Events

Chili Cookoff. Annual statewide event, held at City Market. For information contact Roanoke Special Events Committee, 210 Reserve Ave SW, 24016; 981-2889. 1st Sat May.

Festival in the Park. Art exhibits, crafts, sports, food, parade, entertainment. 2 wkends beginning Fri before Memorial Day.

Seasonal Event

Mill Mountain Theatre. Center in the Square. Musicals, comedies, dramas. Nightly exc Mon; Sat, Sun matinees. For res phone 342-5740. Regular season, Oct-Aug.

(See Salem)

Motels

✔ ★ ★ **DAYS INN-AIRPORT/INTERSTATE.** 8118 *Plantation Rd (24019), I-81 exit 146.* 703/366-0341; FAX 703/366-3935. 123 rms, 2 story. S $36-$48; D $52-$58; each addl $6; suites $80; under 12 free. Crib avail. TV; cable. Pool. Restaurant 6-10:30 am, 5-10 pm. Bar 4:30-11 pm. Ck-out noon. Meeting rms. Valet serv. Free airport transportation. Cr cds: A, C, D, DS, MC, V.

≈ ✕ 🔥 SC

★ **HAMPTON INN-TANGLEWOOD.** 3816 *Franklin Rd SW (24014).* 703/989-4000; FAX 703/989-0250. 70 rms, 2 story. May-Nov: S $46-$54; D $52-$62; family rates; higher rates conventions; lower rates rest of yr. Crib free. TV; cable. Complimentary continental bkfst, coffee in lobby. Restaurant adj 10:30 am-10 pm; wkends from 8 am. Ck-out 11 am. Coin lndry. Meeting rm. Valet serv. Some refrigerators. Cr cds: A, C, D, DS, MC, V.

D ✕ 🔥 SC

★ ★ **HOLIDAY INN-AIRPORT.** 6626 *Thirlane Rd (24019), near Municipal Airport.* 703/366-8861; FAX 703/366-8861, ext. 190. 163 rms, 2 story. S $60-$70; D $65-$80; each addl $4-$6; under 18 free; wkend rates. Crib free. Pet accepted, some restrictions. TV; cable. Pool; wading pool, lifeguard in summer. Complimentary coffee in rms. Restaurant 6 am-10 pm. Rm serv. Bar. Ck-out noon. Coin lndry. Meeting rms. Bellhops. Valet serv. Sundries. Airport, bus depot transportation. Tennis, golf privileges. Some bathrm phones. Cr cds: A, C, D, DS, ER, JCB, MC, V.

[D] [♥] [🏃] [🎿] [≈] [✈] [⇄] [🔥] [SC]

★ ★ **HOLIDAY INN-CIVIC CENTER.** *501 Orange Ave at Williamson Rd (24016). 703/342-8961; FAX 703/342-8961, ext. 121.* 153 rms, 2 story. S $45-$59; D $57-$71; each addl $5; some wknd rates. Crib free. TV; cable. Pool; wading pool. Restaurant 6 am-10 pm. Rm serv from 7 am. Bar from 11 am. Ck-out noon. Bellhops. Valet serv. Cr cds: A, C, D, DS, ER, JCB, MC, V.

[≈] [⇄] [🔥] [SC]

✔ ★ **JEFFERSON LODGE.** *616 S Jefferson St (24011). 703/342-2951; res: 800/950-2580; FAX 703/342-2951, ext. 270.* 100 rms, 3 story. S $40.95; D $45.95; each addl $5; family, wkly rates. Crib avail. TV. Pool; poolside serv. Restaurant 7 am-3 pm. Rm serv. Ck-out noon. Coin lndry. Cr cds: A, C, D, DS, MC, V.

[≈] [⇄] [🔥] [SC]

★ **SLEEP INN.** *4045 Electric Rd (24014). 703/772-1500; res: 800/628-1929; FAX 703/772-1500, ext. 499.* 103 rms, shower only, 2 story. No elvtr. S $49.95-$55.95; D $55.95-$61.95; each addl $8; under 18 free. Crib free. TV; cable, in-rm movies. Complimentary continental bkfst. Restaurant nearby. Ck-out noon. Meeting rm. Valet serv. Cr cds: A, C, D, DS, ER, JCB, MC, V.

[D] [⇄] [🔥] [SC]

✔ ★ **TRAVELODGE-NORTH.** *(2444 Lee Hwy S, Troutville 24175) I-81 exit 150-A. 703/992-6700; FAX 703/992-3991.* 109 rms. S $32.95-$38; D $42-$50; each addl $6; kit. units $50; under 18 free; wkly rates. Crib free. Pet accepted; $6. TV; cable. Pool. Playground. Complimentary continental bkfst, coffee. Restaurant nearby. Ck-out 11 am. Meeting rms. Cr cds: A, D, DS, MC, V.

[D] [♥] [≈] [⇄] [🔥]

Motor Hotels

★ ★ **HOLIDAY INN-TANGLEWOOD.** *4468 Starkey Rd SW (24014). 703/774-4400; FAX 703/774-1195.* 196 rms, 5 story. S, D $88-$102; suites $128-$153; under 18 free; wkend rates. Crib free. Pet accepted; $10. TV; cable. Pool; poolside serv. Restaurant 6:30 am-10 pm. Rm serv. Bar noon-2 am; entertainment, dancing. Ck-out noon. Convention facilities. Bellhops. Valet serv. Concierge. Free airport, bus depot transportation. Golf privileges. Health club privileges. Some wet bars. *LUXURY LEVEL : CONCIERGE LEVEL.* 17 rms, 1 suite. S, D $94-$102; suites $153. Private lounge, honor bar. In-rm movies. Complimentary continental bkfst, refreshments. Cr cds: A, C, D, DS, JCB, MC, V.

[D] [♥] [🏃] [≈] [⇄] [🔥] [SC]

★ ★ **SHERATON INN AIRPORT.** *2727 Ferndale Dr (24017), near Municipal Airport. 703/362-4500; FAX 703/362-4500, ext. 113.* 148 rms, 5 story. S $69-$150; D $79-$160; each addl $12; suites $115-$180; under 18 free; wkend rates. Crib free. Pet accepted; $50. TV; cable. Indoor/outdoor pool; whirlpool. Restaurant 6 am-10:30 pm. Rm serv. Complimentary coffee in rms. Bar 11:30 am-midnight. Ck-out noon. Meeting rms. Bellhops. Valet serv. Sundries. Free airport transportation. Lighted tennis. 18-hole golf privileges. Bathrm phones. Cr cds: A, C, D, DS, ER, MC, V.

[D] [♥] [🏃] [≈] [✈] [⇄] [🔥] [SC]

Hotels

★ ★ **MARRIOTT-ROANOKE AIRPORT.** *2801 Hershberger Rd NW (24017), near Municipal Airport. 703/563-9300; FAX 703/563-9300, ext. 7776.* 320 rms, 8 story. S, studio rms $64-$110; D $64-$120; each addl $10; suites $199-$250; under 18 free; golf, wkend rates. Crib free. Pet accepted, some restrictions; $10. TV; cable. 2 pools, 1 indoor; poolside serv. Restaurant 6:30 am-10 pm. Rm serv 24 hrs. 2 bars 11-2

am; dancing. Ck-out noon. Convention facilities. Concierge. Gift shop. Free airport transportation. Lighted tennis. Golf privileges. Exercise equipt; weights, bicycles, whirlpool, sauna. Some refrigerators. Private patios, balconies. *LUXURY LEVEL.* 34 rms, 4 floors. S $109-$119; D $109-$129; suite $200-$305. Concierge. Private lounge, honor bar. Complimentary continental bkfst, refreshments. Cr cds: A, C, D, DS, ER, JCB, MC, V.

[D] [♥] [🏃] [🎿] [≈] [✈] [⇄] [🔥] [SC]

★ ★ ★ **RADISSON PATRICK HENRY.** *Box 2241 (24009), 617 S Jefferson St. 703/345-8811; FAX 703/342-9908.* 120 kit. units, 10 story. S $89; D $99; each addl $10; suites $150-$250; monthly rates. Crib avail. TV; cable. Pool privileges. Restaurant 6:30 am-10 pm. Bar 4 pm-2 am. Ck-out noon. Guest lndry. Meeting rms. Barber, beauty shop. Free airport transportation. Health club privileges. Refrigerators. Cr cds: A, C, D, DS, ER, JCB, MC, V.

[D] [⇄] [🔥] [SC]

Restaurants

★ ★ **CHARCOAL STEAK HOUSE.** *5225 Williamson Rd. 703/366-3710.* Hrs: 11 am-2 pm, 4-11 pm; Sat from 4 pm. Closed Sun; major hols. Res accepted. Greek, Amer menu. Bar. Semi-a la carte: lunch $3.95-$11.95, dinner $10.50-$30. Child's meals. Specializes in prime rib, steak, seafood. Entertainment. Parking. Cr cds: A, C, D, DS, MC, V.

[D]

★ ★ **KABUKI.** *3503 Franklin Rd SW. 703/981-0222.* Hrs: 5-10:30 pm; Fri, Sat 4:30-11 pm. Closed some major hols; also Jan 2, Super Bowl Sun. Res accepted; required Fri, Sat. Japanese menu. Bar. Complete meals: dinner $9.95-$23.95. Child's meals. Specializes in steak, chicken, shrimp, flounder tempura. Teppanyaki cooking. Parking. Japanese antique display. Cr cds: A, C, D, DS, MC, V.

[D]

★ ★ ★ **LA MAISON.** *5732 Airport Rd. 703/366-2444.* Hrs: 11 am-2 pm, 5-11 pm. Closed Jan 1, Dec 24-25; also Sun & Mon of Memorial Day & Labor Day wkends. Res accepted. French, continental menu. Bar. Semi-a la carte: lunch $4.50-$9.95, dinner $9.95-$29.95. Child's meals. Specializes in prime rib, broiled seafood, veal Oscar. Own baking. Pianist Fri, Sat evenings. Parking. Outdoor dining. Old Georgian mansion. Cr cds: A, C, D, DS, MC, V.

[D]

★ ★ ★ **LIBRARY.** *3117 Franklin Rd, in Piccadilly Sq Shopping Ctr. 703/985-0811.* Hrs: 6 pm-midnight. Closed Sun; major hols. Res accepted. French, Amer menu. Bar. Wine cellar. Semi-a la carte: dinner $18.95-$24.95. Specialties: roast rack of lamb, Dover sole. Own pastries. Parking. Antique books on display. Jacket. Cr cds: A, C, D, MC, V.

✔ ★ **SUNNYBROOK INN.** *7342 Plantation Rd NW. 703/366-4555.* Hrs: 7 am-8 pm; Fri & Sat to 9 pm; Sun to 7 pm. Closed Dec 25. Res accepted. Wine, beer. Semi-a la carte: bkfst $2-$4, lunch $3-$7.45, dinner $5-$15. Buffet: (Fri & Sat) dinner $5.50-$14.99; (Sun) lunch & dinner $8. Child's meals. Specializes in oysters, country ham, fresh mountain trout. Salad bar. Parking. Outdoor dining. In colonial-revival farmhouse (1912). Cr cds: D, DS, MC, V.

[D]

Salem (E-5)

Founded: 1802 **Pop:** 23,756 **Elev:** 1,060 ft **Area code:** 703 **Zip:** 24153

Salem, part of the industrial complex of the Roanoke Valley, shares with Roanoke the beautiful setting between the Blue Ridge and Allegheny Mountains. Historic markers throughout Salem indicate the city's colonial heritage.

What to See and Do

1. **Dixie Caverns.** Off I-81 at exit 132. Stalactites in lofty chambers; modern lighting system makes 45-min tour comfortable as well as interesting. (Daily; closed Dec 25) Pottery shop and mineral shop (all yr). Camping facilities (fee). Phone 380-2085. ¢¢¢

2. **Roanoke College** (1842). (1,600 students) College Ave, off I-81. One of the few Southern colleges to remain open during Civil War. Many historic buildings, some antebellum. Olin Hall, fine arts building, has theater, art gallery and sculptures. Excellent exhibit of paintings, photographs and other items concerning Mary, Queen of Scots (by appt only; phone 375-2487). Tours. Phone 375-2282.

(For further information contact the Salem/Roanoke County Chamber of Commerce, 9 N College Ave, PO Box 832; 387-0267.)

(See Roanoke)

Motels

★ **ECONO LODGE.** *1535 E Main St. 703/986-1000.* 72 rms, 3 story. S $32.95; D $42.95; each addl $5; under 12 free. Crib free. TV; cable. Restaurant adj. Ck-out 11 am. Sundries. Cr cds: A, D, DS, MC, V.

D ⊠ 🐾 SC

★★ **HOLIDAY INN.** *1671 Skyview Rd, I-81 exit 137. 703/389-7061; FAX 703/389-7061, ext. 134.* 102 rms, 3 story. S $52-$72; D $62-$82; each addl $6; under 19 free. Crib free. TV; cable. Pool; wading pool. Restaurant 6 am-10 pm. Rm serv. Bar 5 pm-closing. Ck-out noon. Meeting rms. Bellhops. Valet serv. Sundries. Cr cds: A, C, D, DS, ER, JCB, MC, V.

D 🏌 ≈ ⊠ 🔥 SC

✔ ★★ **QUALITY INN.** *179 Sheraton Dr. 703/562-1912; res: 800/221-2222; FAX 703/562-0507.* 120 rms, 2 story. S $45-$50; D $48-$56; each addl $6; under 18 free. Crib free. TV; cable. Pool. Restaurant 6:30 am-1 pm, 5-9 pm. Bar 5 pm-11 pm. Ck-out 11 am. Meeting rms. Airport transportation. Putting green. Balconies. Cr cds: A, C, D, DS, ER, JCB, MC, V.

🏌 ≈ ⊠ 🔥 SC

Shenandoah National Park (C-7 - D-7)

About 450 million years ago the Blue Ridge was at the bottom of a sea. Today it averages about 2,000 feet above sea level; some 300 square miles of the loveliest Blue Ridge area are included in Shenandoah National Park.

The park is 80 miles long and from 2 to 13 miles wide. Running its full length is the 105-mile Skyline Drive. Main entrances are the North Entrance (Front Royal), from I-66, US 340, US 522 and VA 55; Thornton Gap Entrance (31.5 miles south), from US 211; Swift Run Gap Entrance (65.7 miles south), from US 33; and the South Entrance (Rockfish Gap), from I-64, US 250 and the Blue Ridge Parkway (see). The Drive, twisting and turning along the crest of the Blue Ridge, is one of the finest scenic trips in the East. Approximately 70 overlooks give views of the Blue Ridge, the Piedmont and, to the west, the Shenandoah River Valley and the Alleghenies.

The Drive offers much, but the park offers more. Exploration, on foot or horseback, attracts thousands of visitors who return again and again. Most of the area is wooded, predominantly in white, red and

chestnut oak, with hickory, birch, maple, hemlock, tulip poplar and nearly 100 other species scattered here and there. At the head of Whiteoak Canyon are hemlocks more than 300 years old. The park bursts with color and contrast in the fall, which makes this season particularly popular with visitors. The park is a wildlife sanctuary; deer, bear, fox and bobcat are here, along with more than 200 varieties of birds.

Accommodations in the park are limited, with lodge and cabins at Big Meadows and Skyland, and housekeeping cabins at Lewis Mountain. For reservations and rates (which vary), contact ARA Virginia Sky-Line Co, Inc, PO Box 727, Luray 22835-9051; 800/999-4714. Nearby communities provide a variety of accommodations, also. There are restaurants at Panorama, Skyland and Big Meadows; light lunches and groceries are available at Elkwallow, Lewis Mountain, Big Meadows and Loft Mountain Waysides.

The park is open all year; lodge and cottage accommodations, usually Mar-Dec; phone ahead for schedule. Skyline Drive is occasionally closed for short periods during Nov-Mar. As in all national parks, pets must be on a leash. The speed limit is 35 miles per hour. $5/car/week, annual permit $15; Golden Age and Golden Eagle passports accepted (see INTRODUCTION).

Park Headquarters is five miles east of Luray on US 211. Detailed information and pamphlets may be obtained by contacting Superintendent, Shenandoah National Park, Rte 4, Box 348, Luray 22835-9051; phone 703/999-3483.

What to See and Do

1. **Points of special interest on Skyline Drive.** (Mileposts are numbered north to south, starting at Front Royal. Periods of operation are estimated—phone ahead.)

   Dickey Ridge Visitor Center. 4.6 mi. Exhibits, programs, information, book sales; picnic grounds. (Apr-Oct, daily)

   Mathews Arm (2,800 ft). 22.2 mi. Camping, hiking, programs. (Usually May-Oct)

   Elkwallow (2,445 ft). 24.1 mi. Picnic grounds; food, gas. (May-Oct, daily)

   Panorama (2,300 ft). 31.5 mi, at jct US 211. Dining room, gift shop. Trail to Marys Rock. May be closed in winter.

   Marys Rock Tunnel (2,545 ft). 32.4 mi. Drive goes through 600 feet of rock (clearance 13 ft).

   Pinnacles (3,500 ft). 36.7 mi. Picnic grounds.

   Skyland (3,680 ft). 41.7 mi. Accommodations, restaurant; guided trail rides; Stony Man Nature Trail.

   Byrd Visitor Center. 51.1 mi. Museum exhibits, information, book sales, orientation programs, maps. (Usually Mar-Dec, daily)

   Big Meadows Wayside and Big Meadows (3,500 ft). 51.2 mi. At Wayside are a coffee shop, service station, campers' store. (Daily) At Big Meadows are accommodations, restaurant, tent and trailer sites; picnic grounds; nature trail. (Mar-Dec)

   Lewis Mountain (3,390 ft). 57.5 mi. 1-2 bedroom cabins with heat; tent and trailer sites; picnic grounds. (Usually late May-Oct)

   South River (2,940 ft). 62.8 mi. Picnic grounds, 2½-mile round trip to falls.

   Loft Mountain (3,380 ft). 79.5 mi. Picnicking, camping (May-Oct); wayside facility; service station, store (May-Oct).

2. **Naturalist program.** Guided walks, illustrated campfire talks. (Usually mid-Apr-mid-Oct; rest of yr, on a limited basis) Obtain schedule at Park HQ, entrance stations, visitor centers and concessions.

3. **Hiking.** 500 miles of trails include 94 mi of Appalachian Trail. Along the trail, which winds 2,028 miles from Maine to Georgia, are numerous side trails to mountain tops, waterfalls and secluded valleys. Trail crosses Skyline Drive at several points and can be entered at many overlooks. Overnight backcountry use requires a permit. No open fires are allowed. Regulations and

permits may be obtained at any park entrance station, visitor center or at Park HQ. Backcountry may be closed during periods of high fire danger.

Visitor Centers and lodges post schedules of evening programs and ranger-led hikes. Self-guided walks, ranging from 1/2 to 2 hours, are at Dickey Ridge (4.6 mi), Mathews Arm (22.2 mi), Skyland (41.7 mi), Big Meadows (51.1 mi) and Loft Mt (79.5 mi).

4. **Riding.** 25 mi of horseback trails. Trail rides (ponies for children) for rent at Skyland; wagon rides at Big Meadows.

5. **Fishing.** Trout. Regulations and directions at entrance stations, Panorama, Skyland, Elkwallow, Big Meadows. (Late Mar-mid-Oct) State or 5-day nonresident license necessary. ¢¢¢¢

6. **Camping.** First-come, first-serve tent and trailer sites (no hookups) at Mathews Arm, Big Meadows (res avail thru Ticketron late May-Oct), Lewis Mountain, Loft Mountain. 14-day limit. Campers must register and check out. (Spring-fall) Write Park Superintendent, Rte 4, Box 348, Luray 22835, for information. ¢¢¢-¢¢¢¢

7. **Picnicking.** Near Dickey Ridge Visitor Center, Elkwallow, Pinnacles, Big Meadows, Lewis Mountain, South River, Loft Mountain.

(See Front Royal, Luray, New Market, Waynesboro)

Motels

★ ★ **BIG MEADOWS LODGE.** *(Box 727, Luray 22835) 19 mi S of US 211, 15 mi N of US 33 on Skyline Dr. 703/999-2221; res: 800/999-4714.* 103 units: 73 motel rms, 20 lodge rms, 10 cabins. No A/C. Mid-May-Oct: lodge S, D $40-$69; motel S, D $57-$88; cabins $52-$60; suites $80-$90; each addl $5; under 16 free. Closed rest of yr. Crib free. Playground. Restaurant 7:30-10 am, noon-2 pm, 5:30-8:30 pm. Box lunches. Bar 4-11 pm; entertainment. Ck-out noon. Gift shop. Private patios, balconies. Panoramic view of Shenandoah Valley. Cr cds: A, DS, MC, V.

✔ ★ ★ **SKYLAND LODGE.** *(Box 727, Luray 22835) 10 mi S of US 211, 25 mi N of US 33 on Skyline Dr. 703/999-2211; res: 800/999-4714; FAX 703/999-2231.* 186 rms. No A/C. Mid-May-Oct: S, D $41-$82; each addl $5; suites $90-$120; under 16 free; lower rates Apr-mid-May & Nov. Closed rest of yr. Crib free. TV avail. Playground. Restaurant 7:30-10:30 am, noon-3 pm, 5:30-8:30 pm. Box lunches avail. Bar 3-11 pm. Ck-out noon. Meeting rms. Sundries. Gift shop. Private patios. Balconies. Cr cds: A, DS, MC, V.

Skyline Drive (C-7 - D-7)

(see Shenandoah National Park)

South Boston (F-6)

Pop: 6,997 **Elev:** 407 ft **Area code:** 804 **Zip:** 24592

What to See and Do

Staunton River State Park. 8 mi NE on VA 304, then 11 mi SE on VA 344. Approx 1,300 acres of woods, meadows and lengthy shoreline on John H. Kerr Reservoir (Buggs Island Lake). Swimming pool, wading pool, bathhouse; fishing; boating (rentals, ramp). Hiking, nature trails; tennis courts. Picnic facilities, shelters; children's playground; concession. Tent and trailer sites, 7 cabins (May-Sept). Visitor center, interpretive programs. Standard fees. Phone 572-4623.

(For accommodations see Clarksville, Danville)

South Hill (F-7)

Pop: 4,217 **Elev:** 440 ft **Area code:** 804 **Zip:** 23970

(See Clarksville)

Motels

✔ ★ **COMFORT INN.** *918 E Atlantic St, I-85 exit 12. 804/447-2600; FAX 804/447-2590.* 40 rms, 2 story. S $34.95-$48; D $38-$48; under 12 free. Crib $6. Pet accepted. TV; cable, in-rm movies. Continental bkfst. Complimentary coffee. Restaurant opp 6 am-10 pm. Ck-out 11 am. Whirlpool. Cr cds: A, C, D, DS, JCB, MC, V.

★ ★ **HOLIDAY INN.** *Box 594, jct I-85, US 58. 804/447-3123; FAX 804/447-4237.* 152 rms, 2 story. S $51-$58; D $57-$64; each addl $6; under 19 free. Crib free. TV; cable. Heated pool; wading pool. Restaurant adj open 24 hrs. Bar 5 pm-1 am. Ck-out noon. Coin lndry. Meeting rms. Valet serv. Free airport, bus depot transportation. Health club privileges. Game rm. Cr cds: A, C, D, DS, JCB, MC, V.

Springfield (C-8)

Pop: 23,706 **Elev:** 300 ft **Area code:** 703

(See Alexandria, Arlington County, Fairfax, Mount Vernon; also see District of Columbia)

Motel

✔ ★ ★ **DAYS INN-SPRINGFIELD MALL.** *6721 Commerce St (22150), I-95 exit 169A. 703/922-6100; FAX 703/922-0708.* 179 rms, 6 story. Apr-Oct: S, D $50-$65; each addl $6, ages 13-18, $3; under 12 free; lower rates rest of yr. Crib free. TV. Pool; lifeguard. Restaurant 6 am-2 pm, 4-9 pm. Ck-out noon. Meeting rms. Valet serv. Health club privileges. Cr cds: A, C, D, DS, ER, MC, V.

Hotel

★ ★ **BEST WESTERN SPRINGFIELD INN.** *6550 Loisdale Court (22150), I-95 exit 169A. 703/922-9000; FAX 703/922-9000, ext. 313.* 265 rms. S, D $63-$89; each addl $6; suites, kit. units $115-$175; under 16 free; wkend, cherry blossom festival packages. TV; cable. Pool. Complimentary continental bkfst. Ck-out noon. Meeting rms. Gift shop. Free National Airport transportation. Game rm. Cr cds: A, C, D, DS, MC, V.

Staunton (D-6)

Settled: 1736 **Pop:** 24,461 **Elev:** 1,385 ft **Area code:** 703 **Zip:** 24401

To historians, Staunton (STAN-ton) is known as the birthplace of Woodrow Wilson, and to students of government, as the place where the city-manager plan was first conceived and adopted. Set in fertile Shenandoah Valley fields and orchards, between the Blue Ridge and Allegheny mountain ranges, the area around Staunton produces poultry, livestock and wool. Manufacturing firms in the city make air conditioners, razors, candy and clothing.

A Ranger District office of the George Washington National Forest is located here.

What to See and Do

1. **Woodrow Wilson Birthplace and Presidential Museum.** 24 N Coalter St, near I-81, I-64 & US 11. Restored Greek-revival manse with period furnishings and Wilson family mementos from 1850s; museum building on grounds houses seven-gallery presidential exhibit, "The Life and Times of Woodrow Wilson," and his 1919 Pierce-Arrow limousine. Victorian gardens. (Daily; closed Jan 1, Thanksgiving, Dec 25) Sr citizen rate. Phone 885-0897. ¢¢¢

2. **Museum of American Frontier Culture.** I-81 exit 222, US 250 W and follow signs. Living history museum consists of working farms brought together from England, Germany, Northern Ireland and an American farm. The European farms represent what America's early settlers left; the American farm, from the Valley of Virginia, reflects the blend of the various European influences. Visitors are able to see and take part in life as it was lived on these 18th- and 19th-century farmsteads. The American and Scotch-Irish farms are complete; German and English farms under construction. Costumed interpreters demonstrate daily life at all four. sites. Interpretive center. (Daily; closed Jan 1, Thanksgiving, Dec 25) Sr citizen rate. Phone 332-7850. ¢¢¢

3. **McCormick Memorial Wayside.** 16 mi SW via US 11, I-81; 1 mi E of I-81 on VA 606 near Steeles Tavern. Cyrus McCormick's first reaper is displayed here. Picnic grounds. (Daily) Phone 377-2255. **Free.**

4. **Trinity Episcopal Church** (1855). 214 W Beverley St. Founded as Augusta Parish Church (1746), original building on this site served as Revolutionary capitol of state for 16 days in 1781. Open on request (Mon-Fri). Phone 886-9132.

5. **Augusta Stone Church** (1747). 7 mi N on US 11 in Ft Defiance. Oldest Presbyterian church in continuous use in state. Once used as fort during Indian raids. Museum of early church artifacts (by appt). Phone 248-2634.

6. **Gypsy Hill Park.** Off Churchville and Thornrose Aves. Lake stocked with fish; swimming (late May-Labor Day, fee); lighted softball field with concession stand, outdoor basketball courts; tennis; 18-hole golf; picnicking; miniature train ride, playgrounds; fairgrounds. (Daily) Phone 332-3945.

(For further information contact the Travel Information Center, 1303 Richmond Ave; 332-3972.)

Seasonal Event

Jazz in the Park. Gypsy Hill Park. Thurs nights. July-Sept.

(See Harrisonburg, Waynesboro)

Motels

✔ ★ **ECONO LODGE-HESSIAN HOUSE.** *Rte 2, Box 364, 1/2 mi S of jct I-81 & 64 exit 213/213A Greenville. 703/337-1231; FAX 703/337-0821.* 32 rms, 2 story. May-Nov: S $32-$35.95; D $35.95-$49.95; each addl $5; under 12 free; wkly rates; lower rates rest of yr. Crib free. Pet accepted, some restrictions; $5. TV; cable, in-rm movies. Pool; wading pool. Playground. Complimentary coffee in lobby. Restaurant nearby. Ck-out 11 am. Refrigerators. Private patios, balconies. Picnic tables. Cr cds: A, DS, MC, V.

★ ★ **SHONEY'S INN.** *Rte 4, Box 99E, jct US 250 & I-81 exit 222. 703/885-3117; FAX 703/885-5620.* 91 rms, 2 story. S $43.50; D $48; each addl $6; suites $45-$50; under 18 free. Crib $4. TV; cable. Indoor pool. Restaurant 6 am-11 pm; Fri, Sat to 1 am. Bar 4-10:30 pm. Ck-out noon. Valet serv. Sundries. Exercise equipt; weights, bicycles,

whirlpool, sauna. Some in-rm whirlpools. Cr cds: A, C, D, DS, ER, MC, V.

Motor Hotel

★ ★ ★ **HOLIDAY INN GOLF & CONFERENCE CENTER.** *Box 3209, I-81 exit 225, at Woodrow Wilson Pkwy. 703/248-6020; FAX 703/248-2902.* 113 rms, 4 story. Mid-Mar-mid-Nov: S $56-$70; D $62-$76; each addl $6; suites $91-$121; under 17 free; golf plans; lower rates rest of yr. Crib free. TV; cable. Indoor/outdoor pool; poolside serv. Restaurant 6:30 am-10 pm. Rm serv. Bar 4 pm-12:30 am; entertainment, dancing Fri-Sat. Ck-out noon. Meeting rms. Valet serv. Sundries. Free airport transportation. Lighted tennis. 18-hole golf, greens fee $30, pro, putting green, driving range. Health club privileges. Refrigerator, wet bar in suites. Some balconies. Cr cds: A, C, D, DS, ER, JCB, MC, V.

Inns

★ ★ **BELLE GRAE.** *515 W Frederick St. 703/886-5151.* 15 rms, 2 story. Some rm phones. S, D $69-$79; each addl $25; suites $99; higher rates wkends. Children over 10 yrs preferred. TV in parlor, some rms. Complimentary full bkfst, sherry. Dining rm 7:30-9:30 am, 6-9 pm; closed Mon & Tues. Ck-out 11 am, ck-in 3 pm. Meeting rms. Airport, RR station, bus depot transportation. Tennis, golf privileges. Fireplaces. Private patios, balconies. 1870s restored Victorian mansion. Each rm individually decorated; antiques. Cr cds: A, MC, V.

✔ ★ ★ **BUCKHORN.** *(HCR 33, Box 139, Churchville 24421) 12 mi W on US 250. 703/337-6900; res: 800/369-4242.* 6 rms, 3 story. No rm phones. S $35-$55; D $45-$75; each addl $10. Closed Dec 24, 25. Crib free. Complimentary full bkfst. Restaurant (see BUCKHORN INN RESTAURANT). Ck-out 11 am, ck-in 1 pm. Located in Shenandoah Valley of the George Washington National Forest. Restored 1811 inn. Cr cds: C, MC, V.

★ ★ **FREDERICK HOUSE.** *28 N New St. 703/885-4220; res: 800/334-5575.* 14 units, 2 story, 6 suites. S, D $55-$95; each addl $20; suites $85-$95; wkly rates. Crib $10. TV; cable. Pool privileges avail. Free full bkfst. Rm serv 24 hrs. Ck-out 11 am, ck-in 3-10 pm. Tennis, golf privileges. Private patios, balconies. Picnic tables. Encompasses 5 adj town houses built 1885-1919. Antiques and period furnishings. Across from Mary Baldwin College. Totally nonsmoking. Cr cds: A, D, DS, MC, V.

★ ★ **THORNROSE HOUSE.** *531 Thornrose Ave. 703/885-7026.* 5 rms, 2 story. No rm phones. S $45-$65; D $55-$75. Complimentary full bkfst. Complimentary coffee in rms. Ck-out 11 am, ck-in 3 pm. Georgian-revival house (1912); wrap-around veranda. Antiques; four poster and brass beds. Opp park with swimming, tennis, golf. Totally nonsmoking. No cr cds accepted.

Restaurants

✔ ★ ★ **BUCKHORN INN.** *(See Buckhorn Inn) 703/337-6900.* Hrs: 11 am-8 pm; Sat from 4 pm. Closed Mon; Dec 24, 25; also Tues in Jan, Feb. Semi-a la carte: lunch $1.75-$7.95. Complete meals: lunch, dinner $4.50-$7.95. Sun brunch $10.50. Child's meals. Specializes in regional country dishes. Salad bar. Parking. Located in colonial-era country inn in Shenandoah Valley. Cr cds: C, MC, V.

★ **McCORMICK'S PUB.** *41 N Augusta St. 703/885-3111.* Hrs: 11:30 am-midnight; Sat 5 pm-1 am; Sun 5 pm-midnight. Closed some major hols. Res accepted. Bar. Semi-a la carte: lunch $3-$6.95, dinner $3.75-$23.95. Child's meals. Specializes in prime rib, steamed shrimp, pasta. In old YMCA building (1915) funded by Cyrus Hall McCormick family. Cr cds: A, MC, V.

D

Strasburg (C-7)

Founded: 1761 **Pop:** 3,762 **Elev:** 578 ft **Area code:** 703 **Zip:** 22657

Lying at the base of Massanutten Mountain and on the north fork of the Shenandoah River, Strasburg was the earliest settlement in the Shenandoah Valley. German settlers, who arrived around 1740, first named the spot Stony Lick. The community prospered through trade and the milling of flour. In the years before the Civil War, it was identified with the manufacture of pottery. During the war, Strasburg's proximity to the Valley Pike and the Manassas Gap railroad spur led to the town being held, at various times, by both Northern and Southern forces; it was used by both sides as a base of operations.

Today, Strasburg, which is located near the entrance to the Skyline Drive, attracts visitors with its antebellum and Victorian architecture and many antique shops. The town calls itself the "antique capital of Virginia," and is the home of a burgeoning art community.

What to See and Do

1. **Belle Grove** (1794). 4 mi N on US 11. The design of this limestone mansion reflects the influence of Thomas Jefferson. Used as Union headquarters during the Battle of Cedar Creek, Oct 19, 1864. Unusual interior woodwork; herb garden in rear. Guided tours. (Apr-Oct, daily) National Trust for Historic Preservation property. (See ANNUAL EVENTS) Sr citizen rate. Phone 869-2028. ¢¢

2. **Strasburg Museum.** E King St. Blacksmith, cooper and potter shop collections; displays from colonial homes; relics from Civil War and railroad eras; Native American artifacts. Housed in Southern Railway Depot. (May-Oct, daily) Phone 465-3175. ¢

3. **Hupps Hill Walking Tour.** Signs point the way to historic sites and features of interest in town.

(For further information contact the Chamber of Commerce, PO Box 42; 465-3187.)

Annual Events

Mayfest. Celebration of town's German heritage with parade, entertainment and arts, crafts, antiques and foods fairs. 3rd wkend May.

Battle of Cedar Creek Re-Enactment. Belle Grove (see #1). Mid-Oct.

Seasonal Event

Wayside Theatre. On US 11, I-81 exit 302. Professional performances; legitimate theater. Wed-Sun. Res required. Phone 869-1776. Late May-mid-Oct & Dec.

(See Front Royal, Winchester, Woodstock)

Inns

★ ★ **HOTEL STRASBURG.** *201 S Holliday St, 2 mi E of I-81 exit 298. 703/465-9191; res: 800/348-8327; FAX 703/465-4788.* 27 rms, 3 story. S, D $69-$99; each addl $15; suites $149; under 16 free. Crib free. TV; cable. Restaurant (see HOTEL STRASBURG). Bar. Ck-out 11 am, ck-in 2 pm. Tennis privileges. Health club privileges. Some in-rm whirlpools. Beach nearby; swimming privileges. Cr cds: A, C, D, MC, V.

🏄 🦘 🎿 🔥 SC

★ ★ ★ **WAYSIDE INN.** *(7783 Main St, Middletown 22645) I-81 exit 302. 703/869-1797; FAX 703/869-6038.* 29 rms, 3 story. S, D $70-$125; each addl $20; suites $125; under 12 free. Crib free. TV in some rms; cable. Restaurant (see WILKINSON'S TAVERN). Bar 11 am-midnight. Ck-out 11 am, ck-in 2 pm. Meeting rms. Boating, swimming nearby. Restored colonial-era bldg; antiques. An inn since 1797. Cr cds: A, C, D, MC, V.

D 🎿 🔥 SC

Restaurants

★ ★ ★ **HOTEL STRASBURG.** *(See Hotel Strasburg Inn) 703/465-9191.* Hrs: 11:30 am-2:30 pm, 5-9 pm; Fri, Sat 8 am-2:30 pm, 5-10 pm; Sun 8 am-9 pm. Res accepted. Continental menu. Bar from 11 am. Semi-a la carte: bkfst $3.25-$5.95, lunch $4.25-$6.50, dinner $9.95-$18.95. Buffet lunch Mon-Fri: $4.95. Sun brunch $8.95. Child's meals. Continental bkfst only Mon-Thurs; full bkfst Fri, Sat. Specialties: Tournados Zinfidel, chicken Shenandoah. Parking. Victorian building, decorations. Cr cds: A, C, D, MC, V.

★ ★ **WILKINSON'S TAVERN.** *(See Wayside Inn) 703/869-1797.* Hrs: 7 am-3 pm, 5-9 pm; Sat to 10 pm; Sun 7 am-8 pm. Res accepted; required Sat. Bar 11 am-midnight. Semi-a la carte: bkfst $1.75-$6.95, lunch $4.95-$7.95, dinner $13.95-$19.95. Child's meals. Specializes in fresh seafood, chicken, veal. Guitarist Fri & Sat. Parking. In restored Colonial-style inn; many antiques. Cr cds: A, C, D, MC, V.

D

Suffolk (F-9)

(see Portsmouth)

Surry (E-9)

Pop: 192 **Elev:** 122 ft **Area code:** 804 **Zip:** 23883

What to See and Do

Chippokes Plantation State Park. 6 mi E via VA 10, 634. Across James River from Jamestown. Plantation continuously operated since 1619. Approx 1,600 acres. Swimming pool; fishing; Hiking, bicycle paths; interpretive tour road. Picnicking, concession. Visitor center, programs. Tours of mansion, carriage house, kitchen and formal gardens (Memorial Day-Labor Day, Wed-Sun). (See ANNUAL EVENT) Standard fees. Phone 294-3625 (park) or -3439 (museum). Farm & Forestry Museum ¢

Annual Event

Pork, Peanut and Pine Festival. Chippokes Plantation. Pork products, peanuts, crafts, pine decorations. 2 days mid-July.

(For accommodations see Newport News, Williamsburg, also see Colonial Parkway, Jamestown)

Tangier Island (E-10)

Settled: 1666 **Pop:** 659 **Elev:** 3 ft **Area code:** 804 **Zip:** 23440

Bought from the Indians for two overcoats, Tangier was first settled by a mainland family named West. In 1686 John Crockett moved here with his four sons and four daughters. They were later joined by a few other families. Descendants of these families now populate the island. Life is simple and lacks most urban complexities. Most of the men are fishermen, oystering and clamming in one season, crabbing in another.

This tranquil little island (approximately 4 miles long) is 12 miles out in Chesapeake Bay. The island offers good duck hunting, fishing, swimming and relaxation. There is an airfield here, and there are excursion boats from Reedville and Onancock, Virginia, and Crisfield, Maryland. Accommodations include a boarding house, Chesapeake House, with 8 rooms, family-style meals. Contact PO Box 194; 891-2331 for reservations.

Tappahannock (D-9)

Founded: 1680 **Pop:** 1,550 **Elev:** 22 ft **Area code:** 804 **Zip:** 22560

Bartholemew Hoskins patented the first land here in 1645. Following his lead, others came and a small village soon sprang up, known at that time as Hobbes His Hole. Formally chartered in 1682 as New Plymouth, the town was to experience yet another name change. Built around the Rappahannock River, which means "running water," the town port became known as Tappahannock or "on the running water." Four hundred men gathered here in 1765 to protest the Stamp Act.

Today, the area around Prince, Duke and Water Sts of Tappahannock has been declared a historic district. Highlights include the Ritchie House; the Anderton House, once used for the prizing of tobacco into hogsheads; and Scot's Arms Tavern.

(For further information contact the Chamber of Commerce, PO Box 481; 443-5241.)

(See Lancaster, Montross, Richmond)

Motels

✔ ★ **DAYS INN.** *PO Box 1356, jct US 17, 360. 804/443-9200.* 60 rms, 2 story. S, D $44-$49; each addl $6; under 12 free. Crib free. TV; cable. Complimentary continental bkfst. Ck-out 11 am. Cr cds: A, D, DS, MC, V.

⬛ ⬛ ⬛ **SC**

★ **SUPER 8.** *PO Box 1748, jct US 360 & US 17. 804/443-3888; FAX 804/443-3888, ext. 400.* 43 rms, 2 story. Apr-Sept: S $38.88; D $44.88; each addl $4; under 12 free; lower rates rest of yr. TV; cable. Complimentary continental bkfst, coffee. Restaurant opp 6 am-11 pm. Ck-out 11 am. Meeting rms. Some refrigerators. Cr cds: A, C, D, DS, ER, JCB, MC, V.

⬛ ⬛ ⬛ **SC**

Restaurant

★ ★ **LOWERY'S.** *On US 17, 360. 804/443-4314.* Hrs: 7:30 am-9 pm. Closed Dec 25. Semi-a la carte: bkfst $1.75-$6.75, lunch $3.25-$19, dinner $7-$19. Specializes in fresh local seafood. Own salad dressing. Parking. Antique cars on display. Cr cds: A, DS, MC, V.

⬛ **D**

Triangle (D-8)

Pop: 4,740 **Elev:** 150 ft **Area code:** 703 **Zip:** 22172

Quantico Marine Corps Base is three miles east of town.

What to See and Do

1. **Marine Corps Air-Ground Museum.** 2 mi E, in OCS area on Quantico Marine Corps Base. Chronological presentation of the Marine Corps Air-Ground Team's role in American history; artifacts on exhibit include aircraft, engines, armor, tracked & wheeled vehicles, artillery, small arms, uniforms, dioramas and photographs in pre-World War II aviation hangars. (Apr-late Nov, daily exc Mon) Phone 640-2606. **Free.**

2. **Prince William Forest Park.** From I-95, 1/4 mi W on VA 619. Consists of 17,000 acres. Hiking, bicycling. Picnicking. Camping (14-day limit; no hookups; fee; group cabins by res only); trailer campground off VA 234 (fee; hookups, showers, lndry). Naturalist programs. (Daily) Phone 221-7181. Per vehicle ¢¢

(For further information contact the Prince William County Conference & Visitors Bureau, 4349 Ridgewood Center Dr, Suite 100, Prince William 22192; 792-6680 or 800/432-1792.)

(For accommodations see Alexandria, Fredericksburg; also see District of Columbia)

Tysons Corner (C-8)

Pop: 13,124 **Area code:** 703

This Virginia suburban area of Washington, DC is the location of one of the largest shopping centers in the nation.

(For information about this area contact the Fairfax County Visitor Center, 7764 Armistead Rd, Suite 160, Lorton 22079; 550-2450 or 800/7-FAIRFAX.)

(See Arlington County, Fairfax, Falls Church, McLean; also see District of Columbia)

Motels

★ ★ **COMFORT INN.** *(1587 Springhill Rd, Vienna 22182)* 1 1/2 mi W of I-495, exit 10B. 703/448-8020; FAX 703/448-0343. 250 rms, 3 story. S $55-$65; D $59-$69; each addl $6; under 18 free. Crib free. Pet accepted, some restrictions. TV; cable. Pool; lifeguard. Complimentary continental bkfst. Coffee in rms. Ck-out noon. Meeting rms. Valet serv. Free Dulles Airport, Metro transportation. Cr cds: A, C, D, DS, ER, JCB, MC, V.

⬛ ⬛ ⬛ ⬛ ⬛ **SC**

★ ★ **RESIDENCE INN BY MARRIOTT.** *(8616 Westwood Center Dr, Vienna 22182)* I-495 exit 10B to VA 7, then 2 mi W. 703/893-0120; FAX 703/790-8896. 96 kit. suites, 2 story. Kit. suites $132-$172; each addl $10; under 18 free; wkend rates. Crib free. Pet accepted; $85 non-refundable and $5 per day. TV; cable, in-rm movies avail. Pool; whirlpool, lifeguard. Complimentary full bkfst 6:30-9 am; Sat, Sun 7:30-10 am. Restaurant nearby. Ck-out noon. Coin lndry. Meeting rm. Valet serv. Lighted tennis. Many fireplaces. Picnic tables, grills. Cr cds: A, C, D, DS, MC, V.

⬛ ⬛ ⬛ ⬛ ⬛ ⬛ ⬛ **SC**

Hotels

★ ★ ★ EMBASSY SUITES. *(8517 Leesburg Pike, Vienna 22182) I-495 exit 10B to VA 7, then 2 mi W.* 703/883-0707; FAX 703/883-0694. 232 suites, 8 story. S, D $164-$174; each addl $10; under 12 free; wknd rates. Crib free. TV; cable. Indoor pool. Complimentary full bkfst, coffee. Restaurant 11 am-10 pm. Bar. Ck-out noon. Gift shop. Exercise equipt; bicycles, rowers, whirlpool, sauna. Refrigerators, wet bars. Cr cds: A, C, D, DS, MC, V.

D ≈ ✕ ⊠ 🔥 SC

★ ★ ★ HILTON McLEAN AT TYSONS CORNER. *(7920 Jones Branch Dr, McLean 22102) S on VA 123, turn right at Tysons Blvd, right on Galleria Dr/Westpark Dr, then right on Jones Branch Dr and continue 2 blks.* 703/847-5000; FAX 703/761-5100. 456 units, 9 story. S $110-$170; D $130-$190; each addl $20; suites $275-$575; wkly, wkend rates. Crib free. TV; cable. Indoor pool; lifeguard. Restaurant 6:30 am-11 pm. Rm serv to 2 am. Bar 11-2 am; entertainment, dancing. Ck-out noon. Convention facilities. Drugstore. Exercise rm; instructor, weights, bicycles, sauna. Minibars. Atrium lobby; marble floors, fountain. *LUXURY LEVEL : TOWERS.* 38 rms, 8 suites. S $155-$200; D $170-$215; each addl $20. Concierge. Private lounge, honor bar. Bathrm phones. Complimentary continental bkfst, refreshments. Cr cds: A, C, D, DS, ER, JCB, MC, V.

D ≈ ✕ ⊠ 🔥 SC

✔ ★ ★ HOLIDAY INN OF TYSONS CORNER. *(1960 Chain Bridge Rd, McLean 22102) 2 blks W of I-495 exit 11B.* 703/893-2100; FAX 703/893-2227. 315 rms, 9 story. S $99-$132; D $109-$142; each addl $10; studio rms $103; family rates; wkend rates. Crib free. TV; cable. Indoor pool. Restaurant 6:30 am-10 pm. Bar; entertainment. Ck-out 1 pm. Meeting rms. Notary. Gift shop. Exercise equipt; weights, bicycles, whirlpool. Balconies. Cr cds: A, C, D, DS, JCB, MC, V.

D ≈ ✕ ⊠ 🔥 SC

★ ★ ★ MARRIOTT-TYSONS CORNER. *(8028 Leesburg Pike, Vienna 22182) 1 blk W of I-495 exit 10W.* 703/734-3200; FAX 703/442-9301. 390 units, 15 story. S, D $134-$169; suites $250; family rates; wknd packages. Crib free. TV; cable. Indoor pool; poolside serv, lifeguard. Restaurant 6:30 am-10 pm. Bar 4:30 pm-1 am, Fri to 2 am, Sat 7 pm-2 am, closed Sun. Ck-out noon. Convention facilities. Gift shop. Some covered parking. Exercise equipt; weights, rowing machine, whirlpool, sauna. Refrigerators avail. *LUXURY LEVEL :* 26 rms, 1 suite. S $144; D $179. Concierge. Private lounge, honor bar. Complimentary refreshments. Cr cds: A, C, D, DS, ER, JCB, MC, V.

D ≈ ✕ ⊠ 🔥 SC

★ ★ ★ RAMADA-TYSONS CORNER. *(7801 Leesburg Pike, Falls Church 22043) On VA 7 at I-495 exit 10E.* 703/893-1340; FAX 703/847-9520. 404 rms, 11 story. S $99-$109; D $109-$129; each addl $20; suites $175-$250; under 18 free; wknd rates, packages. Crib free. Pet accepted, some restrictions. TV; cable. Indoor pool; lifeguard. Restaurant 6:30 am-11 pm. Bar 4 pm-2 am, Sun to 1 am; entertainment, dancing. Ck-out noon. Coin lndry. Convention facilities. Gift shop. Exercise equipt; weights, bicycles, whirlpool, sauna. Cr cds: A, C, D, DS, ER, JCB, MC, V.

D 🐾 ≈ ✕ ⊠ 🔥 SC

★ ★ ★ ★ THE RITZ-CARLTON, TYSONS CORNER. *(1700 Tysons Blvd, McLean 22102) N via I-495 exit 11B, adj Tysons II Mall.* 703/506-4300; FAX 703/506-4305. 399 units, 24 story, 32 suites. S, D $139-$179; each addl $30; suites $325-$1,200; under 16 free; wknd family package; lower rates some wknds. Crib free. Pet accepted, some restrictions. Garage parking; valet $6. TV; cable. Indoor pool; lifeguard. Supervised child's activities. Restaurant (see THE RESTAURANT). Rm serv 24 hrs. Bar 11:30-1 am; entertainment. Ck-out noon. Convention facilities. Concierge. Gift shop. Airport transportation. Tennis privileges. 18-hole golf privileges, greens fee $65, pro, putting green, driving range. Exercise rm; instructor, weight machine, bicycles, whirlpool, sauna, steam rm. Masseuse. Bathrm phones, minibars. Antiques, 18th-century oil paintings in lobby. *LUXURY LEVEL :*

RITZ-CARLTON CLUB. 24 rms, 2 floors. S, D $210. Concierge. Private lounge. Complimentary continental bkfst, lunch, afternoon tea, refreshments. Cr cds: A, C, D, DS, JCB, MC, V.

D 🐾 🏹 ⛷ ≈ ✕ ⊠ 🔥 ⊠

★ ★ ★ SHERATON PREMIERE. *8661 Leesburg Pike (22182), I-495 exit 10B, then 2½ mi W on VA 7.* 703/448-1234; FAX 703/893-8193. 455 rms, 24 story. S $125-$155; D $155-$175; each addl $15; suites $325-$750; under 17 free; wkly rates; lower rates wknds, hols. Crib free. TV; cable, in-rm movies avail. 2 pools, 1 indoor; poolside serv, lifeguard. Restaurant 6:30 am-midnight. Rm serv 24 hrs. Bars 11-1 am; dancing exc Sun. Ck-out noon. Convention facilities. Concierge. Gift shop. Drugstore. Free Dulles, National airport transportation. Lighted tennis privileges. 18-hole golf privileges, pro, greens fee. Exercise rm; instructor, weights, bicycles, whirlpool, sauna. Bathrm phones, minibars; some refrigerators. Cr cds: A, C, D, DS, ER, JCB, MC, V.

D 🏹 ⛷ ≈ ✕ ⊠ 🔥 SC

Restaurants

✔ ★ ★ AMERICAN CAFE. *(8601 Westwood Center Dr, Vienna) I-495 exit 10B, then 2 mi W on VA 7.* 703/848-9476. Hrs: 11 am-11 pm; Fri & Sat to 1 am; Sun from 10:30 am; Sun brunch to 3 pm. Res accepted. Bar. A la carte entrees: lunch, dinner $4.95-$12.95. Sun brunch $6.45-$6.95. Child's meals. Specializes in salads, sandwiches, grilled dishes. Parking. Patio dining. Take-out gourmet market. Cr cds: A, MC, V.

D SC

★ ★ ★ BONAROTI. *(428 Maple Ave E, Vienna) 3 mi W on I-495 on VA 123, in Wolf Trappe Shopping Center.* 703/281-7550. Hrs: 11:30 am-10:30 pm; Sat 5-11 pm. Closed Sun; some major hols. Res accepted. Italian menu. Bar. Wine cellar. Semi-a la carte: lunch $6.25-$9.95, dinner $11.95-$18.95. Child's meals. Specializes in veal, pasta, seafood. Own pastries. Italian art throughout. Cr cds: A, C, D, MC, V.

✔ ★ ★ CLYDE'S. *(8332 Leesburg Pike, Vienna) 10 blks W of I-495 exit 10W on VA 7, then right.* 703/734-1901. Hrs: 11-2 am; Sun brunch 10 am-4 pm. Res accepted. Bar 11-2 am. A la carte entrees: lunch $4.95-$9.95, dinner $4.95-$15.95. Child's meals. Specializes in pasta, seafood, sandwiches. Entertainment Fri & Sat. Parking. Original art collection. Cr cds: A, C, D, DS, MC, V.

D SC

★ ★ DA DOMENICO. *1992 Chain Bridge Rd, 2 blks W of I-495 exit 11B.* 703/790-9000. Hrs: 11:30 am-11 pm; Sat from 5 pm. Closed Sun; major hols. Res accepted; required Fri, Sat. Northern Italian menu. Bar. Semi-a la carte: lunch $7-$11.95, dinner $9.95-$16.95. Specializes in veal chop, seafood, fresh pasta. Parking. Cr cds: A, C, D, MC, V.

D

★ ★ FEDORA CAFE. *(8521 Leesburg Pike, Vienna)* 703/556-0100. Hrs: 11:30 am-3 pm, 5:30-10:30 pm; Fri & Sat to 11:30 pm; Sun 10:30 am-2:30 pm, 4:30-9:30 pm. Res accepted. Bar to 12:30 am. Semi-a la carte: lunch $6.95-$9.95, dinner $8.95-$19.95. Specializes in rotisserie chicken, spit-roasted duck, fresh fish. Own desserts. Pianist Wed, Thurs & Sat (in season). Parking. Cr cds: A, C, D, DS, MC, V.

D

★ ★ ★ HUNAN LION. *(2070 Chain Bridge Rd, Vienna) S of I-495 on VA 123.* 703/734-9828. Hrs: 11:30 am-10:30 pm; Fri, Sat to 11 pm. Closed Thanksgiving. Res accepted. Chinese menu. Bar. Semi-a la carte: lunch $6-$8, dinner $12-$16. Specializes in triple delicacy prawns, orange beef, General Tso's chicken, Peking duck. Parking. Cr cds: A, D, MC, V.

D

★ ★ J.R.'S STOCKYARDS INN. *(8130 Watson St, McLean)* ½ mi W of I-495 exit 10B. 703/893-3390. Hrs: 11:30 am-3 pm, 5:30-

10:30 pm; Fri to 11 pm; Sat 5:30-11 pm; Sun 5-9:30 pm. Closed July 4, Thanksgiving, Dec 25. Res accepted; required Fri, Sat. Bar. Semi-a la carte: lunch $4.50-$8.95, dinner $12.95-$19.95. Child's meals. Specializes in marinated sirloin, prime aged beef, fresh seafood. Parking. Western-style chop house. Cr cds: A, C, D, DS, MC, V.

D

★ ★ ★ **LE CANARD.** *(132 Branch Rd, Vienna) VA 123 at Branch Rd, in Danor Shopping Center. 703/281-0070.* Hrs: 11:30 am-2:30 pm, 5:30-10:30 pm; Fri to 11 pm; Sat 6-11 pm. Closed Sun; Jan 1, Thanksgiving, Dec 25. Res accepted; required Fri, Sat. French menu. Bar to 2 am. Wine list. Semi-a la carte: lunch $4.75-$10, dinner $12.75-$21. Specializes in fresh seafood, veal, pasta. Own pastries. Piano bar Tues-Sat. Cr cds: A, C, D, DS, MC, V.

D

★ ★ **MARCO POLO.** *(245 Maple Ave W, Vienna) 2¹/₂ mi N of I-66 exit 62. 703/281-3922.* Hrs: 11:30 am-10:30 pm; Fri, Sat to 11 pm. Closed Sun exc Mother's Day. Res accepted. French, Northern Italian menu. Serv bar. Semi-a la carte: lunch $6-$9, dinner $11-$18. Buffet: lunch (Tues-Fri) $8.25, dinner (Thurs) $14.50. Child's meals. Specializes in fresh seafood, fresh pasta. Parking. Cr cds: A, C, D, MC, V.

D

★ ★ ★ **MORTON'S OF CHICAGO.** *(8075 Leesburg Pike, McLean) I-495 exit 10W, then 1/4 mi W on VA 7 (Leesburg Pike). 703/883-0800.* Hrs: 11:30 am-2:30 pm, 5:30-11 pm; Sat from 5:30 pm; Sun 5-10 pm. Closed major hols. Res accepted. Bar. Wine list. Semi-a la carte: lunch $7.95-$29.95. A la carte entrees: dinner $15.95-$29.95. Specializes in steak, seafood. Valet parking. Jacket. Cr cds: A, C, D, MC, V.

D

★ ★ **NIZAM'S.** *(523 Maple Ave W, Vienna) In Village Green Shopping Ctr. 703/938-8948.* Hrs: 11 am-3 pm, 5-10 pm; Fri, Sat 5-11 pm; Sun 4-10 pm. Closed Mon; Thanksgiving. Res accepted. Turkish menu. Bar. Semi-a la carte: lunch $5.25-$10.50, dinner $11.95-$17.50. Specializes in lamb, chicken, fresh salmon. Turkish lanterns, artwork. Cr cds: A, DS, MC, V.

D

✔ ★ ★ **PANJSHIR II.** *(224 W Maple Ave, Vienna) 3 mi W on I-495; on VA 123. 703/281-4183.* Hrs: 11:30 am-2 pm, 5-10 pm; Sun 5-9 pm. Closed Jan 1, July 4, Thanksgiving. Res accepted. Afghan menu. Bar. Semi-a la carte: lunch $5.95-$7.25, dinner $9.95-$13.25. Specializes in kebabs, saffron rice, vegetarian dishes. Parking. Upscale atmosphere. Cr cds: A, MC, V.

★ ★ ★ **PIERRE ET MADELEINE.** *(246 E Maple Ave, Vienna) 2 mi N of I-66 exit 62. 703/938-4379.* Hrs: 11:30 am-2:30 pm, 5:30-10 pm; Fri to 11 pm; Sat 5:30-11 pm. Closed Sun. Res accepted. French menu. Bar. Semi-a la carte: lunch $4.75-$12.25, dinner $15-$22. Complete meals: dinner (Fri & Sat) $33.95. Specialties: fresh Maine lobster with whiskey sauce, seasonal dishes, veal with seafood. Parking. Cr cds: A, C, D, DS, MC, V.

★ ★ **PRIMI PIATTI.** *(8045 Leesburg Pike, Vienna) W of I-45 exit 10W. 703/893-0300.* Hrs: 11:30 am-2:30 pm, 5:30-10 pm; Fri to 10:30 pm; Sat 5:30-10:30 pm. Closed Sun; most major hols. Res accepted; required Fri, Sat. Italian menu. Bar. Semi-a la carte: lunch $7-$12.95, dinner $10.95-$18.95. Complete meals: lunch $12.95-$19.95, dinner $25-$35. Specialties: agnolotti a la creme, veal involtini. Valet parking. Outdoor dining. Cr cds: A, C, D, MC, V.

D

★ ★ ★ **THE RESTAURANT.** *(See The Ritz-Carlton, Tysons Corner Hotel) 703/506-4300.* Hrs: 6:30 am-10 pm; Sun 6:30-11 am, 5-10 pm; Sun brunch 11:30 am-3 pm. Res accepted. Extensive wine list. Semi-a la carte: lunch $7.50-$18, dinner $14-$30. Sun brunch $32. Child's meals. Specializes in seafood, grilled salmon, lamb chops,

prime aged beef. Pianist, harpist. Valet parking. Cr cds: A, C, D, DS, JCB, MC, V.

D

✔ ★ **WU'S GARDEN.** *(418 Maple Ave E, Vienna) 3 mi W off I-495 exit 11A. 703/281-4410.* Hrs: 11:30 am-10 pm; Sat noon-11 pm. Closed Thanksgiving. Res accepted. Chinese menu. Bar. Semi-a la carte: lunch $4-$7, dinner $7.95-$12. Specialties: kang pao chicken, crispy shrimp with walnuts. Parking. Oriental screens and artwork. Cr cds: A, D, DS, MC, V.

D

Virginia Beach (F-10)

Pop: 393,069 **Elev:** 12 ft **Area code:** 804

For those who seek summertime recreation, Virginia Beach is the answer. Its boardwalks, bays and beaches offer surf and pool swimming, superb fishing, boating, waterskiing, surf-riding; bowling, tennis, golf, bicycling; amusement park fun, the social life of sundeck and nightclub; and good seafood, notably the famous Lynnhaven oyster.

With 3 miles of concrete boardwalk, 28 miles of fine public beach and hundreds of places to stay in all price ranges, Virginia Beach is one of the most popular resorts on the East Coast.

What to See and Do

1. **Fishing.** In the Lynnhaven and Rudee Inlets for channel bass, speckled trout, spots, croakers, flounder and whiting in season; in the Back Bay area, 18 mi S on VA 615, for largemouth black bass, pickerel and perch. Pier fishing and surf casting from two piers jutting into the Atlantic and two piers in the Chesapeake Bay. Reef, deep-sea and Gulf Stream fishing from charter boats, for sea bass, weakfish, flounder, cobia, bonito, tuna, marlin, false albacore, blue and dolphin. Lake and stream fishing at Lake Smith, Lake Christine and the inland waterways of the Chesapeake and Albemarle Canal. Crabbing for blue crabs in Lynnhaven waters, Linkhorn Bay and Rudee Inlet. (No license or closed season for saltwater fishing.)

2. **Center for the Arts.** 2200 Parks Ave. This 32,000-square-foot facility is devoted to presentation of 20th-century art through exhibitions, education, performing arts and special events. (Tues-Sat, also Sun afternoons; closed major hols) Phone 425-0000.

3. **Adam Thoroughgood House** (ca 1680). 1636 Parish Rd. One of the oldest remaining brick houses in US; restored, furnished; restored gardens. (Apr-Dec, daily exc Mon; rest of yr, Tues-Sat; closed some major hols) Phone 460-0007. ¢

4. **Francis Land House** 3131 Virginia Beach Blvd, on the S side of the boulevard, just E of the Princess Anne Plaza Shopping Center. Once residence of prominent family of planters, this 18th-century Dutch-gambrel-roof structure represents the architecture and lifestyle enjoyed by the gentry of colonial Virginia. Tour includes period rooms, changing thematic exhibits and gardens. (Tues-Sun; closed major hols) Phone 340-1732. ¢

5. **Upper Wolfsnare** (1759). 2040 Potters Rd. Brick home in a country setting; built by Thomas Walke III. Period furniture and china, portraits of early Walke relatives, and an authentic 18th-century herb garden. Continuing restoration. Tours focus on lifestyle of 18th-century Princess Anne County. (June-Sept, Wed & Thurs; rest of yr, by reservation) Phone 491-0127. ¢

6. **Lynnhaven House** (ca 1725). 4405 Wishart Rd, 4 mi N of Independence Blvd (US 255). This stately story-and-a-half masonry structure is a well-preserved example of 18th-century architecture and decorative arts. (Mid-Apr-Oct, daily exc Mon) Phone 460-1688. ¢

7. **Life-Saving Museum of Virginia.** 24th St and Oceanfront. Former Life-Saving/Coast Guard Station (1903); visual exhibits of numerous shipwrecks along the Virginia coastline tell of past bravery and disaster. "The War Years" exhibit relates United States Coast Guard efforts during World Wars I and II. Photographs, ship models, artifacts. Gift shop. (Memorial Day-Oct, daily; rest of yr, daily exc Mon; closed Jan 1, Thanksgiving, Dec 25, 31) Sr citizen rate. Phone 422-1587. ¢¢

8. **Virginia Marine Science Museum.** 717 General Booth Blvd, just S of the Rudee Inlet Bridge. Houses more than 60 hands-on exhibits depicting the state's marine environment. Aquariums; simulated dive to the ocean floor. An outdoor boardwalk takes visitors through a salt marsh for a view of waterfowl and other marsh animals. Chesapeake Bay aquarium with scuba diving exhibitions. (Daily; closed Thanksgiving, Dec 25) Sr citizen rate. Phone 425-FISH. ¢¢

9. **Association for Research and Enlightenment.** 67th St & Atlantic Ave. Headquarters for study and research of work of psychic Edgar Cayce. Visitor Center has bookstore, displays, ESP testing machine, movie and daily lecture. (Daily; closed Thanksgiving, Dec 25) Phone 800/333-4499. **Free.**

10. **Ocean Breeze Fun Park.** 849 General Booth Blvd. Family fun park includes MotorWorld, with various driving tracks; Wild Water Rapids, a water park with slides, wave pool, rapids, and children's water amusements (late May-early Sept); Shipwreck Golf miniature golf course; Strike Zone batting cages. (Memorial Day-Labor Day, daily; mid-Apr-May & Sept-Oct, wkends) Sr citizen rate. Phone 425-1241 (recording) or 422-0718. Combination ticket ¢¢¢¢¢

11. *Discovery* **Sightseeing Cruise.** 550 Laskin Rd. Luncheon and dinner sightseeing cruises aboard 80-foot luxury yacht. Reservations. (June-Aug, daily) Phone 491-8090 or 422-2900. ¢¢¢¢¢

12. **Norwegian Lady Statue.** 25th St & Oceanfront. A gift to Virginia Beach from the people of Moss, Norway. The statue commemorates the tragic wreck of the Norwegian bark *Dictator* off the shores of Virginia Beach in 1891.

13. **Cape Henry Memorial** (see) **and Lighthouse.** 6 mi N on US 60.

14. **Seashore State Park.** 5 mi N on US 60 near Cape Henry. More than 2,700 acres with lagoons, cypress trees and sand dunes. Swimming at own risk; fishing; boating (ramp). Hiking, bicycle and self-guided nature trails. Picnicking, concession. Tent & trailer sites (Mar-Nov; fee); 20 cabins (May-Sept). Visitor center, interpretive programs. Access for disabled to nature trail. (Daily) Standard fees. Phone 481-2131. **Free.**

(For further information contact the Visitor Information Center, 2100 Parks Ave, 23451; 800/VA-BEACH.)

Annual Events

Pungo Strawberry Festival. 2 days late May.

Boardwalk Art Show. Works by more than 350 artists from US and abroad. 4 days June.

Can-Am Festival. Mid-July.

East Coast Surfing Championship. 2 days late Aug.

Neptune Festival. Late Sept.

Seasonal Event

Virginia Saltwater Fishing Tournament. The Commonwealth of Virginia sponsors this annual Saltwater Fishing Awards Program. No entry fee or registration requirements; open to everyone who fishes in tournament waters and complies with tournament rules. For information about this program contact Virginia Saltwater Fishing Tournament, 968 S Oriole Dr, Suite 102, 23451; 491-5160. Mar-Dec.

(See Chesapeake, Hampton, Newport News, Norfolk, Portsmouth)

Motels

★ **CAPTAIN'S QUARTERS RESORT.** *304 28th St (23451). 804/491-1700; res: 800/333-6020.* 74 rms, 3 story, 37 kit. suites. July-early Sept: S, D $75-$85; each addl $10; kit. suites $95-$220; under 12 free (up to 2); wkly rates; golf plans; higher rates: Memorial Day, July 4, Labor Day; lower rates rest of yr. Crib avail. TV; cable. Heated pool, whirlpool. Restaurant nearby. Ck-out 11 am. Coin lndry. Meeting rms. Ocean 2 blks. Cr cds: A, C, D, DS, MC, V.

★★ **COURTYARD BY MARRIOTT.** *5700 Greenwich Rd (23462). 804/490-2002; FAX 804/490-0169.* 146 rms, 3 story. S, D $70-$80; suites $85-$95; under 12 free; wkly, wkend rates. Crib free. TV; cable. Heated pool. Coffee in rms. Restaurant 6:30 am-2 pm, 5-10 pm; wkend hrs vary. Bar 4-10 pm. Ck-out noon. Meeting rms. Valet serv. Exercise equipt; weights, bicycles, whirlpool. Some refrigerators. Cr cds: A, C, D, DS, JCB, MC, V.

✔ ★★ **FAIRFIELD INN BY MARRIOTT.** *4760 Euclid Rd (23462). 804/499-1935; FAX 804/499-1935, ext. 709.* 134 rms, 3 story. Mid-May-Labor Day: S, D $49.95-$63.95; each addl $3; under 18 free; lower rates rest of yr. Crib free. TV; cable. Pool. Complimentary continental bkfst, coffee. Restaurant nearby. Ck-out noon. Meeting rms. Cr cds: A, C, D, DS, MC, V.

✔ ★★ **HAMPTON INN.** *5793 Greenwich Rd (23462). 804/490-9800; FAX 804/490-3573.* 122 rms, 4 story. June-Aug: S $55; D $61-$65; under 18 free; lower rates rest of yr. Crib free. TV; cable. Pool. Complimentary continental bkfst, coffee. Restaurant adj 6:30 am-11 pm. Ck-out noon. Meeting rm. Exercise equipt; weight machine, bicycles. Cr cds: A, C, D, DS, MC, V.

★★ **SEA GULL.** *Atlantic Ave at 27th St (23451), on oceanfront. 804/425-5711; res: 800/426-4855; FAX 804/425-5710.* 51 units, 4 story, 9 kit. units. Memorial Day-Labor Day: S, D $95-$110; each addl $10; kit. units $110-$125; family, wkly rates; lower rates rest of yr. Crib $5. TV; cable. Indoor pool; whirlpool, poolside serv. Restaurant 7 am-10 pm. Rm serv. Bar. Ck-out 11 am. Refrigerators. On ocean, swimming beach. Cr cds: D, DS, MC, V.

Motor Hotels

★ **BREAKERS RESORT INN.** *16th St at Oceanfront (23451). 804/428-1821; res: 800/237-7532; FAX 804/422-9602.* 55 rms, 9 story, 15 kit. suites. Mid-June-late Aug: S, D $106; kit. suites $145-$155; wkly rates off-season; lower rates rest of yr. Crib $3. TV; cable. Heated pool. Coffee in rms. Restaurant 7 am-3 pm (Mar-Oct). Ck-out noon. Coin lndry. Meeting rms. Bicycles. Refrigerators. Balconies. On ocean. Cr cds: A, D, DS, MC, V.

★★ **COMFORT INN-OCEANFRONT.** *2105 Atlantic Ave (23451). 804/425-8200.* 83 kit. suites, 10 story. Memorial Day-Labor Day: S, D $165; each addl $7; under 12 free; lower rates rest of yr. Crib free. TV; cable. Indoor pool. Continental bkfst. Restaurant adj 6:30 am-10 pm. Ck-out 11 am. Bellhops. Exercise equipt; weights, bicycles, whirlpool. Private patios. On ocean. Cr cds: A, C, D, DS, ER, JCB, MC, V.

★★ **DAYS INN-OCEANFRONT.** *32nd St & Atlantic Ave (23451). 804/428-7233; FAX 804/491-1936.* 121 units, 8 story, 9 kit. suites. Late June-early Sept: S, D $125-$145; each addl $5; kit. suites $145-$160; under 12 free; golf plans; lower rates rest of yr. Crib free. TV; cable. Indoor pool; whirlpool. Restaurant 7 am-2 pm, 5-9 pm; in season to midnight. Rm serv. Bar from 5 pm. Ck-out 11 am. Coin lndry. Meeting rms. Golf privileges. Game rm. Some refrigerators. Balconies. On ocean; beach. Cr cds: A, C, D, DS, MC, V.

⊡ ⌖ ⩲ ⨯ ⊠ SC

★★★ **HILTON INN.** *8th St & Atlantic Ave (23451). 804/428-8935; FAX 804/425-2769.* 120 rms, 6 story. Memorial Day-Labor Day: S $126; D $149; each addl $10; under 12 free; lower rates rest of yr. Crib free. TV; cable. Indoor/outdoor pool; whirlpool, sauna, poolside serv. Restaurant 7 am-10 pm. Rm serv. Bar noon-1:30 am. Ck-out 11 am. Meeting rms. Bellhops. Valet serv. Lawn games. On ocean; beach. Cr cds: A, C, D, DS, ER, MC, V.

⩲ ⨯ ⊠ SC

★★ **HOLIDAY INN OCEANSIDE.** *Atlantic Ave & 21st St (23451). 804/491-1500; FAX 804/491-1945.* 138 rms, 12 story. June-Sept: S, D $85-$150; each addl $9; under 18 free; lower rates rest of yr. Pet accepted, some restrictions. TV; cable. Indoor pool; whirlpool. Restaurant 7 am-10 pm. Rm serv. Bar 11-2 am. Ck-out 11 am. Meeting rms. Bellhops. Valet parking. Many refrigerators. Balconies. On ocean; swimming beach. Cr cds: A, C, D, DS, JCB, MC, V.

⊡ ⇆ ⌖ ⩲ ⨯ ⊠ SC

✔ ★★★ **HOLIDAY INN ON THE OCEAN.** *39th St & Oceanfront (23451). 804/428-1711; FAX 804/425-5742.* 266 rms, 7 story, 55 kits. S, D $49-$149; each addl $10; kit. units $69-$169; under 19 free. Crib free. TV; cable. Indoor/outdoor pool; poolside serv (summer). Free supervised child's activities (Memorial Day-Labor Day). Restaurant 6:30 am-2 pm, 4-11 pm (in season), to 10 pm rest of yr. Rm serv. Bar 4-11 pm. Ck-out 11 am. Meeting rms. Bellhops. Gift shop. Some refrigerators. Balconies. On ocean. Cr cds: A, C, D, DS, JCB, MC, V.

⊡ ⩲ ⨯ ⊠ SC

Hotels

★★ **BEST WESTERN OCEAN FRONT.** *11th & Atlantic Ave (23451). 804/422-5000.* 110 rms, 8 story. Memorial Day-Labor Day: S, D $99-$140; each addl $7; suites $140-$225; under 12 free; lower rates rest of yr. Crib free. TV; cable. Pool; poolside serv. Coffee in rms. Restaurant (in season) 7 am-11 pm. Bar 11-1:30 am; entertainment, dancing. Ck-out 11 am. Valet parking. Some refrigerators. Balconies. On ocean; swimming beach. All rms with ocean view. Cr cds: A, C, D, DS, ER, MC, V.

⊡ ⩲ ⨯ ⊠ SC

★★★ **CAVALIER.** *42nd St at Oceanfront (23451). 804/425-8555; res: 800/446-8199; FAX 804/428-7957.* 400 rms, 11 story, 18 suites. Mid-May-mid-Sept: S, D $89-$160; each addl $20; suites $189-$640; under 18 free; varied lower rates rest of yr. Crib free. TV; cable. 2 pools, 1 indoor; wading pool, poolside serv; lifeguard in summer. Free supervised child's activities (Memorial Day-Labor Day). Restaurant 7 am-11 pm; 3 dining rms. Bar 11-1 am; entertainment in season, dancing. Ck-out 11 am. Convention facilities. Concierge (summer). Gift shop. Lighted tennis, pro. Putting green. Exercise equipt; weights, bicycles. Private beach. Game rm. Rec rm. Lawn games. Some refrigerators. Private balconies. Cr cds: A, C, D, DS, MC, V.

⊡ ⌖ ⩲ ⨯ ⊁ ⨯ ⊠ SC

★★★ **FOUNDERS INN CONFERENCE CENTER.** *5641 Indian River Rd (23463). 804/424-5511; res: 800/926-4466; FAX 804/366-0613.* 249 rms: 20 rms in Founders Inn, 229 rms in 2 lodge buildings located on grounds. S, D $110-$130; each addl $15; suites $150-$900; family, wkly rates; golf plans. Crib free. TV; cable. 2 pools, 1 indoor; poolside serv (summer); lifeguard. Playground. Supervised child's activities. Complimentary coffee in rms. Restaurant 6 am-10 pm. Rm serv to midnight. Ck-out noon. Meeting rms. Concierge. Shopping arcade. Free valet parking. Free airport, RR station, bus depot transportation. Lighted tennis, pro. Golf privileges, greens fee $36, pro. Exercise rm; instructor, weights, rowers, sauna. Lawn games. Bicycle rentals.

Bathrm phones, refrigerators, minibars. Balconies. Picnic tables, grills. Cr cds: A, C, D, DS, MC, V.

⊡ ⌖ ⨯ ⩲ ⨯ ⊁ ⨯ ⊠ SC

★★ **PARK INN INTERNATIONAL RESORT HOTEL.** *424 Atlantic Ave (23451). 804/425-2200; FAX 804/491-7751.* 95 kit. suites, 9 story. Memorial Day-Labor Day: 1 bedrm kit. suites $75-$125; each addl $10; under 16 free; wkly rates; golf, fishing plans; lower rates rest of yr. Crib avail. TV; cable. Indoor pool; poolside serv. Restaurant 7 am-10 pm. Bar. Ck-out 11 am. Coin lndry. Meeting rms. Concierge (in season). Exercise equipt; weights, bicycles, whirlpool. Some balconies. Beach opp. Cr cds: A, C, D, DS, ER, JCB, MC, V.

⊡ ⩲ ⨯ ⨯ ⊠ SC

★★★ **PLAZA HOTEL.** *4453 Bonney Rd (23462), VA 44 exit Pembroke 3B. 804/473-1700; FAX 804/552-0477.* 149 rms, 8 story. S, D $99-$109; each addl $10; suites, studio rms $109-$139; under 12 free; higher rates special events. Crib free. TV; cable. Indoor pool; whirlpool, sauna, poolside serv. Restaurant 6:30 am-2:30 pm, 5-10 pm. Bars 2 pm-2 am; entertainment Wed-Sat, dancing. Meeting rms. Gift shop. Free airport transportation. Cr cds: A, C, D, DS, MC, V.

⊡ ⩲ ⨯ ⊠ SC

★★ **QUALITY INN OCEAN FRONT.** *PO Box 328 (23458), 2207 Atlantic Ave. 804/428-5141; FAX 804/422-8436.* 111 rms, 14 story. Late May-Labor Day: S, D $115-$131; each addl $7; under 12 free; higher rates Memorial Day wkend; lower rates rest of yr. Crib free. TV; cable. Heated pool; whirlpool. Restaurant (in season) 7 am-11 pm. Bar (in season) 11-2 am. Ck-out 11 am. Coin lndry. Refrigerators. Private patios; balconies. On beach. Cr cds: A, C, D, DS, ER, JCB, MC, V.

⊡ ⩲ ⨯ ⊠ SC

✔ ★★★ **RADISSON.** *1900 Pavilion Dr (23451). 804/422-8900; FAX 804/425-8460.* 296 rms, 12 story. Late May-early Sept: S $79-$119; D $89-$129; each addl $10; suites $179-$350; under 17 free; wkend rates; lower rates rest of yr. Crib free. TV; cable. Indoor pool; poolside serv. Restaurant 6:30-10 pm. Bar from 4 pm; DJ, dancing Fri & Sat. Ck-out noon. Convention facilities. Concierge. Gift shop. Oceanfront transportation. Tennis. Exercise equipt; weights, bicycles, whirlpool, steam rm, sauna. Some refrigerators, minibars. Ocean 6 blks. Cr cds: A, C, D, DS, ER, JCB, MC, V.

⊡ ⌖ ⩲ ⨯ ⨯ ⊠ SC

★★★ **RAMADA OCEANFRONT TOWER.** *57th & Ocean Front (23451). 804/428-7025; FAX 804/428-2921.* 215 rms, 17 story. May-Sept: S, D $125-$170; suites $230-$280; each addl $8; under 18 free; lower rates rest of yr. TV; cable. Indoor/outdoor pool; poolside serv, lifeguard in season. Restaurant 7 am-10 pm. Bar 3 pm-1 am. Ck-out noon. Meeting rms. Concierge. Gift shop. Exercise equipt; weights, bicycles, whirlpool, sauna, hot tub. Balconies. On ocean; oceanfront deck, swimming beach. Most rms with ocean view. *LUXURY LEVEL :* 24 rms, 3 floors. S, D $170. Private lounge. Complimentary continental bkfst, refreshments. Cr cds: A, C, D, DS, ER, JCB, MC, V.

⊡ ⇆ ⩲ ⨯ ⨯ ⊠ SC

★★ **TRAVELODGE-ATLANTIC.** *2109 Atlantic Ave (23451). 804/428-2403; FAX 804/422-2530.* 55 rms, 10 story. Memorial Day-Labor Day: S, D $95-$150; each addl $10; kit. units $115-$165; under 17 free; wkly rates; lower rates rest of yr. Crib free. TV; cable. Indoor pool; poolside serv. Restaurant 7 am-2 pm. Bar 5 pm-1 am. Ck-out 11 am. Meeting rm. Free garage parking. Cr cds: A, C, D, DS, ER, JCB, MC, V.

⊡ ⇆ ⩲ ⨯ ⊠ SC

★★★ **VIRGINIA BEACH RESORT & CONFERENCE CENTER.** *2800 Shore Dr (23451). 804/481-9000; res: 800/468-2722 (exc VA), 800/422-4747 (VA); FAX 804/496-7429.* 295 suites, 8 story. Memorial Day-Labor Day: S, D $136-$269; each addl $10; under 18 free; lower rates rest of yr. Crib free. TV; cable. Indoor/outdoor pool; poolside serv. Supervised child's activities (Memorial Day-Labor Day). Restaurant 6:30 am-10 pm. Bar. Ck-out 11 am. Coin lndry. Convention facilities. Airport, bus depot transportation. Tennis, golf privileges.

Exercise equipt; weights, whirlpool, sauna. Private beach. Boat, jet ski rentals. Bicycles. Refrigerators. Balconies. On bay. Cr cds: A, C, D, MC, V.

Restaurants

★ **ALDO'S RISTORANTE.** *1860 Laskin Rd, at La Promenade shopping center.* 804/491-1111. Hrs: 11 am-11 pm; Fri & Sat to 12:30 am; Sun 4-11 pm. Closed Jan 1, Thanksgiving, Dec 25. Res accepted Fri & Sat. Italian menu. Bar. A la carte entrees: lunch, dinner $2.99-$19.95. Child's meals. Specializes in seafood pasta, pizza, filet mignon. Entertainment exc Sun. Outdoor dining. Contemporary decor. Cr cds: A, MC, V.

D

★ ★ **BLUE PETE'S SEAFOOD & STEAK.** *1400 N Muddy Creek Rd.* 804/426-2005. Hrs: 5:30-10 pm. Closed Sun off season. Res accepted off season. Bar. Semi-a la carte: dinner $12.95-$25.95. Child's meals. Specializes in fresh seafood, sweet potato biscuits, Angus steak. Own desserts. Parking. Outdoor dining. Located on creek in wooded area. Cr cds: A, D, MC, V.

★ ★ **CAPTAIN GEORGE'S SEAFOOD.** *2272 Pungo Ferry Rd.* 804/721-3463. Hrs: 5-10 pm; Sat from 4:30 pm; Sun from noon. Closed Dec 25. Bar. Semi-a la carte: dinner $7.50-$26.95. Buffet: dinner $16.95, $17.95. Specializes in seafood, steamed shrimp. Nautical decor. Located on beach at Intracoastal Waterway. Cr cds: A, MC, V.

D

★ ★ **COASTAL GRILL.** *1427 N Great Neck Rd.* 804/496-3348. Hrs: 5:30-11 pm; Sat 5 pm-midnight. Closed Sun; most major hols. Bar. Semi-a la carte: dinner $2.95-$14.95. Child's meals. Specializes in fresh fish, roast chicken. Parking. Light, airy surroundings; window seating. Smoking at bar only. Cr cds: A, DS, MC, V.

D

★ **FOGG'S.** *415 Atlantic Ave.* 804/428-3644. Hrs: 11:30 am-10 pm; Fri, Sat to 11 pm. Closed Thanksgiving, Dec 24 evening, 25. Res accepted. Bar. A la carte entrees: lunch $2.95-$9.95, dinner $5.95-$21. Child's meals. Specializes in seafood, beef. Parking. Outdoor dining. Four dining areas, all with ocean view. Cr cds: A, C, D, DS, MC, V.

D SC

★ ★ **HENRY'S SEAFOOD.** *3319 Shore Dr, at US 60 & E end of Lessner Bridge.* 804/481-7300. Hrs: 11-2 am; Nov-Feb 5-11 pm. Res accepted. Bar. Semi-a la carte: lunch $3.95-$8.95, dinner $7.95-$19.95. Child's meals. Specializes in fresh seafood. Lobster tank. Raw bar. Entertainment (in season). Valet parking. Outdoor dining. On Lynnhaven Inlet; 2-story saltwater aquarium in dining area. Cr cds: A, D, DS, MC, V.

D SC

★ ★ **IL GIARDINO.** *910 Atlantic Ave, at 10th St.* 804/422-6464. Hrs: 5-11:30 pm; Fri & Sat to midnight. Closed Dec 25. Res accepted. Italian menu. Bar. Semi-a la carte: dinner $8.95-$25. Child's meals. Specializes in seafood, veal. Entertainment nightly in season. Valet parking. Outdoor dining. Wood-burning pizza oven. Cr cds: A, D, MC, V.

★ ★ **LA CARAVELLE.** *1040 Laskin Rd, 5 blks W of oceanfront.* 804/428-2477. Hrs: 5:30-10:30 pm. Closed Sun. Res accepted; required Fri & Sat. French, Vietnamese menu. Bar. Semi-a la carte: dinner $3.95-$19.95. Specializes in seafood, fowl. Pianist evenings. Parking. Country French decor. Cr cds: A, MC, V.

★ ★ ★ **LE CHAMBORD.** *324 N Greatneck Rd.* 804/498-1234. Hrs: 11-1 am. Closed Jan 1, Thanksgiving, Dec 25. Res accepted; required wkend. French, continental menu. Bar. Wine list. Semi-a la carte: lunch $4.95-$6.95, dinner $4.50-$18.95. Specialties: rack of lamb, poached salmon, veal chops. Valet parking. Modern Mediterranean-style decor; fireplaces in lounge area, dining rm. Former post office building. Cr cds: A, C, D, DS, MC, V.

D

✔ ★ ★ **LUCKY STAR.** *1608 Pleasure House Rd.* 804/363-8410. Hrs: 5:30-10 pm. Closed Sun; some major hols. Res accepted; required Fri & Sat. Bar. A la carte entrees: dinner $4-$16.50. Specialties: tuna Stremberg, Chesapeake Bay crab cakes (in season), bayou banana split. Parking. Local artwork. Smoking at bar only. Cr cds: A, MC, V.

D

★ ★ **LYNNHAVEN FISH HOUSE.** *2350 Starfish Rd, next to Westminster Canterbury.* 804/481-0003. Hrs: 11:30 am-10:30 pm. Closed Thanksgiving, Dec 25. Res accepted. Bar. A la carte entrees: lunch $5.95-$8.95, dinner $13.95-$22.95. Child's meals. Specializes in seafood, Belgian whiskey pudding. Raw bar, lobster tank. Valet parking. On Lynnhaven fishing pier. Cr cds: A, C, D, DS, MC, V.

D

✔ ★ **PUNGO GRILL.** *1785 Princess Anne Rd.* 804/426-6655. Hrs: 11 am-9 pm; Fri, Sat to 10 pm. Closed Mon; Jan 1, Dec 24, 25. Regional Amer, continental menu. Bar. Semi-a la carte: lunch $4.50-$12.50, dinner $8.95-$12.95. Child's meals. Specializes in Cajun soups, homemade desserts, French roast coffee. Parking. Outdoor dining. Dining rm on enclosed porch of 1919 "Aladdin" house. Cr cds: DS, MC, V.

D

★ **RUDEE'S.** *227 Mediterranean Ave.* 804/425-1777. Hrs: 11-2 am. Closed Dec 25. Bar. Semi-a la carte: lunch, dinner $4.95-$24.95. Sun brunch $4.95-$9.95. Child's meals. Specializes in fresh seafood, steamed shrimp, handcut steak. Raw bar. Valet parking. Outdoor dining. Nautical decor; casual atmosphere. On inlet; transient slips avail for boats. Cr cds: A, C, D, DS, MC, V.

✔ ★ **SAN ANTONIO SAM'S ICE HOUSE.** *604 Norfolk Ave.* 804/491-0263. Hrs: 11 am-midnight; Fri, Sat to 1 am. Closed Jan 1, Thanksgiving, Dec 24, 25. Tex-Mex menu. Bar. Semi-a la carte: lunch, dinner $3.95-$9.95. Specializes in fajitas, enchiladas, chili. Parking. Casual dining rm in renovated 1898 ice house. Cr cds: A, D, DS, MC, V.

★ ★ **TANDOM'S PINE TREE INN.** *2932 Virginia Beach Blvd.* 804/340-3661. Hrs: 11:30 am-2:30 pm, 5-9 pm; Fri, Sat to 10 pm; Sun noon-9 pm; Sun brunch 10:30 am-2:30 pm. Closed Memorial Day, Labor Day. Res accepted. Bar. Semi-a la carte: lunch $3.95-$8.95, dinner $9.95-$17.95. Sun brunch $7.95-$10.95. Child's meals. Specializes in fresh seafood, prime rib, veal Oscar. Salad bar. Raw bar. Pianist. Parking. Cr cds: A, C, D, DS, MC, V.

D

★ ★ **THREE SHIPS INN.** *3800 Shore Dr.* 804/460-0055. Hrs: 5-10 pm. Res accepted. Continental menu. Bar. Semi-a la carte: dinner $14.95-$18.95. Child's meals. Specializes in fresh seafood, steak, fowl. Lobster tank. Parking. Colonial decor. Cr cds: A, MC, V.

Unrated Dining Spot

CUISINE AND COMPANY. *3004 Pacific Ave.* 804/428-6700. Hrs: 10 am-8 pm; summer 9 am-9 pm. Closed Jan 1, Thanksgiving, Dec 25. Continental menu. Wine, beer. A la carte entrees: lunch, dinner $1.25-$12. Specializes in pasta, salads, specialty desserts. Parking. Cr cds: A, MC, V.

D

Warm Springs (D-5)

Pop: 425 (est) **Elev:** 2,260 ft **Area code:** 703 **Zip:** 24484

Nestled at the foot of Little Mountain (3,100 ft), the spring wildflowers or groves of fall foliage make Warm Springs a very scenic spot for sightseeing, hiking or taking the waters. Visitors also enjoy walking tours to view the many historic buildings.

(See Clifton Forge, Covington, Hot Springs, Monterey)

Inn

★ ★ ★ **INN AT GRISTMILL SQUARE.** *Box 359, 2 blks W of US 220.* 703/839-2231; FAX 703/839-5770. 16 units, 1 & 2 bedrm. Rms: S, D $80-$95; inn apts: S $85-$110; D $85-$125; each addl $8-$12; under 10 free. Crib free. TV; cable. Pool; sauna. Complimentary continental bkfst. Restaurant (see WATERWHEEL). Bar 5-10 pm. Ck-out noon, ck-in 2 pm. Tennis. 18-hole golf privileges, pro. Downhill/x-country ski 5 mi. Refrigerators, fireplaces. Private patios. Picnic tables. Consists of 5 restored 19th-century buildings. Cr cds: DS, MC, V.

Restaurant

★ ★ ★ **WATERWHEEL.** *(See The Inn At Gristmill Square)* 703/839-2231; FAX 703/839-5770. Hrs: 6-9 pm; Fri, Sat to 10 pm; Sun brunch 11 am-2 pm. Res accepted. Continental menu. Bar. Wine list. Semi-a la carte: dinner $18-$24. Specializes in fresh local trout, veal, homegrown vegetables. Own baking. Parking. In gristmill dating from the turn of the century. Cr cds: DS, MC, V.

Warrenton (C-8)

Pop: 4,830 **Elev:** 560 ft **Area code:** 703 **Zip:** 22186

The seat of Fauquier County, Warrenton was named for General Joseph Warren, who fought at Bunker Hill in the Revolutionary War. The town is situated in the valley of the Piedmont near the foothills of the Blue Ridge Mountains and is known for its cattle and Thoroughbred horse farms. Many old buildings and houses provide for an interesting walking tour of the town.

(For further information contact the Fauquier County Chamber of Commerce, PO Box 127; 347-4414.)

Seasonal Event

Flying Circus. 7 mi S on US 15/29, then 7 mi SE on US 17 near Bealeton. Flying shows of the barnstorming era, from comedy acts to precision & stunt flying. Rides, picnic area. Phone 439-8661. Sun. May-Oct.

(See Culpeper, Fairfax, Front Royal, Manassas)

Motels

★ ★ **COMFORT INN.** *US 29 Bypass N.* 703/349-8900; FAX 703/347-5759. 97 rms. S, D $49-$66; addl $8; suites $89-$125; under 17 free; mid-wk rates. Crib free. Pet accepted, some restrictions. TV; cable. Pool. Complimentary continental bkfst. Ck-out 11 am. Coin lndry. Meeting rm. Exercise equipt; weight machine, stair machine. Refrigerators. Cr cds: A, C, D, DS, MC, V.

★ ★ **HAMPTON INN.** *501 Blackwell Rd.* 703/349-4200; FAX 703/349-4200, ext. 307. 100 rms, 2 story. S, D $55-$69; under 18 free. Crib free. TV; cable. Pool. Complimentary continental bkfst, coffee. Ck-out noon. Meeting rms. Coin lndry. Exercise equipt; bicycle, stair machine. Refrigerators avail. Picnic tables, grill. Cr cds: A, C, D, DS, MC, V.

Restaurants

★ ★ **FANTASTICO RISTORANTE ITALIANO.** *640 Warrenton Center, 2 mi NW jct US 29 Business & US 17, in shopping center.* 703/349-2575. Hrs: 11:30 am-2 pm, 5-9:30 pm; Fri to 10 pm; Sat 5-10 pm. Closed Sun; most major hols. Res accepted. Northern Italian menu. Bar. Semi-a la carte: lunch $5.95-$9.75, dinner $9.95-$16.95. Child's meals. Specializes in seafood, veal. Own bread, pastries, pasta. Cr cds: A, DS, MC, V.

[D]

★ **LEGEND'S.** *380 Broadview Ave.* 703/347-9401. Hrs: 11 am-10 pm; Fri, Sat to 11 pm; Sun brunch 9 am-2 pm. Closed Dec 25. Res accepted. Continental menu. Bar. Semi-a la carte: lunch, dinner $3.95-$15.95. Complete meals: lunch $4.95-$6.95, dinner $10.95-$14.95. Sun brunch $3.95-$8.25. Specializes in prime rib, crab cakes. Parking. Cr cds: A, MC, V.

✔ ★ **NAPOLEON'S.** *67 Waterloo St.* 703/347-1200. Hrs: 11 am-midnight; Fri, Sat to 2 am. Closed Dec 25. Res accepted. Continental menu. Bar. Semi-a la carte: lunch $4.95-$7.95, dinner $9.95-$14.95. Specializes in veal, fresh fish, seafood fettucine. Parking. Outdoor dining. Cr cds: D, MC, V.

Washington (C-7)

Founded: 1796 **Pop:** 198 **Elev:** 690 ft **Area code:** 703 **Zip:** 22747

The oldest of more than 25 American towns to be named after the first president, this town was surveyed in 1749 by none other than George Washington himself. The streets remain laid out exactly as surveyed, and still bear the names of families who owned the land on which the town was founded. It is romantically rumored that Gay St was named by the 17-year-old Washington after the lovely Gay Fairfax.

The town, seat of Rappahannock County, is situated in the foothills of the Blue Ridge Mountains, which dominate the western horizon.

(For information about this area contact the Town of Washington, PO Box 7; 675-3428.)

(See Warrenton)

Inns

★ ★ ★ **BLEU ROCK.** *Rte 1, Box 555, on US 211.* 703/987-3190; res: 800/537-3652; FAX 703/987-3193. 5 rms, 2 story. No rm phones. S, D $130-$165. Complimentary full bkfst 8-10 am. Complimentary sherry in rms. Restaurant (see BLEU ROCK INN). Ck-out 11 am, ck-in 3 pm. Balconies. Restored farmhouse (1899) on lake; rustic setting; vineyard. Cr cds: A, MC, V.

★ ★ ★ ★ ★ **THE INN AT LITTLE WASHINGTON.** *Middle & Main Sts.* 703/675-3800; FAX 703/675-3100. 12 rms in 2 bldgs, 2 story. D $240-$370; suites $390-$490; higher rates: Fri, Sat, hols & Oct. Inn closed Tues (exc May & Oct); also Dec 24, 25. Complimentary continental bkfst. Restaurant (see THE INN AT LITTLE WASHINGTON RESTAURANT). Rm serv. Serv bar. Ck-out noon, ck-in 3 pm. Bellhops. Gift shop. Minibars. Some balconies. English country house atmosphere; elegant antique furnishings; library on 2nd floor. Rms individually decorated; some with balcony overlooking garden courtyard. Complimentary tea service, fruit and cookies upon arrival. Cr cds: MC, V.

⊠ ⊠

★ ★ **SYCAMORE HILL.** *Rte 1, Box 978, on US 211. 703/675-3046.* 3 rms, 2 story. No rm phones. S, D $115-$155; higher rates wkends, hols and month of Oct (2-day min). Children over 12 yrs only. Complimentary full bkfst, afternoon refreshments. Ck-out 11 am, ck-in 2 pm. Luggage handling. Lawn games. On top of hill, view of mountains. Gardens. Totally nonsmoking. Cr cds: MC, V.

D ⊠ ⊠

Restaurants

★ ★ ★ **BLEU ROCK INN.** *(See Bleu Rock Inn) 703/987-3190.* Hrs: 5:30-9:30 pm; Sat to 10 pm; Sun 5:30-9 pm; Sun brunch 11:30 am-3 pm. Closed Mon; Dec 25. Res accepted. French, Amer menu. Bar. Semi-a la carte: dinner $15-$22. Complete meals (Nov-Apr): dinner (4-course) $19.95. Sun brunch $4.95-$13. Specialties: eggplant terrine, filet of beef, apple frangipane tart. Parking. Outdoor dining. French provincial decor; fireplaces, antiques. Family-owned. Cr cds: A, MC, V.

D

★ ★ ★ ★ ★ **THE INN AT LITTLE WASHINGTON.** *(See The Inn At Little Washington Inn) 703/675-3800.* Hrs: 6-9:30 pm; Sat 5:30-10 pm; Sun 4-9:30 pm. Closed Tues (exc May & Oct); also Dec 24, 25. Res accepted; required Fri, Sat. Eclectic regional cuisine. Extensive wine cellar. Prix fixe: dinner $78, Fri $88, Sat $98. Specialties: timbale of Virginia lump crabmeat, barbecued rack of lamb. Valet parking. Country inn; distinctive English country decor. Chef-owned. Smoking permitted in lounge and garden only. Cr cds: MC, V.

D

Waynesboro (D-6)

Settled: ca 1739 **Pop:** 18,549 **Elev:** 1,300 ft **Area code:** 703 **Zip:** 22980

Waynesboro is at the southern end of the Skyline Drive and the northern end of the Blue Ridge Parkway.

What to See and Do

1. **Shenandoah Valley Art Center.** 600 W Main St. Art galleries, studios. Working artists; performing arts. Donation. (Daily exc Mon) Phone 949-7662.
2. **Sherando Lake Recreation Area.** 16 mi SW on Blue Ridge Pkwy, in George Washington National Forest. Facilities include 21-acre lake with sand beach and bathhouses. Swimming, fishing. Picnicking. Camping (Apr-Oct, fee). Amphitheater, campfire programs. (Apr-Nov, daily) Sr citizen rate. Phone 942-5965 (summer) or 261-6105. Day use ¢¢
3. **Shenandoah National Park** (see). 1 mi E to Skyline Dr.

(For further information contact the Waynesboro-East Augusta Chamber of Commerce, 301 W Main St; 949-8203.)

Annual Event

Fall Foliage Festival. 1st & 2nd wkend Oct.

(See Charlottesville)

Motels

✔ ★ ★ **COMFORT INN WAYNESBORO.** *640 W Broad St. 703/942-1171.* 75 rms. S $38-$55; D $42-$65; each addl $5; under 18 free. Crib free. Pet accepted, some restrictions. TV; cable. Pool; wading pool. Ck-out noon. Valet serv. Downhill ski 20 mi. Health club privileges. Cr cds: A, C, D, DS, ER, JCB, MC, V.

D ⊯ ⊠ ≈ ⊠ ⊠ SC

★ **DAYS INN.** *2060 Rosser Ave, I-64 & US 340 S. 703/943-1101; FAX 703/949-7586.* 98 rms, 2 story. May-Oct: S $45-$60; D $50-$75; each addl $5; higher rates fall foliage; lower rates rest of yr. Crib free. Pet accepted; $4. TV; cable. Pool; whirlpool. Restaurant adj 6 am-midnight. Ck-out 11 am. Meeting rms. Valet serv. Game rm. Lawn games. Picnic tables. Cr cds: A, C, D, DS, MC, V.

D ⊯ ≈ ⊠ ⊠ SC

★ ★ **HOLIDAY INN.** *Box 849, 4 mi E on US 250 at jct Skyline Dr & I-64 exit 99. 703/942-5201; FAX 703/943-8746.* 118 rms, 2-3 story. No elvtr. May-Oct: S $55-$70; D $60-$75; each addl $6; under 18 free; lower rates rest of yr. Crib free. Pet accepted. TV; cable. Heated pool. Restaurant 7 am-2 pm, 5-10 pm. Rm serv. Bar 5 pm-12:30 am; entertainment Fri-Sat, dancing exc Sun. Ck-out noon. Meeting rms. Valet serv. Downhill ski 18 mi. Cr cds: A, C, D, DS, JCB, MC, V.

D ⊯ ⊠ ≈ ⊠ ⊠

Restaurant

★ ★ ★ **FOX AND HOUNDS PUB.** *533 W Main St. 703/946-9200.* Hrs: 11:30 am-2:30 pm, 5-9:30 pm; Sun to 2:30 pm. Res accepted. Continental menu. Semi-a la carte: lunch $5.25-$9.75, dinner $9.95-$18.75. Child's meals. Specialties: tenderlion of veal, chicken cordon bleu, lamb chops. Parking. In restored 1837 house, used as hospital by both sides during Civil War. English club-like atmosphere. Cr cds: A, MC, V.

D

Williamsburg (E-9)

Settled: 1633 **Pop:** 11,530 **Elev:** 86 ft **Area code:** 804

After the Indian massacre of 1622, this Virginia colony built a palisade across the peninsula between the James and York rivers. The settlement that grew up around the palisade was called Middle Plantation and is now the site of Colonial Williamsburg.

Middle Plantation figured prominently in Bacon's Rebellion against Governor Berkeley. In 1693, it was chosen as the site of the College of William and Mary, and in 1699, the seat of Virginia government was moved here. The capitol was built to replace the Jamestown statehouse, which had burned the year before. Renamed in honor of William III of England, the new capital gradually became a town of about 200 houses and 1,500 residents. For 81 years, Williamsburg was the political, social and cultural capital of Virginia.

The colony's first successful printing press was established here by William Parks, and in 1736 he published Virginia's first newspaper. The capitol was the scene of such stirring colonial events as Patrick Henry's Stamp Act speech (1765),

The First Continental Congress was called from here by the dissolved House of Burgesses in 1774. Two years later, the Second Continental Congress was boldly led by delegates from Virginia to declare independence; George Mason's Declaration of Rights, which became the basis for the first ten amendments to the Constitution, was adopted here.

Williamsburg's exciting days came to an end in 1780, when the capital was moved to Richmond for greater safety and convenience during the Revolution. For a century and a half it continued as a quiet little college town, its tranquility interrupted briefly by the Civil War. In 1917, when a munitions factory was built near the town and cheap housing for the factory's 15,000 workers was hastily erected, Williamsburg seemed destined to live out its days in ugliness.

In 1926, however, John D. Rockefeller, Jr and Dr. W.A.R. Goodwin, rector of Bruton Parish Church, who saw the town as a potential treasure house of colonial history, shared the broad vision that inspired the restoration of Williamsburg. For more than 30 years, Rockefeller devoted personal attention to the project and contributed funds to accomplish this nonprofit undertaking.

Today, after many years of archaeological and historical research, the project is near completion. The Historic Area, approximately a mile long and a half-mile wide, encompasses most of the 18th-century capital. Eighty-eight of the original buildings have been restored; 50 major buildings, houses and shops and many smaller outbuildings have been reconstructed on their original sites; 45 of the more historically significant buildings contain more than 200 exhibition rooms, furnished either with original pieces or reproductions and open to the public on regular seasonal schedules.

Visitors stroll Duke of Gloucester Street and mingle with people in 18th-century attire. Craftsmen at about 20 different shops ply such trades as wigmaking and blacksmithing, using materials, tools and techniques of pre-Revolutionary times.

Williamsburg is beautiful year-round. November through March is an excellent time to visit, when it is less crowded and the pace is more leisurely; some holiday weekends may be busy. The Historic Area is closed to private motor vehicles 8 am-6 pm, later during summer and special events.

What to See and Do

(Please note that Colonial Williamsburg is only a part of the town of Williamsburg. Other attractions are listed for which there are separate admission fees.)

1. Colonial Williamsburg.

Colonial Williamsburg Visitor Center. Colonial Pkwy and VA 132. Ticket sales, sightseeing information; orientation film; lodging and dining assistance; bookstore; transportation. Center (daily). Contact the Colonial Williamsburg Foundation, PO Box 1776, 23187; 800-HISTORY or 220-7645.

Ticket information. An admission ticket is necessary to enjoy the full scope of Colonial Williamsburg. Three types of general admission tickets are available: The **Basic Ticket** provides admission on the Colonial Williamsburg transportation system and entrance to the exhibits in the Historic Area for one day. (This ticket does *not* provide admission to the Governor's Palace, the DeWitt Wallace Decorative Arts Gallery, Carter's Grove or the Abby Aldrich Rockefeller Folk Art Center.) The **Royal Governor's Pass** (valid up to 3 days) provides admission on the transportation system and entrance to all exhibits in the Historic Area, including the Governor's Palace and the DeWitt Wallace Decorative Arts Gallery. (It does *not* provide admission to Carter's Grove.) The **Patriot's Pass** (valid one yr) provides admission on the transporation system and entrance to all historic buildings, colonial houses, craft shops, Governor's Palace, Carter's Grove (see #2), DeWitt Wallace Decorative Arts Gallery, Abby Aldrich Rockefeller Folk Art Center and historical film. Ticket prices vary. Phone 800-HISTORY for exact prices.

Disabled Visitor Information. Efforts are made to accommodate the disabled while still retaining the authenticity of colonial life. Many buildings have wheelchair access once inside, but it should be noted that most buildings are reached by steps. Visitor Center has a list detailing accessibility of each building; wheelchair ramps may be made available at some buildings with advance notice. In addition, there are wheelchair rentals and parking. A hands-on tour of several historic trades may be arranged for the visually impaired and sign language tours are available with advance notice. Phone 220-7644.

Exhibition buildings.

The Capitol. E end of Duke of Gloucester St. House of Burgesses met here (1704-79); scene of Patrick Henry's speech against Stamp Act. North of capitol, across Nicholson St is

Public Gaol. Where debtors, criminals and pirates (including Blackbeard's crew) were imprisoned. A few steps west and back to Duke of Gloucester St is

Raleigh Tavern. Frequent meeting place for Jefferson, Henry and other Revolutionary patriots; a social center of the Virginia Colony. Opposite is

Wetherburn's Tavern. One of the most popular inns of the period.

Governor's Palace and Gardens. N end of Palace Green. Residence of Royal Governor, one of the most elegant mansions in colonial America; set in 10-acre restored gardens. ¢¢¢¢

Brush-Everard House. Home of early mayor has carved staircase, boxwood gardens. Southeast is

Peyton Randolph House (1716). Home of president of First Continental Congress. Rochambeau's headquarters prior to Yorktown campaign. Southwest is

James Geddy House. Once home of a prominent silversmith with working brass, bronze, silver and pewter foundry. Across Palace Green at corner of Prince George St is

Wythe House. Home of George Wythe, America's first law professor, teacher of Jefferson, Clay and Marshall. This was Washington's headquarters before siege of Yorktown, Rochambeau's after.

The Magazine. Duke of Gloucester St, 1 blk E of Palace Green. Arsenal and military storehouse of Virginia Colony; authentic arms exhibited.

Abby Aldrich Rockefeller Folk Art Center. York St 1/2 block SE of capitol. Outstanding collection of American folk art. Items in this collection were created by artists not trained in studio techniques, but who faithfully recorded aspects of everyday life in paintings, sculpture, needlework, ceramics, toys and other media. ¢¢¢

Historic trades. Craftsmen in 18th-century costume pursue old trades of apothecary, printer, bookbinder, silversmith, wigmaker, shoemaker, blacksmith, harnessmaker, cabinetmaker, miller, milliner, gunsmith, wheelwright, basketmaker, cook, cooper and carpenter.

Public Hospital. Reconstruction of first public institution in the English colonies devoted exclusively to treatment of mental illness.

DeWitt Wallace Decorative Arts Gallery. Modern museum adjoining Public Hospital, features exhibits, lectures, films and related programs centering on British and American decorative arts of the 17th-early 19th-centuries. ¢¢¢

Bruton Parish Church. Duke of Gloucester St, just W of Palace Green. One of America's oldest Episcopal churches, in continuous use since 1715. Organ recitals (July-Sept & Dec, Tues, Thurs & Sat; Jan-Feb, Sat; other months, Tues & Sat). (Daily; no tours during services) Phone 229-2891.

Courthouse. Duke of Gloucester St, E of Palace Green. County and city business was conducted here from 1770 until 1932. The interior has been carefully restored to its original appearance. Visitors often participate in scheduled re-enactments of court sessions.

Play Booth Theater. Scenes from 18th-century plays in open-air theater. Open to all Colonial Williamsburg ticket holders. (Spring-fall, daily)

Special focus and orientation tours. Orientation tours for first-time visitors; special tours include African American life, gardens, religion and women of Williamsburg. Reservations are available at the **Lumber House,** located next to Greenhow Store at the south end of Palace Green.

Carriage and wagon rides. A drive through Historic Area in carriage or wagon driven by costumed coachman. General admission ticket holders may make reservations on day of ride at Lumber House ticket office. (Daily, weather permitting) ¢¢-¢¢¢

Lanthorn Tour. A costumed interpreter conducts evening walking tour of selected shops that are illuminated by candlelight. Tickets may be purchased at the Visitor Center or Lumber House ticket office. (Daily) ¢¢¢

Children's Tours. Special programs, tours and experiences exclusively for children and families are offered in the summer.

Evening entertainment. The Virginia Company of Comedians presents "rollicking 18th-century plays" throughout the year; wide variety of cultural events, concerts and historical re-enactments (fees vary). Chowning's Tavern offers colonial "gambols" (games), music, entertainment and light food and drink (evenings).

Shopping. Superior wares typical of the 18th century are offered in nine restored or reconstructed stores and shops; items include silver, jewelery, herbs, candles, hats and books. Two craft houses sell approved reproductions of the antiques on display in the houses and museums.

2. **Carter's Grove** (part of Colonial Williamsburg). 7 mi SE. This James River site includes the Winthrop Rockefeller Archaeology Museum, the partially reconstructed Wolstenholme Towne and an early 18th-century slave quarter. Also a 1755 mansion, located on 80-foot bluff overlooking the James River, that has been restored to its 1930s splendor. A one-way country road begins here and winds through woods, meadows and marshes back to Williamsburg, or visitors may return via US 60. (Mid-Mar-Dec, daily exc Mon) ¢¢¢

3. *Ride With Me to Williamsburg.* Informative and entertaining 90-min audio cassette describes events from Williamsburg's colorful colonial, revolutionary and Civil War past. The town's famous restoration is summarized by one of the architects who worked on the project. Contact RWM Associates, PO Box 1324, Bethesda MD 20817; phone 301/299-7817 or 800/752-3195. ¢¢¢

4. **Busch Gardens Williamsburg.** 3 mi E on US 60. European-style themed park on 360 acres features re-created 17th-century German, English, French, Italian, Scottish and Canadian villages. Attractions include more than 30 thrill rides, including Drachen Fire roller coaster, one of the nation's largest; 3-D movie *Haunts of the Olde Country,* with in-theater special effects; live shows, antique carousel, celebrity concerts, miniature of Le Mans racetrack, rides for small children. Themed restaurants; shops. Transportation around the grounds by sky ride or steam train. A computer-operated monorail links the park with the Anheuser-Busch Hospitality Center; brewery tour. Park (mid-May-Labor Day, daily; spring & fall, wkends only). Phone 253-3000. ¢¢¢¢

5. **College of William and Mary** (1693). (7,000 students) W end of Duke of Gloucester St. America's 2nd oldest college (only Harvard is older). Initiated honor system, elective system of studies, schools of law, modern languages; second to have school of medicine (all in 1779). Phi Beta Kappa Society founded here (1776). Phone 221-4000. On campus are

Wren Building. Oldest (1695-99, restored 1928) academic building in America; designed by the great English architect Sir Christopher Wren. Tours (daily). **Free.**

Earl Gregg Swem Library. Houses College Museum. Large display honoring the college's 300th anniversary. (Mon-Fri; closed most hols).

Muscarelle Museum of Art. Traveling displays and exhibitions from an extensive collection. (Daily; closed Jan 1 & 2, Mar 26) Phone 221-2700. **Free.**

6. **York River State Park.** 8 mi NW via I-64, exit 231B, then 1 mi N on VA 607 to VA 606E. A 2,500-acre park along the York River and its related marshes. Includes the Taskinas Creek National Estuarine Research Reserve. Fishing; boating (launch), canoe trips. Hiking, bridle trails. Picnicking. Interpretive center, programs; nature walks. (Daily) Standard fees. Phone 566-3036.

(For further information contact the Colonial Williamsburg Foundation, PO Box 1776, 23187; 800/HISTORY or 220-7645.)

Annual Events

Antiques Forum. Colonial Williamsburg. Early Feb.

Washington's Birthday Celebration. Colonial Williamsburg. Feb.

Learning Weekend. Colonial Williamsburg. Family-oriented weekend of discovery on a single topic. Mar.

Garden Symposium. Colonial Williamsburg. Lectures and clinics at Colonial Williamsburg. Apr.

Prelude to Independence. Colonial Williamsburg. May 15.

Publick Times. Colonial Williamsburg. Re-creation of colonial market days; contests, crafts, auctions, military encampment. Labor Day wkend.

Traditional Christmas Activities. Colonial Williamsburg. Featuring grand illumination of city; fireworks. Early Dec-early Jan.

Seasonal Events

Colonial Weekends. Package wkends on 18th-century theme, features introductory lecture, guided tours, banquet at Colonial Williamsburg. Jan-early Mar.

18th-Century Comedy. Williamsburg Lodge Auditorium. Sat nights. Mar-Dec.

Military Drill. On Market Square Green. Costumed wkly drill by Williamsburg Independent Company. Mid-Mar-Oct.

Fife-and-Drum Corps. Colonial Williamsburg. Performances in the Historic Area. Sat. Apr-Oct.

Living History Programs at Colonial Williamsburg include *An Assembly, Cross or Crown* and *Cry Witch!* Varying schedule wkly. Spring, summer & fall.

(See Colonial Parkway, Jamestown, Newport News, Surry, Yorktown)

Motels

(Rates may be higher holiday seasons)

✔ ★ **FAIRFIELD INN BY MARRIOTT.** 6493 Richmond Rd (23188). 804/565-1111; FAX 804/564-3033. 129 rms, 2 story. Mar-Labor Day: S, D $50-$69; max 4 persons/rm; higher rates Grand Illumination, July 4 wkend; lower rates rest of yr. Crib free. TV; cable. Pool. Complimentary continental bkfst. Complimentary coffee in lobby. Restaurant adj 7 am-10 pm. Ck-out noon. Refrigerators avail. Cr cds: A, DS, MC, V.

D ≈ ✕ 🔥 **SC**

★ **GOVERNOR'S INN.** 506 N Henry St (23185). 804/229-1000; res: /800-HIST; FAX 804/220-7019. 200 rms, 3 story. May-Aug: S, D $80; each addl (after 4th person) $8; family rates; lower rates rest of yr. Closed Jan-mid-Mar. Crib $8. TV; cable. Pool. Complimentary coffee. Restaurant nearby. Sundries. Gift shop. Free transportation to historic area. Tennis, golf privileges. Game rm. Cr cds: A, DS, MC, V.

D 🐕 🏃 🕴 ≈ ✕ 🔥 **SC**

★ ★ **HAMPTON INN.** 201 Bypass Rd (23185). 804/220-0880; FAX 804/229-7175. 122 rms, 4 story. Mid-June-Labor Day: S, D $79-$89; lower rates rest of yr. Crib free. TV. Indoor pool; whirlpool, sauna. Complimentary continental bkfst. Ck-out 11 am. Meeting rm. Game rm. Cr cds: A, C, D, DS, MC, V.

D ≈ ✕ 🔥 **SC**

★ ★ **HOLIDAY INN 1776.** 725 Bypass Rd (23185), 1 mi N. 804/220-1776; FAX 804/222-3124. 202 rms, 2 story. Mid-June-late Aug: S, D $59-$109; each addl $6; suite $150; under 18 free; lower rates rest of yr. Crib free. TV; cable. Pool; wading pool, poolside serv. Playground. Restaurant 7 am-2 pm, 5-10 pm. Rm serv. Bar from 4 pm;

Sat, Sun from 1 pm.. Ck-out 11 am. Coin lndry. Meeting rms. Bellhops. Valet serv. Concierge. Sundries. Gift shop. Lighted tennis. Game rm. Lawn games. Picnic tables. Colonial Williamsburg 1 mi. Cr cds: A, C, D, DS, JCB, MC, V.

[icons]

★ **HOLIDAY INN EXPRESS.** *119 Bypass Rd (23185).* *804/253-1663; FAX 804/220-9117.* 132 rms, 2 story. Mid-June-Labor Day: S, D $45-$87; each addl $6; under 19 free; lower rates rest of yr. Crib free. TV; cable. Pool. Complimentary continental bkfst. Ck-out 11 am. Meeting rms. Valet serv. Cr cds: A, C, D, DS, ER, JCB, MC, V.

[icons]

✔ ★ ★ **QUALITY INN LORD PAGET.** *901 Capitol Landing Rd (23185).* *804/229-4444; res: 800/537-2438; FAX 804/220-9314.* 94 rms, 1-2 story. May-Oct: S $35-$65; D $45-$70; suites $75-$125; lower rates rest of yr. Crib $6. TV; cable. Pool; wading pool. Restaurant 7 am-11 pm. Ck-out 11 am. Coin lndry. Bellhops. Putting green. On 7½ wooded acres with small lake. Cr cds: A, C, D, DS, ER, JCB, MC, V.

[icons]

★ ★ **QUALITY INN MOUNT VERNON.** *1700 Richmond Rd (23185).* *804/229-2401.* 65 rms, 1-2 story. June-Aug: S, D $69-$75; each addl $5; under 18 free; lower rates rest of yr. Crib $5. TV; cable. Pool. Continental bkfst. Restaurant adj open 24 hrs. Ck-out 11 am. Extensive grounds. Cr cds: A, C, D, DS, MC, V.

[icons]

★ **QUARTERPATH INN.** *620 York St (23185).* *804/220-0960; res: 800/446-9222.* 130 rms, 2 story. Apr-Oct: S, D $62-$69; each addl $6; under 18 free; packages avail; lower rates rest of yr. Crib free. Pet accepted, some restrictions. TV; cable. Pool. Restaurant adj 7 am-10 pm. Ck-out noon. Meeting rm. Some in-rm whirlpools. Cr cds: A, C, D, MC, V.

[icons]

★ ★ **WILLIAMSBURG WOODLANDS.** *Box 1776 (23187), 1 mi SE of I-64, exit 238, opp Visitor Ctr.* *804/229-1000; res: 800/447-8679; FAX 804/221-8942.* 219 rms. Apr-Dec: S, D $81-$100; each addl $8; studio rms $89-$105; golf, tennis packages; lower rates rest of yr. Crib free. TV. 2 pools; wading pool, lifeguard. Playground. Supervised child's activities (mid-June-Aug). Restaurant 7 am-9 pm. Ck-out noon. Meeting rms. Bellhops. Valet serv. Sundries. Barber, beauty shop. Tennis. Golf privileges, putting green. Health club privileges. Lawn games. Miniature golf. Picnic tables. Cr cds: A, DS, MC, V.

[icons]

Motor Hotels

★ ★ **COURTYARD BY MARRIOTT.** *470 McLaws Circle (23185).* *804/221-0700; FAX 804/221-0741.* 151 rms, 4 story. Memorial Day-Labor Day: S, D $92; suites $120; lower rates rest of yr. Crib free. TV; cable. Indoor/outdoor pool; poolside serv (seasonal). Complimentary coffee in rms. Restaurant 6:30 am-noon. Bar 4-11 pm. Ck-out noon. Coin lndry. Meeting rms. Valet serv. Concierge. Sundries. Exercise equipt; weight machine, bicycles, whirlpool. Game rm. Refrigerator in suites. Balconies. Cr cds: A, C, D, DS, MC, V.

[icons]

✔ ★ ★ **DAYS INN EAST.** *90 Old York Rd (23185).* *804/253-6444; FAX 804/253-0986.* 210 rms, 8 story. Memorial Day-Labor Day: S, D $44-$81; each addl $5; under 18 free; lower rates rest of yr. Crib avail. TV; cable. Pool; poolside serv. Restaurant 7-11 am, 5-9:30 pm. Rm serv. Bar from 5 pm. Ck-out 11 am. Coin lndry. Meeting rms. Valet serv. Concierge. Sundries. Game rm. Near Busch Gardens. Cr cds: A, D, DS, MC, V.

[icons]

★ ★ **FORT MAGRUDER INN & CONFERENCE CENTER.** *Rte 60E, Box KE (23187), 6945 Pochanontas Trail.* *804/220-2250; res:*

800/582-1010; FAX 804/220-3215. 303 rms, 4 story. Apr-Oct: S $64-$108; D $72-$118; each addl $10; suites $160-$300; under 16 free; lower rates rest of yr. Crib free. Pet accepted; $25. TV; cable. 2 pools, 1 indoor; wading pool. Playground. Restaurant 7 am-10 pm. Rm serv. Bar 11:30-1 am; entertainment, dancing Tues-Sat. Ck-out noon. Coin lndry. Convention facilities. Bellhops. Concierge. Sundries. Gift shop. Lighted tennis. Golf privileges, greens fee $53-$80. Exercise equipt; weights, bicycles, whirlpool, sauna. Game rm. Bicycles. Some in-rm whirlpools. Balconies; many private patios. Cr cds: A, C, D, DS, MC, V.

[icons]

★ ★ **HILTON.** *50 Kingsmill Rd (23185).* *804/220-2500; FAX 804/220-2500, ext. 7601.* 291 rms, 6 story. Apr-mid-Nov: S $93-$115; D $108-$135; each addl $15; suites $250-$500; family rates; Williamsburg, Busch Gardens plans; lower rates rest of yr. Crib $5. TV; in-rm movies. Indoor/outdoor pool; poolside serv. Restaurant 6:30 am-10:30 pm. Rm serv. Bar; entertainment, dancing. Ck-out noon. Convention facilities. Bellhops. Concierge. Shopping arcade. Tennis. Exercise rm; instructor, weights, bicycles, whirlpool, sauna. Game rm. Rec rm. Refrigerators avail. Private patios, balconies. Cr cds: A, C, D, DS, ER, JCB, MC, V.

[icons]

★ ★ **HOLIDAY INN DOWNTOWN.** *814 Capitol Landing Rd (23185).* *804/229-0200; FAX 804/220-1642.* 139 rms, 3 story. Apr-Oct: S, D $79-$95; each addl $6; suites $158-$190; under 18 free; wknd rates; golf plan; lower rates rest of yr. Crib free. TV; cable. Indoor pool; poolside serv. Restaurant 7 am-10 pm. Rm serv. Bar 5-11 pm. Ck-out noon. Coin lndry. Meeting rms. Bellhops. Concierge. Gift shop. Exercise equipt; weights, bicycles, whirlpool, sauna. Holidome. Game rm. Refrigerators avail. Cr cds: A, D, DS, MC, V.

[icons]

Hotels

★ ★ ★ **WILLIAMSBURG HOSPITALITY HOUSE.** *415 Richmond Rd (23185).* *804/229-4020; res: 800/932-9192; FAX 804/220-1560.* 297 rms, 4 story. Mid-Mar-Dec: S, D $123-$133; each addl $10; suites $253-$303; under 18 free; wknd rates; lower rates rest of yr. Crib free. TV; cable. Heated pool; poolside serv. Restaurant 6:30 am-11 pm. Rm serv 7 am-10 pm. Bar 11:30-1 am; entertainment, dancing. Ck-out noon. Meeting rms. Concierge. Gift shop. Golf privileges. Some bathrm phones. Cr cds: A, C, D, DS, MC, V.

[icons]

★ ★ ★ ★ ★ **WILLIAMSBURG INN.** *Francis St (23185), in historic area.* *804/229-1000; res: 800/HISTORY; FAX 804/220-7798.* 102 rms, 2 story. S, D $245-$325; each addl $12; suites $375-$575; package plans. Crib $12. TV. 3 pools, 1 indoor; wading pool, poolside serv, lifeguard. Family activities program summer months & hols. Restaurant 7 am-10 pm (also see REGENCY ROOM). Complimentary tea 4 pm. Rm serv 24 hrs. Bar 11:30 am-11 pm; entertainment nightly, dancing Fri, Sat. Ck-out noon, ck-in 3 pm. Meeting rms. Concierge. Airport transportation. Tennis, pro. 9-hole & 2 18-hole golf courses, greens fee $85, pro, putting green. Exercise rm; instructor, weights, bicycles, whirlpool, sauna, steam rm. Massage. Lawn games. Bicycle rentals. Card rm. Some refrigerators. Balcony, fireplace in suites. The inn is furnished in regency style; spacious lounges; shaded terrace. At edge of restored area. Cr cds: A, DS, MC, V.

[icons]

★ ★ ★ **WILLIAMSBURG LODGE.** *S England St (23185).* *804/229-1000; res: 800/447-8976; FAX 804/220-7799.* 316 rms, 3 story. Mar-Dec: S, D $165-$225; each addl $12; suites $215-$450; lower rates rest of yr. TV. 3 pools; wading pool, poolside serv, lifeguard. Restaurant 7 am-10 pm. Bar; pianist. Ck-out noon. Meeting rms. Airport transportation. Gift shop. Beauty shop. Tennis, pro. 45-hole golf, greens fee $68, pro, putting green. Exercise rm; instructor, weights, bicycles, whirlpool, steam rm, sauna. Lawn games. Bicycle rentals.

Some fireplaces. Some private patios. Lounge, verandas. Gardens; at edge of Colonial Williamsburg historic district. Cr cds: A, DS, MC, V.

D ✕ ⚒ 🏊 ⚓ 🏃 ➘ 🔥

Inns

★ ★ ★ **COLONIAL HOUSES.** *Francis St (23185), in historic area.* 804/229-1000; *res:* 800/HISTORY; *FAX* 804/220-7798. 85 rms in 26 colonial houses and taverns, 1-2 story; ck-in/ck-out service at Williamsburg Inn Hotel (see). Apr-Dec: S, D $155-$245/rm; 2-8 persons $285-$625/house; lower rates rest of yr. Crib $12. TV. Pool privileges. Dining facilities at Williamsburg Inn Hotel (see). Rm serv 24 hrs. Ck-out noon, ck-in 3 pm. Airport transportation. Recreational facilities avail at Williamsburg Inn Hotel (see). Some of the houses are more than 200 yrs old; furnished in the period. Cr cds: A, DS, MC, V.

🏃 🏃 ➘ 🔥

★ ★ ★ **LEGACY OF WILLIAMSBURG TAVERN.** *930 Jamestown Rd (23185).* 804/220-0524; *res:* 800/962-4722; *FAX* 804/220-2211. 4 rms, 2 story, 2 suites. Mar-Dec: S, D $85-$130; suites $130; lower rates rest of yr. Adults only. TV in sitting rm; cable. Complimentary full bkfst. Restaurant nearby. Ck-out 10:30 am, ck-in 4:30 pm. Rec room. Some balconies. Built in 18th-century style; period antiques, furnishings; library. Large rear deck overlooks small ravine. Totally nonsmoking. Cr cds: A, MC, V.

➘ 🔥

★ ★ ★ **LIBERTY ROSE.** *1022 Jamestown Rd (23185).* 804/253-1260; *res:* 800/545-1825. 4 rms, 2 story. No rm phones. S, D $105-$165; each addl $40. Children over 12 yrs only. TV; in-rm movies. Complimentary full bkfst; afternoon refreshments. Restaurant nearby. Ck-out 11 am, ck-in 3 pm. Free RR station transportation. Picnic tables. Built 1920; many antiques. Wooded grounds. Totally nonsmoking. Cr cds: MC, V.

➘ 🔥

✔ ★ **WAR HILL.** *4560 Long Hill Rd (23188).* 804/565-0248; *res:* 800/743-0248. 5 rms, 2 suites. No rm phones. S, D $65-$85; each addl $15; suites $85-$100. Crib free. TV; cable. Playground. Complimentary full bkfst. Restaurant nearby. Ck-out noon, ck-in 4 pm. On a working farm; built 1969 in colonial style. Totally nonsmoking. Cr cds: A, MC, V.

➘ ➘ 🔥

★ ★ **WILLIAMSBURG SAMPLER.** *922 Jamestown Rd (23185).* 804/253-0398; *res:* 800/722-1169. 4 rms, 3 story. Rm phones avail. S, D $85-$90. TV; cable. Complimentary full bkfst. Restaurant nearby. Ck-out 11 am, ck-in 1 pm. Picnic tables. Plantation-style house; antiques, colonial-style furnishings; gardens. Near William and Mary College; walking distance to historic area. Totally nonsmoking. Cr cds: MC, V.

➘ 🔥

Resort

★ ★ ★ **KINGSMILL.** *1010 Kingsmill Rd (23185).* 804/253-1703; *res:* 800/832-5665; *FAX* 804/253-3993. 407 rms, 2 story. Mid-Mar-mid-Nov: S, D $128-$161; 1-bedrm suites $191-$217; 2-bedrm suites $319-$378; 3-bedrm suites $447-$539; family rates; golf, tennis, vacation package plans; lower rates rest of yr. Crib free. TV; cable. Indoor/outdoor pools. Dining rm 6 am-9:30 pm. Rm serv to midnight. Bar from 10 am. Ck-out noon, ck-in 4 pm. Meeting rms. Concierge. Free village, Colonial Williamsburg, Busch Gardens transportation. Lighted tennis, pro. Four 18-hole golf courses (1 par 3), pro, driving range, putting green. Paddle boats. Marina privileges. Racquetball courts. Entertainment. Exercise rm; instructor, weights, bicycles, whirlpool, steam rm, sauna. Massage. Some refrigerators, fireplaces. Picnic tables, grills. Cr cds: A, C, D, DS, JCB, MC, V.

D ➘ 🏃 🏃 🏊 ⚓ 🏃 🏃 ➘ 🔥 SC

Restaurants

★ ★ **ABERDEEN BARN.** *1601 Richmond Rd.* 804/229-6661. Hrs: 5-9:30 pm; Fri, Sat to 10 pm. Closed Thanksgiving, Dec 25; also first 2 wks Jan. Res accepted. Bar. Semi-a la carte: dinner $13.95-$34.95. Child's meals. Specializes in roast prime rib, seafood, barbecue baby back ribs. Parking. Open-hearth grill. Cr cds: A, DS, MC, V.

D

★ ★ **BERRET'S.** *199 S Boundary St, on Merchant's Square.* 804/253-1847. Hrs: 11:30 am-9 pm. Closed Jan 1, Dec 25; also Mon in Jan & Feb. Res accepted. Regional Amer menu. Bar. Semi-a la carte: lunch $2.50-$7.50, dinner $2.50-$18.95. Child's meals. Specialties: Virginia crab cakes, lobster & crabmeat combo, seafood & herbs baked in parchment. Raw bar. Parking. Outdoor dining. Casual dining rm; fireplace, nautical decor. Cr cds: A, DS, MC, V.

D SC

★ ★ **COACH HOUSE TAVERN.** *(12604 Harrison Landing Rd, Charles City) Approx 25 mi W on VA 5.* 804/829-6003. Hrs: 11 am-3 pm, 6-9 pm; Sun brunch 11 am-4 pm. Closed Dec 25. Res accepted; required Wed-Sun. Bar. Semi-a la carte: lunch $2.95-$11.95. Complete meals: dinner $15-$25. Sun brunch $2.95-$12.95. Child's meals. Specializes in seafood, game, rum pound cake with berries & cream. Parking. In coach house of Berkeley Plantation; view of grounds and plantation house. Cr cds: A, MC, V.

★ ★ **DYNASTY.** *1621 Richmond Rd.* 804/220-8888. Hrs: noon-midnight. Res accepted. Chinese menu. Bar. Semi-a la carte: lunch $2.95-$4.75, dinner $3.95-$18.95. Child's meals. Specialties: steamed whole fish, General Tso's chicken, Peking duck. Parking. Outdoor dining. Large dining area decorated with Chinese screens and art objects. Fish pond. Cr cds: A, C, D, DS, MC, V.

D SC

★ ★ ★ **FORD'S COLONY COUNTRY CLUB.** *240 Ford's Colony Dr, 4 mi W on Long Hill Dr, then left; in club house.* 804/258-4100. Hrs: 5:30-9:30 pm; Sun brunch 11:30 am-3 pm. Closed Mon; also early Jan. Res recommended. Regional Amer menu. Bar. Wine cellar. Semi-a la carte: dinner $18-$30. Sun brunch $15.95. Child's meals. Specializes in fresh seafood, rack of lamb. Parking. Outdoor dining. Within country club in residential area. Traditional decor; Georgian-style paneling; beamed ceiling, fireplace. Jacket (dinner). Cr cds: A, MC, V.

D

✔ ★ **GIUSEPPEI'S.** *5601 Richmond Rd (23188).* 804/565-1977. Hrs: 11:30 am-2 pm, 5-9 pm; Sat from 5 pm. Closed Sun; major hols. Italian menu. Bar. Semi-a la carte: lunch, dinner $4.25-$13.95. Child's meals. Specialties: pasta primavera, seafood fettuccine, chicken Provencale. Parking. Patio dining. Cr cds: DS, MC, V.

D

★ ★ **INDIAN FIELDS TAVERN.** *(9220 John Tyler Memorial Hwy, Charles City) Approx 21 mi W on VA 5.* 804/829-5004. Hrs: 11 am-4 pm, 5-9 pm; Fri & Sat to 10 pm. Sun brunch to 4 pm. Closed Dec 24 & 25; also Mon in Jan & Feb. Res accepted. Bar. Semi-a la carte: lunch $5.50-$11.95, dinner $14-$21. Sun brunch $7-$11.95. Child's meals. Specialties: crab cakes Harrison, pasta jambalaya, bread pudding. Parking. Screened porch dining area. Turn-of-the-century farmhouse on working farm. Cr cds: DS, MC, V.

★ ★ **JEFFERSON INN.** *1453 Richmond Rd.* 804/229-2296. Hrs: 4-11 pm. Closed Jan 1, Thanksgiving, Dec 24, 25. Res accepted. Italian, continental menu. Semi-a la carte: dinner $6.95-$17.95. Child's meals. Specializes in steak, fresh seafood, southern dishes. Parking. Family-owned. Cr cds: A, C, D, MC, V.

D

★ ★ **KING'S ARMS TAVERN.** *Duke of Gloucester St.* 804/229-2141. Hrs: 11:30 am-2:30 pm, 5:15-9:30 pm. Closed Jan 2-Feb 15; also Tues exc July & Mon Nov-Mar. Res accepted. Bar. Semi-a la carte: lunch $1.95-$10.95, dinner $18.25-$25.95. Child's meals. Specializes in game pie, peanut soup, Virginia ham. Garden bar serv. Own apple cider. Garden dining. Colonial balladeers. Restored 18th century tavern; colonial decor. Cr cds: A, DS, MC, V.

★ ★ ★ **KITCHEN AT POWHATAN.** *3601 Ironbound Rd, on grounds of Powhatan Plantation.* 804/220-1200. Hrs: 5:30-10 pm. Closed Mon. Res accepted. Bar. Semi-a la carte: dinner $13-$20. Specializes in game, seafood, regional cuisine. Parking. In 1737 structure near James River. Cr cds: C, D, MC, V.

★ ★ ★ **LE YACA.** *1915 Pocohantas Trail, US 60E in Kingsmill Village shops.* 804/220-3616. Hrs: 11:30 am-2 pm, 6-9:30 pm. Closed Sun. Res accepted. Southern French menu. Bar. Wine cellar. Semi-a la carte: lunch $5.95-$10.95. Complete meals: dinner $17-$39. Specialties: open-spit leg of lamb, marquise au chocolat. Salad bar (lunch). Own pastries. Parking. Cr cds: A, C, D, MC, V.

[D]

✔ ★ **OLD CHICKAHOMINY HOUSE.** *1211 Jamestown Rd, at jct VA 199 and 315.* 804/229-4689. Hrs: 8:30 am-2:15 pm. Closed Thanksgiving, Dec 25; also 2 wks mid-Jan. Wine, beer. Semi-a la carte: bkfst 95¢-$6.25, lunch $1.95-$5.75. Specializes in ham on hot biscuits, Brunswick stew, chicken & dumplings. Parking. 18th-century stagecoach stop atmosphere. Totally nonsmoking. Cr cds: MC, V.

✔ ★ ★ **PEKING.** *122-A Waller Mill Rd.* 804/229-2288. Hrs: 11:30 am-10 pm; Fri & Sat to 11 pm; Sun brunch noon-2:30 pm. Closed Thanksgiving. Res accepted; required wknds. Chinese menu. Bar. A la carte entrees: lunch $3.25-$5.95, dinner $5.95-$12.95. Sun brunch $6.95. Specialties: General Tso's chicken, Emperor's shrimp, Peking chicken. Cr cds: A, D, MC, V.

[D]

★ ★ ★ **REGENCY ROOM.** *(See Williamsburg Inn Hotel)* 804/229-2141. Hrs: 7-10 am, noon-2 pm, 6-9:30 pm; Sun brunch noon-2 pm. Res accepted. Continental menu. Bar. Wine list. Semi-a la carte: bkfst $3.50-$12.50, lunch $7.25-$13.50. A la carte entrees: dinner $19.50-$32. Sun brunch $19.50-$25. Specializes in snapper or veal with crabmeat, rack of lamb. Own baking. Combo Fri & Sat. Valet parking. Full serv at pool. Cocktail patio. Jacket. Cr cds: A, DS, MC, V.

[D]

★ **SHIELDS TAVERN.** *Duke of Gloucester St (23187).* 804/229-2141. Hrs: 8:30-10 am, 11:30 am-3 pm, 5-9:30 pm; Sun brunch 10 am-2:30 pm. Closed Wed; also mid-Feb-Mar. Res accepted. Bar. Semi-a la carte: bkfst $4.25-$10.95, lunch $3.50-$12.95, dinner $3.50-$23.50. Sun brunch $6.25-$10.95. Child's meals. Specialties: peppercorn steak, cream of crayfish soup, fresh local seafood. 18th-century balladeers. Outdoor dining. Eight dining rms in authentically restored Colonial building. Totally nonsmoking. Cr cds: A, DS, MC, V.

[D]

★ **THAT SEAFOOD PLACE.** *1647 Richmond Rd.* 804/220-3011. Hrs: 11:30 am-2:15 pm, 4:30-9 pm (to 10 pm in summer); Fri & Sat 4:30-10 pm (to 11 pm in summer); Sun noon-9 pm. Closed Dec 25. Res accepted. Bar. Semi-a la carte: lunch $4.95-$6.95, dinner $8.25-$29.75. Child's meals. Specialties: shrimp sampler, sautéed shrimp & scallops. Salad bar. Parking. Outdoor dining. Nautical decor. Cr cds: A, C, D, DS, MC, V.

[SC]

★ ★ ★ **TRELLIS.** *Box 287, Duke of Gloucester St, in Merchant's Square.* 804/229-8610. Hrs: 11 am-9:30 pm; Sun brunch to 2:30 pm. Closed Jan 1, Thanksgiving, Dec 24, 25, 31. Res accepted. Bar 11:30 am-10:30 pm. Semi-a la carte: lunch $4.75-$10.95, dinner $14.95-$22. Sun brunch $4.75-$11.95. Specializes in fresh seafood, mesquite grilling. Own ice cream, pasta. Entertainment wknds. Outdoor dining under trees. Cr cds: A, MC, V.

[D]

★ ★ **WHALING COMPANY.** *494 McLaw Circle.* 804/229-0275. Hrs: 11:30 am-10 pm; Fri to 11 pm; Sat 4-11 pm; Sun 4:30-10 pm; early-bird dinner Sun-Fri 4:30-6 pm. Res accepted. Bar. Semi-a la carte: lunch $3.95-$8.95, dinner $9.95-$26.95. Child's meals. Specializes in fresh seafood. Parking. Cr cds: A, C, D, DS, MC, V.

[D] [SC]

★ ★ **YORKSHIRE STEAK & SEAFOOD HOUSE.** *700 York St.* 804/229-9790. Hrs: 4-10 pm; summer to 10:30 pm. Closed Dec 25. Res accepted. Bar. Semi-a la carte: dinner $10.95-$22.95. Child's meals. Specializes in beef shish kebab, prime rib, seafood. Parking. In Colonial-style building. Cr cds: A, MC, V.

[SC]

Winchester (C-7)

Settled: 1732 **Pop:** 21,947 **Elev:** 720 ft **Area code:** 703

This is the oldest colonial city west of the Blue Ridge, a Civil War prize that changed hands 72 times (once, 13 times in a day). Sometimes called the "apple capital of the world," it is located at the northern approach to the Shenandoah Valley.

George Washington, a red-haired 16-year-old, blithely headed for Winchester and his first surveying job in 1748. He began a decade of apprenticeship for the awesome military and political responsibilities he would later assume as a national leader. During the French and Indian Wars, Colonel Washington made the city his defense headquarters while he built Ft. Loudoun in Winchester. Washington was elected to his first political office as a representative from Frederick County to the House of Burgesses.

At the intersection of travel routes, both east-west and north-south, Winchester grew and prospered. By the time of the Civil War, it was a major transportation and supply center, strategically located to control both Union approaches to Washington and Confederate supply lines through the Shenandoah Valley. More than 100 minor engagements and 6 battles took place in the vicinity. General Stonewall Jackson had his headquarters here during the winter of 1861-62. From his headquarters in Winchester, Union General Philip Sheridan started his famous ride to rally his troops at Cedar Creek, 11 miles away, and turn a Confederate victory into a Union rout.

Approximately 3.5 million bushels of apples are harvested annually in Frederick County and are one of Winchester's economic mainstays today. The world's largest apple cold storage plant and one of the world's largest apple processing plants are here.

What to See and Do

1. **Washington's Office-Museum.** Corner Cork and Braddock Sts. Building used by George Washington in 1755-56 during erection of Ft Loudoun. Housed in this museum are French and Indian, Revolutionary and Civil War relics. (Apr-Oct, daily; rest of yr by appt, weather permitting) Sr citizen rate. Phone 662-4412, -6550. ¢¢

2. **Stonewall Jackson's Headquarters.** 415 N Braddock St. Jackson's headquarters Nov, 1861-Mar, 1862; now a museum housing Jackson memorabilia and other Confederate items of the war years. (Apr-Oct, daily; Nov-Dec & Mar, wkends; rest of yr by appt, weather permitting) Inquire about combination ticket for all 3 museums (also see #1, #3). Sr citizen rate. Phone 667-3242 or 662-6550. ¢¢

3. **Abram's Delight and Log Cabin** (1754). 1340 S Pleasant Valley Rd. Oldest house in city, restored, furnished in 18th-century style; boxwood garden; log cabin, basement kitchen. (Apr-Oct, daily; rest of yr, by appt, weather permitting) Inquire about combination ticket for all 3 museums (also see #1, #2) Sr citizen rate. Phone 662-6519 or -6550. ¢¢

4. **Old Stone Presbyterian Church** (1788). 306 E Piccadilly St. Building has been used as a church, a stable by Union troops in Civil War, a public school and an armory; restored in 1941. (Daily) Phone 662-3824.

5. **The Handley Library and Archives.** Braddock & Piccadilly Sts. Completed in 1913, the public library was designed in the Beaux-arts style. The rotunda is crowned on the outside with a copper-covered dome and on the inside by a dome of stained glass. Interesting features of the interior include wrought iron staircases and glass floors. Historical archives are housed on the lower level. (Daily exc Sun; closed hols) Phone 662-9041.

6. **Winchester-Frederick County Chamber of Commerce and Visitor Center,** 1360 S Pleasant Valley Rd, near I-81 & US 50, is located in the Hollingsworth Mill House (1833). "Welcome to the Top," an 18-min video about the area is shown on request. Tourist information, maps, brochures, calendar of events and self-guided driving and walking tours are available (Daily; closed major hols) Phone 662-4135.

(For further information contact the Winchester-Frederick County Visitor Center, 1360 S Pleasant Valley Rd, 22601; 662-4135.)

Annual Events

Historic Garden Tour. Open house and gardens in historic Winchester. Apr.

Shenandoah Apple Blossom Festival. Apple Blossom Queen, parades, arts and crafts, band contests, music, food and attractions. Phone 662-3863. Wkend before Mother's Day.

Apple Harvest Arts & Crafts. Jim Barnett Park. Pie contests, apple butter-making, music, arts & crafts. 3rd wkend Sept.

(See Front Royal)

Motels

(Rates may be higher during Apple Blossom Festival)

✔ ★ **APPLE BLOSSOM MOTOR LODGE.** *2951 Valley Ave (22601), I-81 exit 310, then 2¹/4 mi N on US 11.* 703/667-1200; res: 800/468-8837; FAX 703/667-7128. 66 rms, 2 story. Apr-Oct: S $39; D $46; each addl $6; under 16 free; lower rates rest of yr. Crib free. TV; cable. Pool. Restaurant 6:30 am-9 pm. Rm serv. Bar. Ck-out noon. Meeting rms. Valet serv. Refrigerators avail. Cr cds: A, C, D, DS, MC, V.

D ≈ ⊠ ⚑ SC

★ ★ **BEST WESTERN LEE-JACKSON MOTOR INN.** *711 Millwood Ave (22601).* 703/662-4154; FAX 703/662-2618. 140 rms, 2 story. Apr-Oct: S $46.50; D $51.50; each addl $5; suites $60-$65; kit. units $35 (14-day min); under 13 free; lower rates rest of yr. Crib avail. Pet accepted. TV; cable. Pool. Restaurant 6 am-10 pm. Rm serv. Bar 4-10:30 pm. Ck-out noon. Coin Indry. Meeting rms. Valet serv. Free airport transportation. Health club privileges. Some refrigerators. Picnic tables, grills. Cr cds: A, C, D, DS, MC, V.

D ⚐ ≈ ⊠ ⚑ SC

✔ ★ **BOND'S.** *2930 Valley Ave (22601), I-81 exit 310, 2 mi N on US 11.* 703/667-8881. 16 rms. Apr-Oct: S $28; D $34; each addl $4; lower rates rest of yr. Crib $3. TV; cable. Complimentary coffee. Restaurant nearby. Ck-out 11 am. Cr cds: A, DS, MC, V.

D ⊠ ⚑ SC

★ ★ **COMFORT INN STEPHENS CITY.** *(167 Town Run Ln, Stephens City 22655) I-81 exit 307.* 703/869-6500; FAX 703/869-2558. 60 rms, 2 story. S $43-$70; D $49-$80; each addl $6; under 18 free. Crib free. TV; cable, in-rm movies avail. Pool. Complimentary continental bkfst, coffee. Restaurant adj 11 am-9 pm. Ck-out noon. Sundries. Some in-rm whirlpools. Cr cds: A, C, D, DS, ER, JCB, MC, V.

D ≈ ⊠ SC

★ **DAYS INN.** *1601 Martinsburg Pike (22603), I-81 exit 317.* 703/667-4400; FAX 703/667-2818. 85 rms, 2 story. S, D $39-$51; each addl $5; under 18 free; higher rates Oct. Crib free. TV; cable. Pool. Complimentary continental bkfst. Restaurant adj open 24 hrs. Ck-out

noon. Coin Indry. Meeting rms. Sundries. Downhill ski 20 mi. Health club privileges. Balconies. Picnic tables. Cr cds: A, D, DS, MC, V.

D ⚐ ≈ ⊠ ⚑ SC

✔ ★ **ECONO LODGE-NORTH.** *1593 Martinsburg Pike (22603).* 703/662-4700; FAX 703/665-1762. 50 rms, 2 story. S $39-$44; D $46-$49; each addl $5; under 19 free. Crib free. TV; cable. Complimentary coffee in lobby. Restaurant adj. Ck-out 11 am. Cr cds: A, C, D, DS, JCB, MC, V.

D ⊠ ⚑ SC

★ ★ **HAMPTON INN.** *1655 Apple Blossom Dr (22601), I-81 exit 313, Apple Blossom Mall.* 703/667-8011; FAX 703/667-8033. 103 rms, 4 story. S $42-$46; D $47-$54; under 18 free. Crib free. TV; cable. Pool. Complimentary continental bkfst. Restaurant nearby. Ck-out noon. Meeting rms. Valet serv. Golf privileges. Health club privileges. Cr cds: A, C, D, DS, MC, V.

D ⚑₁ ≈ ⊠ ⚑ SC

★ ★ **HOLIDAY INN.** *1017 Millwood Pike (22602), at jct I-81 & US 50E.* 703/667-3300; FAX 703/722-2730. 175 rms, 2 story. S $47-$63; D $47-$71; each addl $6; under 18 free. Crib free. Pet accepted. TV; cable. Pool. Restaurant 6:30 am-10 pm. Rm serv. Bar 5:30 pm-midnight. Ck-out noon. Meeting rms. Bellhops. Valet serv. Sundries. Tennis. Health club privileges. Some refrigerators. Balconies. Cr cds: A, C, D, DS, JCB, MC, V.

D ⚐ ⚑₁ ≈ ⊠ ⚑ SC

★ ★ **SHONEY'S INN.** *1347 Berrywine Ave (22601), jct I-81 & VA 7.* 703/665-1700; FAX 703/665-3037. 98 rms (4 with shower only), 3 story. May-Oct: S $42-$45; D $48-$51; each addl $6; under 18 free; lower rates rest of yr. Crib free. TV; cable. Indoor pool. Restaurant 6 am-11 pm. Bar from 4 pm. Ck-out noon. Meeting rms. Sundries. Valet serv. Exercise equipt; weight machine, rowers, whirlpool, sauna. Some refrigerators. Cr cds: A, C, D, DS, ER, MC, V.

D ≈ ⚑₁ ⊠ ⚑ SC

✔ ★ ★ **TRAVELODGE.** *160 Front Royal Pike (22602), I-81 exit 313.* 703/665-0685; FAX 703/665-0689. 149 rms, 3 story. S $35-$51; D $41-$57; each addl $5; suites $95; under 17 free. Crib free. Pet accepted. TV; cable, in-rm movies. Heated pool. Complimentary continental bkfst. Complimentary coffee in rms. Restaurant nearby. Ck-out 11 am. Coin Indry. Health club privileges. Refrigerators avail. Cr cds: A, C, D, DS, ER, JCB, MC, V.

D ⚐ ≈ ⊠ ⚑ SC

Inns

★ ★ ★ **ASHBY.** *(Rte 1, Box 2A, Paris 22130) 18 mi SE on US 50, exit VA 759.* 703/592-3900; FAX 703/592-3781. 10 rms, 8 with bath, 3 story. Rm phones avail. S, D $90-$200. Children over 10 yrs only. TV in some rms. Complimentary full bkfst. Restaurant (see ASHBY INN). Ck-out noon, ck-in 3 pm. Tennis, golf privileges. Lawn games. Library/sitting rm. Converted residence (1829) and one-rm schoolhouse; stone fireplace; antique furnishings. Cr cds: MC, V.

⚑₁ ⚐ ⊠ ⚑

★ ★ ★ **L'AUBERGE PROVENÇALE.** *(PO Box 119, White Post 22663) 9 mi E on US 50, then 1 mi S on VA 340.* 703/837-1375; res: 800/638-1702; FAX 703/837-2004. 10 rms, 2 story. No rm phones. S $100-$150; D $130-$190; each addl $25. Children over 10 yrs only. Complimentary full bkfst. Restaurant (see L'AUBERGE PROVENÇALE). Rm serv to midnight. Ck-out 11 am, ck-in 3 pm. Bellhops. Free airport transportation. Tennis privileges. 36-hole golf privileges. Health club privileges. Balconies. Originally a sheep farm (1753) owned by Lord Fairfax. Victorian decor. Totally nonsmoking. Cr cds: A, C, D, MC, V.

D ⚑₁ ⚐ ⊠ ⚑ ⚑

★ ★ **RIVER HOUSE.** *(US 50 at County 622, Boyce 22620) 15 mi SW on US 50.* 703/837-1476; FAX 703/837-2399. 5 rms (2 with shower only), 3 story. D $80-$115; under 15 free; higher rates wkends (2-day min). Crib $5. TV lounges. Playground. Complimentary full bkfst. Ck-out noon, ck-in by arrangement. Tennis & golf privileges. Fireplaces. On 15-acres at Shenandoah River. Original part of house built 1780 as slave quarters; used as field hospital during Civil War. Cr cds: MC, V.

Restaurants

★ ★ ★ **ASHBY INN.** (See Ashby Inn) 703/592-3900. Hrs: 6-9 pm; Sun noon-2:30 pm. Closed Mon, Tues; Jan 1, July 4, Dec 25. Res required. Serv bar. Semi-a la carte: dinner $13.95-$23.95. Sun brunch $17.50. Specialties: roasted lamb loin, smoked seafood, crab cakes. Menu changes daily. Parking. Virginia hunt country atmosphere; antiques. Plank flooring dates back to original inn (1829). Cr cds: MC, V.

D

★ ★ ★ **L'AUBERGE PROVENÇALE.** (See L'auberge Provençale Inn) 703/837-1375. Hrs: 6-10:30 pm; Sun 4-9 pm. Closed Mon, Tues; July 4, Dec 25. Res accepted; required Fri-Sun. French Provençale menu. Bar. Wine cellar. Prix fixe: dinner $50. Specialties: ris de veau au porto, le lapin fume aux champignons, game dishes. Parking. Outdoor dining. Country inn with extensive art collection. Cr cds: A, C, D, MC, V.

D

Wise (F-2)

Pop: 3,193 **Elev:** 2,454 ft **Area code:** 703 **Zip:** 24293

What to See and Do

Recreation Areas. In Jefferson National Forest (see MARION). **High Knob,** 4 mi S on US 23 to Norton, then 3 mi S via VA 619, 1½ mi E on FS Road 238. Camping, swimming, picnicking. **Bark Camp,** 4 mi S on US 23 to Norton, then 6 mi E on US 58A to Tacoma, then 4 mi S off VA 706, 3 mi S on VA 822. Camping, boating, fishing, picnicking. **Cave Springs,** 7 mi W of Big Stone Gap on US 58A, then 1 mi N on VA 622, then 3 mi W on VA 621. Camping (fee). Swimming. Entrance fee. **North Fork of Pound Lake,** US 23 to Pound, then W on VA 671. Camping (fee), picnicking, swimming, boat ramp, hiking. Clinch Ranger District office is in Wise. Phone 328-2931.

(For accommodations see Big Stone Gap, Breaks Interstate Park)

Woodstock (C-7)

Founded: 1761 **Pop:** 3,182 **Elev:** 780 ft **Area code:** 703 **Zip:** 22664

A German immigrant, Jacob Müller received a land grant from Lord Fairfax and came here in 1752 with his wife and six children. A few years later he set aside 1,200 acres for a town, first called Müllerstadt, later Woodstock. In a small log church here, John Peter Gabriel Mühlenberg, in January, 1776, preached his famous sermon based on Ecclesiastes 3:1-8: "There is a time to every purpose . . . a time to war and a time to peace," at the end of which he flung back his vestments to reveal the uniform of a Continental colonel and began to enroll his parishioners in the army that was to overthrow British rule.

The *Shenandoah Valley-Herald,* a weekly newspaper established in 1817, is still published here.

What to See and Do

1. **Shenandoah County Court House** (1792). Main St. Oldest courthouse still in use west of the Blue Ridge Mountains; interior restored to original design. (Mon-Fri)

2. **Woodstock Tower.** 4 mi E on Mill road, crest of Massanutten Mt. Panoramic view of seven horseshoe bends of the Shenandoah River.

3. **Shenandoah Vineyards.** From I-81 exit 279 at Edinburg, W on VA 675, make first right on VA 686, go 1½ mi to winery. Valley's first winery. Premium wines; hand-picked and processed in the European style. Picnic area. Tours, free tastings available. (Daily; closed Jan 1, Thanksgiving, Dec 25) Phone 984-8699. **Free.**

(For further information contact the Chamber of Commerce, PO Box 605; 459-2542.)

Annual Event

Shenandoah County Fair. One of the oldest county fairs in the state. Harness racing last 4 days. Late Aug-early Sept.

Seasonal Event

Shenandoah Valley Music Festival. Outdoor pavilion on grounds of historic Orkney Springs Hotel in Orkney Springs. Symphony pops, classical, folk, jazz, country & big band concerts. Pavilion & lawn seating. Contact Festival, PO Box 12; 459-3396. 4 wkends, mid-July-Labor Day wkend.

(See Basye, Front Royal, Luray, New Market)

Motels

✔ ★ **BUDGET HOST INN.** US 11 S & I-81, exit 283. 703/459-4086. 43 rm (13 with shower only), 1-2 story. S $30; D $33-$39; each addl $4; under 6 free; wkly rates. Crib $4. Pet accepted, some restrictions. TV; cable. Pool. Restaurant 6:30 am-9 pm; Sun from 7 am. Ck-out 11 am. Coin lndry. Gift shop. Downhill ski 20 mi. Picnic tables. Cr cds: A, C, D, DS, MC, V.

★ ★ **RAMADA INN.** 1130 Motel Dr, I-81 exit 283. 703/459-5000; FAX 703/459-8219. 126 rms, 3 story. May-Oct: S $58; D $66; each addl $8; under 18 free; lower rates rest of yr. Crib free. TV; cable. Heated pool. Restaurant 6 am-2 pm, 5-9 pm; Sat from 7 am. Rm serv. Bar 5 pm-midnight. Ck-out 11 am. Meeting rms. Valet serv. Sundries. Some refrigerators. Cr cds: A, C, D, DS, JCB, MC, V.

D

Inns

★ ★ **INN AT NARROW PASSAGE.** PO Box 608, US 11S, 2 mi S of I-81 exit 283. 703/459-8000; FAX 703/459-8001. 12 rms, 10 with bath, 2 share bath, 2 story. Rm phones avail. S $75; D $85-$95; each addl $8. Crib $8. TV. Complimentary full bkfst, coffee. Ck-out 11 am, ck-in 2 pm. On river; canoeing. Historic inn (1740), used as a headquarters by Gen. Stonewall Jackson during Civil War. Cr cds: MC, V.

★ ★ **RIVER'D INN.** Rte 1, Box 217-A1, N on US 11 to VA 663, then E. 703/459-5369; res: 800/637-4561. 7 rms, 2 share bath, 2 story, 5 suites. No rm phones. S, D $80-$110; each addl $15; suites $125-$175. Children over 12 yrs only. TV in lounge; cable. Heated pool; whirlpool. Complimentary full bkfst. Dining rm Wed-Sat 5-9 pm; Sun 11 am-7 pm. Ck-out 11 am, ck-in 2 pm. Fireplaces. On one of the famous 7 bends of the Shenandoah River. Cr cds: MC, V.

Restaurant

★ ★ **SPRING HOUSE.** *325 S Main St (US 11). 703/459-4755.* Hrs: 9 am-9 pm; Fri, Sat to 10 pm. Closed Jan 1, Dec 25. Res accepted. Bar from 4 pm. Semi-a la carte: bkfst $3.25-$4.25, lunch $2.99-$6.99, dinner $8.99-$16.75. Child's meals. Salad bar. Parking. Garden rm. Log cabin with early American antiques, artifacts. Cr cds: A, C, D, MC, V.

⊡ ⊠ SC

Wytheville (F-4)

Founded: 1792 **Pop:** 8,038 **Elev:** 2,284 ft **Area code:** 703 **Zip:** 24382

With lead mines and the only salt mine in the South nearby, Wytheville was a Union target during the Civil War. One story states a detachment of Union Cavalry attempted to take the town in July, 1863, only to be thwarted by Molly Tynes, who rode 40 miles over the mountains from Rocky Dell to tell the countryside that the Yankees were coming. The alerted home guard turned them away. A transportation center today, Wytheville is a vacationland nestled between the Blue Ridge and Allegheny mountains. Rural Retreat Lake is nearby. Wythe Ranger District office for the Jefferson National Forest (see MARION) is located here.

What to See and Do

1. **Shot Tower Historical Park** (1807). At Jackson's Ferry, 6 mi E on I-81, then 7 mi S on US 52; or I-77 S, Poplar Camp exit. On bluff overlooking New River. One of three shot towers still standing in US; fortress-like stone shaft has 2½-foot-thick walls, rising 75 feet above ground and boring 75 feet below to a water tank. Molten lead was poured through sheet-iron colanders from the tower top; during the 150-foot descent it became globular before hitting the water. Pellets were then sorted by rolling them down an incline; well-formed shot rolled into a receptacle; faulty ones zig-zagged off and were remelted. Visitor center, programs; hiking trails, picnicking. (Memorial Day-Labor Day, daily) Standard fees. Phone 699-6778 (New River Trail State Park). Park **Free.** Tower ¢

2. **Big Walker Lookout.** 12 mi N on US 52; on Big Walker Mountain Scenic Byway. A 120-foot observation tower at 3,405-foot elevation; swinging bridge. Gift shop; snack bar. (Apr-Oct, daily) Phone 228-4401. ¢¢

3. **Wytheville State Fish Hatchery.** 12 mi SE on US 52 to VA 629. Approx 150,000 lbs of rainbow trout produced annually. Five-tank aquarium; displays. Self-guided tours. (Daily) Phone 637-3212. **Free.**

(For further information contact the Wytheville-Wythe-Bland Chamber of Commerce, 150 Monroe St, PO Box 563; 228-3211.)

Annual Event

Chautauqua Festival. Held over a 9-day period. Includes parade, educational events, performing arts, art shows, children's activities, music, food, entertainment. 3rd wk June.

(See Marion)

Motels

★ ★ **BEST WESTERN WYTHEVILLE INN.** *355 Nye Rd, I-77N exit 41. 703/228-7300; FAX 703/228-4223.* 99 rms, 2 story. Apr-Oct: S $42-$60; D $48-$66; each addl $6; whirlpool units $85-$105; under 17 free; higher rates special events; lower rates rest of yr. Crib free. TV. Pool. Restaurant 6-11 am, 5-8:30 pm. Rm serv. Ck-out noon.

Meeting rms. Valet serv. Sundries. Gift shop. Some in-rm whirlpools. Cr cds: A, C, D, DS, MC, V.

⊭ ⊠ ⊠ ⊠ SC

★ ★ **COMFORT INN.** *PO Box 567, Holston Rd, I-81 exit 70. 703/228-4488; FAX 703/228-4092.* 80 rms, 2 story. S, D $38-$65; each addl $5; under 18 free. Crib free. TV; cable. Pool. Complimentary continental bkfst, coffee. Restaurant nearby. Ck-out 11 am. Cr cds: A, C, D, DS, ER, JCB, MC, V.

⊡ ⊠ ⊠ ⊠ SC

★ ★ **DAYS INN.** *150 Malin Dr. 703/228-5500; FAX 703/228-6301.* 118 rms, 2 story. Apr-Oct: S $36-$45; D $40-$49; each addl $5; under 12 free; higher rates hols, Bristol auto races; lower rates rest of yr. Crib avail. TV; cable. Complimentary continental bkfst. Restaurant adj 6 am-midnight. Ck-out noon. Game rm. View of mountains. Cr cds: A, C, D, DS, MC, V.

⊡ ⊠ ⊠ SC

★ **ECONO LODGE.** *Box 530, 1190 E Main St. 703/228-5517.* 72 rms, 2 story. S $30; D $35-$44; each addl $5; under 18 free. Crib free. TV; cable. Complimentary coffee. Restaurant adj 6 am-9:30 pm. Ck-out 11 am. Cr cds: A, C, D, DS, MC, V.

⊡ ⊭ ⊠ ⊠ SC

★ ★ **RAMADA INN.** *955 Pepper's Ferry Rd. 703/228-6000; FAX 703/228-6000, ext. 151.* 154 rms, 2 story. S $44-$52; D $52-$57; each addl $5; under 18 free; wkly rates. Crib free. Pet accepted. TV; cable, in-rm movies. Pool. Restaurant 6 am-10 pm. Rm serv. Bar 5 pm-midnight. Ck-out noon. Coin lndry. Meeting rms. Cr cds: A, C, D, DS, ER, JCB, MC, V.

⊡ ⊭ ⊠ ⊀ ⊠ ⊠ SC

Restaurant

★ **LOG HOUSE.** *520 E Main St. 703/228-4139.* Hrs: 11 am-10 pm. Closed Sun; Dec 25. Res accepted. Wine, beer. Semi-a la carte: lunch $2.99-$7.95, dinner $5.95-$14.95. Child's meals. Specialties: beef stew, stuffed chicken breast, tenderloin steak. Parking. Outdoor dining. Colonial motif; structure built 1776. Cr cds: MC, V.

Yorktown (E-9)

Founded: 1691 **Pop:** 390 (est) **Elev:** 54 ft **Area code:** 804

Free land offered in 1630 to those adventurous enough "to seate and inhabit" the 50-foot bluffs on the south side of the York River "formerly known by ye Indyan name of Chiskiacke," brought about the beginning of settlement. When the Assembly authorized a port, built there in 1691, the town quickly expanded and in the following years became a busy shipping center, with prosperity reaching a peak about 1750. From then on, the port declined along with the Tidewater Virginia tobacco trade.

Yorktown's moment in history came in 1781. British commander Cornwallis, after raiding up and down Virginia almost without resistance (and almost without effect), was sent here to establish a port in which British ships-of-the-line could winter. The Comte de Grasse's French fleet effectively blockaded the British, however, by controlling the mouth of the Chesapeake Bay. At the Battle of the Capes on September 5, 1781, a British fleet sent to relieve Cornwallis was defeated by the French. Cornwallis found himself bottled up in Yorktown by combined American and French forces under Washington, which arrived on September 28.

Shelling began Oct 9. The siege of Yorktown ended on Oct 17 with Cornwallis requesting terms of capitulation. On Oct 19, Cornwallis' troops marched out with flags and arms cased, their band playing.

Then they laid down their arms, bringing the American Revolution to a close.

Yorktown Battlefield, part of Colonial National Historical Park, surrounds the village. Though Yorktown itself is still an active community, many surviving and reconstructed colonial structures supply an 18th-century atmosphere.

What to See and Do

1. **Yorktown Battlefield.** Surrounds and includes part of town. Remains of 1781 British fortifications, modified and strengthened by Confederate forces in Civil War. Reconstructed American and French lines lie beyond. Roads lead to headquarters, encampment areas of Americans, French. Stop first at

   Visitor Center. E side of town, at end of Colonial Pkwy. Information; special exhibits, General Washington's field tents. (Daily; closed Dec 25) Phone 898-3400. **Free.**

   Self-guided battlefield tour. Markers, displays aid in visualizing siege. Highlights include headquarters sites of Lafayette, von Steuben, Rochambeau, Washington; American Battery #2; Grand French Battery; a key point is

   Moore House. 1 mi E on Old VA 238 at edge of battlefield. In this 18th-century house the "Articles of Capitulation" were drafted. These were signed by the Americans and French in the captured British Redoubt #10 on Oct 19. (Mid-June-mid-Aug, daily; spring & fall, wkends) Phone 898-3400. **Free.** West of here on VA 704 is

   Yorktown National Civil War Cemetery. 2,183 interments (1,436 unknown).

   Yorktown Victory Monument. E end of Main St. Elaborately ornamented 95-foot granite column memorializes American-French alliance in Revolution. Then proceed to

   Nelson House. Nelson & Main Sts. Original restored mansion built by "Scotch Tom" Nelson in the early 1700s. Home of his grandson, Thomas Nelson, Jr, a signer of the Declaration of Independence. Impressive example of Georgian architecture. (Mid-June-mid-Aug, daily) **Free.**

2. **York County Courthouse.** Main St. Reconstructed in 1955 to resemble 1733 courthouse. Clerk's office has records dating from 1633. (Mon-Fri; closed hols) **Free.**

3. **Grace Episcopal Church** (1697). Church St. Walls of local marl (a mixture of clay, sand and limestone); damaged in 1781, gutted by fire in 1814. A 1649 communion service is still in use. (Daily) Phone 898-3261.

4. **Yorktown Victory Center.** 1/2 mi W on VA 238. Chronicles the American Revolution through a combination of time line, exhibits, living history military camp and colonial farm site; docudrama on final days of the Revolution. (Daily; closed Jan 1, Dec 25) Combination ticket with Jamestown Settlement (see JAMESTOWN COLONIAL NATIONAL HISTORICAL PARK) avail. Phone 887-1776. Museum ¢¢ Combination ticket ¢¢¢¢

(For further information contact Colonial National Historical Park, PO Box 210, 23690; 898-3400.)

Annual Event

Yorktown Day. Commemorates surrender of General Cornwallis in 1781. Wreath-laying ceremony, military parade and patriotic exercises. Oct 19.

(See Colonial Parkway, Gloucester, Jamestown, Newport News, Williamsburg)

Motel

★ ★ **DUKE OF YORK.** *PO Box E (23690), 508 Water St, 1 blk E of bridge.* 804/898-3232. 57 rms, 2-3 story. Memorial Day-Labor Day: S, D $64; each addl $6; lower rates rest of yr. TV. Pool. Restaurant (hrs vary). Ck-out noon. Balconies. Opp beach. Overlooks river; shady lawn. Cr cds: A, C, D, MC, V.

Restaurant

★ ★ **NICK'S SEAFOOD PAVILION.** *On VA 238 (Water St) at S end of bridge.* 804/887-5269. Hrs: 11 am-10 pm. Closed Dec 25. Continental menu. Semi-a la carte: lunch, dinner $7-$30. Child's meals. Specializes in lobster, seafood kebab. Parking. Grecian atmosphere; art collection. Family-owned. Cr cds: A, C, D, MC, V.

West Virginia

Population: 1,793,477

Land area: 24,282 square miles

Elevation: 240-4,863 feet

Highest point: Spruce Knob (Pendleton County)

Entered Union: June 20, 1863 (35th state)

Capital: Charleston

Motto: Mountaineers are always free

Nickname: Mountain State

State flower: Rhododendron

State bird: Cardinal

State tree: Sugar maple

State fair: August 11-19, 1995, in Lewisburg

Time zone: Eastern

The wild, rugged topography that made settlement of this area difficult in the early days has today made West Virginia a paradise for outdoor enthusiasts. The state's ski industry has taken advantage of the highest total altitude of any state east of the Mississippi River by opening several alpine and nordic ski areas. Outfitters offer excellent whitewater rafting on the state's many turbulent rivers. Rock climbing, caving and hiking are popular in the Monongahela National Forest, and West Virginia also boasts an impressive state park system, as well as extensive hunting and fishing areas.

The nickname "mountain state" gives only a hint of West Virginia's scenic beauty, which is unsurpassed in the East. West Virginia is also a land of proud traditions, with many festivals held throughout the year as tributes to the state's rich heritage. These events include celebrations honoring the state's sternwheel riverboat legacy, its spectacular autumn foliage and even its strawberries, apples and black walnuts.

The occupation of West Virginia began with the Mound Builders, a prehistoric Ohio Valley culture that left behind at least 300 conical earth mounds that challenge the imagination. Many have been worn away by erosion, but excavations in some have revealed elaborately adorned human skeletons and artifacts of amazing beauty and utility.

Pioneers who ventured into western Virginia in the 18th century found fine vistas and forests, curative springs and beautiful rivers. George Washington and his family frequented the soothing mineral waters of Berkeley Springs (see); and White Sulphur Springs (see) later became a popular resort among the colonists. But much of this area was still considered "the wild West" in those days, and life here was not easy.

The Commonwealth of Virginia largely ignored its western citizens—only one governor was elected from the western counties before 1860. When the counties formed their own state during the Civil War, it was the result of many years of strained relations with the parent state. The move had been debated during those years, and the war finally provided the opportunity the counties needed to break away from

Virginia. Although many sentiments in the new state remained pro-South, West Virginia's interests were best served by staying with the Union.

The first land battle of the Civil War took place in the western counties (see PHILIPPI) soon after Fort Sumter was fired upon in April, 1861. Through the rest of 1861 and into 1862, Union forces under Generals George McClellan and William S. Rosecrans chased the Confederates back toward rebel Virginia. Succeeding battles were fought farther and farther south until major Confederate resistance became impossible. For the rest of the war, Confederate Army activity in the state was limited to destructive lightning raids designed to wreck railroad lines and damage Union supply sources.

The war left West Virginia a new state, but, like other war-ravaged areas, it had suffered heavy losses of life and property. The recovery took many years, but West Virginians eventually rebuilt their state; new industry was developed, railroads were built, and resources like coal, oil and natural gas brought relative prosperity.

Today, West Virginia still is an important source of bituminous coal and a major producer of building stone, timber, glass and chemicals. The state is also the home of such technological wonders as the National Radio Astronomy Observatory (see MARLINTON), where scientists study the universe via radio telescopes, and the New River Gorge Bridge (see GAULEY BRIDGE), the world's longest steel span bridge.

National Park Service Areas

West Virginia has one of the largest systems of federally protected rivers in the East; included are the New River Gorge National River (see HINTON), the Gauley River National Recreation Area (see SUMMERSVILLE) and the Bluestone National Scenic River. Also here are Harpers Ferry National Historical Park (see HARPERS FERRY), part of Chesapeake and Ohio Canal National Historical Park (see under MARYLAND), and part of the Appalachian National Scenic Trail, a 2,000-mile trail that winds through the Appalachian Mountains from Maine to Georgia.

National Forest

Monongahela National Forest (see ELKINS): Forest Supervisor in Elkins; Ranger offices in Bartow*, Marlinton, Parsons*, Petersburg, Richwood*, White Sulphur Springs.

*Not described in text

State Recreation Areas

The following towns list state recreation areas in their vicinity under What to See and Do; refer to the individual town for directions and park information.

Listed under **Beckley:** see Babcock and Twin Falls Resort state parks.

Listed under **Berkeley Springs:** see Berkeley Springs and Cacapon Resort state parks.

Listed under **Buckhannon:** see Audra State Park.

Listed under **Clarksburg:** see Watters Smith Memorial State Park.

Listed under **Davis:** see Blackwater Falls and Canaan Valley Resort state parks.

Listed under **Fairmont:** see Pricketts Fort State Park.

Listed under **Gauley Bridge:** see Hawks Nest State Park.

Listed under **Grafton:** see Tygart Lake State Park.

Listed under **Hillsboro:** see Watoga State Park.

Listed under **Hinton:** see Bluestone and Pipestem Resort state parks.

Listed under **Huntington:** see Beech Fork State Park.

Listed under **Marlinton:** see Cass Scenic Railroad State Park and Seneca State Forest.

Listed under **Moorefield:** see Lost River State Park.

Listed under **Parkersburg:** see North Bend State Park.

Listed under **Princeton:** see Camp Creek State Park.

Listed under **Webster Springs:** see Holly River State Park and Kumbrabow State Forest.

Listed under **Weirton:** see Tomlinson Run State Park.

Listed under **Weston:** see Cedar Creek and Stonewall Jackson Lake state parks.

Water-related activities, hiking, riding, various other sports, picnicking and visitor centers, as well as camping, are available in many of these areas. There is a small fee for swimming and game court use. Campgrounds with picnic facilities are available in 22 state parks and forests; all have drinking water and sanitary facilities; some have showers, coin laundries, utility hookups; 2-wk limit; $6-$14/night for 6 persons or less, $1 each addl person. Camping season runs from mid-April-October in all parks except Canaan Valley and Pipestem Resorts, which are open year round. Campground reservations may be made at Babcock, Beech Fork, Blackwater Falls, Bluestone, Canaan Valley Resort, Cedar Creek, Chief Logan, Holly River, North Bend, Pipestem Resort, Stonewall Jackson Lake, Tomlinson Run, Twin Falls Resort, Tygart Lake and Watoga state parks and at Greenbrier and Kanawha state forests. There is a $5 handling fee; reservations must be made 7-14 days in advance. Camping at all other state parks is on a first-come, first-served basis. Pets on leash only. Many cabins and lodges are available for seasonal or year-round use; 7-day minimum second Monday in June-Labor Day. Most parks are open daily, 8 am-sunset. For information and reservations contact individual parks or phone 800/225-5982 (exc AK and HI).

Fishing & Hunting

In addition to a million acres of prime federal hunting and fishing land, West Virginia has 45 wildlife management areas. Nonresident state-wide fishing license $25; 3-day license $5. Nonresident (exc KY, OH, PA) hunting, basic license, $70; archery deer, muzzleloader deer and turkey stamps $10; 6-day, small-game license $20. Nonresident migratory waterfowl stamp $5. A conservation stamp is required in addition to all regular hunting and fishing licenses (nonresident $5). For further information contact the Department of Natural Resources, Wildlife Resources Division, State Capitol Complex, Building 3, Charleston 25305; 304/558-2771.

Skiing

The following towns list ski areas in their vicinity under What to See and Do; refer to the individual town for directions and information.

Listed under **Aurora:** see Alpine Lake Ski Resort†.

Listed under **Beckley:** see WinterPlace Ski Resort.

Listed under **Davis:** see Canaan Valley Resort State Park†, Timberline Four Seasons Resort and White Grass Touring Center‡.

Listed under **Marlinton:** see Elk River Touring Center‡ and Snowshoe Mt Resort.

Listed under **Wheeling:** see Oglebay Resort Park.

† Also cross-country trails
‡ Only cross-country trails

Safety Belt Information

Children under 9 years must be in an approved passenger restraint anywhere in vehicle: ages 3-8 may use a regulation safety belt; children under 3 yrs must use an approved safety seat. For further information phone 304/746-2121.

Interstate Highway System

The following alphabetical listing of West Virginia towns in *Mobil Travel Guide* shows that these cities are within 10 miles of the indicated interstate highways. A highway map, however, should be checked for the nearest exit.

INTERSTATE 64: Beckley, Charleston, Huntington, Lewisburg, Nitro, White Sulphur Springs.

INTERSTATE 70: Wheeling.

INTERSTATE 77: Charleston, Parkersburg, Princeton, Ripley; also see WV Tpke.

INTERSTATE 79: Charleston, Clarksburg, Fairmont, Morgantown, Sutton.

INTERSTATE 81: Martinsburg.

Additional Visitor Information

Travel materials, including information on accommodations, skiing, caving, rock climbing, whitewater rafting and other activities, are available from the West Virginia Division of Tourism & Parks, State Capitol Complex, Charleston 25305; 800/225-5982. The Information & Education Section, Department of Natural Resources, State Capitol, Charleston 25305, publishes a monthly magazine, *Wonderful West Virginia*.

Information on hiking along the completed portion of the Allegheny Trail, including a hiking guide (fee), is available from the West Virginia Scenic Trails Association, 633 West Virginia Ave, Morgantown 26505. The trail runs north-south from the Pennsylvania state line near Coopers Rock State Forest to Peters Mountain, southeast of Lindside, at the Virginia state line.

There are several welcome centers in West Virginia; visitors who stop by will find information and brochures most helpful in planning stops at points of interest. Their locations are as follows: on I-64, westbound near White Sulphur Springs and eastbound near Huntington; on I-81, southbound by the West Virginia-Maryland border and northbound near the West Virginia-Virginia border; on I-79, southbound north of Morgantown; on I-77, southbound near Mineral Wells; on I-70, westbound near the West Virginia-Pennsylvania border. The West Virginia Information Center is located at Harpers Ferry. All centers are open (daily, 9 am-5 pm; closed Jan 1, Thanksgiving, Dec 25). Personnel at any of these locations will also assist visitors in making lodging reservations. In addition, information may be obtained at the Capitol Guides Desk in the rotunda of the State Capitol at Charleston (Mon-Fri, 8:30 am-4:30 pm; Sat from 9 am; also Sun, noon-4:30 pm from Memorial Day-Labor Day).

Aurora (C-6)

Settled: 1787 **Pop:** 150 (est) **Elev:** 2,641 ft **Area code:** 304 **Zip:** 26705

Located at the summit of Cheat Mountain, Aurora offers visitors clean air and high altitude.

What to See and Do

1. **Cathedral State Park.** 1 mi E on US 50. Hiking trails through 132 acres of deep, virgin hemlock forest. Cross-country skiing. Picnicking. Standard hrs. Phone 735-3771.

2. **Americana Museum.** 10 mi N, at 401 Aurora Ave in Terra Alta. Exhibits housed in five buildings include old-time doctor's office, country store, blacksmith shop, church, old kitchen, parlor and bedroom furnished with antiques; carriage house with more than 20 horse-drawn vehicles. (Late June-mid-Oct, Sun) Phone 789-2361. ¢

3. **Alpine Lake Ski Resort.** 10 mi N on unnumbered road to Terra Alta, then approx 1 mi E on WV 7, follow signs. 2 Pomalifts, 1 pony lift, T-bar; patrol, rentals; snowmaking; restaurant, bar; lodging. Longest run 2,200 ft; vertical drop 700 ft. (Late Nov-Mar, Thurs-Sun & hols) 18 mi of cross-country trails (late Dec-Mar, daily). Phone 800/752-7179. ¢¢¢¢¢

(For accommodations see Davis, Grafton)

Beckley (E-4)

Founded: 1838 **Pop:** 18,296 **Elev:** 2,416 ft **Area code:** 304 **Zip:** 25801

The "smokeless coal capital of the world" is a center for more than 200 small mining and farming towns. Beckley is situated on a high plateau surrounded by fertile valleys. During the Civil War, the village was held at various times by both armies; Union troops shelled it in 1863. Coal was found here in 1774, but was not mined until 1890. Smokeless coal became the standard bunker fuel during World War I, and the demand continued for years thereafter. Beckley now serves as a commercial, medical and tourist center.

What to See and Do

1. **Youth Museum of Southern West Virginia.** Ewart Ave, in New River Park. Hands-on exhibits, planetarium, log house; John Henry exhibit features more than 100 carved figures depicting railroad work in the 1880s. (May-Labor Day, daily; rest of yr, Tues-Sat) Phone 252-3730. ¢¢

2. **Beckley Exhibition Coal Mine.** In New River Park, 1½ mi SE off I-77 exit 44 on Ewart Ave. Riding tours in coal cars through 1,500 feet of underground passageways, constant 56°F temperature; museum, campground. (Apr-Oct, daily) Phone 256-1747. ¢¢

3. **Lake Stephens.** W of town. A 303-acre lake with swimming; fishing; boating. Trailer camping (hookups). Phone 934-5323.

4. **Plum Orchard Lake Wildlife Management Area.** 11 mi N on I-77 to Pax exit, then E on RR 23. More than 3,200 acres with rabbit, grouse, squirrel hunting. Also 202-acre lake with more than 6 miles of shoreline; boating; fishing for bass, channel catfish, crap-

pie and bluegill. Picnicking, playground, camping. Phone 469-9905.

5. **WinterPlace Ski Resort.** 17 mi S via I-77 exit 28 (Ghent/Flat Top), follow signs. On southern West Virginia's highest peak. 3 triple chairlifts, 1 double chairlift, 2 surface lifts; school, rentals; snowmaking; cafeteria, lounge; restaurants; entertainment; children's program; sporting good shops. Night skiing. 24 runs; longest run 1¼ mi; vertical drop 603 ft. (Thanksgiving-late Mar, daily) Phone 787-3221. ¢¢¢¢¢

6. **Grandview Unit of New River Gorge National River.** 5 mi SE on US 19, then 5 mi NE via Airport, Glen Hedrick and Grandview Rds. Nearly 900 wooded acres at the northern end of the New River Gorge National River area (see HINTON); offers spectacular overlooks of New River Gorge and Horseshoe Bend; rhododendron gardens. Hiking trails, game courts (some fees). Cross-country skiing. Picnicking, playgrounds, concession. Outdoor dramas (June-Labor Day, daily exc Mon). Contact Superintendent, Rte 9, Box 149, Beaver 25813; 763-3145 or 465-0508.

7. **Twin Falls Resort State Park.** 25 mi SW via WV 16 & WV 54, then W on WV 97, near Maben. Approximately 4,000 acres with restored pioneer house and farm. Swimming pool. Hiking trails; 18-hole golf course, clubhouse; tennis, game courts. Picnicking, playground, restaurant, lodge. Camping, 13 cabins (equipment rentals). Recreation center, programs. Standard hrs, fees. Phone 294-4000 or -6000.

8. **Babcock State Park.** 23 mi NE via US 19 to WV 41, near Landisburg. More than 4,100 acres of rugged mountain scenery with trout stream and waterfalls, views of New River Canyon, rhododendrons (May-July); restored operating gristmill. Swimming pool; lake and stream fishing; boating (rowboat, paddleboat rentals). Hiking trails, horseback riding; game courts (equipment rentals). Cross-country skiing. Picnicking, playground, concession; restaurant (seasonal). Camping (electrical hookups), 26 cabins. Nature and recreation programs (summer). Standard hrs, fees. (Mid-Apr-Oct) Phone 438-3004 or -3003.

9. **Whitewater rafting.** Many outfitters offer guided trips on the New and Gauley rivers. For a list of outfitters contact the West Virginia Division of Tourism & Parks, Telemarketing Dept, State Capitol Complex, Bldg 6, Rm 564, 1900 Kanawha Blvd E, Charleston 25305; 800/225-5982.

(For further information contact the Southern West Virginia Convention & Visitors Bureau, PO Box 1799, 25801; 252-2244 or, outside of WV, 800/VISIT-WV.)

Annual Event

Appalachian Arts & Crafts Festival. Raleigh County Civic Center. Exhibitions and demonstrations of native crafts; entertainment; food. Phone 252-7328. Late Aug.

Seasonal Event

Theatre West Virginia. Cliffside Amphitheatre, Grandview Park, W on I-64, follow signs. Outdoor musical dramas. Contact PO Box 1205, 25802; phone 256-6800 or 800/666-9142. Mid-June-late Aug.

(See Gauley Bridge, Hinton)

Motels

★ ★ **BECKLEY HOTEL AND CONFERENCE CENTER.** *1940 Harper Rd (WV 3). 304/252-8661; res: 800/274-6010; FAX 304/253-4496.* 200 rms, 2-4 story. S $65-$80; D $70-$90; each addl $5; under 18 free; suites $100-$200; some wknd rates; higher rates special events. Crib free. Pet accepted, some restrictions. TV; cable. Indoor pool; whirlpool. Restaurant 6:30 am-10 pm. Rm serv 5-10 pm. Bar; closed Sun. Ck-out noon. Coin lndry. Meeting rms. Bellhops. Sundries.

Shopping arcade. Heliport. Some in-rm steam baths. Cr cds: A, C, D, DS, MC, V.

D 🐾 ⛵ 🏊 ⛷ 🔥 SC

✔ ★ **COMFORT INN.** *1909 Harper Rd (WV 3). 304/255-2161; FAX 304/255-2161, ext. 100.* 130 rms, 3 story. S $47-$62; D $52-$67; each addl $5; under 19 free. Crib free. Pet accepted; $10. TV; cable. Complimentary continental bkfst. Restaurant opp. Ck-out noon. Coin lndry. Sundries. Downhill ski 15 mi. Exercise equipt; weights, bicycle. Some refrigerators. Cr cds: A, C, D, DS, ER, JCB, MC, V.

D 🐾 ⛷ 🏃 🏊 ⛷ 🔥 SC

★ ★ **HOLIDAY INN.** *1924 Harper Rd (WV 3). 304/255-1511; FAX 304/255-1511, ext. 476.* 105 rms, 3 story. No elvtr. Apr-Oct: S $71; D $71-$77; each addl $6; under 19 free; lower rates rest of yr. Crib free. TV; cable, in-rm movies. Pool. Restaurant 6 am-2 pm, 5-10 pm. Rm serv. Private club 3 pm-3 am, Sun to 1 am. Ck-out 1 pm. Free lndry. Meeting rms. Downhill ski 15 mi. Some refrigerators. Cr cds: A, C, D, DS, ER, JCB, MC, V.

D ⛷ 🏊 ⛷ 🔥 SC

Berkeley Springs (B-7)

Founded: 1776 **Pop:** 735 (est) **Elev:** 612 ft **Area code:** 304 **Zip:** 25411

Popularized by George Washington, who surveyed the area for Lord Fairfax in 1748, Berkeley Springs is the oldest spa in the nation. Fairfax later granted the land around the springs to Virginia. The town is officially named Bath, for the famous watering place in England, but the post office is Berkeley Springs. The waters, which are piped throughout the town, are fresh and slightly sweet, without the medicinal flavor of most mineral springs. Washington and his family returned again and again. The popularity of the resort reached its peak after the Revolution, becoming something of a summer capital for Washingtonians in the 1830s. But like all resort towns, Berkeley Springs declined as newer, more fashionable spas came into vogue. The Civil War completely destroyed the town's economy. Today, the town is again visited for its healthful waters, and again, it prospers.

What to See and Do

1. **View from Prospect Peak.** On WV 9, near town. Potomac River winds through what the National Geographic Society has called one of the nation's outstanding vistas.

2. **Berkeley Springs State Park.** Center of town. Famous resort with health baths of all types (fees); five warm springs. Main bathhouse (daily; closed Jan 1, Dec 25). Roman bathhouse with second-floor museum (Memorial Day-mid-Oct, daily). Swimming pool (Memorial Day-Labor Day, daily; fee). Phone 258-2711 or -5860. Overlooking park is

   The Castle (1886). English-Norman castle, built by Colonel Samuel Taylor Suit for his fiancee, has the flavor of England's famous Berkeley Castle, where King Edward II was murdered in 1327. The battlement tower walls are indented with the cross of St George. The castle is furnished with 17th- and 18th-century antiques and contains a pine-paneled library, carved staircase, interesting collections. Gift shop. Tours. (Daily) Phone 258-3274. ¢¢¢

3. **Cacapon Resort State Park.** 10 mi S off US 522. More than 6,100 acres with swimming, sand beach; fishing, boating (rowboat and paddleboat rentals). Hiking, bridle trails, horseback riding; 18-hole golf course, tennis, game courts. Cross-country skiing. Picnicking, playground, concession, restaurant, lodge (see RESORTS). No camping; 30 cabins. Nature, recreation programs. Arts & crafts center. Standard hrs, fees. Phone 258-1022.

4. **Sleepy Creek Wildlife Management Area.** 15 mi SE, E of US 522. Approximately 23,000 acres of rugged forest offers wild turkey, deer, grouse and squirrel hunting. Boating, bass fishing on 205-

acre lake. Primitive camping (fee). Also 70 miles of hiking trails crossing 2 mountains, several valleys. Phone 754-3855.

(For further information contact the Berkeley Springs-Morgan County Chamber of Commerce, 304 Fairfax St; 258-3738.)

Annual Event

Apple Butter Festival. Crafts demonstrations, music, contests. Columbus Day wkend.

(See Martinsburg)

Inns

★ ★ ★ **THE COUNTRY INN & RENAISSANCE SPA.** *207 S Washington St. 304/258-2210; res: 800/822-6630; FAX 304/258-3986.* 70 rms, 58 baths, 3 story. S, D $35-$85; each addl $5; suites $80-$145; hol wknds 2-night min; some wkday rates. Crib $5. TV; cable. Dining rm 7 am-2 pm, 5-9 pm; Fri & Sat to 10 pm. Private club 11 am-11 pm; entertainment Fri-Sun. Ck-out noon, ck-in 3 pm. Gift shop. Colonial design. Mineral baths & spa. Cr cds: A, C, D, DS, MC, V.

D ⛷ 🔥 SC

★ ★ **HIGHLAWN.** *304 Market St. 304/258-5700.* 10 rms in 2 bldgs, 2-3 story. No rm phones. S, D $70-$105. Adults only. TV; cable. Complimentary full bkfst, refreshments. Ck-out noon, ck-in 2 pm. Victorian mansion; built 1897. Antiques. Cr cds: MC, V.

D 🔥

Resorts

✔ ★ **CACAPON LODGE.** *Rte 1, Box 304, on US 522, in Cacapon Resort State Park. 304/258-1022; res: 800/225-5982.* 49 rms, 2 story, 30 kit. cabins. Apr-Oct: S $52; D $58; each addl $6; kit. cabins for 1-8, $330-$621/wk; some wkend rates; lower rates rest of yr. Crib free in lodge, $4 in cabins. TV in lodge only. Dining rm 7 am-9 pm; winter to 8 pm. Ck-out noon, ck-in 3 pm. Gift shop. Tennis. 18-hole golf, greens fee $13-$22, putting green, driving range. Rec rm. Lawn games. Picnic tables. Near lake; boat rentals, sandy beach. Hiking trails. Naturalist program (Apr-Oct). State-operated. Cr cds: A, MC, V.

D 🐾 ⛷ 🏃 ⛷ 🏊 🔥 SC

★ ★ **COOLFONT RESORT.** *Rte 1, Box 710, 4 mi W on WV 9, then left on Cold Run Valley Rd. 304/258-4500; res: 800/888-8768 (exc WV); FAX 304/258-5499.* 59 rms in main bldg, 2 story, 34 kit. cottages, 17 A/C. Some rm phones. MAP, Oct: S $105-$145; D $150-$230; each addl $75-$115; kit. cottages $425-$575; family rates; wkend rates; wkends, hols (2-3 night min); lower rates rest of yr. Crib avail. Indoor pool. Playground. Supervised child's activities (wknds). Complimentary coffee in rms. Dining rm 8 am-2 pm, 5:30-8:30 pm; Fri, Sat to 9:30 pm; Sun 8-11:30 am, 12:30-2:30 pm, 5-8 pm. Box lunches. Snacks. Picnics. Bar; entertainment Sat. Ck-out noon, ck-in 4 pm. Gift shop. Coin lndry. Grocery 5 mi. Meeting rms. Bellhops. Tennis. Swimming beach; boats. X-country ski on site. Sleighing. Hiking. Lawn games. Social dir. Game rm. Exercise rm; instructor, weight machine, bicycles, whirlpool, sauna. Masseuse. Refrigerators. Some balconies. Picnic tables. Secluded woodland resort on 1,200 acres. Cr cds: A, C, D, DS, MC, V.

D 🐾 ⛷ 🏃 🏊 🎿 🎣 ⛷ 🔥

Restaurant

✔ ★ **MARIA'S GARDEN.** *201 Independence St. 304/258-2021.* Hrs: 9 am-9 pm; Sun 8 am-7 pm. Closed Wed. Res accepted. Italian, Amer menu. Wine, beer. Semi-a la carte: bkfst $1.99-$3.95, lunch $3-$5, dinner $5.45-$13.95. Complete meals: bkfst $1.99-$5.75, lunch $3.50-$5, dinner $5.95-$13.95. Child's meals. Specializes in pasta, lasagne. Parking. Informal, garden atmosphere; overlooks grotto. Rms avail. Cr cds: D, DS, MC, V.

Bethany (A-5)

Pop: 1,139 **Elev:** 932 ft **Area code:** 304 **Zip:** 26032

What to See and Do

Bethany College (1840). (850 students) Founded by Alexander Campbell, the leading influence in the 19th-century religious movement that gave rise to the Disciples of Christ, Churches of Christ and Christian Churches. Historic buildings on 300-acre campus include Old Main, styled after the University of Glasgow in Scotland; Pendleton Heights, a 19th-century house used as the college president's residence; Old Bethany Meeting House (1852), Delta Tau Delta Founder's House (1858) and the

Campbell Mansion, a 24-room house where Campbell lived; antique furnishings. On property is is hexagonal brick study, one-room schoolhouse and smokehouse. The Campbell family cemetery, "God's Acre," is across from the mansion. (Apr-Oct, daily exc Mon; rest of yr, by appt) For tour of all buildings, phone 829-7285 or -7000. Full tour ¢¢¢; Campbell Mansion only ¢¢

(For accommodations see Wheeling, also see Weirton)

Bluefield (E-4)

Founded: 1889 **Pop:** 12,756 **Elev:** 2,611 ft **Area code:** 304 **Zip:** 24701

Named for the bluish chicory covering the nearby hills, Bluefield owes its existence to the Pocahontas Coal Field. The town came to life in the 1880s, when the railroad came through to transport the coal. This commercial and industrial center of southern West Virginia is known as nature's "air-conditioned city" because of its altitude—one-half mile above sea level. Bluefield has a sister city by the same name in Virginia, directly across the state line.

What to See and Do

1. **Eastern Regional Coal Archives.** In Craft Memorial Library, 600 Commerce St. Center highlights the history of West Virginia coal fields; exhibits, photographs, mining implements; films, research material. (Mon-Fri afternoons; closed most hols) Phone 325-3943. **Free.**

2. **Pinnacle Rock State Park.** 7 mi NW on US 52. The approximately 250-acre park contains a 15-acre lake and interesting sandstone formations, which resemble a giant cockscomb. Hiking. Picnicking. Standard hrs, fees. Phone 589-5307.

3. **Panther State Forest.** 50 mi NW off US 52 near Panther. More than 7,800 acres of rugged hills. Swimming pool (Memorial Day-Labor Day); fishing, hunting. Hiking trails. Picnicking, playground, concession. Camping. Standard hrs, fees. Phone 938-2252.

(For further information contact the Convention & Visitors Bureau, 500 Bland St, PO Box 4099; 325-8438.)

(See Princeton)

Motels

✔ ★ **ECONO LODGE.** *3400 Cumberland Rd. 304/327-8171.* 48 rms, 2 story. S $36.99; D $42.99; each addl $5; under 18 free. Crib free. Pet accepted. TV; cable. Coffee in lobby. Restaurant nearby. Ck-out 11 am. Cr cds: A, C, D, DS, MC, V.

★ ★ **HOLIDAY INN.** *US 460/52 Bypass, 3 mi W of I-77, Bluefield exit 1, via US 460/52. 304/325-6170; FAX 304/325-6170, ext. 324.* 118 rms, 2 story. S $53-$57; D $59-$70; each addl $6; suites $120; under 19 free. Crib free. Pet accepted. TV; cable. Heated pool; saunas, poolside serv. Restaurant 6 am-10 pm. Ck-out noon. Meeting rms. Gift shop. Golf privileges. Cr cds: A, C, D, DS, JCB, MC, V.

Buckhannon (C-5)

Settled: 1770 **Pop:** 5,909 **Elev:** 1,433 ft **Area code:** 304 **Zip:** 26201

What to See and Do

1. **West Virginia Wesleyan College** (1890). (1,600 students) College Ave & Meade St. An 80-acre campus featuring Georgian architecture. Wesley Chapel, the largest place of worship in the state, contains a Casavant organ with 1,474 pipes. Phone 473-8000.

2. **Audra State Park.** 8 mi N on US 119, then 6 mi E on WV 11. Approximately 360 acres offer swimming in a natural mountain stream surrounded by tall timber; bathhouse. Hiking trails. Picnicking, playground, concession. Tent and trailer camping. Standard hrs, fees. Phone 457-1162.

3. **West Virginia State Wildlife Center.** 12 mi S on WV 4, 20. Fenced-in habitats of approximately 50 species of birds and animals native to West Virginia, including deer, elk, buffalo, timber wolf, mountain lion and black bear. Loop walkway (1¼ mi). Trout pond. Picnicking, concession. (May-Oct, daily; Apr & Nov, wkends & hols only; Dec-Mar, days vary) Phone 924-6211 or 800/225-5982. Apr-Nov ¢

(For further information contact the Buckhannon-Upshur Chamber of Commerce, 16 S Kanawha St, PO Box 442; 472-1722.)

Annual Event

West Virginia Strawberry Festival. Parades, dances, exhibits, air show, arts & crafts, other activities. Phone 472-9036. Usually wk before Memorial Day.

(See Elkins, Philippi, Weston)

Motels

★ ★ **BICENTENNIAL.** *PO Box H, 90 E Main St. 304/472-5000; res: 800/762-5137.* 55 rms, 2 story. S $39.95; D $45.95; each addl $6; under 12 free. Crib free. TV; cable. Pool; wading pool, lifeguard. Playground. Restaurant 6 am-9 pm. Rm serv. Private club 4 pm-1 am; entertainment Fri, Sat. Ck-out noon. Meeting rms. Sundries. Gift shop. Some refrigerators. Picnic tables, grills. Cr cds: A, C, D, DS, MC, V.

✔ ★ **CENTENNIAL.** *Box 507, 22 N Locust St. 304/472-4100.* 24 rms. S $27.95-$39.95, D $39.95; each addl $6; apt. $175/wk; under 12 free. Crib free. TV; cable. Complimentary coffee. Restaurant nearby. Ck-out noon. Cr cds: A, C, D, DS, MC, V.

SC

Charleston (D-3)

Settled: 1794 **Pop:** 57,287 **Elev:** 601 ft **Area code:** 304

Charleston, capital of the state, is the trading hub for the Great Kanawha Valley, where deposits of coal, oil, natural gas and brine have greatly contributed to this region's national importance as a production center for chemicals and glass. Two institutions of higher learning, West Virginia State College and the University of Charleston, are located in the metropolitan area. Charleston is also the northern terminus of the spectacular West Virginia Turnpike.

Daniel Boone lived around Charleston until 1795. During his residence he was appointed a lieutenant colonel in the county militia in 1789 and was elected to the Virginia assembly the same year. The area became important as a center of salt production in 1824, when steam engines were used to operate brine pumps. After Charleston became the capital of West Virginia in 1885, following a dispute with Wheeling, the town came into its own. During World War I, an increased demand for plate and bottle glass, as well as for high explosives, made Charleston and the nearby town of Nitro (see) boom.

What to See and Do

1. **State Capitol** (1932). On river at E Kanawha Blvd between Greenbrier St & California Ave. One of America's most beautiful state capitols, the building was designed by Cass Gilbert in Italian-Renaissance style. Within the gold leaf dome, which rises 300 feet above the street, hangs a 10,080-piece, hand-cut imported chandelier weighing more than 2 tons. Guided tours avail. (Memorial Day-Labor Day, daily; rest of yr, daily exc Sun) Phone 558-3809 or 800/225-5982. **Free.** Across the grounds is the

   Governor's Mansion (1925). 1716 Kanawha Blvd E. Beautiful Georgian structure of red Harvard brick with white Corinthian columns. Tours (Thurs & Fri; also by appt). Phone 348-3588. **Free.**

2. **The Cultural Center.** Next to State Capitol, on Greenbrier St. The Center houses the Division of Culture and History and Library Commission; West Virginia crafts shop (daily); archives library (daily exc Sun); state museum; special events, changing exhibits. (Daily; closed hols) Phone 558-0220. **Free.** Also here is

   Mountain Stage. Live public radio show heard on more than 115 stations nationwide; features jazz, folk, blues and rock. Visitors may watch show; afternoon performances (Sun). Phone Ticketmaster at 342-5757. **¢¢¢**

3. **Sunrise Museum.** 746 Myrtle Rd, across South Side Bridge. On 16 acres of wooded grounds with gardens and trails, the museum is housed in two historic mansions built by William MacCorkle, ninth governor of West Virginia. (Daily exc Mon; closed major hols). Guided tours by appt. Phone 344-8035. **¢¢**

   Art Museum. American paintings, graphics and sculpture from 19th through 20th centuries; films and lectures. Sr citizen rate. **¢**

   Science Museum. Exhibits in natural sciences and technology; nature center with animals; planetarium, programs lectures. Nature walks; the Garden Trail of the Five Senses. Sr citizen rate. **¢**

4. **West Virginia State College** (1891). (4,635 students) 8 mi W via I-64 exit 50, in Institute. On campus are Davis Fine Arts Bldg with periodic exhibits (daily exc Sun; closed hols); Asian art collection in library (daily; closed hols); and East Hall (1895), formerly president's residence. Tours. Phone 766-3000.

5. **Elk River Scenic Drive.** Beautiful drive along the Elk River from Charleston northeast to Sutton (approx 60 mi). Begins just north of town; take US 119 northeast to Clendenin, then WV 4 northeast to Sutton.

6. **Coonskin Park.** 3/4 mi N off WV 114. Recreation area includes swimming; fishing for bass and catfish; pedal boating. Hiking trails; 18-hole golf, miniature golf; tennis. Picnicking, play-ground, concession. (Daily; closed Dec 25; some activities seasonal) Fees. Phone 341-8000.

7. **Kanawha State Forest.** 7 mi S off US 119. Approximately 9,300 acres with swimming pool, bathhouse (Memorial Day-Labor Day); hunting. Hiking, interpretive trail for the disabled. Horseback riding. Cross-country skiing. Picnicking, playground, concession. Camping. Standard hrs, fees. Phone 346-5654.

8. **Whitewater rafting.** Many outfitters offer guided rafting, canoeing and fishing trips on the New and Gauley rivers. For a list of outfitters contact the West Virginia Division of Tourism and Parks, Telemarketing Dept, State Capitol Complex, Bldg 6, Rm 564, 1900 Kanawha Blvd E, 25305; 800/225-5982.

(For further information contact the Convention & Visitors Bureau, Charleston Civic Center, 200 Civic Center Dr, 25301; 344-5075 or 800/733-5469.)

Annual Events

Vandalia Gathering. A festival of traditional arts; craft demonstrations, clogging, gospel music, fiddling, banjo picking, special exhibits. Phone 558-0220. Memorial Day wkend.

Sternwheel Regatta Festival. Stern-wheeler and towboat races, parades, contests, hot-air balloon race, fireworks; nationally known entertainers nightly; arts & crafts. Phone 348-6419. Late Aug-early Sept.

(See Nitro)

Motels

★ **KANAWHA CITY MOTOR LODGE.** *3103 MacCorkle Ave SE (25304).* 304/344-2461. 50 rms, 2 story. S $38.99; D $43.99; each addl $5; kit. units $44.95-$58.95; under 13 free. Crib free. TV; cable. Restaurant nearby. Ck-out noon. Charleston Memorial Hospital opp. Cr cds: A, C, D, DS, MC, V.

D ⊗ 🖐 🔥 SC

✔ ★ **RED ROOF INN.** *6305 MacCorkle Ave SE (25304).* 304/925-6953; FAX 304/925-8111. 109 rms, 2 story. Apr-Oct: S $37.99-$43.99; D $47.99-$50.99; each addl $7; under 18 free; higher rates special events; lower rates rest of yr. Crib free. Pet accepted, some restrictions. TV; cable. Complimentary coffee in lobby. Restaurant adj 6 am-10:30 pm. Ck-out noon. Cr cds: A, C, D, DS, MC, V.

D 🖐 🔥 ⊗ 🖐

Motor Hotel

★ ★ **HOLIDAY INN-CIVIC CENTER.** *100 Civic Center Dr (25301).* 304/345-0600; FAX 304/343-1322. 200 rms, 6 story. S $66-$70; D $72-$76; each addl $6; under 18 free; wkend rates; package plans. Crib free. TV; cable, in-rm movies. Heated pool. Restaurant 7 am-2 pm, 5-10 pm. Rm serv. Bar. Ck-out noon. Coin lndry. Meeting rms. Bellhops. Valet serv. Some refrigerators. Cr cds: A, C, D, DS, JCB, MC, V.

D ≈ 🖐 🔥 SC

Hotels

★ ★ **HOLIDAY INN-CHARLESTON HOUSE.** *600 Kanawha Blvd E (25301).* 304/344-4092; FAX 304/345-4847. 256 rms, 12 story. S $78-$81; D $80-$83; each addl $6; under 18 free; suites $150-$305; 4-day min Labor Day wkend; wkend rates; package plans. Crib free. Pet accepted. TV; cable. Heated pool. Restaurant 6:30 am-2 pm; dining rm 5-10 pm. Bar 4 pm-2 am, closed Sun; pianist. Ck-out noon. Convention facilities. Barber, beauty shop. Garage. Airport transportation. Exercise equipt; weights, bicycles. Some wet bars. Some rms with river view. Cr cds: A, C, D, DS, JCB, MC, V.

★ ★ ★ **MARRIOTT TOWN CENTER.** *200 Lee St E (25301). 304/345-6500; FAX 304/353-3722.* 352 rms, 16 story. S, D $95-$140; suites from $250; under 18 free; wkend rates. Crib free. TV; cable. Indoor pool; poolside serv. Restaurant 6:30 am-11 pm; Sun 7 am-10 pm; dining rm 5:30-11 pm. Bar 11-1 am. Ck-out noon. Coin lndry. Tennis. Exercise equipt; weights, bicycles, whirlpool, sauna. Game rm. Rec rm. Some refrigerators. *LUXURY LEVEL : CONCIERGE LEVEL.* 27 rms. S, D $134. Concierge. Private lounge, honor bar. Bathrm phones. Complimentary continental bkfst, refreshments. Cr cds: A, C, D, DS, ER, JCB, MC, V.

Restaurants

★ ★ **ESQUIRE.** *16 Capitol St. 304/345-1414.* Hrs: 11 am-11 pm. Closed Sun; major hols. Res accepted. Private club. Semi-a la carte: lunch $5-$10, dinner $9.95-$22.50. Child's meals. Specializes in veal, steak, seafood. Parking (dinner only). Tableside cooking. Cr cds: A, C, D, MC, V.

★ **FIFTH QUARTER.** *201 Clendenin St. 304/345-2726.* Hrs: 11 am-4 pm, 5-10 pm; Fri & Sat to 11 pm; Sun 4-9 pm. Closed Dec 25. Bar. Semi-a la carte: lunch $5.49-$11.99, dinner $8.69-$19.99. Child's meals. Specializes in prime rib. Salad bar. Entertainment Tues-Sat. Parking. Rustic decor. Cr cds: A, DS, MC, V.

★ ★ **JOE FAZIO'S.** *1008 Bullitt St. 304/344-3071.* Hrs: 5-10:30 pm. Closed Mon; Jan 1, Easter, Dec 24. Res accepted. Italian, Amer menu. Serv bar. Semi-a la carte: dinner $4.50-$18.50. Child's meals. Specializes in veal, chicken, steak. Parking. Family-owned. Cr cds: A, D, MC, V.

★ ★ **LAURY'S.** *14¹/₂ Capitol St. 304/343-0055.* Hrs: 11 am-2 pm, 5-11 pm. Closed Sun; major hols. Res accepted. French, continental menu. Bar 11 am-11 pm. Semi-a la carte: lunch $4.50-$11.50, dinner $12.50-$29.95. Child's meals. Specialties: châteaubriand, veal. Pianist exc Sun. Near Kanawha River. Cr cds: A, C, D, DS, MC, V.

Charles Town (C-8)

Founded: 1786 **Pop:** 3,122 **Elev:** 530 ft **Area code:** 304 **Zip:** 25414

Charles Town is serene, aristocratic and full of tradition, with orderly, tree-shaded streets and 18th-century houses. It was named for George Washington's youngest brother, Charles, who laid out the town and named most of the streets after members of his family. The Charles Washingtons lived here for many years. Charles Town is also famed as the place where John Brown was jailed, tried and hanged in 1859 after his raid on Harpers Ferry.

What to See and Do

1. **Jefferson County Courthouse** (1836). Corner of N George & E Washington Sts. This red-brick, Georgian-colonial structure was the scene of John Brown's trial, one of three treason trials held in the US before World War II. The courthouse was shelled during the Civil War but was later rebuilt; the original courtroom survived both the shelling and fires and is open to the public. In 1922, leaders of the miners' armed march on Logan City were tried here;

one, Walter Allen, was convicted and sentenced to 10 years. (Mon-Fri; closed hols) Phone 725-9761. **Free.**

2. **Jefferson County Museum.** N Samuel & E Washington Sts. Houses John Brown memorabilia, old guns, Civil War artifacts. (Apr-Nov, daily exc Sun) Donation. Phone 725-8628.

3. **Site of the John Brown Gallows.** S Samuel & Hunter Sts. Marked by pyramid of three stones supposedly taken from Brown's cell in Charles Town jail. At execution, 1,500 troops were massed around the scaffold. Some were commanded by Major Thomas (later "Stonewall") Jackson; among them was John Wilkes Booth, Virginia militiaman.

4. **Zion Episcopal Church** (1852). E Congress between S Mildred & S Church Sts. Buried in cemetery around church are about 75 members of Washington family, as well as many Revolutionary and Confederate soldiers. (Interior by appt only) Phone 725-5312.

5. **Horse racing. Charles Town Races.** 1 mi E on US 340. Thoroughbred racing; clubhouse, dining rm. (Mon, Wed & Fri-Sun; closed major hols) Phone 725-7001 or 800/795-7001. ¢-¢¢

(For further information contact the Jefferson County Chamber of Commerce, 200 E Washington, PO Box 426; 725-2055.)

Annual Event

Jefferson County Fair. Livestock show, entertainment, amusement rides, exhibits. Late Aug.

(See Harpers Ferry, Martinsburg, Shepherdstown; also see Winchester, VA)

Motels

✔ ★ **TOWNE HOUSE.** *549 E Washington St. 304/725-8441; res: 800/227-2339; FAX 304/725-5484.* 112 rms, 2-3 story. Apr-Dec: S $28-$42; D $35-$42; each addl $4; suites $90; lower rates rest of yr. Crib $4. TV; cable. Pool. Restaurant adj 7 am-8 pm; Fri, Sat to 9 pm. Ck-out 11 am. Refrigerators. Cr cds: A, C, D, MC, V.

★ **TURF.** *608 E Washington St, 1 mi E on US 340. 304/725-2081; res: 800/422-8873; FAX 304/728-7605.* 46 rms, 2 story, 6 kits. June-Labor Day: S $32-$56; D $46-$56; each addl $2-$5; suites $75-$150; kit. units $55-$75; lower rates rest of yr. Crib $3. Pet accepted. TV; cable. Pool. Restaurant 6:30 am-9 pm; Fri, Sat to 10 pm. Rm serv. Bar 10-2 am. Ck-out noon. Free RR station, racetrack transportation. Cr cds: A, C, D, DS, MC, V.

Inn

★ ★ **HILLBROOK.** *Rte 2, Box 152, 5 mi SW on WV 13 (Summit Point Rd). 304/725-4223; FAX 304/725-4455.* 6 rms, 2 story. No rm phones. MAP: S $250-$300; D $330-$380; wkend rates. Dining rm (public by res) dinner (1 sitting) 8 pm. Ck-out noon, ck-in 3 pm. Lawn games. Some balconies, fireplaces. Large, half-timbered manor house surrounded by romantic English garden. Interior furnished in English country manor-style with eclectic collection of antiques, Oriental rugs, original art. Unique, individually decorated guest rms. Cr cds: DS, MC, V.

Chesapeake And Ohio Canal National Historical Park (B-7 - C-8)

(see Maryland)

Clarksburg (C-5)

Settled: 1773 **Pop:** 18,059 **Elev:** 1,007 ft **Area code:** 304 **Zip:** 26301

Clarksburg, in the heart of the West Virginia hills, is the trading center for an area of grading lands, coal mines and oil and gas fields. During the Civil War it was an important supply base for Union troops. The famous Civil War general "Stonewall" Jackson was born in Clarksburg in 1824. His statue stands before the courthouse.

What to See and Do

1. **Watters Smith Memorial State Park.** 8 mi S on US 19, then SE on unnumbered road. More than 500 acres on Duck Creek with visitor center/museum and 19th-century pioneer homestead. Swimming pool (seasonal). Hiking, game courts. Picnicking, playground, concession. Recreation building. Standard hrs, fees. Phone 745-3081.

2. **Stealey-Goff-Vance House** (1807). 123 W Main St. House restored by Harrison County Historical Society as museum with period rooms, antique furniture, tools, Native American artifacts. (May-Sept, Fri, limited hrs) Phone 842-3073. ¢

3. **Salem-Teikyo University** (1888). (750 students) 12 mi W in Salem. On campus is the Jennings Randolph Center (fee), which houses papers and memorabilia of the former senator. Phone 782-5011 or -5378. Also here is

   Fort New Salem. Collection of 20 log houses from throughout the state were relocated to campus; pioneer history is re-created through crafts and folklore. Special events throughout the year (fee); summer concerts (mid-June-July, Sat evenings). (Memorial Day wkend-Oct, Wed-Sun) Phone 782-5245. ¢¢

(For further information contact the Harrison County Chamber of Commerce, 348 W Main St; 624-6331.)

Annual Event

West Virginia Italian Heritage Festival. Italian arts, music, contests, entertainment. Phone 622-7314. Labor Day wkend.

(See Fairmont, Grafton, Weston)

Motels

★ **COMFORT INN.** *250 Emily Dr. 304/623-2600; FAX 304/622-5240.* 112 rms, 2 story. S, D $47.95; each addl $5; kit. units $51.95; under 18 free. Crib free. TV. Complimentary continental bkfst 6-10 am. Restaurant adj 6 am-11 pm. Ck-out noon. Meeting rm. Gift shop. Cr cds: A, D, DS, MC, V.

D 🏊 🐾 SC

✔ ★ ★ **DAYS INN.** *(112 Tolley Dr, Bridgeport 26330)* 1 mi E of I-79 exit 119. *304/842-7371; FAX 304/842-3904.* 62 rms, 2 story. S $43-$68; D $48-$68; each addl $8; family rates; higher rates: Buckhannon Festival, graduation, Italian Festival, football games. Crib free. TV; cable. Indoor pool; whirlpool. Complimentary full bkfst. Restaurant

6:30-10:30 am. Bar 5 pm-midnight; entertainment, dancing Fri, Sat. Ck-out 11 am. Meeting rms. Cr cds: A, D, DS, MC, V.

D 🏊 🐾 🔥

★ ★ ★ **HOLIDAY INN.** *(100 Lodgeville Rd, Bridgeport 26330)* 2¹/₂ mi E on US 50E, just E of I-79 exit 119. *304/842-5411; FAX 304/842-7258.* 160 rms, 2 story. S, D $60-$70; suites $80; under 19 free; wkend rates. Crib free. TV; cable. Pool; wading pool. Restaurant 6 am-2 pm, 5-10 pm; Sun 6:30 am-10 pm. Rm serv. Private club 2 pm-midnight, Sun 4-11 pm. Ck-out noon. Meeting rms. Valet serv. Sundries. Cr cds: A, C, D, DS, JCB, MC, V.

D 🏊 🐾 🔥 SC

Restaurant

★ ★ ★ **JIM REID'S.** *(1422 Buckhannon Pike, Nutter Fort)* US 50 W to Joyce St exit, then ¹/₂ mi S on WV 20. *304/623-4909.* Hrs: 11 am-2 pm, 5-11 pm; Tues & Sat from 5 pm; Sun noon-8 pm. Closed Mon; Jan 1, Dec 24-26. Res accepted. Bar. Wine list. Complete meals: lunch $4.25-$6.50, dinner $8.95-$16.95. Child's meals. Specializes in fresh seafood, prime rib, steak. Parking. Family-owned. Cr cds: MC, V.

Davis (C-6)

Founded: 1883 **Pop:** 799 **Elev:** 3,099 ft **Area code:** 304 **Zip:** 26260

Davis, the highest town in the state, was founded by Henry Gassaway Davis, US senator between 1871 and 1883. Senator Davis established the first night train in America (1848). He and his son-in-law, Senator Stephen B. Elkins, became wealthy from coal, lumber and railroading.

What to See and Do

1. **Blackwater Falls State Park.** 2 mi W off WV 32. This 1,688-acre park includes deep river gorge with 66-foot falls of dark, amber-colored water. Swimming in lake (fee), bath houses (Memorial Day-Labor Day); fishing; boating (rowboat and paddleboat rentals). Nature trails, horseback riding. Cross-country ski trails, center (rentals, school); sledding. Picnicking, playground, concession, lodge, cabins (see RESORTS). Tent and trailer campground. Nature, recreation programs. Paved falls viewing area for the disabled. Standard hrs, fees. Phone 259-5216.

2. **Canaan Valley Resort State Park.** 9 mi S on WV 32. Approximately 6,000 acres includes valley 3,200 feet above sea level, which is surrounded by spectacular mountain peaks. Swimming pool, bathhouse; fishing; boating. Hiking trails; 18-hole golf course, tennis courts. Skiing (see #3), ice rink. Playground, lodge, cabins (see RESORTS). Camping (dump station). Nature, recreation programs. Standard hrs, fees. Phone 866-4121.

3. **Skiing.**

   Canaan Valley Resort State Park (see #2). 1 quad, 2 triple chairlifts, 1 Pomalift; patrol, school, rentals; snowmaking; restaurant, cafeteria; lodging, nursery; night skiing. 21 trails; vertical drop 850 ft. (Dec-Mar, daily) 18 mi of cross-country trails. Chairlift rides (Early May-end of foliage season, daily exc Mon) Special programs for the disabled. Phone 866-4121. ¢¢¢¢¢

   Timberline Four Seasons Resort. 8 mi S off WV 32. Triple, 2 double chairlifts; patrol, school, rentals; snowmaking; restaurant, bar; nursery; lodging. 24 trails; longest run 2¹/₄ mi; vertical drop 1,000 ft. (Thanksgiving-mid-Apr, daily) Cross-country skiing. Chairlift rides (Memorial Day-Oct, Sat & Sun) Phone 866-4801 or -4828 (snow conditions). ¢¢¢¢¢

   White Grass Touring Center. 9 mi S on WV 32 to Freeland Rd; ¹/₂ mi N of Canaan Valley Resort State Park. 36 mi of cross-country trails, some machine-groomed; patrol, school, rentals; snowmaking; restaurant, beer; night skiing; telemark slopes, guided tours. (Late Nov-Mar, daily) Phone 866-4114. **¢¢¢**

4. **Whitewater rafting.** Many outfitters offer guided trips on the Cheat River. For a list of outfitters contact the West Virginia Division of Tourism and Parks, Telemarketing Dept, State Capitol Complex, Bldg 6, Rm B-564, 1900 Kanawha Blvd E, Charleston 25305; 800/225-5982.

(For further information contact the Potomac Highland Convention & Visitors Bureau, 113 Executive Office Plaza, Elkins 26241; 636-8400.)

Annual Event

Tucker County Alpine Winter Festival. Governor's Cup ski races. Phone 866-4121. 1st wkend Mar.

(See Aurora, Elkins)

Motel

 ✔ ★ ★ **BEST WESTERN ALPINE LODGE.** *Box 520, on WV 32, near Blackwater Falls State Park entrance.* 304/259-5245. 46 rms, 1-2 story. S $42-$44; D $48-$50; each addl $5. Crib $5. TV; cable. Pool; whirlpool. Restaurant 6 am-9 pm. Ck-out 11 am. Coin lndry. Meeting rms. Sundries. Downhill ski 10 mi; x-country ski 2 mi. Refrigerators. Cr cds: A, D, DS, MC, V.

Resorts

★ ★ **BLACKWATER LODGE.** *3 mi SW off WV 32 in Blackwater Falls State Park.* 304/259-5216; FAX 304/259-5881. 55 rms in lodge, 1-2 story, 25 kit. cabins (1, 2 & 4 bedrm). S $55; D $63; each addl $6; cabins for 2-8, $88-$116 (1st night); $66-$101 (addl nights), $418-$621/wk. Crib $4; free in lodge. TV in lodge. Playground. Dining rm 7 am-9 pm. Lodge: ck-out noon, ck-in 3 pm. Cabins: ck-out 10 am, ck-in 4 pm. Coin lndry. Meeting rms. Tennis. Downhill ski 10 mi; x-country ski on site. Lawn games. Game rm. Picnic tables, grills. All state park facilities avail. Cr cds: A, MC, V.

★ ★ ★ **CANAAN VALLEY.** *Rte 1, Box 330, via WV 33, then 10 mi N on WV 32 in Canaan Valley Resort State Park.* 304/866-4121; res: 800/622-4121; FAX 304/866-2172. 250 rms, 2 story. Mid-May-mid-Oct, mid-Dec-mid-Mar: S $64; D $70; each addl $6; suites $98; 2-4 bedrm cabins $515-$669/wk; family rates: ski, golf, tennis plans; lower lodge rates rest of yr. Deposit required. Crib $6; free in lodge. TV; cable. 2 pools, 1 indoor; lifeguard. Playground. Supervised child's activities. Dining rm 7:30 am-10 pm. Snack bars; box lunches, picnics. Private club 4 pm-midnight. Ck-out noon, ck-in 4 pm. Coin lndry. Convention facilities. Sports dir. Lighted tennis, pro. 18-hole golf, greens fee $24, pro, putting green, driving range, miniature golf. Downhill/x-country ski on site. Naturalist program. Bicycles. Lawn games. Entertainment, dancing, movies. Rec rm. Game rm. Exercise equipt; weight machine, bicycles, whirlpool, sauna. Fishing privileges. Some refrigerators. Fireplace in cabins. Picnic tables. Camping sites avail. Cr cds: A, D, DS, MC, V.

Elkins (C-5)

Founded: 1890 **Pop:** 7,420 **Elev:** 1,830 ft **Area code:** 304 **Zip:** 26241

Elkins was named for US Senator Stephen B. Elkins, an aggressive politician and powerful industrial magnate who was Secretary of War under Benjamin Harrison (1888-92). This town is in a coal and timber region, and is also a railroad terminus and trade center. Some of the finest scenery in the state can be seen in and around Elkins.

What to See and Do

1. **Monongahela National Forest.** Entrance is E of town on US 33. This 901,000-acre forest, in the heart of the Alleghenies, has some of the loftiest mountains in the East. Spruce Knob (4,862 ft) is the highest point in the state. Headwaters of the Ohio and Potomac rivers are here. The forest is a meeting ground of northern and southern plant life, with stands of red spruce and northern hardwoods joining with oak, hickory and other southern hardwoods. There are also many interesting secondary and tertiary plants and wildflowers. Several recreation areas, including five wilderness areas, Spruce Knob/Seneca Rocks National Recreation Area, near Petersburg (see), and Blue Bend and Lake Sherwood recreation areas, near White Sulphur Springs (see), are all located within the forest. Swimming; fishing, hunting; boating. Hiking, rock climbing, spelunking. Picnicking. Camping (fee). Fees charged at the more developed recreation sites. Part of the Greenbrier River Trail (see MARLINTON) runs through the southern section of the forest. Forest headquarters are in Elkins; the Cranberry Mountain Visitor Center is near Marlinton (see); and the Seneca Rocks Visitor Center is in Seneca Rocks (see PETERSBURG). For further information contact Supervisor, US Department of Agriculture Building, 200 Sycamore St; 636-1800.

2. **Bowden National Fish Hatchery.** 10 mi E on Old US 33. Produces brook, brown and rainbow trout for stocking in state and national forest streams; also striped bass for Chesapeake Bay restoration project. Hatchery (daily). Visitor center (Memorial Day-mid-Oct, daily). Phone 636-2823. **Free.**

3. **The Old Mill** (1877). 25 mi E via US 33 to WV 32 N, in Harman. A gristmill powered by water turbines rather than a waterwheel. It was also used for planing wood and for producing white flour. Today it still uses water power to grind corn, wheat, rye and buckwheat. West Virginia crafts shop on second floor. (June-Sept, daily exc Sun) Phone 227-4466. **¢**

(For further information contact the Potomac Highland Convention & Visitors Bureau, 113 Executive Office Plaza; 636-8400.)

Annual Events

Augusta Festival. On campus of Davis & Elkins College, 100 Sycamore St. Celebration of traditional folk life and arts, featuring local and national performers, dances, juried craft fair, storytelling sessions, children's activities and homemade foods. Phone 636-1903. Mid-Aug.

Mountain State Forest Festival. Some events on campus of Davis & Elkins College. Queen Silvia is crowned; carnival, parades; entertainment; tilting at rings on horseback; sawing and woodchopping contests; marksmanship tests; State Championship Fiddle and Banjo Contest; juried craft fair and art exhibit. Phone 636-1824. Early Oct.

(See Buckhannon, Davis, Philippi)

Motels

★ ★ **BEST WESTERN.** *PO Box 1878, US 219/250S.* 304/636-7711. 63 rms, 2 story. S $38-$42; D $45-$49; each addl $5; suites, kit. suites $67-$77; under 12 free. Pet accepted. TV; cable. Indoor pool. Complimentary coffee in lobby. Restaurant nearby. Ck-out noon. Sundries. Cr cds: A, C, D, DS, MC, V.

★ ★ **ECONO LODGE.** *4533 US 33E, near Randolph County Airport.* 304/636-5311. 72 rms, 1-2 story. S $35-$40.95; D $38-$45; each addl $3; suites $38.95-$70.95; kit. units $42-$45; under 18 free; wkly rates; higher rates: college graduation, Forest Festival. Crib free. TV; cable. Indoor pool; whirlpool. Complimentary continental bkfst. Ck-out 11 am. Coin lndry. Meeting rms. Sundries. Airport transportation. Some bathrm phones. Picnic tables. Cr cds: A, C, D, DS, MC, V.

✔ ★ ★ **ELKINS MOTOR LODGE.** *Box 46, Harrison Ave, 5 blks W.* 304/636-1400. 54 rms. S $33-$39; D $36-$42; each addl $3; suites $50. Crib $3. TV; cable. Restaurant 5-10 pm. Rm serv. Private club 4:30 pm-1 am. Ck-out noon. Meeting rms. Free airport transportation. Cr cds: A, D, DS, MC, V.

D ⊬ ⊠ ⊠

★ **FOUR SEASONS.** *1091 Harrison Ave, on US 33 & 250.* 304/636-1990; res: 800/367-7130. 14 rms, 1-2 story. S $24-$26; D $28-$30; each $3; under 12 free; wkly rates. Crib free. TV; cable. Complimentary coffee in lobby. Restaurant nearby. Ck-out 11 am. Cr cds: DS, MC, V.

⊠ SC

✔ ★ **SUPER 8.** *Rte 3, Box 284, 2 mi S on US 219/250.* 304/636-6500; FAX 304/636-6500, ext. 300. 43 rms, 2 story. S $36.88-$42.88; D $42.88; each addl $6; under 12 free; higher rates: Forest Festival, graduation, ski wk. Crib free. TV; cable. Complimentary coffee in lobby. Restaurant opp 7 am-10 pm. Ck-out 11 am. Near Randolph County Airport. Cr cds: A, C, D, DS, JCB, MC, V.

D ⊠ ⊠ SC

Restaurant

★ **CHEAT RIVER INN.** *US 33E.* 304/636-6265. Hrs: 11 am-10 pm. Closed Mon; Dec 25. Res accepted. Bar. Semi-a la carte: lunch $2.50-$4.25, dinner $8.95-$16. Specializes in trout, steak. Parking. Outdoor dining. Mounted fish on display. Cr cds: MC, V.

D

Fairmont (B-5)

Settled: 1793 **Pop:** 20,210 **Elev:** 883 ft **Area code:** 304 **Zip:** 26554

Fairmont was a Union supply depot plundered by Confederate cavalry in April, 1863. General William Ezra Jones' division swept through town, took 260 prisoners, destroyed the $500,000 bridge across the Monongahela River and raided the governor's residence. After the war, resources in the region were developed, and coal became the mainstay. Today Fairmont manufactures aluminum, mine machinery and other products.

What to See and Do

1. **Fairmont State College** (1867). (6,600 students) Locust Ave. On campus is a one-room schoolhouse with original desks, books and other artifacts related to early era of education. (May-Oct, days vary; free) Phone 800/641-5678.

2. **Marion County Museum.** Adams St, adj to courthouse. Displays of B & O china, five furnished rooms covering 1776-1920s, doll, train and toy collection. (Daily exc Sun; closed hols) Phone 367-5398. **Free.**

3. **Pricketts Fort State Park.** I-79 exit 139, then 2 mi W. Approx 200 acres with reconstructed 18th-century log fort, colonial trade and lifestyle demonstrations by costumed interpreters, outdoor historical drama (July, Wed-Sat). Boating (ramps). Picnicking. Visitor center. Fort and museum (mid-Apr-Oct, daily). Museum (fee). Phone 367-2731 or 363-3030 (museum).

(For further information contact the Marion County Convention & Visitors Bureau, 316 Monroe St, PO Box 1258; 363-7037.)

Annual Event

Three Rivers Festival and Regatta. Entertainment, parade, clipper ship cruises, carnival, games. Phone 363-2625. Memorial Day wkend.

(See Clarksburg, Morgantown)

Motels

★ ★ **DAYS INN.** *1185 Airport Rd.* 304/367-1370; FAX 304/367-1806. 98 rms, 2 story. S $43-$60; D $48-$65; each addl $5; suites $57-$100; wkly rates; higher rates: WVU football games, graduation. Crib free. TV; cable. Pool. Complimentary continental bkfst. Restaurant nearby. Ck-out noon. Meeting rms. Sundries. Game rm. Refrigerator in suites. Cr cds: A, C, D, DS, MC, V.

D ⊠ ⊠ ⊠ SC

★ ★ **HOLIDAY INN.** *Old Grafton Rd, 1¹⁄₂ mi E on I-79 exit 137.* 304/366-5500; FAX 304/363-3975. 106 rms, 2 story. S, D $50-$80; each addl $4; under 18 free; higher rates: WVU football games, graduation. Crib free. TV; cable. Pool. Restaurant 6 am-2 pm, 5-10 pm. Rm serv. Private club. Ck-out noon. Meeting rms. Bellhops. Valet serv. Sundries. Cr cds: A, C, D, DS, ER, JCB, MC, V.

D ⊠ ⊠ ⊠ SC

✔ ★ **RED ROOF INN.** *Rte 1, Box 602, jct I-79 & US 250.* 304/366-6800; FAX 304/366-6812. 109 rms, 2 story. S $29.99-$39.99; D $40.99-$50.99; each addl $3; under 12 free. Crib free. TV. Complimentary coffee in lobby. Restaurant nearby. Ck-out 11 am. Cr cds: A, D, DS, MC, V.

D ⊠ ⊠ SC

Restaurants

✔ ★ ★ **MURIALE'S.** *(1742 Fairmont Ave, South Fairmont) 2 mi S on US 250; 2 mi N of I-79 exit 132.* 304/363-3190. Hrs: 11 am-9 pm; Sun from 9 am. Closed Dec 25. Italian, Amer menu. Beer. Semi-a la carte: lunch $3-$5.25, dinner $5-$15.50. Sun bkfst buffet $7.85. Child's meals. Specializes in lasagne, ravioli, steak. Own pasta. Parking. Family-owned. Cr cds: A, D, DS, MC, V.

D SC

★ ★ ★ **TIFFANY'S CONTINENTAL KEY CLUB.** *N Bellview Blvd, 1¹⁄₂ mi N of US 19N.* 304/363-7859. Hrs: 11 am-11 pm; early-bird dinner 4:30-6:30 pm. Closed Sun; major hols. Italian, continental menu. Res accepted; required Sun, Mon. Serv bar. Wine list. Semi-a la carte: lunch $2.95-$6.95, dinner $5.95-$18.95. Child's meals. Specialties: beef Wellington, veal parmigiana. Own baking. Valet parking. Braille menu. Family-owned. Cr cds: A, C, D, DS, MC, V.

D SC

Franklin (C-6)

Settled: 1794 **Pop:** 914 **Elev:** 1,731 ft **Area code:** 304 **Zip:** 26807

What to See and Do

Seneca Caverns. Approx 17 mi NW on US 33 to Riverton, then 3 mi E. Caves, which contain magnificent stalagmites and stalactites, were used as a refuge by the Seneca Indians. (Apr-Oct, daily) Phone 567-2691. ¢¢¢

(For further information contact the Potomac Highland Convention & Visitors Bureau, 113 Executive Office Plaza, Elkins 26241; 636-8400.)

Annual Event

Treasure Mountain Festival. Square dancing, clogging; parade; gospel & mountain music, drama; rifle demonstration, cross-cut sawing contest; children's contests, games; trail rides; craft exhibits; country food. Phone 249-5422. 3rd wkend Sept.

(For accommodations see Petersburg; also see Harrisonburg, VA)

Gauley Bridge (D-4)

Pop: 691 **Elev:** 680 ft **Area code:** 304 **Zip:** 25085

This town, at the junction of the New and Gauley rivers, was the key to the Kanawha Valley during the Civil War. In November, 1861, Union General W.S. Rosecrans defeated Confederate General John B. Floyd, a victory that assured Union control of western Virginia. Stone piers of the old bridge, which was destroyed by retreating Confederates in 1861, can be seen near the present bridge.

What to See and Do

1. **Hawks Nest State Park.** 6 mi E on US 60. Approximately 280 acres on Gauley Mt, with fine views of New River Gorge from rocks 585 feet above the river. A 600-foot aerial tramway carries passengers to canyon floor. Swimming pool; fishing. Hiking trails; tennis. Picnic area, playground, concession, restaurant, lodge (see LODGE). Log museum with early West Virginia artifacts (May-Nov, daily; free). Standard hrs, fees. Phone 658-5212 or -5196.

2. **Contentment Museum Complex** (ca 1830). 7 mi E on US 60, 1 mi W of Ansted. Former residence of Confederate Colonel George W. Imboden contains original woodwork, period furniture, toy collection. Adjacent Fayette County Historical Society Museum features displays of Native American relics, local artifacts, Civil War items; restored one-room schoolhouse. (June-Sept, daily; May, Sun; rest of yr, by appt) Phone 658-5695 or 465-0165. ¢

3. **Whitewater rafting.** Many outfitters offer guided trips on the New and Gauley rivers. For a list of outfitters contact the West Virginia Division of Tourism and Parks, Telemarketing Dept, State Capitol Complex, Bldg 6, Rm 564, 1900 Kanawha Blvd E, Charleston 25305; 800/225-5982.

4. **New River Gorge Bridge.** 13 mi SE on US 60, then 6 mi SW on US 19, near Fayetteville. A masterpiece of engineering, this four-lane, single-arch, steel-span bridge rises 876 feet above the New River Gorge National River (see HINTON), making it the second highest bridge in the US, and at 3,030 feet, the longest bridge of its type in the world. Just north of the bridge, on US 19, is the Canyon Rim Visitors Center (daily; closed Dec 25). The visitors center provides 2 overlooks of the bridge and river, a 70-foot descending boardwalk, slide presentation, exhibits and guided walks (May-Oct). Phone 574-2115. (See ANNUAL EVENT)

(For further information contact the Fayette County Chamber of Commerce, 310 Oyler Ave, Oak Hill 25901; 465-5617.)

Annual Event

Bridge Day. New River Gorge Bridge (see #4). Bridge is opened to pedestrians; parachutists test their skills by jumping off the bridge and floating to the bottom of gorge. 3rd Sat Oct.

(See Beckley, Charleston, Summersville)

Lodge

★ ★ **HAWKS NEST LODGE.** *(Box 857, Ansted 25812)* 10 mi E on US 60, in Hawks Nest State Park. 304/658-5212; FAX 304/658-4549. 31 rms, 4 story. Late May-early Sept: S $54; D $60; each addl $6; suites $66-$122; under 13 free; lower rates rest of yr. Crib free. TV; cable. Pool. Dining rm 7 am-9 pm; Dec-Feb to 8 pm. Ck-out noon. Meeting rm. Tennis. Balconies. View of mountains. 1,100-ft vertical tramway to marina. Cr cds: A, MC, V.

Inn

★ ★ **GLEN FERRIS.** *(PO, Glen Ferris 25090)* 1¹/₂ mi W on US 60. 304/632-1111; res: 800/924-6093 (WV). 16 rms. S, D $60-$65; suite $160. TV; cable. Dining rm 6 am-9 pm; Sun from 8 am. Private club. Ck-out 1:30 pm. Meeting rm. Renovated 1840s inn, originally Federal style in design; built by grandson of one of signers of Declaration of Indepedence. Overlooks Kanawha Falls. Cr cds: A, D, DS, MC, V.

Grafton (B-5)

Founded: 1856 **Pop:** 5,524 **Elev:** 1,004 ft **Area code:** 304 **Zip:** 26354

Mother's Day started in Grafton in 1908 when Anna Jarvis observed the anniversary of her mother's death during a religious service. The idea caught on nationally, and in 1914 President Woodrow Wilson issued a proclamation urging nationwide observance. The International Shrine to Motherhood in the original Mother's Day church is located at 11 E Main Street.

During the Civil War, Grafton was an important railroad center; 4,000 Union troops camped here before the Battle of Philippi in 1861. General McClellan also had his headquarters in the town. The first land soldier killed in the war, T. Bailey Brown, fell at Grafton. He is buried in the Grafton National Cemetery.

What to See and Do

Tygart Lake State Park. 2 mi S off US 119, 250. This scenic 2,100-acre park contains one of the largest concrete dams east of the Mississippi (1,900 ft by 209 ft). Swimming, waterskiing; fishing; boating (ramp, rentals, marina). Hiking, game courts. Picnic area, playground, concession, lodge (see MOTELS). Tent and trailer camping, 10 cabins. Nature and recreation programs, dam tours (summer; phone 265-1760). Standard hrs, fees. Phone 265-3383.

(For further information contact the Grafton-Taylor County Convention & Visitors Bureau, 220 W Main St; 265-3938.)

Annual Event

Taylor County Fair. Fairgrounds, US 50. Horse racing, livestock shows, auctions, carnival, crafts. Phone 265-4155. Last wk July.

(See Clarksburg, Fairmont, Morgantown, Philippi)

Motels

✔ ★ **CRISLIP MOTOR LODGE.** 300 Moritz Ave, 1 mi NE on US 50, 1 blk W of jct US 119. 304/265-2100. 56 rms, 2 story. S $30; D $38; each addl $5; bridal suites $38-$40. Crib $5. TV; cable. Pool. Complimentary coffee in rms. Restaurant nearby. Ck-out 11 am. Sundries. Cr cds: A, D, DS, MC, V.

★ ★ **TYGART LAKE STATE PARK LODGE.** Rte 1, Box 260, 4 mi S off US 119. 304/265-3383. 20 rms, 2 story. May-Oct: S $51; D $56; each addl $6; cabins $418-$540/wk; under 13 free (max of 5). Closed rest of yr. Crib free. TV. Free supervised child's activities (Memorial Day-Labor Day). Restaurant 8 am-8 pm. Ck-out noon. Meeting rm. Rec rm. Lawn games. Picnic tables. Rms overlook lake. Cr cds: A, MC, V.

Harpers Ferry (C-8)

Settled: 1732 **Pop:** 308 **Elev:** 247 ft **Area code:** 304 **Zip:** 25425

Harpers Ferry, the scene of abolitionist John Brown's raid in 1859, is at the junction of the Shenandoah and Potomac rivers, where West Virginia, Virginia and Maryland meet. A US armory and rifle factory made this an important town in early Virginia; John Brown had this in mind when he began his insurrection. He and 16 other men seized the armory and arsenal the night of October 16 and took refuge in the engine house of the armory when attacked by local militia. On the morning of the 18th, the engine house was stormed, and Brown was captured by 90 marines from Washington under Brevet Colonel Robert E. Lee and Lt J.E.B. Stuart. Ten of Brown's men were killed, including two of his sons. He was hanged in nearby Charles Town (see) for treason, murder and inciting slaves to rebellion.

When war broke out, Harpers Ferry was a strategic objective for the Confederacy, which considered it the key to Washington. "Stonewall" Jackson captured 12,693 Union prisoners here before the Battle of Antietam in 1862. The town changed hands many times in the war, during which many buildings were damaged. In 1944, Congress authorized a national monument here, setting aside 1,500 acres for that purpose. In 1963, the same area was designated a National Historical Park, now occupying more than 2,200 acres.

What to See and Do

1. **Harpers Ferry National Historical Park.** On US 340. Here the old town has been restored to its 19th-century appearance; exhibits and interpretive presentations explore the park's relation to the water-power industry, the Civil War, John Brown and Storer College, a school established for freed slaves after the war. A Visitor Center is located just off US 340. From there a bus takes visitors to Lower Town. Contact the Visitor Center, PO Box 65; 535-6298. Park entrance fee: per person ¢; per vehicle ¢¢ A walking tour of the park follows.

Master Armorer's House Museum (1859). South side of Shenandoah Street near High Street. Restored federalist house built by US government as residence for the master armorer of the US Armory. During the Civil War it was used as headquarters by various commanding officers. It now houses a museum containing exhibit on gunmaking. Also on this street is the site of the US Armory that John Brown attempted to seize; it was destroyed during the Civil War. Farther down Shenandoah Street and right under the trestle is

The Point, where three states, West Virginia, Virginia and Maryland, and two rivers, the Shenandoah and Potomac, meet at the Blue Ridge Mountains. Back under the trestle is

John Brown's Fort, on Arsenal Square. Where John Brown made his last stand; rebuilt and moved near original site. Across the street is the

John Brown Museum. Contains an exhibit and film on John Brown and a 10-minute slide presentation on the history of the park. Exiting the museum to the right is High Street, which has two Civil War museums and two black history museums. Up the stone steps from High Street is

Harper House. Three-story, stone house built between 1775 and 1782 by founder of town; both George Washington and Thomas Jefferson were entertained as overnight guests. Restored and furnished with period pieces. Behind this house is

Marmion Row. Four restored, private houses built between 1832-50. Continue up the hill to the

Ruins of St John's Episcopal Church. Used as a guardhouse and hospital during the Civil War. Approximately 100 yards farther is

Jefferson's Rock, from which Thomas Jefferson, in 1783, pronounced the view "one of the most stupendous scenes in nature." Further along, above the cemetery is

Lockwood House (1848). Greek-revival house used as a headquarters, barracks and stable during Civil War; later used as a classroom building by Storer College (1867), which was founded to educate freed men after the war.

Other buildings open to the public during the summer are the dry goods store, provost office and blacksmith shop.

2. **John Brown Wax Museum.** High St. Sound and animation depict Brown's exploits, including the raid on Harpers Ferry. (Mid-Mar-early Dec, daily; Jan-Mar, Sat & Sun) Phone 535-6342 or -2792. ¢¢

3. **Whitewater rafting.** Many outfitters offer guided trips on the Shenandoah and Potomac rivers. For a list of outfitters contact the West Virginia Division of Tourism and Parks, Telemarketing Dept, State Capitol Complex, Bldg 6, Rm 564, 1900 Kanawha Blvd E, Charleston 25305; 800/225-5982.

(For further information contact the Jefferson County Chamber of Commerce, 200 E Washington, PO Box 426, Charles Town 25414; 725-2055.)

Annual Events

Mountain Heritage Arts and Crafts Festival. More than 190 craftspeople and artisans demonstrate quilting, wool spinning, pottery throwing, vegetable dyeing and other crafts; concerts. 2nd full wkend June & last full wkend Sept.

Election Day 1860. More than 100 people in 19th-century clothing re-enact the 1860 presidential election. 2nd Sat Oct.

Old Tyme Christmas. Caroling, musical programs, children's programs, taffy pull, candlelight walk. 1st 2 wkends Dec.

(See Charles Town, Martinsburg, Shepherdstown; also see Frederick, MD)

Motel

★ **COMFORT INN.** PO Box 980, Union St & WV 340. 304/535-6391; FAX 304/535-6395. 51 rms, 2 story. Apr-Oct: S $49-$60; D $56-$60; each addl $6; under 18 free; lower rates rest of yr. Crib $6. TV; cable. Coffee in rms. Complimentary continental bkfst. Restaurant nearby. Ck-out 11 am. Cr cds: A, C, D, DS, JCB, MC, V.

D ⊠ 🐾 SC

Hillsboro (D-5)

Settled: 1765 **Pop:** 188 **Elev:** 2,303 ft **Area code:** 304 **Zip:** 24946

Civil War troops marched through Hillsboro, and Confederates camped in town before the decisive Battle of Droop Mountain. Novelist Pearl Buck was born in her grandparents' house (see #1) while her parents, missionaries on leave from China, were visiting.

What to See and Do

1. **Pearl S. Buck Birthplace Museum** (Stulting House). 1/2 mi N on US 219. Birthplace of Pulitzer and Nobel prize-winning novelist, restored to its 1892 appearance; original and period furniture; memorabilia. Exhibit of antique tools and farm implements in restored barn. Sydenstricker House, home of Pearl Buck's father and his ancestors, was moved 40 miles from its original site and restored here. Guided tours. (May-Oct, Mon-Sat, also Sun afternoons) Sr citizen rate. Phone 653-4430. ¢¢

2. **Droop Mountain Battlefield State Park.** 3 mi S on US 219. Encompasses approximately 285 acres on site where, on Nov 6,

1863, Union forces under General William W. Averell defeated Confederates under General John Echols, destroying the last major rebel resistance in the state. Park features graves, breastworks and monuments. Hiking. Picnic areas, playground. Observation tower. Museum. Battle re-enactments (Oct). Standard hrs. Phone 653-4254.

3. **Watoga State Park.** 1 mi N on US 219, then SE. More than 10,100 acres make this West Virginia's largest state park. Watoga, derived from the Cherokee *watauga*, means "river of islands." It aptly describes the Greenbrier River, which forms several miles of the park's boundary. Swimming pool, bathhouses; fishing; boating on 11-acre Watoga Lake (rentals). Hiking, bridle trails, horseback riding; tennis, game courts. Cross-country skiing. Picnicking, playground, concession, restaurant (seasonal). Tent and trailer camping, 33 cabins. Brooks Memorial Arboretum; nature, recreation programs (summer). Standard hrs, fees. Phone 799-4087. Adjacent to the park is

Calvin Price State Forest. This vast, undeveloped forest has more than 9,400 acres for fishing, deer and small game hunting, hiking and primitive camping. Phone 799-4087.

4. **Beartown State Park.** 10 mi S off US 219. Approximately 110 acres of dense forest with unique rock formations created by erosion; boardwalk with interpretive signs winds through park. Standard hrs. Phone 653-4254.

(For further information contact the Potomac Highland Convention & Visitors Bureau, 113 Executive Office Plaza, Elkins 26241; 636-8400.)

(See Marlinton)

Hinton (E-4)

Founded: 1873 **Pop:** 3,433 **Elev:** 1,382 ft **Area code:** 304 **Zip:** 25951

Hinton, a railroad town on the banks of the New River, is the seat of Summers County, where the Bluestone and Greenbrier rivers join the scenic and protected New River.

What to See and Do

1. **New River Gorge National River.** One of the oldest rivers on the continent, the New River rushes northward through a deep canyon with spectacular scenery. The 52-mile section from Hinton to Fayetteville is popular among outdoor enthusiasts, especially whitewater rafters and hikers. The Hinton Visitor Center is located along the river at WV 3 Bypass (Memorial Day-Labor Day, daily); phone 466-0417. A year-round visitor center is located on US 19 near the New River Gorge Bridge (see GAULEY BRIDGE). For further information and a list of whitewater outfitters contact Superintendent, PO Box 246, Glen Jean 25846; 465-0508.

2. **Bluestone State Park.** 5 mi S on WV 20. More than 2,100 acres on Bluestone Lake, which was created by the Bluestone Dam. Swimming pool (Memorial Day-Labor Day), wading pool, bathhouses, waterskiing; fishing; boating (ramps, marina nearby; canoe, rowboat and motorboat rentals). Hiking trails; game courts. Picnicking, playground. Gift shop. Tent and trailer camping (dump station), 25 cabins. Nature, recreation programs (summer). Standard hrs, fees. Phone 466-2805.

3. **Pipestem Resort State Park.** 12 mi SW on WV 20. More than 4,000 acres with 3,600-foot aerial tramway to Bluestone River complex. Swimming, bathhouses; fishing; canoeing, paddleboating. Hiking trails, horseback riding; 9- and 18-hole golf courses, miniature golf, tennis, archery, lighted game courts. Cross-country skiing, sledding. Playground, 2 lodges (see RESORT), 4 restaurants. Tent and trailer camping (dump station), 25 cabins. Visitor center; nature, recreation programs. Aerial tramway, arboretum, observation tower. Amphitheater; dances. Standard hrs, fees. Phone 466-1800.

(For further information, including a walking tour of Hinton and a driving tour of Summers County, contact the Summers County Chamber of Commerce, 206 Temple St; 466-5332.)

(See Beckley)

Inn

★ ★ **PENCE SPRINGS HOTEL.** *(Box 90, Pence Springs 24962) 14 mi E on WV 3. 304/445-2606; res: 800/826-1829.* 15 units, 3 story, 1 cottage. Apr-Dec: S $49-$59; D $59-$69; cottage $300; under 10 free; wkly rates; lower rates rest of yr. Crib free. Complimentary full bkfst. Dining rm 8-10 am, 5-8 pm; wkend hrs vary. Bar 5 pm-midnight. Ck-out 11 am, ck-in 1 pm. Meeting rms. Lawn games. Picnic tables. Resort hotel, built in 1918 for guests who came to "take the waters" of Pence Springs, was closed in 1935 due to the Depression. In 1947, resort was turned into a women's prison, which was closed in 1985. Restored structure retains flavor of rambling country house; sunroom, portico, gallery. On high plateau overlooking Greenbrier River valley. Cr cds: A, C, D, MC, V.

Resort

★ ★ ★ **PIPESTEM.** *(PO Box 150, Pipestem 25979) 12 mi SW via WV 20, in Pipestem Resort State Park, 3 mi from park entrance. 304/466-1800; res: 800/225-5982.* 143 units in 2 bldgs, 7 story, 30 lodge rms, 25 kit. cottages. May-Sept: S $62; D $68; lodge rms (Nov-Mar only): S $46; D $52; each addl $6; under 13 free; suites $72-$94; 2-4 bedrm cottages $575-$754/wk; varied lower rates rest of yr. Crib free. TV; cable. 2 pools, 1 indoor; wading pool, sauna, lifeguard. Playground. Dining rm 7 am-2 pm, 5:30-9 pm. Bar. Snack bars. Ck-out noon, ck-in 4 pm; cottages ck-out 10 am, ck-in 4 pm. Grocery 3 mi. Lighted tennis. 18-hole golf. X-country ski on site; sleighing, tobogganing. Lawn games. Soc dir. Rec rm; entertainment in summer. Many balconies. Picnic tables. Mt Creek Lodge (open May-Oct) located at foot of Bluestone Canyon; accessible only by aerial tram. Resort stateowned, operated; all state park facilities avail to guests. Cr cds: A, MC, V.

Restaurants

★ ★ **OAK SUPPER CLUB.** *(Just N of Pipestem Park entrance, in Pipestem) 12 mi SW on WV 20. 304/466-4800.* Hrs: 5:30-9 pm. Closed Dec 25. Res accepted. Bar. Semi-a la carte: dinner $10.95-$24.95. Child's meals. Specializes in barbecued pork, duckling, fresh mountain trout, country cooking. Parking. Named for 800 year-old white oak on grounds. Dining rm overlooks mountains. Family-owned. Cr cds: MC, V.

★ ★ ★ **RIVERSIDE INN.** *Pence Springs (24962), 14 mi E on WV 3. 304/445-7469.* Hrs: 5-9 pm. Closed Sun-Tues; also Jan-Mar; Wed-Thurs during Apr-May & Nov-Dec. Res required. No A/C. English country menu. Bar. Semi-a la carte: dinner $15-$38. Complete meals: dinner $18-$25. Child's meals. Specializes in colonial meat pies, duck, bread pudding. Own baking. Parking. Porch dining. Rustic log lodge built early 1900s; pewter table settings, kerosene lamps; fireplace. Colonial atmosphere. Cr cds: A, C, D, MC, V.

Huntington (D-2)

Founded: 1871 **Pop:** 54,844 **Elev:** 564 ft **Area code:** 304

The millionaire president of the Chesapeake & Ohio Railroad, Collis P. Huntington, founded this city and named it for himself. Originally a rail and river terminus, commerce and industry have made it the second largest city in the state. Thoroughly planned and meticulously laid out, Huntington is protected from the Ohio River by an 11-mile floodwall equipped with 17 pumping stations and 45 gates. Glass, railroad products and metals are important city industries.

What to See and Do

1. **Huntington Museum of Art.** 2033 McCoy Rd; I-64 exit 8. Museum with American and European paintings, prints and sculpture; Herman P. Dean Firearms Collection; Georgian silver; Oriental prayer rugs; pre-Columbian art; Appalachian folk art; Ohio Valley historical and contemporary glass. Complex includes exhibition galleries, library, studio workshops, amphitheater, auditorium, sculpture garden, observatory, art gallery for young people, nature trails. (Tues-Sat, also Sun afternoons; closed some major hols) Sr citizen rate. Free on Wed. Phone 529-2701. ¢

2. **Camden Park.** US 60 W. Amusement park with 27 rides, games, concession; boat and train rides, log flume, miniature golf, roller rink, picnicking. (May-Labor Day, daily; Apr & after Labor Day-mid-Oct, Sat & Sun) Rides individually priced; also unlimited ride plan. Phone 429-4321. Admission ¢¢¢ Docked at the park is the

   Camden Queen. Riverboat custom-crafted to resemble packet boats of 1890 makes one-hour cruises on Ohio River. (May-Labor Day, daily exc Tues) Phone 429-4321 or 523-9936. ¢¢

3. **Heritage Village.** 11th St and Veterans Memorial Blvd. Restored Victorian B & O Railroad yard surrounding brick courtyard. Restaurant (see RESTAURANTS) in original passenger station (1887), restored Pullman car, shops in renovated freight and box cars, warehouses. (Daily exc Sun) Phone 696-5954. **Free.**

4. **Beech Fork State Park.** Approx 15 mi SE via WV 10, then 7 mi W on Hughes Branch Rd, near Bowen. Nearly 4,000 acres on 720-acre Beech Fork Lake. Fishing; boating (ramp, marina). Hiking trails, physical fitness trail; tennis, game courts. Picnicking. Camping; store. Visitor center; nature, recreation programs (summer). Meeting rms. Standard hrs, fees. Phone 522-0303.

5. **East Lynn Wildlife Management Area.** 15 mi SE via WV 152 & WV 37, near East Lynn. Almost 23,000 acres used primarily by sportsmen; trails, primitive camping (fee). Phone 675-0871.

6. **Industrial tours.**

   Blenko Glass Co, Inc. 16 mi E via US 60, in Milton; I-64 exit 28. Famous glass factory; makers of Country Music Award, presidential gifts and original supplier to Colonial Williamsburg. Visitor center (daily; closed hols) has stained glass from nine leading studios; observation gallery for viewing hand-blown glassmaking and blown stained glass. (Mon-Fri; closed hols; also 1st 2 wks July, Dec 25-Jan 1). Museum of Historical Glass; Garden of Glass beside three-acre lake. Phone 743-9081. **Free.**

   Pilgrim Glass Corp. 5 mi W off I-64 exit 1, adj to Tri-State Airport on Airport Rd, in Ceredo. Observation deck to watch making of hand-blown glassware, including cranberry, cobalt and crystal glass. Gift shop. (Mon-Fri; closed hols, also last wk June & 1st wk July). Phone 453-3553. **Free.**

(For further information contact the Cabell-Huntington Convention & Visitors Bureau, PO Box 347, 25708; 525-7333 or 800/635-6329.)

Seasonal Event

Tri-State Fair & Regatta. Various events held in tri-state area of Kentucky, Ohio and West Virginia. Highlights include Regattafest, Central Park Festival, Budweiser Jet Ski Races, Huntington Miller Classic Power Boat Races and the Industrial Fun O-Limp-ics. Phone 525-8141 or 606/329-8737. June-Aug.

Motels

★ ★ **HOLIDAY INN GATEWAY.** *Box 2528 (25726), 6007 US 60E.* 304/736-8974; FAX 304/736-8974, ext. 726. 208 rms, 1-2 story. S $53-$72; D $59-$78; each addl $6; under 19 free; wkend packages. Crib free. TV. Indoor pool. Playground. Restaurant 6 am-10 pm. Rm serv. Bar; dancing. Ck-out noon. Coin lndry. Meeting rms. Bellhops. Valet serv. Barber, beauty shop. Lighted tennis. Exercise equipt; weights, bicycles, sauna. Cr cds: A, C, D, DS, JCB, MC, V.

[D] [⚕] [≈] [✕] [⊠] [♨] [SC]

✔ ★ **RED ROOF INN.** *5190 US 60E (25705).* 304/733-3737; FAX 304/733-3786. 109 rms, 2 story. S $37.99-$44.99; D $40.99-$47.99; each addl $3; under 18 free. Crib free. TV; cable. Cr cds: A, C, D, DS, MC, V.

[D] [⊠] [♨]

Motor Hotels

★ ★ **HOLIDAY INN-DOWNTOWN/UNIVERSITY.** *1415 4th Ave (25701).* 304/525-7741; FAX 304/525-3508. 138 rms, 4 story. S $55-$60; D $60-$65; each addl $6; suites $90-$100; under 18 free. Crib free. Pet accepted. TV; cable. Pool; wading pool. Restaurants 6:30 am-10 pm; Fri, Sat to 11 pm. Rm serv. Bar 4 pm-midnight, Fri, Sat to 1 am; dancing exc Sun. Ck-out noon. Meeting rms. Exercise equipt; weights, bicycle. Cr cds: A, C, D, DS, JCB, MC, V.

[D] [⚕] [≈] [✕] [⊠] [♨] [SC]

★ **RAMADA INN.** *Box 999 (25713), 5600 US 60E.* 304/736-3451; FAX 304/736-3451, ext. 706. 159 rms, 3 story. S $42-$56; D $47-$60; each addl $5; suites $54; under 18 free. Crib free. Pet accepted. TV; cable. Pool. Restaurant 6:30 am-9 pm. Private club 5 pm-2 am; dancing exc Sun. Ck-out noon. Meeting rms. Sundries. Airport transportation. Exercise equipt; weight machine, bicycles. Private patios, balconies. Cr cds: A, C, D, DS, JCB, MC, V.

[D] [⚕] [≈] [✕] [⊠] [♨] [SC]

Hotel

★ ★ ★ **RADISSON.** *1001 3rd Ave (25701).* 304/525-1001; FAX 304/525-1001, ext. 2041. 200 rms, 11 story. S, D $88-$108; each addl $5; suites $160-$375; under 18 free; wkend rates. Crib free. Pet accepted, some restrictions. TV; cable. Heated pool; poolside serv. Restaurant 6:30 am-11 pm. Bar 3 pm-1 am. Ck-out noon. Meeting rms. Shopping arcade. Valet parking. Airport, RR station, bus depot transportation. Exercise equipt; weight machine, stair machine. On Ohio River. Cr cds: A, C, D, DS, ER, JCB, MC, V.

[D] [⚕] [≈] [✕] [⊠] [♨] [SC]

Restaurants

✔ ★ ★ **HERITAGE STATION.** *11th St & Veterans Memorial Blvd.* 304/523-6373. Hrs: 11:30 am-11 pm. Closed Sun; July 4, Thanksgiving, Dec 25. Res accepted. Bar. Semi-a la carte: lunch $5.25-$10.95, dinner $9.95-$14.95. Specializes in seafood, pasta, steak. Salad bar. Parking. Outdoor dining. Former railroad station built 1887; memorabilia, antiques. Cr cds: A, MC, V.

★ ★ ★ **REBELS & REDCOATS TAVERN.** *412 West 7th Avenue.* 304/523-8829. Hrs: 11:30 am-2:30 pm, 5:30-10:30 pm; Sat to 11:30 pm. Closed Sun; major hols; also wk of July 4. Res accepted. Continental menu. Bar to midnight, Fri, Sat to 2 am. Wine cellar. Semi-a la carte: lunch $6-$9, dinner $11-$39. Specialties: veal Oscar, châteaubriand bouquetière, rack of lamb. Entertainment exc Sun. Parking. Colonial decor; fireplace. Family-owned. Cr cds: A, C, D, DS, MC, V.

[D]

Unrated Dining Spot

BAILEY'S CAFETERIA. *410 9th St, on plaza. 304/522-3663.* Hrs: 11 am-8 pm. Closed Sun; major hols. Avg ck: lunch $3.75-$5.50, dinner $4.75-$6. Specialties: scalloped eggplant, stewed tomatoes with bread. Own baking. No cr cds accepted.

D

Lewisburg (E-5)

Founded: 1782 **Pop:** 3,598 **Elev:** 2,099 ft **Area code:** 304 **Zip:** 24901

At the junction of two important Indian trails, the Seneca (now US 219) and the Kanawha (now US 60), Lewisburg was the site of colonial forts as well as a Civil War battle. The town's 236-acre historic district has more than 60 buildings from the 18th and 19th centuries, in a variety of architectural styles.

What to See and Do

1. **Old Stone Presbyterian Church** (1796). 200 Church St. Original log church (1783) was replaced by present structure. (Daily) Phone 645-2676. **Free.**
2. **North House Museum.** 101 W Church St, at Washington. Colonial and 19th-century objects and artifacts. (Tues-Sat) Phone 645-3398. ¢¢
3. **Organ Cave.** 9 mi S on US 219 in Ronceverte. Rustic, historic cave (visited since 1835) was once used by Robert E. Lee as a refuge and ammunition factory. Limestone formations, 37 saltpeter hoppers. One of the largest caves in the United States. (Daily) Phone 647-5551 or 800/258-CAVE. ¢¢¢
4. **Lost World Caverns.** 1 mi N on Fairview Rd. Scenic trail over subterranean rock mountain; prehistoric ocean floor; stalagmites, stalactites; flow stone, ribbons, hex stones. Guided tours (daily; closed some major hols). Phone 645-6677. ¢¢¢

(For further information and a free guidebook to the historic district contact the Lewisburg Visitors Center, 105 Church St; 645-1000.)

Annual Event

State Fair. Fairgrounds, 2 mi S on US 219. Exhibitors from a number of other states; horse shows, harness racing. Phone 645-1090. Mid-Aug.

(See White Sulphur Springs)

Motels

(Rates are generally higher during state fair)

★ ★ **BRIER INN.** *540 N Jefferson, jct US 219 & I-64 exit 169. 304/645-7722; FAX 304/645-7865.* 162 units, 2 story, 2 kit. units. S $42; D $47; each addl $5; suites $70-$75; kit. units $62-$67; under 12 free; higher rates state fair. Crib $5. Pet accepted; $10. TV; cable. Pool. Restaurant 11 am-10 pm; Fri & Sat to 11 pm. Rm serv. Bar 10-2 am; entertainment Fri, dancing. Ck-out 11 am. Meeting rms. Free airport transportation. Exercise equipt; weights, bicycles. Cr cds: A, D, DS, MC, V.

D ✔ ≋ 🖈 🛇 🅰 SC

✔ ★ **BUDGET HOST-FORT SAVANNAH INN.** *204 N Jefferson St. 304/645-3055; res: 800/678-3055.* 64 rms, 2 story. S $32-$65; D $38-$85; each addl $4; under 18 free. Crib free. Pet accepted; $3-$5. TV; cable. Pool; whirlpool. Restaurant 6 am-9 pm. Rm serv. Ck-out noon. Balconies. Cr cds: A, C, D, DS, MC, V.

✔ ≋ 🛇 🅰 SC

★ **DAYS INN.** *635 N Jefferson St. 304/645-2345.* 26 rms. S $40-$60; D $45-$80; each addl $5; higher rates special events. Crib $5. Pet accepted, some restrictions; $10. TV; cable. Complimentary coffee in lobby. Restaurant nearby. Ck-out 11 am. Airport transportation. 18-hole golf privileges, pro, putting green, driving range. Cr cds: A, D, DS, MC, V.

✔ 🖈 🛇 🅰 SC

Inn

★ ★ ★ **GENERAL LEWIS.** *301 E Washington St. 304/645-2600; res: 800/628-4454.* 25 rms, 2 story. S $50-$70; D $75-$100; each addl $10; family rates; winter package plan avail. Crib free. Pet accepted; $10. TV; cable. Dining rm 7 am-9 pm. Rm serv. Bar 11 am-9 pm. Ck-out 11 am. Part of building dates from 1834. Antiques; gardens. Cr cds: A, MC, V.

D ✔ 🛇 🅰

Marlinton (D-5)

Settled: 1749 **Pop:** 1,148 **Elev:** 2,130 ft **Area code:** 304 **Zip:** 24954

Marlinton is the seat of Pocahontas County, an area known for its wide variety of outdoor recreational opportunities. A Ranger District office of the Monongahela National Forest (see ELKINS) is located in the town.

What to See and Do

1. **Pocahontas County Historical Museum.** On US 219 S, at WV 39. Displays on history of the county from its beginnings to present. Extensive photo collection. (Early June-Labor Day, daily; after Labor Day-Oct, Sat & Sun) Phone 799-4973. ¢
2. **Cass Scenic Railroad State Park.** 5 mi E on WV 39, then 19 mi N on WV 28 to WV 66 in Cass. Steam train makes 8-mile round trip (1½ hr) up the mountain to Whittaker and 22-mile round trip (4½ hr) to top of Bald Knob; picnic stopover; dinner trains (some Sat). On 1,089-acre property are 2 museums, a country store and 12 renovated logging camp houses now serving as tourist cottages. Picnicking. Camping. Steam train (Memorial Day-Labor Day, days vary). Standard hrs, fees. Phone 456-4300. Train ride ¢¢¢¢-¢¢¢¢¢
3. **National Radio Astronomy Observatory.** 5 mi SE on WV 39, then 21 mi N on WV 28, 92 in Green Bank. Study of universe by radio telescopes. Slide show, exhibits and one-hour bus tour of site. (Mid-June-Labor Day wkend, daily; Memorial Day wkend-mid-June & after Labor Day-Oct, Sat & Sun) Phone 456-2209. **Free.**
4. **Cranberry Mountain Visitor Center-Monongahela National Forest.** Approx 7 mi NW of Mill Point via US 219 & WV 39. Exhibits, films and publications on conservation and forest management. (June-Aug, daily; Jan-Apr, Oct-Nov, Sat-Sun; May & Sept, Fri-Sun) Phone 653-4826 or 846-2695 (off-season). **Free.** Two miles west is

   Cranberry Glades. A USDA Forest Service botanical area. Approximately 750 acres featuring open bog fringed by forest and alder thicket. Boardwalk with interpretive signs. Guided tours leave from visitor center (June-Labor Day, wkends). Glades (all-yr, weather permitting). **Free.**
5. **Seneca State Forest.** 5 mi E via WV 39, then 10 mi NE on WV 28. Approximately 12,000 acres with fishing and boating on 4-acre lake; hunting. Hiking trails. Picnicking, playground. Camping, 7 rustic cabins. Standard hrs, fees. Phone 799-6213.
6. **Greenbrier River Trail.** Part of the state park system, this 76-mile trail runs along the Greenbrier River from the town of Cass, on the north, through Marlinton to North Caldwell, on the south; passes through small towns, over 35 bridges and through 2 tunnels.

Originally the trail was part of the Chesapeake & Ohio Railroad. Activities include backpacking, bicycling and cross-country skiing; trail also provides access for fishing and canoeing. No developed sites. Phone 799-4087.

7. Skiing.

Snowshoe Mountain Resort. 26 mi N on US 219, near Slatyfork. 7 triple chairlifts; patrol, school, rentals; snowmaking; restaurants and lodging (all-yr), cafeteria, lounges, bar, nursery; health club, swimming pool. 33 trails; longest run 6,200 ft; vertical drop 1,500 ft. (Mid-Nov-mid-Apr, daily) Summer activities include horseback riding, fishing, hiking. Phone 572-1000 or -4636 (ski report). ¢¢¢¢¢

Elk River Touring Center. 16 mi N on US 219, follow signs, near Slatyfork. Features 34 miles of cross-country trails in the Monongahela National Forest; patrol, school, rentals; restaurant; lodging. Night skiing. Guided tours. (All-yr, daily) Also guided mountain bike tours, cave tours in season. Phone 572-3771. Skiing ¢¢¢

(For further information contact the Potomac Highland Convention & Visitors Bureau, 113 Executive Office Plaza, Elkins 26241; 636-8400.)

Annual Event

Pioneer Days. Craft exhibits and demonstrations; horse pulling contests, frog and turtle races; bluegrass and mountain music shows; "4 X 4" pulling; parade; antique car show. Phone 799-4315. Early or mid-July.

(See Hillsboro)

Martinsburg (B-7)

Settled: 1732 **Pop:** 14,073 **Elev:** 457 ft **Area code:** 304 **Zip:** 25401

Martinsburg is located in the center of an apple and peach-producing region in the state's eastern panhandle. Because of its strategic location at the entrance to the Shenandoah Valley, the town was the site of several battles during the Civil War. The famous Confederate spy Belle Boyd was a resident. Officially chartered in 1778, Martinsburg is recognized for the preservation of its many 18th- and 19th-century houses and mercantile and industrial buildings.

What to See and Do

1. General Adam Stephen House (1789). 309 E John St. Restored residence of Revolutionary War soldier and surgeon Adam Stephen, founder of Martinsburg. Period furnishings; restored smokehouse and log building. (May-Oct, Sat & Sun, limited hrs; other times by appt) Phone 267-4434. **Free.** Adjacent is

Triple-Brick Building. Completed in three sections just after the Civil War, the structure was used to house railroad employees. A museum of local history is located on the top two floors. (May-Oct, Sat & Sun, limited hrs; other times by appt) **Free.**

2. Old Green Hill Cemetery. E Burke St. Patterned after a Parisian cemetery; buried here are Confederate and Union soldiers, the parents of Belle Boyd, Ward Hill Lamon, who served as President Lincoln's bodyguard during the Civil War, and David Hunter Strother (also known as Porte Crayon), writer and artist for *Harper's Weekly*.

(For further information contact the Martinsburg-Berkeley County Chamber of Commerce, 198 Viking Way; 267-4841 or 800/332-9007.)

Annual Event

Mountain State Apple Harvest Festival. Parade, celebrity breakfast, contests, entertainment, Apple Queen coronation, square dancing, grand ball, arts & crafts show. Phone 263-2500. 3rd wkend Oct.

(See Berkeley Springs, Charles Town, Harpers Ferry, Shepherdstown; also see Hagerstown, MD)

Motels

★ **ARBORGATE INN.** *1599 Edwin Miller Blvd.* 304-267-2211; res: 800/843-5644; FAX 304/267-9606. 59 rms, 1-2 story, 6 kits. Apr-Dec: S $38.95; D $39.95-$45.95; each addl $5; kits. $45.95-$50.95; under 17 free; lower rates rest of yr. Crib free. Pet accepted. TV; cable. Complimentary coffee in lobby. Restaurant adj 6 am-11 pm. Ck-out noon. Meeting rms. Sundries. Refrigerators avail. Cr cds: A, C, D, DS, ER, MC, V.

★★ **COMFORT INN.** *2800 Aikens Center, exit 16E.* 304/263-6200; FAX 304/263-6200, ext. 113. 110 rms, 4 story, 11 suites. May-Oct: S $51-$66; D $57-$72; each addl $6; suites $72-$79; under 18 free; wknd, hols rates; lower rates rest of yr. Crib free. TV; cable, in-rm movies avail. Pool. Complimentary continental bkfst. Complimentary coffee in lobby. Restaurant adj 6 am-10 pm. Ck-out noon. Coin lndry. Meeting rms. Sundries. Gift shop. Valet serv. Health club privileges. Some refrigerators, minibars. Cr cds: A, C, D, DS, MC, V.

✔ ★ **WHEATLAND.** *1193 Winchester Ave (US 11), I-81 exit 12.* 304/267-2994. 22 rms. S $28-$30; D $30-$32; each addl $2. Crib free. TV; cable. Pool. Restaurant adj 6-7:30 am, 11 am-2 pm, 5-11 pm; closed Sun. Ck-out 11 am. Picnic tables, grills. Cr cds: A, D, DS, MC, V.

★ **WINDEWALD.** *1022 Winchester Ave (US 11), I-81 exit 12.* 304/263-0831. 16 rms. S $28; D $32-$34; each addl $3. Crib $2. TV. Pool. Restaurant nearby. Ck-out 11 am. Gift shop. Picnic tables. Cr cds: A, DS, MC, V.

Hotel

★★ **SHERATON INN.** *301 Foxcroft Ave, I-81 exit 13.* 304/267-5500; FAX 304/264-9157. 120 rms, 5 story. Apr-Oct: S $74-$100; D $84-$110; each addl $10; under 17 free; lower rates rest of yr. Crib free. TV; cable. Indoor/outdoor pool; lifeguard. Restaurant 6:30 am-10 pm; Sun 7 am-9 pm. Bar 11-1 am, Sun 1-11 pm; entertainment Thurs-Sat. Ck-out noon. Meeting rms. Indoor & lighted tennis, pro. Exercise rm; instructor, weight machines, bicycles, whirlpools, saunas. Lawn games. Some refrigerators. Cr cds: A, C, D, DS, ER, MC, V.

Resort

★★★ **THE WOODS RESORT & CONFERENCE CENTER.** *(Box 5, Hedgesville 25427)* 10½ mi W of I-81 exit 16W via WV 9, then left on Mt Lake Rd 2½ mi. 304/754-7977; res: 800/248-2222 (eastern US); FAX 304/754-8344. 60 rms in 3-bldg lodge, 14 kit. cabins. MAP: D $82-$99/person; EP: S, D $94-$127; each addl $11; kit. cabins $138; under 5 free; wkends 2-night min. Crib free. TV; cable. 3 pools, 1 indoor; wading pools, lifeguard. Dining rm 7 am-3 pm, 5-9 pm; Fri 5-10 pm; Sat 3-10 pm; Sun 3-9 pm. Box lunches, picnics. Bar noon-midnight; entertainment Sat. Ck-out noon, ck-in 4 pm. Grocery 2½ mi. Coin lndry. Package store 12 mi. Meeting rms. Indoor/outdoor lighted tennis. 27-hole golf privileges, greens fee, pro. Exercise rm; weights, bicycles, whirlpool, sauna. Some fireplaces. Private patios. Cr cds: A, C, D, MC, V.

Moorefield (C-6)

Settled: 1777 **Pop:** 2,148 **Elev:** 821 ft **Area code:** 304 **Zip:** 26836

What to See and Do

Lost River State Park. 18 mi E on WV 55 to Baker, then 13 mi S on WV 259, near Mathias. More than 3,700 acres where Lee's White Sulphur Springs was once a famous resort; an original cabin still stands; museum. Swimming pool, wading pool (Memorial Day-Labor Day). Hiking trails, horseback riding; tennis, game courts. Picnicking, playground, restaurant; 24 cabins. Recreation building; nature programs (summer); scenic overlooks. Standard hrs, fees. Phone 897-5372 or 800/CALL-WVA.

(For further information contact the Potomac Highland Convention & Visitors Bureau, 113 Executive Office Plaza, Elkins 26241; 636-8400.)

Annual Event

Hardy County Heritage Weekend. Tours of antebellum houses, medieval jousting, crafts, traditional events. Phone 538-6560. Last full wkend Sept.

(For accommodations see Petersburg)

Morgantown (B-5)

Settled: 1776 **Pop:** 25,879 **Elev:** 892 ft **Area code:** 304 **Zip:** 26505

Morgantown is both an educational and industrial center. West Virginia University was founded here in 1867, the Morgantown Female Collegiate Institute in 1839. Known internationally for its glass, Morgantown is home to a number of glass plants, which produce wares ranging from lamp parts to decorative paper weights and crystal tableware. The town is also home to a number of research laboratories that are maintained by the Federal government.

What to See and Do

1. **West Virginia University** (1867). (22,712 students) University has 15 colleges. Tours (daily exc Sun; for reservation phone 293-3489). The Visitors Center in the Communications Bldg on Patterson Dr has touch-screen monitors and video presentations about the university and upcoming special events (phone 293-6692 for 24-hr event information). Of special interest on the downtown campus are Stewart Hall and the university's original buildings, located on Woodburn Circle. In the Evansdale area of Morgantown are the Creative Arts Center, the 75-acre Core Arboretum, the 63,500-seat Coliseum and the

   Cook-Hayman Pharmacy Museum. Health Sciences Center North, Room 1136. Re-creates pharmacy of yesteryear with old patent medicines. (Mon-Fri; wkends by request; closed hols) Donation. Phone 293-5101.

   Personal Rapid Transit System (PRT). A pioneering transit system, the PRT is the world's first totally automated system. Operating without operators or ticket takers, computer-directed cars travel between university campuses and downtown Morgantown. (Daily exc Sun; may not operate certain hols and univ breaks) Phone 293-5011. One-way ¢

2. **Coopers Rock State Forest.** 10 mi E on I-68. More than 12,700 acres. Trout fishing, hunting. Hiking trails to historical sites; Henry Clay iron furnace (1834-36). Cross-country ski trails. Picnicking, playground, concession. Tent and trailer camping. Standard hrs, fees. Phone 594-1561. Adj is

   Chestnut Ridge Regional Park. Swimming beach; fishing. Tent and trailer camping (hookups, dump station), rustic cabins, lodge (fees). Hiking. Picnicking. Cross-country ski trails (Dec-Feb). Nature center. Park (daily). Phone 594-1773.

3. **Whitewater rafting.** Many outfitters offer guided trips on the Cheat and Tygart rivers. For a list of outfitters contact the West Virginia Division of Tourism and Parks, Telemarketing Dept, State Capitol Complex, Bldg 6, Rm 564, 1900 Kanawha Blvd E, Charleston 25305; 800/225-5982.

(For further information contact the Northern West Virginia Convention & Visitors Bureau, 709 Beechurst Ave, 292-5081 or 800/458-7373.)

Annual Events

Mountaineer County Glass Festival. More than 50 glass companies present shows and exhibits; arts, entertainment. Mid-June.

Mason-Dixon Festival. Morgantown Riverfront Park. River parade, boat races, arts & crafts, concessions. Mid-Sept.

Mountaineer Balloon Festival. Morgantown Municipal Airport. Hot-air balloon races, carnival, music, food. Phone 296-8356. Mid-Oct.

(See Fairmont)

Motels

★ ★ **COMFORT INN.** *Rte 9, Box 225, at jct US 68, US 119.* 304/296-9364; FAX 304/296-0469. 81 rms, 2 story. S $40-$80; D $46-$80; each addl $6; suites $80-$100; kit. units $40-$80; under 18 free; higher rates: football wkends, graduation. Crib free. TV; cable. Heated pool. Complimentary continental bkfst. Restaurant 11 am-9 pm. Ck-out noon. Meeting rm. Valet serv. Sundries. Exercise equipt; weights, bicycles, whirlpool. Cr cds: A, C, D, DS, ER, JCB, MC, V.

D ≈ ✕ ✕ ⚲ SC

★ ★ **DAYS INN.** *(366 Boyers Ave, Star City) 1 mi N on US 19, WV 7.* 304/598-2120; FAX 304/598-3272. 102 rms, 3 story. Apr-Oct: S, D $60; each addl $8; under 12 free; higher rates: football games, graduation; lower rates rest of yr. Crib free. TV; cable. Indoor pool. Complimentary full bkfst. Restaurant 6:30 am-9:30 pm. Rm serv. Bar 5 pm-midnight; entertainment, dancing Wed-Sat. Ck-out 11 am. Meeting rm. Gift shop. Exercise equipt; weight machines, bicycles, whirlpool, steam rm. Cr cds: A, C, D, DS, MC, V.

D ≈ ✕ ✕ ⚲ SC

★ **ECONO LODGE.** *(15 Commerce Dr, Westover) I-79 exit 152.* 304/296-8774. 81 rms, 2 story. S $42; D $48; each addl $5; under 18 free. Crib free. TV. Restaurant nearby. Ck-out noon. Cr cds: A, DS, MC, V.

D ✕ ⚲ SC

✔ ★ **ECONO LODGE-COLISEUM.** *3506 Monongahela Blvd.* 304/599-8181; FAX 304/599-4866. 71 rms, 2 story. S $40-$49; D $42-$50; each addl $5; higher rates: football wkends, graduation. Crib $5. TV. Restaurant adj 6 am-midnight. Ck-out 11 am. Meeting rm. Sundries. Cr cds: A, D, DS, MC, V.

D ✕ ⚲ SC

✔ ★ **FRIENDSHIP INN-MOUNTAINEER.** *452 Country Club Rd.* 304/599-4850; FAX 304/599-4866. 30 rms, 1-2 story. S $30-$38; D $35-$43; each addl $5; wkly, monthly rates; higher rates: football wkends, graduation. Crib $5. TV; cable. Restaurant adj 7 am-11 pm. Ck-out 11 am. Valet serv. Some bathrm phones, refrigerators. Near University Medical Center. Cr cds: A, D, DS, MC, V.

D ✕ ⚲ SC

★ ★ **HAMPTON INN.** *1053 Van Voorhis Rd, I-79 exit 155.* 304/599-1200. 108 rms, 5 story. S $48-$53; D $52-$58; suites $100; under 18 free; higher rates special events. Crib free. TV; cable. Complimentary continental bkfst. Restaurant nearby. Ck-out noon. Meeting rms. Valet serv. Cr cds: A, C, D, DS, MC, V.

★ ★ **HOLIDAY INN.** *1400 Saratoga Ave.* 304/599-1680; FAX 304/598-0989. 147 rms, 2 story. S, D $39-$65; under 12 free; higher rates: graduation, athletic events. Crib free. Pet accepted; TV; cable. Pool. Restaurant 6 am-2 pm, 5-10 pm. Rm serv. Bar 4 pm-2 am. Ck-out noon. Meeting rms. Balconies. Cr cds: A, C, D, DS, ER, MC, V.

Motor Hotel

★ ★ **RAMADA INN.** *Box 1242, 3 mi S on US 119 at jct US 68 & I-79 exit 148.* 304/296-3431; FAX 304/296-3431, ext. 481. 164 rms, 4 story. S $55-$85; D $60-$85; each addl $5; suites, studio rms $100; under 18 free; higher rates: special events, graduation. Crib free. TV. Pool; lifeguard. Restaurant 6 am-10 pm. Private club 11-2 am; entertainment, dancing exc Sun. Ck-out noon. Meeting rms. Sundries. Gift shop. Free airport transportation. Exercise equipt; weights, bicycles. Game rm. Cr cds: A, C, D, DS, JCB, MC, V.

Hotel

✔ ★ **MORGAN.** *127 High St.* 304/292-8401; FAX 304/292-4601. 40 rms, 7 story, 27 kit. suites. S, D $40-$45; kit. suites $60-$100; under 12 free; wkly, monthly rates; higher rates: football season, graduation. TV; cable. Restaurants 6 am-10 pm; closed Sun. Bar. Ck-out 11 am. Meeting rms. Some refrigerators. Historic brick hotel (1925). Cr cds: A, DS, MC, V.

Resort

★ ★ ★ **LAKEVIEW RESORT AND CONFERENCE CENTER.** *(Box 88A, WV 6) 7 mi N, 1/4 mi S off WV 857; 1/4 mi N of US 68 exit 10.* 304/594-1111; FAX 304/594-9472. 187 rms, 1-3 story. Apr-Nov: S $129; D $139; each addl $10; suites $215-$375; under 18 free; summer, winter rates; golf plans; lower rates rest of yr. Crib free. TV; cable. 4 pools, 2 indoor; wading pool, poolside serv, lifeguard. Dining rms 6:30 am-10 pm. Bar 11-1 am, Sun from 1 pm; entertainment, dancing exc Sun. Ck-out 2 pm, ck-in 4 pm. Meeting rms. Valet serv. Gift shop. Free airport transportation. Indoor/outdoor tennis. Two 18-hole golf courses, greens fee $20-$40, pro. Rec rm. Exercise rm; instructor, weight machines, weights, whirlpool, sauna. Massage. Some refrigerators. On 400 acres. Cr cds: A, C, D, DS, MC, V.

Restaurants

★ ★ **BACK BAY.** *1869 Mileground, near airport.* 304/296-3027. Hrs: 11 am-9:30 pm; Fri to 10:30 pm; Sat 4-10:30 pm; Sun noon-9 pm. Closed major hols. Bar. Semi-a la carte: lunch $3.95-$7.95, dinner $5.95-$19.95. Specializes in fresh seafood, Cajun dishes. Nautical atmosphere. Cr cds: A, DS, MC, V.

★ ★ **THE FLAME STEAK HOUSE.** *76 High St.* 304/296-2976. Hrs: 5-11 pm. Closed major hols. Res accepted. Private club. Complete meals: dinner $6.45-$21.95. Child's meals. Specializes in steak, fresh seafood, Italian dishes. Parking. Colonial decor. Family-owned. Cr cds: A, D, DS, MC, V.

Nitro (D-3)

Founded: 1918 **Pop:** 6,851 **Elev:** 604 ft **Area code:** 304 **Zip:** 25143

Nitro experienced explosive growth around a huge smokeless powder plant during World War I, when the town's population reached 35,000 overnight and some 3,400 buildings were erected. When the war ended, the demand for smokeless powder fizzled, and the town dried up; factory buildings were scrapped, and whole houses were shipped down the river. Now a western suburb of Charleston, Nitro produces chemicals.

What to See and Do

1. **Tri-State Greyhound Park.** E via I-64 exit 47 to Goff Mountain Rd, then to Greyhound Dr in Cross Lanes. Indoor grandstand, clubhouse, concessions. (Mon & Wed-Sat evenings; matinees Sat, Sun & hols) Must be 18 to wager. Phone 776-1000.

2. **Waves of Fun.** W via I-64 exit 39, then 3 mi S on WV 34, at Valley Park in Hurricane. Water park featuring three water slides, wave pool, swimming areas; bathhouse, tube rentals (fee), lockers, concessions. (Memorial Day-Labor Day, daily) Sr citizen rate. Phone 757-7572 or 562-0518. ¢¢¢

(For further information contact the Putnam County Chamber of Commerce, PO Box 553, Teays 25569; 757-6510.)

(See Charleston)

Motels

✔ ★ **BEST WESTERN MOTOR INN.** *4115 1st Ave.* 304/755-8341; FAX 304/755-2933. 26 rms, 1-3 story. No elvtr. S $34; D $39; each addl $5; under 12 free. Crib free. TV; cable. Restaurant open 24 hrs. Ck-out noon. Cr cds: A, C, D, DS, MC, V.

★ **COMFORT INN.** *(102 Racer Dr, Cross Lanes 25313)* E on I-64 exit 47 to Goff Mountain Rd. 304/776-8070; FAX 304/776-6460. 114 rms, 2 story. S $45-$50; D $50-$60; each addl $5; under 18 free. Crib free. TV; cable. Pool; whirlpool. Complimentary continental bkfst. Restaurant adj 7 am-midnight. Bar 4 pm-1 am; Fri, Sat to 2 am; dancing. Ck-out noon. Meeting rms. Sundries. Cr cds: A, C, D, DS, ER, MC, V.

Restaurant

★ ★ ★ **CHILTON HOUSE.** *(#2 6th Ave, St Albans)* S across Nitro-St Albans Bridge to 2nd St in St Albans, S to 6th Ave. 304/722-2918. Hrs: 6-10 pm. Closed Sun; major hols. Res accepted. Continental menu. Wine list. Semi-a la carte: dinner $12-$23. Child's meals. Specialties: steak Diane, Caesar salad, seafood. Parking. In restored Gothic-revival house (1847); antiques, original art. Cr cds: A, DS, MC, V.

Parkersburg (C-3)

Settled: 1785 **Pop:** 33,862 **Elev:** 616 ft **Area code:** 304 **Zip:** 26101

In 1770, George Washington came to this area to inspect lands awarded to him by Virginia for his military services. After the Revolution, Blennerhassett Island, in the Ohio River west of Parkersburg, was the scene of the alleged Burr-Blennerhassett plot. Harman Blennerhassett, a wealthy Irishman, built a lavish mansion on this island. After killing Alexander Hamilton in a duel, Aaron Burr came to the island, allegedly with the idea of seizing the Southwest and setting up an empire; Blennerhassett may have agreed to join him. On December 10, 1806, the plot was uncovered. Both men were acquitted of treason but were, in the process, ruined financially. The Blennerhassett mansion burned in 1811, but was later rebuilt.

Today, Parkersburg is the center for many industries, including glass, chemicals, petrochemicals and ferrous and other metals. Fishing is popular in the area, especially below the Belleville and Willow Island locks and dams on the Ohio River.

What to See and Do

1. **Blennerhassett Island Historical State Park.** 2 mi S in Ohio River. A 500-acre island accessible only by sternwheeler (see #$$XR19075450). There are self-guided walking tours of the island; horse-drawn wagon rides; tours of the Blennerhassett mansion. Bicycle rentals. Picnicking, concession. (May-Labor Day, daily exc Mon, also hols; Sept-Oct, Sat & Sun) Tickets avail for boat ride, mansion tour and Blennerhassett Museum (see #2). Phone 428-3000. Mansion tour ¢¢

2. **Blennerhassett Museum.** 2nd & Juliana Sts. Features archaeological and other exhibits relating to history of Blennerhassett Island and Parkersburg area; includes artifacts dating back 12,000 years. Theater with video presentation. (May-Oct, daily exc Mon; rest of yr, Sat & Sun; closed Jan 1, Thanksgiving, Dec 25) Phone 428-3000. ¢

3. **Rubles Sternwheelers Riverboat Cruises** to Blennerhassett Island. Depart from Point Park, 2nd & Ann Sts. (Early May-early Sept, daily exc Mon; early Sept-Oct, Sat & Sun) Phone 614/423-7268. ¢¢

4. **City Park.** Park Ave & 23rd St. A 55-acre wooded area with the Centennial Log Cabin Museum, which dates from 1804. Swimming pool; fishing; paddle boats. Miniature golf, tennis. Shelters and picnic facilities.

5. **Parkersburg Art Center.** 220 8th St. Changing exhibits. (Daily exc Mon; closed hols) Phone 485-3859. ¢

6. **Actors Guild Playhouse.** 8th & Market Sts. Musical, comedic and dramatic performances. (Fri-Sun) Sr citizen rate. Phone 485-1300. ¢¢¢

7. **Industrial tour. Middleton Doll Company.** 2 mi W via US 50, at 1301 Washington Blvd in Belpre, OH. Tour of vinyl and porcelain doll factory (20 min). Factory store (daily exc Sun). (June-Aug, Tues-Sat; rest of yr, Mon-Fri; closed hols) Phone 614/423-1481 or 800/843-9572. **Free.**

8. **Mountwood Park.** 12 mi E via US 50 to Volcano Rd. Wooded area with fishing, boating (no gasoline motors); hiking, nature trails; picnic area. Phone 679-3611. **Free.**

9. **North Bend State Park.** 22 mi E on US 50, then 7 mi SE on WV 31, near Cairo. Approximately 1,400 acres in the wide valley of the North Fork of the Hughes River; scenic overlooks of famous horseshoe bend. Swimming pool, bathhouse; fishing. Miniature golf; tennis, game courts. Hiking, bicycle, bridle trail. Picnicking, playground, concession, restaurant, lodge (see MOTELS). Tent and trailer camping (dump station), eight cabins. Nature, recreation programs. Nature trail for disabled. Standard hrs, fees. Phone 643-2931.

(For further information contact the Parkersburg/Wood Co Convention & Visitor's Bureau, 215 First St; 428-1130 or 800/752-4982.)

Annual Events

Parkersburg Homecoming. Point Park, just off WV 68 at foot of 2nd St. Riverfront celebration features entertainment, parade, sternwheeler races, waterskiing show, miniature car races, fireworks. Phone 422-3588. 3rd wkend Aug.

West Virginia Honey Festival. City Park (see #4). Honey-related exhibits, baking, food, arts and crafts. Last full wkend Sept.

Motels

✔ ★ ★ **ECONO LODGE.** 26101, 3¹/₂ mi E on US 50, at jct I-77 exit 176. 304/422-5401; FAX 304/422-5418. 102 rms, 2 story. S $31.95-$36.95; D $36.95-$42.95; each addl $5; under 18 free. TV; cable. Pool. Restaurant 11am-2 pm, 5-10 pm. Bar. Ck-out noon. Meeting rms. Valet serv. Sundries. On hilltop. Cr cds: A, C, D, MC, V.

[icons] SC

★ ★ ★ **HOLIDAY INN.** 26101, 3¹/₂ mi E on US 50, at jct I-77. 304/485-6200; FAX 304/485-6200, ext. 350. 148 rms, 2 story. S $55-$67; D $61-$73; each addl $6; under 19 free; wkend packages. Crib free. TV. Indoor/outdoor pool; sauna, hot tub. Restaurant 7 am-2 pm, 5-10 pm. Rm serv. Bar 11-2 am; entertainment. Ck-out noon. Coin lndry. Meeting rms. Bellhops. Shopping arcade. Some refrigerators. Some balconies. Cr cds: A, D, DS, JCB, MC, V.

[icons] D SC

★ ★ **NORTH BEND LODGE.** (US 1, Cairo 26337) 22 mi E on US 50, then 7 mi SE on WV 31, in North Bend State Park. 304/643-2931; res: 800/225-5982. 29 rms, 2 story, 8 cabins. Apr-Oct: S $56; D $62; each addl $6; 2-3 bedrm cabins $548-$627/wk; under 13 free; slightly lower rates rest of yr. TV. Pool. Playground adj. Free supervised child's activities (June-early Sept). Restaurant 6:30 am-9 pm. Ck-out noon (lodge), 10 am (cabins). Sundries. Tennis. Picnic tables, grills. On river. View of mountains. State owned, operated. Cr cds: A, MC, V.

[icons] D SC

★ **RED ROOF INN.** 3714 7th St. 304/485-1741; FAX 304/485-1746. 107 rms, 2 story. S $34.99-$43.99; D $39.99-$46.99; each addl $3; under 18 free. Crib free. Pet accepted. TV; cable. Ck-out noon. Meeting rms. Cr cds: A, C, D, DS, MC, V.

[icons] D SC

Hotel

★ ★ ★ **CLARION CARRIAGE HOUSE INN-BLENNERHASSETT.** 4th & Market Sts. 304/422-3131; FAX 304/485-0267. 104 rms, 5 story. S, D $45-$62; each addl $6; suites $75-$95; under 18 free. Crib free. TV; cable. Coffee in rms. Restaurant 6 am-10 pm. Bar 11-1 am. Ck-out noon. Meeting rms. Gift shop. Valet parking. Free airport transportation. Health club privileges. Restored Victorian hotel built 1889. Cr cds: A, C, D, DS, ER, MC, V.

[icons] D SC

Restaurants

✔ ★ **MOUNTAINEER.** 4006 Seventh St, at jct US 50 & I-77. 304/422-0101. Open 24 hrs. Closed Dec 25. Semi-a la carte: bkfst $1.95-$4.95, lunch $1.95-$5.95, dinner $3.95-$9.95. Child's meals. Specializes in steak, seafood, chicken. Parking. No cr cds accepted.

[icons] D SC

★ ★ **POINT OF VIEW.** Riverhill Rd, 3 mi SW via WV 68, Star Ave exit. 304/863-3366. Hrs: 11:30 am-2 pm, 5-9:30 pm. Closed Sun; major hols. Continental menu. Semi-a la carte: lunch $4-$8, dinner $9-$22. Child's meals. Specializes in prime rib, fresh seafood, steak. Own baking. Parking. Open-hearth grill; fireplace. View of Blennerhasset Island. Family-owned. Cr cds: A, D, DS, MC, V.

[icons] SC

Petersburg (C-6)

Settled: 1745 **Pop:** 2,360 **Elev:** 937 ft **Area code:** 304 **Zip:** 26847

A Ranger District office (phone 257-4488) of the Monongahela National Forest (see ELKINS) is located in Petersburg.

What to See and Do

1. **Smoke Hole Caverns.** 8 mi S on WV 28 & 55. Caverns were used centuries ago by Seneca Indians both for shelter and the smoking of meat. During the Civil War, they were used by troops on both sides for storing ammunition. Later, they hid the illegal distillation of corn whiskey. It is claimed the caverns contain the longest ribbon stalactite and the second highest cave room in the world. Large gift shop with wildlife exhibits; concessions. Tours. (Daily; closed Thanksgiving, Dec 25) Phone 257-4442. ¢¢¢

2. **Seneca Rocks Visitor Center-Monongahela National Forest.** 20 mi S on WV 28/55 at Seneca Rocks, in the Spruce Knob/Seneca Rocks National Recreation Area. Center features geological exhibits, films and publications; picnic area; and interpretive programs (summer). Seneca Rocks, a 960-foot-high formation of Tuscarora sandstone, is a challenge for rock climbers. Recreation area is also popular for canoeing, hiking and other outdoor sports. Visitor center (mid-Apr-Nov, daily; rest of yr, Sat & Sun). Phone 567-2827 or 257-4488. **Free.**

(For further information contact the Potomac Highland Convention & Visitors Bureau, 113 Executive Office Plaza, Elkins 26241; 636-8400.)

(See Franklin, Moorefield)

Motels

★ ★ **HERMITAGE MOTOR INN.** *Box 1077, 203 Virginia Ave. 304/257-1711; FAX 304/257-4330.* 39 rms, 2 story. S $32-$40; D $38-$45; each addl $5; under 12 free. Crib $8. TV; cable. Pool; whirlpool. Restaurant 11 am-9 pm; Fri-Sat to 10 pm. Ck-out noon. Airport transportation. Craft shop, bookstore in 1840s inn. Cr cds: A, C, D, DS, MC, V.

★ **SMOKE HOLE CAVERNS MOTEL.** *(HC 59, Box 39, Seneca Rocks 26884) 12 mi S on WV 28/55. 304/257-4442; res: 800/828-8478; FAX 304/257-2745.* 13 rms, 3 suites, 18 cottages. S $25-$45; D $45-$55; each addl $10; kit. cottages $59.50-$99.50; family, wkly rates; varied lower rates. TV; cable. Pool. Playground. Ck-out 11 am. Gift shop. Lawn games. Some refrigerators. Adj Smoke Hole Caverns. Cr cds: DS, MC, V.

Philippi (C-5)

Settled: 1780 **Pop:** 3,132 **Elev:** 1,307 ft **Area code:** 304 **Zip:** 26416

The first land battle of the Civil War, a running rout of the Confederates known locally as the Philippi Races, was fought here on June 3, 1861. A historical marker on the campus of Alderson-Broaddus College marks the site. The Union attacked to protect the Baltimore & Ohio Railroad, whose main line between Washington and the West ran near the town.

What to See and Do

1. **Covered bridge.** Spanning Tygart River since 1852; restored in recent years; believed to be the only two-lane bridge of its type still in daily use on a federal highway (US 250).

2. **Barbour County Historical Society Museum.** 146 N Main St. This B & O Railroad station (1911), used until 1956, is now restored as a museum; also local arts & crafts. (Limited hrs) For further information contact the Chamber of Commerce.

(For further information contact the Philippi-Barbour County Chamber of Commerce, PO Box 5000; 457-1958.)

Annual Events

Blue & Gray Reunion. Commemorates the first land battle of the Civil War; reenactment, parade, crafts. Early June.

Barbour County Fair. Fairgrounds, 5 mi SE on US 250. Horse and antique car shows, quilt and livestock exhibits, carnival rides, nightly entertainment, parade and more. Phone 457-3254. Wk before Labor Day.

(For accommodations see Buckhannon, Clarksburg, Grafton)

Restaurant

✔ ★ **PHILIPPI INN.** *On US 250S. 304/457-2140.* Hrs: 6 am-9 pm; Fri, Sat to 10 pm; Sun 7 am-9 pm. Closed Dec 25. Res accepted. Semi-a la carte: bkfst, lunch $1.95-$5.95, dinner $3.95-$7.95. Child's meals. Specializes in honey-dipped chicken, steak. Own pies. Parking. Family-owned. Cr cds: A, DS, MC, V.

D **SC**

Point Pleasant (C-3)

Settled: 1774 **Pop:** 4,996 **Elev:** 569 ft **Area code:** 304 **Zip:** 25550

On October 10, 1774, British-incited Shawnees under Chief Cornstalk fought a battle here against 1,100 frontiersmen. The colonists won and broke the Indian power in the Ohio Valley. Historians later argued that this, rather than the battle at Lexington, Massachusetts, was the first battle of the Revolutionary War. In 1908, the United States Senate rewrote history by recognizing this claim.

What to See and Do

1. **Point Pleasant Battle Monument State Park.** 1 Main St, in Tu-Endie-Wei Park (Native American for "where two rivers meet"). An 84-foot granite shaft was erected here in 1909, after the US Senate agreed to a claim made by historians that the first battle of the Revolutionary War was fought here. Park also contains a marker where Joseph Celeron de Bienville buried a leaden plate in 1749, claiming the land for France, and the graves of Chief Cornstalk and "Mad Anne" Bailey, noted pioneer scout. Phone 675-0869. **Free.** Also here is

   Mansion House (1796). Oldest log building in Kanawha Valley, restored as a museum. (May-Oct, daily) Phone 675-0869. **Free.**

2. **Krodel Park and Lake.** 1 mi SE via WV 62/2. A 44-acre park with a replica of Fort Randolph (ca 1775). Fishing; paddle boats (fee). Miniature golf (fee). Playground. Camping (mid-Apr-Oct; fee). Phone 675-1068 (seasonal). **Free.**

3. **McClintic Wildlife Management Area.** 7 mi NE off WV 62. Approximately 2,800 acres with primitive camping (fee). Phone 675-0871.

4. **West Virginia State Farm Museum.** 4 mi N via WV 62, adj to county fairgrounds. Contains more than 30 farm buildings depicting early rural life, including a log church, one-room schoolhouse, kitchen and store. Barn contains mount of one of the largest horses in the world; also animals. (Apr-Dec, daily exc Mon) Phone 675-5737. **Free.**

(For further information contact the Mason County Area Chamber of Commerce, 305 Main St; 675-1050.)

Annual Event

Mason County Fair. County Fairgrounds. Livestock show, arts & crafts, contests, Nashville entertainers. Phone 675-5463. Mid-Aug.

(For accommodations see Ripley)

Princeton (E-4)

Settled: 1826 **Pop:** 7,043 **Elev:** 2,446 ft **Area code:** 304 **Zip:** 24740

Princeton is the southern terminus of the spectacular 88-mile West Virginia Turnpike and a trade center for an agricultural, industrial and coal mining area.

What to See and Do

Camp Creek State Park. 13 mi N on I-77, then 2 mi NW, near Camp Creek. Approximately 500 acres. Fishing. Hiking trails, game courts. Picnicking, playgrounds. Camping. Standard hrs, fees. Phone 425-9481.

(For further information contact the Princeton-Mercer County Chamber of Commerce, 910 Oakvale Rd; 487-1502.)

(See Bluefield)

Motels

✔ ★ ★ **COMFORT INN.** *Rte 4, Box 222, Ambrose Lane & US 460W.* 304/487-6101; FAX 304/425-7002. 51 rms, 2 story. S $42-$60; D $48-$75; each addl $6; under 18 free. Crib free. TV; cable. Complimentary continental bkfst. Restaurant nearby. Ck-out noon. Downhill ski 20 mi. Whirlpool. Cr cds: A, C, D, DS, ER, JCB, MC, V.

D ✇ ⊠ ⋈ ⚲ SC

★ **DAYS INN.** *PO Box 830, at jct I-77 exit 9 & US 460.* 304/425-8100. 122 rms, 2 story. S $47-$52; D $52-$58; kit. units $60-$70; under 15 free. Crib free. TV. Indoor pool. Complimentary continental bkfst, coffee. Restaurant adj 6 am-10 pm. Ck-out 11 am. Meeting rms. Sundries. Downhill ski 15 mi. Cr cds: A, C, D, DS, MC, V.

D ✔ ✇ ⊠ ⋈ ⚲ SC

Restaurant

★ **JOHNSTON'S INN.** *On US 460 (Old Oakvale Rd).* 304/425-7591. Hrs: 6:30 am-10:30 pm; Sun to 10 pm. Closed Dec 25. Res accepted. Bar from 11:30 am; Sun 3-10 pm. Semi-a la carte: bkfst $2-$4.50, lunch $5-$6, dinner $8-$15.95. Child's meals. Specializes in steak, seafood, desserts. Salad bar. Own salad dressings. Parking. Tiffany lamps, artwork, antiques. Family-owned. Cr cds: A, C, MC, V.

Ripley (C-3)

Settled: 1768 **Pop:** 3,023 **Elev:** 616 ft **Area code:** 304 **Zip:** 25271

What to See and Do

Washington's Lands Museum and Park. 6 mi N via I-77 exit 146 to Ravenswood, then 2½ mi S on WV 68. Housed in converted river lock building and restored Sayre Log House; exhibits trace the pioneer and river history of the area. Park, on the Ohio River, has picnicking and boat launching facilities. Museum (Memorial Day-Labor Day, Sun, limited hrs). Donation. Phone public library, 372-5343.

Annual Events

Mountaineer State Art & Craft Fair. Cedar Lakes Conference Center. Features traditional crafts, art, folk music and foods. Phone 372-7860 or -7866. Late June-early July.

West Virginia Black Walnut Festival. 25 mi E on US 33/119 in Spencer. Parade, carnival, band festival, car show, contests, livestock show, arts & crafts. Phone 927-1780. Mid-Oct.

(See Point Pleasant)

Motels

★ ★ **BEST WESTERN McCOYS.** *701 W Main St (US 33), I-77 exit 138.* 304/372-9122; FAX 304/372-4400. 127 rms, 2 story. S $46-$49; D $48-$52; each addl $4; under 12 free. Crib $3. TV; cable. Pool. Restaurant 5-10 pm. Rm serv. Private club; entertainment. Ck-out 11 am. Coin lndry. Meeting rms. Sundries. Cr cds: A, C, D, DS, ER, JCB, MC, V.

✇ ⋈ ⋈ ⚲ SC

✔ ★ **ECONO LODGE.** *1 Hospitality Dr, I-77 exit 138N.* 304/372-5000; FAX 304/372-5600. 43 rms, 2 story. S $36-$40; D $40-$44; each addl $4; under 12 free; higher rates Mountain State Arts & Crafts Fair. TV; cable. Complimentary continental bkfst, coffee. Restaurant adj 6:30 am-11 pm. Ck-out 11 am. Cr cds: A, C, D, DS, ER, JCB, MC, V.

D ⋈ ⚲ SC

Shepherdstown (B-8)

Settled: ca 1730 **Pop:** 1,287 **Elev:** 406 ft **Area code:** 304 **Zip:** 25443

In 1787, Shepherdstown was the site of the first successful public launching of a steamboat. James Rumsey, inventor of the craft, died, however, before he could exploit his success. Rival claims by John Fitch, and Robert Fulton's commercial success with the *Clermont* 20 years later, have beclouded Rumsey's achievement.

The state's first newspaper was published here in 1790, and Shepherdstown almost became the national capital. (George Washington considered it as a possible site, according to letters in the Library of Congress.) Shepherdstown is also the location of one of the early gristmills, which is believed to have been constructed around 1739 and finally ceased production in 1939. This is the oldest continuously settled town in the state.

What to See and Do

Historic Shepherdstown Museum. In old Entler Hotel (1786), German & Princess Sts. Artifacts dating to 1700s, including many items concerning the founding of the town. (Apr-Oct, Sat & Sun) Phone 876-0910. **Free.**

(For further information contact the Jefferson County Chamber of Commerce, 200 E Washington, PO Box 426, Charles Town 25414; 725-2055.)

(See Charles Town, Harpers Ferry, Martinsburg; also see Frederick, Hagerstown, MD)

Inns

★ ★ ★ **BAVARIAN INN AND LODGE.** *Rte 1, Box 30, ¼ mi N on WV 480 at the Potomac Bridge.* 304/876-2551; FAX 304/876-9355. 42 rms, 2 in main building, 1-3 story, 4 chalets. S, D $75-$145; each addl $10; under 12 free; wkday package rates; golf package. Crib $10. TV; cable. Heated pool. Complimentary coffee & tea avail. Dining rm (see BAVARIAN INN AND LODGE RESTAURANT). Bar 5 pm-midnight; Sun from 1 pm. Ck-out noon, ck-in 3 pm. Meeting rms. Tennis. Golf privileges, putting green. In-rm whirlpools, fireplaces. Many balconies. Main lodge is a converted greystone mansion overlooking Potomac River; 4 chalets reminiscent of old Bavarian inns. Cr cds: A, C, D, MC, V.

★ ★ ★ **THOMAS SHEPHERD INN.** *PO Box 1162, 300 W German St.* 304/876-3715. 6 rms, 2 story. S, D $85-$125. Children over 12 yrs only. Complimentary full bkfst, coffee & sherry. Restaurant nearby. Ck-out 11 am, ck-in 3 pm. Tennis & golf privileges. Fireplaces. Federal-style house (1868) on land originally owned by town founder Thomas Shepherd. Totally nonsmoking. Cr cds: A, DS, MC, V.

Restaurants

★ ★ ★ **BAVARIAN INN AND LODGE.** *(See Bavarian Inn And Lodge)* 304/876-2551. Hrs: 7:30-10:30 am, 11:30 am-2:30 pm, 5-10 pm; Sat from 4 pm; Sun noon-9 pm. Res accepted. German, continental menu. Bar 5 pm-midnight; Sun from 1 pm. Wine list. Semi-a la carte: bkfst $4.50-$8.50, lunch $4.75-$10.50, dinner $9.50-$22. Child's meals. Specialties: sauerbraten, vegetarian dishes, game specialties in season, fresh seafood. Own baking. Entertainment. Parking. Fireplaces. Antiques. Overlooks Potomac River. Family-owned. Cr cds: A, C, D, MC, V.

★ ★ **YELLOW BRICK BANK.** *201 German at Princess St, downtown.* 304/876-2208. Hrs: 11:30 am-10 pm; Sun brunch to 4 pm. Closed Thanksgiving, Dec 25. Res accepted. Bar. A la carte: lunch $5-$10, dinner $10-$20. Sun brunch $5-$10. Specializes in seafood, pasta. Own desserts. In 1910 bank building in historic commercial district. Overnight stays avail. Cr cds: C, D, MC, V.

Summersville (D-4)

Founded: 1824 **Pop:** 2,906 **Elev:** 1,894 ft **Area code:** 304 **Zip:** 26651

Twenty-year-old Nancy Hart led a surprise Confederate attack on Summersville in July of 1861, captured a Union force and burned the town. She was captured, but her jail guard succumbed to her charms. The guard was then disarmed and killed by the young woman. She escaped to Lee's lines. After the war, she returned to Summersville.

What to See and Do

1. **Gauley River National Recreation Area.** Designated a federally protected area in October, 1988, the 25-mile stretch of the Gauley from the Summersville Dam west to just above the town of Swiss is famous for whitewater rafting. There are no developed sites. Large tracts of land along river are privately owned. For further information and a list of whitewater outfitters contact Superintendent, New River Gorge National River, PO Box 246, Glen Jean 25846; 465-0508.

2. **Carnifex Ferry Battlefield State Park.** 12 mi W on WV 39, then SE on WV 129, near Kesslers Cross Lanes. Here on September 10, 1861, 5,000 Union troops under General William S. Rosecrans fought and defeated a lesser number of Confederates under General John B. Floyd. The 156-acre park includes Patteson House Museum, which displays Civil War relics. Hiking trails. Picnicking; game courts, playgrounds; concession. War re-enactments (June-Sept). Park (May-early Sept, daily). Phone 872-0825. **Free.**

3. **Summersville Lake.** 5 mi S on US 19. A 2,700-acre lake. Swimming, waterskiing; fishing; boating. Hiking. Picnicking. Battle Run

Campground is three miles west on WV 129 (fee/site/night). (May-Oct, daily) Fee for some activities. Phone 872-3459.

(For further information contact the Chamber of Commerce, 801 W Webster Rd, Suite 1, Box 567; 872-1588.)

Annual Events

Nicholas County Fair. 3 mi N at Nicholas County Memorial Park. Midway; flower show; agricultural and crafts exhibits. July.

Nicholas County Potato Festival. Citywide. Includes parades, entertainment, volleyball tournament, arts & crafts show, bed races. 2nd wk Sept.

(See Gauley Bridge)

Motels

✔ ★ **BEST WESTERN SUMMERSVILLE LAKE.** *1203 Broad St.* 304/872-6900. 59 rms, 3 story. May-Sept: S $43; D $46; each addl $5; under 12 free; lower rates rest of yr. Crib free. TV; cable. Complimentary continental bkfst. Restaurant 5-10 pm. Rm serv. Bar. Ck-out 11 am. Cr cds: A, C, D, DS, ER, JCB, MC, V.

★ ★ **COMFORT INN.** *903 Industrial Dr, 2 mi N on US 19 at jct WV 41.* 304/872-6500. 99 rms, 2 story. June-Oct: S $45-$60; D $50-$70; each addl $5; suites $85-$100; under 18 free; lower rates rest of yr. Crib free. Pet accepted, some restrictions; $5. TV; cable. Heated pool; wading pool. Complimentary continental bkfst. Restaurant nearby. Ck-out 11 am. Coin lndry. Meeting rm. Bellhops. Exercise equipt; weight machine, bicycles, whirlpool, sauna. Refrigerator in suites. Picnic tables. Cr cds: A, C, D, DS, ER, JCB, MC, V.

Restaurant

★ **COUNTRY ROAD INN.** *Country Rd, 8 mi W on WV 39.* 304/872-1620; res: 800/439-8852 (WV). Hrs: 5-8 pm; Fri & Sat to 8:30 pm; Sun 2-6 pm. Closed major hols. Res required. Italian menu. Wine. Complete meals: dinner $12.95-$23.95. Child's meals. Specialties: shrimp scampi, fettucine, lasagne. Own pasta. Parking. In restored 19th-century farmhouse; country setting. Cr cds: A, MC, V.

Sutton (C-4)

Settled: 1826 **Pop:** 939 **Elev:** 840 ft **Area code:** 304 **Zip:** 26601

What to See and Do

Sutton Lake. Dam is one mile east. Swimming in designated areas. Boat launch. Camping (May-Dec; some electric hookups; fees) at Gerald R. Freeman Campground, 16 miles east on WV 15; and at Mill Creek-Bakers Run Area, 16 miles southeast on WV 17. Phone 765-2816 or -2705 (recording).

Motel

✔ ★ **SUTTON LANE.** *4 mi N on US 19 (WV 4), just off I-79, Flatwoods exit 67.* 304/765-7351. 31 rms, 2 story. S $28.50; D $33; each addl $5; higher rates: hols, special events. TV; in-rm movies. Restaurant open 24 hrs. Ck-out 11 am. Meeting rm. Sundries. Private patios, balconies. Cr cds: A, D, MC, V.

Motor Hotel

★ ★ **DAYS INN.** *2000 Sutton Lane, I-79 exit 67. 304/765-5055; FAX 304/765-2067.* 100 units, 5 story. Mar-Nov: S $49.95-$54.95; D $54.95-$59.95; each addl $5; suites $100-$105; under 13 free; lower rates rest of yr. Crib free. TV; cable. Pool. Complimentary continental bkfst. Restaurant adj 6 am-10 pm. Bar 5 pm-midnight. Ck-out 11 am. Meeting rms. Sundries. Many balconies. Cr cds: A, C, D, DS, MC, V.

Webster Springs (D-5)

Settled: 1860 **Pop:** 990 (est) **Elev:** 1,509 ft **Area code:** 304 **Zip:** 26288

Once a resort famed for its medicinal "lick" or spring, the town is now a trading center and meeting place for sportsmen.

What to See and Do

1. **Holly River State Park.** 20 mi N on WV 20 to Hacker Valley, then 1 mi E. More than 8,000 acres of heavy forest with excellent trout fishing in Laurel Fork. Swimming pool, bathhouse. Hiking trails to waterfalls and Potato Knob; tennis, game courts. Picnicking, playground; restaurant (seasonal). Camping (dump station), 9 cabins. Nature, recreation programs (summer). Standard hrs, fees. Phone 493-6353.
2. **Kumbrabow State Forest.** 25 mi NE on WV 15, then 5 mi N, near Monterville. More than 9,400 acres of wild, rugged country with trout fishing and deer, turkey and grouse hunting. Hiking trails. Cross-country skiing. Picnicking, playground. Tent and trailer camping, 5 rustic cabins. Standard hrs, fees. Phone 335-2219.

(For further information contact the Mayor's Office, 146 McGraw Ave; 847-5411.)

Annual Events

Webster Springs Woodchopping Festival. Southeastern World Woodchopping Championships; state championship turkey calling contest, draft horse pull, horse show, fireman's rodeo; arts & crafts, music, parades, concessions. Phone 847-7666. Memorial Day wkend.

Webster County Fair. 11 mi S on WV 20 to 4-H Camp Caesar. Rides, agricultural exhibits, entertainers, horse show. Labor Day wk.

Weirton (A-5)

Founded: 1910 **Pop:** 22,124 **Elev:** 760 ft **Area code:** 304 **Zip:** 26062

Weirton has been a steel-producing town since its founding in 1910 by Ernest T. Weir, who also founded the Weirton Steel Company. In 1984, Weirton Steel became the largest employee-owned steel company in the world. Modern plants produce tin plate and hot-rolled, cold-rolled and galvanized steels for containers, automobiles, appliances and other products.

What to See and Do

1. **Tomlinson Run State Park.** 15 mi N off WV 8. Approximately 1,400 acres. Swimming pool, bathhouse; fishing, boating on 27-acre lake (rowboat and paddleboat rentals). Hiking trails; miniature golf, tennis. Picnicking, playground. Tent and trailer camping (dump station). Nature, recreation programs (summer). Standard hrs, fees. Phone 564-3651.

2. **Horse racing. Mountaineer Racetrack & Resort.** 12 mi N on WV 2. Thoroughbred racing on one-mile track; three restaurants. (Fri-Mon) Phone 387-2400.
3. **Industrial Tours. Weirton Steel Corp and Half Moon Industrial Park.** Tours of Weirton Steel Corp, Alpo and others. Contact Chamber of Commerce for details.

(For further information contact the Chamber of Commerce, 3147 West St; 748-7212.)

Annual Event

International Food & Arts Festival. Ethnic foods, circus, entertainment, amusement rides, arts & crafts, antique car show, exhibits. 3 days late June or early July.

(For accommodations see Wheeling; also see Pittsburgh, PA)

Weston (C-5)

Settled: 1784 **Pop:** 4,994 **Elev:** 1,009 ft **Area code:** 304 **Zip:** 26452

Surveyed originally by "Stonewall" Jackson's grandfather, Weston today is a center for coal, oil and gas production, as well as the manufacture of glass products. The Weston State Hospital, completed in 1880 and said to be the largest hand-cut stone building in the nation, is located in town.

What to See and Do

1. **Stonewall Jackson Lake & Dam.** Just S off I-79 exit 96, follow signs to dam. Approx 2,500-acre lake, with over 82 miles of shoreline, created by impounding the waters of the West Fork River. Swimming, scuba diving, waterskiing; fishing; boating (ramps, rentals, marinas). Picnicking. Camping. Visitor center. Phone 269-4588 or -0523.
2. **Stonewall Jackson Lake State Park.** 11 mi S on US 19. West Virginia's newest state park, with approximately 3,000 acres. Fishing; boating (launch, marina). Nature, fitness trails. Picnicking; playground. Camping (hookups). Visitor center. Standard hrs, fees. Phone 269-0523.
3. **Jackson's Mill State 4-H Conference Center.** 4 mi N off US 19. First camp of its kind in US; with 35 buildings, gardens, swimming pool, amphitheater, interfaith chapel. Picnicking. Phone 269-5100. Also here is

   Jackson's Mill Museum. "Stonewall" Jackson lived and worked here as a boy. Museum exhibits represent grist and saw milling, agriculture and home arts of the area as practiced 100 years ago. (June-Aug, daily) ¢
4. **Cedar Creek State Park.** 31 mi SW off US 33/119, near Glenville. More than 2,400 acres. Swimming pool, bathhouse; fishing; boating (rentals). Hiking trails; miniature golf; tennis, game courts. Picnicking, playground, concession. Tent and trailer camping (dump station). Park office in restored log cabin. Standard hrs, fees. Phone 462-7158.

(For further information contact the Lewis County Convention & Visitors Bureau, PO Box 379; 269-7328.)

Annual Events

Horse show. Trefz Farm, 3 mi E on US 33. Saddle, walking, harness, pony, western and Arabian riding. Phone 269-3257. Mid-July.

Stonewall Jackson Heritage Arts & Crafts Jubilee. Jackson's Mill State 4-H Camp (see #3). Mountain crafts, music, dance and food. Phone 269-1863. Labor Day wkend.

(See Buckhannon, Clarksburg)

Motel

✔ ★ ★ **COMFORT INN.** *Box 666, at jct US 33 & I-79. 304/269-7000.* 60 rms, 2 story. S $35-$44; D $47; each addl $6; under 16 free. Crib free. TV; cable. Heated pool. Restaurant 6 am-10 pm. Bar 5-11 pm. Ck-out noon. Meeting rm. Balconies. Cr cds: A, C, D, DS, ER, JCB, MC, V.

≋ ⇊ 🔥 SC

Wheeling (A-4)

Settled: 1769 **Pop:** 34,882 **Elev:** 678 ft **Area code:** 304 **Zip:** 26003

Wheeling stands on the site of Fort Henry, built in 1774 by Colonel Ebenezer Zane and his two brothers, who named the fort for Virginia's Governor Patrick Henry. In 1782, the fort was the scene of the final battle of the Revolutionary War, a battle in which the valiant, young pioneer Betty Zane was a heroine. The fort had withstood several Indian and British sieges during the war. However, during the last siege (after the war was officially ended), the defenders of the fort ran out of powder. Betty Zane, sister of the colonel, volunteered to run through the gunfire to the outlying Zane cabin for more. With the powder gathered in her apron, she made the 150-yard trek back to the fort and saved the garrison. Zane Grey, a descendant of the Zanes, wrote a novel about Betty and her exploit.

Today, Wheeling is home to many industries, including producers of steel, iron, tin, chemical products, pottery, glass, paper, tobacco, plastics and coal.

What to See and Do

1. **Site of Fort Henry.** Main St, near 11th St. Bronze plaque marks location of fort that Betty Zane saved.

2. **Oglebay Resort Park.** 3 mi NE of I-70, on WV 88. A 1,500-acre municipal park. Indoor, outdoor swimming pools; fishing, boating on 3-acre Schenk Lake. Three 18-hole golf courses, miniature golf; tennis courts. Picnicking, restaurant, snack shop. Cabins, lodge (see RESORT). Miniature train ride; 65-acre Good Children's Zoo (fee) with animals in natural habitat. Benedum Natural Science Theater; garden center; arboretum with four miles of walking paths; greenhouses; observatory. Fee for most activities. Phone 243-4000 or 800/624-6988. (See ANNUAL and SEASONAL EVENTS) Also in park are

    Ski area. 3 Pomalifts; rentals, snowmaking; snack shop. (Dec-Mar, daily) Phone 243-4000. ¢¢¢¢

    Mansion House Museum. Period rooms, exhibits trace history from 1835 to present. (Daily) Phone 242-7272. ¢¢

3. **Jamboree, USA.** Capitol Music Hall, 1015 Main St. Live country music shows presented by WWVA Radio since 1933. (Sat; 2 nightly performances) Phone 234-0050 (ticket reservations). ¢¢¢¢

4. **Wheeling Park.** 5 mi E on US 40. Approximately 400 acres. Swimming pool, water slide; boating on Good Lake. Golf, miniature golf, indoor/outdoor tennis. Ice-skating (rentals). Picnicking, playground, refreshment area with video screen and lighted dance floor. Aviary. Fees for activities. (Daily; some facilities seasonal) Phone 242-3770.

5. **West Virginia Independence Hall-Custom House** (1859). 16th & Market Sts. Site of meeting at which Virginia's secession from the Union was declared unlawful, and the independent state of West Virginia was created. The building, used as a post office, custom office and Federal court until 1912, has been restored. It now houses exhibits and events relating to the state's cultural heritage, including an interpretive film and rooms with period furniture. (Mar-Dec, daily; rest of yr, daily exc Sun; closed state hols) Phone 238-1300. **Free.**

6. **Grave Creek Mound State Park.** 9 mi S via WV 2, on Jefferson Ave in Moundsville. Features nation's largest prehistoric Adena burial mound—79 feet high, 900 feet around, 50 feet across the top. Some excavating was done in 1838; exhibits in Delf Norona Museum & Cultural Center (daily; fee). Phone 843-1410.

(For further information contact the Convention & Visitors Bureau, 1233 Main St, Suite 1000; 233-7709.)

Annual Events

Jamboree In The Hills. 15 mi W off I-70 exit 208 or 213, in St Clairsville, OH. A 4-day country music festival featuring more than 30 hours of music; top country stars. Camping avail. Phone 800/624-5456. 3rd wkend July.

Oglebayfest. Oglebay Resort Park (see #2). Country fair, artists' market, fireworks, parade, ethnic foods, contests, square & round dancing, entertainment. Phone 243-4000. 1st wkend Oct.

Seasonal Event

Festival of Lights. Oglebay Resort Park (see #2). A 350-acre lighting display featuring lighted buildings, holiday themes with more than 500,000 lights, including 28-foot candy canes and giant swans on Schenk Lake. Winter Fantasy in Good Zoo. Nov-Feb.

Motel

(Rates are usually higher for Jamboree In The Hills)

★ ★ **DAYS INN.** *(RD 1, Box 292, Triadelphia 26059) 9 mi E, at I-70 exit 11. 304/547-0610; FAX 304/547-9029.* 106 rms, 2 story. S, D $44-$52; each addl $6; under 18 free. Crib free. Pet accepted. TV. Pool. Restaurant 7 am-2 pm, 5-10 pm. Rm serv. Bar 5 pm-1 am, closed Sun. Ck-out noon. Meeting rm. Valet serv. Cr cds: A, C, D, DS, MC, V.

D 🐾 ≋ ⇊ 🔥 SC

Hotel

✔ ★ **BEST WESTERN WHEELING INN.** *949 Main St. 304/233-8500.* 80 rms, 5 story. S $44.75-$57.75; D $51.75-$57.75; each addl $8; suites $105.50; under 12 free. Crib free. TV; cable. Complimentary continental bkfst. Restaurant 11 am-10 pm. Bar 11-2 am; dancing. Ck-out noon. Free valet parking. Whirlpool, sauna. Cr cds: A, C, D, DS, JCB, MC, V.

⇊ 🔥 SC

Resort

★ ★ ★ **OGLEBAY'S WILSON LODGE.** *WV 88, 3 mi NE of I-70 exit 2A. 304/243-4000; res: 800/624-6988; FAX 304/243-4070.* 204 rms in 2-story lodge, chalets; 36 kit. cabins (2-6 bedrm). S $78-$110; D $88-$122; suites $95-$140; kit. cabins $520-$1,195/wk; ski, golf packages. Crib $5. TV. 2 pools, 1 indoor; wading pool, poolside serv, lifeguard. Playground. Supervised child's activities (June-Sept). Dining rm 7:30-11 am, noon-2:30 pm, 5-9 pm. Box lunches, snack bar. Private club noon-midnight. Ck-out 1 pm, ck-in 3 pm. Grocery ½ mi. Package store 2 mi. Meeting rms. Airport, bus depot transportation. 11 lighted tennis courts, pro. Two 18-hole golf courses, greens fee $15-$28, par-3 golf, pro, driving range, miniature golf. Stocked lake. Paddleboats. Downhill ski ½ mi. Sleighing, tobogganing. Lawn games. Children's zoo. Stables. Exercise rm; instructor, weight machine, stair machine, whirlpool. Some fireplaces. Some private patios, balconies. Picnic tables, grills. Mansion museum, garden center. Rustic setting in Oglebay Park. Cr cds: A, D, DS, MC, V.

D 🐾 ⛷ 🏃 ⛸ 🎿 🚶 ⛸ ⇊ 🔥 SC

Restaurants

★ ★ **CORK'N BOTTLE.** *39 12th St. 304/232-4400.* Hrs: 11 am-midnight; Fri, Sat to 2 am; major hols from 5 pm. Closed Dec 25. Res accepted. Bar 11-2 am; Sun 5 pm-midnight. Semi-a la carte: lunch $2.95-$4.95, dinner $5.95-$19.95. Child's meals. Specialties: coquilles, Greek kebab. Salad bar. Entertainment. New Orleans decor; paddle fans. Family-owned. Cr cds: A, D, DS, MC, V.

D

★ ★ ★ **ERNIE'S ESQUIRE.** *Bethlehem Blvd, 1¼ mi off I-70 on WV 88S. 304/242-2800.* Hrs: 11 am-midnight; Fri to 1 am; Sat to 2 am; Sun to 10:30 pm; Sun brunch to 2 pm. Closed Dec 25. Res accepted. Continental menu. Bar. Wine list. Semi-a la carte: lunch $3.75-$8.45, dinner $8.95-$26.95. Sun brunch $7.95. Child's meals. Specialties: lobster Fra Diavolo, fresh seafood, beef. Own baking. Entertainment Fri & Sat. Valet parking. 6 rms, each with different decor. Family-owned. Cr cds: A, C, D, DS, MC, V.

D

White Sulphur Springs (E-5)

Settled: 1750 **Pop:** 2,779 **Elev:** 1,923 ft **Area code:** 304 **Zip:** 24986

In the 18th century White Sulphur Springs became a fashionable destination for rich and famous colonists, who came for the "curative" powers of the mineral waters. It has, for the most part, remained a popular resort ever since. A number of US presidents summered in the town in the days before air conditioning made Washington habitable in hot weather. The John Tylers spent their honeymoon at the famous "Old White" Hotel. In 1913 the Old White Hotel gave way to the present Greenbrier Hotel (see RESORT), where President Wilson honeymooned with the second Mrs. Wilson. During World War II the hotel served as an internment camp for German and Japanese diplomats and, later, as a hospital.

The first golf course in America was laid out near the town in 1884, but the first game was delayed when golf clubs, imported from Scotland, were held for three weeks by customs men, who were suspicious of a game played with "such elongated blackjacks or implements of murder."

A Ranger District office of the Monongahela National Forest (see ELKINS) is located in the town.

What to See and Do

1. **Fishing, swimming, boating, camping, hiking.** In Monongahela National Forest (see ELKINS): Blue Bend Recreation Area, 6 mi N on WV 92, then 4 mi W on WV 16/21 ; Lake Sherwood Recreation Area, 23 mi N via WV 92, then 11 mi NE on WV 14. Phone 536-2144. Camping ¢¢¢-¢¢¢¢

2. **National Fish Hatchery.** 400 E Main St, on US 60. Rainbow trout in raceways and ponds. Visitor center has display pool, aquariums and exhibits. (Memorial Day-Labor Day, daily) Phone 536-1361. **Free.**

3. **Memorial Park.** Greenbrier Ave. Swimming pool (Memorial Day-Labor Day; fee). Tennis courts, ball fields, track, horseshoe pits, playground. (Daily) **Free.**

4. **Greenbrier State Forest.** 3 mi W on US 60, then 1½ mi S on Harts Run Rd. More than 5,100 acres. Swimming pool (Memorial Day-Labor Day); bass fishing in Greenbrier River; hunting. Hiking trails. Picnicking, playground. Tent and trailer camping, 12 cabins. Nature, recreation programs (summer). Standard hrs, fees. Phone 536-1944.

(For further information contact the Chamber of Commerce, PO Box 11; 536-2500.)

(See Lewisburg; also see Covington, VA)

Motel

(Rates are generally higher during state fair)

 ★ ★ **OLD WHITE.** *Box 58, 865 E Main St. 304/536-2441.* 26 rms. S $35; D $46; each addl $3. Crib free. Pet accepted, some restrictions. TV; cable. Heated pool. Restaurant adj 11 am-11 pm. Ck-out noon. Cr cds: A, D, DS, MC, V.

Resort

★ ★ ★ ★ ★ **THE GREENBRIER.** *½ mi W on US 60. 304/536-1110; res: 800/624-6070; FAX 304/536-7834.* 699 rms in hotel, 6 story, 103 guest house rms. MAP, Apr-Oct: S, D, guest rms, cottages $189-$273/person; each addl $115; children under 18 free; tennis, golf, wkend package plans; lower rates rest of yr. Service charge $14.25 per person. Crib free. TV; cable. 2 pools, 1 indoor; wading pool, poolside serv, lifeguard. Playground. Supervised child's activities. Dining rm 7:30 am-6 pm; restaurant (see THE GREENBRIER MAIN DINING ROOM, public by res). Box lunches, snack bar. Rm serv 24 hrs. Private club noon-1 am; entertainment, dancing. Ck-out noon, ck-in 3 pm. Convention facilities. Airport, RR station, bus depot transportation. Sports dir. 5 indoor, 15 outdoor tennis courts, pro. Lighted, heated platform tennis. Three 18-hole golf courses, greens fee $80, cart $35, pro, 2 putting greens, driving range. X-country ski on site. Ice-skating. Horse-drawn sleighing. Fitness trail. Bicycling. Lawn games. Trap shooting. British regulation croquet court. Stables; English saddles. Soc dir; movies, dancing, entertainment. Bowling; indoor games. Full-service health spa. Exercise rm; instructor, weight machines, bicycles, whirlpool, sauna, steam rm. Massage. Some refrigerators; fireplace in cottages. Private patios, balconies. Elegant furnishings, decor. Cr cds: A, C, D, DS, MC, V.

Restaurant

★ ★ ★ ★ **THE GREENBRIER MAIN DINING ROOM.** *(See The Greenbrier Resort) 304/536-1110.* Hrs: 7:30-10 am, 6:30-9 pm. Res required. Continental menu. Private club noon-1 am. Wine cellar. Prix fixe: bkfst $18.25, dinner $57.50. Service charge 15%; addl service charge for alcoholic beverages. Child's meals. Specialties: veal medallions with creamed morrels, roast Long Island duckling, fresh North Carolina seafood. Own baking. Chamber music at dinner. Valet parking. Formal dining. 1880s decor; sculptures, artwork, floral art. Jacket, tie evenings. Cr cds: A, C, D, DS, MC, V.

D

Index

Establishment names are listed in alphabetical order followed by a symbol identifying their classification, and then city, state and page number. Establishments affiliated with a chain appear alphabetically under their chain name, followed by the state, city and page number. The symbols for classification are: [H] for hotels; [I] for inns; [M] for motels; [L] for lodges; [MH] for motor hotels; [R] for restaurants; [RO] for resorts, guest ranches, and cottage colonies; [U] for unrated dining spots. States are arranged alphabetically as are the cities and towns within each state.

OVERLOOK INN [R] *Canadensis PA*, 231
OWENS' [R] *Nags Head (Outer Banks) NC*, 200
OX YOKE INN [M] *Galeton PA*, 242
OYSTER POINT [H] *Red Bank NJ*, 149
P.J. SKIDOO'S [R] *Fairfax VA*, 371
PADDLEWHEEL [M] *Crisfield MD*, 94
PAGE HOUSE [I] *Norfolk VA*, 397
THE PALACE [H] *Myrtle Beach SC*, 337
PALISADIUM [R] *Fort Lee NJ*, 130
PALLADIN BY JEAN-LOUIS [R] *Washington DC*, 71
PALM [R] *Washington DC*, 71
THE PALM [R] *Philadelphia PA*, 282
PALM COURT [U] *Pittsburgh PA*, 291
PALM CREST [M] *Myrtle Beach SC*, 335
PALMETTO DUNES [RO] *Hilton Head Island SC*, 333
PALOMINO [M] *Sanford NC*, 208
PAMLICO HOUSE [I] *Washington NC*, 212
PAN AMERICAN HOTEL [M] *Wildwood & Wildwood Crest NJ*, 158
PAN AMERICAN MOTOR INN [MH] *Myrtle Beach SC*, 336
PAN TAI [R] *Wilmington DE*, 50
PANDA RESTAURANT [R] *Gaithersburg MD*, 100
PANJSHIR [R] *Falls Church VA*, 372
PANJSHIR II [R] *Tysons Corner VA*, 415
PAOLO'S [R] *Washington DC*, 71
PAPILLON [R] *Charleston SC*, 321
THE PARK HOTEL [H] *Charlotte NC*, 176
PARK INN INTERNATIONAL
    South Carolina
        Anderson, [M] 313
    Virginia
        Virginia Beach, [H] 417
PARK LANE HOTEL/FOUR SEASONS [MH] *Greensboro NC*, 187
PARKER'S BAR-B-QUE [R] *Greenville NC*, 188
PARKHURST [R] *Luray VA*, 387
PARKWAY INN [M] *Waynesville NC*, 212
PARSONAGE INN [I] *St Michaels MD*, 110
THE PASADENA INN [I] *St Michaels MD*, 110
PASTA & COMPANY [R] *Willow Grove PA*, 308
PASTA HOUSE [R] *Anderson SC*, 313
PASTA PIATTO [R] *Pittsburgh PA*, 290
PAT & MIKE'S [R] *Gaithersburg MD*, 100
PATISSERIE-CAFE DIDIER [U] *Washington DC*, 73
PATUXENT INN [MH] *St Mary's City MD*, 110
PAVILION [M] *Ocean City NJ*, 144
PEACHES AT SUNSET [R] *Cape May NJ*, 125
PEACOCK INN [I] *Princeton NJ*, 148
PEAKS OF OTTER [R] *Blue Ridge Parkway VA*, 358
PEAKS OF OTTER LODGE [M] *Blue Ridge Parkway VA*, 358
PECAN TREE INN [I] *Beaufort NC*, 166
PEERCE'S PLANTATION [R] *Towson MD*, 113
PEKING [R] *Williamsburg VA*, 425
PEKING DUCK HOUSE [R] *Atlantic City NJ*, 120
PEKING GARDEN [R] *Raleigh NC*, 206
PEKING GOURMET INN [R] *Falls Church VA*, 372
PEKING PALACE [R] *Cumberland MD*, 95
PEKING PAVILION [R] *Richmond VA*, 406
PENCE SPRINGS HOTEL [I] *Hinton WV*, 442
PENGUIN ISLE [R] *Nags Head (Outer Banks) NC*, 200

PENN ALPS [R] *Grantsville MD*, 100
PENN HARRIS INN [M] *Harrisburg PA*, 248
PENN'S VIEW [I] *Philadelphia PA*, 280
PENN-WELLS [H] *Wellsboro PA*, 305
PENN-WELLS LODGE [M] *Wellsboro PA*, 305
PER FAVORE [R] *Pittsburgh PA*, 290
PERFECT REST [M] *Gettysburg PA*, 244
PERIWINKLE INN [M] *Cape May NJ*, 124
PERNA'S [R] *Hawley PA*, 249
PERSEPOLIS [R] *Bethesda MD*, 90
PETITTO'S RISTORANTE D'ITALIA [R] *Washington DC*, 71
THE PHARMACY [R] *Southport NC*, 210
PHILIPPI INN [R] *Philippi WV*, 449
PHILLIPS BEACH PLAZA [MH] *Ocean City MD*, 106
PHILLIPS CRAB HOUSE [R] *Ocean City MD*, 107
PHILLIPS FLAGSHIP [R] *Washington DC*, 71
PHILLIPS SEAFOOD HOUSE [R] *Ocean City MD*, 107
PHILLIPS WATERSIDE [R] *Norfolk VA*, 398
PHOENIX PARK [H] *Washington DC*, 66
PICCADILLY CAFETERIA
    South Carolina
        Charleston, [U] 321
PICCOLO MONDO [R] *Pittsburgh PA*, 290
PIER 4 ON THE BAY [M] *Ocean City NJ*, 144
PIER 61 LTD [R] *Charleston SC*, 321
PIERRE ET MADELEINE [R] *Tysons Corner VA*, 415
PILOT HOUSE [R] *Wilmington NC*, 215
PINE ACRES LODGE [M] *Laurinburg NC*, 194
PINE BARN [I] *Danville PA*, 236
PINE BARN INN [R] *Danville PA*, 236
PINE CREST [I] *Pinehurst NC*, 203
PINE CREST [I] *Tryon NC*, 211
PINE CREST INN [R] *Tryon NC*, 211
PINE HILL FARM [I] *Milford PA*, 266
PINE KNOB [I] *Canadensis PA*, 231
PINE NEEDLES [RO] *Southern Pines NC*, 209
PINE RIDGE INN [I] *Pilot Mountain NC*, 202
PINEHURST RESORT AND COUNTRY CLUB [RO] *Pinehurst NC*, 203
PINES [M] *Crisfield MD*, 94
PINNACLE INN [M] *Banner Elk NC*, 166
PIPESTEM [RO] *Hinton WV*, 442
PIRANHA-AN EATING FRENZY [R] *Norfolk VA*, 398
PISGAH VIEW RANCH [RO] *Asheville NC*, 165
PITTSBURGH PLAZA [M] *Pittsburgh Intl Airport Area PA*, 291
PIXIE MOTOR INN [M] *Linville NC*, 195
PIZZERIA PARADISO [R] *Washington DC*, 71
PIZZERIA UNO [U] *Pittsburgh PA*, 291
PLAIN & FANCY FARM [R] *Bird-in-Hand PA*, 227
THE PLANTATION INN RESORT [M] *Raleigh NC*, 204
PLANTERS [I] *Charleston SC*, 320
PLAZA HOTEL [H] *Virginia Beach VA*, 417
PLAZA NINE [R] *Dover DE*, 42
PLIM PLAZA [MH] *Ocean City MD*, 106
POCONO FOUNTAIN [M] *Mount Pocono PA*, 267
POCONO GARDENS LODGE [RO] *Mount Pocono PA*, 267
POCONO MANOR [RO] *Mount Pocono PA*, 267
POCONO MOUNTAIN LODGE [M] *White Haven PA*, 306
POINT BEACH [M] *Spring Lake NJ*, 153
POINT OF VIEW [R] *Parkersburg WV*, 448

POINT VIEW INN [R] *Oakland (Garrett Co) MD*, 104
POLI'S [R] *Pittsburgh PA*, 290
PONY ISLAND [M] *Ocracoke (Outer Banks) NC*, 202
POOGAN'S PORCH [R] *Charleston SC*, 321
PORT [M] *Southport NC*, 210
PORT ARTHUR [R] *Newport News VA*, 395
PORT O' CALL [R] *Kill Devil Hills (Outer Banks) NC*, 193
PORT ROYAL [M] *Wildwood & Wildwood Crest NJ*, 158
PORT-O-CALL [MH] *Ocean City NJ*, 144
POSITANO [R] *Wilmington DE*, 50
PRIME RIB [R] *Washington DC*, 71
PRIME RIB [R] *Baltimore MD*, 87
PRIMI PIATTI [R] *Washington DC*, 71
PRIMI PIATTI [R] *Tysons Corner VA*, 415
PRIMO [R] *Hilton Head Island SC*, 334
PRINCESS ROYALE [H] *Ocean City MD*, 106
THE PRIORY [I] *Pittsburgh PA*, 289
PROSPECT HILL PLANTATION [I] *Charlottesville VA*, 361
PUFFERBELLY [R] *Erie PA*, 241
PUMP HOUSE [I] *Canadensis PA*, 231
PUMP HOUSE INN [R] *Canadensis PA*, 231
PUNGO GRILL [R] *Virginia Beach VA*, 418
QUAKER STEAK & LUBE [R] *Sharon PA*, 296
QUALITY INN
    Delaware
        New Castle, [M] 45
    District of Columbia
        Washington, [MH] 62, [H] 66
    Maryland
        Ocean City, [M] 105; Pocomoke City, [M] 108
    New Jersey
        Atlantic City, [H] 119; Jersey City, [MH] 134; Rutherford, [M] 150; Toms River, [M] 154
    North Carolina
        Asheville, [MH] 164; Boone, [H] 169; Fayetteville, [M] 183; Nags Head (Outer Banks), [M] 199; Raleigh, [MH] 204; Wilkesboro, [M] 213
    Pennsylvania
        Bedford, [M] 225; Bloomsburg, [M] 228; Breezewood, [M] 228; Gettysburg, [M] 244; Lebanon, [MH] 262; Williamsport, [M] 307
    South Carolina
        Charleston, [MH] 318; Greenville, [M] 329; Spartanburg, [MH] 341
    Virginia
        Arlington County (National Airport Area), [MH] 352, [H] 353; Falls Church, [M] 372; Front Royal, [M] 376; New Market, [M] 394; Petersburg, [M] 399; Salem, [M] 409; Virginia Beach, [H] 417; Williamsburg, [M] 423
QUARTERPATH INN [M] *Williamsburg VA*, 423
QUEEN ANNE'S REVENGE [R] *Manteo NC*, 197
QUEEN BEE [R] *Arlington County (National Airport Area) VA*, 354
QUEEN VICTORIA [I] *Cape May NJ*, 125
QUO VADIS [I] *Franklin (Venango Co) PA*, 242
RADISSON
    Maryland
        Baltimore, [H] 86

Mobil Travel Guide

Order Form

If you would like other editions of the MOBIL TRAVEL GUIDES that might not be available at your local bookstore or Mobil dealer, please use this order form or call the toll-free number below.

Ship to:

Name _____

Address _____

City _____ State _____ Zip _____

☐ My check is enclosed.

☐ Please charge my credit card

    ☐ VISA ☐ MasterCard ☐ American Express

Credit Card # _____

Expiration _____

Signature _____

Please send me the following 1995 Mobil Travel Guides:

☐ 0-679-02851-X
California and the West (Arizona, California, Nevada, Utah)
$13.95 (Can $18.95)

☐ 0-679-02852-8
Great Lakes (Illinois, Indiana, Michigan, Ohio, Wisconsin, Canada: Ontario)
$13.95 (Can $18.95)

☐ 0-679-02853-6
Mid-Atlantic (Delaware, District of Columbia, Maryland, New Jersey, North Carolina, Pennsylvania, South Carolina, Virginia, West Virginia)
$13.95 (Can $18.95)

☐ 0-679-02854-4
Northeast (Connecticut, Maine, Massachusetts, New Hampshire, New York, Rhode Island, Vermont, Canada: New Brunswick, Nova Scotia, Ontario, Prince Edward Island, Québec)
$13.95 (Can $18.95)

☐ 0-679-02857-9
Northwest and Great Plains (Idaho, Iowa, Minnesota, Montana, Nebraska, North Dakota, Oregon, South Dakota, Washington, Wyoming, Canada: Alberta, British Columbia, Manitoba)
$13.95 (Can $18.95)

☐ 0-679-02855-2
Southeast (Alabama, Florida, Georgia, Kentucky, Mississippi, Tennessee)
$13.95 (Can $18.95)

☐ 0-679-02856-0
Southwest & South Central (Arkansas, Colorado, Kansas, Louisiana, Missouri, New Mexico, Oklahoma, Texas)
$13.95 (Can $18.95)

☐ 0-679-02858-7
Frequent Traveler's Guide to Major Cities (Detailed coverage of 46 major U.S. cities, plus airport maps)
$14.95 (Can $19.95)

Total cost of book(s) ordered $ _____

Shipping & Handling (please add $2 for first book, $.50 for each additional book) $ _____

Add applicable sales tax* $ _____

TOTAL AMOUNT ENCLOSED $ _____

*To ensure that all orders are processed efficiently, please apply sales tax in Canada and in the following states: CA, CT, FL, IL, NJ, NY, TN and WA.

Please mail this form to:

Mobil Travel Guides
Random House
400 Hahn Rd.
Westminster, MD 21157
**or call toll-free, 24 hours
a day 1-800-533-6478**

Mobil Travel Guide

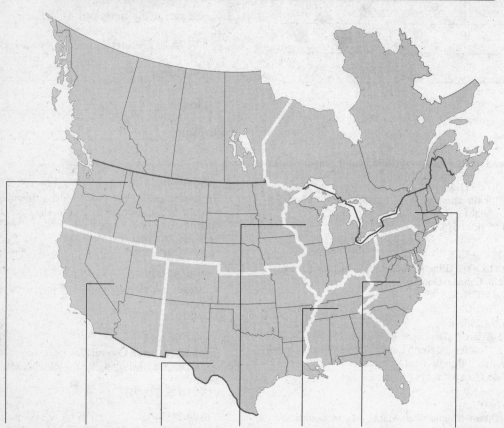

Northwest and Great Plains
Idaho
Iowa
Minnesota
Montana
Nebraska
North Dakota
Oregon
South Dakota
Washington
Wyoming
Canada:
Alberta
British Columbia
Manitoba

California and the West
Arizona
California
Nevada
Utah

Southwest and South Central
Arkansas
Colorado
Kansas
Louisiana
Missouri
New Mexico
Oklahoma
Texas

Great Lakes
Illinois
Indiana
Michigan
Ohio
Wisconsin
Canada:
Ontario

Southeast
Alabama
Florida
Georgia
Kentucky
Mississippi
Tennessee

Middle Atlantic
Delaware
District of Columbia
Maryland
New Jersey
North Carolina
Pennsylvania
South Carolina
Virginia
West Virginia

Northeast
Connecticut
Maine
Massachusetts
New Hampshire
New York
Rhode Island
Vermont
Canada:
Atlantic Provinces
Ontario
Quebec

YOU CAN HELP MAKE THE *MOBIL TRAVEL GUIDES* MORE ACCURATE AND USEFUL

ALL INFORMATION WILL BE KEPT CONFIDENTIAL

Your Name_____
(Please Print)

Street_____

City, State, Zip_____

Were children with you on trip? ☐ Yes ☐ No

Number of people in your party _____

Your occupation_____

1.

Establishment name_____

Hotel ☐ Resort ☐ Cafeteria ☐
Motel ☐ Inn ☐ Restaurant ☐

Street_____ City_____ State _____

Do you agree with our description? ☐ Yes ☐ No If not, give reason_____

Please give us your opinion of the following:

ROOM DECOR	CLEANLINESS	SERVICE	FOOD
☐ Excellent	☐ Spotless	☐ Excellent	☐ Excellent
☐ Good	☐ Clean	☐ Good	☐ Good
☐ Fair	☐ Unclean	☐ Fair	☐ Fair
☐ Poor	☐ Dirty	☐ Poor	☐ Poor

1995 *GUIDE* RATING _____ ★
CHECK YOUR SUGGESTED RATING BELOW:
☐ ★ good, satisfactory ☐ ★★★★ outstanding
☐ ★★ very good ☐ ★★★★★ one of best
☐ ★★★ excellent in country
☐ ✓ unusually good value

Comments:_____

Date of visit_____

First visit? ☐ Yes ☐ No

2.

Establishment name_____

Hotel ☐ Resort ☐ Cafeteria ☐
Motel ☐ Inn ☐ Restaurant ☐

Street_____ City_____ State _____

Do you agree with our description? ☐ Yes ☐ No If not, give reason_____

Please give us your opinion of the following:

ROOM DECOR	CLEANLINESS	SERVICE	FOOD
☐ Excellent	☐ Spotless	☐ Excellent	☐ Excellent
☐ Good	☐ Clean	☐ Good	☐ Good
☐ Fair	☐ Unclean	☐ Fair	☐ Fair
☐ Poor	☐ Dirty	☐ Poor	☐ Poor

1995 *GUIDE* RATING _____ ★
CHECK YOUR SUGGESTED RATING BELOW:
☐ ★ good, satisfactory ☐ ★★★★ outstanding
☐ ★★ very good ☐ ★★★★★ one of best
☐ ★★★ excellent in country
☐ ✓ unusually good value

Comments:_____

Date of visit_____

First visit? ☐ Yes ☐ No

3.

Establishment name_____

Hotel ☐ Resort ☐ Cafeteria ☐
Motel ☐ Inn ☐ Restaurant ☐

Street_____ City_____ State _____

Do you agree with our description? ☐ Yes ☐ No If not, give reason_____

Please give us your opinion of the following:

ROOM DECOR	CLEANLINESS	SERVICE	FOOD
☐ Excellent	☐ Spotless	☐ Excellent	☐ Excellent
☐ Good	☐ Clean	☐ Good	☐ Good
☐ Fair	☐ Unclean	☐ Fair	☐ Fair
☐ Poor	☐ Dirty	☐ Poor	☐ Poor

1995 *GUIDE* RATING _____ ★
CHECK YOUR SUGGESTED RATING BELOW:
☐ ★ good, satisfactory ☐ ★★★★ outstanding
☐ ★★ very good ☐ ★★★★★ one of best
☐ ★★★ excellent in country
☐ ✓ unusually good value

Comments:_____

Date of visit_____

First visit? ☐ Yes ☐ No

FOLD AND TAPE (OR SEAL) FOR MAILING–DO NOT STAPLE

CUT ALONG DOTTED LINE

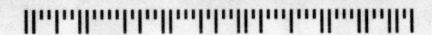

95

Revised editions are now being prepared for publication next year:

California and the West: Arizona, California, Nevada, Utah

Northeast: Connecticut, Maine, Massachusetts, New Hampshire, New York, Rhode Island, Vermont; Eastern Canada.

Mid-Atlantic: Delaware, District of Columbia, Maryland, New Jersey, North Carolina, Pennsylvania, South Carolina, Virginia, West Virginia.

Southeast: Alabama, Florida, Georgia, Kentucky, Mississippi, Tennessee.

Great Lakes: Illinois, Indiana, Michigan, Ohio, Wisconsin; Ontario, Canada.

Northwest: Idaho, Iowa, Minnesota, Montana, Nebraska, North Dakota, Oregon, South Dakota, Washington, Wyoming; Western Canada.

Southwest: Arkansas, Colorado, Kansas, Louisiana, Missouri, New Mexico, Oklahoma, Texas.

Frequent Traveler's Guide to Major Cities: Detailed coverage of 46 Major Cities, plus airport maps.

Mobil Travel Guides are available at Mobil Service Stations, bookstores, or by mail from Mobil Travel Guides, Random House, 400 Hahn Rd., Westminster, MD 21157, or call toll-free, 24 hours a day, 1-800-533-6478.

HOW CAN WE IMPROVE *MOBIL TRAVEL GUIDES*?

Mobil Travel Guides are constantly revising and improving. All attractions are updated and all listings are revised and evaluated annually. You can contribute to the accuracy and usefulness of the guides by sending us your reactions to the places you have visited. Your suggestions for improvement of the guides are also welcome. Just complete this prepaid mailing form or address letters to: *Mobil Travel Guide,* 4709 West Golf Rd., Suite 803, Skokie, IL 60076. The editors of the *Mobil Travel Guides* appreciate your useful comments.

Have you sent us one of these forms before?   ☐ Yes   ☐ No

Please make any general comment here. Thanks! _____

_____

_____

_____

Mobil Travel Guide.

The Guide That Saves You Money When You Travel.

Read each coupon carefully before using. Discounts only apply to the items and terms specified in the offer at participating locations. Remove the coupon you wish to use.

CHOICE HOTELS
INTERNATIONAL

Friendship | Econo Lodge | RODEWAY

With your 10% Mobil Traveler's Discount, the Choices - and savings - are better. So, call **1-800-4-CHOICE** today!

TASTE PUBLICATIONS INTERNATIONAL

Terms and Conditions: 1) Receive a One Car Class Leisure Upgrade when you reserve a Compact 2-Door (Class A) through Full Size 2-Door (Class D) car on any Hertz Leisure daily, weekly or weekend rate. 2) Maximum upgrade is from Full Size 2-Door (Class D) to Full Size 4-Door (Class F). 3) This offer is redeemable at participating Hertz corporate airport locations in the U.S. and participating licensee locations, subject to vehicle availability, and advance reservation is required. Request PC# 52021 at time of reservation. 4) Standard blackout dates apply. 5) This coupon has no cash value, must be surrendered at the time of rental pick-up and may not be used with any other coupon, offer, promotion, or discount. 6) Hertz rate and rental conditions for renting location apply and the car must be returned to that location. 7) Minimum rental age is 25 and Hertz standard driver qualifications apply. 8) Only one coupon will be honored per rental transaction; taxes and optional items, such as refueling are extra. 9) Coupon expires December 31, 1995.

TASTE PUBLICATIONS INTERNATIONAL

Sea World
California • Florida • Ohio • Texas

SESAME PLACE

TASTE PUBLICATIONS INTERNATIONAL

---

sbarro®

TASTE PUBLICATIONS INTERNATIONAL

Mail check for $91.98* for each set to: Merchandise Order Center, 929 N Plum Grove Road, Schaumburg, IL 60173-9797 1-800-788-1808 (8am - 4pm CT)

Name: _____

Address: _____

City: _____ State: _____ Zip: _____

VISA   MasterCard   (please circle one)

Acct. #: _____

Exp. Date: _____ Signature: _____

TASTE PUBLICATIONS INTERNATIONAL

Please indicate: Black, Green, or Gray
* IL residents add sales tax.   004   109/82

❑ Yes! I want to preserve and protect our National Parks by becoming a National Parks and Conservation Association Member.
  ❑ I enclose a check for $15 for my one-year membership.
❑ Charge my annual dues to my ❑ Visa ❑ MasterCard ❑ Amex

Acct. #: _____

Signature: _____

Name: _____

Address: _____

City: _____ State: _____ Zip: _____

Phone: _____

TASTE PUBLICATIONS INTERNATIONAL

Make checks payable and mail to:
NPCA, 1776 Massachusetts Ave. NW
Washington, DC 20036-1904 **GRA95**

ONE HOUR
MOTO*PHOTO*®

TASTE PUBLICATIONS INTERNATIONAL

TASTE PUBLICATIONS INTERNATIONAL

Mobil Travel Guide®
The Guide That Saves You Money When You Travel.

THE COMFORTABLE LANDMARK™
Plazas · Hotels · Park Square Inns · Lodges · HoJo Inns

SAVE UP TO $150

You can save 10% off our standard rates, for up to 7 nights, at any of 600 Howard Johnson Plazas, Hotels, Park Square Inns, Lodges, and HoJo Inns in the United States, Canada and Mexico. Kids always stay free and can play free with Sega™ video games all summer long. Just call 1-800-I-GO-HOJO (800-446-4656) for reservations and request the TravelDeal discount, code "STD".

Advance reservations recommended. Offer may not be available during holidays and special events; cannot be combined with other offers and discounts. Certain restrictions apply.

OFFER EXPIRES DECEMBER 31, 1995

$1.00 OFF

This coupon entitles you to $1.00 off any Footlong Sub.

Valid at participating locations. Offer cannot be combined or used in conjunction with any other promotion. One coupon per visit, please.

© 1994 Doctor's Associates, Inc.

OFFER EXPIRES DECEMBER 31, 1995

Museum of Science and Industry

57th Street and Lake Shore Drive, Chicago, IL (312) 684-1414

FREE CHILD GENERAL ADMISSION

The Museum of Science and Industry invites you to enjoy one free child general admission per coupon when accompanied by a paying adult. While in Chicago, don't miss the world's largest and most popular "hands-on" museum of contemporary science and technology.

This coupon may not be used in conjunction with any other discount or promotion.
MOP 07

OFFER EXPIRES DECEMBER 31, 1995

SAVE $10 OFF YOUR NEXT WEEKLY RENTAL

You can save an extra $10 off Avis weekly rates when you rent any Intermediate through Full Size 4-door car for a week. Just present this certificate at an Avis corporate or participating licensee location in the contiguous U.S. It's good through December 31, 1995. To take advantage of this offer, call your travel consultant, or the Avis Special Promotion reservation number: **1-800-831-8000**. Be sure to mention your Avis Worldwide Discount (AWD) number: **A291806**.

OFFER EXPIRES DECEMBER 31, 1995

$1.00 OFF
reg. price

This coupon entitles you to $1.00 off the regular price of any Supreme Burger or Sandwich.

Valid at all participating Jack In The Box® restaurants. Served after 10:30 a.m. Please present this coupon when ordering. One coupon per guest. One offer per coupon. Not valid in combination with any other offer. © Foodmaker, Inc. 1994.
J732

OFFER EXPIRES DECEMBER 31, 1995

Six Flags Theme Parks
SAVE UP TO $24 AT SIX FLAGS THEME PARKS
($4 per ticket, up to 6 admissions)

Present this coupon at the ticket booth of any Six Flags Theme Park for $4.00 off adult admissions.

Offer cannot be combined with any other discount or promotion. Not valid on already discounted tickets including season, consignment and after 4pm tickets. Limit six discounted admissions per coupon. Offer valid through 1995 operating season. Park schedules vary and are subject to change without notice. It is strongly recommended that you contact the specific park you will be attending for operating schedule information. **NLU 37254 T   NLU 37255 C**

OFFER EXPIRES DECEMBER 31, 1995

Pro Football Hall of Fame

2121 George Halas Drive, Northwest
Canton, Ohio 44709 • (216) 456-8207

UP TO THREE FREE ADMISSIONS

The Pro Football Hall of Fame invites you to enjoy up to three free admissions when accompanied by three paid admissions.

This coupon may not be used in conjunction with any other discount or promotion. Maximum of three free admissions.

OFFER EXPIRES DECEMBER 31, 1995

RAMADA LIMITEDS · INNS · HOTELS · RESORTS · PLAZA HOTELS
10% OFF

We invite you to stay at any of our over 700 Ramada Limiteds, Inns, Hotels, Resorts and Plaza Hotels throughout the United States. Present this coupon at check-in and we'll take 10% off your rack room rate. For reservations call your travel consultant or **1-800-228-2828** and mention this Ramada 10% discount coupon

This coupon cannot be combined with other promotions, group rates, or packages. Availability may be limited and advance reservations are required, so call now.

OFFER EXPIRES DECEMBER 31, 1995

The Place

Where Fresh is the Taste.™

TASTE PUBLICATIONS INTERNATIONAL

Plazas · Hotels · Park Square Inns · Lodges · HoJo Inns

THE COMFORTABLE LANDMARK™

TASTE PUBLICATIONS INTERNATIONAL

Offer valid on an Intermediate (Group C) through a Full Size 4-door (Group E) car for a 5 day rental. Certificate must be surrendered at time of rental; one per rental. May be used in conjunction with Taste Publications International rates and discounts. May not be used in conjunction with any other coupon, promotion or offer. Certificate valid at Avis corporate and participating licensee locations in the contiguous U.S. Offer not available during holiday and other blackout periods. Offer may not be available on all rates at all times. Cars subject to availability. Taxes, local government surcharges and optional items, such as LDW, additional-driver fee and refueling, are extra. Renter must meet Avis age, driver and credit requirements. Minimum age is 25. Offer expires December 31, 1995.

Rental Sales Agent Instructions:
At Checkout: In AWD, enter **A291806** In CPN, Enter **MUGC150**.
Complete this information: RA# _____
Rental Location: _____
Attach COUPON to tape.   © 1994 Wizard Co., Inc.

TASTE PUBLICATIONS INTERNATIONAL

Museum of Science and Industry

Some of the Latest Exhibits at the Museum of Science and Industry • Chicago

"Navy: Technology at Sea" -Step on board partial recreations of three ships, then fly on a top-gun mission in our F-14 Tomcat flight simulators.

"IMAGING: The Tools of Science" -See sound, marvel at 6-foot thermal images of yourself and experience virtual reality.

"Take Flight" -An actual 727 inside the museum provides a unique setting for learning the principles of flight.

MOP 07

TASTE PUBLICATIONS INTERNATIONAL

**No matter where you travel,
there is a Six Flags Theme Park near you.**

Houston
Six Flags AstroWorld
(713) 799-8404

NJ/NY/Philadelphia
Six Flags Great Adventure
(908) 928-2000

Los Angeles
Six Flags Magic Mountain
(805) 255-4100

Atlanta
Six Flags Over Georgia
(404) 948-9290

St. Louis
Six Flags Over Mid-America
(314) 938-5300

Dallas/Fort Worth
Six Flags Over Texas
(817) 640-8900

Chicago/Milwaukee Six Flags Great America
(708) 249-1776

TASTE PUBLICATIONS INTERNATIONAL

TASTE PUBLICATIONS INTERNATIONAL

RAMADA

RAMADA LIMITEDS · INNS · HOTELS · RESORTS · PLAZA HOTELS

Ramada Limiteds, Inns, Hotels, Resorts and Plaza Hotels offer you the value and accommodations you expect... And so much more! Over 700 convenient locations. Children under 18 always stay free. Non-smoking and handicap rooms available. Four people can share a room for the price of one at participating locations.
For reservations call 1-800-228-2828.

TASTE PUBLICATIONS INTERNATIONAL

 Pro Football Hall of Fame

Prices effective January 1, 1994:
Adult - $6.00 • Child - $2.50

TASTE PUBLICATIONS INTERNATIONAL

Mobil Travel Guide®
The Guide That Saves You Money When You Travel.

GENERAL CINEMA THEATRES

UNITED ARTISTS
LOEWS

THEATRE DISCOUNT

Valid at all participating theatres. Please order all tickets in one order.
Enclose 1 check for entire order. Please send me:

____ Loews at $4.25 each = _____
____ United Artists at $4.25 each = _____
____ General Cinemas at $4.50 each = _____
    Add $1.00 for handling   + $1.00
    TOTAL   _____

Make check payable to: Taste Publications International.
Complete application on reverse side.

OFFER EXPIRES DECEMBER 31, 1995

DAYS INN — The Best Value Under The Sun®

10% SPECIAL DISCOUNT

Now you can save even more at any of
our over 1,500 Days Inns throughout the United States and
internationally. Just present this coupon upon check-in and
we'll take 10% off your regular room rate for your entire
length of stay! Advance reservations required so call now!
For reservations and location information call:
1-800-DAYS INN
Available at participating properties. This coupon cannot be combined with
any other special discount offer. Limit one coupon per room, per stay.

OFFER EXPIRES DECEMBER 31, 1995

Las Vegas TRAVEL

20% OFF
PLUS 2 FREE TICKETS

Call Las Vegas Travel for a 20% discount for most major
casino hotels in Las Vegas. Mention this coupon to receive
2 free tickets to the Imperial Palace Antique and Classic
Auto Collection (a $14 value). **Call 1-800-992-7454.**
Valid Sunday - Thursday only. Holidays/City-Wide Conventions excluded.
Discount requires advance reservations.
For show - wedding - casino info: 1-900-RESORT CITY.
For golf reservations: 1-800-627-4465.

SAFE FIT™ $5.00 OFF

Save $5.00 on SAFE-FIT™ shoulder belt adjuster.
Our soft padded SAFE-FIT™ allows any shoulder belt to
be positioned comfortably and safely to fit the child who
has outgrown the infant seat. Retails for $15.00.
Please enclose a check or money order for $11.95
(includes $1.95 for shipping and handling)
with coupon and mail to:
P.O. Box 730, Skyland, NC 28776

OFFER EXPIRES DECEMBER 31, 1995

---

100 ROLLS OF FILM AND
35mm CAMERA FOR $9.95

From U.S. Express, a participating national Colorwatch System
lab. Simply fill out the coupon on the back and as a special
thanks we'll send you a photo finishing package that offers you
fresh Kodak film (your choice) returned with your pictures.
Save 40% off dealing direct with our national lab. Get a
Camtec camera and Kodak film for life too...plus a lot more!

© 1993 U.S. Express. Void where prohibited. Film offer valid with
purchased processing. This offer not affiliated with Eastman Kodak Co.

OFFER EXPIRES DECEMBER 31, 1995

FREE CAMPING STAY

Camp free when you rent a KOA Deal Motor Home
from Cruise America. Call 800-327-7778 and request a
KOA Deal Motor Home rental and learn how to camp
free at participating KOA Kampgrounds.

OFFER EXPIRES DECEMBER 31, 1995

DOLLAR RENT A CAR

ONE
FREE DAY

Add one free day to any seven-day rental or two-day weekend
rental upon presentation of this certificate. For worldwide
reservations, call your professional travel agent or
1-800-800-4000 and mention this code:
MOBIL.

This offer is valid for any economy through intermediate car and may not be used in conjunction
with any other offer. One certificate per transaction. Tax, gas and LDW not included. Offer
subject to availability at participating Dollar locations only. This certificate has no cash value.

OFFER EXPIRES DECEMBER 31, 1995

Harrah's CASINOS

TWO FREE
SHOW TICKETS

Harrah's invites you to enjoy two free show tickets
at Harrah's Lake Tahoe or Harrah's Reno.
For show schedule and reservations,
call **1-800-HARRAHS** (1-800-427-7247).

Coupon redeemable Sunday through Friday.   **MB2**

OFFER EXPIRES DECEMBER 22, 1995

Mobil Travel Guide®

The Guide That Saves You Money When You Travel.